# Adolescence
and
Youth

# ADOLESCENCE AND YOUTH
## PSYCHOLOGICAL DEVELOPMENT IN A CHANGING WORLD

**JOHN JANEWAY CONGER**
University of Colorado School of Medicine

**ANNE C. PETERSEN**
Pennsylvania State University

**THIRD EDITION**

*1817*

**HARPER & ROW, PUBLISHERS, New York**
Cambridge, Philadelphia, San Francisco,
London, Mexico City, São Paulo, Sydney

**Cover photo** and pages i, iii, vii, xi, xv, 693, 697, 723: **Michel Craig**

Photo credits: Page 1, Fitzhugh, Boston; 3, © 1978, Vilms, Jeroboam; 9, Granger; 14, © Jean-Claude Lejeune; 31, © 1983, Joel Gordon; 40, © 1981, Siteman, Jeroboam; 47, Grimes, Leo de Wys Inc.; 49, Silverman, Leo de Wys Inc.; 55, © Jean-Claude Lejeune; 63, © Jean-Claude Lejeune; 75, © George W. Gardner; 78, Compagnone, Jeroboam; 83, Montaris, Leo de Wys Inc.; 91, © 1982, Joel Gordon; 97, © 1980, Dietz, Stock, Boston; 101, Vandermark, Stock, Boston; 105, Michel Craig; 111, Burnett, Stock, Boston; 120, Harbutt, Archive Pictures; 127, © 1978, Falk, Jeroboam; 145, Harbutt, Archive Pictures; 151, © McQueen, Stock, Boston; 159, Anderson, Monkmeyer; 163, © Jean-Claude Lejeune; 183, Dunn, DPI; 186, Laping, DPI; 190, Wolinsky, Stock, Boston; 198, © Marjorie Pickens; 200, Brown, Stock, Boston; 205, Leinwand, Monkmeyer; 213, © 1981, Joel Gordon; 218, Shelton, Monkmeyer; 227, © 1982, Anderson, Stock, Boston; 234, Wolinsky, Stock, Boston; 238, Busselle, DPI; 271, Serbin, Leo de Wys Inc.; 273, © 1981, Russel, International Stock Photo; 280, Forsyth, Monkmeyer; 297, Mark, Archive Pictures; 314, Skytta, Jeroboam; 323, © Jean-Claude Lejeune; 335, Grimes, Leo de Wys Inc.; 337, © Jean-Claude Lejeune; 349, © Dorfman, Jeroboam; 373, Menzel, Stock, Boston; 379, Grimes, Leo de Wys Inc.; 395, Grimes, Leo de Wys Inc.; 417, O'Neil, Stock, Boston; 445, © 1978, Preuss, Jeroboam; 448, © Paris, Picture Group; 450, Harrison, Stock, Boston; 474, © 1980, Druskis, EPA; 487, Mahon, Monkmeyer; 503, Dietz, Stock, Boston; 509, Mendoza, Stock, Boston; 510, Southwick, Stock, Boston; 518, © 1974, Joel Gordon; 540, © 1973, Joel Gordon; 555, © 1979, Anderson, Black Star; 570, © Ivers, Jeroboam; 572, Shackman, Monkmeyer; 585, © 1981, Lapides, Design Conceptions; 597, Franken, Stock, Boston; 602, Harbutt, Archive Pictures; 609, Strickler, Monkmeyer; 612, International Stock Photo; 621, © 1981, Hoffman, Archive Pictures; 643, Lejeune, Stock, Boston; 652, © 1981, Joel Gordon; 681, Bellerose, Stock, Boston; 682, Tress, Photo Researchers.

Sponsoring Editor: Kathy Robinson
Project Editor: Holly Detgen
Designer: Michel Craig
Production Manager: Willie Lane
Photo Researcher: Mira Schachne
Compositor: York Graphic Services, Inc.
Printer and Binder: R. R. Donnelley & Sons Company
Art Studio: Vantage Art, Inc.

**ADOLESCENCE AND YOUTH: Psychological Development in a Changing World, Third Edition**

Library of Congress Cataloging in Publication Data

Conger, John Janeway.
  Adolescence and youth.

  Includes index.
  1. Adolescence. I. Petersen, Anne C. II. Title.
HQ796.C76 1983     305.2′35     83-10674
ISBN 0-06-041357-3

*I have sent forth my prayers.*
*Our children,*
*Even those who have erected their shelters*
*At the edge of the wilderness,*
*May their roads come in safely,*
*May the forests*
*And the brush*
*Stretch out their water-filled arms*
*To shield their hearts;*
*May their roads come in safely;*
*May their roads all be fulfilled,*
*May it not somehow become difficult for them*
*When they have gone but a little way.*

*May all the young boys,*
*All the young girls,*
*And those whose roads are ahead,*
*May they have powerful hearts,*
*Strong spirits;*
*On roads reaching to Dawn Lake*
*May they grow old.*

*—Zuñi Indian Prayer*

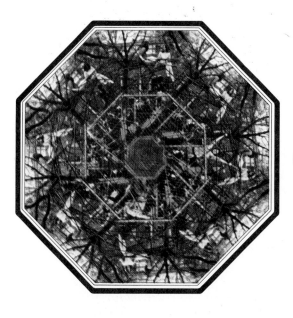

# Contents

# *Preface*

The first edition of this book was published exactly a decade ago. At that time, we observed that young people were coming to maturity in a rapidly changing, complex society whose future directions were shrouded in uncertainty. Today's young people still face a challenging and uncertain future; social change, while not as rapid in the late sixties and early seventies, is likely to involve even more fundamental dislocations and readjustments—personal, social, and economic. The challenges faced by the family as a social institution have increased and become still more complex. Political and social activism have declined markedly, but other legacies of the youth culture of the 1960s have clearly persisted, though not always in the same form, or with the same results. Thus, the so-called sexual revolution of the sixties has not only endured, but broadened. Paradoxically, the greater emphasis on self-expression and self-realization that helped to fuel the political and social activism of the 1960s often took the form of a greater preoccupation with self and a diminished concern with the well-being of others during the "me-decade" of the 1970s. Despite the decline in political activism during the past decade, skepticism toward many social institutions, including government, has actually increased—not only among the young, but even more dramatically among their elders.

The apparently affluent society of a decade ago, with an overabundance of jobs for economically privileged youth, has been replaced by "a society of lowered expectations," with historically high unemployment rates. Many workers—young and old alike—have become victims, in the jargon of economists, of "structural unemployment," as we have moved from a production economy toward one based largely on services and specialized knowledge (e.g., computer sciences). As Daniel Yankelovich recently observed, "In a matter of a few years we have moved from an uptight culture set in a dynamic economy to a dynamic culture set in an uptight economy" (Yankelovich, 1981, p. 22).

If young people are going to be ready to meet the challenges of these new economic realities, many will need to shift their vocational sights away from traditional occupations to newly emerging ones. And our educational institutions will have to play a major role in preparing them to do so. Yet reduced budgets, social tensions, and ideological differences regarding the fundamental purposes of education have created increasingly critical problems for our schools. Changing sex roles, particularly for women, are leading to changes in educational and vocational opportunities, and in many instances, to reappraisals of personal and social goals.

All these changes, and others, have affected the individual adolescent's development and the challenges he or she faces in the search for a stable, workable sense of identity. Much of the new material in this edition reflects the influence of these changes. This is particularly the case in the chapters on the family, parent-adolescent relationships, sexual attitudes and behavior, the schools, vocational choice, drug use, alienation and delinquency, and psychological problems.

More broadly, the book as a whole reflects the remarkable progress in the caliber of research on adolescent development that has taken place in the past decade—in areas as diverse as hormonal influences on behavior, cognitive processes, sex roles, and patterns of family interaction. After years of lagging behind the explosion of productive research in infancy and early childhood, research on adolescence, and especially early adolescence, is finally coming into its own. Inasmuch as the biological, psychological, cognitive, and social changes taking place in the years surrounding puberty are greater than at any other age since the second year of life, recent progress seems overdue—though no less welcome.

In an effort to make the book maximally useful to undergraduate students in developmental psychology and other behavioral sciences and to interested parents and adolescents, as well as to advanced students and established professionals, we have tried to combine thorough, current coverage of the research literature and detailed bibliographic references with a straightforward and, hopefully, well-organized and integrated presentation of the text. If desired, most chapters can be read or assigned separately as a coherent, self-contained presentation of the topic under consideration.

In preparing the third edition, we have been fortunate to have had the help of a group of excellent reviewers. Michael Berzonsky, SUNY, Cortland; Lou Fusilli, Monroe Community College; Harold Perkins, Shippensburg State College; Lee Ross, Frostburg State College; Kathy Smith, Portland State University; Gerald Winer, Ohio State University, reviewed the second edition and provided helpful suggestions. Mark Grabe, University of North Dakota; Stan Henson, Arkansas Technical University; Anthony Olejnick, Northern Illinois University; W. E., Scoville, University of Wisconsin-Oshkosh read and commented on the early drafts of the third edition.

A book such as this inevitably reflects not only the current status of an area of scientific investigation, but, at least to some extent, the outlook of the authors—their own values, hopes and fears, their perceptions and blind spots. To the extent that the hopes outweigh the fears and that, despite the blind spots, there is some understanding, our greatest single debt is to our families. For they have provided not only pleasure and love, but equally important, a meaningful link between the best of the past, present, and future.

Among the many others to whom we are indebted, including our students and colleagues, we especially want to express our appreciation to Dorothy Townsend and Ruth Runeborg, who played an indispensable role in putting together the manuscript, correcting errors, and making helpful editorial suggestions.

**John Janeway Conger**
**Anne C. Petersen**

# Acknowledgments

**Grateful acknowledgment is made to the individuals and publishers who granted permission to reprint portions of their material.**

**Joseph Adelson,** "The Development of Ideology in Adolescence." In *Adolescence in the Life Cycle: Psychological Change and Social Context,* edited by S. E. Dragastin and G. H. Elder, Jr., 1975. Reprinted by permission of the publisher, Hemisphere Publishing Corporation.

**Joseph Adelson,** "Rites of Passage." *American Educator,* Summer 1982. Reprinted by permission.

**Jerald G. Bachman, Lloyd D. Johnston,** and **Patrick M. O'Malley,** *Monitoring the Future: Questionnaire Responses from the Nation's High School Seniors, 1980.* Institute for Social Research, 1981. Reprinted by permission.

**Jerald G. Bachman, Patrick M. O'Malley,** and **Lloyd D. Johnston,** *Youth in Transition, Vol. VI: Adolescence to Adulthood—Change and Stability in the Lives of Young Men.* Institute for Social Research, 1978. Reprinted by permission.

**Jerald G. Bachman** and **Lloyd D. Johnston,** *Fewer Rebels, Fewer Causes: A Profile of Today's College Freshmen.* Institute for Social Research, 1979, 1982. Reprinted by permission.

**Nancy Bayley,** "Development of Mental Abilities." In *Carmichael's Manual of Child Psychology, Vol. I,* edited by P. H. Mussen, 1970. Reprinted by permission of Wiley and Sons.

**Nancy Bayley,** "Learning in Adulthood: The Role of Intelligence." In *Analysis of Conceptual Learning,* edited by H. J. Klausmeier and C. W. Harris, 1966. Reprinted by permission of Academic Press.

**Lee G. Burchinal,** "Trends and Prospects for Young Marriages in the U.S.," *Journal of Marriage and the Family,* 1965. Reprinted by permission.

**Nancy W. Burton** and **Lyle V. Jones,** "Recent Trends in Achievement Levels of Black and White Youth," *Educational Researcher,* 1982. Copyright © 1982, American Educational Research Association, Washington, D.C.

**Theodore Caplow** and **Howard Bahr,** "Half a Century of Change in Adolescent Attitudes: Replication of a Middletown Survey by the Lynds," *Public Opinion Quarterly,* 1979. Copyright 1979 by the Trustees of Columbia University. Reprinted by permission.

**Francis G. Caro,** "Social Class and Attitudes of Youth Relevant for the Realization of Adult Goals," *Social Forces,* 1966. Copyright © The University of North Carolina Press. Reprinted by permission.

**Lucius F. Cervantes,** "Family Background, Primary Relationships and the High School Dropout," *Journal of Marriage and the Family,* 1965. Reprinted by permission.

**Philip R. Costanzo,** "Conformity Development as a Function of Self-Blame," *Journal of Personality and Social Psychology,* 1970. Copyright 1970 by the American Psychological Association and reproduced by permission.

**John C. Coleman,** *Relationships in Adolescence,* 1974. Reprinted by permission of Routledge & Kegan Paul Ltd.

**College Entrance Examination Board,** *National College-Bound Seniors, 1982.* Copyright © 1982 by College Entrance Examination Board. Reprinted by permission.

**William C. Crain** and **Ellen F. Crain,** "The Growth of Political Ideas and Their Expression Among Young Activists," *Journal of Youth and Adolescence,* 1974. Reprinted by permission of Plenum Publishing Corporation.

**Glen H. Elder, Jr.,** "Structural Variations in the Child Rearing Relationship," *Sociometry,* 1962. Reprinted by permission.

**Delbert S. Elliott** and **Suzanne S. Ageton,** "Reconciling Race and Class Differences in Self-Reported and Official Estimates of Delinquency," *American Sociological Review,* 1980. Reprinted by permission.

**Erik H. Erikson,** *Identity: Youth and Crisis.* Copyright © 1968 by W. W. Norton & Company, Inc., Reprinted by permission.

**L. Erlenmeyer-Kimling** and **Lissy F. Jarvik,** "Genetics and Intelligence: A Research Review," *Science,* 1963. Copyright © 1963 by the American Association for the Advancement of Science. Reprinted by permission.

**Margaret S. Faust,** "Somatic Development of Adolescent Girls," *Monographs of the Society for Research in Child Development,* 1977. Copyright © 1977 by the Society for Research in Child Development, Inc. Reprinted by permission.

**Judith F. Fischer,** "Transitions in Relationship Style from Adolescence to Young Adulthood," *Journal of Youth and Adolescence,* 1981. Reprinted by permission.

**Anna Freud,** *The Ego and the Mechanisms of Defense.* Copyright © 1946 by International Universities, Hogarth Press, London, 1968. Reprinted by permission.

**George Gallup, Jr.,** "Gallup Poll," *Denver Post,* 1978. Reprinted by permission.

**Martin Gold,** *Delinquent Behavior in an American City.* Copyright © 1970 by Wadsworth Publishing Company, Inc. Reprinted by permission of the publisher, Brooks/Cole Publishing Company.

**Paul V. Gump,** *Big Schools, Small Schools,* 1966. Reprinted by permission of the Stanford University Press.

**Derek D. Gupta, Andrea Attanasio,** and **Susanne Raaf,** "Plasma Estrogen and Androgen Concentrations in Children during Adolescence," *Journal of Clinical Endocrinology and Metabolism,* 1975. By permission of Williams & Wilkins Company.

**Thomas W. Harrell** and **Margaret S. Harrell,** "Army General Classification Test Scores for Civilian Occupations," *Educational and Psychological Measurements,* 1945. Reprinted by permission.

**E. Mavis Hetherington,** "Effects of Father Absence on Personality Development in Adolescent Daughters." Reprinted from *Developmental Psychology,* 1972. Copyright 1972 by the American Psychological Association and reproduced by permission.

**Marjorie P. Honzik, Jean W. Macfarlane,** and **Lucille Allen,** "The Stability of Mental Test Performance between Two and Eighteen Years," *Journal of Experimental Education,* 1948. Adapted by P. H. Mussen and M. R. Rosenzweig et al. in *Psychology: An Introduction,* 1973. Reprinted by permission of D. C. Heath & Co.

**Arthur R. Jensen,** *Educability and Group Differences,* 1973. Reprinted by permission of Harper & Row, Publishers, Inc.

**Arthur T. Jersild,** *The Psychology of Adolescence,* 1963. Reprinted by permission of Dembar Educational Research Services.

**Denise Kandel,** "Inter- and Intragenerational Influences on Adolescent Marijuana Use," *Journal of Social Issues,* 1974. Reprinted by permission.

**Denise Kandel** and **Gerald S. Lesser,** "Parental and Peer Influences on Educational Plans of Adolescents," *American Sociological Review,* 1969. Reprinted by permission.

**Suzanne M. Kavrell** and **Anne C. Petersen,** "Patterns of Achievement in Early Adolescence." In *Women and Science,* edited by M. L. Maher and M. W. Steinkamp, in press. Reprinted by permission of Jai Press, Inc.

**Seymour Kessler,** "Psychiatric Genetics." In *American Handbook of Psychiatry, Vol. VI: New Psychiatric Frontiers,* edited by D. A. Hamburg and S. K. Brodie, New York, Basic Books, Inc. 1975. Reprinted by permission of the publishers.

**Alfred C. Kinsey, Wardell B. Pomeroy,** and **Clyde E. Martin,** *Sexual Behavior in the Human Male,* Philadelphia, W. B. Saunders Company. 1948. Reprinted by permission.

**Lawrence Kohlberg,** "Moral Stages and Moralization." In *Moral Development and Behavior,* edited by T. Lickona, 1976. Reprinted by permission.

**Gerald S. Lesser** and **Denise Kandel,** "Parent-Adolescent Relationships and Adolescent Independence in the United States and Denmark," *Journal of Marriage and the Family,* 1969. Reprinted by permission.

**J. Kenneth Little,** "The Occupations of Non-College Youth," *American Educational Research Journal,* 1967. Reprinted by permission.

**Hart M. Nelsen, Richard H. Potvin,** and **Joseph Shields,** *The Religion of Children.* Copyright © 1977, United States Catholic Conference. Reprinted by permission.

**Marita P. McCabe** and **John K. Collins,** "Sex Role and Dating Orientation,"

*Journal of Youth and Adolescence,* 1979. Reprinted by permission of Academic Press.

**Patricia Y. Miller** and **William Simon,** "Do Youth Really Want to Work: A Comparison of the Work Values and Job Perceptions of Younger and Older Men," *Youth and Society,* 1979. Reprinted by permission.

**William R. Morrow** and **Robert C. Wilson,** "Family Relations of Bright High-Achieving and Underachieving High School Boys," *Child Development,* 1961. Copyright 1961 by the Society for Research in Child Development, Inc. Reprinted by permission.

**Jeylan T. Mortimer,** "Social Class, Work, and the Family: Some Implications of Father's Occupation for Familial Relationships and Sons' Career Decisions," *Journal of Marriage and the Family,* 1976. Reprinted by permission.

**Michael Rutter, Philip Graham, Oliver Chadwick,** and **William Yule,** "Adolescent Turmoil: Fact or Fiction?" *Journal of Child Psychology and Psychiatry,* 1976. Reprinted by permission.

**Stanley Schachter.** *Emotion, Obesity, and Crime,* 1971. Copyright 1971 by Academic Press and reproduced by permission.

**Earl S. Schaefer,** "A Circumplex Model for Maternal Behavior," *Journal of Abnormal and Social Psychology,* 1959. Copyright 1959 by the American Psychological Association and reproduced by permission.

**Farida Shah** and **Melvin Zelnik,** "Parent and Peer Influence on Sexual Behavior, Contraceptive Use, and Pregnancy Experience of Young Women," *Journal of Marriage and the Family,* 1981. Reprinted by permission.

**Eric Single, Denise Kandel,** and **Richard Faust,** "Patterns of Multiple Drug Use in High School," *Journal of Health and Social Behavior,* 1974. Copyright 1974 by the American Psychological Association and reproduced by permission.

**Leon Speroff** and **Raymond L. Vande Wiele,** "Variations in Hormonal Levels during the Menstrual Cycle," *American Journal of Obstetrics and Gynecology,* 1971. Reprinted by permission.

**Lorene H. Stone, Alfred C. Miranne,** and **Godfrey J. Ellis,** "Parent-Peer Influence as a Predictor of Marijuana Use," *Adolescence,* 1979. Reprinted by permission of the publisher.

**June L. Tapp** and **Felice J. Levine,** "Compliance from Kindergarten to College: A Speculative Research Note," *Journal of Youth and Adolescence,* 1972. Reprinted by permission of Plenum Publishing Corporation.

**E. Paul Torrance** and **D. C. Dauw,** "Attitude Patterns of Creatively Gifted High School Seniors," *Gifted Child Quarterly,* 1966. Reprinted by permission.

**Michael A. Wallach** and **Nathan Kogan,** *Modes of Thinking in Young Children: A Study of the Creativity-Intelligence Distinction.* Copyright 1965 by Holt, Rinehart and Winston, Inc. Reprinted by permission.

**Allan W. Wicker,** "Undermanning, Performance, and Students' Subjective Experiences in Behavior Settings of Large and Small High Schools," *Journal of Personality and Social Psychology,* 1968. Copyright 1968 by the American Psychological Association and reproduced by permission.

**Edwin P. Willems,** "Sense of Obligation to High School Activities as Related to

School Size and Marginality of Student,'' *Child Development,* 1967. Copyright 1967 by the Society for Research in Child Development, Inc. Reprinted by permission.

**Ronald S. Wilson** and **Eileen B. Harpring,** "Mental and Motor Development in Infant Twins,'' *Developmental Psychology,* 1972. Copyright by the American Psychological Association and reproduced by permission.

**Melvin Zelnik** and **John F. Kantner,** "Sexual Activity, Contraceptive Use and Pregnancy among Metropolitan-Area Teenagers: 1971–1979, *Family Planning Perspectives,* 1980. Reprinted by permission.

**Melvin Zelnik, Young J. Kim,** and **John F. Kantner,** "Probabilities of Intercourse and Conception among U.S. Teenage Women, 1971–1976,'' *Family Planning Perspectives,* 1979. Reprinted by permission.

Introduction

CHAPTER 1

# Introduction

*H*umankind has long been preoccupied with its youth. In the collective life of societies, each new generation of young people has been rightly perceived as the rather fragile vessel by which the best of the past—the hard-won fruits of our painful and slippery steps up from the primordial mists—is transmitted into the present. And in the faces of each new generation we have long seen written the future of nations and cultures—the future of humanity itself. Despite a decline in our concern with the problems of children and adolescents in our society during the "me-decade" of the 1970s (20), we still recognize that young people are our hostages to fortune and that the human drama is, in the last analysis, the story of successive generations of young men and women.

But there is a more personal and subjective side to our fascination with youth. Over the centuries (among Egyptians and the early Greeks, as well as in modern existentialists) there has been a tendency to conceptualize our own individual lives largely in terms of our adolescent years. Childhood is perceived by most of us, perhaps with more nostalgia and sentiment than sometimes is justified, as the period of *becoming.*

In contrast, adolescence is remembered as the time when our identities were established, when potentialities for accomplishment—though not the accomplishments themselves—were at their height. For many, like Joseph Conrad, it is remembered as the period of being most alive: "a flick of sunshine upon a strange shore, the time to remember, the time for a sigh . . ." (21). The friendships formed in these years, and the first loves, have a kind of special permanence in our minds.

When we think about whether we have changed over the years, whether we have been true to our hopes and dreams, whether we have realized our potentials, the inevitable comparison is not with the years of childhood or intervening adulthood, but rather with the few short years of our youth. The more mature among us may no longer wish to be young, but despite the frequent heartaches of the adolescent period, we treasure its memory, and indeed we cannot conceive of not having been young.

Consequently, when we look at adolescents we see not merely a necessary generational link between the past, the present, and the future, but also *ourselves.* In

many ways, it seems, our reactions to adolescents are much like those to a projective personality test, such as the vaguely defined Rorschach inkblots. We see in youth not merely what is actually there, but the mirror of our own desires, hopes, satisfactions, frustrations, fears, and disappointments.

## A NEW GENERATION

In the view of some observers, young people are more rootless, more troubled emotionally, more promiscuous sexually, and less idealistic than their peers in earlier generations. As evidence, they point to rising rates of delinquency, drug use, and adolescent suicide, the current epidemic of adolescent pregnancy, and a growing preoccupation with self-fulfillment at the expense of societal concerns (20, 119). Other observers assure us that today's youth are better informed about the world in which they live than any generation in history; no less idealistic, though more pragmatic and less sentimental; more open, honest, and tolerant, and less given to viewing others in terms of simplistic stereotypes; no more, and perhaps less promiscuous than their elders were at the same age; and more caring and responsible, but less hypocritical, obsessed, or troubled in their sexual attitudes and beliefs. We are informed by these optimistic observers that youth today have, if anything, a clearer sense of their own identity and are less emotionally conflicted than their parents were at the same age. Yet another group of observers feels that presumed differences—good or bad—between today's adolescents and those of earlier generations are largely illusory and more a matter of form than substance; or that they stem from unwarranted generalizations based on the behavior of numerically small numbers of atypical young people. Proponents of this latter view remind us "that there have always been differences between generations in social and political beliefs, tastes and fashions, and fundamental liberalism or conservatism" (88, *543*).

It will be one of the aims of this book to examine the evidence for or against these conflicting views and to try to arrive at a balanced judgment about the problems confronting today's adolescents and their responses to these problems. In the process we may also learn a little more about ourselves and about the human condition in these troubled and challenging times.

## HISTORICAL ROOTS

Although concerns with adolescence and youth became especially intense during the "youth revolution" of the 1960s, singling out the years surrounding puberty as a distinguishable and noteworthy period in the life span is by no means new. Comments on the presumably distinctive characteristics of youth occurred in the writings of influential Egyptians many centuries before the emergence of Christianity and, then as now, often served as the basis for dire predictions.

Reflecting the early Greek concern with human nature, Plato offered advice on the socialization of children from the earliest years through adolescence and young adulthood. He pointed out that during the developmental years "more than at any other time the character is engrained by habit" (99, *359*). However, he also acknowledged that "the characters of young men are subject to many changes in the course of their lives" (99, *359*). He advised that boys not be allowed to drink until they were 18 because of their easy excitability: "Fire must not be poured on fire." And he warned that adolescents were prone to arguments for argument's sake (99). In their enthusiasm they would, he commented, "leave no stone unturned, and in their delight at the first taste of wisdom, they would annoy everyone with their arguments" (89, *14*).

But, as Norman Kiell notes in his book *The Universal Experience of Adolescence* (68), perhaps the best early characterization of the period that we now recognize as adolescence is contained in the words of another perceptive observer:

> The young are in character prone to desire and ready to carry any desire they may have formed into action. Of bodily desires it is the sexual to which they are most disposed to give way, and in regard to sexual desire they exercise no self-restraint. They are changeful too, and fickle in their desires, which are as transitory as they are vehement; for their wishes are keen without being permanent, like a sick man's fits of hunger and thirst.
>
> They are passionate, irascible, and apt to be carried away by their impulses. They are the slaves, too, of their passion, as their ambition prevents their ever brooking a slight and renders them indignant at the mere idea of enduring an injury. . . . They are fonder both of honor and of victory than of money, the reason why they care so little for money being that they have never yet had experience of want.
>
> They are charitable rather than the reverse, as they have never yet been witnesses of many villainies; and they are trustful, as they have not yet been often deceived. . . . They have high aspirations; for they have never yet been humiliated by the experience of life, but are unacquainted with the limiting force of circumstances. . . .
>
> If the young commit a fault, it is always on the side of excess and exaggeration for they carry everything too far, whether it be their love or hatred or anything else. They regard themselves as omniscient and are positive in their assertions; this is, in fact, the reason of their carrying everything too far [68, *18–19*].

These words sound as though they might have been written by any number of today's social critics, but the fact is that they were written 2300 years ago—by Aristotle.

In Aristotle's view, children and animals alike were under the control of what today would be called Freud's pleasure principle ("children and brutes pursue pleasures") (6, *1053*); and though they had the capacity for voluntary action, they did not have the capacity for choice ("acts done on the spur of the moment we describe as voluntary, but not as chosen") (6, *967–968*).

In contrast, an important characteristic of adolescence was the development of the ability to choose. Aristotle's emphasis on voluntary and deliberate choice as necessary to achieving maturity is not unlike "that of some current social critics who have stated that today with prolonged education and prolonged dependency we have reduced choices for adolescents to the extent that we interfere with their attainment of maturity" (90, *17*).

Much of the kind of astute logical reasoning and empirically based observations that characterized Aristotle and other Greek philosophers became obscured under the impact of early Christian theology. Nevertheless, a preoccupation with the "ages of life" occupied a prominent place in the pseudoscientific treatises of the Middle Ages (4). Some flavor of this preoccupation is given in *Le Grand Propriétaire de toutes choses,* a kind of encyclopedia of "scientific" knowledge published in 1556:

> Afterwards [i.e., after infancy and childhood] follows the third age, which is called adolescence, which ends according to Constantine in his viaticum in the twenty-first year, but according to Isidore it lasts till twenty-eight . . . and it can go on until thirty or thirty-five. This age is called adolescence because the person is big enough to beget children, says Isidore. In this age the limbs are soft and able to grow and receive strength and vigour from natural heat. And because the person grows in this age to the size allotted to him by Nature [4, *21*].

In reading such pseudoscientific and, in retrospect, rather pretentious speculations (the ages of life were delineated by the author of the foregoing treatise to correspond to the planets—in a manner not too different from that of some of the astrologically enchanted youth of the 1970s), one is reminded of current discussions about the "proper" duration of adolescence in our culture, and the effects of an extended "psychosocial moratorium" (25)—a period of prolonged freedom from adult responsibilities. And, in a sense, we too have our own 35-year-old adolescents!

In a seventeenth-century volume entitled *The Office of Christian Parents* (112), life was divided into six stages: infancy (from birth to age 7), childhood (ages 7 to 14), youth (ages 14 to 28), manhood (28 to 50), gravity (50 to 70), and old age (over 70). It is interesting to note that "youth" was viewed as extending from 14 to 28 years, or what we would currently call young adulthood. It seems likely that this reflected the social and economic circumstances of the time. Typically an older youth who had already completed a period of apprenticeship in a vocation was still likely to be a journeyman, unmarried and living in the home of his master (105). For seventeenth-century males, marriage and the setting up of a separate household typically occurred at about age 27 (105).

It appears that the clergy of the time were greatly concerned about the need of these unsettled youth for guidance, and groups of young journeymen were often subjected to prolonged sermons (in one recorded instance, by a "relay team" of six successive ministers, extending over many hours). That their self-assigned task was not viewed as an easy one and frequently missed the mark was drily noted by John Bunyan (17; 105, *496*):

> Our ministers, long time by word and pen,
> Dealt with them, counting them not boys but men:
> Thunderbolts they shot at them, and their toys:
> But hurt them not, 'cause they were girls and boys.

It was commonly agreed that young people were fickle, vain, unsettled, susceptible to peer pressure, unreasonable, and "unconcerned about the big questions of life" (105, *497*). One clergyman, in a funeral sermon for a young man, compared youth to "a new ship launching out into the main ocean without a helm and ballast or pilot to steer her" (105, *497*). Another observed that man is sinful at all ages, but youth "is carried with more headlong force into vice, lust, and vain pleasures of the flesh" (105, *498*).

More sanguine souls were also impressed, however, with the positive side of youth (39, 105): "Now your parts are lively, senses fresh, memory strong, and nature vigorous" (105, *498*). In *Words to Give to the Young Man Knowledge and Discretion* (39), we learn that youth is the best time in life "for action, both as to the natural and moral frame of the body and mind," because it is a period of "strength and vigor, of purer conscience, and a softer heart than an old man" (105, *498*). The principal danger for youth in the seventeenth century was viewed as "sinfulness," and religious conversion (usually after age 20) was seen as the antidote. Steven Smith (105) notes that "the early modern conception of youth seems to have some similarity [despite important differences] with the modern conception in that both recognize some sort of 'identity crisis.' Furthermore, there is in the early modern conception some foreshadowing of the modern romanticization of youth" (105, *513*).

Nevertheless, the principal theme of seventeenth-century writings by clergymen and others was helping essentially undependable youth to develop mastery of their unruly impulses. The kind of romantic preoccupation with the psychological complexities and special needs of adolescence that we see today was still largely absent. Young people were still not important enough to be taken as seriously as older and wiser adults.

Indeed, not until the declining years of the nineteenth century do we encounter precursors of the modern concern with adolescence as a socially significant and psychologically complex period. The reasons are both demographic and cultural. Perception of adolescence as a truly distinctive stage of development is at least partially dependent on the existence of communities of young people sharing common experiences at similar ages, and isolated in varying degrees from the adult world. It is not surprising that much of the so-called youth culture of the late 1960s and early 1970s centered around schools and colleges, where large numbers of young people were congregated in age-segregated groups.

Such conditions did not exist prior to the latter part of the nineteenth century.

The idea of a large city school with, for example, five hundred or more tenth-grade students living, studying, and interacting in relative isolation from younger children and older adults (not uncommon today) would have seemed incomprehensible. For one thing, most of the population lived in rural areas or in small towns and cities, both in the United States and in other Western countries. Furthermore, there was far less segregation of adults and young people. Most young people in the 1700s and 1800s became involved in the world of work somewhere between the age of 7 and the onset of puberty, whether on the family farm, as "boys (girls) of all work" in other households, as helpers (and after puberty, perhaps, as apprentices for skilled craftsmen and shopowners, or as workers in mills and small factories). In many instances, sending children away from home at an early age was an economic necessity—because of too many mouths to feed, or the death of parents (in the first half of the nineteenth century only 20 percent of mothers survived their youngest child's maturity) (17, *43*). Even among the upper classes, however, the practice of sending young children away from home was not uncommon; wealthy merchants, for example, "often sent their sons out as cabin boys at 8 or 9 or as supercargo at 15 or 16 as part of a process of growing that was to lead to a junior partnership at 21" (67, *23*).

Few children continued their education into the adolescent years. Even for those who did, however, the experience was far different from that of a junior high or high school student today. Attendance was generally sporadic; for example, at Pinkerton Academy in Massachusetts in 1850, of thirty students enrolled for the winter term, only ten were in attendance for the spring term. Furthermore, there was little of the age grading found in modern schools. At Exeter Academy in 1812, the age range was from 10 to 28; the age range of students in public district schools was equally broad (67). Many students wandered casually back and forth between school and work over the years.

Such circumstances of work and education obviously did little to encourage the development of a special youth culture, or a perception of adolescence as a distinctive stage of development. As the historian Joseph Kett comments, "If adolescence is defined as the period after puberty during which a young person is institutionally segregated from casual contacts with a broad range of adults, then it can scarcely be said to have existed at all, even for those young people who attended school beyond age 14" (67, *36*).

### The growth of industrialization

By the latter part of the nineteenth century, the situation began to change, largely as a result of increasing migration to the cities and the growth of industrialization. Although the mass of young people continued to work, the nature of work was changing. The problem was partly one of scale. The relation of an individual craftsman, shopkeeper, or even small mill owner to a younger helper or apprentice was qualitatively different—more personal and direct—from that of a factory owner employing scores of "bobbin boys" (or girls).

Furthermore, with growing mechanization, the division between dead-end jobs and those with the possibility of future advancement became more sharply defined. Young people—both boys and girls—soon learned that the least skilled occupations carried little hope of advancement. Even worse, they frequently discovered that when they reached the usual "adult" age of 17 or 18, and began asking for adult wages, they would be replaced by younger children. In contrast, fewer young people were available to fill the growing number of more complex, higher-level jobs, and those who did qualify were more richly rewarded. These latter positions, however, required greater maturity and more education.

Consequently, increased education and delayed entrance into the work force became more highly valued. But for the mass of families these goals were unachievable. Too many of them needed the earnings of their young for family survival, and the generational cycle of poverty and despair that was to become one of the bitter fruits of the industrial revolution gained momentum. For the upper classes and the developing middle classes, however, the story was different. Greater wealth and a marked decrease in family size permitted what they perceived as an investment in the future—education. Parental attitudes toward children were altered in the process.

"Increasingly, each individual child was treated (according to sex) without prejudice to his or her place in the birth order. 'Give the boys a good education and a start in life,' wrote J. E. Panton in 1889, 'and provide the girls with £150 a year, either when they marry or at your own death, and you have done your duty by your children. The girls cannot starve on that income, and neither would they be prey of any fortune hunter; but no one has a right to bring children into the world in the ranks of the upper middle class and do less'" (43, *99*).

The result was a rapid relative increase in the number of schools, academies, and colleges. Furthermore, these institutions quickly became less casual, more tightly organized, and more academically demanding, with a sharp narrowing of the age ranges included at each level. Thus the preconditions were set for the self-conscious delineation of an adolescent stage of development: age segregation, a separate pattern of expectations for—and demands upon—youth, and increased isolation from adults and the world of work. As we have noted, this phenomenon was largely restricted initially to an economically favored minority. But it established a model that was eventually to be democratized and considered normal for young people generally.

### The "era of adolescence"

Once broad economic and social conditions began to create a visible group of segregated youth, the time was ripe for speculations about its presumably unique psychological nature, for concerns about how it should be controlled, and for prognoses about its future. Each of these would vary over the years as society itself changed. The important fact, however, is that by 1900, the "era of adolescence" in the modern sense of the term had begun.

Although middle- and upper-class youth were the initial beneficiaries of this discovery (including the idea that adolescents were still developing and required special nurturance), it gradually came to benefit poorer youth as well. Incredible as it may seem, in America in 1904, only 17 states had any age limits on coal mining, and in those that did, the *oldest* minimum age was 14. But many desperate 12-year-olds lied about their ages in order to work 10 to 12 hours a day in the mines for 35 cents a

day. The 1900 U.S. census showed over three-quarters of a million children, aged 10 to 13, employed in sweatshops, factories, mines, and the like. In England in 1902, only 9 percent of young people were still in school at age 14. Subsequent child labor laws and later school-leaving ages were a product of both a new view of the nature of childhood and adolescence, as well as social and religious pressures and a more enlightened view of the value of individual human life generally.

Widespread popular awareness of youth really came into its own, however, only after World War I, when young people became actively aware of a group consciousness, and when a foreshadowing of the 1960s generational conflicts over the war in Indochina could be seen in the solid opposition of young veterans to the older generations in the rear (4). From that point on, popular notions of, and preoccupation with, adolescence exploded: "It encroached upon childhood in one direction and maturity in the other" (4, *30*). As Philippe Aries comments: "It is as if, to every period of history, there corresponded a privileged age and a particular division of human life: 'youth' is the privileged age of the seventeenth century, childhood of the nineteenth, adolescence of the twentieth" (4, *32*).

## SCIENTIFIC STUDY OF ADOLESCENCE

Although there had already developed serious and sophisticated literary concern with the phenomenon of adolescence, modern scientific investigation of adolescence as a separate and distinct phase in human development really began with the work of G. Stanley Hall, who published his epochal two-volume work *Adolescence* in 1904 (49). Though now largely relegated with vague respect to the dusty archives of psychological history, Hall was, in his day, a most remarkable man: America's first PhD in psychology, the founder of the American Psychological Association, father of the child-study movement in this country, and president of Clark University from its inception until his retirement. It was he who invited Sigmund Freud to Clark, in the only journey that the founder of psychoanalysis made to this country. Although Hall and his students did much to introduce scientific techniques into the study of adolescence, and, as we have said, to delineate it as a substantive field of study in its own right, his ultimate interests were far more global—some would say grandiose.

Enchanted by Darwin's concepts of evolution, and by the related biological notion that "ontogeny [i.e., individual development] is a brief and rapid recapitulation of phylogeny [i.e., the evolutionary development of the race]" (46, *35*), Hall developed an analogous psychological and social theory of *recapitulation* in which "the experiential history of the human species had become part of the genetic structure of the individual" (90, *32*). According to this theory, the individual organism during its development passes through stages comparable to those that occurred during the history of humankind. "That is, the individual relived the development of the human race from early animal-like primitivism, through periods of savagery [i.e., later childhood and prepubescence], to the more recent civilized ways of life which characterize maturity" (90, *32–33*).

Many psychological writers have been led by Hall's recapitulation theory to view him as a one-sided exponent of a strictly biological, maturational concept of adolescence that ignores the effects of culture (46). Such an interpretation is erroneous, however. "Although Darwinism committed Hall to an emphasis on the genetic determinants of behavior, he believed firmly that at adolescence the process of recapitulating instincts gave way to the primacy of cultural influences" (46, *12*). "Young children," he maintained, "grow despite great hardships, but later adolescence is more dependent upon favoring conditions in the environment, disturbances of which more readily cause arrest and prevent maturity" (49, *47*). Elsewhere, he states, "The processes last to be attained are least assured by heredity and most dependent upon individual effort, in aid of which nature gives only propulsion, often less defined the later it can be acquired" (49, *94*).

Scornful of "the dead level of the average man," Hall believed that adolescents, properly encouraged, constituted the primary source of recruitment for a new elite that would create a collective society in which mankind could be directed toward evolutionary perfection (46). Although Hall extolled such "unique" assets of the adolescent as a second "birth of love in the largest Christian sense, psychologically free from all selfish motive" (46, *11*) (what romantic apologist for contemporary youth could ask for more?), his elitist notions seem at times painfully prescient to those who have lived to witness the subsequent development of Hitler's elite youth or, indeed, some of the more extreme and arrogant self-styled elitist youth groups of the late 1960s and early 1970s, whether of the far right or far left.

It is likely that, in part because of his Germanically inspired romanticism (he was influenced by the works of Schiller and the early Goethe) and in part because of his lofty expectations for adolescents, "Hall juxtaposed his concept of what he believed the environment could do for the adolescent with his concept of what it was doing to the adolescent" (46, *13*). The resulting hiatus led to what probably was his most controversial concept regarding adolescent development, namely, that it was a period of extreme "storm and stress" (Sturm und Drang)—suggestive of some ancient time "when old ways were broken and a high level attained" (49, *xiii*).

Contrary to popular interpretations, cultural influences were considered by Hall to play at least as large a role as maturational factors in the resulting oscillations of behavior that he viewed as characterizing this period: energy alternating with lethargy; exaltation, with depressive gloom; childish selfishness, with altruistic selflessness; conceit, with humility; tenderness, with cruelty; and curiosity, with apathy. As we shall see in some detail in this book, not only the presumed bases for adolescent storm and stress but the extent of the phenomenon itself have been, and remain, sources of considerable controversy.

Finally, in addition to his advocacy of recapitulation theory and his concept of adolescent storm and stress, Hall also provoked controversy by his assertion that adolescent physical growth was "saltatory" (rapid and abrupt), rather than part of an essentially continuous process—an assertion vigorously denied by Edward Thorndike and other eminent psychologists even in Hall's day (45, 113).

### Influence of Hall's concepts

However anachronistic some of the notions of this rather strange but vigorous and gifted man may seem today, they set the stage for the subsequent development of a scientific psychology of adolescence (which is still emerging) and for a clearer delineation of many of the most important theoretical and empirical questions facing the field. These include: (1) What is the relative importance of biological and cultural influences in adolescent development, and what is the nature of their interaction? (2) Is adolescence for most young people a relatively placid time characterized by essentially benign "normative crises" or is it a period characterized by clinically demonstrable psychological disturbance that is qualitatively similar to persisting emotional disorders in adulthood? (3) What are the nature and course of physical and physiological development in adolescence? (4) Should adolescent development be viewed as basically continuous with earlier and later development or considered a separate, discriminable *stage* or *critical period* in development (whether in terms of inherent physiological and psychological processes, a special set of culturally defined "developmental tasks," or both)?

## ISSUES IN ADOLESCENT DEVELOPMENT

### Biological versus cultural
### determinants of adolescent behavior

Although many behavioral scientists since Hall have felt that the weight of mounting empirical evidence fails to support his rather turgid conceptions of extreme adolescent storm and stress (at least for the average adolescent), most have agreed that adolescence does represent a difficult developmental period in our society. They have, however, been far from unanimous about the principal sources of this difficulty. The biologically oriented view adolescent behavior primarily as a reflection of the unfolding of additional sequences in a biologically "programmed" process of maturation—either directly or in terms of the psychological adjustments required by the physiological changes of puberty, including increases in sex hormones and changes in body structure and function (88, 90). Furthermore, according to some of these theorists, interindividual differences in adolescent adjustment are largely due to biologically determined, usually genetic, differences in basic temperament (9, 88, 90).

In contrast, others view adolescent adjustment problems as principally cultural in origin. Such theorists emphasize the many, highly concentrated demands made upon youth by society during this period—for independence, for peer and heterosexual adjustments, for educational and vocational preparation, and for the development of a workable set of personal and social values. They assert that in cultures in which these demands are "neither as complex, nor as restricted to one limited age, as in our society, adolescence is not viewed as a particularly difficult period of adjustment" (88, *605*).

Arnold Gesell (42), a pioneer in the systematic, detailed empirical observation of infant and child development, basically held the first of these views, although he did not deny the role of culture. "The culture inflects and channelizes, but it does not generate the progressions and trends of development" (42, *19*). For Gesell, development involved maturationally determined, recurring cycles of "innovation, integration, and equilibrium." Each major advance in development disturbed a previously existing equilibrium, and required an often awkward period of integration—characterized by partial regressions increasingly yielding to mastery—until a new equilibrium could be established.

> This mechanism is so fundamental that it governs the passing growth events of the day, the succession of behavioral phases of the years, and even the major rhythms of the grand cycle of human growth. The cycle moves onward in time and space. The consolidating stages of increased equilibrium stand out as they recur at progressive intervals, as though the cycle pursued a spiral-like course [42, *20*].

In the progression of these recurring cycles, Gesell also notes pendulumlike swings, in which "one extreme of behavior [is counterbalanced] by offsetting or pairing it with its opposite" through a continuous process of "reciprocal interweaving" (42, *19*). He cites the analogy of a tightrope walker who maintains "a balance by leaning first left, then right, then left in rapid reciprocation. He returns toward a golden mean after each shift; this enables him to step forward even though he fluctuates from side to side" (42, *20*).

Gesell's famed descriptions of modal behaviors at various ages—descriptions that so often served as a kind of bible for middle-class American parents, at least until the advent of Benjamin Spock's *Pocket Book of Baby and Child Care* (106)—reflect this rather reassuring model. Whether a particular age promises a difficult or placid experience for parent and child depends on the child's position in one or another of these recurring cycles of equilibrium and disequilibrium. In periods of innovation and still unresolved integration, greater difficulty can be expected; in periods of equilibrium, on the other hand, parent and child experience a rewarding respite from the developmental struggle.

Thus, in Gesell's view: "Ten [is a year of] consummation as well as of transition—an amiable, relatively relaxed interlude in which the organism assimilates, consolidates, and balances its attained resources. Only mildly does he foreshadow the tensions of later youth. In a frank, unself-conscious manner he tends to accept life and the world as they are with free and easy give-and-take. It is a golden age of developmental equipoise" (42, *37*). In contrast: "Eleven, like Five-and-a-half to Six is 'loosening up,' 'snapping old bonds' " (42, *19*). He is restive, investigative, talkative, argumentative; his moods are likely to be intense and to fluctuate rapidly—gay and enthusiastic at one moment, gloomy or angry the next. But peace gradually returns and "Twelve [becomes] more positive in mood, smoother in relationships" (42, *19*). And so it goes: "Thirteen pulls inward; Fourteen thrusts out; Fifteen specifies and organizes; Sixteen again achieves a more golden mean. (And we would venture to guess that the process does not stop with age sixteen and that sixteen is another modal age" [41, *19*]).

Gesell made valuable contributions to developmental psychology by his insistence on careful and detailed observations of behavior, rather than reliance on anecdotal or clinical impressions, and by his development and application of ingenious techniques for detailed study of infant and child development (41, 42). His theoretical model, however, appears somewhat simplistic, especially when applied to older age groups. Although his observations are often perceptive, his generalizations sometimes appear overly broad and inclusive, and suffer the disadvantage of failing to account adequately for deviations from established norms. More important, his model does not provide a means for conceptualizing in detail the *processes* by which biological, psychological, and cultural factors may interact to produce deviant as well as normative behavior.

As noted, some biologically oriented investigators have tended to view interindividual differences in adolescent adjustment as due primarily to biologically determined, usually genetic, differences in basic temperament (9, 88, 90). This view is reflected in the work of Ernst Kretschmer (71) in Europe and William H. Sheldon (104) in the United States. These investigators employed theories of "body types" (or "physiques") to explain individual variations in the course of development. The assumption is that basic bodily configurations are biogenetically related to major temperamental characteristics. For example, persons with a thin, fragile ("asthenic") body build were claimed to have a "schizoid," introspective temperament, while those with a soft, round, stocky ("pyknic") build were thought to have a "cycloid" temperament, characterized by mood swings between happiness and sadness.

In Kretschmer's view, adolescence itself was a developmental phase with schizoid characteristics (71). Consequently, a youth with an asthenic body type would already have a tendency toward a schizoid personality and would, therefore, be more likely to experience adolescence as a turbulent period. In contrast, "a child with a stocky body constitution, who is inclined toward cycloid personality characteristics, would not experience adolescence as a very disturbing phase in his development" (9, *74–75*). As yet there is little dependable empirical evidence to support such assertions.

It seems likely that a more fruitful biological approach to development will

involve research into the complex interactive effects of hormones and other influ-ences on physical and psychological development, both prenatally and throughout the life span (98). We need to know much more, for example, about the possible effects of rapidly changing levels of sex hormones on affective (i.e., emotional) states during puberty (98), as well as on sexual and other behaviors (see pages 307–309). There is new evidence, for example, that extensive exercise during pu-berty alters growth patterns among girls (36, 114), demonstrating that experiences affect hormone production. These interactive effects are likely to be important in cognitive and psychosocial development as well (97).

**Cultural and sociological influences** In contrast to such biogenetically oriented approaches to adolescent behavior, other theorists—including cultural an-thropologists and social psychologists and psychiatrists—have emphasized the im-portance of cultural influences (11, 51, 59, 88, 110). Utilizing comparative studies of different preliterate cultures (10, 84, 86, 117, 118), historical approaches to social change (37), and clinical observations of our own society (38, 58), these theorists have demonstrated that human personality and behavior may vary within remark-ably wide limits. And these variations frequently emerge as functions of the social structure of a culture, which include its patterns of child-rearing.

Many differing behavior patterns may be considered psychologically normal and adaptive within the context of particular cultures. Sometimes, however, the social structure of a culture may produce neurotic or destructive personality types. Erich Fromm and Karen Horney, for example, have emphasized the maladaptive consequences of societal and family structures in which love is lacking; in which a sense of community is absent; in which individuals are emotionally isolated, deprived of roots, and treated impersonally; and in which competition is emphasized at the expense of cooperation. Such conditions, they believe, violate man's "essential nature" (37, 58) and are likely to lead to neurotic distortions in relations with the self and others.

Among such possible distortions in our own society, Horney, for example, cites "overdetermined" and exaggerated needs for affection and approval, for dependence, for power, for exploiting others, for personal admiration, for a false kind of defensive independence that leads one to become a "lone wolf," or for restricting "one's life within narrow borders" (58, 59). Long before the advent of the youth revolution of the 1960s, both Horney and Fromm called attention to the internal contradictions inherent in much of contemporary society: the contradiction between rewards for "competition and success on the one hand and brotherly love and humility on the other" (58); the conflict between stimulation of the individual's needs in a marketing society and the frustrations he or she encounters in trying to satisfy them; and the contradiction between our emphasis on "freedom of the individual"—being told that one is free, and that the "great game of life" is open to one—on the one hand and finding that for the majority of people the possibilities actually are quite limited (58).

Perhaps the most immediately relevant (even though one of the earliest) illustrations, for our purposes, of the dependence on cultural influences of personality development and functioning is to be found in Margaret Mead's classic study, *Coming of Age in Samoa* (85). After intensively following the course of development of girls in Samoan society earlier in this century, Mead noted that she had "the proper conditions for an experiment" regarding hypotheses about adolescent storm and stress: "Is adolescence a period of mental and emotional distress for the growing girl as inevitably as teething is a period of misery for the small baby?" (85, *196*). Mead's answer is no:

> The adolescent girl in Samoa differed from her sister who had not reached puberty in one chief respect, that in the older girl certain bodily changes were present which were absent in the younger girl. There were no other great differences to set off the group passing through adolescence from the group which would become adolescent in two years or the group which had become adolescent two years before [85, *196*].

But if storm and stress are likely to be present in the adolescence of many American girls, but not of Samoan girls, what, Mead asked, could account for the differences? The answer, she concluded, lay in the general casualness of Samoan society and its unhurried pace; in a looseness of family and other interpersonal bonds; in the absence of economic, social, or other crises; and, to a considerable extent, in the absence of a necessity for individual choice—vocationally, socially, or morally. Mead notes, for example, that young people in our society are confronted with conflicting standards of sexual morality, and that even those standards that are most widely professed are constantly and visibly violated, often leaving the adolescent anxious and confused. In contrast,

The Samoan child faces no such dilemma. Sex is a natural, pleasurable thing; the freedom with which it may be indulged in is limited by just one consideration, social status. Chiefs' daughters and chiefs' wives should indulge in no extra-marital experiments. Responsible adults, heads of households and mothers of families should have too many important matters on hand to leave them much time for casual amorous adventures. Everyone in the community agrees about the matter; the only dissenters are the missionaries who dissent so vainly that their protests are unimportant [85, *201–202*].

Mead did not find the greater ease of adjustment of the Samoan girls an unmixed blessing, however. She noted the absence of deep feeling and a "low level of appreciation of personality differences" (85, *221*) that Samoan child-rearing produced. But she also did not consider the increasingly common American "tiny, ingrown, biological family opposing its closed circle of affection to a forbidding world" (85, *212*) a satisfactory alternative, either. Such "specialization of affection" did not appear to her worth the price "of many individuals' preserving through life the attitudes of dependent children, of ties between parents and children which successfully defeat the children's attempts to make other adjustments, of necessary choices made unnecessarily poignant because they become issues in an intense emotional relationship" (85, *212*). She noted that the Samoan parent "would reject as unseemly and odious an ethical plea made to a child in terms of personal affection. 'Be good to please mother.' 'Go to church for father's sake.' 'Don't be so disagreeable to your sister, it makes father so unhappy'" (85, *214*).

As we shall see in succeeding chapters, many aspects of development—from the growth of independence and the development of sexual attitudes and behavior to the formation of moral values and cognitive styles—are all dependent, at least in part, on cultural influences. As we shall also see, the question of the relative influence of nature and nurture has not one but many answers, depending on the characteristics under consideration, the individual involved, and his or her biological and cultural heritage.

### *"Genetic" versus situational determinants of adolescent behavior*

Another important theoretical dimension of adolescent personality and behavior is "genetic" (i.e., historical) versus situational determinism, that is, the extent to which an individual's behavior is elicited by his or her biological and experiential past, as opposed to the influence of the particular situation in which he or she is presently functioning. Just as there are few behavioral scientists who would take an exclusively biological or cultural approach to the understanding of adolescent behavior, there are few who would take an exclusively genetic or situational one.

Nevertheless, there are differences among behavioral scientists in the degree to which they look toward the individual's past or to influences in the current situation for an understanding of his or her behavior and personality characteristics. To what extent, for example, is an outburst of violent, destructive behavior by a student on a member of another ethnic group in a racially troubled high school, or by a young gang member in an urban ghetto, a consequence of the kind of person he has become—the personality traits, motives, psychological defenses, and perceptions of the world that he has acquired throughout the course of his development? To what extent are they the result, instead, of influences peculiar to the particular situation in which the individual finds himself or herself?

One observer might look primarily (though probably not exclusively) to a youth's developmental history for experiences that may have predisposed him to violence—hostility toward parents, peers, or a society that have denigrated and abused him—or that have deprived him of love and the opportunity to develop rewarding relationships with others. Another observer might say that although each of us reflects the effects of our unique developmental histories, we all have a capacity for violence toward others; consequently, in the examples cited, all of which involve the operation of special social pressures, we must look primarily to the unique aspects of the individual's current situation for an understanding of his behavior. Such an observer might argue, for example, that a young soldier who has killed children and raped defenseless women in a remote jungle village was perceived as a kind and considerate individual in his own family and community, and therefore the explanation for his violent behavior must be found primarily in social determinants peculiar to his present situation.

Classical psychoanalytic theory emphasized the importance of biological pro- gramming and the enduring effects of early childhood experience. There was *rela- tively* little emphasis on the significance of social and cultural variation. It may thus be viewed as an example of a theoretical system that is primarily *genetic* in orienta- tion. It should be noted, however, that later analytic theorists, such as Erik Erikson and a number of psychoanalytically oriented "ego psychologists"—and even Freud himself to some extent in later years—gave increasing importance to cultural and even to immediate situational determinants of behavior, and to the modifiability of personality in important ways well beyond childhood. Thus, Anna Freud made an important contribution in her stress on the opportunities that adolescence may pro- vide, under favorable conditions, for undoing the effects of prior adverse experience (31, 33). And Erikson, in his discussions of the development of "ego identity" and "identity crisis" in adolescence, emphasizes that the adolescent's chances for estab- lishing a stable identity and *for finding meaning in life* depend on the ethical sound- ness, credibility, and rational consistency of the society and the world of the adolescent, as well as on the psychological assets and liabilities that the young per- son brings to the adolescent experience (26, 27).

Otto Rank (100), though initially an orthodox psychoanalyst in the classical tradition, later broke with Freud and developed his own theoretical constructs. In addition to stressing the creative and productive aspects of human nature over the repressed and neurotic, and placing greater emphasis on the conscious ego as com- pared to unconscious forces, Rank asserted that "the past is of importance only to the degree that it acts in the present to influence behavior" (90, 45–46). In this emphasis, he foreshadowed some of the thinking of the individual who will be dis- cussed next in considering situational determinants of behavior.

In contrast to classical psychoanalytic theory, we may cite as one important example of a theoretical system that led many psychologists to a more thoughtful and sophisticated exploration of situational determinants of behavior the *field theory* of Kurt Lewin (74). This remarkable man, one of the handful of truly innovative psychologists of the twentieth century, came to the United States from Germany, where he had been a student of the early Gestalt school of psychology (87) at the University of Berlin. Undoubtedly he was influenced by this theoretical system (with its assertion, derived largely from studies of perception, that the dynamic unity of the whole is greater than the sum of its parts), but he probably also was moved by his personal observations of the rise of Hitlerism in Europe—observations that revealed how easily, often tragically, human behavior can be swayed by the social climate of the times.

Lewin developed, as a core concept of his theory, the formula "behavior (B) is a function (f) of the person (P) and his environment (E)" (76, *34*). Thus, $B = f(PE)$. In this formula, P and E are viewed as *interdependent* variables. "An unstable psychological environment during adolescence brings about instability in an individual" (78, *89*). Therefore, to understand a child's or adolescent's behavior, one must consider both the individual *and his or her environment* as a constellation of dynamically interacting, interdependent factors. It should be noted that P is an essential part of the formula, and further that Lewin would not have denied that the state of P at any point in time is influenced by a long developmental history—by "genetic" influences.

But his primary emphasis is on searching for an understanding of current behavior in the current "dynamic" interaction between P and E. A change in E therefore will produce a change in P; consequently, a sophisticated understanding of E at a particular point in time is essential to an understanding of B (behavior).

It is impossible, in this short space, to convey adequately the richness of Lewin's work, or of his many additional theoretical constructs, such as that of the "life space"—the sum of all the environmental and personal factors in interaction. The concept of life space—or psychological space—as distinguished from physical or "real" external space enabled Lewin to account theoretically for the growing complexity of the child's psychological development and his or her expanding awareness; for increasing differentiation of reality and fantasy as the child grows older; for an increase in time perspective with age; and for differences between the way an individual views the world and the so-called objective realities of that world (78).

Lewin's concepts, and his personal breadth of vision, curiosity, charm, and infectious enthusiasm, had a wide-ranging effect on the development of social psychology and its movement in the direction of "real-life experiments" in the field—from studies of integrating housing developments successfully, combating race prejudice, improving worker morale, and forming group decisions (87), to the effects of authoritarian, democratic, and laissez-faire leadership upon individual and group behavior in boy's clubs, and even to the beginnings of a system of ecological psychology (78, 79, 90).

Less well known, however, is the extent to which Lewin developed a relatively integrated and specific theory of adolescent development (75, 90). In Lewin's view, many American adolescents know that it is important for them to get somewhere in a hurry, but they know only roughly where, and have an even poorer idea of how to proceed. As he pointed out, they have no real status in our society during this period (75). The adolescent has renounced childhood, but has not yet been fully accepted as an adult. Partly accepted and partly rejected by the privileged group, he has

> . . . a position somewhat similar to what is called in sociology the "marginal" [i.e., underprivileged] man. To some extent behavior symptomatic for the marginal man can be found in the adolescent. He too is oversensitive, easily shifted from one extreme to the other, and particularly sensitive to the shortcomings of his younger fellows. Indeed, his position is sociologically the same as that of the marginal man; he does not wish to belong any longer to a group which is, after all, less privileged than the group of adults; but at the same time he knows that he is not fully accepted by the adult [75, *882–883*].

Lewin's emphasis on the importance of understanding the "dynamic" interaction between the growing person and his or her environment laid the theoretical groundwork for contemporary development in *ecological psychology,* as exemplified by the work of Roger Barker (8), Urie Bronfenbrenner (16), and others (24, 109). Barker and his colleagues, for example, have shown how behavior is influenced by the social setting, such as a school, in which it occurs (see pages 388–392). More broadly, Bronfenbrenner's work "focuses on the progressive accommodation, throughout the life span, between the growing human organism and the changing environments in which it actually lives and grows" (16, *513*)—including both such immediate settings as the home, family, or peer group and the larger social and economic systems of society. Bronfenbrenner is interested, for example, in what urban living, poverty, current welfare policies, or employment procedures do to family life and parent-child relationships, and in whether there are better alternatives.

### Adolescence as a stage of development

Still another important theoretical and empirical question—in addition to the biological-cultural and the genetic-situational—is whether adolescence should be viewed as a *stage* or *critical period* in development. To the extent to which one views development throughout the growth process as steady, continuous, and gradual, with little in the way of rapid change, either quantitatively or qualitatively, a concept of adolescence as a *stage* of development would be likely to appear redundant and misleading. Such a view was well expressed early by Leta Hollingworth (56), who took sharp exception to Hall's views of adolescence as a "period of second birth" (46), involving dramatic storm and stress:

> A child grows by imperceptible degrees into an adolescent, and the adolescent turns by gradual degrees into the adult. . . . [The] widespread myth that every child is a changeling, who at puberty comes forth as a different personality, is doubtless a survival in folklore of the ceremonial rebirth, which constituted the formal initiation of our savage ancestors into manhood and womanhood [56, *16–17*].

To the degree that such a theoretical position emphasizes that there are important continuities in development which might otherwise be ignored, it may perform a useful function. Thus, for example, longitudinal research on personality development (65) has shown that there are some basic psychological characteristics (e.g., passive withdrawal from stressful situations, dependency, involvement in intellectual mastery) which show a remarkable degree of stability and consistency from the early school years through adolescence (although other characteristics reveal discontinuities).

However, although most theorists do not deny the existence of significant continuities, they have been impressed with what they perceive as crucial changes during puberty and the years immediately thereafter. These changes can be viewed quantitatively in terms of an accelerated rate of change, and qualitatively in terms of personality organization and defense mechanisms; the emergence of new needs, motives, capabilities, and concerns; and new developmental tasks that must be confronted. For such theorists, the concept of adolescence as a stage of development is considered useful because it serves to focus attention on the importance of these perceived changes. The *nature* of the postulated stage, however, varies from one theorist to another, depending on what each considers to be the essential aspects of this developmental period.

Thus, for Sigmund Freud, the father of psychoanalysis, and Ernest Jones, a distinguished psychoanalytic pioneer, adolescence was viewed as a stage of development in which, largely as a result of the physiological changes accompanying puberty, the sexual impulses break through to produce the "subordination of all sexual component-instincts under the primacy of the genital zone" (35, *337*). This phase of development, following earlier "oral," "anal," and "phallic" stages, was referred to as the "genital" stage, and involved (among other important matters) a revival of earlier oedipal attachments and rivalries, and the need to resolve them in the direction of greater independence from parents and a shifting of attachments to new "love objects," perhaps through initial same-sex "crushes" and, ultimately, increasingly mature heterosexual involvement (29). "It has been customary to examine the youth's oedipal transition and to seek to understand his adolescent problems largely as recrudescences of the oedipal difficulties. . . . The intense sexual drives of adolescents tend to follow earlier attachments in seeking outlets, and the oedipal configurations must be reworked and once again resolved" (80, *105–106*). Unlike some later psychoanalytically oriented theorists (e.g., Erik Erikson, Erich Fromm, Karen Horney, Harry Stack Sullivan, and to some extent Anna Freud), Freud tended to place less stress on uniquely new, qualitatively different, problems of adolescent adjustment (29, 35).

Erikson (25, 26, 27, 28), while acknowledging his debt to Freud's biologically oriented "genetic" conceptions, has stressed what for him are the relatively unique *psychological tasks* of the adolescent period. Strongly influenced by the findings of cultural anthropology, and by his own humanistic background as artist, writer, and educator of young people, as well as psychoanalyst, Erikson has viewed as the quintessential task of adolescence the establishment of a sense of one's own identity as a unique person ("ego identity"), and the avoidance of role (identity) confusion. Erikson's "eight stages of man" (25, 26) are summarized in Table 1.1. Each stage is viewed as having two possible resolutions, one positive and one negative. Failures at any stage may be expected to affect development adversely at later stages (26).

For Peter Blos—like Erikson, a psychologist and psychoanalyst—the onset of puberty, accompanied by increased sexual drive, disturbs the relative psychological equilibrium of middle childhood, and the resulting "instinctual tensions" lead (most conspicuously in boys) to *regression*—to a reactivation of infantile needs and behavior, such as messiness, bathroom humor, restless activity, impulsiveness, and sudden episodes of childish dependency. For Blos this regression, far from being

**TABLE 1.1 ERIKSON'S EIGHT STAGES OF MAN**

| DEVELOPMENTAL STAGES | BASIC COMPONENTS |
|---|---|
| I. Infancy | Trust vs. mistrust |
| II. Early childhood | Autonomy vs. shame, doubt |
| III. Preschool age | Initiative vs. guilt |
| IV. School age | Industry vs. inferiority |
| V. Adolescence | Identity vs. identity confusion |
| VI. Young adulthood | Intimacy vs. isolation |
| VII. Adulthood | Generativity vs. stagnation |
| VIII. Senescence | Ego integrity vs. despair |

Source: *Childhood and society* by Erik H. Erikson. Copyright 1950, © 1963 by W. W. Norton & Company, Inc. And *Identity: Youth and crisis* by Erik H. Erikson. © 1968 by W. W. Norton & Company, Inc. By permission.

negative in its effects, is not only positive, but necessary: "Adolescent development progresses via the detour of regression" (15, *58*). By "revisiting," as it were, earlier experiences and conflicts (e.g., an unconsciously distorted perception of what parents are like), but now with a more mature ego and greater cognitive ability, the young adolescent has an opportunity to rework and resolve long-standing, but inappropriate and maladaptive, ways of responding that may be impeding his or her continued development. This, then, opens the way to what Blos calls a "second individuation" (the first being the realization in early childhood of the distinction between self and other), an effort to define who and what one is and is not, frequently through such "adolescent" means as opposition to parental dictates, trying out different roles, or developing sudden and transitory loves and hates. The ultimate aim of individuation—which may be accompanied by feelings of isolation, loneliness and confusion, and a painful realization of the finality of the end of childhood—is consonant with Erikson's view, namely the development of a stable sense of identity (14, 15, 26).

Other theorists emphasize other distinctive characteristics or processes of an adolescent stage (or stages). For Gesell, they are "negativism, introversion, and rebellion"; for Lewin, "marginality," ideological instability, extremism, expansion, and increasing differentiation of the "life space"; for Hall, "storm and stress" and a "second birth"; for Anna Freud, "psychological disequilibrium" resulting from sexual maturity and arousal of ego-defense mechanisms (e.g., intellectualism, asceticism); for Otto Rank, a "striving for independence"; for Kretschmer and his followers (71, 104), an increase in "schizoid" characteristics; for Remplein (9, 102), "a second period of negativism, followed by ego experimentation and the formation of a new self-concept."

For Jean Piaget, the distinguished Swiss psychologist whose theory of cognitive development we will examine in detail in Chapter 5, adolescence is characterized by development of the capacity to think abstractly, and to generate alternative hypotheses and test them against the evidence (the stage of "formal operations," replacing the "concrete operations" of middle childhood). For Lawrence Kohlberg, whose stages of moral development (see Chapter 13) have been strongly influenced by Piagetian thinking, adolescence involves reaching what he calls the postconventional stages of moral development, characterized by "a major thrust toward autonomous moral principles which have validity and application apart from authority of the groups or persons who hold them and apart from the individual's identification with those persons or groups" (70, *1066–1067*).

All postulated stages of adolescent development have a certain arbitrary quality about them (64, 65). Although some theorists and their followers tend to view their formulations as having a kind of independent existence, a reality somewhat in the manner of Plato's absolutes, the fact is that each represents only the theorist's judgment (often astute) of what is *most* important about a particular developmental period. Such judgments must by their nature be relative, and they cannot be exclusive.

Interestingly, Eduard Spranger (107, 108), the German philosopher-psychologist whose *Geisteswissenschaftliche* theory of adolescence has had great influence in Europe, took a position compatible both with stage theory and with notions, such as Hollingworth's, of gradual, continuous, harmonious, "imperceptible" development. He distinguishes three patterns of adolescent development (108):

> The first pattern, which corresponds to Hall's idea of adolescent development, is experienced as a form of rebirth in which the individual sees himself as another person when he reaches maturity. This is a period of storm, stress, strain, and crisis, and results in personality change. It has much in common with a religious conversion, also emphasized by Hall.
>
> The second pattern is a slow, continuous growth process and a gradual acquisition of the cultural values and ideas held in the society, without a basic personality change.
>
> The third pattern is a growth process in which the individual himself actively participates. The youth consciously improves and forms himself, overcoming disturbances and crises by his own energetic and goal-directed efforts. This pattern is characterized by self-control and self-discipline, which Spranger relates to a personality type that is striving for power. This system of the three forms of developmental rhythm incorporates older, controversial issues, such as Hall's "erratic form" of adolescent development as well as Hollingworth's "gradual form." It considers them both possible. It allows for various developmental rhythms within a given culture [90, *59*].

It is also important to recognize that some characteristics which may appear at any one time as an inevitable accompaniment of an adolescent stage of development may in fact be reflecting to an important degree the effects of social change. The proverbial man from Mars, asked to bring back a report of what earthly adolescents were like psychologically, would probably have brought back somewhat different reports in 1950, in 1968 (at the height of the youth revolution), and in 1980 (91).

***Critical periods***    Closely allied with stage theory is the concept of *critical periods* in development. This concept, which will be discussed in some detail in the following chapter, involves the notion that certain kinds of psychological or physiological events should occur at a particular stage of development, and that if these events do not occur at the appropriate time, developmental progress will be hindered. Attempts to make up for the deficit at a later (or earlier) period will be either ineffective or not very successful. As we shall see, for example, mounting empirical evidence indicates that the absence of sensory stimulation in infancy may have adverse effects on later cognitive and emotional development (60). Freud was particularly concerned that, following the onset of increased sexual drive at puberty, the adolescent avoid "missing the opposite sex" (34, *95*). "There exists the danger that friendship ties that are too strong will bind boys and girls to their own sex" (90, *40*), with the possibility of developing a predominantly homosexual orientation.

Despite important differences in their orientation and emphasis, most theorists also reveal commonalities:

> The most widely accepted assumption is that childhood, adolescence, and adulthood are three periods which can be recognized psychologically and sociologically, and even physiologically. It is also accepted that there are individual as well as cultural differences in the length of adolescence and in the age at onset and end. The earlier maturing of girls is generally recognized. The physiological changes of pubescence are frequently used to determine the beginning, while sociological criteria, namely adult status, duties, and privileges as well as marriage, end of education, and economic independence are most frequently cited for the end of that period. Termination of adolescence depends primarily on the requirements and conditions of the culture. It occurs earlier in primitive cultures and later in more civilized ones [90, *189*].

### *Normal adolescent turmoil versus psychological disorder*

One of the problems that has long plagued clinicians in their efforts to classify, diagnose, and establish prognostic criteria for psychological disorders in adolescents stems from the fact that adolescence is a period of transition and rapid change. In contrast to more stable periods in the life cycle, such as middle childhood and adulthood, adolescence is characterized, as we shall see, by accelerated physical, physiological, and cognitive development, and by new and changing social demands. As a consequence of these changes, it is asserted, many essentially normal adolescents, in their efforts to deal with them, may display alterations of mood; distressing, turbulent, and unpredictable thoughts; manifestations of anxiety and exaggerated defenses against anxiety; and impulsive, inappropriate or inconsistent behaviors that in an adult would often be considered symptomatic of psychological disorders of varying degrees of severity. This raises two basic questions: (1) Should adolescent turmoil be viewed as a disturbed state? (2) How widespread, in fact, is adolescent turmoil?

**Adolescence as a disturbed state** Although dating back to G. Stanley Hall and his conceptions of adolescent Sturm und Drang, current formulations of adolescence as at least a transiently disturbed, maladjusted state stem primarily from psychoanalytic conceptualizations such as those of Anna Freud and others (30, 31, 33). In the words of one theorist:

> The fluidity of the adolescent's self-image, his changing aims and aspirations, his sex drives, his unstable powers of repression, his struggle to readapt his childhood

standards of right and wrong to the needs of maturity bring into sharp focus every conflict, past and present, that he has failed to solve. The protective coloring of the personality is stripped off, and the deeper emotional currents are laid bare [1, *227–228*].

Similarly, Irene Josselyn (61, 63), a prominent psychoanalyst experienced in the treatment of adolescents, asserts that, although as a result of further development the adolescent has a greater "ego capacity" than he or she had at an earlier age, the magnitude of the developmental tasks that confront the young person are likely to exhaust this newfound resource:

> The behavior of the adolescent is typical of that of individuals, of whatever age, who have not found an adequate integrative pattern with which to reconcile their own impulses, the demands of conscience, and the demands of reality. Adolescence, as is equally true of the neuroses and psychoses, is characterized by the relative failure of the ego. Demands placed upon it have caused a strain it cannot meet [61, *225*].

Despite the apparent severity of this description of adolescence, Josselyn nevertheless emphatically differentiates this state of relative "ego failure" from psychopathology: "The normal adolescent is inevitably a mixed-up person, but not at all in the sense of being a psychologically sick person" (62, *43*). Most adolescents, she maintains, actually have "sufficient inherent personality strengths to emerge from their confusion as relatively healthy adults" (62, *43*).

The equation of adolescent disturbance with normal adolescent development may have interesting semantic implications. Thus, as Irving Weiner (115) notes, a number of analytic theorists have presented the view that adolescent disturbance is sufficiently normal that its *absence* may be more of a source of concern than its presence. One writer (12), for example, suggests that the adolescent "who does not experience a state of flux and uncertainty is likely to suffer premature crystallization of his response patterns that may presage serious psychopathology" (55, *89*).

Anna Freud, daughter of the founder of psychoanalysis, in discussing the normality (and desirability) of "adolescent upheaval," remarks:

> We all know individual children who as late as the ages of 14, 15, or 16 show no such outer evidence of inner unrest. They remain, as they have been during the latency [i.e., middle childhood] period, "good" children, wrapped up in their family relationships, considerate sons of their mothers, submissive to their fathers, in accord with the atmosphere, ideas, and ideals of their childhood background. Convenient as this may be, it signifies a delay of normal development and is, as such, a sign to be taken seriously. The first impression conveyed by these cases may be that of a quantitative deficiency of drive endowment, a suspicion which will usually prove unfounded. . . . These are children who have built up excessive defenses against their drive activities and are now crippled by the results, which act as barriers against a normal maturational process of phase development. They are perhaps, more than any others, in need of therapeutic help to remove the inner restrictions and clear the path for normal development, however "upsetting" the latter may prove to be [32, *14*].

In our view, whether to label *normative* transient adolescent upheavals as a *disturbed state* is an open and, to some extent, semantic, question. To the degree that transient variations in mood, thought, and action do occur in the "normal" course of adolescence, and to the degree that they bear a resemblance to more serious psychiatric symptomatology in adults, it may be valuable to identify these similarities in disturbance, and then to note explicitly the differences in their significance for adolescents as opposed to adults.

On the other hand, there is the inherent danger that, in identifying normative adolescent phenomena as disturbed, we may be tempted to view *nonnormative, nontransient* disturbed manifestations as normal, when, in fact, they may indicate the presence of serious and potentially chronic disturbances requiring prompt attention. Such confusion is not likely to occur in the case of experienced and skilled clinicians like Anna Freud and Irene Josselyn, but others less skilled may be tempted to ignore or dismiss serious signs of psychopathology on the assumption that they represent normal adolescent disturbance and will pass.

This view is supported by the findings of several investigators (82, 83, 103, 115, 116) who followed up samples of adolescents initially diagnosed as "transient situational personality disorder" or "situational adjustment reaction of adolescence." In a significant number of cases (approximately 50 percent in one study), these young people either ended up in psychiatric treatment or showed continued, and in some instances more serious, problems several years later.

**Extent of adolescent turmoil** A more crucial empirical question than the proper labeling of adolescent turmoil, however, is how much adolescent turmoil the average young person actually undergoes. Available data suggest that the storm and stress of adolescence first postulated by Hall may, in fact, be exaggerated. This is not to say that some essentially normal adolescents may not undergo considerable turmoil during this period. In fact, it is the authors' conviction that this is the case. What is questioned is the presumed universality of these phenomena.

Contrary to the assertions of many influential clinicians, a considerable body of data is accumulating to suggest that "the modal teenager is a reasonably well-adjusted individual whose daily functioning is minimally marred by psychological incapacity" (115, *48*). The longitudinal investigation by Daniel Offer and Judith Offer (92, 93, 94) of middle-class Midwestern adolescent boys revealed little evidence of a high degree of "turmoil" or "chaos" in the average boy. Of the sample selected to be in the modal range of psychological functioning, only about one subject in five displayed the extent of adolescent turmoil (anxiety, depression, distrust, extreme mood swings, lack of self-confidence) assumed to be typical by some clinicians and others. "Many were highly sensitive and introspective individuals who took great interest in exploring their inner world" (94, *212–213*). About one-third of these subjects had received some form of therapy or counseling. Separation from their sons tended to be painful for the parents of this group, and many appeared unsure of their own values, and hence unable to confidently present well-defined values to their children.

Most of the remaining subjects fell into one of two groups: a *continuous growth* group and a *surgent growth* group. Members of the continuous growth group (about 25 percent) had strong egos, "were able to cope well with internal and external stimuli, and had mastered previous developmental stages without serious setbacks. They had accepted general cultural and societal norms, and felt comfortable within this context" (94, *212*). Although they had reasonably active fantasy lives, subjects in this group tended to be basically reality and action oriented. "The balance between the intensity of the drives and the ego capacity to tolerate new impulses was good. They had a realistic self-image, a sense of humor, and were relatively happy human beings" (94, *212*).

Parents of these subjects were generally able to tolerate their children's growth and gradual assumption of independence. "Throughout the eight years of the study, there was mutual respect, trust, and affection between the generations" (94, *212*). Members of the surgent group (about 35 percent), although reasonably well adjusted and capable of meeting successfully the developmental demands of adolescence, tended to have somewhat greater difficulty in dealing with unexpected stresses. "There was a tendency to use projection and anger at such times and regression took place before consolidation" (94, *212*). Among parents of this group, there were more likely to be value conflicts between mother and father, and maternal difficulty in separating from children.

Similar conclusions were reached by Roy Grinker and his colleagues in an intensive study of two samples of lower-middle- and middle-class Midwestern males (47, 57). Most reported an absence of serious adolescent turbulence, although there was some increase in conflict with their parents during adolescence. In general, however, "they reported positive, affectionate, and warm relationships with both parents, and experienced continued communication with them. Sociability, general contentment in a setting of striking conventionality were typical" (57, *282*). The general good adjustment, absence of psychopathology, freedom from serious social and work failures that characterized these subjects, whom Grinker labels "homoclites," persisted through a 15-year follow-up period, ending in the middle 1970s (47).

In an extensive study of a representative national sample of 3000 adolescents of both sexes, Elizabeth Douvan and Joseph Adelson concluded that the traditional psychoanalytic view of adolescence as a period in which the adolescent "responds to the instinctual and psychosocial upheaval of puberty by disorder, by failures of ego-synthesis, and by a tendency to abandon earlier values and object attachments" (23, *351*) is based largely on the sensitive, articulate, upper-middle-class adolescent. Indeed, they express some dismay at the relative absence of turmoil in many adolescents—attributing much of it to a "premature identity consolidation, ego and ideological construction, and a general unwillingness to take psychic risks" (23, *351*).

It appears from these and other studies (13, 22, 65) that the stresses adolescence imposes on the individual, particularly in our culture, do not, for the great majority, lead to the high degree of emotional turmoil, violent mood swings, and threatened loss of control suggested by some clinical theorists. All these consequences clearly characterize some adolescents, but the evidence suggests that there has been an unwarranted tendency on the part of some clinicians to generalize too readily to the average adolescent findings obtained from a limited segment of the population. While many adolescents face occasional periods of uncertainty and self-doubt, of loneliness and sadness, of anxiety and concern for the future, they are also likely to experience joy, excitement, curiosity, a sense of adventure, and a feeling of competence in mastering new challenges.

As will become apparent, many of the issues summarized briefly in this chapter are still with us in one form or another. In many instances, however, the recent explosion of research in adolescence has succeeded in reducing the areas of uncertainty, and in better defining still unanswered questions.

### REFERENCES

1. Ackerman, N. W. *The psychodynamics of family life.* New York: Basic Books, 1958.
2. Adelson, J. (ed.). *Handbook of adolescent psychology.* New York: Wiley, 1980.
3. Adelson, J., & Doehrman, M. J. The psychodynamic approach to adolescence. In J. Adelson (ed.), *Handbook of adolescent psychology.* New York: Wiley, 1980. Pp. 99–116.
4. Aries, P. *Centuries of childhood: A social history of family life.* (R. Baldick, trans.) New York: Random House (Vintage Books), 1962.
5. Arieti, S. Schizophrenia: Other aspects, psychotherapy. In S. Arieti, *American handbook of psychiatry* (Vol. I). New York: Basic Books, 1959. Pp. 485–507.
6. Aristotle. Ethica Nicomachea. In R. McKeon (ed.), *The basic works of Aristotle.* (W. D. Ross, trans.) New York: Random House, 1941.
7. Baltes, P. B., Reese, H. W., & Lipsitt, L. P. Life-span developmental psychology. In M. R. Rosenzweig & L. W. Porter (eds.), *Annual Review of Psychiatry* (Vol. 31). Palo Alto, Calif.: Annual Reviews, Inc., 1980. Pp. 65–110.
8. Barker, R. *Ecological psychology.* Stanford, Calif.: Stanford University Press, 1968.
9. Beller, E. K. Theories of adolescent development. In J. F. Adams (ed.), *Understanding adolescence: Current developments in adolescent psychology.* Boston: Allyn & Bacon, 1968.
10. Benedict, R. *Patterns of culture.* Boston: Houghton Mifflin, 1934.
11. Benedict, R. Continuities and discontinuities in cultural conditioning. In W. E. Martin & C. B. Stendler (eds.), *Readings in child development.* New York: Harcourt Brace Jovanovich, 1954. Pp. 142–148.
12. Beres, D. Character formation. In S. Lorand & H. I. Schneer (eds.), *Adolescents: Psychoanalytic approach to problems and therapy.* New York: Harper & Row, 1961. Pp. 1–9.
13. Block, J. *Lives through time.* Berkeley, Calif.: Bancroft Books, 1971.
14. Blos, P. The child analyst looks at the young adolescent. *Daedalus,* Fall 1971, 961–978.
15. Blos, P. *The adolescent passage: Developmental issues.* New York: International Universities Press, 1979.
16. Bronfenbrenner, U. Toward an experimental ecology of human development. *American Psychologist,* 1977, **32,** 513–531.
17. Bunyan, J. A book for boys and girls (London, 1686). Cited in S. R. Smith, *History of Childhood Quarterly: The Journal of Psychohistory,* 1975, **2,** 496.
18. Conger J. J. A world they never knew: The family and social change. *Daedalus,* Fall 1971, 1105–1134.
19. Conger, J. J. Parent-child relationships, social change and adolescent vulnerability. *Journal of Pediatric Psychology,* 1977, **2,** 93–97.
20. Conger, J. J. Freedom and commitment: Families, youth, and social change. *American Psychologist,* 1981, **36,** 1475–1484.
21. Conrad, J. *Youth: A narrative and two other stories.* Edinburgh and London: Blackwood, 1902. Cited in J. Bartlett, *Familiar quotations.* Boston: Little, Brown, 1968 (14th ed.). P. 843.
22. Cox, R. D. *Youth into maturity.* New York: Mental Health Materials Center, 1970.
23. Douvan, E., & Adelson, J. *The adolescent experience.* New York: Wiley, 1966.
24. Elder, G. H., Jr. Adolescence in historical perspective. In J. Adelson (ed.), *Handbook of adolescent psychology.* New York: Wiley, 1980. Pp. 3–46.

25. Erikson, E. H. *Childhood and society.* New York: Norton, 1950.
26. Erikson, E. H. *Identity: Youth and crisis.* New York: Norton, 1968.
27. Erikson, E. H. *Dimensions of a new identity.* New York: Norton, 1974.
28. Evans, R. I. *Dialogue with Erik Erikson.* New York: Harper & Row, 1967.
29. Fenichel, O. *The psychoanalytic theory of neurosis.* New York: Norton, 1945.
30. Freud, A. *The ego and the mechanisms of defense.* (C. Baines, trans.) New York: International Universities Press, 1946.
31. Freud, A. *Adolescence: Psychoanalytic study of the child* (Vol. 13). New York: International Universities Press, 1958.
32. Freud, A. Adolescence. In A. E. Winder & D. L. Angus (eds.), *Adolescence: Contemporary studies.* New York: American Book, 1968. Pp. 13–24.
33. Freud, A. Adolescence as a developmental disturbance. In G. Caplan & S. Lebovici (eds.), *Adolescence: Psychosocial perspectives.* New York: Basic Books, 1969.
34. Freud, S. Three contributions to the sexual theory. *Nervous and Mental Diseases Monographs,* 1925, **7.**
35. Freud, S. *A general introduction to psychoanalysis.* (Joan Riviere, trans.) New York: Permabooks, 1953.
36. Frisch, R. E. Fatness, puberty, and fertility: The effects of nutrition and athletic training on menarche and ovulation. In J. Brooks-Gunn & A. Petersen (eds.), *Girls at puberty: Biological, psychological, and social perspectives.* New York: Plenum, in press.
37. Fromm, E. *Escape from freedom.* New York: Holt, Rinehart and Winston, 1941.
38. Fromm, E. *The sane society.* New York: Holt, Rinehart and Winston, 1955.
39. Fuller, F. Words to give to the young man knowledge and discretion (London, 1685). Cited in P. Aries, *Centuries of childhood: A social history of family life.* New York: Random House (Vintage Books), 1962. P. 498.
40. Gesell, A. *Studies in child development.* New York: Harper & Row, 1948.
41. Gesell, A., & Ilg, F. L. *Infant and child in the culture of today.* New York: Harper & Row, 1943.
42. Gesell, A., Ilg, F. L., & Ames, L. B. *Youth: The years from ten to sixteen.* New York: Harper & Row, 1956.
43. Gillis, J. R. *Youth and history.* New York: Academic Press, 1974.
44. Glueck, S., & Glueck, E. T. *Physique and delinquency.* New York: Harper & Row, 1956.
45. Grinder, R. E. (ed.). *Studies in adolescence: A book of readings in adolescent development.* New York: Macmillian, 1969 (2nd ed.).
46. Grinder, R. E., & Strickland, C. E. G. Stanley Hall and the social significance of adolescence. In R. E. Grinder (ed.), *Studies in adolescence: A book of readings in adolescent development.* New York: Macmillan, 1969 (2nd ed.).
47. Grinker, R. R., & Werble, B. Mentally healthy young men (homoclites): Fourteen years later. *Archives of General Psychiatry,* 1974, **30,** 701–704.
48. Haeckel, E. *Evolution of man* (Vol. 2). London: C. Kegan Paul, 1879.
49. Hall, G. S. *Adolescence: Its psychology and its relations to physiology, anthropology, sociology, sex, crime, religion, and education* (Vol. I). Englewood Cliffs, N.J.: Prentice-Hall, 1904, 1905.
50. Hall, G. S. *Life and confessions of a psychologist.* Englewood Cliffs, N.J.: Prentice-Hall, 1923.
51. Hall, G. S., & Lindzay, G. *Theories of personality.* New York: Wiley, 1970 (2nd ed.).
52. Hall, G. S., & Saunders, F. H. Pity. *American Journal of Psychology,* 1900, **11,** 590–591.
53. Hathaway, S. R., & Monachesi, E. D. *Adolescent personality and behavior.* Minneapolis: University of Minnesota Press, 1963.
54. Heath, D. *Explorations in maturity.* Englewood Cliffs, N.J.: Prentice-Hall, 1965.
55. Hirsch, E. A. *The troubled adolescent as he emerges on psychological tests.* New York: International Universities Press, 1970.
56. Hollingworth, L. S. *The psychology of the adolescent.* Englewood Cliffs, N.J.: Prentice-Hall, 1928.

57. Holzman, P. S., & Grinker, R. R., Sr. Schizophrenia in adolescence. In S. C. Feinstein and P. L. Giovacchini (eds.), *Adolescent psychiatry: Developmental and clinical studies* (Vol. V). New York: Aronson, 1977. Pp. 276–290.

58. Horney, K. *The neurotic personality of our time.* New York: Norton, 1937.

59. Horney, K. *Neurosis and human growth.* New York: Norton, 1950.

60. Hunt, J. McV. Psychological development: Early experience. In M. R. Rosenzweig & L. W. Porter (eds.), *Annual Review of Psychiatry* (Vol. 30). Palo Alto, Calif.: Annual Reviews, Inc., 1979. Pp. 103–144.

61. Josselyn, I. M. The ego in adolescence. *American Journal of Orthopsychiatry,* 1954, **24,** 223–227.

62. Josselyn, I. M. Psychological changes in adolescence. *Children,* 1959, **6,** 43–47.

63. Josselyn, I. M. *Adolescence.* Washington, D.C.: Joint Commission on Mental Health of Children, 1968.

64. Kagan, J. A conception of early adolescence. *Daedalus,* Fall 1971, 997–1012.

65. Kagan, J., & Moss, H. A. *Birth to maturity: The Fels study of psychological development.* New York: Wiley, 1962.

66. Kett, J. F. Adolescence and youth culture in nineteenth-century America. *Journal of Interdisciplinary History.* 1971, **2,** 285–297.

67. Kett, J. F. *Rites of passage.* New York: Basic Books, 1977.

68. Kiell, N. *The universal experience of adolescence.* Boston: Beacon Press, 1967.

69. King, S. H. Coping mechanisms in adolescents. *Psychiatric Annals,* 1971, **1,** 10–46.

70. Kohlberg, L., & Gilligan, C. The adolescent as a philosopher: The discovery of the self in a postconventional world. *Daedalus,* Fall 1971, 1051–1086.

71. Kretschmer, E. *Korperbau und Character.* New York: Springer-Verlag, 1951.

72. Lasch, C. *The culture of narcissism: American life in an age of diminishing expectations.* New York: Norton, 1978.

73. Levinson, D. J., et al. *The seasons of a man's life.* New York: Knopf, 1978.

74. Lewin, K. *A dynamic theory of personality.* New York: McGraw-Hill, 1935.

75. Lewin, K. Field theory and experiment in social psychology: Concepts and methods. *American Journal of Sociology,* 1939, **44,** 868–897.

76. Lewin, K. Studies in topological and vector psychology: I. Formalization and progress in psychology. *University of Iowa Studies in Child Welfare,* 1940, **16,** 9–42.

77. Lewin, K. Behavior and development as a function of the total situation. In L. Carmichael (ed.), *Manual of child psychology.* New York: Wiley, 1946.

78. Lewin, K. *Field theory and social science.* New York: Harper & Row, 1951.

79. Lewin, K., Lippitt, R., & White, R. K. Patterns of aggressive behavior in experimentally created social climates. *Journal of Social Psychology,* 1939, **10,** 271–299.

80. Lidz, T. The adolescent and his family. In G. Caplan & S. Lebovici (eds.), *Adolescence: Psychosocial perspectives.* New York: Basic Books, 1969.

81. Masterson, J. F. *The psychiatric dilemma of adolescence.* Boston: Little, Brown, 1967.

82. Masterson, J. F. The psychiatric significance of adolescent turmoil. *American Journal of Psychiatry,* 1968, **124,** 1549–1554.

83. Masterson, J. F., & Washburne, A. The symptomatic adolescent: Psychiatric illness or adolescent turmoil? *American Journal of Psyychiatry,* 1966, **122,** 1240–1248.

84. Mead, M. *Growing up in New Guinea.* New York: New American Library (Mentor Books), 1953.

85. Mead, M. *Coming of age in Samoa.* New York: Morrow, 1961.

86. Mead, M. *New lives for old: Cultural transformation—Manus, 1928–1953.* New York: New American Library, 1961.

87. Morrow, A. J. *The practical theorist: The life and work of Kurt Lewin.* New York: Basic Books, 1969.

88. Mussen, P. H., Conger, J. J., & Kagan, J. *Child development and personality.* New York: Harper & Row, 1974 (4th ed.).

89. Muus, R. E. The nature, theory, and historical roots of theories of adolescence. In R. E. Muus (ed.), *Adolescent behavior and society: A book of readings.* New York: Random House, 1971.

90. Muus, R. E. *Theories of adolescence.* New York: Random House, 1975 (3rd ed.).
91. Nesselroade, J. R., & Baltes, P. B. Adolescent personality development and historical change: 1970–1972. *Monographs of the Society for Research in Child Development,* 1974, **39,** Serial No. 154.
92. Offer, D. *The psychological world of the teen-ager: A study of normal adolescent boys.* New York: Basic Books, 1969.
93. Offer, D., Marcus, D., & Offer, J. L. A longitudinal study of normal adolescent boys. *American Journal of Psychiatry,* 1970, **126,** 917–924.
94. Offer, D., & Offer, J. Normal adolescent males: The high school and college years. *Journal of the American College Health Association,* 1974, **22,** 209–215.
95. Offer, D., & Offer, J. *From teenage to young manhood.* New York: Basic Books, 1975.
96. Ostow, M. The biological basis of human behavior. In S. Arieti (ed.), *American handbook of psychiatry* (Vol. I). New York: Basic Books, 1959. Pp. 58–87.
97. Petersen, A. C. Pubertal change and cognition. In J. Brooks-Gunn & A. C. Petersen (eds.), *Girls at puberty: Biological, psychological, and social perspectives.* New York: Plenum, in press.
98. Petersen, A. C., & Taylor, B. The biological approach to adolescence. In J. Adelson (ed.), *Handbook of adolescent psychology.* New York: Wiley, 1980.
99. Plato. Laws. (B. Jewett, trans.) *The dialogues of Plato* (Vol. 4). New York: Oxford University Press (Clarendon Press), 1953 (4th ed.).
100. Rank, O. *Will therapy and truth and reality.* New York: Knopf, 1945.
101. Rees, L. Physical characteristics of the schizophrenic patient. In D. Richter (ed.), *Schizophrenia: Somatic aspects.* New York: Macmillan, 1957.
102. Remplein, H. *Die seelische Entwicklung in der Kindheit und Reinfezert.* Munich: Ernst Reinhard, 1956.
103. Rutter, M., Graham, P., Chadwick, O., & Yule, W. Adolescent turmoil: Fact or fiction. *Journal of Child Psychology and Psychiatry,* 1976, **17,** 35–56.
104. Sheldon, W. H. *Varieties of human physique.* New York: Harper & Row, 1940.
105. Smith, S. R. Religion and the conception of youth in seventeenth century England. *History of Childhood Quarterly: The Journal of Psychohistory,* 1975, **2,** 493–516.
106. Spock, B. *Baby and child care.* New York: Pocket Books, 1946.
107. Spranger, E. *Types of men.* Halle-Saale: Max Niemeyer, 1928.
108. Spranger, E. *Psychologic des Jugendalters.* Heidelberg: Queller and Meyer, 1955 (24th ed.).
109. Stokols, D. Environmental psychology. In M. R. Rosenzweig and L. W. Porter (eds.), *Annual Review of Psychology* (Vol. 29). Palo Alto, Calif.: Annual Reviews, Inc., 1978. Pp. 253–296.
110. Sullivan, H. S. *The interpersonal theory of psychiatry.* New York: Norton, 1953.
111. Tanner, J. M. Physical development. In P. H. Mussen (ed.), *Carmichael's manual of child psychology* (Vol. I). New York: Wiley, 1970. Pp. 77–156.
112. The office of Christian parents (Cambridge, 1616). Cited in P. Aries, *Centuries of childhood: A social history of family life.* New York: Random House (Vintage Books), 1962. Pp. 18–22.
113. Thorndike, E. L. *The original nature of man.* New York: Teachers College, Columbia University, 1930.
114. Warren, M. P. Physical and biological aspects of puberty. In J. Brooks-Gunn & A. Petersen (eds.), *Girls at puberty: Biological, psychological, and social perspectives.* New York: Plenum, in press.
115. Weiner, I. B. *Psychological disturbance in adolescence.* New York: Wiley, 1970.
116. Weiner, I., & DelGaudio, A. Psychopathology in adolescence. *Archives of General Psychiatry,* 1976, **33,** 187–193.
117. Whiting, B. B. (ed.). *Six cultures: Studies of child rearing.* New York: Wiley, 1963.
118. Whiting, J. W. M., & Child, I. L. *Child training and personality: A cross-cultural study.* New Haven, Conn.: Yale University Press, 1953.
119. Wolfe, T. The "me" decade and the third great awakening. *New York,* August 23, 1976, pp. 26–40.

Principles of
development:
Person-environment
interaction

CHAPTER 2

# Principles of development I. Person-environment interaction

**A**dolescence is a period of rapid change—physical, physiological, psychological, and social. If we are to begin to understand the nature of these changes and their relations to each other and to prior and subsequent developments in the life of the individual, it is necessary to set forth briefly some basic principles and concepts of development that relate not only to adolescence, but to the entire life span. Unless we do so, we will encounter difficulty in placing the complex and often confusing phenomena of adolescence in meaningful perspective.

If there is one fundamental assumption underlying our conceptions not only of adolescent development, but of development in general, it is that *an individual becomes the kind of person he or she is as a result of continuing and continuous interaction between a growing, changing biological organism and its physical, psychological, and social environment.* Even in the earliest stages of prenatal development, when the future poet, actress, business executive, or scientist is represented by only a few, seemingly simple and identical cells, all the long history of genetic inheritance and maturational potential is already interacting with a nurturant or harmful physical environment. Future development may be affected, for good or ill, by the adequacy or inadequacy of the mother's nutritional status; by the effects of drugs she may take; by diseases she may contract (e.g., rubella, or German measles); even by her emotions, which during pregnancy liberate soothing or irritating chemicals into her own and her unborn baby's bloodstreams (1, 2, 15, 43, 60, 91). Recent lawsuits, for example, have drawn attention to the fact that a significant number of the daughters of women who took the drug stilbestrol (an estrogenic compound) during pregnancy to prevent miscarriages have developed cancer of the vagina during adolescence, as well as other problems (43).

As growth and development proceed, this biological organism becomes increasingly complex as a function both of maturation itself and of prior organism-environment interactions. So, too, does the environment, first within the womb, and later in an ever-expanding world outside it—from initial encounters with the mother and father and a relatively simple world of sight, sound, and touch; to those with family, peers, and community; and, ultimately, to those with a far wider world in which, through satellites and television, he or she may be affected immediately by events occurring on distant continents.

# ANTECEDENT-CONSEQUENT RELATIONSHIPS

Implicit in this view of development is the concept of antecedent-consequent relationships—the idea that the effects of events occurring at any one stage of development depend on and proceed from the developmental events that preceded them
and will, in turn, influence the individual's responses to future events. In this respect,
development may be viewed much like a growing tree, where the possibilities of
present and future growth, flexible and varied though they may be, are still dependent on and, to some extent at least, limited by the nature of the tree and by patterns
of prior growth. Or, as one adolescent patient in psychotherapy recently remarked,
"without a past, there can be no future."

The importance of prior events to present functioning is clearly evident in the
study of adolescents. Under the stresses of seemingly constant change and increased
environmental demands, older regressive patterns of responding (see Chapter 3) are
frequently reawakened, rising like ghosts to haunt the present. The young person
who, during the more placid and stable years of middle childhood, apparently came
to terms with extreme dependency on the mother and learned to function reasonably independently, may have dependency needs—and the anxiety they provoke—
aroused again by the uncertainties and accelerated demands of adolescence. Old
hostilities toward parents or siblings may recur to compound and intensify new ones.

On a broader level, the readiness of the adolescent to cope with the vastly
increased demands of the adolescent period, psychological and social, depends in
great measure on the whole array of intellectual, physical, and social competencies
and the feelings of personal security, confidence, and self-esteem that he or she has
acquired in the years between infancy and the onset of puberty. In turn, the degree of
success with which young people are able to master the tasks of the adolescent
period and to develop a stable, clearly defined sense of their own identity will
strongly affect their future chances for a rewarding, self-fulfilling adult life—whether
as worker, lover, husband, wife, parent, or citizen (see page 74).

In this connection it is important to stress that, although the chances of achieving these goals will be heavily influenced by the young person's inherent resources
and by the facilitating or inhibiting effects of prior experience, he or she is far from
completely bound by them. Despite popular notions that the early years of childhood
are all-important in determining future adjustment, and that, as one worried mother
remarked, "the game is over by the age of 6," the adolescent years present critically
important opportunities for continued growth and development and for the repair of
many of the damaging effects of adverse prior experience.

> Rectifications and reparative changes can be instituted spontaneously at a develop-
> mental phase as advanced as late adolescence. Studies (7) of children who suffered
> extreme deprivation in infancy have indicated that the "distortion of psychic struc-
> ture" which they had experienced was "not immutably fixed." As late as adoles-
> cence reparative processes counteracted, at least partially, early deficits, and
> considerable growth in ego functions took place [13, *190*].

Heinz Hartmann, a pioneer in the application of "ego psychology" to psychoanalysis, makes a similar point: "The potentialities for formation of personality, dur-

ing latency [i.e., middle childhood] and adolescence, has been underrated in psychoanalytic writing" (36). So, too, to a degree, does Anna Freud when she suggests that "adolescence brings about occasionally something in the nature of a spontaneous cure" (29, *15*).

In many respects, what Erik Erikson calls a "psychosocial moratorium"—a period in which the adolescent has an opportunity to develop an identity of his or her own, relatively free of adult responsibilities—may represent for some the last sustained opportunity for significant psychological change and restructuring before the onset of adulthood and entrance into the world of work, marriage, and social and personal responsibility.

## CRITICAL PERIODS IN DEVELOPMENT

This leads us to an additional concept, derived in part from ethology as well as observations of child development, of what may be called sensitive or *critical* periods in development. The essential notion here is that there are specific periods or stages in development during which the organism is particularly prepared for certain crucial psychological or physiological events that can have important effects on future development. If these events do not occur at the appropriate time, development will be hindered and subsequent efforts to make up for the omission will be either ineffective or only partially effective.

Konrad Lorenz, the distinguished animal ethologist, has applied this notion to the "imprinting" phenomenon found in the social behavior of precocial birds (i.e., those capable of independent activity from birth). Lorenz observed the behavior of newly hatched geese, both in the presence of their natural parents and when he presented himself to the young animals "as a parental object before they had any opportunity to associate with their own parents" (38, *25*). The animals that had Lorenz as a parental substitute went on later in life to treat him and other human beings as members of their own species, whereas the animals hatched in the presence of their parents confined their social interactions to their own species. Lorenz concluded that species recognition was "imprinted" (Prägung) on the nervous system of these young during the first period of exposure after hatching (38, *57*).

Under natural conditions imprinting appears to play an adaptive role in the organism's survival. The first object seen is normally the parent. And it is the parent that, during the first days of life, "broods the young, protects it from predators, leads it away from dangerous situations, and takes it to food objects in the environment" (38, *25*).

Although the existence of such critical periods in human development has been clearly shown at a *neurophysiological* level (38, 82, 94), (e.g., the importance of maternal sex hormones in determining sexual differentiation during prenatal life—see Chapter 8), critical *psychological* periods are more difficult to demonstrate unequivocally. However, a number of findings appear consistent with this idea. Recent research suggests that interaction between mothers and their infants very early in life may facilitate communication and mutual emotional attachment (49, 86). Conversely, young children who are neglected or abused appear especially likely to have difficulty in forming intimate and trusting emotional relationships: "They relate indiscriminately, quickly making superficial friendships but ready to discard them at the first sign of rejection" (47, *38*). Studies of children born with disorders that lead parents to mistake their sex are more likely to develop a gender identity based on sex of rearing, rather than their genetic sex; furthermore, it appears that this gender identity becomes relatively fixed early in life (23, 69). Finally, many therapists are aware of the great difficulty encountered in efforts to help young adults to develop adequate same- and opposite-sex peer relationships when the individual, for whatever reason, has been severely deprived of age-appropriate peer experiences in childhood or adolescence.

These examples and others do not establish that specific psychological critical periods exist in human development. But they do at least suggest that certain intellectual and social competencies and emotional response patterns, normally acquired at certain ages, may be much more difficult, and perhaps in some cases impossible, to acquire at earlier or later stages of development. And they suggest that further investigation of the concept of critical periods is amply justified.

## LEARNING: THE PRINCIPLES OF INDIVIDUAL-ENVIRONMENT INTERACTION

The continuing interaction that takes place between the growing, changing individual and his or her environment is not a random one. It is governed by specific principles and conditions commonly referred to as principles, or laws, of learning. Although we still have much to discover about how learning takes place, there is also much we do know. Only those learning principles that are most basic and indispensable for present purposes will be dealt with here; more detailed discussions are available elsewhere (40).

### What is learning?

To the average person, learning means something that he or she does in school or while acquiring a vocational skill (e.g., "learning" to be a mechanic or an airline pilot). As the term is employed by psychologists, however, its connotations are far broader. Stated in its simplest form, *learning is the process by which behavior or the potentiality for behavior is modified as a result of experience.* It represents the establishment of new relationships—bonds or connections—between stimuli and responses that were not previously associated. Let us consider an extremely simple example: Prior to learning, the sight of a red traffic light (stimulus), though it may attract attention, does not produce any organized motor response. After learning, however, the sight of a red light will produce in the experienced driver a virtually automatic, often unconscious, braking response. An association has been *learned* between a visual stimulus (the light) and a motor response (braking).

Contrary to much popular opinion, stimuli and responses may be of many kinds. Thus, stimuli to which responses can be learned are not restricted to such obvious *cues* (a term used to denote distinctive stimuli) as traffic lights, stop signs, or fire alarms. The sight of a mother's face and the sound of her voice (as even casual observation of infants makes clear) are stimuli. And there are also internal stimuli, such as thoughts, images, feelings, and bodily sensations (70).

Responses may be equally varied, obviously including motor acts, such as talking, walking, or driving a car. But as recent experiments indicate, they may also include physiological responses, even those traditionally described as involuntary, such as changes in heart rate, blood pressure, or electrical activity of the brain; release of hormones by endocrine glands; and constriction or dilation of blood vessels (vasoconstrictors). Or they may include thoughts and images. It should be noted that internal responses like thinking and feeling can serve either as cues or responses. This means that any example of ongoing behavior, such as solving a problem or learning a poem, involves a complex, continuous series of cues and responses.

## LEARNING AND INNATE RESPONSES

Not all behavior is learned. Some innate or "preprogrammed" response tendencies, such as the pupillary reflex (contraction of the pupil in response to light), grasping when pressure is applied to the palm, or shuddering in response to a bitter taste, have been observed even in premature infants (70). Erection of the penis in male infants and children may occur reflexively in response to physical or physiological stimulation, or even generalized body tensions (48, 61).

In animals, ethologists have demonstrated that highly specific external stimuli may "release" complex patterns of behavioral response in the absence of any opportunity for prior learning (38). Thus, in the case of the male stickleback, the sight of the red underbelly of another fish will provoke complex fighting behavior. Even dummies that look very little like sticklebacks will provoke the response as long as the essential elements of the key stimulus or stimuli are present (57, 59). In many instances, much of the gentle art of mothering appears to be unlearned. Thus animals ranging from the humble rat to birds will build nests in preparation for their young, even though they may never have witnessed such activities themselves.

Obviously, it is far more difficult to isolate and study possible instances of complex human behavior that may have been innately programmed and not learned, and most of our knowledge comes from experimental work with animals. It appears likely that complex behavior in humans is generally much more dependent on learning and much less dependent on innate response tendencies. However, the possibility exists that at least some types of human behavior previously assumed to be learned may turn out to be at least partially dependent on such innate response tendencies (70). For example, in the course of evolution, primary and secondary sex characteristics may have come to serve, at least to some degree, as key stimuli in attracting members of the opposite sex (97). Other investigators suggest that some of the psychological and physiological responses of females to "babyishness" in appearance (whether in children or animals) may be innately programmed (38).

Anke Ehrhardt and Susan Baker (24) note that "hormonal manipulation during the critical time of differentiation of the CNS [central nervous system] has resulted in some animals in 'masculinizing' or 'feminizing' the type of response to small offspring" (24, *120*). In their own work with humans, they have found that fetally androgenized girls (those exposed abnormally to male hormones during prenatal life) displayed a lack of interest in small infants and in doll play compared to hormonally normal girls. "Although, understandably, social factors influence this kind of behavior to a large degree, our studies suggest that fetal hormones may play a part in the intensity of response in maternal behavior, or some aspects of it" (24, 120).

## TYPES OF LEARNING

### Classical conditioning

Probably the most basic and easily understood category of learning is that of *classical* or *respondent conditioning*. In this form of learning, a reflexive response (i.e., one that is automatically, or innately, elicited by a specific—"unconditioned"—stimulus) becomes associated with a previously neutral stimulus. The response can be an *overt action* (e.g., a child's withdrawal of her hand from a hot stove) or a *physiological reaction* (e.g., a change in heart rate as a consequence of electric shock). But the response must be a naturally occurring reaction to an existing stimulus.

In a pioneering experiment, Pavlov, the great Russian physiologist, demonstrated that a dog can be taught the *response* of salivation to the *stimulus (cue)* of a buzzer by repeated pairing of the sound of a buzzer with the presentation of food (*unconditioned stimulus*). Eventually, the buzzer alone (*conditioned stimulus*) becomes capable of eliciting the salivation response.

Similar conditioning takes place in humans. For example, within a few weeks after birth, the infant's sucking reflex, an innate (unconditioned) response to a nipple in the mouth, is readily conditioned to previously neutral stimuli, such as the sight, smell, and sound of the mother as she prepares to feed the infant. Through association with the unconditioned stimulus of the nipple, these stimuli become capable of eliciting sucking.

### Operant or instrumental conditioning

Obviously, many instances of learning in older children and adolescents are not so simple. A more complex kind of learning that also involves establishment of a new relation between a stimulus and a response is called *operant* or *instrumental conditioning* (89, 90). Here the response to be learned or conditioned is not automatically elicited by a known stimulus but must be gradually and painstakingly developed. A familiar example is teaching a dog to play dead, roll over, or shake hands. In essence, this technique involves rewarding appropriate responses whenever they happen to occur. In this procedure, the subject's own response is *instrumental* to the production of the reward—it *operates* to bring about the reward; hence the term *instrumental* or *operant conditioning*.

In some learning situations, particularly those in which the desired response is a fairly simple one, the experimenter or teacher may simply wait for the response to occur by chance. In other situations, he or she may not rely on chance alone but may take steps to increase the likelihood of the response occurring, either in the interest of time and efficiency or because the response, often a complicated one, is not likely to occur without assistance. (In the case of the dog training cited, the trainer may first physically guide the dog through the desired trick, while giving the proper command, and then promptly reward him, either with praise or with some other reinforcing agent, such as a dog biscuit.) Using such operant "shaping" procedures, animals can often be taught surprisingly complex sequences of learned behaviors (recently, for example, dolphins were gradually taught, by the use of operant conditioning procedures, to deliver equipment in undersea explorations).

**Behavior modification**  Of considerably greater importance, similar techniques are currently being applied to humans as well, under the general rubric of *behavior modification* or *behavior therapy* (8, 32, 46, 84). Gerald Patterson and his associates at the Oregon Social Learning Center have had remarkable success in helping parents learn to deal with excessive aggression in children and adolescents (75, 76, 77). They began by studying families referred to clinics because one or more of their children had displayed very high levels of aggressive, disruptive, unruly behavior, both at home and at school. When these families were compared with a control group of families similar in age, socioeconomic status, and number of children, but whose children were not excessively aggressive, significant differences emerged. Unlike the control group families, the families of highly aggressive children were found to be reinforcing (rewarding) aggressive behavior, albeit unwittingly. For example, members of the aggressive children's families were five times as likely to respond to the child's actions in ways that were aggression maintaining. Thus, a sister who teased her brother after he yelled acted in a way that incurred the probability of the brother's making another hostile response, such as hitting, often setting in motion an escalating exchange.

Parents of the problem children and adolescents tended to be inconsistent in their handling of aggressive responses. At times, they reinforced these actions by approving, paying attention, or complying with the child's wishes; at other times, they would threaten the child with punishment, although they often failed to back up these threats (77). In contrast, the parents of non-problem children tended to be evenhanded and consistent in their use of punishment.

Based on such findings, Patterson and his colleagues concluded that parents can control a child's aggressive behavior if they apply specific techniques, based on learning principles, when interacting with the child. After introducing parents of the problem children to these basic principles, the investigators showed the parents how to identify undesirable aggressive behaviors and to keep accurate records of their occurrence and the conditions surrounding them. Modeling and role-playing procedures were used to demonstrate the application of both positive and negative consequences in shaping the child's behavior. In consultation with professional staff, parents prepared and implemented programs to modify their children's behavior.

The effectiveness of the program was tested systematically over a 12-month period with twenty-seven families with boys between the ages of 5 and 15 who were considered severe cases of aggression. The progam was highly successful. Following treatment, approximately three-fourths of the boys showed major reduction from an initial baseline period in the amount of aggression expressed and in the number of "bursts" of aggressive behaviors. Furthermore, when the program was completed, *all* members of the family showed less aggression and provided fewer of the kinds of stimuli that originally provoked the problem child's aggressive behavior.

Other investigations have reported considerable progress in getting deviant and disruptive adolescents to function adequately in a classroom situation by systematically reinforcing specific relevant responses, such as sitting quietly, responding appropriately to questions, and so on (46, 74). In still other studies, behavior-modification procedures have been employed to overcome social withdrawal and increase social interaction in children, to decrease stammering, to treat enuresis and insomnia, to discourage smoking or drug use, and to increase the incidence of socially appropriate behavior among adolescent delinquents (8, 9, 12, 20, 21, 46, 72, 81, 83, 84).

**Token economies**  Token economy programs represent one of the more recent applications of the operant conditioning approach to modifying behavior in a broad social setting (e.g., a school, a residential treatment center, an institution for delinquents). At the simplest level, "a token economy program involves the setting up of a contingent reinforcement program with three aspects" (52, *636*). First, it is necessary to decide what kinds of behavior are necessary or desirable. Second, there must be a *medium of exchange,* an object (e.g., a poker chip, or slip of paper, even green stamps!). Third, there must be a way of using the tokens to obtain rewards or reinforcements that are meaningful to the individual (52).

The kinds of behaviors selected for reinforcement may be rather simple, as in the case of seriously retarded children and adults who are reinforced for self-grooming, getting to meals, and straightening up their rooms (46, 52, 83, 84). Or they may be complex. Thus, in a number of residential treatment centers for emotionally disturbed adolescents, tokens or chips may be provided for trying to talk over one's angry feelings rather than losing control and attacking another adolescent or staff person; for demonstrating a capacity to take responsibility for one's own behavior (getting chores done, getting to school, avoiding drugs); or for trying to provide support and help to peers (9, 10, 33, 37, 46, 79). The reinforcements may then be increased privileges, such as being able to go outside the institution, alone or with others, for increased periods of time, to go walking, or to a shop or a movie. Some token economy programs have been attacked recently as simply "big brother" efforts to produce conformity and the avoidance of behaviors troublesome to staff members (28, 100). The result, it is asserted, is likely to be increased dependence, rather than the promotion of independence. Certainly, this can be, and unfortunately sometimes has been, the case. But it need not be, and in the better programs is not.

It is essential that the behaviors to be reinforced, and the kinds of reinforcers employed, be ones that will benefit the individual involved and lead to increased growth and the capacity to take increased responsibility for one's own life, with a subsequent *decrease* in rules imposed by others. For this reason, in a complex setting such as a residential treatment center, a token program should be designed to meet the needs of a particular adolescent. Different programs may be employed for different individuals. For example, in one case the program may be designed to help a young person acquire and feel confidence in his or her capacity to establish internal (rather than external) controls over impulsive, self-defeating behavior; in another instance, the goal may be gradually to establish interactions with others, which

though difficult and anxiety-producing at first, are ultimately rewarding and promote increased self-esteem. Often the program is worked out and the goals set jointly by the young person and his or her therapist or counselor. Frequently, too, token programs are simply one part of the total treatment or educational program.

It should also be recognized that in a sense we all live in token economies; many of our daily actions are reinforced positively or negatively by others, whether they be parents, peers, teachers, or employers. In the absence of planning, however, the procedure is likely to be haphazard, and the signals we get confused and sometimes contradictory (83). For example, a teacher who has never heard of operant conditioning or token economies may still operate on the principle that "the best student is a quiet, orderly student" and consistently reinforce such behaviors, whether appropriately or not. He or she may thus conceivably be helping a restless, impulsive student to learn some needed controls, but not be serving the needs of a shy, insecure, withdrawn child or adolescent who needs to learn that a reasonable degree of assertiveness and self-expression may be rewarding rather than anxiety-producing and self-defeating. The use of token economies will be discussed further in subsequent chapters.

**Biofeedback**  The use of operant conditioning techniques is not restricted to behavioral responses, but may include a variety of so-called involuntary physiological responses involving the autonomic nervous system (66, 67, 68, 88, 96).

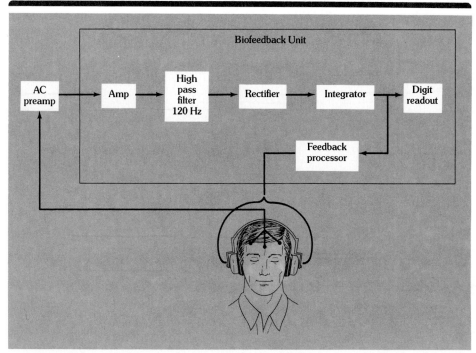

***Figure 2.1*** Schematic diagram of auditory biofeedback from the frontalis (forehead) muscle. (From J. Stoyva. Biofeedback techniques and the conditions for hallucinatory activity. Paper delivered at symposium on the Psychophysiology of Thinking, Hollins College, Virginia, October 17–21, 1971. By permission.)

Operant conditioning techniques have been employed in the treatment of a number of physiological disorders in which psychological factors play a role, such as tension (frontal) headaches, hypertension (high blood pressure), gastric ulcers, and migraines. For example, experimental psychologists at the University of Colorado School of Medicine have shown that it is possible to teach patients to control previously intractable and incapacitating tension headaches by using a biofeedback technique. Although the electronic instrumentation involved is rather complex, the experimental procedure itself is relatively simple. Because tension headache is produced by sustained contraction of the neck and scalp muscles (17, 18, 101), these investigators applied electrodes to the frontalis (forehead) muscle in their subjects, all of whom were chronic tension headache sufferers.

Minute variations in the amount of electrical energy resulting from contraction or relaxation of this muscle (electromyographic activity, or EMG) were translated electronically into variations in auditory stimuli that could be "fed back" to the patient (hence the term *biofeedback* for this kind of research) (see Figure 2.1). When muscle tension was high, the patient heard a high-pitched tone in a set of earphones; when tension decreased, the frequency of the tone also decreased. Patients were simply instructed to keep the pitch of the tone low.

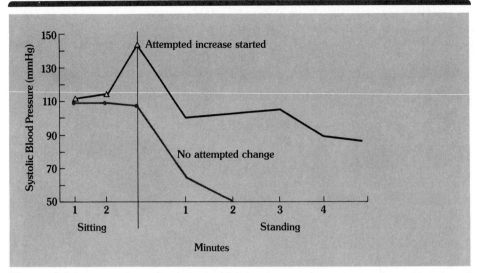

**Figure 2.2** Sitting and standing systolic blood pressure of a patient with severe postural hypotension due to a spinal cord lesion, during conditions of no attempted control of pressure and attempted increase in pressure. (From B. S. Brucker and L. P. Ince. Biofeedback as an experimental treatment for postural hypotension in a patient with spinal cord lesion. In J. Stoyva et al. [eds.], *Biofeedback and self-control.* Chicago: Aldine Publishing Co., 1979. By permission.)

Most subjects were able to learn this task, and when it was supplemented with daily self-induced periods of relaxation (i.e., without biofeedback), most also proved capable of avoiding incapacitating headaches over a follow-up period of several months. In one study, patients receiving such biofeedback training were compared with two control groups of similar patients (one of which received pseudofeedback, the other no treatment). The true biofeedback group showed a steady decline in headache activity over the training period and, of greater importance, over a 12-week follow-up period. In addition, many subjects reported less tension generally in their daily lives, more sensitivity to subtle cues of impending stress, and better sleep patterns. More recent studies have obtained similar findings (78, 95).

Other investigators are making progress in control of blood pressure and cardiac arrhythmias (irregular heartbeats) in a number of abnormal states by feeding back to the subject information on cardiovascular functioning (66, 67, 68, 80, 87). In one such study, patients with spinal cord lesions (who characteristically suffer from hypotension, or low blood pressure) have been taught to increase their blood pressure (16, 68). In some cases, individuals who were previously unable to maintain an erect posture because of a precipitous drop in blood pressure were able to resume fairly normal activities (see Figure 2.2). Currently, other researchers appear to be making progress in reducing seizures and improving brain-wave (EEG) functioning in epileptics by biofeedback training of sensorimotor rhythm (27, 92). Other possible future applications of biofeedback include rehabilitation of physical function following injury, therapy for speech disorders, sexual dysfunctions, and various muscular disorders (20, 56, 66, 68, 88, 96).

## Observational or vicarious learning

Not all learning depends on conditioning. Many human activities, especially complex responses, are acquired by observing the behavior of others (4, 6, 40). Thus, the teacher may interrupt a student's unsuccessful approach to a problem in order to demonstrate the correct response. Adolescents, in particular, are likely to carefully observe the behavior of peers in order to learn which ways of dressing, talking, and acting lead to approval or accomplishment and which to failure. *Social learning theorists,* such as Albert Bandura and his colleagues (4, 5, 6), have stressed the importance of observational learning and the factors that influence the likelihood of an individual's subsequently performing responses acquired through observation.

For example, they have found that subjects are more likely to imitate the behavior of prestigious than nonprestigious models. Models who are similar to the individual himself or herself have a greater effect on behavior than dissimilar models. Thus, an adolescent boy is more likely to imitate the behavior of a male peer whom he views as having similar interests and abilities, and who belongs to the same social clique or group, than he is the behavior of a younger girl with different interests and talents.

Social learning theorists tend to place greater emphasis on the importance of cognitive processes than do learning theorists whose primary interest lies in the nature of basic conditioning. Because humans can think and represent situations symbolically in their minds, they are able to foresee the probable consequences of their actions and alter their behavior accordingly (5). "Anticipated consequences, represented symbolically in one's thoughts, can motivate behavior in much the same way that actual consequences can" (39, *318*). Because they can foresee similar consequences for themselves, children and adolescents are more likely to imitate the behavior of models who are rewarded for their actions than those who are punished or not rewarded.

> Observational learning and learning by conditioning of overt responses, either classically or instrumentally, often supplement each other. One would not permit an adolescent to learn to drive a car or an army recruit to handle firearms solely through trial-and-error procedures. On the other hand, in these, as in many other instances of complex learning requiring novel responses, actual corrective practice combined with reward for correct responses is necessary. For example, simply telling a youth who is learning to shoot a rifle not to blink his eyes when he fires and not to grab the trigger will not be sufficient [70, *34*].

Observational learning is likely to be of less value when it involves responses that are complex and largely new. In contrast, it appears most effective when it involves fairly simple combinations, or responses that have already been acquired, although the new learning situation may require putting these responses together in new or novel sequences or in response to new stimuli. Behavior shaping appears most effective where the response pattern is sufficiently complex or unusual as to constitute, at least in its totality, new and difficult behavior. Optimal learning in many situations requires a skillful combination of the two elements: "It is the introduction of just such skillful combinations that has produced so many remarkable educational advances in recent years, as, for example, in the newer forms of language training used in our schools" (70, *57*).

## BASIC CONDITIONS OF LEARNING

Although learning plays an indispensable role in the overall development of the child and adolescent, it is not inevitable. It does not always occur even under circumstances where we might most expect it. It appears that certain basic conditions must be met if learning is to take place. What do we know about the nature of these conditions?

A few basic points seem obvious. In the first place, unless a stimulus is distinctive enough to be discriminable, it will be difficult, if not impossible, to attach a response to it. (As we have seen, this point is clearly recognized in biofeedback procedures.) Further, even a *distinctive stimulus* (*or cue*) may be of little value unless the subject can be induced to attend to or notice it. Even a bright, capable adolescent girl may have difficulty in her academic work if she is too preoccupied with her own private concerns or worries to pay attention to the task at hand.

It also appears clear that if a particular response is to be attached to a stimulus, the individual must be capable of making that response—either because it is already available and can easily be evoked by presenting some other appropriate stimulus (as in classical conditioning) or because it is developed and perfected in the course of the current learning experience (as in behavior shaping in operant conditioning). It does little good, for example, simply to encourage an adolescent to be more socially assertive or to study more effectively if he or she is unable to perform the relevant responses.

### Internal states

The physiological and psychological state of the individual is also important. Learning does not take place in a vacuum, but in a living, changing organism. Obviously, then, the biological state of a child or adolescent will affect capacity for learning. Earlier theories of learning tended to ignore or minimize the importance of the state of the organism doing the learning (40).

Recent evidence, however, points increasingly to the influence of the individual's biological state on learning ability. There are many factors that affect this state. One that is especially important in the field of child and adolescent development is the individual's degree of physical and physiological maturation. A young child may be incapable of succeeding in a particular learning task (e.g., drawing a square) at one stage of development, even though the stimulus may be distinctive and uncomplicated and the required response relatively simple. A few weeks or months later he or she may learn to make the response relatively easily. Sometimes, of course, increased readiness may be aided by other learning that has taken place in the meantime, but very often it is primarily a function of advances in neurophysiological and physical maturation. Not even a bright, highly motivated 6-year-old who is given the most efficient and advanced training will be able to achieve the capacity for abstract thought and logical reasoning displayed by many adolescents. As Barbel Inhelder and Jean Piaget observed, learning is subordinate to the laws of development, and development follows laws that are both logical and biological (44).

Other biological factors, both stable and transient, may also affect learning. Thus, the individual's capacity for learning may be affected by brain damage, physiological disorders, fatigue, or the effects of drugs, as well as by anxiety, elation, or other emotional states. For example, children with disturbances in neurophysiological functioning resulting from congenital disorders or subsequent disease may be hyperactive and have great difficulty in maintaining sustained attention, thus making learning difficult. Many adolescents have difficulty in performing to the level of their capabilities in academic work because of high levels of anxiety and fears of failure (11). Although mild levels of anxiety may actually aid learning, or at least not interfere with it appreciably, high levels of anxiety can be extremely disruptive and may significantly impair learning ability (85).

In short, it appears clear that learning is a function of the nature of the *stimulus,* the nature of the *response,* and the *state of the learning organism.* What other factors may be important? Two that are often cited by many, though by no means all, theorists are *motivation* and *reinforcement.* The contention of these theorists is that learning is more likely to occur (1) when the organism wants or needs to obtain a certain goal (i.e., when he or she is *motivated*) and (2) when the response he or she makes results in acquisition of the goal (i.e., the response is *rewarded* or *reinforced*).

### The role of reinforcement

You have probably noted that in several of the examples of learning already cited, the subject was provided a reward or reinforcement whenever he or she made the desired (i.e., correct) response to a stimulus (e.g., a dog given a biscuit when he raised his paw to the command to shake hands). The presumption in these instances was "that a reward or *reinforcement,* if given promptly when the subject makes a correct response to a stimulus, strengthens the stimulus-response bond and increases the likelihood that the proper response will again be made the next time the stimulus is presented" (70, *58*).

How important is reinforcement or reward in facilitating learning? Psychologists differ in their answers to this question. Some argue that reinforcement is not a necessary condition for learning at all and that its apparent importance in some cases is really only incidental—in helping to motivate the individual, and in ensuring that the appropriate response will take place in the presence of the stimulus and not under other conditions (40, 99).

In contrast, other psychologists assert that reinforcement is always necessary for learning, and that instances in which conditioning appears to take place without reinforcement are deceptive. In their view, it is not that reinforcement was absent in these cases, but merely that the psychologist was not aware of the reinforcement that was occurring. Although these *reinforcement theorists* (99) often differ among themselves regarding the specific ways reinforcement or reward operates, they agree that some sort of reinforcement is necessary for learning.

Still other psychologists—perhaps a majority—maintain that although reinforcement may not be a necessary concomitant of all learning (e.g., some conditioned responses that involve the autonomic nervous system), it is important for many and perhaps most forms of learning, particularly social learning (40, 70). They note, for example, that a child or adolescent who finally makes the correct response in a complicated learning problem is more likely to repeat it the next time it is presented if he or she is rewarded for it and not for other (incorrect) responses. The

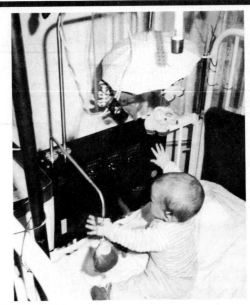

**Figure 2.3** Infant manipulating a control panel to produce varied environmental stimulation. (By permission of J. Meier.)

reward may be a piece of candy, a grade of A, or simply a congratulatory statement such as "very good"—just as long as the "reward" actually is rewarding for the particular child.

Unfortunately, in our present state of knowledge none of these questions regarding the role of reinforcement can be definitively settled. However, it is our view that reward or reinforcement does play an important role in most of the kinds of social learning with which we shall be especially concerned throughout this book.

**The nature of reinforcement** What do we actually mean by reward or reinforcement? An operational definition is relatively easy: A reward is an event that follows a response and increases the likelihood that the response will occur the next time the eliciting stimulus is presented. In a sense, however, such a definition, while admittedly useful, begs the question. It does not tell us ahead of time whether a particular event is likely to promote learning. We have to wait to find out whether this is the case.

Many experiments have been conducted in an effort to arrive at a more independent definition of the nature of reinforcement. Studies of learning under conditions of intense hunger, thirst, and pain indicate that organisms (including humans) do indeed learn to do things that reduce high levels of tension or overstimulation.

In other cases, however, *increases* in stimulation appear reinforcing or rewarding. For example, studies of infants (62) indicate that children under a year old will

learn to manipulate a rather elaborate control panel in their cribs in order to produce varied environmental stimulation, such as increasing illumination level, turning on a movie projector, and playing music (see Figure 2.3).

The fact that both increases and decreases in stimulation (or tension) sometimes appear rewarding has led still other psychologists, such as J. McVicker Hunt of the University of Illinois, to postulate that active, normal biological organisms, including children and adolescents, require a moderate amount of variety in stimulation and that such variety will be reinforcing, although the optimum amount may vary from time to time (42, 53).

It is unlikely that such theoretical arguments concerning the "true" nature of reinforcement will be settled in the near future. Nevertheless, two things are evident: Reward or reinforcement, as operationally defined, can play a significant role in many kinds of learning, and we do not need to wait for any final resolution of theoretical problems regarding the nature of reinforcement to gain much valuable information about the kinds of events likely to serve as rewards in many kinds of learning situations important to the individual's development. Fortunately, much is already known, as we shall see, and much more is being learned by psychologists who are unwilling to wait until all the theoretical issues are solved before getting on with the job of finding out more about what children and adolescents can learn at various ages, and what sorts of conditions facilitate appropriate learning and limit maladaptive learning—including the most effective use of various kinds of rewards (70).

## *MOTIVATION*

The term *motivation* is a general one that refers to the needs, goals, and desires that provoke an individual to action (50). More specifically, there are basic biological needs, commonly called *primary needs,* which require gratification if the individual is to survive. These include the need for food, water, warmth, and oxygen as well as other needs (e.g., sex). A primary need is viewed as an internal state of the organism and not a set of responses. For example, the young child has to *learn* to eat or seek food when he or she is hungry. It is true that nature sometimes helps in this process by providing the child with a response that is appropriate to a certain need. Thus, the response of sucking is typically elicited automatically when a nipple is placed in an infant's mouth. However, he or she learns to suck more efficiently with practice, and with age learns how to drink from a glass and eat from a spoon. In similar fashion, although many components of sexual responses are elicited by appropriate stimulation, nevertheless, complex human sexual response patterns have to be learned.

There are, of course, other sources of motivation besides primary needs. There is nothing innate about the need for social status, for security, for love from one's parents, for money, or for acceptance by one's friends. These needs are learned (70). In common with primary needs, however, *learned needs* (or *motives* as they are usually called) may serve to motivate future learning. Moreover, as with primary needs, the individual has to learn a set of behaviors to gratify the learned needs. One of the common sources of tension and anxiety in human beings is the chronic presence of a learned need—for love, for dominance, for social status—but no means of gratifying it.

Like other learned responses, motives may be learned as a function of the reinforcement of primary (biological) needs. Thus, a young boy may initially develop love for his mother as a result of her meeting his primary needs through such acts as feeding, tactile and kinesthetic stimulation, and the like. Once developed, however, learned needs or motives may play an important role in the acquisition of further complex motives. For example, if a mother gives love to her son only if he is orderly and conscientious, the child may develop needs for orderliness and conscientiousness that will be manifested even when the mother is not around. He may even learn to do many complex acts, such as always putting his toys away carefully, never getting his clothes dirty, washing his hands frequently, and always doing what he is told, in order to satisfy these needs.

One of the important characteristics of needs or motives (both primary and learned) is as an *energizer* of behavior. When an individual is hungry or thirsty, or anxious or in need of nurturance ("tender loving care"), he or she tends to become active and to make a variety of responses, some of which may be reinforced and lead to learning.

### *Primary and learned rewards*

Just as there are primary needs, there are primary rewards. Food, water, sleep, and warmth are called primary rewards because they satisfy basic biological requirements. In addition, however, there is increasing evidence to suggest that certain kinds of *stimulation* are innately rewarding, although they are not directly necessary

for the survival of the organism. Tactile contact in infancy, visual and auditory stimulation from the surrounding environment, and genital stimulation are examples of additional primary rewards (35, 62, 70).

Furthermore, just as there are learned needs or motives (e.g., for love, recognition, power), there are learned rewards. Money has no reward value for a baby, although it certainly has for many adolescents. A *learned reward* is one that has acquired positive value because it gratifies a motive (70). Thus, in the case of the motive for academic achievement, the reward may be the acquisition of a good report card. Similarly, in the case of an adolescent girl's need for social approval, a learned reward may be the admiration of her peers. Obviously, by the time an individual reaches adolescence, a seemingly endless number of objects, persons, and experiences have acquired learned reward value. Learned rewards act as incentives, and any response that leads to the acquisition of a learned reward will be strengthened.

If something is to acquire reward value, it must be associated with an already functioning reward (i.e., primary rewards or previously learned rewards) (40, 63). For a young child, candy may provide strong reinforcement, and money, at least initially, no reinforcement at all. But because the child soon discovers that money can buy candy, it acquires learned reward value. Many things that function as rewards for individuals appear to acquire reward value in this fashion (63, 70).

We have already pointed out that a particular object (or person or experience) cannot function as a reward unless there is a need or motive operating at the moment that will be satisfied by the object. Although we are likely to recognize this principle in the case of primary rewards (e.g., no one thinks of offering food to an individual who needs sleep), we often fail to recognize it in the case of learned rewards. We often assume, for example, that an event is intrinsically rewarding because it is rewarding for many children or adolescents. But because no two individuals have had identical learning experiences in the course of their development, they will not have exactly the same motives. Consequently, they will not always be equally satisfied by the same rewards. For example, although parental approval may serve as a reward for many adolescents, it is not likely to do so in the case of a boy whose need is to convince himself and others that he is tough and independent, and not simply "a good child." Similarly, an adolescent girl whose dominant need is for social recognition by same- or opposite-sex peers is not likely to find this motive satisfied by receiving all A's on her report card. To be rewarding, an event must, as we have said, be able to satisfy, at least to some degree, a need or motive operating at the moment.

## OTHER INFLUENCES ON LEARNING

Thus far we have discussed several types of learning: *classical* or *respondent conditioning, instrumental* or *operant conditioning,* and *observational* or *vicarious learning,* each of which has been illustrated with a number of straightforward examples. We have also discussed the role of four basic factors that appear to be involved in many forms of learning: *stimulus* (or *cue*), *response, motivation,* and *reinforcement* (or *reward*), as well as the influence of the biological and psychological *state of the learning organism.* Several additional principles affecting learning must be considered briefly before we can proceed to an analysis of some of the more complex forms of learned behavior that are important in adolescent development.

### The principle of generalization

Obviously, if an individual could profit from past learning only when he or she encountered *exactly* the same situation again, opportunities for continued development would be severely limited. Fortunately, as we all know, this is not the case. Thus, for example, when a young boy has been trained to avoid a particular hot radiator or stove in his own home, he will also tend to avoid similar, even though not identical, radiators or stoves in other houses (70). But how does this happen? If the cues presented are not identical, why doesn't the child have to learn all over again to make the appropriate response in the new situation? The answer to this question requires an additional learning principle—that of *stimulus generalization.* This principle states that when a response has been learned to one cue or stimulus, it is likely to occur to similar stimuli. The greater the degree of similarity between the original stimulus and that in the new situation, the greater the likelihood that the response will occur, and the stronger it will be (70). This is called the *gradient of generalization.*

Stimulus generalization is not confined to physical stimuli. Once language has been acquired, generalization may also take place in terms of the meaning of words. "Conditioning a response to the meaning of a word (as opposed to the configuration or sound of a word) is called *semantic conditioning*" (39, *196*). In an ingenious experiment by a Russian psychologist (98), children were taught to respond to the word "good" with salivation, much in the manner of Pavlov's dog (in this case, however, the *unconditioned stimulus* was cranberry puree!). Once this conditioned response had been established, the investigator then "tested for generalization by reciting some Russian sentences that could be construed as communicating something 'good' and some that could not" (39, *196–197*). It was found that the children salivated to sentences like "The pioneer helps his comrade" and "Leningrad is a wonderful city," but not to ones like "The pupil was rude to the teacher" and "My friend is seriously ill" (39, *197*).

As will become evident, generalization of previously learned responses may play a crucial role in the young person's adjustment to the developmental demands of adolescence. A girl who has learned to fear a father who throughout the course of her development was harsh and punitive or who continually criticized and ridiculed her will be likely to have difficulty in relating to male peers during adolescence. Her deeply ingrained (i.e., "overlearned") responses to her father will be likely to generalize to her male contemporaries, and lead (consciously or unconsciously) to an anticipation of similar treatment from them—even though these peers may, in fact, be kindly, considerate, and admiring. The fact that she may know, intellectually and rationally, that such responses are inappropriate and unrealistic may be of little help in ameliorating the situation. A boy who has learned to fear a dominating father may later find himself reacting with fear and submissiveness to his male employer, even though the employer may actually wish to encourage initiative and independence.

**Discrimination**  Initially, generalization is likely to be extensive. A young child who has learned to attach the label "dog" to the family pet is apt to extend the label to all four-footed animals he meets, including sheep, cows, and horses. Gradually, however, through a process called *discrimination,* the child will learn to limit this label only to dogs.

Similarly, at a more sophisticated level, the adolescent girl who initially generalizes negative responses to a punitive father to nonpunitive male peers may, under favorable circumstances, learn through discrimination to limit such responses to the father. A primary aim in much psychotherapy is to help undo the effects of inappropriate, self-limiting generalizations based on unfortunate learning experiences earlier in life.

Whereas generalization involves "reaction to similarities, discrimination is reaction to differences" (39, *197*). Discrimination is brought about by the selective reinforcement of responses that have been appropriately generalized and by the elimination, or *extinction,* of incorrectly generalized responses.

**Extinction**  The fact that a response is learned does not mean that it will always remain strong. "If the response is not followed by a reward, the association between the stimulus and response becomes weak, and eventually the stimulus will fail to elicit the response" (70, *63*). Consider the matter of getting a young boy to go to sleep. The child may have found that if he cries after he has gone to bed, his mother will come in, pick him up, and give him additional attention. As a result, he is rewarded for crying, and will likely adopt this response in this situation, rather than go to sleep, even though he may be tired. If, however, the mother stopped respond-ing to the child's cries (except, of course, in real emergencies), the crying response probably would eventually cease—it would have undergone *extinction*. Likewise, an adolescent who is loud and aggressive in her behavior in order to attract attention is more likely to abandon these responses if they are ignored.

### Response heirarchy

Because lack of reward is not the only condition that can result in a decreased likelihood of the occurrence of a response, we are led to the notion of a *response hierarchy*, a term that refers to the fact that in most new situations, an individual is potentially capable of a variety of responses (22). However, not all potential re-sponses are of equal strength; some are stronger than others, and thus have a greater probability of being elicited. "The relative strength of each of these responses determines the response hierarchy" (70, 63). With age, the relative strength of two responses may change—through decreased reinforcement or punishment of one response, through increased reinforcement of the other, or both. To use a simple illustration, a young boy, when hit by a classmate in a fight, may fight back or he may run home to his mother. Initially, perhaps, the second response may be stronger, and thus more likely to occur (after all, Mother has often provided comfort in the past). However, if as the boy grows older, his parents increasingly express disap-proval of this response while rewarding all evidences (however tentative) of standing his ground, the latter response may gradually increase in relative strength and be-come more likely to occur.

The concept of response hierarchy is useful in efforts to understand the appar-ently unpredictable shifts that often occur in early adolescent behavior. The boy who has learned to become a model of neatness during middle childhood may suddenly become sloppy and indifferent. The girl who has been showing increasing poise and apparent self-sufficiency may suddenly revert to childlike dependency. In many instances, what happens is that more mature responses lose some of their reward value, perhaps because such responses lead to expectations for other responses with which the adolescent is not yet prepared to cope (e.g., separation from family sup-port, heterosexual behavior, academic achievement, vocational choice). Conse-quently, earlier learned, more childlike responses once again become *relatively* stronger. As we shall see, a return to older, more primitive forms of responding is called *regression*. Furthermore, early adolescent regressions, rather than being solely negative, may, in fact, serve a valuable restorative or safety-valve function in adolescent development (see page 20).

Although the learning principles just outlined are by no means exhaustive and are, in and of themselves, insufficient to explain some instances of learning—particu-larly some forms of complex verbal learning (31, 39, 41, 55, 93)—they nevertheless help us better understand many of the processes involved in psychological and social development during childhood and adolescence.

### Complexity of adolescent needs and motives

The newborn's repertoire of needs is limited and largely restricted to primary (i.e., basic biological) needs, such as those for food, sleep, physical contact, environmental stimulation, and protection from extremes of heat or cold. In contrast, the adolescent has had many years in which to develop an elaborate set of learned needs or motives—for social approval, friendship, love from parents and others (including opposite-sex peers), independence (or dependence), nurturance of others, achievement, a sense of self-esteem, and a sense of identity. Even the adolescent's biologically based needs are likely to be more numerous and more inextricably intertwined with socially learned motives (e.g., tastes for special foods rather than simply food per se; sexual attraction to a particular kind—physical and psychological—of girl or boy).

It should be emphasized that the individual need not be, and probably never is, fully aware of all his or her motives. Many remain at least partially—and sometimes completely—*unconscious.* For example, the adolescent girl who astounds and shocks both herself and her parents by suddenly "blowing up" at her mother, and who is unable to provide any reason for her behavior (even to herself), may be motivated by unconscious aggressive needs. Many adolescents are puzzled or alarmed by such evidences of unconsciously motivated behaviors. Indeed, some may even be led to wonder if they are "losing their minds" because of what may appear, even to themselves, to be irrational, unmotivated thoughts or acts.

Obviously, motives are most likely to remain unconscious when they involve thoughts or feelings that are inconsistent with the individual's self-concept, or that are unacceptable to his or her conscience (superego). As we shall see in the following section, awareness of such motives would probably lead to painful feelings of anxiety, guilt, or self-blame.

## ANXIETY

Anxiety is of central importance as a determinant of human behavior, for it is most likely to arouse internal responses (thoughts, feelings, psychophysiological reactions) or behaviors that conflict with the satisfaction of other needs or motives. A young child wants to jump off a diving board like her friends, but she is afraid. An adolescent boy would like to ask a girl for a date, but he is fearful of being rebuffed. A college student wants to do well on an examination, but the anxiety aroused by her fear of failure makes her unable to order her thoughts and concentrate on the task at hand.

At a more complex level, a dutiful adolescent son may resent the "unreasonable" demands of parents, but fear retribution or loss of their love if he acknowledges his resentment, even to himself. A father may feel hostile toward, and critical of, his daughter's boyfriends, because he unconsciously views them as rivals for her affection; a mother may have similar feelings toward her daughter-in-law. In each of these instances, life might be easier, the air might be cleared, and psychological tensions reduced if the individual could admit these secret feelings to himself or herself; but even thinking such "unacceptable" thoughts would produce too much anxiety. Therefore, the individual learns to avoid these thoughts and acts because avoidance is rewarding (i.e., it is reinforced by a reduction in the anxiety aroused by the thoughts and behaviors). As we shall see later, this may involve adoption of a variety of techniques, commonly referred to as *defense mechanisms* (see Chapter 3).

Anxiety involves both a subjective or cognitive component and a physiological component. How does anxiety begin? What produces the feelings of acute discomfort, the perspiration, the trembling, the exaggerated startle response, the dryness of the throat and mouth, and other indicators of anxiety? Objectively, as these illustrations demonstrate, the physiological components of anxiety are not learned, but are part of the constitutional makeup of the individual (64). What he or she *learns* is an association between a person, object, or situation, and the combined feelings, images, and physiological reactions that characterize anxiety (63). It is the *arousal* of anxiety that is learned.

Furthermore, because anxiety is a learned response, it follows the same principles of learning (such as extinction and generalization) that apply to other behaviors. For example, if an adolescent has had humiliating experiences with the first few girls that he has attempted to date, and has learned to fear them, he may generalize this reaction to girls in general, even though by any objective appraisal these other girls might be far less likely to humiliate him. At a more profound level, a girl who as a child learned to fear a punitive or seductive father may generalize this response to all males and be unable, even as an adolescent, to relate to boys her own age with pleasure rather than with anxiety.

### Sources of anxiety in adolescents

Although the potential for becoming anxious exists within the physiology (i.e., the constitutional makeup) of the individual, many of the kinds of situations or events to which anxiety may become attached are a function of the individual's learning experiences. It is important to be aware of these differential learning situations, for use of the term *anxiety* alone, without further stipulation of anxiety over what, is not helpful in understanding or predicting behavior.

Many of the sources of potential anxiety in adolescents are similar to, and indeed may represent, carry-overs from, earlier years. Thus, both the adolescent and child may be anxious about potential physical harm; loss of parental love; inability to master the environment or to meet personal, parental, or cultural standards; or about aggressive or sexual impulses. (Of course this anxiety might be relatively realistic or largely unrealistic and subjective.) Guilt, a special form of anxiety that may occur as early as 3 or 4 years of age, is elicited by the anticipation of violating a rule or standard, or following the violation of an internal standard or value. It is characterized by feelings of self-derogation and unworthiness.

Although many sources of adolescent anxiety reveal continuities with the individual's past (often indeed the distant past), differences may also be evident. Some of these may be quantitative differences (a heightening of previous anxieties) and others may be qualitative differences (the source of anxiety may be new or it may have a special quality, even though in some respects it may be similar to earlier sources of anxiety).

Anna Freud (29) and others (13, 14, 36) emphasize that the physiological changes of adolescence and their subjective manifestations bring about a psychological disequilibrium—a disruption of whatever balance may previously have been achieved between the individual's basic needs and impulses (what psychoanalysts

refer to as instinctual drives), and between external and internal demands (i.e., social demands and internal standards or the demands of conscience or superego—see Chapter 13). In this new situation, the ego, that aspect of the self responsible for arbitrating internal conflicts as well as the demands of external reality, may be hard pressed to restore equilibrium and to prevent "decompensation" or disorganization. In Erikson's words, "all previous sameness and continuities" may be lost (25, *261*).

Thus, among the potential sources of adolescent anxiety is a *fear of loss of control* and of a breakdown in the organization of the self. Most adults can recall some time in their adolescence when they experienced such ego anxiety—frequently expressed subjectively as a fear of "going crazy."

This broader source of anxiety may be accompanied by, and related to, more specific anxieties. Although all normal children will have learned a socialized *anxiety about the expression of aggression,* this anxiety is likely to be heightened in adolescence as a consequence of the increase in the strength (and hence the potential danger) of aggressive impulses or feelings following puberty. In fact, an intensive longitudinal study of normal, middle-class adolescent boys indicated that aggressive and angry feelings and problems of controlling or coping with them were most strongly manifested around the ages of 12 and 13, although they extended beyond these ages in somewhat attenuated form.

> We found that a large number of our subjects experienced the affect of anger directly, often without any reason that would satisfy them. The students were rarely overwhelmed by their angry feelings and even more rarely lost control of their im-

pulses, i.e., acted on the basis of their angry feelings alone, even though they were worried about this alternative [73, *101*].

*Anxiety over sexuality* is obviously another prominent source of potential anxiety for adolescents. Sometimes anxiety may be aroused by the sexual impulses themselves (viewed as "evil," "bad," or "dirty" in their own right); sometimes the anxiety may be a function not so much of the impulses themselves, as of the objects toward which they are directed. Thus, the girl who has been "daddy's little darling," and has always had a close and affectionate relationship with him, may become extremely anxious if, as a consequence of her sexual maturation, she finds erotic elements intruding into the relationship. Usually, of course, although by no means always, such unacceptable feelings remain unconscious, although they continue to influence behavior.

Sometimes, too, sexual impulses may arouse anxiety because in their intensity they threaten to overwhelm the sense of self-control, thus posing the danger of ego disorganization or the danger of acting out sexual behavior that violates self-imposed internal standards or conscience (superego).

*Anxiety over dependence-independence* is likely to be intensified at adolescence. As we shall see (Chapter 7), demands (and rewards) for achieving independence are accelerated by society during the adolescent years. Whereas young persons may truly desire these rewards, they may also be anxious about their ability to achieve independence, to "stand on their own two feet" and take responsibility for their actions, including the consequences of ill-considered ventures. Faced by such unaccustomed challenges, the adolescent may seek a regressive return to the security (and limitations) of childhood dependency. But overly intense dependency needs may also provoke anxiety for several reasons. They may preclude the rewards of independence, and may impair the individual's self-image as an increasingly mature person and reduce self-esteem. Furthermore, as conceptualized psychoanalytically (34), the adolescent may need to achieve independence not only for its own sake, but as a way of resolving or overcoming overly intense emotional ties to parents and redirecting emotions to new love objects outside the "hothouse" of the family (34, 54). Thus, continued dependence, though appealing in some respects, poses the danger of being unable to cope with the intense and psychologically unacceptable feelings that may be associated with it.

*Anxiety over rationality*, though not usually conceptualized as such, may represent a significant source of anxiety for the adolescent. In our society it is assumed, despite considerable evidence to the contrary, that the normal person is *rational,* and can give lucid reasons and justifications for his or her motives, moods, and behaviors (70). Thus, any indication of an inability to provide some logical accounting to himself, or herself, or others threatens the self-image of the adolescent or adult and generates anxiety. For the adolescent who oscillates from euphoria to depression, from lethargy to frantic activity, from purposeful determination to paralyzing doubt, or from careful, sometimes almost compulsive, planning to impulsive action, without any clearly ascertainable basis in his or her own mind for such fluctuations, anxiety over rationality can at times be very real.

*Anxiety over acceptance by peers* is, of course, not confined to adolescents.

But with the continued loosening of parental ties and emancipation of the adolescent from the comfort and protection, as well as the restrictions, of the family, acceptance by peers becomes more urgent. This is so not only because the adolescent emotionally is placing more eggs in one basket, but objectively, because of the increased power of the peer group to affect future opportunities, status, and well-being (see Chapter 9).

The heightened societal demands made upon the adolescent for achievement and mastery of varied, often complex, developmental tasks may initiate or intensify *anxiety over competence*. For boys, anxiety over competence has traditionally centered around mastery of objective tasks or skills; for girls, it has tended to involve competence in interpersonal relationships, although sex-related distinctions are currently lessening somewhat.

As we shall see in the following chapter, the rapid physical maturation that takes place in adolescents is likely to precipitate *anxiety over one's body image*, manifested in concerns for the temporary, but often painful, instability of this image, as well as in concerns about real or fancied deficiencies in one's physical self.

Demands for a clearly defined *sexual identity* increase during adolescence. This developmental change has been labeled "gender intensification" (41): Pubertal changes, leading to more differentiated male or female appearance, are accompanied by changes in degree of sex-role orientation as masculine or feminine (45, 50). The individual needs to feel secure in, and comfortable about, his or her status as a male or female. Especially in adolescence, the need for conformity, together with heightened awareness of body image and sex, can create confusion, leading to anxiety over the extent to which one is "male enough," or "female enough." The individual whose prior developmental experiences have failed to foster a secure, stable sexual identity may encounter increased *anxiety over sexual identity* in adolescence.

Probably at no other time in life is concern about developing a meaningful set of values and guiding moral standards more acute than during adolescence. For reasons that will be explored in some detail in Chapter 13, adolescents have what Erik Erikson calls "almost an instinct of fidelity—meaning that when you reach a certain age you can and must learn to be faithful to some ideological view" (26, *30*). Needless to say, in this present era of rapid social change and ideological diversity, adolescent (and adult) *anxiety about values* is widespread.

As will become evident in Chapter 5, the important changes that take place in cognitive development during adolescence—including the capacity to think abstractly, formulate hypotheses and alternatives, compare what might be with what is, and to extend one's time perspective both backward and forward—add to the adolescent's ability to deal with his or her environment and to cope with anxieties. But they also increase the young person's capacity for self-criticism, and for comparison of the self with others and with his or her own emerging ego ideal—the hypothetical best self one might become.

Obviously, these potential sources of special adolescent anxiety are by no means an exhaustive list, and are not intended to be. Other instances will become evident in the course of the book. But these examples should serve to emphasize our initial point in this discussion—namely, that anxiety is an important determinant of adolescent (indeed, human) behavior.

**REFERENCES**

1. Annis, L. F. *The child before birth.* Ithaca, N.Y.: Cornell University Press, 1978.
2. Apgar, V., & Beck, J. *Is my baby all right?* New York: Pocket Books, 1974.
3. Bandura, A. Psychotherapy based upon modeling principles. In A. E. Bergin & S. L. Garfield (eds.), *Handbook of psychotherapy and behavior change: An empirical analysis.* New York: Wiley, 1971. Pp. 653–708.
4. Bandura, A. Self-efficacy: Toward a unifying theory of behavioral change. *Psychological Review,* 1977, **84,** 191–215.
5. Bandura, A. *Social learning theory.* Englewood Cliffs, N.J.: Prentice-Hall, 1977.
6. Bandura, A., & Walters, R. H. *Social learning and personality development.* New York: Holt, Rinehart and Winston, 1963.
7. Beres, D., & Obers, S. J. The effects of extreme deprivation in infancy on psychic structure in adolescence: A study of ego development. *Psychoanalytic Study of the Child,* 1950, **5,** 212–235.
8. Bergin, A. E., & Garfield, S. L. (eds.). *Handbook of psychotherapy and behavior change: An empirical analysis.* New York: Wiley, 1971.
9. Bergin, A. E., & Suinn, R. M. Individual psychotherapy and behavior therapy. In M. R. Rosenzweig & L. W. Porter (eds.), *Annual review of psychology* (Vol. 26). Palo Alto, Calif.: Annual Reviews, Inc., 1975. Pp. 509–556.
10. Berkowitz, I. H. (ed.). *Adolescents grow in groups: Experiences in adolescent group psychotherapy.* New York: Brunner/Mazel, 1972.
11. Birney, R. C., Burdick, H., & Teeran, R. C. *Fear of failure.* New York: Van Nostrand, 1969.
12. Blanchard, E. B., & Johnson, R. A. Generalization of operant classroom control procedures. *Behavior Therapy,* 1973, **4,** 219–229.
13. Blos, P. *On adolescence.* New York: Free Press, 1962.
14. Blos, P. *The adolescent passage: Developmental issues.* New York: International Universities Press, 1979.
15. Brackbill, Y. Longterm effects of obstetric medication. Paper delivered at the biennial meeting of the Society for Research in Child Development, San Francisco, March 15–18, 1979.
16. Brucker, B. S., & Ince, L. P. Biofeedback as an experimental treatment for postural hypotension in a patient with spinal cord lesion. In J. Stoyva, J. Kamiya, T. X. Barber, N. E. Miller, & D. Shapiro (eds.), *Biofeedback and self-control.* Chicago: Aldine, 1979. Pp. 557–561.
17. Budzynski, T., Stoyva, J., & Adler, C. Feedback-induced muscle relaxation: Application to tension headache. *Journal of Behavior Therapy and Experimental Psychiatry,* 1970, **1,** 205–211.
18. Budzynski, T. H., Stoyva, J. M., Adler, C. S., & Mullaney, D. J. EMG biofeedback and tension headache: A controlled outcome study. *Psychosomatic Medicine,* 1973, **35,** 484–496.
19. Budzynski, T. H., Stoyva, J. M., & Peffer, K. E. Biofeedback techniques in psychosomatic disorders. In A. Goldstein & E. B. Foa (eds.), *Handbook of behavioral interventions: A clinical guide.* New York: Wiley, 1980. Pp. 186–205.
20. Burns, D., & Brady, J. P. The treatment of stuttering. In A. Goldstein & E. B. Foa (eds.), *Handbook of behavioral interventions: A clinical guide.* New York: Wiley, 1980. Pp. 673–722.
21. Davidson, W. S., II, & Seidman, E. Studies of behavior modification and juvenile delinquency: A review, methodological critique, and social perspective. *Psychological Bulletin,* 1974, **81,** 998–1011.
22. Dollard, J., & Miller, N. E. *Personality and psychotherapy: An analysis in terms of learning, thinking, and culture.* New York: McGraw-Hill, 1950.
23. Ehrhardt, A. A. Biological differences: A developmental perspective. Master lecture series on psychology. Washington, D.C.: American Psychological Association, 1979.

24. Ehrhardt, A. A., & Baker, S. W. Hormonal aberrations and their implications for the understanding of normal sex differentiation. In P. H. Mussen, J. J. Conger, & J. Kagan (eds.), *Basic and contemporary issues in developmental psychology.* New York: Harper & Row, 1975. Pp. 113–121.

25. Erikson, E. H. *Childhood and society.* New York: Norton, 1950.

26. Evans, R. I. *Dialogue with Erik Erikson.* New York: Harper & Row, 1967.

27. Finley, W. W., Smith, H. A., & Etherton, M. D. Reduction of seizures and normalization of the EEG in a severe epileptic following sensorimotor biofeedback training: A preliminary study. *Biological Psychology,* 1975, **2,** 189–203.

28. Franks, C. M., & Wilson, G. T. (eds.). *Annual review of behavior therapy and practice* (Vol. 3). New York: Brunner/Mazel, 1975.

29. Freud, A. Adolescence as a developmental disturbance. In G. Caplan & S. Lebovici (eds.), *Adolescence: Psychosocial perspectives.* New York: Basic Books, 1969. Pp. 5–10.

30. Freud, S. Three contributions to the sexual theory. *Nervous & Mental Diseases Monographs,* 1925, **7.**

31. Gagne, R. M. *The conditions of learning.* New York: Holt, Rinehart and Winston, 1965.

32. Garfield, S. L., & Bergin, A. E. (eds.). *Handbook of psychotherapy and behavior change: An empirical analysis.* New York: Wiley, 1978.

33. Graziano, A. M. (ed.). *Behavior therapy with children.* Chicago: Aldine, 1975.

34. Group for the Advancement of Psychiatry. *Normal adolescence.* New York: Scribner, 1968.

35. Harlow, H. F., & Suomi, S. J. Nature of love—simplified. *American Psychologist,* 1970, **25,** 161–168.

36. Hartmann, H., Kris, E., & Loewenstein, R. M. Comments on the formation of psychic structure. *Psychoanalytic Study of the Child,* 1946, **2.**

37. Hersen, M., Eisler, R. M., Smith, B., & Agras, W. A token reinforcement reward for young psychiatric patients. *American Journal of Psychiatry,* 1972, **129,** 228–233.

38. Hess, E. H. Ethology and developmental psychology. In P. H. Mussen (ed.), *Carmichael's manual of child psychology* (Vol. I). New York: Wiley, 1970. Pp. 1–38.

39. Hilgard, E. R., Atkinson, R. L., & Atkinson, R. C. *Introduction to psychology.* New York: Harcourt Brace Jovanovich, 1979 (7th ed.).

40. Hilgard, E. R., & Bower, G. H. *Theories of learning.* Englewood Cliffs, N.J.: Prentice-Hall, 1975 (4th ed.).

41. Hill, J. P., & Lynch, M. E. The intensification of gender-related role expectations during early adolescence. In J. Brooks-Gunn & A. C. Petersen (eds.), *Girls at puberty: Biological, psychological, and social perspectives.* New York: Plenum, in press.

42. Hunt, J. McV. Experience in the development of motivation: Some reinterpretations. *Child Development,* 1960, **31,** 489–504.

43. Illingworth, R. S. *The development of the infant and young child: Normal and abnormal.* Edinburgh: Churchill Livingstone, 1975.

44. Inhelder, B., & Sinclair, H. Learning cognitive structures. In P. Mussen, J. Langer, & M. Covington (eds.), *New directions in developmental psychology.* New York: Holt, Rinehart and Winston, 1969.

45. Kavrell, S. M., & Petersen, A. C. Influences on cognition and achievement in early adolescent boys and girls. In M. L. Maehr & M. W. Steinkamp (eds.), *Women in science.* Greenwich, Conn.: JAI Press Inc., in press.

46. Kazdin, A. E. The application of operant techniques in treatment, rehabilitation, and education. In S. L. Garfield & A. E. Bergin (eds.), *Handbook of psychotherapy and behavior change: An empirical analysis.* New York: Wiley, 1978. Pp. 549–590.

47. Kempe, R. S., & Kempe, C. Henry. *Child abuse.* Cambridge, Mass.: Harvard University Press, 1978.

48. Kinsey, A. C., Pomeroy, W. B., & Martin, C. E. *Sexual behavior in the human male.* Philadelphia: Saunders, 1948.

49. Klaus, M. H., & Kennell, J. H. *Maternal-infant bonding.* St. Louis: Mosby, 1976.
50. Koch, S. The logical character of the motivation concept: I. *Psychological Review,* 1941, **48,** 15–38.
51. Koff, E., Rierdan, J., & Silverstone, E. Changes in representation of body image as a function of menarcheal status. *Developmental Psychology,* 1978, **14,** 635–642.
52. Krasner, L. The operant approach in behavior therapy. In A. E. Bergin & S. L. Garfield (eds.), *Handbook of psychotherapy and behavior change: An empirical analysis.* New York: Wiley, 1971. Pp. 612–652.
53. Leuba, C. Toward some integration of learning theories: The concept of optimal stimulation. *Psychological Review,* 1955, **1,** 27–33.
54. Lidz, T. The adolescent and his family. In G. Caplan & S. Lebovici (eds.), *Adolescence: Psychosocial perspectives.* New York: Basic Books, 1969. Pp. 105–112.
55. Lindsay, P. H., & Norman, D. A. *Human information processing.* New York: Academic Press, 1977 (2nd ed.).
56. LoPiccolo, J., & Hogan, D. R. Sexual dysfunction. In O. F. Pomerleau & J. P. Brady (eds.), *Behavioral medicine: Theory and practice.* Baltimore: Williams & Wilkins, 1979. Pp. 177–204.
57. Lorenz, K. Z. *King Solomon's ring.* London: Methuen, 1952.
58. Lorenz, K. Z. *Evolution and modification of behavior.* Chicago: University of Chicago Press, 1965.
59. Lorenz, K. Z. *On aggression.* New York: Harcourt Brace Jovanovich, 1966.
60. Lubchenco, L. O. *The high risk of infants.* Philadelphia: Saunders, 1976.
61. Masters, W. H., & Johnson, V. E. *Human sexual response.* Boston: Little, Brown, 1966.
62. Meier, J., Segner, L., & Grueter, A. An educational system for high-risk infants: A preventive approach to developmental and learning disabilities. In J. Hellmuth (ed.), *Disadvantaged child ( Vol. III). Compensatory education: A national debate.* New York: Brunner/Mazel, 1970. Pp. 405–444.
63. Miller, N. E. Learnable drives and rewards. In S. S. Stevens (ed.), *Handbook of experimental psychology.* New York: Wiley, 1951. Pp. 435–472.
64. Miller, N. E. Laws of learning relevant to its biological bases. *Proceedings of the American Philosophical Association,* 1967, **3,** 315–325.
65. Miller, N. E. Biofeedback and visceral learning. *Annual Review of Psychology,* 1978, **29,** 373–404.
66. Miller, N. E. Fact and fancy about biofeedback and its clinical implications. Master lecture series on psychology. Washington, D.C.: American Psychological Association, 1978.
67. Miller, N. E., & Dworkin, B. R. Critical issues in therapeutic applications of biofeedback. In G. Schwartz & J. Beaty (eds.), *Biofeedback theory research.* New York: Academic Press, 1977.
68. Miller, N. E., & Dworkin, B. R. Effects of learning on visceral functions: Biofeedback. *New England Journal of Medicine,* 1977, **296,** 1274–1278.
69. Money, J., & Ehrhardt, A. A. *Man and woman, boy and girl: The differentiation and dimorphism of gender identity from conception to maturity.* Baltimore: Johns Hopkins University Press, 1972.
70. Mussen, P. H., Conger, J. J., & Kagan, J. *Child development and personality.* New York: Harper & Row, 1979 (5th ed.).
71. Muus, R. E. *Theories of adolescence.* New York: Random House, 1969.
72. O'Connor, R. D. Relative efficacy of modeling, shaping, and the combined procedures for modification of social withdrawal. *Journal of Abnormal Psychology,* 1972, **79,** 327–334.
73. Offer, D. *The psychological world of the teenager: A study of normal adolescence.* New York: Basic Books, 1969.
74. Patterson, G. R. Behavioral intervention procedures in the classroom and in the home. In A. E. Bergin & S. L. Garfield (eds.), *Handbook of psychotherapy and behavior change: An empirical analysis.* New York: Wiley, 1971. Pp. 751–775.

75. Patterson, G. R. Reprogramming the families of aggressive boys. In C. E. Thoresen (ed.), *Behavioral modification in education.* (Yearbook of the National Society for the Study of Education.) Chicago: University of Chicago Press, 1972. Pp. 154–194.
76. Patterson, G. R. A basis for identifying stimuli which control behaviors in natural settings. *Child Development,* 1974, **45,** 900–911.
77. Patterson, G. R. The aggressive child: Victim and architect of a coercive system. In L. A. Hamerlynck, L. C. Handy, & E. J. Mash (eds.), *Behavior modification and families: 1. Theory and research.* New York: Brunner/Mazel, 1976.
78. Phillips, C. The modification of tension headache pain using EMG biofeedback. In J. Stoyva, J. Kamiya, T. X. Barber, N. E. Miller, & D. Shapiro (eds.), *Biofeedback and self control.* Chicago: Aldine, 1979. Pp. 69–79.
79. Phillips, E. L., Phillips, E. A., Wolf, M. M., & Fixsen, D. L. Achievement place: Development of the elected manager system. *Journal of Applied Behavior Analysis,* 1973, **6,** 541–561.
80. Pickering, T. G., & Miller, N. E. Learned voluntary control of heart rate and rhythm in two subjects with premature ventricular contractions. In J. Stoyva, J. Kamiya, T. X. Barber, N. E. Miller, & D. Shapiro (eds.), *Biofeedback and self-control.* Chicago: Aldine, 1979. Pp. 562–569.
81. Pomerleau, O. F., & Brady, J. P. (eds.). *Behavioral medicine: Theory and practice.* Baltimore: Williams & Wilkins, 1979.
82. Riesen, A. H. Sensory deprivation. In *Progress in physiological psychology* (Vol. I). New York: Academic Press, 1966. Pp. 117–147.
83. Risley, T. R., & Baer, D. M. Operant behavior modification: The deliberate development of behavior. In B. M. Caldwell & H. N. Ricciuti (eds.), *Review of child development research ( Vol. III). Child development and social policy.* Chicago: University of Chicago Press, 1973. Pp. 283–329.
84. Ross, A. O. Behavior therapy with children. In S. L. Garfield & A. E. Bergin (eds.), *Handbook of psychotherapy and behavior change: An empirical analysis.* New York: Wiley, 1978. Pp. 591–620.
85. Sarason, I. G. Test anxiety, general anxiety, and intellectual performance. *Journal of Counseling Psychology,* 1957, **21,** 485–490.
86. Schaffer, R. *Mothering.* Cambridge, Mass.: Harvard University Press, 1977.
87. Seer, P. Psychological control of essential hypertension: Review of the literature and methodological critique. *Psychological Bulletin,* 1979, **86,** 1015–1043.
88. Shapiro, D., & Surwit, R. S. Biofeedback. In O. F. Pomerleau & J. P. Brady (eds.), *Behavioral medicine: Theory and practice.* Baltimore: Williams & Wilkins, 1979. Pp. 45–74.
89. Skinner, B. F. *The behavior of organisms.* Englewood Cliffs, N.J.: Prentice-Hall, 1938.
90. Skinner, B. F. *Contingencies of reinforcement.* Englewood Cliffs, N.J.: Prentice-Hall, 1969.
91. Sontag, L. W. The significance of fetal environmental differences. *American Journal of Obstetrics and Gynecology,* 1941, **42,** 996–1003.
92. Sterman, M. B. Effects of sensorimotor EEG feedback training on sleep and clinical manifestations of epilepsy. In J. Stoyva, J. Kamiya, T. X. Barber, N. E. Miller, & D. Shapiro (eds.), *Biofeedback and self-control.* Chicago: Aldine, 1979. Pp. 323–356.
93. Stevenson, H. W. *Children's learning.* Englewood Cliffs, N.J.: Prentice-Hall, 1972.
94. Stone, L. J., Smith, H. T., & Murphy, L. B. *The competent infant: Research and commentary.* New York: Basic Books, 1973.
95. Stoyva, J. M. Musculoskeletal and stress-related disorders. In O. F. Pomerleau & J. P. Brady (eds.), *Behavioral medicine: Theory and practice.* Baltimore: Williams & Wilkins, 1979. Pp. 155–176.
96. Stoyva, J., Kamiya, J., Barber, T. X., Miller, N. E., & Shapiro, D. (eds.). *Biofeedback and self-control.* Chicago: Aldine, 1979.
97. Tanner, J. M. Physical growth. In P. H. Mussen (ed.), *Carmichael's manual of child psychology* (Vol. I). New York: Wiley, 1970. Pp. 77–156.

98. Volkova, V. D. On certain characteristics of conditioned reflexes to speech stimuli in children. *Fiziologicheski Zhurnal* SSSR, 1953, **39,** 540–548.

99. Wilcoxon, H. C. Historical introduction to the problem of reinforcement. In J. C. Tapp (ed.), *Reinforcement and behavior.* New York: Academic Press, 1969.

100. Winett, R. A., & Winkler, R. C. Current behavior modification in the classroom: Be still, be quiet, be docile. *Journal of Applied Behavior Analysis,* 1972, **5,** 499–504.

101. Wolff, H. G. *Headache and other pains.* New York: Oxford University Press, 1963.

102. Ziesat, H. A., Jr., Rosenthal, T. L., & White, G. M. Behavioral self-control in treating procrastination of studying. *Psychological Reports,* 1978, **42,** 59–69.

Principles of
development
II. Identification,
identity, and
mechanisms of
defense

**CHAPTER 3**

# Principles of development II. Identification, identity, and mechanisms of defense

**S**ome years ago, the poet W. H. Auden labeled our era the Age of Anxiety; and recent events have done little to lessen the appropriateness of this description. But though the climate of the times has increased its pervasiveness in our society, anxiety has always been a part of the human condition. Furthermore, as we saw in the previous chapter, anxiety is likely to be heightened during periods of rapid developmental change, such as adolescence, when older, more familiar ways of responding tend to lose their adaptational value, and new, still untried responses must be sought and learned.

## ANXIETY AND THE MECHANISMS OF DEFENSE

Because anxiety represents a painful state of heightened tension that markedly disturbs psychological equilibrium, responses that lead to a reduction in anxiety (i.e., that are reinforcing) tend to be learned. In the course of the individual's development, he or she acquires a variety of such techniques of coping with, or defending against, anxiety. One of the principal contributions of psychoanalytic theory to our knowledge of personality development has been its careful and perceptive elucidation of a variety of these techniques, or *defense mechanisms* (20, 21, 31).

Initially, the conceptualization of many of these defenses came from the study of psychopathology, in an effort to rationalize otherwise inexplicable, seemingly senseless behaviors (e.g., amnesia, phobias, severe obsessions and compulsions, and apparent physical disabilities for which no organic impairment could be found). In many instances it was found that the source of these symptoms lay in unconscious thoughts, feelings, or impulses that the individual could not admit, even to himself or herself, without producing painful increases in anxiety, sometimes even panic. The seemingly senseless symptoms, it was found, often served to protect or defend the individual from such awareness. Thus, for example, a painful episode may not be remembered *precisely because* it was so painful. Frequently, the anxiety also includes guilt, in that it involves impulses, thoughts, or fears that are unacceptable to the individual's conscience or superego—that is, to the internal standards he or she has developed about what is right and wrong, good and wicked. A young combat infantryman may become extremely fearful of getting killed. But to admit such feelings to himself would produce acute anxiety, since "cowardice" would violate his internalized standards of acceptable behavior. Consequently, he may *repress* any awareness of this fear, and solve the dilemma by developing a hysterical paralysis of his leg. This then enables him to continue repressing his unacceptable fear, while still avoiding the original anxiety-producing situation.

As this illustration implies, whereas the basic function of defense mechanisms is to help the individual avoid painful feelings of anxiety without conscious awareness that he or she is doing so, some defense mechanisms possess the additional advantage of allowing gratification of unconscious needs or impulses while permitting the individual to remain unaware of them. In effect, such defense mechanisms are doubly reinforcing. A classic example is that of the bluestocking censor of pornographic literature or films, who is able to reassure herself by virtue of her obvious dedication to suppressing such material that she has no illicit sexual impulses herself. Simultaneously, however, she gains secret satisfaction from reading the suspect books or viewing the films in order to "protect" others.

Although many of the symptoms in psychological disorders reflect the presence of defense mechanisms (or the consequences of their failure, as in the case of acute anxiety when defenses break down), most of these mechanisms also play a role in the development and functioning of "normal" individuals. The kinds of defense mechanisms a particular person is most likely to employ vary, depending on personality structure, specific learning experiences, age, and level of cognitive development. Some defense mechanisms are most easily seen in children, because of their relative lack of sophistication and the immaturity of their egos. Others, as we shall see later in this discussion, depend on the acquisition of a fairly advanced level of intellectual and cognitive functioning, and for that reason are most likely to assume prominence in adolescents.

### *Repression*

*Repression,* which serves as a basis for many other defenses, is apparent at all ages from early childhood on. In repression, anxiety-producing impulses, memories, and the like are kept from conscious awareness. When the individual's associations begin to encroach on such painful areas, anxiety is increased, and associations move off in another, safer direction—with the consequence that anxiety then decreases. In this fashion, repression as a defense tends to be learned and employed, unconsciously, because it is rewarded by a reduction in anxiety (20). Repression may be limited or pervasive, temporary or persistent. Thus, one may experience a transient block in remembering the name of a familiar person whom one dislikes. In contrast, an entire period of childhood may be repressed in order to avoid the discomfort of remembering painful instances of maltreatment or unacceptable desires or behaviors (e.g., sexual or aggressive impulses or encounters) associated with this period.

When repression is used, the individual blots out the anxious or frightening event by removing it completely from awareness. Repression is neither a refusal to remember an event nor a denial of its reality. Rather, the thought or event has been removed from consciousness by forces beyond the individual's control. For example, a girl may repress her memory of a violent argument between her parents, or of resentful thoughts she has felt toward one of them. Although she once was clearly aware of these thoughts, after repression she is unaware of them, and questioning her will not bring them to light.

Repression is one of the reasons that middle-aged adults, including parents, frequently have difficulty in achieving empathy with their adolescent sons and daughters and in appreciating the turbulent emotions and exquisite sensitiveness of many young people during this period:

> For more of the population than we may care to recognize, adulthood, with the settling of impulse and identity problems, brings with it an encapsulation and even retrenchment of the personality. The adult loses both the misery and the advantages that arise from the adolescent's peculiar openness to inner experience; thus, there is little need to examine and share the internal world with others. Adulthood all too often brings with it a retreat into extroversion and, paradoxically, a loss of sensitivity to the other. Aside from those whose work or style of life allows or encourages introspection and insight, the tendency is to abandon the inner resources. To be intimate with another endangers the repression of drives and affects [22, *178*].

## *Denial*

In a closely related, but more primitive defense, *denial,* obvious reality factors are treated by the child or young person as if they did not exist. An amusing, if touching, example might be the little girl who, while sobbing her heart out, keeps insisting, "I am not unhappy!"

In denial, the individual insists that an anxiety-arousing event or situation is not true, and believes it. For example, a boy who has been openly rejected by his mother may deny that she is hostile, and insist that she is a kind and loving person. Some children who have been rejected by their families deny that these people are their parents. They insist that they are adopted and that their true parents love them.

There is a subtle, but important, distinction between denial and repression. In repression, the child has no awareness of the frightening or painful thought (e.g., he or she cannot recall the parents' heated argument); in denial, the anxiety-arousing thought is rejected (e.g., the child actively negates having heard the argument). Because denial is "at once so simple and so supremely efficacious" (31, *85*) in eliminating anxiety and pain, it is used extensively. This is often the case with young children, and, as Anna Freud points out, adults may even foster it:

> It is a curious thing that adults are so ready to make use of this very mechanism in their intercourse with children. Much of the pleasure which they give to children is derived from this kind of denial of reality. It is quite a common thing to tell even a small child "what a big boy" he is and to declare, contrary to the obvious facts, that he is as strong "as father" . . . or as "tough" as his "big brother." It is more natural that, when people want to comfort a child, they resort to these reversals of the real facts. The grown-ups assure him, when he has hurt himself, that he is "better now" or that some food which he loathes "isn't a bit nasty" or, when he is distressed because somebody has gone away, we will tell him that he or she will be "back soon" [31, *90*].

Even in adult life, wish-fulfilling daydreams may still play a part in our defensive apparatus, "sometimes enlarging the boundaries of a too narrow reality and sometimes completely reversing the real situation" (31, *86*). But in normal adolescents and adults, such fantasies are more like games, and are not to be confused with reality. In the case of younger children, the adult who encourages the child's fantasies sets limits on them. For example, a boy who has just been a horse, running about on all fours and neighing, must be prepared at a moment's notice to take his place at the dinner table and be quiet and well behaved (31). In Anna Freud's words,

> It seems that the original importance of the day-dream as a means of defence against objective anxiety is lost when the earliest period of childhood comes to an end. For one thing, we conjecture that the faculty of reality-testing is objectively reinforced, so that it can hold its own in the sphere of affect; we know also that, in later life, the ego's need for synthesis makes it impossible for opposites to coexist; perhaps, too, the attachment of the mature ego to reality is in general stronger than that of the infantile ego, so that, in the nature of the case, phantasy ceases to be so highly prized as in earlier years. At any rate, it is certain that in adult life gratification through phantasy is no longer harmless. As soon as more considerable quantities [of emotional investment] are involved, phantasy and reality become incompatible: it must be one or the other [31, *86–87*].

If persistent use of denial occurs in adult life, the individual's capacity for dealing effectively with reality may be seriously impaired (31).

### Projection and displacement

In projection and displacement, an unacceptable feeling or impulse is acknowledged but attributed to other sources. *Projection* is the ascription of an undesirable thought or action of one's own to another person. The plea, "He started the fight, Mother, not me," is one of the more common examples of projection in young children. At a more serious level, the troubled adolescent who ascribes overwhelming hostility, blatant self-serving, or sexual license to peers or adults when there is no objective evidence to support these claims is likely to be projecting his or her own unacceptable impulses onto these other people. To the extent that the individual employs projection as a defense, "his ability to see the world truly, accurately, is in some degree diminished" (31, *90*). Carried to a *pathological* extreme, projection can result in paranoid, delusional thinking.

In *displacement,* the individual has the appropriate emotional response, but it is not attributed to its true source. A boy's fear of his father, for example, may be too painful for him to acknowledge consciously, but he *is* fearful and needs to account for his condition. As a result, he may attribute the fear to an acceptable symbolic substitute for the father (e.g., lions, robbers lurking in the neighborhood). As we shall see in Chapter 15, displacement plays an important part in *school phobias,* in which unconscious fears, such as fear of separation from parents or fear of some particular aspect of the school situation, are displaced onto the school situation as a whole. In such a situation, simply forcing the child or adolescent to go to school, without exploring and dealing with the real underlying reasons for his or her fears, may result in acute (and eventually chronic) anxiety.

### Rationalization

*Rationalization* is a comforting defense that all of us—children, adolescents, and adults as well—engage in. It involves "providing one's self with socially acceptable reasons for his behavior or attitudes, when the real reason would not be acceptable to one's conscience, and hence, would, if permitted into awareness, lead to painful anxiety and guilt" (70, *349*). The father who harshly punishes his son because of his own intense anger toward him, but who then says he is doing it for the child's own good, is engaging in a rationalization. The adolescent who has become bored with his long-time girlfriend and wants to be free to pursue other girls, but who finds such a motive unacceptable to his conscience and too guilt-inducing to acknowledge, may tell himself—and the girl—that he isn't a good influence on her, that she would be better off without him, or that she needs the experience of dating other boys, while she is still young. Whereas such assertions might or might not be true, the fact is that, for this boy, they do not reflect his actual motivation, and hence he is simply rationalizing. So, too, is the mother who sends her adolescent daughter off to boarding school "to broaden her opportunities and foster her independence," when the real reason is that she can't stand having her at home.

### Reaction formation

*Reaction formation,* as it is labeled by psychoanalysts, has already been illustrated in the case of the censor of pornographic films and books. Similarly, the child or adolescent who is overly preoccupied with being spotlessly clean and tidy may actually be defending himself or herself against strong and unacceptable wishes to be dirty and messy, either literally or symbolically (e.g., sexually). It is as though the child were saying, "I can't have any desire to be messy or dirty, because look how preoccupied I am with being clean." By the same token, the conspicuous adolescent who assiduously pursues being dirty, even to the extent of considerable personal inconvenience, may be engaging in reaction formation; that is, this youth may be trying to say to himself or herself, "I'm not hung-up on my parents' sterile, middle-class notions; being dirty doesn't bother me."

### Withdrawal

*Withdrawal* is a defense that may be used by young children, or by adolescents and adults; it involves the direct avoidance of, or flight from, threatening situations or people. A young boy may hide his eyes or run to his room when a stranger enters the house or refuse to approach a group of strange children, despite his desire to play with them. The adolescent boy who fears being rebuffed by girls or who doubts his ability to gain recognition from male peers may withdraw into a solitary world of his own. Withdrawal may temporarily remove the individual from feared situations, but there is the danger that through reinforcement (i.e., reduced anxiety) the response may become increasingly strong each time it is resorted to. "This defense is, therefore, maladaptive, for the child [or adolescent] who refuses to cope with stressful situations may eventually become fearful of all problems and stresses, and may never learn to handle adequately the crises that are inevitable in the course of development" (70, *349*). This currently appears to be a danger in some, though by no means all, adolescent users of alcohol and drugs.

### Regression

As we have seen in our discussion of response hierarchies in Chapter 2, *regression* involves the adoption—or, more accurately, the readoption—of a response that was characteristic of an earlier phase of development. The schoolage child who resorts to bedwetting or thumbsucking when threatened by the arrival of a new baby and the greater attention it is getting from his or her parents is engaging in regressive behavior. Finding that later, more mature responses are no longer effective in getting the desired amount of the parents' attention, he or she resorts to the earlier, less mature means that were formerly successful. As Anna Freud notes, "regressive tendencies can be shown to occur with regard to all the important achievements of the child" (35, *98*), including social behavior, ways of handling frustration (e.g., temper tantrums), approaches to intellectual tasks, methods of dealing with anxiety, sexual behavior, even responses to the demands of conscience for honesty or fairness in dealing with others (35).

A number of psychoanalysts (10, 33) assert that some of the reemergence of infantile or childish behaviors that may occur in early adolescence is due to regression. Faced on the one hand by the problem of coping with rapid physical and sexual changes and the anxiety that they may create, and on the other hand by greatly increased social demands, including demands for greater independence, the adolescent may temporarily abandon anxiety-producing and not always successful efforts at more mature responding, and retreat to more "primitive" responses that were successful and rewarding in an earlier, simpler period.

Within limits, regression can be adaptive, a fact recognized in the popular saying, "Children take two steps forward and one step backward." In the young child, "nonsense talk or even babbling have a rightful place in the child's life, alongside rational speech and alternating with it. . . . Constructive play with toys alternates with messing, destructiveness, and erotic body play" (35, *99*). In older children, pressures toward social adaptation may be relieved occasionally by reversals to pure self-centeredness.

Periodic regression may also play an important role in the adolescent's efforts to achieve maturity. Indeed, Peter Blos (see pages 20–21) comments, "Adolescent development progresses via the detour of regression" (10, *58*). By revisiting, as it were, "lingering infantile dependencies, anxieties, and needs," but now with a more mature ego and greater cognitive ability, the adolescent has an opportunity to rework long-standing, but inappropriate and maladaptive, ways of responding that may be impeding his or her continued development. Such normative regression Blos calls "regression in the service of development" (10, 11). Not all regression serves such positive functions, however. For the young person who enters adolescence unprepared to meet its demands, use of regression may be purely defensive, leading to "developmental arrest and symptom formation" (11, *484*).

### Asceticism and intellectualization

More than 30 years ago, Anna Freud (31) called attention to two additional defense mechanisms that, in contrast to those of younger children, appeared particularly characteristic of adolescents: *asceticism* and *intellectualization*. Asceticism involves "an attempt to deny entirely the instinctual drives" (41, *25*). An adolescent boy or girl may—perhaps outwardly in the name of religious dedication or self-discipline—seek to avoid any semblance of giving in to sexual desires, tastes in food or drink, sometimes even such basic bodily needs as sleep or protection from cold. Unlike some individuals with specific neurotic problems, who may need to repress specific impulses (e.g., sexual, oral, aggressive), but may be free to express others, the adolescent ascetic appears to have a need to repress all "instinctual" impulses:

> Adolescents are not so much concerned with the gratification or frustration of specific instinctual wishes as with instinctual gratification or frustration as such. Young people who pass through the kind of ascetic phase which I have in mind seem to fear the quantity rather than the quality of their instincts. They mistrust enjoyment in general and so their safest policy appears to be simply to counter more urgent desires with more stringent prohibitions. Every time the instinct says, "I will," the ego retorts, "Thou shalt not," much after the manner of strict parents in the early training of little children [31, *168*].

It is as though the disruptions of psychological equilibrium and previously workable controls that accompany the onset of puberty create conflicts and anxieties that the young person attempts to counteract by making avoidance of all such basic impulses a positive value. Up to a point, in Anna Freud's view, ascetic responses to adolescent anxiety and confusion can be considered normal. However, when carried to extremes, asceticism may go beyond normal limits—as in the case of the adolescent girl who not only gives up "frivolous entertainment," sexual pleasures, or indulgence in favorite foods, but who attempts to deprive herself of sleep, reduces all food to a minimum, constantly tests her capacity to withstand pain or cold, and may even in extreme instances attempt to defer urination or defecation as long as possible "on the grounds that one ought not immediately to give way to all one's physical needs" (31, *169*). This defense appears to serve to control what seems to the adolescent to be an out-of-control outer and, especially, inner world. Such a defense is likely involved in an extreme way with disorders such as anorexia nervosa (see Chapter 15).

Intellectualization may also be employed by some adolescents to deal with troubling anxieties that may be too painful to deal with directly. Thus, apparently impersonal, highly intellectual discussions of the philosophical basis of a single committed sexual relationship versus "open" sexual relationships, of the role of aggression in human affairs, of responsibility versus freedom, of the nature of friendship, of the existence of God—the possibilities are almost limitless—may in fact reflect deep-seated personal concerns. Thus, they may indicate strong concern with how to handle the unfamiliar and insistent stirring of sexual or aggressive feelings; or conflicts between childlike gratification of desires, on the one hand, and an increasingly demanding conscience, on the other. Or they may reflect a concern for acceptance by others, despite doubts of one's own worth; or a feeling of existential abandonment, based on losing the protection and nurturance not only of one's parents, but even of a "Heavenly Father."

None of these statements should be interpreted as implying that the content of the abstract, philosophical, highly intellectualized discussions of some adolescents may not be valuable, or that the motivations involved are necessarily restricted to concerns with highly personal needs, doubts, and conflicts. Discussions of this sort may give the adolescent practice in exercising a newfound capacity for abstract thought and for formulating and testing hypotheses (see Chapter 5), and may at times lead to conclusions that are valid and useful *in their own right.* Furthermore, a significant part of the motivation (and reinforcement) for such discussions may come simply from the pleasure of finding that one is now *able* to engage in higher-level cognitive tasks than was the case during the earlier years of childhood.

Dramatic examples of both asceticism and intellectualization are frequently found in the writings of gifted adolescents (e.g., poems, diaries) and in the behavior of some intelligent, well-educated young people (like many of Anna Freud's own patients). There is, however, increasing reason to believe that the extent to which both of these defenses are employed by contemporary adolescents in general has been exaggerated.

A variety of recent, representative investigations of normal adolescents, both intensive (73) and extensive (22), suggest that the average adolescent appears to make relatively little use of these defenses. Two possible explanations come to mind, for which there appears to be some empirical support. In the first place, the *average* adolescent appears to suffer less from the kind of turmoil that is likely to produce the use of these defenses.

Second, intellectualization and, to a lesser extent, asceticism seem to require the development in adolescence of the kind of higher-level cognitive functioning—the capacity for abstract, hypothetical thinking—that Piaget refers to as "the stage of formal operational thought" (see Chapter 5). And whereas this stage is not likely to be reached much before adolescence, even in highly intelligent children, it is reached—at least in full measure—*after* adolescence by only a minority of young people and adults. Thus, many young people may fail to invoke these defenses not only because they have less need to do so than some others, but also because they are ill-equipped, in terms of the level of their cognitive development, to do so.

When the more typical adolescent is confronted with troubling emotional problems and conflicts, he or she is more likely to ". . . retreat from introspectiveness of any sort. We find more commonly a marked use of character defenses, such as ego restriction, and a heavy reliance on interpersonal conformity" (22, *11*). Despite their social acceptability, these adjustments may represent defensive reactions to the tensions of adolescence (22).

Nevertheless, any of the defenses summarized here *may* be resorted to in adolescence. In fact, as a result of the constant shifting of internal forces and external pressures that characterize adolescence and the disruption of equilibrium that they produce, there is "some reason to believe that a greater variety of defenses is employed in adolescence than in more placid periods of the human career" (22, *9*). Furthermore, flexibility and variety in the use of defenses in response to changing pressures at this stage of development appear to provide greater insurance against the development of longer-term or chronic psychopathology than rigid and inflexible reliance on particular defenses that are, as Anna Freud states, "overused, overstressed, or used in isolation" (33, *23*).

# THE CONCEPT OF IDENTIFICATION

One of the most important, but still incompletely understood, processes in child and adolescent development is that of identification (29, 47, 53, 69). This term, originated by Freud (29, 36, 37), refers to the hypothesized process by which an individual is led to think, feel, and behave as though the characteristics of another person (or "model") belong to that individual (70). Although identification may involve imitation of a model (e.g., a boy who identifies with his father may imitate his father's verbal expressions or copy his habit of reading the sports page of the local newspaper), the two terms are not synonymous. Simple imitation learning may involve nothing more than the emulation of a specific behavior of a model (e.g., operating a lawn mower or baking a cake), which, if it is rewarded (reinforced), may persist.

In contrast, identification is a far more complex process. It involves, to varying degrees, responding as though one *were* the other person. Thus, the young girl who is identified with her mother is likely to feel sad when her mother receives bad news; a young boy identified with his father will respond with the proud and pleasant emotions associated with victory when his father defeats a rival on the tennis court. In simple imitation learning, the individual may acquire a learned imitative response from a model without such extensive emotional involvement. Furthermore, responses based on identification with a model are likely to be more widespread and pervasive and may persist "without any specific training or direct rewards for imitation" (70, *330*). In addition, although simple imitative responses are likely to involve conscious awareness, identification responses frequently occur unconsciously, and have an emotional intensity lacking in simple imitation (15).

## Development of identification

How does identification develop? Following the principles of reinforcement learning theory, Jerome Kagan (53) has hypothesized that for identification to occur, the individual must perceive that the model "possesses or commands goals and satisfactions" that the individual desires. This desire then leads the individual to want (whether consciously or unconsciously) to possess the characteristics of the model because he or she believes that similarity to the model would be likely to enable him or her to achieve these goals. As Kagan notes, this subjective association, or link, between sharing the model's characteristics and gaining access to "the model's desired goal states" is often encouraged by parents and others in a child's social environment. Thus, a child may be told, "You have your father's eyes," and, almost in the next breath, "You'll grow up to be big and strong just like Daddy" (53).

As this example also demonstrates, parents and others may facilitate the child's assumption that he or she does, indeed, possess attributes similar to those of the model. In other instances the child may be able to make the observation; thus, a young boy or girl may note similarities to the same-sex parent in physical appearance, sexual anatomy, dress, interests or skills (53). With each addition in perceived similarity to the model, identification may increase. As Freud remarked,

> Identification . . . may arise with every new perception of a common quality shared with some other person who is not an object of the sexual instinct. The more im-

portant this common quality is, the more successful may this partial identification become, and it may thus represent the beginning of a new tie (37, *65*).

It should be obvious from our discussion of reinforcement and extinction that if an identification is to be maintained, there must be some continuing reinforcement or reward; being like the other person must prove rewarding, even if only vicariously. Otherwise, the identification response "should extinguish just as any other habit does in the absence of positive reinforcement" (53, *303*). Should the model no longer appear to be achieving shared goals or desirable emotional states, or should identification with the model prove otherwise unrewarding, or even frustrating, "then both the motivation for the identification and the intensity of the positive reinforcement should decrease" (53, *303*).

### *Motivations for identification*
Obviously, there may be a wide variety of motivations for wanting to possess characteristics similar to the model (and hence to increase the likelihood of sharing the model's control over goal states). Two of the most prominent appear to be a desire for power and mastery over the environment, and a need for nurturance and affection (53, 70). To a young child, parents appear to control many desirable goal states not readily accessible to the child. Parents can decide what a child (or they themselves) will eat, when to go to bed, whether to attend a movie or the circus, where to go on a vacation. They appear to have the power to acquire money, to buy things, to make others do their bidding (although often the child may exaggerate the actual extent of parental power and control, especially in situations not relating directly to the child).

Another prominent motivation for identification is the need for nurturance and affection. In his initial formulations regarding identification and the so-called oedipus complex, Freud hypothesized that the child was motivated to identify with the same-sex parent in order to receive vicariously the affection of the opposite-sex parent (37). Obviously, however, identifications based on the need for love and affection may, and do, extend to others (e.g., identification with older siblings).

In summary, children may become aware of the discrepancies between their perceptions of their parents' power, privileges, and desirable characteristics and their perceptions of themselves. They begin to behave as though they believe that if they were similar to the parents they would share vicariously in their emotions and possess some of their envied qualities. They may therefore imitate and adopt parental actions in order to increase the similarity between themselves and their parents. This process is aided by others telling the child that he or she is similar to the parent, and by the child's own perception of similarity to that parent. "As the child's identification becomes stronger, he begins to behave as though he does indeed possess some of the model's characteristics. The behaviors that he imitated earlier become automatic and are more firmly entrenched aspects of his character and personality" (70, *397*).

It might be added that the child, particularly the boy, may also be motivated to identify with the same-sex parent because of that parent's perceived power and

*power*
*+ older*

control, even when the power might be directed partially, at least, against the child and even though it might at times provoke fear or anxiety in the child. This phenomenon, referred to by Anna Freud as "identification with the aggressor" (31), has been observed not only among children, but also among adults (e.g., in some concentration camp prisoners who, paradoxically, appeared to identify with their oppressors). In our terms, this identification would result not only from a desire for power and control similar to that of their oppressors, but also from the reduction in anxiety that results from conceiving of one's self as having the oppressor's power. Anna Freud cites an amusing anecdote about a little girl who was afraid of ghosts and suddenly began to make peculiar gestures as she ran. She told her perplexed brother, "there is no need to be afraid, you just have to pretend that you're the ghost that might meet you" (31, *119*).

Finally, it should be emphasized that identification is not an all-or-none phenomenon. A child identifies, to some degree, with both parents, and with adults and peers outside the family as his or her social contacts become wider (70). Furthermore, many of a younger child's identifications may be partial, transient, unrealistic, even contradictory. A younger child's identifications, far more than those of an adolescent or adult, may also have an indulgent, playful quality, because in a relatively structured world characterized by limited choices and responsibility, he or she is far less likely to have to pay the piper for behaviors resulting from identifications.

Furthermore, during the years of rapid physical and social development, the child's identifications are changing as he or she becomes exposed not only to parents, but to an ever wider array of other significant figures—from younger siblings at one end of the age spectrum to grandparents at the other. Increasingly, as the child becomes involved in the wider world outside the family, peers, older young people, teachers, and cultural or countercultural figures (e.g., prominent athletic figures, popular singers, television or movie personalities, some governmental or minority-group leaders) may become, to varying degrees, objects of identification. Under favorable conditions, these successive and interrelated identifications help to provide a child with "some kind of a set of expectations as to what he is going to be when he grows older, and very small children identify with a number of people in a number of respects and establish a kind of hierarchy of expectations which then seeks 'verification' in life" (27, *159*). As Erikson comments, "The fate of childhood *identifications,* in turn, depends on the child's satisfactory interactions with trustworthy representatives of a meaningful hierarchy of roles as provided by the generations living together in some form of family" (27, *159*).

As we shall see in the next section, patterns of childhood identifications, though essential as core ingredients, are not, in and of themselves, capable of providing the adolescent with a coherent, reasonably stable and consistent image of the self—a sense of identity.

## IDENTITY

An essential problem of adolescence, and one under which many other adolescent problems can be subsumed, is that of finding a workable answer to the question, "Who am I?" Although this problem has preoccupied humankind for many centu-

ries, only in recent decades has it become the focus of systematic psychological concern—principally through the writings of Erik Erikson (25, 26, 27). Perhaps it is no coincidence that Erikson came to psychoanalysis with a broad background in art, literature, and education.

In an effort to maintain links with, but also to expand, traditional psychoanalytic theory, Erikson employed the concept of what he has called "ego identity" (25, 26, 27). The term is somewhat lacking in precision, a situation that Erikson himself recognizes, and indeed intends—preferring, as he says, to let "the term identity speak for itself in a number of connotations." Erikson would rather have the concept remain elusive than to have it lose some of its richness and integrating capacity by overly rigid and explicit definition. Nevertheless, its main outlines emerge rather clearly.

The adolescent or adult with a strong sense of ego identity sees himself or herself as a separate, distinctive individual. Indeed, the very word *individual,* as a synonym for *person*, implies a universal need to perceive oneself as somehow separate from others, no matter how much one may share motives, values, and interests with others. Closely related is the need for self-consistency—for a feeling of wholeness (26). When we speak of the *integrity* of the self, we imply both a separateness from others and unity of the self—a workable integration of one's needs, motives, and patterns of responding. In order to have a clear sense of ego identity, the adolescent or adult also requires a sense of continuity of the self over time. In Erikson's words, "The younger person, in order to experience wholeness, must feel a progressive continuity between that which he has come to be during the long years of childhood and that which he promises to become in the anticipated future" (26, *91*).

Finally, for Erikson, the individual needs to have a sense of *psychosocial reciprocity* (26)—a consistency "between that which he conceives himself to be and that which he perceives others to see in him and expect of him" (26, *91*). Erikson's assertion that one's sense of identity is tied, at least partly, to social reality is important; it emphasizes the fact that societal or individual rejection can seriously impair a child's or adolescent's chances of establishing a strong, secure sense of personal identity—an all-too-frequent occurrence.

Any developmental influences that contribute to confident perceptions of oneself as separate and distinct from others, as reasonably consistent and integrated, as having a continuity over time, and as similar to the way one is perceived by others, also contribute to an overall sense of ego identity. By the same token, influences that may impair any of these self-perceptions foster what Erikson initially referred to as "identity diffusion," but which he now prefers to call "identity confusion—a failure to achieve the integration and continuity of self-images" (27, *212*).

### Identity problems of adolescence

As we have already noted in our discussion of Erikson's postulated "eight stages of man," he considers the problem of identity versus identity diffusion—or confusion—as particularly characteristic of, and central to, adolescence. It is not surprising that the search for identity should become particularly acute at this stage of development, when rapid change and the challenges it presents to a feeling of self-consistency are the order of the day.

The change that occurs during the middle childhood years is for the most part gradual and regular, without abrupt shifts from day to day, or month to month. However, as we shall see in the following chapter on physical and physiological development, "in puberty and adolescence all sameness and continuities relied on earlier are more or less questioned again, because of a rapidity of body growth which equals that of early childhood and because of the new addition of genital maturity" (25, *261*). The very rapidity of these changes—both quantitative and qualitative—increases the difficulty of achieving and maintaining a perception of the self as clearly defined and consistent, both internally and over time.

Furthermore, a well-defined sense of identity is at least partially dependent on the capacity to conceptualize oneself in abstract terms, at times almost like a spectator—"to take one's own thought as object and reason about it." But, as we shall see in Chapter 5, it is only with the onset during adolescence of what Jean Piaget calls the "formal operations" stage of cognitive development that thinking becomes sophisticated enough for the young person to be fully capable of such a high level of abstract thinking. In addition, it is with the onset of the stage of formal operations that the adolescent becomes truly capable of "scientific" reasoning—of systematically generating all logically possible hypotheses applicable to a given situation and testing these hypotheses against the available evidence. Once the younger child has thought of one possible solution to a problem, he or she is likely immediately to adopt it as fact. In contrast, the adolescent can consider not merely one possible answer to a problem, one possible course of action, or one explanation of a situation, but many possible alternatives. This newfound capability aids the adolescent's search for an individual identity but at the same time increases its difficulty. As Erikson recently observed, "such cognitive orientation forms not a contrast but a complement to the need of the young person to develop a sense of identity, for, from among all possible and imaginable relations, he must make a series of ever-narrowing selections of personal, occupational, sexual, and ideological commitments" (27, *245*).

In short, at a time when young people are confronted with very rapid physical, physiological, and cognitive changes within themselves, they must also consider how they are going to deal with the varied intellectual, social, and vocational demands of adulthood that lie directly ahead. It is hardly surprising, then, that the search for an individual identity should be particularly prominent during adolescence, and that the young person at this stage of development should be vitally concerned with the question of how to connect the roles and skills cultivated earlier with the demands of tomorrow. Nor is it surprising that

> in their search for a new sense of continuity and sameness, adolescents have to refight many of the battles of earlier years, even though to do so they must artificially appoint perfectly well-meaning people to play the roles of adversaries; and they are ever ready to install lasting idols and ideals as guardians of a final identity [25, *261*].

### Identity formation

Whereas the problem of identity is likely to be most critical during adolescence, it does not begin then. Nor, despite frequent misinterpretations to the contrary, does Erikson imply that this is the case. In discussing his eight-stage theory of development, he explicitly states that: (1) "each item of the vital personality to be discussed is systematically related to all others, and . . . they all depend on the proper development in the proper sequence of each item; and (2) each item exists in some form before 'its' decisive and critical time normally arrives" (27, *93–95*).

Thus, in Erikson's view, the beginnings of the child's ultimate identity are already being shaped during the earlier periods of life, starting with the infant's initial orientations of basic trust or mistrust of the people and world around him. Nor is the individual's sense of identity, or even its overall strength, necessarily cast in final form in adolescence or early adulthood. As Helen Lynd has observed, "Some men and women as they grow older become less differentiated from more and more replicas of, or masks formed by, their society. Advancing years means to them more need of the protection of being like others, less of the risk involved in the search for their own way of life" (59, *228–229*). In contrast, others become genuinely individual and more deeply self-assured in relation to the world (59). This was clearly true of such people as Eleanor Roosevelt and Albert Einstein, but it is equally true of many others who, while unknown to the world at large, exert a profound influence on those whose daily lives they touch.

### Identifications and identity

How does a sense of identity develop? In Erikson's view, it develops gradually out of the successive identifications of childhood. These may include *individuals,* such as parents, peers, teachers, and folk heroes. Or they may include *groups* or *cultural categories*—for example, "my gang," "our generation," other blacks (or

Italians, or Jews), other Americans (30). "Is identity, then, the mere sum of earlier identifications, or is it merely an additional set of identifications?" (27, *158*). For Erikson, the answer to his own question is no. Rather, "identity includes, but is more than the sum of, all the successive identifications of those earlier years when the child wanted to be, and often was forced to become, like the people he depended on" (26, *91–92*). Elsewhere he asserts that "the limited usefulness of the mechanism of identification becomes obvious at once if we consider the fact that none of the identifications of childhood . . . could, if merely added up, result in a functioning personality" (27, *158*). Although prior, continuing, and future identifications all play a part in, and may importantly affect, an individual's sense of identity (whether for good or ill), they alone do not produce it. Something more is needed. And that something more is *the capacity to synthesize successive identifications into a coherent, consistent, and unique whole.*

Perhaps this notion can be clarified by means of an illustration of what may happen when this process of synthesis is still incomplete: An adolescent girl had three distinctly different handwriting styles. When asked why she did not simply have one consistent style, she replied, "How can I only write one way till I know who I am?" (70, *495*). Although she had a number of identifications, as indicated by her varied handwriting styles, she had not yet synthesized them into a coherent whole that was uniquely her own.

Similarly, Ibsen's *Peer Gynt* is essentially a depiction of Peer's search for identity. In his encounter with the Onion Man, Peer felt threatened because he felt himself, like an onion, to be merely a series of layers, of transient and shifting roles. When all the layers were peeled off, Peer wondered, would there be any central core, or true identity, left? Many adolescents have similar feelings. Not only do they find themselves playing roles that shift from one situation, or one time, to another, and worry about "which, if any, is the *real* me," but they also self-consciously try out different roles in the hope of finding one that seems to fit. This role experimentation may be more active in some areas than in others. For example, a girl might remain a good student but experiment with participation in various kinds of peer groups. Or a boy might continue his role as a good athlete but experiment with various sexual roles. Limited or sequential role experimentation may be an adaptive means for adolescents to cope with the diversity of available roles.

The younger child may be able to develop satisfactorily without a consistent, well-defined sense of identity. In the relatively protected world of childhood, with limited cognitive abilities and a limited time perspective and few critically important choices to make, the child may be perfectly able to be a cowboy or astronaut at one moment, and at the next, a miniature version of father worrying about the stock market or the fate of the Oakland Raiders. But such luxuries are less possible for adolescents. There are simply too many changes occurring within them, too many present and future demands facing them, too many critically important choices to be made. Unless they can somehow achieve a workable integration of prior and current identifications, they will become, as many older adolescents and adults unfortunately are, increasingly like rudderless ships, changing course with each passing wave, but going nowhere—in short, victims of *identity confusion.* Or, as Biff, the son in *Death of a Salesman,* put it, "I just can't take hold, Mom. I can't take hold of some kind of life."

## VARIATIONS IN IDENTITY FORMATION

Thus far we have spoken of identity formation as though it were a relatively unitary, all-or-nothing task at which the individual succeeds or fails. However, this is not the case. Patterns of identity formation may vary widely among particular adolescents or groups of adolescents as a result of many influences, ranging from individual parent-child relationships to cultural or subcultural pressures, and even the *rate* of social change (9, 10, 27, 42, 44, 60, 62). Thus, identity formation may be, at least relatively, simple or complex; normative, ascribed, or deviant; positive or negative; prematurely foreclosed or indefinitely extended; successful, strong, and coherent or unsuccessful, weak, and confused.

Whether the process of identity formation will be relatively simple or complex depends, at least in part, on the number and compatibility of the various identifications that must be synthesized, on the variety of individual choices and social roles open to the adolescent, and on the difficulty of the demands made upon him or her. In a relatively simple, static, preliterate society, identification models may be few and compatible, role opportunities extremely limited, and demands few and straightforward. Consequently, identity formation may constitute a relatively simple task and one that is rather quickly accomplished. But by the same token, the resultant identity might be viewed in our culture as lacking in subtlety, richness, and adaptability. In contrast, in a rapidly changing, fragmented, complex society, identity formation may become for many a difficult and extended task.

Within a particular society identities may also be *normative* (i.e., in accord with the overall values and expectations of the individual's cultural milieu) or socially *deviant.* And in each case, the motivations involved may be primarily *positive* or *negative* (22, 26, 27). Sometimes a normative identity may have to be *achieved*, as in the case of a self-made man like Al Smith, who worked his way up from the tenements of New York's Lower East Side to become governor of the state and Democratic candidate for the presidency. Sometimes, however, the route to a normative identity may be carefully engineered by the individual's parents and other significant members of his or her particular social group. As Douvan and Adelson (22) note, in the latter case, the individual's identity may be both *normative* and *ascribed*. Malvina Reynold's song of the 1950s, *Little Boxes*, about the people who live on the hillside in "little boxes" and who "all look just the same" is a classic, if extreme, example of an identity formation that is both normative and ascribed:

> And they all play on the golf course
> And drink their martinis dry,
> And they all have pretty children
> And the children go to school,
> And the children go to summer camp
> And then to the university,
> Where they are put in boxes
> And they come out all the same.[1]
>
> *Malvina Reynolds*

[1] From the song "Little Boxes." Words and music by Malvina Reynolds. ©1962 Schroder Music Co. (ASCAP). Used by permission. All rights reserved.

It should be noted, however, that normative, even ascribed, identities are not necessarily insensitive, unimaginative, or limiting of the individual's potential. Even though an individual's identity formation may be ascribed or expected, it may possess a rewarding richness and depth, if it is natural and appropriate for him or her. Not all children of physicians who also become physicians are simply doing someone else's thing.

In contrast to a *normative* identity, some individuals may adopt a *deviant* identity—one that is at odds with, or at least not systematically reinforced by, the values and expectations of their society. Obviously, the reasons for adopting such an identity may differ widely from one person to another. In some instances, adolescents may seek a deviant identity, either temporarily or permanently, in order to ward off being programmed into a premature crystallization of an *ascribed* identity they feel they have had little part in defining, and that may not represent their potential real self. In other instances, more pathological factors may be involved. A deviant identity may be adopted not for positive reasons, but because the young person feels guilty about, or is fearful of, failure if he or she attempts a more normative, socially valued identity. The reader may well wonder what can be the possible reinforcement, or reward value, of such a *negative identity*. However, as Erikson notes,

> Such vindictive choices of a negative identity represent of course a desperate attempt at regaining some mastery in a situation in which the available possible identity elements cancel each other out. The history of such a choice reveals a set of conditions in which it is easier for the . . . [individual] to derive a sense of identity out of a total identification with that which he is least supposed to be than to struggle for a feeling of reality in acceptable roles which are unobtainable with his inner means (27, *176*).

In short, the reward value lies in "the relief following the total choice of a negative identity" (27, *176*). On the other hand, a socially advantaged adolescent boy may adopt a deviant identity and reject the kind of identity formation his father represents not because the latter is inconsistent with his own potentialities, but because of disturbed parent-child relationships. He may be deeply angry at his father, or feel guilty, consciously or unconsciously, about appearing to compete with him. Or he may fear the threat to his ego—and the dangers of identity confusion—represented by failing where his father succeeded.

Among contemporary adolescents who seek, or in some cases passively accept—either temporarily or permanently—a deviant identity, the motivations involved may be either positive or negative, or a mixture of the two. Indeed, the ultimate degree of success in identity formation that such a person is able to achieve—whether he or she is a political or social activist, a member of a youth counterculture, a poet or artist, a delinquent, or a member of a drug culture—is likely to reflect the ratio of positive (seeking) to negative (avoiding) motivations involved.

Identity formation may be prematurely foreclosed (i.e., crystallized), or indefinitely extended (2, 21, 61, 62, 63, 66, 80, 81, 92, 96, 98). "Identity foreclosure is . . . an interruption in the process of identity formation. It is a premature *fixing* of one's self-images, thereby interfering with one's development of other potentials and possibilities for self-definition. An individual does not emerge as 'all he could be'" (22, *35*).

Studies of late adolescents, particularly college students, have found that individuals whose identities have been prematurely foreclosed are more likely than those who are struggling with, or have already achieved, a clear sense of identity to be highly approval-oriented, to base their sense of self-esteem largely on recognition by others, to have a high degree of respect for authority, to be more conforming and less autonomous (12, 13, 61, 64, 66, 68, 96). They are also likely to be more interested in traditional religious values, less thoughtful and reflective, less anxious, and more stereotyped and superficial, as well as less close and intimate in same-sex and heterosexual relationships (12, 13, 68, 75, 77, 90). Although they do not differ from their peers in overall intelligence, identity foreclosure youth become more constricted and impulsive, and less reflective, when confronted with stressful cognitive tasks (41). They are also more likely to keep regular hours, study diligently, avoid drug use, and in general welcome structure in their lives, while eschewing expression of strong feeling, positive or negative (21, 23, 41, 78). They tend to have close relationships with their parents (especially in the case of sons and their fathers), and to adopt parental values; in turn, their parents generally appear to be accepting and encouraging (12, 13, 49), while exerting considerable pressure and support for conformity to family values (41, 49, 68).

In contrast, there are other adolescents who may go through a prolonged period of identity confusion. These are adolescents who "cannot 'find themselves,' who keep themselves loose and unattached, committed to a bachelorhood of pre-identity" (22, *16*). In some instances the problem of identity definition is ultimately worked out after much trial and error—sometimes resulting in an identity that is not only clearly defined, self-consistent, and whole, but also subtle, rich, and varied in its resources.

Several studies suggest that individuals who have achieved a strong sense of identity after a period of active searching are likely to be more autonomous, less dependent on the views of others, more complex in their thinking, less constricted, more resistant to stress, and more creative (12, 13, 21, 61, 68, 90, 93). They are also likely to show a greater capacity for intimacy with same- and opposite-sex peers, a more confident sexual identity, a more positive self-concept, a higher level of moral reasoning, and greater cultural sophistication (12, 13, 41, 46, 50, 51, 75, 77, 81, 85, 95). In addition, they tend to be better liked by their peers, especially by those who have achieved a strong sense of identity themselves (39). While their relationships with their parents are generally positive, they have also achieved considerable independence from their families (see pages 237–240) (12, 64, 77).

In other instances, however, the person may never truly develop a strong, clearly defined sense of ego identity, remaining in a state of identity diffusion. Like Biff, in *Death of a Salesman,* or Lenny, the anti-hero of Romain Gary's *The Ski Bum,* who "opts for total detachment from family, country, home, and work," he or she may exhibit "a pathologically prolonged identity crisis" (99, 47), never achieving any consistent loyalties or commitments.

In a recent study of identity status and interpersonal style, it was found that many identity diffusion individuals "were not satisfied with their parents' way of life, but neither could become productively involved in fashioning one of their own" (21, *51*). In the words of one such subject:

Let's say I'm a Psych. major. I have no idea what I will do with it. I try not to plan more than a week in advance. My parents would like me to settle down and get married. That seems pretty far off right now. Mother would love it, if I stayed right at home. . . . I have plans to go to Africa this summer, go to Europe by myself in the fall. After that I don't know [21, *51*].

Identity diffusion youth tend to have lower underlying self-esteem, a less advanced level of moral reasoning, and less self-directedness, and are less likely to take responsibility for their own lives (14, 41, 71, 80, 84). They are also more likely to be impulsive, less organized in their thinking, more likely to be involved in drug use and less likely to stop, more likely to be isolated from others, and less likely to be capable of intimate interpersonal relationships (23, 41, 77, 78, 96).

All these variations in identity formation may and do occur among contemporary adolescents, and for a variety of reasons. However, the currently popular stereotype of a *typical* process of identity formation, among the public generally and many professional therapists as well, is that of an intense period of identity confusion—an acute *identity crisis*—characterized by marked emotional turmoil and upheaval. So fashionable, in fact, is this view that Erikson himself was recently moved to ask, ". . . Would some of our youth act so openly confused and confusing if they did not *know* they were *supposed* to have an identity crisis?" (27).

Nevertheless, as we have seen, there is a widespread tendency, particularly among clinicians dealing with upper-middle-class, "elite" youth, to consider a period of acute identity confusion and struggle as typical (33, 52, 72, 73, 74, 99). Indeed, many have come to consider an absence of an acute period of adolescent turmoil as almost automatically indicative of impending emotional disturbance (7, 32, 57, 72). However, for reasons discussed elsewhere (see page 25), we consider that these theorists have tended to exaggerate both the frequency and especially the extent of serious identity crises among youth in general, and that, in some instances at least, they have misinterpreted the psychological significance of the absence of serious adolescent turmoil.

### Sexual identity

An important part of a person's overall identity is *sexual* (or *gender*) *identity*—an awareness and acceptance of one's basic biological nature as a male or female (88). Except for the severely retarded or disturbed (and a small minority with physical abnormalities in sexual development—see Chapter 8), children become aware of their own and others' biological gender (and of the constancy of gender) relatively early in life (55, 86, 88)—although initially gender assignment tends to be based on such superficial characteristics as clothing or hair styles, rather than anatomical distinctions, and the child does not yet have a concept of gender stability and constancy, a realization that boys will remain boys and girls will remain girls, even if they change their hair style, attire, and even interests (55, 86). Children appear to understand gender labels by about age 3, but do not acquire gender constancy until about ages 5 to 7 (19, 24, 86, 91). (Interestingly, children typically become convinced of their own gender constancy earlier than they do that of other children.) However, sex-typed play and interest emerge as early as 2 or 3 (67). Sandra Bem (5) thinks that children acquire a sex-typed self-concept by gradually integrating what she calls a gender schema—a societally induced set of sex-linked associations—with their evolving self-concept: "As children learn the contents of the society's gender schema, they learn which attributes are to be linked with their own sex, and, hence, with themselves" (4, 355). This is not simply a matter of learning who is supposed to be better at a particular skill, for example, that boys are "supposed" to be better than girls at mathematics. In addition, there are some characteristics that do not even apply to both boys and girls. For example, girls usually do not think of themselves in terms of strength. Similarly, nurturance is not a concept that boys typically integrate into their identities.

In addition to this cognitive awareness, most individuals also acquire what Richard Green describes as a basic emotional conviction of being male or female (40). However, a notable exception to this occurs among transsexuals, who typically report having felt, even as children, that they were trapped in a body of the wrong sex.

Individuals may "vary in the degree to which they enjoy or resent their biological gender (a reaction that should be distinguished from individuals' enjoyment or resentment of the roles and opportunities that society makes available to their gender)" (40, *12*). As we shall see, parent-child relationships play an important part in determining the way adolescents feel about belonging to their sex (see pages 251–253). Nevertheless, the great majority, including most homosexuals, appear content with being male or female and have no desire to change. In view of the fact that one's gender is a biological fact, about which one can do little (short of radical surgery and hormone maintenance), this is fortunate. Conflicts about sexual or gender identity are not only difficult to deal with as such, but are likely to create significant problems in the development of a confident, secure *overall* identity.

It is important, however, especially in view of current controversies and confusion, to distinguish between *gender identity* and conformity to *sex-typed characteristics* or *stereotypes* (personality traits, interests, and behaviors traditionally associated primarily with one sex or the other). Appropriate behavior as a man or woman need not mean rigid conformity to sex-role stereotypes—such as that of the ambitious, self-reliant, assertive, but not very sensitive male, and the affectionate, gentle, sensitive, but not very assertive female (3, 4, 87). There is no basic biological reason why both men and women should not be capable of independence and a reasonable kind of assertiveness *and* of nurturant feelings and sensitivity. Indeed, there is evidence to suggest that such individuals tend to be highly competent, effective, and well adjusted (4, 56, 88, 89).

What appears more important in the development of a secure, positive sexual identity than whether an individual conforms, or does not conform, to sex-role stereotypes is the nature of his or her relationships with both parents—in particular, the extent to which the parents are confident of their own sexual identity and the degree to which identification with parents is a positive, rewarding experience for the child or adolescent.

**Gender intensification** In early adolescence, the emergence of adult male and female characteristics at puberty typically leads to a process of *gender intensification* (45). To the extent that gender has become an important aspect of the young person's identity earlier in development, through gender-based schematic processing, it will become intensified after puberty, when accommodation to a new appearance is required. During this time, young adolescents may exaggerate their behavior in sex-typed ways, in an effort to find themselves in such stereotypes. Recent research indicates that adolescents do, in fact, develop increasingly divergent views of what constitutes sex-appropriate behavior for males and females, and do increase their own adherence to sex-typed roles (45). While this process seems natural and benign enough, if carried too far it may foreclose opportunities for both boys and girls; academic and occupational choices may then be limited to sex-typed choices rather than focusing on true interests and talents. The extent of sex-typed decisions currently appears to be declining—there are more women becoming physicians and mathematicians and more men taking an active part in child rearing (see Chapter 11). Nevertheless, today's adolescents—particularly younger adolescents—still tend to make predominantly sex-typed choices (79).

## REFERENCES

1. Adams, G. R., Shea, J., & Fitch, S. A. Toward the development of an objective assessment of ego-identity status. *Journal of Youth and Adolescence,* 1979, **8,** 223–237.
2. Andrews, J. The relationship of values of identity achievement status. *Journal of Youth and Adolescence,* 1973, **2,** 133–138.
3. Baumrind, D. Are androgynes better persons and parents? *Child Development,* 1982, **53,** 44–75.
4. Bem, S. L. Sex-role adaptability: One consequence of psychological androgyny. *Journal of Personality and Social Psychology,* 1975, **31,** 634–643.
5. Bem, S. L. Gender schema theory: A cognitive account of sex-typing. *Psychological Review,* 1981, **88,** 354–364.
6. Benson, P. L., & Vincent, S. M. Development and validation of the Sexist Attitudes Toward Women Scale (SATWS). *Psychology of Women Quarterly,* 1980, **5,** 276–291.
7. Beres, D. Character formation. In S. Lorand & H. I. Schneer (eds.), *Adolescents: Psychoanalytic approaches to problems and theory.* New York: Harper & Row, 1961. Pp. 1–9.
8. Block, J. H. Conceptions of sex role: Some cross-cultural and longitudinal perspectives. *American Psychologist,* 1973, **28,** 512–526.
9. Blos, P. *The young adolescent: Clinical studies.* New York: Free Press, 1970.
10. Blos, P. The child analyst looks at the young adolescent. *Daedalus,* Fall 1971, 961–978.
11. Blos, P. *The adolescent passage: Developmental issues.* New York: International Universities Press, 1979.
12. Bourne, E. The state of research on ego identity: A review and appraisal. Part I. *Journal of Youth and Adolescence,* 1978, **7,** 223–251.
13. Bourne, E. The state of research on ego identity: A review and appraisal. Part II. *Journal of Youth and Adolescence,* 1978, **7,** 371–392.
14. Breuer, H. Ego identity status in late-adolescent college males as measured by a group-administered incomplete sentences blank and related to inferred stance toward authority. Unpublished doctoral dissertation. New York University, 1973.
15. Bronfenbrenner, U. Freudian theories of identification and their derivatives. *Child Development,* 1960, **31,** 15–40.
16. Chandler, M. J., Paget, K. F., & Koch, D. A. The child's demystification of psychological defense mechanisms: A structural and developmental analysis. *Developmental Psychology,* 1978, **14,** 197–205.
17. Conger, J. J. A world they never knew: The family and social change. *Daedalus,* Fall 1971, 1105–1138.
18. Constantinople, A. An Eriksonian measure of personality development in college students. *Developmental Psychology,* 1969, **1,** 357–372.
19. DeVries, R. Constancy of generic identity in the years three to six. *Monographs of the Society for Research in Child Development,* 1969, **34** (3, Serial No. 127).
20. Dollard, J., & Miller, N. E. *Personality and psychotherapy: An analysis in terms of learning, thinking, and culture.* New York: McGraw-Hill, 1950.
21. Donovan, J. M. Ego identity status and interpersonal style. *Journal of Youth and Adolescence,* 1975, **4,** 37–56.
22. Douvan, E., & Adelson, J. *The adolescent experience.* New York: Wiley, 1966.
23. Dufresne, J., & Cross, J. H. Personality variables in student drug use. Unpublished master's thesis. University of Connecticut, 1972.
24. Emmerich, W., & Goldman, K. S. Boy-girl identity task (technical report). In V. Shipman (ed.), *Disadvantaged children and their first school experiences* (Technical Report PR-72-20). Educational Testing Service, 1972.
25. Erikson, E. H. *Childhood and society.* New York: Norton, 1950.
26. Erikson, E. H. The problem of ego identity. *Journal of the American Psychoanalytic Association,* 1956, **4,** 56–121.
27. Erikson, E. H. *Identity: Youth and crisis.* New York: Norton, 1968.
28. Evans, R. I. *Dialogue with Erik Erikson.* New York: Harper & Row, 1967.

29. Fenichel, O. *The psychoanalytic theory of neurosis.* New York: Norton, 1945.
30. Fox, D. J., & Jordan, V. B. Racial preference and identification of black, American Chinese, and white children. *Genetic Psychology Monographs,* 1973, **88,** 229–286.
31. Freud, A. *The ego and the mechanisms of defense.* New York: International Universities Press, 1946.
32. Freud, A. Adolescence. *Psychoanalytic Study of the Child,* 1958, **13,** 255–278.
33. Freud, A. Adolescence. In A. E. Winder & D. L. Angus (eds.), *Adolescence: Contemporary studies.* New York: American Book, 1968.
34. Freud, A. Adolescence as a developmental disturbance. In G. Caplan & S. Lebovici (eds.), *Adolescence: Psychosocial perspectives.* New York: Basic Books, 1969, Pp. 5–10.
35. Freud, A. *Normality and pathology in childhood: Assessment of development.* New York: International Universities Press, 1977 (6th ed.).
36. Freud, S. *The ego and the id.* London: Hogarth, 1927.
37. Freud, S. *Group psychology and the analysis of the ego.* London: Hogarth, 1949.
38. Gerzon, M. *The whole world is watching.* New York: Paperbook Library, 1970.
39. Goldman, J. A., Rosenzweig, C. M., & Lutter, A. D. Effect of similarity of ego identity status on interpersonal attraction. *Journal of Youth and Adolescence,* 1980, **9,** 153–162.
40. Green, R. *Sexual identity conflict in children and adults.* New York: Basic Books, 1974.
41. Group for the Advancement of Psychiatry. *Normal adolescence.* New York: Scribner, 1968.
42. Hauser, S. T. *Black and white identity formation.* New York: Wiley, 1971.
43. Hauser, S. T. Ego development and interpersonal style in adolescence. *Journal of Youth and Adolescence,* 1978, **7,** 333–352.
44. Heilbrun, A. B., Jr. Identification and behavioral ineffectiveness during late adolescence. In E. D. Evans (ed.), *Adolescents: Readings in behavior and development.* New York: Holt, Rinehart and Winston, 1970.
45. Hill, J. P., & Lynch, M. E. The intensification of gender-related role expectations during early adolescence. In J. Brooks-Gunn & A. C. Petersen (eds.), *Girls at puberty: Biological, psychological, and social perspectives.* New York: Plenum, in press.
46. Hodgson, J. W., & Fischer, J. L. Sex differences in identity and intimacy development in college youth. *Journal of Youth and Adolescence,* 1979, **8,** 37–50.
47. Hoffman, M. L. Moral development. In P. H. Mussen (ed.), *Carmichael's manual of child psychiatry* (Vol. II). New York: Wiley, 1970. Pp. 261–360 (3rd ed.).
48. Hudson, W. H. *Far away and long ago.* New York: Dutton, 1918.
49. Jordan, D. Parental antecedents and personality characteristics of ego identity statuses. Unpublished doctoral dissertation. State University of New York—Buffalo, 1971.
50. Josselson, R. L., Greenberger, E., & McConochie, D. Phenomenological aspects of psychosocial maturity in adolescence. Part I: Boys. *Journal of Youth and Adolescence,* 1977a, **6,** 25–55.
51. Josselson, R., Greenberger, E., & McConochie, D. Phenomenological aspects of psychosocial maturity in adolescence. Part II: Girls. *Journal of Youth and Adolescence,* 1977b, **6,** 145–167.
52. Josselyn, I. M. The ego in adolescence. *American Journal of Orthopsychiatry,* 1954, **24,** 223–227.
53. Kagan, J. The concept of identification. *Psychological Review,* 1958, **65,** 296–305.
54. Kavrell, S. M., & Petersen, A. C. Patterns of achievement in early adolescent boys and girls. In M. L. Maehr & M. W. Steinkamp (eds.), *Women in Science.* Greenwich, Conn.: JAI Press, in press.
55. Kohlberg, L. A. A cognitive-developmental analysis of children's sex-role concepts and attitudes. In E. E. Maccoby (ed.), *The development of sex differences.* Stanford, Calif.: Stanford University Press, 1966. Pp. 82–173.
56. Leary, T. *Interpersonal diagnosis of personality.* New York: Ronald Press, 1957.
57. Lindemann, E. Adolescent behavior as a community concern. *American Journal of Psychotherapy,* 1964, **18,** 405–417.

58. Locksley, A. C., & Colten, M. C. Psychological androgyny: A case of mistaken identity? *Journal of Personality and Social Psychology,* 1979, **37,** 1017–1031.

59. Lynd, H. On shame and the search for identity. New York: Science Editions, Inc., 1966.

60. Lynn, D. B. *Parental and sex-role identification: A theoretical formation.* Berkeley, Calif.: McCutchan, 1969.

61. Marcia, J. E. Development and validation of ego identity status. *Journal of Personality and Social Psychology,* 1966, **3,** 551–558.

62. Marcia, J. E. Ego identity status: Relationship to change in self-esteem, "general maladjustment," and authoritarianism. *Journal of Personality,* 1967, **35,** 118–133.

63. Marcia, J. E. The case history of a construct: Ego identity status. In E. Vinacke (ed.), *Readings in general psychology.* New York: Van Nostrand Reinhold, 1968.

64. Marcia, J. E. Identity six years after: A follow-up study. *Journal of Youth and Adolescence,* 1976, **5,** 145–160.

65. Marcia, J. E. Identity in adolescence. In J. Adelson (ed.), *Handbook of adolescent psychology.* New York: Wiley, 1980. Pp. 159–187.

66. Marcia, J. E., & Friedman, M. L. Ego identity status in college women. *Journal of Personality,* 1970, **38,** 249–263.

67. Marcus, D. E., & Overton, W. F. The development of cognitive gender-constancy and sex-role preferences. *Child Development,* 1978, **49,** 434–444.

68. Matteson, D. R. Exploration and commitment: Sex differences and methodological problems in the use of identity status categories. *Journal of Youth and Adolescence,* 1977, **6,** 353–374.

69. Mischel, W. Sex-typing and socialization. In P. H. Mussen (ed.), *Carmichael's manual of child psychology* (Vol. II). New York: Wiley, 1970. Pp. 3–72 (3rd ed.).

70. Mussen, P. H., Conger, J. J., & Kagan, J. *Child development and personality.* New York: Harper & Row, 1975 (4th ed.).

71. Neuber, K. A., & Genthner, R. W. The relationship between ego identity, personal responsibility, and facilitative communication. *Journal of Psychology,* 1977, **95,** 45–49.

72. Nixon, R. E. Psychological normality in adolescence. *Adolescence,* 1966, **1,** 211–223.

73. Offer, D. *The psychological world of the teen-ager: A study of normal adolescence.* New York: Basic Books, 1969.

74. Offer, D., & Offer, J. *From teenage to young manhood.* New York: Basic Books, 1975.

75. Orlofsky, J. L. Intimacy status: Relationship to interpersonal perception. *Journal of Youth and Adolescence,* 1976, **5,** 73–88.

76. Orlofsky, J. L. Identity formation, achievement, and fear of success in college men and women. *Journal of Youth and Adolescence,* 1978, **7,** 49–62.

77. Orlofsky, J. L., Marcia, J. E., & Lesser, I. M. Ego identity status and the intimacy vs. isolation crisis of young adulthood. *Journal of Personality and Social Psychology,* 1973, **27,** 211–219.

78. Pack, A. T., Brill, N. Q., & Christie, R. L. Quitting marijuana. *Diseases of the Nervous System,* 1976, **37,** 205–209.

79. Petersen, A. C. Biopsychosocial interactional processes influencing sex differences in cognition: No one is looking. Invited presentation at a Conference on Gender Role at the National Institute for Child Health and Human Development, September 30–October 2, 1981, Bethesda, Md.

80. Podd, M. H. Ego identity status and morality: The relationship between two developmental constructs. *Developmental Psychology,* 1972, **6,** 497–507.

81. Podd, M. H., Marcia, J. E., & Rubin, B. M. The effects of ego identity and partner perception on a prisoner's dilemma game. *Journal of Social Psychology,* 1970, **82,** 117–126.

82. Pomerantz, S. C. Sex differences in the relative importance of self-esteem, physical self-satisfaction, and identity in predicting adolescent satisfaction. *Journal of Youth and Adolescence,* 1979, **8,** 51–61.

83. Raphael, D. Identity status in university women: A methodological note. *Journal of Youth and Adolescence,* 1977, **6,** 57–62.

84. Rowe, I. Ego identity status, cognitive development, and levels of moral reasoning. Master's thesis. Simon Fraser University, 1978.
85. Rowe, I., & Marcia, J. E. Ego identity status, formal operations, and moral development. *Journal of Youth and Adolescence,* 1980, **9,** 87–99.
86. Slaby, R. G., & Frey, K. S. Development of gender constancy and selective attention to same-sex models. *Child Development,* 1975, **47,** 849–856.
87. Spence, J. T. Traits, roles, and the concept of androgyny. Paper presented at the Conference on Perspectives on the Psychology of Women. Michigan State University, May 13–14, 1977.
88. Spence, J. T., & Helmreich, R. L. *Masculinity and femininity: Their psychological dimensions, correlates, and antecedents.* Austin, Texas: University of Texas Press, 1978.
89. Spence J. T., & Helmreich, R. L. The many faces of androgyny: A reply to Locksley and Colten. *Journal of Personality and Social Psychology,* 1979, **37,** 1032–1046.
90. St. Clair, S., & Day, H. D. Ego identity status and values among high school females. *Journal of Youth and Adolescence,* 1979, **8,** 317–326.
91. Thompson, S. K. Gender labels and early sex-role development. *Child Development,* 1975, **46,** 339–347.
92. Toder, N. L., & Marcia, J. E. Ego identity status and response to conformity pressure in college women. *Journal of Personality and Social Psychology,* 1973, **26,** 287–294.
93. Waterman, A. S., & Archer, S. Ego identity status and expressive writing among high school and college students. *Journal of Youth and Adolescence,* 1979, **8,** 327–341.
94. Waterman, A. S., & Goldman, J. A. A longitudinal study of ego identity development at a liberal arts college. *Journal of Youth and Adolescence,* 1976, **5,** 361–369.
95. Waterman, A. S., & Waterman, C. K. A longitudinal study of changes in ego identity status during the freshman year in college. *Developmental Psychology,* 1971, **5,** 167–173.
96. Waterman, A. S., & Waterman, C. K. A longitudinal study of changes in ego identity status during the freshman to the senior year in college. *Developmental Psychology,* 1974, **10,** 387–392.
97. Waterman, C. K., & Nevid, J. S. Sex differences in the resolution of the identity crisis. *Journal of Youth and Adolescence,* 1977, **6,** 337–342.
98. Waterman, C. K., & Waterman, A. S. Ego identity status and decision styles. *Journal of Youth and Adolescence,* 1974, **3,** 1–6.
99. Weiner, J. B. *Psychological disturbance in adolescence.* New York: Wiley, 1970.

Biological changes
in adolescence

CHAPTER 4

# Biological changes in adolescence

**A**dolescence, it has been said, begins in biology and ends in culture. The biological changes that come with adolescence are inevitable: rapid acceleration of height and weight, changing bodily dimensions, development of secondary sex characteristics, mature reproductive capacity, and further growth and differentiation of cognitive ability. These biological changes and the young person's need to adjust to them give adolescence such universal qualities as it possesses, and differentiate it from earlier periods of development. In contrast, culture will determine whether the period we call adolescence is long or short, and whether its social demands represent an abrupt change or only a gradual transition from earlier periods of development.

The culture may facilitate or hinder the young person's adjustment to the biological changes of puberty and it may influence whether these changes become a source of pride or of anxiety and confusion. But it cannot change the fact that these changes will occur, and that, in one way or another, the adolescent must cope with them. Furthermore, were it not for the accelerated biological maturation that characterizes the adolescent years, young people would not be capable of meeting many of the social demands made upon them during this period in most cultures—whether these demands are for academic or intellectual competence; for physical or vocational skills; for heterosexual relationships, marriage and parenthood; even, unfortunately, for fighting their elder's wars.

For all these reasons, and because, as we remarked at the outset of this book, the development of personality and behavior results from the continuing, complex interaction between a biological organism and its environment, it is important to consider in some detail the nature of the biological changes that accompany adolescence and their effects on the individual. In this chapter we will be concerned primarily with physical and physiological development—the external and internal aspects of biological development. Later we will consider intellectual and cognitive development and the psychological and behavioral consequences of sexual maturation.

## PUBERTY

The term *puberty* refers to the first phase of adolescence when sexual maturation becomes evident. Strictly speaking, puberty begins with hormonal increases and their manifestations, such as gradual enlargement of the ovaries in females and testicular cell growth in males. But because these changes are not outwardly observable, the onset of puberty is often measured by such events as the emergence of pubic hair in boys and girls, beginning elevation of the breasts in girls, and penis and testicular growth in boys. Another major aspect of puberty is an acceleration in height and weight, which usually lasts about four years.

### Hormonal factors in development

As we shall see, the timing of onset and the course of the varied developmental phenomena that surround puberty—such as the growth spurt and sexual maturation—are markedly interrelated. This should not be surprising, in view of the fact that hormones from the endocrine glands are among the principal agents "for translating the instructions of the genes into the reality of the adult form" (115, *112*). And the actions of these hormones in stimulating physical growth, sexual maturation, and other physiological aspects of development are themselves closely interrelated.

Of critical importance in the orderly regulation of growth is the pituitary gland, located immediately below the brain, to which it is connected by nerve fibers. When the cells of the hypothalamus, a central regulating nerve center in the brain, mature (which may occur at different ages in different individuals), signals are sent to the pituitary gland to begin releasing previously inhibited hormones (47, 89). Activating hormones released by the pituitary have a stimulating effect on most other endocrine glands, including the thyroid and adrenal glands and the testes and ovaries, activating their own growth-related and sex-related hormones. The latter include androgens (masculinizing hormones), estrogens (feminizing hormones), and progestins (pregnancy hormones) (75). These and other hormones interact with each other in complex ways to stimulate the orderly progression of the many physical and physiological developments of puberty and adolescence (75, 112). For example, the development of pubic and other body hair is linked to the production of adrenal androgens, while the development of fluctuating levels of estrogen and progesterone are involved in menarche (the onset of the menstrual cycle) (5, 75).

### The timing of puberty

Exactly when puberty will begin depends on a variety of factors, only some of which are currently understood. Genetic influences obviously play a role; for example, the onset of puberty, and subsequent events such as menarche, occur closer together in time among identical twins than among nonidentical (dizygotic) twins (115). Chinese girls begin menstruation earlier than do those of European origin. Nutrition and general health also play a part; deprived adolescents mature later than those who are well cared for. Recent research (47) suggests that a critical rate of metabolism (see page 103) may have to be achieved for puberty to begin. There is some evidence that for menarche to begin, and to continue, fat must make up about 17 percent of body weight (39, 40). If this turns out to be true, it could help explain

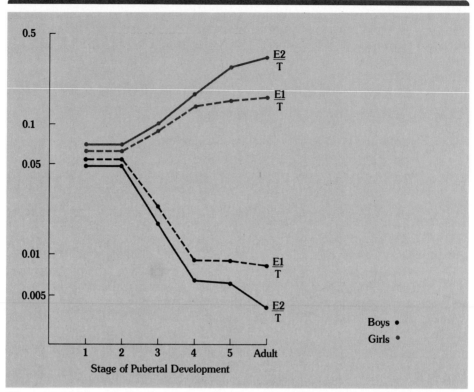

**Figure 4.1** Mean trends in estrogen/testosterone ratios during pubertal development for girls and boys. Two measures of estrogen level are shown, estrone (E1) and the more potent estradiol (E2). (From D. Gupta, A. Attanasio, and S. Raaf. Plasma estrogen and androgen concentrations in children during adolescence. *Journal of Clinical Endocrinology and Metabolism,* 1975, **40,** 636–643. By permission.)

why adolescent anorexics who starve themselves (see pages 665–668) and female athletes who train heavily and maintain a low weight, as is required in certain sports such as gymnastics, may become *amenorrheic* (cease menstruation). Indeed, some recent evidence suggests that female athletes who are close to or below the critical weight and associated metabolic level, may "turn on" their menstrual cycles when they cease training due to an injury, but become amenorrheic again when they resume training (40).

### Hormonal dimorphism

In the early days of sex-hormone research, when sex differences were conceived of as dichotomous and absolute, it was assumed that females produce only female sex hormones and males only male sex hormones. Indeed, the sex hormones were named accordingly. Actually, however, there is overlap, and the hormones of both sexes are present in both men and women (63, 75). All three kinds of sex hormones are closely related in chemical structure, and the site of production may be the ovary or testis, the cortex of the adrenal gland, or other glands or tissues (89). The hormonal difference between the sexes, and corresponding differences in sexual characteristics, is not a matter of either-or, but of the proportion between masculinizing and feminizing hormones. As may be seen in Figure 4.1, as puberty proceeds, the ratio of estrogen levels to testosterone levels increases for girls and decreases in boys (45).

## ADOLESCENT GROWTH SPURT

The term *growth spurt* refers to the accelerated rate of increase in height and weight that occurs with the onset of adolescence. This increase varies widely in intensity, duration, and age of onset from one child to another, even among perfectly normal children—a fact often poorly understood by adolescents and their parents and, consequently, too often a source of needless concern.

In both boys and girls, the adolescent growth spurt takes about $4\frac{1}{2}$ years (7, 30, 117). For the average boy, peak growth occurs at age 13; in girls it is about 2 years earlier, at age 11. While in the average boy the adolescent growth spurt begins a few months before his eleventh birthday, it may begin as early as age 9; similarly, the adolescent growth spurt is usually completed in the boy shortly after age 15, but it may continue until age 17. In girls, the entire process begins, and ends, about 2 years earlier. Further slow growth may continue for several years after the spurt is completed (see Figure 4.2) (30, 70, 113, 115).

Because the onset of the growth spurt is so variable, some young people will complete the pubertal growth period in height before others have begun. Figure 4.2 illustrates how widely the onset, pattern, and end of the growth spurt can vary among normal adolescent girls; as can be seen, girl A's growth spurt was completed a year before girl B's began. Clearly, as these examples show, *normal* does not mean *average*.

Events occurring within the growth spurt cycle are not independent of one another. For example, girls with an early growth spurt tend to reach menarche earlier than those with a later growth spurt (30, 80, 87, 113, 115). Similarly, in boys the period of most rapid growth tends to be closely related to the development of secondary sex characteristics, such as the emergence of axillary (body) and pubic hair (102, 113).

One of the matters likely to concern both adolescents and their parents at this time is that of ultimate height (106). In view of current masculine and feminine stereotypes, this is especially likely to be true of boys who are short and girls who are afraid of growing too tall. Much of the concern of adolescents and their parents about ultimate height is, however, exaggerated. Height before the growth spurt is correlated with ultimate height, which means, for example, that a young person who is in the twenty-fifth percentile in height prior to the growth spurt is most likely to be at the twenty-fifth percentile after puberty (30, 115). However, girls who are early maturers tend to be somewhat shorter at pubertal onset than late maturers, but they also show more rapid growth in height during the growth period, and their growth period tends to be longer. Conversely, late maturers tend to be somewhat taller at onset, but they also tend to have shorter, less intense periods of growth. The net

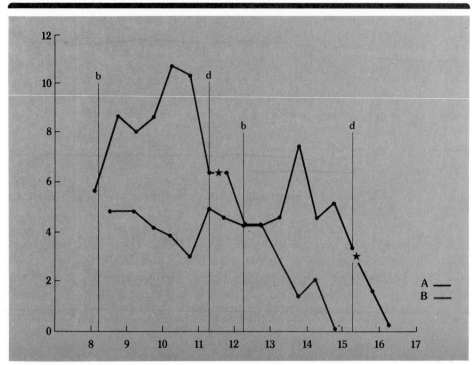

**Figure 4.2** Differences in timing of the pubertal growth period in height. The early developing girl reached the end (d) of the pubertal period before the late-developing girl reached onset (b). Stars indicate onset of menarche. (From M. S. Faust. Somatic development of adolescent girls. *Monographs of the Society for Research in Child Development*, 1977, **42**, 1, Serial No. 169. By permission.)

result is that early maturers as a group "do not end up any taller or shorter than do girls who are older upon reaching onset" (30, *15*). Once an early-maturing girl and her late-maturing peers have passed the period of rapid adolescent growth, their comparative standings in height are most likely to return to those of preadolescence. Similar developmental phenomena appear to occur with boys.

Although increases in weight tend to follow the general curve for height in both males and females, there are some differences. While increased weight obviously reflects skeletal growth, it also reflects increases in muscle and fat tissue and in the size of various body organs. As we shall see, a number of these systems, though not unrelated to increased skeletal development, have their own characteristic timetables. Because weight reflects a combination of developmental events, it may not be too informative. For example, an increase in weight may reflect increased bone or muscle development or it may simply reflect an increase in fat (115). Thus an adolescent's weight curve may suggest continued normal development when this is not, in fact, the case. Similarly, as every parent and adolescent knows, failure to gain weight or even actual loss of weight in an adolescent may merely reflect increased attention to diet and exercise. In contrast, failure to gain height and muscle would call for immediate investigation (112, *438*).

Environmental conditions, such as malnutrition, disease, and even severe psychological stress may affect growth rate, final height, and (to a lesser extent) body shape (92, 115). Under optimal environmental conditions, however, genetic factors appear to play a major role. Nancy Bayley (4) has shown that there is an increasingly significant correlation between midparent height (average height of the two parents) and the heights of their children at increasing ages from 6 to 18 years (4, 25, 26). Rather interestingly, correlations appear highest between fathers and daughters, followed by fathers and sons, mothers and daughters, and, lowest of all, mothers and sons (4).

### The shape of things to come

Rapid acceleration in height and weight is accompanied by changes in body proportions in both males and females. Although virtually all parts of the skeletal and muscular structures take part in the growth spurt, they do so to differing extents and according to different timetables. The parts of the body that achieve adult size and form earliest are the head, hands, and feet. In turn, increases in arm and leg length reach their peak before body width (including shoulder width). Adult trunk length is achieved last, although it accounts for the greatest proportion of the total increase in height occurring during the growth spurt (26, 113, 115). The effect is that "a boy stops growing out of his trousers (at least in length) a year before he stops growing out of his jackets" (115, 94).

These disparate rates of growth in the various parts of the skeletal structure (which can be still further exaggerated in some atypical young people) can be a source of concern, and can produce feelings of awkwardness in adolescents. They

## TODAY'S ADOLESCENTS: BETTER FED, HEALTHIER, AND TALLER

Today's young people are better fed, healthier, and less vulnerable to childhood diseases than their grandparents, or even their parents. At least partly as a result, they are also taller. The table below shows the average height of American boys and girls at each age from 12 to 17 in the most recent national survey conducted by the U.S. Public Health Service. Equally important, it shows how much variability there is among normal boys and girls at each age. At age 14, for example, approximately half of all boys are shorter than 60.9 inches or taller than 68.1 inches, with the remainder distributed between these two figures.

### HEIGHT IN INCHES OF YOUTHS AGED 12–17 YEARS BY SEX AND AGE AT LAST BIRTHDAY

| | | PERCENTILE | | | | | | |
|---|---|---|---|---|---|---|---|---|
| SEX AND AGE | MEAN | 5TH | 10TH | 25TH | 50TH | 75TH | 90TH | 95TH |
| *Male* | | | | | | | | |
| 12 years | 60.0 | 54.6 | 55.7 | 57.8 | 60.0 | 61.9 | 64.0 | 65.2 |
| 13 years | 62.9 | 57.2 | 58.3 | 60.4 | 62.8 | 65.4 | 68.0 | 68.7 |
| 14 years | 65.6 | 59.9 | 60.9 | 63.2 | 66.1 | 68.1 | 69.8 | 70.7 |
| 15 years | 67.5 | 62.4 | 63.7 | 65.7 | 67.8 | 69.3 | 71.0 | 72.1 |
| 16 years | 68.6 | 64.1 | 65.2 | 67.0 | 68.7 | 70.4 | 72.1 | 73.1 |
| 17 years | 69.1 | 64.1 | 65.7 | 67.2 | 69.2 | 70.9 | 72.6 | 73.7 |
| *Female* | | | | | | | | |
| 12 years | 61.1 | 55.8 | 57.4 | 59.5 | 61.2 | 63.0 | 64.6 | 65.9 |
| 13 years | 62.5 | 57.8 | 58.9 | 60.7 | 62.6 | 64.4 | 66.0 | 66.9 |
| 14 years | 63.5 | 59.6 | 60.5 | 61.9 | 63.5 | 65.2 | 66.7 | 67.4 |
| 15 years | 63.9 | 59.6 | 60.3 | 62.0 | 63.9 | 65.8 | 67.2 | 68.1 |
| 16 years | 64.0 | 59.7 | 60.7 | 62.4 | 64.2 | 65.6 | 67.2 | 68.1 |
| 17 years | 64.1 | 60.0 | 60.9 | 62.3 | 64.3 | 65.9 | 67.4 | 68.1 |

*Source:* U.S. Public Health Service. *Vital and health statistics,* Series 11, No. 124, Height and weight of youths, 12–17 years, United States: January 1973.

may feel at one juncture that their hands and feet are too big or at another that they are "all legs."

More subtle changes in physique also occur during this period. The last residuals of the baby face of childhood begin to disappear. The low forehead becomes higher and wider; the mouth widens and the relatively flat lips of childhood become fuller; the slightly receding chin of earlier years begins to jut out (77). And, of course, as head growth diminishes while other parts of the skeletal system continue to grow, the large head characteristic of childhood becomes smaller in relation to total body size (see Figure 4.3).

Such changes as those described for head shape reflect the fact that, as skeletal structures increase in length during the growth spurt, they also change in width, proportions, and composition. Thus, bone width, as well as length, increases during this period. Interestingly, bone width differences between boys and girls are minimal during childhood, although from birth onward girls are slightly ahead of boys in bone age (72, 75, 113). However, growth is clearly greater in the male during adolescence

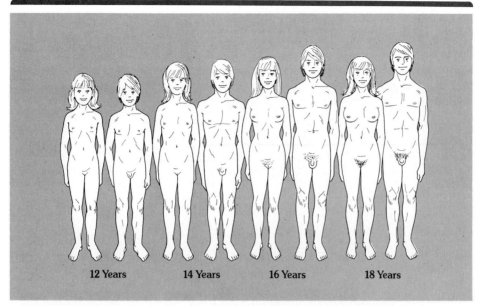

**12 Years**      **14 Years**      **16 Years**      **18 Years**

***Figure 4.3*** Body growth and development from ages 12 to 18 years.

(113). The composition of the skeletal structure also changes. During early childhood, the bones have relatively more cartilage and fibrous tissues and less mineral
matter than is found later. This makes the bones somewhat spongy and soft and also
more flexible. But as the skeletal structures increase in size, the cartilage begins to
calcify, making the bones harder, more dense, and more brittle (115).

Although prior to puberty the ratio of shoulder width to hip width is—perhaps
surprisingly—higher for girls than for boys, the picture reverses dramatically soon
after the onset of the growth spurt, and the size of difference continues to expand
until adult height is reached. However, the variability in hip width among girls is
significantly greater than among boys at all stages of development (30, 115).

***Differential development of muscle and fat***   Changes in adolescent
physique reflect changes in the development of muscle and body fat, as well as in
skeletal structure. In both boys and girls muscular development proceeds rapidly as
height increases, reaching a peak rate of growth slightly after the point of peak
velocity in height. Boys, however, show a more rapid rate of increase than girls, with
the result that their overall gain in muscle tissue during this period is greater than
that for girls (114, 115)—an advantage they retain throughout the adult years.

Conversely, both boys and girls show a decline in the rate of development of fat
during the adolescent growth spurt—a decline that reaches its maximum velocity at
the point of maximum growth in height. In girls the decreased velocity of growth in
fat is not so great as to eliminate a modest absolute gain in fat during this period (as
many girls are only too well aware). In boys, however, the rate of decline is so great

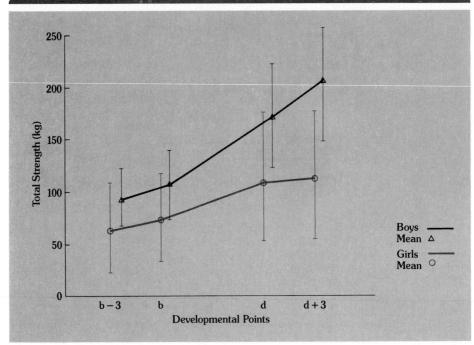

**Figure 4.4** Sex differences in strength, showing extreme scores and mean values at four developmental points: beginning of prepuberty (b − 3), onset (b) and end (d) of pubertal period, and end of postpubertal period (d + 3). (From M. S. Faust, Somatic development of adolescent girls. *Monographs of the Society for Research in Child Development,* 1977, **42,** 1, Serial No. 169. By permission.)

that it produces an actual (though temporary) loss of fat in the months preceding and following the point of peak velocity in height (113, 115).

Although both muscle and fat are influenced by the sex hormones, they are also both influenced by exercise, an activity that also shows sex differences. Studies that control for the amount of exercise still find male-female differences in the percentage of body weight due to fat, but the differences are much smaller than in the more sedentary society at large (121).

**Changes in strength and exercise tolerance**  The acceleration of muscular development that takes place during this period is, not surprisingly, accompanied by increases in strength, as measured by such indices as pulling and pushing strength in the arms and hand grip (14, 27, 30, 68, 113). On the average, the greatest overall increment in strength occurs about one year after peak height and weight velocity (30). Also, not surprisingly, the relative increases are much greater for boys than for girls, although the distribution of overall strength scores (arm pull, arm thrust, hand grips) of boys and girls overlap at every point in development (see Figure 4.4). For the most part, prepubescent boys and girls are similar in strength,

but after adolescence boys are, and remain, much stronger. This greater strength is principally a function of greater muscular development; however, it is probably due partly to a number of other related developmental factors. Thus, relative to their size, boys develop larger hearts and lungs, higher systolic blood pressure, a greater capacity for carrying oxygen in the blood, a lower heart rate while at rest, and interestingly, "a greater power for neutralizing the chemical products of muscular exercise, such as lactic acid," which makes itself felt in fatigue (115, *95*). It also seems likely that some of the greater increase in strength and exercise tolerance among boys has been due, at least up until very recently, to more physical exercise. "Until recently, there have been strong sociocultural pressures on girls to cease such 'masculine' activity at adolescence" (89).

Increases in strength during adolescence are probably reflected in the greater emphasis on athletic activities (as well as general physical restlessness) that is likely to occur at this time, particularly in boys. In this connection, Tanner lays to rest the popular notion of a boy outgrowing his strength during these years. As he comments,

> A short period may exist when the adolescent, having completed his skeletal and probably also muscular growth, still does not have the strength of a young adult of the same body size and shape. But this is a temporary phase; considered absolutely, power, athletic skill, and physical endurance all increase progressively and rapidly throughout adolescence. It is certainly not true that the changes accompanying adolescence enfeeble, even temporarily. If the adolescent becomes weak and

## SEX DIFFERENCES AND SPORTS

In the past decade, there has been an explosion in women's competitive sports (121). Although almost everyone is aware of the accomplishments of a small band of female "superstars" in such activities as gymnastics, figure skating, swimming, tennis, and golf (in 1976, Nadia Comaneci was the first Olympic gymnast of either sex to win a perfect 10), many still do not realize how widespread has been the recent growth of women's athletics. Since 1970, for example, the number of female tennis players has risen from 3 million to 11 million. In 1980, more than a million girls under the age of 19 were playing soccer, compared to almost none in 1970. Currently 33 percent of all high school athletes are female—a 600-percent increase in less than 10 years (121).

What are the implications of adolescent sex differences in physical development for this revolution in women's athletics? Clearly, in some sports men have a physical advantage. On average, they are 10 percent bigger than women. Because they have broader and stronger shoulders, as well as larger arms with more (hormonally induced) muscle fiber, they have an obvious advantage in sports involving throwing and hitting. And because their legs are generally larger and stronger, and their hips narrower, they are able to run faster.

On the other hand, women often have an advantage where endurance is a factor. Because sustained activity begins to convert body fat to energy, and because women's bodies have a higher percentage of body fat (25 percent of body weight, as compared to about 14 percent for men), they have a relatively greater reserve to draw on. Women also appear able to tolerate heat better than men because of a more efficient system for bringing blood to the body surface for cooling; "although the male sweats sooner the female sweats better" (121, *98*). Ever since Gertrude Ederle set a new record for swimming the English Channel, women have dominated the sport of long-distance swimming. In addition to serving as an energy reserve, their body fat provides better buoyancy and insulation against the cold. And their narrower shoulders cut more easily through the water. Similarly, in marathon running, slight-shouldered, strong-legged women have less upper body weight to carry around. In many sports, of course, skill counts more than other factors. This is clearly true of equestrian sports, diving, figure skating, ballet, and most gymnastics.

Such comparisons as these are interesting physically and physiologically; in a larger sense, however, they are irrelevant. The challenge in all competitive sports, as in many other activities, is to achieve as nearly perfect, coordinated use of one's resources of body and mind as possible. Whether a male basketball player is stronger or a female gymnast more graceful is basically beside the point. As Dr. Dorothy Harris, director of the Center for Women in Sports at Pennsylvania State University says, "Sports are not for men or women; they are for people" (121, *31*).

*Source:* P. S. Wood. Sex differences in sports. *New York Times Magazine,* May 18, 1980, p. 31ff.

easily exhausted it is for psychological reasons and not physiological ones [115, 96–97].

### Other aspects of adolescent growth

While such visible characteristics of the growth spurt as increased height and weight and changes in muscle and fat are taking place, other less readily apparent, but equally important, changes are also occurring. As already noted, a number of these changes, though related to the onset and course of the spurt in height, have their own timetables within the overall development sequence.

***Growth of the heart*** During the adolescent years the heart's transverse diameter increases by about half and its weight almost doubles (69). In the earlier years of childhood, boys' hearts are slightly larger than girls'. Although acceleration in the growth rate of the heart occurs earlier in girls (in accordance with their earlier overall growth spurt), the total growth is not as great for girls as for boys. The result is that by late adolescence boys have significantly larger hearts than girls. Whereas heart rate in both boys and girls falls gradually during the entire period of growth, the decline during adolescence is slightly faster for boys, so that by age 17 the average boy's heart rate is about 5 beats per minute slower than the average girl's (25, 48). Heart rate is, of course, related to overall size.

Conversely, systolic blood pressure rises steadily throughout childhood, accelerating rapidly during the years immediately prior to puberty and for about 6 months thereafter. It then tends to settle at a somewhat lower level: "Apparently sexual maturity operates to stabilize the upward trend of blood pressure" (42, 54). Pulse rate also increases during the prepubescent years, reaching a maximum prior to puberty and declining thereafter (48).

***Growth of the lungs*** Lung growth is similar to heart growth. The steady gradual increase of the childhood years gives way to a rapid acceleration during the years of maximum growth in both boys and girls, with growth greatest for boys. On measures of vital capacity (the amount of air that can be exhaled after a deep breath), boys exceed girls up until about 10 years of age, at which point there is no significant difference between the two. However, beginning at about $11\frac{1}{2}$ years, boys again exceed girls, and the difference continues to increase throughout the growth years, as a function both of boys' larger hearts and their typically greater amount of exercise (33, 34, 42).

***Development of the brain*** In contrast to the marked increases in the heart and lungs that accompany adolescence, there is little further growth in the size of the brain during this period. Where the average child has acquired only about 50 percent of total adult weight by the age of 10, he or she has acquired 95 percent of adult brain weight (115).

***Basal metabolism*** Another change occuring during this period is the rather sudden decline in basal metabolism (the energy turnover of the body at a standard low level of activity). Although both boys and girls show a continuous decrease in metabolic rate following puberty, boys retain a higher rate than girls, probably partly as a function of greater muscular development requiring greater consumption of oxygen, but perhaps also because of hormonal differences between boys and girls (113, 115).

***Nutritional needs*** The nutritional needs of the young person during the years of accelerated growth clearly increase considerably, although there is wide variation from one individual to another, depending on both body size and activity level. As can be seen in Table 4.1, the nutritional needs of the average boy consistently exceed those of the average girl, although sex differences are far greater follow-

**TABLE 4.1 RECOMMENDED DAILY DIETARY ALLOWANCES (CALORIES)**

| | AGE | WEIGHT (POUNDS) | HEIGHT (INCHES) | CALORIES |
|---|---|---|---|---|
| Boys | 11–14 | 97 | 63 | 2800 |
| | 15–18 | 134 | 69 | 3000 |
| | 19–22 | 147 | 69 | 3000 |
| Girls | 11–14 | 97 | 62 | 2400 |
| | 15–18 | 119 | 65 | 2100 |
| | 19–22 | 128 | 65 | 2000 |

*Source:* National Academy of Sciences, National Research Council. *Recommended dietary allowances, revised, 1974.* Washington, D.C.: National Academy of Sciences, National Research Council, 1974.

ing the growth spurt, due primarily to size differences. Nevertheless, at any age, a large, extremely active girl will obviously have a greater nutritional need than a small, relatively inactive boy. The needs of early and late maturers will also differ. Both consistent overeating and chronic loss of appetite (anorexia nervosa) may result from emotional problems during the adolescent years (see Chapter 15).

## SEXUAL MATURATION

As we have already noted, the adolescent growth spurt is accompanied by sexual maturation in both boys and girls. The rapidity of all these changes—the greater part of which take place in a period of only about 4 years—are likely at times to give young people a feeling of being spectators of their own growth and development, waiting, sometimes self-consciously, to find out what will happen next.

### Sexual maturation in boys

Although testicular cell growth and secretion of male sex hormone begin earlier—typically about age $11\frac{1}{2}$ (102, 113)—the first outward sign of impending sexual maturity in boys is usually an increase in the growth of the testes and scrotum (the baglike structure enclosing the testes). There may also be beginning, but perhaps slowly, growth of pubic hair at about the same time or shortly thereafter. Approximately a year later, an acceleration in growth of the penis accompanies the beginning of the growth spurt in height. Axillary (body) and facial hair usually make their first appearance about 2 years after the beginning of pubic hair growth, although the relationship is sufficiently variable so that a few children's axillary hair actually appears first (26, 115). The ultimate amount of body hair developed by both males and females appears to depend largely on genetic factors.

Although the process begins earlier, a definite lowering of the voice usually occurs fairly late in puberty (113, 115). In some boys this voice change is rather abrupt and dramatic, whereas in others it occurs so gradually that it is hardly perceptible. During this process, the larynx (or Adam's apple) enlarges significantly, and the

vocal cords (which it contains) approximately double in length, with a consequent drop in pitch of about an octave: ". . . It takes two or more years for boys to achieve control in the lower register, and during that time the roughness of their tones may become a source of embarrassment. This can be observed in boys whose shifts of pitch suddenly jump from a deep bass to a high squeak" (42, 62).

The insensitivity of adults who take advantage of the boy's voice change, beginning growth of facial or pubic hair, or of other primary or secondary sex characteristics in order to ridicule him, in a supposedly friendly fashion, is obvious. The event of beginning shaving may be a welcome sign of adulthood for some boys, or an embarrassing experience, depending upon whether parents treat it as a matter of course or poke fun at him.

During adolescence the male breast also undergoes changes. The diameter of the areola (the area surrounding the nipple) increases considerably (although not as much as in girls) and is accompanied by an elevation of the nipple. In some boys (perhaps 20 to 30 percent), there may also be a distinct enlargement of the breast

## MATURATION IN BOYS

Although there may be some individual—and perfectly normal—variations in the sequence of events leading to physical and sexual maturity in boys, the following sequence is typical:

1. Testes and scrotum begin to increase in size.
2. Pubic hair begins to appear.
3. Adolescent growth spurt starts; the penis begins to enlarge.
4. Voice deepens as the larynx grows.
5. Hair begins to appear under the arms and on the upper lip.
6. Sperm production increases, and nocturnal emission (ejaculation of semen during sleep) may occur.
7. Growth spurt reaches peak rate; pubic hair becomes pigmented.
8. Prostate gland enlarges.
9. Sperm production becomes sufficient for fertility; growth rate decreases.
10. Physical strength reaches a peak.

about midway through adolescence (5, 103, 115), although usually it disappears within a year or so, depending on its degree of development (109). That this enlargement (though usually temporary and quite normal) superficially resembles feminine breast development can be a source of needless anxiety to both a boy and his parents because of their preoccupation with "masculinity."

Prepubescent boys may also show a tendency to adiposity of the lower torso, which, again, may suggest feminine body contours to the apprehensive adolescent or adult. Although this bodily configuration typically disappears with the growth spurt in height, it also may represent a source of unnecessary concern (102). There is no evidence that either of these conditions (in the absence of specific pathology) is related to any deficiency in sexual functioning. As in so many other areas of adolescent development, a minimum amount of accurate basic knowledge could frequently eliminate a great deal of unnecessary anxiety, and even misery.

### Sexual maturation in girls

Although hormonal stimulation of the sex glands begins earlier, at about 9 or 10 (28), initial appearance of unpigmented, downy *pubic* hair is usually the first outward sign of sexual maturity in girls. However, in about 17 percent of girls beginning elevation of the breast (the so-called bud stage of breast development) may precede it (30, 95). Budding of the breast is accompanied by the emergence of downy, unpigmented *axillary* (body) hair, and increases in estrogen (female sex hormone) secretion. In the following year, the uterus and vagina show accelerated growth; the labia and clitoris also enlarge (89). Pubic hair becomes moderately well developed, and vaginal secretion begins. By age 12, nipples show pigmentation and the breasts show further development toward mature form. About $12\frac{1}{2}$ (fairly late in the developmental sequence) the first menstruation occurs. By this time, most girls are in the final stages of pubic hair development, and are approaching the final stages of breast development and axillary hair development (30, 123).

## MATURATION IN GIRLS

Although, as in the case of boys, there may be normal variations in the sequence of physical and sexual maturation in girls, a typical sequence of events is:

1. Adolescent growth spurt begins.
2. Downy (nonpigmented) pubic hair makes its initial appearance.
3. Elevation of the breast (the so-called bud stage of development) and rounding of the hips begin, accompanied by the beginning of downy axillary (body) hair.
4. The uterus and vagina, as well as labia and clitoris, increase in size.
5. Pubic hair is growing rapidly and becoming slightly pigmented.
6. Breasts develop further; nipple pigmentation begins; areola increases in size. Axillary hair is becoming slightly pigmented.
7. Growth spurt reaches peak rate and then declines.
8. Menarche, or onset of menstruation, occurs (almost always *after* the peak rate of growth in height has occurred).
9. Pubic hair development is completed, followed by mature breast development and completion of axillary hair development.
10. Period of "adolescent sterility" ends, and girl becomes capable of conception (up to a year or so after menarche).

There is frequently a period that may last up to a year or year and a half following the beginning of menstruation (109), during which the adolescent girl is not yet physiologically capable of conception. Similarly, boys are able to have intercourse long before the emergence of live spermatozoa (59). Obviously, however, because of significant individual differences, assuming that they are still "safe" from conception because of their age is an extremely risky form of birth control for sexually active young adolescents to employ. Some girls are capable of conception within the first year after menarche, the period formerly thought to be "safe" (123).

### Normal variations in development

It should be emphasized that the average developmental sequences for boys and girls as discussed here are just that—*average*. Among perfectly normal boys and girls there are wide variations in the age of onset of the developmental sequence. (There may also be significant, though generally much smaller, variations in the interrelation of various events within the sequence [26].) For example, while maturation of the penis may be complete in some boys by $13\frac{1}{2}$, for others it may not be complete until as late as 17, or even older. Pubic hair development may vary even more (30). The bud stage of breast development may occur as early as age 8 in some girls, as late as 13 in others (30, 95). Age of menarche may vary from about age 9 to $16\frac{1}{2}$. The great differences that occur among normal boys and girls in their rates of development are dramatically illustrated in Figure 4.5, which shows the differing degrees of pubertal maturity among three normal boys, all aged $14\frac{3}{4}$ years, and three normal girls, all age $12\frac{3}{4}$ years.

As we have noted, whereas the ages of onset of the developmental sequence may vary widely, there is much less variation within individual sequences—the order in which various developmental changes occur. For example, in a developmental

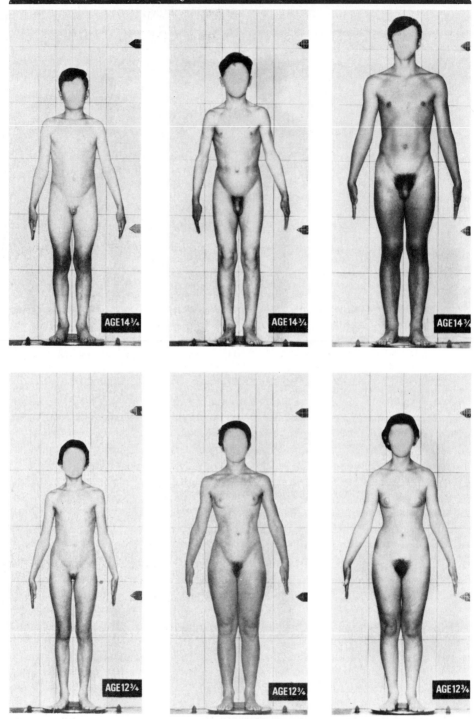

**Figure 4.5** Different degrees of pubertal development at the same chronological age. Upper row: three boys, all aged 14¾ years. Lower row: three girls, all aged 12¾ years. (From J. M. Tanner. Growth and endocrinology of the adolescent. In L. J. Gardner [ed.], *Endocrine and genetic diseases of childhood.* Philadelphia: Saunders, 1969. By permission.)

study of forty-nine normal girls at the Fels Research Institute, the correlation obtained between age at appearance of breast buds and age at subsequent menarche was .86, a very high correlation for biological events. Similar relationships were obtained among various developmental measures for boys (96, 107). Nevertheless, even such high correlations allow room for a fair amount of individual variation within developmental sequences (26). For example, in the Fels study, genital maturation in boys began before the appearance of pubic hair in 70 percent of cases; the two events occurred at approximately the same age in 16 percent; and in 14 percent the order of appearance was reversed (96).

## PSYCHOLOGICAL ASPECTS OF ADOLESCENT GROWTH AND DEVELOPMENT

Many adults have managed to repress potentially anxiety-producing memories of the needs, desires, and fears associated with their own adolescence. Even college students are better at remembering events from earlier years than from the prepubertal years. Consequently, adults are likely to have only a vague realization of how acutely aware the average adolescent is of the entire growth process. That such intense awareness is characteristic of the adolescent is, however, hardly surprising. As discussed earlier, a central problem of the adolescent period is the development of one's own identity as a person. In turn, this sense of identity requires, among other things, a feeling of *consistency over time*—of being similar to, and having consistent links with, the person one was yesterday and will be tomorrow (see pages 75–76). The adolescent (particularly the younger one) is faced with rapid increases in height,

### CHILDREN AS MOTHERS?

During the past century, there has been a trend toward earlier physical and sexual maturation among both boys and girls, including a slower rate of change among U.S. adolescents. Does this mean, as a number of social scientists have concluded, that a relentless evolutionary trend is at work, and that we can expect the average girl in the next century to begin menstruation at 9 or 10, with all the concomitant psychological and social problems this would entail?

Fortunately, the answer is no. When age of menarche is compared across generations reared under nearly identical conditions, no dramatic downward trend in menarcheal age is found. Rather than being due to a continuing evolutionary trend, earlier maturation appears to be the result of the individual's general health and nutrition throughout the entire developmental period. For example, during World War II, age of menarche was significantly retarded in a number of European countries with temporarily inadequate diets.

Furthermore, although good nutrition, health care, and an optimal physical environment may accelerate maturation, it appears clear they can do so only within the ultimate, genetically determined limits for a particular population. Current estimates of the biological limit for age of menarche for the *average* girl are around $12\frac{1}{4}$ years. While we can and should be concerned about the recent "epidemic" of adolescent pregnancies, we are not likely to have to set up prenatal classes for 9-year-olds!

*Sources:* (1) *A history of the study of human growth.* Cambridge, England: Cambridge University Press, 1981. (2) A. F. Roche (ed.). Secular trends in human growth, maturation, and development. *Monographs of the Society for Research in Child Development,* 1979, Serial No. 179. (3) Bullough, V. L. Age at menarche: A misunderstanding. *Science,* 1981, **213,** 365–366.

changing bodily dimensions, and the objective and subjective changes related to sexual maturation. Obviously, all these developments threaten the feeling of self-consistency, and the adolescent needs time to integrate them into a slowly emerging sense of a positive, self-confident personal identity.

Developmental change and the need to adjust to it cause adolescents to focus concern on physical aspects of the self. However, the nature of these concerns is influenced by a number of additional factors. With the onset of adolescence and the accelerated shift away from dependence on the family and toward the peer group as a major source of security and status, conformity, not only in social behavior but in appearance and physical skills, becomes increasingly emphasized (77). Like any marginal group concerned about where it currently stands and, even more important, where it is going, the adolescent peer group tends to be more harshly critical of deviation than groups that are more secure and confident in their social identity. Although there have been recent signs of a somewhat greater tolerance of diversity among some groups of today's youth, deviance in rate of development and physical appearance can still be an agonizing experience for many adolescents, particularly younger ones.

Probably at least partly in anticipation of their future roles as adult men and women, adolescents tend to have idealized norms for physical appearance and skills that conform largely to culturally determined stereotypes of masculinity and femininity. An analysis of advertisements in several popular magazines recently reveals stereotypes that provide a difficult model for boys to attain—a muscular mesomorph— but an impossible one for adolescent girls to attain—that of a prepubertal girl (31). "Marked variations may adversely influence how a person is treated by others and how he thinks of himself" (22, *101*).

Thus, it is not surprising to find that even the average adolescent is sensitive to, and often critical of, his or her changing physical self (15, 26, 73, 106). The important role that physical characteristics play in the younger adolescent's self-evaluation has been demonstrated in a number of studies (21, 36, 64, 66, 97, 105, 106) in which adolescents were asked what they did and did not like about themselves. Physical characteristics were mentioned more often than either intellectual or social ones. Concerns included skin problems; wanting to be taller, shorter, thinner, or heavier; and wanting a better figure or a more athletic body build. Interestingly, the proportion of things liked to things disliked shifted increasingly in a favorable direction from junior high school to senior high school and from senior high school to college.

The adolescent who perceives himself or herself as deviating physically from cultural stereotypes is likely to have an impaired self-concept. Thus, among adolescent boys those with slim, athletic builds tend to have a higher self-concept, to be more self-assured, and to see themselves more often as leaders than do heavy-set, chubby youths or those with slight, angular body builds. Furthermore, they are more likely to be viewed by peers as popular, dominant, enthusiastic, active, aggressive, and daring, and as leaders (64, 65, 66). The bodies that are favored among boys tend to be those associated with earlier maturation. Among girls, the earlier maturers tend to have the worst self- and body-image. The best timing is to be right on pace with everyone else, with late maturers being a close second best (118). These results

are consistent with the finding that the media stereotype of an attractive young woman is a leggy, slim, prepubertal body shape.

It should be stressed, however, that such self-perceptions are not always simply a result of objective realities. Adolescents' perceptions of their physical self (body image) may be influenced by prior experiences that have led them to view themselves as attractive or unattractive, strong or weak, masculine or feminine—regardless of the actual facts of their adolescent physical appearance and capabilities.

Thus, a boy with low self-esteem who is of average overall size and strength may view himself as smaller and weaker than he is. Not infrequently, the boy or girl who feels guilty, consciously or unconsciously, about masturbation may find "evidence" of resulting physical "abnormalities," ranging from acne, circles under the eyes, or fatigue to supposed deformities in appearance of the sexual organs—none of which have any objective basis. A girl who, in terms of current cultural stereotypes, is really quite beautiful may view herself as unattractive because she has been told for years that she looks like a parent or other relative whom she resents, or whom others have denigrated.

Whereas the perceptions that adolescents have of their physical appearance can be influenced by their more general image of themselves as people—by their overall self-esteem or the lack of it—the reverse can also be the case. The young person who meets cultural standards of physical appearance and ability, and receives approval from peers and adults for these characteristics, may gain a better self-image in other respects as well, unfair as this may seem.

Adolescent girls tend to be even more concerned about their physical development than boys for a number of reasons (20, 23, 64, 66, 105). The societal stereotype of feminine beauty is impossible for most girls to attain. For girls, outward appearance and their inner self-image are often more closely bound together than for males. They are more likely than boys to interpret objective remarks about appearance, such as "You look awful," to mean "You are awful" (20, 21, 22, 23). Furthermore, despite recent changes in sex-role concepts, resulting in more flexibility and greater allowance for individual differences, the average girl's self-esteem is still anchored to interpersonal relations more than is the case for boys (20, 64, 71, 105). "Both individual and overall ratings of assumed body parts attractiveness accounted for more variation in the self-concepts of females than males" (64, *315*). A more recent study, however, revealed similar contributions of body image to self-image in both boys and girls (58).

Conformity to cultural stereotypes regarding appearance may be a social asset, but it may also present problems. Extremely attractive adolescents may receive special treatment they have not earned; as a result, they may fail to recognize the need for establishing competence in other areas of life. Being a high school beauty queen may be a very pleasant experience, but it does little to prepare one for the many and varied demands and stresses of adult life (23).

### Psychological aspects of menstruation

Menstruation is much more to the adolescent girl than just a physiological readjustment. It is a symbol of sexual maturity—of her future status as a woman. Because a girl's reaction to menstruation may generalize, it is vital that her initial experiences be as favorable as possible.

Increasing numbers of contemporary girls view the onset of menstruation calmly, and some look forward to it as a symbol of increased status—of becoming a woman. In the words of one older adolescent girl, "It seemed that all my friends had gotten their period already, or were just having it. I felt left out. I began to think of it as a symbol. When I got my period, I would be a *woman*." Unfortunately, however, many other girls view this normal—and inevitable—development negatively. In a recent study (101), a majority of preadolescent and adolescent American girls saw the effects of menstruation as either negative, or at best neutral: Only 39 percent expressed the view that it was something to be happy about. Most felt that menstruation "is something women just have to put up with."

Why do so many adolescent girls seem to react negatively to the onset of menstruation? One frequent reason is the negative attitude of others. If a girl's parents and friends act as though she requires sympathy for her "plight"—an attitude indicated by such euphemisms as "the curse"—the girl herself is likely to react in a similar fashion. Another reason is lack of adequate preparation for menarche (the onset of menstruation). If a mother or other primary caretaker waits until menstruation has actually started to explain its functions, the girl may be surprised and shocked by the sudden appearance of menstrual blood, and think that she has injured herself; some girls have even thought they were dying, though fortunately such events are much rarer in today's more open climate regarding sexual matters. Recent research shows that premenarcheal girls *expect* more menstrual difficulties than postmenarcheal girls of the same age (10). The same data also show that

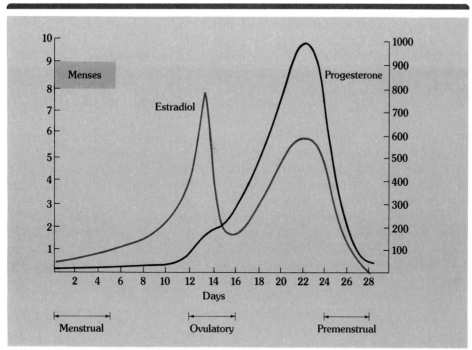

**Figure 4.6** Variations in hormonal levels during the menstrual cycle. (Adapted from L. Speroff and R. L. Vande Wiele. *American Journal of Obstetrics and Gynecology,* 1971, **109,** 234–247. By permission.)

expectations are related to later experiences of premenstrual pain. At particular risk, however, are early-maturing girls, who are less likely to be informed about menarche and more vulnerable to feeling different from their peers (88).

Some reactions to menstruation are, of course, related to actual experiences of pain. Dysmenorrhea, or cramps experienced before or during menses, was reported by almost 60 percent of the 7000 adolescents (aged 12 to 17 years) studied in the National Health Examination Survey, Cycle III (61). This study provides the first data on dysmenorrhea in adolescence in a national probability sample of American youth. Contrary to the popular belief that cramps and other menstrual symptoms are worst during the early postmenarcheal years, reports of at least mild pain increase from 31 percent to 78 percent over the first 5 postmenarcheal years and then plateau at about 70 percent (62). Only 14 percent of those in pain describe it as "severe," and relief is now available from several drugs, including aspirin, that inhibit the primary substance that produces cramps (62).

### Personality and the menstrual cycle

The common belief that most women show mood fluctuations linked to hormonal changes of the menstrual cycle has been challenged by recent research (83, 84). The patterns of monthly variations that take place in the female hormones estrogen and progesterone are shown in Figure 4.6. While some women do show cyclic patterns of mood fluctuation presumably related to hormone changes, most do not. And the kind of pattern observed is not consistent from study to study: Some have found negative moods premenstrually (49) while others have found more positive moods at this time (84). The prevalent beliefs about such changes were reinforced by studies using extreme clinical samples (17). An experiment where some girls were led to believe that they were premenstrual while others were told that their period was two weeks off revealed that beliefs about menstrual cycle effects are stronger than changes that are actually experienced (100). Longitudinal studies (19, 84) of day-to-day changes in mood, personality, or activity levels have failed to find the cyclic fluctuations seen in studies relying on retrospective reports (44, 98). In one study where husbands and wives were studied, the only mood variable showing a different pattern between the two was hostility. Moreover, husbands and wives differed only in the pattern of changes, but not in overall amount of hostility (19).

Studies with adolescents have found that boys and premenarcheal girls describe the stereotypic patterns of changes, with stronger negative effects assumed than are reported by girls who are actually menstruating (10). While there is no doubt that some girls and women do experience physiologically based psychological effects of menstruation, traditional strong beliefs about changes have exaggerated the prevalence and perhaps the intensity of menstrual effects.

While the effects of hormonal variations in females (and in a less clearly understood fashion in males) (93) are of considerable interest, they provide no scientific basic for what Karen Paige (81, 82) refers to as the "raging hormone" theory. In earlier generations, many girls were brought up expecting to feel weak, sick, or depressed before and during their periods, and to be unable to engage in normal activities, including vigorous physical exercise. Not surprisingly, many girls responded as expected. In reality, the only danger is not likely to be failing to avoid exercise, but using menstruation as an excuse for retreating from normal activities, for gaining attention, or for avoiding other problems. "A healthy girl can exercise, go to classes, work, go to parties, or do anything else she likes while she menstruates" (16, *24*).

There are, of course, other reasons why an adolescent girl may react negatively to menstruation. If she resents or fears growing up, or if she has been unable to establish a satisfactory feminine identification, she may be disturbed by the unmistakable message that menstruation provides—that she is a developing woman and there is nothing she can do to change that fact.

Recent educational materials for girls such as *Period* (41) and *Our Bodies, Ourselves* (8) describe the changes of menarche and menstruation more accurately than previous descriptions. But accurate educational materials cannot do the job alone; parents are essential to the process. Many negative reactions to menstruation could be avoided or alleviated if parents employed a wise and understanding approach. By explaining to the girl the naturalness of the phenomenon, by seeing that she receives adequate medical care in case of any physical difficulties, and by showing pride and pleasure in her greater maturity, parents can help to make the onset of menstruation a rewarding, rather than a feared or hated, event. While the mother usually plays the major part in this, the father can be very helpful too. Dr. Wardell Pomeroy, a clinical psychologist and one of the original authors of the Kinsey Report, describes one father "who observed the occasion of his daughter's first menstruation by bringing her flowers and making a little ceremony of the fact that she had now become a young lady. That daughter could not help feeling proud and good about becoming an adolescent" (91, 47).

### Erection, ejaculation, and nocturnal emission

As the onset of menstruation may cause concern to the pubescent girl, so may uncontrolled erection and initial ejaculation surprise and worry the pubescent boy. The penis is, of course, capable of erection from birth on, and erection is frequently seen in male infants during bathing or prior to elimination. Most often it results from local stimulation or related physical events (such as a full bladder). Although genital stimulation (as well as other forms of bodily stimulation) is clearly pleasurable for male (and female) infants and children, neither erection nor genital stimulation usually carries with it the sense of sexual urgency that characterizes it during puberty, and frequency of erection is much less. Prior to puberty, boys may produce an erection and are capable of penetration, though without ejaculation. During pubescence, however, the penis begins to tumesce very readily, either spontaneously or in response to a variety of stimuli: "provocative sights, sounds, smells, language, or whatever—the [younger] male adolescent inhabits a libidinized life-space where almost anything can take on a sexual meaning" (108, 424). Although boys may be proud of their capacity for erection, they may also be worried or embarrassed by an apparent inability to control this response. They may become apprehensive about dancing with a girl, or even having to stand up in a school classroom to give a report. They may wonder if other boys show a similar apparent lack of control.

Initial ejaculation of seminal fluid may also be a source of concern. The adolescent boy's first ejaculation is likely to occur within a year of the onset of the growth spurt (around age 14, although it may occur as early as 11 or as late as 16) (12, 102). "At this point the youth is usually sterile; only in a year to three years does spermatogenesis advance far enough for sufficient numbers of motile sperm to appear in the ejaculate so that the boy is fertile" (102, 31). First ejaculation may occur as a result of masturbation or nocturnal emission (ejaculation of seminal fluid during sleep)—or even of spontaneous waking orgasm. A boy who has previously masturbated, with accompanying pleasant sensations but without ejaculation, may wonder if the ejaculation of seminal fluid is harmful or is an indication that something is physically wrong with him.

According to Kinsey (59), approximately 83 percent of males report experiencing nocturnal emissions at some time in their lives, usually beginning a year or two after the onset of puberty. Frequently, but by no means always, these emissions are accompanied by erotic dreams. Nocturnal emission occurs more frequently among youth without other sexual outlets, such as masturbation, petting to orgasm, or intercourse (59, 75, 94). The female equivalent of nocturnal emissions, nocturnal dreams with orgasm, is far less frequent (probably never exceeding 10 percent) and tends not to occur at all until after adolescence (59, 75).

It appears that contemporary adolescents are better informed and less likely to be concerned about such developmental events as menstruation or nocturnal emission than those of earlier generations. Nevertheless, many boys and girls, especially in the early years of adolescence, do not gain proper instruction from parents, schools, or peers, and torture themselves with unnecessary fears (90, 91).

### Pubertal hormones and their effects on sexual interest and behavior

The hormonal changes accompanying puberty play an important, but by no means exclusive, role in fostering increased sexual interest and activity during this period, most clearly for males. In males, "the onset of sex drive (manifested in nocturnal emissions and masturbation) and of sociosexual behavior (dating and falling in love) correspond with the rapid rise in testosterone levels between 12 and 14" (47, *480–481*). Decline in the frequency of sexual activity with age also tends to parallel decreasing testosterone levels (59, 75). Administration of antiandrogen drugs can reduce sex drive in males (9, 47).

In females, relationships between hormonal levels and psychosexual functioning are more complex and are still incompletely understood (47, 89). As in boys, androgen (testosterone) levels increase in girls during puberty, but much less (see Figure 4.7). Nevertheless, androgens appear to play some role in the female sex drive; administration of testosterone can result in increased sexual interest and activity, as can androgen-producing tumors of the ovary (47).

It was previously thought that fluctuating levels of sexual interest and activity in women were due to hormonal changes of the menstrual cycle (3, 6, 17, 49, 111). Recent research, based upon a 30-year-old hypothesis of Clelland Ford and Frank Beach, pioneers in this field of research (35), has suggested that the changes in sexual interest and activity are based upon anticipated deprivation during menstruation, with a rebound effect after menses (43). Such an explanation may also account for studies that find that sexually aggressive dreams and fantasies are more frequent during the menstrual phase of the cycle, while those involving acceptance and receptivity are more frequent during the ovulatory phase (47, 49, 76, 98, 99).

As we shall see in Chapter 8, although hormones play a role in the *level* of sexual interest and arousal, environmental factors (particularly sex of rearing) appear to play the principal role in determining gender identity and the *direction* of sexual preference.

Psychoanalytic theory emphasizes an upsurge in both sexual *and* aggressive impulses with the onset of adolescence, particularly in males (32, 37, 38). Social and clinical observation also calls attention to the apparent greater restlessness of younger adolescent boys, as well as their greater preoccupation with sexual activity. The magnitude of the sex difference in testosterone levels following puberty, seen in conjunction with our knowledge that testosterone level is related to activity levels and aggressive (including sexual) behavior (3, 24, 46, 85), may help to account in part not only for the relatively greater physical aggressiveness of adolescent males, but also for the apparently more imperious and less easily suppressed quality of the male sexual drive during adolescence (3, 46, 59). It is important, however, in discussing greater aggressiveness among adolescent males to emphasize that, as Elea-

*Figure 4.7* Androgens during pubertal development. Mean trends in plasma concentrations of (a) dihydrotestosterone and (b) testosterone related to pubertal developmental stages. (From D. Gupta, A. Attanasio, and S. Raaf. Plasma estrogen and androgen concentrations in children during adolescence. *Journal of Clinical Endocrinology and Metabolism*, 1975, **40,** 636–643. By permission.)

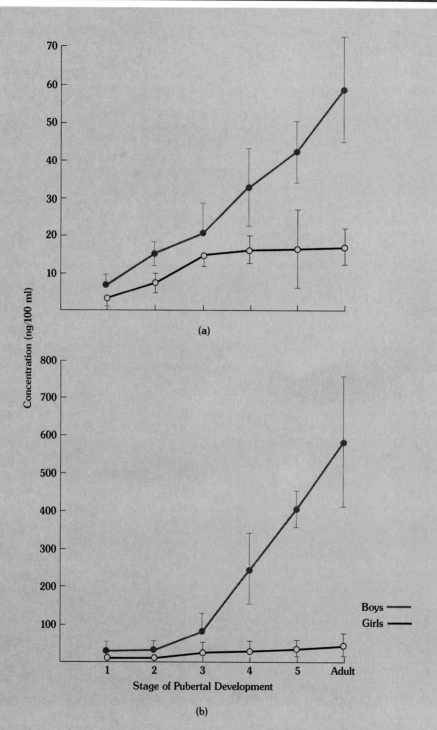

(a)

(b)

Concentration (ng/100 ml)

Stage of Pubertal Development

Boys ———
Girls ———

nor Maccoby and Carol Jacklin point out, this does not mean that females are either angelic or weak:

> Women share with men the human capacity to heap all sorts of injuries upon their fellows. And in almost every group that has been observed, there are some women who are fully as aggressive as the men. Furthermore, an individual's aggressive behavior is strengthened, weakened, redirected, or altered in form by his or her unique pattern of experiences. All we mean to argue is that there is a sex-linked differential readiness to respond in aggressive ways to the relevant experiences [67, *247*].

### Early and late maturers

As we have already seen, young people vary widely in the ages at which they reach puberty. At age 15, one boy may be small, with no pubertal development of reproductive organs or pubic hair. Another boy of the same age may appear to be virtually a grown man, with broad shoulders, strong muscles, adult genitalia, and a bass voice (115). Even though such variations are perfectly normal, and do not either help or interfere with the eventual achievement of full physical and sexual maturity, they can affect the way adolescents view themselves—and the way they are viewed by others.

### Early versus late maturation in boys

In general, the effects of early or late maturing appear to be more direct among boys, and easier to understand; for girls, timing of maturation has more complex effects. Adults and other adolescents tend to think of the 14- or 15-year-old boy who looks 17 or 18 as older than he actually is. They are likely to expect more mature behavior from him than they would from a physically less developed boy of the same age. Because there is less of a physical discrepancy between an early-maturing boy and most girls his own age (because of the earlier growth spurt in girls), he may become involved sooner and with more self-confidence in boy-girl relationships. Furthermore, a physically more developed boy has an advantage in many activities, especially athletics. Although a boy who matures much faster than most of his peers may feel somewhat different, he is not likely to feel insecure about the difference. After all, with his more rugged physique, increased strength, and greater sexual maturity, he can assure himself that he is simply changing in the direction society expects and approves.

In contrast, the late-maturing boy is more likely to be treated as a child—a fact which may infuriate him, even though he may continue to behave immaturely. He is likely to have a harder time in achieving recognition in athletics and other activities, and in his relations with girls. Perhaps most painful of all, he may wonder when, if ever, he will reach full physical and sexual maturity.

Not surprisingly, all of this results—on the average—in personality differences between early and late maturers. Extensive, long-term research studies at the University of California found that boys who matured late tended to be less poised, more tense and talkative, and more self-conscious and affected in their manner (15, 51, 53, 54, 55, 56, 57, 78, 79, 86). They were also likely to be more restless, more overeager, more impulsive, more bossy, and more attention-seeking. Though obviously there are exceptions, late maturers tended to be less popular with peers, and fewer of them were leaders.

Early maturers, on the other hand, appeared more reserved, self-assured, and matter-of-fact, and more likely to engage easily in socially appropriate behavior. They were also more likely to be able to laugh at themselves.

On psychological tests, late maturers were found to have more feelings of inadequacy, poorer self-concepts, and more feelings of being rejected or dominated by others. Somewhat paradoxically, they were more likely to combine persisting dependency needs with a seemingly rebellious search for independence and freedom from parental and social restraints (78). In other words, late maturers appeared more likely to prolong the typical adolescent independence-dependence conflict than early maturers (120). Recent research with young adolescents (118) supports the finding of better outcomes among earlier-maturing boys.

Such differences can easily persist into adulthood. When the subjects of the California investigation were followed up at age 33, the average late maturer still emerged as less self-controlled, less responsible, and less dominant in relations with others; and more likely to turn to others for support and help. Early maturers, on the other hand, tended to be more conventional, conforming, dominant, and concerned with making a good impression (15, 77). However, by age 38, the two groups showed relatively few differences, principally a tendency for early maturers to be more conventional and to take pride in seeing themselves as reasonable and objective (15).

Much can be done by parents, teachers, and others to minimize the anxiety and other negative psychological effects of late maturing. They can make a conscious effort to avoid the trap of treating a late maturer as younger than he actually is. They can help him to realize that his slower maturation is perfectly normal—that he will indeed grow up and be just as physically and sexually masculine as his peers. And they can help him to achieve success in activities where physical size and strength are not a handicap. For example, while immaturity and smaller physical size can be a handicap for a potential football player, it can often be an asset for a diver or tumbler. In many hobbies, relative maturity makes absolutely no difference whatever.

### Early versus late maturation in girls

Although early or average maturation appears generally advantageous to boys, among girls overall differences are much less, as well as more variable (11, 15, 29, 57, 118). Some studies have found early-maturing girls to be slightly more relaxed, more secure in their view of themselves and the world, and better adjusted, while late-maturing girls appeared somewhat more anxious. Others, however, have found late-maturing girls to be slightly more outgoing, confident, and self-assured, while early-maturing girls appeared more restless, moody, listless, and lacking in poise (29, 86, 120).

How can we explain these discrepancies, as well as the fact that overall differences between early and late maturation are much less for girls than for boys? It seems likely that the *meaning* of early or late maturation is dependent on more different factors than is the case with boys. One such factor is age. In an ingeniously

designed study, it was found that in the sixth grade, early maturers (girls who had already achieved menarche) had less prestige among their peers than those who were developmentally "in phase" (prepubertal). However, beginning with the seventh grade, when most girls had begun to cope with the demands of puberty, and continuing through junior high school, the picture shifted. At the seventh grade, postpubertal girls scored most favorably, and at eighth and ninth grades, girls in late adolescence (4 to 6 years beyond menarche) scored most favorably.

In brief, "it appears that prestige is more likely to surround those in the sixth grade who are developmentally 'in phase' (prepubertal) whereas during the junior high school years being ahead of the group developmentally seems to be an advantage" (29, *97*). That girls who had not yet experienced puberty should assign the most prestige to others like themselves does not appear too surprising. Nor does the fact that once these girls had entered puberty and begun to look ahead to new social-sexual roles, they ascribed prestige increasingly to those among their peers who were furthest along in role-related development. However, the *rapidity* of the shift in prestige from prepubertal to postpubertal and late-adolescent stages can pose significant problems. The investigator herself describes the case of a girl who was popular and commanded prestige at the age of 12, but who at age 14 or 15 was still developmentally immature: "She is now one of the very few little girls; she seemed like a child in the midst of adults with a group of girls; tended to avoid large mixed groups of boys and girls and their activities" (29, *98*).

In a recent study of young adolescents (118), seventh-grade girls who were "on time" relative to their peers had the most positive views of themselves and their bodies, while late maturers had the next most positive images.

Another factor appears to be social class—or probably more precisely, the effect of social class on the meaning to the girl of early or late maturation. In one extensive study (15, 89), it was found that for middle-class girls early maturation was positively related to self-confidence, while for working-class girls, there was a negative relationship between early maturation and self-confidence. It may be that middle-class parents were better able to help their daughters to handle early maturation and to shield them from confusing pressures from older peers to engage in premature heterosexual and other social activities engaged in by older adolescents.

More importantly, however, society's expectations for adolescent boys tend to be clearer and less ambiguous than for girls. In boys, early maturing means greater strength and physical prowess—and, eventually, active sexual behavior. In girls, the expectations are less clearly defined. Is early sexual maturity a help or a hindrance? Is sexual activity at an earlier age than peers good or bad? Is the girl's adjustment aided by having to deal with the complex feelings aroused by the onset of menstruation and the adaptations it requires, when most of her peers are still more like little girls? Society often gives girls mixed messages on these matters, as do peers. The girl who is sexually attractive at an early age will be more likely to attract the attention of older boys. But is this desirable? There is always the danger that she may be lured by the immediate rewards of dating older boys into failing to continue developing mature relationships with other girls her age, or developing as an individual in her own right. She may also come to feel that she is gaining attention merely as a sex object, rather than for who she really is—a complex person. Perhaps worse, she may come to believe that being pretty and sexy, and having superficial social skills, are all that is needed to be truly grown-up.

In the final analysis, a girl's adjustment to the changes of puberty will probably depend more on the kinds of support, encouragement, and guidance she receives from parents, and the values and expectations of her own particular peer group, than it will on whether maturation is early, average, or late.

In the case of the early-maturing girls, parents and others should be careful to avoid pressing the girl too early into heterosexual relationships. They can help her to realize that popularity and being grown-up at an early age can be a two-edged sword, and that the most important assets one can have are self-reliance, competency, and a clear, abiding sense of one's own identity as a total person. Girls have less need than boys for engaging in rebellion against the family in early adolescence, and it has been our clinical experience over the years that attempts to push younger adolescent girls out of the nest into premature, and often largely superficial, heterosexual relationships are likely to be destructive, and to interfere with, rather than foster, eventual true maturity.

Of course, at the same time, parents and others need to assure the late-maturing girl of her ultimate physical and sexual maturity, just as in the case of boys. If they can help her to realize that there is really no need to rush things along—that, in fact, gradual maturation can even be useful in allowing her to devote her energies to other important developmental tasks—many unnecessary concerns can be alleviated.

**REFERENCES**

1. Acheson, R. M. Maturation of the skeleton. In F. Falkner (ed.), *Human development.* Philadelphia: Saunders, 1966.

2. Adelson, J. (ed.). *Handbook of adolescent psychology.* New York: Wiley, 1980.

3. Bardwick, J. *Psychology of women: A study of bio-cultural conflicts.* New York: Harper & Row, 1971.

4. Bayley, N. Some increasing parent-child similarities during the growth of children. *Journal of Educational Psychology,* 1954, **45,** 1–21.

5. Bell, R. *Changing bodies, changing lives: A book for teens on sex and relationships.* New York: Random House, 1980.

6. Benedek, T. F., & Rubenstein, B. *The sexual cycle in women: The relation between ovarian function and psychodynamic processes.* Washington, D.C.: National Research Council, 1942.

7. Bock, R. D., Wainer, H., Petersen, A., Thissen, D., Murray, J., & Roche, A. A parameterization for individual human growth curves. *Human Biology,* 1973, **45,** 63–80.

8. The Boston Women's Health Book Collective. *Our bodies, ourselves: A book by and for women.* New York: Simon & Schuster, 1976 (2nd ed.).

9. Brecher, E. M. *The sex researchers.* New York: New American Library, 1971.

10. Brooks-Gunn, J., & Ruble, D. N. The experience of menarche from a developmental perspective. In J. Brooks-Gunn & A. C. Petersen (eds.), *Girls at puberty: Biological, psychological, and social perspectives.* New York: Plenum, in press.

11. Buck, C., & Stavraky, K. The relationship between age of menarche and age at marriage among childbearing women. *Human Biology,* 1967, **39,** 93–102.

12. Burgess, A. P., & Burgess, H. J. L. The growth pattern of East African school girls. *Human Biology,* 1964, **36,** 177–193.

13. Burrell, R. S. W., Healy, M. J. R., & Tanner, J. M. Age at menarche in South African Bantu schoolgirls living in the Transkei reserve. *Human Biology,* 1961, **33,** 250–261.

14. Carron, A. V., & Bailey, D. A. Strength development in boys from 10 through 16 years. *Monographs of the Society for Research in Child Development,* 1974, **39,** No. 4, 1–36.

15. Clausen, J. A. The social meaning of differential physical and sexual maturation. In S. E. Dragastin & G. H. Elder, Jr. (eds.), *Adolescence in the life cycle: Psychological change and social context.* New York: Wiley, 1975. Pp. 25–47.

16. Conger, J. J. *Adolescence: Generation under pressure.* New York: Harper & Row, 1979.

17. Dalton, K. *The premenstrual syndrome.* Springfield, Ill.: Thomas, 1964.

18. Dalton, K. The influence of mother's menstruation on her child. *Proceedings of the Royal Society for Medicine,* 1966, **59,** 1014.

19. Dan, A. J. Free-associative versus self-report measures of emotional change over the menstrual cycle. In A. J. Dan, E. A. Graham, & C. P. Beecher (eds.), *The menstrual cycle, Volume I, A synthesis of interdisciplinary research.* New York: Springer Publishing Co., 1980.

20. Douvan, E., & Adelson, J. *The adolescent experience.* New York: Wiley, 1966.

21. Douvan, E. A., & Kaye, C. *Adolescent girls.* Ann Arbor: Survey Research Center, University of Michigan, 1957.

22. Dwyer, J., & Mayer, J. Variations in physical appearance during adolescence. Part 1. Boys. *Postgraduate Medicine.* 1967, **41,** 99–107.

23. Dwyer, J., & Mayer, J. Variations in physical appearance during adolescence. Part 2. Girls. *Postgraduate Medicine,* 1967, **42,** 91–97.

24. Ehrhardt, A. A., & Baker, S. Hormonal aberrations and their implications for the understanding of normal sex differentiation. In P. H. Mussen, J. J. Conger, & J. Kagan (eds.), *Basic and contemporary issues in developmental psychology.* New York: Harper & Row, 1975. Pp. 113–121.

25. Eichorn, D. H. Physiological development. In P. H. Mussen (ed.), *Carmichael's manual of child psychology* (Vol. 2). New York: Wiley, 1970 (3rd ed.).

26. Eichorn, D. H. Asynchronizations in adolescent development. In S. E. Dragastin & G. H. Elder, Jr. (eds.), *Adolescence in the life cycle: Psychological change and social context.* New York: Wiley, 1975. Pp. 81–96.
27. Espenschade, A. Motor performance in adolescence. *Monographs of the Society for Research in Child Development,* 1940, **5,** No. 1.
28. Faiman, C., & Winter, J. S. D. Gonadotropins and sex hormone patterns in puberty: Clinical data. In M. M. Grumbach, G. D. Grave, & F. E. Mayer (eds.), *Control of the onset of puberty.* New York: Wiley, 1974.
29. Faust, M. S. Developmental maturity as a determinant in prestige of adolescent girls. *Child Development,* 1960, **31,** 173–184.
30. Faust, M. S. Somatic development of adolescent girls. *Monographs of the Society for Research in Child Development,* 1977, **42,** No. 1, 1–90.
31. Faust, M. Alternative constructions of adolescent growth. In J. Brooks-Gunn & A. C. Petersen (eds.), *Girls at puberty: Biological, psychological, and social perspectives.* New York: Plenum, in press.
32. Fenichel, O. *The psychoanalytic theory of neurosis.* New York: Norton, 1945.
33. Ferris, B. G., & Smith, C. W. Maximum breathing capacity and vital capacity of female children and adolescents. *Pediatrics,* 1953, **12,** 341–353.
34. Ferris, B. G., Whittenberger, J. L., & Gallagher, J. R. Maximum breathing capacity and vital capacity of male children and adolescents. *Pediatrics,* 1952, **9,** 659–670.
35. Ford, C., & Beach, F. *Patterns of sexual behavior.* New York: Harper & Row, 1951.
36. Frazier, A., & Lisonbee, L. K. Adolescent concerns with physique. *School Review,* 1950, **58,** 397–405.
37. Freud, A. Adolescence. *Psychoanalytic Study of the Child,* 1958, **13,** 255–278.
38. Freud, S. *A general introduction to psychoanalysis* (Joan Riviere, trans.). New York: Permabooks, 1953.
39. Frisch, R. E. Critical weight at menarche, initiation of the adolescent growth spurt, and control of puberty. In M. M. Grumbach, G. D. Grave, & F. E. Mayer (eds.), *Control of the onset of puberty.* New York: Wiley, 1974.
40. Frisch, R. E. Fatness, puberty, and fertility. In J. Brooks-Gunn & A. C. Petersen (eds.), *Girls at puberty: Biological, psychological, and social perspectives.* New York: Plenum, in press.
41. Gardner-Loular, J., Lopez, B., & Quackenbush, M. *Period.* San Francisco: New Glade Publications, Inc., 1979.
42. Garrison, K. C. Physiological changes in adolescence. In J. F. Adams (ed.), *Understanding adolescence: Current development in adolescent psychology.* Boston: Allyn & Bacon, 1968.
43. Gold, A. R., & Adams, D. B. Motivational factors affecting fluctuations of female sexual activity at menstruation. *Psychology of Women Quarterly,* 1981, **5,** 670–680.
44. Golub, S. Premenstrual changes in mood, personality, and cognitive function. In A. J. Dan, E. A. Graham, & C. P. Beecher (eds.), *The menstrual cycle, Volume I, A synthesis of interdisciplinary research.* New York: Springer Publishing Co., 1980.
45. Gupta, D., Attanasio, A., & Raaf, S. Plasma estrogen and androgen concentrations in children during adolescence. *Journal of Clinical Endocrinology and Metabolism,* 1975, **40,** 636–643.
46. Hamburg, D., & Trudeau, M. B. (eds.). *Biobehavioral aspects of aggression.* New York: Alan R. Liss, Inc., 1981.
47. Higham, E. Variations in adolescent psychohormonal development. In J. Adelson (ed.), *Handbook of Adolescent Psychology.* New York: Wiley, 1980.
48. Iliff, A., & Lee, V. A. Pulse rate, respiratory rate, and body temperature of children between two months and eighteen years of age. *Child Development,* 1952, **23,** 237–245.
49. Ivey, M. E., & Bardwick, J. M. Patterns of affective fluctuation in the menstrual cycle. *Psychosomatic Medicine,* 1968, **30,** 336–345.
50. Jersild, A. T. *In search of self.* New York: Columbia University Press, 1952.

51. Jones, H. E. The California adolescent growth study. *Journal of Educational Research,* 1938, **31,** 561–567.

52. Jones, H. E. *Motor performance and growth: A developmental study of state dynamometric strength.* Berkeley, Calif.: Unviersity of California Press, 1949.

53. Jones, H. E. The environment and mental development. In L. Carmichael (ed.), *Manual of child psychology.* New York: Wiley, 1954. Pp. 631–698.

54. Jones, M. C. The later careers of boys who were early or late maturing. *Child Development,* 1957, **28,** 113–128.

55. Jones, M. C. A study of socialization patterns at the high school level. *Journal of Genetic Psychology,* 1958, **92,** 87–111.

56. Jones, M. C., & Bayley, N. Physical maturing among boys as related to behavior. *Journal of Educational Psychology,* 1950, **41,** 129–148.

57. Jones, M. C., & Mussen, P. H. Self-conceptions, motivations, and interpersonal attitudes of early and late maturing girls. *Child Development,* 1958, **29,** 491–501.

58. Kavrell, S. M., & Jarcho, H. Self-esteem and body image in early adolescence. Presented in a symposium, "The psychological significance of pubertal charges," at the annual meeting of the American Psychological Association, Montreal, 1980.

59. Kinsey, A. C., Pomeroy, W. B., & Martin, C. E. *Sexual behavior in the human male.* Philadelphia: Saunders, 1948.

60. Kinsey A. C., Pomeroy, W. B., Martin, C. E., & Gebhard, P. H. *Sexual behavior in the human female.* Philadelphia: Saunders, 1953.

61. Klein, J. R., & Litt, I. F. Epidemiology of adolescent dysmenorrhea. *Pediatrics,* in press (a).

62. Klein, J. R., & Litt, I. F. Menarche and dysmenorrhea. In J. Brooks-Gunn & A. C. Petersen (eds.), *Girls at puberty: Biological, psychological, and social perspectives.* New York: Plenum, in press (b).

63. Korenman, S. G., Perrin, L. E., & McCallum, T. P. A radio-ligand binding assay system for estradiol measurement on human plasma. *Journal of Clinical Endocrinology and Metabolism,* 1969, **28,** 879–883.

64. Lerner, R. M., & Karabenick, S. A. Physical attractiveness, body attitudes, and self-concept in late adolescents. *Journal of Youth and Adolescence,* 1974, **3,** 307–316.

65. Lerner, R. M., Karabenick, S. A., & Stuart, J. L. Relations among physical attractiveness, body attitudes, and self-concept in male and female college students. *Journal of Psychology,* 1973, **85,** 119–129.

66. Lerner, R. M., & Korn, S. J. The development of body-build stereotypes in males. *Child Development,* 1972, **43,** 908–920.

67. Maccoby, E., & Jacklin, C. *The psychology of sex differences.* Stanford, Calif.: Stanford University Press, 1974.

68. Malina, R. M. Adolescent changes in size, build, composition and performance. *Human Biology,* 1974, **46,** 117–131.

69. Maresh, M. M. Growth of the heart related to bodily growth during childhood and adolescence. *Pediatrics,* 1948, **2,** 382–404.

70. Maresh, M. M. Variations in patterns of linear growth and skeletal maturation. *Journal of the American Physical Therapy Association,* 1964, **44,** 881–890.

71. Marshall, J. M., & Karabenick, S. A. Self-esteem, fear of success, and occupational choice in female adolescents. In C. Guardo (ed.), *Readings in adolescence.* New York: Harper & Row, 1975.

72. Marshall, W. A., & Tanner, J. M. Variations in the pattern of pubertal changes in boys. *Archives of Disease in Childhood,* 1970, **45,** 13.

73. Minahan, N. Relationships among self-perceived physical attractiveness, body shape, and personality of teen-age girls. *Dissertation Abstracts International,* 1971, **32,** 1249–1250.

74. Money, J. Psychosexual differentiation. In J. Money (ed.), *Sex research: New developments.* New York: Holt, Rinehart and Winston, 1965. Pp. 3–23.

75. Money, J., & Ehrhardt, A. A. *Man and woman, boy and girl: The differentiation and*

*dimorphism of gender identity from conception to maturity.* Baltimore: Johns Hopkins University Press, 1972.

76. Money, J., & Higman, E. Sexual behavior and endocrinology. In G. Cahill, L. DeGroat, L. Martini, D. Nelson, W. Odell, J. Potts, E. Steinberger, & A. Winegrad (eds.), *Metabolic basis of endocrinology.* New York: Grune & Stratton, 1979.

77. Mussen, P. H., Conger, J. J., & Kagan, J. *Child development and personality.* New York: Harper & Row, 1979 (5th ed.).

78. Mussen, P. H., & Jones, M. C. Self-conceptions, motivations, and interpersonal attitudes of late and early maturing boys. *Child Development,* 1957, **28,** 243–256.

79. Mussen, P. H., & Jones, M. C. The behavior-inferred motivations of late and early maturing boys. *Child Development,* 1958, **29,** 61–67.

80. Onat, T., & Ertem, B. Adolescent female height velocity: Relationships to body measurements, sexual and skeletal maturity. *Human Biology,* 1974, **46,** 199–217.

81. Paige, K. E. The effects of oral contraceptives on affective fluctuations associated with the menstrual cycle. *Psychosomatic Medicine,* 1971, **33,** 515–537.

82. Paige, K. E. Beyond the raging hormone: Women learn to sing the menstrual blues. *Psychology Today,* 1973, **7,** 41–46.

83. Parlee, M. B. The premenstrual syndrome. *Psychological Bulletin,* 1973, **80,** 454–465.

84. Parlee, M. B. Positive changes in moods and activation levels during the menstrual cycle in experimentally naive subjects. In A. J. Dan, E. A. Graham, & C. P. Beecher (eds.), *The menstrual cycle, Volume I, A synthesis of interdisciplinary research.* New York: Springer Publishing Co., 1980.

85. Persky, H., Smith, K. D., & Basu, G. K. Relation of psychologic measures of aggression and hostility to testosterone production in man. *Psychosomatic Medicine,* 1971, **33,** 265–277.

86. Peskin, H. Pubertal onset and ego functioning. *Journal of Abnormal Psychology,* 1967, **72,** 1–15.

87. Petersen, A. C. Female pubertal development. In M. Sugar (ed.), *Female adolescent development.* New York: Brunner/Mazel, 1979. Pp. 23–46.

88. Petersen, A. C. Menarche: Meaning of measures and measuring meaning. In S. Golub (ed.), *Menarche.* Lexington, Mass.: D. C. Heath, 1983.

89. Petersen, A. C., & Taylor, B. The biological approach to adolescence: Biological change and psychological adaptation. In J. Adelson (ed.), *Handbook of adolescent psychology.* New York: Wiley, 1980. Pp. 117–155.

90. Pomeroy, W. B. *Boys and sex.* New York: Dell (Delacorte Press), 1968.

91. Pomeroy, W. B. *Girls and sex.* New York: Dell (Delacorte Press), 1969.

92. Powell, G. F., Brasel, J. A., & Blizzard, R. M. Emotional deprivation and growth retardation simulating idiopathic hypopituitarism. I. Clinical evaluation of the syndrome. *New England Journal of Medicine,* 1967, **276,** 1271–1278.

93. Ramey, E. Discussion. *Annals of the New York Academy of Sciences,* 1973, **208,** 251.

94. Reevy, W. R. Adolescent sexuality. In A. Ellis & A. Abarbanel (eds.), *The encyclopedia of sexual behavior* (Vol. I). New York: Hawthorn Books, 1961.

95. Reynolds, E. L., & Wines, J. V. Individual differences in physical changes associated with adolescence in girls. *American Journal of Diseases of Children,* 1948, **75,** 329–350.

96. Reynolds, E. L., & Wines, J. V. Physical changes associated with adolescence in boys. *American Journal of Diseases of Children,* 1951, **82,** 529–547.

97. Rosen, G. M., & Ross, A. O. Relationship of body image to self-concept. *Journal of Consulting & Clinical Psychology,* 1968, **32,** 100.

98. Rossi, A. S. Mood cycles by menstrual month and social week. In A. J. Dan, E. A. Graham, & C. P. Beecher (eds.), *The menstrual cycle, Volume I, A synthesis of interdisciplinary research.* New York: Springer Publishing Co., 1980.

99. Rossi, A., & Rossi, P. Body time and social time: Mood patterns are affected by menstrual cycle phase and day of week. University of Massachusetts. Unpublished manuscript, 1977.

100. Ruble, D. N. Premenstrual symptoms. *Science,* 1977, **197,** 291–292.
101. Ruble, D. N., & Brooks, J. Attitudes about menstruation. Paper presented at the Biennial Meeting of the Society for Research in Child Development, New Orleans, March 17–20, 1977.
102. Schonfeld, W. A. The body and the body-image in adolescents. In G. Caplan & S. Lebovici (eds.), *Adolescence: Psychosocial perspectives.* New York: Basic Books, 1969. Pp. 24–53.
103. Shipman, W. G. Age at menarche and adult personality. *Archives of General Psychiatry,* 1964, **10,** 155–159.
104. Shuttleworth, F. K. Sexual maturation and the physical growth of girls age six to nineteen. *Monographs of the Society for Research in Child Development,* 1937, **2,** No. 5, Serial No. 12.
105. Simmons, R. G., & Rosenberg, F. Sex, sex roles, and self-image. *Journal of Youth and Adolescence,* 1975, **4,** 229–258.
106. Stoltz, H. R., & Stoltz, L. M. Adolescent problems related to somatic variation. In N. B. Henry (ed.), *Adolescence: Forty-third yearbook of the National Committee for the Study of Education.* Chicago: Department of Education, University of Chicago, 1944.
107. Stoltz, H. R., & Stoltz, L. M. *Somatic development of adolescent boys.* New York: Macmillan, 1951.
108. Stone, L. J., & Church, J. *Childhood and adolescence: A psychology of the growing person.* New York: Random House, 1973 (3rd ed.).
109. Stuart, H. C. Normal growth and development during adolescence. *New England Journal of Medicine,* 1946, **234,** 666–672, 693–700, 732–738.
110. Stunkard, A., & Burt, V. Obesity and the body image. II. Age at onset of disturbances in the body image. *American Journal of Psychiatry,* 1967, **123,** 1443–1447.
111. Sutherland, H., & Stewart, I. A critical analysis of the premenstrual syndrome. *Lancet,* 1965, **1,** 1180–1183.
112. Tanner, J. M. *Education and physical growth. Implications of the study of children's growth for educational theory and practice.* London: University Press, 1961.
113. Tanner, J. M. *Growth at adolescence.* Philadelphia: Davis, 1962 (2nd ed.).
114. Tanner, J. M. Growth of bone, muscle and fat during childhood and adolescence. In G. A. Lodge (ed.), *Growth and development of mammals.* London: Butterworth, 1968.
115. Tanner, J. M. Physical growth. In P. H. Mussen (ed.), *Carmichael's manual of child psychology* (Vol. 2). New York: Wiley, 1970 (3rd ed.).
116. Tanner, J. M. Sequence, tempo, and individual variation in the growth and development of boys and girls aged twelve to sixteen. *Daedalus,* 1971, **100,** No. 4, 907–930.
117. Thissen, P., Bock, R. D., Wainer, H., & Roche, A. F. Individual growth in stature: A comparison of four growth studies in the U.S.A. *Annals of Human Biology,* 1976, **3,** 529–542.
118. Tobin-Richards, M., Boxer, A., & Petersen, A. C. The psychological impact of pubertal change: Sex differences in perceptions of self during early adolescence. In J. Brooks-Gunn & A. C. Petersen (eds.), *Girls at puberty: Biological, psychological, and social perspectives.* New York: Plenum, in press.
119. Valenstein, E. S. Steroid hormones and the neuropsychology of development. In R. L. Isaacson (ed.), *The neuropsychology of development: A symposium.* New York: Wiley, 1968. Pp. 1–39.
120. Weatherley, D. Self-perceived rate of physical maturation and personality in late adolescence. *Child Development,* 1964, **35,** 1197–1210.
121. Woods, P. D., Haskell, W. L., Stern, S. L., & Perry, C. Plasma lipoprotein distributions in male and female runners. *Annals of the New York Academy of Sciences,* 1977, **301,** 748–763.
122. Young, W. C., Goy, R. W., & Phoenix, C. H. Hormones and sexual behavior. *Science,* 1964, **143,** 212–218.
123. Zabin, L. S., Kantner, J. F., & Zelnik, M. The risk of adolescent pregnancy in the first months of intercourse. *Family Planning Perspectives,* 1979, **11,** 215–222.

# Intelligence and cognitive development

## CHAPTER 5

# Intelligence and cognitive development

*T*he impressive gains in physical and physiological development that take place during adolescence are accompanied by equally impressive gains in intellectual and cognitive development. This is obvious to experienced teachers; it is also revealed in tests of intelligence. For example, if asked why we should keep away from bad company, a 15-year-old might say, "They will lead you into temptation," or "To keep from being influenced by them." The younger child might say, " 'Cause they're bad," or "My mother wouldn't like it." When asked to listen to a series of numbers and then to repeat them, the average 15-year-old will be able to remember more numbers in the correct order. Similar results will be found on a variety of indices of mental ability, ranging from measures of general information, abstract verbal reasoning, and commonsense understanding of everyday events, to tests of arithmetic skill and mechanical ability. Although parents may sometimes express consternation about the apparent inability of their adolescent sons and daughters to follow seemingly simple instructions about straightening up a bedroom, taking out the garbage, or putting the cap back on the toothpaste, the fact is that adolescents are clearly more advanced cognitively than their younger brothers and sisters.

As David Elkind, an authority on adolescent cognitive development, has observed, the gains that occur during this period can be viewed both quantitatively and qualitatively (60). They are quantitative in the sense that the adolescent becomes capable of accomplishing more easily, more quickly, and more efficiently intellectual tasks that as a child or preadolescent he or she was able to accomplish only slowly, inefficiently, and with great difficulty, if at all. They are qualitative in the sense that significant changes also occur in *the nature of the adolescent's underlying mental processes*—in the ways in which he or she is able to define problems and reason about them (60, 65).

For many years, the primary focus of psychologists was on the quantitative aspects of cognitive development, as exemplified by traditional intelligence testing, with its emphasis on individual and age differences in the ability to perform a variety of verbal and performance tasks. Only in recent decades has there been a comparable emphasis on the qualitative aspects—the underlying processes—involved in cognitive development, as exemplified by the newer developmental psychology of Jean

Piaget and others (77, 120, 156, 157). Obviously, distinctions between the quantitative and qualitative aspects of cognitive development are somewhat arbitrary, and primarily reflect differences in emphasis. The quantitative approach "does not deny that modes of thought differ with age" (60, *129*). Similarly, the qualitative approach "does not deny that individual differences in brightness exist, and such differences are used to account for the finding that some children attain particular mental abilities before or after the majority of their age mates" (60, *129*). In brief, the quantitative and qualitative approaches to cognitive development represent, as it were, two sides of the same coin, which complement, rather than contradict, each other.

If it were not for these quantitative and qualitative gains in cognitive capability, adolescents would be incapable of confronting and dealing successfully with many of the important demands made upon them during this period. This may appear obvious in the case of demands for educational accomplishment and the development of vocational skills; but, as we shall see, it is equally true in the case of such nonacademic tasks as the development of personal, social, and political values, and a sense of ego identity.

## THE COURSE OF MENTAL GROWTH

The quantitative approach to intellectual development dates back at least to the pioneer work of Alfred Binet, a prominent French psychologist who was the father of the modern intelligence test. In 1904, the French government became concerned about the many nonlearners in the schools of Paris, and asked Binet to develop a test to detect those children who were too dull to profit from ordinary schooling. In collaboration with another French psychologist, Theodore Simon, Binet set about devising a test that would "separate the generally dull from those who had adequate educability" (40, *103*). Their responsibility was not to devise a measure of *intellectual achievement,* but a measure of *intelligence, or intellectual ability.* That is, they were to assess not what students *had* accomplished, but what they *might be able* to accomplish. This is not a simple task, and requires the adoption of a number of assumptions about the nature of intelligence and how it develops. To understand what Binet and Simon faced, it is necessary to explore somewhat further what is actually meant by the term *intelligence,* and to distinguish tests of intelligence from tests of achievement.

### The meaning of intelligence

What do we actually mean by *intelligence?* To the ordinary person, the answers may seem obvious. We seem satisfied that we understand the meaning of the term when we say in everyday conversation, "He is not very bright," or "As any normally intelligent person can see . . . ," and so on. However, the matter is more complex than it may at first appear. In attempting to clarify the issue, it is probably best to begin by stating what intelligence is *not.*

There is a tendency for people to think that because many words stand for things, all words do. This idea is false. Many words, such as the concepts of time and force in physics, are simply useful scientific fictions (i.e., hypothetical constructs) that help us to explain observable events. But they do not stand for objects, or classes of objects, in the way words such as *tree* and *chair* do. In the same way, no one has ever seen, heard, or touched *intelligence*. It too is a hypothetical construct—invented to help explain and predict behavior (37). And because intelligence is hypothetical, there is no single correct definition of the term, although one definition may be more useful for particular purposes than another. Over the years a number of psychologists have defined intelligence, and though they differ in terminology, most would probably agree that it is best defined as the ability to benefit from experience, to learn new ideas or new sets of behaviors easily (89, 195, 210). For example, David Wechsler, developer of the widely used Wechsler Intelligence Scales for children, adolescents, and adults, prefers to define intelligence as "the aggregate or global capacity of the individual to act purposefully, to think rationally, and to deal effectively with his environment" (210, 211).

It is generally assumed that everyone has a ceiling, a point above which he or she will not be able to profit from experience in a particular activity, and that this ceiling is set by hereditary factors (152). How nearly any individual approaches that potential ceiling, and the rate at which he or she does so, is determined by a variety of factors, including rate of physiological *maturation* and the richness of the *environment* to which he or she is exposed.

Conversely, a person's potential ceiling may be lowered in the course of development, from conception on, by a variety of external and internal events. Obvious examples include such physiological events as brain injury or disease. Less obviously, it may be that if the developing biological organism does not receive a certain amount of psychological and physical stimulation from its environment during certain *critical periods* in its development (50, 109, 110, 111), it may be temporarily or permanently handicapped in its *future* ability to profit from subsequent learning opportunities.

There is, however, an additional point that needs to be stressed at this juncture, which is of critical importance in any consideration of intelligence, and particularly of intelligence *testing* (i.e., the determination of IQs): *There is no way to measure directly* an individual's intellectual potential (his or her ultimate "ceiling"). We can only measure what a person can *do* (whether the task be a verbal or psychomotor one). This means that we can measure only the results of an *interaction* between the individual, with whatever potential he or she may have, and the environment. To take an extreme example, a young child raised from birth in silence in a dark room by a psychotic mother (and there have been such cases) would obviously be unable to perform any of the tasks on a standard intelligence test. But this does not mean that his or her intellectual potential is zero. As will become evident, we may attempt *indirectly* to estimate a child's or adolescent's intellectual potential, and indeed that is one of the purposes of an intelligence test as distinguished from an achievement test. The manner in which this is done is best illustrated by considering an example of intelligence-test construction. And here we return to the task facing Alfred Binet at the turn of the century.

### Intelligence-test construction

Binet assumed that a dull child was like a normal one but retarded in his or her mental growth; he reasoned that the dull child would perform on tests like a normal child of younger age. He therefore decided to scale intelligence as the kind of change that occurs in the course of a child's maturation.

Accordingly, he set about constructing a scale of units of *mental age* (MA). Average mental-age scores would correspond to *chronological age* (CA) (i.e., the age determined from date of birth). A bright girl's MA would be above her CA; a retarded child would have an MA below her CA. The mental-age scale is easily interpreted by teachers and others who deal with children differing in mental ability (98).

**Item selection** Because Binet, like most of his successors in the development of intelligence tests, conceived intelligence broadly as an individual's global capacity to profit from experience, he attempted to sample a wide range of mental abilities. Included were measures of verbal ability, perceptual-motor coordination, memory, perception, logical reasoning, and the like.[1] Scores on these individual measures could then be combined to form an estimate of *overall* ability.

Because he was attempting, albeit indirectly, to measure intellectual ability or potential rather than achievement, Binet tried to select tasks that would not unduly favor individuals with specific training, nor unduly penalize those without it. His assumption was that if the kind of task selected did not favor a child with specific training, then differences in children's levels of performance would be more likely to reflect differences in their basic potential. "There are two chief ways to find items on which success is uninfluenced by special training. One way is to choose *novel items* with which an untaught child has as good a chance to succeed as one who has been taught at home or in school" (98, *350*). Figure 5.1 illustrates novel items. In this example, the child is directed to select figures that are alike, the assumption being that the designs are unfamiliar to all children (172, 201).

The second way is to select *familiar items,* "so that all those for whom the test is designed will be presumed to have had the requisite prior experience to deal with the items" (98, *350*). To illustrate, the Wechsler Adult Intelligence Scale (WAIS), a test widely used with adolescents and adults, contains an *information* subtest, which includes the following item: "How many weeks are there in a year?" The assumption is that virtually all children in our society (for which the test was designed) would have been exposed to this information. Whether they were then able to go on to incorporate it into their store of knowledge is assumed to depend on their underlying level of mental ability. A similar rationale applies to the following item involving "commonsense" reasoning, from another Wechsler subtest (*comprehension*): "If you were lost in the woods in the daytime, how would you go about finding your way out?" (210).

---

[1] Although we are unable to pursue the matter here, it should also be noted that various psychologists—and hence their tests—differ with respect both to the number of specific primary mental abilities they assume and to the extent to which each is viewed as separate and distinct, or linked to a general, or *g*, factor of overall intellectual competence. For example, Thurstone (199, 201) has isolated what he believes to be 7 "primary abilities," whereas Guilford (88, 89) envisages 120 factors or combinations of factors. Other psychologists believe that mental abilities become increasingly differentiated with age (1). According to this hypothesis, mental ability is relatively undifferentiated and global in childhood, then shows increasing differentiation and specification with age, particularly in adolescence (91, 106, 151). (For further discussion of these issues, see 76, 85, 88, 91, 98, 104, 106, 120, 151, and 172.)

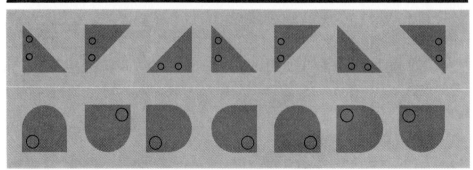

**Figure 5.1** Novel items used in intelligence tests. The following instructions accompany the test: "Here are some cards for you to mark. In each row mark every card that is like the first card in the row." (From L. L. Thurstone and T. G. Thurstone. Factorial studies of intelligence. *Psychometric Monographs* [No. 2]. Chicago: University of Chicago Press, 1941. By permission.)

Unfortunately, in its effort to measure indirectly differences in underlying potential, an intelligence test cannot provide for differences among individual experiences. Thus, in this example, environmental exposure may indeed be more or less equal for most children. However, even a relatively dull child or adolescent who had just spent a summer at a camp that taught camping and mountaineering would be likely to come up with the correct answer, if only because he or she had been specifically and repeatedly instructed on what to do in such a situation.

Conversely, the experience of a disadvantaged ghetto child or one raised in relative isolation in a remote rural area may be such that he or she will be penalized to some extent on tests basically designed for, and standardized on, a representative sample of children or adolescents in the society (7, 42, 43). The intelligence test is in some respects a crude instrument, for its assumptions can never be strictly met:

> The language spoken in one home is never exactly that of another, the reading matter available to the subjects differs, and the stress upon cognitive abilities varies. Even the novel items depend upon perceptual discriminations that may be acquired in one culture and not in another. Despite the difficulties, items can be chosen that work reasonably well. The items included in contemporary intelligence tests are those that have survived in practice after many others have been tried and found defective [98, *351*].

Once the test maker has chosen a large number of items for possible use, he or she is ready to begin construction of the test. Binet and his immediate successors did this by noting the changes in proportions of children of different ages correctly answering a particular item. Binet reasoned that "unless older children are more successful than younger ones in answering the item, the item is unsatisfactory in a test based on the concept of mental growth" (97, *363*). On other tests, such as the Wechsler scales for children and adults, difficulty is determined by the percentage of subjects in a given population passing a particular item. Thus, within each of the

**TABLE 5.1 TESTS COMPRISING THE WECHSLER ADULT INTELLIGENCE SCALE AND THE WECHSLER INTELLIGENCE SCALE FOR CHILDREN**

| VERBAL | PERFORMANCE |
|---|---|
| Information | Digit symbol[a] |
| Comprehension | Picture completion |
| Arithmetic | Block design |
| Similarities | Picture arrangement |
| Digit span[b] | Object assembly |
| Vocabulary | Coding[c] |
| | Mazes[d] |

*Source:* Data from D. Wechsler. *Wechsler intelligence scale for children.* New York: Psychological Corp., 1952; *The measurement of adult intelligence.* Baltimore: Williams & Wilkins, 1958. By permission.
[a] Adult scale only.
[b] Adult scale; alternate test for children.
[c] Scale for children only.
[d] Alternate test for children.

subtests of which the Wechsler is composed (see Table 5.1), the items passed by almost all subjects are listed first and the items passed by almost none listed last. Items that everybody passed or failed would, of course, be of no help and consequently would be thrown out, as would ambiguous or poorly worded questions. The assumption here is that the more items a person passes, the higher his or her ability is.

**Determination of intelligence quotient** In 1916, Lewis Terman of Stanford University published a completely revised, well-standardized intelligence test for children and younger adolescents based on the pioneering work of Binet and Simon, and known as the Stanford-Binet (150, 195). A subsequent revision of this test, providing for two alternate forms, was published by Terman and Maud Merrill in 1937, and there have been subsequent revisions in 1960 and 1972 (196, 197). A significant feature of Terman's original Stanford-Binet was the expression of the results not merely in terms of mental age (as Binet and Simon had done), but also as an *intelligence quotient,* or IQ. As the term itself implies, this quotient was determined by computing a ratio of the individual's mental age to his or her chronological age:

$$IQ = 100 \times \frac{\text{Mental age (MA)}}{\text{Chronological age (CA)}}$$

How does this formula work out? As the reader is aware, a person with an IQ of 100 is considered to be of average intelligence. If an adolescent boy of 13 is able to pass test items passed by other 13-year-olds, but not items passed by 14-, 15-, or 16-year-olds, his mental age is 13. If we then divide this number by his chronological

**TABLE 5.2 INTELLIGENCE CLASSIFICATIONS**

| IQ | CLASSIFICATION | PERCENT INCLUDED |
|---|---|---|
| 130 and above | Very superior | 2.2 |
| 120–129 | Superior | 6.7 |
| 110–119 | Bright normal | 16.1 |
| 90–109 | Average | 50.0 |
| 80– 89 | Dull normal | 16.1 |
| 70– 79 | Borderline | 6.7 |
| 69 and below | Retarded | 2.2 |

*Source:* D. Wechsler. *Manual of the Wechsler Adult Intelligence Scale.* New York: Psychological Corp., 1955. By permission.

age (also 13) and multiply by 100, we do indeed obtain an IQ of 100. On the other hand, if this 13-year-old is brighter and can pass all 15-year-old items, applying the same arithmetical procedure would yield an IQ of 115, clearly above average.[2]

On the Wechsler scales and similar tests, mental age as such has not been introduced (partly because the concept of mental age tends to lose its usefulness later in life). Instead, the individual's level of accomplishment is simply compared with that of others in the same age group. Thus, a 20-year-old and a 40-year-old would both receive an IQ of 100 if they performed better than half of their contemporaries and not as well as the other half. Although current Binet- and Wechsler-type tests use somewhat different procedures for computing IQ, the results are similar. The higher an individual's IQ, the smaller the percentage of his or her contemporaries who perform at or about this level (see Table 5.2). As can be seen in Figure 5.2, the distribution of IQs follows the form of a curve found for many differences among individuals (e.g., height); namely, the bell-shaped normal distribution curve, in which most individuals cluster around the midpoint, with only a few scoring at either extreme.

### Constancy of the IQ

The practical utility of an intelligence-test score depends partly upon its stability or constancy—that is, upon its capacity to predict scores on future tests. How confidently can we predict that a child or adolescent who obtains a superior score at one age will obtain a comparable score at a later age? Whereas tests given to infants under 2 years of age have little value for the prediction of future intelligence scores, tests given to older children and adolescents are more highly predictive.

Table 5.3 shows the correlations between intelligence test scores during the middle-childhood years and at ages 10 and 18. During the middle-school years, the correlation between Stanford-Binet test scores given 1 or 2 years apart is very high (around .90). Moreover, tests given during this period are fairly good predictors of

[2] In the 1960 and 1972 versions of the Stanford-Binet, the IQ is obtained directly from tables. The meaning of the IQ remains basically the same as previously, but the tables permit somewhat greater precision by adjusting scores for variability (differences in standard deviation) at each age level (195, 196).

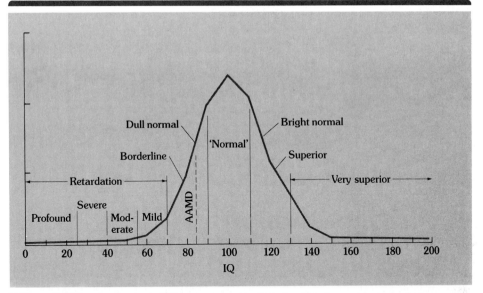

**Figure 5.2** The distribution of IQ test categories. Subclassifications of the retarded group are based on criteria adopted by the American Association on Mental Deficiency. (From J. D. Matarazzo. *Wechsler's measurement and appraisal of adult intelligence.* Baltimore: Williams & Wilkins, 1972 [5th ed.]. By permission.)

intellectual status in later adolescence (age 18). Nevertheless, despite the fact that the IQ becomes more stable in later ages, we must be cautious in using test scores for predicting the future status of individual children because the correlations are not high enough to preclude the possibility of marked changes in individual IQs (102, 103, 191). Repeated testings of large groups of children between the ages of 6 and 18 revealed that the IQs of over half the children showed a variation of 15 or more points at some time during the school years, and a third varied as much as 20 points.

## TABLE 5.3 CORRELATIONS AMONG INTELLIGENCE TEST SCORES AT DIFFERENT AGES

| TEST AGE (YEARS) | RETEST AGE (YEARS) | | | |
|---|---|---|---|---|
|  | 7 | 10 | 14 | 18 |
| 2 | .46 | .37 | .28 | .31 |
| 7 |  | .77 | .75 | .71 |
| 10 |  |  | .86 | .73 |
| 14 |  |  |  | .76 |

*Source:* A. R. Jensen. *Educability and group differences.* New York: Harper & Row, 1973. By permission.

*Note:* Table entries show correlation between IQs obtained from the same individuals at different ages.

Variations as great as 50 IQ points were obtained for 0.5 percent of subjects (102, 103, 191).

In general, children and adolescents showing IQ gains with age are most likely to come from socioeconomically favored environments (9, 96, 103, 143, 174, 191), whereas those showing decreases are most likely to come from culturally isolated environments (remote rural mountain villages) or "disadvantaged" settings (inner-city slums) (3, 49, 143, 174). A wide range of more specific factors has also been found to be related to IQ changes during the course of development. For example, results of several investigations (23, 102, 143) indicate that parents displaying interest and encouragement regarding educational achievement in a child's preschool years are more likely to have children who show gains in IQ. One study (143), however, strongly suggests that the effects of parental encouragement and efforts at acceleration can be vitiated if they are combined with either very harsh or very weak and ineffective discipline. In contrast, "parents of children who show gains in IQ provide their children with acceleration and encouragement for intellectual tasks *and* take a moderate, rationally structured approach to discipline" (143, *71;* emphasis added).

Other studies have found that children who increased in IQ, compared with those who decreased, were more independent, competitive, and verbally aggressive (117, 191). Although no relationship was obtained between the pattern of IQ changes and the degree of friendliness with age-mates, those who gained in IQ worked harder in school, showed a strong desire to master intellectual problems, and were not likely to withdraw from difficult problem situations. Apparently children and adolescents who attempt to master challenging problems are more likely to show increases in IQ than those who withdraw from such situations (191).

More individual, idiosyncratic influences, detectable only through detailed case histories, may also result in IQ changes upward or downward. Figure 5.3 shows the results of repeated tests of three subjects from the longitudinal Guidance Study at the Institute of Human Development at the University of California, Berkeley (101). As may be seen, each of these subjects showed markedly different patterns of change in the years from 3 to 18. Their individual histories suggest some of the factors that may have been involved:

> Case 783 changed very little in I.Q. through the years, although he had poor health, was insecure, did poorly in school, and had a number of symptoms of emotional disturbance. Case 946 scored as low as 87 and as high as 142. She was the daughter of unhappily married immigrant parents who were divorced when the girl was seven. When she was nine her mother remarried but the girl was very insecure and unhappy at home. When she became better adjusted in her family, her I.Q. scores rose. Case 567 showed consistent improvement. In her early years she was sickly and shy, but after age ten her social life expanded and she became very much involved in music and sports. These changes were reflected in her improved test scores [154, *365*].

Nevertheless, despite such variations, prediction of adult intelligence is more reliable at adolescence than at any earlier ages. In one study (8), 111 boys and girls were tested as preschoolers, as adolescents, and as adults. Preschool and adult IQs showed a correlation of .65 (Stanford-Binet), and adolescent and adult IQs corre-

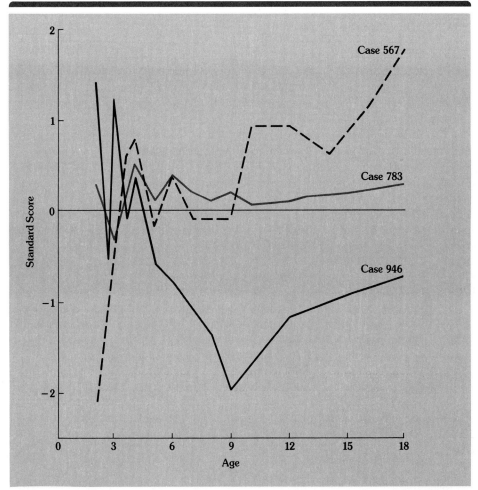

**Figure 5.3** IQ scores of three children on successive tests (plotted in standard scores with the mean for children in the overall study taken as 0). (From M. P. Honzik, J. W. Macfarlane, and L. Allen. The stability of mental test performance between 2 and 18 years. *Journal of Experimental Education,* 1948, **17,** 309–324. Adapted by P. H. Mussen and M. R. Rosenzweig et al. in *Psychology: An introduction.* Lexington, Mass.: Heath, 1973. By permission.)

lated .85 (Stanford-Binet) and .80 (Stanford-Binet and WAIS). In general, adolescent measures of IQ appear to be fairly good predictors of adult IQs.

**The usefulness of IQs** What do we actually know when a child or adolescent obtains an IQ of, for example, 119 on the Wechsler Adult Intelligence Scale? At the very least, we know that he or she can do the items on this test better than approximately two-thirds of persons the same age on whom the test was standardized. And we know that these items are probably representative of a large variety of tasks commonly met by people in their daily lives.

In this sense, the author of the test feels justified in calling it a measure of *general intelligence*. But how useful is such knowledge? Few teachers or potential employers, for example, are particularly interested in whether an adolescent can put a manikin together, assemble blocks, or tell you how many weeks there are in a year. They want to know if he or she will be able to do satisfactory academic work or perform a particular kind of job.

In the former case, the only way of settling the question is by examination of the actual relationship between IQ and school success. In general, IQ scores have been found to be fairly good predictors of academic performance (20, 46, 144, 148). Of course, the fairly high correlation between school success and IQ scores may be attributed partly to the similarity of the kinds of behavior measured in both cases. Indeed, when it comes to predicting success in less related fields—such as mechanical trades, music, and art—the intelligence test does a far less adequate job, although *on the average* there are IQ differences between persons holding different kinds of jobs (see Table 5.4).

Interestingly, in both academic and vocational performance, the spread in IQs is greater at lower than at higher levels (19, 28). Thus, whereas the mean IQ of unskilled workers is below 90, individual workers may score in the very superior range of intelligence. On the other hand, among physicians and other professionals whose mean scores are in the superior or very superior range, one does not find individuals scoring in the 80s (28, 95). The obvious implication is that whereas certain tasks—academic or vocational—require a certain minimum level of intellectual capability, intelligence alone is not sufficient to produce success; other factors, ranging from motivation and personality characteristics to environmental stimulation and opportunity, may be necessary as well.

## COGNITIVE DEVELOPMENT IN ADOLESCENCE

Although the average individual's IQ remains fairly stable, particularly as he or she grows older, mental ability does not. This is a frequent source of confusion to the student new to this area. The explanation, of course, is that a mental-ability score is an *absolute* measure (i.e., an average 15-year-old can pass more and harder items than an average 5-year-old). IQ, however, is, as we have seen, a *relative* measure, based on the individual's ability in relation to that of contemporaries. Thus, both the 5- and 15-year-old may have the same IQ, but the 15-year-old will obviously be able to do many tasks that the 5-year-old cannot—his or her mental ability is greater.

It is clear from any number of investigations that *mental ability,* as distinguished from IQ, increases rapidly from birth through adolescence (see Figure 5.4) (10, 102). Furthermore, some specific components of overall mental ability appear to mature more rapidly than others. Thus, so-called fluid measures, which appear to depend most heavily on flexibility, adaptability, and speed of information processing (e.g., perceptual speed, conceptualizing the relationship of objects in space, psychomotor speed and coordination) tend to develop more rapidly than so-called crystallized measures, which are influenced more by experience and acquired knowledge

**TABLE 5.4 AVERAGE AGCT SCORES OF PERSONS IN VARIOUS CIVILIAN OCCUPATIONS**

| RANK IN LIST OF 72 OCCUPATIONS | CIVILIAN OCCUPATION | AVERAGE SCORE |
|---|---|---|
| 1 | Accountant | 128.1 |
| 2 | Lawyer | 127.6 |
| 4 | Public relations man | 126.0 |
| 6 | Chemist | 124.8 |
| 9 | Teacher | 122.8 |
| 10 | Draftsman | 122.0 |
| 15 | Manager, sales | 119.0 |
| 18 | Photographer | 117.6 |
| 20 | Clerk-typist | 116.8 |
| 25 | Radio repairman | 115.3 |
| 27 | Salesman | 115.1 |
| 31 | Tool maker | 112.5 |
| 39 | Airplane mechanic | 109.3 |
| 41 | Electrician | 109.0 |
| 49 | Auto serviceman | 104.2 |
| 51 | Cabinetmaker | 103.5 |
| 53 | Butcher | 102.9 |
| 54 | Plumber | 102.7 |
| 55 | Bartender | 102.2 |
| 61 | Chauffeur | 100.8 |
| 65 | Cook and baker | 97.2 |
| 67 | Truck driver | 96.2 |
| 68 | Laborer | 95.8 |
| 70 | Lumberjack | 94.7 |
| 72 | Farmhand | 91.4 |

Source: Adapted from T. W. Harrell and M. S. Harrell. Army General Classification Test scores for civilian occupations. *Educational and Psychological Measurement*, 1945, **5**, 229–239. By permission.

(e.g., word fluency, general information, and verbal comprehension) (32, 34, 104, 105, 200) and less on immediate adaptability. Thus, the average young person's score on perceptual speed reaches 80 percent of his or her ultimate peak score by age 12; in contrast, the 80-percent level for verbal comprehension is not reached until age 18, and for word fluency later than age 20 (98, 200).

On measures of *overall* intelligence there appears to be a leveling off during young adulthood, with a slight decline in middle age, and a more rapid decline in old age (5, 10, 11, 21, 32, 104, 106, 178, 179). However, these overall results can be deceptive. They mask the fact that some abilities improve well into the middle years, while others reach a peak in the early adult years and then decline. For example, in the Berkeley Growth Study (11), which involved repeated measurements of the same subjects over the years, scores on such crystallized measures from the Wechsler intelligence test scales as vocabulary and information and verbal comprehension were still continuing to improve at age 36. In contrast, scales that appear to depend more on "fluid" abilities, such as object assembly and block design (jigsaw-type

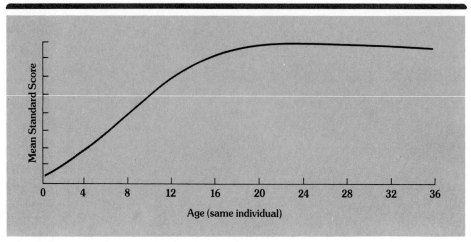

**Figure 5.4** Theoretical curve of the growth of intelligence based on repeated examination of the same individuals in the Berkeley Growth Study with infant and preschool intelligence tests, the S-B, W-B, and WAIS. $N = 61$ cases; the number of cases tested at each of 42 ages averaged 54 per age. (Adapted from N. Bayley. Development of mental abilities. In P. H. Mussen [ed.], *Carmichael's manual of child psychology* [Vol. 1]. New York: Wiley, 1970. P. 1176, Fig. 3 [3rd ed.]. By permission.)

tasks, both of which involve speed of perception and response and the ability to conceptualize objects in space) and digit symbol (a coding task in which speed of response is important), peaked in early adulthood and then began to decline (see Figure 5.5).

In the light of such findings, it is perhaps not too surprising that significant contributions of people in fields like mathematics and physics tend to occur relatively early in life (in their twenties for mathematicians). These fields require "pure ability," flexibility, and intellectual adaptability. The great historians and social philosophers tend to reach their height in middle age (48, 89, 115, 130), for in these fields experience, distilled knowledge, and judgment play a relatively greater role.

What happens in later life is less clear, although recent longitudinal and quasilongitudinal research suggests that more abilities than previously thought hold up reasonably well into the sixties and beyond (4, 21, 32, 104, 178, 179). Not surprisingly, this is particularly true of abilities in which experience, knowledge, and judgment play a major role. Elderly people do less well on tasks that depend heavily on perceptual and response speed, speed of information processing, and the necessity of encoding information, storing it in memory for moderate lengths of time, and then retrieving it (2, 31, 32, 108, 153). Even here, however, there is some evidence that performance can be improved through specific training and practice (5, 32).

In summary, a considerable amount of further research will be needed to determine conclusively the exact rates of development and decline of various specific mental functions. Nevertheless, it appears clear that the level of intellectual functioning achieved by late adolescence or early adulthood, and the extent to which this

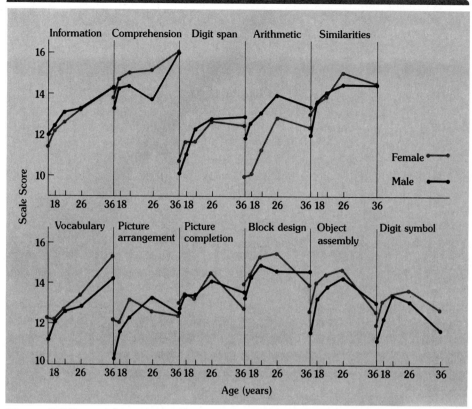

**Figure 5.5** Curves of mean scores by sex and age for the eleven Wechsler subtests, Berkeley Growth Study. (From N. Bayley. Learning in adulthood: The role of intelligence. In H. J. Klausmeier and C. W. Harris [eds.], *Analysis of conceptual learning.* New York: Academic Press, 1966. By permission.)

capacity is exploited during this period, will determine in great measure the future course of adult cognitive functioning (60). As Alfred North Whitehead once remarked, "the imagination is most active between the ages of nineteen and thirty-five and we must keep going thereafter on whatever fizz we have experienced then" (60, *132*).

### Sex differences

There has been a great deal of interest in intellectual differences between males and females for about as long as there has been interest in intellect. The study of sex-related differences in cognition has been highly controversial and often has involved more opinion than science (140, 167, 183). The publication in 1974 of *The Psychology of Sex Differences* by Eleanor Maccoby and Carol Jacklin established a point of reference, since it reviewed all research on sex differences to that date.

Writing on the topic since that time uses their conclusions as a starting point for comparison with any new views or data to be presented.

These investigators, in their review of intelligence and cognitive abilities, concluded that although males and females show no consistent differences in *overall* intelligence, there are some *average* sex differences on some specific cognitive abilities, all emerging by early adolescence and continuing into adulthood.

Beginning at about 10 to 11 years of age, girls outscore boys on a variety of measures of verbal ability such as language production, creative writing, comprehension of difficult written material, and verbal fluency (139, 140). Contrary to some earlier formulations, "in most population groups the two sexes perform very similarly until adolescence" (140, *88*).

Boys overtake girls at about the same time on measures of spatial ability and mathematics (146, 147, 194). Spatial ability requires skill in visual transformation of some kind. This ability has been studied a great deal, with many different measures used (140, 146, 147, 149, 204). All of the measures are interrelated, but most investigators think of at least two conceptually distinct abilities: (1) *spatial visualization* (the ability to conceptualize a transformed visual arrangement—for example, imagining how an object in space would look from a different angle, or deducing from a drawing of a set of gears how movement in one gear would affect the direction and speed of movement in another gear); and (2) *spatial relations or spatial orientation* (comprehension of the arrangement of elements within a visual stimulus pattern—for example, looking at complex designs and seeing if they are the same, or, if not, how they differ) (90, 147). Visual-spatial tasks, such as those involved in architecture, engineering, geometry, or graphic arts, use these two abilities to varying degrees.

The ability to judge horizontality and verticality, originally conceptualized as a Piagetian task of concrete operations, is strongly related to both types of spatial ability and shows similar sex differences (79, 133, 187).

Field independence, the capacity to orient oneself to a stimulus ignoring the background, or to discern a previously seen shape, even though it is imbedded in a confusing background, is highly correlated with both aspects of spatial ability (90, 147, 149). Indeed, field independence had been originally conceptualized as an overall cognitive style (220), but it now appears that the sex differences in field independence are due to those in spatial visualization (165). The existence of sex differences could explain many of the findings linking field independence to personality factors, since the personality factors (such as independence-dependence) are linked to societal sex roles. Variations in sex roles across cultures as well as cultural variations in spatial skill could then explain the cross-cultural variations in field independence. This view of field independence is further supported by a study that found that when the stimulus in one field independence task was changed to a human figure rather than a rod, girls' performance increased substantially and was better than that of boys on the same task (155).

The conclusion that during adolescence boys begin to perform better, on the average, than girls on tests of mathematics (71, 140), has been borne out by more recent studies as well (166). There has been a great deal of research recently on sex differences in mathematics (26, 69, 185) with a focus on why such differences exist.

Some studies (72, 185) have found that the sex differences disappear once the number of mathematics courses that the adolescent has taken have been considered. However, more boys than girls are identified as mathematically precocious *prior* to the time that mathematics courses become elective (14). While this result may be due to biological factors, it is also the case that children sex-type mathematics as a male domain (185).

Although many of the scholars who write about sex differences are careful to place their inferences in the appropriate context (112, 140, 167), misinterpretations of these results, particularly with respect to spatial ability and mathematics, are commonplace. The average differences between boys and girls are often no more than a point or two on a test (161). *Reliable* findings on sex differences (and in the Maccoby and Jacklin volume this usually means in about half the studies) are often interpreted as *large*. In all cases, boys and girls obtain scores over the same range of points with the averages for each group differing from one-fourth to one-half of a standard deviation, or small- to medium-sized effects, with sex accounting for between 1 and 5 percent of the variation in scores (112). Thus, sex is a poor predictor of performance even in those areas where there tend to be group differences between males and females.

It is also clear that these sex differences do not explain the different numbers of men and women seen in certain occupations. For example, even if we assume that a very high level of spatial ability (ninety-fifth percentile) is required for engineering—and this is the case for only a few kinds of engineering—the ratio of men to women in the occupation on the basis of spatial ability would be 2:1 rather than 99:1 as is seen presently (112).

The focus on sex differences often overshadows the fact that in most areas of cognitive ability—including concept mastery, reasoning, level of moral judgment, and analytic cognitive style—there do not appear to be differences between adolescent boys and girls (140).

## GENETIC DETERMINANTS OF MENTAL ABILITY

If the measures employed on intelligence tests reflect underlying ability and not simply the results of specific learning opportunities (at least for the average individual in the population on which the test was standardized), and if the potential ceiling on an individual's ability is, as assumed, set by heredity, then we might expect to find evidence of genetic influences on intelligence-test performance.

To what extent are the kinds of abilities measured by intelligence tests in fact influenced by heredity? The topic is a controversial one, and discussions of it are frequently characterized by a good deal more heat than light. Some authorities assert that genetic influences play a dominant role in determining intellectual abilities; other claim that evidence for such an assertion is at most slight. How can these conflicting views be resolved?

If genetic factors do play a significant role in determining an individual's intellectual abilities, we would expect to find that a child's or adolescent's IQ is more highly correlated with the IQs of his or her parents and other immediate relatives than with those of randomly selected nonrelatives. This is indeed the case. Unfortunately for investigators, however, the matter is not so simple. Parents who may have provided their children with a superior genetic endowment may be providing them with other advantages that may also be related to intellectual ability—good health, a stimulating home environment, superior educational opportunity. Thus, if we are to isolate the potential contributions of heredity, a way must be found to control for the potential effects of such other variables.

### Adoptive parents

One way to control for the effect of other variables is to study children and adolescents raised from a very early age by adoptive parents and to compare the IQs of these children with those of their biological and adoptive parents. In a comprehensive analysis (151) of a broad range of investigations, it was found that when all subjects from these studies were combined, a correlation of .19 was obtained between adoptive parents' intelligence-test scores (obtained by averaging mother's and father's scores) and those of their adopted children. In contrast, the correlation between the scores of the adopted children and those of their biological parents was .48. (The correlation between parents' and childrens' scores when children were raised by their biological parents was .58.)

It appears clear that the hereditary influence on IQ of these adopted children's biological parents was much greater than the environmental influences of their adoptive parents. However, the correlation (.58) was highest in the case of children raised by their biological parents, where the effects of heredity *and* environment were combined (151).

### Twin studies

Investigation of the effects of heredity on intellectual ability may be greatly aided by comparing *monozygotic* (i.e., identical) twins with ordinary brothers and sisters from different births and with *dizygotic* (i.e., nonidentical, or fraternal) twins. The latter, although more likely to have been subjected to similar experiences, having been conceived and born at the same time, "are no more alike genetically than ordinary siblings. They need not be of the same sex nor do they necessarily resemble each other" (97, *390*). If genetic influences play an important role in the determination of intellectual ability, we would expect the IQs of monozygotic twins to be more highly correlated than those of dizygotic twins or nontwin siblings. If both heredity and environmental influences play a significant role, we might also expect that dizygotic twins, while revealing a lower correlation than monozygotic twins, would show a higher correlation than nontwin siblings born and reared at different times.

Both hypotheses have been confirmed. As may be seen from Figure 5.6, which summarizes the results of a large number of studies of pairs of persons differing in degree of genetic similarity, the correlation in IQ of one-egg (monozygotic) twins reared together is significantly higher than that of two-egg (dizygotic) twins (who were also reared together), and of nontwin siblings. In turn, the correlation between dizygotic twins is higher than that of nontwin siblings.

One fascinating investigation (216, 291) has found that even *variations* in developmental test scores at early ages (which, as we have seen, tend to limit predic-

tion of later IQ) may have a genetic component. When repeated measurements during the first two years of life on 261 monozygotic (MZ) and dizygotic (DZ) twins were analyzed, it was found that the profiles of the developmental spurts and lags were very similar, especially for MZ twins (see Figure 5.7 and Table 5.5).

> In a predictive sense, Twin A's developmental score is a better estimate of Twin B's score at the same age than it is of Twin A's developmental score several months later. . . . [It] appears that the developmental sequence is an expression of timed gene action which may produce spurts or lags between ages, but which remains coordinated for both twins in proportion to the number of genes they hold in common [219, *280*].

In a follow-up study (217, 218) of these same subjects during the preschool years, similar within-pair correlations for monozygotic and dizygotic twins were found. Not surprisingly, the ability of an individual's score at one age to predict his or her score at a later age was much better than during the earlier period, but these correlations were still less impressive than the within-pair correlations.

In summary, correlations in IQ are highest between persons most closely re-

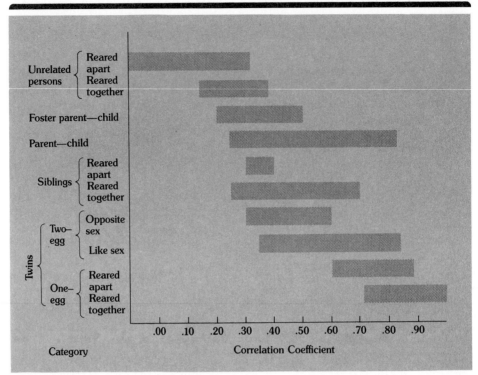

**Figure 5.6** Genetic relationships and IQ. Correlation coefficients in IQ between persons of various relationships, based on the results of 52 studies. The horizontal lines give the range of the coefficients obtained in various studies and the vertical lines show the median (middle) coefficients. (From L. Erlenmeyer-Kimling and L. F. Jarvik. Genetics and intelligence: A research review. *Science*, 1963, **142**, 1477–1479. Copyright 1963 by the American Association for the Advancement of Science. By permission.)

lated genetically (i.e., monozygotic twins) and lowest between those who are unrelated. However, there is a low positive correlation between the IQs of foster parents and their children (who are not genetically related), and a higher correlation between dizygotic twins than between siblings (who are equal in genetic similarity, though probably not in environmental influences). Thus it appears that environmental as well as genetic factors are important in raising or lowering a child's level of intellectual performance. Of course, environmental forces are effective only within the ultimate limits set by heredity.

## MINORITY-GROUP STATUS AND INTELLIGENCE

A variety of investigations have indicated that the *average* IQ scores of some minority groups (7, 53, 54, 174, 186) tend to be lower than those of socioeconomically advantaged whites and of the U.S. population as a whole. These findings, coupled

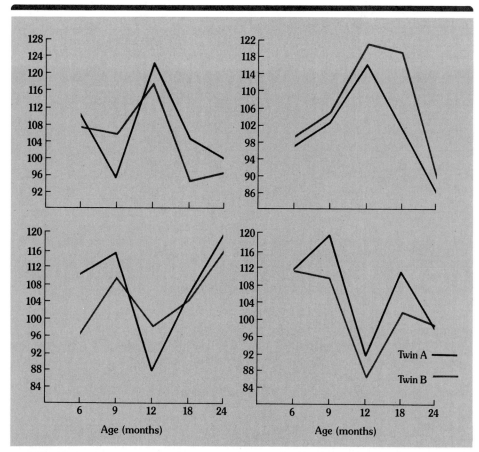

**Figure 5.7** Bayley score profiles for four pairs of twins illustrating concordance in developmental status at each age and congruence for the pattern of changes over age. (From R. S. Wilson and E. B. Harpring. Mental and motor development in infant twins. *Developmental Psychology*, 1972, **7,** 277–287. Copyright, 1972, American Psychological Association. By permission.)

with the results of studies of the role of genetic factors in intelligence, have led some people, such as Arthur Jensen, an educational psychologist at the University of California, to conclude that these groups, *on the average,* are genetically limited in their intellectual capacities in comparison to advantaged whites and that they have lower IQ scores at least partly because of less underlying potential ability. Jensen's principal argument is that, although environmental factors may contribute to socio-economic and racial differences in IQ, a significant portion of these differences is likely to be due to genetic influences, and therefore chances for boosting IQ or scholastic achievement are rather limited (53, 114).

What can we say about the emotion-laden topic of race and intelligence? On the basis of the available evidence, it appears that *at least* a significant part of the

**TABLE 5.5 WITHIN-PAIR CORRELATIONS
FOR SCORES ON THE MENTAL AND MOTOR SCALES**

| AGE (MONTHS) | MENTAL SCALE | | MZ (TRUE SCORE RELIABILITY) | MOTOR SCALE | | MZ (TRUE SCORE RELIABILITY) |
| | MZ (PAIRS) | DZ (PAIRS) | | MZ (PAIRS) | DZ (PAIRS) | |
|---|---|---|---|---|---|---|
| 3 | .84[b] | .67 | .91 | .50 | .41 | .67 |
| 6 | .82 | .74 | .90 | .87[b] | .75 | .93 |
| 9 | .81[b] | .69 | .89 | .84[b] | .61 | .91 |
| 12 | .82[b] | .61 | .90 | .75[a] | .63 | .86 |
| 18 | .76 | .72 | .86 | .70 | .77 | .82 |
| 24 | .87[b] | .75 | .93 | — | — | |

*Source:* R. S. Wilson and E. B. Harpring. Mental and motor development in infant twins. *Developmental Psychology,* 1972, **7,** 277–287. Copyright, 1972, American Psychological Association. By permission.
*Note:* MZ = monozygotic; DZ = dizygotic. The numbers of pairs at each age on the Mental Scale were 57–109 for MZ pairs and 65–116 for DZ pairs. On the Motor Scale, numbers of pairs of each age were 71–93 for MZ pairs and 77–91 for DZ pairs.
[a] $p < .10$.
[b] $p < .05$.

average difference between the majority population and some racial or ethnic minorities is the result of environmental factors. Although we undoubtedly have not as yet identified all these factors, the possibilities include a number of variables associated with generally lower overall class and/or caste status: poorer prenatal and postnatal nutrition; poorer health generally; less stimulating early family experiences, including less stimulation of language development and less varied parent-child interactions; less motivation for the development of intellectual skills; poorer and less experientially relevant schooling; fewer culturally enriching opportunities outside the home and the school; and the psychological effects of discrimination and second-class status (21, 23, 35, 39, 52, 126, 132, 136, 184, 198). Where efforts are undertaken to equalize some of these influences on black and white young people, differences between them are consistently reduced (7, 19, 23, 78, 93, 152, 174).

Furthermore, there is increasing evidence to indicate that matching on broad demographic variables, such as socioeconomic status, may fail truly to equate environmental opportunities (23, 50, 93, 177). Even within a particular socioeconomic group (e.g., disadvantaged, middle-class), there is considerable variation in the nature of the child's home environment, as measured by such indices as: mother's involvement with the child, and her degree of emotional and verbal responsiveness; opportunities for creative play and varied cultural experiences; parents' educational aspirations for the child; degree of academic guidance and supervision of the child's study habits; shared family activities; and intellectuality of the home. (Furthermore, at least among middle-class families, the amount of variation is greater among blacks than whites.) Home environment consistently correlates more highly with IQ and measures of academic achievement than does socioeconomic status (23).

Whether proper control of all relevant environmental influences would eliminate all differences—both in overall intelligence and in the distribution of specific component abilities—cannot be conclusively demonstrated at present. Despite contrary claims, although genetic studies demonstrate in the general population a significant contribution of heredity to level of intellectual functioning (as well as to the upper limits of an individual's mental ability), they do not establish that differences in mean IQ between selected racial or ethnic groups are determined, even in part, by genetic factors: "Whether or not the variation in IQ within either race is entirely genetic or entirely environmental has no bearing on the question of the relative contributions of genetic factors and environmental factors to the differences [if any] between races" (19, 27). The extrapolation of "heritability" estimates to racial differences "assumes that the environmental differences between the races are comparable to the environmental variation within them" (19, 27), and there is currently no basis for making such an assumption (19, 22).

It appears, therefore, that this question can ultimately be answered—if indeed it can ever be conclusively answered—only by making certain that all potentially relevant environmental differences between racial or ethnic groups have been equalized or adequately controlled for, a goal that we have not thus far been able to reach (19, 35, 126). In view of the extent and apparent subtlety of some current environmental differences in the backgrounds of, for example, blacks and whites, probably the most appropriate

> . . . approach applicable to the study of the IQ difference between the races is that of working with black children adopted into white homes and vice versa. The adoptions would, of course, have to be at an early age to be sure of taking into account any possible effects of the early home environment. The IQ's of black children adopted into white homes would also have to be compared with those of white children adopted into comparable homes [19, 29].

While no such comprehensive, adequately controlled studies have thus far been conducted, a beginning has been made in one study (177) that examined the IQ test performance of black children of educationally average parents who were adopted by advantaged white families. The investigators found that these children obtained an average IQ of 106, which is above that for all children (100 IQ), and above the average for comparable nonadopted black children in the same community (90 IQ). Those children within this group who were adopted early (in the first year of life) scored higher. However, adopted children did not score as high as the natural children of these adoptive parents, perhaps at least partly because of poorer prenatal and postnatal nutrition and health care, and early postnatal stimulation.

Despite these encouraging results, more—and more adequately controlled— research is obviously needed. And any optimally designed study would have to find ways to carefully control for such possible prenatal environmental influences as nutritional and health care deficiencies and maternal stress—something easier said than done. Furthermore, even if this were accomplished, it would "not remove the effects of prejudice directed against black people in most white communities. . . . The question of a possible genetic basis for the race IQ difference will be almost impossible to answer satisfactorily before the environmental differences between U.S. blacks and whites have been substantially reduced" (19, 29).

In the meantime, however, assertions that differences in IQ scores between black children and adolescents (or other significantly disadvantaged minorities) and their majority peers can be attributed primarily to genetic differences in intellectual potential should be viewed with considerable suspicion. One of the issues addressed by Jensen was a preliminary finding that a variety of compensatory education programs, such as Head Start, had proved to be of little benefit to disadvantaged minority children, in terms of later school achievement and IQ. Jensen concluded that such efforts are unlikely ever to be very successful because of genetic ceilings limiting the potential of most of these children. More recent studies, however, have challenged a number of these findings (127, 173).

It has been found, for example, that by the end of grade school, Head Start children are more likely than their non-Head Start peers to be in the correct grade for age and less likely to be in special education classes (41, 128, 159, 173, 181). The one program that followed former Head Start students into high school found that they have lower rates of juvenile delinquency (181). It is likely, moreover, that many programs were not intensive enough to overcome the effects of countervailing influences (e.g., lack of early and continuing stimulation) (41, 107, 127, 222).

Recently, a major collaborative study (127) employed combined data from the projects of twelve different investigators who had conducted studies on the effects of infant and preschool programs. The investigators found that early education programs for children from low-income families had long-lasting effects in a number of areas. Compared to control groups of children, children exposed to these programs were less likely subsequently to be assigned to special education classes, and were less likely to be retained in grade. There was some indication that program graduates performed better over time on achievement tests, particularly mathematics; they also performed better on IQ tests for several years after the program, but apparently not permanently. In terms of attitudes and values, children who had attended early education programs were more likely than controls to give achievement-related reasons, such as school or work accomplishments, for being proud of themselves. Furthermore, these programs tended to have a positive effect on the attitudes of the children's mothers toward their children's school performance and vocational aspirations (127).

It should also be added that it is hard to see how the results of the most definitive study could affect the way members of either majority or minority racial or ethnic groups *should* reasonably act (although by fueling or perhaps reducing prejudice, they might affect how they *would* act). In either case, there would be no justification for abandoning efforts—through improved environmental opportunity and reduction of environmental hazards—to maximize the intellectual potential of all individuals for coping with an increasingly complex world.

Finally, and most important, it should not be forgotten that, even under present social conditions, variations in IQ within any racial or ethnic (or social class) group are far larger than any differences that might exist between them, and that there is a wide overlap in their distribution curves.

Therefore "it is impossible to predict an individual's IQ by the color of his skin" (7, *13*). And this will always be the case, regardless of the possible findings of any future genetic research. There will always be many black adolescents who are brighter than many white (or brown or red) adolescents, as well as the reverse.

The only possible conclusion, in our view, is that each individual must be

judged on his or her own merits—which is, after all, the presumed aim of any truly democratic society. But as long as residuals of racial or ethnic discrimination persist, attempts to apply comparative IQ data inappropriately must be resisted while we seek social conditions that will provide every individual "with equal opportunities to develop all his potential qualities, both intellective and nonintellective" (7, *13*).

## *CREATIVITY*

Despite the difficulties encountered in attempting to define the term objectively (15, 16, 81, 203, 208), *creativity* nevertheless impresses us as a useful concept, distinguishable from intelligence, and meaningful in its own right. We all know people, including adolescents, whom we acknowledge to be intelligent, but who appear singularly lacking in creativity. Similarly, we know people who appear highly creative, even though they may not obtain particularly outstanding scores on an intelligence test. But what exactly do we mean by creativity, and can it be distinguished from overall intelligence?

Perhaps the best way to search for clues to the most useful definition of creativity is to consider the introspections of successful artists and scientists (209). When we do this, one major focus emerges:

> The majority of the available introspective accounts have in common a concern with associative freedom and uniqueness. These accounts consistently stressed the ability to give birth to associative content that is abundant and original, yet relevant

to the task at hand rather than bizarre. The writer's classical fear of "drying up" and of never being able to produce another word, the composer's worry over not having another piece of music within him, the scientist's concern that he won't be able to think of another experiment to perform—these are but indications of how preoccupied creative individuals can become with the question of associative flow. Introspections about times of creative insight also seem to reflect a kind of task centered, permissive, or playful set on the part of the person doing the associating. Einstein refers to the "associative play" or "combinatory play." The person stands aside a bit as associative material is given freedom to reach the surface [209, *88*].

This kind of "playful," uninhibited associative freedom is similar to what a number of psychoanalysts, notably Ernst Kris (123), have in mind when they speak of "regression in the service of the ego"—the ability to relinquish conscious controls and allow free expression of previously subconscious association—as an essential element in creative production. A variety of investigators have used one or another measure of this associative freedom as indicators of creativity in studies of the relationship between creativity and personality characteristics, familial influences, and the like (74, 87, 89, 208).

One such study (209) aimed at determining whether creativity could be differentiated from intelligence per se, and investigating the relationship of personality characteristics and social behavior to creativity. The subjects, preadolescent fifth-grade boys and girls, were given standard intelligence tests as well as tests of creativity. The creativity measures required generating many unusual hypotheses. For example, in one test the subject was told a characteristic and then asked to name as many objects as he or she could that had that characteristic (e.g., "Name all the things you know that are *sharp*"). Subjects were also asked to think up varied uses for objects (e.g., "Tell me all the different ways that you would use a *newspaper*"). In a third test, the young people were shown line drawings (see Figure 5.8a, b) and asked to think up all the things the drawings might be. They were also shown nonsense line designs (see Figure 5.8c, d) and asked to enumerate all the things the nonsense designs made them think of. Subjects were classified as creative if they gave many answers to each of the tests, some of which were unusual or unique in comparison to the answers given by the other children. These measures of creativity correlated highly with one another, but they showed little correlation with the various measures of intelligence employed in the study—suggesting that creativity and intelligence can indeed be meaningfully differentiated.[3]

Subjects were then grouped into four categories: high creativity–high intelligence, high creativity–low intelligence, low creativity–high intelligence, and low creativity–low intelligence. Using observations of the subjects' classroom behavior over a 2-week period, as well as such other supplementary information as the results of tests of emotional sensitivity and anxiety, the investigators found a number of significant differences among the four groups of subjects. Those high in both creativity and

---

[3] Results of other investigations (6, 36, 141, 207) indicate that a moderately high level of intellectual ability is essential for creativity, "but beyond a given 'floor' which varies in different fields, there is no relationship between intellectual abilities and creativity" (207, *114*). For example, in several investigations of creative writing (4), modest correlations between creativity and intelligence scores were obtained over the total range of intelligence, but beyond an IQ level of 120, intelligence was a negligible factor in creativity.

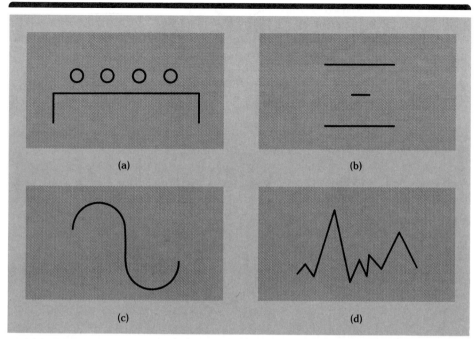

**Figure 5.8** Drawings used to test creativity. (From *Modes of thinking in young children: A study of the creativity-intelligence distinction,* by M. A. Wallach and N. Kogan. Copyright © 1965 by Holt, Rinehart and Winston, Inc. Reprinted by permission of Holt, Rinehart and Winston, Inc.)

intelligence appeared self-confident, independent, and able to "exercise within themselves both control and freedom, both adult-like and child-like kinds of behavior" (209, *98*). Those high in creativity but low in intelligence appeared to be in angry conflict with themselves and with their school environment. They were "beset by feelings of unworthiness and inadequacy. In a stress-free context, however, they can blossom forth cognitively" (209, *98*). In contrast, subjects low in creativity but high in intelligence emerged as conspicuously loath to "stick their necks out," and to try anything that was "far out," or unconventional and, hence, possibly wrong. Their social behavior, their academic efforts, their emotional responses, and their thinking all tended to be cautious, conventional, and concerned primarily with "correctness." Finally, subjects low in both creativity and intelligence appeared basically bewildered. They engaged in "various defensive maneuvers ranging from useful adaptations such as intensive social activity to regressions such as passivity or psychosomatic symptoms" (209, *98*).

Of special interest were the findings on anxiety in the four groups. Anxiety level was highest in the low-creativity–low-intelligence group, and lowest in the low-creativity–high-intelligence group, with the two high-creativity groups scoring in the middle range. These latter findings support those of other investigations, which have indicated that creativity tends to be "maximal in the presence of an intermediate level of anxiety. If anxiety is either too low or too high, the creativity is reduced" (209, *97–116*). It appears, as the authors note, that "creativity need not be all sweetness and light . . . but may well involve a tolerance for and understanding of sadness and pain. To think otherwise is to fall prey to the rather widespread American stereotype that suffering is always a bad thing and is to be avoided at all cost" (209, *97*). By "playing it safe," the high-intelligence–low-creativity group was more able to avoid anxiety, but at the cost of seriously limiting its creative potential and inner freedom (131, 209).

Other recent studies (99, 214, 215) have found that even among gifted adolescents, there are differences between those who score higher on originality than intellectual mastery and those who score higher on intellectual mastery. The former tend to be more sociable, impulsive, and nonconforming; their thinking is generally less precise and more fantasy-based. In contrast, those who score higher on intellectual mastery than on originality tend to be more shy and guarded and more conventional; their thinking is more deliberate, logical, and narrowly analytical—focused more on individual trees than on the forest as a whole (99).

### Age and area of interest

Whereas some personality characteristics appear to distinguish more or less creative individuals generally, there are also significant variations associated with age and area of interest. For example, personality measures (84) were given to adults in various occupations judged as more or less creative (writing, mathematics, research science, and architecture), and to high school seniors selected from the Annual Science Talent Search (45) and rated similarly by two judges, using such criteria of creativity as relative degree of novelty and effectiveness (162).

In both the adult and adolescent samples, and regardless of field of interest, more creative individuals scored higher on a cluster of traits summarized as *adaptive autonomy*—individuality, spontaneity, self-reliance, introspection, emotional lability, interpersonal perspicacity, and high motivation to work independently. They also scored higher on another cluster of traits summarized as *assertive self-assurance*—measures of poise, ascendancy or dominance, and self-assurance. On the other hand, more creative adults and adolescents did not differ significantly from those rated as less creative on a third cluster of traits summarized as *humanitarian conscience,* or *superego strength*—breadth of interest, sensitivity, and conscientiousness (162).

On a fourth general personality dimension, however, adults and adolescents differed markedly. Among adults, more creative individuals scored significantly *lower* on a cluster of traits summarized as *disciplined effectiveness*—self-control, achievement via conformity, sense of well-being—whereas more creative adolescents scored *higher* on this cluster. Although this reversal of direction may appear paradoxical, it emerges as more reasonable when one considers the differences between adults and adolescents, both in their stage of psychological development and in their social status and acceptance in the broader society.

Creativity appears to require, as we have already implied, an ability to free oneself from conventionality and inhibition in search of wellsprings of originality that are often unconscious—of new and spontaneous associations, however loosely organized ("regression in the service of the ego"). But to be creatively productive also requires a further ability to impose order, organization, and discipline (whether aesthetic or scientific) on the novel material that emerges as a result of this associative freedom. A poem, for example, may be highly original in its raw material, but it will fail as art unless this material can be distilled to meet the needs of aesthetic discipline and communication. Conversely, a poem may be technically flawless, but without genuine originality of perception, it will also fail.

If one accepts this concept, it becomes easier to see why adolescents, who are still in a very fluid state in terms of their psychological development and defense mechanisms (i.e., who are closer and more vulnerable to unconscious influences) may need *more* disciplined thinking to be creatively effective; adults, who are more likely to be more "set in their ways"—more staled, as Shakespeare says, by custom—may need to break away from the tyranny of too much discipline in their search for greater spontaneity and associative freedom.

Furthermore, the social positions of creative adolescents and adults may be different. As the investigators themselves speculate,

> The adolescent, unlike the adult, is faced with the practical necessity of coping with a world in which his success is, in fact, dependent upon his ability to maintain a reasonable degree of cooperation with those who control the resources he needs to achieve his goals. Society is understandably more tolerant of the demands, eccentricities, and flouting of convention of adults who have demonstrated their creativity than it is of similar behavior from the "brash," unrecognized adolescent. The adolescent who is unwilling to make appropriate allowances for this reality may perforce have to devote much of his effort to struggle and rebellion, with a resultant loss of energy which might otherwise have been available for creative productivity [70, *364–365*].

These findings characterized creative adolescents and adults generally, but there were also differences in relative emphasis from one field of interest to another. For example, creative adult writers tended to be lower in *disciplined effectiveness* than their less creative colleagues; for research scientists, the reverse was the case. Creative writers were also significantly lower overall in disciplined effectiveness than creative research scientists—probably reflecting differences in the kinds of creative demands imposed by the two occupations.

In the case of adolescents, at least, this study has the limitation of focusing on "scientific" creativity. Therefore, it is interesting to consider the results of another study that employed a more general population of adolescents (203). In this investigation, the attitude patterns of 115 high school seniors scoring high on measures of creativity (202) were compared with those of 100 unselected adolescents of similar age, socioeconomic status, and parental occupation.

Interestingly, the results were generally compatible with those of the earlier study on creativity, despite the fact that the creative students in this latter investigation represented a far wider range of interests outside the sciences (e.g., art, music, writing, dancing, politics). "As a group our creatively gifted seniors can be described as high in Freedom Orientation, low *in* Control Orientation, high in Achievement Orientation, high in Recognition Orientation and high in Anxiety Orientation" (203, *137*). In contrast, the comparison group emerged as oriented much more toward

**TABLE 5.6 COMPARISON OF HIGH PATTERNS OF HIGHLY CREATIVE HIGH SCHOOL SENIORS AND A SIMILAR UNSELECTED GROUP ON THE RUNNER STUDIES OF ATTITUDE PATTERNS**

| ATTITUDE OR ORIENTATION | CREATIVE SENIORS (N = 115) | | UNSELECTED (N = 100) | |
|---|---|---|---|---|
| | NUMBER | PERCENT | NUMBER | PERCENT |
| Experimental | 94 | 82 | 23 | 23[a] |
| Intuitive | 105 | 91 | 56 | 56[a] |
| Rules and tradition | 22 | 19 | 40 | 40[a] |
| Planfulness (structure) | 17 | 15 | 44 | 44[a] |
| Power and authority | 18 | 17 | 18 | 18 |
| Passive compliance | 38 | 33 | 56 | 56[a] |
| Extraversiveness | 51 | 44 | 44 | 44 |
| Hostility and blame | 47 | 41 | 59 | 59[b] |
| Resistance to social pressure | 76 | 66 | 35 | 35[a] |
| Social anxiety | 91 | 79 | 70 | 70 |
| Pleasure in tool-implemented hand skills | 66 | 57 | 78 | 78 |
| Performance anxiety | 88 | 76 | 70 | 70 |

*Source:* E. P. Torrance and D. C. Dauw. Attitude patterns of creatively gifted high school seniors. *Gifted Child Quarterly,* Summer 1966, 53–57. By permission.
  [a] Difference in percentages is significant at better than .01 level.
  [b] Difference in percentages is significant at better than .05 level.

rules and tradition, a need for structure, and passive compliance (see Table 5.6). On most attitude patterns there were few sex differences associated with creativity.

Other studies have yielded largely similar results. Depending somewhat on area of talent, creative adolescents have been found variously to be more independent, dominant, autonomous, and unconventional (33, 47); more self-reliant, efficient, perceptive, imaginative, and rebellious about rules and constraints (161); more spontaneous and energetic (33); more capable of tolerating the tension that comes from holding strongly opposed values, as well as more capable of reconciling them to some degree (142); more capable of tolerating ambiguity (124); more open to feelings (47); and generally more socially poised, mature, ambitious, intellectually motivated, and self-confident than their less creative peers (100, 120, 193).

### Sex differences

Although one can easily think of many exceptionally creative women, both past and present, who have made unique contributions to science and the arts, the fact remains that women have been, and still are, underrepresented among the outstanding figures in these fields. Why have fewer women gained such recognition?

A recent survey of male and female performances shows no consistent sex differences on a wide variety of measures of creativity, including the ability to generate a variety of hypotheses and to produce unusual ideas (140). Thus it appears that we must look elsewhere for answers to the question posed. One obvious factor involves traditional societal attitudes and practices, which historically have had the effect of limiting opportunity, encouragement, and recognition for women to a greater degree than for men.

It seems highly likely, however, that more complex and subtle influences have also been involved. Creative individuals tend to be distinguished from their less creative peers by being more independent, nonconforming, adventurous, and resistant to social pressures (in addition to being more imaginative, perceptive, and open to feelings). Traditionally, the former characteristics have been encouraged more for males, whereas conformity, capacity for intimacy, caution, and working for social approval have been emphasized to a greater extent for females. It may be, therefore, that personal predispositions, as well as societal restrictions, have played a significant role in limiting the number of outstandingly creative women. As social change proceeds—as greater emphasis on both personal autonomy and social oportunity for girls and women occurs—we may well see an increase in the number of outstandingly creative women who are recognized as such. This desirable goal, even when achieved, does not necessarily mean, however, that the numbers of highly creative males and females will be distributed equally in all fields, or that the particular kinds of contributions will necessarily be the same, *on average,* within fields. Creative productions requiring verbal fluency and awareness of psychological nuances may conceivably engage the interests and talents of more females; those emphasizing spatial abilities, more males; and so on. In poetry, more males may continue to confront the cosmos, more females may continue to address the more immediate complexities of the self and its relation to others. As noted earlier, there may be *average* sex differences that have a partial biological basis, and there may (or may not) continue to be some sex-related cultural preferences. But there is no convincing evidence to suggest that one sex is inherently more potentially creative than the other (140).

Finally, it should be noted that neither excessive "masculinity" nor "femininity" fosters creativity. A growing number of studies suggest that those who are most likely to be creative are those who combine, within their own personalities, traits traditionally stereotyped as masculine (e.g., autonomy) and feminine (e.g., sensitivity) (20, 129, 130, 135, 144, 192, 203).

Whether creative thinking can be facilitated among contemporary adolescents appears to depend on a variety of external as well as internal factors—including family influences and the attitudes and behaviors of teachers and administrators in our schools. Creativity appears likely to be fostered in direct proportion to the extent that parents and the schools value creative thinking, respect curiosity and unusual questions and interests, recognize and reward unusual skills and talents, provide opportunities for self-initiated learning, take the ideas of adolescents seriously, and try to provide as rich and varied a cultural and educational atmosphere as possible (44, 99, 138, 202, 206, 207). In one investigation (209), for example, it was found that parents of high-intelligence–low-creativity adolescents tended to emphasize academic grades, conformity, cleanliness, and good manners. In contrast, parents of high-intelligence–high-creativity adolescents were less critical of their children, and encouraged openness, enthusiasm, and interest in new experiences. A variety of studies (55, 94, 188, 202, 209) suggest that factors such as the following are likely to inhibit the development of creative thinking: "an extremely peer-oriented culture, sanctions against questioning exploration, overemphasized or misplaced emphasis on sex roles, the equation of divergency with abnormality or delinquency, and a work-play dichotomy" (202, 236).

Adolescence is, as we shall see, the stage in development when the individual, with greatly expanded cognitive skills, is most open to curiosity, exploration, and a sense of adventure—intellectually, as well as in other areas. For this reason, failure to take advantage of the adolescent's creative potential during this period of development (or worse, to actively discourage it), as is too often the case, is disheartening and wasteful.

## QUALITATIVE ASPECTS OF ADOLESCENT COGNITIVE DEVELOPMENT

As we have already noted, the changes that take place in cognitive functioning during adolescence are both qualitative and quantitative. Although for many years the greatest emphasis (largely as a function of the impact of the intelligence-test movement) was primarily on quantitative aspects, in recent years there has been a rapidly growing interest in the qualitative aspects of mental development—the maturational changes in the kinds of fundamental processes underlying improvements in intellectual performance. Inherent in the idea of qualitative changes with age is the concept of *stages* in mental functioning, and the further assumption of a necessary progression, or sequence, from one stage to another (76, 116). In other words, regardless of the age at which a particular child or adolescent reaches a particular stage (with its associated gain in intellectual capability), he or she cannot reach that stage without having first mastered earlier stages.

The newer emphasis on stages of cognitive development owes more to the Swiss psychologist Jean Piaget (see photo on page 159) than to any other single theorist or investigator. According to Piaget, there are four major stages in cognitive development: the *sensorimotor* stage (from birth to 18 months), the *preoperational* stage (18 months to 7 years), the stage of *concrete operations* (7 to 12 years), and the stage of *formal operations* (from about age 12 onward) (76, 113, 168). In this theoretical system, thought is viewed as developing through the gradual internalization of action (and true thought is not considered to emerge before the age of 6 or 7, with the onset of the stage of concrete operations) (113). During the sensorimotor stage (conceived as the period prior to the acquisition of language), the child is developing rather simple generalized responses ("schemas of action") to the objects and persons in the world around him or her. He or she may discover that already acquired responses may be applied to new objects (i.e., shaking or banging an unfamiliar toy), a process called *assimilation*. However, the child's developing relationships with objects during this period is not a one-way street. In addition to incorporating new objects into existing schemas or response systems, the young child is also learning to modify existing responses in order to adjust to the unique characteristics of new objects; this process is called *accommodation:*

> The 2-year-old child who has never been exposed to a magnet may initially assimilate it to prior schemata and act toward the magnet as he or she does toward a familiar toy. The child may bang it, bounce it, throw it, or try to make it produce a

noise. But once the child discovers the unique quality of the magnet, that it attracts metal, he or she will now accommodate to that quality and begin to apply the magnet to a variety of objects to see if they will adhere to it [152, *17*].

Obviously, unless the young child is capable of accommodation as well as assimilation, progress in mental development would not be possible. Assimilation provides for continuity in development and enables the child to profit from past experiences; accommodation provides for meaningful growth and change. Much of mental development, in Piaget's view, involves the resolution of tensions between the opposing processes of assimilation and accommodation (168).

In the preoperational stage, children's mental growth advances significantly, for they have now the tool of language and can manipulate meanings as well as objects. They can deal with objects as symbols for other objects (e.g., pretend that a block of wood is a toy car, or that a doll is a baby girl). But their conceptual ability is still relatively rudimentary, although recent research indicates that when dealing with relatively simple and *familiar* events and objects, preschool children are likely to display greater cognitive ability than Piagetian theory—which is generally based on more complex, less familiar tasks—would predict (80).

### The stage of concrete operations

The child's thought in middle and late childhood (roughly 7 to 11 years) shows impressive advances over the earlier preoperational period. The preoperational child functions largely in terms of "the phenomenal, before-the-eye reality" (76,

*203*). Even when the child is treating an object symbolically (e.g., pretending that a block of wood is a toy car), he or she is still dealing with it primarily in terms of actual, unsystematic (Piaget calls it "intuitive") physical manipulation in the here and now. For example, the child does not systematically explore mentally the potential situations in which the "car" might logically become involved. In contrast, in the period of concrete operations the child begins to extend thought from the *actual* toward the *potential* (61, 76). This extension is aided by—indeed it may be said to be a natural consequence of—the development of concrete-operational structures. Unlike preoperational children, who are basically limited to responding directly to the absolute properties of objects themselves, 7- to 11-year-olds become increasingly capable of dealing with the properties of objects and relationships among them.

The child in the stage of concrete operations begins to utilize a new set of rules (called groupings) for dealing with these relationships—rules that greatly increase the flexibility and power of the child's thinking. One rule is that of equivalence: If A is equal to B in some way (e.g., length), and if B is equal to C, then it must be true that A is equal to C. Given this information, the child does not have to measure A and C to know that this is the case.

Another rule that the child recognizes—although in most cases it is unlikely that he or she could state it formally—is that there are certain fixed relationships among objects (or properties of objects). For example, the concrete-operational child can appreciate that if A is longer than B, and B is longer than C, then A must be longer than C. The child at this stage also realizes that objects (or their qualities) can belong to more than one category, or *class* (e.g., a chocolate bar can belong both to a class of objects that are sweet and to a class of objects that are brown in color). In addition, he or she begins to recognize that classes can be *hierarchical*—although the child would be most unlikely to use this term. (For example, the concrete-operational child can accept the idea that an orange belongs to the class *fruit* which, in turn, belongs in the larger class *food*.)

Finally, the concrete-operational child comes to understand that intellectual operations are *reversible*. For example, he or she recognizes that if four poker chips are removed from a pile of six chips, and these four are further subdivided in two piles of two each, after which the whole procedure is reversed, the final pile must contain the original number of chips. "Reversibility means that one can always get back to the starting point of a series of operations" (60, *140*).

The development of this system of concrete operations makes possible a kind of reasoning that does not appear in the preschool child (60, 61, 76). Thus, children become increasingly able to think in *relational terms*. Where previously they might have been able to describe an object in absolute terms as dark, they now become able to think *relatively* as well, so that they can also describe the object as darker than or lighter than another object. Because they are less limited by the absolute properties of objects, concrete-operational children can also deal with the problem of what Piaget calls *class inclusion* (76, 113, 168): They can reason simultaneously about part of the whole and the whole. If younger children are shown ten red blocks and five yellow blocks and asked whether there are more red blocks or more blocks, they are likely to reply that there are more red blocks. As soon as they deal with subclasses the larger class is destroyed, since they cannot conceive that a particular object can belong to two classes at the same time. The 6- or 7-year-old child, on the other hand, will be able to view "red blocks" as included in the more general class "blocks," and will give the correct answer (57).

Another important operation of which the school-age child becomes capable is *conservation*. The idea that liquids and solids can be changed in shape without changing their volume or mass is a result of concrete-operational thinking. For example, "it is not until about age six or seven that the child is able to grasp the fact that an amount of liquid poured from a large glass into two smaller glasses remains the same" (60, *141*). The 4- or 5-year-old believes that if you change the shape of an object you also change its amount; he or she does not realize that its amount is *conserved*.

> The concrete operational child solves the problem by taking account of *both* the width of the container and the levels of the liquids at the same time. He thus comes to realize that for *every* change in the level of the liquids there is a corresponding change in the widths of the containers which exactly compensates for change in level. This awareness of reversibility, thanks to the concrete operational system, allows the child to discover the conservation of quantities [60, *141*].

Similarly, in the greater ability to depart from the isolated, absolute properties of objects, the concrete-operational child also becomes capable of *serialization* (or *serial ordering*)—the ability to arrange objects along some abstract dimension, such as size, weight, or brightness (e.g., to arrange dolls in order of height from shortest to tallest). The older child is able to do this because he or she can comprehend that a particular doll (B) must be viewed *both* as taller than doll A and shorter than doll C if it is to fit into its proper place. "The young child fails because he cannot compose these relations and recognize that one and the same element can stand in two different relations at the same time" (60, *141*).

Piaget notes that the concrete-operational child's ability to begin to move from the *actual* to the *potential* is a logical consequence of just such processes as these (76, 113). For example, once a child can view doll A as shorter than doll B, which, in turn, is shorter than doll C, it represents "a simple potential prolongation of the actions or operations applied to the given content" to extend thought to the *possibility* of a doll D, which would be taller than doll C (113, *249*). In John Flavell's words, "The structures of concrete operations are, to use a homely analogy, rather like parking lots whose individual parking spaces are now occupied and now empty; the squares themselves endure, however, and lead their owner to look beyond the cars actually present towards potential, future occupants of the vacant and to-be-vacant spaces" (76, *203*).

Obviously, the child's thought makes many significant advances during the concrete-operational period, and these advances will continue to play an important role throughout life. At the same time, however, thinking is still clearly limited when contrasted to that of the adolescent. As Bärbel Inhelder and Piaget note, "concrete thought remains essentially attached to empirical reality. . . . Therefore, it attains no more than a concept of 'what is possible,' which is a simple (and not very great) extension of the empirical situation" (113, *250*). In other words, the starting point for the concrete-operational child is always the real rather than the potential, and he or she can only reason about those things with which he or she has had direct personal experience (60, 76). Furthermore,

> He has difficulty as soon as he has to deal with any hypothetical or contrary-to-fact proposition. In addition, while he can deal with two classes, relations, or quantitative dimensions at the same time, this is about the limit of his capabilities. As soon as more variables than two have to be taken into account in a systematic way, he flounders because he lacks an operational system appropriate to such situations. This is the fundamental deficiency of concrete operational thought [60, *141*].

### *The stage of formal operations*

With the advent of formal operations—usually around age 12 but with marked individual variations (56, 77, 120, 156, 157, 169, 175)—the adolescent is likely to gain a number of important capabilities not present in the middle-childhood years. In Piaget's view, the most basic of these involves a shift of emphasis in the adolescent's thought from the *real* to the *possible:*

> In formal thought there is a reversal of the direction of thinking between *reality* and *possibility* in the subject's method of approach. *Possibility* no longer appears merely as an extension of an empirical situation or of actions actually performed. Instead, it is *reality* that is now secondary to *possibility* [113, *251*].

Unlike the concrete-operational child, the normative adolescent is able to approach a problem by trying to imagine all the possible relationships that might obtain in a given body of data. Then, through a careful process that combines logical analysis and experimental verification, he or she is able to determine which of these possible relationships actually holds true (76, 113). "Reality is thus conceived as a special subset within the totality of things which the data would admit as hypotheses; it is seen as the 'is' portion of a 'might be' totality, the portion it is the subject's job to discover" (76, *205*). In short, the adolescent becomes more capable of *hypothetico-deductive* thinking, much like that of the scientist. The process of deduction is no longer confined to perceived realities, but extends to hypothetical statements. "It refers to propositions which are formulations of hypotheses or which postulate facts or events independently of whether or not they actually occur" (113, *251*).

The development of hypothetico-deductive thinking and related aspects of formal operations makes adolescent thought much richer, broader, and more flexible than that of the concrete-operational child. Although the latter is capable of a rudimentary form of hypothesis formation closely linked to concrete experience, the limits of this capability are readily apparent. For example, younger children are much more likely, once they have thought of one possible explanation for a problem situation, to immediately accept it as true. In contrast, adolescents are more likely to recognize the arbitrary nature of hypotheses. Consequently, they will tend systematically to exhaust all possible explanations, even those which may be rather fanciful, and to examine the evidence for or against each, before adopting one of them. Even then, as we shall see, they may be hesitant to commit themselves.

This fundamental difference in approach between the younger child and the average adolescent has been clearly shown in an experiment by Elkind (58). Two groups of subjects, children 8 to 9 years old and adolescents 13 to 14 years old, were

presented with a concept-formation problem involving pictures of wheeled and nonwheeled tools, and wheeled and nonwheeled vehicles. The pictures were presented in pairs, with each pair including both a wheeled and a nonwheeled object. In each case, the subject was asked to choose one member of the pair. Choosing a wheeled object always made a light go on, whereas choosing a nonwheeled object never did. The problem for the subject was to determine the kind of picture that would make the signal light go on every time.

Differences in the manner in which adolescents and younger children handled the task were clearly demonstrated:

> Only half of the children were able to arrive at the notion that it was the choice of wheeled objects which made the light go on. Furthermore, it took those children who did succeed almost all of the allotted 72 trials to arrive at a correct solution. On the other hand, *all* of the adolescents solved the problem and many did so in as few as 10 trials [60, *145*].

The tendency of adolescents to raise alternative hypotheses successively, test each against the facts, and discard those that prove wrong was apparent in their spontaneous verbalizations during the experiment (e.g., "Maybe it's transportation . . . no, it must be something else, I'll try . . ." (61, *145*). In this fashion, adolescents quickly solved the problem. The children, on the other hand, appeared to become fixated on an initial hypothesis that was strongly suggested by the data (e.g., tool versus nontool or vehicle versus nonvehicle). They then clung to this hypothesis even though they continued to fail on most tests. Although the adolescents also might have considered such likely hypotheses initially, they quickly discarded them when they were not substantiated by subsequent experience. It appears that an important part of the child's greater inflexibility is an inability to clearly differentiate his or her hypotheses from reality (60). Once a hypothesis was adopted, it became "true" and the child then felt no need to test it further (60, 213). "Indeed, he seems unaware of the hypothetical quality of his strategy and seems to feel that it is imposed from without rather than constructed from within" (60, *146*). In Piaget's view, it is the adolescent's awareness of *possibility* that enables him or her to distinguish thought from reality (113).

Other related differences distinguish adolescent thought from that of the concrete-operational child. Unlike the child, the adolescent can "take his own thought as an object and reason about it" (50, *141*). Formal thinking is above all *propositional thinking* (76). As Piaget comments, "When verbal statements are substituted for objects, a new type of thinking—propositional logic—is imposed on the logic of classes and relations relevant to these objects" (113, *253*):

> The important entities which the adolescent manipulates in his reasoning are no longer the raw reality data themselves, but assertions or statements—propositions— which "contain" these data. What is really achieved in the 7–11 year period is the organized cognition of concrete objects and events *per se* (i.e., putting them into classes, seriating them, setting them into correspondence, etc.). The adolescent performs these first-order operations, too, but he does something else besides, a necessary something which is precisely what renders his thought formal rather than concrete. He takes the *results* of these concrete operations, casts them in the form of propositions, and then proceeds to operate further upon them, i.e., make various logical connections between them. . . . Formal operations, then, are really operations performed upon the results of prior (concrete) operations [76, *205*].

### *Other characteristics of adolescent thought*

In addition to those aspects of adolescent thinking emphasized by Piaget, there are a number of other related changes to which psychologists have recently called attention (77, 120). In comparison to younger children, adolescents are more likely to be aware of the distinction between simply perceiving something and storing it in memory; they are also more likely to be aware of their own memory capacities and limitations, and to use increasingly sophisticated techniques (mnemonic schemes) as aids to remembering (77, 120, 156). "The common thread is the individual's awareness and knowledge about cognitive activity itself and about the mechanisms that can make it more or less efficient" (120, *215*).

Adolescents are also more likely to use efficient problem-solving strategies in approaching a wide variety of tasks. A good example is the familiar game of "Twenty Questions," in which one player has to determine what the other player is thinking of, using as few questions as possible. The adolescent or adult is far more likely than the younger child to adopt an overall planful strategy that involves asking a series of increasingly narrower categorical questions (e.g., "Is it alive?," "Is it an animal?"). In contrast, the younger child is likelier to adapt the more concrete-minded and considerably less efficient procedure of asking specific questions from the outset (e.g., "Is it a dog?") (77).

The future time perspective of adolescents is greater than that of younger children (77, 120). Adolescents begin to think about what they will be doing with their lives—whether they will go to college, what kind of work they may be doing, whether they will marry, what the world will be like in 5 or 10 years. For the younger child, the prospect of 3 months of summer vacation may seem like an eternity; his or her attention is likely to be focused on an upcoming birthday party or a trip to the zoo.

In general, adolescents and adults are more likely than younger children to have what Flavell calls "a sense of the game" (77)—an awareness that much of life consists of anticipating, formulating, and developing strategies for dealing with problems—whether this involves developing a household budget to avoid financial crisis, or estimating the interactions and probable behavior of other people.

### The generality of formal operations

There is fairly widespread agreement that there is a level of cognitive development beyond that of the concrete-operational child, and that it conforms generally to the description of formal operational thinking provided here (77, 156, 157). There is considerably more question, however, about how universal and age-specific it is. Doubts have also been raised about the extent to which the various specific competencies that presumably reflect the development of formal operational thinking develop together and represent a distinct departure from earlier modes of thinking, as the theory would suggest (77, 82, 120).

Investigators have found some aspects of formal thinking in highly intelligent younger children (118, 120). Furthermore, the development of formal thought among adolescent 12-, 14-, and 16-year-olds has been found to result from "an interaction of age and intelligence with significant gains being made by adolescents of average intelligence from 12 to 14 and by low-intelligence adolescents from 14 to 16. [Subjects] of superior intelligence show an almost linear development" (221, 707).

Some adolescents and adults never acquire true formal operational thought, because of either limited ability or cultural limitations, in both our own and other countries (56, 77, 113, 120, 156, 169, 175). For example, it was found that rural villagers in Turkey and a number of other countries never reached this stage, though it was reached by urbanized educated persons in these same countries (122).

Furthermore, even very bright adolescents and adults do not always employ their capacity for formal operational thinking. Even well-educated, intelligent adults appear to do better when thinking abstractly about "real, concrete problems, even scientific ones, than when thinking abstractly about abstract wholly logical problems that seem to have no reality outside of a logic textbook" (156, *116*). They are also likely to do better with problems whose content is familiar, or in which they are interested. And they do better when they are not bored, tired, frustrated, or overly involved emotionally. Take the familiar example of an intelligent young woman searching for a missing earring while late for an important date. Frustrated by her failure to find it, she is likely to end up looking in the same place repeatedly, despite the certain knowledge that it is not there. Even supposedly objective scientists may be inclined to look for evidence confirming their hypotheses, while ignoring equally solid evidence that appears to contradict them (157).

Finally, it should be realized that formal operational thought is not an all-or-none affair, although for simplicity in exposition we may have appeared to suggest otherwise. The really gifted adolescent girl or boy is likely to display greater imagination, greater flexibility, and more precision in the exercise of formal operational thinking than less gifted peers, although the basic processes involved may be similar (121, 122).

### Social cognition

If deviations from formal operational thinking often occur—even among those who presumably know better—in dealing with physical, scientific, or primarily intellectual problems, what may we expect when the far more elusive and emotion-laden problems of human beings and human affairs are involved? The scientific investigation of this kind of problem solving is called *social cognition* (77). It implies attempts to understand in what manner, to what extent, and how accurately people of different ages and differing levels of ability are able to infer what others are thinking or feeling, what they are like psychologically, how they view the world, what their intentions are, and what characterizes their relationships with others (e.g., friendship, love, power, fear, admiration?) (77, 182).

Research has shown that children tend to improve in all of these capabilities as they grow older. Preschoolers can identify certain simple emotions in others through facial and other cues, but they appear unable to anticipate another's thoughts, and they tend to describe others in terms of physical appearances or shared activities rather than psychological or social characteristics (134, 182).

During middle childhood dramatic advances occur in the child's social understanding. "First, social inferences now progress to the level of the child's understanding that his own thoughts, feelings, and intentions can be the object of another's thinking. He can view simple social episodes from the position of each participant and maintain a consistency among viewpoints on the episode. . . . In addition, the child shows an ability to infer the feelings of others when others are in situations largely unfamiliar to him" (182, *312*).

Furthermore, beginning in early middle childhood, children "describe others less in terms of their 'surface' characteristics and more in terms of their covert attributes—attitudes, abilities, interests" (182, *312*). And they begin to attend less to the physical aspects of interpersonal interactions, and more to the inferred inner experiences and social relations between the participants.

Social cognition continues to develop during adolescence:

> The perspective of the adolescent extends further to include himself, the other person, the inner experiences of each, and the relation between himself and the other as a third-party observer might understand it. In social episodes, the adolescent is much more oriented toward and accurate in making inferences about the thoughts, intentions, and feelings of each participant in the episode. Particularly, there is a spontaneous tendency to try to *explain* such thoughts and feelings, not merely to describe them. Likewise, the descriptions of others show much greater subtlety and refinement in the use of traits, the recognition of contradictory tendencies within an individual, and relating situational factors to another's behavior. The refinement, breadth, and depth of understanding others does not have, of course, an "end point" [182, *312–313*].

Despite these remarkable advances in cognitive capacity, both adolescents and adults can, and not infrequently do, fail to perceive accurately the thoughts, feelings, and intentions of others, and the nature of interactions with them (59, 77). This may occur for a variety of reasons, including a simple lack of relevant information on which to base their inferences. Most often, however, it is likely to result from *egocentrism*—a failure to distinguish sufficiently clearly between one's own point of view and that of others: "My assessment of your opinions and feelings is egocentric to the degree that I have unwittingly misattributed my own opinions and feelings to you" (77, *124*).

## EFFECTS OF ADOLESCENT MENTAL GROWTH ON PERSONALITY AND SOCIAL DEVELOPMENT

It would be difficult to overestimate the importance of the quantitative and qualitative changes in cognitive development (particularly the shift in the direction of formal operations) that take place during adolescence. It is not difficult to appreciate the critical role that these changes play in helping the adolescent to deal with increasingly complex educational and vocational demands; it would be virtually impossible to master such academic subjects as calculus or the use of metaphors in poetry without a high level of abstract thinking.

Further reflection, however, should make it clear that many other aspects of adolescent development are also dependent on the cognitive advances occurring during this period. Changes in the nature of parent-child relationships, emerging personality characteristics and psychological defense mechanisms, planning of future educational and vocational goals, mounting concerns with social, political, and personal values, even a developing sense of ego identity—all are strongly influenced by these cognitive changes.

As we have noted, one of the most important aspects of the emergence of formal operational thought is the ability to entertain hypotheses or theoretical propositions that depart from immediately observable events. In contrast to the child, who for the most part is preoccupied with learning how to function in the world of here and now, the adolescent is able "not only to grasp the immediate state of things but also the possible state they might or could assume" (60, *152*). The implications of this change are vast (38, 61).

For example, the adolescent's newfound and frequently wearing talents for discovering his or her previously idealized parents' feet of clay—for questioning their values, for comparing them with other, "more understanding" parents, and for accusing them of hypocritical inconsistencies between professed values and behavior—all appear to be at least as dependent on the adolescent's changes in cognitive ability as on such widely emphasized events as the revival of oedipal rivalries or conflicting identifications. "The awareness of the discrepancy between the actual and the possible also helps to make the adolescent a rebel. He is always comparing the possible with the actual and discovering that the actual is frequently wanting" (60, *152*).

The relentless criticism by many adolescents of existing social, political, and religious systems and their preoccupation with the construction of often elaborate or highly theoretical alternative systems is dependent on their emerging capacity for formal operational thought. The fact that such concerns tend to be most characteristic of our brightest young people appears to be due at least as much (and quite possibly more) to their greater cognitive capability as to their more "permissive upbringing," "affluence," or other favorite whipping boys of politicians and the popular press.

The fact that a good deal of an adolescent's concern with the deficiencies of parents and the social order and with the creation of alternatives often turns out to be more a matter of word than deed is perhaps a reflection of the fact that this stage of development is still relatively new and not yet fully integrated into the adolescent's total adaptation to life. The adolescent frequently voices devotion to humanitarian causes, but often does little to implement them:

> Likewise, his acute dissatisfaction with his parents does not in most cases cause him to break from them and go out on his own. It is just because of this discrepancy between the adolescent's ability to conceptualize ideals and his lack of awareness as to what implementing these ideals entails in the way of action, that he is able to be so adamant (and apparently hypocritical) in his demands [60, *152–153*].

Only as the end of adolescence approaches is the young person likely to assume a less militant, more tolerant, and more understanding stance toward society in general, and parents in particular (60).

At the same time, it is important to recognize the positive aspects of the adolescent's newly acquired ability to conceptualize and reason abstractly about what may often appear to the weary adult to be a seemingly endless series of hypothetical possibilities and instant convictions. As Paul Osterrieth, a psychologist at the University of Brussels, comments:

> To reason is for the young person a need and a pleasure; the "constructs of the mind" are a delight. He reasons every which way, about subjects that are most unreal and farthest from his experience. . . . The arrival at abstraction permits the individual to delve into the systems of collective representation that are offered to him by the culture in which he is growing up, and he will gradually be carried away by ideas, ideals, and values [158, *15*].

The younger adolescent's enthusiasm often appears initially to have little order or system, as though it were an uncritically accepted game of ideas, but it is important for adults to recognize that the exercise is, nevertheless, a vitally important and productive one:

> Everything will be food for thought, for spoken thought, for passionate discussion, for endless discussions, for peremptory affirmation, and the adult, losing his footing a little in this tidal wave, will often fail to perceive that what he takes to be vain rehashing or sterile questioning of old worn-out problems corresponds in reality, for the youngster, to youthful explorations and true discoveries [158, *15*].

### Cognitive aspects of
### adolescent personality development

Adolescent cognitive development is reflected not only in attitudes and values with respect to parents and society, but also in attitudes toward the self, and in the personality characteristics and defense mechanisms likely to assume prominence during this period. With increasing ability to consider hypothetical possibilities and to take his or her own thought as object and reason about it, and guided by the irresistible, sometimes painful, self-awareness that stems from the rapid physical, physiological, and psychological changes of this period, the adolescent boy or girl is likely to become more *introspective* and *analytical*. Many adolescents at this stage are concerned with such issues as whether the world that they perceive actually exists, and indeed whether they themselves are real or a product of consciousness. Many readers will probably feel a nostalgic empathy for the young adolescent who remarked, "I found myself thinking about my future, and then I began to think about why I was thinking about my future, and then I began to think about why I was thinking about why I was thinking about my future" (51, *367*). Such preoccupation with thought itself is characteristic of the emergence of the stage of formal operations.

In a related vein, the adolescent's thought and behavior may appear *egocentric*. Whereas the older child also displays egocentric characteristics, there are important qualitative differences in the way egocentrism is manifested in the child and in the adolescent. In one study (163), children and adolescents were read a passage about Stonehenge, and then were asked questions. One had to do with whether "Stonehenge was a place for religious worship or a fort. The children (ages 7 to 10) answered the question with flat statements, as if they were stating a fact. When they were given evidence that contradicted their statements, they rationalized the evidence to make it conform with their initial positions. Adolescents, on the other hand, phrased their replies in probabilistic terms and supported their judgments with material gleaned from the passage" (59, *1028*).

As shown in this experiment, children who are still in the stage of concrete operations tend to believe that their initial interpretations must be correct, because they are the product of their own reasoning (61). In contrast, the more sophisticated adolescent, although freer of the arbitrary quality of the child's egocentrism, is likely to become involved in a special egocentrism of his or her own.

> Formal operational thought not only enables the adolescent to conceptualize his thought, it also permits him to conceptualize the thought of other people. It is this capacity to take account of other people's thought, however, which is the crux of adolescent egocentrism [59, *1029*].

As Elkind asserts in a perceptive essay on the subject (59), this particular kind of egocentrism apparently develops because, although the adolescent can conceptualize the thoughts of others, "he fails to differentiate between the objects toward which the thoughts of others are directed and those which are the focus of his own concern" (59, *1029*). And because the focus of the adolescent's concern during this period of rapid change is likely to be upon himself, he is likely to conclude that other people are equally obsessed with his behavior and appearance. "It is this belief that others are preoccupied with his appearance and behavior that constitutes the ego-centrism of the adolescent" (59, *1029*).

One of the consequences of this egocentrism is the adolescent's feeling of being on stage, and much time is spent "constructing, or reacting to, *an imaginary audience*" (59, *1030*). It is an audience because the adolescent feels that all eyes are focused upon him or her and it is imaginary because this is so seldom the case. In Elkind's view, the construction of such imaginary audiences helps to account, at least to some degree, for a variety of adolescent behaviors and experiences, including the adolescent's sometimes excruciating self-consciousness (59). When the adolescent is feeling self-critical, he or she is likely to anticipate that the audience will be similarly critical:

> And, since the audience is of his own construction and privy to his own knowledge of himself, it knows just what to look for in the way of cosmetic and behavioral sensitivities. The adolescent's wish for privacy and his reluctance to reveal himself may, to some extent, be a reaction to the feeling of being under the constant critical scrutiny of other people. The notion of an imaginary audience also helps to explain the observation that the effect which most concerns adolescents is not guilt but, rather, shame, that is, the reaction to an audience [59, *1030*].

By the same token, when the adolescent is in an ebullient, self-admiring mood, he or she also may project *these* feelings onto peers or adults. The younger adolescent boy who stands before the mirror flexing his muscles and admiring his profile, or the girl who spends hours applying her makeup or trying one hair style or dress after another, may be dreaming of the dramatic impression that he or she will make on a date or at a party that evening (59). It is perhaps one of the minor tragedies of adolescent life that when these young people actually meet, each is likely to be more preoccupied with himself or herself than with observing others. "Gatherings of young adolescents are unique in the sense that each young person is simultaneously an actor to himself and an audience to others" (59, *1030*).

It has been found, as Elkind's concept of imaginary audience would imply, that self-consciousness does tend to be greatest in early adolescence (around age 12) and declines in later years (190). In an interesting extension of this formulation, Elkind and Robert Bowen distinguished between two aspects of the self: the *transient self* (referring to temporary appearances and behaviors, such as a bad haircut, soiled clothing, or inadvertent words or acts) and the *abiding self* (consisting of long-lived personal characteristics, such as personality traits or mental ability) (63, 64). In a study of fourth-, sixth-, eighth-, and twelfth-grade boys and girls, they found that early adolescents (eighth graders) were more self-conscious and less willing to reveal *both* their transient and abiding selves to an audience than younger or older subjects, although they were slightly more reluctant to reveal their abiding selves than their transient selves (64).

Elkind also postulates a complementary mental construction to the imaginary audience, which he refers to as the "personal fable."

> While the adolescent fails to differentiate the concerns of his own thought from those of others, he at the same time overdifferentiates his feelings. Perhaps because

he believes he is of importance to so many people, the imaginary audience, he comes to regard himself, and particularly his feelings, as something special and unique. Only he can suffer with such agonized intensity, or experience such exquisite rapture. How many parents have been confronted with the typically adolescent phrase, "But you don't know how it feels. . . ." [59, *1031*].

Several investigators (64, 66, 67) have attempted recently to test Elkind's constructs empirically. In one such effort (66, 67), scales were developed for *personal fable, imaginary audience,* and *focus on the self* (e.g., one item on the imaginary audience scale asked how important the individual considered "being able to daydream about great successes and thinking of other people's reactions"). It was predicted that these three aspects of adolescent egocentrism should be correlated with one another, and that all three should decline with age. Two additional scales measured *sociocentrism* (concerns with society, such as "knowing what society's laws are") and *nonsocial focus* (personal concerns that do not directly involve others, such as "having lots of money," "watching television"). It was predicted that there would be a decline in the importance of nonsocial activities, and an increase in sociocentric activity, from early to later adolescence.

As predicted, both imaginary audience and personal fable declined from early to late adolescence. The findings on self-focus, on the other hand, were more complex. Instead of a steady decline, a curvilinear relationship was found; that is, self-focus was highest at the sixth-grade and college levels, and lower during eighth, tenth, and twelfth grades. The investigators' interpretation is that rather than simply an overall decline in self-focus from early to late adolescence, there is a change in the nature of the self-focus: "It should be noted that this late adolescent focus on the self appears to be without a self-conscious expectation of other's reactions or an insistence on considering oneself totally unique and special. Most likely it is an unself-conscious stirring for betterment of the self in the college years which tends to overshadow other concerns" (66, *694*). Furthermore, in early adolescence, self-focus appears to take place at the expense of sociocentric concerns, while in late adolescence this is not necessarily the case. This view is supported, at least partly, by the fact that in this investigation sociocentrism reached its highest level in the college sample, and that nonsocial focus decreased from sixth grade to college (67).

A number of other characteristics of the adolescent appear related, at least in part, to his or her level of cognitive development. Thus, the adolescent's frequent use of irony—of the sometimes elaborate "put-on" or "put-down"—while clearly serving other motivations as well, can be understood partly as an exercise of his or her newfound talents for thinking at the symbolic level of the metaphor, the "as if," and the manifestly absurd. The delight of the younger adolescent (and some rather adolescent adults) in the use of double entendres appears to represent not merely an exhilarating tasting of forbidden fruit, but an opportunity to demonstrate a new cognitive skill. The same may be said of the older adolescent's appreciation of political and social satire and his or her skill "in making the apparently innocent yet cutting remark" (61, 62).

The psychological defense mechanisms employed by adolescents may also reflect their level of cognitive development. Indeed, an awareness of the role of cognitive factors in the adolescent's use of defenses may help to explain an apparent inconsistency in the findings of various clinical investigations. A number of psychoanalysts (17, 18, 78) have stressed the importance of such characteristically adolescent defenses as intellectualization and asceticism, which they encountered both in the literature of youth and in their analyses of intelligent, sensitive adolescent patients (see Chapter 3). Other investigators, however, on the basis of studies of more representative samples of young people in general, believe that the frequency of use of such defenses by adolescents has been exaggerated. Whereas these discrepancies may reflect differences in the severity of the emotional conflicts encountered in different samples of adolescents, they may also reflect differences in cognitive level. At any rate, it appears that the use of such "primitive" defenses as denial, so frequently found in younger children, requires a far lower level of cognitive development than does the use of more sophisticated defenses, such as intellectualization.

The emerging awareness of how things might be in contrast to how they are that accompanies the development of formal operations may help explain some of the "recurrent adolescent feelings of depression and dissatisfaction (*Weltschmerz*)" (60, *152*). It is most often in adolescence, for example, that adopted children are likely to feel compelled to seek out their real parents. Similarly, "it is only in adolescence that previously happy, cheerful and 'gutty' handicapped and crippled children experience their first real depression" (60, *152*).

The adolescent's cognitive development also plays an important role in the emergence of a well-defined *sense of ego identity*. It seems likely that the degree of a differentiation and definiteness that an individual is able to achieve in the development of a sense of identity will depend upon cognitive capability. As Osterrieth eloquently observes,

> By getting away from the concrete, by reasoning, by "concentrating," by trying out hypotheses, he meets up with himself. Who is he, this person who thinks, who adopts an attitude, who speaks his opinion? What is he? What is it in him, what is this center where his ideas are shaped, where his thoughts are produced, where his assumptions are formulated? Is it not himself? And doubtless he will have an impression of interior freedom, of profound originality, of authenticity, and also, therefore, of responsibility: he will feel himself involved by the fact of this freedom. It is apparent that intellectual transformations bring the youngster to ask himself questions about himself, to wonder, to acknowledge himself, just as much as do the physical transformations and just about at the same time. The values that the adolescent is "trying out," not without paradoxes and sophisms, the opinions that he defends sometimes with as much fire as thoughtlessness, are these not just so many ways of looking for himself, of defining himself, so many attempts to be and to become himself? [158, *15–16*]

Furthermore, as we shall see later, the level and complexity of the adolescent's political thinking, value systems, and conceptions of morality are all dependent to a significant extent on his or her degree of cognitive development (see Chapter 13).

Finally, Inhelder and Piaget (113) assert that, even when it comes to falling in love, much of the special character of adolescent love depends on the cognitive changes related to the development of formal operations:

What distinguishes an adolescent in love from a child in love is that the former generally complicates his feelings by constructing a romance or by referring to social or even literary ideals of all sorts. But the fabrication of a romance or the appeal to various collective role models is neither the direct product of the neurophysiological transformations of puberty, nor the exclusive product of affectivity. Both are also indirect and specific reflections of the general tendency of adolescents to construct theories and make use of the ideologies that surround them. And this general tendency can only be explained by taking into account the two factors which we will find in association over and over again—the transformations of thought and the assumption of adult roles. The latter involves a restructuring of the personality in which the intellectual transformations are parallel or complementary to the affective transformations [113, *336*].

## REFERENCES

1. Adelson, J. *Handbook of adolescent psychology.* New York: Wiley, 1980.
2. Arenberg, D. Cognition and aging: Verbal learning, memory, and problem solving. In C. Eisdorfer & M. P. Lawton (eds.), *The psychology of adult development and aging.* Washington, D.C.: American Psychological Association, 1973.
3. Asher, E. J. The inadequacy of current intelligence tests for testing Kentucky mountain children. *Journal of Genetic Psychology,* 1935, **46,** 480–486.
4. Baltes, P. B. (ed.). *Life-span developmental psychology* (Vol. 1). New York: Academic Press, 1978.
5. Baltes, P. B., Reese, H. W., & Lipsitt, L. P. Life-span developmental psychology. *Annual Review of Psychology,* 1980, **31,** 65–110.
6. Barron, F. Creative vision and expression in writing and painting. In D. W. MacKinnon (ed.), *The creative person.* Berkeley: Institute of Personality Assessment Research, University of California, 1961.
7. Baughman, E. E. *Black Americans.* New York: Academic Press, 1971.
8. Bayley, N. Consistency and variability in the growth of intelligence from birth to eighteen years. *Journal of Genetic Psychology,* 1949, **75,** 165–196.
9. Bayley, N. Behavioral correlates of mental growth: Birth to thirty-six years. *American Psychologist,* 1968, **23,** 1–17.
10. Bayley, N. Development of mental abilities. In P. Mussen (ed.), *Carmichael's manual of child psychology* (Vol. I). New York: Wiley, 1970. Pp. 1163–1209 (3rd ed.).
11. Bayley, N. Learning in adulthood: The role of intelligence. In M. C. Jones, N. Bayley, J. W. Macfarlane, & M. P. Honzik (eds.), *The course of human development.* Waltham, Mass.: Xerox Publishing Co., 1971.
12. Beller, E. K. Early intervention programs. In J. D. Osofsky (ed.), *The handbook of infant development.* New York: Wiley, 1979.
13. Beller, E. K. The impact of preschool on disadvantaged children: Twelve year follow-up study. Paper presented at the International Congress of Early Childhood Education, Tel Aviv, January 1980.
14. Benbow, C. P., & Stanley, J. C. Sex differences in mathematical ability: Fact or artifact? *Science,* 1980, **210,** 1262–1264.
15. Bennet, S. N. Divergent thinking abilities: A validation study. *British Journal of Educational Psychology,* 1973, **43,** 1–7.
16. Bloomberg, M. (ed.). *Creativity.* New Haven, Conn.: College & University Press, 1973.
17. Blos, P. *On adolescence.* New York: Free Press, 1962.
18. Blos, P. *The young adolescent: Clinical studies.* New York: Free Press, 1970.
19. Bodmer, W. F., & Cavalli-Sforza, L. L. Intelligence and race. *Scientific American,* 1970, **4,** 19–29.
20. Bond, E. A. *Tenth grade abilities and achievements.* New York: Columbia University Press (Teachers College, Bureau of Publications), 1940.

21. Botwinick, J. Intellectual abilities. In J. E. Birren, & K. W. Schaie, (eds.), *Handbook of the psychology of aging.* New York: Van Nostrand Reinhold, 1977. Pp. 580–605.
22. Bouchard, T. J., Jr., & McGee, M. G. Sex differences in human spatial ability: Not an X-linked recessive gene effect. *Social Biology,* 1977, **24,** 332–335.
23. Bradley, R. H., Caldwell, B. M., & Elardo, R. Home environment, social status, and mental test performance. *Journal of Educational Psychology,* 1977, **69,** 697–701.
24. Bradway, K. P., & Thompson, C. W. Intelligence at adulthood: A twenty-five-year follow-up. *Journal of Educational Psychology,* 1962, **53,** 1–14.
25. Broadhurst, P. L., Fulker, D. W., & Wilcock, J. Behavioral genetics. In M. R. Rosenzweig & L. W. Porter (eds.), *Annual review of psychology* (Vol. 25). Palo Alto, Calif.: Annual Reviews, Inc., 1974.
26. Brush, L. *Encouraging girls in mathematics: The problem and the solution.* Cambridge, Massachusetts: Abt Books, 1980.
27. Buffery, A. W. H., & Gray, J. H. Sex differences in the development of spatial and linguistic skills. In C. Ounstead & D. C. Taylor (eds.), *Gender differences: Their ontogeny and significance.* London: Churchill, 1972.
28. Burt, C. Intelligence and social mobility. *British Journal of Statistical Psychology,* 1961, **14,** 3–24.
29. Caldwell, B. M. The fourth dimension in early childhood education. In R. D. Hess & R. M. Bear (eds.), *Early education: Current theory, research, and action.* Chicago: Aldine, 1968. Pp. 71–81.
30. Canavan, D. Field dependence in children as a function of grade, sex, and ethnic group membership. In H. B. Gerard (Chair), *School desegregation and achievement-related attitudes.* Symposium presented at the 77th annual convention of the American Psychological Association, Washington, D.C., August 1969.
31. Canestrari, R. E. Paced and self-paced learning in young and elderly adults. *Journal of Gerontology,* 1963, **18,** 165–168.
32. Carroll, J. B., & Maxwell, S. E. Individual differences in cognitive abilities. *Annual Review of Psychology,* 1979, **30,** 603–640.
33. Cashdan, S., & Welsh, G. S. Personality correlates of creative potential in talented high school students. *Journal of Personality,* 1966, **34,** 445–455.
34. Cattell, R. B. Theory of fluid and crystallized intelligence: An initial experiment. *Journal of Educational Psychology,* 1963, **105,** 105–111.
35. Cavalli-Sforza, L. L. Problems and prospects of genetic analysis of intelligence at the intra- and inter-racial level. In J. Hellmuth (ed.), *Compensatory education: A national debate.* New York: Brunner Mazel, 1970. P. 460.
36. Chambers, J. A. A multidimensional theory of creativity. *Psychological Reports,* 1969, **25,** 779–799.
37. Conger, J. J. The meaning and measurement of intelligence. *Rocky Mountain Medical Journal,* June 1957, **54,** 570–576.
38. Cottle, T. J., Howard, P., & Pleck, J. Adolescent perceptions of time: The effect of age, sex, and social class. *Journal of Personality,* 1969, **37,** 636–650.
39. Cravioto, J., et al. (eds.). *Early malnutrition and mental development; Symposium of the Swedish Nutrition Foundation XII.* Stockholm: Almquist and Wiskell, 1974.
40. Cronbach, L. J. *Essentials of psychological testing.* New York: Harper & Row, 1949.
41. Darlington, R. B., Royce, J. M., Snipper, A. S., Murray, H. W., & Lazar, I. Preschool programs and later school competence of children from low-income families. *Science,* 1980, **208,** 202–204.
42. Davis, A. *Social class influences upon learning.* Cambridge, Mass.: Harvard University Press, 1948.
43. Davis, A., & Eells, K. *Davis-Eells games.* New York: Harcourt Brace Jovanovich, 1953.
44. Davis, G. A. Teaching creativity in adolescence: A discussion of strategy. In R. E. Grinder, *Studies in adolescence.* New York: Macmillan, 1969 (2nd ed.).
45. Davis, W. *National Science Youth.* Washington, D.C.: Science Service, 1963.

46. Day, H. Role of specific curiosity in school achievement. *Journal of Educational Psychology*, 1968, **59**, 37–43.

47. Dellas, M., & Gaier, E. L. Identification of creativity: The individual. *Psychological Bulletin*, 1970, **73**, 55–73.

48. Dennis, W. Age and productivity among scientists. *Science*, 1956, **123**, 724–725.

49. Deutsch, C. P. Social class and child development. In B. M. Caldwell and H. N. Ricciuti (eds.), *Review of child development research* (Vol. 3). Chicago: University of Chicago Press, 1973. Pp. 233–282.

50. Deutsch, M. On the education of the disadvantaged. In M. Deutsch, I. Katz, & A. R. Jensen. *Social class, race, and psychological development.* New York: Holt, Rinehart and Winston, 1968.

51. *Developmental psychology today.* Delmar, Calif.: CRM Books, 1971.

52. Dobbing, J., & Smart, J. L. Vulnerability of the developing brain and behavior. *British Medical Bulletin*, 1974, **30**, 104–168.

53. Dreger, R. M., & Miller, K. S. Comparative psychological studies of Negroes and whites in the United States. *Psychological Bulletin*, 1960, **57**, 361–402.

54. Dreger, R. M., & Miller, K. S. Comparative psychological studies of Negroes and whites in the United States: 1959–1965. *Psychological Bulletin Monograph Supplemental*, 1968, **70**, No. 3, Part 2.

55. Drews, E. M. A critical evaluation of approaches to the identification of gifted students. In A. Traxler (ed.), *Measurement and evaluation in today's schools.* Washington, D.C.: American Council on Education, 1961. Pp. 47–51.

56. Dulit, E. Adolescent thinking à la Piaget: The formal stage. *Journal of Youth and Adolescence*, 1972, **1**, 281–302.

57. Elkind, D. The development of the additive composition of classes in the child. *Journal of Genetic Psychology*, 1961, **99**, 51–57.

58. Elkind, D. Conceptual orientation shifts in children and adolescents. *Child Development*, 1966, **37**, 493–498.

59. Elkind, D. Egocentrism in adolescence. *Child Development*, 1967, **38**, 1025–1034.

60. Elkind, D. Cognitive development in adolescence. In J. F. Adams (ed.), *Understanding adolescence.* Boston: Allyn & Bacon, 1968. Pp. 128–158.

61. Elkind, D. *Children and adolescents: Interpretive essays on Jean Piaget.* New York: Oxford University Press, 1970.

62. Elkind, D. Measuring young minds. *Horizon*, 1971, **13**, No. 1, 35.

63. Elkind, D. *The child's reality: Three developmental themes.* Hillsdale, N.J.: Erlbaum, 1978.

64. Elkind, D., & Bowen, R. Imaginary audience behavior in children and adolescents. *Development Psychology*, 1979, **15**, 38–44.

65. Elkind, D., & Weiner, I. B. *Development of the child.* New York: Wiley, 1978.

66. Enright, R. D., Lapsley, D. K., & Shukla, D. G. Adolescent egocentrism in early and late adolescence. *Adolescence*, 1979, **14**, 687–695.

67. Enright, R. D., Shukla, D. G., & Lapsley, D. K. Adolescent egocentrism-sociocentrism and self-consciousness. *Journal of Youth and Adolescence*, 1980, **9**.

68. Erlenmeyer-Kimling, L., & Jarvik, L. F. Genetics and intelligence: A research review. *Science*, 1963, **142**, 1477–1479.

69. Ernest, J. *Mathematics and sex.* Santa Barbara: University of California Press, 1976.

70. Evans, E. D. *Adolescents: Readings in behavior and development.* New York: Holt, Rinehart and Winston, 1970.

71. Fennema, E. Mathematics learning and the sexes: A review. *Journal for Research in Mathematics Education*, 1974, **5**, 126–139.

72. Fennema, E. Influence of selected cognitive, affective and educational variables on sex-related differences in mathematics learning and studying. In J. Shoemaker (ed.), *Women and mathematics: Research perspectives for change* (N.I.E. Papers in Education and Work: No. 8). Washington, D.C.: Education and Work Group, The National Institute of Education, U.S. Department of Health, Education and Welfare, 1977.

73. Fennema, E., & Sherman, J. Sex-related differences in mathematics achievement, spatial visualization and affective factors. *American Educational Research Journal,* 1977, **4,** 51–71.

74. Flanagan, J. C. The definition and measurement of ingenuity. In C. W. Taylor & F. Barron (eds.), *Scientific creativity: Its recognition and development.* New York: Wiley, 1963.

75. Flanagan, J. C., Dailey, J. T., Shaycoft, M. F., Gorham, W. A., Orr, D. B., Goldberg, I., & Neyman, C. A., Jr. *Counselor's technical manual for interpreting test scores.* Project Talent, Palo Alto, Calif., 1961.

76. Flavell, J. H. *The developmental psychology of Jean Piaget.* New York: Van Nostrand, 1963.

77. Flavell, J. H. *Cognitive development.* Englewood Cliffs, N.J.: Prentice-Hall, 1977.

78. Freud, A. *The ego and the mechanisms of defense.* New York: International Universities Press, 1946.

79. Geiringer, E. R., & Hyde, J. S. Sex differences on Piaget's water-level task: Spatial ability incognito. *Perceptual and Motor Skills,* 1976, **42,** 1323–1328.

80. Gelman, R. Cognitive development. *Annual Review of Psychology,* 1978, **29,** 297–332.

81. Getzels, J. W., & Jackson, P. W. The highly intelligent and the highly creative adolescent: A summary of some research findings. In C. W. Taylor (ed.), *The third University of Utah research conference on the identification of creative scientific talent.* Salt Lake City: University of Utah Press, 1959.

82. Ginsberg, H., & Koslowski, B. Cognitive development. *Annual Review of Psychology,* 1976, **27,** 29–61.

83. Gordon, I. J., & Jester, R. E. *Middle school performance as a function of early intervention.* Final report to the Child Welfare Research & Demonstration Grants Program Administration for Children, Youth, and Families, May 1980.

84. Gough, H. G. *California psychological inventory manual.* Palo Alto, Calif.: Consulting Psychologists Press, 1957.

85. Gray, S. W., Klaus, R. A., & Ramsey, B. K. Participants in Early Training Project, 1962–1977. In M. Begab, H. C. Haywood, & H. Gerber (eds.), *Prevention of mental retardation in psychosociologically disadvantaged children.* Baltimore: University Press, in press.

86. Gray, S. W., Ramsey, B. K. The Early Training Project: A lifespan view. *Human Development,* in press.

87. Guilford, J. P. A factor analytic study across a domain of reasoning, creativity, and evaluation. I: Hypothesis and description of tests. *Reports from the psychology laboratory.* Los Angeles: University of California, 1954.

88. Guilford, J. P. Theories of intelligence. In B. B. Wolman (ed.), *Handbook of general psychology.* Englewood Cliffs, N.J.: Prentice-Hall, 1973. Pp. 630–643.

89. Guilford, J. P. *The nature of human intelligence.* New York: McGraw-Hill, 1967.

90. Guilford, J. P., Fruchter, B., & Zimmerman, W. S. Factor analysis of the Army Air Forces, Shepphard Field battery of experimental aptitude tests. *Psychometrika,* 1952, **16,** 45–68.

91. Harris, L. J. Sex differences in spatial ability: Possible environmental, genetic, and neurological factors. In M. Kinsbourne (ed.), *Asymmetrical function of the brain.* New York: Cambridge University Press, 1978.

92. Heber, F. R. *Rehabilitation of families at risk for mental retardation: A progress report.* University of Wisconsin, 1971 (mimeographed).

93. Heber, F. R. Sociocultural mental retardation: A longitudinal study. In D. G. Forgays (ed.), *Primary prevention of psychopathology, Vol. II: Environmental influences.* Hanover, N.H.: University Press of New England, 1978. Pp. 39–62.

94. Helson, R. Sex differences in creative style. *Journal of Personality,* 1969, **36,** 33–48.

95. Herrnstein, R. J. I.Q. *Atlantic,* February, 1971, 43–64.

96. Hilden, A. H. A longitudinal study of intellectual development. *Journal of Psychology,* 1949, **28,** 187–214.

97. Hilgard, E., Atkinson, R. C., & Atkinson, R. L. *Introduction to psychology.* New York: Harcourt Brace Jovanovich, 1971 (5th ed.).

98. Hilgard, E. R., Atkinson, R. L., & Atkinson, R. C. *Introduction to psychology.* New York: Harcourt Brace Jovanovich, 1979 (7th ed.).

99. Hogan, R. The gifted adolescent. In J. Adelson (ed.), *Handbook of adolescent psychology.* New York: Wiley, 1980. Pp. 536–559.

100. Hogan, R., & Weiss, D. Personality correlates of superior academic achievement. *Journal of Counseling Psychology,* 1974, **21,** 144–149.

101. Honzik, M. P. Developmental studies of parent-child resemblance in intelligence. *Child Development,* 1957, **28,** 215–228.

102. Honzik, M. P. The development of intelligence. In B. B. Wolman (ed.), *Handbook of general psychology.* Englewood Cliffs, N.J.: Prentice-Hall, 1973. Pp. 644–655.

103. Honzik, M. P., Macfarlane, J. W., & Allen, L. The stability of mental test performance between two and eighteen years. *Journal of Experimental Education,* 1948, **17,** 309–324.

104. Horn, J. L. Human abilities: A review of research and theory in the early 1970s. *Annual Review of Psychology,* 1976, **27,** 437–485.

105. Horn, J. L., & Cattell, R. B. Age differences in primary ability factors. *Journal of Gerontology,* 1966, **21,** 210–220.

106. Horn, J. L., & Donaldson, G. Cognitive development II: Adult development of human abilities. In O. G. Brim & J. Kagan (eds.), *Constancy and change in human development: A volume of review essays.* Cambridge, Mass.: Harvard University Press, 1980. Pp. 445–529.

107. Horowitz, F. D., & Paden, L. Y. The effectiveness of environmental intervention programs. In B. M. Caldwell & H. N. Ricciuti (eds.), *Review of child development research* (Vol. 3). Chicago: University of Chicago Press, 1973. Pp. 331–402.

108. Hulicka, I. M., & Grossman, J. L. Age group comparisons for the use of mediators in paired-associate learning. *Journal of Gerontology,* 1967, **22,** 46–51.

109. Hunt, J. *Intelligence and experience.* New York: Ronald Press, 1961.

110. Hunt, J. McV. Psychological development: Early experience. *Annual Review of Psychology,* 1979, **30,** 103–143.

111. Hunt, J. McV., Mohandessi, K., Ghodssi, M., & Akiyama, M. The psychological development of orphanage-reared infants: Interventions with outcomes (Tehran). *Genetic Psychological Monographs,* 1976, **94,** 117–226.

112. Hyde, J. S. How large are cognitive gender differences? A meta-analysis using $\Omega$ and *d. American Psychologist,* 1981, **36,** 892–901.

113. Inhelder, B., & Piaget, J. *The growth of logical thinking from childhood to adolescence.* New York: Basic Books, 1958.

114. Jensen, A. R. How much can we boost IQ and scholastic achievement? *Harvard Educational Review,* 1969, **39,** 1–123.

115. Kagan, J. Personality development. In I. Janis (ed.), *Personality dynamics.* New York: Harcourt Brace Jovanovich, 1969.

116. Kagan, J. A conception of adolescence. *Daedalus,* Fall 1971, 997–1012.

117. Kagan, J., Sontag, L. W., Baker, C. T., & Nelson, V. L. Personality and I.Q. change. *Journal of Abnormal and Social Psychology,* 1958, **56,** 261–266.

118. Keating, D. P. Precocious cognitive development at the level of formal operations. *Child Development,* 1975, **46,** 276–280.

119. Keating, D. P. (ed.). *Intellectual talent: Research and development.* Baltimore: Johns Hopkins University Press, 1976.

120. Keating, D. P. Thinking processes in adolescence. In J. Adelson (ed.), *Handbook of adolescent psychology.* New York: Wiley, 1980. Pp. 211–246.

121. Kohlberg, L., & Gilligan, C. The adolescent as a philosopher: The discovery of the self in a postconventional world. *Daedalus,* Fall 1971, 1051–1086.

122. Kohlberg, L., & Kramer, R. Continuities and discontinuities in childhood and adult moral development. *Human Development,* 1969, **12,** 93–120.

123. Kris, E. *Psychoanalytic explorations in art.* New York: International Universities Press, 1952.

124. Kurtzman, K. A. A study of school attitudes, peer acceptance, and personality of creative adolescents. *Exceptional Children,* 1967, **33,** 157–162.

125. Lachman, J. L., Lachman, R., & Thronesbery, C. Metamemory through the adult life span. *Developmental Psychology,* 1979, **15,** 543–551.

126. Layzer, D. Heritability analyses of IQ scores: Science or numerology? *Science,* 1974, **183,** 1259–1266.

127. Lazar, I., & Darlington, R. Lasting effects of early eduction: A report from the consortium for longitudinal studies. *Monographs of the Society for Research in Child Development,* in press.

128. Lazar, I., et al. The persistence of preschool effects. A long-term follow-up of fourteen infant and preschool experiments. (Final Report Grant No. 18-76-07843). U.S. Department of Health, Education and Welfare, Administration on Children, Youth, and Families, September, 1977.

129. Leahy, A. M. Nature-nurture and intelligence. *Genetic Psychology Monographs,* 1935, **17,** 235–308.

130. Lehman, H. C. *Age and achievement.* Princeton, N.J.: Princeton University Press, 1953.

131. Leith, G. The relationships between intelligence, personality, and creativity under two conditions of stress. *British Journal of Educational Psychology,* 1972, **42,** 240–247.

132. Lewin, R. Starved brains. *Psychology Today,* 1975, **9,** 29–33.

133. Liben, L. S. Performance of Piagetian spatial tasks as a function of sex, field dependence and training. *Merrill Palmer-Quarterly,* 1978, **24,** 97–110.

134. Livesley, W. J., & Bromley, D. B. *Person perception in childhood and adolescence.* New York: Wiley, 1973.

135. Ljung, B. O. *The adolescent spurt in mental growth.* Stockholm Studies in Educational Psychology. Uppsala (Sweden): Alinquist and Wiksell, 1965.

136. Loehlin, J. C., Lindzey, G., & Spuhler, J. N. *Race differences in intelligence.* San Francisco: Freeman, 1975.

137. Loehlin, J. C., Sharan, S., & Jacoby, R. In pursuit of the "spatial gene": A family study. *Behavior Genetics,* 1978, **8,** 27–41.

138. Lytton, H. *Creativity and education.* New York: Schocken Books, 1972.

139. Maccoby, E. E. Sex differences in intellectual functioning. In E. E. Maccoby (ed.). *The development of sex differences.* Stanford, Calif.: Stanford University Press, 1966a.

140. Maccoby, E. E., & Jacklin, C. N. *The psychology of sex differences.* Stanford, Calif.: Stanford University Press, 1974.

141. MacKinnon, D. W. Creativity in architects. In D. W. MacKinnon (ed.), *The creative person.* Berkeley: Institute of Personality Assessment Research, University of California, 1961.

142. MacKinnon, D. W. Identifying and developing creativity. *Journal of Secondary Education,* 1963, **38,** 166–174.

143. McCall, R. B., Appelbaum, M. I., & Hogarty, P. S. Developmental changes in mental performance. *Monographs of the Society for Research in Child Development,* 1973, **38,** No. 3, 1–84.

144. McCandless, B. *Adolescents: Behavior and development.* New York: Holt, Rinehart and Winston, 1971.

145. McGee, M. G. Interfamilial correlations and heritability estimates for human spatial abilities in a Minnesota sample. *Behavior Genetics,* 1978, **8,** 77–80.

146. McGee, M. G. *Human spatial abilities.* New York: Praeger, 1979.

147. McGee, M. G. Human spatial abilities: Psychometric studies and environmental, genetic, hormonal, and neurological influences. *Psychological Bulletin,* 1979, **86,** 889–918.

148. Meyer, W. J., & Bendig, A. W. A longitudinal study of the Primary Mental Abilities Test. *Journal of Educational Psychology,* 1961, **52,** 50–60.

149. Money, J., Alexander, D., & Walker, H. T., Jr. *A standardized test of direction sense.* Baltimore: Johns Hopkins University Press, 1965.

150. Morrow, R. S., & Morrow, S. The measurement of intelligence. In B. B. Wolman (ed.), *Handbook of general psychology.* Englewood Cliffs, N.J.: Prentice-Hall, 1973. Pp. 656–672.

151. Munsinger, H. The adopted child's IQ: A critical review. *Psychological Bulletin,* 1975, **82,** 623–659.

152. Mussen, P. H., Conger, J. J., & Kagan, J. *Child development and personality.* New York: Harper & Row, 1979 (5th ed.).

153. Mussen, P. H., Conger, J. J., Kagan, J., & Geiwitz, J. *Psychological development: A life-span approach.* New York: Harper & Row, 1979.

154. Mussen, P. H., & Rosenzweig, M. R., et al. *Psychology: An introduction.* Lexington, Mass.: Heath, 1973.

155. Naditch, S. F. *Sex differences in field dependence: The role of social influence.* Paper presented at Symposium on Determinants of Gender Differences in Cognitive Functioning, American Psychological Association meeting, Washington, D.C., 1976.

156. Neimark, E. D. Intellectual development during adolescence. In F. D. Horowitz (ed.), *Review of child development research* (Vol. 4). Chicago: University of Chicago Press, 1975a.

157. Neimark, E. D. Longitudinal development of formal operations thought. *Genetic Psychology Monographs,* 1975b, **91,** 171–225.

158. Osterrieth, P. A. Adolescence: Some psychological aspects. In G. Caplan & S. Lebovici (eds.), *Adolescence: Psychosocial perspectives.* New York: Basic Books, 1969.

159. Palmer, F. H. The effects of early childhood educational intervention on school performance. Paper prepared for the President's Commission on Mental Health, 1977.

160. Palmer, F. H., Semlear, T., & Fischer, M. One-to-one. In M. J. Begab, H. C. Haywood, & H. L. Garber (eds.), *Prevention of retarded development in psychosocially disadvantaged children.* Baltimore, Md.: University Park Press, 1979.

161. Parloff, M. B., & Datta, L. E. Personality characteristics of the potentially creative scientist. *Science and Psychoanalysis,* 1965, **8,** 91–106.

162. Parloff, M. B., Datta, L., Kleman, M., & Handlon, J. H. Personality characteristics which differentiate creative male adolescents and adults. *Journal of Personality,* 1968, **36,** 528–552.

163. Peel, E. A. *The pupil's thinking.* London: Oldbourne Press, 1960.

164. Petersen, A. C. Biopsychosocial processes in the development of sex-related differences. In J. Parsons (ed.), *The psychobiology of sex differences and sex roles.* New York: Hemisphere Publishing Corporation, 1980.

165. Petersen, A. C. & Gitelson, I. B. *Toward understanding sex-related differences in cognitive performance.* New York: Academic Press, in press.

166. Petersen, A. C., Tobin-Richards, M. H., & Crockett, L. Sex differences. In H. E. Mitzel (ed.), *Encyclopedia of educational research.* New York: Free Press, in press.

167. Petersen, A. C., & Wittig, M. A. Sex-related differences in cognitive functioning: An overview. In M. A. Wittig & A. C. Petersen (eds.), *Sex-related differences in cognitive functioning: Developmental issues.* New York: Academic Press, 1979.

168. Piaget, J. *The construction of reality in the child.* New York: Basic Books, 1954.

169. Piaget, J. Intellectual evolution from adolescence to adulthood. *Human Development,* 1972, **15,** 1–12.

170. Raspberry, W. Studying genes and I.Q. *Voice for Children.* Washington, D.C.: Day Care and Developmental Council of American and Washington Post, 1971.

171. Ray, W. J., Georgiou, S., & Rawizza, R. Spatial abilities, sex differences, and lateral eye movements. *Developmental Psychology,* 1979, **15,** 455–459.

172. Reinert, G. Comparative factor analytic studies of intelligence throughout the human life span. In L. R. Goulet & P. B. Baltes (eds.), *Life-span methodology: Research and theory.* New York: Academic Press, 1970.

173. Report of the Task Panel on Mental Health and American Families: Sub-Task Panel on Infants, Children, and Adolescents. In *Task Panel reports submitted to the President's Commission on Mental Health* (Vol. III). Washington, D.C.: U.S. Government Printing Office (No. 040-000-00392-4), 1978. Pp. 612–660.

174. Roberts, J. *Intellectual development of children by demographic and socioeconomic factors.* Washington, D.C.: Department of Health, Education and Welfare, Publication No. (HSM) 72-1012 (Data from National Health Survey, Series 11, No. 110), 1971.

175. Ross, R. J. Some empirical parameters of formal thinking. *Journal of Youth and Adolescence,* 1973, **2,** 167–177.

176. Saltz, R. Effects of part-time "mothering" on IQ and SQ of young institutionalized children. *Child Development,* 1973, **44,** 166–170.

177. Scarr, S., & Weinberg, R. A. IQ test performance of black children adopted by white families. *American Psychologist,* October 1976, 726–739.

178. Schaie, K. W., & Labouvie-Vief, G. Generational versus autogenetic components of change in adult cognitive behavior: A fourteen-year cross-sequential study. *Developmental Psychology,* 1974, **10,** 305–320.

179. Schaie, K. W., & Parnham, J. A. Cohort-sequential analysis of adult intellectual development. *Developmental Psychology,* 1977, **13,** 649–653.

180. Schweinhart, L., & Weikart, D. Perry preschool effects in adolescence. Paper presented at the Biennial Meetings of the Society for Research in Child Development, San Francisco, March, 1979.

181. Schweinhart, L., & Weikart, D. Young children grow up: The effects of the Perry preschool program on youths through age 15. *Monographs of the High Scope Educational Research Foundation,* 1980, **7,** No. 4.

182. Shantz, C. U. The development of social cognition. In E. M. Hetherington (ed.), *Review of child development research* (Vol. 5). Chicago: University of Chicago Press, 1975.

183. Shields, S. A. Functionalism, Darwinism, and the psychology of women: A study in social myth. *American Psychologist,* 1975, **30,** 739–754.

184. Shneour, E. A. *The malnourished mind.* Garden City, N.Y.: Doubleday (Anchor Books), 1975.

185. Shoemaker, J. (ed.). *Women and mathematics: Research perspectives for change* (N.I.E. Papers in Education and Work: No. 8). Washington, D.C.: Education and Work Group, The National Institutes of Education, U.S. Department of Health, Education and Welfare, 1977.

186. Shuey, A. M. *The testing of Negro intelligence.* New York: Social Science Press, 1966.

187. Signorella, M. L., & Jamison, W. Sex differences in the correlations among field dependence, spatial ability, sex role orientation, and performance on Piaget's water-level task. *Developmental Psychology,* 1978, **14,** 689–690.

188. Silberman, C. E. *Crisis in the classroom: The remaking of American education.* New York: Random House, 1970.

189. Silverman, J., Bucksbaum, M., & Stierlin, H. Sex differences in perceptual differentiation and stimulus intensity control. *Journal of Personality and Social Psychology,* 1973, **25,** 309–318.

190. Simmons, R., Rosenberg, F., & Rosenberg, M. Disturbance in the self-image at adolescence. *American Sociological Review,* 1973, **38,** 553–568.

191. Sontag, L. W., Baker, C. T., & Nelson, V. L. Mental growth and personality: A longitudinal study. *Monographs of the Society for Research in Child Development,* 1958, **23,** No. 68, 1–143.

192. Spence, J. T., & Helmreich, R. L. *Masculinity and femininity: Their psychological dimensions, correlates, and antecedents.* Austin, Texas: University of Texas Press, 1978.

193. Stanley, J. S., Keating, D. P., & Fox, L. H. (eds.). *Mathematical talent: Discovery, description, and development.* Baltimore: Johns Hopkins University Press, 1974.

194. Teitelbaum, M. S. *Sex differences: Biological and social perspectives.* New York: Doubleday (Anchor Press), 1976.

195. Terman, L. M., & Merrill, M. A. *Stanford-Binet intelligence scale. Manual for 3rd revision.* Boston: Houghton Mifflin, 1960.

196. Terman, L. M., & Merrill, M. A. *Stanford-Binet intelligence scale. Manual for the third revision from L-M* (1972 Norms edition). Boston: Houghton Mifflin, 1973.

197. Terman, L. M., & Tyler, L. E. Psychological sex differences. In L. Carmichael (ed.), *Manual of child psychology.* New York: Wiley, 1954 (2nd ed.).

198. Thoday, J. M., & Gibson, J. B. Environmental and genetical contributions to class difference: A model experiment. *Science,* 1970, **167,** 990–992.

199. Thurstone, L. L. Primary mental abilities. *Psychometric Monographs* (No. 1). Chicago: University of Chicago Press, 1938.

200. Thurstone, L. L. *The differential growth to mental abilities.* Chapel Hill, N.C.: Psychiatric Laboratory, University of North Carolina, 1955.

201. Thurstone, L. L., & Thurstone, T. G. Factorial studies of intelligence. *Psychometric Monographs* (No. 2). Chicago: University of Chicago Press, 1941.

202. Torrance, E. P. *Torrance tests of creative thinking.* Princeton, N.J.: Personnel Press, 1966.

203. Torrance, E. P., & Dauw, D. C. Attitude patterns of creatively gifted high school seniors. *Gifted Child Quarterly,* Summer 1966, 53–57. Reprinted in R. E. Muus (ed.), *Adolescent behavior and society: A book of readings.* New York: Random House, 1971. Pp. 133–138.

204. Unger, R. K. *Female and male: Psychological perspectives.* New York: Harper & Row, 1979.

205. Waber, D. P. Sex differences in mental abilities, hemispheric lateralization, and rate of physical growth at adolescence. *Developmental Psychology,* 1977, **87,** 29–38.

206. Walberg, H. J. Physics, femininity, and creativity. *Developmental Psychology,* 1969, **1,** 47–54.

207. Walberg, H. J. Varieties of adolescent creativity and the high school environment. *Exceptional Children,* 1971, **38,** 111–116.

208. Wallach, M. A., & Kogan, N. *Modes of thinking in young children.* New York: Holt, Rinehart and Winston, 1965.

209. Wallach, M. A., & Kogan, N. A new look at the creativity-intelligence distinction. In J. P. Hill & J. Shelton (eds.), *Readings in adolescent development and behavior.* Englewood Cliffs, N.J.: Prentice-Hall, 1971.

210. Wechsler, D. *The measurement of adult intelligence.* Baltimore: Williams & Wilkins, 1944.

211. Wechsler, D. *Wechsler intelligence scale for children.* New York: The Psychological Corporation, 1952.

212. Weikart, D. P., Bond, J. T., & McNeil, J. T. The Ypsilanti Perry preschool project: Preschool years and longitudinal results. *Monographs of the High/Scope Educational Research Foundation,* 1978, No. 3.

213. Weir, M. W. Developmental changes in problem-solving strategies. *Psychological Review,* 1964, **71,** 473–490.

214. Welsh, G. S. *Creativity and intelligence: A personality approach.* Chapel Hill, N.C.: Institute for Research in Social Science, 1975.

215. Welsh, G. S. Personality correlates of intelligence and creativity in gifted adolescents. In J. C. Stanley, W. C. George, & C. H. Solano (eds.), *The gifted and the creative: A fifty-year perspective.* Baltimore: Johns Hopkins University Press, 1977.

216. Wilson, R. S. Twins: Early mental development. *Science,* 1972, **175,** 914–917.

217. Wilson, R. S. Twins: Mental development in the preschool years. *Developmental Psychology,* 1974, **10,** 580–588.

218. Wilson, R. S. Twins: Patterns of cognitive development as measured on the Wechsler Preschool and Primary Scale of Intelligence. *Developmental Psychology,* 1975, **11,** 126–134.

219. Wilson, R. S., & Harpring, E. B. Mental and motor development in infant twins. *Developmental Psychology,* 1972, **7,** 277–287.

220. Witkin, H. A., Dyk, R. B., Faterson, H. F., Goodenough, D. R., & Karp, S. A. *Psychological differentiation: Studies of development.* New York: Wiley, 1962.
221. Yudin, L. W. Formal thought in adolescence as a function of intelligence. *Child Development,* 1966, **37,** 697–708.
222. Zigler, E., & Valentine, J. (eds.). *Project Head Start: A legacy of the war on poverty.* New York: Free Press, 1979.

Adolescence, the family, and social change

CHAPTER 6

# Adolescence, the family, and social change

**P**hysical and cognitive maturation, and adaptation to them, do not occur in a vacuum. Both play a necessary role in the transition from childhood to adult status in all societies, but maturity—psychological and social—requires that the adolescent successfully master a number of other critically important and interrelated developmental tasks (2, 14). There are, of course, wide variations from one society and culture to another in the specific nature of these tasks, and in the ease with which they can be met. Nevertheless, despite these variations, there are also broad and important commonalities.

## DEVELOPMENTAL DEMANDS OF ADOLESCENCE

If an adolescent is to become truly adult, and not just physically mature, he or she must gradually achieve independence from parents, adjust to sexual maturation, establish cooperative and workable relationships with peers without being dominated by them, and decide on and prepare for a meaningful vocation.

In the process of meeting these challenges, the young person must also gradually develop a philosophy of life, a view of the world, and a set of guiding moral beliefs and standards that, however simple and basic, are "nonnegotiable." A basic philosophy is essential in lending order and consistency to the many decisions the individual will have to make and the actions he or she will have to take in a diverse, changing, often seemingly chaotic world. And the person must develop a sense of identity. "Before the adolescent can successfully abandon the security of childhood dependence on others, he must have some idea of who he is, where he is going, and what the possibilities are of getting there" (40, 556).

The adolescent's capacity and readiness to meet these demands is a function of many factors, past and present, including, of course, rapid physical and physiological development and markedly expanded cognitive abilities. Without these capabilities it would be impossible, even under the most favorable conditions, for the adolescent to master these increasingly complex demands. However, other factors also play an important role: the kind of overall society the adolescent has grown up in, and the complexity of the adaptational challenges it presents; the characteristics—ethnic, socioeconomic, and other—of the individual's subculture and the society's attitudes and behaviors toward it; and the family structure and parental influences to which he or she has been exposed over the course of development. As will become apparent, though all these additional factors may affect significantly the adolescent's present and future adaptations, none plays a more critical role than the family.

Obviously, the establishment of autonomy is itself one of the major developmental tasks of adolescence. But the role of the family does not cease there. The ways in which the adolescent approaches the other developmental tasks of this age period, the degree of difficulty these tasks present, and his or her relative success in mastering them, will all be importantly affected by prior and continuing parent-child relationships. Therefore, it becomes essential to consider the effects on development, not only of individual variations in parent-child relationships, but also of the broader changes that are currently taking place in the nature and function of the contemporary family and in its relationships to other social institutions and to the society at large.

In our culture, adolescence has traditionally been viewed as a more difficult period in the lives of children and their parents than either the middle-childhood years or the years of emerging adulthood. Although a number of recent investigations suggest that the *extent* of adolescent and parental turmoil during this period has frequently been exaggerated (see Chapter 1), there is general agreement that adolescence, and particularly early adolescence, has traditionally been a challenging and sometimes trying time for both the young and their parents (40, 44, 62).

Furthermore, the difficulties of this period appear to have increased over the past two decades, partly as a consequence of continuing changes in the family itself and in its relations to society, and partly because of the accelerated rate of these changes (14). In this chapter we will examine briefly the nature of some of these changes and consider their effects on contemporary adolescents and their parents.

## THE CHANGING AMERICAN FAMILY

The nature of the American family, and its role in society and in the lives of its members, are significantly different from what they were less than half a century ago (7, 14, 18, 30, 52). Furthermore, the rate of change in recent years has been increasing rather than decreasing. Although the picture is complicated by socioeconomic, ethnic, religious, and other factors, certain general trends are nevertheless apparent.

Increased *urbanization* and *geographic mobility* have altered the face of the country and the nature of our social institutions to a rather astonishing degree. In 1900, nearly two out of every three persons in America lived in a rural area. Today that figure has declined to only about one person in four. Although the rate of immigration to urban areas has slowed in recent years, approximately three-fourths of the entire population is still living in urban areas on only 1.5 percent of the land (58, 59, 60).

Even for those already living in urban areas, mobility has not ceased. Incredible

as it may seem, approximately half of all families in the United States move every 5 years, and the average American may expect to move 13 or 14 times in the course of a lifetime (57, 58). Even though almost half of all moves are within the same county, they still may tend to diminish personal, extended family, and neighborhood ties, though obviously not as much as more distant moves. Furthermore, the fact that moves are between or within large metropolitan areas means that there is less opportunity for experiencing the informal, more direct communication between the family and such social institutions as the schools, churches, neighborhood groups, and local government, including law enforcement officials, which traditionally characterized small cities and towns (7, 11, 18).

These changes have tended to weaken the stability and interdependence of communities, as well as to leave the modern family more isolated from personal, familial, and community support systems, and more dependent on its own resources in an increasingly complex world. We have become to a considerable extent, in Vance Packard's phrase, "a nation of strangers" (46).

### Functions of the family

At the same time, the nature of the family itself, and its functions, have been changing rapidly, resulting in additional demands for adaptation on the part of family members. In the nineteenth century, marriages tended to be later and family size larger (between 1800 and 1930, for example, "the birth rate declined from an average of 8 children per mother to slightly less than three" (30, 60), and is now only 2 (61). Life expectancy, on the other hand, was far shorter than it is today. Consequently, marriage was frequently broken by the death of a spouse before the end of the child-rearing period, and few couples experienced the luxury (or the problems) of the "empty nest stage" so common today, when most couples who remain married can look forward to as many years together without children as with them. Despite nostalgic notions to the contrary, the likelihood of a grandfather or grandmother being around to take a young adolescent fishing or to help with the first party dress was even more remote.

On the other hand, because of higher mortality and fertility rates, "functions within the family were less specifically tied to age, and members of different age groups were consequently not so segregated by the tasks they were required to fulfill. . . . Children were accustomed to growing up with large numbers of siblings and were exposed to a greater variety of models from which to choose than they would have been in a small nuclear family" (30, 62). Older children, particularly girls, often took care of younger siblings.

The family's functions differed also. In a world in which early parental death, illness, and economic insecurity were far more prevalent, family members, including children, of both the nuclear family and the parents' families of origin, as well as relatives, had to depend more on each other for survival, and it was expected that they would. The effects of this greater interdependence, not surprisingly, were both positive and negative.

Having the support of other family members tended to promote family solidarity and feelings of belonging. In addition, life transitions—the time one is expected to be a dependent child, to go to school, to go to work, to leave home, to marry—were generally more flexible and less regularized than they tend to be today. On the other hand, the freedom to take each of these steps was often limited. If a child's help with work was needed, he or she left school; if a younger daughter was needed to care for an aging parent, she might have to defer or abandon marriage plans. The time simply was not ripe for the contemporary idea that decisions about work and marriage and how to live one's life are *individual*—not family—matters. "Individualistic patterns of family behavior first appeared in the 19th century among the urban class, and with them came patterns of segregation in family roles" (30, 67). Middle-class families were the first to initiate a regular, carefully timed progression for their children's entering school, graduating, preparing for a vocation, leaving home, marrying, and forming a new family. In part, this was a consequence of the greater affluence and increased parental longevity that permitted it; in part, it was a function of the "discovery" of childhood and, later, of adolescence as distinctive stages of development with their own special needs.

As America entered the twentieth century, however, these middle-class patterns began to spread across the social spectrum. In part this was due to the migration of rural and small-town residents into increasingly homogenized metropolitan areas, and to the gradual assimilation of second-generation immigrants. But other social changes also played a major role. In the words of historian Tamara Harevan, "As state institutions gradually took over the functions of welfare, education, and social control that had previously lodged in the family, there was greater conformity in timing [of life transitions]" (30, 67). The gradual introduction of compulsory school attendance, child labor legislation, age-segregated schools, social and recreational activities aimed at particular age groups, and mandatory retirement all combined to impose more rigid patterns of timing, both in the larger society and in family behavior.

### The rise of the nuclear family

All of these forces—increasingly depersonalized relations between the family and other social institutions, greater age segregation, less economic interdependence of family members, smaller families, greater rigidity in the timing of transitions from one life stage to another, and increased differentiation of the roles and functions of individual family members—combined to foster the emergence of the so-called nuclear family, which has played such a central role in society through much of the present century.

As Edward Shorter has observed in *The Making of the Modern Family,* the nuclear family is as much a state of mind as it is a formal structure (52): "What really distinguishes the nuclear family—father, mother, and children—from other patterns of family life in Western society is a special sense of solidarity that separates the domestic unit from the surrounding community. Its members feel they have much more in common with one another than they do with anyone else on the outside— that they enjoy a privileged emotional climate they must protect from outside intrusion, through privacy and isolation" (52, *205*).

In contrast to other family forms, the nuclear family tends to be child-centered, and to place emphasis on the family as a center of nurture and affection—"a warm shelter of domesticity from the cold, inhospitable night," rather than as a means of economic survival (52, *205*). As the necessity of women's and children's labor diminished, greater role differentiation of family members increased. "Wives were expected instead to be the custodians of the family and to protect the home as a refuge from the world of work, and children, although expected to help with household tasks, were freed from serious work responsibility until their late teens" (30, *67*).

It seems likely that the stereotypical nuclear family reached its peak in popular acclaim and social influence in the years following the Second World War and continuing through the 1950s. Returning veterans of World War II and their spouses longed for a period of normality. They felt an urgent need to resume their interrupted lives—to set about choosing a career, achieving financial security, getting married, buying a home, and raising a family. And in a period of rising prosperity, such symbols of the American dream appeared achievable, at least for the dominant majority. This was also, however, the period of the cold war and heightened fears of nuclear destruction. Confronted by an inhospitable world, America began turning in more upon itself and developing a suspicion of "foreign subversives" and of nonconformity among its citizens. It was, as 1970s nostalgia had it, the period of *American Graffiti*—of drive-ins, "cruising," and the birth of rock-and-roll; but it was also the period of McCarthyism, "witch hunts," and that strangest of nonwars—the Korean "episode" (18).

Not surprisingly, the family followed suit. In the pursuit of emotional security and "the good life"—symbolized by what one social critic of the time called "the split-level trap" (29)—parents were willing to accept what in retrospect may appear as an excessive conformity in their social, political, sexual, and vocational roles. This was also the period, some may recall, of the "organization man" (63), and the "man in the gray flannel suit" (64). Children, too, went along. They were the Silent Generation of young people about whom philosopher-theologian Paul Tillich complained at the time that they showed "an intensive desire for security both internal and external, the will to be accepted at any price and an unwillingness to show individual traits, acceptance of a limited happiness without serious risk" (65, *84*). A study of college students in the late 1950s found them to be models of the status quo (26). They had few real commitments and valued a happy family life above everything else, with the security of employment (preferably in a large corporation) running a close second. In the areas of politics and government, the dominant traits were apathy and conservatism (26).

If there was intergenerational friction, as to some extent there always is, it was of a familiar and comfortable sort—a conviction on the part of youth that they could do a better job of running society than their more "old-fashioned" parents, not the kind of frontal attack on the basic values of the society and its social institutions that we were to see in the sixties. In its way, it was an era of a certain kind of innocence, characterized by a fundamental faith in existing social institutions and in prescribed social, sexual, and vocational roles. Even when the Korean conflict intruded, and even though it was the first unpopular war in this century, those unlucky enough to be called up were simply told (and told themselves), "That's the way the ball bounces"; the rest of the nation continued its pursuit of "the good life" and material success undisturbed.

In its more positive aspects, the period from World War II through the 1950s can be viewed as one of relative tranquility, of an acceptance of the way things were, in which those who were psychologically capable of it could, and did, make personal commitments—to husbands, wives, and children, and to a way of life. Marriage vows still contained the words "for better or worse, for richer, for poorer, in sickness and in health, till death us do part"—instead of "as long as we continue to feel the way we do about each other," which was heard at a recent wedding of two "liberated" young people.

In other respects, however, it was an era of suppressed individuality, of national paranoia, and of largely unrecognized discrimination—against minorities,

women, the poor, "foreigners," homosexuals, and, indeed, most of those who dared to be different. In a number of respects, the era that came to an end with the onset of the 1960s was a time bomb waiting to explode (18).

And explode it did.

### The turbulent sixties

It is likely that no decade in our nation's history, with the possible but not probable exception of the Civil War, contained as many shocks to a sense of cultural order, continuity, and national purpose as the period between the mid-1960s and the early 1970s. Consider for a moment what parents and their children went through after John Kennedy announced "the passing of the torch to a new generation": the rise and abortive demise of the much-heralded War on Poverty—a victim of an impossible goal of guns and butter too; the escalation of the peaceful civil rights movement under Martin Luther King, Jr., into inner-city riots stemming from an increased sense of frustration at the lack of progress; the assassinations of a president, a presidential candidate, and our most important and charismatic civil rights leader; the forced retirement of two other presidents and a vice-president, two of them under threat of impeachment or criminal prosecution; the increasing evidence that we were destroying at an irreversible rate the water, land, and air of the only planet we have to leave to our children; and, most recently, the series of events summed up in the word Watergate, with its revelations of duplicity, deception, attempted corruption of federal agencies intended to protect our freedom, and outright criminal behavior at the highest levels of the executive branch of government.

More important than any of these, however, in its effect on our nation, including its adolescents and their parents, was the war in Indochina (15, 16, 69). No other issue did so much to divide the nation, to set formerly respected national leaders—and even neighbors—at each other's throats, or to alienate some of our brightest and most promising young people from their elders. Once the war had passed (at least for Americans), much of the feeling of urgency and outrage that it lent not only to antiwar protest, but also to the struggle for civil rights and against poverty, discrimination, and deception and hypocrisy in politics and government, declined significantly. This decline, it should be noted, occurred even though young people's perceptions of what they had come to view as serious flaws in our society did not undergo a corresponding change (see Chapter 14). In short, what was to have been a new era turned into what Andrew Hacker has called the Age of Rubbish, characterized by violence, separatism, and a rudderless morality. To a virtually unprecedented degree, young people were exposed to a deeply divided adult society.

***Decline of adult authority*** One of the inevitable, and most important, consequences of these conditions was a decline in adult authority (14, 16, 17, 18). In earlier periods in this country, and in other, less fragmented and less rapidly changing cultures, adolescents were able to view adult society as relatively homogeneous. Although adolescents may have felt that the adults were misguided, compromising, apathetic, or just plain wrong, there was an identifiable, reasonably self-confident, confrontable "they." And parents, particularly fathers, could be viewed with considerable justification as the adult society's resident ambassadors in the family court. As such, parents derived authority and wisdom—implied or real—from their position as representatives of the adult power structure, and could serve as sympathetic guides to its mysteries and as effective models for success in gaining entry into it.

In the sixties and early seventies, a majority of adolescents in this country were denied such coherent perceptions. From childhood on, they were exposed to deep divisions among prestigious adults on almost every front, from the broadest social issues to the most intimate questions of personal standards and morality. Even to the limited extent that adolescents were able to view adult society as speaking with one voice and planning a unified attack on the country's mounting problems, the evidence of its capacity to achieve success was hardly reassuring. Consequently, the authority of the adult culture became compromised in the eyes of many adolescents, and with it, the authority derived by parents from their position as family representatives of this culture (14, 68).

The phenomenon, of course, was not restricted to America or to its dominant middle class. As other countries have faced similar problems, the authority of adults also declined—in England, Japan, France, a number of Soviet-bloc countries, and on across the globe—although in many instances not at the pace, nor as pervasively, as in this country (14).

All this is not to say that parents were no longer able to serve as effective role models for their children. But it does suggest that their authority could no longer be derived simply from their status as representatives of a unified adult society. It had to come from their own individual strengths and resources or from their position as representatives of only a limited segment of adult society. This, of course, did not make the task of the parent any easier, for he or she too was confronted with "a world I never made," despite some sixties' adolescents' rather naive and occasionally arrogant assertions to the contrary.

At any rate, the older assertion that "father (i.e., adult society) knows best" was likely to be met—not merely for psychodynamic, but for increasingly reality-based reasons as well—with the adolescent response of, "Who's kidding whom?" It was not so much that the young were incapable of respecting authority, as that they had so little reason to do so (6).

**The rise of youth culture**    A related difference between the worlds in which parents of the 1960s and early 1970s and their adolescent sons and daughters developed lay in the ascent of the so-called youth culture and its effects on adolescents. In the days when a majority of young people went to work at 17 or 18, after graduation from high school or before, there were two discernible groups—adolescents in the traditional sense, and adults. During the 1960s, however, increased visibility was assumed by a third group, variously identifiable as postadolescents or, more simply, as youth. With greater numbers of these young people in our society than ever before (58), and with more and more of them denied access to full adult status for longer and longer periods of time (whether as college or graduate students in the case of the advantaged, or as the rootless unemployed or underemployed in the case of the disadvantaged), the size of this group grew, along with its visibility and social impact on both adults and younger adolescents. It is interesting to note that the most rapid increase since 1900 in the number of persons aged 15 to 24 (52 percent) took place in the decade from 1960 to 1970, although the number of adolescents and youth continued to grow, though at a slower rate, throughout the seventies (9, 13, 33). Only now, in the decade of the 1980s, will there be a modest (8 percent) absolute decline in the number of adolescents and youth and a corresponding increase in the number of young adults—with as yet unforeseeable consequences.

As a result of these trends, younger adolescents in particular were exposed to the influences not only of age-mate peers and of an older adult society, but also to those of an older adolescent youth culture as well, a culture that was frequently viewed (and portrayed by the media) as being in conflict with these other groups for the loyalty and emulation of younger adolescents. The situation was further complicated by the fact that this youth culture as *perceived* by adolescents (and to a large extent also by adults) often bore little resemblance to the *actual* behavior, attitudes, and value systems of the average postadolescent or youth (13, 16). What the younger adolescent perceived was influenced in part by personal observation, but he or she was also influenced to a significant degree by popular stereotypes of this group.

Because of such stereotypes, some younger adolescents were led to see the so-called youth culture as more influential, homogeneous, and active in a wider variety of behaviors (e.g., sexual activities, use of drugs) than was actually the case for many of its members. In an effort, often mistaken, to emulate older youth, some younger adolescents plunged into life-styles and behaviors that many older youth were not prepared to engage in.

**Age segregation** Accompanying the growth of a more visible adolescent peer culture was a further reduction of interaction among age groups, both within the family and in the community. In part, this was a consequence of accelerated changes in residential patterns, a trend that had already received considerable impetus from the "flight to the suburbs" following World War II. Increasingly, in the 1960s (and continuing into the 1970s) young single adults began to cluster in recreational apartment complexes for "singles only." Young marrieds, particularly those in the middle class, tended to congregate in newer suburban areas, where the financing of subdivisions permitted the purchase of homes with a minimal down payment and where they could find schools and age-mate peers for their children.

Couples with grown children tended to remain in older neighborhoods, where other couples were also older and where things were generally quieter, or they moved to apartments where children were not allowed, or to "planned environments" for "senior citizens," if they could afford it.

Educational patterns also contributed to increased age segregation both of the young from adults and of young persons of different ages from one another (12). At the turn of the century, only a small minority of the high school age group could be found in school; the great majority was already out of the system and at work. During the sixties, not only were most adolescents in school (between 1950 and 1976, the percentage of young people completing high school rose from 52 percent to 85 percent), the schools they were attending were growing ever larger, as school consolidations increased, and became more age-segregated (see pages 388–392). Even within a particular school (e.g., a junior high school), it was (and is) not uncommon to find a thousand tenth graders interacting "largely with others of the same level, much as any segregated social stratum with well defined boundaries" (12, *82*). In addition, the length of the school year continued to increase, and participation in work settings when not in school continued to decline. As one social critic of the time observed:

> This absorption of adolescent time by the school has contributed greatly to the dominance of the student role among the many roles that a young person might have. His family role has been diminished as the family has declined in size and strength. The delaying of work until after the completion of schooling gives the adolescent no place in the work force. The mass media have entered the lives of the young, but the media remain remote from the specific social setting of the young person and largely provide him with the passive role of mass spectator and some activity as consumer. The school is where we find the adolescent: for at least ten years and usually longer the school is the only regular place provided by society. This has become so much the case one can speak of the family as closing its doors to the young during the day when they are "supposed to be in school" [12, *80–81*].

*Requiem for the sixties*   Clearly, the period from the early 1960s through the beginning of the 1970s was a difficult one, both for parents and their adolescent young. Although even at the height of the 1960s' so-called youth revolution, the generation gap between the average adolescent and his or her parents was much less than the journalistic "pop sociology" of the time would have had us believe, there can be little doubt that these years were difficult, too, for the integrity of the family itself. Like all revolutions, the "revolution" of the sixties produced its share of casualties and walking wounded, of shattered families, of broken-hearted parents, and of rootless, alienated, confused youth, some of whom even today as young adults are still trying to "find themselves," if they have not given up and settled for marginal existences far below their original promise and potential (see Chapter 14). For the more fortunate majority of families who survived intact, in some cases with greater understanding and closeness than ever, many had to struggle hard to keep open the lines of communication between generations, and to undergo "agonizing reappraisals" of their individual values and beliefs, in the face of incredibly rapid social change (18).

## NEW CHALLENGES: THE SEVENTIES AND BEYOND

Although some of the challenges faced by the family in the 1960s abated during the 1970s, others continued, and new, qualitatively different, challenges were born. Political and social divisions between generations eased for a variety of reasons—including the end of the war in Indochina, a realization on the part of young people that social change was both more complex and harder to achieve than it had once appeared, and a new and more sobering economic climate. Equally significant, a majority of adults who had once castigated youth for its suspicion and distrust of established social institutions came to share this skepticism in the wake of the war and Watergate, and of the nation's apparent inability to deal with such problems as inflation, energy shortages, pollution, and increased balance of payment deficits (69, 70).

Other challenges to the family, however, have continued. As America enters the 1980s, the relative isolation of the family from effective communication with and influence over other institutions has, if anything, increased. Age segregation—in education, in housing, and in social activities—shows little change. In addition, there have been several significant, perhaps even revolutionary, social changes in the decade of the 1970s that are creating new challenges to traditional concepts of the nuclear family, and to which, in one way or another, the family must adapt.

### The women's movement

One of these changes has been the rise of the women's movement, perhaps the single most significant event of the decade. A logical extension of earlier struggles for individual and group rights, beginning with the civil rights struggles of minorities in the early 1960s, this development has already produced major changes in contemporary society.

It has fundamentally altered the way that women, and particularly younger women, view themselves, but it has also changed the way that men view women—and themselves. Traditional gender-related stereotypes of the psychological, social, and emotional characteristics of men and women are breaking down, as are notions of what can properly be considered "women's (or men's) work," or the appropriate roles of men and women in the broader society. Increasing numbers of women are insisting (with support from increasing numbers of men) on being viewed by society as equals and—just as important—as individuals, each with her own unique set of talents, interests, psychological and social needs, and personal idiosyncrasies.

Accomplishment of these goals is far from complete, and there remain strong pockets of resistance, from women as much as from men. Nevertheless, it appears that an evolutionary process has been set in motion that is unlikely to be reversed, despite slowdowns and occasional setbacks.

### Women's participation in the labor force

Another major change that has accelerated in the past decade—one that has at the same time been both a stimulus to, and to some extent a product of, the women's movement—has been the increase in the number of women working outside the home (see pages 457–460). In 1950, only a third of all women were engaged in outside employment; by 1970, that figure had increased to 43 percent; and by 1980, to 51 percent (59).

Currently, two-thirds of childless married women with a husband present in the home are in the labor force. Among those with school-age children, 58 percent are employed outside the home, and among those with children under 6, the figure is 42 percent (see page 458). It is estimated that by the end of the present decade, 70 percent of the mothers of school-age children, and 55 percent of the mothers of preschoolers, will be in the labor force (54, 59). By 1990, the stereotype of a wife as someone who stays home and looks after the children will fit only about one quarter of all American wives (54).

The reasons for the increase in the number of women working outside the home are, of course, varied. For some, particularly those who are single parents or whose husbands are unemployed or underemployed, it is often an economic necessity. For others, it may be a way of improving a family's living standards, coping with inflation, or remaining in contact with the world outside the home. For an increasing number of women, particularly those with interesting jobs or professions, it is a way of fulfilling deeply prized vocational interests or career goals. Regardless of the particular reasons, or set of reasons, for women's increased participation in the labor force, the implications for the family as a social institution, and for the lives of its members, are likely to be profound.

### The "me-decade"

Still another social force was at work in the decade just ended. Although subtler, and more difficult to define (perhaps partly because we are still so close to it in time), its impact on the family—even on our conceptions of the family—is nevertheless likely to be marked.

In our characteristic predilection for attempting to find simple terms to describe complex phenomena, we have sometimes labeled this force the "new narcissism"

(36) or the "me-decade" (66). But neither phrase seems adequate. What are we really talking about?

Most centrally, we think that what is involved is a greater preoccupation with the self and a diminished concern with the needs of others, particularly strangers, in the confusing world in which we live today. This preoccupation manifested itself in many ways as we entered the 1980s, some positive, some negative. Many Americans showed a renewed interest in their own physical well-being—in jogging, conditioning programs, weight control, yoga, modern dance, and concern for nutrition and the contents of the food they ate. The pursuit of pleasure was reified, whether in the form of hot tubs (originating, not surprisingly, in California), disco dancing, or "the joy of sex." New religious cults, self-improvement programs, and so-called psychological therapies mushroomed—sometimes indistinguishable from one another in their apparent aims (18). Terms like est, the Moonies, Krishna Consciousness, Esalen, mantra, Mind Control, sex therapy, making it, being Number One, laid back, consciousness raising, finding my own space, knowing where you're coming from, getting my act together, assertiveness training, bioenergetics, primal scream, and rolfing entered the language in seemingly endless profusion—along with bumper stickers exhorting fellow drivers to "Honk if you love Jesus," or proclaiming ecstatically, "I found it!" (18). Slogan embossed T-shirts to express one's individuality became a minor industry, leading Fran Lebowitz, the young author of *Metropolitan Life,* to wonder, "If people don't want to talk to me, why would they want to talk to my T-shirt?" (37).

So-called self-realization—physical, psychological, spiritual, or material—appeared to be the predominant message, along with a desire to be "free." But was this simply an expression of narcissism, as some have maintained, or a reaction, as others believe, to frustration—to a perceived inability to influence events in the surrounding world or to establish intimate and lasting relationships with others? It seems likely that all of these factors were involved, and, further, that this development was not a cultural accident, but evolved as a logical culmination of events we have already described (18).

With the rise of the nuclear family, decreased economic interdependence, and a greater emphasis on defining life stages came a greater concern for people as *individuals,* rather than primarily as necessary members of a collective effort. Initially, however, the individual was expected to earn his or her share of the good life through rather rigidly defined, if unlabeled, conformity to societal expectations. The values of society, and the social institutions that supported them, were not basically in question, and part of the price of success in the late forties and the 1950s was "not rocking the boat."

All of this changed, of course, in the 1960s and early 1970s, as Americans—first the young, and then their elders—began to lose faith in government and other social institutions. The immediate results, stated simply, were twofold: an increase in political and social activism, spearheaded, as might be expected, by the young; and, when the effectiveness of activism began to be questioned, at least by some, a rejection of the social structure as a whole, and a retreat (or escape) into "doing your own thing." This was the era of the hippie movement, which reached its height (and began its fall) in the 1967 Summer of Love in the Haight-Ashbury district of San

Francisco (see pages 603–605). By the middle of the 1970s, skepticism about government and other institutions had spread from the young to their elders, and generational conflicts, at least in the political arena, had declined (18, 70). The end of the Vietnam war had removed a major impetus to youthful revolt, and both young people and their elders began to sense an intractability in seemingly ever more complex social problems, and in the capacity of either individuals or government to produce dramatic or immediate changes.

In addition, we had begun to enter a period of economic slowdown combined with increased inflation—a delayed legacy of the Johnson administration's policy of "guns and butter, too." The days when young people could freely choose—or reject—jobs, as in the sixties, were ending, and personal economic well-being became an increasing concern of both young and old. Most recently, of course, has come a long-suppressed awareness of declining global natural resources, and the likelihood that we are entering an era of lowered expectations, nationally and internationally. There seems little doubt that a feeling of diminished ability to influence events has played a significant part in the movement away from social concerns to a greater concern for the self.

At the same time, however, the greater "freedom to be me," to do one's own thing, that emerged from the 1960s was a genie that, though it might be restrained, was not going to be put back in the bottle. Newly established sexual and social life-styles were not to be abandoned in favor of the 1950s' gray flannel suit and "selling one's soul to the company store"—or to the more rigidly defined roles of family members in the nuclear family of an earlier day.

Unfortunately, however, at least in our view, a nagging question remains—for adults, for adolescents, and for families: To what or to whom *does* one entrust one's soul? Greater self-realization and self-awareness can be positive goals, as Freud recognized early in the present century. But if they become a person's only goals they can lead only to the kind of banality that has characterized so many of the current fads in religion, self-improvement books and seminars, and so-called therapies—or even worse, to self-destructiveness (18).

The problem is, as Freud was also aware, that without love for someone else—or for some transcendent purpose—it is not possible in any but the most superficial sense to love one's self. With considerable foresight, Philip Slater commented in the early 1970s on what he called the delusions of individualism, and the dangers of abandoning collective activities in life for the disappointments of "structured narcissism" (38). In a similar vein, Richard Sennett, in *The Fall of Public Man,* argues for restoring a better balance between private and public life (51). Social stability and personal expression, he maintains, can better come through the assumption of public responsibilities and convictions than merely through taking one's own emotional temperature.

In what can be productive efforts to reexamine old stereotypes about family, sex, and social roles—to realize oneself—it is important also to be aware that self-realization is not synonymous with self-indulgence, that concern for others is a necessary ingredient of concern for self, and that there can be no true freedom without responsibility and commitment. With such awareness, perhaps the "me-decade" of the 1970s can become the "us-decade" of the 1980s.

## *CONSEQUENCES OF SOCIAL CHANGE*

Recent and continuing changes in the nature of the family and its relations to society, and the rate of these changes, undoubtedly have increased the stresses on today's nuclear family. In a number of ways, they have also altered the kinds of adaptations that family members must make if they are to survive and prosper.

### *Isolation of the nuclear family*

For many modern parents, geographic isolation from members of the extended family—brothers and sisters, mothers and fathers, cousins, aunts, and uncles—and lifelong friends, both of their own and their parents' generation, has significantly increased the stresses of child-rearing and other family responsibilities. Furthermore, parents in contemporary, relatively isolated nuclear families often have to learn about, select, and master techniques for raising their children and adolescents virtually unaided (1, 15, 29, 46). In an earlier day, the puzzled parent could more readily turn for help to family members or close friends or others of similar cultural background. In today's nuclear family, living in a mobile community, with transient acquaintances from diverse cultural and geographic backgrounds, parents frequently lack such support. They are likely only to be confused by all the conflicting advice they read in magazines or hear from neighbors (29).

Of course, it is not simply a matter of the parents gaining a greater feeling of security and direction from living in a close-knit, relatively homogeneous community. Their children are also more likely to accept parental rules, standards, and beliefs when they see that these are shared by other significant adults (see Chapter 9). When the parents of adolescent peers are in communication with one another, and when all of them expect adolescents to observe certain rules about, for example, use of a car, dating, drinking, smoking, marijuana use, or standards of social and sexual behavior, the individual adolescent is less likely to question his or her parents' advocacy of these rules, and the task of the parents is thus made easier. In this fashion, parents from different families can effectively reinforce one another.

On the other hand, where, as is often the case today, parents either are unable to communicate closely with other parents, or where these other parents follow widely varying practices, the opportunities for such familiar adolescent "blackmail" techniques as, "But all the other kids are allowed to do it," or, "Susie's parents don't act that way," are increased significantly. Furthermore, the adolescents themselves may be genuinely confused or skeptical about the diversity they observe in the values, beliefs, and practices among peers' parents.

Isolation of the nuclear family is likely to be stressful for all members of the family, but it appears to have its greatest impact on wives and mothers during the child-rearing years. A study (27, 28, 29) comparing the incidence of psychiatric and psychosomatic symptoms (e.g., high blood pressure, peptic ulcer) in two rural areas, a relatively stable suburban county and a highly transient, socially mobile suburban county (both on the east coast of the United States), found that the incidence of such disorders was greatest for both sexes in the highly mobile surburb and least in the rural county, that the frequency of such symptoms increased rapidly in the highly mobile suburb over a period of a decade in which the county grew rapidly and its stability decreased, and that the greatest increase occurred among wives and mothers aged 18 to 44.

Isolation of the nuclear family may intensify other problems as well. The more the intimate emotional relationships of both parents and children are confined to the nuclear family, and the smaller this family unit is, the more intense family relationships are likely to be, and the more difficult and stressful to modify (3, 19, 50). Consequently, during age periods such as adolescence, when significant modifications are necessary—when dependence must yield increasingly to independence, when bonds to parents must be loosed and new ties established with peers, and when intergenerational conflicts and resentments are likely to reach their peak—the isolated nuclear family is likely to be subject to special stress. The necessary adjustments of both parents and adolescents to changing circumstances are sometimes made more difficult than might be the case in an extended family setting in a close-knit community.

### *Rapidity of social change*
The rapidity of the rate of social change in the past several decades has also magnified the difficulties of the adolescent period, both for parents and for their adolescent daughters and sons. It has meant that adolescents and their parents have grown up in markedly different worlds. When the developmental experiences that

shape our personalities and the social changes that must be confronted vary mark-edly from adults to young people, from parents to their children, generational differ-ences in cultural values and outlook—even in knowledge—tend to be magnified (14, 17, 34). Thus, to the extent that today's parents look only to their own experience as adolescents for expectations about their children's behavior or for guidance in un-derstanding their needs, outlooks, and goals, they are bound to encounter frustra-tion, bewilderment, or disappointment.

As we shall see, the psychological, social, sexual, political, and economic cli-mate in which today's adolescents are coming to maturity, and the pressures they face, are different in significant ways from those encountered by their parents, who were adolescents in the late 1950s and early 1960s, when John Kennedy was pro-claiming the "passing of the torch to a new generation" who would establish a bold "New Frontier." Unless parents can understand the nature of these differences, efforts to help their children to fulfill their potential and to avoid self-destructive actions are likely to fall wide of the mark. The task is not an easy one, and establish-ing effective communication between parents and children is not made any easier by continued age segregation and the persistence of a separate youth culture with values and social pressures of its own.

Rapid social change has also not been easy for parents themselves to adapt to, and for many has required an "agonizing reappraisal" of their own values, beliefs, and expectations. Confronted with a world in which natural resources appear to be diminishing; pollution of air, land, and water are increasing; and seemingly intractable inflation is threatening present and future hopes for a better life, many can be forgiven if President Kennedy's New Frontier now seems more like the Last Frontier. Bigger is no longer better, and "small is beautiful." Rather than finding ways to put a man on the moon, they face the problem of how to distribute equitably the slices of a shrinking economic pie.

**Changes within the family** Even more importantly, however, changes that have been taking place within the family in recent years have presented the parents of adolescents with new challenges to their capacity to adapt, and also have raised questions about the kinds of models parents can and should provide their children.

As we have seen, in the homes in which today's parents of adolescents grew up, the stereotypical ideal (however much it might be breached on occasion) was that of a father who was the family's economic provider and protector, and a mother who provided nurturance for the children and took care of the home. Unmarried couples did not proclaim to the world that they were living together; marriage was supposed to be forever; and divorce, when it occurred, was generally considered a sign of personal failure. Boys were supposed to be little men—outgoing and assertive—and girls were supposed to be dainty, feminine, and conforming. The work ethic was strong, and instant gratification was certainly not a socially approved goal.

Today the situation is a far different one. As a consequence of the women's movement and increasing female employment, previously accepted sex-role standards and relations between spouses are being reevaluated, and many marriages have felt the strain. A husband may not be able to accept easily his wife's newfound need for a more equal sharing of family decision making, household tasks, and child-rearing responsibilities, or her desire to have a career of her own outside the home. In some instances, a wife may be troubled by a newly "liberated" husband's desire to leave a "safe" job in order to "fulfill himself" by starting a risky small business of his own, becoming a poet or painter, or living on a sailboat. In other instances, parents may simply be confused; in a recent symposium on alternative family life styles at Tulane University, one young woman tentatively asked the panel: "I just want to get married and have children. Is that still O.K.?" (56).

Although a majority of married women, including those with young children, will be employed outside the home, the desirability of this arrangement is a source of continuing debate. In a New York *Times*–CBS News poll, Americans were asked, "What kind of marriage do you think makes the more satisfying kind of life?" The choice was: one in which the husband provides for the family and the wife takes care of the home and children, or one in which both have jobs, both do housework and both take care of the children. In the youngest age group, 18- to 29-year-olds, only 27 percent preferred the traditional marriage. However, in the age groups most likely to be the parents of adolescents, 30- to 44-year-olds, 44 percent chose the traditional marriage; and among those 45 and older, this figure increased to 55 percent (39). Obviously, views of marriage and the family are in transition, and it is among those who are currently the parents of adolescents that opinions regarding the merits of "traditional" versus "liberal" or "modern" arrangements are most likely to be divided, and hence most likely to be sources of stress. Opinions about whether women working outside the home make better or worse mothers are also divided. While 43 percent of working women believe that employed women make better mothers, and only 24 percent think they make worse mothers (the remainder opting for no difference), approximately 45 percent of both men and nonworking women think they make worse mothers (only 21 percent of men and 14 percent of nonworking women think they make better mothers) (39). Again, younger age groups are more likely than older age groups to believe that working women make better mothers.

Among high school seniors in the United States in 1980, only 13 percent of boys and 4 percent of girls considered an employed husband and a wife who remains at home desirable if they have no children (5). However, where they had one or more preschool children, 44 percent of boys and 39 percent of girls considered this traditional arrangement desirable. Only 11 percent of boys and 15 percent of girls considered having the mate work part-time desirable, and less than 6 percent considered both spouses working either full time or both part-time desirable (see Chapter 11).

**Home and family life**    What are the actual effects on marriage and the family of increased participation of women in the labor force? The available evidence suggests that working women are more likely to postpone marriage than nonworking women, but they are only slightly less likely not to marry at all (54). They are, however, likely to have fewer children. Although divorce rates in general are increasing dramatically, there is no clear-cut body of evidence indicating that employment of the wife leads to divorce or separation. It appears that in some cases (e.g., working wives with relatively high incomes, particularly in those cases where the husband earns less) divorce rates are somewhat higher; in other cases (e.g., where husband and wife are in agreement about the wife's employment, where the wife finds satisfaction in her work, and where the family's overall standard of living benefits) divorce rates are lower (54).

What about marital satisfaction? Again, it is difficult to make generalizations. Overall, there is a tendency for working wives to be somewhat more satisfied than nonworking wives (54). Conversely, husbands of working wives report somewhat less satisfaction than those of nonworking wives, despite the fact that working places heavier burdens on the typical wife's schedule, in terms of household tasks and child-rearing responsibilities, than on the husband's. (Although husbands of working wives participate slightly more in household and child-rearing tasks than those of nonworking wives, wives still typically retain the major responsibility for these tasks.) However, this working versus nonworking dichotomy is too simplistic. Marital satisfaction for both partners appears to be enhanced when the wife works by choice rather than necessity, has an interesting job, works part-time, or works when children are no longer of preschool age (54). On the other hand, satisfaction appears to suffer when the wife works by necessity rather than preference, when the work is uninteresting or poorly paid, and when the burden of home responsibilities is great and little relief or external help is possible.

Inasmuch as most wives and mothers will be working throughout the remainder of this century, it is important that efforts be made to ease the difficulties involved—through greater division of labor in the home, more adequate maternity benefits and leave allowances, increased availability of part-time jobs and more flexible work schedules, greater availability of high-quality day care, and more equal pay and benefits for women and men (18, 54).

Ultimately, however, the success of a majority of couples in creating an enduring, mutually rewarding, and growth-enhancing family life will probably depend as much or more on the individuals themselves as on these needed social accommodations. Even under the best of external circumstances, successful marriage and child rearing are not easy. They require personal maturity, a capacity for true intimacy, an ability to change, patience, tolerance, and above all commitment—a willingness when necessary to subordinate one's own immediate desires to the welfare of another human being. As Michael Novak has observed, "Marriage presupposes a willingness to grow up." In the aftermath of the "me-decade," with its emphasis on self-realization and a lessened concern for others, achieving this degree of developmental maturity can be more difficult. As Judy Collins sings in the title song of one of her record albums,

> These are hard times for lovers,
> Everyone wants to be free.
> Ain't these hard times for lovers,
> Everyone's singin' I got to be me.[1]

> *Hugh Prestwood*

Achieving a sense of identity is an important developmental stage, as Erik Erikson observes. But maturity also requires the development of a capacity for intimacy and what Erikson calls "generativity"—satisfaction gained from contributing to the development of others, and particularly the young (20).

### *Separation, divorce, and the single-parent family*

As the functions of the family have changed and its stresses have mounted, parental separation, desertion, and divorce have also increased (9, 10, 25, 59). After a flurry of both marriages and divorces following World War II, the divorce rate declined throughout the 1950s. Since 1960, however, it has more than doubled (see Figure 6.1). Demographers are predicting that 40 to 50 percent of children born during the 1970s will experience divorce or death of a parent (9, 25). Although the overall rate of remarriage is high (despite a modest decline in the past decade), the rate for single parents with children (95 percent of whom are women) is much lower (10, 25). In addition, the percentage of births to unmarried women has increased over four times since 1950, and has more than doubled since 1965 (61). As a result of all these factors, only 63 percent of all children under 18 in 1978 were living with both natural parents in their first marriage, and nearly one in five was living in a single-parent family, almost double the number 25 years ago. Most of the remainder were living with one natural parent and one stepparent, or with relatives (25).

[1]© 1978 Hugh Prestwood, Careers Music, Inc.

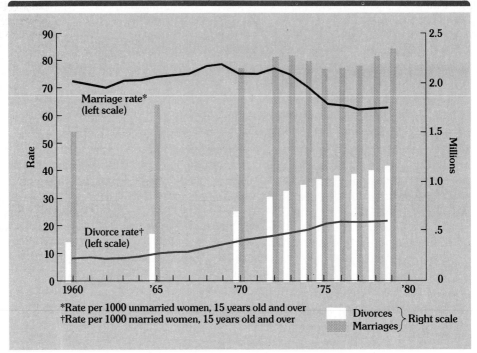

**Figure 6.1** Rates of marriages and divorces from 1960 to 1979. (From U.S. Department of Commerce, Bureau of the Census, *Statistical abstract of the United States.* Washington, D.C.: U.S. Government Printing Office, 1980 [101st ed.].)

Coping with the fact of divorce or separation places special psychological stresses on both parents and children. In addition, single parenthood is likely to be difficult, both for parent and child, even in the absence of financial strain and even when external assistance, such as quality day care, is available. The difficulties are compounded, however, when—as is typically the case—the single parent is poor. Among families headed by women with children (whether as a result of desertion, separation, divorce, never having been married), over 42 percent are currently living below the poverty level, in contrast to only about 12 percent for all women with children (61).

In brief, the heightened responsibilities of single parenthood are most likely to fall on those least equipped to handle them. When one realizes that in such families the mother is more likely to be working (two-thirds of those with school-age children and nearly 50 percent for those with children under 3), that the number of children in the family is likely to be larger, and that the family is likely to be faced with all the other burdens of poverty, including inadequate housing and deteriorating neighborhoods, the strain on the family unit becomes particularly evident. Interestingly, although single parenthood is significantly more frequent among blacks than whites, these differences fade rapidly when residential setting and income are controlled for;

". . . regardless of color, families in similar circumstances are affected in the same way for better or for worse" (7, *18*).

### *The future of the family*

In view of all the buffeting they have been subjected to on many fronts, it is not surprising that many of today's nuclear families are showing signs of stress. The social trends that we have reviewed in this chapter have clearly increased the difficulties of the adolescent period, both for parents and for young people. But have they also produced, as was so often asserted in the past two decades, a largely unbridgeable generation gap between today's average parents and their adolescent young? Has the contemporary nuclear family become obsolete? Have parents become irrelevant as models for their children's psychological and social development? And have contemporary adolescents forsaken their parents' values, and become the captives of a pervasive peer culture? Each of these questions will be considered, in this and succeeding chapters, in the hope of restoring some perspective to a topic that has become unduly burdened by rhetorical extremes.

## DIMENSIONS OF THE GENERATION GAP

Is there a generation gap, and if so, how extensive is it? On the basis of the available evidence, the best answer appears to be that there *is* a gap between the average parent and his or her adolescent young, but that it is neither as wide nor as novel as we have been led by popular stereotypes to believe. Even at the height of the so-called counterculture of the late 1960s, when generational conflicts were most apparent, approximately two out of three young people and seven out of ten parents expressed the view that a gap existed, but that it had been exaggerated (31, 41, 44, 45, 68). Only about one young person in four, and a like percentage of parents, felt that there was a large gap; only a small minority of both groups (about one in twenty) felt that there was no gap (31, 68).

When asked to describe their relationships with their parents, a majority of both younger and older adolescents of the late 1960s and early 1970s (57 percent) stated that they got along fine with their parents and enjoyed their company. Approximately one in three said that they were fond of their parents but had trouble communicating with them. Interestingly, among the third who felt they had trouble communicating, only 18 percent expressed the view that it was their parents' fault; 6 percent said it was their own fault; and an overwhelming majority (74 percent) said it was "both our faults." Furthermore, when asked if they felt that their upbringing had been "too strict, too permissive, or about right," over 80 percent felt that it had been about right (31).

When these same subjects were asked if they thought that their values and ideals differed markedly from those of their parents, most said they did not (31, 68). About three-fourths of adolescents stated that they accepted and agreed with their parents' values and ideals; most stated that such differences as existed were either moderate (49 percent) or slight (35 percent) (31, 68). It is interesting, in view of popular stereotypes, that parents (perhaps remembering their own youth) were even less likely than their children to perceive significant differences in ideals and values. Thus, less than one parent in ten (9 percent) felt that differences between their children and themselves were great; a majority (55 percent) felt that they were slight; and the remainder (36 percent) felt that they were moderate (68).

### Recent studies

More recent surveys—although not as extensive as some earlier studies—have yielded comparable results (4, 5, 23, 42, 43). In one representative survey of American adolescents aged 13 to 18, young people were asked, "How well do you get along with your parents?" Most said they got along very well (52 percent) or fairly well (45 percent); only 3 percent said they did not get along well at all. There were no sex differences, but younger adolescents, those with an above-average academic standing, and whose parents were college educated were slightly more likely to say that they got along very well or fairly well (23). When asked if they felt that their parents had been too strict with them, or not strict enough, 24 percent felt their parents had been too strict, while 20 percent felt they had not been strict enough; 54 percent said that their parents' discipline had been about right (see Table 6.1). (Although the latter figure represents a decline from that obtained in 1970 [80 percent], it may be due, at least partly, to the form in which the question was asked; in the earlier study, "about right" was given as an alternative, while in the most recent survey this answer had to be volunteered.) Perhaps not surprisingly, 63 percent of adolescents who felt their parents' discipline had been about right said they got along very well with their parents, compared to 49 percent of those who felt

**TABLE 6.1 PARENTS TOO STRICT OR NOT STRICT ENOUGH**

| | TOO STRICT | NOT STRICT ENOUGH | ABOUT RIGHT (VOLUNTEERED) | NO OPINION |
|---|---|---|---|---|
| National | 24% | 20% | 54% | 2% |
| Boys | 21 | 20 | 56 | 3 |
| Girls | 26 | 21 | 51 | 2 |
| Both Sexes | | | | |
| 13–15 years old | 25 | 19 | 54 | 2 |
| 16–18 years old | 22 | 21 | 54 | 3 |
| Academic Standing | | | | |
| Above average | 23 | 17 | 57 | 3 |
| Average or below | 24 | 24 | 50 | 2 |
| Occupation | | | | |
| Blue collar | 23 | 16 | 59 | 2 |
| White collar | 25 | 24 | 49 | 2 |
| Father's Education | | | | |
| College or more | 22 | 17 | 58 | 3 |
| High school or less | 24 | 21 | 52 | 3 |

Source: G. Gallup. Gallup poll. *Denver Post*, January 22, 1978. By permission.

discipline had not been strict enough, and only 29 percent of those who felt it had been too strict (23).

In another national survey, 88 percent of all adolescents (87 percent of boys and 89 percent of girls) stated that they had a lot of respect for their parents as people; and 80 percent stated that they had a lot of respect for their parents' ideas and opinions. The percentage acknowledging "a lot of respect" was somewhat higher for girls than for boys, and higher for younger girls than for older. Only a relatively small minority (21 percent) stated that they did not feel any strong affection for their parents, and only 6 percent felt that "my parents don't really like me" (55, *380*). Obviously, a troubling minority of young people feel unable to understand their parents, to communicate with them, to respect their values (even where they may disagree), or even, in some cases, to like, or to feel liked by, their parents. But such situations are not characteristic of the average adolescent.

In addition, there was in the late sixties and early seventies—and still remains—a rather surprising degree of agreement among both parents and their young regarding the validity of such traditional values as self-reliance, hard work, and the importance of the family (see Chapter 12). On the other hand, there are, as we shall see, important differences between generations in their attitudes toward sex, education, marriage, the role of women, female employment, drugs, and social justice, as well as in such obvious areas as personal tastes in dress, music, art, and social customs. But although such differences exist—with adolescents generally emerging as somewhat more liberal and more inclined to let people do their own thing—the extent of the differences often appears to have been exaggerated, at least in the case of the *average* adolescent and his or her parents (5, 17, 43, 69, 70).

In a national survey of high school seniors in 1980 (5), students were asked how closely their ideas agreed with those of their parents on a wide range of topics. Most (over 70 percent) indicated that their ideas were "very similar" or "mostly similar" to those of their parents on what the young person should do with his or her life, what values in life are important, the value of education, religion, and what are appropriate roles for men. There was somewhat less, though still substantial, agreement about politics, racial issues, conservation and pollution issues, and use of drugs other than marijuana. The least agreement was found on such topics as use of leisure time, how the young person spent his or her money, drinking and marijuana use, and what things are OK to do on a date; even here, however, approximately 50 percent of the students indicated that their views were mostly or very similar (5). In still other areas, such as the need for reform of social institutions (ranging from government and the military to business, education, industry, and the communications media), there is considerable intergenerational agreement—primarily because adults themselves have become increasingly critical of these institutions in today's post-Watergate world (18, 42, 69, 70). In summary, it appears that, at least for the average adolescent and his or her parents, there are generation gaps, but they are not nearly as wide nor as pervasive as we have been led to think.

How can we reconcile the discrepancies, not only between the apparent facts and popular stereotypes about the size and nature of the so-called generation gap, but also between these facts and what we might expect theoretically, on the basis of the nature and rate of social change? There appear to be a number of relevant factors which are often overlooked.

For one thing, there is a tendency to overgeneralize from the behavior of relatively small minorities of young people to adolescents and youth as a whole. This was particularly the case during the late sixties and early seventies when the mass media tended to picture young people (whether favorably or unfavorably) in terms of the attitudes and behavior of visible, controversial, sometimes highly articulate minorities (white middle-class activities, minority-group militants, hippies and teeny-boppers—even, at times, delinquents (21, 22, 24, 47, 67). In contrast, adults of that period were most commonly characterized as members of a "silent majority" of middle Americans (14, 38).

Although there is less emphasis currently on such simplistic and misleading stereotypes as societal conflicts have lessened and as the obsession of the media and the public with "the youth problem" has receded, we still frequently hear blanket statements—whether positive or negative—about "today's youth." Recently, the notion that youth are returning to the values of the 1950s has enjoyed considerable popularity in some circles, despite substantial evidence to the contrary (see Chapter 13). Less sanguine souls still deplore what they view as virtually universal involvement among young people with drug use and sexual promiscuity, in contrast to their presumably drug-free, sexually monogamous parents.

Such simplistic adolescent-adult comparisons ignore the fact that ours has long been a heterogeneous society, rather than simply a melting pot, both for adults and adolescents (32, 48, 68, 69). As we shall see in succeeding chapters, variations among important subgroups of adolescents are at least as great as and frequently greater than those between the average adult and the average adolescent. This holds in the areas of political and social values, sexual attitudes and behavior, patterns of drug use, and educational and vocational goals.

Popular stereotypes also confuse and confound comparisons between adults and adolescents generally with those between individual parents and their adolescent sons and daughters, despite the fact that these may differ significantly. Two-thirds of adolescents 15 years of age and older in one national study replied yes to the question "Do your parents approve of your values and ideals?" but a majority of them responded negatively to the question "Do they approve of the way *your generation* expresses their ideals?" (31). Adolescents also tend to be more critical, generally in rather stereotyped terms, of the older generation as a whole than of their own parents (5, 14, 31, 43, 55). In some instances, adolescents may come into conflict with the values of some adult authority figures in their society *precisely because* those values conflict with values the young person has acquired from, and shares with, his or her parents.

Finally, there is a widespread tendency to overlook the possibility that parents and adolescents may be able to differ in some of their values and modes of behavior, and still remain capable of mutual understanding and respect. For example, in a national survey of adolescent sexuality in contemporary America (55), 80 percent of all adolescents stated that they had "a lot of respect" for their parents' ideas and opinions, while disagreeing with them on specific issues. Thus, only 38 percent of this same sample of young people (28 percent of boys and 49 percent of girls) agreed that "when it comes to sex, my attitudes and my parents' attitudes are pretty much the same" (55, *388*).

### *Generational differences and the life cycle*

> To everything there is a season
> And a time to every purpose under heaven. . . .
>
> *Ecclesiastes 3:1*

The extent of generational differences may be expected to vary from one era to another, largely as a result of the speed and pervasiveness of social change. Nevertheless, there will always be some sort of generation gap—if for no other reason than that successive generations occupy differing positions in the life cycle (14, 16). The adolescent who is just becoming aware of the insistent stirring of sexual impulses will inevitably differ from the middle-aged adult who perceives their urgency waning. Adolescents need ways to consume their energy; adults look for ways to conserve it. Young people are concerned about where they are going; adults are concerned about where they have been. Adults, having personally experienced the many partial victories and defeats and the inevitable compromises of living, tend to be tempered in their enthusiasms and cautious in their moral judgments. Young people, in contrast, tend to be impatient, impulsive, and given at times to imperious moral judgments that allow little room for shades of gray. They are more likely to move rapidly from profound joy to despair. Adults must worry more about their children; adolescents must worry more about themselves. The psychological defense mechanisms of adolescents are in flux, and only partially effective; those of adults tend, like arteries, to harden with age (14).

Despite such differences, adolescents and their elders can—and indeed need to—communicate with and learn from each other. How successfully they will be able to do so may depend on many factors, including the social, economic, and political climate and the kind and rate of social change. But most of all, their success is likely to depend on the nature of parent-child relationships and the continued viability of the family as society's most basic—and enduring—social unit.

### REFERENCES

1. Adams, B. N. *The American family: A sociological interpretation.* Chicago: Markham, 1971.
2. Aldous, J. *The family developmental approach to family analysis.* Minneapolis: Family Study Center, University of Minnesota, 1967.
3. Anthony, E. J., & Benedek, T. (eds.). *Parenthood: Its psychology and psychopathology.* Boston: Little, Brown, 1970.
4. Bachman, J. G., Johnston, L. D., & O'Malley, P. M. *Monitoring the future: Questionnaire responses from the nation's high school seniors 1978.* Ann Arbor, Mich.: Institute for Social Research, University of Michigan, 1979.
5. Bachman, J. G., Johnston, L. D., & O'Malley, P. M. *Monitoring the future: Questionnaire responses from the nation's high school seniors 1980.* Ann Arbor, Mich.: Institute of Social Research, University of Michigan, 1981.
6. Baumrind, D. Early socialization and adolescent competence. In S. E. Dragastin & G. H. Elder, Jr.(eds.), *Adolescence in the life cycle: Psychological change and social context.* New York: Wiley, 1975. Pp. 117–143.
7. Bronfenbrenner, U. *Two worlds of childhood: U.S. and U.S.S.R.* New York: Russell Sage Foundation, 1970.
8. Bronfenbrenner, U. The challenge of social change to public policy and developmental research. Paper presented at the bi-annual meeting of the Society for Research in Child Development, Denver, April 2, 1975.
9. Calhoun, J. A., Grotberg, E. H., & Rackey, W. F. *The status of children, youth, and families 1979.* DHHS Publication No. (OHDS) 80-30274. Washington, D.C.: U.S. Government Printing Office, 1980.
10. Carter, H., & Glick, P. C. *Marriage and divorce: A social and economic study.* Cambridge, Mass.: Harvard University Press, 1976 (Rev. ed.).
11. *Children and parents: Together in the world.* Report of Forum 15, 1970 White House Conference on Children. Washington, D.C.: U.S. Government Printing Office, 1971.
12. Clark, B. Current educational institutions. In J. S. Coleman et al. (eds.), *Youth: Transition to adulthood.* Report of the Panel on Youth of the President's Science Advisory Committee. Chicago: University of Chicago Press, 1974. Pp. 76–90.
13. Coleman, J. S., et al. *Youth: Transition to adulthood.* Report of the Panel on Youth of the President's Science Advisory Committee. Chicago: University of Chicago Press, 1974.
14. Conger, J. J. A world they never knew: The family and social change. *Daedalus,* Fall 1971, 1105–1138.
15. Conger, J. J. A world they never made: Parents and children in the 1970s. Invited address, American Academy of Pediatrics meeting, Denver, April 16, 1975.
16. Conger, J. J. Current issues in adolescent development. JSAS *Catalog of Selected Documents in Psychology,* 1976, **6,** 96. (Ms. No. 1, 334.)
17. Conger, J. J. Parent-child relationships, social change, and adolescent vulnerability. *Journal of Pediatric Psychology,* 1977, **2,** No. 3, 93–97(b).
18. Conger, J. J. Freedom and commitment: Families, youth, and social change. *American Psychologist,* 1981, **36,** 1475–1484.
19. Cooper, D. *Death of the family.* New York: Pantheon, 1970.

20. Erikson, E. H. *Identity: Youth and crisis.* New York: Norton, 1950.
21. Feigelson, N. *The underground revolution.* New York: Funk & Wagnalls, 1970.
22. Fort, J. *The pleasure seekers: The drug crisis, youth and society.* New York: Grove Press, 1969.
23. Gallup, G. Gallup poll. *Denver Post,* January 22, 1978.
24. Gerzon, M. *The whole world is watching.* New York: Paperback Library, 1970.
25. Glick, P. C., & Norton, A. J. Marrying, divorcing, and living together in the U.S. today. *Population Bulletin,* 1979, **32,** 1–40.
26. Goldsen, R., Rosenberg, M., Williams, R., & Suchman, I. *What college students think.* New York: Van Nostrand, 1960.
27. Gordon, R. E., & Gordon, K. K. Psychiatric problems of a rapidly growing suburb. *Archives of Neurological Psychiatry,* 1958, **79.**
28. Gordon, R. E., & Gordon, K. K. Social psychiatry in a mobile suburb. *International Journal of Social Psychiatry,* 1960, **6,** 1–2.
29. Gordon, R. E., Gordon, K. K., & Gunther, M. *The split-level trap.* New York: Dell, 1962.
30. Harevan, T. K. Family time and historical time. In A. S. Ross, J. Kagan, & T. K. Harevan (eds.), *The family.* New York: Norton, 1978.
31. Harris, L. Change, yes—upheaval, no. *Life,* January 8, 1971, 22–27.
32. Harris, T. G. The young are captives of each other: A conversation with David Riesman. *Psychology Today,* October 1969, 28ff.
33. Havighurst, R. J. Youth in social institutions. In R. J. Havighurst & P. H. Dreyer (eds.), *Youth: The seventy-fourth yearbook of the National Society for the Study of Education.* Chicago: University of Chicago Press, 1975. Pp. 115–144.
34. Keniston, K. *The uncommitted: Alienated youth in American society.* New York: Dell, 1960.
35. Kett, J. F. *Rites of passage: Adolescence in America 1790 to the present.* New York: Basic Books, 1977.
36. Lasch, C. *The culture of narcissism: American life in an age of diminishing expectations.* New York: Norton, 1979.
37. Lebowitz, F. *Metropolitan life.* New York: Dutton, 1978.
38. Man and woman of the year: The middle Americans. *Time,* January 5, 1970.
39. Meislin, R. J. Poll finds more liberal beliefs on marriage and sex roles, especially among the young. New York *Times,* November 27, 1977, 75.
40. Mussen, P. H., Conger, J. J., & Kagan, J. *Child development and personality.* New York: Harper & Row, 1974 (4th ed.).
41. *New Times,* October 3, 1975, 12.
42. Norback, C. *The complete book of American surveys.* New York: New American Library (Signet), 1980.
43. Norman, J., & Harris, M. *The private life of the American teenager.* New York: Rawson, Wade, 1981.
44. Offer, D. *The psychological world of the teen-ager: A study of adolescent boys.* New York: Basic Books, 1969.
45. Offer, D., Marcus, D., & Offer, J. L. A longitudinal study of normal adolescent boys. *American Journal of Psychiatry,* 1970, **126,** 917–924.
46. Packard, V. *A nation of strangers.* New York: Pocket Books, 1974.
47. Roszak, T. *The making of a counter culture.* Garden City, N.Y.: Doubleday (Anchor Books), 1969.
48. Scammon, R., & Wattenberg, B. J. *The real majority.* New York: Coward, McCann & Geoghegan, 1970.
49. Scanlon, J. *Self-reported health behavior and attitudes of youths 12–17 years.* Washington, D.C.: Department of Health, Education and Welfare, Publication No. (HRA) 75-1629 (Data from National Health Survey, Series 11, No. 147), 1975.
50. Sebald, H. *Adolescence: A sociological analysis.* Englewood Cliffs, N.J.: Prentice-Hall, 1968.
51. Sennett, R. *The fall of public man.* New York: Knopf, 1977.

52. Shorter, E. *The making of the modern family.* New York: Basic Books, 1975.
53. Slater, P. *Pursuit of loneliness: American culture at the breaking point.* Boston: Beacon Press, 1971.
54. Smith, R. E. (ed.). *The subtle revolution: Women at work.* Washington, D.C.: The Urban Institute, 1979.
55. Sorensen, R. C. *Adolescent sexuality in contemporary America: Personal values and sexual behavior ages 13–19.* New York: Abrams, 1973.
56. The family in transition: Challenge from within. *New York Times,* November 27, 1977, 1, 74.
57. U.S. Department of Commerce, Bureau of the Census, Current Population Reports, Series P-20, No. 353. *Geographic mobility: March 1975 to March 1979.* Washington, D.C.: U.S. Government Printing Office, 1980.
58. U.S. Department of Commerce, Bureau of the Census, Current Population Reports, Series P-23, No. 49. *Population of the United States, trends and prospects: 1950–1990.* Washington, D.C.: U.S. Government Printing Office, 1974.
59. U.S. Department of Commerce, Bureau of the Census, Current Population Reports, Series P-20, No. 363. *Population profile of the United States, 1980.* Washington, D.C.: U.S. Government Printing Office, 1981.
60. U.S. Department of Commerce, Bureau of the Census. Projections of the population of the United States: 1977 to 2050. In *Current Population Reports,* Series P-25, No. 704. Washington, D.C.: U.S. Government Printing Office, 1977.
61. U.S. Department of Commerce, Bureau of the Census. *Statistical abstract of the United States.* Washington, D.C.: U.S. Government Printing Office, 1980 (101st ed.).
62. Weiner, I. B. *Psychological disturbance in adolescence.* New York: Wiley, 1970.
63. Whyte, W. *The organization man.* New York: Simon & Schuster, 1956.
64. Wilson, S. *The man in the gray flannel suit.* New York: Simon & Schuster, 1955.
65. Wolensky, R. P. College students in the fifties: The silent generation revisited. In S. C. Feinstein & P. L. Givacchini (eds.), *Adolescent psychiatry: Developmental and clinical studies* (Vol. 5). New York: Aronson, 1977.
66. Wolfe, T. The "me" decade and the third great awakening. *New York,* August 23, 1976, 26–40.
67. Yablonsky, L. *The hippie trip.* New York: Pegasus, 1968.
68. Yankelovich, D. *Generations apart.* New York: Columbia Broadcasting System, 1969.
69. Yankelovich, D. *The new morality: A profile of American youth in the 70's.* New York: McGraw-Hill, 1974.
70. Yankelovich, D. *New rules: Searching for self-fulfillment in a world turned upside down.* New York: Random House, 1981.

Parent-child relationships and adolescent socialization

CHAPTER 7

# Parent-child relationships and adolescent socialization

**A**s America entered the 1980s, "the future of the family" began to replace the obsessive concern of the 1960s and 1970s with "today's youth" as a primary focus of popular sociology and political rhetoric. A White House Conference on Families was held, and it became the subject of considerable unanticipated conflict and divisiveness. Magazine articles and television reports on "Saving the Family" and "The Family in Transition: A Challenge from Within" appeared in seemingly endless profusion (9, 57, 196). Social scientists argued not only about whether the family as a basic social unit could survive the pressures to which it was being subjected, but even about whether it should. What are the issues, and what can we reasonably conclude about them?

### The family in transition

Whether or not one agrees that the family as a social unit is endangered, it is clearly changing. As a result of the kinds of social changes discussed in the previous chapter, only about one family in four now conforms to the traditional stereotype of the one-marriage, two-parent family, with the father as the breadwinner and the mother as the homemaker and primary caretaker of several dependent children. Two-income families, single-parent families, one-child families, "blended families" (resulting from remarriages), and childless couples are all becoming more common. Though relatively rare, combined households (most frequently of two women with children), group marriages, and communal rearing of children can also be found.

For some, such trends are testimony to the decline of the family (84, 128, 225). Those sharing this view are likely to also point to increases in delinquency, adolescent pregnancies, runaways, reported cases of child abuse and family violence, and the number of children placed outside the home in foster care or institutions. In contrast, others see the increasing variety of family forms more optimistically as a necessary, even positive, adaptation to social change. Those with this perspective see the family not as declining, but as evolving creative new forms within the basic structure (128, 196, 225). In the words of Alice Rossi, a sociologist at the University of Massachusetts, "What was defined a decade ago as 'deviant' is today labeled 'variant,' in order to suggest that there is a healthy experimental quality to current social explorations 'beyond monogamy' or 'beyond the nuclear family'" (225, *1*).

In our view, passionate advocates of both positions are apt to ignore some important considerations. Those anticipating the imminent demise of the family tend to overlook the fact that in one form or another, the family—parents and children—has proved remarkably durable over many centuries. Furthermore, despite current pressures on the family, the fact remains that 98 percent of children are still raised in families and that 79 percent of these are living with two parents. In addition, nearly two-thirds of all couples remain married until death, and of those who divorce, 75 percent of the women and 83 percent of the men remarry within 3 years (91, 255). In brief, despite all the difficulties, most people—adults and children alike—still prefer to live in families.

Those who tend to see most variations in family structure simply as creative responses to changing times may also be guilty of oversimplification. It is certainly the case, in our view, that some variations from traditional family structure, such as the small, two-career family, can be both creative and rewarding for both parents and children. It also seems clear that children can be successfully reared in single-parent and "blended" families, particularly where parents are psychologically mature and where sufficient social support systems are available. Indeed, not infrequently children in such families may prosper more than those in traditional families torn by dissent and individual frustration.

As will become evident in more detail in subsequent discussions, however, variations from traditional family structure can also be disruptive and painful or damaging. Many single adolescent mothers, for example, are emotionally immature, economically disadvantaged, and ill prepared to cope with the responsibilities of parenthood, and their children are at high risk for child abuse and problems of physical and mental health (see pages 297–298). Even mature, socially and economically successful single parents—especially those who are divorced, abandoned, or widowed—are likely to suffer from loneliness and a sense of isolation. In the words of the task panel on families of the President's Commission on Mental Health,

> These feelings of isolation are often associated with lack of social contact with other adults and feelings of being locked into a child's world and with having no one to consult or help with personal, economic, and rearing problems. The difficulty is compounded by task overload since many single parents have to fulfill the work role as well as the roles of homemaker and parent. Clinical depression is a major mental problem for single parents [128, *575–576*].

Although much can be done to minimize the adverse effects of divorce on both children and parents (121, 122, 258, 261), people, particularly children and adolescents, emerge from the experience untroubled. As one expert on family therapy states, "The child learns the rules of human relationships in the immediate household. When the child sees that world splitting up, he feels his world is shattered. His learned rules no longer make sense or are true" (84, *59*). In the words of child psychologist Lee Salk, "Children sense a deep loss and feel they are suddenly vulnerable to forces beyond their control" (84, *58*). Depending on age and sex, children may regress, withdraw, become aggressive, feel guilty and responsible for the divorce, blame one or both parents, or suffer conflict of loyalties. Most common, however, at all ages is an obsessive desire to reunite the parents. Even though her parents had been separated for 4 years, a 13-year-old girl in Virginia was adamant that they not get a divorce. "Once all the papers are signed, I wouldn't have a chance," she said. "Now I have hope" (84, *61*). The child's or adolescent's problems are often aggravated by the fact that the divorced parents are preoccupied with their own problems, especially during the first year, and have difficulty in responding to the child's needs. Although the situation is likely to improve within a year or two (121, 122) (and although divorce no longer carries the social stigma it once did), a significant number of children continue to have difficulty adjusting (258, 259, 260, 261). In one study (258), it was found that 5 years after separation, a third of the children appeared resilient, relaxed, and self-reliant; another third appeared to be coping fairly well; while the rest had significant psychological problems and still looked back with intense longing to life before the divorce. It is difficult to disagree with Albert Solnit, director of the Yale Child Study Center, when he says: "Divorce is one of the most serious and complex mental health problems facing children in the '80s" (84, *58*).

Remarriages can also be difficult for all concerned, accounting perhaps for the fact that 40 percent of such marriages currently fail, compared to about one in three first marriages. Children may resent the stepfather or stepmother who has displaced the original parent, or they may resent the intrusion of a new competitor for a parent's love and attention after a prolonged period of having a single parent all to themselves. Stepparents may feel insecure in handling newly acquired stepchildren. Where two sets of children are involved in a "blended" family, there may be rivalries between them. In short, such variations in family structure may frequently be better for children's development than their remaining in a crisis-ridden family with both original parents present. But it appears somewhat ingenuous to view these variations simply as "creative alternatives," as a number of social scientists seem currently bent on doing—perhaps as an overreaction to the kind of stigma and discrimination unfairly associated with such variations in the past.

Despite their differing perspectives, most advocates of both of these views of the family share a common concern for its survival in one form or another, and view it as playing a vital and constructive role in child-rearing. Consequently, both groups are deeply concerned with providing a greater degree of societal and community support for strengthening families than currently exists.

In contrast, there is another group of social critics who assert that the nature and rate of recent social change have made parents largely irrelevant as models or guides for the current and future development of their adolescent sons and daughters (59, 63, 225). Indeed, some of these critics, such as David Cooper, the British psychiatrist and author of *Death of the Family* (59), have gone so far as to proclaim that the family has become not simply irrelevant to the needs of children and adolescents, but a malignant force that acts only to frustrate the fulfillment of these needs. In Cooper's view, today's nuclear family frustrates the development of a "free sense of identity" by forcing the individual to perceive herself or himself in terms of predetermined family roles, even in later interactions with other social institutions, and makes the person feel incomplete, except as he or she is "glued together" with others in a continuing family system. Furthermore, through guilt, it imposes an elaborate system of nonfunctional taboos not merely against overt sexual expression, but also against physical—and even verbal—expressions of feelings (59).

In a similar vein, Simone de Beauvoir, in her autobiography, *All Said and Done* (63), urges the abolition of the family and endorses instead communal rearing of children (234). Somewhat ironically, however, in the same book she repeatedly stresses the importance of her own mother, father, and sister in her development as a woman and as a writer (224).

In a more moderate vein, Margaret Mead argued that today's parents of adolescents are pioneers, immigrants in an unexplored land—the "country of the young." In this new terrain, the young person will have to chart his or her own path, without significant assistance from either parents or peers. Under such circumstances, about all that parents can provide are love and trust, although these are of vital importance (175).

It appears clear that a background of love and trust is, as Erik Erikson (77, 78) also asserts, fundamental. Without these, the child's chances of becoming a reasonably happy, effective, contributing adult, of developing a positive self-image and a sense of identity, are seriously impaired, as clinical experience and any number of more systematic investigations make abundantly clear (9, 21, 78, 266). But there is little or no evidence to support the notion that the young have little else to learn from parents. As will also become evident, the role that parental models play in fostering or hindering their children's and adolescents' psychological development and in preparing them to meet the challenges of emerging adulthood extends far beyond these essential ingredients.

### Parent-child relationships and the developmental tasks of adolescence

What often tends to be lost sight of in our current concern about the nature and rate of social change is that, though the rapidity of change has increased the difficulties of adolescent adaptation for both parent and child, there are still basic developmental tasks that the adolescent must master if he or she is to become a competent, autonomous, responsive, and responsible adult (53). The period between puberty and adulthood may be relatively short (as in the case of the blue-collar youth who may be employed, married, and a parent at 19) or relatively long (as in the case of the upper-middle-class youth who may still be involved in obtaining an education, unmarried, and largely dependent on parents at 25). It may also be relatively simple or complex, depending on cultural and familial circumstances.

Nevertheless, as we have noted, adolescence still involves the accomplishment of a number of critically important developmental tasks: adjustment to the changes of puberty that bring adult size and appearance as well as reproductive capacity; the development of autonomy from parents and other caretakers; the establishment of effective social and working relationships with same- and opposite-sex peers; preparation for a vocation; and, withal, the development of a system of values and a sense of identity—a personal answer to the age-old question, "Who am I?"

The fact that in today's world these tasks may be more complex, and that both parent and child have fewer consistent blueprints to guide them in their accomplishments, does not fundamentally alter the situation. Social roles of men and women

may change, as indeed they are changing today, and the transitions into adult roles may be more difficult and prolonged (195); the responsibilities and privileges associated with independence may change; the difficulties of projecting the vocational needs of the future may increase; and the kind of personal and social identity that will be viable in both today's and tomorrow's world may alter. But regardless of the particular forms assumed, each remains a critical and indispensable task of adolescent development.

The question then becomes one of what factors increase the likelihood that a young person will be able to accomplish these tasks successfully and get through the adolescent period without excessive turmoil, without a highly disruptive relationship with parents, and with a reasonable degree of resilience to internal psychological difficulties and to destructive external pressures, including deviant peer-group influences. It should be obvious that we cannot look only to individual psychodynamic or intrafamilial factors for answers; social factors are also clearly of major importance, particularly in a period of rapid social change such as the present. Even growing up in a relatively isolated and homogeneous small town, where common values are largely shared and taken for granted by the community as a whole, and where generally acceptable and shared models of adult identity are to be found, the adolescent faces complex developmental demands in identity formation (209). The task may be different, and somewhat less difficult, than that of an adolescent growing up in a heterogeneous, frequently conflict-ridden, avant-garde, rapidly changing urban complex or in the socially disorganized and deteriorated ethnic ghettos of our large cities, but the realities of the broader society, extensively communicated by the mass media, communicate the messages of the times everywhere.

Similarly, adolescents growing up in the 1980s face complex demands in achieving personal and social identity formation, but for most it is a less conforming, less conflict-ridden task than was the case in the latter half of the turbulent 1960s (56, 57). Nevertheless, an increasing body of empirical data indicates that the single most important external influence in aiding or hindering the average adolescent (particularly the younger one) in the accomplishment of the developmental tasks of adolescence—at least in today's relatively isolated nuclear family—is his or her parents (19, 41, 53, 56, 166). The real question is not whether parental models are any longer important; rather, it is what kinds of parental models are necessary and appropriate in preparing contemporary adolescents to cope with the largely unpredictable world of tomorrow.

## *MODELS OF PARENT-CHILD INTERACTION*

In the face of increasing change in today's world, parents are likely to feel somewhat unprepared to be the parent of an adolescent. The 1970s saw a rapid proliferation in the number of books, magazine articles, and even television programs devoted to infant care and child-rearing, and many parents came to rely on them. While providing much valuable new information, based on recent research, such parental aids tended to imply that expert advice is essential to the task of being the parents of such complex beings.

Consequently, when confronted with another challenging age—adolescence— many of these same parents have tended to again seek the advice of "experts." Unfortunately, however, they are considerably less likely to find the kind of help they are seeking. This relative dearth of relevant information may increase further the anxieties of parents as their children approach adolescence.

In our view, an overemphasis on expert advice can be counterproductive, serving to reduce the confidence of parents in their own resources. If the task is, in fact, so complex that expert advice is needed, then those lacking such advice will understandably fear failure. But the evidence suggests that while expert advice can be helpful at times, much of what is required to be a competent parent was well understood by our grandparents, and consists primarily of common sense about, and sensitivity to, matters of human interaction. This is not to suggest that many parents do not need help to fulfill their parental roles; in fact, many could profit from such assistance. Our point is simply that approaches that serve to strengthen and support the parents' own resources are more promising than those that suggest that experts are always necessary, and therefore that parents are inadequate.

In the case of adolescents, the question of what kinds of parental models are most helpful involves the effects not simply of current patterns of parent-child interaction, but of a long history of prior interactions, extending back to early childhood. Parents may be loving or rejecting; calm or anxious; involved or uninvolved; rigid or flexible; controlling, guiding but encouraging of autonomy, or very permissive. All these qualities have been found, singly and in combination, to influence the child's subsequent behavior and adjustment (21, 56, 166, 190).

### Parental warmth or hostility

Particular attention has been focused on two major dimensions of parental behavior (166, 231). The first dimension may be termed *love-hostility,* although the exact labels employed have varied from one investigator to another (e.g., "warmth-hostility" [21, 166], "acceptance-rejection" [230, 231], "loving-rejecting" [53, 59]. At its positive end, this dimension refers generally to such characteristics as "accepting, affectionate, approving, understanding, child-centered, frequent use of explanations, positive response to dependency behavior, high use of reasons in discipline, high use of praise in discipline, low use of physical punishment" (21, *174*). At its negative end, it refers to the opposite characteristics.

It is to the positive end of this dimension that Erikson and Mead are referring when they speak of the child's need for love and trust. Indeed, any number of studies make clear that without strong and unambiguous manifestations of parental love, the child (or adolescent) has far more difficulty developing self-esteem, constructive and rewarding relationships with others, and a confident sense of his or her own identity (61, 166, 220, 226, 227). Parental hostility, rejection, or neglect consistently occur more frequently than acceptance, love, and trust in the backgrounds of children with a very wide range of problems. These range from cognitive and academic difficulties (7, 111, 241, 244, 266) and impaired social relationships with peers and adults, to neurotic disorders, psychophysiological and psychosomatic disturbances, and character problems such as delinquency (5, 7, 8, 56, 111, 124, 166, 200, 226, 227, 228, 244, 266). Most studies indicate that parents' hostility or rejection tends to produce counterhostility on the part of their children—regardless of how it may be expressed (or not expressed) (21, 49, 56, 166, 190).

**Abusing parents**    In some cases, parental hostility becomes extreme, or out of control, and serious abuse of the child or adolescent occurs. Unfortunately, child abuse is widespread, and it appears to be increasing, although it is difficult to obtain accurate data on incidence. Many cases are still unreported or unrecognized by authorities, although the situation has clearly improved in recent years, and all states now have laws requiring health professionals to report cases of suspected child abuse (113, 150, 151). Over half a million cases of confirmed or suspected cases of abuse are reported annually, and actual incidence is in all likelihood much higher (113, 150). Although child abuse occurs somewhat more often among parents, particularly mothers, who are poorly educated and economically deprived, it occurs with disturbing frequency among both sexes at all socioeconomic levels (150, 151).

Much more needs to be learned about the factors that predispose a parent to child abuse. Nevertheless, certain salient characteristics stand out. The most consistent trend in the histories of abusive parents is the repetition, from one generation to the next, of a pattern of abuse, neglect, and parental loss or deprivation: "In each generation we find, in one form or another, a distortion of the relationship between parents and children that deprives the children of the consistent nurturing of body and mind that would enable them to develop fully" (151, *13*).

Abusing parents, for the most part, have not been exposed to models of successful parenting—models that they could then apply in rearing their own children. Many abusing parents, including many adolescent mothers, have extremely unrealis-

## CHILD ABUSE

Drs. Henry and Ruth Kempe, of the National Center for Child Abuse in Denver, have had long experience with the detection and treatment of child abuse. They point out that once a case of child abuse has been identified, medical staff and social workers need some means of assessing the likelihood of future abuse by parents. They report that the following checklist of factors in the parents' background and behavior can predict that risk with a high degree of accuracy:

1. As a child was the parent repeatedly beaten or deprived?
2. Does the parent have a record of mental illness or criminal activities?
3. Is the parent suspected of physical abuse in the past?
4. Is the parent suffering lost self-esteem, social isolation, or depression?
5. Has the parent experienced multiple stresses, such as marital discord, divorce, debt, frequent moves, significant losses?
6. Does the parent have violent outbursts of temper?
7. Does the parent have rigid, unrealistic expectations of the child's behavior?
8. Does the parent punish the child harshly?
9. Does the parent see the child as difficult and provocative (whether or not the child is)?
10. Does the parent reject the child or have difficulty forming a bond with the child?

*Source:* Ruth S. and C. Henry Kempe. *Child abuse.* Cambridge, Mass.: Harvard University Press, 1978.

tic ideas about the kinds of behavior that can be expected of a child at a particular stage of development. Consequently when an infant soils its diapers or does not stop crying, or when a child does not perform a task well enough, the parent (like his or her own parents) views the child as willfully misbehaving, and resorts to punishment, without success, leading to a downward spiral of a deteriorating parent-child relationship interspersed with additional punishment.

If a lack of knowledge about child development were the only problem, however, assistance would be easier to provide. Such help can often be useful, but the problem usually goes much deeper. Having been deprived of love and care themselves, abusing parents are hungry for love and acceptance (245, 246). Furthermore, they are often socially isolated, view themselves as bad or unlovable, and lack the ability to make friends (at least partly because of being overdemanding) or to develop broader social support systems. Consequently, they may leap at the opportunity to marry and have a family as a way of finally satisfying their urgent need for love and approval. When it turns out that successful family life, especially in the case of young children, requires as much or more giving of love and care as the parent receives, frustration and a sense of betrayal are likely to be the result. If the problem is then aggravated by other adverse conditions—such as developmental difficulties, or chronic illness of the child, loss of a job, financial crises, lack of basic homemaking skills, marital disputes, or an inability to establish extrafamilial support systems— then the stage is likely to be set for child abuse. As Brandt Steele, one of the first clinical investigators to study the causes and treatment of child abuse systematically, notes:

Physical abuse is usually not a constant or daily occurrence. . . . There are four conditions which seem necessary for abuse to occur:

1. A caretaker who has the predisposition for abuse related to the psychological residues of neglect or abuse in his or her own early life
2. A crisis of some sort placing extra stress on the caretaker
3. Lack of lifelines or sources of help for the caretaker, either because he or she is unable to reach out or the facilities are not available
4. A child who is perceived as being in some way unsatisfactory

These four factors interact in a mutually reinforcing way. Abusive parents live in a state of precarious balance between emotional supply and demand. They are more needy because of their low self-esteem, but less able to reach out for pleasure and support, and so turn with the increased need to those who are least able to provide full satisfaction, their infants. Any crisis, even a small one such as a broken washing machine, becomes unmanageable because of the parent's poor coping techniques and inability or reluctance to seek help [246, *58*].

**Effects of abuse**  Many abused children, aided by the ameloriating effects of beneficial experiences during development, "grow up to be essentially normal citizens and average parents" (151, *19*). Unfortunately, however, many show continuing adverse effects of abuse. Abused children and adolescents characteristically find it difficult to trust adults, and not infrequently other children as well (150, 151, 245). Even in psychotherapy where a good relationship with the therapist seems to be developing, they tend to relapse into distrust at the slightest disappointment (151, 245, 246). As Ruth Kempe and Henry Kempe, pioneers in the recognition, study, and treatment of child abuse, note:

> Abused children often continue to find relationships very difficult, even beyond the question of trust. They relate indiscriminately, quickly making superficial friendships but ready to discard them at the slightest sign of rejection. They come eagerly to treatment hours, but when the time is up they seem unable to deal with separation and quickly depart as if there were no next time. It seems to us that their early experiences have made it hard for them to acquire what is called object constancy—that is, the ability to see the people they love as always in existence and always basically the same no matter what. With these children it seems to be "out of sight, out of mind" [151, *38*].

Abused children and adolescents tend to be lonely and friendless, already showing the same absence of joy and spontaneity as their parents. "They may yearn for substitutes to love and often make great efforts to find a friend among youngsters of their own sex. But these attempts tend to fail because their demands are excessive and are not understood by the friend or his parents" (151, *40*).

In addition, abused children all too often come to accept—at least consciously—that their parents' "discipline" for "bad behavior" was justified, and that such discipline is the right way to bring up recalcitrant children. At the same time, they are likely to suffer a strong underlying resentment and anger toward their parents—as much for their lack of care and understanding as for their physical abuse. Not surprisingly, a history of child abuse and neglect is common among adolescent runaways and delinquents (245, 246). Many adolescents "begin to express the anger they have felt for so long, not at home, but in delinquent behavior elsewhere" (151, *42*). Belonging to a group, which can provide a feeling of belonging and being wanted, can help the young person to deal with feelings of emotional deprivation, while at the same time offering a means of discharging pent-up aggression in group-approved delinquent activities (see pages 621–622). In one recent study (151, 245) of 100 adolescent runaways and delinquents brought to a juvenile detention center (the sole facility of its type in that county) for the first time, 84 had been neglected or abused before the age of 6, and 92 had been maltreated or sexually abused in the past 18 months. "The great majority of families . . . were intact, and very few children came from an environment that in any way resembled the crowded inner city milieu of poverty and violence. . . ." (245, *20*). Other studies of delinquent children and violent youthful criminals confirm a strong link between the experience of being abused as a child and subsequent antisocial behavior (150, 151, 245). These findings do not mean that most abused children become delinquent, but they do indicate that a history of prior abuse is common among those who later commit aggressive offenses.

**Sexual abuse**  The effects of sexual abuse during childhood or adolescence are not uniform, either in kind or severity. Much depends on the child's age at the time of abuse, the nature of the abusive act, the amount of aggression or physical abuse involved, the relationship between the abuser and the abused, and the kinds of relationships with nonabusing caretakers before, during, and after the episodes of sexual abuse (186, 187). In general, parental and sexual abuse, especially where it is accompanied by coercion, physical abuse, or general family disorganization, is likely to be more traumatic and to create more pervasive and lasting difficulties than abuse by a stranger when the child has a healthy, loving family available for support. Approximately 75 percent of incest and other family sexual involvement is between father and daughter, with the remaining 25 percent divided between mother-son, mother-daughter, father-son, and brother-sister involvement.

Among the longer-term effects that sexual abuse may have are: feelings of having been exploited or abandoned; a sense of helplessness and inability to control one's own destiny; depression, anxiety, and insomnia or nightmares; and, most predictably, distortion in the development of a normal association of pleasure with sexual activity. There may be a total withdrawal from sexual relationships; in less severe instances, there may be problems of sexual dysfunction. Adolescent girls involved in father-daughter incest often will eventually forgive their fathers, but rarely will they forgive the mothers (typically passive, intimidated, or inadequate) who failed to protect them (151, 186, 187).

If begun soon enough and sustained long enough, treatment of sexual abuse, including incest, can often have surprising success—including development of the capacity to enjoy normal, trusting sexual relationships. Without intervention, however, serious long-term consequences may occur. Particularly in the case of sexually exploited adolescent girls, but also boys, there may be severe loss of self-esteem ("I guess I'm a slut," "I guess I never was any good"), chronic depression, and social isolation or reckless promiscuity.

### Parental control

Besides *love-hostility,* the other major dimension emerging from studies of parent-child relationships may be broadly termed *autonomy-control,* although again, precise labels have varied from one investigator to another (e.g., "permissiveness-restrictiveness" [21, 166, 218]. At its restrictive or controlling end, this dimension refers generally to parental behaviors that involve "many restrictions and strict enforcement of demands" (21, *174*), including rigid insistence on neatness, orderliness, obedience, and inhibition of aggression (verbal or otherwise) toward parents, siblings, or peers. Restrictiveness fosters inhibition not only in such obvious areas as social behavior, but also in curiosity (169), creativity (147, 265), initiative (21, 147), and flexibility in approaching intellectual, academic, and practical everyday problems (21, 190). It should be emphasized that a high level of restrictiveness, in the sense in which the term is used here, does not refer to clear parental expectations of socially appropriate behavior or achievement, which, although they may be viewed in one sense as restricting the child's freedom to do what he or she wants, actually are encouraging the child to develop capabilities and talents, rather than limiting him or her (17, 19) (see pages 226–227).

Although it has proved possible to make meaningful though limited generalizations about the probable effects of variations in parental behavior on each of these dimensions, more precise and meaningful generalizations become possible when *interactions* between, or *combinations* of, these two dimensions are considered (see Figure 7.1). For example, a child who is subjected to covertly hostile, *restrictive* parental child-rearing practices is more likely to internalize angry feelings (as in the case of many neurotic children and adolescents) (19, 21, 166); in contrast, the child who is reared under hostile but lax conditions is more likely to act out resentment (as in the case of many delinquents) (21, 58, 228).

The behavior of the child whose parents are high on the dimension of love (warmth) may also vary, depending on coexisting conditions. Thus, children reared in warm but restrictive (as opposed to autonomy-encouraging) homes are likely to be compliant, polite, and neat, but also more dependent and conforming; less aggressive, dominant, and competitive with peers; less friendly; less creative; and more hostile in their fantasies (21, 147, 166, 236). In contrast, those reared in homes where parental love is evident though not cloying, and where the children are given considerable age-appropriate autonomy, are likely to emerge as more active, outgoing, socially assertive, independent, friendly, creative, and lacking in hostility toward others and themselves (21, 73, 147, 190, 235). Such children may also tend to be somewhat disobedient, disrespectful, and rebellious on occasion, but these behaviors appear to result largely from feelings of security and lack of severe punitive responses from parents, and are "more easily turned on and off in response to reinforcing conditions" (21, *197*). They do not reflect chronic anger and frustration or uncontrollable expressions of deep-seated or dammed-up feelings of hostility.

### Parental styles

Especially in conducting research on areas related to values, it is important to define carefully the terms employed. For example, the terms *permissiveness* and *authoritarianism* have frequently aroused controversy (41, 53). Does permissiveness

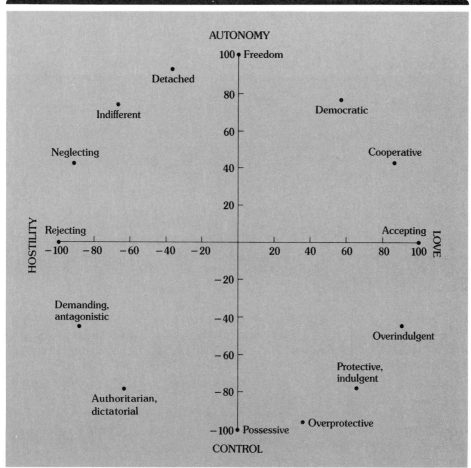

**Figure 7.1** A hypothetical model for parental behavior patterns. (From E. S. Schaefer. A circumplex model for maternal behavior. *Journal of Abnormal and Social Psychology,* 1959, **59**, 232. Copyright 1959 by the American Psychological Association. By permission.)

mean indulgence, intimidation of parents by children, a laissez-faire parental attitude, or simple neglect (41)? Or does this term as employed by some authoritarian adults really refer to *any* encouragement of adolescents' autonomy and participation in decision making, albeit under parental guidance and ultimate authority? The presumed alternative to so-called permissiveness in the minds of some vociferous critics seems to be a "return" to an authoritarian or autocratic model, which might (or might not) have prepared an adolescent for some simpler era, but not for today's unpredictable world, where change, and readiness for change, are central (53, 54, 55). Many adults would apparently prefer to create a simpler society than to face the task of preparing our young people for the complex challenges of today's world.

Indeed, what some adults seem to be crying out against is not so much the changing behavior of youth as the changing nature of society itself. Clearly, adolescents in tomorrow's world will require discipline (ultimately self-discipline), but they will also require independence, self-reliance, adaptability, creativity, and the ability to distinguish between assertiveness and hostility—not to mention a sense of humor. And these characteristics are fostered neither by permissiveness nor parental neglect, nor by autocratic or authoritarian child-rearing methods:

> Authoritarian control and permissive noncontrol may both shield the child from the opportunity to engage in vigorous interaction with people. Demands which cannot be met or no demands, suppression of conflict or sidestepping of conflict, refusal to help or too much help, unrealistically high or low standards, all may curb or understimulate the child so that he fails to achieve the knowledge and experience which could realistically reduce his dependence upon the outside world. The authoritarian and the permissive parent may both create, in different ways, a climate in which the child is not desensitized to the anxiety associated with nonconformity. Both models minimize dissent, the former by suppression and the latter by diversion or indulgence. To learn how to dissent, the child may need a strongly held position from which to diverge and then be allowed under some circumstances to pay the price for nonconformity by being punished. Spirited give and take within the home, if accompanied by respect and warmth, may teach the child how to express aggression in self-serving and prosocial causes and to accept the partially unpleasant consequences of such actions [175, *904*].

A major source of confusion in many discussions of the role of adult authority in contemporary child-rearing appears to involve a failure to distinguish clearly between authoritarian and authoritative parental behaviors. And yet, the distinction is a valid and important one.

As Diana Baumrind (17) has observed, the *authoritarian* or, in more extreme form, *autocratic* parent "attempts to shape, control, and evaluate the behavior and attitudes of the child in accordance with a set standard of conduct, usually an absolute standard [often], theologically motivated and formulated by a higher authority" (17, *261*). Such a parent values obedience per se as an absolute virtue, and "favors punitive, forceful measures to curb self-will at points where the child's actions or beliefs conflict with what [the parent] thinks is right conduct" (17, *261*). He or she believes in reinforcing such instrumental values as "respect for authority, respect for work, and respect for the preservation of order and traditional structure" (17, *261*). Any sort of two-way interaction between parent and child—any encouragement of verbal give and take—is negatively reinforced in the conviction that the child should accept unquestioningly the parents' word for what is right (17).

In contrast, the *authoritative* (democratic but not permissive) parent assumes ultimate responsibility for the child's activities, but in a rational, issue-oriented manner. Such a parent values both autonomous self-will and disciplined behavior. Verbal give and take are encouraged, and the parent attempts to provide "legitimacy" (71, 216, 217) in the exercise of parental authority by frequent explanations of reasons for demands or prohibitions (71). Under authoritative or democratic child-rearing methods, the child or adolescent "contributes freely to discussions of issues relevant to his behavior, and may even make decisions" (50, *242*); however, the parent does not abdicate ultimate responsibility, and any final decision must meet with parental sanction.

Whereas the distinction between authoritarian and authoritative parental behaviors is important in the case of children, it assumes special significance in the case of adolescents—because they are capable of assuming increasingly greater responsibility for their own behavior and because they will need to do so if they are to become mature, self-reliant adults (74). Because the adolescent can imagine viable alternatives to parental directives, the parent must be ready to defend his or her directives on rational grounds (19). The nature of adolescent development and the specific developmental tasks of adolescence add a special emphasis to the impact of parenting styles.

Furthermore, adolescents demonstrate clearly that they are able to distinguish between authoritarian and authoritative parental behavior, and to respond accordingly. A study of 656 Swedish adolescents showed that significant differences occurred in their acceptance of parental authority, depending on the reason for the directive (212). Authority based on rational concern for the young person's welfare was accepted well, whereas authority "based on the adult's desire to dominate or exploit" was rejected. Interestingly, in another investigation (177), it was found that parental discipline which the young person viewed as either very strict (authoritarian) or very permissive tended to be associated with a lack of closeness between parent and child and with rebellion against the parent's political and social views. Similarly, another study (71) found that junior and senior high school students were more likely to model themselves after their parents and to associate with parent-approved peers if their parents used reason to explain decisions and demands.

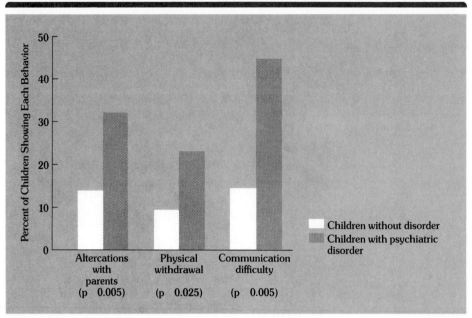

**Figure 7.2** Parent-child alienation and psychiatric disorder at 14 years. (From M. Rutter, O. F. D. Graham, and W. Yule. Adolescent turmoil: Fact or fiction? *Journal of Child Psychology and Psychiatry*, 1976, **17**, 35–56. By permission.)

### Communication patterns

Studies of parent-child interaction in troubled families, or in families with a mentally ill parent or child, have often found distortions in the capacity of parent and child to communicate with one another, and to do so effectively (95, 183, 227, 229, 274). For example, in one comprehensive study of adolescents on the Isle of Wight (227, 229), altercations with parents, physical withdrawal (e.g., going off to his or her room, staying out of the house), and communication difficulties all occurred more frequently in the families of adolescents with psychological disorders (see Figure 7.2). In detailed studies of parent-child interactions in troubled families, it often seems that family members are talking past each other (95, 227, 274). The failure of parents to respond in a meaningful—even a rational—way in such situations is well illustrated in the following excerpt from a family therapy session:

> *Daughter* (the patient): Nobody will listen to me. Everybody is trying to still me.
> *Mother:* Nobody wants to kill you.
> *Father:* If you're going to associate with intellectual people, you're going to have to remember that still is a noun and not a verb [274, *195*].

Adolescents whose problems become more severe, or who fail to get better, are more likely to have at least one parent who says confusing things, is overly critical, or hostile, and overly intrusive. These deviant communication patterns have been found between adolescent and parents in cases where the adolescent was, or later became, schizophrenic (96, 97, 142, 143). Of course, having a schizophrenic child in a family could as easily precipitate communication difficulties as the reverse. However, recent research provides some evidence that problems with communication exist in families where an adolescent *later* becomes mentally ill or manifests less serious psychological difficulties (98).

Disordered communication patterns have also been seen in families where adolescents have other kinds of problems. Families of delinquent boys, for example, have higher rates of defensive communications—those where the purpose is to defend oneself—than families of normal boys (2, 124). Defensive communications are more likely to be reciprocated between delinquent and parent, probably reflecting greater feelings of anger and hostility in families of delinquents. By contrast, in families with normal adolescents, supportive, loving, and encouraging communications occur more often, and are more often reciprocated.

Studies of families with disturbed adolescents have found a greater frequency of communications revealing negative feelings, particularly critical evaluations of the adolescent (139, 267). For example, one study (267) found that a negative emotional quality in verbal interactions between parent and child—such as harsh criticism, excessive intrusiveness, and guilt inducement—was related to lower self-esteem, increased sense of isolation, and increased negative or contrary responses on the part of the adolescent.

Other research (81, 200) suggests that families with a disturbed adolescent showed less mutual understanding in their relationships than families without a disturbed adolescent. In one investigation (81), parents and adolescents tended to agree about what the adolescents' needs were, but disturbed adolescents did not agree with their parents about the parents' needs. The authors concluded that adolescent disturbance is likely to be related to the unwillingness of the parents to adjust their own needs to meet the needs of the troubled young person. These results suggest that in families with healthy adolescents, the parents are better able to respond to the needs of the developing adolescent.

Inasmuch as a negative emotional quality is also seen in adolescents' families where there is a disturbed parent (214), it appears that a disturbed family member of any age is likely to produce strained interactions among family members. Evidently, the way the family works—the family system of interactions—exaggerates the effects of a disturbed family member. One study found that more positive *and* negative interactions were reciprocated in such families (214). It is quite clear that the family *system*—and the complex interactions between family members that are involved— plays an important part in adolescent socialization and development, and we need to know more about what goes on in families without a disturbed member, using similar measures.

### Adolescent transitions

Parental support and guidance, in addition to meeting the basic need of developing young people for nurturance, are especially crucial in the face of the stressful nature of adolescent transitions. The transition from childhood into adolescence, marked by the dramatic changes of puberty, is one difficult period. Similarly difficult is the transition out of adolescence into adulthood, a time when youth typically leave the parental home to begin independent lives. It is clear that parent-child relationships affect the relative ease with which the young person adjusts to the changed role and new demands of adolescence. The overprotected child, who may have achieved a workable *modus vivendi* within the family during middle childhood, may find coping with the demands of others for independence and self-reliance during adolescence extremely difficult to handle. Similarly, as the overindulged child approaches adolescence, he or she may find frustrating the society's unwillingness to provide a like degree of indulgence. The child of hostile parents may have controlled counter-hostility reasonably well until adolescence, only to lose this control under conditions of increased stress, conflict, and opportunities for acting-out behavior.

Furthermore, the appropriateness of particular patterns of parental behavior may vary with the age of the child or adolescent. It has been noted that, during early childhood, "power is asymmetrical in the family unit. That is, the parent's ability to exercise control over the child and to restrict his autonomy exceeds that of the child, in reciprocal interaction with his parent" (17, *263*):

> When a young child refuses to obey, his parent can persist until he does obey, giving him a reason based upon a principle which he may not understand or a reason based upon the asymmetry of power, which he is sure to understand. She can say, "you must do it because I say so"; and the child will accept such a parental maneuver as legitimate even if he continues to have objections on hedonistic grounds, because he is not yet capable of principled objections.
>   An adolescent, on the other hand, is capable of principled objections. When an adolescent refuses to do as his parent wishes, it is more congruent with his construction of reality for the parent simply to ask him "why not?" Through the dialogue that ensues, the parent may learn that her directive was unjust; or the adolescent may learn that his parent's directive could be legitimated. In any case, a head-on confrontation is avoided. While head-on confrontations serve to strengthen authority in the Authority Inception Period, it undermines authority during adolescence [17, *256–266*].

Several investigators (138, 139, 247, 248) have found that the nature of parent-child interactions varies over the early adolescent years. These studies, all conducted with sons, show that parents respond to physical maturation in their children regardless of the age or abstract reasoning skills of the young adolescent. Before the physical changes of puberty become visible, the interactions between child and parents are dominated by parents, with mothers and fathers showing equal dominance. By the end of puberty, the son typically has become more dominant than his mother in family interactions.

Evidence from the study of interruptions in conversations suggests that conflict between mothers and sons arises as soon as puberty begins, with the conflict strongest at the peak of adolescent growth (247). The father is likely to enter into the conflict at this point. From here on, the mother yields to her son more often in discussions, and gradually becomes less influential in decision making. Boys also engage their fathers in conflict, but show a deference toward their fathers that is lacking in their relationships with their mothers. Whether these changes in relationships are due to boys' increasing size relative to their mothers, or to the more complex set of meanings attached to pubertal change, or both, is not yet known.

These results, if they can be generalized to girls, suggest that early adolescence is a time when parents and their children must learn to establish new kinds of relationships with each other. Such adjustments are not easy. The data cited earlier about troubled families suggest that these families are unable to adapt to the new demands that having an emerging adult in the family requires. As John Hill, a developmental psychologist asserts, adolescence generates family stress; in response to the stress, problem families disintegrate while normal families adapt (126).

### Autonomy

The development of autonomy is central to any discussion of the tasks of adolescence, not only because autonomy itself is important but also because it is intimately related to the accomplishment of other tasks. Thus, if the adolescent does not ultimately resolve the conflict between the continuing, potentially regressive dependence on the family and the newer demands and privileges of independence, he or she will encounter difficulties in most other areas as well. Without the achievement of a reasonable degree of emotional separation and autonomy, the adolescent can hardly be expected to achieve mature heterosexual or peer relationships, confident pursuit of a vocation, or a sense of identity, which requires a positive image of the self as separate, unified, and consistent over time (see Chapter 3).

The change in parent-child relationships during adolescence is probably best described as a *transformation* (127), rather than as a radical change for most young people. An overemphasis on the development of separation and independence can be misleading inasmuch as continuing social contact between child and parent is maintained throughout the life cycle in most subgroups in our society (1, 85, 237), as well as in other Western countries (276). What is expected in every culture is that the developing adolescent should achieve an *appropriate balance* of independence from, and dependence on, parents, in a manner that facilitates mutually rewarding reciprocal interactions between generations (52).

Similarly, parents must be able to recognize—and encourage—the adolescent's need for increased independence. Continuing to think of their adolescent young simply as "our darling little girl" or "our cute little boy," and treating them accordingly, is a prescription for later disaster—whether it takes the form of explosive rebellion or continued and increasingly inappropriate dependence. At the same time, however, it is vital for parents to recognize that true independence is not achieved in a day, and that dependence needs coexist—often in uneasy and fragile alliance— along with independence needs. Partly because so many things are changing in the adolescent's world, he or she urgently needs a base of security and stability in home and parents. Along with increasing independence comes an inevitable shift in the emotional relationships between parent and child. If the young person is eventually going to achieve emotional, social, and sexual maturity, he or she must gradually begin shifting to peers—to "best friends" and girlfriends or boyfriends—some of the intimate emotional attachment previously reserved largely for parents. Obviously, as we shall see, adapting to these new kinds of relationships is more difficult for some kinds of parents—and adolescents—than for others (see pages 247–251).

### *Adolescent socialization in other cultures*

In a number of preliterate societies and even in some culturally isolated areas of more technologically advanced societies, the task of establishing independence may be less difficult than it is in our own complex, socially fragmented, and rapidly changing culture. Among the mountain Arapesh people of New Guinea, for example, there is a very gradual transition from a high degree of dependence and indulgent care in infancy and early childhood to increasing independence as the child grows older, with no discernible spurt during puberty or adolescence. Furthermore, "the mildness of the transition in this case is facilitated by the fact that the change is not very great" (174, *95*).

Although the Arapesh adolescent begins to take over much of the responsibility for supporting and managing a household, there are few marked changes in basic family relationships at this time. The Arapesh girl does not suddenly leave home during adolescence to go to live in a strange household with strange people in order to undergo the joint uncertainties of married life, sex, and childbearing (174). Rather, she has been chosen as a wife by her husband's parents many years prior to consummation of the marriage, and she has been allowed during the interim to wander confidently back and forth between her own home and that of her future husband. Similarly, the Arapesh adolescent boy does not need to go out into a new community on his own, obtain an unfamiliar job, and complete emotional independence from his parents. He continues, but with new responsibility, to till the family's garden. He still sees his parents daily, and when at last he consummates his marriage, it is with a girl he has known, cared for, and adjusted to over a long period of time (174, 190).

Among the Mixtecan Indians of Mexico, socialization is also a gradual and informal process (178). Around the sixth or seventh year, girls begin caring for younger siblings, going to market, helping to serve food and wash the dishes, and perhaps caring for small domestic animals. At about the same age, boys begin gathering produce or fodder in the fields and caring for large animals such as goats or burros.

In such informal ways, and largely through example, Mixtecan children gradually learn to take increasing responsibility and to perform the tasks they will assume as adults. There is little anxiety about the children's learning these tasks, on the part of either parents or children. Parents assume that their children will learn to do such basic jobs adequately, and there is no demand or expectation for achievement beyond this. Aggressive competition would be considered unseemly, and nurturance plays a strong role among these people.

In contrast to the Arapesh and Mixtecan young, children and adolescents in some other preliterate societies may find the establishment of independence a stressful and anxiety-producing task. The extent of the shift required by a particular society may be relatively great, such as from extreme dependency and indulgence early in life to equally extreme demands for independence in later childhood, adolescence, or adulthood. Or the transition from dependence to independence may be compressed into a relatively short period, or characterized by short breaks or discontinuities. For example, the Kwoma, close neighbors of the Arapesh in New Guinea, are "exceedingly indulgent of the infant's needs, and develop through learning strong drives for dependence upon the mother" (270, *94*). This process continues until weaning at about age 3, only to be followed by a sharp and virtually immediate rejection by the mother of continued dependent behavior (269).

In other societies, similar rapid shifts may occur late in development—as, for example, following puberty rites intended to mark the transition from childhood to some degree of adult status. The Mundugumor adolescent of the South Seas, for example, finds the problem of orderly transition to an independent household infinitely more difficult partly because "Mundugumor social organization is based on a theory of a natural hostility between all members of the same sex" (174, *176*) Fathers and sons view each other almost as natural enemies, as do mothers and daughters. Moreover, relations between husband and wife are notably poor. Fathers band together with daughters while mothers band together with sons. Between the two subfamily groups rivalry and distrust are typical. Consequently, the Mundugumor boy approaches adolescence psychologically close only to his mother, hostile toward his father, and distrustful of girls his own age. The girl, on the other hand, has strong ties to her father, resentment toward her mother, and distrust of her male contemporaries. Furthermore, the girl's problem is magnified because of the jealous father's attempt to keep his hold on her as long as possible.

There seems little doubt that Mundugumor children, who grow up in a culture that contains so much hostility and so little tenderness, early develop a kind of hearty independence that prepares them somewhat for the demands they must face in adolescence. But this advantage is virtually negated by the fact that the independence demanded of the Mundugumor adolescent is so much more extreme than in most cultures. The prospect of establishing independence is unpleasant, and in most ways threatening. In fact, its only really attractive aspect seems to be escape from the hostility of the same-sex parent (190).

## DEVELOPING AUTONOMY
## IN AMERICAN CULTURE

Today's American adolescents and their counterparts in other technologically advanced nations clearly encounter greater stress in developing autonomy than the Arapesh or Mixtecan youth, although in most families they are spared much of the violence and hostility of the Mundugumor's struggle for autonomy. In contrast to the Arapesh adolescent and those in many other primitive cultures (178, 268, 270), the American adolescent is expected, in the limited period between puberty and adulthood, to pass from a state of relatively great dependence on the family to one of considerable independence. As John Whiting and Irvin Child (270) and others (178, 268) have found in cross-cultural investigations of child training practices in a wide variety of preliterate cultures, most societies begin independence training somewhat later than the American middle-class culture, but they also complete it sooner, and few have anything approaching the kind of extended freedom from adult responsibilities characteristic of many American young people today.

The complexity of achieving autonomy for the American adolescent is due, at least in part, to the gradual manner in which responsibilities and freedoms are granted. There is no single point at which an adolescent in our society achieves adult

status. Adult status is achieved sphere by sphere over a broad span of years, extending up to 15 years in some cases. Among the first signs of adult status are mature size and reproductive capacity. Some religious traditions grant adult status at about the same time through confirmation or Bar and Bas Mitzvah. Schools and parents require increasing responsibility on the part of their sons and daughters over the adolescent years, but the role of student or child living at home can hardly be considered conducive to the development of full autonomy or independence. Only with employment, a separate place of residence, and intimate extrafamilial relationships, is the young person, in most cases, able to acquire the full responsibilities and privileges related to his or her actions. Given this extended period of dependency, we ought to be less surprised at the recent increases in adolescent sexual behavior and childbearing; perhaps these changes are related in part to the adolescents' wishes for independent adult status in the face of prolonged dependency. Clearly, adult status is meaningless without the capacity for responsible behavior in that role.

### Rites of passage

As mentioned above, our society provides no clear pattern of transition to adulthood, and this appears to be becoming more, rather than less, the case. For example, there are now fewer traditional timetables for the transitions to adult roles such as parenthood. In contrast, many primitive societies have formalized *rites of passage*, or initiation ceremonies, to mark the adolescent's assumption of new, more adult social roles. Such ceremonies typically exist for both boys and girls.

Among the Zuñi Indians, the initiation rites of adolescents serve an important psychological function. Younger children are taught to fear the displeasure of "scare Kachinas," or "punitive masked gods," employed in tribal ceremonies, if they behave improperly (25). Traditionally, when a boy is about 14 and considered responsible, he undergoes an initiation rite at which he is ceremonially whipped with strands of yucca by these "masked gods"—not as a physical punishment, of which the Zuñi disapprove, but as a rite of exorcism, "to take off the bad happenings," and to make future events propitious.

> It is at this initiation that the Kachina mask is put upon his head, and it is revealed to him that the dancers, instead of being the supernaturals from the sacred lake, are in reality his neighbors and his relatives . . . the priests lift the masks from their heads and place them upon the heads of the boys. It is a great revelation. The boys are terrified. The yucca whips are taken from the hands of the scare Kachinas and put in the hands of the boys who face them, now with the masks upon their heads. They are commanded to whip the Kachinas. *It is their first object lesson in the truth that they, as mortals, must exercise all the functions which the uninitiated ascribe to the supernaturals themselves* [25, 69–70; italics added].

Similar *rites de passage* for adolescent boys occur in many other tribal societies (42, 188, 192, 271, 275).

Among girls, initiation ceremonies are likely to center around the onset of menstruation, "which furnishes an obvious and dramatic signal of approaching physiological maturity" (83, *174*). A common feature of such ceremonies in a large number of societies is the seclusion of the girl, especially from men. This seclusion may last for only a few days or continue for several months (83). In many instances the secluded girl receives special instruction from an older woman in matters pertaining to sex and marriage. The teaching generally "includes an explanation of the social regulations governing proper conduct in sexual affairs, a description and sometimes demonstration and pantomime of the techniques of lovemaking, advice on how to get along in married life, methods of avoiding pregnancy, and what to expect in childbirth" (83, *174*). Typically, the conclusion of the period is marked by a feast or dance, at which the girl, after bathing or going through ritual purification, publicly dons the clothes of a mature woman.

A complementary view of puberty rites, particularly those for young girls, describes the political and economic functions of these transitional rites in various societies (204). In this view, the primary function of such rites for a girl is to mark her transition from her family of origin to the family of her husband. Girls are seen as valuable in many cultures for the children they are able to bear; therefore, it is important to fathers that a marriage be arranged early. Similarly, prospective husbands are interested in finding a wife who can bear as many children as possible; although in some cultures actual evidence of fertility is required (as demonstrated by the birth of a child), in many others menarche is taken as sufficient evidence of fertility, and the goal is to arrange a marriage as soon after menarche as possible so that opportunities for bearing children are not lost. In any case, puberty rites for girls in these societies mark the transition to adult status in that society, as they do for boys.

In contrast, a variety of laws, often internally inconsistent, are about all that our own society has in the way of institutionalized patterns of recognizing the adolescent's increasing independence. Furthermore, they vary a great deal in their content from one area of the country to another. For example, there are significant variations from state to state in the age at which a young person can drink alcohol, drive a car, marry, and own property. One of the ironies of our times is that until the 1970s, young people who were considered old enough to do most of the fighting in the armed services in this country were not considered mature enough to vote.

As a consequence of this extended and sequential process of status changes, adolescents who must face the problems of transition to adulthood are likely to be impressed not with the solidarity of the expectations of adult society, but with their apparent confusion and divisiveness. In one instance or with one set of people, they are likely to find that independent responses are rewarded. In other instances, or with other people, they will find that they are punished. The church, the school, the members of various social classes, even an adolescent's own parents may have different notions as to the time when adult protection and guidance should be relinquished in favor of greater individual responsibility.

Contemporary adolescents are likely to observe that some of their peers are allowed by their parents to decide how to earn and spend their own money, to obtain a car, to choose their companions, to go off alone on dates, to take trips by themselves or with friends, and to make their own educational and vocational plans. In contrast, other peers may be allowed to do none of these things.

Furthermore, today's adolescents often find inconsistencies in the way people react to them as individuals. The young high school student's employer usually expects him or her to be independent and responsible more often than do parents. Same- and opposite-sex peers may also have different expectations. Even within the same family, a mother and father may have differing expectations in regard to responsibilities and privileges of their children. Finally, either or both parents may possess mixed feelings about their child's growing independence. These feelings are likely to be reflected in inconsistent patterns of parental behavior—as, for example, demanding independence and at the same time punishing it when it occurs (190).

Another manifestation of the ambivalence of adults over the increasing autonomy of adolescents is seen in adults' failure to provide appropriate instruction or guided experiences in areas where adolescents need to be able to function responsibly. Issues related to sexuality, as well as drug and alcohol use, for example, cause particular difficulties for many adolescents. These are aspects of adult functioning, and adolescents must learn at some point how to be responsible sexual partners, and how to approach situations where alcohol or drugs are available. Adolescents sometimes find themselves in a double bind: unprepared for these experiences by parents or other adults, yet criticized if they behave irresponsibly. These socialization practices—or lack of them—stand in dramatic contrast to the institutionalized practices of some of the primitive societies described earlier in which appropriate behavior is taught.

# PARENT-CHILD RELATIONSHIPS
# AND THE DEVELOPMENT OF AUTONOMY

The severity of the adolescent's independence-dependence conflicts and the ease with which they are resolved in the direction of greater autonomy depend to a large extent on previous and current parent-child relationships. The parent who encourages increasing autonomy as the child grows older, but who still retains an interest in, and some responsibility for, the adolescent's decisions, is likely to encourage both responsibility and independence (17, 70, 71, 74). Autocratic or authoritarian parents, on the other hand, tend to stifle the orderly acquisition of independence; indifferent or completely permissive parents may fail to encourage the development of responsibility.

In a study by Glen Elder (70) of 7400 adolescents in a Southern and a Midwestern state, adolescent ratings of parents' behavior were employed to study parental variations in child-rearing techniques, ranging from complete parental domination to complete self-direction. Seven parental structures were defined:

> *Autocratic.* No allowance is provided for youth to express their views on a subject nor for them to assert leadership or initiative in self-government.
>
> *Authoritarian.* Although the adolescent contributes to the solution of problems, the parents always decide issues according to their own judgment.
>
> *Democratic.* The adolescent contributes freely to discussions of issues relevant to his or her behavior, and may even make decisions; however, in all instances the final decision is either formulated by parents or meets their approval.
>
> *Equalitarian.* This type of structure represents minimal role differentiation. Parents and the adolescent are involved to a similar degree in making decisions pertaining to the adolescent's behavior.
>
> *Permissive.* The adolescent assumes a more active and influential position in formulating decisions that concern him or her than do the parents.
>
> *Laissez-faire.* The position of the adolescent in relation to that of the parents in decision making is clearly more differentiated in terms of power and activity. In this type of relationship the youth has the option of either subscribing to or disregarding parental wishes in making decisions.
>
> *Ignoring.* This type of structure, if it can be legitimately considered as such, represents actual parental divorcement from directing the adolescent's behavior.

Moving from the autocratic to the ignoring structure involves a gradual increase in the participation of the adolescent in self-direction and a concurrent decrease in the participation of parents in making decisions concerning him or her. Just as these types of interdependence, as perceived by adolescents, represent variations in the allocation of power between parents and the adolescent, they also represent different patterns of communication. Communication is primarily from parent

*parent*

to child in the autocratic structure and from child to parent in the permissive structure (70).

A number of other interesting findings emerged from this study. As might be expected, fathers were more likely to be rated as authoritarian or autocratic (35 percent) than mothers (22 percent). This is consistent with findings from other studies that indicate that most adolescents tend to view their fathers as stricter and more aggressive, and their mothers as more emotionally supportive, expressive of affection, child-centered, and protective (62, 104, 190, 208, 215). Also, as one might anticipate, both mothers and fathers tended to treat older adolescents more permissively than younger ones, although there was a greater shift toward permissiveness with age in the case of mothers than with fathers. Parents in larger families tended to be slightly more autocratic or authoritarian than those in smaller families, even when social class was held constant.

How did adolescents respond to these varying patterns of parental control ("child rearing structures")?[1] Subjects were asked, "Do you think your (mother's/father's) ideas, rules, or principles about how you should behave are good and

---

[1] Inasmuch as the classification of parental behaviors was based on adolescent reports rather than independent measures, there is a possibility that the subjects' perceptions of parental child-rearing practices may have been influenced by their reactions to their parents (as fair, unfair, etc.). However, in similar research (148, 157), where independent measures of parental practices were obtained, adolescent perceptions of these practices appeared generally consonant with parental reports. Nevertheless, the lack of independent measures of parental practices remains a methodological limitation of the research.

### TABLE 7.1 FEELINGS OF MATERNAL AND PATERNAL REJECTION AS RELATED TO TYPES OF CHILD-REARING STRUCTURES

| PARENT | PERCENTAGE OF ADOLESCENTS BY TYPES OF CHILD-REARING STRUCTURES | | | | | |
| --- | --- | --- | --- | --- | --- | --- |
| | AUTO-CRATIC | AUTHORI-TARIAN | DEMO-CRATIC | EQUALI-TARIAN | PER-MISSIVE | LAISSEZ-FAIRE IGNORING |
| Mother | 41.7 (277) | 25.7 (239) | 10.9 (283) | 11.0 (143) | 11.1 (190) | 56.8 |
| Father | 40.1 (525) | 17.6 (220) | 8.4 (193) | 11.1 (117) | 11.0 (140) | 58.0 |

Source: G. H. Elder, Jr. Structural variations in the child rearing relationship. *Sociometry,* 1962, **25,** 259. By permission.

reasonable, or wrong and unreasonable?" Children exposed to *democratic* practices considered their parents most fair (approximately 95 percent for both mother and father). Autocratic parents (those who "just tell" their children what to do) ranked lowest. These results are consistent with other findings (21, 60, 166) and with the hypothesis that communication between parents and children (e.g., democratic, equalitarian) fosters *identification,* whereas a unilateral exercise of power without communication (e.g., autocratic) is more likely to produce resentment (35).

Interestingly, however, more favorable ratings on fairness were given to authoritarian fathers than to authoritarian mothers; in contrast, more favorable ratings were given to permissive mothers than to permissive fathers. Inasmuch as these results held up when sex and social class were controlled, it appears that a father, even though he makes the basic decisions, will generally be considered fair if he is willing to listen (authoritarian), but not if he lays down the law without listening (autocratic). In other words, acceptance of parental dictates is greater if the parent makes some effort to "legitimize" his or her power (132). Further, being the lawgiver (provided he is willing to listen) is generally considered by adolescents as a more socially appropriate role for fathers than for mothers. In contrast, permissiveness is considered a somewhat more appropriate role for mothers. This, of course, is consistent with other findings (69, 198, 257).

Adolescents were also asked whether they ever thought that their parents made them feel unwanted. As Table 7.1 shows, by far the largest percentages of adolescents who reported that they felt unwanted were found among youths with autocratic or laissez-faire and ignoring parents. Thus, about 40 percent of the youths with either an autocratic mother or father reported that they had felt unwanted by that parent, whereas only about 10 percent of adolescents with democratic, equalitarian, or permissive parents expressed similar feelings. This relationship was also analyzed with the age, sex, and social class of the adolescent controlled, and the nature and strength of the relationship remained essentially unchanged. "In essence, child rearing structures which represent considerable adolescent participation in self-direction appear least provocative of rejection feeling" (70, *260*).

Interestingly, another study (104) indicates that adolescents perceiving their parents as authoritarian are more likely to view them as unhappy, whereas those perceiving their parents as democratic are more likely to view them as happy. In a related study, Elder (71) found that democratic and permissive parents *who also provide frequent explanations for their rules of conduct and expectations* were most likely to have adolescent sons and daughters who are *confident* in their own values, goals, and awareness of rules, and who are *independent* (desiring to make up their own minds, with or without listening to others' ideas). In contrast, autocratic, nonexplaining parents were most likely to have adolescent young who are dependent and lacking in self-confidence.

Similar results were obtained in an investigation (148, 157) of several thousand American and Danish adolescents and their parents. In both countries, democratic parents were significantly more likely than either authoritarian or permissive parents to have adolescents who felt independent and considered themselves to be treated in an adult manner by their parents (see Table 7.2). Furthermore, feelings of independence were highest among adolescents whose parents provided frequent explanations for their rules of conduct (see Table 7.3).

> In both countries, feelings of independence are enhanced when parents have few rules, when they provide explanations for their rules, and when they are democratic and engage the child actively in the decision-making process. Furthermore, feelings of independence from parents in both countries, far from leading to rebelliousness, are associated with closeness to parents and positive attitudes toward them [157, *357*].

Other studies (61, 110, 220) have yielded similar results. Confidence and self-esteem were found to be highest among adolescents whose parents expressed strong interest in, and knowledge about, their opinions and activities and who encouraged autonomous behavior and active participation in family affairs (220). Similarly, Bachman (6), in a national sample of tenth-grade boys, found significantly higher self-esteem among boys with positive family relations, as indicated by the extent of perceived close, nonpunitive relationships with democratic, explaining parents (see Figure 7.3).

### Laissez-faire parents

Early in this chapter, we described how parent-child communications of a confused or conflicted nature seem to be related to adjustment problems or psychopathology in adolescents. Parents who are laissez-faire, neglecting, or who assume a false and exaggerated equalitarianism appear to have effects on their adolescents that are as strong as those seen in the disturbed families described earlier. Among middle-class adolescents, high-risk drug use and other forms of socially deviant behavior occurred most frequently among those whose parents, while outwardly expressing such values for themselves and their children as individuality, self-understanding, readiness for change, maximizing one's human potential, and stressing the need for equalitarianism in the family, were actually using those proclaimed values to avoid assuming parental responsibility. Motivation to avoid responsibility stemmed variously from uncertainties about their own convictions, indecision about how to handle their children, needs to be liked or to feel youthful, or, as often

## TABLE 7.2 FEELINGS OF INDEPENDENCE BY JOINT PARENTAL AUTHORITY PATTERN AND COUNTRY

| | UNITED STATES | | | DENMARK | | |
| | JOINT PARENTAL AUTHORITY | | | JOINT PARENTAL AUTHORITY | | |
| PERCENTAGE OF ADOLESCENTS | AU-THORI-TARIAN | DEMO-CRATIC | PER-MIS-SIVE | AU-THORI-TARIAN | DEMO-CRATIC | PER-MIS-SIVE |
|---|---|---|---|---|---|---|
| Who feel both parents give them enough freedom | 58 | 82 | 68 | 60 | 88 | 78 |
| Total N | (239) | (164) | (76) | (83) | (345) | (120) |
| Who feel parents should treat them more like adults | 63 | 44 | 64 | 46 | 21 | 39 |
| Total N | (201) | (133) | (63) | (59) | (276) | (105) |

Source: G. S. Lesser and D. Kandel. Parent-adolescent relationships and adolescent independence in the United States and Denmark. *Journal of Marriage and the Family*, 1969, **31**, 348–358. By permission of the National Council on Family Relations.

Note: Chi-square differences within countries significant at .001.

## TABLE 7.3 FEELINGS OF INDEPENDENCE BY JOINT PARENTAL EXPLANATIONS FOR RULES AND COUNTRY

| | UNITED STATES | | | DENMARK | | |
| | JOINT FREQUENCY OF EXPLANATIONS[a] | | | JOINT FREQUENCY OF EXPLANATIONS[a] | | |
| PERCENTAGE OF ADOLESCENTS | BOTH PARENTS HIGH | ONE HIGH ONE LOW | BOTH PARENTS LOW | BOTH PARENTS HIGH | ONE HIGH ONE LOW | BOTH PARENTS LOW |
|---|---|---|---|---|---|---|
| Who feel both parents give them enough freedom | 79 | 57 | 50 | 85 | 70 | 63 |
| Total N | (300) | (293) | (224) | (558) | (176) | (107) |
| Who feel parents should treat them more like adults | 47 | 51 | 68 | 26 | 40 | 54 |
| Total N | (249) | (180) | (186) | (447) | (147) | (80) |

Source: G. S. Lesser and D. Kandel. Parent-adolescent relationships and adolescent independence in the United States and Denmark. *Journal of Marriage and the Family*, 1969, **31**, 348–358. By permission of the National Council on Family Relations.

Note: Chi-square differences within countries significant at .001.

[a] Frequency of parental explanations was defined as follows: high: parents explain "usually" or "always"; low: parents explain "sometimes," "once in a while," or "never."

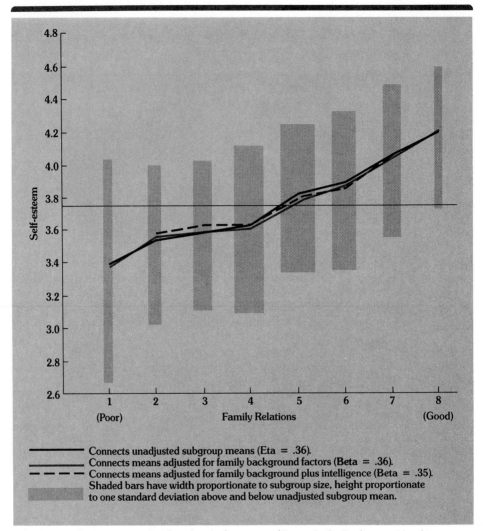

**Figure 7.3** Self-esteem related to family functions. (From J. G. Bachman. *Youth in transition, Vol. 2: The impact of family background and intelligence on tenth-grade boys.* Ann Arbor: Institute for Social Research, University of Michigan, 1970. By permission.)

appeared to be the case, their own antagonism, or at least ambivalence, toward authority—parental or social.

These parents "find it hard to make decisive value judgments that require the exercise of power over their children and prefer to escape from the obligation of being an authority figure—an untenable position if authority is distrusted in general or if there has been no identification in childhood with an admired authority" (37, 52). But by placing themselves on the footing of peers, they end up leaving their children to drift essentially alone in an uncharted sea, without any dependable models of responsible adult behavior. Ironically, despite their protestations of parent-child togetherness, parents of high-risk drug users actually spent less time in family activities with their children, enjoyed their company less, and were less able to handle problems that arose than the more traditional parents of low-drug-risk adolescents (37).

In another study (140), high school students exhibiting a relative absence of problem behavior (e.g., drug use, sexual activities, problem drinking) were found to have mothers who had firm, relatively traditional values of their own; made clear their disapproval of deviant behaviors (e.g., stealing, lying, drug use, drinking, extramarital sex); and exerted reasonable controls (e.g., being in at night, doing homework)—but who also manifested a high level of affectionate interaction with their children.

Obviously, the degree of parental control that is appropriate and consistent with the development of responsible autonomy, will vary with age. In the study of Danish and American adolescents previously cited (see page 240), Danish adolescents emerged as somewhat more mature and independent than their American counterparts. It appeared that Danish parents exercised greater control during childhood, but imposed fewer rules during adolescence. Consequently, Danish adolescents appeared more able to behave in a mature fashion without external constraints (19). In the United States, "parents treat their children as adolescents longer than in Denmark. Danish adolescents are expected to be self-governing; American adolescents are not" (157, *358*).

### Sociocultural influences and parental power practices

**Sociocultural influences and parental power practices** In several of the foregoing studies, the relationship of parental power practices to social class was also investigated (19, 70, 71). Overall there was a slight tendency for middle-class parents to be viewed as more democratic, equalitarian, or permissive, and for lower-class parents to be viewed as more autocratic and authoritarian (19, 70). Rural families have been shown to be more authoritarian, and to delay independence longer than urban families, both in the United States and in other Western countries (72, 207).

### Summary

**Summary**
In brief, it appears that democratic practices, with frequent explanations by parents of their rules of conduct and expectations, foster responsible autonomous behavior in several ways: (1) by providing opportunities for increasing autonomy, guided by interested parents who communicate with the child and exercise appropriate degrees of control; (2) by promoting positive identification with the parent, based on love and respect for the child, rather than rejection or indifference; and (3) by themselves providing models of reasonable independence, that is, autonomy within the framework of democratic order. In contrast, the child of autocratic or indifferent parents is not presented with models of responsible, cooperative independence; he or she is not so likely to be encouraged by parental acceptance to identify with adults; and he or she is not given age-graded experiences in the orderly assumption of responsible autonomy (15, 17, 251).

Although a number of these studies were conducted some years ago, they appear, if anything, more rather than less relevant today. The democratic child-rearing structure (as defined here), providing as it does for perceptions of parental fairness, for feelings of personal security and being wanted, and for the development of both responsibility and increasing autonomy, seems especially important in a period of rapid social change such as the present, when the need for adult autonomy is at a premium, when there are few clear-cut social guidelines for behavior and responsibility must come largely from within, and when the opportunities for generational conflict, hostility, and alienation are legion (53).

Autocratic, or at least authoritarian, patterns of parental behavior may have been more workable in other times and other cultures where the adolescent could expect to be reasonably successful simply by following in a father's or mother's footsteps. Under such cultural conditions, carefully defined, even rigid, channels were also more likely to be provided by the society for coping with the greater intergenerational hostility than an autocratic structure may provoke. Furthermore, in such situations the autocratic posture of the parent, though it may have been frustrating to the adolescent, was more legitimate in the sense that the parent really did "hold all the cards" and was the repository of most of the relevant power and skills the adolescent was seeking. Today, however, parents can, under favorable circumstances, provide models of successful, autonomous, flexible, problem-solving behavior, and they can provide love and a fundamental underlying security; they can also teach their children how to think about and deal with challenging situations; but they cannot provide detailed blueprints for mastering the demands of a constantly changing society. Unlike the Mixtecan or Zuñi societies described earlier, we cannot teach young people the specific content of what they will be doing as adults. But we can teach them strategies or processes for approaching life.

The laissez-faire or ignoring parent makes the task of achieving responsible independence or autonomy especially difficult in the current world. Despite contrary claims, other influences on adolescent behavior—age-mate peers, the older adolescent youth culture, the adult world in general—frequently cannot provide adequate or consistent guidelines for assuming the kind of responsible behavior required by our changing times. Indeed, parents often model behavior as confused and as dependent upon their adult peer group norms as do their adolescent children. Rather than providing models for mature adult behavior, they often model adolescent behavior instead. This situation stands in distinct contrast to that noted by Urie Bronfenbrenner (41) in his thoughtful study of American and Soviet child-rearing practices. Where there is a systematic, consistent, and supervised effort by adults to employ the peer group as models of adult standard setting, peers may play such a role (as they do in the Soviet Union). Bronfenbrenner argues that one of the reasons for the relatively higher rates of antisocial behavior in the United States and England is that, to an increasing extent, parents have been isolated from their children—and from child-rearing—without having provided planned substitutes adequate to the task (e.g., schools, the church, peers or older adolescents, and extended family and neighbors). We might speculate that such isolation from children leads adults to lose sight of what constitutes appropriate role behavior as adults. The benefits of child-rearing can go both ways—to provide adult models for children and adolescents, and to remind adults of the distinctions between, and responsibilities of adults relative to, children and adolescents.

### Sex-role socialization and
### the development of autonomy

A study of sex differences in socialization in a large number of preliterate, principally tribal, societies throughout the world (13) found that whereas sex-role differences were relatively unimportant in infancy—with both sexes being treated simply as babies—the picture soon changed. By 4 or 5 years of age, and persisting through adolescence, there was, as has traditionally been the case in our own society, "a widespread pattern of greater pressure toward nurturance, obedience, and responsibility in girls, and towards self-reliance and achievement striving in boys" (13, *332*). Although continued dependence tended to be acceptable for girls, independence was increasingly stressed for boys. Interestingly, the greatest sex differences on these variables occurred in societies with "an economy that places a high premium on the superior strength, and superior development of motor skills requiring strength, which characterize the male" (13, *330*), and also in societies with large family groups characterized by a high degree of cooperative interaction.

These findings appear to have particular relevance currently in our society, in view of the emphasis on less rigidly defined sex-role behaviors among an increasing number of young people. Greater differentiation of sex roles may be more important in societies where the work on which the economy depends requires heavy physical labor. Rigid differentiation of sex roles may be neither necessary nor socially desirable in other cultural settings, however. In our own increasingly technological, automated, and geographically mobile society, jobs are becoming ever more dependent on education and intellectual skills rather than physical strength. Furthermore, the fact of increasing numbers of women in the work force makes it more important that many roles within the family unit be interchangeable and cooperative, rather than complementary as in the past. Under such circumstances, decreased emphasis on gender specificity of family roles appears likely to prove more adaptive, and may also provide greater room for a more realistic expression of individual differences among both males and females.

Mothers are now more likely than before to be employed outside the home, and fathers are more likely now to participate in household work and child-rearing (213) (see pages 457–461). Contrary to earlier predictions of maladjustment, sons and daughters of employed mothers appear generally *better* adjusted than children of mothers not working outside the home (14, 93, 131). This may be due to the current positive valuation placed on such employment, as well as the fact that many more women are now employed out of economic necessity (93).

Many parents still appear more apprehensive about venturesome, risk-taking activities, and more likely to reward dependent behavior, in girls, and they seem more inclined to stress competitiveness and career goals in boys (34, 119, 134). For example, recent research on achievement in mathematics indicates that parents tend to have lower expectations for girls' performance in mathematics than they do for that of boys, even when both are equally good students (204). Furthermore, they view mathematics as less valuable for girls. There is also still a tendency, beginning as early as 7 or 8, to allow girls significantly less freedom than boys (134).

Nevertheless, there appears to be an increasing effort, particularly among educated, middle-class parents, to treat boys and girls in a similar manner, especially with respect to such matters as freedom in pursuing educational and career goals.

Several recent studies (88, 238) have found that although adolescents perceive that their mothers and fathers have different parental styles, neither parent is viewed as treating boys and girls differently. Although parents of younger children still tend to reinforce "sex-appropriate" play and other sex-related behaviors, aggressive behavior is not intentionally encouraged in either sex, although aggressive behavior is still more common among young boys than girls (79, 137, 154).

### *Sex differences in the achievement of autonomy*

The past decade was marked by significant changes in women's roles, and, more recently, in the roles of men. These changes can be seen in behavior—for example, the increase in the number of women in the work place—as well as in attitudes, such as beliefs about whether specific functions should more appropriately be performed by men or women. We expect that this societal change will have an increasing impact upon the development of autonomy and the resolution of independence-dependence conflicts, particularly in adolescent girls. And indeed, this already appears to be happening.

A major study published in 1966 (68) was consistent with the views of other writers on this topic (11, 36) in concluding that girls in our culture appeared to experience fewer and less stressful conflicts over the development of independence than boys, particularly during the earlier years of adolescence. In a national sample of adolescents, boys were significantly more likely to be "actively engaged in establishing independence from parental control" than girls (68, *115*), were more concerned with issues of self-esteem and achievement of responsibility for their own actions, and (probably partly as a consequence) were more preoccupied with problems of self-control (e.g., control of temper and impulsiveness). In contrast, they found, somewhat to their surprise, that adolescent girls (particularly younger ones) were not as likely to be deeply involved with these issues. Girls were more likely to consider their parents' rules to be fair, right, and lenient (68). They were also more likely to progress from a rather passive childhood acceptance of parental authority to a more independent identification with the point of view of that authority without an intervening phase "in which the girl defiantly asserts her own values and controls before moving closer to those of the parents" (68, *109*).

Since the time of that study, there have been important changes in the socialization and development of adolescent girls (87, 136, 213). Greater autonomy and self-reliance—socially and economically—are meeting with increased approval among peers and in society generally, and this may be reflected in parent-child relations. For example, a recent study (208) found that adolescent girls, compared to boys, were *less*, rather than more, likely to consider their parents' rules to be lenient. Other studies have also found fewer sex differences in attitudes related to autonomy and independence (156, 201). In one recent investigation (156), no differences were found between adolescent boys and girls in the extent to which they employed an "agentic style" (characterized by assertion of the individual's self-interests, and usually considered more typical of males) or a "communal style" (characterized by a concern for harmony and sensitivity to the needs of others, and usually considered more typical of females). At this point, it appears we should be cautious about concluding that contemporary adolescent girls are less concerned than boys with the development of autonomy and less likely to become involved in independence-dependence conflicts with parents.

Part of the explanation for these apparent changes may be provided by earlier studies which found that female adolescents and young women who are more independent, self-reliant, and achievement-oriented than their peers tend to have parents who, while they may have been fundamentally loving and caring, were not passively accepting of, or overprotective toward, their daughters, and indeed made strong demands for maturity, self-reliance, and a reasonable (and possible) level of achievement (19, 129, 166). It seems likely that such parents, particularly the mothers, promoted these characteristics in their daughters both by positively reinforcing evidences of such behavior (while failing to reinforce, or negatively reinforcing, dependence and lack of instrumental competence), and by themselves providing models of independent, self-confident, achieving behavior (16, 18, 19, 129). For example, one investigator (197) found that the same-sex parents of gifted achieving children had significantly lower conformity and higher independence scores themselves than did the same-sex parents of nonachieving gifted children. In a study of children who grew up during the Depression, girls from families that had to cope with moderate to severe economic deprivation achieved more effective adjustments as adults than did boys (75). The fact that in many of these studies the correlations between parental behaviors and adolescent independence, achievement orientation, and self-reliance were stronger for girls than for boys suggests that models of parental independence are far more crucial for girls in our society, and also that a greater and more clearly defined effort to foster independence is necessary in girls if traditional, societal, and familial influences are to be mitigated. The nature of these associations may change in future studies, reflecting current societal changes.

What appears most clear is that excessive sex-role stereotyping tends to limit the potential development of individual members of both sexes (23, 24, 67, 133, 213, 232). Neither the "supermale"—aggressive, but lacking nurturance and interpersonal sensitivity—nor the supposedly fragile and delicate female—lacking instrumental independence and self-reliance, and forced to rely on a manipulative, subtly controlling "aggressive dependency"—is well prepared for the demands of rapidly changing society or capable of sustaining mature, mutually supportive, but growth-encouraging heterosexual relationships. Furthermore, among both males and females, those who are most likely to be creative are those who combine, within their own personalities, traits traditionally stereotyped as masculine (e.g., autonomy) and feminine (e.g., sensitivity) (12, 67, 133, 243). They may also achieve more mature levels of moral development (34). These results suggest that rigid sex-role stereotyping is dysfunctional for our society (213). The ultimate aim of any process of socialization should be, in our view, to permit each adolescent to develop his or her *unique* potential as a human being, consistent with the rights of others.

## PARENTAL STRESS AND ATTITUDES TOWARD ADOLESCENT AUTONOMY

As we have noted, there are likely to be contradictions in attitudes toward adolescent autonomy not only between various agents of the adult culture but also within the individual parent. It is the second type of contradiction that is likely to be most difficult for the adolescent to cope with because of its elusiveness. When one voice of the culture, such as the church, issues a particular set of directives for adolescent behavior, and another voice, such as the peer group, issues another, the adolescent may be in conflict, and may be forced to choose between them. But at least in this situation the young person has clear recognition of the attitudes with which he or she is dealing. However, when a father proclaims that he wants his own son to be independent but covertly does everything he can to prolong dependency, the result is likely to be confusing for the adolescent. The son's position becomes similar to Alice in her encounter with the Mad Hatter—nothing is quite what it seems. Because of the difficulty of identifying and labeling parental attitudes correctly, he may find it virtually impossible to deal with them rationally.

Parental inconsistencies with regard to emancipation may simply reflect confusion on the part of parents as to the roles society expects them to play (53, 190). In a society that is changing as rapidly as ours and that is as deeply divided internally, this is seldom a simple matter. (When *should* a parent permit a child to go out alone on dates—and with whom; to go to parties where adults may be absent and alcohol and marijuana may be present; to have his or her own spending money, and how much; to drive a car—where and when; to make his or her own decisions?) As we have observed, many of these matters were and are simpler in traditional societies characterized by the continued presence of extended family and neighborhood ties. In such communities, fundamental values and social customs have tended to be more firmly held and widely shared among both adults and adolescents (53). Therefore, where the parent's confusion stems primarily from such rational concerns, the problems involved are more easily resolved.

Frequently, however, parents' inconsistencies may stem from their own contradictory needs—needs that are deeply rooted and frequently unconscious. Many parents genuinely want their children to become able to handle their own affairs because they realize that ultimately this will be necessary. But, at the same time, they are likely to want to continue to protect their children from the unpleasant realities of existence—an impossible task. There are, of course, many other possible sources of a parent's inconsistencies, including his or her own emotional problems and conflicts, particularly at this critical period in the life cycle.

### Parental stress in the adolescent years

Much is made these days of adolescent identity problems. But adults, too, may have their own identity crises, and for a majority most crises are likely to occur during the period when their children are coming to maturity. Indeed, as one observer has noted, one reason that the adolescent years are more likely to be difficult ones for the family "is that everyone concerned is apt to be at a 'dangerous stage' in his or her development" (48).

The average parental marriage is most likely to be at midstage when the children are adolescents. At this juncture in the life of the average family of today, the wife is about 40 years of age, and her husband is about 2 years older. They have been married for approximately 20 years. They have three children, the oldest a little over 18, and the youngest about 12 (48, 89). In about 6 more years, the youngest child will leave home, and the parents, after some 25 years devoted to child-rearing, can anticipate almost that many more years without children (48). It is easy to see how this might be a difficult "developmental stage" for parents, entirely apart from the problems of child-rearing per se. For both husband and wife, it is likely to be a time of reappraisal. In the case of the husband, whatever dreams he may have had of vocational or social glory either have usually been realized by age 42 or shortly thereafter, or are not likely ever to be realized. If he has not been successful in his own eyes or others' eyes or if his job security is threatened, he will be only too well aware of the difficulties involved in obtaining or changing employment in the "over-forty" group. A number of studies indicate that this is likely to be a period of occupational restlessness, when a man may wonder if he has chosen the wrong vocational field, either in terms of personal fulfillment or economic opportunity (48, 158, 256).

Similarly, the wife, who may have suppressed other life goals through her involvement in child-rearing, or worse, who may have used her relationship with her children as a compensation for other disappointments, must face the fact her children will soon be gone. What will she do then; indeed, *who* will she be then? A number of studies have indicated that bright, educated women who have followed the typical homemaker lifestyle have greater difficulty during their middle years in adjusting to the prospective and actual loss of children than those who have combined marriage and career. This tends to be especially true of those noncareer women who have built their lives around "muting of self-assertion" (31, 4) and a relatively single-minded preoccupation with child-rearing, to the exclusion of outside interests and activities (32, 93, 94, 129, 240).

Furthermore, both parents are likely to become increasingly aware of the fact that they have passed the height of their physical prime, and that the rest of the road slopes downhill, however gently at first. In a society as obsessed with youthfulness as our own, where old people may be ignored, condescended to, or treated as useless; where, instead of sitting in a position of honor in the family council, surrounded by children and grandchildren, they may be distant from families and loved ones, the prospect can be chilling for many, especially the poor. Parents' growing awareness of physical and mental aging is likely to be heightened by the obvious contrasts between themselves and their adolescent young, who are just now beginning to approach the height of their physical, sexual, and mental capabilities.

None of these problems of adjustment is made easier by the sexual revolution that accompanied the explosion of the youth population (the products of the 1947 to 1958 baby boom) with its strong emphasis throughout society on sexual adequacy and sexual expression (48). Significant numbers of middle-aged adults, particularly women who may only recently have rediscovered their "sexual birthright," may feel that precious years have been wasted, and that time is running out (43, 48, 76, 159).

For all these reasons, there is typically a substantial decrease in marital satisfaction during the child-rearing years (38, 44, 48, 99, 211, 225). In view of such potential stresses, it is not surprising that significant numbers of parents may demonstrate greater inconsistencies in their attitudes toward their sons' and daughters' growing autonomy than might otherwise be the case (4, 5, 76). A father with strong needs to be all-powerful and all-wise in the eyes of others may in reality have gained little recognition from the world at large. As a result, he may be unwilling to foster autonomy in his child because the inevitable corollary of autonomy is a renunciation of the idea that anyone, including one's parent, is always right and can be trusted to run one's life adequately (5, 190).

Similarly, both mothers and fathers who feel unloved by their marriage partners or their friends may be reluctant to see their children begin leading their own lives. For they know, either with or without conscious awareness, that another of the inevitable consequences of autonomy is a shift in primary affectional goals from parents to other important life figures. Allowing a child to achieve emancipation "will be difficult in proportion as the parent has achieved satisfaction, knowingly or not, for his own wants by loving and controlling his child. If the child is providing gratification and compensation for frustrations arising elsewhere, he will be surrendered reluctantly, surrendered at a cost, or not surrendered at all" (176, *252*).

The parent who possesses secret needs for sexual delinquency may project these desires onto the child, and then become fearful of what the child may do if left to his or her own devices. As a result, the parent may become unduly repressive in controlling the child's activities (4, 76). Some parents, while consciously desiring that their children lead happy and rewarding lives, keep them tied to their apron strings through jealousy. Unconsciously, they do not want their children to enjoy good times that they themselves have missed or would like to have again (76). Such problems are likely to be magnified in today's social climate, when many young people are, in fact, more free of social, sexual, academic, vocational, and economic constraints than their parents were at the same ages. Nor, as we have already noted, is the problem ameliorated by the nation's obsession with youth.

It may appear that a bleak picture of potential parental stress has been painted. Clearly, there is another side as well. For one thing, various studies indicate that for the vast majority of parents whose marriages survive this period, there is an increase in marital satisfaction after the children leave home (48, 51). This is particularly likely after the arrival of grandchildren. More importantly, there are wide individual differences in the extent to which these years are viewed as threatening. For many parents who have lived full lives up to this point and who have been reasonably successful vocationally, socially, in their marriage, and as parents, the compensations of greater security, other interests, and continuing contact with—and pleasure in—their children outweigh the disadvantages. Erik Erikson observes that whereas the stage of young adulthood centrally involves "the search for intimacy," the proper concern of a psychologically minded, mature adult of middle age involves making the transition to what he calls "generativity" (78):

> Evolution has made man a teaching as well as a learning animal, for dependency and maturity are reciprocal: mature man needs to be needed, and maturity is guided by the nature of that which must be cared for. Generativity, then, is primarily the concern for establishing and guiding the next generation. There are, of course, people who, from misfortune or because of special and genuine gifts in other directions, do not apply this drive to offspring of their own, but to other forms of altruistic concern and creativity which (for) many absorb their kind of parental drives. And indeed, the concept of generativity is meant to include productivity and creativity, neither of which, however, can replace it as designations of a crisis in development. For the ability to lose oneself in the meeting of bodies and minds leads to a gradual expansion of ego-interests and to a libidinal investment in that which is being generated [78, *138*].

The middle-aged adult who can gain satisfaction from using experience, resources, security, and a position in society and in the family—in short, his or her *maturity*—in caring for others (whether his or her own adolescent young, his or her parents, or those of any age in the larger society that are often in need of care) has perhaps the best insurance against the approaching fall and winter of life. However, even the fortunate father and mother who have achieved the maturity of generativity—meeting their own needs through an increasing concern for others, including their own adolescent young—are not likely to be free of all conflict regarding the prospects of their children's increasing autonomy. Perhaps the most common source of parental ambivalence toward the child's development of autonomy is the realization that the child must some day stand on his or her own feet and the coexistent fear that in learning to do so he or she will be deeply hurt. A great many of these fears, however, are unfounded.

Children will, of course, make mistakes; and they may even be hurt. This is unfortunate. But the chances of their being seriously harmed seem smaller if they are allowed to learn autonomous responses gradually, while they are still able to turn to their parents for needed support, than if they are suddenly thrust out into the world at the age of 21, totally unprepared to act independently.

The kinds of conflicts to which middle-aged parents are exposed during their children's adolescent years and the ways in which they cope with them can profoundly affect their children's chances of mastering the developmental tasks of adolescence successfully and without undue difficulty—whether the task involves the development of autonomy, heterosexual adjustment, vocational choice, or even the development of a sense of identity.

## PARENT-CHILD RELATIONSHIPS AND IDENTITY FORMATION

The ease with which adolescents are able to achieve a clear sense of identity depends on many factors, including the kinds of previous identifications they have developed and their ability to integrate these identifications with their newfound sexual maturity, the aptitudes and skills they have developed out of their ability and experience, and the opportunities provided by changing social roles (77, 190). Perhaps most critically, however, it depends on the kinds of relationships they have had and continue to have with their parents (190). Establishing a strong sense of identity will be facilitated if a sufficiently rewarding, interactive relationship exists between the child or adolescent and *both* parents, and if both parents provide models of competent problem-solving behavior, a confident sense of their own identity, including gender identity, and mutually supportive relationships with one another (34, 35, 55, 130, 166). Within this general framework, the model provided by the same-sex parent, and the degree of approval and acceptance of this model by the opposite-sex parent, may play an important role (78, 109, 129, 130, 189).

Under such circumstances, the adolescent or young adult will be likely to have a favorable and clearly defined perception of himself or herself, and will also be less likely to encounter conflicts between self-perceptions and both the internal demands of approaching sexual maturity and the external demands of society. Consistent with this reasoning, it has been shown that nurturance and warmth on the part of the same-sex parent facilitate the development of a clearer, more consistent sense of their personal identity—as individuals and as members of their own sex—among both boys and girls (117, 123, 191). Furthermore, it has been found that the adolescent boy's sense of identity is likely to be stronger when both parents are similar in their behavior toward him, when the father is seen as strong but affectionate and exercises moderate controls, and when the mother supports the boy's identification with the father, while herself avoiding an intrusive, demanding kind of orientation to the boy (165, 203, 211).

Similarly, among adolescent girls, a strong sense of identity is facilitated by having a mother who serves as a nurturant, personally effective role model with whom the girl can identify, as well as a father who is an effective person, who is affectionate, attentive, and supportive of his daughter's development as an individual in her own right, and who manifests approval of the girl's mother as a marriage partner and as a desirable role model for her daughter (68, 117, 123).

As both of these sets of findings suggest, the development of a sense of identity—including sexual identity—is influenced by the kinds of role models that both parents provide, as well as the kinds of relationships that they have with one another. When relationships between the parents are distorted or conflict-ridden, the task that the young person faces in identity formation becomes more difficult (34). Domination of one parent by the other, mutual hostility, inadequacy in either parent, or parental role reversals that emphasize the most negative aspects of sex-role stereotypes of both sexes, all increase the difficulty of adolescent identity development (34, 56, 123, 243).

### Sex typing and sexual identity

As we have already noted (see page 85), appropriate behavior as a man or woman need not involve rigid conformity to sex-role stereotypes. Furthermore, identification with the same-sex parent and with the model he or she provides need not imply the adoption of traditional or exaggerated sex-role stereotypes. From the point of view of the development of a relatively conflict-free *sexual identity* (as distinguished from sex-role stereotypes), the outward forms that role behavior takes are less important than the kind of parental identification on which it is at least in part based and whether, despite cultural variations, one's role behavior is consistent with one's basic biological nature as a girl or boy.

For example, the girl who is identified with a traditionally very feminine mother *and* the girl who is identified with a socially assertive, intellectual, highly independent mother may both achieve a relatively conflict-free adjustment and a strong sense of ego identity, even though the latter girl may score low on a stereotyped measure of femininity. On the other hand, a girl whose sex-role behavior is based on rejection of a nonnurturant mother (regardless of whether the mother is "traditional" or "modern"), or on identification with a mother who rejects her basic biological identity (e.g., resents her sexual nature or her childbearing capability, or who is hostile to her own or the opposite sex), will have difficulty in establishing a stable, secure sense of identity (34, 56, 68). Fathers who are uninvolved, ineffectual, or hostile can also make the development of a secure sense of identity more difficult, as well as fostering problems in forming long-lasting heterosexual relationships (27, 28, 30, 100, 101, 165). Sexual responsiveness and positive attitudes toward marriage and child-rearing have been found to be related in women to having had a warm, supportive father (82, 123, 141). Among boys, having a passive, ineffective father and a dominant, intrusive mother is especially likely to be destructive to identity development, including the development of a confident sense of a masculine sexual identity (34).

### Parent-child relationships and identity status

Identity status (see pages 80–84), and changes in status, have been found to vary with degree of independence from the family and overall level of cultural sophistication (78, 254, 262, 263, 264). In one series of studies (262, 263, 264), incoming college freshmen were categorized (where possible) on the basis of intensive structured interviews into one of four initial categories: (1) *identity achievement* (an individual who has been through a period of crisis and has apparently developed relatively firm commitments); (2) *moratorium* (a person who "is currently in a state of crisis and is actively seeking among alternatives in an attempt to arrive at a choice" [263, 167]); (3) *identity foreclosure* (a person who has not experienced an identity crisis, but nevertheless is committed in his or her goals and beliefs apparently largely as a result of parental influences); and (4) *identity diffusion* (an individual who is not committed to anything and who does not appear to be actively trying to make a commitment) (78, 163, 164, 202, 254).

When these same students were reevaluated in the spring of their freshman year, about half were found to have changed their identity status in some fashion. This was true even of a substantial number of students initially placed in the identity achievement category, suggesting that apparently stable resolutions of identity conflicts at the high school or beginning college level may be deceptive. However, when these subjects were recently studied again at the end of the senior year (262), much more stability was evident. Those who had reached identity achievement by the end of the freshman year (11 percent) maintained that status throughout college and were joined by others, so that by the end of senior year, approximately 45 percent of students had reached identity achievement status. Few students were still in the moratorium group, and about one in five had settled on life goals and beliefs without experiencing an identity crisis (identity foreclosure group). Unhappily, however, about one-third remained in a state of identity diffusion, virtually the same number as at the end of freshman year (262).

What is perhaps most interesting, however, in the findings of this investigation are factors associated with one or another identity status category and the usefulness of these factors in predicting a student's likelihood of changing status during the freshman year. Thus, for example, when these subjects were tested independently on measures of family independence and cultural sophistication (211), it was found that students initially classified in the identity achievement category scored relatively high on both family independence and cultural sophistication; in contrast, foreclosure students scored relatively low on these variables. It was further found that subjects most likely to change status during the course of the year "have scores on personality scales inconsistent with the scores usually associated with their particular identity status" (263, *173*). Thus, among subjects initially characterized as identity achievers, those who scored *lower* on family independence and cultural sophistication were most likely to change status; conversely, among foreclosure subjects, those scoring *higher* on these variables were most likely to change (263).

In other studies (165, 168), parent-child relationships appeared related to identity status among youth. Thus, among males, those with *identity achievement* status were most likely to have had fathers who were masculine, spent a lot of time interacting with their sons, praised their sons' efforts, and exerted only moderate control over them (155, 165). In contrast, the families of youth whose identities appeared prematurely *foreclosed* tended to be accepting and protective, but to exert considerable pressure for conformity to family values. Fathers in this group appeared to dominate their sons, but not to encourage emotional expression (168). *Moratorium* sons appeared to have more ambivalent relations with their parents than those in either of the first two groups and, in particular, appeared to be struggling to free themselves from maternal domination; they were also more likely to see their parents as disapproving or disappointed in them (165). Of all the four identity categories among males, *identity diffusion* youth were most likely to see themselves as experiencing rejection and/or detachment, particularly on the part of their fathers (165).

Among female youth, the picture differs somewhat. *Identity achievement* college women appeared in one study (185) to have reestablished ties with non-possessive mothers, after having in effect been pushed out of the nest; while close to their mothers, they were also very aware of the differences between them. *Foreclosure* females, like their male counterparts, seemed to come from close, child-centered, conformity-encouraging families. *Moratorium* females appeared to be "the most critical of their mothers and saw themselves as least like them" (165, *177*), but still felt affection for their mothers. In contrast, young women characterized by *identity diffusion* generally felt so distant from their mothers that no rapprochement seemed possible. Of all groups, the identity diffusion group emerged as most confused about their sexual identity, and preoccupied with infantile fantasies (144). As adults, they "see their mothers as nonemulatable or discouraging and their fathers as idealized but unobtainable. In the company of inadequate husbands and boyfriends, they dream of Prince Charmings. Extremely afraid of being hurt or betrayed, any consistent 'identity' is a negative one" (165, *177–178*).

*Identity achievement* youth of both sexes rank high in self-esteem, resistance to stress, and capacity for expressing affection, but relatively low in hostility, emotional distress, and either submission or exaggerated domination (66, 165). Young women who have reached identity achievement status "have weighed occupational and ideological alternatives and have arrived at conclusions to which they appear committed, yielded least of the statuses to conformity pressures, and were also less uncomfortable in resisting them" (254, *292*). They also manifested the fewest negative feelings (along with identity foreclosure subjects), and they tended to choose more difficult college majors (165). Women without a firm identity status (identity diffusion subjects) conformed most and showed the greatest amount of negative feelings (i.e., anxiety, hostility, and depression (165, 254).

## ONE-PARENT FAMILIES

Thus far we have been discussing the effects of parental influences in the intact family setting. However, as we saw in the previous chapter, one-parent families are becoming increasingly frequent: currently one out of every five children under 18 years of age is living in a one-parent family—in 90 percent of cases the mother. What then do we know about the effects of father absence?

### Effects of father absence on boys

Boys are more likely than girls to live with both parents (90). In addition, of children living with only one parent, boys are more likely than girls to be living with their fathers (90). Nevertheless, the majority of boys with one parent are likely to live with their mothers. Boys from father-absent homes are more likely than boys from father-present homes to encounter difficulties in social, emotional, and cognitive development. They are more likely to score lower on tests of intellectual performance (28, 29, 33, 64, 142) and academic aptitude (29, 236) and to perform below grade level on measures of academic achievement (33, 64, 65). Interestingly, the patterning of their intellectual performance also differs significantly from that of father-present boys and is more similar to that of girls. For example, father-absent adolescent boys are more likely to obtain higher scores in verbal ability than in mathematics, in contrast to the usual male pattern of higher mathematics scores (45). The longer the absence of the father, and the earlier the age at which the separation took place, the greater is the likelihood of "feminine" patterning. Father-absent adolescent boys are also more likely to display a global (or field-dependent) conceptual style, usually more characteristic of girls, as opposed to an analytical (field-independent) style (10, 29, 47, 252). Similar results have been obtained for boys whose fathers are present in the home, but who are ineffective, passive, neglecting, or rejecting (27, 28, 29, 45). Paternal hostility and rejection are found far more frequently among academically underachieving boys than among those with warm, supportive fathers who display an active interest and involvement with their sons (28, 126).

On the other hand, the presence of a supportive stepfather may help to remedy the effects of the loss of the father due to death or divorce. A recent study of the cognitive performance of college students (47) has shown that father-absent college males with stepfathers have a more analytical, field-independent cognitive style and score higher on the Scholastic Aptitude Test (SAT) than father-absent males without stepfathers. However, they are less analytical and score lower on the SAT than students from two-parent homes.

In brief, it appears that having a father present in the home who serves as a competent, effective role model, and who expresses interest in his son and interacts with him, facilitates the development of intellectual potential and influences its development in a "masculine" direction. In contrast, not having a father, or having one who is ineffective or distant from the child, is likely to handicap the boy in cognitive development. Obviously, the presence or absence of the father is not the only factor influencing this development, and much of the father-absent boy's ultimate success or failure will depend on the qualities of the mother as the remaining parent.

Adolescent boys from father-absent homes are also more likely than those from father-present homes to have emotional and social problems. They are more likely to be impulsive and to have difficulty in delaying gratification and assuming social responsibility (29, 179, 180, 181, 182). It has been suggested that fathers are more likely than mothers in our society to represent such values as discipline, order, and punctuality. Further, mothers whose husbands are absent may be more indulgent and overprotective toward their sons than would otherwise be the case (28, 29, 253). Father-absent boys are also generally more immature psychologically, have more difficulty in forming satisfying peer relations, and are less popular with their peers (20, 27, 29, 30, 184, 250, 253). Boys in single-parent homes are also more likely to have a lower self-concept than girls in such a situation or adolescents from two-parent homes (223).

Finally, boys from father-absent homes are significantly more likely than other boys to drop out of school and to become involved in delinquent activities (3, 28, 40, 92, 103, 170). One study showed a significantly higher than average rate of delinquency among boys living with their mothers following the loss of the father through death, parental separation, or divorce (102). When the boy lived with his father following the loss of the mother, however, only an average rate of delinquency was found. In an effort to explain the relation of delinquency to father absence among boys, a number of investigators have concluded "that the exaggerated toughness, aggressiveness, and cruelty of delinquent gangs reflects the desperate effort of males in lower-class culture to rebel against their early overprotective, feminizing environment and to find a masculine identity" (40, *915*).

The age of separation from father also appears to be important. One investigator (116) found that both early-separated (age 4 or earlier) black and white preadolescent boys and late-separated boys (after age 6) were more dependent on their peers and somewhat less dependent on adults than were boys whose fathers lived at home. But only early-separated boys differed significantly from father-present boys on a number of measures of sex typing. The former had lower scores in masculine aggressiveness, masculine sex-role preference, and involvement in competitive physical contact games. The results of this study suggest that boys who lose their fathers early, before identification can be assumed to have been clearly established, have greater difficulty in establishing a masculine identification, whereas absence of the father after the child reaches age 5 has far less effect.

### Effects of father absence on girls

The effects of father absence on girls have not been studied as extensively as in the case of boys. Available research data suggest that girls from father-absent homes have higher than average dependency on their mothers (161), especially if the girl has only older sisters as siblings, rather than brothers (28, 29). These girls are also more likely to have emotional problems, to encounter school maladjustment, and to engage in antisocial "acting-out" behavior (108, 223). In contrast, Mexican-American girls from one-parent families were not different from those in two-parent families in terms of egocentrism or antisocial behavior (46). Father absence during the first 10 years of life is associated with deficits in quantitative ability, a finding that appears to parallel the findings for boys in the area of cognitive development (153).

**TABLE 7.4 MEANS FOR DAUGHTER INTERVIEW MEASURES**

| | FATHER ABSENT | | FATHER PRESENT | F | P |
| INTERVIEW VARIABLE | DIVORCED | DEATH | | | |
| --- | --- | --- | --- | --- | --- |
| Security around male peers | 2.71 | 2.62 | 3.79 | 4.79 | .01 |
| Security around male adults | 2.12 | 2.12 | 3.66 | 11.25 | .001 |
| Heterosexual activity | 4.83 | 2.62 | 3.83 | 12.96 | .001 |
| Conflict with mothers | 5.08 | 3.63 | 4.08 | 5.64 | .005 |
| Positive attitude toward father | 3.08 | 4.66 | 4.21 | 7.57 | .001 |
| Father's warmth | 3.33 | 4.50 | 3.87 | 2.82 | .06 |
| Father's competence | 3.16 | 4.75 | 4.12 | 6.65 | .002 |
| Conflict with father | 4.43 | 2.25 | 3.46 | 7.03 | .002 |
| Relations with other adult males | 3.29 | 3.12 | 4.54 | 5.08 | .009 |
| Self-esteem | 2.87 | 3.58 | 4.04 | 3.34 | .04 |

Source: E. M. Hetherington. Effects of father absence on personality development in adolescent daughters. Reprinted from *Developmental Psychology*, 1972, **7**, 313–326. Copyright © 1972 by the American Psychological Association. Reprinted by permission.

Note: All row means which do not share a common subscript differ at least a $p < .05$ with two-tailed *t* tests.

Father-absent girls are also more dependent as adults, but they show little apparent deviation from other women in sex-typed behaviors, in preference for the female role, or in relationships with other females (118). As adolescents they do, however, show anxiety about and difficulty in relating to males. However, the kinds of problems, and the ways in which they are manifested, differ for girls who have lost their fathers through death and those who have been separated by divorce. E. Mavis Hetherington, a psychologist at the University of Virginia, studied three groups of adolescent girls in a neighborhood recreation center: father-present girls, girls whose fathers had died, and girls whose fathers had left the home due to divorce. Using a variety of observational measures, psychological tests, and interviews, she found that daughters of widows tended to be shy and withdrawn, to become physically tense, and to avoid close proximity to male peers and adults. They also tended to start to date later than other girls and to be sexually inhibited.

In contrast, daughters of divorcées, while also anxious (as evidenced by such behaviors in the presence of males as nail biting and hair pulling), tended to seek out male peers constantly at the expense of activities with other females. They were also more likely than father-present girls to begin to date earlier and to have sexual intercourse at earlier ages (118, 193). As may be seen from Table 7.4, both groups of father-absent girls felt less secure around male peers and adults than did father-present girls. But although girls whose parents were divorced revealed more conflict with their mothers than did father-present girls, those whose fathers had died showed less maternal conflict. Girls whose fathers were absent due to death also had the most positive views about the father's warmth and competence, and reported having had less conflict with him. Father-present girls felt most confident about relations with other adult males, and they tended to have the highest level of self-esteem (118). As in the case of boys, the effects of separation from fathers during early childhood were more marked than effects of later separation. Apparently, for father-absent girls, "lack of opportunity for constructive interaction with a loving attentive father has resulted in apprehension and inadequate skills in relating to males" (118, *324*).

In a related study of adolescent girls living in a lower-income environment (193), girls whose fathers were absent due to divorce were found to engage in more precocious dating behavior and to display greater sexual knowledge than otherwise similar girls from father-present homes. A recent investigation of middle-class, urban college women (105) found that daughters of widows, particularly those who were widowed early, were more likely to be disapproving of sexual intercourse, even in a love relationship, than either daughters of divorcées or father-present subjects. As in Hetherington's study, these father-absent young women appeared similar to those with fathers present in sex-typed behaviors and in attitudes toward their mothers and toward femininity. In other respects, however, fewer differences emerged between father-present women and father-absent women (either through divorce or death) than in Hetherington's study. For example, there was little evidence in any of these groups of subjects of the kind of tension and anxiety in the presence of males found in Hetherington's study—suggesting, perhaps, that increased age and experience may lessen the effects of father absence found in younger adolescent girls.

In general, it appears that a girl's acquisition of feminine behavior and of the specific skills involved in interacting with males is at least partly based on learning experiences and reinforcements received in interaction with the father (117, 118, 191). It should be emphasized, however, that having a father present is not likely to be beneficial if the father is inadequate, passive, neglectful, or harsh and rejecting. Paternal rejection, for example, is associated with deficits in adolescent girls' cognitive and academic functioning. Even if a father is highly nurturant, he can inhibit his daughter's cognitive and psychological development if he reinforces such "feminine" stereotypes as dependence, timidity, and conformity (28, 47).

On the other hand, a father who is nurturant and caring, and who also praises and rewards intellectual and creative efforts on the part of his daughter may facilitate both her personal and cognitive development (28). Such a father clearly serves as an effective role model; equally important, however, he is demonstrating by his behavior and expectations that he (as a male) does not view independent-mindedness, creativity, and intellectual accomplishment as inconsistent with successful feminine development, including heterosexual development. A number of studies "indicate that high paternal expectations in the context of a warm father-daughter relationship are conducive to the development of autonomy, independence, achievement, and creativity among girls" (28, *139*). The effects of father absence appear stronger and more pervasive in the case of boys than in the case of girls, possibly due partly to the fact that father-absent girls still have a same-sex identification figure in the home, whereas father-absent boys do not. All of these effects may change along with the changing patterns in our society. One recent study (249) found no difference in sex-role identity or self-concept among adolescent girls from mother-absent, father-absent, or intact families. There was some evidence of diminished identification with the mother in father-absent families, but no other effects on parental identification.

It should be stressed at this point that the effects of absence of either parent are by no means either universal or inevitable. Much depends on the psychological strengths, interest, talents, and skills of the remaining parent. An intensive investigation of adults whose fathers had died when they were children concluded that the mother's ego strengths were a major determinant of her child's subsequent adjustment as an adult (125). Mothers who were able to assume some of the roles of both mother and father with little conflict about their basic feminine identity were able to deal constructively with the problem of running a fatherless family. As Henry Biller, an expert on parental deprivation, emphasizes, "the mother's ego strength rather than her warmth or tenderness seemed to be the essential variable in her child's adjustment. If a child is paternally deprived, excessive maternal warmth and affection may be particularly detrimental to his personality development. A close-binding, overprotective relationship can severely hamper his opportunities for interpersonal growth" (28, *100*).

A mother can also foster her father-absent son's sex-role development by showing a positive attitude toward the absent father and males in general, and by consistently encouraging competency and independence in her son. Father-absent young boys whose mothers accepted and reinforced assertive, aggressive, and independent behavior were more confidently masculine (as measured by game preferences and peer interactions) than father-absent boys whose mothers disapproved of such behavior (26).

Furthermore, the remaining parent may be able to help to compensate for the other parent's absence by finding parent surrogates (as in the case of Big Brothers, Brownies, Boy and Girl Scouts, YMCA and YWCA, athletic teams, camps, and so on). In the case of young children, group settings, such as day-care centers, may sometimes be able to provide father surrogates (28). Several studies have indicated that use of father surrogates where the father is absent, ineffective, or antisocial may help to reduce the incidence of delinquent behavior in boys (28, 29, 92). Continued presence of either parent in the home will do little to help and may, in fact, serve only to hinder the child's development if the parent is inadequate, rejecting, neglectful, or emotionally disturbed, or if there is extreme tension and conflict between the parents.

There are few systematic studies at this point on the effects of mother absence, though studies may appear increasingly in the future, with current increases in father custody. Because of this dearth, it is difficult to determine the extent to which some of the findings in father-absent studies are due to single as opposed to double parenting, rather than to father absence as such (120). One study suggested that the presence of a second adult in the home may play a protective role in reducing psychological, social, and other risks to the child's development (149). In this study, involving a mainly lower-income black community, it was found that adolescents from mother-grandmother families did as well as those from mother-father families in terms of school achievement, mental health status, and other indicators of successful adjustment. Youth from mother-alone families consistently showed the poorest adjustment. Few studies have included the variety of adults in the family setting that this one did—89 distinct combinations of adults were identified! But there does appear to be a trend for more recent studies to focus on the number of parents in the home rather than simply on the gender of the missing parent (46, 120, 149, 222, 223).

As described in this and the preceding chapter, there are many kinds of families in our present society. We know all too little about the effects on adolescent development of joint custody, reconstituted families, or other arrangements. The variety of kinds of families demands that we give thought to the aspects of parenting that are likely to be most important. How important is the frequency or duration of time spent with children? Or the regularity of contact? What qualities of interaction are important? Our focus on "intactness" has obscured the importance of those issues that differentiate families, whether or not both parents live with the adolescent. These are questions, however, that are now being asked by the many parents who are trying to continue to be effective parents while not living continually with their children.

### REFERENCES

1. Adams, B. *Kinship in an urban setting.* Chicago: Markham Publishing Co., 1968.
2. Alexander, J. F. Defensive and supportive communications in normal and deviant families. *Journal of Consulting and Clinical Psychology,* 1973, **40,** 223–231.
3. Anderson, R. E. Where's Dad? Paternal deprivation and delinquency. *Archives of General Psychiatry,* 1968, **18,** 641–649.
4. Anthony, E. J. The reaction of parents to adolescents and to their behavior. In E. J. Anthony & T. Benedek (eds.), *Parenthood: Its psychology and psychopathology.* Boston: Little, Brown, 1970. Pp. 307–324.
5. Anthony, E. J., & Benedek, T. *Parenthood: Its psychology and psychopathology.* Boston: Little, Brown, 1970.
6. Bachman, J. G. *Youth in transition, Vol. II: The impact of family background and intelligence on tenth-grade boys.* Ann Arbor: Institute for Social Research, University of Michigan, 1970.
7. Bachman, J. G., O'Malley, P. M., & Johnston, J. *Adolescence to adulthood: Change and stability in the lives of young men.* Ann Arbor, Mich.: Institute for Social Research, University of Michigan, 1978.
8. Baittle, B., & Offer, D. On the nature of adolescent rebellion. In S. C. Feinstein, P. Giovacchini, & A. Miller (eds.), *Annals of adolescent psychiatry* (Vol. 1). New York: Basic Books, 1971.
9. Bane, M. J. *Here to stay: American families in the twentieth century.* New York: Basic Books, 1977.
10. Barclay, A. G., & Cusumano, D. Father-absence, cross-sex identity, and field-dependent behavior in male adolescents. *Child Development,* 1967, **38,** 243–250.
11. Bardwick, J. *Psychology of women: A study of bio-cultural conflicts.* New York: Harper & Row, 1971.
12. Barron, F. X. *Creative person and creative process.* New York: Holt, Rinehart and Winston, 1969.
13. Barry, H., III, Bacon, M. K., & Child, I. L. Cultural survey of some sex differences in socialization. *Journal of Abnormal and Social Psychology,* 1957, **3,** 327–332.
14. Baruch, G. K. Maternal influences upon college women's attitudes toward women and work. *Developmental Psychology,* 1972, **6,** 32–37.
15. Baumrind, D. Effects of authoritative control on child behavior. *Child Development,* 1966, **37,** 887–907.
16. Baumrind, D. Child care practices anteceding three patterns of preschool behavior. *Genetic Psychology Monographs,* 1967, **75,** 43–83.
17. Baumrind, D. Authoritarian vs. authoritative control. *Adolescence,* 1968, **3,** 255–272.
18. Baumrind, D. Current patterns of parental authority. *Developmental Psychology Monographs,* 1971, **4,** No. 1, Part 2.

19. Baumrind, D. Early socialization and adolescent competence. In S. E. Dragastin and G. H. Elder, Jr. (eds.), *Adolescence in the life cycle.* New York: Wiley, 1975.

20. Beck, A. T., Sehti, B. B., & Tuthill, R. W. Childhood bereavement and adult depression. *Archives of General Psychiatry,* 1963, **9,** 295–302.

21. Becker, W. C. Consequences of different kinds of parental discipline. In M. L. Hoffman & L. W. Hoffman (eds.), *Review of child development* (Vol. I). New York: Russell Sage Foundation, 1964.

22. Bem, S. L. The measurement of psychological androgyny. *Journal of Consulting and Clinical Psychology,* 1974, **42,** 155–162.

23. Bem, S. L. Androgyny vs. the tight little lives of fluffy women and chesty men. *Psychology Today,* September 1975, 58–62.

24. Bem, S. L. Sex role adaptability: One consequence of psychological androgyny. *Journal of Personality and Social Psychology,* 1975, **31,** 634–643.

25. Benedict, R. *Patterns of culture.* Boston: Houghton Mifflin, 1934.

26. Biller, H. B. Father-absence, maternal encouragement, and sex-role development in kindergarten-age boys. *Child Development,* 1969, **40,** 539–546.

27. Biller, H. B. *Father, child, and sex-role.* Lexington, Mass.: Heath, 1971.

28. Biller, H. B. *Paternal deprivation.* Lexington, Mass.: Lexington Books, 1974.

29. Biller, H. B., & Bahm, R. M. Father-absence, perceived maternal behavior, and masculinity of self-concept among junior high school boys. *Developmental Psychology,* 1971, **4,** 178–181.

30. Biller, H. B., & Davids, A. Parent-child relations, personality development, and psychopathology. In A. Davids (ed.), *Issues in abnormal and child psychology.* Monterey, Calif.: Brooks/Cole, 1973. Pp. 48–76.

31. Birnbaum, J. A. Life patterns, personality style and self-esteem in gifted family-oriented and career-committed women. (Unpublished doctoral dissertation. University of Michigan, 1972).

32. Birnbaum, J. A. Life patterns and self-esteem in gifted family oriented and career committed women. In M. T. S. Mednick, S. S. Tangri, & L. W. Hoffman (eds.), *Women and achievement.* Washington, D.C.: Hemisphere, 1975.

33. Blanchard, R. W., & Biller, H. B. Father availability and academic performance among third-grade boys. *Developmental Psychology,* 1971, **4,** 301–305.

34. Block, J. H. Conceptions of sex role: Some cross-cultural and longitudinal perspectives. *American Psychologist,* 1973, **28,** 512–526.

35. Block, J., & Turula, E. Identification, ego control, and adjustment. *Child Development,* 1963, **34,** 945–953.

36. Blos, P. The child analyst looks at the younger adolescent. *Daedalus,* Fall 1971, **100,** 961–978.

37. Blum, R. H. et al. *Horatio Alger's children.* San Francisco: Jossey-Bass, 1972.

38. Bossard, J. H. S., & Bell, E. S. Marital unhappiness in the life cycle. *Marriage and Family Living,* 1955, **17,** 10–14.

39. Boxer, A. M., Solomon, B., Offer, D., Petersen, A. C., & Halprin, F. Parents' perceptions of their young adolescents. In R. Cohen, B. J. Cohler, & S. J. Weissman (eds.), *Parenthood as an adult experience.* New York: Guilford Press, in press.

40. Bronfenbrenner, U. The psychological costs of quality and equality in education. *Child Development,* 1967, **38,** 909–925.

41. Bronfenbrenner, U. *Two worlds of childhood: U.S. and U.S.S.R.* New York: Russell Sage Foundation, 1970.

42. Brown, J. K. Adolescent initiation rites among preliterate people. In R. E. Grinder (ed.), *Studies in adolescence.* New York: Macmillan, 1969 (2nd ed.).

43. Burr, W. R. Satisfaction with various aspects of marriage over the life cycle: A random middle-class sample. *Journal of Marriage and the Family,* 1970, **32,** 29–37.

44. Campbell, A., Converse, P., & Rodgers, W. *The quality of American life: Perceptions, evaluations, and satisfactions.* New York: Russell Sage Foundation, 1976.

45. Carlsmith, L. Effect of early father-absence on scholastic aptitude. *Harvard Educational Review,* 1964, **34,** 3–21.

46. Castellano, V., & Dembo, M. H. The relationship of father absence and antisocial behavior to social egocentrism in adolescent Mexican American females. *Journal of Youth and Adolescence,* 1981, **10,** 77–84.
47. Chapman, M. Father absence, stepfathers, and the cognitive performance of college students. *Child Development,* 1977, **48,** No. 3, 1155–1158.
48. Chilman, C. S. Families in development at mid-stage of the family life cycle. *Family Coordinator,* 1968, **17,** 297–331.
49. Chorost, S. B. Parental child-rearing attitudes and their correlates in adolescent hostility. *Genetic Psychology Monographs,* 1962, **66,** 49–90.
50. Clark, M., & Seligmann, J. Bringing up baby: Is Dr. Spock to blame? *Newsweek,* September 23, 1968, 68–72.
51. Cohler, B. J., & Boxer, A. M. Settling into the world: Person, time and context in the middle-adult years. In D. Offer & M. Sabshin (eds.), *Normality and the life cycle.* New York: Basic Books, in press.
52. Cohler, B. J., & Geyer, S. Autonomy and interdependence in the family. In F. Walsh (ed.), *Normal family processes: Implications for clinical practice.* New York: Guilford Press, in press.
53. Conger, J. J. A world they never knew: The family and social change. *Daedalus,* Fall 1971, 1105–1138.
54. Conger, J. J. A world they never made: Parents and children in the 1970s. Invited address, American Academy of Pediatrics meeting, Denver, April 17, 1975.
55. Conger, J. J. Current issues in adolescent development. Master lectures series, annual meeting of the American Psychological Association, Chicago, August 28, 1975.
56. Conger, J. J. Parent-child relationships, social change and adolescent vulnerability. *Journal of Pediatric Psychology,* 1977, **2,** 93–97.
57. Conger, J. J. Freedom and commitment: Families, youth, and social change. *American Psychologist,* 1981, **36,** 1475–1484.
58. Conger, J. J., & Miller, W. C. *Personality, social class, and delinquency.* New York: Wiley, 1966.
59. Cooper, D. *Death of the family.* New York: Pantheon Books, 1970.
60. Cooper, J. B. Parent evaluation as related to social ideology and academic achievement. *Journal of Genetic Psychology,* 1962, **101,** 135–143.
61. Coopersmith, S. *The antecedents of self-esteem.* San Francisco: Freeman, 1967.
62. Dahlem, N. W. Young Americans' reported perceptions of their parents. *Journal of Psychology,* 1970, **74,** 187–194.
63. De Beauvoir, S. *All said and done.* New York: Warner, 1975.
64. Deutsch, M. Minority group and class status as related to social and personality factors in scholastic achievement. *Monographs in Social and Applied Anthropology,* 1960, **2,** 1–32.
65. Deutsch, M., & Brown, B. Social influences in Negro-white intelligence differences. *Journal of Social Issues,* 1964, **20,** 24–35.
66. Donovan, J. M. Ego identity status and interpersonal style. *Journal of Youth and Adolescence,* 1975, **4,** 37–55.
67. Douvan, E. New sources of conflict at adolescence and early adulthood. In J. M. Bardwick et al. (eds.), *Feminine personality and conflict.* Monterey, Calif.: Brooks/Cole, 1970. Pp. 31–43.
68. Douvan, E. A., & Adelson, J. *The adolescent experience.* New York: Wiley, 1966.
69. Droppleman, L. F., & Schaefer, E. S. Boys' and girls' reports of maternal and paternal behavior. Paper presented at the meeting of the American Psychological Association, New York, August 29, 1961.
70. Elder, G. H., Jr. Structural variations in the child-rearing relationship. *Sociometry,* 1962, **25,** 241–262.
71. Elder, G. H., Jr. Parental power legitimation and its effect on the adolescent. *Sociometry,* 1963, **26,** 50–65.
72. Elder, G. H., Jr. Parent-youth relations in cross-national perspective. *Social Science Quarterly,* 1968, **49,** 216–228.

73. Elder, G. H., Jr. *Adolescent socialization and personality development.* Skokie, Ill.: Rand McNally, 1971.

74. Elder, G. H., Jr. Adult control in family and school: Public opinion in historical and comparative perspective. *Youth and Society,* September 1971, 5–34.

75. Elder, G. Historical change in life patterns and personality. In P. Baltes & O. G. Brim, Jr. (eds.), *Life-span development and behavior* (Vol. II). New York: Academic Press, 1979.

76. English, O. S., & Pearson, G. H. J. *Emotional problems of living.* New York: Norton, 1955.

77. Erikson, E. H. *Childhood and society.* New York: Norton, 1963 (2nd ed.).

78. Erikson, E. H. *Identity: Youth and crisis.* New York: Norton, 1968.

79. Fagot, B. Sex-determined parental reinforcing contingencies in toddler children. Paper presented at the biennial meeting of the Society for Research in Child Development, New Orleans, 1977.

80. Faw, T. T., & Goldsmith, D. F. Interpersonal perceptions within families containing behavior problem adolescents. *Journal of Youth and Adolescence,* 1980, **9,** 553–556.

81. Fischer, J. L. Reciprocity, agreement, and family style in family systems with a disturbed and nondisturbed adolescent. *Journal of Youth and Adolescence,* 1980, **9,** 391–406.

82. Fischer, S. F. *The female orgasm: Psychology, physiology, fantasy.* New York: Basic Books, 1973.

83. Ford, C. W., & Beach, F. A. *Patterns of sexual behavior.* New York: Harper & Row, 1951.

84. Francke, L. B. Children of divorce. *Newsweek,* February 11, 1980, 58–66.

85. Gans, H. *The urban villagers: Group and class in the life of Italian-Americans.* New York: Free Press, 1962.

86. Garbarino, J., & Crouter, A. Defining the community context for parent-child relations: The correlates of child maltreatment. *Child Development,* 1978, **49,** 604–616.

87. Gilligan, C. Woman's place in man's life cycle. *Harvard Educational Review,* 1979, **49,** 431–446.

88. Gitelson, I. The relationship of parenting behavior to adolescents' sex and spatial ability. Presented as a symposium paper at the American Psychological Association Annual Meeting, Montreal, September 1980.

89. Glick, P. C. Demographic analysis of family data. In H. T. Christensen (ed.), *Handbook of marriage and the family.* Skokie, Ill.: Rand McNally, 1964. Pp. 300–334.

90. Glick, P. C. Children from one-parent families: Recent data and projections. Paper presented at the Special Institute on Critical Issues in Education, sponsored by the Charles F. Kettering Foundation, Washington, D.C., June 1981.

91. Glick, P. C., & Norton, A. J. Marrying, divorcing, and living together in the U.S. today. *Population Bulletin,* 1979, **32,** 1–40.

92. Glueck, S., & Glueck, E. T. *Unraveling juvenile delinquency.* New York: Commonwealth Fund, 1950.

93. Gold, D., & Andres, D. Developmental comparisons between ten-year-old children with employed and nonemployed mothers. *Child Development,* 1978a, **49,** 75–84.

94. Gold, D., & Andres, D. Comparisons of adolescent children with employed and nonemployed mothers. *Merrill-Palmer Quarterly,* 1978b, **24,** 242–254.

95. Goldstein, M. J., Baker, B. L., & Jamison, K. R. *Abnormal psychology: Experiences, origins, and interventions.* Boston: Little, Brown, 1980.

96. Goldstein, M. J., & Jones, J. E. Adolescent and familial precursors of borderline and schizophrenic conditions. In *Borderline personality disorders: The concept, the syndrome, the patient.* New York: International Universities Press, 1977.

97. Goldstein, M. J., & Rodnick, E. The family's contribution to the etiology of schizophrenia: Current status. *Schizophrenia Bulletin,* 1975, **14,** 48–63.

98. Goldstein, M. J., Rodnick, E. H., Jones, J. E., McPherson, S. R., & West, K. L. Familial precursors of schizophrenia spectrum disorders. In L. D. Wynne, R. L. Cromwell, & S. Matthysse (eds.), *The nature of schizophrenia.* New York: Wiley, 1978.

99. Gove, W., & Peterson, C. An update of the literature on personal and marital satisfac-

tion: The effect of children and the employment of wives. *Marriage and Family Review,* 1980, **3,** 63–96.

100. Green, R. *Cross-sexed identity in children and adults.* New York: Basic Books, 1973.
101. Green, R. Homosexuality. In H. I. Kaplan, A. M. Freedman, & B. J. Sadock (eds.), *Comprehensive textbook of psychiatry* (Vol. 2). Baltimore: Williams & Wilkins, 1980. Pp. 1762–1770 (3rd ed.).
102. Gregory, I. Studies of parental deprivation in psychiatric patients. *American Journal of Psychiatry,* 1958, **115,** 432–442.
103. Gregory, I. Anterospective data following childhood loss of a parent: I. Delinquency and high school drop out. *Archives of General Psychiatry,* 1965, **13,** 99–109.
104. Gulo, E. V. Attitudes of rural school children toward their parents. *Journal of Educational Research,* 1966, **59,** 450–452.
105. Hainline, L., & Feig, E. The correlates of childhood father absence in college-aged women. *Child Development,* 1978, **49,** No. 2, 37–42.
106. Harevan, T. K. Family time and historical time. In A. S. Rossi, J. Kagan, & T. K. Harevan (eds.), *The Family.* New York: Norton, 1978. Pp. 33–56.
107. Harris, I. D., & Howard, K. I. Phenomenological correlates of perceived quality of parenting: A questionnaire study of high school students. *Journal of Youth and Adolescence,* 1979, **8,** 171–180.
108. Heckel, R. V. The effects of fatherlessness on the preadolescent female. *Mental Hygiene,* 1963, **47,** 69–73.
109. Heilbrun, A. B., Jr., & Fromme, D. K. Parental identification of late adolescents and level of adjustment: The importance of parent-model attributes, ordinal and sex of the child. *Journal of Genetic Psychology,* 1965, **107,** 49–59.
110. Heilbrun, A. B., & Gillard, B. J. Perceived maternal childrearing behavior and motivational effects of social reinforcement in females. *Perceptual and Motor Skills,* 1966, **23,** 439–446.
111. Heilbrun, A. B., Orr, H. K., & Harrell, S. N. Patterns of parental childrearing and subsequent vulnerability to cognitive disturbance. *Journal of Consulting Psychology,* 1966, **36,** 51–59.
112. Heilbrun, C. G. *Toward a recognition of androgyny.* New York: Knopf, 1973.
113. Helfer, R. E., & Kempe, C. H. (eds.). *Child abuse and neglect: The family and the community.* Cambridge, Mass.: Ballinger, 1982.
114. Helson, R. Sex differences in creative style. *Journal of Personality,* 1969, **35,** 214–233.
115. Henggeler, S. W., Borduin, C. M., Rodick, J. D., & Tavormina, J. B. Importance of task content for family interaction research. *Developmental Psychology,* 1979, **15,** 660–661.
116. Hetherington, E. M. Effects of paternal absence on sex-typed behavior in Negro and white preadolescent males. *Journal of Personality and Social Psychology,* 1960, **1,** 87–91.
117. Hetherington, E. M. The effects of familial variables on sex typing, on parent-child similarly and on imitation in children. In J. P. Hill (ed.), *Minnesota symposia on child psychology* (Vol. 1). Minneapolis: University of Minnesota Press, 1967. Pp. 82–107.
118. Hetherington, E. M. Effects of father absence on personality development in adolescent daughters. *Developmental Psychology,* 1972, **7,** 313–326.
119. Hetherington, E. M. Mothers' and fathers' responses to appropriate and inappropriate dependency in sons and daughters. Unpublished manuscript, 1978.
120. Hetherington, E. M. Divorce: A child's perspective. *American Psychologist,* 1979, **34,** 851–858.
121. Hetherington, E. M., Cox, M., & Cox, R. The aftermath of divorce. In J. H. Stevens, Jr., & M. Matthew (eds.), *Mother-child, father-child relations.* Washington, D.C.: National Association for the Education of Young Children, 1978.
122. Hetherington, E. M., Cox, M., & Cox, R. Family interaction and the social, emotional and cognitive development of children following divorce. Johnson and Johnson Conference on the Family, Washington, D.C., May 1978.

123. Hetherington, E. M., & Parke, R. D. *Child psychology: A contemporary viewpoint.* New York: McGraw-Hill, 1979.
124. Hetherington, E. M., Stouwie, R. J., & Redberg, E. H. Patterns of family interaction and child rearing attitudes related to three dimensions of juvenile delinquency. *Journal of Abnormal Psychology,* 1971, **75,** 160–176.
125. Hilgard, J. R., Neuman, M. F., & Fisk, F. Strength of adult ego following bereavement. *American Journal of Orthopsychiatry,* 1960, **30,** 788–798.
126. Hill, J. P. The family. In *Toward adolescence: The middle school years. Seventy-ninth Yearbook of the National Society for the Study of Education.* Chicago: University of Chicago Press, 1980.
127. Hill, J. P., & Steinberg, L. D. The development of autonomy during adolescence. In *Jornadas sobre problemática juventil.* Madrid, Spain: Fundación Faustino Orvegozo Eizaguirra, 1976.
128. Hobbs, N., et al. Report of the Task Panel on Mental Health and American Families: General Issues and Adult Years. In *Task panel reports submitted to the President's Commission on Mental Health* (Vol. 3). Washington, D.C.: U.S. Government Printing Office, 1978.
129. Hoffman, L. W. Effects of maternal employment on the child—A review of the research. *Development Psychology,* 1974, **10,** 204–228.
130. Hoffman, L. W. Changes in family roles, socialization, and sex differences. *American Psychologist,* 1977, **32,** 644–657.
131. Hoffman, L. W. Maternal employment: 1979. *American Psychologist,* 1979, **34,** 859–865.
132. Hoffman, M. L. Power assertion by the parent and its impact upon the child. *Child Development,* 1960, **31,** 129–143.
133. Horner, M. S. Feminity and successful achievement: A basic inconsistency. In J. M. Bardwick et al., *Feminine personality and conflict.* Monterey, Calif.: Brooks/Cole, 1970. Pp. 45–73.
134. Houston, A. Sex typing. In P. H. Mussen (ed.), *Handbook of child psychology* (Vol. 4, *Socialization,* E. M. Hetherington [ed.]). New York: Wiley, in press.
135. Hurley, J. R. Parental malevolence and children's intelligence. *Journal of Consulting Psychology,* 1967, **31,** 199–204.
136. Huston-Stein, A., & Higgens-Trenk, A. Development of females from childhood through adulthood: Career and feminine role orientations. In P. Baltes (ed.), *Life-span development and behavior* (Vol. I). New York: Academic Press, 1978.
137. Jacklin, C. N., DiPietro, J. A., & Maccoby, E. E. Sex-typing behavior and sex-typing pressure in child-parent interaction. *Archives of Sexual Behavior,* in press.
138. Jacob, T. Patterns of family conflict and dominance as a function of age and social class. *Developmental Psychology,* 1974, **10,** 1–12.
139. Jacob, T. Family interaction in disturbed and normal families: A methodological and substantive review. *Psychological Bulletin,* 1975, **82,** 33–65.
140. Jessor, S. L., & Jessor, R. Maternal ideology and adolescent problem behavior. *Developmental Psychology,* 1974, **10,** 246–254.
141. Johnson, N. N., Stockard, J., Acker, J., & Naffziger, C. Expressiveness reevaluation. Paper presented at the meeting of the American Sociological Association, August 1974.
142. Jones, F. A 4-year follow-up of vulnerable adolescents. *Journal of Nervous and Mental Disease,* 1974, **159,** 20–39.
143. Jones, J., Rodnick, E., Goldstein, M. J., McPherson, S., & West, K. Parental transactional deviance as a possible indicator of risk for schizophrenia. *Archives of General Psychiatry,* 1977, **34,** 71–74.
144. Josselson, R. L. Psychodynamic aspects of identity formation in college women. *Journal of Youth and Adolescence,* 1973, **2,** 3–52.
145. Josselyn, J. M. Sexual identity arises in the life cycle. In G. H. Seward & R. C. Williamson (eds.), *Sex roles in changing society.* New York: Random House, 1970. Pp. 67–92.

146. Kagan, J. *The growth of the child: Reflections on human development.* New York: Norton, 1978.

147. Kagan, J., & Moss, H. A. *Birth to maturity: The Fels study of psychological development.* New York: Wiley, 1962.

148. Kandel, D. B., & Lesser, G. S. Youth in two worlds. San Francisco: Jossey-Bass, 1972.

149. Kellam, S. G., Engsminger, M. E., & Turner, R. J. Family structure and the mental health of children. *Archives of General Psychiatry,* 1977, **34**, 1012–1022.

150. Kempe, C. H., & Helfer, R. E. (eds.). *The battered child.* Chicago: University of Chicago Press, 1980 (2nd ed.).

151. Kempe, R. S., & Kempe, C. H. (eds.). *Child abuse.* Cambridge, Mass.: Harvard University Press, 1978.

152. Korbin, J. E. *Child abuse and neglect: Cross cultural perspectives.* Berkeley, Calif.: University of California Press, 1981.

153. Landy, F., Rosenberg, B. G., & Sutton-Smith, B. The effect of limited father-absence on cognitive development. *Child Development,* 1969, **40**, 941–944.

154. Langlois, J., & Downs, C. Mothers, fathers and peers as socialization agents of sex-typed play behavior in young children. *Child Development,* 1980, **7**, 1237–1247.

155. LaVoie, J. C. Ego identity formation in middle adolescence. *Journal of Youth and Adolescence,* 1976, **5**, 371–385.

156. Lerner, R. M., Sorrell, A. T., & Brackney, B. E. Sex differences in self-concept and self-esteem in late adolescents: A time-lag analysis. *Sex Roles,* 1981, **7**, 709–722.

157. Lesser, G. S., & Kandel, D. Parent-adolescent relationships and adolescent independence in the United States and Denmark. *Journal of Marriage and the Family,* 1969, **31**, 348–358.

158. Levinson, D. J., Darrow, C. N., Klein, E. B., Levinson, M. H., & McKee, B. *The seasons of a man's life.* New York: Knopf, 1978.

159. Lidz, T. *The person: His development throughout the life cycle.* New York: Basic Books, 1968.

160. Lowenthal, M., & Chiriboga, D. Transition to the empty nest: Crisis, challenge, or relief? *Archives of General Psychiatry,* 1972, **26**, 8–14.

161. Lynn, D. B., & Sawrey, W. L. The effects of father-absence on Norwegian boys and girls. *Journal of Abnormal and Social Psychology,* 1959, **59**, 258–262.

162. Maccoby, E. E., & Jacklin, C. N. *The psychology of sex differences.* Stanford, Calif.: Stanford University Press, 1974.

163. Marcia, J. E. Development and validation of ego-identity status. *Journal of Personality and Social Psychology,* 1966, **3**, 551–558.

164. Marcia, J. E., Ego identity status: Relationship to change in self-esteem, "general maladjustment," and authoritarianism. *Journal of Personality,* 1967, **35**, 118–123.

165. Marcia, J. E., Identity in adolescence. In J. Adelson (ed.), *Handbook of adolescent psychology.* New York: Wiley, 1980. Pp. 159–187.

166. Martin, B. Parent-child relations. In F. D. Horowitz (ed.), *Review of child development research* (Vol. 4). Chicago: University of Chicago Press, 1975. Pp. 463–540.

167. Martin, H. *The abused child.* Cambridge, Mass.: Ballinger, 1976.

168. Matteson, D. R. Alienation vs. exploration and commitment: Personality and family corollaries of adolescent identity statuses. Report from the Project for Youth Research. Copenhagen: Royal Danish School of Educational Studies, 1974.

169. Maw, W. H., & Maw, E. W. Children's curiosity and parental attitudes. *Journal of Marriage and the Family,* 1966, **28**, 343–345.

170. McCord, J., McCord, W., & Thurber, E. Some effects of paternal absence on male children. *Journal of Abnormal and Social Psychology,* 1962, **64**, 361–369.

171. McDonald, G. W. A reconsideration of the concept "sex-role identification" in adolescent and family research. *Adolescence,* 1978, **13**, 215–220.

172. McDonald, G. W. Determinants of adolescent perceptions of maternal and paternal, power in the family. *Journal of Marriage and the Family,* 1979, **41**, 757–770.

173. McDonald, G. W. Parental power and adolescents' parental identification: A reexamination. *Journal of Marriage and the Family,* 1980, **42**, 289–296.

174. Mead, M. *From the south seas: Part III. Sex and temperament in three primitive societies.* New York: Morrow, 1939.

175. Mead, M. *Culture and commitment: A study of the generation gap.* Garden City, N.Y.: Doubleday, 1970.

176. Meyers, C. E. Emancipation of adolescents from parental control. *Nervous Child,* 1946, **5,** 251–262.

177. Middleton, R., & Snell, P. Political expression of adolescent rebellion. *American Journal of Sociology,* 1963, **68,** 527–535.

178. Minturn, L., & Lambert, W. W., et al. *Mothers of six cultures: Antecedents of child rearing.* New York: Wiley, 1964.

179. Mischel, W. Preference for delayed reinforcement: An experimental study of cultural observation. *Journal of Abnormal and Social Psychology,* 1958, **56,** 57–61.

180. Mischel, W. Delay of gratification, need for achievement, and acquiescence in another culture. *Journal of Abnormal and Social Psychology,* 1961, **62,** 543–522(a).

181. Mischel, W. Father-absence and delay of gratification. *Journal of Abnormal and Social Psychology,* 1961, **62,** 116–124(b).

182. Mischel, W. Preference for delayed reward and social responsibility. *Journal of Abnormal and Social Psychology,* 1961, **62,** 1–7.

183. Mishler, E. G., & Waxler, N. E. *Interaction in families: An experimental study of family processes and schizophrenia.* New York: Wiley, 1968.

184. Mitchell, D., & Wilson, W. Relationship of father-absence to masculinity and popularity of delinquent boys. *Psychological Reports,* 1967, **20,** 1173–1174.

185. Morse, B. Identity status in college women in relation to perceived parent-child relationships. Unpublished doctoral dissertation. Ohio State University, 1973.

186. Mrazek, P. B., & Kempe, C. H. *Sexually abused children and their families.* Elmsford, N.Y.: Pergamon Press, 1981.

187. Mrazek, P. B., & Mrazek, D. A. The effects of child sexual abuse. In R. S. Kempe and C. H. Kempe, *Child abuse.* Cambridge, Mass.: Harvard University Press, 1978. Pp. 223–245.

188. Munroe, R. L., & Munroe, R. H. *Cross-cultural human development.* Monterey, Calif.: Brooks/Cole, 1975.

189. Mussen, P. H. Long-term consequents of masculinity of interests in adolescence. *Journal of Consulting Psychology,* 1962, **26,** 435–440.

190. Mussen, P. H., Conger, J. J., & Kagan, J. *Child development and personality.* New York: Harper & Row, 1979 (5th ed.).

191. Mussen, P., & Rutherford, E. Parent-child relations and parental personality in relation to young children's sex-role preferences. *Child Development,* 1963, **34,** 489–607.

192. Muus, R. E. Puberty rites in primitive and modern societies. *Adolescence,* 1970, **5,** 109–128.

193. Nelson, E. A., & Vangen, P. M. Impact of father absence on heterosexual behaviors and social development of preadolescent girls in a ghetto environment. *Proceedings, 79th Annual Convention of the American Psychological Association,* 1971, **6,** 165–166.

194. Nesselroade, J. R., & Baltes, P. B. *Adolescent personality development and historical change: 1970–1972,* SRCD Monograph (Vol. 39, No. 154). Chicago: University of Chicago Press, 1974.

195. Neugarten, B. L., & Hagestad, G. O. Age and the life course. In R. H. Binstock & E. Shanas (eds.), *Handbook of aging and the social sciences.* New York: Van Nostrand Reinhold, 1976.

196. Nordheimer, J. The family in transition: A challenge from within. *New York Times,* November 27, 1977.

197. Norman, R. D. Interpersonal values of parents of achieving and nonachieving gifted children. *Journal of Psychology,* 1966, **64,** 49–57.

198. Nye, I. Adolescent-parent adjustment: Age, sex, sibling, number, broken homes and employed mothers as variables. *Marriage and Family Living,* 1952, **14,** 327–332.

199. Offer, D. *The psychological world of the teenager.* New York: Basic Books, 1969.

200. Offer, D., Marohn, R. C., & Ostrov, E. *The psychological world of the juvenile delinquent.* New York: Basic Books, 1979.

201. Offer D., Ostrov, E., & Howard, K. I. *The adolescent: A psychological self-portrait.* New York: Basic Books, 1981.

202. Oshman, H., & Manosevitz, M. The impact of the identity crisis on the adjustment of late adolescent males. *Journal of Youth and Adolescence,* 1974, **3,** 207–216.

203. Pable, M. W. Some parental determinants of ego identity in adolescent boys. *Dissertation Abstracts,* 1965, **26,** 3480–3481.

204. Paige, K. E., & Paige, J. M. *The politics of reproductive ritual.* Berkeley, Calif.: University of California Press, 1981.

205. Parsons, J. E., Adler, T. F., & Kaczala, C. M. Socialization of achievement attitudes and beliefs: Parental influences. *Child Development,* 1982, **53,** 310–321.

206. Patterson, G. R., & Reid, J. B. Reciprocity and coercion: Two facets of social systems. In C. Neuringer & J. L. Michael (eds.), *Behavior modifications in clinical psychology.* Englewood Cliffs, N.J.: Prentice-Hall, 1970.

207. Pearlin, L. J., & Kohn, M. L. Social class, occupation, and parental values: A cross-national study. *American Sociological Review,* 1966, **31,** 466–479.

208. Petersen, A. C., & Gitelson, I. B. *Toward understanding sex-related differences in cognitive performance.* New York: Academic Press, in preparation.

209. Petersen, A. C., Offer, D., & Kaplan, E. The self-image of rural adolescent girls. In M. Sugar (ed.), *Female adolescent development.* New York: Brunner/Mazel, 1979.

210. Peterson, R. E. *Technical manual: College student questionnaires.* Princeton, N.J.: Educational Testing Service, 1965.

211. Pietz, K. R. Parent perception and social adjustment among elementary and high school students. *Journal of Clinical Psychology,* 1968, **24,** 165–171.

212. Pikas, A. Children's attitudes toward rational versus inhibiting parental authority. *Journal of Abnormal and Social Psychology,* 1961, **62,** 315–321.

213. Pleck, J. *The myth of masculinity.* Cambridge, Mass.: MIT Press, 1981.

214. Prinz, R. J., Rosenblum, R. S., & O'Leary, K. D. Affective communication differences between distressed and nondistressed mother-adolescent dyads. *Journal of Abnormal Child Psychiatry,* 1978, **6,** 373–383.

215. Rabin, A. I. *Growing up in the kibbutz.* New York: Springer-Verlag, 1965.

216. Raven, B. H., & French, J. R. P., Jr. Group support, legitimate power and social influence. *Journal of Personality,* 1958, **26,** 400–409.

217. Raven, B. H., & French, J. R. P., Jr. Legitimate power, coercive power, and observability in social influence. *Sociometry,* 1958, **21,** 83–97.

218. Roe, A., & Siegelman, M. A parent-child relations questionnaire. *Child Development,* 1963, **34,** 355–369.

219. Rollins, B., & Galligan, R. The developing child and marital satisfaction of parents. In R. Lerner & G. Spanier (eds.), *Child influences on marital and family interaction: A life-span perspective.* New York: Academic Press, 1978.

220. Rosenberg, M. *Society and the adolescent self-image.* Princeton, N.J.: Princeton University Press, 1965.

221. Rosenberg, M., & Simmons, R. G. *Black and white self-esteem: The urban school child.* Rose Monograph series. Washington, D.C.: American Sociological Association, 1972.

222. Rosenthal, D., & Hansen, J. Comparison of adolescents' perceptions and behaviors in single- and two-parent families. *Journal of Youth and Adolescence,* 1980, **9,** 407–417.

223. Rosenthal, D. M., Peng, C. J., & McMillan, J. M. Relationship of adolescent self-concept to perceptions of parents in single- and two-parent families. *International Journal of Behavioral Development,* 1980, **3,** 441–453.

224. Rossi, A. S. Review of S. De Beauvoir, All said and done. *Psychology Today,* October 1975, **9,** 16–17.

225. Rossi, A. S. A biosocial perspective on parenting. In A. S. Rossi, J. Kagan, & T. K. Harevan (eds.), *The family.* New York: Norton, 1978. Pp. 1–31.

226. Rutter, M. Maternal deprivation 1972–1978: New findings, new concepts, new approaches. *Child Development,* 1979, **50,** 283–305.

227. Rutter, M. *Changing youth in a changing society: Patterns of adolescent development and disorder.* Cambridge, Mass.: Harvard University Press, 1980.

228. Rutter, M., & Giller, H. *Juvenile delinquency: Trends and perspectives.* Baltimore: Penguin, in press.

229. Rutter, M., Graham, O. F. D., & Yule, W. Adolescent turmoil: Fact or fiction? *Journal of Child Psychology and Psychiatry,* 1976, **17,** 35–56.

230. Schaefer, E. S. A circumplex model for maternal behavior. *Journal of Abnormal and Social Psychology,* 1959, **59,** 226–235.

231. Schaefer, E. S. A configurational analysis of children's reports of parent behavior. *Journal of Consulting Psychology,* 1965, **29,** 552–557.

232. Schaeffer, D. L. *Sex differences in personality: Readings.* Monterey, Calif.: Brooks/Cole, 1971.

233. Schram, R. Marital satisfaction over the family life-cycle: A critique and proposal. *Journal of Marriage and the Family,* 1979, **41,** 7–12.

234. Schulterbrandt, J. G., & Nichols, E. J. Ethical and ideological problems for communal living: A caveat. In M. E. Lasswell & T. E. Lasswell (eds.), *Love, marriage, family.* Glenview, Ill.: Scott, Foresman, 1973. Pp. 441–445.

235. Sears, R. R. The relation of early socialization experiences to aggression in middle childhood. *Journal of Abnormal and Social Psychology,* 1961, **63,** 466–492.

236. Sears, R. R., Maccoby, E. E., & Levin, H. *Patterns of child rearing.* New York: Harper & Row, 1957.

237. Shanas, E. Family-kin networks and aging in cross-cultural perspective. *Journal of Marriage and the Family,* 1973, **35,** 505–511.

238. Shepard, W. Mothers and fathers, sons and daughters: Perceptions of young adults. *Sex Roles,* 1980, **6,** 421–433.

239. Signorella, M. L., Vegega, M. E., & Mitchell, M. E. Subject selection and analyses for sex-related differences: 1968–1970 and 1975–1977. *American Psychologist,* 1981, **30,** 988–990.

240. Simmons, R. G., & Rosenberg, F. Sex, sex roles, and self-image. *Journal of Youth and Adolescence,* 1975, **4,** 229–257.

241. Skeels, H. M. Adult status of children with contrasting early life experiences. *Monographs of the Society for Research in Child Development,* 1966, **31,** No. 105, 1–13, 54–59.

242. Spence, J. T. Traits, roles, and the concept of androgyny. Paper presented at the Conference on Perspectives on the Psychology of Women, Michigan State University, May 13–14, 1977.

243. Spence, J. T., & Helmreich, R. L. *Masculinity and feminity: Their psychological dimensions, correlates and antecedents.* Austin: University of Texas Press, 1978.

244. Staats, A. W. *Child learning, intelligence, and personality.* New York: Harper & Row, 1971.

245. Steele, B. Violence within the family. In R. E. Helfer & C. H. Kempe (eds.), *Child abuse and neglect: The family and the community.* Cambridge, Mass.: Ballinger, 1976. Pp. 3–24.

246. Steele, B. Psychodynamic factors in child abuse. In C. H. Kempe and F. E. Helfer (eds.), *The battered child.* Chicago: University of Chicago Press, 1980. Pp. 49–85.

247. Steinberg, L. D. Transformations in family relations at puberty. *Developmental Psychology,* 1981, **17,** 833–840.

248. Steinberg, L. D., & Hill, J. P. Patterns of family interaction as a function of age, the onset of puberty, and formal thinking. *Developmental Psychology,* 1978, **14,** 683–684.

249. Stephen, N., & Day, H. D. Sex-role identity, parental identification, and self-concept of adolescent daughters from mother-absent, father-absent, and intact families. *Journal of Psychology,* 1979, **103,** 193–202.

250. Stolz, L. M. *Father relations of warborn children.* Stanford, Calif.: Stanford University Press, 1954.

251. Straus, M. A. Conjugal power structure and adolescent personality. *Marriage and Family Living,* 1962, **24,** 17–25.

252. Sutton-Smith, B., Rosenberg, B. G., & Landy, F. Father-absence effects in families of different sibling compositions. *Child Development,* 1968, **38,** 1213–1221.

253. Tiller, P. O. Father-absence and personality development of children in sailor families. *Nordisk Psyckologi's Monograph Series,* 1958, **9,** 1–48.

254. Toder, N. L., & Marcia, J. E. Ego identity status and response to conformity pressure in college women. *Journal of Personality and Social Psychology,* 1973, **26,** 287–294.

255. U.S. Department of Commerce, Bureau of the Census, *Statistical Abstract of the United States.* Washington, D.C.: U.S. Government Printing Office, 1981 (102nd ed.).

256. Valliant, G. *Adaptation to life.* Boston: Little, Brown, 1977.

257. Vogel, W., & Lauterbach, C. G. Relationships between normal and disturbed sons' percepts of their parents' behavior and personality attributes of the parents and sons. *Journal of Clinical Psychology,* 1963, **19,** 52–56.

258. Wallerstein, J. S. Children of divorce: The long-term impact. *Medical Aspects of Human Sexuality,* 1981, **15,** 36–47.

259. Wallerstein, J., & Kelly, J. The effects of parental divorce: The adolescent experience. In A. J. Koupernik (ed.), *Children at psychiatric risk.* New York: Wiley, 1974.

260. Wallerstein, J. S., & Kelly, J. B. Effects of divorce on the visiting father-child relationship. *American Journal of Psychiatry,* 1980, **137,** 1534–1539.

261. Wallerstein, J. S., & Kelly, J. B. *Surviving the break-up: How children and parents cope with divorce.* New York: Basic Books, 1980.

262. Waterman, A. S., Geary, P. S., & Waterman, C. K. Longitudinal study of changes in ego identity status from the freshman to the senior year at college. *Developmental Psychology,* 1974, **10,** 387–392.

263. Waterman, A. S., & Waterman, C. K. A longitudinal study of changes in ego identity status during the freshman year in college. *Developmental Psychology,* 1971, **5,** 167–173.

264. Waterman, A. S., & Waterman, C. K. Relationship between freshman ego status and subsequent academic behavior: A test of the predictive validity of Marcia's categorization system for identity status. *Developmental Psychology,* 1972, **6,** 179.

265. Watson, G. Some personality differences in children related to strict or permissive parental discipline. *Journal of Psychology,* 1957, **44,** 227–249.

266. Weiner, I. B. *Psychological disturbance in adolescence.* New York: Wiley, 1970.

267. West, K. L. Assessment and treatment of disturbed adolescents and their families: A clinical research perspective. In M. Lansky (ed.), *Major psychopathology and the family.* New York: Grune & Stratton, 1981.

268. Whiting, B. B. (ed.). *Six cultures: Studies of child rearing.* New York: Wiley, 1963.

269. Whiting, J. W. M. *Becoming a Kwoma.* New Haven, Conn.: Yale University Press, 1941.

270. Whiting, J. W. M., & Child, I. L. *Child training and personality.* New Haven, Conn.: Yale University Press, 1953.

271. Whiting, J. W. M., Klucholm, R. C., & Anthony, A. The function of male initiation ceremonies at puberty. In E. Maccoby, T. M. Newcomb, & E. L. Hartley (eds.), *Readings in social psychology.* New York: Holt, Rinehart and Winston, 1958.

272. Wohlford, P., & Liberman, D. Effects of father absence on personal time, field independence, and anxiety. *Proceedings of the 78th Annual Convention of the American Psychological Association,* 1970, **5,** 263–264.

273. Wynne, L. C., & Singer, M. T. Thought disorder and family relations of schizophrenics. I. A research study. *Archives of General Psychiatry,* 1963, **9,** 191–198.

274. Wynne, L. C., Singer, M. T., Bartko, J. J., & Toohey, M. Schizophrenics and their families: Recent research on parental communication. In J. M. Tanner (ed.), *Psychiatric research: The widening perspective.* New York: International Universities Press, 1976.

275. Young, F. W. The function of male initiation ceremonies: A cross-cultural test of an alternate hypothesis. *American Journal of Sociology,* 1962, **67,** 379–396.

276. Young, M., & Wilmott, P. *Family and kinship in East London.* Boston: Routledge & Kegan Paul, 1957.

# Adolescent sexuality

# CHAPTER 8

# Adolescent sexuality

**A**mong the many developmental events that characterize puberty and the onset of adolescence, none is more dramatic, or more challenging to the young person's emerging sense of identity, than the changes associated with sexual development. Bodily dimensions of boys and girls become increasingly differentiated, as boys develop broader shoulders and show a greater overall gain in muscle development, and girls undergo breast development and develop more rounded hips. Girls experience their first menstruation and boys their first ejaculation. In both sexes genital organs—the penis and scrotum in boys, the clitoris, vagina, and labia in girls—increase in size, and pubic hair develops. All of these physical changes (see Chapter 4) require new adjustments on the part of the young person and lead to a changing self-image. As one 16-year-old girl expressed it, "When I was 14 my body started to go crazy" (16).

Furthermore, although sexuality in the broadest sense is a lifelong part of being human (even babies love to be held and may fondle their genitals), the hormonal changes that accompany puberty lead to stronger sexual feelings, although there may be considerable diversity in the ways these feelings are expressed in different individuals and in the same individual at different times. Adolescents may find themselves "thinking more about sex, getting sexually aroused more easily, even at times feeling preoccupied with sex" (16, 73). Or they may find themselves excited by and involved in other interests, and not be particularly aware of sexual feelings. At the same age, one adolescent may be involved in sexual experimentation, another may not; one may be in love and going steady, another may feel that it is much too early for such commitments and may prefer to play the field (16). Despite such individual variations, integrating sexuality meaningfully, and with as little conflict and disruption as possible, with other aspects of the young person's developing sense of self and of relations with others is a major developmental task for both boys and girls. How adequately this task is ultimately handled—the extent to which it becomes a source of joy or despair, of challenge and success, or failure and defeat—depends on many factors, ranging from the complexities of early parent-child relationships to contemporary social standards and values.

## SEX DIFFERENCES

For most boys, the rapid increase in sexual drive that accompanies puberty is difficult to deny, and tends to be genitally oriented (25, 38, 105). Increased frequency of erections in response to a wide variety of sexualized stimuli (see page 115) clearly calls attention to sexual arousal (at times under awkward social circumstances). Self-perceived sex drive in males reaches a peak during adolescence, as does the frequency of total sexual outlet (primarily through masturbation except for the minority of married adolescents who are having intercourse) (25, 86).

Among adolescent girls, there appears to be a much wider range of individual differences (25, 87). While some girls experience sexual desire in much the same way as the average boy, for a majority sexual feelings tend to be more diffuse, as well as more closely related to the fulfillment of other needs, such as self-esteem, reassurance, affection, and love (16, 25, 87, 104, 105). "For most girls, the overall relationship with the individual boy whom she loves—the extent to which this relationship is characterized by trust, concern, and a mutual sharing of life experiences—takes precedence over specific sexual release. Consequently, control of impulses is likely to constitute a considerably less urgent problem for girls" (38, *635*).

Although there is a significant increase in sexual interests and behavior among both boys and girls during adolescence, sexual activity in general—and masturbation in particular—is greater among boys than girls, although the size of the differences has narrowed in recent years (25, 30, 62, 74, 86, 87, 137) (see pages 284–286). Subjective awareness of specifically sexual pressure also appears greater among boys, particularly in the earlier years of adolescence. The average adolescent boy experiences nocturnal emissions during sleep, whereas the average girl does not have orgasm dreams during adolescence, particularly early adolescence (86, 87, 107). Among sexually experienced American male and female adolescents, ages 13 to 15 and 16 to 19, only in the case of 13- to 15-year-old adolescent boys did a majority of any subgroup reply affirmatively to the statement, "Sometimes I think I am addicted to sex, the way some people are addicted to drugs" (137). Furthermore, in studies of sexual morality (e.g., attitudes toward premarital intercourse, the importance of love in a sexual relationship, avoidance of promiscuity, respect for parental or societal wishes), girls have displayed in the past—and continue to display—more conservative attitudes. For example, among American college freshmen in 1980, two-thirds of all males, but only one-third of females agreed with the statement, "Sex is okay if people like each other" (4). On the other hand, when there is deep involvement, as in living together prior to marriage, differences are much smaller (only 32 percent of American adolescent girls and 21 percent of boys said they would not do so) (114). When adolescents, aged 15 to 18, were recently asked "Do you feel you have to be romantically involved with a girl (boy) before you have sexual contact with her (him)?", 68 percent of girls, but only 41 percent of boys said yes (62).

Obviously, we are speaking here only of *relative* differences. More girls than boys would agree with the girl in the study cited above who stated, "I feel you have to be romantically involved because if you are not then the only motive behind the contact is sexual and has nothing to do with your emotional feelings" (62, *15*). Nevertheless, many boys would agree with the boy who stated, "I don't feel cheap sex accomplishes anything. If I am romantically involved, I feel it is somehow a statement of my affection" (62, *16*). Conversely, a significant minority of girls would agree with the girl in the study who stated, "If two people are physically attracted to each other, I don't see the necessity for a romantic relationship as long as both people understand the relationship is purely physical and there are no ties connected" (62, *17*).

Findings of continuing adolescent sex differences in attitudes, values, and behavior, despite the advent of the so-called sexual revolution, do not come as a surprise, but the underlying reasons for them are still far from clear. A number of theories have been advanced—some primarily physiological, others primarily cultural. Recent changes in adolescent sexual interests, values, and behavior in our society, particularly among girls, as well as the findings from other cultures (see below), provide impressive evidence that cultural influences play a significant role.

The part played by physical, physiological, and endrocrinological factors is less immediately obvious. One hypothesis is that females are less likely than males to discover sexual responses spontaneously because the girl's sexual organs are less prominent and hence less subject to spontaneously learned manipulation (16, 25, 97, 102). It has also been asserted that there may be basic physiological differences between males and females in the levels of their sexual drive and responsiveness or in the capacity of various stimuli to arouse them, or both. For the Victorians, of course, the question was not even considered to be open to discussion; it was simply assumed that normal women did not have strong sexual drives or responses.

A majority of today's adolescent girls, however, do not subscribe to such views. More than two-thirds of adolescent girls, aged 13 to 19, express the belief that "women enjoy sex as much as men" (73, *96*). Only one out of every ten adolescent girls believes that "women have innately less capacity for sexual pleasure than men" (73). This predominant contemporary view receives strong support from William Masters and Virginia Johnson, the gynecologist-psychologist team of investigators, who were the first scientists to study human sexual responses comprehensively and objectively (97, 98). They comment that the female's basic "physiological capacity for sexual response . . . surpasses that of man" (98, *219–220*). It has also been clearly documented (86, 87, 97) that sexual behavior (e.g., frequency of orgasm) may vary over much wider ranges among girls than boys, and even within a particular girl at different times.

A still more complex question than the relative physiological capacity of males and females for sexual response involves the conditions under which arousal of the response is likely to occur. It has been argued that boys are more easily aroused than girls by a wider variety of external "psychosexual stimuli," such as provocative behavior, erotic art, films, and literature (25, 86, 87, 96, 97, 105, 110, 129, 152, 153, 163). Here, too, however, simplistic hypotheses appear inadequate. A wide-ranging series of experimental investigations showed that while males still emerge as more responsive in an overall survey, the differences are smaller than originally supposed (144). Furthermore, in some situations, some groups of adolescent and young adult females, that is, the younger, more liberal, and more sexually experienced, reported greater "sexual excitement" in response to various kinds of sexual stimuli than some groups of males, that is, the older, more conservative, more inhibited, and less experienced (87, 129, 144, 152, 153). It is also interesting to note that several more recent studies found that although males more frequently reported subjective feelings of arousal, direct measurements of physiological-sexual response did not show substantial differences. This may suggest that conflicts between feelings of arousal and defenses against feelings may occur more frequently among females. One German study found that "women have a stronger tendency to react with avoidance and an emotional defense reaction to pictorial and narrative stimuli than men," even when physiologically aroused (129, *126*).

It is also possible that, even in the absence of defensive reactions, physiological sexual arousal—at least below a certain level—is more difficult for females to identify, whereas in males it can hardly fail to be noticed. Thus, in one study (67, 68), sexually experienced young women (although they had reported themselves strongly aroused by frankly erotic stimuli) nevertheless had more difficulty than males in identifying physiological arousal which for some unknown, personal reasons they were experiencing, but which was not accompanied by erotic or erotic-romantic stimuli. As soon as the women did not have extended erotic cues linked to their arousal, they had more difficulty recognizing physiological excitement (68). Also, as one of the authors has noted elsewhere, in the absence of socially ascribed meaning, or a girl's personal learning experiences, there may not be any necessary link between bodily sensations and particular responses to them: "A young adolescent girl may feel attraction for a boy and may experience bodily sensations that could be labelled as desire for sex or desire for a relationship, depending upon the girl's values and attitudes, as well as those of her parents and peers" (117).

The fact that significantly more females (particularly younger females) are reporting feelings of arousal (and demonstrating physiological arousal) today than at the time of Kinsey's studies 30 years ago may be due in large measure to "cultural desensitization" in recent years regarding sexual expression for women (and perhaps also more opportunities for specific learning of sexual responses). This, in turn, may have lowered psychological defenses against arousal and awareness of arousal. In the past, strong sexual responsiveness was generally less accepted by society and less clearly acknowledged in girls than in boys. This situation has recently changed significantly in the direction of greater permissiveness. However, it should also be recognized that "this permissive message has been given in a limited context. Information about what it means to be sexual and how it is integrated with other aspects of life have been missing" (117). Furthermore, many girls are still brought up to be less accepting and proud of their sexuality than boys are. Though less rigid than in the past, vestiges of a double standard still remain:

> A teenage boy finds that his sexual adventures are usually tolerated or even encouraged. (Of course, this is often hard for the boys who aren't interested!) A girl, however, is told she must be the one to say "No!" and to hold off a boy's sex drive. She rarely hears about her own sex drive. So it can be hard for her to let her sexual responses flow freely. . . . [16, *83*].

It may also be that sexuality tends to be more intimately bound up with other aspects of personality in the case of girls, and, therefore, the conditions that must be satisfied if psychosexual stimulation is to produce arousal, or for arousal to be subjectively recognized, may be more complex than is generally the case for boys. Stimulation that cannot be related to the self as a total person because it is perceived as threatening, conflicts with existing value systems, is impersonal, or is aesthetically offensive, may be more likely to "turn off" the average adolescent girl than her male peer (25, 28, 105, 135, 141). Fantasies of both male and female college students during sexual arousal were most likely to involve petting or having intercourse, with "someone you love or are fond of" (105). However, fantasies of sexual activity with strangers for whom they had no particular emotional attachment were almost as frequent for males (79 percent), but not for females (22 percent). Indeed, "doing nonsexual things with someone you are fond of or in love with" was second in frequency for females (74 percent), but not for males (48 percent). As Patricia Miller and William Simon comment, for females, "the investment of erotic meaning in both explicitly sexual and nonsexual symbols appears to be contingent on the emotional context. The two genders evaluate the meaning of potentially erotic symbols using distinctive sets of criteria. For males, the explicitly sexual is endowed with erotic meaning regardless of the emotional context. For females, the emotional context is endowed with erotic meaning without regard for the presence or absence of explicitly sexual symbols" (105, *403*).

Finally, it may also be that the greater sexual aggressiveness generally manifested by adolescent males is related, at least in part, to vastly greater increases in testosterone levels among males at puberty. It has been demonstrated that this hormone increases sexual and aggressive behavior in both sexes under experimental conditions (63, 103, 111).

Regardless of the ultimate significance of these and other factors, it nevertheless appears abundantly clear that the lesser sexual activity of female adolescents, and probably to some extent its qualitatively different nature, is *at least partially* attributable to our culture's more restrictive social attitudes toward sexual expression for girls (30).

## CULTURAL DIFFERENCES IN SEXUAL ATTITUDES AND BEHAVIOR

Learning appears to play a critical role in determining the sexual response patterns that are adopted to satisfy sexual drives (12, 45, 46, 87). Hence, we would expect to find rather wide variations in sexual attitudes and behavior from one culture to another. There are some widespread generalities, even universals, which reflect commonalities in the human condition, for example, some form of incest taboo, but there are also marked differences between cultures, not only in the amount and type of sexual behavior that is socially accepted, but also in the consistency of the society's sexual standards as development proceeds.

Some cultures are restrictive with regard to sexual activity throughout childhood, adolescence, and even to some extent in adulthood. Others are thoroughly permissive at all ages. Still others are highly restrictive during childhood and adolescence, and then suddenly become much more permissive about, and even demanding of, sexual activity in adulthood.

Among the Cuna of the coast of Panama, children "remain ignorant of sexual matters (as far as adult information is concerned) until the last stages of the marriage ceremony. They are not even allowed to watch animals give birth" (46, *180*). The Ashanti of the west central coast of Africa believe that sexual intercourse with a girl who has not undergone the puberty ceremony is so harmful to the community that the offense is punishable by death for both partners (46).

In contrast, sexual experience in some societies is carefully nurtured from early childhood on. The Chewa of Africa believe that unless children begin to exercise themselves sexually early in life, they will never beget offspring. "Older children build little huts some distance from the village, and there, with the complete approval of their parents, boys and girls play at being husband and wife. Such child matings may extend well into adolescence, with periodic exchanges of partners until marriage occurs" (46, *190*). Similarly, the Lepcha of India believe that girls "will not mature without benefit of sexual intercourse. Early sex play among boys and girls characteristically involves many forms of mutual masturbation and usually ends in attempted copulation. By the time they are eleven or twelve years old, most girls regularly engage in full intercourse" (46, *191*).

Among the Siriono of central South America, intercourse before puberty is forbidden, but premarital relations are customary once the girl has menstruated (46). Somewhat the reverse occurs among the Alorese of Oceania. Here the young child enjoys relatively complete sexual freedom. Alorese mothers may fondle the genitals of their infants while nursing them; Alorese boys and girls are allowed to masturbate freely, and occasionally they may imitate intercourse. But as these children grow older, "sexual activity is frowned upon and during late childhood such behavior is forbidden to both boy and girl" (46, *189*).

Until recently, the Manus boy of the Admiralty Islands north of New Guinea was in much the same position in sexual matters as American middle-class adolescent males were at the turn of the century (6, 111). Whereas the male physiological sex drive was recognized as natural among these people, sexual behavior was strongly tabooed until marriage. Apparently, such relief of sexual tension as did occur was achieved primarily through covert homosexual activity and through solitary masturbation surrounded by shame (6). In turn, the Manus girl's position was highly reminiscent of that of a female of the Victorian era. She was taught that sex is not gratifying to women, and, in fact, that it is loathsome, shameful, and repugnant (6). The consequent difficulties in adjusting to intercourse after marriage can easily be imagined.

In our own society, despite the advent of the recent "sexual revolution," many parents still spend a great many years teaching children and adolescents to inhibit and control sexual behavior, presumably in order to prepare them for a time when they will be expected to make these responses! Many children are still taught, consciously or unconsciously, to be anxious about sex, and then, upon marriage, are expected to be able to respond without inhibition or anxiety. What we have frequently tended to teach, in fact, is not sexual adaptation but rather sexual concern.

### Sexual attitudes in relation to broader cultural values

The kind and timing of sexual training that boys or girls receive during childhood and adolescence can be of major importance in determining whether they will show great or little interest in sexual behavior. Sex training also determines whether they will tend to view sex as a pleasant and matter-of-fact affair, as sinful and dangerous, as extremely exciting, or as a manifestation of aggressive conquest. Socialization practices with respect to sex may also have broader and more generalized effects upon the adolescent's or adult's personality and his or her perceptions of the larger society. In societies that begin training in inhibition of heterosexual behavior relatively late in childhood and avoid using excessively severe training methods, people are less likely to show propensities toward guilt about sex than members of societies which institute early and relatively harsh training (151).

Such relationships between sexual training and broader characteristics of the individual and of his or her culture are not unidirectional. Sex training practices may be generalized to affect other aspects of social behavior, but they are also affected by and reflect broader cultural attitudes. Thus, among the Zuñi, the relations—sexual and otherwise—between husband and wife tend to be pleasant, cooperative, and untainted by feelings of guilt. Sexual intercourse is a cooperative, rather than a competitive, matter to the Zuñis, "not simply because of specific sex training, but because cooperation is an integral part of the whole Zuñi way of life" (19).

A similar set of cultural values characterizes the Mixtecan Indians of Mexico

(150). When a man takes a post of public responsibility in the barrio, his wife shares the honor and responsibility. Exploitation of one sex by the other is rare, and children are not disciplined primarily by physical or other heavy punishment. One seldom encounters bickering and fighting among either adults or children. "From the barrio point of view, the use of sex for exploitative purposes is inconsistent with their attitudes, just as are all other forms of exploitation of human beings. Sexual power does not add to the luster of the individual within the barrio" (150, 565–566). In contrast, in societies such as the Mundugumor (see pages 232–233), aggression and competition play an important part in the individual's sexual relations largely because they pervade the whole Mundugumor way of life (101).

## SEXUAL ATTITUDES AND VALUES OF CONTEMPORARY ADOLESCENTS

It has been apparent for some years now that the sexual attitudes and values of adolescents have been changing significantly, that a "new morality" has been developing in the United States and other Western countries (30). In comparison to their peers of earlier generations, they have both a greater openness and honesty about sex and an increasing tendency to base decisions about appropriate sexual behavior more on personal values and judgment, and less on conformity to institutionalized social codes (25, 30, 74, 137, 156, 161). This change has manifested itself in a variety of ways, ranging from greater openness about sexuality and sexual relationships, to a greater tolerance of variations in the sexual values and behavior of others, to a desire for more and better sex education, including access to birth control information.

### Sex education

Despite an overall increase in openness about sexual matters since the 1960s, the subject of sex education remains highly controversial in many areas of the country. In the view of some (particularly members of the militant right and some fundamentalist religious groups), sex education, even at the high school level, is either dangerous and premature for "impressionable" adolescents and likely to lead to indiscriminate promiscuity, or should be taught only by parents in the privacy of their own homes. Members of these groups tend to have highly traditional—some would say stereotyped—views regarding women's roles, the family, and sexuality (125), and many feel excluded generally from influence over the social institutions, including schools and government, that nevertheless affect their lives (95). Other adults appear to have reached the awesome conclusion that contemporary adolescents have nothing left to learn about sex (certainly nothing their *parents* could teach them).

Opponents of sex education have received national support from the current administration, which has announced its strong opposition to federal participation in the development of programs of sex education, as well as to continued use of Medicaid funds for providing birth control information or assistance (131). On the other hand, a recent (1981) poll by the National Broadcasting Company found that 75 percent of American adults (and 80 percent of the parents of minor children) favor

sex education, and more than two-thirds think it fosters a healthy attitude toward sex (112).

In the light of statistics on current adolescent premarital intercourse, pregnancy, and abortion, as well as the general social climate, it is difficult to see how sex education for adolescents could be viewed as "premature." When asked if sex education is likely to encourage sexual activity, 82 percent of American adults (and 87 percent of the parents of minor children) expressed the view that young people are likely to become involved anyway (112). Whether or not such education should be done primarily by parents, the fact is that, despite current trends toward greater freedom of discussion in our society, parents are still not providing the knowledge their children need in a majority of cases (5, 20, 62, 114, 137, 152). Friends rank first as the source of most sex information among both boys and girls in the United States; among girls, mothers rank second and school third, while among boys, school ranks second and fathers third (5, 152). In one national study (137), American adolescents were asked whether they and their parents talked "pretty freely" about sex; over 70 percent of both boys and girls, virgins and nonvirgins, replied that they did not. Nearly two-thirds stated that their parents thought that their sexual activities were "pretty much my own personal business." When asked specifically whether their parents had ever discussed such topics as masturbation, venereal disease, or contraceptive methods with them, two-thirds or more said they had not (137).

In another recent survey (62), adolescents were asked if they had ever tried to talk openly with either of their parents about sex; 44 percent of boys and 54 percent of girls reported that they had at one time or another. When asked how the parents responded, a minority responded positively, as in the case of a 16-year-old girl:

> Whenever I have sexual problems or questions I often consult my parents (usually my mother, but sometimes my father too). Our views aren't always the same. Sometimes we feel very different about some things. However, whether we agree or disagree, it's always nice to know that they will always be there and give their opinion if I have a question [62, *177*].

Or this from a 15-year-old boy:

> I feel I can be very open to them about sex because I know they would always try to help me. I know that not many kids can tell their parents anything, but I can. I know that if I did anything wrong, like getting a girl pregnant, they would be upset, but in the end they would help [62, *176*].

More often, however, parents responded with denial, avoidance, teasing, or disapproval. Frequently, the young person felt lectured to, instead of listened to; in the words of a 15-year-old boy, "She [his mother] began to preach about what is right and what is wrong. She just didn't understand" (62, *176*). A recent study of 1400 parents of adolescent girls in Cleveland, Ohio, found that 60 percent of their mothers had never explained menstruation and 92 percent had never discussed sex (91).

The notion of some adults that adolescents have nothing left to learn about sex also is not supported by the facts. Many adolescents think they cannot become pregnant if it is their first intercourse, if they do not have an orgasm, or if they do not want to become pregnant (78, 137, 159). In one study, nearly one-third of all adolescents, and about 25 percent of older adolescents (age 16 to 19) expressed the belief that "If a girl truly doesn't want to have a baby, she won't get pregnant though she may have sex without taking any birth control precautions" (137). The fact that more nonvirgins than virgins (both male and female) subscribed to this fallacy is hardly reassuring. In another representative study (78), less than 40 percent of 15- to 19-year-old adolescent American girls clearly understood the time of greatest pregnancy risk in the menstrual cycle; among those who had never had a sex education course, only 27 percent of 15- to 17-year-olds were correct (see Figure 8.1).

Unlike a vocal minority of their elders, adolescents themselves are strongly in favor of expanded and improved sex education courses (66, 73, 137, 153). In a recent Gallup poll, 84 percent of teenage youth (and 77 percent of adults) wanted such courses taught (50, 91). In another survey (137) representative of all American adolescents aged 13 to 19, 85 percent of girls and 75 percent of boys agreed on the need for properly taught sex education courses in the nation's schools. In a study (73) of the confidential opinions of 1500 middle-class adolescent girls in this same age group, 98 percent said they wanted sex taught in schools. Asked whether they thought that "discussion of physical intimacy may provoke curious young people to experiment sexually," the great majority claimed they had little or no such fear. When asked what was currently being taught and what *should* be taught, most girls responded that such topics as the anatomy and physiology of the female reproduc-

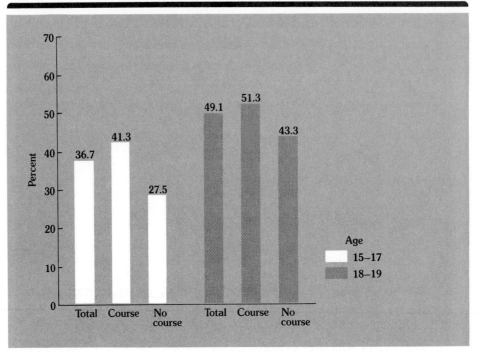

***Figure 8.1*** Percentage of never-married women aged 15–19 who correctly perceived time of greatest risk for pregnancy by whether they have had a sex education course. (From Planned Parenthood Federation of America. *Teenage pregnancy: The problem that hasn't gone away.* New York: Alan Guttmacher Institute, 1981. By permission.)

tive system and the menstrual cycle not only should be taught, but that they *were* being covered. Most girls also felt strongly that sex education classes should deal with such philosophical or scientific issues as premarital ethics, abortion, birth control and contraception, male and female sex drives, masturbation, homosexuality, loss of virginity, impotence and frigidity, fertility, and the nature of the orgasm. In all these important areas, however, only a small minority reported having had school instruction. In 1980, only three states and the District of Columbia mandated sex education in the public schools (91, 143).

### *Sexual morality*

In addition to greater openness and honesty, there is a growing tendency to view decisions about individual sexual behavior as more a private and less a public concern (7, 30, 31, 157). In 1980, American high school seniors were asked their reactions to a man and woman living together without being married (7). About one in five said that they were experimenting with "a worthwhile alternate life style," and smaller minorities felt either that they were violating a basic principle of human morality or that they were living in a way that was destructive to society. In contrast, nearly half expressed the view that they were "doing their own thing and not affecting anyone else" (7, *190*). In part, this trend appears to reflect a decline within our society since the 1960s in the perceived credibility and influence of established social, political, and religious institutions (31, 155). But it also appears to reflect a greater emphasis on the quality of the relationships that couples share. In one study (137), for example, nearly 75 percent of American adolescents concurred with the statement, "When it comes to morality in sex, the important thing is the way people treat each other, not the things they do together" (137). What many adolescents appear to be saying is that the morality of sexual behavior can often be judged not so much by the nature of the act itself, but by its meaning to the persons involved.

Approximately three-fourths of contemporary adolescents believe that "It's all right for young people to have sex before getting married if they are in love with each other" (137), and an equal number would consider living with a prospective spouse before marrying him or her (114). Less than a quarter of older adolescents think that sex outside of marriage is necessarily immoral (7, 114, 149). However, in one national survey 75 percent of all girls maintained, "I wouldn't want to have sex with a boy unless I loved him." Although only 47 percent of boys stated this stringent a requirement, 69 percent said, "I would not want to have sex with a girl unless I liked her as a person" (115). Other studies have yielded similar findings (4, 62, 137).

As we have already noted (see page 274), among college freshman in 1980, two-thirds of all males, but only one-third of females agreed with the statement, "Sex is okay if people like each other" (4). Most adolescents clearly oppose exploitation, pressure, or force in sex; sex solely for the sake of physical enjoyment without a personal relationship; and sex between people too young to understand what they are getting into (94, 116, 137).

Despite a growing emphasis among contemporary adolescents on openness and honesty, there is little evidence of an increased preoccupation with sex, as many parents and other adults seem to think. Indeed, it may well be that the average adolescent of today is less preoccupied and concerned with sex than prior generations of young people, including his or her parents when they were the same age. Greater acceptance of sex as a natural part of life may well lead to less preoccupation than did anxious concern in an atmosphere of secrecy and suppression. Most adolescents (87 percent) agree that "All in all, I think my head is pretty well together as far as sex is concerned" (137). Nor has sex displaced or become synonymous with love in the eyes of most young people (28). Most adolescents (67 to 80 percent in various surveys) disagree with the notion that the most important thing in a love relationship is sex, with older adolescents (both male and female) disagreeing more often than young adolescents (30, 62, 114, 137). Interestingly, the percentage disagreeing is higher for nonvirgins than for virgins. Among those having a steady sexual relationship with one boy or girl, 92 percent disagree (137).

Finally, in ranking the relative importance of various goals, younger adolescent boys and girls (aged 13 to 15) cited as most important: "preparing myself to earn a good living when I get older," "having fun," and "getting along with my parents," and for younger girls, "learning about myself." Older adolescents of both sexes (aged 16 to 19) stressed "learning about myself" as most important, followed by "being independent so that I can make it on my own" and "preparing myself to accomplish useful things." Among all age groups, "having sex with a number of different boys (girls)" and "making out" consistently ranked at or near the top among goals considered *least* important (137).

In other recent studies (62, 114), among both younger and older girls and boys, "having sex with someone" ranked last behind having friendships with members of the same and opposite sex, doing well in school, being very romantically involved with someone, and athletics.

## EFFECTS OF CHANGING VALUES ON SEXUAL BEHAVIOR

How are the continuing changes in sexual attitudes and values among contemporary adolescents reflected in behavior? The answer depends on *what* behaviors one is referring to, among *which* adolescents, and *how recently.*

Available information indicates that among boys the number who have engaged in masturbation by age 19 has remained fairly stable since their parents' generation at around 85 to 90 percent (3, 25, 28, 62, 74, 86, 149). But it also appears that the number involved at younger ages is increasing significantly. In Kinsey's original sample (86), only 45 percent of males reported masturbating by age 13; in contrast, in recent surveys (62, 74), that number had increased to between 52 and 65 percent. Among girls, recent data indicate that there has been an increase in masturbation at all age levels, with incidences currently of around 33 percent by age 13 (in contrast to 15 percent, or less than half as many in Kinsey's [87] study); and about 60 percent by age 20 (compared to about 30 percent for their mothers at age 20 [28, 62, 74, 87, 137]).

Even with recent changes, however, girls as a whole appear to engage in masturbation during adolescence only about half as often as boys. Furthermore, among those with masturbation experience, girls masturbate less frequently, on the average, though with wider variability (74, 86, 87, 137). One might be tempted to conclude that masturbation would occur most commonly among adolescents lacking other outlets. Interestingly, however, current masturbation experience among contemporary adolescents occurs about three times as frequently among those engaged in sexual intercourse or petting to orgasm as among the sexually inexperienced (137).

Petting does appear to have increased somewhat in the past few decades, and it tends to occur slightly earlier (25, 62, 74, 86, 87, 94, 137, 147). The major change, however, has probably been in frequency of petting, degree of intimacy of techniques involved, the frequency with which petting leads to erotic arousal or orgasm, and, certainly, frankness about this activity (25, 30, 62, 74, 137, 147).

Currently, the topic of greatest interest to adolescents and their parents, and the source of the most heated social and political controversy, is the extent of premarital sexual intercourse among contemporary adolescents and youth. Until the last few years, opinions were rife, but comprehensive data were scarce (except in the case of college students—see page 288). Consequently, some observers claimed that a "sexual revolution" was taking place, while others asserted that today's young people were actually no more sexually active than their parents had been at the same ages, but were simply more open and honest.

However, the situation began to become clearer with the publication in 1973 of

## TABLE 8.1 PERCENTAGE OF WOMEN AGED 15 TO 19 WHO EVER HAD INTERCOURSE BEFORE MARRIAGE, BY MARITAL STATUS AND RACE, UNITED STATES, 1979, 1976 AND 1971

| MARITAL STATUS AND AGE | 1979 | | | 1976 | | | 1971 | | |
|---|---|---|---|---|---|---|---|---|---|
| | TOTAL | WHITE | BLACK | TOTAL | WHITE | BLACK | TOTAL | WHITE | BLACK |
| *All* | | | | | | | | | |
| % | 49.8 | 46.6 | 66.2 | 43.4 | 38.3 | 66.3 | 30.4 | 26.4 | 53.7 |
| (N) | (1717) | (1034) | (683) | (1452) | (881) | (571) | (2739) | (1758) | (981) |
| *Ever married* | | | | | | | | | |
| % | 86.7 | 86.2 | 91.2 | 86.3 | 85.0 | 93.9 | 55.0 | 53.2 | 72.7 |
| (N) | (146) | (106) | (40) | (154) | (121) | (33) | (227) | (174) | (53) |
| *Never married*[a] | | | | | | | | | |
| Total | 46.0 | 42.3 | 64.8 | 39.2 | 33.6 | 64.3 | 27.6 | 23.2 | 52.4 |
| 15 | 22.5 | 18.3 | 41.4 | 18.6 | 13.8 | 38.9 | 14.4 | 11.3 | 31.2 |
| 16 | 37.8 | 35.4 | 50.4 | 28.9 | 23.7 | 55.1 | 20.9 | 17.0 | 44.4 |
| 17 | 48.5 | 44.1 | 73.3 | 42.9 | 36.1 | 71.0 | 26.1 | 20.2 | 58.9 |
| 18 | 56.9 | 52.6 | 76.3 | 51.4 | 46.0 | 76.2 | 39.7 | 35.6 | 60.2 |
| 19 | 69.0 | 64.9 | 88.5 | 59.5 | 53.6 | 83.9 | 46.4 | 40.7 | 78.3 |
| *Age at First Intercourse* (All) | | | | | | | | | |
| Mean | 16.2 | 16.4 | 15.5 | 16.1 | 16.3 | 15.6 | 16.4 | 16.6 | 15.9 |
| (N) | (933) | (478) | (455) | (726) | (350) | (376) | (936) | (435) | (501) |

*Source:* M. Zelnik and J. F. Kantner. Sexual activity, contraceptive use and pregnancy among metropolitan-area teenagers: 1971–1979. *Family Planning Perspectives,* 1980, **12,** 230–237. By permission.

*Note:* In this and subsequent tables, figures refer to the household population of SMSAs. Base excludes those for whom no information was obtained on premarital intercourse. Percentages are computed from weighted data. "White" includes the relatively small number of women of races other than black. Except where indicated, the base excludes those who did not respond to the question analyzed in the table. Absolute numbers shown in parentheses are unweighted sample Ns.

[a] Ns are not shown for each single year of age in order to simplify the presentation; $N \geq 87$ for each age-race cell among the never married.

a national survey of adolescents aged 13 to 19 by Robert Sorensen (137). He found that 44 percent of boys and 30 percent of girls had sexual intercourse prior to age 16. These figures increased to 72 percent of boys and 57 percent of girls by age 19.

More recently, Melvin Zelnik and John Kantner, population experts at the Johns Hopkins University, found that by 1979, 38 percent of unmarried 16-year-old girls in metropolitan areas in the United States had engaged in premarital intercourse (up from 21 percent in 1971 and 29 percent in 1976—see Table 8.1) (161). Among unmarried 19-year-olds in 1979, 69 percent had engaged in intercourse (up from 46 percent in 1971 and 59 percent in 1976). In 1979, 50 percent of all 15- to 19-year-old females reported having engaged in premarital intercourse, compared to 30 percent in 1971 and 43 percent in 1976. Not surprisingly, rates were highest for the relatively small number who were married. We know that premarital intercourse is most likely with future spouses, and further, that pregnancy often precedes marriage among teenage brides.

**TABLE 8.2 PERCENTAGE OF MEN AGED 17 TO 21
WHO EVER HAD INTERCOURSE BEFORE MARRIAGE, BY
MARITAL STATUS AND RACE, 1979**

| MARITAL STATUS AND AGE | TOTAL | WHITE | BLACK |
|---|---|---|---|
| **All** | | | |
| % | 70.3 | 69.6 | 74.6 |
| (N) | (917) | (567) | (350) |
| **Ever-married** | | | |
| % | 82.7 | 83.3 | 72.8 |
| (N) | (74) | (58) | (16) |
| **Never-married**[a] | | | |
| Total | 68.9 | 67.8 | 74.7 |
| 17 | 55.7 | 54.5 | 60.3 |
| 18 | 66.0 | 63.6 | 79.8 |
| 19 | 77.5 | 77.1 | 79.9 |
| 20 | 81.2 | 80.7 | 85.7 |
| 21 | 71.2 | 68.0 | 89.4 |

Source: M. Zelnik and J. F. Kantner. Sexual activity, contraceptive use and pregnancy among metropolitan-area teenagers: 1971–1979. *Family Planning Perspectives*, 1980, **12**, 230–237. By permission.
[a] $N \geq 33$ for each age-race cell among the never married.

Among males aged 17 to 21 in 1979, these investigators found that 70 percent had engaged in premarital intercourse (see Table 8.2). Of these, 56 percent had intercourse by age 17, and 77 percent by age 19 (161). Comparable results have been obtained recently in another large, but somewhat less systematically controlled, national sample of adolescents, aged 13 to 18. Among 13- to 15-year-olds, 41 percent of boys and 21 percent of girls reported having had sexual intercourse; among those aged 16 to 18, 70 percent of boys and 46 percent of girls had done so (114).

When compared with females of their mother's generation in Kinsey's investigation (only 3 percent of whom had engaged in premarital intercourse by age 16 and less than 20 percent by age 19), these findings indicate very large increases, particularly at the younger age level (87, 114, 161). Furthermore, they demonstrate dramatically that the so-called sexual revolution of the late 1960s has not only continued into the present, but has expanded in scope. When compared with males of their father's generation (approximately 39 percent of whom had engaged in premarital intercourse by age 16, 61 percent by age 17, and 72 percent by age 19), contemporary adolescent boys as a whole show little change, mainly a tendency to have first intercourse at a slightly younger age (86, 114, 137, 161). However, as we shall see in the following section, these *overall* findings for boys obscure significant changes taking place among boys of higher socioeconomic and educational levels.

# *DIVERSITY OF SEXUAL ATTITUDES AND BEHAVIOR*

Up to this point, our focus has been on *overall* trends in sexual attitudes and behavior among contemporary adolescents and youth. Such group trends have meaning and usefulness in their own right, but they should not be allowed to distract our attention from an equally important phenomenon: the diversity of sexual attitudes and behavior in different sectors of the adolescent and youth population. Such factors as age, sex, socioeconomic and educational level, race, religion, and even geographical area appear to be related to sexual attitudes, values, and behavior. For this reason, the results of almost any survey dealing with adolescent sexuality will inevitably seem exaggerated to some young people and adults and minimized to others.

What do we know about some of these variations? As we have already noted, a majority of American adolescents aged 13 to 19 currently report having engaged in premarital sexual intercourse. As significant as this evidence of a trend toward greater sexual freedom clearly is, it should not be allowed to obscure the complementary finding that a very substantial minority of young people have not as yet had such experience. Furthermore, neither of these broad groups is homogeneous. Thus, adolescents who have not had intercourse range from those with virtually no sexual experience to those with a variety of experiences short of intercourse itself, including petting to orgasm (114, 137). As we have also noted (see pages 273–274), girls still tend to be more conservative than boys in attitudes, values, and behavior, although sex differences have narrowed in recent years (4, 25, 62, 74, 114, 137, 161). In view of current peer pressures on many adolescents to become involved early in premarital sexual relationships, it is important to keep this diversity in mind.

### *Serial monogamists and sexual adventurers*

Among youthful nonvirgins, the majority are currently involved with only one person, with whom they share strong affectionate bonds. Thus, in Sorensen's study, two major subgroups of nonvirgins emerged: *serial monogamists,* who were the most frequent, and *sexual adventurers,* who comprised only 15 percent of all adolescents and 6 percent of girls. The former generally have a relationship with only one partner for a period of time and have intercourse only with that partner during that time. The term serial is used because one such relationship is often succeeded by another (137). The sexual adventurer, on the other hand, "moves freely from one sex partner to the next and feels no obligation to be faithful to any sex partner" (137, *121*). (Among the minority of adolescents in Sorensen's study who were sexual adventurers, 80 percent were male; in contrast, 64 percent of serial monogamists were female.)

Not surprisingly, the two groups tended to vary significantly in attitudes as well as in behavior. Most monogamists believe they love and are loved by their partners, believe in openness and honesty between partners, and deny that sex is the most important thing in a love relationship—although they also express greater satisfaction than adventurers with their sex lives. At the same time, their code stresses personal freedom without commitment to marriage, although more than half believe they will or may marry their partner eventually.

Sexual adventurers, in contrast, are primarily interested in variety of experience for its own sake, do not believe that love is a necessary part of sexual relationships, and feel no particular personal responsibility for their partners, although neither do they believe in hurting others. For many adventurers, sex itself is viewed as an avenue to communication; as one young adventurer stated, "Having sex together is a good way for two people to become acquainted."

As a group, monogamists tended to be more satisfied with themselves and life in general, to get along better with parents, and to be more conventional in social, political, and religious beliefs. Despite their greater emphasis on sex as a goal in itself, female adventurers report having orgasm during intercourse less frequently than monogamists.

### Socioeconomic and educational status

Economically privileged, more highly educated adolescents and youth are less conservative in their sexual attitudes and values than their less economically favored peers of the same age, although the differences currently appear to be decreasing (25, 30, 156) (see Chapter 13). Also, it is among economically favored college or college-bound adolescents and youth, especially females, that the greatest changes in sexual behavior have occurred since their parents' generation (25, 30, 105, 154, 156). In the 1940s, by the age of 21, the incidence of premarital experience among college-educated persons was 49 percent for males and 27 percent for females. In contrast, several representative investigations of contemporary American college and university students of comparable ages (25, 30, 86, 87, 149) indicate a substantial upward shift for both sexes, but particularly among women. Thus, for males, incidence of premarital intercourse ranged up to a high of 82 percent; comparable percentages for females ranged up to a high of 76 percent. While the incidence for males appeared to reach a plateau in the early 1970s, the incidence for females continued to increase throughout the decade (30, 74, 149).

Other factors are also related to sexual attitudes, values, and behavior. Younger adolescents are more *conservative* about sexual matters than older adolescents (30, 62, 66, 73, 137). Significantly fewer 13- to 14-year-olds than 16- to 19-year-olds agree that "It's all right for young people to have sex before getting married if they are in love with each other" (137). Politically conservative and religiously oriented youth are more conservative in sexual attitudes and behavior than liberal or religiously inactive young people (25, 30, 74, 75, 77, 140). Black adolescents are more active sexually than whites of the same age (77, 78, 159, 161, 162). Cultural differences also exist (26, 30, 92, 94). For both sexes, premarital intercourse is less common in Canada and the United States than in England, West Germany, and the Scandinavian countries (94).

## PARENT-CHILD CONFLICTS IN SEXUAL VALUES

The sexual attitudes and values of parents are generally more conservative than those of their adolescent young. Parents are more likely to disapprove of premarital sexual relations and of making birth control information and contraceptive devices available to adolescents, although such differences have narrowed significantly in recent years (15, 30, 137). Adults generally are also somewhat more likely to view sexual behavior in terms of prevailing social codes, and less likely to be influenced by the nature of the relationship between the persons involved (15, 30).

In one national survey (50), nearly half of all adults felt that living together outside of marriage was always wrong, and only a quarter approved of the idea. In other recent national surveys (53, 136), 59.6 percent of adults ages 35 to 44, and 44.6 percent of those ages 45 to 64, indicated that premarital sexual relations were not wrong, at least under some circumstances. Those who were younger, male, urban residents, divorced or never married, college educated, high-income, or lacking in religious affiliation were most permissive (136). Those who were older, female, nonurban, widowed, low-income, or religiously affiliated, or had less than high school education were most disapproving. In contrast, as we have seen, three out of four adolescents approve of living together prior to marriage, and of having premarital sexual relations, at least under some circumstances (see page 283). It is interesting to note that the only age group of adults whose views became more conservative during the 1970s was the 18- to 25-year-old group, though they remained by far the most liberal. All other age groups, including those over 65, became more liberal than they had been early in the decade (136).

Although most adolescents say they have respect for their parents' views generally, including their ideas and opinions about sex, there does not appear to be much communication on the subject between adolescents and their parents in a majority of instances (20, 62, 74, 114, 137). In only a little over one-third of cases do adolescents and their parents indicate that they find it easy to discuss sex with each other (62, 114, 137).

Why are the views of parents on sexual behavior generally more conservative than those of their adolescent young? One obvious factor is the speed of social change; the social standards that middle-aged and older adults grew up with were significantly more conservative than is the case today. Although, as we have seen, there has been some shift in the past decade among these adults in the direction of greater permissiveness, it would be surprising if the change from previously acquired beliefs had been a radical one. Another related factor may be ambivalence. Even in those instances in which the grandparents and parents of today's youth engaged in generally similar sexual behavior, they probably did so with more conflicting emotions and more of a sense of guilt. After all, their break with *their* parents was more clearly revolutionary as far as actual behavior was concerned. Consequently, it seems reasonable to assume that it was accompanied by more doubt and anxiety, and such indeed appears to have been the case (121). Thus, it should not be too surprising to find less consonance between behavior, on the one hand, and values and attitudes, on the other hand, in the older generation than among their children.

In contrast, anxiety and guilt appear significantly lower among contemporary adolescents who have had premarital intercourse (30, 74, 137, 140). Eighty-six percent of all sexually experienced adolescents (including 91 percent of serial monogamists and 89 percent of sexual adventurers) believe that their own sex life is "pretty normal for a person my age" (137). Only a little over one-third acknowledged that they sometimes feel guilty about their sexual behavior; interestingly, monogamists are least likely to feel guilty.

Some of today's young people may be perceiving a lack of consonance between feelings and behavior when they accuse adults of being hypocritical in their sexual attitudes and values. It should be recognized, however, that parents and children stand in a different relationship to one another and differ in their responsibilities. As Robert R. Bell notes in a thoughtful article on parent-child conflicts in sexual values,

> Given their different stages in the life cycle, parents and children will almost always show differences in how they define appropriate behavior for a given role. Values as to single "proper" premarital sexual role behavior from the perspective of the parents are greatly influenced by the strong emotional involvement of the parent with his child. Youth, on the other hand, are going through a life cycle stage in which the actual behavior occurs, and they must relate the parent values to what they are doing or may do. There is a significant difference between defining appropriate role conduct for others to follow and defining proper role conduct to be followed by one's self. Even more important for actual behavior, there is often more than one significant group of role definers to which the young person can turn as guide for his sex role behavior [15, *34*].

Young people who have only to decide their own values and behavior are in a very different position from parents concerned about the welfare of their children. In addition to being freer of the strong pressures (both physiological and social) that their adolescent sons and daughters are confronted with, they have, as Bell says, "a strong emotional involvement with their children." They do not wish to see them hurt, either by becoming involved in sexual and emotional relationships they may not be prepared to handle, or by becoming pregnant or involved in early, ill-considered marriages. In many respects, these concerns of parents are part of the larger problem of independence-dependence. Parents want their children ultimately to grow up and be independent, but they do not wish to see them hurt in the process.

These assertions receive some support from findings that childless couples are significantly more permissive in their attitudes toward adolescent sexual behavior than couples with children—even when they are comparable in other respects, including age (123). Similarly, the more daughters a father has, the more conservative are his attitudes; conversely, the more sons he has, the more permissive are his attitudes (123).

Even among adolescents themselves, feelings of responsibility for others seem to affect attitudes. Thus, adolescents with siblings are significantly less permissive in their own attitudes than only children; and among siblings, first-borns (who presumably feel greater responsibility) are least likely to approve of premarital intercourse, whereas the youngest are the most likely to approve of it (123).

## INFLUENCE OF PARENTS AND PEERS ON ADOLESCENT SEXUAL ATTITUDES AND BEHAVIOR

Recently Farida Shah and Melvin Zelnik (132), population specialists at the Johns Hopkins University, used the data from a comprehensive survey (159) of young unmarried women in the United States, aged 15 to 19 (see pages 285–286), to determine the influence of parents and peers on the views of the participants, and to find how this influence was related to premarital sexual behavior and other issues. They found that on such issues as going to college and having a career, these young women were influenced more by parents than by friends. On the other hand, with respect to their attitudes toward premarital sex, these young women's views resembled those of their friends much more than those of their parents. Participants were asked, "Which one of these statements best describes how you feel about intercourse before marriage?":

1. Sexual intercourse is okay, even if the couple has no plans to marry.
2. Sexual intercourse is okay, but only if the couple is planning to marry.
3. Sexual intercourse is never okay before marriage.

They were also asked whether their views were more like those of their parents, their peers, both, or neither.

The data were analyzed in two ways: distribution by *source of influence* and by *respondents' views* (see Table 8.3). To illustrate, under *source of influence,* we find that among black adolescents who felt that premarital sex was okay whether the participants were engaged or not, 56.6 percent said their views were most like those of their friends, while 10 percent said their views were most like those of their parents. Even among black adolescents who felt that premarital sex was never acceptable, 38.1 percent said their views were most like their friends, although 27.9 percent said their views were most like their parents, and 8.4 percent said they were like both parents and friends. Under distribution by *respondents' views,* we find, for example, that among white adolescents who said that their views were most like their parents (rather than their friends or both parents and friends), only 3.5 percent considered premarital sex acceptable, regardless of whether they were engaged; 27.6 percent considered it acceptable only if engaged, and 68.9 percent considered it unacceptable. In contrast, among white adolescents whose views were most like those of their friends, one-third (33.4 percent) considered premarital sex acceptable, regardless of whether they were engaged; almost half (47 percent) considered it acceptable if engaged; and less than one in five (19.6 percent) considered it never acceptable.

In sum, it appears (1) that, while parents' views are more influential than those of peers on some issues (such as career plans), peer influence is clearly stronger for the average adolescent on attitudes toward premarital sex; (2) that peer views are generally, but not always, more permissive than those of parents; and (3) that black adolescents (and to a lesser extent their parents) are generally more permissive than whites. Other less comprehensive studies have yielded similar results (75, 76, 106, 122).

In general, the attitudes of these adolescents were reflected in their sexual behavior. Thus, among those believing that premarital sex was acceptable whether engaged or not, 84 percent of blacks and 73.5 percent of whites had, in fact, had such experience. However, of those who viewed premarital sex as unacceptable under any circumstances, 24 percent of blacks and 7 percent of whites had nevertheless had some experience. Rates of premarital sexual experience were lowest for

**TABLE 8.3 PERCENTAGE DISTRIBUTION OF 15- TO
19-YEAR-OLD WOMEN, BY OPINION ON SEX BEFORE
MARRIAGE AND BY SIMILARITY OF VIEWS ON SEX TO
SIGNIFICANT OTHERS, BY RACE**

| | BLACK | | | | |
| | RESPONDENTS' VIEWS LIKE: | | | | |
| SEX BEFORE MARRIAGE | PARENTS | FRIENDS | BOTH | NEITHER | N |
|---|---|---|---|---|---|
| *Percentage Distribution by Source of Influence* | | | | | |
| Acceptable | 10.0 | 56.6 | 11.5 | 21.8 | 339 |
| Only if engaged | 12.8 | 58.0 | 6.9 | 22.3 | 188 |
| Never acceptable | 27.7 | 38.1 | 8.4 | 25.8 | 155 |
| *Percentage Distribution by Respondents' Views* | | | | | |
| Acceptable | 33.7 | 53.3 | 60.0 | 47.4 | |
| Only if engaged | 23.8 | 30.3 | 20.0 | 26.9 | |
| Never acceptable | 42.6 | 16.4 | 20.0 | 25.6 | |
| N | 101 | 360 | 65 | 156 | |

young women whose views on sex before marriage were like their parents' views and highest for those with views like those of their friends (see Table 8.4). Furthermore, particularly for whites, those with views like those of their parents were more likely to

**TABLE 8.4 PERCENTAGE OF 15- TO 19-YEAR-OLD
WOMEN WITH PREMARITAL SEXUAL EXPERIENCE,
BY SIMILARITY OF VIEWS ON SEX TO SIGNIFICANT
OTHERS, BY RACE**

| | BLACK | | WHITE | |
| VIEWS ON SEX LIKE: | PERCENTAGE | N | PERCENTAGE | N |
|---|---|---|---|---|
| Parents | 50.5 | 103 | 17.1 | 286 |
| Friends | 69.4 | 359 | 54.0 | 654 |
| Both | 63.1 | 65 | 28.4 | 225 |
| Neither | 63.0 | 154 | 34.6 | 301 |
| All | 64.5 | 681 | 38.9 | 1466 |

*Source:* F. Shah and M. Zelnik. Parent and peer influence on sexual behavior, contraceptive use, and pregnancy experience of young women. *Journal of Marriage and the Family,* 1981, **43,** 339–348. By permission.

| | | WHITE | | | |
|---|---|---|---|---|---|
| | | RESPONDENTS' VIEWS LIKE: | | | |
| PARENTS | FRIENDS | BOTH | NEITHER | *N* | |
| 3.2 | 71.4 | 13.0 | 12.3 | 308 | |
| 13.7 | 53.6 | 9.4 | 23.4 | 577 | |
| 33.7 | 22.1 | 22.6 | 21.6 | 584 | |
| 3.5 | 33.4 | 17.7 | 12.7 | | |
| 27.6 | 47.0 | 23.9 | 45.2 | | |
| 68.9 | 19.6 | 58.4 | 42.1 | | |
| 286 | 658 | 226 | 299 | | |

*Source:* F. Shah and M. Zelnik. Parent and peer influence on sexual behavior, contraceptive use, and pregnancy experience of young women. *Journal of Marriage and the Family,* 1981, **43,** 339–348. By permission.

have had intercourse only once; they also were more likely to have had only one partner ever (132).

### A "new morality"

It appears clear that adolescent attitudes and values regarding sex and sexual behavior itself have changed dramatically since the early 1960s, although the extent of the change still varies widely from one segment of the youth population to another. Indeed, as in other areas of social concern, the differences between some subgroups of youth appear wider than those between youth in general and adults in general.

There is a real and often ignored danger in generalizing too widely from specialized subgroups (e.g., a particular college campus or a particular small-town high school) to youth in general. Furthermore, the greatest relative changes in both attitudes and behavior since their parents' generation have occurred among middle- and upper-class adolescents, particularly girls. Not surprisingly, it is among this socio-economically favored segment of the youth population that the "youth culture" of the 1960s took root and found its initial sustenance.

Although the "new morality" of today's adolescents has many positive aspects—a greater emphasis on openness and honesty, more mutual respect and less exploitation, and a more "natural" and somewhat better-informed approach to

Greatest change middle upper girls

sex—it would be a mistake to conclude that the picture is unclouded. Many experienced adolescents, particularly older adolescents and youth, appear able to handle their sexual involvement and their relationships with themselves without undue stress. (Four out of five nonvirgins report getting "a lot of satisfaction" out of their sex lives; two-thirds of all nonvirgins and four out of five monogamists state that sex makes their lives more meaningful.) However, significant minorities report feelings of conflict and guilt, find themselves exploited or rejected, or discover belatedly that they have gotten in over their heads emotionally (16, 137). Especially after the first experience of intercourse, girls are far more likely to experience negative feelings (16, 62, 114, 137). Whereas boys are most likely to report being excited, satisfied, and happy, many girls most frequently report being afraid, guilty, worried, or embarrassed after their initial intercourse experience.

There are obviously dangers in assuming that sexual involvement is "okay as long as you're in love." Encouraged by such a philosophy among peers, a girl or boy may become more deeply involved emotionally than she or he can handle responsibly at a particular stage of maturity. An adolescent may also consciously think that his or her attitudes are more liberal than they actually are, and involvement may lead to unanticipated feelings of guilt, anxiety, or depression.

## PREGNANCY AND CONTRACEPTION

There also still remain very practical problems, such as the possibility of pregnancy. Despite significant progress during the past decade, in 1979 only 34 percent of sexually active young women, aged 15 to 19, reported always using contraceptives (up from 17 percent in 1971 and 29 percent in 1976) (77, 78, 160, 161, 162). Less than half used any form of contraceptive in their first intercourse (see Figure 8.2). Compared to younger adolescents (aged 15), older adolescents (age 19) are twice as likely to have used contraception in their last intercourse (78, 143, 159, 160). Among those using some form of contraception, the most popular methods used initially are, in order of frequency, the male-controlled methods of the condom and withdrawal (each about 35 percent of total use), followed by the pill. Intrauterine devices (IUDs) and other methods accounted for only a relatively small percentage of the total. However, the pill is most likely to be the method most recently used (41 percent, down from 48 percent in 1976) (161). Probably largely as a result of health-related concerns, use of the pill and IUD declined 16 percent in only a 3-year period; the biggest relative gains were for the diaphragm, rhythm, and withdrawal, in that order (see Table 8.5).

As a result of this widespread lack of proper contraceptive measures, and the continuing increase in premarital intercourse among adolescents by 1975, over one million 15- to 19-year-old girls in the United States alone (10 percent of this entire age group) were becoming pregnant each year. (Two-thirds of these pregnancies were conceived out of wedlock.) In addition, some 30,000 girls under the age of 15 were becoming pregnant annually (25, 41, 162). In 1979, 16.2 percent of all girls aged 15 to 19 in metropolitan areas of the United States had become pregnant at least once before marriage (161) (up from 13 percent in 1976 and 8.5 percent in 1971).

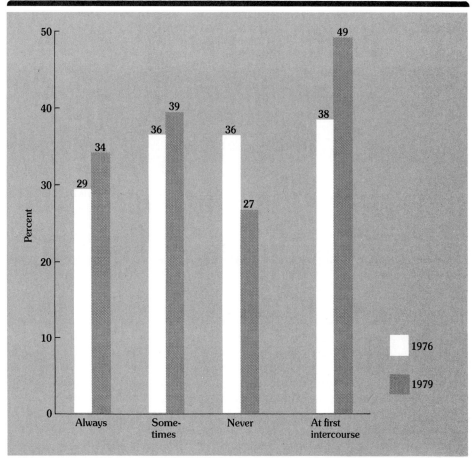

**Figure 8.2** Percentage of premaritally sexually active women aged 15–19 from metropolitan areas who always, sometimes, and never practiced contraception, and percentage who practiced at first intercourse, 1976 and 1979. (Adapted from M. Zelnik and J. F. Kantner. Sexual activity, contraceptive use and pregnancy among metropolitan-area teenagers: 1971–1979. *Family Planning Perspectives,* 1980, **12,** 230–237. By permission.)

Among sexually active adolescent girls, the figures are even more sobering. For example, among sexually active 15-year-olds in 1976, 16 percent had already had a premarital conception, while among 19-year-olds, this figure rose to 34.7 percent—one girl in every three; among black adolescents, rates were higher than among their white peers (see Table 8.6). Furthermore, these rates have risen slightly; between 1976 and 1979, overall pregnancy rates for all sexually active adolescents, aged 15 to 19, increased from 30 percent in 1976 to 33 percent in 1979 (161).

The consequences of this epidemic of adolescent pregnancies are serious indeed. More than a quarter are terminated by induced abortion; 10 percent result in marital births that were conceived premaritally; and over one-fifth result in out-

**TABLE 8.5 PERCENTAGE DISTRIBUTION OF WOMEN AGED 15 TO 19 WHO EVER USED A CONTRACEPTIVE METHOD, BY MOST RECENT METHOD USED,[a] ACCORDING TO RACE, 1979 AND 1976**

| METHOD LAST USED | 1979 | | | 1976 | | |
|---|---|---|---|---|---|---|
| | TOTAL (N = 665) | WHITE (N = 374) | BLACK (N = 291) | TOTAL (N = 440) | WHITE (N = 228) | BLACK (N = 212) |
| Pill | 40.6 | 38.2 | 50.6 | 47.8 | 46.0 | 53.3 |
| IUD | 2.0 | 1.8 | 2.8 | 3.2 | 3.3 | 2.8 |
| Diaphragm | 3.5 | 3.7 | 2.5 | 0.9 | 1.0 | 0.5 |
| Condom | 23.2 | 23.1 | 24.2 | 22.9 | 23.7 | 20.4 |
| Foam | 3.9 | 4.4 | 2.2 | 3.8 | 4.0 | 3.2 |
| Douche | 2.1 | 1.7 | 4.0 | 2.8 | 0.9 | 8.8 |
| Withdrawal | 18.8 | 21.4 | 7.5 | 14.6 | 17.2 | 6.6 |
| Rhythm | 5.8 | 5.7 | 6.2 | 3.8 | 3.9 | 3.5 |
| Total | 100.0 | 100.0 | 100.0 | 100.0[b] | 100.0 | 100.0[b] |

*Source:* M. Zelnik and J. F. Kantner. Sexual activity, contraceptive use and pregnancy among metropolitan-area teenagers: 1971–1979. *Family Planning Perspectives,* 1980, **12,** 230–237. By permission.

[a] Most recent method for those never-married women covered in Figure 8.2; for the ever-married, most recent method is last premarital use.

[b] Does not add to 100.00 because the 0.9 percent of blacks reported as sterilized are excluded.

of-wedlock births. Fourteen percent lead to miscarriages (28). Even among the 27 percent of adolescent pregnancies that occur postmaritally each year, problems are more frequent than among older women.

Adolescent pregnancies are more likely to endanger the physical health of both mother and child, although, as a number of investigations have shown, the risks could be reduced if more adequate prenatal and postnatal care, and better nutrition, were provided to all pregnant adolescents (117). In fact, several investigations have

**TABLE 8.6 ESTIMATED PERCENTAGE OF SEXUALLY ACTIVE WOMEN, AGES 15 TO 19, WHO HAD EVER HAD A PREMARITAL CONCEPTION (1976)**

| AGE | TOTAL | WHITE ADOLESCENTS | BLACK ADOLESCENTS |
|---|---|---|---|
| 15 | 16.0 | 11.2 | 25.2 |
| 16 | 21.6 | 16.9 | 33.9 |
| 17 | 25.8 | 21.3 | 39.9 |
| 18 | 31.0 | 27.1 | 45.3 |
| 19 | 34.7 | 30.7 | 52.8 |

*Source:* M. Zelnik, Y. J. Kim, and J. F. Kantner. Probabilities of intercourse and conception among U.S. teenage women, 1971–1976. *Family Planning Perspectives,* 1979, **11,** No. 3, 177–183. By permission.

shown that *older* adolescents who bear children fare no worse—in terms of maternal and infant outcomes—than other age groups, once social class and quality of care are controlled (56, 61, 117). Under current circumstances, however, babies of teenage mothers are more likely to have low birth weights, a major cause of infant mortality, as well as neurological defects and childhood illnesses (see Figure 8.3). And adolescent mothers are more likely to have complications of pregnancy (such as toxemia and anemia); among very young teenagers, pregnancy tends to deplete nutritional requirements needed for their own growth, and this places them at higher risk for a variety of illnesses (41).

In addition, teenage mothers—90 percent of whom currently keep their babies—generally face significant problems in other areas; they are twice as likely as their peers to drop out of school, less likely to gain employment, and more likely to end up on welfare (41, 48, 83, 142). Many are still psychologically in need of mothering themselves, and ill prepared to take on the psychological, social, and economic responsibilities of motherhood; their knowledge of an infant's needs and capabilities is often unrealistic—leading to expectations and demands that their infants cannot meet (25, 54). Because of their immaturity and the greater stress they are subjected to, adolescent mothers have a higher risk of child abuse (124). Fur-

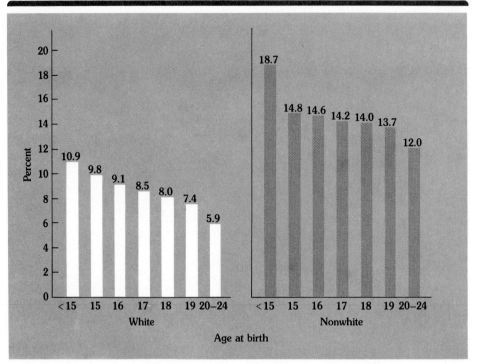

**Figure 8.3** Percentage of babies of low birth weight (less than 2500 grams), by age of mother, according to race, 1978. (From Planned Parenthood Federation of America. *Teenage pregnancy: The problem that hasn't gone away.* New York: Alan Guttmacher Institute, 1981. By permission.)

thermore, the single adolescent mother has less chance of getting married than her peers, and a much greater chance of divorce if she does marry (24, 41, 54). Even adolescents who are already married when they become pregnant, or who marry prior to the birth of their child, have a far higher divorce rate than those who become mothers after age 20 (see pages 356–360).

Why do so many adolescent girls and younger women fail to use contraceptive measures? In recent surveys, the major reasons given for not using contraceptives were that the teenagers (usually mistakenly) thought that they could not become pregnant because of time of month, age, or infrequency of intercourse, or because contraceptives were not available when they needed them. As the Planned Parenthood Federation notes: "The first set of reasons could be remedied with better education, the second with more adequate service programs." Yet only one in three high schools currently teach about birth control methods, despite the fact that eight out of ten Americans old enough to have children of junior high or high school age favor such teaching (41). Substantial progress has been made in recent years in making contraceptive services available to adolescents, and nearly one-third of sexually active teenagers currently at risk of unintended pregnancy have visited an organized clinic program (32). Nevertheless, additional comprehensive services are still needed for the more than 1.6 million sexually active adolescents who have not visited a clinic or private physician for counseling and contraceptive services (32, 143).

Psychological studies comparing sexually active adolescent girls who do and do not use contraceptives (or use them rarely) have found that those not using them tend more often to hold fatalistic attitudes: They are more likely to feel powerless to control the events of their lives, to have a low sense of personal competence, and to have a passive, dependent approach to male-female relationships. They are also more inclined generally to take risks, and to cope with anxiety by attempting to deny possible dangers, rather than by facing up to them (25). Some adolescents avoid contraceptive use because they fear it will spoil the spontaneity of the relationship, or because they think it would indicate that they expected to have intercourse. Interestingly, girls who frankly accept their sexuality are more likely to use contraceptives than those who deny it—to themselves or others (24, 25, 72).

In addition, consistent contraceptive use is more likely among female adolescents who are older, who are in love and involved in an ongoing relationship, who have high self-esteem and self-confidence, who are making normal school progress, who have positive attitudes toward parents, and who received sex education early and at home, rather than from an acquaintance (24, 54, 72, 78, 82, 132, 159, 160, 161). Among male adolescents, those most likely to employ contraceptive measures are older, more experienced in dating, and more organized and responsible in their general approach to life, and have parents who approve of their sexual involvement. Males least likely to employ contraception tend to be either sexually naive or to be permissively reared and "exploitative," believing that contraception is the female's responsibility (25, 54, 72, 82).

Contrary to some popular opinion on the subject, only one in fifteen pregnant adolescents stated that she did not use contraceptives because she was trying to have a baby, and only one in eleven indicated she "didn't mind" getting pregnant (see Figure 8.4). However, among adolescents either seeking or not objecting to pregnancy, a common theme is that of emotional deprivation. In the words of one pregnant 15-year-old: "I guess for once in my life, I wanted to have something I could call my own, that I could love and that would love me." Other related motivations may include being accepted as an adult, getting back at one's parents, "holding" a boyfriend, gaining attention from peers, escaping from school, or just looking for some change in an unrewarding existence (25).

It seems unlikely that the trend toward premarital intercourse as an accepted practice, and especially toward serial monogamy as the most frequent and the most socially approved pattern among sexually experienced adolescents, will be reversed. Of all residuals of the youth culture of the 1960s, greater sexual freedom and openness appear to be the most enduring. What one must hope is that those adolescents who do enter sexual relationships can be helped to become mature enough, informed enough, responsible enough, sure enough of their own identities and value systems, and sensitive and concerned enough about the welfare of others so that the inevitable casualties in the sexual revolution can be reduced to a minimum, and sex as a vital part of human relationships can promote, rather than hinder, growth toward maturity and emotional fulfillment (30).

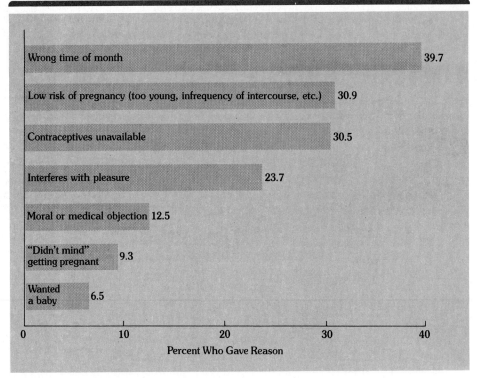

**Figure 8.4** Reasons given by female adolescents aged 15–19 for not using contraception. (From Planned Parenthood Federation of America. *Eleven million teenagers: What can be done about the epidemic of adolescent pregnancies in the United States?* New York: Alan Guttmacher Institute, 1976.)

## SEXUAL BEHAVIOR AND ADOLESCENT ADJUSTMENT

### Masturbation

There are wide cultural differences in attitudes toward masturbation and in masturbatory behavior. Among the Apinaye of northeastern South Africa, for example, boys and girls "are warned from infancy not to masturbate and a severe thrashing awaits the child suspected of such behavior" (46, *180*). Kwoma boys in New Guinea "are constantly warned not to finger their genitals; if a woman sees a boy with an erection she will beat his penis with a stick, and boys soon learn to refrain from touching their genitals even while urinating" (46, *180*). In contrast, in some permissive societies adults have actively participated in the sexual stimulation of infants and young children (46). Among the Hopi and and Siriono, parents were found to masturbate their children frequently (46).

In America, and in many other technologically developed Western countries, masturbation has traditionally been condemned, often "as a perversion on a par with homosexual relations" (45, *308*). Even as late as the beginning of the present century, many prominent physicians, teachers, and even health publications of the United States government warned—and apparently believed—that masturbation weakened the individual or caused a variety of diseases, and might even end in insanity if practiced to excess (84, 118, 119, 138). Despite such dire warnings, most boys (and a much smaller number of girls) continued to engage in this activity, so it is not difficult to imagine the widespread anxiety, conflict, and depression that frequently ensued—sometimes extending over a period of years, and in some cases even resulting in suicide.

Even G. Stanley Hall, the distinguished father of the modern scientific study of adolescence, was not spared. The considerable personal misery he experienced and the elaborate psychological defense mechanisms that he resorted to as a late-nineteenth-century adolescent in attempts to deal with conflicts over masturbation are painfully evident:

> So great was my dread of natural phenomena [i.e., masturbation and nocturnal emission] that in the earliest teens I rigged an apparatus and applied bandages to prevent erethism while I slept, which very likely only augmented the trouble. If I yielded to any kind of temptation to experimentation upon myself I suffered intense remorse and fear, and sent up many a secret and most fervent prayer that I might never again break my resolve. At one time I feared I was abnormal and found occasion to consult a physician in a neighboring town who did not know me. He examined me and took my dollar, and laughed at me, but also told me what consequences would ensue if I became unchaste. What an untold anguish of soul would have been saved me if someone had told me that certain experiences while I slept were as normal for boys in their teens as are monthly phenomena for girls. I did not know that even in college and thought myself secretly and exceptionally corrupt and not quite worthy to associate with girls. This had probably much, if not most, to do with my abstention from them and was, I think, the chief factor that brought about my [religious] "conversion" in my sophomore year, although this made the struggle for purity far more intense, though I fear but little more successful. . . .
>
> Perhaps, again, my profound sense of inferiority here prompted me to compensate by striving all the harder for excellence in other lines, although there was always a haunting sense that if I succeeded in making anything of myself it would be despite this private handicap. I should certainly never dare to marry and have children. It was ineffable relief, therefore, to learn as I did only far too late, that my life in this sphere had, on the whole, been in no sense abnormal or even exceptional [84, *185*].

Fortunately, general attitudes, and especially the views of acknowledged experts on sexual behavior, have changed markedly in recent years (27, 29, 64, 114, 118). In one recent survey, among 15- and 16-year-olds, 76 percent of boys and 70 percent of girls said they believed that "it is okay for boy (girl) my age to masturbate" (62, *84*). Among 17- and 18-year-olds, agreement increased to 85 percent for boys and 72 percent for girls. Nevertheless, many adolescents continue to have at least occasional feelings of guilt, anxiety, or depression regarding their masturbating experience (74, 137). In the words of one 15-year-old girl, "When I was really little, my best girlfriend and I would sleep over at each other's house and we'd masturbate together in the same room. We even had our own name for it. We certainly didn't think there was anything wrong with what we were doing: it was just something we did that felt good. But in about fourth grade I found out more about sex and I realized that masturbating was *sexual*. Then, as far as I was concerned, it was definitely not OK to do anymore—especially not with somebody else in the same room. After that I used to feel guilty when I was doing it, like it was kind of humiliating, and I tried to stop myself. Then last year when I heard from a lot of my girlfriends that they do it too, I felt better about it" (16, *80–81*). Furthermore, investigators of sexual behavior among adolescents and adults still find that participants had more difficulty in discussing masturbation than any other sexual topic (62, 74, 137). And there are still clinicians who, while avoiding the dire predictions of yesteryear, nevertheless assert that masturbation among children or adolescents is likely to make it difficult for the individual subsequently to transfer to heterosexual sources of gratification (74, 118, 119).

What is the actual evidence? Obviously, at least in boys, earlier predictions that masturbation would seriously impair physical and psychological health have been clearly demonstrated to be erroneous, since the practice is virtually universal. Furthermore, in the absence of previously acquired guilt or anxiety, masturbation may be both enjoyable and tension-reducing. It may also provide an opportunity for rehearsal of sexual responses that will later be required in heterosexual intercourse, and for learning to establish associations between appropriate cues (actual or fantasied) and sexual response (8, 27, 29, 118).

Learning techniques of sexual arousal may be valuable in female adolescents as well, since the relatively "automatic" arousal of this response and subsequent orgasm that occurs among boys does not take place as readily among many girls (although the ultimate strength of the response, once it occurs, may be as strong or stronger than that of boys) (97, 98, 119). Masters and Johnson (97, 98) and other experts on sexual response (86, 87) have found that orgastic adequacy among females is dependent not only on the absence of culturally or parentally invoked patterns of anxiety and conflict, but upon the availability of appropriate techniques for learning to respond, and subsequent practice—whether through masturbation or the use of a heterosexual partner, or both—in these techniques. They and other sex therapists have been able to successfully treat a majority of cases of orgasmic dysfunction in women referred to them, largely through training in methods of sexual arousal and anxiety reduction (8, 79).

The notion that masturbation reduces the likelihood of achieving orgasm in later heterosexual intercourse also lacks empirical support. Kinsey found that among females who had never engaged in masturbation prior to marriage or whose masturbation had never led to orgasm, approximately one-third failed to reach orgasm during intercourse in the first year of marriage, and in most instances in the first 5 years of marriage. In contrast, "among those who had masturbated to the point of orgasm before marriage, only 13 to 16 percent had been totally unresponsive in the early years of marriage" (87, *172–173*). As Kinsey concedes, a selective factor may have been involved in these results because the more responsive females may have been the ones who masturbated before marriage and who had responded more often in their marital intercourse. On the other hand, his analyses of specific histories appeared to indicate that the quality of the marital response was "furthered by the female's previous knowledge of the nature of a sexual orgasm" (87, *173*). The findings of Masters and Johnson and others also appear to support this interpretation. In any event, it seemed clear that "the capacity to respond in orgasm in marital coitus had not been lessened by the premarital masturbatory experience of the females in the sample" (87, *173*).

It is sometimes argued that masturbation, though not physically harmful, may be psychologically maladaptive because it may lead to a preoccupation with sex. However, as the not atypical example provided by G. Stanley Hall indicates, preoccupation with sex is generally far more likely to result from constant, conflict-ridden attempts to avoid masturbation, particularly on the part of males. At the same time, there can be little doubt that in some instances masturbatory activities may be related to problems of adolescent adjustment. The adolescent whose masturbatory activities serve as a substitute for other activities in which he or she feels inadequate—whether involving peer-group projects or recreation, or more individual pursuits, such as hobbies or intellectual interests—has a problem. So also does the adolescent who engages in masturbation, not in addition to, but as a substitute for, efforts to establish pleasant and meaningful social relationships with opposite-sex peers. But in each of these instances, the masturbatory activity is not primarily a *cause* of the individual's problems, but rather a *response* to them.

### *Petting and premarital intercourse*

Premarital experience in petting to orgasm may perform many of the functions ascribed to masturbation. Kinsey found that among females who had never engaged in petting to orgasm prior to marriage, slightly over a third did not reach orgasm in the first year of marriage (87). In contrast, among those "who had reached orgasm in at least some of their premarital petting, only 10 percent had failed to achieve it in the first year of marriage. Similar differences were apparent for some 15 years after marriage" (87, *265*).

Similarly, more than 50 percent of females in Kinsey's investigation who had premarital intercourse that led to orgasm reached orgasm in virtually all their experiences of marital intercourse during the first year of marriage. Among those who had not had any premarital experience of intercourse and had not reached orgasm from any source before marriage, less than a third "had approached a 100-percent response in the first year of marriage" (87, *329*).

Again, these correlations may have depended on selective factors, at least to some extent. Females who had abstained before marriage may have been "physiologically less responsive individuals" (87, *329*). However, it also appears likely, in view of the therapeutic experiences of Masters and Johnson and others (17, 97, 98), that the experiences themselves promoted learning of sexual responsiveness to appropriate stimuli. Petting to orgasm can also provide young people who are ready to share a more intimate relationship an opportunity for mutual pleasure and release of tension without their having to worry about pregnancy, if they are careful. On the other hand, premarital sexual experiences for which the individual is emotionally unprepared, that arouse guilt and anxiety, or that are traumatic in themselves or lead to unfortunate consequences may tend to inhibit rather than facilitate the young person's capacity for subsequent successful marital response.

### Homosexuality and heterosexuality

Many young people fail to distinguish between homosexual *experience* and *homosexuality* (or, more accurately, a primarily homosexual *orientation*). Because they have found themselves having sexually tinged fantasies or dreams about a member of the same sex, have engaged in mutual sexual experimentation, or had a crush on a teacher or friend, they conclude that they are gay. And in a society that still has a strong fear of homosexuality and that tends to view gay males and lesbians as immoral or "sick," this conclusion can lead to considerable anxiety, to the formation of elaborate psychological defenses of asceticism or masochistic self-denial, or even, on occasion, to suicide (114).

The fact of the matter, however, is that such concerns are usually groundless. Although many young people have had such experiences, most of them go on to establish satisfying heterosexual adjustments. Kinsey (86, 87) found that more than half of all older boys and adults recalled some sort of preadolescent sex play, mostly between the ages of 8 and 13, and he considered this figure low because 70 percent of the preadolescent boys he interviewed acknowledged such experiences. Among girls, one-third acknowledged having engaged in sex play prior to the onset of adolescence.

Among preadolescent boys, same-sex play most commonly involved exhibition of the genitalia, self-masturbation with one or more others (frequently in the form of exhibitionistic "contests"), or mutual masturbation. Among preadolescent girls, genital exhibitions and examinations, and "manual manipulation of the genitalia of one or both of the girls" (87, *114*) were most frequent. Insertion of objects, including fingers, into the vagina was relatively rare (87). Girls were far less likely than boys to be involved in group activities. Although preadolescent sex play, both same- and opposite-sex, may clearly involve pleasurable sexual stimulation, a great deal of it is primarily motivated by curiosity about one's self and others.

During adolescence itself, a significant number of boys have at least occasional active sexual contacts with other males. Kinsey (86) found that by age 16, over 20 percent—and by age 20 about 25 percent—of males had engaged in homosexual activity to the point of orgasm. Perhaps not surprisingly, the incidence was higher among boys maturing early than among those maturing late. In Sorensen's more recent (1973) national study (see page 285), 5 percent of boys aged 13 to 15, and 17 percent of those aged 16 to 19, reported having had homosexual experiences (137).

Among Kinsey's sample of adolescent girls, "not more than 2 to 3 percent had reached orgasm in their homosexual relations during adolescence and their teens, although five times that many may have been conscious of homosexual arousal and three times that many may have had physical contacts with other girls which were specifically sexual" (87, *454*). In Sorensen's study, 6 percent of girls aged 13 to 15, and a like percentage of those aged 16 to 19, reported having had homosexual experiences (137).

A recent extensive study of homosexual and heterosexual adults by investigators at the Kinsey Institute for Sex Research (14) suggests that having *predominantly or exclusively* homosexual feelings in childhood and adolescence is more closely related to adoption of a homosexual orientation in adulthood than having had homosexual experiences during the developmental years. For example, among white males, 21 percent of heterosexuals had engaged in mutual masturbation with other males prior to age 19, and a considerably larger number (51 percent) had been involved in some kind of sex play. Eighty-four percent of homosexuals had engaged in mutual masturbation; however, because there are so many fewer gay persons in the population, the total number of heterosexuals having such experience is far greater than the number of homosexuals. In contrast, when both groups were asked whether their sexual feelings during childhood and adolescence were predominantly homosexual, 59 percent of homosexuals and only 1 percent of heterosexuals replied affirmatively. It is important to keep in mind the influence that an individual's current situation may have on a retrospective report. Because these differences are so large, it seems highly unlikely that they would have resulted primarily from retrospective bias.

Similar results were obtained among white females, although the overall incidence of homosexual activity was far less. Four percent of heterosexuals reported having engaged in mutual masturbation prior to age 19, compared to 41 percent of homosexuals. As with males, however, the principal characteristic distinguishing those who became homosexual as adults from those who became heterosexual was whether their sexual feelings during childhood and adolescence had been predominantly homosexual (44 percent versus 1 percent). In brief, although homosexual adults are more likely than heterosexuals to have had homosexual experiences in childhood and adolescence, the predominance of homosexual over heterosexual feelings during this developmental period was a considerably better predictor of adult homosexuality.

While most young people (including a significant number who have had some sort of sexual involvement with members of the same sex during childhood and adolescence) develop a heterosexual orientation as adults, a minority do not. Contemporary investigations suggest that about 2 to 3 percent of males and about 1 to 2 percent of females are more or less exclusively homosexual after adolescence, although perhaps 10 to 12 percent of males and about half that number of females have had at least one homosexual experience beyond age 19 (74, 90).

When a national sample of college students in the 1970s was asked to indicate sexual preferences, 93 percent of males and 91 percent of females stated an exclusive interest in the opposite sex; an additional 4 percent of males and 5 percent of females said they were interested mostly in the opposite sex (140). Only 1 percent of males and 2 percent of females indicated an exclusive interest in the same sex. The remainder reported equal interest in either sex or same-sex mostly. These figures appear remarkably consistent with the results of a reanalysis of Kinsey's data on college males obtained more than 30 years ago, which indicated that only about 5 or 6 percent had any real homosexual experience after late adolescence. In brief, contrary to the assertions of some social critics that greater freedom of discussion of homosexuality and increased tolerance of individual homosexual preference is leading to an increase in the number of persons with a predominantly homosexual orientation, it appears clear that "the incidence of homosexuality, if it has not diminished since Kinsey's time, has not demonstrably increased" (74, *313*).

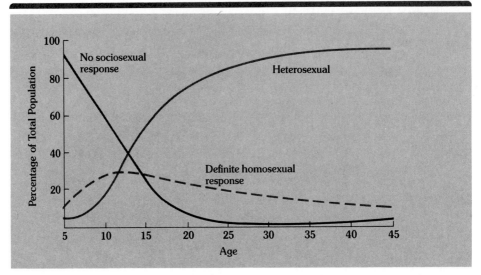

**Figure 8.5** Development of heterosexuality and homosexuality by age periods. Active incidence curves, corrected for U.S. population. Males with no sociosexual response (rating X) rapidly disappear between the ages of 5 and 20. Males whose responses are chiefly heterosexual (rating 0 or 1) rapidly increase in number until they ultimately account for 90 percent of the whole population. Males who are more than incidentally homosexual in response or overt activity (ratings 2–6) are most abundant in preadolescence and through the teens, gradually becoming less abundant with advancing age. (From A. C. Kinsey, W. B. Pomeroy, and C. E. Martin. *Sexual behavior in the human male.* Philadelphia: Saunders, 1948. By permission.)

### Heterosexuality versus homosexuality—a false dichotomy?

We have tended to use the phrase "primarily homosexual in orientation," rather than "homosexual," because the words *heterosexual* and *homosexual* imply, and, indeed, popular thought assumes, that these terms are mutually exclusive and dichotomous. As Kinsey (86, 87) established, however, this is simply not the case. Employing a rating scale that ranged from 0 (exclusively heterosexual in activity and psychic response) to 6 (exclusively homosexual in both)—with an X rating for individuals who did not respond either heterosexually or homosexually—he found that there were individuals who fell at all points along this scale. Among males, significant though small percentages of individuals were to be found at all age levels who, though primarily heterosexual, had had at least incidental homosexual arousal (ratings 1 and 2); who were about evenly divided between heterosexual and homosexual responsiveness (rating 3); or who, though primarily homosexual in orientation, nevertheless had at least incidental heterosexual experience (ratings 4 and 5). As may be seen in Figure 8.5, the percentage of males whose experiences are primarily homosexual (ratings 4, 5, or 6) declines steadily from adolescence onward (63). The same trend is observable among females, although in all instances absolute frequencies are much lower (87).

### Nature versus nurture

How can homosexual orientations, either exclusive or partial, be understood? Are they primarily the result of nature (e.g., chromosomal or hormonal deviations) or of nurture (e.g., sex-role or gender training, atypical patterns of parent-child relationships, unusual sociopsychological experiences), or some combination of the two?

Each of these positions has had, and continues to have, its advocates. Masters and Johnson in their most recent book, *Homosexuality in Perspective* (99), maintain that homosexuality is a result of learning—a view also endorsed by Kinsey (86, 87) and others (11, 46, 107). In their view, sex drive—especially in humans—does not appear initially to be attached inflexibly to any particular object. Consequently, an individual's sexual potential can be channeled by various learning experiences in either a homosexual or heterosexual direction. In contrast, a number of other investigators assert that homosexuality has its roots in hormonal or other biological factors (12, 36, 70, 99). Even among Kinsey's successors, this view finds some support; Alan Bell, Martin Weinberg, and Sue Kiefer Hammersmith of the Kinsey Institute for Sex Research in their recent study of the development of sexual preference in men and women (14) conclude that "our findings are not inconsistent with what one would expect if, indeed, there were a biological basis for sexual preference" (99, *216*).

We still have a great deal to learn, and it seems unlikely that definitive answers regarding the relative roles of nature and nurture in the development of homosexual (and, indeed, heterosexual) behavior will be found quickly. Nevertheless, recent research has begun to provide some clarification of the issues.

### Biological influences on sexual orientation

A number of investigations suggest that deviant hormonal influences acting during prenatal life may subsequently affect sexual and other behavior. In several species of lower animals, it has been found that male and female sexual behavior is largely controlled by particular brain centers (in the area of the hypothalamus) which mature before or shortly after birth (23). If androgens (male hormones) are available during this process of maturation, these brain centers become masculinized.

> When the animal reaches puberty, its hypothalamic control centers react in a male way to male hormones and the animal displays male sexual behavior. If androgens are not available during the maturing process, the hypothalamic centers which control sexual behavior mature in a feminine manner and the animal after puberty exhibits essentially female sexual behavior—even in the presence of male hormones [23, *250*].

Thus, when female guinea pigs were administered male hormones prenatally, they subsequently exhibited male copulatory behavior during adolescence and adulthood (5). Similarly, when male rats were prenatally administered cyproterone, a drug that counteracts the natural masculinizing effect of the animal's own self-produced male hormone (androgen), they later engaged in female copulatory behavior (23, 113). Immature female rhesus monkeys exposed to androgens before birth adopted relatively masculine patterns of infant and youthful play (65).

No such dramatic and clear-cut effects have been observed to date in humans (where learning presumably plays a relatively greater role in development in comparison to biologically predetermined behavior patterns). However, in several studies where girls received excess androgens during prenatal life (either as a result of drugs administered to the mother or because of a genetic abnormality), there was a tendency for these girls to exhibit a higher incidence of "masculine" behaviors than their female peers (39, 40, 60, 145). Thus in one study (39), girls with adrenogenital syndrome (AGS), a genetic defect resulting in an excess of prenatal androgens, showed higher levels of rough-and-tumble play, initiation of fighting, and preference for boys as playmates than a control group of unaffected female siblings. They also appeared less interested in babies and more interested in jobs and careers. In none of these investigations, however, including instances where the participants had entered adolescence, did the girls with fetal hormonal androgenization display any observable lesbian tendency.

Thus, while such *preliminary* findings suggest that deviant hormonal or other biological factors may occasionally play some role in fostering personality characteristics and drive patterns more typical of one sex than another, there is currently no indication that they significantly affect overall heterosexual or homosexual life styles or choice of sexual partners (21, 23, 107).

***Hormonal differences*** Furthermore, efforts to find current hormonal or other biological differences between persons with homosexual versus heterosexual orientations have led to inconsistent or ambiguous results. Several investigators (43, 88, 89) in the early 1970s did report finding homosexual-heterosexual differences in the ratio of androsterone and etiocholanolone (two metabolites of androgen in the urine). Other investigators reported significantly lower average plasma testosterone levels in males who were exclusively or predominantly homosexual (60, 88, 89, 93). Other investigators, however, have been unable to find homosexual-heterosexual differences on either of these sets of measures (60, 146).

Comparisons of female homosexuals and heterosexuals have not been any more consistent. One study found significantly higher plasma testosterone levels among the homosexual females (51), but this conflicted with earlier findings (60). In addition, there is a very real question of the meaning of such hormonal differences even where they are found. A low androsterone-etiocholanolone ratio (comparable to that originally reported for homosexuals) was found in army recruits during the stress of early basic training, and among Green Berets prior to a combat mission (127). Among primates, plasma testosterone level has been shown to be reduced as a result of defeat in a fight or loss of a dominant rank in their social hierarchy (see page 116).

Other factors that may influence plasma testosterone level include tobacco or marijuana intake, anxiety, depression, recovery of sexual arousal, and even time of day (60). Such findings suggest that, even where current homosexual-heterosexual differences in hormonal levels or ratios are found, they may indicate a physiological stress response to societal pressures among some homosexual males rather than a physiological cause for homosexual preference.

More recently several investigators (37, 60) have explored the effects of estradiol (female hormone) on the production of luteinizing hormone (LH), a basic hormone produced by the anterior pituitary gland, which plays an important role in the reproductive cycle in females and in stimulation of testosterone production in males, among other functions (60). Typically, when estradiol is administered to females, there is an initial drop in LH, followed by a return *above the original level*. In males, the return is only to the original level. In one study (37), estradiol was administered to homosexual, bisexual, and heterosexual males, as well as to heterosexual females. The homosexual males' response was more similar to that of the heterosexual females than to the heterosexual males; in contrast, the bisexual males were more like the heterosexual males. However, until such preliminary investigations are repeated and extended, they can be considered at most suggestive.

**Genetic factors**   A number of studies (60, 69) have examined the incidence of homosexuality among the twins of homosexual males. In several studies, the likelihood that the twin would also be homosexual was found to be significantly greater for monozygotic (identical) twins than for dizygotic (nonidentical) twins. The results of some other studies are more ambiguous (60). Furthermore, studies to date have been of twins reared together, thus confounding the possible effects of hereditary and environmental influences. In the absence of reared-together versus reared-apart monozygotic twins, or similarly controlled extended family studies, no conclusive statements can be made about possible genetic influences on the development of a homosexual orientation.

### Psychological and social influences on gender identity and sexual orientation

Research to date indicates rather clearly that psychological and social factors *can* play a dominant role in the development of an individual's gender identity and sexual orientation. Perhaps the most dramatic evidence of this comes from investigations by John Money, a psychologist at the Johns Hopkins University School of Medicine, and his associates. They studied individuals who were assigned the chromosomally incorrect sex at birth, due to various deceptive developmental anomalies (23, 108, 109). In a series of nineteen cases, "babies with a male chromosomal pattern were assigned and reared as girls, while babies with a female chromosomal pattern were assigned and reared as boys" (23, *242*). In all these cases, "the person established a gender role and orientation consistent with assigned sex and rearing and inconsistent with chromosomal sex. Thus, it is convincingly clear that gender role and orientation as male or female evidenced itself independently of chromosomal sex, but in close conformity with assigned sex of rearing" (23, *242*).

Similar results have been obtained in studies of individuals whose sex of assignment and rearing differed from their basic gonadal structure (i.e., testes or ovaries) or their hormonal sex (which affects adolescent development of male and female sex characteristics) (9, 23). Like chromosomal sex and gonadal sex, "hormonal sex *per se* proved a most unreliable prognosticator of a person's gender role and identification as man or woman, boy or girl" (23, *243*).

One particularly interesting study (108) involved what is now called *androgen insensitivity syndrome.* In this condition, the individual begins life with normal male (XY) chromosomes, and normal testes are developed at the usual time in prenatal life and begin their function of secreting male hormones (androgens). However, due apparently to an enzyme deficiency, the fetus is unable to utilize the androgens produced, and continued masculine development is interfered with, so that by birth the testes have failed to descend properly, and the infant appears to have a vagina instead, although it is relatively short. Consequently, the infant usually receives a female sex assignment and rearing. When a number of these individuals were studied from age 14 on, most, despite their male chromosomes and male gonads, "were strongly feminine and unmistakably and immediately recognizable as such. As girls their play preference had been for dolls and other feminine toys. They had not been tomboys. In teenage they had their fair share of boyfriends and dating. Marriage with fulltime homemaking was their career of choice" (23, *244*).

### Psychological factors in homosexual orientation

Although findings such as these indicate that psychological factors *can,* under some circumstances, play a dominant role in the development of sexual orientation, they do not establish that psychological influences are responsible in most cases for the development of a primarily homosexual, rather than a heterosexual, orientation. This can only be done through carefully controlled comparisons of reasonably representative groups of homosexuals and heterosexuals. Most such efforts to date have focused on possible differences in child-rearing and parent-child relationships (14, 22, 42, 60), although peer relationships and other psychological and social functions have also been studied (14, 60).

Until recently, many of the more detailed investigations of predisposing factors in homosexuality were conducted with groups of psychiatric patients. Because these were individuals who were suffering from psychological distress, they could not be assumed to be representative of homosexuals in general. Thus, while some of the findings might be suggestive, their applicability to nonclinical populations could only be determined by further research with these groups.

In one of the more comprehensive clinical investigations (22), a team of psychoanalytically trained investigators conducted a detailed study of 106 self-acknowledged, predominantly homosexual male psychoanalytic patients and a carefully matched group of 100 nonhomosexual control patients. It was found that homosexual patients were more likely than the controls to have had overly protective, dominating, intimacy-encouraging mothers, and detached and/or hostile fathers. Furthermore, parental marital relationships tended to be unsatisfactory and mothers of the homosexual patients were likely to depreciate their husbands (22).

In comparison to the mothers of controls, mothers of homosexuals were significantly more often found by the investigators to discourage masculine activities and attitudes, to have interfered with any initiatives taken by the son in the direction of heterosexual activity, and to have had a mutually shared "confidant" relationship with the son. Compared to the control group, homosexual patients were significantly less likely to feel accepted by their fathers, and to have their father spend time with them. The fathers themselves were less likely to encourage masculine attitudes in their sons and to express affection or respect for them (as compared with other male siblings). These fathers more often manifested contempt for their sons than was the case for fathers of controls. Their sons, in turn, were more likely to "knowingly hate" their fathers, and to lack respect for them.

Subsequently, another investigator attempted to replicate this study, using a more representative, nonpatient population (42). All participants were male volunteers in a study of cardiovascular disease, and the homosexuals were aware that aspects of homosexuality were also being studied. Interestingly, results similar to those of the original study of patients were obtained. More of the homosexuals described themselves as frail or clumsy as children and less often as athletic. "More of them were fearful of physical injury, avoided physical fights, played with girls, and were loners who seldom played baseball and other competitive games" (42, *170*). Their mothers were more likely to be viewed by their sons as puritanical and cold toward men, and as demanding to be the center of the son's attention. They more often made the son their confidant, "were 'seductive' toward him, allied with him against the father, openly preferred him to the father, interfered with his heterosexual activities during adolescence, discouraged masculine attitudes, and encouraged feminine ones" (42, *171*). The fathers of the homosexuals were less likely to encourage masculine attitudes and activities, and spent little time with their sons. The sons, in turn, were more often aware of hating the father and of being afraid that he might physically harm them. They less often were the father's favorite, felt less accepted by him, and, in turn, less frequently accepted or respected the father (42). However, another investigator found that in a similar nonclinical population, the kinds of parent-child relationships described above were likely to be found only among participants scoring high both in neuroticism and in femininity (133), rather than among homosexual participants in general. Furthermore, in all of these studies, significant numbers of homosexuals had positive and rewarding parent-child relationships, while significant numbers of heterosexuals did not.

In a recent extensive study of the development of sexual preference by investigators at the Kinsey Institute for Sex Research (14), the parent-child relationships of heterosexual and homosexual males and females were compared. Among white males, 52 percent of heterosexuals and 23 percent of homosexuals gave a generally or entirely positive description of their fathers; in contrast, 48 percent of homosexuals and 29 percent of heterosexuals expressed negative feelings such as anger, resentment, or fear toward their fathers. More homosexuals than heterosexuals viewed their fathers as detached, hostile, rejecting, or unfair (52 percent versus 37 percent). With respect to identification, a considerably larger percentage of homosexuals felt "very little" or "not at all" like their fathers while growing up (72 percent versus 34 percent); and many more homosexuals said that they felt more similar to their mothers than to their fathers (72 percent versus 37 percent).

Although heterosexual and homosexual males did not differ in the extent of positive or negative feelings expressed toward their mothers, more homosexuals reported feeling particularly close to their mothers while growing up (47 percent versus 21 percent), saw their mothers as stronger and more dominant than their fathers (53 percent versus 30 percent), and felt their mothers had been overprotective (43 percent versus 21 percent).

Less systematic research has been conducted on comparisons of the parent-

child relationships of homosexual and heterosexual females. A number of (principally clinical) studies have described homosexual females as more likely to view their fathers as emotionally withdrawn from their daughters and other family members, or as hostile and exploitative (14, 33, 60). The daughters, in turn, were more likely to report feelings of fear or hostility toward their fathers (14, 18, 34, 60, 81). Poorer relationships of homosexual women with their mothers have also been reported, with homosexual daughters more frequently describing feelings of being unloved, unwanted, or neglected (14, 60, 90, 128).

Among white females in the Kinsey Institute's extensive study of nonclinical participants, 73 percent of heterosexuals and 36 percent of homosexuals gave generally or entirely positive descriptions of their fathers. Forty-five percent of homosexuals and 23 percent of heterosexuals expressed such negative feelings as anger, fear, or resentment toward their fathers. In contrast to the findings for males, more homosexual than heterosexual females viewed their relationships with their mothers as generally or entirely negative (49 percent versus 21 percent). More homosexuals than heterosexuals described their mothers as "bitter," "uncommunicative," or "frustrated" (48 percent versus 20 percent), and fewer described them as warm, pleasant, relaxed, and adequate as mothers (19 percent versus 40 percent). With respect to maternal identification, significantly more homosexual women recalled not feeling at all similar to their mothers while they were growing up (45 percent versus 15 percent), and not wanting to be at all like them (47 percent versus 15 percent).

In another recent study (134) of the parental background of nonclinical samples of homosexual and heterosexual women who scored low on measures of neuroticism, homosexuals described their fathers as less loving and more rejecting. They also depicted their mothers as less loving, more demanding, and more distant, but not more rejecting. In turn, the lesbian daughters reported less closeness than the heterosexuals to both fathers and mothers.

Several considerations need to be kept in mind in attempting to evaluate the results of these studies: (1) Although problems in parent-child relationships are generally reported more frequently in the development of male and female homosexuals than of their heterosexual peers, *virtually all studies have found significant numbers of homosexuals who had satisfactory parent-child relationships, as well as significant numbers of nonhomosexuals who had disturbed relationships* (14, 60, 42); (2) associations between perceived parent-child relationships (e.g., mother-son closeness and father-son distance) and the development of a homosexual orientation do not, in themselves, indicate causality. "Some consideration must be given to the likelihood that the child's innate characteristics at least partially determine parental reactions and attitudes toward him" (42, *170*); and (3) most studies to date have been retrospective, making it difficult to determine the accuracy of the individual's recollections and the extent to which they may have been influenced by the sexual orientation ultimately adopted.

Obviously, much remains to be learned about the factors likely to lead to the development of a predominately homosexual (or, indeed, heterosexual) orientation. At present no definitive conclusions can be reached regarding the role of biological or experiential sets of influences, or of interactions among them. Furthermore, just as homosexuals, like heterosexuals, differ enormously from one another as individuals (13), they may also differ in terms of the roots—biological, psychological, and/or social—of their homosexual orientation.

Several studies, for example, suggest that "feminine" males and "masculine" females who are exclusively homosexual may develop a more deep-seated predisposition toward homosexuality early in life than some other homosexuals or bisexuals. This appears to be reflected in greater early gender nonconformity in interests and activities, and in more frequent feelings of "being different," during childhood; in early emergence of homosexual feelings; and in lack of heterosexual arousal during childhood and adolescence (14). The sexual preferences of bisexuals and some other homosexuals, in contrast, may be "more subject to influence by social and sexual learning" (14, *201*). In this connection, it is interesting to note that individuals who are more or less exclusively homosexual in their orientation, and have not experienced significant heterosexual arousal, are less likely to find their homosexuality "ego-dystonic" (60), are less likely to seek changes in sexual orientation through therapy, and less likely to accomplish this goal if they do try (60).

### *Sexual orientation and psychopathology*

Many young people in such groups as the Gay Liberation movement assert that homosexuality is as normal as heterosexuality (71). They have protested that labeling homosexual behavior "psychopathological" is not only incorrect, but pejorative and indicative of discrimination and oppression. They point out that there have been cultures (e.g., the early Greeks) in which homosexual behavior was accepted along with heterosexual behavior; that significant numbers of professionally, socially, and culturally effective artists, scientists, and leaders in all walks of life have been homosexually oriented (47); and that although some homosexuals may be personally miserable, sexually unsatisfied, and socially ineffective, so are many heterosexuals.

Many of these protests are valid. Labeling of homosexually oriented individuals as "sick" or "pathological" *is* often done pejoratively for a variety of reasons—including hostility and fear, and as a way of reassuring oneself of one's own "normality" and of reinforcing heterosexual impulses and suppressing homosexual ones. It is often true, as one young homosexual movement leader has stated, that "calling homosexuality sick is like calling it sinful" (71, 93). In response to such protests, the American Psychiatric Association has removed homosexuality as such from its diagnostic manual of mental disorders, retaining only a category entitled "ego-dystonic homosexuality" for those individuals who experience "sustained distress" from homosexual arousal and who want to acquire or increase heterosexual arousal, but have difficulty in doing so (1, 60).

A recent extensive study of homosexual and heterosexual men and women concluded that homosexual adults who have come to terms with their homosexuality, who do not regret their sexual orientation, and who can function effectively sexually and socially, are no more distressed psychologically than heterosexual men and women (13). Similar results have been obtained by others (13, 14, 60). Clearly, there are many homosexually oriented individuals who in their overall personal

adjustment and contributions to society are at least as successful as many heterosexually oriented individuals.

Nevertheless, a predominantly or exclusively homosexual orientation is likely to present significant problems of adaptation, at least in our society (114). Despite the development of a greater understanding during the past decade, large segments of the population—younger as well as older—still consider homosexual behavior wrong or disturbed, even though they may oppose legal regulation. Among current college freshmen, nearly half (and a majority of males) state they favor prohibition of homosexual behavior (4, 44). A majority of American adolescents do not favor employment of homosexuals as schoolteachers, clergy, or physicians (49). It seems unlikely that an individual would be motivated to accept the personal restrictions and social difficulties imposed in our culture by a homosexual life-style in the absence of strong arousal by members of the same sex and, especially, an inability to experience heterosexual arousal.

As Alan Bell and his colleagues at the Kinsey Institute recently observed (14), "Neither homosexuals nor heterosexuals are what they are by design. Homosexuals, in particular, cannot be dismissed as persons who simply refuse to conform. There is no reason to think it would be any easier for homosexual men or women to reverse their sexual orientation than it would be for heterosexual readers to become predominantly or exclusively homosexual" (14, *222*).

In view of this fact, legal and social harassment of homosexuals and attempts to picture them as strange beings, utterly different from oneself, are both cruel and unjustified, and only make the homosexually oriented individual's developmental tasks of achieving self-esteem and social adaptation more difficult. It is perhaps worth recalling that often the "unconscious reason why societies have made such harsh laws against such acts that harm no one is people's fear of their own unrecognized . . . impulses" (139, *124–125*).

Fortunately, gay young people today have more reliable sources of support to turn to than in the past (16). Social, professional, religious, and political mutual support groups of gay males and lesbians are expanding, as are groups of gay parents and other interested nongay organizations. More health and mental health professionals are developing special knowledge and skills (as well as abandoning myths and misconceptions) to enable them to deal more effectively with the general—as well as specific—psychological and physical problems of gay persons when they arise. Expert legal and other services are more available, although more are needed.

With additional research, we may gain a better understanding of the genesis of sexual orientation. In the meantime, however, it should be possible, with greater self-understanding and understanding of others, for both homosexuals and heterosexuals to enjoy mature, constructive, and rewarding lives.

### REFERENCES

1. American Psychiatric Association. *Diagnostic and statistical manual of mental disorders.* Washington, D.C.: American Psychiatric Association, 1980 (3rd ed.).
2. Antonovsky, H. F., Shohan, I., Kavenaki, S., Lancet, M., & Modan, B. Gender differences in patterns of adolescent sexual behavior. *Journal of Youth and Adolescence,* 1980, **9,** 127–141.
3. Arafat, I., & Cotton, W. Masturbation practices of males and females. *Journal of Sex Research,* 1974, **9,** 293–307.
4. Astin, A. W. *The American freshman: National norms for fall 1980.* Los Angeles: American Council on Education and Graduate School of Education, University of California at Los Angeles, 1981.
5. Athamasiou, R. A review of public attitudes on sexual issues. In J. Zubin and J. Money (eds.), *Contemporary sexual behavior: Critical issues in the 1970s.* Baltimore: Johns Hopkins University Press, 1973. Pp. 361–390.
6. Ausubel, D. P. *Theory and problems of adolescent development.* New York: Grune & Stratton, 1954.
7. Bachman, J. G., Johnston, L. D., & O'Malley, P. M. *Monitoring the future: Questionnaire responses from the nation's high school seniors.* Ann Arbor, Mich.: Survey Research Center, Institute for Social Research, University of Michigan, 1981.
8. Barbach, L. G. *For yourself: The fulfillment of female sexuality.* New York: Simon & Schuster, 1976.
9. Bardwick, J. *Psychology of women: A study of bio-cultural conflicts.* New York: Harper & Row, 1971.
10. Bardwick, J. M., Douvan, E., Horner, M. S., & Guttman, D. *Feminine personality and conflict.* Monterey, Calif.: Brooks/Cole, 1970.
11. Beach, F. A. (ed.). *Sex and behavior.* New York: Wiley, 1965.
12. Beach, F. A. (ed.). *Human sexuality in four perspectives.* Baltimore: Johns Hopkins University Press, 1977.
13. Bell, A. P., & Weinberg, M. S. *Homosexualities: A study of diversity among men and women.* New York: Simon & Schuster, 1978.

14. Bell, A. P., Weinberg, M. S., & Hammersmith, S. K. *Sexual preference: Its development in men and women.* Bloomington, Indiana: Indiana University Press, 1981.
15. Bell, R. R. Parent-child conflict in sexual values. *Journal of Social Issues,* 1966, **22,** 34–44.
16. Bell, R. *Changing bodies, changing lives: A book for teens on sex and relationships.* New York: Random House, 1980.
17. Belliveau, F., & Richter, L. *Understanding human sexual inadequacy.* New York: Bantam Books, 1970.
18. Bene, E. On the genesis of female homosexuality. *British Journal of Psychiatry,* 1965, **111,** 803–813.
19. Benedict, R. Continuities and discontinuities in cultural conditioning. In W. E. Martin & C. B. Stendler (eds.), *Readings in child development.* New York: Harcourt Brace Jovanovich, 1954. Pp. 142–148.
20. Bennett, S. M., & Dickinson, W. B. Student-parent rapport and parent involvement in sex, birth control, and venereal disease education. *Journal of Sex Research,* 1980, **16,** 97–113.
21. Bermant, G., & Davidson, J. M. *Biological bases of sexual behavior.* New York: Harper & Row, 1974.
22. Bieber, J., et al. *Homosexuality: A psychoanalytic study of male homosexuals.* New York: Random House (Vintage Books), 1962.
23. Brecher, E. M. *The sex researchers.* New York: New American Library, 1971.
24. Chilman, C. S. Why do unmarried women fail to use contraceptives? *Medical Aspects of Human Sexuality,* 1973, **7,** No. 5, 100–168.
25. Chilman, C. S. *Adolescent sexuality in a changing American society: Social and psychological perspectives.* Washington, D.C.: U.S. Government Printing Office, 1978.
26. Christenson, H. T., & Carpenter, G. R. Value-behavior discrepancies regarding premarital coitus in three Western cultures. *American Sociological Review,* 1962, **27,** 66–74.
27. Comfort, A., & Comfort, J. *The facts of love: Living, loving, and growing up.* New York: Crown, 1979.
28. Conger, J. J. Sexual attitudes and behavior of contemporary adolescents. In J. J. Conger (ed.), *Contemporary issues in adolescent development.* New York: Harper & Row, 1975. Pp. 221–230.
29. Conger, J. J. *Adolescence: Generation under pressure.* New York: Harper & Row, 1979.
30. Conger, J. J. A new morality: Sexual attitudes and behavior of contemporary adolescents. In P. H. Mussen, J. J. Conger, & J. Kagan (eds.), *Readings in child and adolescent psychology: Contemporary perspectives.* New York: Harper & Row, 1980.
31. Conger, J. J. Freedom and commitment: Families, youth, and social change. *American Psychologist,* 1981, **36,** 1475–1484.
32. *Contraceptive services for adolescents: United States, each state and county, 1975.* New York: The Alan Guttmacher Institute, 1978.
33. Cory, D. W. Homosexuality. In A. Ellis & A. Abarband (eds.), *The encyclopedia of sexual behavior* (Vol. I). New York: Hawthorn Books, 1961. Pp. 485–493.
34. Deutsch, H. Homosexuality. In *Psychology of women: A psychoanalytic interpretation* (Vol. I). New York: Grune & Stratton, 1944. Pp. 325–393.
35. Diepold, J., & Young, R. D. Empirical studies of adolescent sexual behavior: A critical review. *Adolescence,* 1979, **14,** 45–64.
36. Dorner, G. *Hormone and brain differentiation.* New York: Elsevier, 1976.
37. Dorner, G., Rohde, W., Stahl, R., Krell, L., & Musius, W. Neuroendocrine predisposition to homosexuality in men. *Archives of Sexual Behavior,* 1975, **4,** 1–8.
38. Douvan, E. A., & Adelson, J. *The adolescent experience.* New York: Wiley, 1966.
39. Ehrhardt, A. A., & Baker, S. W. Hormonal orientations and their implications for the understanding of normal sex differentiation. In P. H. Mussen, J. J. Conger, & J. Kagan (eds.), *Basic and contemporary issues in developmental psychology.* New York: Harper & Row, 1975. Pp. 113–121.

40. Ehrhardt, A. A., & Money, J. Progestin-induced hermaphroditism: IQ and psychosocial identity. *Journal of Sex Research,* 1967, **3,** 83–100.

41. *Eleven million teenagers: What can be done about the epidemic of adolescent pregnancies in the United States.* New York: Planned Parenthood Federation of America, 1976.

42. Evans, R. B. Parental relationships and homosexuality. *Medical Aspects of Human Sexuality.* April 1971, 164–177.

43. Evans, R. B. Physical and biochemical characteristics of homosexual men. *Journal of Consulting and Clinical Psychology,* 1972, **39,** 140–147.

44. Fact-file, *Chronicle of Higher Education,* 1981, **21,** 7–8.

45. Ford, C. S. Culture and sex. In A. Ellis & A. Abarband (eds.), *The encyclopedia of sexual behavior* (Vol. I). New York: Hawthorn Books, 1961. Pp. 306–312.

46. Ford, C. S., & Beach, F. A. *Patterns of sexual behavior.* New York: Harper & Row, 1951.

47. Freedman, M. *Homosexuality and psychological functioning.* Monterey, Calif.: Brooks/Cole, 1971.

48. Furstenberg, F. F., Jr. The social consequences of teenage parenthood. *Family Planning Perspectives,* 1976, **8,** 148–164.

49. Gallup, G. Gallup youth survey. *Contemporary, Denver Post,* June 10, 1979, 40.

50. Gallup, G. 1978 Gallup poll cited in C. Norback (ed.), *The complete book of American surveys.* New York: New American Library, 1980.

51. Gartrell, N., Loriaux, D., & Chase, T. Plasma testosterone in homosexual and heterosexual women. *American Journal of Psychiatry,* 1977, **134,** 1117–1119.

52. Gilligan, C., & Belenky, M. F. Crisis and transitions: A naturalistic study of abortion decisions. In R. L. Selman & R. Yando (eds.), *New directions for child development: Clinical-developmental psychology.* San Francisco: Jossey-Bass, 1980.

53. Glenn, N. D., & Weaver, C. N. Attitudes toward premarital, extramarital, and homosexual relations in the U.S. in the 1970s. *Journal of Sex Research,* 1979, **15,** 108–118.

54. Goldfarb, J. L., Mumford, D. M., Schum, D. A., Smith, P. B., Flowers, C., & Schum, D. An attempt to detect "pregnancy susceptibility" in indigent adolescent girls. *Journal of Youth and Adolescence,* 1977, **6,** 127–144.

55. Goy, C. H., Gerall, A. A., & Young, W. C. Organizing action of prenatally administered testosterone proprionate on the tissues mediating mating behavior in the female guinea pig. *Endocrinology,* 1959, **65,** 369–382.

56. Grant, J. A., & Heald, F. P. Complications of adolescent pregnancy: Surveys of the literature on fetal outcome in adolescence. *Clinical Pediatrics,* 1972, **11,** 567–570.

57. Green, R. *Cross-sexed identity in children and adults.* New York: Basic Books, 1973.

58. Green, R. Twenty-five boys with atypical gender identity. In J. Zubin & J. Money (eds.), *Contemporary sexual behavior: Critical issues in the 1970s.* Baltimore: Johns Hopkins University Press, 1973. Pp. 351–360.

59. Green, R. Children's quest for sexual identity. *Psychology Today,* 1974, **7,** 45–51.

60. Green, R. Homosexuality. In H. I. Kaplan, A. M. Freedman, & B. J. Sadock (eds.), *Comprehensive textbook of psychiatry* (Vol. 2). Baltimore: Williams and Wilkins, 1980 (3rd ed.). Pp. 1762–1770.

61. Gunter, N. C., & LaBarba, R. C. The consequences of adolescent childbearing on postnatal development. *International Journal of Behavioral Development,* 1980, **3,** 191–214.

62. Haas, A. *Teenage sexuality: A survey of teenage sexual behavior.* New York: Macmillan, 1979.

63. Hamburg, D. A., & Trudeau, M. B. *Biobehavioral aspects of aggression.* New York: Alan R. Liss, Inc., 1981.

64. Hamilton, E. *Sex, with love: A guide for young people.* Boston: Beacon Press, 1978.

65. Harlow, H. F. Sexual behavior in the rhesus monkey. In F. A. Beach (ed.), *Sex and behavior.* New York: Wiley, 1965. Pp. 234–265.

66. Harris, L. Change, yes—upheaval, no. *Life,* January 8, 1971, **70,** 22–27.

67. Heiman, J. R. Responses to erotica: An exploration of physiological and psychological

correlates of human sexual response. Unpublished doctoral dissertation. State University of New York at Stony Brook, 1975.

68. Heiman, J. R. The physiology of erotica: Women's sexual arousal. *Psychology Today,* 1975, **8,** 90–94.
69. Heston, L., & Shields, J. Homosexuality in twins. *Archives of General Psychiatry,* 1968, **18,** 149–160.
70. Hoffman, M. Homosexuality. In F. A. Beach (ed.), *Human sexuality in four perspectives.* Baltimore: Johns Hopkins University Press, 1977. Pp. 164–189.
71. Homosexuality: A symposium on the causes and consequences—social and psychological—of sexual inversion. *Playboy,* April 1971, 61ff.
72. Hornick, J. P., Doran, L., & Crawford, S. H. Premarital contraceptives usage among male and female adolescents. *The Family Coordinator,* 1979, **28,** 181–190.
73. Hunt, M. Special sex education survey. *Seventeen,* July 1970, 94ff.
74. Hunt, M. *Sexual behavior in the 1970s.* Chicago: Playboy Press, 1974.
75. Jessor, R., & Jessor, S. L. *Problem behavior and psychological development.* New York: Academic Press, 1977.
76. Kaats, G. R., & Davis, K. E. The dynamics of sexual behavior of college students. *Journal of Marriage and the Family,* 1970, **32,** 390–399.
77. Kantner, J. F., & Zelnik, M. Sexual experiences of young unmarried women in the U.S. *Family Planning Perspectives,* 1972, **4,** 9–17.
78. Kantner, J. F., & Zelnik, M. Contraception and pregnancy: Experience of young unmarried women in the United States. *Family Planning Perspectives,* 1973, **5,** 21–35.
79. Kaplan, H. S. *The new sex therapy: Active treatment of sexual dysfunctions.* New York: Bruner/Mazel, 1974.
80. Karlen, A. *Sexuality and homosexuality: A new view.* New York: Norton, 1971.
81. Kaye, H., et al. Homosexuality in women. *Archives of General Psychiatry,* 1967, **17,** 626–634.
82. Kelley, K. Socialization factors in contraceptive attitudes: Roles of affective responses, parental attitudes, and sexual experience. *Journal of Sex Research,* 1979, **15,** 6–20.
83. Kerckhoff, A. C., & Parrow, A. A. The effect of early marriage on the educational attainment of young women. *Journal of Marriage and the Family,* 1979, **41,** No. 1, 97–108.
84. Kiell, N. *The universal experience of adolescence.* Boston: Beacon Press, 1964.
85. Kilman, P. R., Wanlass, R. L., Sabalis, R. F., & Sullivan, B. Sex education: A review of its effects. *Archives of Sexual Behavior,* 1981, **10,** 177–205.
86. Kinsey, A. C., Pomeroy, W. B., & Martin, C. E. *Sexual behavior in the human male.* Philadelphia: Saunders, 1948.
87. Kinsey, A. C., Pomeroy, W. B., Martin, C. E., & Gebhard, P. H. *Sexual behavior in the human female.* Philadelphia: Saunders, 1953.
88. Kolodny, R. C., Jacobs, L. S., Masters, W. H., Toro, G., & Daughaday, W. H. Plasma gonadotrophins and prolactin in male homosexuals. *Lancet,* 1972, **2,** 18–20.
89. Kolodny, R. C., Masters, W. H., Hendryx, J., & Toro, G. Plasma testosterone and semen analysis in male homosexuals. *New England Journal of Medicine,* 1971, **285,** 1170–1174.
90. Kremer, M. W., & Rifkin, A. H. The early development of homosexuality: A study of adolescent lesbianism. *American Journal of Psychiatry,* 1969, **126,** 91–96.
91. Langway, L. Sex ed 101 for kids—and parents. *Newsweek,* September 1, 1980, 50.
92. Linner, B. *Sex and society in Sweden.* New York: Pantheon Books, 1967.
93. Loraine, J. A., Ismail, A. A. A., Adamopolous, D. A., & Dove, G. A. Endocrine function in male and female homosexuals. *British Medical Journal,* 1970, **4,** 406–409.
94. Luckey, E., & Nass, G. A comparison of sexual attitudes and behavior in an international sample. *Journal of Marriage and the Family,* 1969, **31,** 364–379.
95. Mahoney, E. R. Sex education in the public schools: A discriminant analysis of characteristics of pro and anti individuals. *Journal of Sex Research,* 1979, **15,** 276–284.

96. Mann, J. Experimental induction of human sexual arousal. In W. C. Wilson et al., *Technical report of the Commission on Obscenity and Pornography, Vol. I: Preliminary studies.* Washington, D.C.: U.S. Government Printing Office, 1971. Pp. 23–60.

97. Masters, W. H., & Johnson, V. E. *Human sexual response.* Boston: Little, Brown, 1966.

98. Masters, W. H., & Johnson, V. E. *Human sexual inadequacy.* Boston: Little, Brown, 1970.

99. Masters, W. H., & Johnson, V. E. *Homosexuality in perspective.* Boston: Little, Brown, 1979.

100. McCarthy, J., & Menken, J. Marriage, remarriage, marital disruption, and age at first birth. *Family Planning Perspectives,* 1979, **11,** No. 1, 21–30.

101. Mead, M. *From the south seas: Part III. Sex and temperament in three primitive societies.* New York: Morrow, 1939.

102. Mead, M. *Male and female.* New York: Morrow, 1939.

103. *Medical Tribune,* December 26, 1968.

104. Mercer, G. W., & Kahn, P. M. Gender differences in the integration of conservatism, sex urge, and sexual behaviors among college students. *Journal of Sex Research,* 1979, **15,** 129–142.

105. Miller, P. Y., & Simon, W. The development of sexuality in adolescence. In J. Adelson (ed.), *Handbook of adolescent psychology.* New York: Wiley, 1980. Pp. 383–407.

106. Mirande, A. Reference group theory and adolescent sexual behavior. *Journal of Marriage and the Family,* 1968, **30,** 572–577.

107. Money, J., & Ehrhardt, A. A. *Man and woman, boy and girl: The differentiation and dimorphism of gender identity from conception to maturity.* Baltimore: Johns Hopkins University Press, 1972.

108. Money, J., Ehrhardt, A., & Masica, D. N. Fetal feminization induced by androgenic insensitivity in the testicular feminizing syndrome: Effect on marriage and maternalism. *Johns Hopkins Medical Journal,* 1968, **123,** 105–114.

109. Money, J., Hampson, J. G., & Hampson, J. L. An examination of some basic sexual concepts: The evidence of human hermaphroditism. *Bulletin of Johns Hopkins Hospital,* 1955, **97,** 301–319.

110. Mosher, D. L., & Whites, B. B. Effects of committed or casual guided erotic imagery on females' subjective arousal and emotional response. *Journal of Sex Research,* 1980, **16,** 273–299.

111. Mussen, P. H., Conger, J. J., & Kagan, J. *Child development and personality.* New York: Harper & Row, 1974 (4th ed.).

112. NBC News poll, *Today,* National Broadcasting Company, October 8, 1981.

113. Neumann, F., & Elger, W. Proof of the activity of androgenic agents on the differentiation of the external genitalia. *Excerpta Medica International Congress Series,* 1965, **101,** 168ff.

114. Norman, J., & Harris, M. *The private life of the American teenager.* New York: Rawson, Wade, 1981.

115. Packard, V., & the sexual behavior reported by 2100 young adults. In V. Packard, *The sexual wilderness: The contemporary upheaval in male-female relationships.* New York: Pocket Books, 1970. Pp. 166–184.

116. Packard, V. *The sexual wilderness: The contemporary upheaval in male-female relationships.* New York: Pocket Books, 1970.

117. Petersen, A. C., & Boxer, A. Adolescent sexuality. In T. Coates, A. Petersen, & C. Perry (eds.), *Adolescent health: Crossing the barriers.* New York: Academic Press, 1982. Pp. 237–253.

118. Pomeroy, W. B. *Boys and sex.* New York: Dell (Delacorte Press), 1969.

119. Pomeroy, W. B. *Girls and sex.* New York: Dell (Delacorte Press), 1969.

120. Pomeroy, W. B. *Dr. Kinsey and the Institute for Sex Research.* New York: Harper & Row, 1972.

121. Reiss, I. L. *Premarital sexual standards in America.* New York: Free Press, 1960.
122. Reiss, I. L. *The social context of premarital sexual permissiveness.* New York: Holt, Rinehart and Winston, 1967.
123. Reiss, I. L. How and why America's sex standards are changing. In W. Simon & J. H. Gagnon (eds.), *The sexual scene.* Chicago: Trans-action Books, 1970. Pp. 43–57.
124. Report of the Task Panel on Mental Health and American Families: Sub-task Panel on General Issues and Adult Years. In *Task Panel Reports submitted to the President's Commission on Mental Health, 1978, Vol. III.* Washington, D.C.: U.S. Government Printing Office, 1978.
125. Richardson, J. G., & Cranston, J. E. Social change, parental values, and the salience of sex education. *Journal of Marriage and the Family,* 1981, 547–558.
126. Rogel, M. J., & Zuehlke, M. E. Adolescent contraceptive behavior: Influences and implications. In I. R. Stuart & C. F. Wells (eds.), *The pregnant adolescent: Problems and management.* New York: Van Nostrand Reinhold, 1981.
127. Rose, R. M., Bourne, P. G., Poe, R. O., Mougey, E. H., Collins, D. R., & Mason, J. W. Androgen responses to stress. II. Excretion of testosterone, epitestosterone, androsterone, and etiocholanolone during basic combat training and under threat of attack. *Psychosomatic Medicine,* 1969, **31,** 418–436.
128. Saghir, M. T., & Robins, E. *Male and female homosexuality: A comprehensive investigation.* Baltimore: Williams and Wilkins, 1973.
129. Schmidt, G., & Sigusch, V. Women's sexual arousal. In J. Zubin & J. Money (eds.), *Contemporary sexual behavior: Critical issues in the 1970s.* Baltimore: Johns Hopkins University Press, 1973. Pp. 117–145.
130. Schwartz, M. F., Kolodny, R. C., & Mastens, W. Y. Plasma testosterone levels of sexually functional and dysfunctional men. *Archives of Sexual Behavior,* 1980, **9,** 355–366.
131. Schweiker is critical of programs on sex education. *New York Times,* January 30, 1981, 1.
132. Shah, F., & Zelnik, M. Parent and peer influence on sexual behavior, contraceptive use, and pregnancy experience of young women. *Journal of Marriage and the Family,* 1981, **43,** 339–348.
133. Siegelman, M. Parental background of male homosexuals and heterosexuals. *Archives of Sexual Behavior,* 1974, **3,** 3–18.
134. Siegelman, M. Parental background of homosexual and heterosexual women. *British Journal of Psychiatry,* 1974, **124,** 14–21.
135. Simon, W., & Gagnon, J. H. Psychosexual development. In W. Simon & J. H. Gagnon (eds.), *The sexual scene.* Chicago: Trans-action Books, 1970. Pp. 23–41.
136. Singh, B. K. Trends in attitudes toward premarital sexual relations. *Journal of Marriage and the Family,* 1980, **8,** 387–393.
137. Sorensen, R. C. *Adolescent sexuality in contemporary America: Personal values and sexual behavior ages 13–19.* New York: Abrams, 1973.
138. Spitz, R. A. Authority and masturbation: Some remarks on a bibliographical investigation. *Yearbook of Psychoanalysis,* 1953, **9,** 113–145.
139. Spock, B. *A teen-ager's guide to life and love.* New York: Simon & Schuster, 1970.
140. Student survey, 1971. *Playboy,* September 1971, 118ff.
141. Sue, D. Erotic fantasies of college students during coitus. *Journal of Sex Research,* 1979, **15,** 299–305.
142. Sugar, M. At-risk factors for the adolescent mother and her infant. *Journal of Youth and Adolescence,* 1976, **5,** 251–270.
143. *Teenage pregnancy: The problem that hasn't gone away.* New York: Alan Guttmacher Institute, Planned Parenthood Federation of America, 1981.
144. *The report of the Commission on Obscenity and Pornography.* New York: Bantam Books, 1970.
145. Thomas, D. R. Conservatism and premarital sexual experience. *British Journal of Social and Clinical Psychology,* 1975, **14,** 195–196.

146. Tourney, G., & Hatfield, L. M. Androgen metabolism in schizophrenics, homosexuals, and normal controls. *Biological Psychiatry*, 1973, **6**, 23–36.

147. Vener, A., & Stewart, C. Adolescent sexual behavior in America revisited: 1970–1973. *Journal of Marriage and the Family*, 1974, **36**, 728–735.

148. Voss, J. R. Sex education: Evaluation and recommendations for future study. *Archives of Sexual Behavior*, 1980, **9**, 37–59.

149. What's really happening on campus. *Playboy*, 1976, **23,** 128–169.

150. Whiting, B. B. (ed.). *Six cultures: Studies of child rearing*. New York: Wiley, 1963.

151. Whiting, J. W. M., & Child, I. L. *Child training and personality: A cross-cultural study*. New Haven, Conn.: Yale University Press, 1953.

152. Wilson W. C., et al. *Technical report of the Commission on Obscenity and Pornography, Vol. I: Preliminary studies*. Washington, D.C.: U.S. Government Printing Office, 1971.

153. Wilson, W. C., et al. *Technical report of the Commission on Obscenity and Pornography, Vol. VI: National survey*. Washington, D.C.: U.S. Government Printing Office, 1971.

154. Yankelovich, D. *Generations apart*. New York: CBS News, 1969.

155. Yankelovich, D. *Youth and the establishment*. New York: JDR 3rd Fund, 1971.

156. Yankelovich, D. *The new morality: A profile of American youth in the 1970s*. New York: McGraw-Hill, 1974.

157. Yankelovich, D. *New rules: Searching for self-fulfillment in a world turned upside down*. New York: Random House, 1981.

158. Zabin, L. S., Kantner, J. F., & Zelnik, M. The risk of adolescent pregnancy in the first months of intercourse. *Family Planning Perspectives*, 1979, **11,** 215–222.

159. Zelnik, M., & Kantner, J. F. Sexual and contraceptive experience of young unmarried women in the United States, 1976 and 1971. *Family Planning Perspectives*, 1977, **9,** 55–71.

160. Zelnik, M., & Kantner, J. F. First pregnancies to women aged 15–19: 1976 and 1971. *Family Planning Perspectives*, 1978, **10,** 11–20.

161. Zelnik, M., & Kantner, J. F. Sexual activity, contraceptive use and pregnancy among metropolitan-area teenagers: 1971–1979. *Family Planning Perspectives*, 1980, **12,** 230–237.

162. Zelnik, M., Kim, Y. J., & Kantner, J. F. Probabilities of intercourse and conception among U.S. teenage women, 1971 and 1976. *Family Planning Perspectives*, 1979, **11,** 177–183.

163. Zuckerman, M. Physiological measures of sexual arousal in humans. In W. C. Wilson et al., *Technical report of the Commission on Obscenity and Pornography, Vol. I: Preliminary studies*. Washington, D.C.: U.S. Government Printing Office, 1971. Pp. 61–102.

Adolescents and
their peers

HERE COMES
TROUBLE

CHAPTER·9

# Adolescents and their peers

**P**eers play a crucial role in the psychological and social development of most adolescents, especially in age-segregated, technological societies like our own, where entrance into the adult world of work and family responsibility is increasingly delayed. Of course, peer influences do not begin in adolescence. During the years of middle childhood as well, the peer group provides opportunities to learn how to interact with others, to control social behavior, to develop age-relevant skills and interests, and to share similar problems and feelings (79, 123). But the role played by peers in adolescence is especially critical. Relations with both same- and opposite-sex peers during the adolescent years come closer to serving as prototypes for later adult relationships—in social relations, in work, and in interactions with members of the opposite sex. The young man or woman who has not learned how to get along with others of the same sex and to establish satisfactory heterosexual relationships by the time he or she reaches adulthood is likely to face serious obstacles in the years ahead.

Adolescents are also more dependent upon peer relationships than are younger children simply because ties to parents become progressively looser as the adolescent gains greater independence. In addition, relations with family members are likely to become charged with conflicting emotions in the early years of adolescence—dependent yearnings exist alongside independent strivings, hostility is mixed with love, and conflicts occur over cultural values and social behavior. Consequently, many areas of the adolescent's inner life and outward behavior become difficult to share with parents. Parents, in turn, having managed to repress many of the painful emotional ups and downs of their own adolescence, may have difficulty understanding and sharing their adolescent sons' and daughters' problems, even though they make an effort to do so and are truly interested in the welfare of their children.

In some cases, parental warmth and understanding may be lacking, as in the case of a 16-year-old girl who said of her relationship with her father, "I get along, but, I mean, we're really not that close. Like he's got his business and I've got my school work. He just doesn't seem interested in what I do" (101, 69). In other cases, there may be parental hostility, neglect, or exploitation. In such circumstances, interested and competent peers may help to provide not only a physical and psychological escape from a difficult family situation, but a source of understanding and support as well. They may also serve as alternative role models for achieving mutually rewarding interactions with others (39).

As Peter Blos (12, 13), Anna Freud (63), and others (77, 123) have observed, adolescence may provide an important opportunity, sometimes the last major opportunity, for repairing psychological damage incurred during the years of early and middle childhood and for developing new and more rewarding relationships both with one's self and with others. A mature, warm, interested, and above all, nonexploitative adolescent peer may play an important, sometimes crucial, role in helping a boy or girl to gain a clearer concept of self, problems, and goals; a feeling of personal worth; and renewed hope for the future.

For example, a warm, supportive, and nonmanipulative girl may sometimes do a great deal, both intellectually and emotionally, to show the son of a demanding, manipulative mother that relations with women can be rewarding and nonthreatening. A girl whose father has acknowledged her worth only when she has accomplished some socially approved, external goal, such as high grades in school, may learn from a male peer that it is possible to be appreciated for herself alone—for who she is, rather than what she can do. Just by being himself and by being interested, an equalitarian male friend may help to demonstrate to the son of a competitive, authoritarian father that all relationships between males need not be characterized by competition and by patterns of domination and submission.

There is no intention here to minimize the serious handicaps that prior distorted relationships with family members may impose on an adolescent, nor the obvious need in many such cases for psychotherapy. But it is extremely difficult to treat an adolescent successfully, even in intensive individual psychotherapy, when opportunities for reinforcing the corrective experiences of therapy in relationships with peers are absent or inadequate. In such instances, it is more difficult to promote discrimination learning (i.e., the learning of *different* responses to *similar* stimuli). Therefore, overgeneralized (and inappropriate) responses learned in interactions with parents are more likely to persist and be carried over into relationships with others.

Of course, there is another side to the coin. Relations with peers during this vulnerable stage of development may also be harmful. For example, the boy or girl who is put down, laughed at, or rejected in initial efforts to establish heterosexual relationships or to join a high school clique may acquire anxious, avoidant responses in such situations that will prove difficult to extinguish. Furthermore, adolescents may be pressured by a group of their peers into suspending their own better judgment and engaging in behaviors that they may later regret. These may range from relatively minor improprieties to more serious, sometimes tragic, incidents, such as wanton destruction of school property, unintended involvement in group sexual activities, or attacks on isolated members of other social or ethnic groups. In the climate of such situations, the degree of autonomy that an adolescent has previously been able to acquire and his or her self-confidence and personal values may sometimes be severely tried.

Obviously, it is highly desirable that a preponderance of the adolescent's experiences with peers be positive, for more than at any other time in life, the young person needs to be able to share strong and often confusing emotions, doubts, and dreams. "Adolescence is generally a time of intense sociability, but it is also often a time of intense loneliness. Merely being with others does not solve the problem; frequently the young person may feel most alone in the midst of a crowd, at a party or a dance" (87, *253*). Under such circumstances, being accepted by peers generally, and especially having one or more close friends, may make a great difference in the young person's life.

Finally, the role of the peer group in helping an individual to define his or her own identity becomes particularly important during adolescence because at no other stage of development is one's sense of identity so fluid. No longer a child, but not yet fully accepted as an adult, the adolescent must prepare, with few clear guidelines, to meet society's demands for social independence, for new kinds of relationships with peers of both sexes, for vocational competence, for a responsible role as a citizen, and in many cases, for marriage and parenthood (39, 40).

For all these reasons, adolescents need the guidance, support, and communion of their peers. No matter how understanding parents and other adults may be, their role is necessarily limited by the fact that the adolescent and his or her peers are struggling to achieve adult status—adults are already there. Young people may not, indeed often do not, know how they are going to accomplish this task successfully. But they know that previous generations of adolescents have done so, and they reason that if they can stick with their peers who, after all, are "all in the same boat," they too will be successful.

### Conformity to peers

Because of the heightened importance of the peer group during adolescence, motivation for conformity to the values, customs, and fads of peer culture increases during this period. Although evidences of a need for peer-group conformity are clearly observable in middle childhood (79, 123), and although there are wide individual differences at all ages in the strength of this need, most studies indicate that there is a rather rapid rise in conformity needs and behavior during the preadolescent and early adolescent years, followed by a gradual but steady decline from middle through late adolescence (16, 21, 32, 45, 102, 117). Although a number of studies have shown that the need to conform to peers may vary with the sex of the participants, their socioeconomic background, relationships with parents and other adults, school environment, and personality factors, such variations are most likely to be found in the extent of conformity or the exact age at which it peaks, rather than in the overall developmental pattern (16, 21, 32, 36, 45).

For example, one study examined the relationship between conformity and the tendency to blame oneself for adverse happenings in life (45). Conformity to group pressure was assessed by having subjects compare the length of a single blank line (the standard) with reference lines of different lengths. The frequency with which the individual abandoned correct responses in favor of wrong responses apparently selected by peers constituted the measure of conformity. As may be seen in Figure 9.1, children and adolescents with a strong tendency toward self-blame scored significantly higher in conformity than those low or medium in self-blame, but the shape

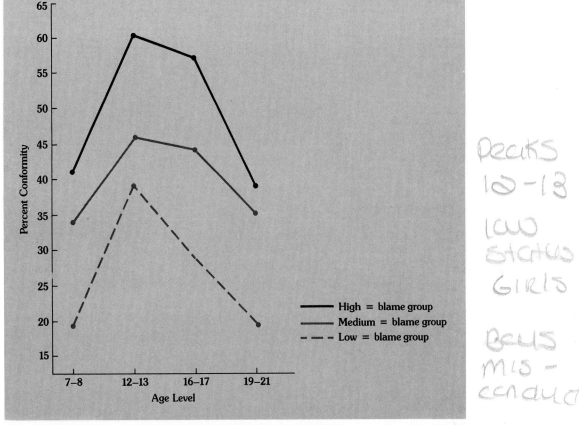

**Figure 9.1** Percentage of conformity as a function of age at different levels of self-blame intensity. (From P. R. Costanzo. Conformity development as a function of self-blame. *Journal of Personality and Social Psychology,* 1970, **14,** 366–374. By prmission.)

of the distribution was quite similar in each case, with conformity reaching a peak in the 12- to 13-age group.

Similar studies have found that young people who have low status among their peers are more conforming than those with high status (32, 80); that girls are slightly more likely to be conforming than boys (32, 80), except where group pressure is toward misconduct, in which case boys appear generally more susceptible (11); that children and adolescents who have favorable attitudes toward adults are less subject to peer group pressures than are those with negative attitudes. Adolescents with high self-esteem and strong feelings of competence are less conforming than their peers (68, 79, 102, 166).

Inasmuch as independence (or autonomy) is in many ways the other side of the coin from conformity, the results of a study by the English psychologist John C. Coleman (31) are interesting. As part of a sentence-completion test, boys and girls,

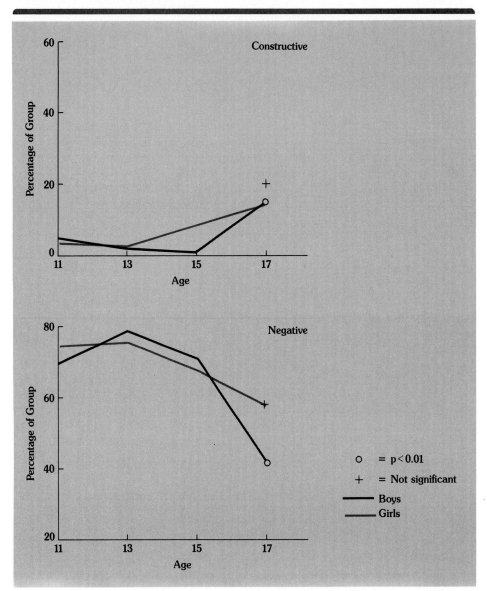

**Figure 9.2** Proportions of each age group expressing constructive and negative themes. (From J. C. Coleman. *Relationships in adolescence*. London: Routledge & Kegan Paul, 1974. By permission.)

aged 11 to 17, were presented with a sentence stem that read: "If someone is not part of the group. . . ." Completions were scored as *constructive* (e.g., "he enjoys it because he is not being a sheep") or *negative* (e.g., "he feels inferior to them"; "he is looked on as an outcast"). As may be seen in Figure 9.2, constructive (autonomous) responses reached a peak at age 17, while negative (conformity) responses reached a peak around age 13, as in other studies.

Recent findings regarding adolescent conformity are generally similar to those obtained some years ago. In short, whereas the *manifestations* of peer group conformity change rapidly in our society, there can be little doubt that the adolescent, and in particular the younger one, has strong needs to conform to peer group norms and pressures, and that these needs are reflected in behavior (32, 79).

Of course, the adolescent may deny or fail to recognize what sometimes appears to the outside observer as an excessive conformity to peer pressures. What appears as conformity to the observer may appear to the young person as a bold exercise in individuality. The explanation of this paradox lies in the different perspectives of the observer and the adolescent. The adolescent may perceive his or her behavior as highly individual because it differs markedly from that of parents and other adults; in contrast, the observer's attention is likely to focus on the similarities of the adolescent's behavior to that of immediate peers.

Needless to say, this is not exclusively an adolescent phenomenon. Parallels exist in the conforming behavior of adults, who may also fail to recognize it. Self-conscious liberal or conservative adults may see themselves as paragons of rugged individualism because their attitudes, beliefs, and behaviors differ from those of the "silent majority" of their fellow citizens. But what they fail to recognize is that they are conforming—sometimes in a fashion as doctrinaire as that of any adolescent—to the myths, customs, fads, and philosophical clichés of their own cultural subgroup. To paraphrase a popular slogan, one person's individualism may well be another's conformity.

Having left the world of childhood forever, but not yet fully admitted to the world of adults, adolescents are virtually forced to create at least a semblance of an interim culture of their own. And obviously, it is important that this culture, whatever form it may take (and forms are likely to change with breathtaking speed), be unambiguously recognizable as different from that of adults if it is to serve its purpose. Once adults have recovered from their anguished cries of imminent disaster and have, rather ironically, gone on to incorporate adolescent fashions and tastes into adult culture (as has happened in dress, in hair styles, in music, and even to some extent in language), adolescents will have to turn to new fads to preserve their separateness.

Parents are frequently mystified, and in some cases deeply threatened, by the shifting external trappings of adolescent peer cultures, from fashions in clothes and music to special and rapidly shifting vocabularies. They may wonder why adolescents need to behave so "bizarrely." But, of course, that is one of the principal reasons for the existence of adolescent fads: to establish, at least superficially, a clear line of demarcation from adults. Parents and other adults might actually take some comfort from the presence of these outward trappings of the "differentness" of adolescents. By achieving the semblance of a group identity of their own in these relatively superficial ways, adolescents may satisfy some of the need to be different from their parents in more fundamental matters (49). Although, as we shall see, adolescent values and behavior are changing and are different, sometimes to an important degree, from those of adults, in most cases there is also a fundamental continuity in many of the values and beliefs of parents and children that often is overlooked.

*Less IA in later/midd Ad.*

## PARENTAL AND PEER INFLUENCES—A FALSE DICHOTOMY?

We should be cautious about being misled by conspicuous but actually rather superficial differences between parents and adolescents (as opposed to divergences on more basic matters, including fundamental moral and social values). The common assertion that parental and peer group values are necessarily mutually incompatible and that an inevitable consequence of heightened peer group dependence during adolescence is a sharp decline in parental influence is untrue, at least in the case of most adolescents.

In the first place, there is usually considerable overlap between the values of parents and peers because of commonalities in their backgrounds—social, economic, religious, educational, even geographic. A Catholic blue-collar adolescent and his peers in one of our larger cities are likely to share more common attitudes and values with their parents than they do with upper- or upper-middle-class WASP contemporaries (39, 40, 62, 109). In this sense, then, peers may actually serve to reinforce parental values—educational, vocational, sexual, social, and political.

Another factor tending to limit potential conflict between parental and peer influences lies in the uncertainty of many parents about the behavior they should expect from adolescents. Parents may feel that social change has been so rapid that they lack the experience to teach their young how to deal with today's world. This was particularly likely to be the case in the late 1960s (when social change was most rapid and frequently disruptive), but it is still true of many parents in the 1980s.

Such a view can easily become a self-fulfilling prophecy. While bemoaning the adolescent's conformity to the peer group, parents may, however unwittingly, be encouraging the child to turn to the peer group for guidance. Furthermore, many parents, particularly upper- and middle-class parents, place a great emphasis on popularity and success, and thus strengthen the adolescent's motivation to conform to peer expectations.

Another important consideration that is frequently overlooked is that neither parental nor peer influence is monolithic, extending to all areas of adolescent decision making and behavior (8, 17, 18, 28, 40, 79, 105, 106). The weight given to either parental or peer opinion depends to a significant degree on the adolescent's appraisal of its relative value in a specific situation. For example, peer influence is more likely to be predominant in such matters as tastes in music and entertainment, fashions in clothing and language, patterns of same- and opposite-sex peer interaction, and the like. Parental influence is more likely to be predominant in such areas as underlying moral and social values, and understanding of the adult world (39, 40). It is also important to recognize that when the peer group assumes an unusually dominant role in the lives of adolescents, often it is due as much, or more, to the lack of attention and concern at home as to the inherent attractiveness of the peer group.

Adolescents who were strongly peer-oriented were found to be more likely than those who were adult-oriented to hold negative views of themselves and the peer group. They saw themselves (and were seen by teachers and their peers) as less dependable, "meaner," more subject to peer group pressure, and more likely to disobey adults (38). They tended to lack positive self-esteem and to take a dimmer view of their future. Their peer group activities were more apt to involve such diffuse activities as teasing and baiting other young people, playing hooky, listening to records, gossiping, going to the movies or parties, and doing something illegal; and less likely to involve such activities as making or building something, playing musical instruments, watching sports, or helping someone. Peer-oriented adolescents were also less interested in and less effective in academic work.

The parents of adult-oriented adolescents were seen as being more *active* (i.e., more nurturant, demanding, giving of companionship and discipline—and, in all of these, more consistent). This was especially likely to be true in the case of boys. Apparently, parents of peer-oriented adolescents are more likely to show a relative lack of concern and affection—a passive neglect, rather than a more active punitiveness. Indeed, they appear to neither support nor control their children to any significant degree, thus leaving them to seek approval and affection elsewhere. In commenting on these findings, Urie Bronfenbrenner concludes:

> The peer-oriented child is more a product of parental disregard than of the attractiveness of the peer group—that he turns to his age-mates less by choice than by default. The vacuum left by the withdrawal of parents and adults from the lives of children is filled with an undesired—and possibly *undesirable*—substitute of an age-segregated peer group [20, 96].

Somewhat similar findings have emerged from an investigation of seventh-, ninth-, and twelfth-grade boys and girls (105, 106). Parental influence was found to be greatest where there was the highest "parent-adolescent affect" (i.e., the quality of the parent-child relationship, as measured by parental interest and understanding, willingness to be helpful, amount of shared family activity, and so on). Furthermore, adolescents with high parent-adolescent affect were significantly less likely than those with low affect to see a need to differentiate between the influence of their parents and that of their best friends.

Not surprisingly, parental influence was found to be greatest at the sixth-grade level and least at the twelfth-grade level. Interestingly, it was also found that at the seventh-grade level the extent of parental influence was only minimally a function of the quality of the parental relationship. At later grade levels, however, where the potential impact of peer group influence had increased significantly, parent-adolescent affect assumed markedly increased importance as a determinant of parental influence (104). In short, parents may be seriously mistaken in thinking that, because they can influence their children at the beginning of adolescence without concerning themselves with the quality of their relationship and their contributions to it, they will continue to be able to do so in middle and later adolescence.

Finally, we tend to overlook the important fact that the need for rigid conformity to *either* parents or peers varies enormously from one adolescent to another (39, 117). Thus, more self-confident, more autonomous (democratically reared) adolescents may be able to profit from the views and learning experiences provided by both parents and peers without being strongly dependent on either or being unduly troubled by parent-peer differences (79, 132). Ironically, the adolescent who has gained the most confidence in his or her own self-image as a result of such child-rearing techniques, and who is least concerned with popularity and most individualistic, may find that peers flock around him or her as a tower of strength (153).

### Sources of difficulty

It appears that serious difficulties are more likely to arise and parents are most likely to find themselves feeling helpless where there is a very strong, homogeneous peer group, with patterns of behavior and attitudes that differ markedly from those of parents (39); there is no rewarding parent-child relationship because of a lack of parental interest and understanding, manifest willingness to be helpful, and shared family activities (16); the parents' own values and behaviors are inconsistent, uninformed, unrealistic, maladaptive, or obviously hypocritical; or where the adolescent lacks either the self-confidence (based on a positive self-image) and the independence training to act autonomously without undue concern. In most cases where young people have forsaken or renounced family values for those of deviant peer groups, one or more of these conditions is likely to obtain (39).

As indicated earlier, the parents' task may be simpler in the traditional, geographically remote small town characterized by extended kinship and neighborly ties and by continual interaction between parents and other adults, peers, the schools, and other social institutions. Under such circumstances, fundamental values and customs are often more firmly held and widely shared among adults and adolescents.

In contrast, the parents' task (as well as that of the adolescent) may be much more difficult in other settings, such as that of a large city, where both the nuclear family and the peer group may be relatively isolated from community-wide interaction or even communication. Where, for example, such an isolated peer group is heavily involved in experimentation with the more serious drugs, with varied forms of early sexual activities or with delinquent behavior, and where the group is homogeneous and exerts strong social pressures for conformity, parents may be confronted with seemingly insurmountable problems (39, 41).

A typical mistake is assuming that such situations either do not exist or are exaggerated—or, conversely, that they are universal, which they are not. But where they do exist, it is most often where the older sense of community has been dissipated, whether in the urban ghetto or, ironically, in a number of our "swinging," affluent suburban "bedroom communities" (39).

The more discrepant or deviant the peer group setting, however, the more important does it appear for parents to attempt to provide the kind of confidence-inspiring, autonomy-inducing democratic child-rearing cited in our discussion of independence training. And the more crucial are efforts at communication and understanding—and active interaction—between parent and child. The laissez-faire parent (who provides neither guidance nor a strong model of basic standards and values with which the adolescent can identify) *and* the authoritarian parent (who is certain of his or her own views and neither understands nor feels any need to understand the views and problems of his or her adolescent son or daughter) are both likely to vitiate whatever influence they might have had, and to leave the adolescent vulnerable to deviant and destructive peer group influences.

## THE CHANGING NATURE OF ADOLESCENT PEER GROUPS

Although we have spoken of the adolescent peer group or peer culture, these terms are an oversimplification. In reality, the developing adolescent is involved in complex ways with a number of overlapping peer groups that vary in size and in the degree of intimacy among group members. Furthermore, the nature of these groups and the functions they serve change with age.

During middle childhood and preadolescence, the child's peer relationships tend to center about neighborhood play groups and same-sex "gangs" (123). Largely informal at first, these children's groups become more highly structured with increasing age (usually from about age 10 on). Aspects of formal organization, such as special membership requirements and elaborate rituals for conducting meetings, appear. Even so, the personnel may change frequently and the group itself may not last long (79, 123).

There are a number of reasons for the predominance of same-sex groupings during this period. Most obviously, there are sex cleavages in interests and activities that are more easily served by same-sex peer groups. Also, from about ages 9 through 11 there is likely to be anxiety over associations with members of the opposite sex or expressions of any interest in them (probably somewhat more so in the case of boys).

Throughout the middle-childhood and preadolescent years, boys tend to be more involved with gangs than do girls. However, girls tend to have more intimate, individual interpersonal relationships than boys even at these ages, a precursor, perhaps, of later lifelong interpersonal orientations (79, 123). The peer group relations of both boys and girls during the middle-childhood years tend to be limited principally to neighborhood acquaintances and schoolmates (who at the elementary school level tend to come from the same or adjoining neighborhoods). However, as the young person enters junior high school and the wider world of adolescence and spends less and less time at home, the range of acquaintances broadens: "Where the school-aged child's peer group was peopled with friends, best friends, and faceless strangers, the adolescent has a wider circle of casual acquaintances as well" (153, *442*).

In general, the adolescent's peer relationships fall into three broad categories: the "crowd" or "set," the "clique," and individual friendships (123). The most inclusive of these categories is the crowd. It is also the least personal: "It is a 'forced group' comprised of individuals selected because of mutual interests, likes, and social ideals. The members meet on the basis of *activities*, not because of mutual attraction as is true of chums and, to a lesser extent of cliques" (85, *126*).

A study of adolescent peer groups in an urban setting confirmed that the two basic groups consisted of relatively large crowds and much smaller cliques (generally about one-third the size of a crowd). The crowd is essentially an association of cliques. "Clique membership appears to be a prerequisite of crowd membership" (55, *234*). Thus, no subject in the study was found to belong to a crowd without also belonging to a component clique. On the other hand, an individual might well be a member of a clique without also belonging to a crowd.

Cliques and crowds perform different functions for their members. The clique, smaller in size (with an upper limit in one study of nine members), permits and encourages a far higher degree of intimacy and group cohesion than the larger crowd. The limited membership of cliques makes possible the strong cohesion which characterizes them. Their similarity in size to the family possibly facilitates the transference of the individual's allegiance to them and allows them to provide an alternative center of security (32, 55). Clique activity centers heavily around talking (especially on the telephone). An analysis of the content of these conversations showed that the clique performs "an important instrumental function in that it is the center for the preparation of crowd activities, for dissemination of information about them, and for their evaluation after they are over" (55, *235*). The crowd, on the other hand, is the center of larger and more organized social activities, such as parties, which provide for interaction between the sexes. The crowd "acts as a reservoir of acceptable associates who can be drawn on to the extent required by any social activity. Thus cliques and crowds are not only different in size; they are also different in function" (55, *235*).

### Stages of peer group development

As adolescence proceeds, structural changes in the nature of peer groups take place; and these in turn are related to the changing socialization processes of adolescence, including, in particular, the development of heterosexual relationships (55). As the young person enters adolescence, the same-sex cliques or "gangs" of preadolescents predominate. Gradually, however, cliques of one sex begin to interact with cliques of the opposite sex, leading to the beginnings of the adolescent crowd. At least initially, such heterosexual interactions are generally rather tentative, "and only undertaken in the security of the group setting where the individual is supported by the presence of his [or her] own sex associates" (55, *237*).

Only in the next stage of group development do we see the formation of genuinely heterosexual cliques, in which individual-to-individual heterosexual interactions are begun (usually by higher-status clique leaders). Adolescents belonging to these emerging heterosexual groups still maintain a membership role in their former same-sex clique; consequently, they possess dual memberships in two intersecting cliques. In the following stage of adolescent group development, however, the situation shifts, and we see the emergence of the fully developed adolescent crowd, made up of a number of heterosexual cliques in close association.

Finally, in late adolescence, loosely associated groups of couples are frequently seen; same-sex friendships continue but become more stable and less intense. The importance of the crowd begins to diminish as the need for conformity to peers lessens and the perceived need for individual identity development grows (32, 54, 55).

Although adolescents currently tend to enter these various stages at somewhat younger ages, the sequence of stages seems to have persisted, despite individual

variations and occasional regressions (54). One of the principal functions served by the crowd is the role that it performs in making possible the transition from the same-sex cliques of early adolescence to the heterosexual cliques of later adolescence. At the same time, however, it should be recognized that associations with individuals and groups of same-sex members continue, though somewhat less in the foreground, throughout adolescence and into adult life—whether in the form of small circles of friends, individual close friends, fraternities, sororities, clubs, or interest groups.

In many instances, socioeconomic status plays a significant role in determining crowd and clique membership. There is usually little cutting across class lines, particularly in the case of girls, whose cliques tend generally to be closer, more exclusive, more impregnable to outsiders, and somewhat more enduring (34, 94, 95, 113, 130). There is somewhat more democracy and flexibility in male groups, where athletic skills and overall sociability tend to have a leveling influence (33). In many high schools, there is a fairly sharp division between students (usually of higher socioeconomic status) planning to go on to college and those planning to go to work. Ethnic group membership may also be involved. Indeed, one of the current disappointments of many who felt that ethnic and socioeconomic integration of the schools would produce a like degree of social interaction of their students has been the extent to which social separation still persists. In many schools (particularly at upper grade levels), it is not infrequently *demanded* by some influential minority and majority students. Some American high schools, of course, are highly homogeneous in their makeup, but most are sufficiently varied to permit a predictable social hierarchy to emerge (35, 45, 153). Other influences may also play a role in crowd or clique formation, including common interests and hobbies; social and athletic skills; degree of personal and sexual maturity; traditionalism versus rebellion in cultural values; participation in or avoidance of drug use, sexual experimentation, or delinquent (or quasi-delinquent) behavior; academic involvement or lack of involvement; personality characteristics; and residential proximity (70, 153). Not infrequently, cliques may exhibit considerable intolerance or contempt for those who are different (32). Individuals—particularly girls—who are most personally secure and emotionally mature are most likely to be able to reach out and establish relationships with members of other cliques (76). In general, older students are also more likely to cross clique boundaries successfully (74, 108).

There are, of course, individuals who, either through choice or, more frequently, through rejection by peers, are isolates—loners who belong neither to cliques nor crowds (81, 103). Although a number of today's adolescents appear to be demonstrating a greater degree of tolerance, concern, and empathy for their peers than earlier generations of young people, the fact remains that many adolescents—self-preoccupied, uncertain of their own worth, and eager to gain security and status through acceptance by the "in-group"—can often be remarkably indifferent or even cruel toward other adolescents who do not fit in. As we shall see, for many of these isolated young people, the adolescent years can be a lonely and difficult time.

## FRIENDSHIPS AND IDENTITY DEVELOPMENT

Among the peer relationships of adolescents, friendships hold a special place. Compared to other broader and more general interactions with peers, friendships typically are more intimate, involve more intense feelings, and are more honest and open and less concerned with self-conscious attempts at role-playing to gain greater popularity and social acceptance (49, 101). Consequently, close friends frequently can contribute to an adolescent's development in ways the broader peer group cannot: "The particular advantage of the adolescent friendship is that it offers a climate for growth and self-knowledge that the family is not equipped to offer, and that very few persons can provide for themselves" (49, *174*). At the same time, because it plays such a vital role in adolescent development, friendship gains an importance and intensity it has never had before and is not likely to have again (49). In his study of adult development in men, *The Seasons of a Man's Life* (110), Daniel Levinson observes that most participants did not have the kind of intimate friend that they recalled fondly from boyhood or youth.

The young person who is attempting to adjust to a changing self (psychologically and physiologically) and to meet rapidly changing societal demands may often experience doubts, anxieties, and, not infrequently, strong resentments. In most situations, these reactions must be concealed. To admit them to any but one's closest friends opens the door to possible misunderstanding, lack of acceptance, or worst of all, amusement, scorn, or rejection. When a meaningful friendship exists, however,

such defensiveness is no longer required. In such a relationship, "there is trust, there is no need to pretend, no necessity for being on guard against betrayal of shared secrets. Adolescents who have a relationship of this kind can reprove each other without condemning each other" (87, *254*).

In view of the sensitivity of adolescents to the potential dangers of revealing their inner feelings, it is not surprising to find that they place particular emphasis on the need for security in discussing the requirements of true friendship: They want the friend to be loyal and trustworthy, and a reliable source of support in any emotional crisis (7, 79, 101). In the words of one 14-year-old girl from an urban ghetto, "A friend don't talk behind your back. If they are a true friend they help you get out of trouble and they will always be right behind you and they help you get through stuff. And they never snitch on you. That's what a friend is" (101, *85*).

Of nearly equal importance in the view of most adolescents is being able to listen and understand at the level of feeling (101). In the words of a 12-year-old rural adolescent, "A friend is someone who I can talk to, who'll understand, and don't turn you down and say they don't want to listen and they don't want to hear what you're having to say" (101, *85*).

Under favorable circumstances, adolescents may reveal a talent for friendships not shared by younger children or most adults. A major distinction between both the younger child and the adult, on the one hand, and the adolescent, on the other, is that the adolescent often enters friendships with a considerable degree of flexibility and readiness for change. Younger children may not be happy with themselves as

Ad enters friendship w/fla

they are, but they tend to accept the situation as an unfortunate fact of life (49). However, with the beginning of adolescence and the onset of the stage of formal operational thinking, young persons become more aware of themselves as social stimuli that can be changed by conscious intent (49, 58). Indeed, their readiness for change—for "self-improvement"—has become the basis for an enormous, and sometimes rather cynically motivated "self-help" industry, ranging from grooming aids to magazine columns on manners and morals. Close friends can often help each other to identify and change behaviors that may turn off others, to develop tastes and social skills, and to learn to articulate and express their ideas.

Along with openness to change, adolescents also reveal an openness to inner states of experience. Adolescents have not yet defined the boundaries of the self; they have not yet made the fixed commitments to a particular way of life that, while resulting in a sharper definition of the self, also tend to limit the individual's openness to other possibilities. As a result, they often exhibit "a psychic flexibility, or vulnerability to conflict, an affective liability which together give adolescent intimacies so much of their characteristic flavor" (49, *180*).

At their best, friendships may help young people to learn to deal with their own complex feelings and those of others. They can serve as a kind of therapy by allowing the freer expression of suppressed feelings of anger or anxiety and by providing evidence that others share many of the same doubts, hopes, fears, and seemingly dangerously strong feelings. As one 16-year-old girl expressed it, "My best friend means a lot to me. We can talk about a lot of things I could never talk about with my parents or other kids—like hassles we're getting or problems we're worried about, and like ideals and things. It really helps to know you're not the only one that has things that bother them" (149, *70*).

Similar thoughts are expressed by this 13-year-old boy: "A best friend to me is someone you can have fun with and you can also be serious with about personal things, about girls, what you're going to do with your life or whatever. My best friend, Jeff, and I can talk about things. His parents are divorced too, and he understands when I feel bummed out about the fights between my mom and dad. A best friend is someone who's not going to make fun of you just because you do something stupid or put you down if you make a mistake. If you're afraid of something or someone, they'll give you confidence" (7, *62*).

Finally, and most broadly, close friendships may play a crucial role in helping young people to develop a sense of their own identity. By sharing their experiences, their plans, their hopes and fears—in brief, by explaining themselves to each other—adolescent friends are also learning to understand themselves. And when a friend who "really understands" you, still likes you and values you, your own confidence and self-esteem are bolstered (128). In short, under favorable circumstances, friendships may help the adolescent both to better define his or her own identity *and* to have confidence and pride in it.

Unfortunately, the circumstances of adolescent friendship are not always so favorable. By virtue of their very intensity, these friendships may sometimes be more easily imperiled than those of most adults, which are likely to involve more modest demands (and to yield more modest returns):

If the youngster is too narcissistic, he may be so sensitive to rejection that he cannot abide friendship, or so obtuse to the needs of others as to be unfit for it. If projection dominates the interaction, it may end in the other being seen as overdangerous. Identifications may become problematic in threatening to blur the all too tentative lineaments of ego identity. These dangers are by no means confined to the adolescent; the adult may avoid close friendships for the same reasons. But the adolescent, generally, will feel these dangers more acutely because of a turbulent intrapsychic situation, and because he has nowhere else to go. If friendship is difficult or dangerous, it is ordinarily less so than isolation, or working these things out in the family [49, *179*].

Even the more stable and enduring—and rewarding—adolescent friendships are likely to blow "hot and cold, responsive to all the rise and fall of feeling in self and others" (49, *179*).

### *Similarity in friendship pairs*

Friendships are most likely to develop between adolescents who share a number of the more obvious demographic characteristics—age, school grade, sex, socioeconomic status, and ethnic background (78, 79). The percentage of close friends who are members of the opposite sex increases with age, but even in later adolescence same-sex friendships predominate, particularly in the case of "best friends" (52, 61, 79, 91, 156). Behavioral and attitudinal similarities between best friends are not as great as those for demographic characteristics; nevertheless, best friends tend to be more similar than acquaintances in intelligence, educational aspirations, sociability, cooperative activities, school grades and school behavior, career goals, conformity to adult expectations, amount of participation in peer group activities, and use of drugs and alcohol (53, 79, 86, 91). Although similarities in personality and —especially—behavior are generally more evident than differences in adolescent friendships (50, 52, 79, 86), this is by no means always the case. Indeed, parents sometimes find their adolescent young's choice of friends incomprehensible. What, they may ask, does their Sally, who has always been so neat, quiet, and studious, see in that noisy, extroverted Barbara, who seems more interested in being constantly on the go than in her schoolwork, or indeed in any serious activity? Where such an attraction of opposites occurs, it is usually because the young person finds in the friend something felt to be desirable but lacking in himself or herself. Thus, extroverted Barbara may be helping Sally to become less inhibited and self-conscious, and to learn to get along more easily with peers. Barbara, in turn, may find in Sally someone to help her understand some of her own previously hidden feelings— someone who is really willing to listen (42).

The fact that in many instances there tend to be similarities in behavior, values, and interests between friends could have two sources: It could be that individuals who share personally relevant similarities are attracted to each other, or it could be that the friendship itself has a socializing effect—that similarity between friends results from the influence they have on each other over the course of their friendship. Although it appears likely that both processes are involved, most studies do not present a clear answer to the question because they are conducted at a single point in time. However, in a longitudinal investigation of New York State high school students (90, 91, 92), Denise Kandel and her colleagues were able to study individuals before they became friends, during the course of their friendship, and in some cases, after their friendship had broken up. They found that both factors played a part. These adolescents tended to choose as friends others who were similar to them in such characteristics as use of legal and illegal drugs, academic interests (educational aspirations, overall grade average, classes cut, and school program), and participation in peer activities (90, 91). However, it was also found that friends tended to resolve any imbalances in such characteristics by becoming more like each other. In those instances where this did not happen, friendships were more likely to be dissolved (90). Others have found that these dual sets of influences also play a part in the formation and maintenance of adolescent cliques (30, 156).

### Variations in friendship patterns

The function, quality, and content of friendship patterns vary with age and sex (49, 79, 150). Prior to the onset of adolescence, friendships tend to be more superficial than they will be later (8, 9, 10, 79, 82). The young person wants a friend who is readily available, who is fun to be with, and who can share interests, activities, and possessions. It is expected that friends will cooperate with and help each other, and there is a growing emphasis on equality in relations between friends. What tends to be lacking "is the sense that friendship can be emotionally relevant" (49, *186*). As the young person moves into and through adolescence, however, there is an increasing emphasis on mutual understanding, empathy, emotional investment, and eventually a sense of shared identities (133, 146, 147, 165), in which "I and you" become "we" (165).

By middle adolescence, "the personality of the other and the other's response to the self become the central themes of the friendship" (49, *188*). During this period, the opportunity for shared thoughts and feelings may help to ease the gradual and initially uncertain transition toward heterosexual relations and a newly defined sex-role identity (49, 158). This is the age when the aforementioned emphasis on a friend's loyalty, trustworthiness, and respect for confidences reaches its peak and when the emotional intensity and vulnerability of friendships are likely to be at their height (49, 128). One study (133) found that the emphasis on intimacy potential, common activities, and loyalty commitment increased until about eighth grade.

In contrast, by late adolescence, the passionate quality of friendship tends to recede and be replaced by a more equable "autonomous interdependence" (146, 147), in which friends can be mutually close yet grant each other autonomy and independence. In the words of one older adolescent, "If you are really close friends and trust each other, you can't hold on to everything. You gotta let go once in a while. Give each other a chance to breathe" (147, *74*). Although having someone to share confidences with is still important, there is a greater, more objective emphasis on the friend's personality and talents—on what he or she can bring to the relationship in the way of interest and stimulation—and a greater degree of tolerance for, and even appreciation of, individual differences. As the adolescent begins to define herself or himself, to find a basis for personal identity, and to develop fairly secure psychological defenses, intense dependence on identification with close friends be-

**TABLE 9.1 COMPARISON OF MALE AND FEMALE
HIGH SCHOOL AND COLLEGE STUDENTS (PERCENT)**[a]

| | MALE | | FEMALE | |
|---|---|---|---|---|
| RELATIONSHIP STYLE | HIGH SCHOOL | COLLEGE | HIGH SCHOOL | COLLEGE |
| Uninvolved | 39 | 28 | 31 | 17 |
| Friendly | 24 | 23 | 26 | 11 |
| Intimate | 15 | 23 | 15 | 30 |
| Integrated | 22 | 26 | 28 | 42 |

*Source:* J. L. Fischer. Transitions in relationship style from adolescence to young adulthood. *Journal of Youth and Adolescence,* 1981, **10,** 11–23. By permission.

[a] School $\times$ gender $\times$ style: $x^2(9) = 21.76$, $p < 0.01$.

comes less vital. Furthermore, more meaningful heterosexual relationships are likely to have begun to develop, thus further diluting the exclusiveness of the adolescent's reliance on same-sex friends (55).

Adolescent friendship patterns also vary with sex. Girls' friendships generally are typically more frequent, deeper, and more interdependent than those of boys; and in their friendships, girls reveal greater nurturance needs, desire for and ability to sustain more intimate relationships, and concern about defection. Boys, in contrast, tend to place relatively more stress on the results of friendship, such as having a congenial companion with whom one shares a common interest in activities oriented to reality.

In one recent study of middle and late adolescence (61), two major aspects of friendships were identified: a *friendship* factor (voluntary involvement in mutual activities with a unique other) and *intimacy* (closeness, ease of communication, attachment and affection, lack of egocentrism). On the basis of these two dimensions, male and female adolescents were divided into four categories: relatively *uninvolved* (below the median on both friendship and intimacy), *friendly* (above the median on friendship, below the median on intimacy), *intimate* (the reverse), and *integrated* (above the median on both intimacy and friendship). It was found that middle-adolescent (high school) males were most likely to be classified as either relatively uninvolved or friendly in their relationship styles, while older adolescent (college) females were most likely to be classified as integrated or intimate (see Table 9.1). Interestingly, when the gender of the subject and his or her friend was taken into account, female-male friendships showed the highest incidence of integrated relationships, followed in order by male-female, female-female, and male-male (see Table 9.2). On the basis of these findings it appears possible "that late adolescent females socialize the males for heterosexual relationships on the basis of their practice in intimacy with their girl friends" (61, *21*).

The differences in emphasis between girls' and boys' friendships are not particularly surprising, because throughout adolescent and adult life women have traditionally tended to maintain a stronger interpersonal orientation in adjusting to life. A girl or woman is more likely than a man to have drives for love and nurturance as

**TABLE 9.2 COMPARISON OF GENDER OF PERSON AND GENDER OF TARGET PERSON BY RELATIONSHIP STYLE (PERCENT)**[a]

| RELATIONSHIP STYLE | GENDER OF SUBJECT–GENDER OF TARGET PERSON | | | |
|---|---|---|---|---|
| | MALE–MALE | MALE–FEMALE | FEMALE–MALE | FEMALE–FEMALE |
| Uninvolved | 46 | 12 | 15 | 28 |
| Friendly | 22 | 27 | 22 | 16 |
| Intimate | 17 | 24 | 15 | 28 |
| Integrated | 15 | 36 | 48 | 29 |

*Source:* J. L. Fischer. Transitions in relationship style from adolescence to young adulthood. *Journal of Youth and Adolescence,* 1981, **10,** 11–23. By permission.

[a] $x^2(9) = 28.91$, $p < 0.001$.

strong motives; when threatened, she is generally less reluctant to appeal for support and nurture from persons important to her. Adolescent and adult males, on the other hand, are more likely than females to be motivated by a need for autonomy, and for relying on one's self or on a broader group of peers (the gang or the clique) in dealing with the competitive demands of the world about them (88, 116, 125, 164). Adolescent boys tend to be more competitive and more hesitant about expressing support or warmth in all-male discussion groups than do girls in female groups; as the study cited above might suggest, boys are somewhat freer in talking about personal feelings in mixed-sex than in same-sex groups (1, 125, 164). Apparently, group discussions centering around interpersonal intimacy are somewhat more threatening to males than to females (124). Whether, and to what extent, such sex differences in relative emphasis may change as sex differences in social and vocational roles are reduced is still an open question.

## SOCIAL ACCEPTANCE, NEGLECT, AND REJECTION

As we have implied, an adolescent's personality characteristics and social behaviors affect the likelihood of being accepted by peers. In general, as indicated by a variety of sociometric studies, adolescents of both sexes who are accepted by their peers are perceived as liking other people and being tolerant, flexible, and sympathetic; being lively, cheerful, good-natured, and possessing a sense of humor; being low in anxiety and having a reasonable level of self-esteem; acting naturally and self-confidently without being conceited; and possessing initiative, enthusiasm, drive, and plans for group activity (2, 15, 32, 71, 75, 77, 79, 107, 114, 118, 161). Adolescents who are viewed favorably tend to be those who contribute to others by making *them* feel accepted and involved, by promoting constructive interaction between peers, or by planning and initiating interesting or enjoyable group activities (2, 96, 123, 144).

Characteristics that are least admired and most likely to lead to neglect or outright rejection are in many ways the opposite of those leading to acceptance and popularity. The adolescent who is ill at ease and lacking in self-confidence and who tends to react to discomfiture by timidity, nervousness, or withdrawal is likely to be neglected by peers and to emerge as a social isolate (2, 123). In contrast, the adolescent who reacts to discomfiture by compensatory overaggressiveness, conceit, or demands for attention is likely to court active dislike and rejection. Similarly, the adolescent who is self-centered and unable or unwilling to perceive and act to meet the needs of others, who is sarcastic, tactless, and inconsiderate, and contributes little to the success of group efforts, is likely to receive little consideration in return.

There are, of course, many other factors that may affect an adolescent's acceptance or rejection by peers—including intelligence and ability, physical attractiveness, special talents, social-class and socioeconomic status, and ethnic-group membership (25, 27, 71, 77, 163). Among boys, athletic ability (79, 123), and among girls, social skills contribute importantly to peer status in most adolescent groups (32, 34). Some characteristics, such as physical size, athletic ability, and physical assertiveness, are more related to group status among younger than among older adolescents; conversely, intelligence, creativity, and social skills play a relatively larger role among older adolescents (43, 144). It is frequently assumed that Americans in general, and adolescents in particular, shun any appearance of being too bright or too intellectual. From this assumption, one might infer that superior intelligence may actually be a detriment to adolescent social acceptance. The reverse, however, appears to be the case (65, 66, 75, 111). Other factors being equal, intelligence is positively and significantly related to acceptance by peers (75, 111). Intelligence and ability may affect social acceptance indirectly as well as directly. An awareness that he or she is of below-average ability and is having school difficulties, and that others are also aware of this, may lead an adolescent to develop personality characteristics—insecurity, withdrawal, compensatory demands for attention, or aggressiveness—that may in themselves lead to rejection (123).

Popularity and social acceptance are also more easily achieved by members of the culturally dominant majority in most peer groups—only partly because they tend, through their greater numbers, to set its norms. Thus members of socioeconomically deprived subgroups are less likely to be accepted not only by more economically favored peers, but by other deprived youth as well (123, 129, 148).

Similar results traditionally have been found in the case of ethnic minorities (19, 131). With the current emphasis, particularly among adolescents and young adults, on ethnic pride and cultural traditions, acceptance and popularity for members of one's own ethnic group have increased rapidly—not only among adolescents, where the trend is currently most pronounced, but, even more important, among younger children as well (5, 83). Perhaps the growth of genuine confidence and pride in one's own cultural identity *and* in one's self as an individual human being may lead to a lack of defensiveness—of a need to "protest too much"—among young people of *all* cultural, racial, and ethnic groups, majority and minority. If this occurs, adolescents will become increasingly free to select friends and acquaintances on the basis of compatible personal characteristics and shared interests, outlooks, and goals (including, but not restricted to, shared ethnic cultural interests).

Influential adults, such as school principals or community leaders, can help to foster a greater degree of constructive interaction between young people who are members of varied ethnic, racial, and socioeconomic groups. Social psychological experiments in summer camps, schools, and other settings (79, 149) have shown that the conditions under which individuals and groups interact can either foster a spirit of togetherness or effectively sabotage it. When diverse groups of children or adolescents are brought together under conditions where cooperating and working together as a total group aid—or are essential to—the accomplishment of common goals, where interactions *within* the group are made rewarding, and where all members are given a sense of belonging, then individual and intragroup rivalries and suspicion diminish and a spirit of "we," rather than "they," emerges. In contrast, under conditions that foster intergroup competition and rivalry, cohesiveness within each group may increase, but, unfortunately, so will stereotyping and hostility between groups. Where superordinate goals can be established and achieved that benefit all individuals, even deep-seated animosities can often be ameliorated. These principles have long been recognized, at least intuitively, by successful religious, political, and military leaders; what we need now is to find better ways to employ them in the schools and other community settings.

Few adolescents (or adults) are unaffected by social neglect or rejection (77, 89). A few individualists, confident of their own goals and interests and possessed of a strong sense of ego identity, may neither need nor seek the approbation of peers. But most adolescents, still judging their own worth to a considerable extent in terms of others' reactions to them, are dependent on the approval and acclaim of prestigious peers. Unfortunately, the unpopular adolescent is likely to be caught in a vicious circle. If already emotionally troubled, self-preoccupied, and lacking in a secure self-concept, he or she is likely to meet with rejection or indifference from peers. In turn, an awareness of not being accepted by peers and a lack of opportunity to participate in and learn from peer group activities only further undermines self-confidence and increases his or her sense of social isolation.

The result is likely to be still further inappropriateness in behavior with peers. Other things being equal, social acceptance by peers is desirable—particularly if it is based on mutual helpfulness and shared interests. In our opinion, however, there is currently an overemphasis, particularly among upper- and middle-class parents, on the pursuit of popularity for their children. A greater emphasis by parents and other significant adults on the importance of being oneself and of remaining faithful to individual values and goals, and a downgrading of the importance of popularity and superficial appearances—of fitting in at all cost—is certainly to be strongly encouraged. But as we have already noted, to expect the average developing adolescent—unsure of his or her own identity and unclear about the demands that will be made in a confused, rapidly changing society—to be immune to the favor of peers would be unrealistic and inappropriate. Most adolescents, at one time or another, feel that they do not belong, and the pain, however temporary, can be very real; parents' overdetermined insistence on popularity can only further compound the adolescent's difficulties.

## *PEER RELATIONS AND SUBSEQUENT ADJUSTMENT*

In view of the important role played by peer relationships in our society, it should not be surprising to find that peer experiences in childhood and adolescence are significantly related to subsequent adjustment during adolescence and adulthood (79). Poor peer relations have been found to be predictive of adult neurotic and psychotic disturbances, as well as conduct disorders and delinquency, and disturbances in sexual behavior and adjustment (72, 79, 100, 119, 136). For example, in one investigation (47) a wide variety of measures were obtained on third-grade children, including intelligence test scores, school grades, achievement test scores, school attendance, and teacher and peer ratings. Eleven years later, those using mental health services were identified through community mental health registers. Of all the measures originally obtained, the best predictors of adult mental health were the peer ratings.

Similarly, delinquency rates among adolescents and young adults and "bad conduct" discharges from the armed services are significantly higher among individuals who had difficulty getting along with others as children (137, 138, 140). In one comprehensive longitudinal study of schoolchildren in a large metropolitan area conducted at the University of Colorado School of Medicine (see page 623), differences between future delinquents and nondelinquents (matched for age, social class, IQ, school attended, residence area, and ethnicity) emerged as early as the period from kindergarten to the third grade (43, 44). Future delinquents showed "more difficulty in getting along with peers, both in individual one-to-one contacts and in group situations, and they were less willing or able to treat others courteously, tactfully, and fairly. In return, they were less well liked and accepted by their peers" (43, *68*). In the period from the fourth to the sixth grade, the future delinquents showed less empathy, were more aggressive, and were less well liked by other children; these differences continued through early adolescence. Self-evaluations from psychological tests revealed that the delinquents did not enjoy close personal relations with other adolescents to the same extent as the nondelinquents, were less interested in organized parties and school organizations, and were more immature. Differences between future delinquents and nondelinquents were no greater in adolescence than in middle childhood, suggesting that poor peer relations emerge early in the social histories of future delinquents and persist through time (43, 79).

In brief, "there is every reason to believe, then, that poor peer relations are centrally involved in the etiology of a variety of emotional and social maladjustments" (79). But whether poor peer relations simply reflect general differences in life course development, or whether they contribute to the development of maladaptive behavior cannot be resolved solely through such "natural experiments." However, experimental studies of monkeys have found that early disturbances in peer relations can have serious adverse effects on long-term adjustment (154). As William Hartup, a psychologist at the University of Minnesota and an expert on peer relations, comments, "It is difficult to believe, however, that trouble with contemporaries does not contribute its own variance to the etiology of psychopathology" (79).

## *RELATIONS WITH OPPOSITE-SEX PEERS*

During preadolescence and very early adolescence, peer relationships in general, and close friendships in particular, tend to be restricted largely to members of the same sex, as we have seen. To some extent, these patterns are culturally imposed and hence subject to variation and modification (as in the case of preadolescents in

some liberally oriented, progressive coeducational boarding schools, where cross-sex friendships are more common than is generally the case). In considerable measure, however, these patterns appear to reflect the needs of the rapidly developing young people themselves. Prior to the onset of adolescent increases in sex drive, the young person is more likely to find others with common concerns, interests, talents, and skills among same-sex peers. Learning culturally sanctioned behaviors (other than those that are specifically heterosexual) may be more easily accomplished in company with others engaged in similar efforts. During a period of rapid physical and psychological change, finding out about one's changing self and, especially, finding out (often with considerable relief) that one is not different or peculiar may be facilitated by communication with, and observation of, same-sex peers.

Further, the awakening of sexual impulses and related physiological and psychological changes is likely to provoke at least a temporary period of self-consciousness and anxiety about sex in general, and about those "strange" (meaning, quite simply, different) peers of the opposite sex. The sex antagonisms common in the preadolescent years appear to be at least partly self-protective and defensive, as though the young person were saying, I must be a real boy (or girl) because I'm certainly not like those strange persons of the opposite sex. Partly, too, antagonisms appear to facilitate an avoidance of premature heterosexual relationships with which the emerging adolescent is unprepared to cope, and which consequently may produce anxiety.

At this stage of development, when narcissistic preoccupations with the self and family ties are still strong, seeking to achieve an embryonic sense of one's own identity through identification with others of the same sex (either through close peer friendships or "crushes" on idealized older persons) appears to be a precondition for later cross-sex friendships, infatuations, and, eventually, mature love (12, 14, 60).

As maturation continues, boys and girls begin to pay more attention to one another. Earlier sex antagonisms and crushes begin to wane, and heterosexual interests increase. Nevertheless, in their early stages, heterosexual relationships still reflect many preadolescent characteristics (49, 50, 152). Self-preoccupation remains strong, deep emotional involvement with opposite-sex peers is rare, and there is usually a superficial, gamelike quality to heterosexual interactions. At this juncture, heterosexual group activities are common and may serve the useful function of providing the security of having familiar same-sex peers present. These activities offer graduated opportunities to learn ways of relating to opposite-sex peers and ensuring that one will not have to cope with being alone in a dating context with an opposite-sex peer for prolonged periods before one is prepared to.

Gradually, however, experience with heterosexual cliques promotes increasing familiarity with, and confidence in, one's ability to relate to individual peers of the opposite sex. At the same time, increased personal maturity—decreased narcissistic self-preoccupation, a clearer sense of self, and a greater capacity to be concerned with others—increases the likelihood that such relationships will themselves be more mature and will involve not only sexual attraction, but feelings of mutual trust and confidence, a genuine sharing of interests, and a serious involvement in the well-being of the other as a person in his or her own right.

## TABLE 9.3 FREQUENCY OF DATING AMONG U.S. HIGH SCHOOL SENIORS, 1980

| | SEX | | COLLEGE-BOUND | |
| --- | --- | --- | --- | --- |
| | MALE | FEMALE | YES | NO |
| Never | 12.4 | 13.7 | 13.0 | 13.0 |
| Once a month or less | 20.5 | 18.0 | 22.1 | 15.7 |
| 2 or 3 times a month | 21.1 | 16.6 | 20.5 | 16.9 |
| Once a week | 17.1 | 13.8 | 16.3 | 14.3 |
| 2 or 3 times a week | 20.3 | 24.2 | 20.4 | 24.5 |
| Over 3 times a week | 8.6 | 13.7 | 7.7 | 15.7 |

Source: J. F. Bachman, L. D. Johnston, and P. M. O'Malley. *Monitoring the future: Questionnaire responses from the nation's high school seniors, 1980.* Ann Arbor, Mich.: Institute for Social Research, 1980. By permission.

### Dating

In our society, the traditional vehicle for fostering individual heterosexual relationships has been the institution of dating. Although dating has an undeniable function in providing a ritualized structure for learning heterosexual interactions, it may also tend to promote a maladaptive superficiality, a lack of genuineness, and even, at times, dishonesty and competitiveness (however well disguised) in relations between the sexes, as an increasing number of young people are aware. Because the dating institution is so ubiquitous in America, we often take it for granted, neglecting the fact that dating tends to occur earlier and to play a more dominant role in adolescent peer relations here than in many other countries. Most girls in the United States begin dating at age 14 and most boys begin between 14 and 15 (49, 84, 152). In a national survey of high school seniors in 1980 (4), approximately half indicated that they went out on a date at least once a week, and one-third said they dated at least two or three times a week (see Table 9.3).

Under favorable conditions, dating presumably serves a number of useful functions: developing social and interpersonal skills in relations with members of the opposite sex, providing an opportunity to meet opposite-sex peers and explore mutual compatibility within a social framework that allows for terminating unwanted relationships (and for finding new ones) with a minimum loss of face (49, 123), aiding in the finding and testing of identity, and providing occasions for sexual experiment and discovery within mutually acceptable limits. Perhaps most important as far as future marriage is concerned, dating may permit the development of reciprocal relationships of genuine trust, love, and mutual concern between opposite-sex peers (49, 58, 123).

Middle-class dating patterns in this country do, in fact, appear to facilitate at least some of these goals. Compared to many of their European contemporaries, American adolescents exhibit "a degree of poise and nonchalance which stands in vivid contrast to the shyness, embarrassment, and even gaucherie of the European youngster of equivalent years" (49, *207*). If the adolescent does not begin going steady with one person too early and for too long a period of time, the dating institution permits him or her to gain experience with a variety of opposite-sex peers.

The depth and maturity of interpersonal relationships encouraged by the dating pattern appear more open to question. Particularly in the earlier years of adolescence, there seems to be less emphasis on the development of warm, spontaneous, meaningful interactions between two individuals and more emphasis on the development of the so-called dating personality. Many aspects of the so-called good date (superficial social and conversational skills; charm; the ability to affect a bright, interested manner without letting mood variations show through; keeping the conversation from getting too serious; manipulating sexual attractiveness) seem somewhat irrelevant if not inimical to later development of more honest, direct, complex, deeper emotional relationships, particularly if dating is begun too early. As we noted earlier, overly eager pursuit of popularity can sometimes work against the development of a richer personal identity and inner resourcefulness.

### Current dating patterns

Although current dating is considerably less formal and structured than it was in earlier generations, the characteristics that today's adolescents say they look for in a prospective date, the dating "rules of the game" that they anticipate or desire, and the personal doubts and anxieties they share, are not nearly as new and different as one might expect (7). Young people are still concerned with such issues as: "Does he like me?" "If I ask her to go out with me, will she turn me down?" "Will he call?" "Will I know what to say and how to act if I go out with her?" "What about making out?"

For the young person who is shy, socially inexperienced, or fearful of rejection, asking someone for a first date is not easy. In the words of one 16-year-old boy, "The way you think about yourself really has a lot to do with how you act. Like you might stop yourself from going up to someone you might want to meet because you think, Oh, I'm not attractive enough or I don't have a good enough personality. You think you won't make a good impression so you're afraid to make an effort. For me, it was always that I was afraid I'd be rejected or—even worse than that—ignored. But what I've learned is that you may have something inside you that the other person would like very much. You have to give yourself a chance because if you put yourself down too quick you never get anywhere" (7, 65).

Despite the so-called sexual revolution and the rise of the women's movement, many traditional stereotypes about dating appear alive and well. For example, in a recent national sample of adolescent girls (66), almost two-thirds (64 percent) said they had never asked a boy out first, and nearly a quarter more said they seldom did; only 2 percent said they did so frequently. Even among female college students, a majority had never asked a boy out first, and just over 10 percent said they did sometimes (66). Ironically, when a comparable national sample of adolescent boys was asked what their reaction is when a girl asks them for a date, most reacted positively (44 percent) or said it didn't matter (43 percent); only 13 percent said it would "turn them off" (65). In the words of one 17-year-old boy, "I think it's great when a girl calls up a guy to ask him out. A lot of guys are shy, like I was shy for a long time. It was hell for me to ask a girl out. And a lot of the girls I know are much

less shy than I am, so it makes me feel wonderful when one of them asks me out" (7, 67).

Nevertheless, the average adolescent, particularly the younger adolescent, still feels constrained by traditional sex-role expectations: "I think boys have it really hard. Once you get to be a teenager, suddenly everybody expects you to start calling up girls and going out with them. But, hey, I think it takes a lot of courage to call a girl up and ask her out. You know, you always worry that she'll say no. . . . It's not so easy for me to just pick up the phone and act cool. I get nervous" (7, 66).

Nor is the position of the girl who has been taught that you are supposed to wait to be asked any more enviable! "Sitting around waiting for the phone to ring is a big part of my life—you know, wondering if some boy's going to call and ask you out for the weekend. Like on Monday night I'll sit there and say to myself, Well, the phone's going to ring by the time I count to twenty-five. Then if it doesn't ring I count to a new number. It makes me so nervous I can't concentrate on anything else and I'm always yelling at everybody else in the family to get off the phone if they're using it" (7, 66). Although nearly 40 percent of boys (65) and nearly 50 percent of girls (66) still think the boys should pay all the expenses of a date, the picture is changing in a more egalitarian direction, especially among older adolescents and youth (66).

Many contemporary adolescents, like their peers of an earlier day, are concerned about what kinds of sexual activity are or are not appropriate at various stages of the dating process, and how to initiate or respond to sex-related behavior—although sexual standards today are generally more liberal (7, 65, 66, 73, 126). Most adolescents still expect boys to take the lead in "making out," despite the fact that less than 22 percent of American adolescent boys said that they would be "turned off" by the girl taking the lead, 36 percent said it made no difference, and a little over 41 percent approved (65). Among adolescent girls, nearly two out of three either agreed strongly (31 percent) or agreed somewhat (33 percent) that they preferred the boy to take the lead in making out, 20 percent said they weren't sure, and 16 percent disagreed to some degree (66).

***Dating preferences*** In a recent national survey (66), adolescent American girls, aged 16 to 21, were asked what qualities in boys "turned them on"—or off. Rated as most important (90 percent or more) were: good personality, kindness, good manners, and a sense of humor; these were followed by compassion, good looks, and charm (over 70 percent). In contrast, the following emerged as the most frequent "turn-offs": heavy drinking, inability to communicate feelings, profanity, and drug use (all over 70 percent), followed by indecisiveness, "super-jock," and "don't kiss goodnight" (40 percent or more). Apparently, these young women wanted boys to be somewhat androgynous—sensitive and compassionate but also reasonably assertive and decisive.

In a similar survey (65) of boys of the same ages, a number of interesting findings emerged. Three-quarters of these adolescents said that the first thing that initially attracts them to a girl is her looks—whether she has an attractive figure and pretty face. However, when asked what they considered most important in a girl, or what would lead them to want to continue dating her, personality and a sense of humor ranked first, followed by beauty and intelligence and personal warmth.

In contrast, the most frequent "turn-offs" for boys included using profanity, refusing a goodnight kiss on the first date, being overly possessive, and being "not smart enough." Whether a girl would take a drink or smoke marijauna didn't matter one way or the other to the great majority of boys. A prominent reason for not wanting a second date was "boredom."

In other surveys, desirable qualities frequently mentioned by both sexes included good looks; intelligence; being friendly, confident, but not conceited; honesty ("not into game playing"); being a good conversationalist; having a sense of humor; being fun to be with.

***Sex role and dating orientation*** It has traditionally been assumed that male and female adolescents and youth differ in their dating orientation, with males placing a greater emphasis on the specifically sexual (psychobiological) aspects and females placing a greater emphasis on the psychoaffectional aspects (e.g., sincerity, understanding, affection, trust, companionship, tenderness, romance, and mutual sharing of life experiences). Recent research, however, suggests that matters are considerably more complex. In one study (115), the investigators obtained separate scores on a psychobiological scale and a psychoaffectional scale for three groups of middle-class young people, ages 16 to 17, 19 to 20, and 24 to 25. Participants were further subdivided into six categories that were based on biological sex and sex-role scores on a measure of psychological androgyny as follows: masculine males, an-

**TABLE 9.4 MEANS OF MALE AND FEMALE PSYCHOBIOLOGICAL SCORES AT VARIOUS STAGES OF THE DATING RELATIONSHIP**

| | MALES | | | FEMALES | | |
|---|---|---|---|---|---|---|
| | FEMI-NINE | ANDROGY-NOUS | MASCU-LINE | FEMI-NINE | ANDROGY-NOUS | MASCU-LINE |
| **16–17 YEARS** | | | | | | |
| First date | 6.8 | 7.0 | 11.6 | 4.2 | 4.8 | 4.0 |
| Several dates | 10.4 | 10.8 | 13.5 | 6.9 | 7.4 | 6.3 |
| Going steady | 11.6 | 13.5 | 13.4 | 9.7 | 10.3 | 9.2 |
| **19–20 YEARS** | | | | | | |
| First date | 4.8 | 6.5 | 10.4 | 3.5 | 4.0 | 4.5 |
| Several dates | 9.8 | 8.7 | 13.4 | 7.3 | 8.5 | 10.1 |
| Going steady | 13.4 | 12.5 | 14.7 | 11.9 | 13.1 | 13.9 |
| **24–25 YEARS** | | | | | | |
| First date | 4.4 | 6.7 | 8.9 | 2.9 | 4.8 | 5.0 |
| Several dates | 9.1 | 11.8 | 13.7 | 8.6 | 10.6 | 11.0 |
| Going steady | 14.1 | 13.6 | 14.1 | 14.5 | 13.8 | 13.7 |

Source: M. P. McCabe and J. K. Collins. Sex role and dating orientation. *Journal of Youth and Adolescence,* 1979, **8,** 407–425. By permission.

drogynous males, and feminine males; masculine females, androgynous females, and feminine females.

A number of interesting findings emerged. With respect to the psychobiological score, four main conclusions can be drawn: First, the sex role adopted by adolescents influences their sexual desires during dating. Irrespective of their biological sex, feminine adolescents do not generally desire as much sexual involvement (i.e., do not have as high psychobiological scores) as masculine or androgynous adolescents (see Table 9.4). Second, young adolescent males score higher than corresponding groups of females at all stages of dating. Third, with increasing age these differences diminish, with females increasing their desire for more sexual involvement. Fourth, both males and females show a desire for greater biological involvement, or greater compatibility of desire, as the dating relationship deepens. As a consequence, there are virtually no differences in the extent of physical intimacy desired among older youth who are going steady (see Table 9.5).

In contrast to findings on the psychobiological scale, only one significant difference emerged on the psychoaffectional scale. The desire for affection increased with all groups of males and females as the commitment to the relationship increased (see Table 9.6). Contrary to some traditional stereotypes, both male and female adolescents and youth "commence dating with an affectional orientation, and the desire for this affectional component increases with increased commitment to the relationship" (115, *422*). In brief, contrary to some earlier assumptions, the desire of younger males for greater physical intimacy early in a dating relationship does not appear to indicate any lack of interest in an affectional orientation. In other words,

**TABLE 9.5 DESIRED PSYCHOBIOLOGICAL BEHAVIORS OF MALES AND FEMALES IN THREE AGE GROUPS AND AT VARIOUS STAGES OF THE DATING RELATIONSHIP (PERCENT)**

| | 16–17 YEARS | | | | | |
| | FIRST DATE | | SEVERAL DATES | | GOING STEADY | |
| BEHAVIOR | M | F | M | F | M | F |
|---|---|---|---|---|---|---|
| Hand holding | 89 | 96 | 93 | 100 | 95 | 100 |
| Light embrace | 94 | 91 | 94 | 100 | 97 | 100 |
| Light kissing | 96 | 94 | 93 | 97 | 89 | 98 |
| General body contact | 76 | 48 | 98 | 93 | 100 | 100 |
| Necking | 67 | 31 | 84 | 79 | 77 | 94 |
| Deep kissing | 60 | 31 | 89 | 79 | 97 | 90 |
| Light breast petting | 55 | 18 | 85 | 55 | 87 | 76 |
| Heavy breast petting | 27 | 3 | 67 | 15 | 93 | 49 |
| Light genital petting—female | 36 | 2 | 67 | 15 | 87 | 52 |
| Heavy genital petting—female | 20 | 2 | 53 | 12 | 80 | 30 |
| Nude embrace | 9 | 6 | 40 | 9 | 70 | 31 |
| Simulated intercourse | 16 | 3 | 44 | 12 | 60 | 31 |
| Mutual masturbation | 18 | 3 | 45 | 12 | 76 | 31 |
| Oral stimulation | | | | | | |
|   Female genitals | 24 | 6 | 44 | 7 | 75 | 31 |
|   Male genitals | 13 | 3 | 27 | 6 | 64 | 31 |
| Intercourse | 16 | 0 | 27 | 4 | 62 | 19 |

**TABLE 9.6 MEANS OF MALE AND FEMALE AFFECTIONAL SCORES AT VARIOUS STAGES OF DATING WITH AGE GROUPS COMBINED**

| | | STAGES OF DATING | | |
| BIOLOGICAL SEX | SEX ROLE | FIRST DATE | SEVERAL DATES | GOING STEADY |
|---|---|---|---|---|
| Males | Feminine | 11.9 | 14.3 | 15.5 |
| | Androgynous | 12.0 | 14.2 | 15.6 |
| | Masculine | 11.6 | 13.7 | 15.6 |
| Females | Feminine | 12.1 | 14.2 | 15.5 |
| | Androgynous | 11.9 | 14.4 | 15.6 |
| | Masculine | 10.6 | 13.9 | 15.0 |
| Males and females combined | Feminine | 12.0 | 14.2 | 15.5 |
| | Androgynous | 11.9 | 14.3 | 15.7 |
| | Masculine | 11.3 | 13.8 | 15.4 |

*Source:* M. P. McCabe and J. K. Collins. Sex role and dating orientation. *Journal of Youth and Adolescence,* 1979, **8,** 407–425. By permission.

| 19–20 YEARS | | | | | | 24–25 YEARS | | | | | |
| FIRST DATE | | SEVERAL DATES | | GOING STEADY | | FIRST DATE | | SEVERAL DATES | | GOING STEADY | |
| M | F | M | F | M | F | M | F | M | F | M | F |
|---|---|---|---|---|---|---|---|---|---|---|---|
| 92 | 76 | 97 | 98 | 100 | 98 | 83 | 75 | 90 | 87 | 90 | 87 |
| 92 | 73 | 97 | 98 | 100 | 98 | 79 | 75 | 93 | 100 | 93 | 100 |
| 92 | 79 | 89 | 92 | 94 | 90 | 83 | 87 | 90 | 92 | 90 | 87 |
| 69 | 29 | 94 | 92 | 97 | 100 | 65 | 33 | 94 | 96 | 100 | 100 |
| 50 | 25 | 75 | 62 | 78 | 82 | 21 | 25 | 69 | 75 | 75 | 92 |
| 58 | 25 | 83 | 73 | 97 | 98 | 45 | 29 | 79 | 71 | 90 | 100 |
| 50 | 19 | 86 | 67 | 94 | 80 | 45 | 25 | 86 | 83 | 93 | 92 |
| 45 | 6 | 58 | 42 | 86 | 77 | 31 | 8 | 27 | 58 | 86 | 96 |
| 36 | 8 | 58 | 44 | 83 | 77 | 38 | 12 | 83 | 54 | 90 | 83 |
| 33 | 2 | 58 | 21 | 78 | 69 | 24 | 4 | 62 | 37 | 86 | 83 |
| 45 | 4 | 53 | 19 | 78 | 71 | 28 | 4 | 69 | 46 | 93 | 92 |
| 25 | 4 | 47 | 29 | 65 | 57 | 24 | 8 | 55 | 33 | 65 | 55 |
| 36 | 8 | 61 | 27 | 81 | 75 | 24 | 4 | 55 | 37 | 79 | 79 |
| 45 | 10 | 61 | 21 | 72 | 50 | 24 | 4 | 48 | 46 | 79 | 87 |
| 36 | 6 | 56 | 21 | 75 | 58 | 3 | 4 | 55 | 29 | 83 | 83 |
| 31 | 2 | 47 | 8 | 78 | 58 | 24 | 4 | 52 | 37 | 86 | 87 |

*Source:* M. P. McCabe and J. K. Collins. Sex role and dating orientation. *Journal of Youth and Adolescence,* 1979, **8,** 407–425. By permission.

psychobiological and psychoaffectional orientation are not, as some have suggested (115), opposite ends of a continuum; each exists in its own right. Whether similar findings would emerge from studies of lower-class youth requires further investigation.

In another study (141), the relationship of sex roles to self-disclosure and openness was studied in college-student dating couples. It was found that both men and women with egalitarian sex-role attitudes were more open with each other than those with traditional attitudes. Not surprisingly, the investigators also found greater self-disclosure and openness among couples who had been dating longer and who were in love, as compared to simply liking each other.

**Going steady** When adolescents in a national survey were asked if they were going steady at the present time, 23 percent of boys and 32 percent of girls said yes. The discrepancy suggests that girls and boys may not always perceive the nature of their relationships in the same way—with girls appearing more constant in their affections; part of the difference may also be due to more girls than boys going steady with someone older (64). Not surprisingly, older adolescents are more likely to say they are going steady; among boys, 11 percent of 13- to 15-year-olds, but 31 percent of 16- to 18-year-olds, were going steady; among girls, the comparable figures were 22 percent for 13- to 15-year-olds, and 40 percent for 16- to 18-year-olds.

Interestingly, when adolescents who were going steady were asked if their parents objected, only 8 percent of boys and 11 percent of girls said that they objected; furthermore, the figures were approximately the same for younger as well as for older adolescents. Despite this evident lack of parental concern, going steady too early may hinder the young person's overall development (64).

The adolescent who begins restricting his or her relations to one member of the opposite sex at too early an age is likely to miss a number of important developmental experiences (42). For one thing, the young person may never achieve the benefits of like-sex friendships discussed in the previous section. Such friendships play a vital role in helping the adolescent to learn to get along with members of the same sex, and to find satisfactions in close relationships with same-sex friends. Having such friends can be very important in adult life, even after marriage. The honeymoon does not go on forever, and having close friends of the same sex can make life richer, fuller, and more rewarding, as well as providing additional sources of support at times of stress. As we have also seen, identification with friends of the same sex helps the adolescent come to a deeper understanding of himself or herself and fosters the process of identity formation.

Furthermore, when young people begin going steady at an age when they are both still emotionally and socially immature, the relationship itself is likely to have these qualities, and their further development in the direction of becoming mature, self-reliant persons in their own right may be jeopardized. They may tend to use their relationship as a way of avoiding other important developmental tasks. Finally, and most obviously, they may miss the invaluable opportunity adolescence provides of getting to know, understand, and enjoy a wide variety of acquaintances of both sexes (42).

An extensive national study of adolescent girls (49) found that girls who begin dating very early (ages 11 to 14) and those who do not date at all—even in late adolescence—are both at a developmental disadvantage. Adolescent girls who begin dating very early tended to be active, energetic, and self-confident, but also immature, superficial, unimaginative, and limited in their interests and friendships, especially with other girls.

Because of the peculiar admixture of positive and negative aspects of dating, late adolescents who have had little experience with dating may also be penalized, though in different ways. The same study found that those who did not date at all tended to be retarded in social development, overly dependent on parents, insecure, and self-absorbed. Clearly, these personality characteristics are not attributable solely to the dating pattern. Preexisting personality characteristics are at least as likely to influence dating practices as the reverse. But once the patterns are begun, a vicious cycle appears to be set in motion, further reinforcing the girls' particular liabilities.

**Stages in dating behavior**   The average girl appears to go through three general stages in dating behavior (49). Preadolescents tend to treat dating almost as an intellectual issue and give "no real indication of emotional involvement with boys except for occasional signs of anxiety about their imminent introduction to dating" (49, *210*). In contrast, early adolescents tend to be very much involved in beginning dating, but are often self-conscious, and somewhat anxious and defensive in their relationships with boys. "Only in late adolescence, as initial anxiety subsides, do girls begin to have true interactive relationships with boys, and bring understanding, sensitivity, and feeling to these relationships" (49, *210*). Somewhat similar patterns exist with boys, although, as in other areas, boys tend to place somewhat less stress on the intimate, emotional, interpersonal aspects of boy-girl relationships, and more on commonly shared activities and interests (49, 123).

**Adolescent love** When American adolescents were asked if they had ever been in love, 56 percent replied that they had been; 39 percent said they had not, and 5 percent were not sure (64). Younger adolescent boys, aged 12 to 15, were least likely to say they had been in love (47 percent), while older adolescent girls, age 16 to 18, were most likely. Among those who said that they had been in love at some point, slightly over half (52 percent) said they were currently in love. Again girls were more likely than boys to say they were currently in love (61 percent versus 42 percent), with older girls having the highest frequency (69 percent), followed by younger girls (49 percent), older boys (43 percent) and younger boys (38 percent).

In some cases, adolescent romances evolve gradually into stable, committed, long-term relationships; more frequently they involve an "intense emotional experience that lasts a while and then changes" (7, *68*). Nevertheless, during the relationship, the feelings can be just as vital, and the capacity for joy or despair just as great, as in adult love affairs. To be in love with someone who does not reciprocate is painful; it is "even more painful when you are still in love with someone who's no longer in love with you"(7, *69*). For adults to discuss adolescent "puppy love" as not serious (or even as amusing) indicates a lack of sensitivity—as well as a short memory. Breaking up with a boyfriend or girlfriend can lead at times to genuine depression; as one 17-year-old girl described her feelings: "I just feel like my life's over, like there's never going to be anything to smile about again" (7, *69*). Fortunately, in most cases, the hurt gradually fades, but having a close friend to talk to can be very helpful at such a time (7).

On the other hand, adolescents may sometimes seek to maintain a relationship simply for the security involved, thus limiting their own continued development:

> It's comforting to know that you'll always have a date for the weekend and that someone cares about you and is choosing to spend time with you. But fear—fear of being alone, fear of going out with new people, fear of hurting the other person's feelings, fear of being rejected—is not a healthy basis for a relationship [7, *70*].

In brief, it appears that the young person who will be best prepared for both social and vocational responsibilities in adult life, and also for the intimate, emotional demands of marriage, will be one who has been able to try out a variety of social and personal roles. Optimally, this means involvement both with opposite-sex peers and with close friends of the same sex in the early years of adolescence; and in the later years of adolescence, an opportunity to develop meaningful, trusting, and mutually supportive relationships with an opposite-sex peer. In this connection, it is interesting to note that up through middle adolescence, young people who have clearly defined educational and vocational plans and who aspire to marriages like those of their parents "tend to be less often in love while in school, are less frequently going steady, and are less apt to plan on being married before they are 21" (56, *228*). Adolescents *not* wanting a marriage like their parents' were significantly more likely to report being in love right now (56). Young women with high self-esteem tended in adolescence to date more often, but to go steady less often than those with low self-esteem (98). Another investigator (99) found that high school seniors who have parents who are living together tend to have a more realistic, less romantic attitude toward love than those whose parents are divorced or who have a deceased parent.

## ADOLESCENT MARRIAGES

In our society, the role requirements associated with marriage are complex and often difficult to fulfill. And they appear to be becoming more so as societal rewards for marriage have diminished and as traditional role relationships have become less clearly defined and more controversial, particularly among some socioeconomically favored, highly educated young people (51, 152). Although more than three-fourths of contemporary adolescents and youth plan to marry, and only 5 percent are sure they do not want to marry, with the remainder uncertain (4, 67), the degree of importance attached to being married and raising a family has declined considerably in the past decade. For example, among all first-year college students in the United States in 1981, 65 percent of both males and females cited "raising a family" as an essential or very important personal objective, down from 78 percent of women and 66.5 percent of men in 1969 (3, 59). Most of this decline in importance occurred among women (from 78 to 64 percent), with only a slight drop among men (from 66.5 to 62.5 percent), probably reflecting the increased importance of careers in women's value systems during the past decade. (The percentage of women desiring administrative responsibility more than doubled during this period, with large increases also in the numbers wishing to succeed in their own businesses, to be an authority in their field, or to be well off financially.)

Similarly, among the small minority of young people aged 13 to 18 planning not to marry, 50 percent of adolescent males, but only 4 percent of females say they do not want the responsibility of marriage (126). In contrast, twice as many girls as boys fear the loss of freedom in marriage (44 percent versus 22 percent); similarly, more than twice as many girls as boys express concern that marriage would interfere with their career plans (19 percent versus 9 percent).

Among American high school seniors in 1980, only about four in ten agreed that "most people will have fuller and happier lives if they choose legal marriage, rather than staying single, or just living with someone" (4)—an idea that was virtually an article of faith in their parents' generation (see Table 9.7).

In addition, the burdens are likely to be greater for married adolescents, who may still be struggling to complete their education, to establish themselves in a vocation, or simply to decide who they really are and what they want to be. Typically,

**TABLE 9.7 AGREEMENT OF 1980 U.S. HIGH SCHOOL
SENIORS WITH THE STATEMENT "MOST PEOPLE WILL
HAVE FULLER AND HAPPIER LIVES IF THEY CHOOSE
LEGAL MARRIAGE RATHER THAN STAYING SINGLE,
OR JUST LIVING WITH SOMEONE" (PERCENT)**

| | SEX | | COLLEGE-BOUND | |
| --- | --- | --- | --- | --- |
| | MALE | FEMALE | YES | NO |
| Disagree | 20.5 | 22.4 | 20.5 | 22.1 |
| Mostly disagree | 13.9 | 14.9 | 13.6 | 15.8 |
| Neither | 26.9 | 22.4 | 25.1 | 23.3 |
| Mostly agree | 16.8 | 15.2 | 17.4 | 15.0 |
| Agree | 22.0 | 25.3 | 23.5 | 23.8 |

*Source:* J. F. Bachman, L. D. Johnston, and P. M. O'Malley. *Monitoring the future: Questionnaire responses from the nation's high school seniors, 1980.* Ann Arbor, Mich.: Institute for Social Research, 1980. By permission.

married adolescents are also economically insecure or dependent on parents for continued financial assistance—either of which may create additional problems (23, 48, 122, 145).

Young married couples have to be far more concerned than their single peers with meeting complicated cultural demands, both in social relationships with others and in the increasingly complex and changing world of work. With the rapid increase in two-job families in recent years (see pages 457–460), the need to juggle work, household work, and childrearing can add to family stress. This is especially likely for wives without extended family support; even among young couples who share an equalitarian view of marriage, in which the husband makes an effort to share household tasks and child care, the burden of these responsibilities is still likely to fall most heavily on the young wife (whether employed or not) (151).

Both husband and wife have to learn to cope with new restrictions on personal freedom, to adjust their personal wishes and habits to those of their partner, and to shift much of their emotional concern from themselves to their spouse and children. This can be particularly difficult if the young people are still preoccupied, as adolescents characteristically are, with their own identity formation. In addition, the emphasis in our society on marriage as a continuing romantic affair may burden with unrealistic expectations what is already a difficult, intimate emotional interaction. Considerable personal maturity and prior integration into other adult roles are desirable if a couple's chances for a successful marriage are to be enhanced.

Adolescent marriages are often complicated by the fact that they are more likely than older marriages to have resulted from pregnancy. The great majority of all premaritally pregnant brides are in their teens (57); nearly half of all marital births to teenagers are conceived premaritally, despite the fact that the percentage of out-of-wedlock births has been increasing each year (see Figure 9.3). Clearly, premarital pregnancy is largely a phenomenon characteristic of the young (112). In such cases, young people may not be marrying the person they would ultimately have chosen,

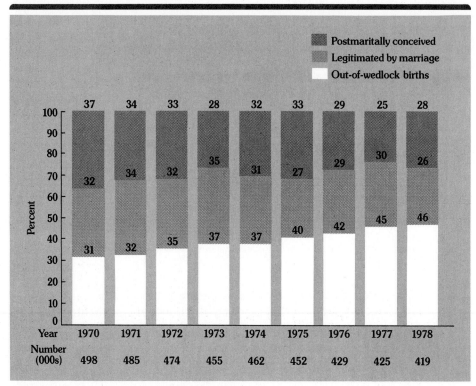

Legend:
- Postmaritally conceived
- Legitimated by marriage
- Out-of-wedlock births

| Year | 1970 | 1971 | 1972 | 1973 | 1974 | 1975 | 1976 | 1977 | 1978 |
|------|------|------|------|------|------|------|------|------|------|
| Postmaritally conceived | 37 | 34 | 33 | 28 | 32 | 33 | 29 | 25 | 28 |
| Legitimated by marriage | 32 | 34 | 32 | 35 | 31 | 27 | 29 | 30 | 26 |
| Out-of-wedlock births | 31 | 32 | 35 | 37 | 37 | 40 | 42 | 45 | 46 |
| Number (000s) | 498 | 485 | 474 | 455 | 462 | 452 | 429 | 425 | 419 |

**Figure 9.3** Percentage distribution of first births to women aged 15–19, by time of conception and marital status at outcome, 1970–1978. (From Planned Parenthood Federation of America. *Teenage pregnancy: The problem that hasn't gone away.* New York: Alan Guttmacher Institute, 1981. By permission.)

and even if they are, they have less time to become adjusted to each other and to the demands of marriage before undertaking the responsibilities and restrictions of parenthood. Most young people would prefer to wait at least 2 years after marriage before having children (4), and for a majority of women this is indeed the case (160).

When to all of these other considerations we add the facts that young marrieds are statistically more likely than persons marrying at later ages to have lower intelligence test scores and lower school grades, to have lower educational levels, to be school dropouts, and to be employed at unskilled and semiskilled jobs (24, 48), it is not surprising to find that adolescent marriages are two to three times more likely to break up than those of couples who marry in their twenties (57). The younger the adolescent partners are when they marry, the greater is the likelihood of divorce or legal separation (24, 57, 112). Brides aged 17 and younger are three times more likely, and their husbands twice as likely, to split up with their spouses as those who marry in their early twenties (see Figure 9.4). "More than one-quarter of first marriages where the bride is 14–17 end in divorce or separation, compared to 10 percent where the bride is 20–24. Marriages in which the husbands are adolescents

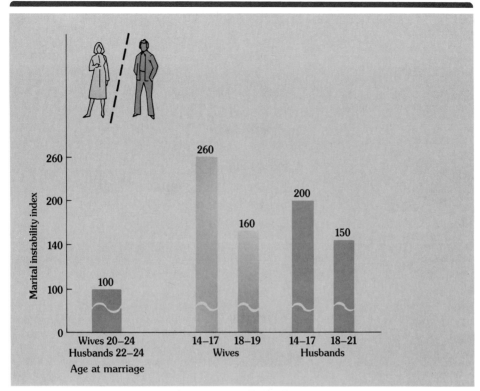

**Figure 9.4** Risk of first marriage ending in divorce or separation where partners married as teenagers and at age 20–24, United States, 1968–1972. (Risk of separation to women married at 20–24, and men married at 22–24 = 100.) (From Planned Parenthood Federation of America. *Eleven-Million teenagers: What can be done about the epidemic of adolescent pregnancies in the United States.* New York: Alan Guttmacher Institute, 1977. By permission.)

show a similar trend of instability (12 percent of teens, vs. six percent who married at 22–24)'' (57, *28*).

Premaritally pregnant adolescent girls are even more likely to suffer marital breakups. One Baltimore study found that three out of five premaritally pregnant mothers aged 17 and younger were separated or divorced within 6 years of the marriage. One-fifth of the marriages were dissolved within 12 months, two and one-half times the proportion of broken marriages among classmates of the adolescent mothers who were not pregnant premaritally. "Even at the end of three years, the premaritally pregnant teenage brides were nearly twice as likely to have separated as their classmates. Those teenage mothers who married the father prior to the child's delivery were more likely to stay married than those who did not marry until after the birth'' (57, *28*).

Nevertheless, significant numbers of adolescent marriages are successful. What makes the difference between those that end in divorce and the larger number

**TABLE 9.8** *HYPOTHESIZED RELATIONSHIPS BETWEEN SELECTED CHARACTERISTICS AND OUTCOMES OF YOUNG MARRIAGES: FORECAST OF MARITAL COMPETENCE AND SATISFACTION*

| CHARACTERISTIC | POOREST |
|---|---|
| Ages at marriage | Both 17 or younger |
| Educational attainment | Both school dropouts |
| Pregnancy | Premarital pregnancy |
| Acquaintance before marriage | Less than 6 months, no engagement period, formal or informal |
| Previous dating patterns | Limited number of dating partners, went steady immediately, or short period between first date and first date with fiancé |
| Personality dynamics | Generally poor interpersonal skills, lacking maturity, limited interests, poor personal and social adjustment |
| Motivation for marrying | Drift into marriage, because of pregnancy, seemed like the thing to do, just wanted to, or other impulsive reasons with no strong emphasis on marital and parental roles |
| Status of families of orientation | Both lower |
| Parental attitudes before marriage | Strongly opposed |
| Wedding | Elopement and civil ceremony |
| Economic basis | Virtually completely dependent upon relatives |
| Residence | Always lived with in-laws or other relatives |
| Postmarriage parental views | Rejecting or punitive, assistance provided as a method of controlling the marriage |

that apparently succeed, despite the difficulties involved? A number of factors appear to significantly differentiate successful young marriages from those that end in failure (see Table 9.8). Obviously, the larger the number of positive factors operating in a particular adolescent marriage, the greater are its chances for survival; conversely, the larger the number of negative factors, the more likely it may create additional problems (23, 122, 145).

| INTERMEDIATE | BEST |
|---|---|
| Female 17, male 20 or older | Female at least 18, male 20 or older |
| Female dropout, male high school graduate | Both high school graduates, male, at last, with some post-high school education |
| No premarital pregnancy, pregnancy immediately following marriage | Pregnancy delayed until at least 1 year following marriage |
| One year, at least, with at least 6 months engagement or understanding to marry | Several years, with at least 6 months engagement or understanding to marry |
| Some dating experience before first dating fiancé | Numerous different dates, played the field, some previous experience with going steady |
| Mixed | Generally competent in interpersonal relations, flexible, mature, maintaining healthy and pleasurable relations with others |
| Mixed, marriage as preferred to career, though had previous post-high school educational aspirations and for females perhaps tentative plans to work, etc. | No post-high school educational aspirations and, for females, marriage, family, and homemaking preferred as career over working, living independently; positive emphasis upon role as wife and mother |
| Mixed, lower, and middle or high | Both middle or high |
| Mildly opposed or resigned acceptance | Supportive once the decision was clear |
| | Conventional, hometown, and church-sanctioned |
| Low dependence upon relatives, mostly independent income, even if near hardship level | At least assured income above self-perceived hardship level |
| Doubled up with relatives some of the time, independent other periods of time | Always maintained own independent place of residence |
| Cool | Psychologically supportive, sincerely want to help the young couple, assistance provided with no strings attached |

*Source:* L. G. Burchinal. Trends and prospects for young marriages in the U.S. *Journal of Marriage and the Family,* May 1965. By permission.

### Current age trends in marriages among youth

Although the number of youthful marriages increased and the average age at first marriage decreased during the first half of this century, during the period from 1950 to the early 1970s, there was little change. Since 1974, however, there has been a steady increase in the age of first marriages among both males and females (see Table 9.9). In 1980, more than three-fourths of all 19-year-old young women

**TABLE 9.9 MEDIAN AGE AT FIRST
MARRIAGE BY SEX: UNITED STATES, 1965–1979**

| YEAR | MALE | FEMALE |
|------|------|--------|
| 1979 | 23.4 | 21.6 |
| 1978 | 23.2 | 21.4 |
| 1977 | 23.0 | 21.1 |
| 1976 | 22.9 | 21.0 |
| 1975 | 22.7 | 20.8 |
| 1974 | 22.5 | 20.6 |
| 1970 | 22.5 | 20.6 |
| 1965 | 22.5 | 20.4 |

*Source:* U.S. Bureau of the Census, *Statistical Abstract of the United States, 1981.* Washington, D.C.: U.S. Government Printing Office, 1981 (102nd ed.).

were single, compared to a little over two-thirds in 1970. Among 20- to 24-year-olds, half were single in 1980, compared to only a little over one-third in 1970 (see Table 9.10).

For most young people, these figures reflect a postponement of marriage, and not, as some have suggested, an abandonment of marriage as an institution. Thus, in 1980 only 9.5 percent of women in their early thirties had never married, compared to 7.5 percent in 1975, and 6.2 percent in 1970. Nevertheless, a small but significant minority (5 to 10 percent) of young people are making a conscious decision not to marry (4, 126, 159).

What accounts for the increasing age of first marriage, particularly among young women? One factor that clearly plays a role is the greater social and personal acceptability of sexual relationships among unmarried youth and young adults, especially those who are going steady or engaged (see page 283). Many more young couples are living together (a threefold increase between 1970 and 1980, and eight-fold among young people under 25) or having fairly stable premarital relationships than ever before (6, 158, 159). It should be noted, however, that apparently successful efforts at living together are rarely the same as being married (134). Marriage entails different societal expectations and more clearly defined responsibilities and commitment. Clinicians are currently encountering an increasing number of young couples who expected marriage to be simply a continuation of their premarital relationship and who, when they find it is not, experience a variety of previously absent tensions and problems.

Increased high school and college attendance also appear to be contributing to a reduction in adolescent marriage rates, and may be expected to play a still larger role in the future (26). Between 1970 and 1980, college enrollment of males increased by 14.2 percent, while among females it increased by an astonishing 71.1 percent (159). As the presumed value of education diffuses further through lower-class subcultures, where early marriage rates are highest, marriage rates among 16- and 17-year-olds may decline further (29).

In addition, a growing concern with material values and "making it" (see page

**TABLE 9.10 PERCENT SINGLE (NEVER MARRIED) WOMEN, BY AGE: 1980, 1975, AND 1970**

| AGE | 1980 | 1975 | 1970 |
|---|---|---|---|
| Total, 15 years and over[a] | 22.4 | 22.8 | 22.1 |
| Under 40 years[a] | 38.7 | 39.5 | 38.5 |
| 40 years and over | 5.1 | 5.1 | 6.2 |
| 15–17 years[a] | 97.0 | 97.1 | 97.3 |
| 18 years | 88.0 | 83.7 | 82.0 |
| 19 years | 77.5 | 71.4 | 68.8 |
| 20–24 years | 50.2 | 40.3 | 35.8 |
| 20 years | 66.5 | 59.1 | 56.9 |
| 21 years | 59.7 | 49.2 | 43.9 |
| 22 years | 48.1 | 38.1 | 33.5 |
| 23 years | 41.8 | 31.0 | 22.4 |
| 24 years | 33.5 | 21.1 | 17.9 |
| 25–29 years | 20.8 | 13.8 | 10.5 |
| 25 years | 28.4 | 20.0 | 14.0 |
| 26 years | 22.7 | 14.6 | 12.2 |
| 27 years | 22.1 | 13.7 | 9.1 |
| 28 years | 15.9 | 10.5 | 8.9 |
| 29 years | 14.5 | 9.4 | 8.0 |
| 30–34 years | 9.5 | 7.5 | 6.2 |
| 35–39 years | 6.2 | 5.0 | 5.4 |
| 40–44 years | 4.8 | 4.8 | 4.9 |
| 45–54 years | 4.7 | 4.6 | 4.9 |
| 55–64 years | 4.6 | 5.1 | 6.8 |
| 65 years and over | 5.9 | 5.8 | 7.7 |

*Source:* U.S. Bureau of the Census, Current Population Reports, Series P-20, No. 287, and unpublished Current Population Survey data.

[a] Figures for 1970 and 1975 include persons 14 years of age.

475), combined with the increased difficulty of achieving financial stability and such goals as home ownership in the face of high rates of inflation, are leading a number of young people to postpone the responsibilities of marriage until they feel more secure. Furthermore, for many young people, especially young women, there are fewer peer pressures to rush into marriage and parenthood and their attendant obligations, and there is increased concern with achieving financial and social independence and becoming well established in a career—in short, with developing a social and vocational identity of their own—before taking on the commitments of marriage and family life. A recent national study (29) found that young women in their early twenties who planned to be working outside the home later in life (at age 35) were more likely to postpone marriage than those planning to be full-time housewives. In the words of an 18-year-old young woman,

> I said to myself a long time ago that I was going to get married when I was eighteen. Well, I'm eighteen now, and I'm not about to get married. Probably by the

time I'm thirty I'll say to myself, "Well, I haven't found the right person yet, so that's okay." There's no special age you have to get married. I know my mother told me when she was twenty-one every girl thought they had to be married or they'd be old maids. Nowadays girls don't feel that way. They can work, have careers, and wait until the right guy comes along. Or never get married if they don't want to. I'd like to be married about twenty-five or twenty-six, but there's no big sweat if I'm not. I think women like my mother used to feel insecure if they weren't married by twenty-one. Like no one would ever want them. I don't feel that way [126, 73–74].

Finally, the continued rise in divorce rates (which doubled just between 1970 and 1980), and the amount of marital conflict young people observe, not only among members of their parents' generation, but among many of their married peers who are struggling with their new responsibilities, may be leading a number of young people to want to be quite sure of their decision before commiting themselves to marriage. Paradoxically, perhaps, recent changes in the life-styles and values of young people relating to marriage may portend a greater marital stability within the next decade: Insofar as low income, low education, and early age at marriage increase the probability of eventual divorce, current trends away from these conditions are consistent with a favorable prognosis of future marital stability (69, 157).

The formidable obstacles faced by many young marriages, their demonstrably higher divorce rates, and the less easily documented premature identity foreclosure that may sometimes result appear to provide substantial justification for generally not encouraging adolescent marriages. At the same time, it is important to realize that "no matter what the circumstances are and no matter how injudicious it may seem, [adolescent marriage] is not a crime and, if used as grounds for punitive reactions, probably will only promote the completion of the self-fulfilling prophecy of greater risks of young marriages" (24, 253). Nevertheless, many apparently well-meaning persons have been prompted to take actions that only increase the obstacles confronting young married couples. For example, some school boards still require the withdrawal or suspension of pregnant girls or of married students in general. Such policies probably are intended to prevent additional marriages among high school students. However, the few available studies indicate that such policies have little, if any, effect on high school marriage rates (22, 24). Instead, they may only help to ensure that young married people will be prevented from acquiring the kind of basic education necessary for employment in today's complex, rapidly changing world.

Far more appropriate are the recent efforts of some high schools to make all students aware of the realistic problems and demands of marriage (93, 127). In one current experimental program (162), senior high school students "marry" for a trimester, during which they learn to face such problems as working out a budget, obtaining housing, providing child care, facing random crises delivered by a "wheel of misfortune" (e.g., coping with the death of a young child), and even—at the end of the course—obtaining a divorce. Most students report becoming strongly involved in the course and believe that it has increased their understanding of the realities of marriage. A number of such couples who were planning early marriage in real life decided to defer it until they were more mature and more secure financially.

## REFERENCES

1. Aries, E. Interaction patterns and themes of male, female, and mixed groups. Paper presented at the annual meeting of the American Psychological Association, New Orleans, August 30–September 3, 1974.

2. Asher, S. R. Children's peer relations. In M. E. Lamb (ed.), *Social and personality development*. New York: Holt, Rinehart and Winston, 1978. Pp. 91–113.

3. Astin, A. W. *The American freshman: National norms for fall 1981*. Los Angeles: American Counsel on Education and Graduate School of Education, University of California at Los Angeles, 1982.

4. Bachman, J. F., Johnston, L. D., & O'Malley, P. M. *Monitoring the future: Questionnaire responses from the nation's high school seniors, 1980*. Ann Arbor, Mich.: Institute for Social Research, 1980.

5. Baughman, E. E. *Black Americans*. New York: Academic Press, 1971.

6. Bayer, A., & McDonald, G. W. Cohabitation among youth: Correlates of support for a new American ethic. *Youth and Society*, 1981, **12**, 387–402.

7. Bell, R. *Changing bodies, changing lives: A book for teens on sex and relationships*. New York: Random House, 1980.

8. Berndt, T. J. Developmental changes in conformity to peers and parents. *Developmental Psychology*, 1979, **15**, 606–616.

9. Bigelow, B. J. Children's friendship expectations: A cognitive developmental study. *Child Development*, 1977, **48**, 246–253.

10. Bigelow, B. J., & LaGaipa, J. J. Children's written descriptions of friendships: A multidimensional analysis. *Developmental Psychology*, 1975, **ii**, 857–858.

11. Bixenstine, V. E., DeCorte, M. S., & Bixenstine, B. A. Conformity to peer-sponsored misconduct at four grade levels. *Developmental Psychology*, 1976, **12**, 226–236.

12. Blos, P. *On adolescence: A psychoanalytic interpretation*. New York: Free Press, 1962.

13. Blos, P. The child analyst looks at the younger adolescent. *Daedalus*, Fall 1971, **100**, 961–978.

14. Blos, P. *The adolescent passage*. New York: International Universities Press, 1979.

15. Bonney, M. E. A sociometric study of some factors relating to mutual friendships on the elementary, secondary, and college levels. *Sociometry*, 1946, **9**, 21–47.

16. Bowerman, C. E., & Kinch, J. W. Changes in family and peer orientation of children between the fourth and tenth grades. *Social Forces*, 1959, **37**, 206–211.

17. Brittain, C. V. Age and sex of siblings and conformity toward parents versus peers in adolescence. *Child Development*, 1966, **37**, 709–714.

18. Brittain, C. V. A comparison of rural and urban adolescents with respect to parent vs. peer compliance. *Adolescence*, 1969, **13**, 59–68.

19. Brody, E. B. *Minority group adolescents in the United States*. Baltimore: Williams & Wilkins, 1968.

20. Bronfenbrenner, U. *Two worlds of childhood: U.S. and U.S.S.R.* New York: Russell Sage Foundation, 1970.

21. Brownstone, J. E., & Willis, R. H. Conformity in early and late adolescence. *Developmental Psychology*, 1971, **4**, 334–337.

22. Burchinal, L. G. Do restrictive policies curb teen marriages? *Overview*, 1960, **1**, 72–73.

23. Burchinal, L. G. School policies and school age marriages. *Family Life Coordinator*, 1960, **8**, 45–46.

24. Burchinal, L. G. Trends and prospects for young marriages in the U.S. *Journal of Marriage and the Family*, 1965, **27**, 243–254.

25. Byrne, D., London, O., & Reeves, K. The effects of physical attractiveness, sex, and attitude similarity on interpersonal attraction. *Journal of Personality*, 1968, **36**, 259–271.

26. Carlson, E. Family background, school and early marriage. *Journal of Marriage and the Family*, 1979, **43**, 341–353.

27. Cavior, N., & Dokecki, P. R. Physical attractiveness, perceived attitude similarity, and

academic achievement as contributors to interpersonal attraction among adolescents. *Developmental Psychology,* 1973, **9,** 44–54.

28. Chand, I. P., Crider, D. M., & Willets, F. K. Parent-youth disagreement as perceived by youth: A longitudinal study. *Youth and Society,* 1975, **6,** 365–373.

29. Cherlin, A. Postponing marriage: The influence of young women's work expectations. *Journal of Marriage and the Family,* 1980, **42,** 355–365.

30. Cohen, J. M. Sources of peer group homogeneity. *Socioeconomic background and achievement.* New York: Seminar Press, 1972.

31. Coleman, J. C. *Relationships in adolescence.* Boston: Routledge & Kegan Paul, 1974.

32. Coleman, J. C. Friendship and the peer group in adolescence. In J. Adelson (ed.), *Handbook of adolescent psychology.* New York: Wiley, 1980. Pp. 408–431.

33. Coleman, J. S. Athletics in high school. *Annals of the American Academy of Political Social Science,* 1961, **338,** 33–43.

34. Coleman, J. S. *The adolescent society.* New York: Free Press, 1961.

35. Coleman, J. S., et al. *Youth: Transition to adulthood.* Report of the Panel on Youth of the President's Science Advisory Committee. Chicago: University of Chicago Press, 1974.

36. Collins, J. K. Age and susceptibility to same-sex peer pressure. *British Journal of Educational Psychology,* 1972, **42,** 83–85.

37. Collins, J. K. Adolescent dating intimacy: Norms and peer expectations. *Journal of Youth and Adolescence,* 1974, **3,** 317–328.

38. Condry, J., & Siman, M. L. Characteristics of peer- and adult-oriented children. *Journal of Marriage and the Family,* 1974, **36,** 543–554.

39. Conger, J. J. A world they never knew: The family and social change. *Daedalus,* Fall 1971, **100,** 1105–1138.

40. Conger, J. J. A world they never made: Parents and children in the 1970s. Invited address, American Academy of Pediatrics meeting, Denver, April 17, 1975.

41. Conger, J. J. Parent-child relationships, social change and adolescent vulnerability. *Journal of Pediatric Psychology,* 1977, **2,** 93–97.

42. Conger, J. J. *Adolescence: Generation under pressure.* New York; Harper & Row, 1979.

43. Conger, J. J., & Miller, W. C. *Personality, social class, and delinquency.* New York: Wiley, 1966.

44. Conger, J. J., Miller, W. C., & Walsmith, C. R. Antecedents of delinquency, personality, social class and intelligence. In P. H. Mussen, J. J. Conger, & J. Kagan (eds.), *Readings in child development and personality.* New York: Harper & Row, 1965.

45. Costanzo, P. R. Conformity development as a function of self-blame. *Journal of Personality and Social Psychology,* 1970, **14,** 366–374.

46. Costanzo, P. R., & Shaw, M. E. Conformity as a function of age level. *Child Development,* 1966, **37,** 967–975.

47. Cowen, E. L., Pederson, A., Babijian, H., Izzo, L. D., & Trost, M. A. Long-term follow-up of early detected vulnerable children. *Journal of Consulting and Clinical Psychology,* 1973, **41,** 438–446.

48. De Lissovoy, V. High school marriage: A longitudinal study. *Journal of Marriage and the Family,* 1973, **35,** 245–255.

49. Douvan, E., & Adelson, J. *The adolescent experience.* New York: Wiley, 1966.

50. Douvan, E., & Gold, M. Modal patterns in American adolescence. In L. W. Hoffman & M. L. Hoffman (eds.), *Review of child development research* (Vol. 2). New York: Russell Sage Foundation, 1966. Pp. 469–528.

51. Dreyer, P. H. Sex, sex roles, and marriage among youth in the 1970s. In R. J. Havighurst & P. H. Dreyer (eds.), *Youth: The seventy-fourth yearbook of the National Society for the Study of Education.* Chicago: University of Chicago Press, 1975. Pp. 194–223.

52. Duck, S. W. Personality similarity and friendship choices by adolescents. *European Journal of Social Psychology,* 1975, **5,** 351–365.

53. Duncan, O. D., Featherman, L., & Duncan, B. *Socioeconomic background and achievement.* New York: Seminar Press, 1972.

54. Dunphy, D. C. Peer group socialisation. In F. J. Hunt (ed.), *Socialisation in Australia.* Sydney: Angus & Robertson, 1972. Pp. 200–217.

55. Dunphy, D. C. The social structure of urban adolescent peer groups. *Sociometry,* 1963, **26,** 230–246.

56. Duvall, E. M. Adolescent love as a reflection of teen-agers' search for identity. *Journal of Marriage and the Family,* 1964, **26,** 226–229.

57. *11 Million teenagers: What can be done about the epidemic of adolescent pregnancies in the United States.* New York: The Alan Guttmacher Institute, 1977.

58. Erikson, E. H. *Identity: Youth and crisis.* New York: Norton, 1968.

59. Fact-file: Characteristics and attitudes of first-year college students, 1969–1979. *The Chronicle of Higher Education,* January 28, 1980, 4–5.

60. Feinstein, S. C., & Ardon, M. S. Trends in dating patterns and adolescent development. *Journal of Youth and Adolescence,* 1973, **2,** 157–166.

61. Fischer, J. Transitions in relationship style from adolescence to young adulthood. *Journal of Youth and Adolescence,* 1981, **10,** 11–23.

62. Floyd, H. H., Jr., & South, D. R. Dilemma of youth: The choice of parents or peers as a frame of reference for behavior. *Journal of Marriage and the Family,* 1972, **34,** 627–734.

63. Freud, A. Adolescence. *Psychoanalytic Study of the Child,* 1958, **13,** 255–278.

64. Gallup, G. Gallup youth survey. *Denver Post,* November 20, 1979, 36.

65. Gaylin, J. What boys look for in girls. *Seventeen,* March 1978, 107–113.

66. Gaylin, J. What girls really look for in boys. *Seventeen,* March 1979, 131–137.

67. Gaylin, J. What you want out of life. *Seventeen,* March 1980, 113–119.

68. Gelfand, D. M. The influence of self-esteem on rate of verbal conditioning and social matching behavior. *Journal of Abnormal and Social Psychology,* 1962, **65,** 259–265.

69. Glick, P. C., & Norton, A. J. Marrying, divorcing, and living together in the U.S. today. *Population Bulletin,* 1979, **32,** 1–40. Washington, D.C.: Population Reference Bureau, Inc.

70. Gordon, C. Social characteristics of early adolescence. In J. Kagan & R. Coles (eds.), *Twelve to sixteen: Early adolescence.* New York: Norton, 1972. Pp. 25–54.

71. Gronlund, N. E., & Anderson, L. Personality characteristics of socially accepted, socially neglected, and socially rejected junior high school pupils. *Educational Administration and Supervision,* 1957, **43,** 329–330.

72. Grubb, T., & Watt, N. F. Longitudinal approaches to promoting social adjustment through public school programs. Paper presented at biennial meetings of the Society for Research in Child Development, San Francisco, 1979.

73. Haas, A. *Teenage sexuality: A survey of teenage sexual behavior.* New York: Macmillan, 1979.

74. Hallinan, M. T. Structural effects on children's friendships and cliques. *Social Psychology Quarterly,* 1979, **42,** 43–54.

75. Hallworth, H. J., Davis, H., & Gamston, C. Some adolescents' perceptions of adolescent personality. *Journal of Social and Clinical Psychology,* 1965, **4,** 81–91.

76. Hansell, S. Ego development and peer friendship networks. *Sociology of Education,* in press.

77. Hartup, W. W. Peer interaction and social organization. In P. H. Mussen (ed.), *Carmichael's manual of child psychology* (Vol. 1). New York: Wiley, 1970. Pp. 361–456 (3rd ed.).

78. Hartup, W. W. The social world of children. *American Psychologist,* 1979, **34,** 944–950.

79. Hartup, W. W. The peer system. In P. H. Mussen (ed.), *Handbook of child psychology* (Vol. 4, *Socialization,* E. M. Hetherington [ed.]). New York: Wiley, in press.

80. Harvey, O. J., & Rutherford, J. Status in the informal group. *Child Development,* 1960, **31,** 337–385.

81. Horrocks, J. E., & Benimoff, M. Isolation from the peer group during adolescence. *Adolescence,* 1967, **2,** 41–52.
82. Horrocks, J. E., & Buker, M. E. A study of the friendship fluctuation of preadolescents. *Journal of Genetic Psychology,* 1951, **78,** 131–144.
83. Hraba, J., & Grant, G. Black is beautiful: A reexamination of racial preference and identification. *Journal of Personality and Social Psychology,* 1970, **16,** 398–402.
84. Hunt, M. *Sexual behavior in the 1970s.* Chicago: Playboy Press, 1974.
85. Hurlock, E. B. *Adolescent development.* New York: McGraw-Hill, 1967 (3rd ed.).
86. Izard, C. E. Personality similarity and friendship. *Journal of Abnormal and Social Psychology,* 1960, **61,** 47–51.
87. Jersild, A. T. *The psychology of adolescence.* New York: Macmillan, 1963 (2nd ed.).
88. Johnson, T. J., & Smith, L. M. Achievement, affiliation, and power motivation in adolescents. *Psychology Reports,* 1965, **16,** 1249–1252.
89. Kagan, J., & Kogan, N. Individual variation in cognitive processes. In P. H. Mussen (ed.), *Carmichael's manual of child psychology* (Vol. I). New York: Wiley, 1970. Pp. 1273–1365.
90. Kandel, D. B. Homophily, selection, and socialization in adolescent friendships. *American Journal of Sociology,* 1978, **84,** 427–436.
91. Kandel, D. B. Similarity in real-life adolescent friendship pairs. *Journal of Personality and Social Psychology,* 1978, **36,** 306–312.
92. Kandel, D. B. Peer influences in adolescence. Paper presented at the biennial meeting of the Society for Research in Child Development, Boston, April 2, 1981.
93. Kantner, J. F., & Zelnik, M. Contraception and pregnancy: Experience of young unmarried women in the United States. *Family Planning Perspectives,* 1973, **5,** 21–35.
94. Keedy, T. C. Factors in the cohesiveness of small groups. *Sociology and Social Research,* 1956, **40,** 329–332.
95. Keislar, E. R. Differences among adolescent social clubs in terms of members' characteristics. *Journal of Educational Research,* 1954, **48,** 297–303.
96. Keislar, E. R. Experimental development of "like" and "dislike" of others among adolescent girls. *Child Development,* 1961, **32,** 59–66.
97. Kerckhoff, A. C., & Panow, A. A. The effect of early marriage on the educational attainment of young men. *Journal of Marriage and the Family,* 1979, **41,** No. 1, 97–108.
98. Klemer, R. H. Self-esteem and college dating experience as factors in mate selection and marital happiness: A longitudinal study. *Journal of Marriage and the Family,* 1971, **33,** 183–187.
99. Knox, D. H. Attitude toward love of high school seniors. *Adolescence,* 1970, **5,** 89–100.
100. Kohn, M., & Clausen, J. Social isolation and schizophrenia. *American Sociological Review,* 1955, **20,** 265–273.
101. Konopka, G. *Young girls: A portrait of adolescence.* Englewood Cliffs, N.J.: Prentice-Hall, 1976.
102. Lanelsbaum, J., & Willis, R. Conformity in early and late adolescence. *Developmental Psychology,* 1971, **4,** 334–337.
103. Lantz, H. R. Number of childhood friends as reported in the life histories of a psychiatrically diagnosed group of 1000. *Marriage and Family Living,* 1956, **18,** 107–108.
104. Larson, L. E. The relative influence of parent-adolescent affect in predicting the salience hierarchy among youth. Paper presented at the annual meeting of the National Council on Family Relations, Chicago, October 1970.
105. Larson, L. E. The influence of parents and peers during adolescence. *Journal of Marriage and the Family,* 1972, **34,** 67–74.
106. Larson, L. E. The relative influence of parent-adolescent affect in predicting the salience hierarchy among youth. *Pacific Sociological Review,* 1972, **15,** 83–102.
107. Laughlin, F. *The peer status of sixth and seventh grade children.* New York: Columbia University Press, 1954.

108. Leinhadt, S. Developmental change in the sentiment structure of children's groups. *American Sociological Review,* 1972, **37,** 302–312.

109. Lerner, R. M., & Knapp, J. R. Actual and perceived intrafamilial attitudes of late adolescents and their parents. *Journal of Youth and Adolescence,* 1975, **4,** 17–36.

110. Levinson, D. J. *The seasons of a man's life.* New York: Knopf, 1978.

111. Lindzey, G., & Byrne, D. Measurement of social choice and interpersonal attractiveness. In G. Lindzey & E. Aronson (eds.), *The handbook of social psychology* (Vol. 2). Reading, Mass.: Addison-Wesley, 1968 (2nd ed.).

112. Lowrie, S. H. Early marriage: Premarital pregnancy and associated factors. *Journal of Marriage and the Family,* 1965, **27,** 48–57.

113. Maccoby, E. E. (ed.). *The development of sex differences.* Stanford, Calif.: Stanford University Press, 1966.

114. Mannerino, A. P. Friendship patterns and altruistic behavior in pre-adolescent males. *Developmental Psychology,* 1976, **12,** 555–556.

115. McCabe, M. P., & Collins, J. K. Sex role and dating orientation. *Journal of Youth and Adolescence,* 1979, **8,** 407–425.

116. McDonald, R. L., & Gynther, M. D. Relationship of self and ideal self descriptions. *Journal of Personality and Social Psychology,* 1965, **1,** 85–88.

117. McGhee, P. E., & Teevan, R. C. Conformity behavior and need for affiliation. *Journal of Social Psychology,* 1967, **72,** 117–121.

118. McGurk, H. *Issues in childhood social development.* London: Methuen, 1978.

119. Mednick, S. A., & Schulsinger, F. Factors related to breakdown in children at high risk for schizophrenia. In M. Roff & D. F. Ricks (eds.), *Life history research in psychopathology.* Minneapolis: University of Minnesota Press, 1970.

120. Mitchell, E. Children's uses and perceptions of friendship. Paper presented at the annual meeting of the American Educational Research Association, Los Angeles, April 13–17, 1981.

121. Montemayor, R., & VanKomen, R. Age segregation of adolescents in and out of school. *Journal of Youth and Adolescence,* 1980, **9,** 371–381.

122. Moore, B. M., & Holtzman, W. H. *Tomorrow's parents: A study of youth and their families.* Austin: University of Texas Press, 1968.

123. Mussen, P. H., Conger, J. J., & Kagan, J. *Child development and personality.* New York: Harper & Row, 1979 (5th ed.).

124. Newman, B. M. Characteristics of interpersonal behavior among adolescent boys. *Journal of Youth and Adolescence,* 1975, **4,** 145–153.

125. Newman, B. M. Interpersonal behavior and preferences for exploration in adolescent boys: A small group study. In J. G. Kelly (ed.), *The socialization process in the high school years.* New York: Behavioral Publications, 1975.

126. Norman, J., & Harris, M. *The private life of the American teenager.* New York: Rawson Wade, 1981.

127. Osofsky, H., & Osofsky, J. Adolescents as mothers: Results of a program for low-income pregnant teenagers with some emphasis upon infant development. *American Journal of Orthopsychiatry,* 1970, **40,** 825–834.

128. Osterrieth, P. A. Adolescence: Some psychological aspects. In G. Caplan & S. Lebovici (eds.), *Adolescence: Psychosocial perspectives.* New York: Basic Books, 1969.

129. Peck, R. F., & Gallini, C. Intelligence, ethnicity and social roles in adolescent society. *Sociometry,* 1962, **25,** 64–72.

130. Phelps, H. R., & Horrocks, J. E. Factors influencing informal groups of adolescents. *Child Development,* 1958, **29,** 69–86.

131. Prohansky, H., & Newton, P. The nature and meaning of Negro self-identity. In M. Deutsch, I. Katz, & A. R. Jensen (eds.). *Social class, race, and psychological development.* New York: Holt, Rinehart and Winston, 1968.

132. Purnell, R. F. Socioeconomic status and sex differences in adolescent reference-group orientation. *Journal of Genetic Psychology,* 1970, **116,** 233–239.

133. Reisman, J. M., & Shorr, S. I. Friendship claims and expectations among children and adults. *Child Development,* 1978, **49,** 913–916.

134. Risman, B., Hill, C. T., Rubin, Z., & Peplau, L. A. Living together in college: Implications for courtship. *Journal of Marriage and the Family,* 1981, **43,** 77–83.

135. Robins, L. *Deviant children grown up.* Baltimore: Williams & Wilkins, 1966.

136. Rodnick, E. H., & Goldstein, M. J. A research strategy for studying risk for schizophrenia during adolescence and early adulthood. In J. Anthony & C. Koupernick (eds.), *The child in his family: Children at psychiatric risk* (Vol. 3). New York: Wiley, 1974.

137. Roff, M. *Some developmental aspects of schizoid personality.* U.S. Army Medical Research and Development Command, Report No. 65-4, March 1965.

138. Roff, M. *Some childhood and adolescent characteristics of adult homosexuals.* U.S. Army Medical Research and Developmental Command, Report No. 66-5, May 1966.

139. Roff, M., & Sells, S. B. Juvenile delinquency in relation to peer acceptance-rejection and socio-economic status. *Psychology in the Schools,* 1968, **5,** 3–18.

140. Roff, M., Sells, S. B., & Golden, M. M. *Social adjustment and personality development in children.* Minneapolis: University of Minnesota Press, 1972.

141. Rubin, Z., Hill, C. T., Peplau, L. A., & Schetter, C. D. Self-disclosure in dating couples: Sex roles and the ethic of openness. *Journal of Marriage and the Family,* 1980, **42,** 305–317.

142. Rutter, M. *Changing youth in a changing society: Patterns of adolescent development and disorder.* Cambridge, Mass.: Harvard University Press, 1980.

143. Savin-Williams, R. C. Dominance hierarchies in groups of late adolescent males. *Journal of Youth and Adolescence,* 1980, **9,** 75–83.

144. Savin-Williams, R. C. Social interactions of adolescent females in natural groups. In H. C. Foot, A. J. Chapman, & J. R. Smith (eds.), *Friendship and social relations in children.* New York: Wiley, 1980.

145. Sebald, H. *Adolescence: A sociological analysis.* Englewood Cliffs, N.J.: Prentice-Hall, 1968.

146. Selman, R. L. *The growth of interpersonal understanding: Developmental and clinical analyses.* New York: Academic Press, 1980.

147. Selman, R. L., & Selman, A. D. Children's ideas about friendship: A new theory. *Psychology Today,* October 1979, **13,** No. 4, 71ff.

148. Sewell, W. H., & Haller, A. O. Factors in the relationship between social status and the personality adjustment of the child. *American Sociological Review,* 1959, **24,** 511–520.

149. Sherif, M., Harvey, O. J., White, B. J., Hood, W. R., & Sherif, C. W. *Intergroup conflict and cooperation: The Robbers Cave experiment.* Norman: University of Oklahoma Press, 1961.

150. Skorepa, C. A., Horrocks, J. E., & Thompson, G. G. A study of friendship fluctuations of college students. *Journal of Genetic Psychology,* 1963, **102,** 151–157.

151. Smith, R. E. (ed.), *The subtle revolution: Women at work.* Washington, D.C.: The Urban Institute, 1979.

152. Sorensen, R. C. *Adolescent sexuality in contemporary America: Personal values and sexual behavior, ages 13–19.* New York: Abrams, 1973.

153. Stone, L. J., & Church, J. *Childhood and adolescence: A psychology of the growing person.* New York: Random House, 1973 (3rd ed.).

154. Suomi, S. J. Differential development of various social relationships by Rhesus monkey infants. In M. Lewis & L. A. Rosenblum (eds.), *The social network of the developing infant.* New York: Plenum, 1978.

155. *Teenage pregnancy: The problem that hasn't gone away.* New York: The Alan Guttmacher Institute, 1981.

156. Tuma, N. B., & Hallinan, M. T. The effects of similarity and status on change in schoolchildren's friendships. Unpublished manuscript, Stanford University, 1977.

157. U.S. Bureau of the Census, Current Population Reports, Series P-23, No. 49. *Popula-*

*tion of the United States, trends and prospects: 1950–1990.* Washington, D.C.: U.S. Government Printing Office, 1974.

158. U.S. Department of Commerce, Bureau of the Census, Current Population Reports, Series P-220, No. 338. *Marital status and living arrangements: March 1978.* Washington, D.C.: U.S. Government Printing Office, 1979.

159. U.S. Department of Commerce, Bureau of the Census, Current population reports, Series P-20, No. 287. Washington, D.C.: U.S. Government Printing Office, 1981.

160. U.S. Department of Commerce, Bureau of the Census, *Statistical Abstract of the United States, 1981.* Washington, D.C.: U.S. Government Printing Office, 1981 (102nd ed.).

161. Van Krevelen, A. Characteristics which identify the adolescent to his peers. *Journal of Social Psychology,* 1962, **56,** 285–289.

162. *The Wall Street Journal,* June 10, 1975.

163. Walster, E., Aronson, V., Abrahams, D., & Rottman, L. Importance of physical attractiveness in dating behavior. *Journal of Personality and Social Psychology,* 1966, **4,** 508–516.

164. Yankelovich, D. *The new morality: A profile of American youth in the 1970s.* New York: McGraw-Hill, 1974.

165. Youniss, J. *Parents and peers in social development: A Sullivan-Piaget perspective.* Chicago: University of Chicago Press, 1980.

166. Yuferova, T. I. The behavior of "affective" children in conflict situations. *Voprosy Psikhologii,* 1975, **2,** 113–123.

Adolescents and the schools

CHAPTER 10

# Adolescents and the schools

*I*n contemporary America, the school is the one major social institution, other than the family, with which nearly everyone is involved during the critical years of childhood and adolescence. Currently over 99 percent of all children in the United States between the ages of 7 and 13, and approximately 95 percent of those between 14 and 17, are enrolled in school (260). These young people spend more working hours in school than in any other activity; as a result, "the schools and colleges have come to provide the general social environment for youth" (66, *2*).

Although this may seem to be merely the normal state of affairs because we and our children are used to it, the fact is that it is a relatively recent development. When ours was still primarily an agrarian society, the level of educational skills required for economic survival were generally less, and the need for young people to become productive members of the labor force early was greater (66). In 1890, only 6.7 percent of all 14- to 17-year-olds were enrolled in school; by 1900 this figure had risen, but only to 11.4 percent (263). The primary institutional settings in which most young people grew up were the home and the work place. "Choices in the occupational sphere were few: the future roles of the children were generally well-exemplified by those of parents. In short, the task of socialization was resolved by early and continual interaction with the parents and nearby adults" (66, *1*).

Furthermore, as our society has become more complex, the influence on the young person's development of other social institutions, including the family, the work place, and the church, has been reduced. This means that more of the burden for the development not only of expanded academic skills, but also of vital non-cognitive capabilities—including the ability to take responsibility for and to manage effectively one's own affairs and life plans—has been increasingly shifted to the schools (43, 66). How well the schools are meeting all these varied responsibilities, and, indeed, whether they can reasonably be expected to accomplish such diverse missions without significant participation by other social institutions, are questions of critical importance.

# THE QUALITY OF AMERICAN EDUCATION

Let us begin by asking how well the schools are meeting their traditional, and in the view of many, their primary responsibility—the development of basic academic skills.[1] From some perspectives, the answer appears to be a positive one. The percentage of young adults who had completed 4 years of high school or more increased from approximately 74 percent in 1970, and 81 percent in 1975, to 86 percent in 1980 (260). Similar trends occurred in the percentages attending and completing college. While the increases were similar for males and females in all of these categories, blacks showed a significantly greater increase than whites or those of Spanish origin (see Table 10.1). Thus, the percentage of blacks completing 4 years of high school rose from approximately 53 percent in 1970 to 76 percent in 1980, a rise of 23 percent, while the percentage of whites increased only 11 percent, from approximately 76 to 87 percent. Young adults of Spanish origin increased from 44 to 57 percent, a gain of 13 percent.

Whether these trends will continue is a matter of conjecture. The percentage of 18-year-olds graduating from high school, as well as the percentage of graduates going on to college, appears to have reached a plateau by the middle 1970s, showing relatively little change since then (260). Indeed, with recent cutbacks in federal, state, and private student support, it appears likely that the percentage of lower-income blacks and whites of both sexes going on to college or beyond will drop significantly in the coming decade unless current policies and priorities are altered.

Nevertheless, more schooling does not necessarily mean better schooling; the critical question is whether students today are learning more (239). Unfortunately, definitive answers are difficult to come by. The existing evidence suggests that an overall increase of about 20 percent occurred in the academic achievement level of American secondary school students in the decade following World War II (239, 266), but that this trend has been reversed since the early 1960s (49, 199, 265).

An intensive nationwide investigation conducted by the National Assessment of Educational Progress (199) found evidence of a continuing decline in reading and writing skills between 1970 and 1980, among both 13-year-olds and 17-year-olds (in each instance, girls performed slightly better than boys). The greatest deficiencies occurred, not in the act of reading itself or in literal reporting of the material read, but in the students' ability to go beyond initial comprehension: to interpret, analyze, and evaluate what they had read—to form critical judgments and to be able to explain and defend their judgments. "Few students could provide more than superficial responses to such tasks, and even the 'better' responses showed little evidence of well-developed problem-solving strategies or critical thinking skills" (199, 2). In writing about a particular passage they had read, students (especially the 13-year-olds) tended to make evaluative judgments (e.g., "that was a good story," "that poem made me feel sad"), but without explaining or supporting these judgments: "Between 1970 and 1980, both 13- and 17-year-olds became less likely to interpret

---

[1] For most adolescents, "the schools" mean one type of organization: the public comprehensive junior and senior high schools. Less than 10 percent of this age group attend private or parochial institutions; fewer still attend so-called alternative schools, private or public (38).

**TABLE 10.1 YEARS OF SCHOOL COMPLETED BY
YOUNG ADULTS, 25 TO 34 YEARS OLD: 1980, 1975, 1970**

| | 1980 | | |
| --- | --- | --- | --- |
| | 4 YEARS OF HIGH SCHOOL OR MORE | 1 YEAR OF COLLEGE OR MORE | 4 YEARS OF COLLEGE OR MORE |
| All persons | 85.7 | 46.1 | 24.3 |
| Males | 86.4 | 50.9 | 27.7 |
| Females | 85.0 | 41.3 | 21.0 |
| White | 86.9 | 47.1 | 25.4 |
| Black | 75.7 | 34.0 | 12.6 |
| Spanish origin[a] | 57.1 | 24.1 | 9.1 |

what they read and more likely to simply make unexplained value judgments about it. One way of characterizing the change during the seventies is to say that 17-year-olds' papers became more like 13-year-olds' papers" (199, 3).

As the authors of this report comment:

> These findings seem to us a direct reflection of current emphases in testing and instruction. In the classroom, teachers following traditional patterns of whole-class teaching and recitation move quickly from student to student so that many students can be involved without any one student dominating. . . .
>    The relatively short responses encouraged in classroom discussion parallel the mutiple-choice and fill-in-the-blank formats that dominate standardized and teacher-developed tests. When doing well in most school contexts requires little beyond short responses, it is not surprising that students fail to develop more comprehensive thinking and analytic skills [199, 2].

In a related investigation of mathematical knowledge, skills, and understanding, performance declined significantly for both 13- and 17-year-olds across the sexes and in all racial-ethnic groups between 1973 and 1978 (198). Similar declines occurred on measures of performance in the physical and biological sciences (263, 264).

In 1981, the much publicized 18-year nationwide decline in average verbal and mathematical scores on the Scholastic Achievement Test (SAT) came to an end (see Figure 10.1). For the second year in a row, scores on this test (which is taken by about one-third of all high school students and by about two-thirds of those planning to go on to college) remained at 424 on the verbal section and 466 on the mathematics section. (The test has a range from 200 to 800.) And in 1982, there was actually a slight increase to a verbal score of 426 and a mathematics score of 467. Whether this signals the end of the score decline and the beginning of a turnaround, or simply an interruption in the 18-year trend, only time will tell (32, 200).

| | 1975 | | | 1970 | | |
|---|---|---|---|---|---|---|
| 4 YEARS OF HIGH SCHOOL OR MORE | 1 YEAR OF COLLEGE OR MORE | 4 YEARS OF COLLEGE OR MORE | 4 YEARS OF HIGH SCHOOL OR MORE | 1 YEAR OF COLLEGE OR MORE | 4 YEARS OF COLLEGE OR MORE |
| 81.1 | 39.4 | 21.4 | 73.8 | 29.8 | 15.8 |
| 82.4 | 45.2 | 25.4 | 74.3 | 34.8 | 19.7 |
| 79.7 | 33.8 | 17.5 | 73.3 | 25.0 | 12.0 |
| 82.3 | 40.4 | 22.2 | 76.1 | 31.2 | 16.6 |
| 69.3 | 25.9 | 10.7 | 53.4 | 15.0 | 6.1 |
| 49.0 | 19.6 | 7.0 | 44.5 | 14.6 | 5.4 |

Source: U.S. Bureau of the Census, Current Population Reports, Series P-20, No. 363, 1980.
[a] Persons of Spanish origin may be of any race.

The reasons for these apparent declines in academic performance in recent years are still unclear. They have been attributed variously to a decline in the quality of teaching, to increased disruption of the academic environment, to less mental stimulation in the home and other nonschool settings (including many thousands of hours spent watching television at the expense of reading), and to changes in the

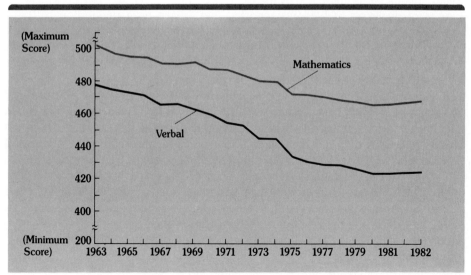

**Figure 10.1** Average scores for senior high school students taking the Scholastic Aptitude Test, 1963–1982. (From *National College-Bound Seniors, 1981,* 1982. Copyright © by the College Entrance Examination Board, New York. By permission.)

**TABLE 10.2 AMOUNT OF TIME SPENT ON HOMEWORK BY U.S. SECONDARY SCHOOL STUDENTS, AGES 13 AND 17, 1979–1980**

| TIME SPENT | AGE 13 (PERCENT) | AGE 17 (PERCENT) |
|---|---|---|
| None | 30.2 | 31.7 |
| Didn't do it | 6.2 | 12.6 |
| Less than 1 hour | 32.6 | 23.8 |
| 1–2 hours | 23.5 | 22.3 |
| 2 hours or more | 7.2 | 9.3 |

*Source:* National Assessment of Educational Progress. *Reading, thinking, and writing: Results for the 1979–80 national assessment of reading and literature.* Denver: Education Commission of the States, 1981. By permission.

*Note:* Columns may not total 100% due to rounding.

socioeconomic mix of students attending school—particularly at the upper secondary school and college levels (204, 205, 253, 278). What does appear clear, however, is that no one factor is adequate in itself to explain current results. Whatever the ultimate findings regarding the academic performance of American students and the variables contributing to them turn out to be, there is rather widespread agreement that the school experience of many young people today leaves a good deal to be desired (32, 199, 223, 239, 254, 276, 278), not only for the poor, who are generally at the greatest disadvantage, but for the socioeconomically favored as well. A blue-ribbon panel appointed by the College Board in 1977 (278) to investigate the causes of declining SAT scores reported that "there have unquestionably been changes over the past 10 to 15 years in the standards to which students at all levels of education are held" (223, *79*). Members of the panel cited as examples: grade inflation (higher grades for poorer work), condoning of absenteeism, and reductions by as much as 50 percent in required homework.

Recent studies appear to substantiate these assessments; in the 1980 study of reading and writing already cited (see page 375), students were asked how much time they had spent on homework the previous day. Less than one-third of both 13- and 17-year-olds reported spending an hour or more, and more than 4 out of 10 17-year-olds said they had spent no time at all (see Table 10.2).

A presidential commission recently reported that only 15 percent of American high school students now study a foreign language—down from 24 percent in 1965 (223). Another major study by the National Science Foundation (203), noting a continuing decline in both the quantity and quality of available courses in mathematics and the sciences, the number of courses required for high school graduation, and the number of students voluntarily enrolling in these courses, warned of "a current trend toward virtual scientific and technological illiteracy. . . ." (223, *80*).

Diane Ravitch, a historian and educator at Teachers College, Columbia University, calls attention to the paradox that "some students finish high school with few skills and less knowledge, and others arrive at college unprepared for college-level

work, while a small minority of the same graduating class has been remarkably well-educated in their special fields of interest" (223, 80). She attributes this disparity in considerable measure to the decline in a common curriculum—including requirements in English, foreign languages, American history, mathematics, biological and physical sciences—that began in the middle 1960s, and a proliferation of electives, such as mass media or career education.

Criticism by the general public and by students themselves has not been as harsh, perhaps partly because expectations have not been as great. Nevertheless, confidence of the public in its schools appears to have declined in the past decade. In 1974, two-thirds of American adults rated the schools in their communities as excellent or good; by 1981, this figure had declined to 47 percent (276). Most frequently cited as deficiencies were needs for a greater emphasis on skills in reading, writing, and computation; more discipline; better educated and concerned teachers and principals; and better parent-teacher relationships. Still, six in ten parents judged their child's education as better than their own elementary and secondary education, and nearly three-fourths rated the performance of their own children's teachers as excellent (29 percent) or good (45 percent). Among U.S. high school seniors in 1980, 42 percent said they liked school very much or quite a lot; girls, whites, nonusers of drugs, and those planning to go on to college were most likely to express approval (see Table 10.3).

Although the many critics of today's schools may agree that something is wrong, they frequently disagree about what it is, or about what remedial steps need to be taken. For example, parents of various majority and minority groups within a

**TABLE 10.3 "SOME PEOPLE LIKE
SCHOOL VERY MUCH. OTHERS DON'T. HOW
DO YOU FEEL ABOUT GOING TO SCHOOL?"**

| PERCENTAGE OF ADOLESCENTS | TOTAL | SEX | | RACE | |
|---|---|---|---|---|---|
| | | BOYS | GIRLS | WHITE | BLACK |
| Weighted No. of Cases: | 3328 | 1530 | 1621 | 2516 | 408 |
| % of Weighted Total: | 100.0 | 46.0 | 48.7 | 75.6 | 12.3 |
| 5. I like school very much | 13.6 | 13.1 | 14.1 | 12.4 | 20.6 |
| 4. I like school quite a lot | 32.5 | 29.3 | 35.4 | 32.7 | 31.3 |
| 3. I like school some | 40.3 | 43.2 | 37.7 | 40.7 | 39.4 |
| 2. I don't like school very much | 9.8 | 10.6 | 9.0 | 10.5 | 6.2 |
| 1. I don't like school at all | 3.8 | 3.8 | 3.9 | 3.8 | 2.6 |

school may differ markedly in their views of the kind of education their children require. One study has shown that school board members often have priorities for the schools that differ from those of parents (166).

### Quality of teaching

What are the facts, insofar as we can ascertain them, about the quality of today's teachers? Clearly, teachers are often held accountable for problems largely beyond their control: bureaucratic rigidity, poorly designed or inappropriate curricula, inadequate staffing and facilities, poorly motivated or unruly students, lack of administrative or parental support, student drug use and absenteeism, even, in some cases, violence and vandalism.

A national study of adolescents aged 13 to 18 years (105) found that nearly one in five were concerned about their personal safety in school. Among nonwhites, one in four expressed such a fear. In another Gallup poll, 25 percent of parents said they were concerned for their children's safety in school (105). Four percent of all adolescents, and 7 percent of boys 16 to 18 years of age, reported having been physically assaulted during the course of the school year; 12 percent reported money stolen, 24 percent had other property stolen, and 11 percent had property damaged or destroyed. Especially in larger inner-city schools, violence against teachers appears to be increasing. In 1980, 5 percent of teachers in the United States reported having been attacked by students, an increase of 57 percent since 1977 (254). In New York City alone, nearly 3400 physical assaults against the system's 68,000 teachers were reported in 1980 (221). More than half of all assaulted teachers felt that school authorities did not take appropriate disciplinary action, for

| 4-YEAR COLLEGE PLANS | | ILLICIT DRUG USE: LIFETIME | | | | |
|---|---|---|---|---|---|---|
| YES | NO | NONE | MARIJUANA ONLY | FEW PILLS | MORE PILLS | ANY HEROIN |
| 1664 | 1274 | 1134 | 874 | 401 | 771 | 17 |
| 50.0 | 38.3 | 34.1 | 26.3 | 12.0 | 23.2 | .5 |
| 16.9 | 9.8 | 18.7 | 11.7 | 12.2 | 8.4 | — |
| 37.0 | 26.9 | 37.4 | 31.7 | 32.8 | 25.2 | 36.6 |
| 37.6 | 43.4 | 34.9 | 42.4 | 42.0 | 45.3 | 43.2 |
| 6.8 | 13.6 | 7.2 | 11.2 | 9.4 | 13.2 | 9.0 |
| 1.7 | 6.3 | 1.9 | 3.0 | 3.7 | 7.9 | 11.1 |

*Source:* J. G. Bachman, L. D. Johnston, and P. M. O'Malley. *Monitoring the future: Questionnaire responses from the nation's high school seniors, 1980.* Ann Arbor: Institute for Social Research, University of Michigan, 1981. By permission.

fear of adverse publicity (254). "Today one in eight high school teachers says he 'hesitates to confront students out of fear.' One in every four reports that he has had personal property stolen at school" (254, *29*). Not surprisingly, under such circumstances, issues of physical security and discipline are likely to take precedence over teaching and learning.

Such pressures as these can significantly increase the difficulties of teaching; nevertheless, many of the problems of today's teachers are not simply the result of such external factors. At a time when the challenges faced by teachers in dealing with an increasingly diverse school population are increasing, the quality of students entering teaching appears to be declining. Although there are many intellectually exciting and highly skilled teachers, there are also too many who lack minimal competency, even in basic communication skills (132, 254, 277). The verbal SAT scores (see above) of high school seniors intending to teach have declined to a current average of 392, compared to 505 for English majors, and 498 for those interested in the physical sciences.

What accounts for these trends? According to J. Myron Atkin, Dean of the School of Education at Stanford University, there are a number of probable causes, including: the success of the women's movement, which has opened up a wider range of careers for talented women; relatively low pay and diminishing job security, as more and more schools are confronted with rising costs and declining federal, state, and local support; repressive and dulling influences of some school bureaucracies and political bodies that stifle creativity and any departure from prescribed routines and lock-step curricula; and a lack of relevance in the curriculum and training methods of schools of education (132). As important a factor as any other, however, in our opinion, is a decline in the value placed on the critically important task of educating our young people in an increasingly self-preoccupied, materialistically oriented society. In the words of the president of the American Federation of Teachers, "Teachers are surrounded by parents who feel they could do as good a job teaching their children if they weren't too busy making more money" (277, *78*). Increasing numbers of teachers "are fed up with a public that howls for accountability at the same time it begs them to virtually raise their children" (277, *78*).

### Students in the electronic age

Despite an impressive number of exceptions, many of today's students "believe they will emerge from school into an electronic world that will require little reading and less writing" (199, *5*). The truth, of course, lies elsewhere; indeed "the information business"—which is currently the fastest-growing sector of the economy—will place a high premium on skills in reducing data to manageable form, distinguishing important from trivial information, interpreting it, packaging it effectively, documenting decisions, and, not least, being able to explain complex matters in simple terms. Furthermore, "Quality of life is directly tied to our ability to think clearly amid the noise of modern life, to sift through all that competes for our attention until we find that we value what will make our lives worth living" (199, *5*).

Unfortunately, however, only a minority of today's junior high and high school students reveal a strong interest in reading for its own sake, and, ironically, their numbers decline as they grow older (199). When American students, ages 9, 13, and 17, were asked how much time they had spent "reading for enjoyment yesterday," three-fourths of all 17-year-olds reported spending either no time, or less than an hour, compared to a little over half of all 9-year-olds (see Table 10.4). Conversely, more than four out of ten 17-year-olds (but only one out of five 9-year-olds) reported spending more time watching television than reading (see Table 10.5).

### Education for docility

As Charles Silberman observed in his nationwide survey of secondary education, *Crisis in the Classroom* (239), too many of our public schools, including many middle-class schools, tend to concentrate on what he called education for docility— an overemphasis on order, discipline, and conformity at the expense of self-expression, intellectual curiosity, creativity, and the development of a humane, sensitive human being who is able and willing to learn for himself or herself.

The situation is likely to be most pronounced at the junior high school and high school levels: "Because adolescents are harder to 'control' than younger children, secondary schools tend to be even more authoritarian and repressive than elementary schools; the values they transmit are the values of docility, passivity, conformity, and lack of trust" (239, *324*). The fact that such dulling and repressive emphases appear stronger at the junior high school level is especially ironic because it is at this time that cognitive changes open wider intellectual and cultural horizons than the younger child is capable of envisioning.

Obviously, not all schools and students fit this rather dismal picture. A growing number (though still too few) are developing competency-based curricula and inno-

**TABLE 10.4 *"HOW MUCH TIME DID YOU SPEND READING YESTERDAY?" 1979–1980***

| TIME SPENT | AGE 13 (PERCENT) | AGE 17 (PERCENT) |
|---|---|---|
| No time | 42.5 | 43.6 |
| Less than 1 hour | 29.8 | 32.2 |
| 1–2 hours | 20.6 | 19.5 |
| 3 or more hours | 5.8 | 4.2 |

*Source:* National Assessment of Educational Progress. *Reading, thinking, and writing: Results for the 1979–80 national assessment of reading and literature.* Denver: Education Commission of the States, 1981. By permission.
*Note:* Columns may not total 100% due to rounding.

vative learning programs addressed flexibly to the needs of individual students from a variety of backgrounds; are successfully combining the development of core knowledge and skills with exciting and creative experiences in the arts and humanities; and are challenging students to work at the peak of their capacities, to think for themselves, and—of critical importance in the long run—to learn how to learn. In most, if not all, of these innovative programs, the key to success appears to lie in the attitudes and commitment of teachers and administrators (supported by students and parents). As we shall see in later sections, probably the single most important situational influence on students in most school environments is the teacher. This appears especially true in some of the more innovative and flexible programs, where absence of rigid controls requires self-reliance, hard work, and mutual confidence and respect on the part of both teachers and students, if programs are to work and chaos is to be avoided.

**TABLE 10.5 *"HOW MUCH TIME DID YOU SPEND WATCHING TELEVISION YESTERDAY?" 1979–1980***

| TIME SPENT | AGE 13 (PERCENT) | AGE 17 (PERCENT) |
|---|---|---|
| None or less than 1 hour | 22.8 | 38.8 |
| 1–2 hours | 28.2 | 30.4 |
| 3 or more hours | 47.9 | 30.4 |

*Source:* National Assessment of Educational Progress. *Reading, thinking, and writing: Results for the 1979–80 national assessment of reading and literature.* Denver: Education Commission of the States, 1981. By permission.
*Note:* Columns may not total 100% due to rounding.

## FROM UP THE DOWN STAIRCASE

There was one heady moment when I was able to excite the class by an idea: I had put on the blackboard Browning's "A man's reach should exceed his grasp, or what's a heaven for?" and we got involved in a spirited discussion of aspiration vs. reality. Is it wise, I asked, to aim higher than one's capacity? Does it not doom one to failure? No, no, some said, that's ambition and progress! No, no, others cried, that's frustration and defeat! What about hope? What about despair?—You've got to be practical!— You've got to have a dream! They said this in their own words, you understand, startled into discovery. To the young, clichés seem freshly minted. Hitch your wagon to a star! Shoemaker, stick to your last! And when the dismissal bell rang, they paid me the highest compliment: they groaned! They crowded in the doorway, chirping like agitated sparrows, pecking at the seeds I had strewn—when who should appear but [the administrative assistant to the principal].

"What is the meaning of this noise?"

"It's the sound of thinking, Mr. McHabe," I said.

In my letter box that afternoon was a note from him, with copies to my principal and chairman (and—who knows—perhaps a sealed indictment dispatched to the Board?) which read:

I have observed that in your class the class entering your room is held up because the pupils exiting from your room are exiting in a disorganized fashion, blocking the doorway unnecessarily and *talking*. An orderly flow of traffic is the responsibility of the teacher whose class is exiting from the room.

The cardinal sin, strange as it may seem in an institution of learning, is talking.

*Source:* From the book *Up the Down Staircase* by Bel Kaufman. © 1964 by Bel Kaufman. Published by Prentice-Hall, Inc., Englewood Cliffs, New Jersey 07632. By permission.

### Education for inequality

More ominous, in both its short- and long-term implications, than inadequacies in the average school is the disparity *among* schools in this country in virtually every respect—from physical facilities, equipment, and curricular strength to teacher and pupil composition (160, 162, 239). Prior to the rapid growth in urbanization and geographic mobility in recent decades, a majority of young people still lived in smaller cities and towns and on farms, where the quality of education was more evenly distributed geographically and socioeconomically (if not racially). Students of varying socioeconomic levels were more likely to attend the same or similar high schools, to interact socially and academically, and to receive similar educational experiences.

This is no longer the case: The differences between a wealthy suburban high school and its counterpart in the city ghetto are so great as to make broad statements about what is wrong with contemporary American education *in general* misleading, and even, in some cases, irrelevant. There is undoubtedly much that needs to be done in many of the "better" (mostly middle- and upper-middle-class) schools to make the educational process more stimulating; more encouraging of creativity, independent and innovative thinking, and self-reliance; and more relevant to the needs of a changing world. However, the more urgent need in these troubled times is clearly to achieve a virtual revolution in the quality of larger urban schools (particularly inner-city schools), and to make them more relevant to the needs of the hundreds of thousands of disadvantaged young people whom they are intended to serve (160). A section later in this chapter is reserved for a consideration of the needs and school experiences of these adolescents, and what may be done to improve their chances of survival in "a world they never made," despite current cutbacks in federal, state, and local funding for education.

First, however, the research evidence concerning a number of factors affecting the school adjustment and academic progress of students generally will be examined—including factors in the school environment itself, the influence of parents and peers, and the personality of the student.

## DO SCHOOLS MAKE A DIFFERENCE?

During the past decade, there was a large body of research whose aim was to identify the qualities of effective schools, schools that seemed to "make a difference" in the lives of youth (14, 64, 127, 146). The general conclusion of much of this research, with some important exceptions that we will describe later, has been that schools do not make a difference in the subsequent achievements of students. Rather, these studies have concluded that home environment, genes, and whatever else a child brings to school are what make the difference in further attainments once high school is completed.

The first of these studies was based on a survey of 645,000 American children in elementary and secondary schools. The report of this survey, published in 1966 by sociologist James Coleman and his colleagues, stimulated the controversy. Subsequent studies have both reanalyzed the same data (146) and collected new information (14). These studies have generally agreed on the conclusion that schools in the United States have little effect on the achievement of their youth, accounting for no more than 15 percent of the variation in student outcomes such as educational or occupational attainment (9, 14, 145, 235).

There are indications that family background is more important than school effects in other countries besides the United States (62, 67, 222, 251). Utilizing data from six countries (Chile, England, Finland, Italy, Sweden, and the United States), researchers found that home background had stronger effects than school effects, but that school effects increased from age 10 years to age 14 years (62). Of all the countries, England had the highest proportion of variance (50 percent) explained by variation in home background. The next highest proportion due to home background (46 percent) was seen in the United States.

One of the studies that focused specifically on high schools (14) utilized longitudinal data and very carefully compared the effects of socioeconomic level among individual students to that of the total body of students in the school. This comparison was made to differentiate the home background of individual students from the school environment itself. The investigators found that about one-fifth of the variation in the family socioeconomic status of individual students is shared with other students in the school, thus contributing to school effects. The remaining variation, however, was specifically related to the home and not the school environment. Furthermore, the socioeconomic level of the school contributed little to outcomes such as college plans or actual years of education. Academic ability of the students prior to entering high school was the next most important variable. An analysis of a second large and more varied sample of students produced similar results.

These investigators (14) reason that two explanations might account for the diminished effect of schools in our society. First, there are many factors apart from school that affect education: the home, churches, youth organizations, and the media (especially television). Some of these factors are strongly linked to home advantages, to the extent that they cost money, or are neighborhood-based. Other factors, such as television, are so widely available as to confer no particular advantage (or disadvantage) on any specific group, again, except for home values that determine the amount of and specific kinds of programs watched. These nonschool influences, it was hypothesized, may swamp any effects that the school itself can have.

A second possible explanation, in their view, for the small effect of schools is that public high schools are more similar than different. Secondary education is widespread in this society, and there has been an emphasis on uniformity. New innovations are likely to be generally adopted rather quickly. Furthermore, the basic structural features of schools—"patterns of course offerings, laboratories, libraries, classrooms with blackboards and rows of seats, masses of students moving from class to class at fifty-minute intervals, hallways lined with lockers, and the like" (14, 51)—are very similar from school to school. Once schools are so similar, it is difficult to identify measures that differentiate schools enough to produce varied student outcomes.

### School processes

Another possible explanation, however, deals with the kinds of measures of school effect employed in these studies. Most have dealt with what Patricia Minuchin and Esther Shapiro (193) call "distal variables," such as socioeconomic status, school size, teacher-student ratios, and physical facilities. There appear to be more powerful ways of examining school effects (45, 89, 231). As we shall see, when the potential effects of other kinds of school variables are examined, particularly those that relate to the *processes* of the school experience, differences in educational outcomes have been found. Furthermore, school effects are stronger with subjects learned primarily at school, such as mathematics (231, 272).

Before we proceed to a closer examination of the effects of such process variables, we must make clear that even the studies reporting negative results on differential school effects do not mean that there are no effects of *schooling*, as some have mistakenly concluded. The studies finding minimal school effects imply that the specific school that a student attends makes no difference in the achievement of that student, apart from advantages or disadvantages that the student brings into the school. But attending some school is clearly important. A major review of 51 studies (143) concluded that the number of years of school is associated with knowledge attainment and knowledge seeking or the capacity to continue learning. Formal schooling also affects the quality of thinking that children engage in (234). It is safe to conclude, therefore, that schooling does influence adolescents in expected ways (123).

We said earlier that one major study produced results different from those showing no school effects. In a recent large-scale study of twelve schools in inner London, child psychiatrist Michael Rutter and his colleagues found that *school processes*—what goes on in schools—appeared to be more important than any other set of variables in explaining secondary school student outcomes (231). This important study showed that schools *do* make a difference in what happens to their students, thus challenging the conclusions of the major studies already cited (64, 146). Although it is clear that some characteristics of education in London are quite different from those in the United States, the educational dimensions studied are generally universal. Other studies had focused on structural variables such as school size, rather than on process. Furthermore, as student outcomes, other studies focused primarily on measures of achievement; the Coleman study, for example, looked at effects only on verbal ability.

The twelve schools in Rutter's study were all from a rather poor area in inner London. Nevertheless, they varied in size (from 450 pupils to just under 2000 students), in physical space per pupil (from 800 to 2000 square feet per child), in availability of sports facilities, in the age of the buildings, and in their condition. Some schools were for boys only, others were for girls only, and some had both boys and girls as students. The schools differed in the style of leadership employed, and in their educational aims. In short, they were quite variable despite the geographic and socioeconomic homogeneity.

The study measured characteristics of pupils upon the beginning of secondary school ("intake") so as to separate these factors from effects of secondary schooling; intake factors included verbal reasoning skill, parental occupation, and teachers' ratings of student behavior. Outcome measures—a much broader set than those typically measured in previous studies of school effects—included the adolescents' behavior in school, the regularity of attendance, the proportion of students who stayed in school beyond the required age, the success of students on public examinations, and delinquency rates. The schools varied on each of the outcome measures.

The main focus of the study was on school processes. Data were collected from staff interviews, pupil questionnaires, and direct observation of teachers and pupils during class time. Several specific school processes turned out to be quite important for at least one of the student outcomes: homework assignments, teachers' expectations, total teaching time spent on lessons, percent of teacher time spent in interaction with the whole class, provision of rewards and incentives and less emphasis on punishments, provision of a pleasant and comfortable environment for the children, provision of opportunities for student responsibility in school life, and continuity of teachers and staff organization. What is striking about this list of school variables is that although some studies have commented on their potential importance, these aspects of schooling typically have not actually been measured except by variables much more distal—such as the use of average self-esteem in a school as a measure of positive feelings about school.

Because this study involved so many different measures, the investigators also identified the key factors overall. School characteristics such as the percent of students with behavioral difficulties or low achievement were not the most important factors influencing pupil behavior. School characteristics that were important included: the degree of academic emphasis, teacher activity and lessons, the availability of incentives and rewards for students, good conditions for students, and the extent of responsibility available to adolescents. As the authors point out, all of these factors may be controlled by the school staff. One uncontrollable factor was also important: the prior achievement of students upon entry to secondary schools; this factor, called "the balance of intake," was unrelated, however, to the school process variables. In this study, factors such as school size, the age of buildings, the amount of space available, and the administrational and organizational qualities of the school were unrelated to student outcome. Of the student outcomes, the effect of the balance of intake—that is, the level of student ability and prior achievement— was most important for delinquency and least important for classroom behavior. The combined measures of school process were more potent than any individual process measure, implying that they operate together to produce a cumulative effect.

What is perhaps most important about Rutter's study is its focus on *processes* in the school. There has been a great deal written about what kinds of educational factors influence student outcomes, but few studies have assessed the *ways* in which various factors might influence students. A second important characteristic of his study is the simultaneous assessment of several kinds of school processes together with structural aspects of education. These features make it the first study to provide information on how various important factors interact and what their importance is relative to each other.

Rutter's research does raise the question, however, of possible differences between English and U.S. schools. Even though his study addresses different aspects of schooling than many other studies, it is also possible that schools in the two countries differ in crucial ways. Some studies conducted in the United States, while not as comprehensive as Rutter's study, suggest that some of the aspects of the schooling process studied by Rutter are also important in U.S. schools. For example, a series of studies (97, 98) showed that the formal and informal organization of the classroom affects student achievement and affective development. Other studies on the academic climate of schools also suggest that these processes are important (40, 191).

## SPECIFIC ATTRIBUTES OF THE SCHOOL ENVIRONMENT

### School size

Although most of the studies cited above have concluded that school size does not have a major effect on education attainment, it appears from other research that the lack of effects is due principally to the uniformly large size of most high schools in the United States (106). The effect of size in schools is not linear, but involves a threshold effect: Beyond a total size of 500 students—some say it can go as high as 1000 students—increases in the numbers of students do not have incremental negative effects (193). Some investigators have concluded that the optimal school size— both physically and psychologically—is 700 to 1000 students (258).

The history of school size provides an important perspective for understanding the issues. As the number and percentage of students enrolled in public secondary education have grown over the past several decades, so too has school size. Whereas the number of students enrolled in public high schools tripled between 1930 and 1970, the number of schools remained virtually unchanged (106). In part, this has been a function of population concentration due to ever-increasing urbanization. In large measure, however, it has been the result of an explicit educational philosophy. The most influential educational reform document of a decade ago, the Conant Report (69),

> . . . pressed hard for the elimination of small high schools on the premise that they could not economically provide the specified courses appropriate to modern expertise. The trend toward largeness has long been stimulated by the influential models and the derived ideologies of school administrators that emphasized management and efficiency [66, 77].

But is bigness really better? With respect to this question, it is interesting to consider the results of recent investigations of the effects of school size upon the personality and behavior of adolescent students (19, 18, 20, 50, 66, 121, 275). Students in small high schools emerged as more likely than their peers in large high schools to report more internal and external pressure to participate in school activities, to actually engage in more different kinds of activities, and to hold more positions of responsibility in activities entered (i.e., to be active participants, rather than merely nominal participants or spectators) (274).

Roger Barker, an ecologically oriented psychologist, and his colleagues assert that the *behavior settings* (e.g., in the context of school, such activities as sports, clubs, student councils, plays, projects, trips) "must be supported by member participation if the settings are to continue to exist. Depending upon the number of people available to perform the essential functions, behavior settings may be *undermanned, optimally manned,* or *overmanned*" (274, *255*).

Behavior settings in small schools are more likely to be undermanned than those in large schools. Even though large schools tend to have a greater total number of activities ("settings"), the number of activities per student is usually higher for the small school (256). Consequently, there is likely to be more encouragement of active student participation for the purpose of keeping a more satisfying activity going in the small school. This leads students to invest more time and effort than they probably would where potential participants are numerous and continuation of the activity is not dependent on their individual participation. Under such circumstances, students are more likely to take positions of responsibility and engage in a wide range of supportive behaviors. "Under pressure to keep activities going, members seek to induce others to participate. Membership requirements are minimized, and attempts are made to bring available personnel to at least a minimal level of performance" (274, *255*).

What are the consequences of the greater involvement of more students in more activities in the small school? Students in small schools were more likely than those in large schools to report that involvement in school activities had helped them to develop skills or abilities, to increase confidence in themselves, to prove themselves, to feel needed, to gain a sense of accomplishment, and to work closely with others (274) (see Table 10.6). These results are consistent with findings that in all

**TABLE 10.6 *SIGNIFICANCE LEVELS FOR MEAN DIFFERENCES IN EXPERIENCE SCALE RATINGS OF STUDENTS OF LARGE AND SMALL SCHOOLS***

| SCALE | KIND OF BEHAVIOR SETTING | | | | | |
|---|---|---|---|---|---|---|
| | GAME | MEETING | PLAY | DANCE | PROJECT | TRIP |
| 1. Helped me develop a skill or ability | b | e | c | a | b | — |
| 2. Helped me have more confidence in myself | b | d | c | — | a | — |
| 3. Gave me a chance to see how good I was | a | e | c | a | a | — |
| 4. People depended on me: I was needed | b | — | c | a | a | — |
| 5. I worked hard | b | — | c | a | c | — |
| 6. I had an important job | c | a | c | a | b | — |
| 7. I was worried whether the activity would be a success | b | a | c | — | a | — |
| 8. I was asked to go and help out | b | b | c | a | c | — |
| 9. I was active in what was going on | c | a | c | — | c | a |
| 10. I felt like I had really accomplished something | a | — | c | a | a | — |
| 11. I spent much time | c | — | c | a | c | b |
| 12. I worked closely with others | b | a | c | a | b | — |

*Source:* A. W. Wicker. Undermanning, performance, and students' subjective experiences in behavior settings of large and small high schools. *Journal of Personality and Social Psychology,* 1968, **10,** 255–261. Copyright 1968 by the American Psychological Association. By permission.

*Note:* Tests are one-tailed. The pole listed was expected to be favored by small-school students.
a = difference in expected direction, but not significant.
b = $p < .05$ in expected direction.
c = $p < .005$ in expected direction.
d = $p < .05$ in unexpected direction.
e = $p < .005$ in unexpected direction.

instances, *performers* (students actively and responsibly involved in an activity) reported more gains than did *nonperformers* (students who were only marginally involved or were spectators) in both large and small schools. Because small schools have a larger percentage of performers participating in a larger number of activities (121, 169), it would be predicted that they would show more gains.

Students in small schools also reported different kinds of satisfactions than large-school students: ". . . Satisfactions in the small schools are more related to improvement of one's capacity, to challenge and action, to close cooperation among peers, and to 'being important'" (121, 3). These students were likely to make comments such as "acting in the play gave me more confidence," "It was a lot of work organizing the dance, but we all thought it was worth it," and "Going on trips with the team helps you learn how to adjust yourself to different surroundings" (121, 3).

In contrast, large-school satisfactions "tended to be more passive; that is, they were derived from somebody else's action. These satisfactions were also connected with belonging to 'something big'" (121, 3). These students tended to make statements such as "I like to watch a good, suspenseful game," "It was very interesting to hear the ideas and arguments of the debaters," and "Pep rallies give you a feeling of school spirit" (121, 3).

Again, it is obvious that most of these differences resulted from the fact that students in small schools had many more performance experiences. As the investigators conclude: "When students in a large school were able to perform, they achieved many of the same satisfactions as did the performers in the small school. Unfortunately, the 'facts of life' in a large school do not allow for nearly as many performance experiences per student" (121, 3). Of particular interest are findings relating to the involvement of marginal students (i.e., those whose IQs, academic performance, and home background appeared "relatively unsuited for academic success") (121, 2). In one such investigation (275), the incidence of a *sense of obligation* for participation in school activities was determined for marginal and regular students in both large and small schools. "Sense of obligation was defined as the personal feeling of 'I ought to . . . ,' or 'I must . . . ,' that is, a personal feeling of constraint, with reference to attending, participating in, or helping with the group activity" (275, *1257*).

> Number of students available per activity, a close correlate of school size, had no marked effect upon regular students, especially when their reports of *sense of obligation were statistically controlled for frequencies of actual participation in positions of leadership and activities*. The picture was quite different for marginal students. . . . In the small schools, where there were relatively few students available for activities, these marginal students reported a sense of obligation that was similar in magnitude to their regular schoolmates. In the large school, the marginal students were a group apart and reported little, if any, sense of obligation. In fact, it would appear that the small-school marginal students were not experientially and behaviorally marginal, while their large-school counterparts were a group of relative outsiders [275, *1257–1258*; italics added].

As Figure 10.2 indicates, almost identical results were obtained in a replication of the study 5 years later. Similar results have been obtained in studies of "personal responsibility," a concept very much like "sense of obligation" (119, 121).

> When one thinks about "instilling a sense of civic responsibility" in our youth, these results should be considered. Here is evidence that the small schools, with their real need for students' participation, are offering experiences that may be quite valuable. . . . It may also be significant that whether one is marginal in the sense of being involved in the enterprises around him depends not only on his talent and background but also on how much he is needed by these enterprises. The large school again seems to have produced its group of "outsiders." Its academically marginal students are also socially marginal. This did not happen in the small school [121, 4].

Probably partly because of their greater experience of participation in school activities and their greater sense of being needed and being important to the success

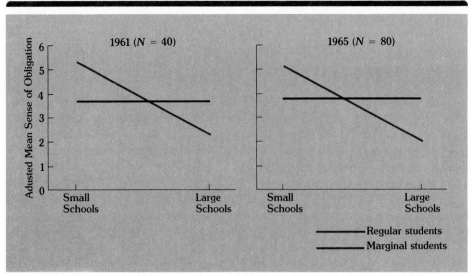

**Figure 10.2** Mean numbers of responses indicating sense of obligation in 1961 and 1965, adjusted for numbers of performances. (From E. P. Willems. Sense of obligation to high school activities as related to school size and marginality of student. *Child Development,* 1967, **38,** 1247–1260. Copyright 1967 by the Society for Research in Child Development. By permission.)

of these activities, marginal students in small schools are less likely to drop out of school than are marginal students in large schools (despite comparable IQs, grades, and home backgrounds) (121).

A more recent study found that anomie and victimization increased as school size increased, and, as in other studies, as participation in school activities decreased (36). A wider age span among the youth in the school also increased the likelihood of negative effects; in this study, the larger schools tended to include more older students.

The principal advantage of large schools is the greater variety of information they offer (see Figure 10.3). However,

> It takes a lot of bigness to get a little added variety. On the average, a 100 percent increase in size yielded only a 17 percent increase in variety. Since size increase, by itself, pays relatively poor dividends, it might be well for educational planners to consider other maneuvers for increasing the richness of the small school's curriculum [121, *1*].

Furthermore, many of the offerings of the large school tend to be used by only a limited number of students. "Although opportunities in the large school seem great, it is the small school that does a better job of translating opportunities into actual experiences for the total student body" (121, *4*). In school size, as in so many other areas of contemporary society, it appears that the traditional American slogan, "bigger is better," is open to considerable question.

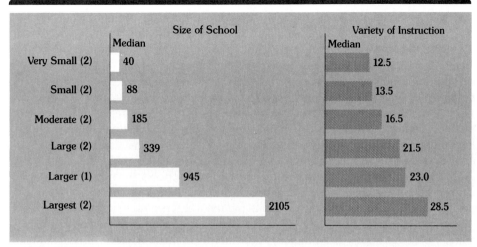

**Figure 10.3** Does increasing school size produce a corresponding increase in variety of instruction? (From P. V. Gump. *Big schools, small schools*. Moravia, N.Y.: Chronicle Guidance Publications, 1966. Source: R. Barker and P. V. Gump. *Big school, small school*. Stanford, Calif.: Stanford University Press, 1964. By permission.)

### The principal

Although unstudied in the major investigations we described earlier, good principals with clear goals have often been cited as a key factor in creating effective schools (27, 182). A strong principal, who acts as an educational leader, is thought to be especially important in schools where the majority of students are socially and economically disadvantaged. In many schools, it is the principal who sets the tone, maintains school values, and reinforces school practices (see pages 420–421).

Although the principal bears a great deal of responsibility, Gordon McAndrew, a scholar on the topic (187), has called the principal "the man in the middle"—of the school board, parents, and teachers and their unions—a position that results in generally diminished authority for principals (and superintendents). One source of this problem has been the excessive reliance on white males for principal positions: There are simply not enough outstanding ones to go around (187). In 1977, 96 percent of the secondary school principals in a national survey were white and 93 percent were male. The percentage of female principals had actually declined from 1965 to 1977 (187). A review of studies of women in school administration since 1974 concludes that factors such as the masculine sex-role stereotyping of positions in school administration, socialization practices that discourage women from seeking such leadership positions, the lack of role models, and discrimination explain the low number of women in school administration (1). Similar factors probably operate for members of minority groups.

### The role of the teacher

Teachers play a highly influential role in schools, since they have the most direct contact with students. The kinds of teachers an adolescent has will determine in great measure whether the school experience will foster overall development or simply increase the adolescent's difficulties and frustrations. The right teachers may help adolescents to overcome handicaps and to make the most of their talents and interests, whereas teachers who are ill suited for working with young people generally, or with particular kinds of young people, may cause serious—sometimes disastrous—consequences. This is especially true in the case of teachers working with culturally disadvantaged, minority-group young people.

As we discussed earlier, teachers, as well as schools themselves, have come in for increasingly harsh criticism recently from many directions: educational critics, legislators, spokespersons for both majority and minority constituencies of schools, activist students, and professional educators themselves (66, 117, 119, 129, 169, 239, 254). Undoubtedly there are teachers in our schools today who are poorly trained or incompetent, who are psychologically ill suited to working with young people, or who are overly concerned with personal and professional self-interest and preservation of a status quo that they find familiar and comfortable. Some teachers suffer from "burnout," from the continual stress on them. There is little evidence, however, to support the frequent assertion that such persons represent a majority of today's teachers (31, 196).

Furthermore, as we have already indicated, in many instances where teachers appear to be failing to meet the needs of students, the ultimate source of the difficulty may lie elsewhere. Overly large classes, impossible work loads, rigid curricula and administrative regulations, poorly prepared or poorly motivated students, extension of community divisions and polarizations into the classroom (including controversies over busing and confrontations between ethnic groups), shortages of proper teaching materials, and lack of agreement on the part of the various constituencies served by the school as to the proper goals of education may all serve to frustrate the best efforts of even the most sensitive, imaginative, and dedicated teacher. In a growing number of instances, particularly in large metropolitan areas, violence and vandalism have been making the jobs of teachers and administrators increasingly difficult (see pages 380–381). In an attempt to address what is perceived as declining teacher competence, some cities and states have begun to require that new teachers attain at least minimal scores on the National Teacher Examination, a move supported by 85 percent of the adults in the United States (254).

The increased criticism of teachers is viewed by many as adding insult to injury. "Many teachers have come to see themselves as casualties in a losing battle for learning and order in an indulgent age. Society does not support them, though it expects them to compensate in the classroom for social prejudice, economic inequality and parental indifference" (254). There has been substantial change in the role of teachers over the past four to five decades (8). Many teachers feel that they *are* teaching less because they have so many other responsibilities that they cannot teach. Since 1965, the number of teachers with 20 or more years experience has dropped by nearly half. College freshmen are now less likely than at any time in the past 30 years to aim toward teaching as a profession. Those who do become teachers now are less talented intellectually than in earlier years. Most pointedly, 40 percent of current teachers would not repeat their choice. Four out of ten claim that they plan to quit before retirement (254).

One result of all this has been an increase in teacher burnout, a psychological condition produced by stress, with the various symptoms typical of psychological stress—ulcers, migraine headaches, colitis, depression. The first national conference on teacher burnout was held in New York City in the spring of 1980. Teachers in small towns and affluent suburbs are afflicted along with their urban colleagues, who are thought to be under the most duress.

As is often the case with social institutions, a specific component of the system—such as teachers—is seldom the sole problem. Many feel that the solution must be sought in the society itself. As one prominent educator has put it, "By and large, society gets what it deserves out of its school system. It gets what it expects. If you don't value things, you don't get them" (254, 63).

### Teacher characteristics and student responses

Despite the general problems confronting teachers, some are, nevertheless, able to teach effectively. Obviously, students in general like and respond to some kinds of teachers better than others. There are also individual differences in the kinds of teachers to whom different kinds of students respond favorably. In general, adolescents appear to place more emphasis on "the teacher's qualities as a human

**TABLE 10.7 RELATIVE FREQUENCY OF MENTION OF VARIOUS CHARACTERISTICS IN DESCRIPTIONS BY STUDENTS OF TEACHERS WHOM THEY "LIKED BEST" AND "LIKED LEAST OR DISLIKED MOST"**

TEACHERS LIKED BEST

| | IV–VI | VII–XII |
|---|---|---|
| Grade level | | |
| Number of persons reporting | 303 | 298 |
| Number of characteristics named | 370 | 604 |
| Human qualities as a person: kind, sympathetic, companionable, "she likes us," cheerful, etc. | 22% | 28% |
| Qualities as director of class and as disciplinarian: fair, impartial, has no pets, discipline strict but firm and fair, does not treat failure to learn as moral wrong, etc. | 24 | 26 |
| Performance as a teacher, teaching: makes things interesting, knows a lot, explains well, helps individuals with their lessons, permits students to express opinions | 27 | 32 |
| Participation in students' games, activities | 6 | 3 |
| Physical appearance, dress, grooming, voice | 7 | 5 |
| Other | 14 | 6 |

TEACHERS DISLIKED MOST

| | | |
|---|---|---|
| Number of persons reporting | 99 | 265 |
| Number of characteristics named | 170 | 459 |
| Human qualities as a person: harsh, unkind, sarcastic, ridicules, "makes fun of you," sour, glum, cross, nervous, "queer," etc. | 21% | 32% |
| Qualities as director of class and disciplinarian: unfair, has pets, punishes too much, rigid, too strict, constant scold, treats failure to learn as moral wrong, preachy, etc. | 43 | 35 |
| Performance as teacher, teaching: dull, dry, poor at making assignments, doesn't know much, no help for individual pupils, too much homework, etc. | 17 | 18 |
| Participation in students' interests and activities | 1 | 1 |
| Physical appearance, grooming, voice, etc. | 8 | 7 |
| Other | 10 | 7 |

*Source:* A. T. Jersild. *The psychology of adolescence.* New York: Macmillan, 1963 (2nd ed.). Adapted from A. T. Jersild. Characteristics of teachers who are "liked best" and "disliked most." *Journal of Experimental Education,* 1940, **9,** 139–151. By permission.

being and the emotional qualities that he brings into his personal relationships with his students far more than his academic competence" (147, *331*). Thus, adolescents in the seventh to twelfth grades (as well as younger children) were asked what qualities of teachers they "liked best" and "liked least or disliked most" (147). As may be seen from Table 10.7,

> The two categories that included mention of the teacher's kindness and friendliness as a person and his tendency to be considerate and thoughtful of the learner when he acts in his role as a disciplinarian include considerably more responses than the category pertaining to the teacher's performance as an instructor and a source of information [147, *331*].

A number of other studies have yielded similar results (16, 34, 74, 93, 104, 125, 126, 144, 167, 192, 220, 238). For example, in one recent national survey of 160,000 American adolescents aged 13 to 18 years (207) young people were asked, "What do you like about a teacher?" The characteristic mentioned most often was "Is fair. Grades fairly and doesn't pick on certain kids." This was followed in order of frequency by: knows the subject he or she is teaching; is enthusiastic about the subject; will help kids with schoolwork or other problems . . . even after school; likes kids; gives almost no homework; and can keep discipline in the classroom.

Taken together, these studies indicate that adolescents in our society tend to prefer and to respond more favorably to teachers who are warm, possessed of a high degree of ego strength, enthusiastic, able to display initiative, creative, reactive to suggestions, poised and adaptable, able to plan, interested in parental and community relations, and aware of individual differences in children and oriented toward individual guidance. Being well organized is important (28), as is having a teaching style that actively involves the students in the learning process (231). In contrast, teachers who are hostile or dominating generally appear to affect pupil adjustment adversely (5, 177, 233).

Although such general characteristics distinguished liked from disliked teachers, it would be inappropriate to conclude that the successful teacher fits some sort of bland stereotype. As most readers will recall, the teachers who influenced students most in a positive direction also tended to be unique human beings. It is also becoming increasingly clear that there are group and individual differences among pupils in the kinds of teachers to whom they respond most favorably or most negatively, although far more research needs to be done in this area.

### Teacher-student interactions

Specific characteristics of students or teachers may enhance or inhibit the effectiveness of the interaction between them. Class, race, or sex stereotypes may create initial barriers to effective communication. More importantly, there is evidence that the expectations teachers have for students exert powerful influences on student behavior (216). If these expectations are based upon stereotypes rather than the behavior that is likely for the student, student behavior will be shaped in the direction of the expectations.

The recent emphasis on teacher-student interaction marks a departure from previous perspectives that sought to identify the characteristics of a good teacher, or of effective teaching. Much of the research previously done on these topics produced inconclusive findings (88, 193). It is now thought that the inconsistent results were due to an inaccurate conceptualization of the problem. Teaching involves few absolutes that *always* hold. It is essential to consider the age or grade of the students, their ethnic and socioeconomic characteristics, the content of the lessons, and other aspects of the school situation. These conclusions are consistent with the larger body of work that recognizes reciprocal interactions between individuals (175) and the influence of the context on human behavior (44).

Nevertheless, there are some aspects of good teaching that are generally effective. For example, "at the least, in order for the children to learn and work, the teacher has to be in charge of the classroom, to provide the conditions that make work possible" (193).

It is quite clear that different children can have quite different experiences in the same classroom. Most of these studies have focused on students in elementary school (51), although the results would seem to apply to older students as well, inasmuch as the findings are quite consistent. "Teachers are generally more attached to students who are achieving, conforming, and make few demands. They show concern for students who make demands appropriate to classroom activity but are indifferent to the invisible and silent children and have little interaction with them. They reject children who make demands considered illegitimate or who tend to be 'behavior problems'" (193, *84*). In several studies, education majors and student teachers were more likely than others (e.g., psychology majors, Teacher Corps interns) to rate highly pupils described as rigid, conforming, and orderly, and to give low ratings to those described as independent, active, and assertive (193). Similar results have been found for both male and female teachers, and at varying grade levels. These studies document clearly "that teacher time, attention, and involvement is differentially distributed" among the students (193).

Although the initial assertions made about the powerful impact of teacher expectations (229) have been modified some, there is no doubt that teachers treat students differently and that differential treatment produces differential outcomes. Usually this differential treatment represents a pattern of reinforcing what is already there; for example, high achievers receive more praise, which causes continued high achievement, thus sustaining this pattern (111). As mentioned earlier, however, differential treatment is sometimes based upon stereotypes rather than actual previous behavior. Therefore, the teacher's expectations may be discrepant from the students' abilities. For example, teachers' ratings of likability conform to social stereotypes: blacks are rated lower than whites and children from low-income families are rated lower than middle-income children (173). These findings have been linked with results showing that low-income black children become less involved with school over time, and manifest decreasing confidence in their ability to achieve.

Boys and girls are also treated differently. Until the last decade, the study of differential effects focused on possible negative consequences for boys (153, 236). More recently, research has focused on the negative effects on girls of differential treatment (216). Consistent with the findings on younger children, studies of young adolescents have found that girls receive less criticism than boys, but they also receive less praise (100, 216). Girls who were in classrooms where they were treated differently from boys had lower expectations for their own achievement (216).

A great deal more, however, needs to be known about the most beneficial teacher characteristics for specific types of students. What information exists suggests that a good "fit" can be very important. For example, one investigation of preadolescents compare the effects of *self-controlled, emotionally turbulent,* and *fearful* types of teachers on the academic and social progress of students. The greatest overall progress was made under self-controlled teachers, and the least under fearful teachers (133). Similarly, growth of the young person in "friendliness" during the course of the year was significantly greater under self-controlled teachers than under either turbulent or fearful ones (133). However, these three types of teachers did not have identical effects on all types of students. When students were also divided into four general types—*conformers, opposers, waverers,* and *strivers*—a number of significant variations were obtained. For example, whereas self-controlled teachers were generally more effective, conforming students (possibly already overly self-controlled, orderly, and so on) made slightly more progress under turbulent teachers. In contrast, opposers made significantly greater progress under self-controlled teachers and showed wider differences than other groups between the effectiveness of self-controlled and fearful teachers. Presumably these young people, unlike the conformers, had a need for control and order that they could not obtain from the fearful, insecure teacher. High-achieving adolescents have been found to be significantly more likely to identify with teachers and to perceive themselves as much more like their teachers than either average or low-achieving students (225, 226). They are also more likely to feel that their teachers care about them (266).

Considerably more attention needs to be paid not only to the personal characteristics of teachers selected to educate and to serve as important identification models for adolescents, but also to the characteristics of teachers assigned to work with particular children or groups of children.

**Student behavior and teacher response**  Certainly, teacher behavior affects student response, but student response affects teacher behavior as well. In one ingenious investigation (135), a "guest lecturer" was presented to each of two introductory psychology classes. It was explained that the "guest" had already had some graduate work in psychology and wanted to teach a class for the experience of teaching.

> Some bogus information, allegedly personality descriptions of him by friends, was given to the students. One class was told that the lecturer's friends considered him to be "quite warm" in his interpersonal relationships; the second class was told that he was "quite cold." The guest lecturer was, of course, an accomplice, albeit one unaware of the true nature of the study [135, *521*].

His "lecture" (a 10-minute speech on schools of psychology) was first presented to a class that had been given the "warm set"; 2 weeks later, it was given to a second class that had been given the "cold set." To determine the effect of student set on his performance, excerpts from the first and second halves of these two talks were played to two other classes, and rated by the students on three dimensions: warm-cold, tense-relaxed, and good teacher–poor teacher. It was found that student expectations did indeed affect teacher behavior.

Students who expected a cold teacher produced one; raters judged the teacher's performance before the cold class to be colder, more tense, less competent at the end of the talk than at the beginning. Furthermore, the *same* speaker giving the *same* talk was judged as warmer, more relaxed, more competent during the last segment of his talk to the warm class than during the final segment of his presentation to the cold class (135).

As the investigator notes, studies such as this one raise an interesting question about the potential effects of the faculty rating guides now in vogue on many campuses:

One can imagine students who have read in the latest installment of the faculty guide that Professor X is uninspiring, paying less attention, participating less in class, and responding less to the professor's efforts to enthuse the class. Professor X, responding to this behavior, may in turn become less enthusiastic, and each side will continue reinforcing the other's negative behavior with predictably regrettable results [135, *522*].

***Variations in teaching methods*** Differences among teachers are not the only factors in the learning environment that may differentially affect students. The effectiveness of different teaching methods may also vary from one student to another. This is illustrated in a study of college students (83) in which types of instruction were distinguished: those that were formally structured and stressed conformity (e.g., classes with formal lectures, assigned papers, and regular examinations) and those that were more informal and placed a premium on student independence and initiative (e.g., small seminars stressing independent planning and study). The students' needs for achievement were then determined independently by psychological testing. Two types of achievement motivation were also identified: a need for achievement through being independent (Ai); and a need for achievement through conforming (Ac).

Students high in achievement motivation, regardless of its sources, performed better in their overall college work than students low in such motivation. Furthermore, students high on the Ai dimension and low on Ac did not differ in *overall* academic performance from students scoring high on Ac and low on Ai. What was of particular interest, however, was the finding that the Ai group performed significantly better in the more informal settings stressing self-reliance and independence, whereas the Ac group performed significantly better in the more formal, structured settings.

Among younger children (116), highly anxious or highly compulsive children were found to be more dependent than were less anxious or less compulsive children on highly structured approaches to teaching reading (i.e., those that stressed phonics, as compared with less structured word-recognition—whole word or look-and-see—approaches). Somewhat similarly, college students (85) who were low in manifest anxiety performed better in more informal, student-centered classes (in which active student participation was encouraged at all times); students high in manifest anxiety performed better in more formal, structured, teacher-centered classes.

We still have a great deal to learn about the appropriateness, both for students in general and for particular types of students, of various teaching methods (119, 239). But studies such as these demonstrate clearly and ingeniously that different teaching methods may well have very different effects on different kinds of children and adolescents. These studies also serve as a needed corrective to the natural tendency of students *and* teachers to assume that a technique that seems to work for *them* individually (or for their school) would automatically be better for others as well, and that only bureaucratic or student intransigency (depending on where one sits) prevents recognition of this obvious "fact."

### Socioeconomic status, educational
### aspiration, and educational attainment

As described earlier, studies conducted in the United States (14, 64, 146) as well as other countries (62, 67, 222, 251) have found that socioeconomic status is significantly related to level and kind of educational aspiration and to educational attainment. Upper-middle- and upper-class youth have traditionally aspired to higher educational levels than their lower-middle- and lower-class peers. Youth from higher socioeconomic levels tend to view education as having intrinsic values quite apart from its function of increasing vocational opportunities and economic rewards (10, 12, 15, 41, 170, 255). Social-class (and minority-group) disparities in educational aspirations, opportunities, and actual performance have been shrinking somewhat recently as the total number of young people completing high school and going on to college has risen and as increased (though still inadequate) efforts have been made to provide greater opportunities for socioeconomically disadvantaged youth (48). For example, the average black-white differences in achievement level declined during the 1970s (48) (see Figure 10.4).

Nevertheless, the association between socioeconomic level and educational attainment, as demonstrated by a recent, continuing study of a representative sample of male youth (14, 15), is still quite large. Thus, young people whose parents are at a high socioeconomic level are more than fifteen times as likely to gain a bachelor's degree as those whose parents' socioeconomic status is low (15). Conversely, they are highly unlikely to drop out of high school (see Figure 10.5). Similar findings have been reported in the area of school achievement (78, 79, 112, 183). Thus, at any particular educational level, socially and economically favored youth, as a group, score somewhat higher than their working-class peers—and much higher than peers seriously deprived socially and economically—in both school grades and scores on standard tests of academic skills. In 1975, the National Assessment of Educational Progress (NAEP) reported initial results from a massive, continuing national effort to evaluate the performance (and progress or decline) of all U.S. students aged 9, 13, and 17 (plus a representative sample of adults aged 26 to 35) in a variety of areas ranging from science, reading, and writing to citizenship and appreciation of music and literature (103, 149; see also pages 375–378). Figures 10.6 and 10.7 show the extent to which American 17-year-olds exceeded or fell below national norms in each of these areas as a function of parental education (defined as highest grade attended by a parent) and residential area—two indices generally related to socioeconomic situation. As may be seen, adolescents and youth whose parents are themselves highly educated and who are from affluent suburban backgrounds have a marked advantage in terms of achievement in all areas over young people whose parents are themselves poorly educated, and who come from poverty areas of inner cities. Unhappily, results of this project to date indicate that these differences tend to be clearly established by age 9 and change little thereafter (103, 149).

Some of the reasons for these persisting disparities are straightforward and reasonably obvious; others are more subtle. The lower-class young person is more likely to face serious economic problems in continuing his or her education. Govern-

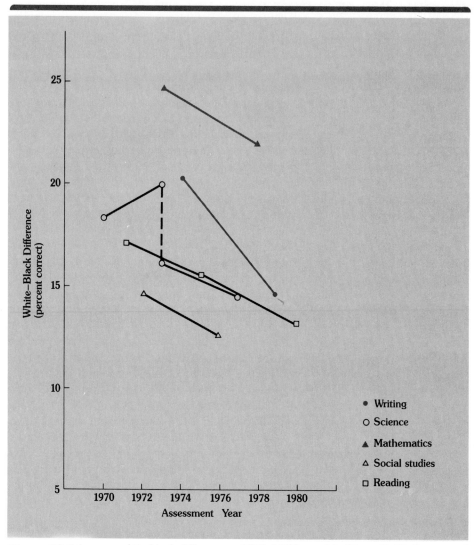

**Figure 10.4** Average white-black differences, 1970–1980, age 13. (From N. W. Burton and L. V. Jones. Recent trends in achievement levels of black and white youth. *Educational Researcher,* 1982, **11,** 10–17. By permission.)

ment and private assistance is grossly inadequate to meet the needs of many students and is becoming more so. Furthermore, lower-class or deprived adolescents are more likely to have had poorer academic preparation throughout their schooling as a result of reliance on local property taxes and obvious discrimination—whether intended or not. Typically, their schools have been physically inferior and poorly equipped, with inadequate curricula and severe shortages of trained teachers and auxiliary personnel.

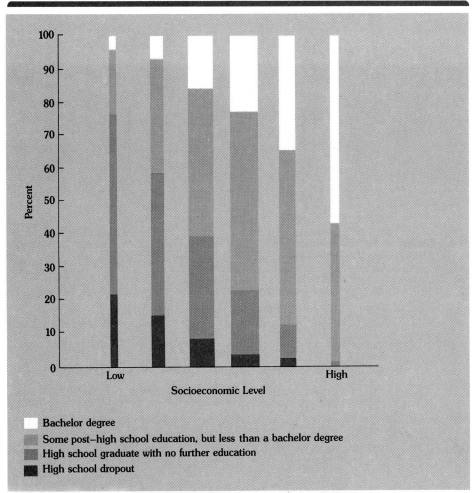

**Figure 10.5** Educational attainment related to parental socioeconomic level. (From J. G. Bachman, P. M. O'Malley, and J. Johnston. *Youth in transition, Vol. VI: Adolescence to adulthood—change and stability in the lives of young men.* Ann Arbor, Mich.: Institute for Social Research, 1978. By permission.)

Because of poor nutrition and inadequate or nonexistent health care, many more children at the lowest economic levels have serious health problems that may interfere with their ability to do academic work (33, 232). There are increasing indications that significant numbers of children *may* be retarded in their mental and psychological development even before or shortly after birth as a result of inadequate maternal diets, lack of prenatal health care, and poor postnatal care (33, 47, 76, 82, 244). Furthermore, many thousands of children still go to school hungry—a condition unlikely to produce maximum alertness and attention to studies.

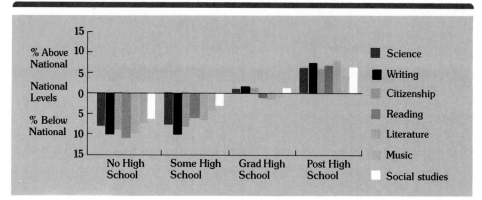

**Figure 10.6** Typical educational achievement of 17-year-olds by parental education. (From S. S. Johnson. *Update on education: A digest of the National Assessment of Educational Progress.* Denver: The Education Commission of the States, 1975. By permission.)

Because many studies have found an association between self-esteem and educational attainment or achievement (73, 109, 227, 228), it has been thought that perhaps socioeconomic status affects educational outcomes through self-esteem (10, 14). With this explanatory model, for example, low socioeconomic status would cause low self-esteem, which would, in turn, cause lower educational outcomes. A recent study (13, 14, 15) showed that this is *not* what happens. Instead, it appears that socioeconomic status affects both self-esteem and educational attainment, with the association between these latter two declining past mid-adolescence, apparently because educational attainment decreases in its importance for self-definition. What is most surprising in the results is that educational success was viewed as least vital by those who were the most successful—the ones who went on to college (14).

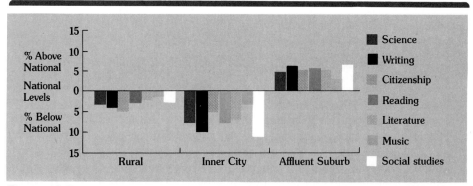

**Figure 10.7** Typical educational achievement of 17-year-olds by type of community. (From S. S. Johnson. *Update on education: A digest of the National Assessment of Educational Progress.* Denver: The Education Commission of the States, 1975. By permission.)

Other, more subtle factors also operate to limit the educational aspirations and accomplishments of working-class and socioeconomically deprived young people, including broad, class-related customs and values and the individual influence of parents and peers.

### The home environment and intellectual growth

Two social psychologists, Robert Zajonc and Hazel Markus, proposed in 1975 that the way that the home environment affects intelligence and achievement is through the intellectual resources in the home. This model, called the *confluence model,* simply sums the intellectual resources (or IQ scores) in the family at any particular time in order to predict the intellectual performance of any child. The rationale for the model is that intellectual stimulation in the home is dependent upon the available resources. A family with one parent and several small children, for example, would have a low level of intellectual stimulation; the model predicts that a child born into such a family will have a lower IQ. This model is consistent with evidence for socioeconomic effects, since lower-status families are also more likely to have more children. In addition, the model is consistent with the research showing birth order effects, where older children in the family tend to be higher achievers than those born later (58). The model also explains spacing effects, since it has been observed that children born closer in age to older siblings tend to have lower IQs than those more distantly separated in years (58).

Subsequent research (29, 186, 281) has tended to provide support for this model. In a recent test of the model using actual IQ data for family members and information on the exact spacing of siblings showed that over half of the variation in children's mental ages could be explained (29). Thus, mental development is predicted by family structure and the mutual influences of family members. This model provides an explanation for at least some of the power of socioeconomic status in predicting school achievement.

### Parental aspirations and rewards for school achievement

Parents of different socioeconomic groups vary in their views of schooling for their children. From school entrance on, middle- and upper-class parents tend to value schooling for the education—both academic and social—that it provides. Parents in lower socioeconomic groups, in contrast, have traditionally looked upon school as necessary for vocational success, because of the skills provided and the credentials earned (128, 130, 196). However, except for the very lowest socioeconomic groups (particularly those subject to ethnic discrimination), all groups of parents have reinforced the value of school to some degree because they have expected the school to do something for their children (196).

Several factors seem to be meaningfully related to the more positive attitudes toward academic success shown by both young people and adults of higher socioeconomic levels. For one thing, most school programs have actually been more relevant to the needs, customs, and expectations of individuals in these classes (188, 196). Indeed, one of their principal functions has traditionally been to prepare (indoctrinate?) succeeding generations of young people for admission to a society dominated and controlled by the middle class (196, 197, 243). As psychologist Boyd McCandless commented, "schools succeed relatively well with upper- and middle-class youngsters. After all, schools are built for them, staffed by middle-class people, and modeled after middle-class people" (188, *295*).

Other factors also play a role in the function of the more positive attitudes traditionally displayed by socioeconomically favored parents and their young: The school child's social-class identification tends to be strong, and threats to his or her membership status in a particular social class will be tremendously anxiety-producing (196). School success is still more important in maintaining class membership in the higher socioeconomic classes than in the lower, and consequently, middle- and upper-class children are likely to be motivated to succeed in school. The middle- or upper-class adolescent is able to see for himself or herself the delayed rewards to which academic skills may lead by noting the important part that they play in the success of a doctor-father, a scientist-aunt, or an accountant-older brother. Of course, we would not expect these distantly anticipated rewards to be effective if the young person's immediate experiences were punishing, but when they are favorable, the prospects of additional future rewards may provide increased impetus to try to do well in school. Moreover, parents of high socioeconomic status are more likely to encourage their children to work hard in school, not simply because of their interest in the child's academic progress, but also because of the threat to their own social status of having a child who "couldn't make the grade." Indeed, one study (77) found that the strongest determinant of parents' aspirations for the education of their children was socioeconomic status; in this study, there was no direct effect of socioeconomic status on the educational aspirations of the adolescent once parental aspirations were considered.

Despite popular stereotypes, social-class differences and attitudes cut across racial, ethnic, and other minority-group lines. For example, among middle- and upper-class blacks, the concern of parents for their child's scholastic success and, consequently, their approval of his or her successful efforts are, if anything, stronger than among middle-class whites. Conversely, ethnic or other differences in attitudes toward education may be found, even when socioeconomic level is held constant or otherwise controlled (e.g., the traditionally greater interest in educational values among Jews).

Perhaps most important of all, there are wide individual differences *within* all socioeconomic, ethnic, racial, and other subgroups in their orientation to education (171, 188, 196). When parents are truly interested in their children and motivated to have them succeed academically, and when relevant educational opportunities exist in the community, the effects of parental influences may override the otherwise limiting effects of lower socioeconomic status or the negative influences of peers. It was demonstrated in a study of high school boys (241) that although middle-class boys, as a group, had higher educational and vocational aspirations than their working-class peers, working-class boys with parents who encouraged and supported educational and occupational mobility had higher aspirations than middle-class boys with parents who did not encourage such striving.

Similarly, in a recent study (77) of parental and peer influences on the educational plans of adolescents, it was found that the educational aspirations that parents had for their children were equaled only by the young person's academic ability as a prediction of adolescent educational aspirations. Interestingly, the effects of parents' actual aspirations were greater than their adolescent young's *perceptions* of their parents' aspirations. "These findings are important, for they document that the interpersonal influences of parents are exerted in subtle ways, and not necessarily with the awareness of the adolescent being influenced" (77, *376*).

In a similar vein, a national study of tenth-grade boys (12) found that *family relations* were a better predictor of school attitudes than was socioeconomic status. Boys whose family relations were positive and rewarding showed more positive and fewer negative attitudes toward school. Other investigators have obtained similar results (39, 101, 116, 154, 180).

## FAMILY INFLUENCES ON EDUCATIONAL ASPIRATIONS AND ACHIEVEMENT

Studies indicate that parents *may* have an important positive influence on the academic aspirations and achievement of their children—an influence that can, under favorable circumstances, transcend the otherwise limiting effects of such factors as lower socioeconomic status. But what determines whether parents will, in fact, exert such a positive influence? There is increasing evidence that the single most important factor is the expectations held by parents for the educational attainments of their child (216). Parental expectations are a function of their attitudes, values, and motivations, all of which may be expressed in their own achievement behavior. The models for achievement presented by parents have been thought to exert influence on the achievement of their children, but this may be a less potent factor than their expectations. In addition, the extent to which adolescents identify positively with parental models undoubtedly plays a role.

What kinds of parents have academically motivated, achieving children? A variety of studies indicate that such parents are likely to place a high value on autonomy and independence (7, 23, 24, 136, 137, 138, 208) and on mastery, competence, and achievement generally (21, 23, 24, 26, 31, 39, 136, 138, 189); to be democratic and encouraging of an active give-and-take interaction with their children (84, 161, 195); and to exhibit curiosity and a respect for knowledge (26, 161, 195, 255). The parents of children with low aspirations and achievements do not share these values or characteristics even if they are like the parents of achieving children in socioeconomic status and intelligence.

In brief, it is clear that the parents of children and adolescents with relatively high educational aspirations and achievement tend to manifest academically relevant attributes themselves. A variety of studies indicate that the parents of academic achievers also manifest personality characteristics and behaviors that seem likely to facilitate the attainment of their expectations. Specifically, such parents have been found to give their children more praise and approval, to show more interest and understanding, to be closer to their children, and to provide them with more of a feeling of family belongingness (195, 224, 252, 270).

One of the more adequately controlled of these studies is an investigation (195) that compared the family relations of bright high-achieving and underachiev-

**TABLE 10.8 FAMILY RELATIONS SCALES: MEDIAN TESTS**

| | | PERCENT ABOVE MEDIAN | | |
| SCALE TITLE | $r^a$ | HIGHS (N = 48) | LOWS (N = 48) | p |
|---|---|---|---|---|
| Family sharing of recreation | .76 | 69 | 44 | .02 |
| Family sharing of confidence and ideas | .84 | 63 | 35 | .01 |
| Family sharing in making decisions | .88 | 60 | 44 | ns |
| Parental approval | .56 | 73 | 33 | .001 |
| Parental affection | .88 | 60 | 42 | ns |
| Parental trust | .73 | 60 | 25 | .001 |
| Parental approval of peer activities | .94 | 71 | 42 | .01 |
| Student acceptance of parental standards | .69 | 52 | 25 | .01 |
| Student affection and respect toward parents | .91 | 58 | 44 | ns |
| Lack of parental overrestrictiveness | .63 | 56 | 29 | .01 |
| Lack of parental severity or discipline | .70 | 69 | 42 | .01 |
| Lack of parental overprotection | .77 | 52 | 56 | ns |
| Lack of parental overinsistence on achievement | .75 | 63 | 46 | ns |
| Parental encouragement of achievement | .74 | 60 | 40 | .05 |
| Harmony of parents (N = 40) | .72 | 63 | 48 | ns |
| Regularity of home routine | .76 | 52 | 46 | ns |
| Overall family morale | .97 | 67 | 33 | .001 |

Source: W. R. Morrow and R. C. Wilson. Family relations of bright high-achieving and under-achieving high school boys. *Child Development*, 1961, **32**, 501–510. Copyright 1961 by The Society for Research in Child Development. By permission.

Note: Tests are two-tailed

[a] Odd-even reliability coefficient, corrected by Spearman-Brown formula.

ing high school boys equated for grade in school, socioeconomic status, and intelligence. As Table 10.8 shows, the families of high achievers were significantly more likely to do things together, to share ideas, and to involve their children in family decision making. They were also more likely to display parental approval, confidence, and trust, and less likely to engage in overrestrictive controls and overly severe discipline. Overall morale in these families was far higher than in the families of underachieving boys.

In contrast, the parents of underachieving children and adolescents have been found to be more domineering (150), more overrestrictive (224, 271), more likely to engage in severe and arbitrary punishment (15, 72, 165, 271), and more likely to be either overly protective of their children *or* to pressure them excessively for achievement (195, 224). In most investigations (150, 195, 252), family tensions and parental disagreement regarding standards of behavior expected of their children were greater in the families of underachieving children and adolescents. Such findings suggest that strong and positive parent-child relationships are more likely in the case of achieving than of underachieving children and adolescents.

This line of research has been interpreted as providing evidence that higher-achieving adolescents identify more strongly with parents than do underachieving youth. For example, one study (237) employing a variety of measures of parental identification (e.g., correspondence between self-descriptions and ratings of parents [or children, in the case of parents] and agreement between students' and parents' self-ratings) in relation to academic achievement among eleventh- and twelfth-grade achievers and underachievers of bright-normal intelligence (IQ of 110) or better, found significant child-parent correlations (thus indicating identification) on virtually all measures between achieving boys and their fathers and between achieving girls and their mothers. No significant positive correlations were found between underachieving boys and girls and either parent. Furthermore, "male achievers . . . identified much more closely with their fathers than they did with their mothers. Female achievers identified much more closely with their mothers than with their fathers. No such distinctions could be made in underachiever groups of either sex" (237, *12*).

It has been generally assumed that identification with parents results, to a great extent, from the quality of the models that parents provide (17, 185). While it may be true in general that high achievers become so to a significant extent because they identify with the models of achievement provided by their parents, this explanation has not been supported for the socialization of sex-typed achievement behavior (e.g., mathematics). In a recent study (216) of 1250 children from grades five through eleven, no support was found for a parental modeling hypothesis. Although mothers and fathers differed in their reports of attitudes toward, as well as experience with, mathematics, these were unrelated to the expectancies and attitudes of their children toward mathematics. Similarly, there was no relation between the parental division of mathematics-related tasks at home and their child's self-concept, task concept, or performance measures. The authors conclude, "Thus, it seems that parental role modeling of mathematical skills does not exert a very strong influence on children's mathematics-related self-perceptions, task perceptions, actual performance, or plans to continue in mathematics courses" (216, *325*).

Parents' *expectations,* in contrast, proved to be strongly related to the child's attitudes about and performance in mathematics. Despite the fact that, prior to the study, the boys and girls had performed equally well in mathematics courses and on their most recent standardized test, parents reported sex differences in the abilities of, and aspirations for, their children. For both mathematics and science, parents of daughters reported that their children had to work harder than did parents of sons. In addition, parents of sons felt that mathematics and science were more important than did parents of daughters. The (apparently erroneous) belief that success for girls is due to effort rather than ability, together with the lesser importance placed on these subjects for girls than boys, is likely to decrease the motivation for girls to continue in these courses, an outcome that has been observed in other studies (99). A causal model, proposing that children's self-concepts and task concepts were more directly related to their parents' beliefs about their mathematics aptitude and potential than to their own past performance, was supported in this study. The model held equally well for boys and girls, although parental beliefs varied for the sexes. In contrast to previous speculation that fathers have a greater influence on their children's attitudes toward mathematics—a task that is sex-typed as masculine—this study found that, in fact, mothers had a stronger influence on their children's achievement beliefs and attitudes, and that fathers had little independent additional influence.

Similar results have been seen in other studies as well. For example, one recent study of high school seniors (6) found that parents had higher educational aspirations for their sons than for their daughters, with mothers differentiating more than fathers. This same study also found that mothers' expectations for the education of their adolescents, both boys and girls, were more strongly related to the goals of the adolescents than were the fathers' expectations. Another study (242) of several thousand adolescents in sixth, eighth, tenth, and twelfth grades also found that the influence of mothers on educational aspirations was greater than that of fathers, at least in terms of the adolescents' perceptions.

We indicated earlier that a potential factor in the extent to which parents influence their adolescent young is the response that the adolescent has to each parent. The quality and strength of the parent-child relationship is surely important. In addition, the adolescent, because of various personality characteristics in the adolescent or parent, may find identification with either parent difficult or impossible. Under these circumstances, the parent's potential influence may be vitiated. Indeed, in the search for a workable identity, the young person may even attempt, consciously or unconsciously, to be as *unlike* the parent as possible. Thus, he or she may reject the parent's academically oriented values, even though under other circumstances he or she might have found them "ego-syntonic" (or psychologically compatible). Every therapist has encountered young people who, seemingly in spite of their basic inclinations and abilities, somehow manage to fail academically because they are so involved with rejecting the academic values and aspirations of their parents. Conversely, an adolescent may be strongly and positively identified with a parental model; but if that model is indifferent to or suspicious and critical of educational values and goals, the young person may adopt the parent's attitudes and motivations. These considerations may help to explain some apparently contradictory findings regarding the role of parental identification in academic aspirations and achievement.

## PEER INFLUENCES ON
## EDUCATIONAL ASPIRATIONS

Acceptance by peers is one of the strong needs of adolescents. Depending upon the particular values of the peer group generally, and of close friends in particular, the adolescent's educational aspirations may be either strengthened or reduced. The educational aspirations of adolescents are clearly consonant with those of their peers (77, 122, 158, 190, 241). Furthermore, the degree of adolescent-peer agreement is directly related to the intimacy of the relationship. One extensive study of high school students (158) made use of several indicators of intensity of friendship: (1) whether or not the friendship choice was reciprocated, (2) how frequently the adolescent saw the friend out of school, and (3) whether the best school friend was also the best friend overall. Friendship pairs characterized by greater intimacy and greater frequency of contact were expected to show greater concordance in academic aspirations.

As shown in Table 10.9, it was found that friends whose choices were reciprocated were in somewhat greater agreement about educational goals than friends involved in unreciprocated choices; adolescents were in greater agreement with

**TABLE 10.9** *CONCORDANCE ON EDUCATIONAL PLANS BETWEEN ADOLESCENT AND BEST SCHOOL FRIEND, BY STRENGTH OF FRIENDSHIP (DYADS)*

| STRENGTH OF FRIENDSHIP | TAU-BETA | N |
|---|---|---|
| Reciprocity of choice | | |
| Reciprocated | .390 | (438) |
| Not reciprocated | .346 | (622) |
| Frequency of contact out of school | | |
| More than once a week | .369 | (732) |
| Once a week-month | .350 | (213) |
| Never | .316 | (114) |
| School friend is best friend overall | | |
| Yes | .406 | (710) |
| No | .291 | (338) |

*Source:* D. B. Kandel and G. S. Lesser. Parental and peer influences on educational plans of adolescents. *American Sociological Review*, 1969, **34,** 213–223. By permission.
*Note:* Concordance as measured by tau-beta, all significant beyond .001 level.

friends they saw frequently out of school than with those they saw rarely. Furthermore, "agreement is higher with school friends who are also the adolescent's very best friend overall (outside school as well as in school) than with those school friends who are not" (158, *221*).

In this investigation the degree of friendship was refined further by considering simultaneously whether the choice was reciprocated *and* whether the friend in school was the best friend overall. "The 'very best friend' in terms of this classification, is the best friend overall whose choice is reciprocated. Concordance on educational plans with reciprocated best friends overall is higher than for any other category of friendship" (158, *221*) (see Table 10.9).

A subsequent study by these investigators (77), as well as others (87), suggests that one should be cautious in assuming that similarity in peer aspirations is solely, or even primarily, the result of peer influence. As longitudinal studies (77, 156, 157) show, similarities in educational aspirations (and other attitudes and behavior), for example, drug use, tend to lead to the development of friendships in the first place. Only subsequently does interaction with the friend strengthen or reduce the young person's existing aspirations or beliefs; furthermore, such peer influences are reciprocal (77). Also, in many situations, common educational aspirations are widely shared in peer groups (often in considerable measure because of socioeconomic homogeneity). Finally, peer influences on educational aspirations appear to be considerably greater for girls than for boys, reaching a peak at the ninth grade, and then declining (77).

### Relative influences of parents and peers

It is often assumed that with educational aspirations, as well as with most other areas, irreconcilable differences are likely to arise between parents and peers, and that in any such confrontation, peer values will win out over those of parents (61).

Actually, however, there is usually considerable overlap between the values of parents and peers because of commonalities in their backgrounds—social, economic, religious, educational, and even geographic (71). With respect to educational goals, in many middle- and upper-class groups, scholastic success—or at least the absence of scholastic failure—is positively valued and explicitly rewarded not only by teachers and parents, but also by young people themselves. In a number of studies primarily involving middle-class children and adolescents (37, 38, 196), those who were most popular in school were also better students and were rated as more conforming and cooperative. Lower-class, and particularly ghetto, children are far less likely to be rewarded either by parents or peers for scholastic achievement.

Furthermore, although peer influences may predominate in some current customs and tastes (94), parental influence is likely to be predominant in more fundamental areas, such as life goals, "underlying moral and social values, and understanding of the adult world" (71, *1129;* 84). Concordance between the aspirations of adolescents and those of parents was found to be greater than that for peers generally, and even for best school friend:

> Far from supporting the notion that adolescents are influenced by their peers more than by their parents, these data suggest the opposite: namely, that parents are more influential than peers as regards future life goals. Furthermore, far from acting at odds with parents' goals, peers seem to reinforce these goals [158, *217*].

It was found that a majority of adolescents (57 percent) held plans that were in agreement with those of their parents *and* their friends. Furthermore, adolescents who agreed with their parents were more likely to be in agreement with their peers (76 percent) than were those who disagreed with their parents (59 percent). "In the area of future life goals, no polarization seems to exist either toward parents or peers" (158, *217*).

In one recent study (77), parental influence on adolescent educational aspirations exceeded peer influence by ratios ranging from 2:1 to 8:1, depending upon the measure of educational aspirations used. Contrary to the popular view, parental influences *increased* over the high school years faster for girls than for boys. Other studies have yielded similar results (71, 210). Obviously, however, there are exceptions to this general finding, as in some cases where deviant peer-group pressures are unusually strong and homogeneous, or where communication between parents and their children has broken down and parental influence is correspondingly vitiated.

## PERSONALITY CHARACTERISTICS, INTELLIGENCE, AND SCHOOL ACHIEVEMENT

Clearly, intellectual level is significantly related to school success. A variety of investigations indicate that "the correlation between intelligence and academic achievement as measured by some external test (standardized rather than teacher constructed and graded) ranged from about .50 to about .70 or .75. There is little

**TABLE 10.10 CORRELATIONS FOR BOYS AND
GIRLS BETWEEN GROUP INTELLIGENCE TEST SCORES
AND STANDARDIZED ACHIEVEMENT TEST SCORES**

| ACHIEVEMENT TEST SCORE | SIXTH GRADE | | EIGHTH GRADE | |
|---|---|---|---|---|
| | BOYS | GIRLS | BOYS | GIRLS |
| Reading | .72 | .77 | .58 | .75 |
| Mathematics | .70 | .79 | .52 | .72 |
| Total achievement[a] | .82 | .75 | .59 | .78 |

Source: S. M. Kavrell and A. C. Petersen. Patterns of achievement in early adolescence. In M. L. Maehr and M. W. Steinkamp (eds.), *Women and science*. Greenwich, Conn.: JAI Press, in press.
[a] Based on other areas besides those listed.

difference between boys and girls in the size of the correlation" (188, *273*). (As we shall see later, the achievement of disadvantaged children and adolescents is less well predicted by standard intelligence tests than is that of advantaged children.)

The results of one investigation (159) are typical. The correlations between IQ scores and achievement test scores for a longitudinal sample at both sixth and eighth grades are shown in Table 10.10. While the correlations are quite similar for boys and girls in sixth grade, by eighth grade, IQ is less related to achievement for boys than for girls.

When teacher grades are used as a measure of achievement, the correlations are usually lower (159, 188, 213). Although boys and girls are generally not different on IQ test scores, differences on achievement tests are sometimes seen on specific scores, with boys higher than girls on mathematics and some science tests, and girls higher than boys on verbal and language tests (185). Girls often earn higher grades than boys until college (185, 230). This sex difference was found in the study cited in Table 10.10; boys and girls did not differ in IQ or achievement test scores, but girls received consistently higher grades from sixth through eighth grade (159). The correlations between IQ and teachers' grades, however, are similar for boys and girls, varying for both from subject to subject (see Table 10.11). An earlier study of adolescents at this same age had found stronger correlations for girls, a result attributed to a variety of teacher and student factors (188), including the possibility that teachers view boys more harshly and estimate their achievement less accurately; this seems unlikely in light of more recent data. More active and often more disruptive behavior on the part of boys (100), however, provides a noncognitive explanation for their lower grades.

As these findings suggest, intelligence is not the only determinant of school achievement, and, indeed, among some students may be far less important than many other factors, including motivation, interest, work habits, and personality characteristics (124, 172). Even when the potential effects of intelligence are controlled for statistically, students of varying levels of academic achievement differ significantly on these other factors. For example, in one investigation of 475 high school seniors (108), students were divided into three subgroups: those whose academic perform-

**TABLE 10.11 CORRELATIONS FOR BOYS AND GIRLS BETWEEN GROUP INTELLIGENCE SCORES AND GRADES IN FIVE BASIC CLASSES**

| SCHOOL SUBJECT | SIXTH GRADE | | EIGHTH GRADE | |
|---|---|---|---|---|
| | BOYS | GIRLS | BOYS | GIRLS |
| Language arts | .49 | .53 | .47 | .50 |
| Literature | .68 | .57 | .62 | .57 |
| Mathematics | .56 | .42 | .17 | .30 |
| Science | .54 | .55 | .65 | .49 |
| Social studies | .55 | .47 | .63 | .66 |

*Source:* S. M. Kavrell and A. C. Petersen. Patterns of achievement in early adolescence. In M. L. Maehr and M. W. Steinkamp (eds.), *Women and science.* Greenwich, Conn.: JAI Press, in press.

ance (in English, science, mathematics, and social science) exceed what would have been anticipated statistically on the basis of their IQs (overachievers); those whose performance was about what would have been anticipated (normal achievers); and those whose performance fell below expected levels (underachievers). When these three groups were compared, a number of significant differences emerged.

Overachievers demonstrated significantly better work habits, greater interest in schoolwork generally, and more persistence in carrying out assignments, and they tended to be more grade-conscious. They also emerged as more responsible, conscientious, and likely to plan than normal achievers, although they were similar to them in many other respects. Underachievers differed markedly from normal achievers and overachievers. They appeared to have more difficulty in "self-regulation," and were more impulsive, uninhibited, pleasure-seeking, and interested in immediate rewards. They also appeared to have greater difficulty in interpersonal relationships with peers, and appeared less cooperative, more selfish, less dependable, less sociable, less respecting of "authority, order, and tradition," and "less diligent in their efforts to attain socially acceptable goals" (108, *153*). They enjoyed both school and home less than normal achievers, manifested more "defensive and resentful" behavior, and were more likely to become disorganized—particularly under pressure. Finally, they displayed greater pessimism about their futures. Perhaps symptomatically, underachievers were less likely than either overachievers or normal achievers to report not having enough time for their studies!

Other studies (247) reveal that overachievers, in comparison with underachieving peers, are more likely to be characterized by: (1) *positive self-value* (e.g., optimism, self-confidence, self-acceptance, high self-esteem); (2) *acceptance of authority* (e.g., conformity to expectations of teachers and parents, eagerness to please them); (3) *positive interpersonal relations* (e.g., interest in, and responsiveness to, the feelings of others); (4) *little independence-dependence conflict* (e.g., freedom to make choices and initiate activities and to lead, although within a generally conforming context); (5) an *academic orientation* (e.g., orderly study habits, high motivation for academic achievement, interest in academic values and subject matter); (6) a *realistic goal orientation* (e.g., a drive to organize and plan their lives, basic serious-ness of purpose, ability to delay short-term pleasures for longer-term goals, effi-ciency and energy); and (7) *better control over anxiety* (e.g., direction of inner ten-sions into organized task-related activities).

In contrast, underachieving students are more likely to be characterized by a high level of free-floating anxiety; negative self-concepts; hostility toward authority; difficulty in relating to peers, combined with excessive dependence on the peer group; a high level of independence-dependence conflict; a social, pleasure-seeking orientation, rather than an academic one; and unrealistic (e.g., emotional, indeci-sive, restless, changeable) goal orientations or no long-term goals at all (247, 271).

Obviously, these findings represent only general trends, and there are many exceptions. For example, whereas many high-achieving students are well adjusted, self-confident, and mature, significant numbers (particularly of excessively over-achieving students) have been found to have feelings of inadequacy and unworthi-ness, to be overly worried about the impressions they make on others, to be con-cerned about loss of parental love if they do not measure up to perceived parental expectations, and to be overly dependent and conforming (86, 114, 139, 140, 141, 194). For such young people, overachieving may be a way of compensating for self-doubts and warding off potential rejection by parents and others. By the same token, some students who are classified as underachieving in the usual academic sense (and history provides some distinguished examples, such as Darwin, Church-ill, and Einstein) may merely be following the sound of a different drummer. It is also clear that the fact of achievement, or underachievement, can influence the develop-mental course of self-esteem and academic self-concept (164). Therefore, achiev-ment is as much a *cause* of psychological characteristics as a *result*.

## SCHOOLS AND THE SOCIOECONOMICALLY DISADVANTAGED ADOLESCENT

During the 1970s, several national task forces and commissions examined schools for adolescents (52, 163, 202, 211, 267). First among the major conclusions of these reports is that "students from minority groups—blacks and Hispanics—suffer most from poorly articulated educational programs and unresponsive school envi-ronments" (96, *20*). The reports concluded that about half of all secondary school students in the United States attend schools with such programs and environments. Inasmuch as minority-group students are more likely than other groups to also be poor, they suffer doubly from their disadvantage. Although many schools that pri-marily serve disadvantaged lower-class and minority-group adolescents have im-proved substantially in recent years (48), most still fail, as Charles Silberman, author of *Crisis in the Classroom* (239), found a decade ago, "to provide the kind of education Negroes, Indians, Puerto Ricans, Mexican Americans, Appalachian whites—indeed, the poor of every color, race, and ethnic background—need and deserve" (239, *62*).

The reasons for this lack of faster progress extend, of course, far beyond the schools themselves. Accelerated migration of the disadvantaged poor into the central cities, the exodus of the middle class to the suburbs, high rates of pupil turnover due to transiency, and attendant breakdowns in community organization (reflected in joblessness, crime and drugs, substandard housing, and the like) have all greatly increased the problems the schools face in attempting to meet their responsibilities to these young people. The situation is frequently exacerbated by inadequate financial, political, and administrative support for the schools' efforts at reform.

The economically disadvantaged adolescent is likely to be poorly prepared for academic work (at least by traditional, largely middle-class standards) even at the time of school entrance. Largely as a result of developmental influences in the family and in the overall social milieu—which are markedly different from those of the middle- and upper-class child—he or she is likely to be handicapped in approaching academic tasks requiring a variety of basic cognitive abilities. Language development is likely to be more limited in comparison to that of the middle-class child (4, 248, 249, 273). Even at this early age, he or she is likely to be less capable of complex sentence construction (196) and of using language "to communicate ideas, relationships, feelings, and attitudes" (112, *13*), rather than simply to communicate signals and directions (196). In addition, disadvantaged minority children are given a double message about school performance: They have to work hard to get ahead, but discrimination will prevent their achievement (212). They may be encouraged to have high aspirations and low expectations.

Consequently, disadvantaged minority-group adolescents have typically performed more poorly than their middle-class white peers, even at the first-grade level, both on the standardized achievement tests and in school grades. Furthermore, the discrepancy is likely to widen during the course of the school years, although there is also substantial overlap (64, 239). (It should be remembered that 50 percent of white children fall below their own median and 50 percent of minority-group children fall above the median for their group.)

Similar results are obtained in various areas of school achievement. Black 17-year-olds, who as a total group have suffered disproportionately in terms of socioeconomic deprivation and ethnic discrimination, scored lower than their white peers in most academic areas, particularly reading, writing, and literature (103, 149, 198, 199). (Significantly, however, middle-class black children who have shared the advantages of middle-class white children do not show this relative pattern.) Much the same picture obtains for other minority groups, such as Spanish-speaking young people and Native Americans (64). Similarly, "relatively high proportions of children who were living in families below the poverty level—whether white, black, or of Spanish Origin—were behind in school" (120, *73*).

The seeming inevitability of declining performance is most discouraging. It has been demonstrated, for example, that by the end of first grade, more than half the children who will later be failing in arithmetic in grade six can be identified on the basis of their social class, their intelligence test scores, and their achievement in arithmetic. By the end of the second grade, two-thirds of failing children can be identified (245).

In general, it appears that disadvantaged children and adolescents "tend to depend more on real life encounters than on symbolic experience in developing ideas and skills" (112, *15*). In this connection, it is interesting to note that although

these young people perform more poorly on measures of language skills and conceptual thinking (273), they perform relatively well on motor tasks, on tasks requiring a short time span, and on tasks that can easily be related to concrete objects and services (196). In addition, they are likely to be less motivated and to have lower aspirations for academic achievement than middle-class young people, and characteristically receive little academic encouragement from either parents or peers. The disadvantaged young person's progress in school may be further limited by feelings of inadequacy and a depressed self-concept resulting from the greater difficulties encountered and from feelings of not belonging in a social setting characterized by unfamiliar or foreign (typically middle-class) goals and codes of behavior (55, 56, 112, 115, 174, 218, 268). Whatever factors may be involved in individual cases, the fact remains that the gap between advantaged and disadvantaged young people is likely to widen, rather than narrow, in the course of their school experience.

Another problem that is likely to arise in any attempt to deal adequately with the disadvantaged child or adolescent in the school setting, particularly in the changing inner-city environment, is that of transiency (152, 176). As some people become more affluent and move out of urban ghettos, their places are taken by a constant stream of newcomers, largely from poor rural backgrounds: blacks, Appalachian whites, Puerto Ricans, Chicanos or Latinos, and others. In some ghetto schools, the turnover of pupils may approach 100 percent in a single year (70, 176).

When one considers the problems that disadvantaged young people face in meeting traditional academic, social, and vocational demands, it seems reasonable to conclude that they should be provided *greater* assistance in school than better-prepared, more advantaged middle-class youth. Yet the fact of the matter is that the reverse is typically the case (70, 162). However, it would be a mistake to conclude that what disadvantaged children and adolescents need is simply more of the traditional educational programs provided for the average middle- and upper-class young person. Certainly, like all children they need decent physical surroundings and educational facilities and dedicated, skillful teachers. But they also need new and imaginative approaches to psychological development in general, and educational development in particular. They need curricula geared to their specific talents, needs, and problems (academic and social), and skilled academic, vocational, social, and personal guidance.

Despite the difficulties involved, educational programs that *work*—not only in developing essential academic, social, and vocational skills, but in fostering self-pride and a sense of meaningful and rewarding cultural identity (see Chapter 3)—are being instituted, even in some of the most crowded ghetto schools. An equally important although little acknowledged fact is that these programs make learning and living joyful and exciting (46, 54, 75, 168, 197, 217, 239, 259). The programs that have been successful all have the essential elements of imaginative, empathic, talented principals and dedicated, enthusiastic teachers.

### *Teachers and the disadvantaged student*

The greater challenges and difficulties encountered in working with disadvantaged children and adolescents demand special skills and understanding on the part of the teacher. Nevertheless, although there are many more superb, dedicated teachers in ghetto schools than is generally recognized (196), working against what must often seem like insurmountable odds to provide their pupils a good start in life, there are still too few. In many school systems, it is the least experienced and least skilled teachers who are most likely to be assigned to ghetto or slum schools—urban or rural. And although some of these teachers may make a permanent adjustment to such a setting, more often they become dissatisfied and frustrated and attempt to leave for advantaged middle-class schools as soon as possible (25, 57, 70, 102, 280).

The reasons for these attitudes are not difficult to understand. As we have observed, the ghetto school is itself likely to be the undernourished stepchild of the school system, physically and financially. Furthermore, these schools are likely to lack prestige and support not only within the administration of the school system and among older teachers, but also in the neighborhood and among parents and pupils (196). Such factors alone may be enough to discourage even an optimistic, dedicated teacher. In addition, given the values and cultural backgrounds of many middle-class teachers, attempts to teach disadvantaged children too often become an exercise in frustration, particularly if the teacher has had no special training in understanding the needs of such students (239).

Teachers in general are most likely to feel rewarded when their efforts to instill traditional academic skills yield the greatest gains; indeed, this is what most perceive as their basic responsibility. When the disadvantaged child or adolescent does not respond to traditional instruction, or when he or she does not appear to share the teacher's own need for achievement, the teacher may become frustrated, discouraged, or resentful (57, 280). Consequently, the results of a study (280) of teacher-student interaction in advantaged and disadvantaged settings, although discouraging, are not surprising. In this investigation, teachers were almost equally divided between those teaching in advantaged middle-class neighborhoods and those teaching in disadvantaged neighborhoods in a variety of communities.

It was found that from the outset of the study teachers of lower-class students tended to "possess traditionalistic and inflexibly negative attitudes toward child control," whereas teachers of middle-class children showed a relatively "more permissive, positive, and flexible attitude toward controlling children" (280, *278*). One consequence of this difference was that teachers in the former group tended to exercise a one-way dominance over lower-class students, whereas among middle-class teachers and students there was more of a give-and-take relationship, involving mutual influence. Still more discouraging, the attitudes of older, more experienced teachers of lower-class young people were generally more negative and more rigid and dominating than those of younger teachers; no such negative effect of experience was apparent in the case of teachers in middle-class, advantaged settings.

Not only did teachers of disadvantaged students manifest more negative and dominating attitudes initially, but the situation continued to deteriorate as the year wore on: "Interaction became more teacher dominated, pupils became more conforming, and classroom atmosphere became colder" (280, *280*). And as teacher behavior became progressively colder, more distant, and less permissive, the attitudes of students became correspondingly less favorable. No such deterioration was observable in the case of advantaged students and teachers. In brief, "education for docility"—whether it works or not—is more likely to be applied to disadvantaged children.

The failures of a considerable number of white, middle-class, Establishment teachers to understand and be able to help—and in some cases even to sympathize with—disadvantaged and minority-group children and adolescents has become a matter for concern in many communities. In some quarters, it has led to demands that such young people should be taught only by teachers with disadvantaged or minority-group backgrounds themselves, on the grounds that only such teachers can adequately serve the needs of these young people.

In our view, it is clearly desirable—even essential—for disadvantaged or minority young people to have significant numbers of teachers who can function not only as understanding aides to learning, but as cultural role models with whom they can identify positively. Nevertheless, there appears to be a danger in adopting a stereotyped view that, for example, black teachers will *inevitably* have a more favorable influence on black children and adolescents or that white teachers are necessarily better for white children. Furthermore, the available evidence (239, 279) does not appear to support such a view. In one investigation (279), equal numbers of black and white lower-class children were administered a variety of tasks designed to assess "social approach and avoidance tendencies, curiosity, and intelligence" (279, *290*). Three black and three white teachers judged independently as effective, and three black and three white teachers judged noneffective, served as examiners. It was found that the performance of children was influenced "by individual variation in the personal characteristics of the adults with whom they were interacting rather than by the adults' race" (279, *290*). Furthermore, this influence was relatively constant for both black and white students.

Also, there is no assurance that teachers from minority or disadvantaged backgrounds will necessarily have more favorable attitudes toward their charges than other teachers. Unfortunately, studies indicate that, although teachers from minority or disadvantaged backgrounds tend to be somewhat less critical and less pessimistic in their evaluations of disadvantaged students, both they *and* white, middle-class teachers are likely to become progressively more dissatisfied working with culturally disadvantaged children and adolescents (113).

Finally, there is no assurance that a teacher will be truly oriented to the needs and problems of disadvantaged students because he or she shares their backgrounds (110, 196). In at least some cases, the lower-class individual (whether a minority-group member or not) who violates class expectancies by becoming a teacher does so because of his or her dedication to stereotyped middle-class values and a need for upward social mobility. As a consequence, he or she may, despite a lower-class background, adopt middle-class expectations of pupils that are not unlike those of middle-class teachers (196). Some of the most successful teachers recently, especially in lower-class schools with imaginative programs, have come from the ranks of a new generation of young people—regardless of race, ethnic, or social-class background—who are energetic, self-confident, concerned with human values, ready to try new ideas, and not overly impressed by traditional middle-class values (197, 239).

### What is needed?

If our rapidly changing society is to remain workable, we can no longer afford a laissez-faire approach to the education of culturally and economically disadvantaged children and adolescents—or an approach based only on traditional middle-class methods, even with better facilities and financial support. What is needed are superior schools, staffed with dedicated teachers and administrators who are trained, motivated, and able to understand the special needs, talents, and difficulties of the particular populations of young people they serve.

Above all, these schools need to provide an overall atmosphere that makes learning a rewarding and relevant experience, one that promotes self-confidence and self-respect, and a sense of cultural identity—particularly for minority students. They cannot serve only to reinforce already existing negative self-concepts and feelings of inadequacy and frustration (55). Furthermore, improved and innovative programs need to begin early (preferably at the preschool level) and continue throughout the entire course of the young person's educational experience (10). If school programs for the socioeconomically disadvantaged are to work, they must gain the confidence of parents and community (112, 162, 239). Decades of discrimination, exploitation, and lack of concern on the part of the middle-class majority have led urban and rural slum dwellers to be suspicious and fearful of, or antagonistic to, the middle-class establishment and its institutions—ranging from welfare and the police to the schools themselves.

These are challenging assignments, and the difficulty of carrying them out successfully should not be underestimated. Nevertheless, the fact is that at all educational levels, some schools—led by imaginative administrators and enthusiastic, dedicated teachers—are succeeding (118, 134, 197, 239). For example, one recent study of 200 desegregated high schools (75) found that the most effective schools were 40 to 75 percent black, had teachers who (regardless of their attitudes) treated students with respect, had an emphasis on race relations, and had a strong extracurricular activity program. Racial tension was not necessarily a disadvantage in terms of effectiveness. Another set of studies (96) concluded that student responsibility for learning and participation in decision making are particularly important. One urban high school, troubled by discipline problems, poor attitudes, high rates of delinquency, and low achievement, was turned around by an emphasis on student decision making (259). In schools, as in laboratory experiments, "it is the successful experiment which is decisive and not the thousand-and-one failures which preceded it. More is learned from the single success than from the multiple failures. A single success proves it can be done" (239, *95*).

How are such results achieved? Several factors appear to play a major role, in the view of recent investigators who have studied these schools: (1) "the atmosphere is a good bit warmer and more humane, and the environment both freer and more supportive, than in most schools" (239, *103*)—kindness and gentleness are evident throughout the school, and unkindness on the part of staff is not tolerated; (2) disruptive behavior is handled more gently and more positively; (3) there is "a conviction that 'disadvantaged' children and adolescents can learn" (239, *105*), and the principal and teachers hold themselves accountable if their students fail; (4) innovative, imaginative, pupil-centered approaches to the development of academic skills are flexibly employed; (5) strong efforts are made "to involve parents in their children's education" (239, *110*); (6) every opportunity is taken advantage of to enhance the young person's self-esteem and pride in his or her cultural heritage.

These innovative schools—the experiments that succeeded—demonstrate that it is possible to reach even seriously disadvantaged students. But unless the number of such schools is expanded significantly, and soon, there is a real question as to whether democracy as we know it can endure. At the very least, unless adequate steps are taken, millions of adolescents will enter adulthood unprepared to lead reasonably happy, self-sustaining, and productive lives.

## SCHOOL DROPOUTS

In 1980, 12 percent of all 14- to 24-year-olds were high school dropouts, down from 12.2 percent a decade before (262). Although overall rates for blacks were still higher than those for whites, the dropout rate declined much more rapidly for blacks than for whites between 1970 and 1980—from 21.6 to 16.0 percent for blacks, and from 11.9 to 11.3 percent for whites. Furthermore, this trend is most pronounced among younger black adolescents (48, 142). Thus, in 1980, only 4.5 percent of black teenagers, ages 14 to 17, had dropped out, while among whites of the same ages, 5.6 percent had dropped out. Although both male and female black adolescents showed a significant decline, the change for black males was much greater (see Figure 10.8).

### Antecedents of dropping out

Both sociological and psychological factors appear to be involved in the adolescent's leaving school prematurely. The dropout rate is highest among ethnically segregated youth living in urban and rural slums. It is higher among the poor in

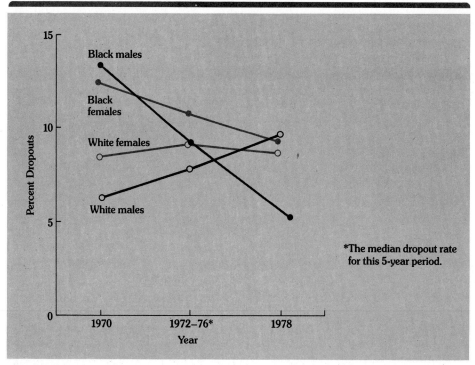

**Figure 10.8** High school dropout percentage by race and sex, ages 16 and 17, from 1970 to 1978. (From N. W. Burton and L. V. Jones. Recent trends in achievement levels of black and white youth. *Educational Researcher*, 1982, **11,** 10–17. By permission.)

general than among the more well-to-do (15, 55, 91). At the highest socioeconomic level, dropping out is extremely rare (probably less than among upper-upper-class families, one youth in fifty). At the lower end of the socioeconomic ladder, nearly one-quarter drop out, and at the very bottom of the ladder, as many as one in two youth may drop out of high school (15, 55).

However, a variety of investigations indicate that economic need per se is often not the major factor in dropping out (55, 68, 269). In one study of a large number of youth dropping out of school in a large urban community, only 3 percent withdrew primarily because of financial need or because they were required at home (55).

### School experience and the dropout

A greater number of dropouts than graduates are below average in intelligence, and the probability of dropping out of school prior to completion of high school varies with intelligence (55, 176, 239, 269). In one investigation (269), almost one-third of dropouts, but only 10 percent of high school graduates, had IQ scores below 85. Fifteen percent of dropouts and 11 percent of graduates fell in the 85 to 89 range. In contrast, 48 percent of dropouts had average IQ scores (90 to 109), and 6 percent had above-average scores (110 or more). These findings suggest that a high level of intelligence favors graduation, but that intelligence per se is not a decisive factor in many cases of dropping out of school, because a majority of dropouts are of at least average intelligence.

A qualification should be added, however. Most studies of intelligence levels among dropouts, including those cited here, do not distinguish between early and later school dropouts. When this distinction is made, the picture shifts significantly (80, 184, 142, 269). In one investigation (269), early dropouts (students dropping out in the seventh grade) were compared with later dropouts (those dropping out at all later grade levels). The findings were dramatic. Whereas approximately one-third of later dropouts had IQ scores below 85, three-fourths of early dropouts scored below this level.

School difficulties, both academic and social, play a prominent role in the histories of most dropouts. The typical dropout, even though of average IQ, is 2 years behind in reading and arithmetic by the time he or she reaches the seventh grade, and a majority of the dropout's grades are below average. Again, as might be expected, the grades of early dropouts are significantly lower than those of later dropouts (269). Also, dropouts are likely to have failed one or more school years (11, 31, 55, 269). Furthermore, although dropouts tend to fall further behind in academic skills during the course of their school experience (15, 89, 131, 239, 250, 273), future dropouts and graduates differ significantly even in the early school years (53, 55). In tests given at grade two, for example, only about 10 percent of future graduates scored below their grade level on measures of reading and spelling in one study, whereas the figure was about 90 percent for future dropouts (53). Students dropped out earlier and more abundantly in direct ratio to their low scholastic ranks and in direct proportion to the number of times that they had been held back in grade level (53).

Interestingly, as these findings suggest, the percentile level of dropouts in reading achievement is characteristically lower than their overall level of intelligence (81). Obviously, there are a variety of reasons for discrepancies between the potential dropout's intelligence and his or her basic academic skills: deficiencies in home background, in motivation, in emotional adjustment, in the appropriateness of teaching, and the like. Once academic difficulties have developed, however, they exert a formidable influence of their own (196).

> The student who cannot keep up academically or who finds much of the curriculum puzzling and irrelevant to his needs is likely to find his school experience frustrating, unrewarding, and in a significant number of instances, humiliating. A frequent theme expressed by dropouts in various studies is "feeling goofy" with those "little kids." In such a situation, the decision to drop out is at least as likely to be guided by a desire to escape from the burdens of his school experience as by any positive attraction of external goals [196, *512*].

Failures in keeping up academically or in finding relevance and challenge in the school curriculum are not the only factors that may make continuance in school a frustrating and unrewarding experience. For many lower-class youth (among whom the largest numbers of dropouts are found), school is an unrewarding experience socially as well as academically. They do not participate to the same degree as other youth in the social life and activities of the school; they do not share the values of their largely middle-class teachers; and they are likely to feel inadequate or resentful when confronted with the social, as well as the academic, demands of the school setting (179). Similar reactions may affect dropouts from other social classes; and they also appear to affect the lower-class dropout more than the lower-class youth who stays in school. Even while still in school, future dropouts tend more frequently than nondropouts to associate with peers who have already dropped out and to avoid participation in school activities (55, 92).

One conclusion appears inescapable at this juncture: "The school experience, as currently constituted, is failing to meet the needs—personal, social, and vocational—of an increasing number of our youth, particularly in the lower-class large urban ghettos" (196, *512*). And the situation for these young people is continuing to deteriorate. This is not to say that the fault lies solely with the schools—obviously, much wider social and personal factors are also involved.

### *Influence of family and peers*

Not all dropouts come from deprived backgrounds, and many deprived students (over 50 percent) successfully complete high school. Furthermore, in one study in which dropouts were matched in age, sex, school background, family socioeconomic status, and minority-group membership, significant differences still emerged in family and peer influences and in individual psychological characteristics of the students themselves (56, 55). Communication between parents and children and mutual acceptance and understanding among family members were significantly poorer in the families of dropouts than of graduates. For example, when asked, "Would you say that your whole family both understands and accepts each other?" 84 percent of dropouts gave responses classified by a panel of three trained raters as "little" or "very little," whereas 82 percent of graduates gave replies ranging from "moderate" to "very much" (56). To this question one dropout responded,

> Very little. Like before you all came. We was having a big argument. My sister keeps dogging me. When I come in she tells me to get out or go to work or something like that. She is stupid. She don't understand me. And my mother doesn't understand me. She just don't have time to understand me. She's got to be worried with my brothers and sisters and I can take care of myself. I can look after myself and make my own decisions and all (56, *219*).

When asked further, "How do you fit into the picture? Would you say that your family both understands and accepts *you?*" four out of five dropouts (79 percent) replied in terms similar to those used by a 17-year-old dropout who confessed that he had never felt understood or accepted: "I always felt left out. But really I think I need the time that the others got. . . . It's just that I felt left out. It seems when I was little I was always left out. I wasn't one of the family, really" (56, *220*).

In contrast, 84 percent of graduates expressed the view that they were both understood and accepted by their families. Almost identical percentages were obtained when subjects were than asked, "And would you say that you both understand and accept them?" (i.e., most dropouts' responses were classified "very little" or "little," whereas most graduates' responses were classified "moderately," "much," or "very much") (56).

**TABLE 10.12 COMMUNICATION
WITHIN THE HOME (IN PERCENTAGES)**

|  | VERY INFREQUENT | INFREQUENT | MODERATE | FREQUENT | VERY FREQUENT |
|---|---|---|---|---|---|
| Dropouts | 43 | 38 | 11 | 6 | 2 |
| Graduates | 3 | 17 | 20 | 24 | 36 |

*Source:* L. F. Cervantes. Family background, primary relationships, and the high school dropout. *Journal of Marriage and the Family*, 1965, **5**, 218–233. By permission.

*Note: N* = 300 (150 dropouts, 150 graduates). Hypothesis: There is less intrafamily communication in the families of dropouts than in the family of graduates. *D* = .633; $x^2$ *(2df)* = 87.48, *p* < .001.

There also appeared to be far less communication within the families of dropouts than within those of graduates (see Table 10.12). Furthermore, the families of graduates were far more likely to share leisure-time activities as a family. In addition, "the different climate of happiness in the homes of the dropouts as contrasted with the graduates is startling. Unhappiness is the characteristic of the one group, happiness that of the other" (56, *222*). The families of dropouts also tended to be more isolated socially than those of graduates. Families of dropouts had fewer friends, and such friendships as they had tended to be more superficial. These families tended to view friends simply as people you "can have fun with" or "who will help you." In contrast, families of graduates tended to view friendships more in terms of *reciprocal* assistance and mutual understanding. Further, friends of graduates' families tended to be more stable themselves and more homogeneous in terms of socioeconomic status, region of origin, religion, and occupational aspirations. Similar results were obtained in another study (142) where parental emphasis on the importance of school, together with a willingness to discuss dropping out, appeared to make dropping out less likely.

### Psychological characteristics of dropouts

In several studies, dropouts have emerged as more troubled emotionally, less confident of their own worth, lower in self-esteem, more lacking in a clearly defined self-image and sense of identity, and less likely to have structured values and goals—personal, social, or occupational—than graduates (11, 15, 30, 55, 56, 151, 250). They are more likely to have hostile, angry feelings and to be resentful of authority in any form—"home authority, civil authority, intellectual authority, occupational authority" (55, *192*). Influenced more by frustrations from which they are trying to escape than by longer-term goals toward which they are striving, these adolescents tend to live more for the moment, responding impulsively, planning little, showing little sustained, goal-directed activity, and seeking immediate gratification (11, 55).

In one nationwide study (68), significant differences between male and female dropouts and control groups of students who completed high school, but did not go on to college, were found, even on group paper-and-pencil personality inventories. Among male adolescents, controls scored significantly higher than dropouts on measures of tidiness, calmness, vigor, self-confidence, cultural interests, emotional maturity, and sociability; dropouts scored higher than controls only in impulsiveness, and, to a lesser extent, interest in leadership. Similarly, among female adolescents, controls significantly exceeded dropouts in all of the measures differentiating males, and in social sensitivity as well. On none of the measures did female dropouts score higher than controls.

According to projective tests and interview material, dropouts are more likely to view the world as an unpredictable place, characterized by violence, hostility, strife, cheating, faithlessness, and exploitation of other people (55). In this world, as perceived by the dropouts, longer-term goals are relatively meaningless; plans are likely to go astray or to be doomed from the start. In this approach to life,

> Human relations are characteristically brittle, haphazard, unpremeditated, affectless, and exploitative. . . . Gratitude is a superfluous theme. Fun, pleasure, spontaneity, and emotional upheavals of various types are much in evidence but not as integrated with the superphysical or with life's goals. Our dropout protocols seem more interlaced with the impulse ridden, the nondeferred gratification, the unconventional (from the host culture's viewpoint), the unrealistically romantic, the loosely structured, the shallow, the predestined, the fateful.
> . . . the mind of the dropout seems to exhale feelings of inadequacy, worthlessness, frustration, and failure. A dropout, by that very fact, is more clearly cast in the role of outcast and pariah [55, *192–193*].

### Consequences of dropping out

The Youth in Transition project had as a special focus the goal of distinguishing between the causes and consequences of dropping out of high school. One entire volume (11), focusing on their sample of over 2000 young men studied longitudinally until 1 year after most had graduated from high school, examined this issue. The investigators concluded that ". . . dropping out does not change things a great deal—at least not in ways that are apparent by the time a young man reaches the age of nineteen or twenty" (11, *175*). A subsequent follow-up, 4 years later, did not alter this conclusion (14, 15).

Among the findings in this investigation were that dropouts had lower self-esteem; higher rates of delinquency; higher use of cigarettes, alcohol, and drugs; and greater fears about unemployment. The differences in self-esteem, delinquency, and drug use, however, predated dropping out from school. Increases in self-esteem among dropouts over the 8 years of the study (from tenth grade on) paralleled those seen among young men who completed high school, except in the immediate post-high school period (see Figure 10.9). This result contradicts the common belief that the self-esteem of dropouts suffers as a result of their leaving school. Similarly, differences in delinquency were stable over the years of the study; if anything, the gap between dropouts and high school graduates decreased over the 8 years of the study.

### Dropping out—Problem or symptom?

It should be obvious from these findings that many of the problems that the dropout is likely to encounter after he or she leaves high school—such as higher unemployment rates, more personality problems, lower aspiration levels, and a

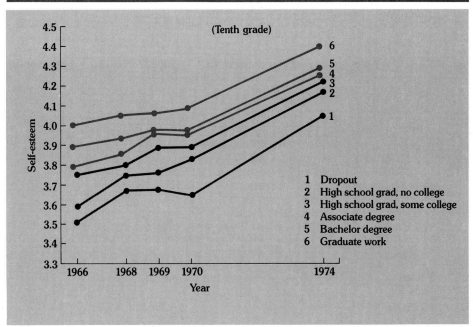

**Figure 10.9** Self-esteem related to educational attainment in young males during the transition from adolescence to young adulthood. (From J. G. Bachman, P. M. O'Malley, and J. Johnston. *Youth in transition, Vol. VI: Adolescence to adulthood—Change and stability in the lives of young men.* Ann Arbor, Mich.: Institute for Social Research, 1978. By permission.)

higher incidence of delinquency—are at least as likely (and probably more likely) to reflect the kinds of problems that led to dropping out in the first place, as they are to result from the act of dropping out itself.

The greatest challenge is not to keep a young person in a school situation that is unrewarding, irrelevant, or destructive, but to ameliorate the conditions that led to dropping out in the first place, beginning as early as possible in the child's life. Indeed, the investigators conclude that about the only negative consequence of dropping out per se is a greater fear of unemployment and a higher actual rate of unemployment. Interestingly, however, when dropouts who were employed were compared with employed peers who had completed high school, it was found that the dropouts did not have worse jobs in terms of status, pay, or job satisfaction. Because this evidence suggests that dropouts can be just as good employees as those with high school diplomas, the authors attribute dropouts' higher rates of unemployment to two factors: (1) lesser ability and/or motivation to work and (2) job discrimination. While acknowledging that the first factor is an important criterion for employment, the authors argue that the second should be addressed, and altered, in our society:

The campaign against dropping out seems based on the assumption that everyone needs at least twelve years of formal education. But the research reported here has led us to question that assumption. We have found that some young men can manage reasonably well on the basis of ten or eleven years of education. Perhaps others would do so if they were not branded as "dropouts."

Certainly there are alternatives to a twelve-year diploma; perhaps one based on ten years would be sufficient. Young people wishing to enter college might spend the years equivalent to grades eleven and twelve in publicly-supported college preparatory academies. Others might enter one-year or two-year vocational training or work-study programs. . . . Still other young people might choose to go directly into the world of work after their tenth-grade graduation—some to return to part-time or full-time education after a year or two or three.

In a world of rapidly changing technology with its emphasis on continuing education and periodic retraining, there is less and less reason to maintain the traditionally sharp boundary between the role of student and the later role of worker. Shortening the prescribed minimum period for full-time uninterrupted schooling might be a positive step toward new patterns of lifetime education in which individuals can choose for themselves among a wide range of "educational life-styles." If such changes would reduce the credential value attached to high school diplomas, all the better. One of the unfortunate side effects of the anti-dropout campaign has been the tendency to confuse education with credentials; any step in the opposite direction could have a salutary effect on our whole educational establishment [11, *181–182*].

## SCHOOLS FOR YOUNGER ADOLESCENTS

We have focused much of our discussion thus far on high schools and the achievement of adolescents at this level. This bias is due primarily to the prevalence of research on high school students, the stereotypic teenagers. Recently, however, greater attention has been drawn to younger or early adolescents (181). Schooling of younger adolescents is more difficult to study, primarily because of the great variability in the kinds of schools. Joan Lipsitz, one major scholar in this area, has identified 34 varieties of schools for young adolescents (182). Some young adolescents are in schools that go through eighth grade (from kindergarten or first grade) and therefore have experiences—in terms of schooling effects—more similar to those of students in elementary schools. A more common kind of school for young adolescents, however, is the junior high school (grades seven and eight, or seven through nine) or, increasingly, middle schools (grades five through seven, five through eight, or six through eight) (2). Junior high schools are more likely to be modeled after high schools, with a primary focus on subject matter, while middle schools have focused more on the specific developmental needs of young adolescents (90).

There is some evidence that the groupings of grades during the early adolescent years affects the nature of adolescent development and the behavior exhibited by young people (35, 36, 240). To some extent, simply changing schools at this age is disruptive. The negative effects of a school transition—for example, from sixth grade in an elementary school to seventh grade in a junior high school—appear to be amplified by a simultaneous transition to pubertal status, when these occur together (209, 240).

In addition, however, there are effects due to the grade levels housed in a single school building. In one recent study (35), all seventh- to ninth-grade students in a school district adding a secondary school were studied before and after the change. The additional school was created by combining grade nine from the junior high with grade ten from the high school, leaving a junior high school of seventh and eighth graders and a high school of juniors and seniors. The influence of older upon younger students was examined in terms of six domains: participation and leadership, substance use, perceptions of school environment, victimization experiences, dating and sexual behavior, and self-evaluation. Both boys and girls were influenced by the presence of older students in their school. Ninth graders were more influenced by being with older students than were seventh- and eighth-grade students. Seventh-grade boys were seldom influenced by older students. Of the six domains within which influence was examined, the students' perceptions of their school environment (measured in terms of the control exercised by adults, the anonymity of students, the extent of concern about being picked on) was the one most negatively affected by the presence of older students. Participation in school activities and substance use were also affected by the presence of older students. For boys only, athletic participation decreased for eighth graders and increased for ninth graders, clearly as a function of a shift in the athletic program to the new school. For boys and girls, substance use decreased among eighth graders and increased among ninth graders with the school change. In addition, younger students were more likely to be victimized (by offers of drugs, thefts, or threats of being beaten) when older students were present. Some aspects of dating and sexual behavior as well as self-evaluations were affected, particularly for seventh-grade girls. Seventh-grade girls dated more but had a lower incidence of intercourse as well as higher self-esteem when the ninth graders were *not* present. The presence of older adolescents always had the effect of increasing the sophistication or precocity of the younger students' behavior.

The National Middle School Association has been particularly interested in creating schools that address the developmental needs of young adolescents. A recent survey of the membership of this organization (59) revealed a desire on the part of at least 90 percent of the respondents for more research on motivations and interests, self-concept, influences of family structure, social factors influencing behavior, how children learn, discipline, moral development, peer influence, social competence, attitudes toward parents and other adults, peers and authority; and involvement with sex, illegal behavior and alcohol, drugs, and tobacco. The same survey (60) revealed a need for research on how to deal with individual differences, how to create a classroom climate that facilitates learning, how to motivate students, interactions between children's aptitudes and teaching networks, and student discipline. Research on effective interpersonal relationships—especially between teacher and child—was also thought to be needed.

It is apparent that teachers of young adolescents are eager for research to help them be more effective. In their eagerness, or perhaps desperation, there is the potential danger of embracing new research prematurely. For example, it has been asserted that the curriculum for young adolescents should not present new material because of the belief that young adolescents cannot learn due to a plateau in brain growth at this age (90, 95, 257). A recent study (219) questions this belief, and the related curricular practice, by presenting evidence that cognitive capacities continue to increase over early adolescence. Any increased learning difficulties during early adolescence may stem more from psychosocial than cognitive change (159).

The National Institute of Education recently commissioned a major effort to identify and examine effective middle-grade schools that foster healthy social development (182). This effort was thought to be crucial because of the numerous problems observed in schools for young adolescents.

> There is no other level of public education for minors that is so poorly defined. Teacher education for this age group is in a state of flux, as are certification standards. Added to this institutional chaos is the personal dismay all too often experienced by teachers who work with this age group, some of whom have been prepared to teach secondary level courses in specific subject areas, with little or no background in child development, and others of whom have been prepared to teach elementary school students, and have few if any areas of academic expertise [182, 2].

Nevertheless, four middle schools were identified as exemplars of effective schools for young adolescents. These schools were all safe and orderly, responsive to the developmental needs of young adolescents, and able to cope with the divisive societal pressures experienced by public schools. The schools had staying power in their communities and their students were completely engaged in learning.

Specific characteristics shared by the four effective schools were: a within-school consensus about their primary purpose, a confidence in their mission, and a clear sense of their place in the overall educational system. Each of the schools had a principal with "a driving vision who imbues decisions and practices with meaning, placing powerful emphasis on why things are done, as well as how" (182, 22). They were practical as well as visionary, showing extensive political savvy and excellent performance. The schools focused on their community nature, with a high level of caring in evidence. While all schools were fairly large, they functioned with units of 100 to 150 students. The climates in these schools were tied to clear reward structures, with several available routes to student success. For example, sports were important in three of the four schools, particularly through intramural programs. In addition, academic excellence was rewarded in all schools, with special programs in two schools for those with specific learning problems. The arts, leadership, decorum, and special events were also rewarded in these schools. As with the students, the teachers received abundant psychological and social rewards. All schools were responsive to their particular social and political milieus; they provided an education wanted and needed by their communities. These schools provide evidence that "contrary to prevalent assumptions, young adolescents need not be experienced by adults as an emotionally and physically assaultive age group to be placed on 'hold' until they 'grow out of it'" (182, 44). These schools were effective in attenuating differences in academic performance and in creating positive environments for social development.

## NEW DIRECTIONS FOR SCHOOLS

As exemplified by the focus of the questions raised by those interested in schools for young adolescents, many educators currently are turning their attention toward identifying "what works." This focus on process is promising, and long overdue. The bulk of the educational research in the decade of the 1970s, particularly the latter part, seemed to suggest that little could be done to create effective schools. This trend in thinking about education coincided with the more general shift in our society away from a belief in the effectiveness of social programs. We have seen, however, that recent studies—such as the study by Rutter and colleagues (231) described earlier—demonstrate that schools can be effective environments for learning and social development, regardless of socioeconomic status. Unfortunately, these studies and other recent promising trends may be too late to influence policy on educational matters.

Indeed, the emphasis for education in the 1980s has clearly shifted. Scott Thompson, executive director of the National Association of Secondary School Principals, said recently: "The theme of the 80's is quality not equality" (206). The recent study of sociologist James Coleman, "Public and Private Schools" (65), is in this same vein, concluding that students in private and parochial high schools learned more than those in public ones. Although the methods and assumptions of this study have been questioned (63, 214, 215), it has nevertheless reinforced the current trend demonstrating a lack of concern for the American ideal of equality of educational opportunity. A shift to voucher systems of financing education, or similarly, providing tax incentives for parents who send their children to private schools, would clearly lead to the demise of public schools. Public schools would be left with those students who were unable to attend elsewhere, because they were either too poor or too inadequately prepared for other schools. This situation would grossly overburden public schools, which are already struggling with increasing demands that they meet a broad variety of needs for the society.

One response that large public school systems have made to these pressures is to offer more diversity among schools in the system. In Chicago, for example, there are a few "academies" that accept students from the entire city but require evidence of specific competencies before granting admission. Such schools are not just a recent phenomenon; the Bronx High School of Science in New York and the former Dunbar High School in the District of Columbia exemplify this long-standing tradition of elite public schools.

Such approaches, however, are unlikely to be the total answer to the ills of today's public schools. A broader problem, as we noted at the beginning of this chapter, is that in recent decades "the nonschool portions of a youth's environment have dwindled in scope and force while the school's portions have increased" (66, 140). In the process, the schools have been assigned an ever-mounting set of responsibilities not only for cognitive development and the development of necessary academic skills, but also for preparing the student for entrance into the work force and for coping independently with the increasingly complex problems of everyday life in our society. In addition, the public seems to expect schools and colleges somehow to solve our most recalcitrant social problems: disenchanted youth, social inequality, unemployables in the work force, and even the breakdown of the community (66). But as a President's Science Advisory Committee panel observed,

> A variety of needs can only be served by a variety of institutions. Up to a point, the variety may be provided within a single comprehensive structure, through internal

elaboration. But there are limits on how far any organization can be asked to stretch and still function effectively, especially when it is vulnerable to a turbulent environment of contradictory and shifting group demands. There are also limits on how comprehensive any educational organization can be without blandness eroding all sense of purpose and enterprise [66, *90-91*].

It may well be that some things are not learned best in the school setting; a major difficulty of schools in handling activities other than academic learning is the position of the young person within the school setting. The student is a dependent, and the school is responsible for guiding his or her development (66). Yet if young people are to develop responsibility and the capacity for independent decision making, "then the responsibility and dependency are in the wrong place. To reorganize a school in such a way that young persons have responsibility and authority appears extremely difficult, because such reorganization is incompatible with the basic custodial function of the school" (66, *142*). Consequently, the panel recommended exploring a number of changes, both in the structure of schools themselves and in the relationship of the schools to other institutions. In the former category, they recommended greater emphasis on curriculum diversity and the development of schools with specialized areas of concentration (e.g., art, science, performing arts, medical services); reductions in school size (see pages 388–392); and greater role diversity for youth in schools (e.g., encouraging involvement and development of responsibility by using adolescents to help in tutoring, teaching, or counseling younger children [42, 43, 66]). In the last category, they recommended bringing young people into work situations sooner (66). This could be done in a variety of ways: alternating periods of work and study; establishing formal programs to give school credit for structured outside work experiences; giving up some school time to permit (and encourage) part-time work; bringing employers and persons actually practicing a variety of trades and professions into the school setting to talk and work with students, and the like.

> A work situation can involve interdependent and collective tasks, experience with others differing in background and in age, and the experience of having others dependent on one's actions. Our general belief is that environments which provide a significant amount of serious and responsible work experience are much more likely to meet these objectives than are the narrower environments of school that most youth find themselves limited to. In addition, such work settings are intended to provide, to a much greater extent than reducing school size, the opportunity for adults outside schools to become enough involved with young persons that they constitute personal resources to whom the young persons can turn in times of stress [66, *147-148*].

As Urie Bronfenbrenner observed, the recent trend toward segregation of the school from the rest of society has been accelerated by the forces of social disorganization, age segregation, the decline of neighborhoods, geographic mobility, and the consequent loss of a sense of community. But when schools become isolated from the community, they become more likely to encourage rather than discourage youthful alienation: "For this reason it is of crucial importance for the welfare and development of school-aged children that schools be reintegrated into the life of the community'' (42, 60). Increased contact with working adults is one way to accomplish this vital goal. We shall have more to say about the importance of work experience for young people—psychologically, socially, and economically—in the following chapter.

## REFERENCES

1. Adkison, J. A. Women in school administration: A review of the research. *Review of Educational Research*, 1981, **51,** 311–343.
2. Alexander, W. M., & George, P. S. *The exemplary middle school.* New York: Holt, Rinehart and Winston, 1981.
3. *The American almanac: The statistical abstract of the United States.* (Bureau of the Census, U.S. Department of Commerce.) New York: Grosset & Dunlap, 1975 (95th ed.).
4. Anastasi, A., & D'Angelo, R. Y. A comparison of Negro and white preschoolers in language development and Goodenough Draw-a-man I.Q. *Journal of Genetic Psychology*, 1952, **81,** 147–165.
5. Anderson, H. H., & Anderson, G. L. Social development. In L. Carmichael (ed.), *Manual of child psychology* (Vol. 1). New York: Wiley, 1954 (2nd ed.).
6. Anderson, K. L. Educational goals of male and female adolescents: The effects of parental characteristics and attitudes. *Youth and Society*, 1980, **12,** 173–188.
7. Argyle, M., & Robinson, P. Two origins of achievement motivation. *British Journal of Social and Clinical Psychology*, 1962, **1,** 107–120.
8. Atkin, J. M. Who will teach in high school? *Daedalus*, 1981, **110,** 91–103.
9. Averch, H., Carroll, S., Donaldson, T., Kiesling, H., & Pincus, J. *How effective is schooling? A critical review of research.* Englewood Cliffs, N.J.: Educational Technology Publications, 1974.
10. Bachman, J. G. *Youth in transition, Vol. II: The impact on family background and intelligence on tenth-grade boys.* Ann Arbor: Institute for Social Research, University of Michigan, 1970.
11. Bachman, J. G., Green, S., & Wirtanen, I. *Dropping out—Problem or symptom.* Ann Arbor: Institute for Social Research, University of Michigan, 1972.
12. Bachman, J. G., Kahn, R. L., Mednick, M. T., Davidson, T. N., & Johnson, L. D. *Youth in transition, Vol. I: Blueprint for a longitudinal study of adolescent boys.* Ann Arbor: Institute for Social Research, University of Michigan, 1967.
13. Bachman, J. G., & O'Malley, P. M. Self-esteem in young men: A longitudinal analysis of the impact of educational and occupational attainment. *Journal of Personality and Social Psychology*, 1977, **35,** 365–380.
14. Bachman, J. G., & O'Malley, P. M. The search for school effects: Some new findings and perspectives. Unpublished manuscript, Institute for Social Research, University of Michigan, 1978.
15. Bachman, J. G., O'Malley, P. M., & Johnston, J. *Youth in transition, Vol. VI: Adolescence to adulthood—change and stability in the lives of young men.* Ann Arbor, Mich.: Institute for Social Research, University of Michigan, 1978.
16. Baird, L. L. Teaching styles: An exploratory study of dimensions and effects. *Journal of Educational Psychology*, 1973, **64,** 15–21.
17. Bandura, A., & Walters, R. H. *Social learning and personality development.* New York: Holt, Rinehart and Winston, 1963.
18. Barker, R. G. Ecology and motivation. In M. R. Jones (ed.), *Nebraska symposium on motivation.* Lincoln: University of Nebraska Press, 1960. Pp. 1–49.
19. Barker, R. G. Ecological units. In R. G. Barker & P. V. Gump (eds.), *Big school, small school.* Stanford, Calif.: Stanford University Press, 1964. Pp. 11–28.
20. Barker, R. G., & Barker, L. S. Structural characteristics. In R. G. Barker & P. V. Gump, *Big school, small school.* Stanford, Calif.: Stanford University Press, 1964. Pp. 41–63.

21. Barton, K., Dielman, T. E., & Cattell, R. B. Child rearing practices and achievements in school. *Journal of Genetic Psychology,* 1974, **124,** 155–165.
22. Baumrind, D. Socialization and instrumental competence in young children. *Young Children,* December 1970, 9–12.
23. Baumrind, D. Current patterns of parental authority. *Developmental Psychology Monographs,* 1971, **4,** No. 1, Part 2.
24. Baumrind, D. Early socialization and adolescent competence. In S. E. Dragastin & G. H. Elder, Jr. (eds.), *Adolescence in the life cycle: Psychological change and social context.* New York: Wiley, 1975. Pp. 117–146.
25. Becker, H. The career of the Chicago public school teacher. *American Sociological Review,* 1952, **17,** 470–476.
26. Bell, G. D. Process in the formation of adolescents' aspirations. *Social Forces,* 1963, **42,** 179–195.
27. Benjamin, R. *Making schools work.* New York: Continuum, 1981.
28. Bennett, S. N. Recent research on teaching: A dream, a belief, and a model. *British Journal of Educational Psychology,* 1978, **48,** 127–147.
29. Berbaum, M. L., & Moreland, R. L. Intellectual development within the family: A new application of the confluence model. *Developmental Psychology,* 1980, **16,** 506–515.
30. Berry, G. L. Self-concept and need factors of inner city high school adolescents and dropouts. *Child Study Journal,* 1974, **4,** 21–31.
31. Bertrand, A. L. School attendance and attainment: Function and dysfunction of school and family social systems. *Social Forces,* 1962, **40,** 228–233.
32. Biemille, L. 18-year decline in aptitude-test scores halted this year, College Board reports. *The Chronicle of Higher Education,* October 7, 1981, 1, 7.
33. Birch, H. G., & Gussow, J. D. *Disadvantaged children: Health, nutrition and school failure.* New York: Grune & Stratton, 1970.
34. Blake, M. T. Factors influencing teacher success. *Dissertation Abstracts,* 1966, **27,** 990.
35. Blyth, D. A., Hill, J. P., & Smyth, C. K. The influence of older adolescents on younger adolescents: Do grade-level arrangements make a difference in behaviors, attitudes, and experiences? *Journal of Early Adolescence,* 1981, **1,** 85–110.
36. Blyth, D. A., Simmons, R. G., & Bush, D. M. The transition into early adolescence: A longitudinal comparison of youth in two educational contexts. *Sociology of Education,* 1978, **51,** 149–162.
37. Booney, M. E. A study of the relation of intelligence, family size, and sex differences with mutual friendships in the primary grades. *Child Development,* 1942, **13,** 79–100.
38. Booney, M. E. Relationships between social success, family size, socioeconomic home background, and intelligence among school children in grades III to V. *Sociometry,* 1944, **7,** 26–39.
39. Bordua, D. J. Educational aspirations and parental stress on college. *Social Forces,* 1960, **38,** 262–269.
40. Bossert, S. T. *Tasks and social relationships in classrooms: A study of instructional organization and its consequences.* New York: Cambridge University Press, 1979.
41. Boyle, R. P. The effect of the high school on students' aspirations. *American Journal of Sociology,* 1966, **131,** 628–639.
42. Bronfenbrenner, U. The origins of alienation. *Scientific American,* August 1974, **231,** 53–61.
43. Bronfenbrenner, U. The challenge of social change to public policy and developmental research. Paper presented at the biennial meeting of the Society for Research in Child Development, Denver, April 2, 1975.
44. Bronfenbrenner, U. *The ecology of human development: Experiments by nature and design.* Cambridge, Mass.: Harvard University Press, 1979.
45. Brookover, W., Beady, C., Flood, P., Schweitzer, J., & Wisenbaker, J. *School social systems and students: Schools can make a difference.* New York: Praeger, 1979.
46. Bryant, B. E. *High school students look at their world.* Columbus, Ohio: Goettler, 1970.

47. Bryant, T. E., et al. *Report to the President from the President's Commission on Mental Health* (Vol. I). Washington, D.C.: U.S. Government Printing Office, 1978.
48. Burton, N. W., & Jones, L. V. Recent trends in achievement levels of black and white youth. *Educational Researcher,* 1982, **11,** 10–17.
49. Calhoun, J. A., Grotberg, E. H., & Rackley, W. R. *The status of children, youth, and families, 1979.* Washington, D.C.: Department of Health and Human Serivces, Office of Human Development Serivces, 1980 (DHHS Publication No. [OHDS] 80-30274).
50. Campbell, W. J. Some effects of high school consolidation. In R. G. Barker & P. V. Gump (eds.), *Big school, small school.* Stanford, Calif.: Stanford University Press, 1964. Pp. 139–153.
51. Carew, J. V., & Lightfoot, S. L. *Beyond bias: Perspectives on classrooms.* Cambridge, Mass.: Harvard University Press, 1979.
52. Carnegie Council on Policy Studies in Higher Education. *Giving youth a better chance: Options for education, work and service.* San Francisco: Jossey-Bass, 1979.
53. Carrino, C. Identifying potential dropouts in the elementary grades. *Dissertation Abstracts,* 1966, **27,** 343.
54. Center for New Schools. Strengthening alternative high schools. *Harvard Educational Review,* 1972, **42,** 313–350.
55. Cervantes, L. F. *The dropout: Causes and cures.* Ann Arbor: University of Michigan Press, 1965.
56. Cervantes, L. F. Family background, primary relationships, and the high school dropout. *Journal of Marriage and the Family,* 1965, **5,** 218–223.
57. Cheyney, A. B. Teachers of the culturally disadvantaged. *Exceptional Children,* 1966, **33,** 83–88.
58. Cicirelli, V. G. The relationship of sibling structure to intellectual abilities and achievement. *Review of Educational Research,* 1978, **48,** 365–379.
59. Clark, D. C., Babich, G., & Burpeau, M. Y. Priorities for research in early adolescent learner characteristics: A report of a national survey. *Journal of Early Adolescence,* 1981, **1,** 385–390.
60. Clark, D. C., Babich, G., & Burpeau, M. Y. Research needs in teacher activities: Results of a national survey. *Journal of Early Adolescence,* 1981, **1,** 391–395.
61. Coleman, J. S. *The adolescent society.* New York: Free Press, 1961.
62. Coleman, J. S. Methods and results in the IEA studies of effects of school on learning. *Review of Educational Research,* 1975, **45,** 335–386.
63. Coleman, J. S. Response to Page and Keith. *Educational Researcher,* 1981, **10,** 18–20.
64. Coleman, J. S., Campbell, E. Q., Hobson, C. J., McPartland, J., Mead, A. M., Weinfeld, F. D., & York, R. L. *Equality of educational opportunity.* Washington, D.C.: U.S. Government Printing Office, 1966.
65. Coleman, J. S., Hoffer, T., & Kilgore, S. *Public and private schools: A report to the National Center for Education Statistics by the National Opinion Research Center.* University of Chicago, March 1981.
66. Coleman, J. S., et al. *Youth: Transition to adulthood.* Report of the Panel on Youth of the President's Science Advisory Committee. Chicago: University of Chicago Press, 1974.
67. Comber, L. C., & Keeves, J. P. *Science education in nineteen countries.* International studies in evaluation, Vol. 1. Stockholm: Almquist & Wiksell, 1973.
68. Combs, J., & Cooley, W. W. Dropouts: In high school and after school. *American Education Research Journal,* 1968, **5,** 343–363.
69. Conant, J. B. *The American high school today.* New York: McGraw-Hill, 1959.
70. Conant, J. B. Social dynamite in our large cities. In *Social dynamite: The report of the conference on unemployed, out-of-school youth in urban areas.* Washington, D.C.: National Committee for Children and Youth, 1961.
71. Conger, J. J. A world they never knew: The family and social change. *Daedalus,* Fall 1971, 1105–1138.

72. Conklin, A. M. Failures of highly intelligent pupils. *Teachers College Contributions to Education,* 1940, No. 792.

73. Coopersmith, S. *The antecedents of self-esteem.* San Francisco: Freeman, 1967.

74. Costin, F., & Grush, J. E. Personality correlates of teacher-student behavior in the college classroom. *Journal of Educational Psychology,* 1973, **65,** 35–44.

75. Crain, R. L., Mahard, R. E., & Narot, R. *Making desegregation work: How schools create social climates.* The Johns Hopkins University Center for Social Organization of Schools, manuscript, 1980.

76. Cravioto, J., et al. (eds.). *Early malnutrition and mental development: Symposium of the Swedish Nutrition Foundation XII.* Stockholm: Almquist & Wiksell, 1974.

77. Davies, M., & Kandel, D. B. Parental and peer influences on adolescents' educational plans: Some further evidence. *American Journal of Sociology,* 1981, **87,** 363–387.

78. Deutsch, M. Minority group and class status as related to social and personality factors in scholastic achievement. *Monographs of the Society for Applied Anthropology,* 1960, **2.**

79. Deutsch, M. The disadvantaged child and the learning process. In A. H. Passow (ed.), *Education in depressed areas.* New York: Columbia University Press, 1963. Pp. 163–179.

80. Dillon, H. *Early school leavers: A major educational problem.* Publication No. 401, National Child Labor Committee, 1949.

81. Division for Youth. *The school dropout problem: Rochester* (Part 1). State of New York, May 1962. Pp. 14–16.

82. Dobbing, J., & Smart, J. L. Vulnerability of the developing brain and behavior. *British Medical Bulletin,* 1974, **30,** 164–168.

83. Domino, G. Differential predication of academic achievement in conforming to independent settings. *Journal of Educational Psychology,* 1968, **59,** 256–260.

84. Douvan, E., & Adelson, J. The psychodynamics of social mobility in adolescent boys. *Journal of Abnormal and Social Psychology,* 1958, **56,** 31–34.

85. Dowaliby, F. J., & Schumer, H. Teacher-centered versus student-centered mode of college classroom instruction as related to manifest anxiety. *Proceedings, 79th Annual Convention, American Psychological Association,* 1971.

86. Drews, E. M., & Teahan, J. E. Parents' attitudes and academic achievement. *Journal of Clinical Psychology,* 1957, **13,** 328–332.

87. Duncan, O. D., Featherman, D. L., & Duncan, B. *Socioeconomic background and achievement.* New York: Seminar, 1972.

88. Dunkin, M. J., & Biddle, B. J. *The study of teaching.* New York: Holt, Rinehart and Winston, 1974.

89. Edmonds, R. Some schools work and more can. *Social Policy,* 1979, **9,** 28–32.

90. Eichorn, D. H. The school. In M. Johnson (ed.), *Toward adolescence: The middle school years.* 79th Yearbook of the National Society for the Study of Education. Chicago: University of Chicago Press, 1980.

91. Elliott, D. S., Voss, H. L., & Wendling, A. Capable dropouts and the social milieu of the high school. *Journal of Educational Research,* 1966, **60,** 180–186.

92. Elliott, D. S., Voss, H. L., & Wendling, A. Dropout and the social milieu of the high school: A preliminary analysis. *American Journal of Orthopsychiatry,* 1966, **36,** 808–817.

93. Elmore, P. B., & LaPointe, K. A. Effect of teacher sex, student sex, and teacher warmth on the evaluation of college instructors. *Journal of Educational Psychology,* 1975, **67,** 368–374.

94. Emmerich, J. J. The influence of parents and peers on choices made by adolescents. *Journal of Youth and Adolescence,* 1978, **7,** 175–180.

95. Epstein, H. T. Growth spurts during brain development: Implications for educational policy and practice. In J. S. Chall & A. F. Mirsky (eds.), *Education and the brain.* 77th Yearbook of the National Society for the Study of Education. Chicago: University of Chicago Press, 1978.

96. Epstein, J. L. *Secondary school environments and student outcomes: A review and annotated bibliography.* Baltimore: The Johns Hopkins University Center for Social Organization of Schools, 1981.

97. Epstein, J. L., & McPartland, J. M. *The effects of open school organization on student outcomes.* Report 194. Baltimore: The Johns Hopkins University Center for Social Organization of Schools, 1975.

98. Epstein, J. L., & McPartland, J. M. Authority structures. In H. Walberg (ed.), *Educational environments and effects: Evaluation and policy.* Berkeley: McCutchan, 1979.

99. Fennema, E. Sex-related differences in mathematics achievement: Where and why. In L. H. Fox, L. Brody, & D. Tobin (eds.), *Women and the mathematical mystique.* Baltimore: The Johns Hopkins University Press, 1980. Pp. 76–93.

100. Fine, J. T. Sex similarities in behavior in a seventh grade classroom. *Journal of Early Adolescence,* 1981, **1,** 233–243.

101. Floud, J. E., Halsey, A. H., & Martin, F. M. (eds.). *Social class and educational opportunity.* London: Heinemann, 1956. Pp. 93–95, 107–108.

102. Foley, W. J. Teaching disadvantaged pupils. In J. M. Beck & R. W. Saxe (eds.), *Teaching the culturally disadvantaged pupil.* Springfield, Ill.: Thomas, 1965. Pp. 89–107.

103. Gadway, C., & Wilson, H. A. *Functional literacy—basic reading performance: Technical summary.* Denver: The Education Commission of the States, 1975.

104. Gage, N. L. Desirable behaviors of teachers. *Urban Education,* 1965, **1,** 85–95.

105. Gallup, G. Gallup youth survey. *Denver Post,* December 18, 1977.

106. Garbarino, J. Some thoughts on school size and its effects on adolescent development. *Journal of Youth and Adolescence,* 1980, **9,** 19–31.

107. Garbarino, J., & Asp, C. E. *Successful schools and competent students.* Lexington: Mass.: Heath, 1981.

108. Gawronski, D. A., & Mathis, C. Differences between over-achieving, normal-achieving, and under-achieving high-school students. *Psychology in the Schools,* 1965, **2,** 152–155.

109. Gergen, K. J. *The concept of self.* New York: Holt, Rinehart and Winston, 1971.

110. Goldenberg, I. Social class differences in teacher attitudes toward children. *Child Development,* 1971, **42,** 1637–1640.

111. Good, T. L. *Teacher expectations, teacher behavior, student perceptions and student behavior: A decade of research.* Paper presented at the annual meeting of the American Educational Research Association, Toronto, 1980.

112. Gordon, E. W., & Wilkerson, D. A. *Compensatory education for the disadvantaged. Programs and practices: Preschool through college.* New York: College Entrance Examination Board, 1966.

113. Gottlieb, D. Teaching and students: The views of Negro and white teachers. *Sociological Education,* 1964, **37,** 345–353.

114. Gowan, J. C. Dynamics of the underachievement of gifted students. *Exceptional Children,* 1957, **24,** 98–101.

115. Greenberg, J. W., Gerver, J. M., Chall, J., & Davidson, H. H. Attitudes of children from a deprived environment toward achievement-related concepts. *Journal of Educational Research,* 1965, **59,** 57–62.

116. Grimes, J. W., & Allinsmith, W. Compulsivity, anxiety and school achievement. *Merrill-Palmer Quarterly,* 1961, **7,** 247–269.

117. Gross, B., & Gross, R. (eds.). *Radical school reform.* New York: Simon & Schuster, 1969.

118. Gross, R. (ed.). *The teacher and the taught: Education in theory and practice from Plato to James B. Conant.* New York: Dell, 1963.

119. Gross, R., & Osterman, P. *High school.* New York: Simon & Schuster, 1971.

120. Grotberg, E. H., et al. *The status of children, youth and families, 1979.* Washington, D.C.: U.S. Government Printing Office, 1980 (DHHS Publication N. [OHOS] 80-30274).

121. Gump, P. V. *Big schools, small schools.* Moravia, N.Y.: Chronicle Guidance Publications, 1966.
122. Haller, A. O., & Butterworth, C. E. Peer influences on levels of occupational and educational aspiration. *Social Forces,* 1960, **38,** 289–295.
123. Hamilton, S. F. Contexts for adolescent development: The interaction of school, home, peer group, and workplace. Paper presented at the Conference on Adolescence and Secondary Schooling, Madison, Wis., November 7–10, 1981.
124. Handel, A. Attitudinal orientations and cognitive functioning among adolescents. *Developmental Psychology,* 1975, **11,** 667–675.
125. Hart, F. W. Teachers and teaching. New York: Macmillan, 1934.
126. Hartlage, L. C., & Schlagel, J. Teacher characteristics associated with student classroom behaviors. *Journal of Psychology,* 1974, **86,** 191–195.
127. Hauser, R. M., Sewell, W. H., & Alwin, D. F. High school effects on achievement. In W. H. Sewell, R. M. Hauser, & D. L. Featherman (eds.), *Schooling and achievement in American society.* New York: Academic Press, 1976.
128. Havighurst, R. J., & Breese, F. H. Relations between ability and social status in a midwestern community. III. Primary mental abilities. *Journal of Educational Psychology,* 1947, **38,** 241–247.
129. Havighurst, R. J., & Dreyer, P. H. (eds.). *Youth: The seventy-fourth yearbook of the National Society for the Study of Education.* Chicago: University of Chicago Press, 1975.
130. Havighurst, R. J., & Janke, L. L. Relations between ability and social status in a midwestern community. I. Ten-year-old children. *Journal of Educational Psychology,* 1944, **35,** 357–368.
131. Heber, R. Rehabilitation of families at risk for mental retardation. *American Education,* 1971, **7,** 3ff.
132. Hechinger, F. M. About education: a warning on the decline of quality in teacher training. *New York Times,* June 16, 1981, 17.
133. Heil, L. M., & Washburne, C. Characteristics of teachers related to children's progress. *Journal of Teacher Education,* 1961, **12,** 401–406.
134. Henssenstamm, F. K. Activism in adolescence: An analysis of the high school underground press. *Adolescence,* 1971, **6,** 317–336.
135. Herrell, J. M. Galatea in the classroom: Student expectations affect teacher behavior. *Proceedings, 79th Annual Convention, American Psychological Association,* 1971.
136. Hoffman, L. W. Early childhood experiences and women's achievement motives. *Journal of Social Issues,* 1972, **28,** 129–155.
137. Hoffman, L. W. Effects of maternal employment on the child—A review of the research. *Developmental Psychology,* 1974, **10,** 204–228.
138. Hoffman, L. W. Work, family, and socialization of the child. In R. D. Parke, et al. (eds.), *The review of child development research, Vol. 7: The family and interdisciplinary perspective.* Chicago: University of Chicago Press, in press.
139. Hoffman, L. W., Rosen, S., & Lippitt, R. Parental coerciveness, child autonomy and child's role at school. *Sociometry,* 1960, **23,** 15–21.
140. Holland, J. L. Creative and academic performance among talented adolescents. *Journal of Educational Psychology,* 1961, **52,** 136–147.
141. Horrall, B. M. Academic performance and personality adjustments of highly intelligent college students. *Genetic Psychology Monographs,* 1957, **55,** 3–38.
142. Howell, F. M., & Frese, W. Early transition into adult roles: Some antecedents and outcomes. *American Educational Research Journal,* 1982, **19,** 51–73.
143. Hyman, H. H., Wright, C. R., & Reed, J. S. *The enduring effects of education.* Chicago: University of Chicago Press, 1975.
144. Isaacson, R. L., McKeachie, W. J., & Milholland, J. E. Correlation of teacher personality variables and student ratings. *Journal of Educational Psychology,* 1963, **54,** 110–117.

145. Jencks, C. S., & Brown, M. D. Effects of high schools on their students. *Harvard Educational Review*, 1975, **45,** 273–324.
146. Jencks, C. S., Smith, M., Acland, H., Bane, M. J., Cohen, D., Gintis, H., Heyns, B., & Michelson, S. *Inequality: A reassessment of the effects of family and schooling in America.* New York: Basic Books, 1972.
147. Jersild, A. T. *The psychology of adolescence.* New York: Macmillan, 1963 (2nd ed.).
148. Johnson, J., & Bachman, J. G. *The transition from high school to work: The work attitudes and early occupational experiences of young men.* Ann Arbor, Mich.: Institute for Social Research, University of Michigan, 1973.
149. Johnson, S. S. *Update on education: A digest of the National Assessment of Education Progress.* Denver: The Education Commission of the States, 1975.
150. Jones, E. S. The probation student: What he is like and what can be done about it. *Journal of Educational Research*, 1955, **49,** 93–102.
151. Jones, W. M. The impact on society of youths who drop out or are undereducated. *Educational Leadership*, 1977, **34,** 411–416.
152. Justman, J. Academic aptitude and reading test scores of disadvantaged children showing varying degress of mobility. *Journal of Educational Review*, 1965, **2,** 151–155.
153. Kagan, J. The child's sex-role classification of school objects. *Child Development*, 1964, **35,** 1051–1056.
154. Kahl, J. A. Educational and ocupational aspirations of "common-man" boys. *Harvard Educational Review*, 1953, **23,** 186–203.
155. Kamens, D. H. Student status aspirations: A research note on the effects of colleges. *Youth and Society*, 1979, **11,** 83–92.
156. Kandel, D. B. Homophily, selection, and socialization in adolescent friendships. *American Journal of Sociology*, 1978, **84,** 427–436.
157. Kandel, D. B. Similarity in real life adolescent friendship pairs. *Journal of Personality and Social Psychology*, 1978, **36,** 306–312.
158. Kandel, D. B., & Lesser, G. S. Parental and peer influences on educational plans of adolescents. *American Sociological Review*, 1969, **34,** 213–223.
159. Kavrell, S. M., & Petersen, A. C. Patterns of achievement in early adolescence. In M. L. Maehr & M. W. Steinkamp (eds.), *Women and science.* Greenwich, Conn.: JAI Press, in press.
160. Keach, E. T., Jr., Fulton, R., & Gardner, W. E. (eds.). *Education and social crisis: Perspectives on teaching disadvantaged youth.* New York: Wiley, 1967.
161. Kelly, J. A., & Worrell, L. The joint and differential perceived contribution of parents to adolescents' cognitive functioning. *Developmental Psychology*, 1977, **13,** 282–283.
162. Kerber, A., & Bommarito, B. (eds.). *The schools and the urban crisis.* New York: Holt, Rinehart and Winston, 1966.
163. Kettering Foundation. *The adolescent, other citizens, and their high schools. Report of Task Force '74.* New York: McGraw-Hill, 1975.
164. Kifer, E. Relationships between academic achievement and personality characteristics: A quasi-longitudinal study. *American Educational Research Journal*, 1975, **12,** 191–210.
165. Kimball, B. The sentence-completion technique in a study of scholastic achievement. *Journal of Consulting Psychology*, 1952, **16,** 353–358.
166. Kirst, M. W. Loss of support for public secondary schools: Some causes and solutions. *Daedalus*, 1981, **110,** 45–68.
167. Kosier, K. P., & DeVault, M. V. Effects of teacher personality on pupil personality. *Psychology in the Schools*, 1967, **4,** 40–44.
168. Kozberg, G. Left out kids in a left out school. *Harvard Graduate School of Education Association Bulletin*, 1980, **25,** 24–26.
169. Kozol, J. *Death at an early age.* Boston: Houghton Mifflin, 1967.
170. Krauss, I. Sources of educational aspirations among working-class youth. *American Sociological Development*, 1964, **29,** 867–879.

171. Kriesberg, L. Rearing children for educational achievement in fatherless families. *Journal of Marriage and the Family,* 1967, **29,** 289–301.

172. Lao, R. C. Differential factors affecting male and female academic performance in high school. *The Journal of Psychology,* 1980, **104,** 119–127.

173. Leacock, E. B. *Teaching and learning in city schools.* New York: Basic Books, 1969.

174. Lefevre, C. Inner-city school—As the children see it. *Elementary School Journal,* 1966, **67,** 8–15.

175. Lerner, R. M., & Busch-Rossnagel, N. A. (eds.). *Individuals as producers of their development: A life-span perspective.* New York: Academic Press, 1981.

176. Levine, M., Wesolowski, J. C., & Corbett, F. J. Pupil turnover and academic performance in an inner city elementary school. *Psychology in the Schools,* 1966, **3,** 153–158.

177. Lewin, K., Lippitt, R., & White, R. K. Patterns of aggressive behavior in experimentally created "social climates." *Journal of Social Psychology,* 1939, **10,** 271–299.

178. Lewin, R. Starved brains. *Psychology Today,* 1975, **9,** 29–33.

179. Lichter, S. O., Rapien, E. B., Seibert, F. M., & Slansky, M. A. *The drop-outs.* New York: Free Press, 1962.

180. Lipset, S. M., & Bendix, R. *Social mobility in industrial society.* Berkeley: University of California Press, 1959.

181. Lipsitz, J. *Growing up forgotten.* Lexington, Mass.: Lexington Books, 1977.

182. Lipsitz, J. Successful schools for young adolescents: A report on a report. Paper presented at the annual meeting of the American Educational Research Association, New York City, March 21, 1982.

183. Little, J. K. Occupations of non-college youth. *American Education Research Journal,* 1967, **4,** 147–153.

184. Livingston, A. Key to the dropout problem: The elementary school. *Elementary School Journal,* 1959, **59,** 267–270.

185. Maccoby, E., & Jacklin, C., *The psychology of sex differences.* Stanford, Calif.: Stanford University Press, 1974.

186. Markus, G. B., & Zajonc, R. B. Family configuration and intellectual development: A simulation. *Behavioral Science,* 1977, **22,** 137–142.

187. McAndrew, G. L. The high-school principal: Man in the middle. *Daedalus,* 1981, **110,** 105–118.

188. McCandless, B. *Adolescents: Behavior and development.* New York: Holt, Rinehart and Winston, 1970.

189. McClelland, D. C. *The achieving society.* New York: Van Nostrand, 1961.

190. McDill, E. L., & Coleman, J. S. Family and peer influence in college plans of high school students. *Sociology of Education,* 1965, **38,** 112–116.

191. McDill, E. L., & Rigsby, L. *Structure and process in secondary schools: The academic impact of educational climates.* Baltimore: Johns Hopkins University Press, 1973.

192. McKeachie, W. J., & Lin, Y. G. Sex differences in student response to college teachers: Teacher warmth and teacher sex. *American Educational Research Journal,* 1971, **8,** 221–226.

193. Minuchin, P. P., & Shapiro, E. K. The school as a context for social development. In P. H. Mussen (ed.), *Handbook of child psychology* (Vol. 3, *Social development,* E. M. Hetherington, ed.). New York: Wiley, in press (4th ed.).

194. Mitchell, J. V. Goal-setting behavior as a function of self-acceptance, over- and under-achievement, and related personality variables. *Journal of Educational Psychology,* 1959, **50,** 93–104.

195. Morrow, W. R., & Wilson, R. C. Family relations of bright high-achieving and underachieving high school boys. *Child Development,* 1961, **32,** 501–510.

196. Mussen, P. H., Conger, J. J., & Kagan, J. *Child development and personality.* New York: Harper & Row, 1974 (4th ed.).

197. Namenwirth, J. Z. Failing in New Haven: An analysis of high school graduates and dropouts. *Social Forces,* 1969, **48,** 23.

198. National Assessment of Educational Progress. *Changes in mathematical achievement 1973–78.* Washington, D.C.: National Institute of Education, 1979.
199. National Assessment of Educational Progress. *Reading, thinking, and writing: Results from the 1979–80 national assessment of reading and literature.* Denver: Education Commission of the States, 1981.
200. *National college-bound seniors, 1981.* New York: College Board, 1981.
201. National Institute on Education. *Violent schools—safe schools* (2 vols.). The safe school study report to the Congress. Washington, D.C.: National Institute of Education, 1978.
202. National Panel on High School and Adolescent Education. *The education of adolescents. Final report.* Washington, D.C.: U.S. Government Printing Office, 1976.
203. National Science Foundation, Office of Program Integration, Directorate for Science Education. *What are the needs in precollege science, mathematics, and social science education? Views from the field.* SE 80-9. Washington, D.C.: U.S. Government Printing Office, 1980.
204. *Newsweek,* November 10, 1975.
205. *The New York Times,* October 4, 1975.
206. *The New York Times,* The high schools: New shapes for the 80's by E. B. Fiske. April 26, 1981, 12, 28.
207. Norman, J., & Harris, M. W. *The private life of the American teenager.* New York: Rawson, Wade, 1981.
208. Norman, R. D. The interpersonal values of achieving and nonachieving gifted children. *Journal of Psychology,* 1966, **64,** 49–57.
209. Nottelman, E. D. Childrens' adjustment in school: The interaction of physical maturity and school transition. Presented at the annual meeting of the American Educational Research Association, March 20, 1982, New York City.
210. Offer, D. *The psychological world of the teen-ager: A study of normal adolescent boys.* New York: Basic Books, 1969.
211. Office of Education. *The urban high school reform initiative. Final report.* Washington, D.C.: U.S. Government Printing Office, 1979.
212. Ogbu, J. *The next generation: An ethnography of education in an urban neighborhood.* New York: Academic Press, 1974.
213. Olson, G. M., Miller, L. K., Hale, G. A., & Stevenson, H. W. Long-term correlates of children's learning and problem-solving behavior. *Journal of Educational Psychology,* 1968, **59,** 227–232.
214. Page, E. B. The media, technical analysis, and the data feast: A response to Coleman. *Educational Researcher,* 1981, **10,** 21–23.
215. Page, E. B., & Keith, T. Z. Effects of U.S. private schools: A technical analysis of two recent claims. *Educational Researcher,* 1981, **10,** 7–17.
216. Parsons, J. E., Kaczala, C. M., & Meece, J. L. Socialization of achievement attitudes and beliefs: Classroom influences. *Child Development,* 1982, **53,** 322–339.
217. Passow, A. H. (ed.). *Developing programs for the educationally disadvantaged.* New York: Teachers College Press, 1968.
218. Pavenstedt, E. A comparison of the child-rearing environment of upper-lower- and very low lower-class families. *American Journal of Orthopsychiatry,* 1965, **35,** 89–98.
219. Petersen, A. C., & Kavrell, S. M. Cognition during early adolescence. Unpublished manuscript, 1982.
220. Price, J. R., & Magoon, A. J. Predictors of college student ratings of instructors. *Proceedings, 79th Annual Convention, American Psychological Association,* 1971.
221. Purnick, J. Rise in crime against teachers is termed a chilling fact of life. *New York Times,* December 15, 1980, 1, 13.
222. Purves, A. C. *Literature education in ten countries.* International studies in evaluation (Vol. 2). Stockholm: Almquist & Wiksell, 1973.
223. Ravitch, D. We have the schools we deserve. *Rocky Mountain News,* May 17, 1981, 79–80.

224. Rickard, G. The relationship between parental behavior and children's achievement behavior. Unpublished doctoral dissertation. Harvard University, 1954.

225. Ringness, T. A. *Differences in attitudes toward self and others of academically successful and non-successful ninth-grade boys of superior intelligence.* Madison: University of Wisconsin, 1963.

226. Ringness, T. A. Identification patterns, motivation, and school achievement of bright junior high school boys. *Journal of Educational Psychology,* 1967, **58,** 93–102.

227. Rosenberg, M. *Society and the adolescent self-image.* Princeton: Princeton University Press, 1965.

228. Rosenberg, M., & Simmons, R. G. *Black and white self-esteem: The urban school child.* Washington, D.C.: Rose Monograph Series, American Sociological Association, 1971.

229. Rosenthal, R., & Jacobsen, L. *Pygmalion in the classroom: Teacher expectation and pupils' intellectual development.* New York: Holt, Rinehart and Winston, 1968.

230. Russell, S. Learning sex roles in the high school. *Interchange,* 1979–80, **10,** 57–66.

231. Rutter, M., Maughan, B., Mortimore, P., & Ouston, J. *Fifteen thousand hours: Secondary schools and their effects on children.* Cambridge, Mass.: Harvard University Press, 1979.

232. Scanlon, J. *Self-reported health behavior and attitudes of youths 12–17 years.* Washington, D.C.: Department of Health, Education, and Welfare, Publication No. (HRA) 75-1629 (Data from National Health Survey, Series 11, No. 147), 1975.

233. Schmuck, R. Some aspects of classroom social climate. *Psychology in the School,* 1966, **3,** 59–65.

234. Scribner, S., & Cole, M. Cognitive consequences of formal and informal education. *Science,* 1973, **182,** 553–559.

235. Sewell, W. H., Hauser, R. M., & Featherman, D. L. (eds.). *Schooling and achievement in American society.* New York: Academic Press, 1976.

236. Sexton, P. *The feminized male: Classrooms, white collars and the decline of manliness.* New York: Random House, 1969.

237. Shaw, M. E., & White, D. L. The relationship between child-parent identification and academic underachievement. *Journal of Clinical Psychology,* 1965, **21,** 10–13.

238. Sherman, B. R., & Blackburn, R. T. Personal characteristics and teaching effectiveness of college faculty. *Journal of Educational Psychology,* 1975, **67,** 124–131.

239. Silberman, C. E. *Crisis in the classroom: The remaking of American education.* New York: Random House, 1970.

240. Simmons, R. G., Blyth, D. A., Van Cleave, E. F. & Bush, D. M. Entry into early adolescence: The impact of school structure, puberty, and early dating on self-esteem. *American Sociological Review,* 1979, **44,** 948–967.

241. Simpson, R. L. Parental influence, anticipatory socialization, and social mobility. *American Sociological Review,* 1962, **27,** 517–522.

242. Smith, T. E. Adolescent agreement with perceived maternal and paternal educational goals. *Journal of Marriage and the Family,* 1981, **43,** 85–93.

243. Speedie, S., Hobson, S., Feldhusen, J., & Thurston, J. Evaluation of a battery of noncognitive variables as long-range predictors of academic achievement. *Proceedings, 79th Annual Convention, American Psychological Association,* 1971, 517–518.

244. Stein, Z., et al. Nutrition and mental performance. *Science,* 1972, **178,** 708.

245. Stodolsky, S. S., & Lesser, G. Learning patterns in the disadvantaged. *Harvard Educational Review,* 1967, **37,** 546–593.

246. Tanner, J. M. Physical growth. In P. H. Mussen (ed.), *Carmichael's manual of child psychology* (Vol. I). New York: Wiley, 1970 (3rd ed.).

247. Taylor, R. G. Personality traits and discrepant achievement: A review. *Journal of Counseling Psychology,* 1964, **11,** 76–82.

248. Templin, M. C. Norms on screening tests for articulation for ages three through eight. *Journal of Speech and Hearing Disorders,* 1953, **8,** 323–331.

249. Thomas, D. R. Oral language, sentence structure and vocabulary of kindergarten children living in low socioeconomic urban areas. *Dissertation Abstracts,* 1962, **23,** 101.

250. Thornburg, H. D. An investigation among minority group potential dropouts during their freshman year in high school. In H. D. Thornburg (ed.), *School learning and instruction: Readings.* Monterey, Calif.: Brooks/Cole, 1973.

251. Thorndike, R. L. *Reading comprehension education in fifteen countries.* International studies in evaluation (Vol. 3). Stockholm: Almquist & Wiksell, 1973.

252. Tibbets, J. R. The role of parent-child relationships in the achievement of high school pupils. *Dissertation Abstracts,* 1955, **15,** 232.

253. *Time,* March 31, 1975.

254. *Time,* June 16, 1980, 54–63.

255. Toby, J. Orientation to education as a factor in the school maladjustment of lower-class children. *Social Forces,* 1957, **35,** 259–266.

256. Todd, D. M. Contrasting adaptations to the social environment of a high school: Implications of a case study of helping behavior in two adolescent subcultures. In J. G. Kelly (ed.), *Adolescent boys in high school.* Hillsdale, N.J.: Lawrence Erlbaum, 1979.

257. Toepfer, C. F., & Mirani, J. V. School-based research. In M. Johnson (ed.), *Toward adolescence: The middle school years.* Seventy-ninth Yearbook of the National Society for the Study of Education, Part I. Chicago: University of Chicago Press, 1980. Pp. 269–281.

258. Turner, C., & Thrasher, M. *School size does make a difference.* San Diego, Calif.: Institute for Educational Management, 1970.

259. Urich, T., & Batchelder, R. Turning an urban high school around. *Phi Delta Kappan,* 1979, **61,** 206–209.

260. U.S. Bureau of the Census, Current Population Reports, Series P-20, No. 363. *Population profile of the United States: 1980.* Washington, D.C.: U.S. Government Printing Office, 1981.

261. U.S. Bureau of the Census, Current Population Reports, Series P-23, No. 114. *Characteristics of American children and youth, 1980.* Washington, D.C.: U.S. Government Printing Office, 1982.

262. U.S. Department of Commerce, Bureau of the Census, *Statistical abstract of the United States.* Washington, D.C.: U.S. Government Printing Office, 1981 (101st ed.).

263. U.S. Department of Education, National Center for Education Statistics. *The American high school: A statistical overview.* Washington, D.C.: U.S. Government Printing Office, 1980.

264. U.S. Department of Education, National Center for Education Statistics. *The condition of education: Statistical report.* Washington, D.C.: U.S. Government Printing Office, 1979.

265. U.S. Department of Education, National Center for Education Statistics. *The condition of education: Statistical report.* Washington, D.C.: U.S. Government Printing Office, 1980.

266. U.S. Department of Health, Education and Welfare. *Toward a social report.* Washington, D.C.: U.S. Government Printing Office, 1969. Pp. 66–70.

267. U.S. President's Science Advisory Committee: Panel on Youth. *Youth: Transition to adulthood.* Chicago: University of Chicago Press, 1974.

268. Vosk, J. S. Study of Negro children with learning difficulties at the outset of their school careers. *American Journal of Orthopsychiatry,* 1966, **36,** 32–40.

269. Voss, H. L., Wendling, A., & Elliott, D. S. Some types of high-school dropouts. *Journal of Educational Research,* 1966, **59,** 363–368.

270. Walsh, A. *Self-concepts of bright boys with learning difficulties.* New York: Columbia University Press, 1956.

271. Weiner, I. B. *Psychological disturbance in adolescence.* New York: Wiley, 1970.

272. Welsh, W. W., Anderson, R. E., & Harris, L. J. The effects of schooling on mathematics achievement. *American Educational Research Journal,* 1982, **19,** 145–153.

273. Whiteman, M., & Deutsch, M. Social disadvantage as related to intellective class, race, and psychological development. In M. Deutsch, I. Katz, & A. Jensen (eds.), *Social*

*class, race, and psychological development.* New York: Holt, Rinehart and Winston, 1968.

274. Wicker, A. W. Undermanning, performances, and students' subjective experiences in behavior settings of large and small high schools. *Journal of Personality and Social Psychology,* 1968, **10,** 255–261.

275. Willems, E. P. Sense of obligation to high school activities as related to school size and marginality of student. *Child Development,* 1967, **38,** 1247–1260.

276. Williams, D. A. Why public schools fail. *Newsweek,* April 20, 1981, 62–65.

277. Williams, D. A. Teachers are in trouble. *Newsweek,* April 27, 1981, 78–84.

278. Wirtz, W., et al. *Report of the advisory panel on the scholastic aptitute test score decline.* Princeton, N.J.: College Board, 1977.

279. Yando, R., Zigler, E., & Gates, M. The influence of Negro and white teachers rated as effective or noneffective on the performance of Negro and white lower-class children. *Developmental Psychology,* 1971, **5,** 290–299.

280. Yee, A. H. Source and direction of causal influence in teacher-pupil relationships. *Journal of Educational Psychology,* 1968, **59,** 275–282.

281. Zajonc, R. B., Markus, H., & Markus, G. B. This birth order puzzle. *Journal of Personality and Social Psychology,* 1979, **37,** 1325–1341.

Vocational choice in a changing world

CHAPTER 11

# Vocational choice in a changing world

*T*he problem of deciding on and preparing for a vocation represents one of the major developmental tasks of adolescence. Indeed, it has been asserted that adolescence can end only with "practical experience in the working world" (168). Prior to this time, the vocational goals of adolescents tend to have a highly theoretical quality (55). With such experience, however, young people begin to learn whether they can, in fact, achieve a workable resolution of the inevitable conflicts between their ideals, values, and goals, and the sometimes harsh realities of adult life. In the process, they begin to reassess the adult world, as well as their own assets and limitations, and tend to become more accepting of both (55).

Opportunities for adolescents to have constructive and appropriate work experiences can provide them a source of purpose and responsibility, help to give them a feeling of meaningful participation in the broader society, and reduce the communication barrier between adults and young people (28, 40, 79, 86). Such work experiences may also provide young people with a chance to learn about vocational possibilities, to develop their interests, and to test their developing skills and talents against the demands of the so-called real world. "If a child is to become a responsible person, he not only must be exposed to adults engaged in demanding tasks, but must himself participate in such tasks" (28, *60*). In our age-segregated, technological society, young people are seldom given such opportunities for interaction with working adults, presumably because "it just isn't practical." However, this need not be the case.

For example, in one school in Chicago, formerly characterized by a high delinquency rate, students spend half of each day studying academic subjects at their own pace, earning credits when they complete a prescribed amount of work. During the other half, they earn money working in business-funded training projects, such as renovating buildings in the community. Among the results have been a high rate of school attendance and elimination of vandalism (167). A limited number of programs around the country are currently providing high school (and college) students with well-planned exposure to the kinds of work actually involved in a variety of health careers, in industry and business, in the arts, and in local government and social service agencies (41, 79, 86, 146, 167).

As we noted in Chapter 10, a major recommendation of the recent youth panel of the President's Science Advisory Committee was that young people be given greater opportunity to become involved in work experiences (41). Among their specific proposals are vocational education programs available to young people ages 16 and over, involving half a day of work and half a day of school; alternation for a period of time, such as a semester, between school and work (a program already in effect at the college level in some institutions); provision for specialized continuing education in some work settings, including academic credits; and greater opportunities for public service participation by young people, for periods up to a year (41).

If such programs are to be of greatest value in helping adolescents to make the transition to the adult world of work, the experiences provided should be meaningful and relevant to their future goals (76, 79). Recent studies (74, 75, 78, 146, 147) suggest that the kinds of jobs most frequently available to adolescents attending school, such as working at drive-in fast food outlets, washing cars, or packing groceries, may promote a greater understanding of money matters, an increased work orientation, and a somewhat greater feeling of independence, but they do little to encourage future educational and vocational aspirations and planning (73, 74, 145, 147). Indeed, for some young people, especially those who work long hours and are poorer students to begin with, such employment may interfere significantly with school performance (73, 144), and for those in highly stressful or hazardous jobs, with health (73, 77). In addition, although under favorable conditions, work experience may help an adolescent to interact more effectively with others, including employers (74, 78, 146), in many of the more frequent kinds of adolescent jobs, opportunities for learning from, or modeling oneself after, a successful adult mentor are actually rather limited (73, 74, 79). Furthermore, in some shoddy or unchallenging work settings, adolescents may become more cynical about the intrinsic rewards side of work and more accepting of marginal business practices (79, 147, 149). Finally, while having had such jobs during adolescence appears to have a positive effect on adult employability for high school dropouts, how much difference it makes in the case of full-time students is still unclear (73, 77, 79, 151, 168, 172).

Obviously, adolescents entering the world of work need adequate protection and safeguards. This was, of course, the purpose of the child labor laws instituted earlier in this century, and, for some, such as the children of some migrant farm workers, stricter enforcement of such laws is still necessary. But it appears that for many adolescents, some of these laws are unduly restrictive. "The evidence indicates that children [and adolescents] acquire the capacity to cope with difficult situations when they have an opportunity to take on consequential responsibilities in relation to others and are held accountable for them" (28, *60*).

As we shall see, a more widespread problem in today's world than protecting young people from unsafe working conditions is that of being able to assure them that meaningful employment opportunities will be available when they are ready for—and need—full-time participation in the work force. In times like the present (1982), when unemployment among young people actively seeking work exceeds 20 percent for all teenagers (and involves nearly one in every two black teenagers), providing such assurances requires considerable temerity, despite political rhetoric to the contrary. Even in more prosperous periods, teenage unemployment in the

United States considerably exceeded that for adults by a wide margin (see pages 482–486).

It is clear that the problem of planning for a vocation represents one of the critical developmental tasks of adolescence. The extent and the kinds of pressure exerted may vary with social class, sex, and ethnic group status, as well as with a number of other factors.

## THE PSYCHOLOGICAL SIGNIFICANCE OF WORK

In our society, choice of a vocation and subsequent participation in it may help to crystallize and reinforce an adolescent's self-concept (23, 34, 156, 181). Indeed, for most people, young and old alike, their vocational identity forms an important part of their overall sense of identity (56, 114). Consequently, it is not surprising that having a job that society values—and doing it well—enhances self-esteem and aids in the development of an increasingly secure, stable sense of identity; conversely, being given an unmistakable, if ambiguously stated, message by society that, in essence, one is not needed and that meaningful employment is not available fosters self-doubt, resentment, and a loss of self-esteem, and may increase the likelihood of identity confusion or even—as in some cases of delinquency or "dropping out"—a negative identity (56; see page 81).

A very important aspect of most people's working lives—and one not readily available to them elsewhere—is the fact that "working gives them a feeling of being tied into the larger system of society, of having something to do, of having a purpose in life" (121). In an investigation in which men were asked, "If by some chance you inherited enough money to live comfortably without working, do you think you would work anyway or not?'' the great majority (80 percent) answered that they would indeed continue to work. Many stated that they would ''feel lost'' if they did not work, ''go crazy with idleness,'' and ''not know what to do'' with their time. Such responses indicated to the investigators that many adults work to ward off the twin threats of loneliness and isolation (117). In 1980, American high school seniors were asked, ''If you were to get enough money to live as comfortably as you'd like for the rest of your life, would you want to work?'' More than 82 percent stated that they would want to work (12).

More recent research (67, 68, 69, 94) indicates that women who are employed outside the home are generally more likely to indicate overall satisfaction with their lives than those employed full time in the role of housewife and mother. Among both white-collar and blue-collar working women, employment may provide additional evidence of self-worth and a sense of challenge.

At the same time, it should be recognized that work that is unrewarding, frustrating, or extremely stressful, or that leads to failure, can have a negative effect on a man's or woman's self-concept, as well as creating stresses in other areas. Thus, ''when maternal employment involves excessive strain from the hassle of juggling two roles, the effects may be disruptive for the family and the child,'' as well as the mother herself (94).

In addition to helping generally to crystallize and strengthen the young person's sense of identity and feelings of self-esteem, choice of a particular vocation may offer adolescents socially approved ways of achieving direct or indirect satisfaction for motives that may have been strong, but not gratified in the course of their earlier development. For example, motives such as dominance over others, aggression, nurturance, and, occasionally, sexual curiosity can be at least partially gratified in one or another occupation (e.g., army officer, police officer, social worker, physician, or nurse).

### *Vocational identity in other cultures*

In many earlier societies, both literate and nonliterate, the problem of vocational choice for an adolescent was considerably simpler than in our own rapidly changing culture. These societies typically supported fewer vocations, and the adolescent was already likely to be familiar with most of them either through observation or apprenticeship. The Arapesh youth, for example, was able gradually to take over from his father responsibility for tilling the family garden as he entered adolescence.

Even in earlier periods in our own society, the rural or small-town youth was far more likely to have observed adults pursuing the occupations he or she was considering entering, and to have opportunities for early apprenticeships, either informal and occasional (e.g., summer or after-school work) or formal and sustained (e.g., blacksmith's or jeweler's apprentice). Small-town youth, even today, may have at least some opportunity for such experiences, in contrast to the present situation in our major cities and sprawling suburbs, where many adolescents have only a vague conception of the work that their own and their friends' fathers and mothers actually

do. This may help to explain the finding (39) that boys in small towns in this country are more likely to follow in their fathers' vocational footsteps than are city or suburban youth.

Furthermore, some, but by no means all, simpler societies lacked the anxiety-producing involvement in extreme competitiveness and concern with social status that has characterized American culture. Among the Zuñi Indians, for example, the aggressive emphasis of our society on winning at all cost, of being number one, would be considered unseemly, if not bizarre. In Zuñi culture, considerable effort traditionally has been made to avoid any appearance of individual superiority or the exercise of power over others; and positions of leadership have been accepted reluctantly, and then only temporarily (21). For the Zuñi, a rational and rewarding existence, in work as in all other areas of life and interpersonal relationships, is built around cooperation rather than competition. One problem that some urbanized minority-group members in the United States (e.g., some rural Indian and Spanish-speaking peoples in the Southwest) encountered was an unfamiliarity with the complex ways of relentlessly competitive, urban American culture. They were also likely to reflect an unfamiliarity with, and frequently a genuine disapproval of, the basic values underlying these ways. For many of these in-migrants, the typical urban "rat race" was perceived as just that (27, 46, 107, 131).

Although in the late 1960s and early 1970s a significant minority of disenchanted young people—typically middle-class and well-educated—began to question seriously what they perceived as a one-sided preoccupation with these values in a society with pressing human needs, in the early 1980s the tide appears to have turned, and concern with "making it" in an increasingly competitive world once again is gaining ascendency, while concern for the welfare of others and for society generally is diminishing (see pages 470–476). In brief, aggressive competition, pressure, and individual recognition continue to play a major role in many, if not most, work settings in American society.

## *VOCATIONAL PROBLEMS OF CONTEMPORARY ADOLESCENTS*

The typical contemporary adolescent in our society does not share the vocational advantages of youth in some earlier or simpler cultures. On the one hand, he or she knows that many important satisfactions will depend upon the ability to find and keep a job—including the chances for full emancipation from parents, for acceptance as an equal by peers, and for getting married and maintaining a home. On the other hand, despite the importance of vocational adjustment for American adolescents, they typically have only a vague idea of the nature of the many different kinds of jobs available in the society. They do not know which they would be able to do successfully and would enjoy doing, the prior training required for a specific job, or the present or future demands for workers in these various occupations.

This problem, rather than becoming easier, is becoming increasingly difficult as our entire society grows more complex, more specialized, and more technologically oriented. The *Dictionary of Occupational Titles* lists more than 47,000 different occupations. It appears safe to state that many of these are totally unfamiliar not only to contemporary adolescents and their parents, but to most school and vocational counselors as well. Furthermore, the kinds of skills society requires are changing ever more rapidly, as new technologies are developed. With the growth of automation, there is less and less room for the unskilled or semiskilled worker; prior education and training are becoming increasingly necessary for admission to the world of work. Since the early 1900s the number of professional jobs has doubled. In contrast, only about 5 percent of today's jobs require an unskilled worker (165, 166).

In addition, as machines take on more of the jobs formerly performed by people, there is a significant movement away from production and into service occupations. We shall have more to say later about some of these critical problems and their implications for today's adolescents, including socioeconomically deprived youth. For the present, we only wish to emphasize the increasing difficulties faced by most adolescents today in planning for their vocational futures.

As adolescents leave childhood behind and the time when they must support themselves approaches, they are likely to spend more of their time thinking about vocational goals. They also become progressively more realistic about these goals.

Three distinguishable periods in the maturation of vocational choice have been suggested by Eli Ginzberg and his colleagues: the fantasy period, the tentative period, and the realistic period (25, 65, 66, 126). In early and middle childhood, occupations are likely to be selected that seem active and exciting, such as cowboy, astronaut, firefighter, nurse, and explorer. These choices are emotional, not practical: They are made within the child's world, not in terms of the actual world in which the adolescent will eventually function (65, 126).

Beginning with preadolescence, however, there is a progression into the tentative period. This period may be subdivided into four stages: interest, capacities, values, and what has been called transition. At the beginning of the tentative period, the influence of adolescents' interests predominates; however, as they mature, they begin to assess their capacity for actually performing the jobs in which they are interested. Still later, they attempt to integrate interests and capacities into a broader, gradually emerging value system.

At this juncture, adolescents are ready for the transition to the period of realistic choice, somewhere around age 17 or 18. Decisions made during this period can have increasingly important consequences for the young person's future and the career options open to him or her. Consequently, there is greater pressure on young people at this time to reassess their aspirational level, their needs and interests, their actual or potential skills and abilities, and the specific requirements of jobs that hold promise of being consonant with their needs, interests, and talents. On this basis, future educational and vocational decisions can be made.

Ginzberg formerly felt that the realistic period ended and vocational stability was completed prior to about age 25 (26, 64). Perhaps reflecting changes in society as a whole, he now believes that there is no fixed cutoff point, and that "occupational choice is a lifelong process of decision-making in which the individual seeks to find the optimal fit between his career preparation and goals and the realities of the world of work" (164, *171*). In brief, as circumstances change, as job experience changes, and as the person himself or herself changes over the years, new choices may be made, though frequently not free of cost—financial, social, or personal.

Empirical research supports the notion of a steady but gradual maturation of the average young person's vocational thinking during the adolescent years (126). Whereas the younger child is not likely to be influenced very much by the social status of a preferred occupation, as he or she grows older, occupations of marked prestige in the adult world begin to be preferred. Finally, as adulthood approaches, young people are likely to settle on some occupation that represents a realistic reconciliation between what they would like to do and what they think they might actually be able to do (25, 26, 66, 126).

As the young person's vocational interests become progressively more realistic and less influenced by glamour and excitement, they also become more stable. For example, the older the adolescent, the less changeable the vocational interests become (as measured by vocational interest tests repeated after a given interval of time) (26, 35, 120). By late adolescence, vocational interest tends to become fairly stable, though changes may still occur (26).

Although adolescents' vocational interests reflect increasing stability and realism, there is considerable evidence that they cannot simply be left to their own devices in coping with vocational problems. In a society as complex as ours, in which the actual requirements of most jobs and their availability in the labor market are not matters of common knowledge, young people clearly need help. Unfortunately, however, the availability of truly knowledgeable, skilled assistance is extremely limited. In our culture, the young person's vocational interests usually develop in a rather unsystematic fashion, guided by such influences as parental desires, relationships with parents, suggestions of school counselors (who are frequently poorly informed), accidental contact with various occupations, and the kinds of jobs friends are going into. Class- and sex-typed standards also play a role, as we shall see in succeeding sections.

## SUBCULTURAL INFLUENCES ON VOCATIONAL CHOICE

Two broad subcultural influences affect vocational goals differentially and are important enough to merit special consideration—social-class and sex-group membership. Each will be discussed in turn.

### Socioeconomic factors and vocational goals

Social-class membership influences vocational goals in a variety of ways. For one thing, it helps to determine the kinds of occupations with which the young person will be familiar, and hence be likely to consider in formulating occupational aims. In addition, it plays an important role in determining the social acceptability (i.e., the reward value) of a given occupation to the young person and to his or her peers. Certain types of occupations are considered appropriate to the members of a particular social class, others inappropriate. The individual who deviates from class expectancies for occupational choice is likely to be subjected to anxiety-producing disapproval from peers, particularly if this deviation is in the direction of jobs associated with lower-class status.

The very young upper-class child who wants to be an ice cream vendor or truck driver may be indulged or even encouraged. After the attainment of adolescence, however, when the problem of vocational choice becomes a serious one with practical implications, the child's parents are not likely to find such notions amusing. Choices of lower-status occupations run counter to the parents' ideas about appropriate behavior for a member of their social class, and consequently are likely to be discouraged (124).

If the reader harbors any doubts that this indeed is the case, just observe the reactions of many otherwise tolerant and reasonably flexible upper- and upper-middle-class parents to the announcement by an adolescent daughter that she intends to raise vegetables and take in sewing on a communal farm, or by a son that he intends to live frugally by taking part-time laboring jobs or driving a cab in order to devote as much time as possible to painting or writing poetry. Parents may also fear that such choices will lead to general social disapproval both of their child and of themselves. Furthermore, when the economic rewards of the occupation selected are meager, parents may fear that the child will not be able to live in the same kind of neighborhood as other members of his or her social class, or to afford the same social, recreational, and educational advantages.

Conversely, aspirations toward higher-social-status occupations may also lead to social disapproval (particularly if they are flaunted) because such aspirations may be viewed as a threat by other members of the individual's social class. In this case, however, the disapproval is likely not to be as strong and, in the adolescent's view, may be more than outweighed by the prospect of increased rewards associated with higher-class status. Actually, most young people aspire to jobs with a somewhat higher socioeconomic status than those of their parents (25, 26, 105).

The relation of social-class membership to vocational aspiration was clearly demonstrated in an investigation (108) of all graduating seniors in Wisconsin's public and private high schools. Students were asked to state the occupations that they hoped eventually to enter. Their choices were then assigned "prestige scores." It was found that subjects in the lower third of the student population in socioeconomic status aspired to high-prestige occupations significantly less often than would be expected by chance; conversely, students in the upper third aspired to such occupations significantly more often than would be expected. Furthermore, the later actual occupational attainments of students of lower socioeconomic status were close to their expectations (see Table 11.1).

Several hypotheses have been offered to account for social-class differences in vocational goals. One is that there are differences in the evaluation of the relative values assigned by adolescents to various occupations, and that these differences account largely for social-class differences in vocational goals (33). Other theorists, however, have argued that both middle-class and working-class youth agree on the relative desirability and prestige of various occupations, and that differences in goals stem not primarily from values, but from class-associated perceptions of differences in opportunities and general life chances (148). Although many adolescents may be somewhat unrealistic about their vocational goals, they nevertheless possess some awareness of practical obstacles that may modify their vocational aspirations, and these are certainly affected by social-class status. A lower-class girl whose parents are unable to help or uninterested in helping her to go to college is less likely to aspire to be a doctor than one whose parents encourage such a vocational choice and who are in a position to help her. Similarly, a boy whose parents expect him to go to work upon completion of the ninth grade is not likely to spend much time contemplating the idea of becoming an engineer (152).

In addition to limiting the adolescent's opportunity for training in a particular occupation, social-class factors may also influence the chances of obtaining some jobs, even if he or she is qualified. Persons in a particular social class tend to pick others from the same social class as their colleagues and successors, although they often do this without conscious awareness. An employer may say that a person from another social class does not have the right sort of personality for a particular job, when he or she means that the person does not have the same sets of class-learned social traits as others in that position.

To a certain extent, such attitudes may be justified in that people with similar social backgrounds may find it easier to deal with one another in the job situation. But it appears that the importance of socially derived personality characteristics is often exaggerated by employers. This may be attributable in part to their need to maintain their own status as members of a particular social class. Somewhat similar arguments may also be used, consciously or not, to justify racial, ethnic, or sex-related discrimination, despite the fact that substantial numbers of minority-group individuals—and women—are currently doing well in previously nearly all-white male occupations and professions (116).

**TABLE 11.1 CHARACTERISTICS OF
GRADUATES IN HIGH- AND LOW-PRESTIGE OCCUPATIONS**

| CHARACTERISTICS | HIGH PRESTIGE | | | LOW PRESTIGE | | |
|---|---|---|---|---|---|---|
| | (1) % | (2) % | (3) DIFF. | (1) % | (2) % | (3) DIFF. |
| **1. Size of community** | | | | | | |
| Counties with cities: | | | | | | |
| Not over 10,000 | 38 | 30 | −8 | 38 | 48 | +10 |
| 10,000–24,999 | 7 | 7 | 0 | 7 | 8 | +1 |
| 25,000–49,999 | 22 | 22 | 0 | 22 | 22 | 0 |
| Metropolitan areas | 33 | 41 | +8 | 33 | 22 | −11 |
| **2. Socioeconomic status** | | | | | | |
| Low $\frac{1}{3}$ | 33 | 20 | −13 | 33 | 40 | +7 |
| Middle $\frac{1}{3}$ | 34 | 33 | +11 | 34 | 40 | +6 |
| High $\frac{1}{3}$ | 33 | 47 | +14 | 33 | 20 | −13 |
| **3. Father's occupation** | | | | | | |
| Farming | 22 | 15 | −7 | 22 | 35 | +13 |
| Unskilled | 39 | 35 | −4 | 39 | 42 | +3 |
| Skilled | 10 | 10 | 0 | 10 | 9 | −1 |
| White collar | 20 | 25 | +5 | 20 | 11 | −9 |
| Professional | 9 | 15 | +6 | 9 | 3 | −6 |
| **4. Father's education** | | | | | | |
| No high school | 46 | 34 | −12 | 46 | 58 | +12 |
| Some high school | 16 | 13 | −3 | 16 | 17 | +1 |
| High-school graduate | 26 | 32 | +6 | 26 | 19 | −7 |
| Some college | 12 | 21 | +9 | 12 | 6 | −6 |
| **5. Scholastic aptitude** | | | | | | |
| Low $\frac{1}{2}$ | 52 | 32 | −20 | 52 | 67 | +15 |
| High $\frac{1}{2}$ | 48 | 68 | +20 | 48 | 33 | −15 |
| **6. High school achievement** | | | | | | |
| Low $\frac{1}{2}$ | 62 | 41 | −21 | 62 | 77 | +15 |
| High $\frac{1}{2}$ | 38 | 59 | +21 | 38 | 23 | −15 |
| **7. Level of education** | | | | | | |
| High school only | 43 | 18 | −25 | 43 | 76 | +33 |
| Vocational school | 16 | 14 | −2 | 16 | 13 | −3 |
| Some college | 41 | 68 | +27 | 41 | 11 | −30 |

*Source:* J. K. Little. The occupations of non-college youth. *American Educational Research Journal,* 1967, **4,** 147–153. Copyright by American Educational Research Association, Washington, D.C. By permission.

*Note:* Column (1), percentage of all graduates in sample; column (2), percentage of all graduates who attained high- or low prestige occupations; column (3), difference and direction of difference.

However, if these trends toward greater diversity continue, such stereotyped attitudes should become more difficult to defend; when, for example, more than one-third of accountants are women—as is currently the case—it becomes harder to defend the notion that "somehow or other," accounting "just doesn't suit" women (164). The greatest danger, particularly in the case of minorities, is that such penetration of additional areas of the job market—and consequently the number of suc-cessful occupational models that are available—will reach a premature plateau. This is already happening in some professional occupations, such as medicine, and with current drastic reductions in federal, state, and private student aid, the situation is likely to get worse, at least in the near term.

***The concept of value stretch*** Rodman introduced a concept of what he called *value stretch,* asserting that "the lower-class person, without abandoning the general values of society, develops an alternative set of values. Without abandoning the values placed upon success . . . he stretches the values so that lesser degrees of success also become desirable (133, *209*). In the stretched value system there is a "low degree of commitment to all values within the range, including the dominant, middle-class values" (133, *209*). The alternative values help the lower-class person to adjust to his or her deprived circumstances.

In a test of this concept, 71 working-class and 73 middle-class male high school seniors were asked to describe the desirability of two sets of occupations on a seven-point scale (33). The first set consisted of such high-prestige positions as lawyer, factory owner, and educator; a second set included such medium-prestige positions as police officer, machine operator, and bookkeeper. Students were then asked to estimate the relative probability of their actually ending up in one group or the other, under various conditions (e.g., with or without a college education). The results indicated that students from both middle- and working-class backgrounds preferred the set of high-prestige positions to those of medium prestige, but middle-class students ranked high-prestige occupations higher and medium-prestige occupations lower than working-class students did (see Table 11.2). It appears that mid-dle-class students have strong preferences for high-prestige occupations, whereas working-class students are more flexible or less immediately concerned about their occupational futures.

With respect to probable job outcome, middle-class students perceived them-selves as more likely than working-class students actually to achieve high-prestige occupations. Incidentally, both groups also viewed college as increasing the chances of a high-prestige job; however, working-class students perceived college as less likely to ensure such a result, and they showed only a slight preference for college over work as an immediate post-high school activity. In contrast, middle-class stu-dents showed a strong preference for college.

Working-class students, perceiving high-prestige occupations as less accessible to them, tend to protect themselves from possible disappointment by placing less value on high-prestige positions and more value on medium-prestige positions (33, 34). Nevertheless, like their middle-class peers, they still tend to view high-prestige positions as more desirable, though the differences are not nearly so wide as in the case of middle-class students.

***The growing underclass*** In contrast to the vocational outlooks of both these middle-class and working-class students is that of a growing *underclass*—individuals who in effect have been, and see themselves, as excluded from participa-tion in "the system" (see pages 601–603). The desperately poor, largely minority,

**TABLE 11.2 DESIRABILITY RATINGS OF
SETS OF OCCUPATIONS BY SOCIAL CLASS (MEANS)**

| | SOCIAL CLASS | | | |
| SETS OF OCCUPATIONS | WORKING (N = 71) | MIDDLE (N = 73) | t | p |
|---|---|---|---|---|
| High prestige | 3.01 | 2.29 | 4.09 | <.01 |
| Medium prestige | 3.49 | 4.30 | 3.90 | <.01 |
| t | 2.12 | 17.60 | | |
| p | <.05 | <.01 | | >.01 |

Source: F. G. Caro. Social class and attitudes of youth relevant for the realization of adult goals. *Social Forces*, 1966, **44**, 495. By permission.
Note: 1 = high desirable; 7 = highly undesirable.

young person, living in the heart of a socially disorganized, crime-ridden inner city who sees that the great majority of his or her peers are out of work—with virtually no prospects of future employment—is more likely either to have no sustainable vocational hopes, or, more rarely, to have highly unrealistic aspirations. And the fact that the size of this group has grown steadily since the early fifties is hardly encouraging.

> Distrust of education, meaningless social reward systems, lack of recognition for intellectual promise, the absence of effective occupational role models in the home environment, and poor school and guidance facilities have been typical conditions with which disadvantaged children and adolescents have had to contend. For many, these have been factors too difficult to circumvent and which, when combined, have militated powerfully against the prospects for adequate career development. The consequences are to be seen in the behavior of those boys and girls who may hold negative self-images as potential workers and who lack realistic pictures of the world of work [26, *511*].

In many cases, these young people appear unable to undertake long-range planning, look for unstable short-term rewards, and "fail to comprehend the conventional work etiquette that employers appear to expect from those seeking work" (26, *511*). But even if these young people were better prepared to enter the world of work, their prospects would still be poor. As the *Wall Street Journal* recently commented about the situation of many unemployed black teenagers living in the inner cities, "new jobs keep emerging farther from inner-city areas" (112, *40*). And with the current efforts to reduce or eliminate federally sponsored youth training and job programs, future prospects appear dimmer still: In the words of Vernon Jordan, recent president of the National Urban League, the situation today "verges on the brink of disaster" (112, *40*).

### Women and work: "The subtle revolution"
One of the most dramatic and significant changes in American society since the end of World War II has been the precipitous rise in the number of women entering the job market. More young women are working prior to marriage, delaying mar-

**TABLE 11.3 MARRIED, SEPARATED, AND DIVORCED WOMEN: LABOR FORCE STATUS, BY PRESENCE AND AGE OF CHILDREN: 1960 TO 1980 (IN PERCENT)**

| ITEM | PARTICIPATION RATE[a] | | | |
| --- | --- | --- | --- | --- |
| | 1960 | 1970 | 1975 | 1980 |
| *Married, husband present, total* | 30.5 | 40.8 | 44.4 | 50.2 |
| No children under 18 | 34.7 | 42.2 | 43.9 | 46.1 |
| Children 6–17 yr only | 39.0 | 49.2 | 52.3 | 61.8 |
| Children under 6 yr | 18.6 | 30.3 | 36.6 | 45.0 |
| *Separated, total* | (NA) | 52.3 | 54.8 | 59.4 |
| No children under 18 | (NA) | 52.3 | 56.4 | 58.7 |
| Children 6–17 yr only | (NA) | 60.6 | 59.0 | 66.4 |
| Children under 6 yr | (NA) | 45.4 | 49.1 | 51.8 |
| *Divorced, total* | (NA) | 70.9 | 72.1 | 74.5 |
| No children under 18 | (NA) | 67.7 | 69.9 | 71.4 |
| Children 6–17 yr only | (NA) | 82.4 | 80.1 | 82.3 |
| Children under 6 yr | (NA) | 63.3 | 65.6 | 68.0 |

riage longer, and returning to work sooner and in ever greater numbers following the birth of children (see Table 11.3). In 1947, only one-third of all women over age 16 were employed outside the home; by 1980 that figure had risen to just over half (60 percent for those aged 18–64). And by 1990, it is estimated that two out of every three married women, and—somewhat surprisingly—three out of every four married women with children living at home will be in the job market (143). "The stereotype of a wife as someone who stays home to look after children will fit only about one quarter of American wives" (45, *1*).

Although a majority of women are still entering traditionally female (and frequently more poorly paid) occupations, more young women are seeking and gaining entrance into jobs, both professional and nonprofessional, that previously were largely male preserves (see pages 485–491), and insisting on equal pay for equal work. And more of them are registering effective protests, both inside and outside the courts, when either of these demands is denied, although, regardless of job type or level, women are still paid about 60 percent of what men receive.

The reasons for these profound social changes are both economic and social. They include: a sharply declining birth rate, increased employment opportunities and higher salaries for women, a family's desire to keep up with inflation by having two wage earners, and changing social and sex roles (22). In a recent national survey (84), the attitudes of high school seniors toward various working arrangements be-

| | UNEMPLOYMENT RATE[b] | | |
|---|---|---|---|
| 1960 | 1970 | 1975 | 1980 |
| 5.4 | 4.8 | 8.5 | 5.2 |
| 4.8 | 3.2 | 7.0 | 4.5 |
| 4.9 | 4.7 | 7.2 | 4.3 |
| 7.8 | 7.8 | 13.9 | 8.0 |
| (NA) | 6.9 | 14.8 | 9.7 |
| (NA) | 4.2 | 10.4 | 8.2 |
| (NA) | 5.9 | 12.9 | 10.3 |
| (NA) | 13.3 | 23.7 | 12.0 |
| (NA) | 5.2 | 8.4 | 6.3 |
| (NA) | 4.7 | 7.2 | 4.5 |
| (NA) | 6.5 | 9.1 | 6.5 |
| (NA) | 5.2 | 10.4 | 13.2 |

*Source:* U.S. Bureau of Labor Statistics, 1982; and U.S. Department of Commerce, Bureau of the Census, *Statistical abstract of the United States, 1981.* Washington, D.C.: U.S. Government Printing Office, 1981 (102nd ed.).

*Note:* NA = Not available.

[a] Percent of women in each specific category in the labor force.

[b] Unemployed as a percent of civilian labor force in specified group.

tween husband and wife were investigated. For couples without children, the most widely preferred working arrangements are those in which the husband is employed full-time and the wife is employed either full-time or half-time—with slightly more females preferring that both partners work full-time and slightly more males preferring that the wife work only half-time. Only 12 percent of the males and 5 percent of the females viewed as desirable the traditional pattern of the husband employed full-time and the wife not employed outside the home. (Except for a very small minority, neither males nor females considered a reversal of this traditional sex-role pattern desirable, or even acceptable.)

The existence of preschool children changes the picture dramatically, however. Under this circumstance, the most preferred arrangement is for the husband to work full-time while the wife remains at home; indeed only 7 percent consider it unacceptable. In contrast, 70 percent considered any arrangement in which the wife works full-time unacceptable. While only 12 percent think it desirable for the wife with young children to work half-time if the husband is working, most (especially females) feel they could at least accept this latter arrangement.

Interestingly, regardless of the particular pattern of husband-wife working arrangements, both males and females show the greatest preference for an equal division of labor in child care, although many consider a somewhat greater proportion of female care acceptable, particularly where the male is working full-time.

The results of this study reflect an interesting mixture of equalitarianism and traditionalism among today's high school seniors. Although in the case of childless couples, both males and females prefer to have the wife work part- or full-time, and although both also believe in sharing child care (and other household duties), where young children are involved there is strong opposition to the wife working full-time—a view shared by both males and females. (Unfortunately, this study did not include attitudes toward wives working where children are of school age or older, although it seems likely that a wife working under these circumstances would be considered more acceptable or desirable.)

In addition, although for childless wives, full-time, half-time, or no outside employment are considered at least acceptable by over 75 percent of seniors (these options are reduced to half-time or no outside employment for women with pre-school children), in the case of males, only full-time employment, regardless of the presence or absence of children, is considered acceptable by a majority of both male and female seniors. In the final analysis, despite a significant liberalization regarding male and female roles in marriage, it appears that for the majority of young people ultimate responsibility for the financial stability of the family still appears to rest more with the husband, and ultimate responsibility for child care more with the wife (although further changes may well occur as the number of women working continues to grow).

It is probably at least partly for this reason that, with a growing number of exceptions, adolescent girls as a group, regardless of social-class status, still tend to set their vocational sights lower than boys, and fewer have a long-term career commitment to vocational goals (61, 62, 89, 109).

***Sex differences in vocational goals*** Despite large increases in women's participation in the labor force, the rise of the women's movement, and decreases in sex-role stereotyping, members of both sexes still tend to have relatively traditional, sex-related occupational aspirations. Thus, the most common career choice for adolescent boys remains that of skilled worker (e.g., carpenter, electrician, mechanic, tool and die worker); for girls, the most frequent choices are still office worker, nurse, or other health service provider, and teacher—although the last has declined in popularity in the last few years as a result of a teacher surplus (61, 62). At the college-entry level, more young women than men are planning to enter such occupations as social worker, laboratory technician, physical therapist, or artist (6, 8). Although the percentages of adolescent girls and young women aspiring to such traditionally male-oriented occupations as business executive, physician, engineer, lawyer, pilot, or telephone line worker have increased dramatically in the past dozen years or so (in some cases tenfold or more), they still are clearly in the minority (6, 8).

At the same time, *more* girls than boys currently choose nontraditional jobs; that is, more girls than boys choose jobs traditionally filled by the opposite sex (8, 115). This appears due partly to the greater economic and other rewards associated with many traditionally male occupations, partly to the greater number and variety of traditionally male jobs in our society, and partly to fewer inhibitions on the part of girls in aspiring to an occupation that is nontraditional for one's own sex.

What determines these sex-related differences in vocational goals? Obviously, a variety of factors play a part, including patterns of sex-role socialization, job availability, and the demands of the labor market. Even among high school students, and even where age and socioeconomic status are controlled, their job experiences provide "a harbinger of things to come": "Girls are less likely to have had steady paid work, typically even lower hourly wages, and to work fewer hours per week" (75). As is the case for adult employment, hourly wages of adolescents are related positively to the degree to which the individual's job classification is dominated by males. Furthermore, combining work with child-rearing can present additional problems (particularly with children in infancy and early childhood) (5, 58, 94, 161). Domestic responsibilities keep significant numbers of women at home, at least temporarily, or limit them to part-time employment.

***Family values and vocational goals*** As noted recently by a number of critics, vocational theorists have tended to ignore the role of values regarding family life and parenthood in vocational orientation—at least in part because these values appear to be related less strongly to the vocational aspirations and behavior of males than to those of females (58, 94, 161). Several recent studies indicate that the occupational aspirations of young women are importantly related to their views about marriage and parenthood (5, 161)—considerably more so than in the case of males (5).

Young women with high-status occupational expectations, typically in full-time careers and often in traditionally male fields, are more likely to have less traditional sex-role attitudes (5). If they are among the more than 90 percent planning to marry, they are more likely than those without such high-status expectations to plan to marry later, to have relatively fewer children, and to work while their children are young (5, 94, 161). Although most want to be involved with both a career *and* child-rearing, they tend to be somewhat more oriented toward a job than toward children, and they are somewhat less likely to view having children and having "someone to rely on" as important needs or satisfactions in deciding to marry (5, 161).

Other studies have shown that female adolescents and youth planning to enter nontraditional careers typically score higher on measures of academic ability (particularly in the physical and biological sciences and in mathematics) and have higher grades (5, 36, 88, 94, 115, 161). They are also likely to be more independent and assertive, and more concerned with exhibiting competence (87, 91, 92, 94). As we shall see in the next section of this chapter, they are also more likely to have working mothers—especially mothers who have a positive orientation toward working (17, 40, 89, 94).

In contrast, the minority of young women planning full-time careers as housewives and mothers tend to strongly endorse traditional values with respect to occupational and domestic roles of men and women, and to have more traditional perceptions of male and female behavior generally (5, 160, 161). They also plan to marry younger and have more children, have lower educational aspirations, and view children and "having someone to rely on" as important family values (5, 94, 160, 161). Occupying a middle ground between these two extremes are adolescents who plan to stay at home while their children are young, but work before having children and when their children are older. On most variables (e.g., desired family size, relative importance of children and jobs, occupational and domestic values, sex-role attitudes), their scores fall between those of full-time homemakers and the high-status career seekers. Not surprisingly, perhaps, these young women are more likely to have relatively traditional occupational expectations (5, 160, 161).

Of considerable interest is the fact that a substantial percentage of high school girls, particularly middle-class girls, are uncertain about how they are going to coordinate job and child-rearing roles (5, 160, 161). In one representative study (5), senior high school girls were asked whether they planned to work outside the home while their children were young. As in other studies (12, 84, 143), approximately 9 percent said it was not at all likely, and another 13.5 percent said it was very likely; however, nearly 60 percent were about equally divided between the categories of "somewhat likely" and "not very likely."

Such uncertainty is hardly surprising, and reflects a genuine dilemma for many. Even for the less traditional women, finding workable solutions to the problems of combining children and a career is not likely to be easy. Young children do require a great deal of intelligent and loving care, which even a more equitable distribution of care between husband and wife cannot fully provide, if both parents are working most of the day. This means outside help, but currently, high-quality comprehensive day care is in short supply nationally and is likely to remain so, at least for the immediate future. At the same time, for those women seeking a long-term career, interruptions of 5 or more years' duration can present a significant obstacle to career advancement (22).

***Sex differences and similarities in vocational values*** In many respects, adolescent boys and girls share similar values with respect to work. As we shall see, in any future employment, both place a high value on having a job that is interesting to do, "where you can see the reality of what you do," and where the best use is made of "your skills and abilities" (see pages 476–482). However, girls are somewhat more concerned with having a job where one can help others, contribute to society, and be creative; boys, in contrast, are somewhat more concerned with having a high-income job that also provides opportunities for leadership (12).

## FAMILY INFLUENCE
## ON VOCATIONAL CHOICE

Family influences of parents and siblings may also play a significant role in vocational choice. One of the more obvious of the former influences is that of *parental motivation,* and a good deal of variation in parental motivation occurs within all social classes. It has been hypothesized that a working-class boy is relatively likely to seek advanced education and occupational mobility if his parents urge him to do so and unlikely to seek mobility if they do not exert pressure in this direction (137; see also 24, 59, 102, 106). Indeed, such a boy with strong parental support may prove more ambitious than a middle-class boy without such parental support and urging.

According to the data of one study (137), ambitious middle-class boys showed the highest percentage of parental support; mobile working-class boys ranked a close second. In contrast, unambitious middle-class boys and nonmobile working-class boys ranked far behind in percentage of parental support. These results provide evidence for the hypothesis that parental influence is associated with mobility aspiration among working-class boys, and also with ambition among middle-class boys. Indeed, as the author points out, parental advice may be a better predictor of high ambition than is the boy's social class alone.

Parental motivation has been found to be significantly related to students' aspiration levels, even when social-class status and IQ are held constant. In general, students whose parents ranked high on aspirational motivations (i.e., held high educational and occupational goals for their children and rewarded good schoolwork) tended to have a high aspiration level themselves (i.e., a "desire for an occupation above that of their parents' social class level") (49, *183*). Interestingly, however, this positive relationship was particularly strong among students scoring high on personality measures of *authoritarianism* and *conformity*. Apparently, nonauthoritarian and nonconforming adolescent males are less susceptible than their more dogmatic, conforming peers to parental influences and goals.

Father's occupation exerts a significant influence on the career choice of sons, though apparently not of daughters. The number of sons following in their father's footsteps greatly exceeds what one would expect by chance, even if social-class influences are taken into account (122, 123, 173, 174). For example, sons of physicians, lawyers, and scientists are far more likely to enter these occupations than are other young men of similar socioeconomic status (123, 173, 174). When the occupational categories are broadened to include the same or similar kinds of occupations, the strength of the relationships between the vocational choices of fathers and sons increase (94, 104, 122, 123).

In part, these findings can probably be accounted for on the basis of such obvious factors as: (1) greater opportunity to become familiar with father's occupation, as compared with others; (2) greater likelihood of access to the occupation; and (3) at least in some cases (e.g., physicians) strong parental motivation—and sometimes pressure—for the son to enter the occupation. However, recent research suggests that more subtle factors play a part, including the communication of values from father to son (123).

It has been hypothesized, for example, that there are value differences in business and professional subcultures and work activities, and that these value differences are transmitted from fathers to their sons and influence their sons' subsequent occupational choices. Professional occupations are considered to place greater emphasis on intrinsic work satisfactions, such as autonomy, expert knowledge, and opportunities for service; business occupations, in turn, have been found to place a greater emphasis on such extrinsic rewards as high income and advancement (123).

One series of studies (122, 123) examined the occupational choices of college students whose fathers were (1) professionals (e.g., physician, scientist, lawyer, teacher); (2) high-prestige businessmen; and (3) lower-prestige businessmen. In addition, degree of closeness between father and son was measured. A number of interesting findings emerged. As predicted, sons of professionals were genuinely more likely than sons of businessmen to choose a profession, while the latter were

**TABLE 11.4** *PERCENTAGE DISTRIBUTIONS OF*
*SENIOR CAREER CHOICES BY CLOSENESS TO FATHER*
*IN BUSINESS AND PROFESSIONAL ORIGIN GROUPS*

|  | SENIOR CAREER CHOICE[a] | | | |
|---|---|---|---|---|
|  | DOCTOR | DENTIST | SCIENTIST | TEACHER |
| **A. *Lower-prestige business origin*** | | | | |
| Close | 16.9 | 4.8 | 9.6 | 8.4 |
| Not close | 14.9 | 1.1 | 3.4 | 6.9 |
| Total | 15.9 | 2.9 | 6.5 | 7.6 |
| **B. *Higher-prestige-business-origin*** | | | | |
| Close | 17.8 | 4.1 | 4.1 | 5.5 |
| Not close | 17.9 | 7.1 | 3.6 | 5.4 |
| Total | 17.8 | 5.4 | 3.9 | 5.4 |
| **C. *Professional origin*** | | | | |
| Close | 48.4 | 3.1 | 1.6 | 4.7 |
| Not close | 30.8 | 7.7 | 11.5 | 3.8 |
| Total | 43.3 | 4.4 | 4.4 | 4.4 |

more likely to choose business. However, following a vocational pattern similar to that of the father was far more likely where (1) the father's job had high prestige, and (2) the son had a close relationship with his father (see Table 11.4). Where the prestige of the father's job was low, even close sons apparently were motivated to look elsewhere, outside business, to find their life's work. "The father's prestigious occupation alone, however, is not enough to motivate occupational inheritance if the relationship between the father and son is not conducive to strong parental identification and value transference" (123, *252*).

For example, among the sons of high-prestige businessmen, those who were close to their fathers were almost twice as likely to choose business as those who were not close. This combination of a son's close relationship with a prestigious father and choice of similar occupation has been found in other studies to be associated with sons' identification and modeling (89, 94, 101).

That basic vocational values, and not merely greater opportunity and support, played a significant mediating part in sons' choices of similar occupations was indicated by the fact that when the values of sons were studied in relation to closeness to the father, it was found in the professional category that closeness to the father was significantly related to the son's concerns with intrinsic rewards, but unrelated to concerns with extrinsic rewards; in the business category, the opposite pattern was found.

One important possibility that is frequently overlooked in research on the ef-

| SENIOR CAREER CHOICE[a] | | | | TOTAL | |
|---|---|---|---|---|---|
| COLLEGE PROFESSOR | GOVERNMENT | LAWYER | BUSINESS | % | N |
| 19.3 | 4.8 | 12.0 | 24.1 | 48.8 | 83 |
| 20.7 | 10.3 | 12.6 | 29.9 | 51.2 | 87 |
| 20.0 | 7.6 | 12.4 | 27.1 | 100.0 | 170 |
| 4.1 | 4.1 | 20.5 | 39.7 | 56.6 | 73 |
| 21.4 | 7.1 | 16.1 | 21.4 | 43.4 | 56 |
| 11.6 | 5.4 | 18.6 | 31.8 | 100.0 | 129 |
| 20.3 | 1.6 | 7.8 | 12.5 | 71.1 | 64 |
| 19.2 | 0 | 11.5 | 15.4 | 28.9 | 26 |
| 20.0 | 1.1 | 8.9 | 13.3 | 100.0 | 90 |

*Source:* J. T. Mortimer. Social class, work, and the family: Some implications of the father's occupation for familial relationships and sons' career decisions. *Journal of Marriage and the Family,* 1976, **38**, No. 2, 241–256. By permission.

[a] Students making other, less popular choices are deleted from the table.

fects of parental identification patterns is the influence of negative as well as positive models. Another is that the relevance of parental models—either positive or negative—may vary considerably with age. Both of these possibilities were investigated in a longitudinal study of 101 male adolescents during the ninth grade (average age 15) and again when they had been out of high school for 7 years (age 25). Using semistructured interviews rated independently (and reliably) by two judges, the investigators attempted in both the earlier and later periods to determine the adolescent's primary role models "overall" and in various "life spheres" (i.e., educational, occupational, personal), as well as the position occupied by the model on a dimension ranging from highly positive to negative. A role model was defined operationally as any person about whom the subject made statements of (1) "similarity" (i.e., acknowledging a similarity, resemblance, or likeness between the subject and that person, or their opposites, as in the case of a negative role model); (2) "imitation" (i.e., statements indicating that the subject wanted to be like, or unlike, the other person); or (3) "assimilation" (i.e., "any specific reference to another person whose ideas, standards, or values" the subject claimed to have adopted or refused to adopt).

Vocational adjustment in adulthood was measured in this study by a variety of criteria, including fulfillment of original adolescent occupational goal, job stability and realism of reasons for changing jobs, occupational level, job competence and success, job satisfaction, and the like. A number of interesting findings emerged:

1. The most frequently mentioned role model, both at ninth grade and in young adulthood, was the father. However, with age the importance of the father decreased and the importance of other figures, including peers, teachers, adult relatives, employers, and other adults increased.

2. Of all the role models that subjects possessed at ninth grade (e.g., father, mother, siblings, adult relatives), only the father's role modeling (both occupational and overall) was related to the son's vocational adjustment and behaviors 10 years later.

3. In general, boys who at age 15 had fathers as strong *and* positive role models—occupationally or overall—tended to achieve higher levels of vocational adjustment than those for whom fathers were either weak or nonexistent role models, or who were negative models.

4. Interestingly, however, the differences in vocational adjustment were generally greater in the former cases (weak or nonexistent role model) than in the latter (negative role model). As the investigators comment:

> This curvilinear relationship is not particularly surprising. Although the usual emphasis has been upon the possession of "positive" role models and its relationship to the formation of a sense of identity, it is possible that "negative" role models can also be helpful in the same identity strivings. It may be as important to have in one's environment those with whom one perceives a dissimilarity, whose attitudes or values one refuses to adopt, or whom one would wish not to imitate [19, *34*].

> Both identification *and* rejection of role models may well serve as determinants of career patterns (19, 155, 156): "Their importance may be more similar than it has been commonly realized. Each may serve as important occasions for self-definition" (19, *34*).

5. Also of considerable interest is the finding that the kinds of relationships between father-modeling at age 15 and subsequent vocational adjustment at 25 are not found at this later age. Indeed, at age 25 moderate use of the father as a positive role model is significantly more often associated with successful vocational adjustment than either strong, positive modeling or negative modeling:

> It would appear that what may be appropriate with regard to the use of fathers as role models in adolescence is no longer so in young adulthood. The latter period has been thought of as involving a trend toward increasing autonomy, as the giving up of internalized parents, as the opportunity for the nonparents emerging as increasingly significant role models as the adolescent subjects moved into young adulthood. And those subjects whose fathers were moderate or even nonscoring role models at this period and whose statuses appeared to denote a disengagement with them on the part of their sons appeared to function more effectively in young adulthood than those subjects whose relationship with their fathers represented a continuing and negative involvement. It may be that adolescents need their fathers as important sources of self-definition even into adolescence but must move on, in young adulthood, to new and different but important experiences of others [19, *34–35*].

## Effects of maternal employment
## on adolescent vocational attitudes

Studies of the father's influence on adolescent vocational values and goals have tended to focus on "the idea that the father's occupation affects the child because the traits required for success in that occupation are valued and passed on to the child" (94, *39*). In contrast, as Lois Hoffman (94) and others (30) have observed recently, in studies of the mother's influence, the focus has been primarily on her employment status per se. Furthermore, the assumption until recently was that maternal employment outside the home was most likely to have an adverse effect, not merely on vocational orientation, but on child and adolescent development generally (94).

Recent research, however, suggests that maternal employment is more likely to have positive effects, particularly for adolescents (94). Furthermore, as maternal employment continues to shift from being the exception to being the norm, and as social and economic arrangements increasingly accommodate to this shift, it seems likely that this trend will continue (94). A number of studies (17, 37, 60, 63, 88, 89, 91, 92, 93, 94, 113, 171) have indicated that the views of girls and young women (and, in some investigations, males as well) regarding appropriate sex and vocational roles for women are influenced by the kinds of maternal role models to which they are exposed. In the middle-childhood years, girls whose mothers work outside the home are more likely than those with nonemployed mothers to view both men and women as typically engaging in a wider variety of adult activities, including those traditionally stereotyped as masculine or feminine (82, 89, 94, 113); to say that they approve of maternal employment (50, 94, 103); and to state that they themselves will want to work when they are mothers (81, 89). Even among preschool children, both sons and daughters of employed mothers are less stereotyped in their views of men and women (69, 94, 118).

Female adolescents and youth whose mothers are employed outside the home are also more likely to view work as something they will want to do if and when they themselves become mothers (13, 20, 89, 94, 142). In a study of the sex-role perceptions of college students, one team of investigators (171) found that young women and young men with employed mothers perceived smaller male-female differences than did the sons and daughters of nonemployed mothers on such generally sex-stereotyped attributes as competence and warmth-expressiveness, with females being more affected by maternal employment than males. In a related study (17), college women were administered a measure (70) in which subjects were given a number of scholarly articles and asked to judge the quality of the article and of the author. Half the articles were attributed to female authors, and half to male authors. It was found that daughters of working mothers were less likely than those of nonemployed full-time homemakers to assume lower competence on the part of female authors. There are also indications that daughters of working mothers tend to be somewhat more autonomous and active (48, 89) and somewhat more likely to consider their mothers as people they admire and want to be like (18, 48). However, the self-esteem of girls does not seem to be related to their mothers' employment status (18, 89).

Finally, the vocational attitudes, aspirations, and accomplishments of girls will be influenced not simply by the fact of maternal employment as such, but by the mother's attitude toward employment, her degree of satisfaction and accomplishment in her work, and her ability to successfully combine the roles of worker, mother, and wife. In one study (17), it was found that whether a girl expresses positive attitudes toward employment combined with homemaking will depend on "whether her mother endorses it and, if the mother works, upon how successfully she has integrated her two roles. Thus, if a subject's mother had worked but had also experienced negative personal consequences because of her career, the subject evaluated women's competence highly but was unfavorable to the dual role pattern" (17, 37). The girl's attitudes were also found to be influenced by whether or not her father indicated acceptance of the idea of having a career-oriented wife. A variety of investigations have found that "highly achieving women and women who aspire to careers, particularly to less conventionally feminine careers, are more likely to be the daughters of educated women and the daughters of employed women. The high-achieving woman has a high-achieving daughter" (88, *213*). Lois Hoffman (87, 88, 89, 92, 93, 94) suggests that there are several reasons why this may be the case. In the first place, the mother herself provides an appropriate role model of achievement for her daughter. Furthermore, such mothers are more likely to encourage independence in their daughters (92, 94), and independence "is particularly important because many girls are handicapped by overprotection and encouragement of dependency. And finally, optimum conditions include a good relationship with the father who encourages the girl's independence and achievement while accepting her as a female" (88, *213*).

While greater encouragement of independence by employed mothers is likely to have positive effects on daughters, it is not clear whether it is an advantage or a disadvantage to sons (94). Sons traditionally have received more independence training than daughters, "and while this seems to have provided them with an advantage in the nonemployed mother family, it may be excessive in the employed mother family" (94, *42*). For both sons and daughters, maternal employment is likely to result in a higher level of adolescent household responsibilities. Though it can obviously be overdone, assumption of such responsibilities has been found to foster ego development and self-esteem (54, 94).

### *Ordinal position and sibling sex status*

Vocational values and goals may also be influenced by the adolescent's ordinal position in the family, by his or her siblings' sex status, and by combinations of the two (134, 157). In part this may be due to a tendency for parents to treat children with different ordinal positions or sibling sex-status patterns differently—to provide them with different learning experiences and different patterns of reinforcement for various behaviors. There is considerable research evidence, for example, to indicate that firstborns are likely to receive a higher degree of achievement and responsibility training than children who are born later, as well as more attention from parents (1, 37, 60, 63, 127). Differential treatment stemming from ordinal position and sibling sex status does not derive solely from parents, however. The siblings themselves, depending on their sex and power in the family, can sometimes have as important an effect as that of the parents (91, 94, 113).

There are indications that firstborns tend to prefer occupations that involve the direction, control, and supervision of others (57, 125, 157, 169). It has been hypothesized that this may be a function of generally greater responsibilities delegated to the oldest child by parents (63). They appear more likely to be "put in charge of other children and of household chores and in general get more extensive experience of playing an adult surrogate role than do non-first-borns" (157, *31*). Among college students in two-child families, firstborns (both male and female, but especially the latter) are significantly more likely than second-borns to score high on vocational interest patterns associated with teaching (157). In contrast, second-borns appear more inclined toward activities requiring sociable, empathic, and sympathetic behavior (125, 135, 138, 153, 169, 170, 180)—possibly because "these characteristics are related to the more relaxed relationship the second child has with his parents as well as the opportunity to seek more varied relationships" (63, *406*).

Sex of sibling also appears to play a role. In general, traditionally "masculine" vocational interests occur more frequently in all-male dyads (i.e., among both older and younger brothers in all-male, two-child families) (157). Similarly, there appears to be a tendency, though not pronounced, for girls in all-girl dyads to score highest on interest patterns associated with traditionally "feminine" occupations (157).

In addition to studying the influence on vocational interest patterns of ordinal position alone or sibling sex status alone, investigators have also been interested in determining the influence of particular combinations of these two variables (e.g., younger boy with an older sister, older boy with a younger brother). For example, in view of the findings regarding "masculine" preferences in two-boy dyads, it is interesting to note that younger girls with older brothers were found to have more masculine vocational interest patterns than girls in older ordinal position-sibling sex-status dyads. This finding appears consistent with prior research indicating that girls in this particular dyad are most likely to display "masculine" personality characteristics and cognitive styles (i.e., higher quantitative and verbal scores on measures of mental ability) (134, 158).

Finally, opposite-sex siblings have been found to affect the masculinity-femininity scores of the subject in the direction of the sibling's sex (157). Interestingly, "the most expressively creative occupations of artist, music performer, author, and architect were preferred most by subjects with opposite sex siblings" (157, *34–35*), and particularly by boys with a younger sister, and girls with an older brother: "The success style of these two dyads is presumably that of creating new solutions and new culture. . . . It is apparently the cross-sex affect . . . which contributes to the interest of these two dyads in the expressive arts" (157, *35*).

Incidentally, vocational interest patterns associated with psychology occurred most frequently among firstborn males with a younger sister and second-born females with an older sister (although in the latter case the trend only approached statistical significance).

### *Personality characteristics and interest patterns*

Clearly, personality characteristics, interests, and needs are related to vocational interests. Adolescent boys with vocational interests in artistic fields are more likely than boys with other interests to perceive themselves as introspective, intuitive, disorderly, imaginative, original, sensitive, unconventional, enthusiastic, rebellious, and impractical (96). In contrast, boys expressing interest in scientific vocations are more likely to perceive themselves as analytical, curious, "hard-headed," imaginative, quiet and reserved, and scholarly. Those with entrepreneurial interests (such as sales manager) are relatively more apt to perceive themselves as aggressive, striving, dominant, conventional, energetic, extroverted, industrious, practical, persuasive, and not particularly interested in artistic, idealistic, scholarly, or scientific pursuits (96). Youth who are not anxious and do not fear failure, and who have a strong need for achievement, tend to choose high-prestige occupations on tests of vocational choice. In contrast, those with a high level of anxiety and fear of failure, but a weak need for achievement, tend to make lower-prestige choices (32, 52, 53). Similarly, introverted adolescents tend to exhibit a narrower, more rigid range of possible vocational choices than do extroverts (139).

Among college women, those majoring in science have been found to have the strongest motives for achievement, with those majoring in languages scoring in the midrange and those majoring in education scoring lowest. Conversely, the latter scored highest in need for affiliation with others (154). Women who are most anxious or least achievement-motivated may not complete a degree at all, but certain fields obviously lend themselves to a less ambivalent success than others (154). Young women choosing an atypical—particularly a high-status, traditionally male—vocation are more likely to be independent, self-confident and able to assert themselves (5, 94, 97, 98, 154, 159). In view of the fact that they are more likely to be subjected to greater competitive and sex-role stresses than their peers in many, more traditional occupations, this is fortunate (14).

Obviously, the adolescent may not consciously recognize all of the motives that help to direct his or her selection of a career. However, most adolescents have a fantasy or stereotyped picture of what an engineer, army officer, physicist, actor, or psychiatrist is like and what he or she does—a daydream that contains some of the gratifications that are being sought, and that usually has at least some relationship to reality (47, 95). To illustrate, the most frequent attributes assigned to engineers by high school seniors of superior ability were found to be (in order of frequency): practical, builders, useful, intelligent, inventive, important, interesting, and hardworking (95). Teachers, in contrast, were seen as underpaid, dedicated, indispensable to society, patient, and helpful. Accountants were seen as dull, precise, mathematically inclined, boring, methodical, and unimaginative, but necessary! Stereotypes obviously can be misleading, and the chances of a student's selecting an occupation consonant with his or her own needs (consciously or unconsciously) will be greatly enhanced by possessing actual knowledge of a variety of careers. Unfortunately, the availability of such knowledge, even on the part of professional high school, college, and independent vocational counselors, is all too limited, and frequently is also influenced by stereotyped thinking.

## VOCATIONAL VALUES AND SOCIAL CHANGE

Much was made during the latter half of the 1960s of a presumed revolution in the vocational values and goals of adolescents and youth. Young people, it was asserted, were no longer interested in such traditional goals of the characteristically American work ethic as power and material success. Furthermore, they were said to view many of the practices of the world of business and industry as exploitative, unjust, and overly concerned with profit at the expense of human need, social values, and the quality of the environment (42, 136, 177). In more personal terms, they were said to consider many traditional Establishment occupations as too demanding of conformity, both on and off the job, too limiting of personal freedom and individual expression, and too likely to involve restriction of opportunities for exercising the full range of one's individual talents and skills in work that is both creative and important in and of itself. In too many jobs, it was asserted, the young person felt that he or she would become simply one cog in a large, impersonal machine—a machine that in the view of such apostles of the then "new consciousness" as Charles Reich, author of the *Greening of America,* was probably not controlled even by its nominal masters (132). As America entered the decade of the 1980s, it was asserted with equal vigor that these trends had been reversed, and that there was a return to the traditional vocational attitudes and values of the 1950s. As we shall see, both views represent oversimplifications and distortions of the actual facts.

What are the facts concerning the vocational values and goals of adolescents and youth then and now, insofar as we have been able to ascertain them? As in so many other areas of adolescent attitudes, values, and behaviors, any blanket generalizations should be viewed with considerable caution. In many respects the variations among adolescents in their vocational values, goals, and beliefs have been at least as great as those among adults, and probably greater than those between the average adolescent and the average adult. If anything, this was probably more clearly the case during the so-called generation-gap era of the 1960s than it was in earlier periods, or has been since.

There is no question that during the late 1960s and early 1970s a significant, but still rather limited, number of young people became profoundly disenchanted with a vocational world they viewed either as exploiting its workers and the public while remaining indifferent to the ills of society, as unduly restricting personal freedom and individual expression, or both. For example, among most of the small minority of American youth classified as revolutionary in a national survey conducted in 1968 (177), disillusionment with "the system" was, as might have been expected, virtually total. Nine out of ten of these young people strongly agreed that "business is overly concerned with profits and not with public responsibility" and that "economic well-being in this country is unjustly and unfairly distributed." Forty-four percent expressed the belief that big business was in need of "fundamental reform," and 42 percent thought that it should be "done away with." A majority said they would reject outright "outward conformity for the sake of career advancement"; "being treated impersonally in a job"; and "having little decision-making power in the first few years of a job." Only 3 percent said that they could "accept easily" the power and authority of the boss in a work situation; 42 percent said they would reject them outright; and a majority (54 percent) said they would accept them only reluctantly.

Although lacking the political commitment of their revolutionary peers, many members of the hippie minority then in flower revealed a strong disdain of their own for Establishment vocational values, which they viewed as false, dehumanizing, "uptight," and incompatible with individual freedom, spontaneity, self-expression, and creativity (31, 128, 129, 140). They did not consider the struggle worth the effort, and were unwilling to compromise their life-styles by conforming to the demands of traditional 9-to-5 employment. Many also expressed the view that their labor was not actually needed in an increasingly automated, consumer-oriented society; ironically, their argument appears, at least superficially, to have gained support from the Establishment itself, through its increasing inability or unwillingness to provide meaningful job opportunities for many adolescents and young adults who have needed and wanted them (42).

Nevertheless, even at the height of the youth movement, a majority of young people still held to many traditional beliefs commonly associated with the Protestant work ethic (see Chapter 13), such as the beliefs that "competition encourages excellence," and that "everyone should save as much as he can regularly and not have to lean on family and friends the minute he runs into financial problems" (136, 177). Although the percentages of young people subscribing to such beliefs were somewhat smaller than the corresponding percentages for their parents, the differences seldom exceeded 10 percent (177). Approximately two out of three 1968 adolescents (52 percent of college students and 70 percent of the considerably larger number of high school youth) expressed the view that hard work led to success and wealth, and that these goals were worth striving for (177). Most of these adolescents and youth believed that young people should earn some of their own money, and two-thirds were actively involved in saving (80). In a nationwide longitudinal study of American high school boys conducted in the late 1960s (9, 10), "having a job with good chances of getting ahead" was considered "very important" by 67 percent. (What the investigators termed "ambitious job attitudes" were particularly likely to characterize youth with good relations with their families, high intelligence, and favorable socioeconomic status.) In contrast, only about 12 percent of youth considered "very important" having a "job where I don't have to have a lot of responsibility" or one "that doesn't mean we learn a lot of new things" (10).

Although a majority of adolescents, even in the late 1960s and early 1970s, still looked forward to their future employment, usually within "the system," they nevertheless appeared to be seeking somewhat different job satisfactions than stereotypes of the success ethic might seem to imply, and there was little question that they were less willing than their predecessors of the 1950s to go along with arbitrary, authoritarian, or impersonal treatment by employers. Thus, although a number of studies conducted at the time (51, 80, 177) indicated that most young people were willing to work hard (less than a third would have welcomed "working less hard") and that they could accept the authority of the boss in a work situation, more than two out of three also stated that they could not easily accept "being treated impersonally on the job" or having to engage in "outward conformity for the sake of career advancement" (177). While most (approximately 70 percent) believed that business made "a major contribution to America" (51), a majority also felt that business placed undue emphasis on competition and was overly concerned with profits at the expense of public responsibility (177). Overall, a majority of late 1960s young people (52 percent) believed that big business was in need of "moderate change" (177). Although unlike their revolutionary peers only 3 percent believed it should be "done away with," only 20 percent of all youth (and only 10 percent of college youth) believed that no substantial change was needed. The remainder (24 percent) believed that "fundamental reform" was needed.

In brief, young people in the late 1960s (particularly college students) were more concerned than their 1950s predecessors with finding work that provided opportunities for individuality, self-expression, and personal growth. Furthermore, the number who felt that this could not be done "within the system" reached an all-time high (177, 178). So, too, did the number of those seeking "alternative occupations"—whether as a means of self-expression (as in art, music, or skilled crafts), achieving a fundamentally new life-style (as in the case of some communal residents), or promoting social change (as in frequently low-paying jobs as counselors of runaway children, or organizers of the poor in urban or rural ghettos) (51, 52). Nevertheless, a clear majority—while more critical of business values and practices than their predecessors, and more insistent on being given recognition as individuals in work that was "more than just a job"—still planned to (and, in fact, did) enter relatively traditional careers. The 1960s led to significant changes in the vocational values of adolescents and youth, particularly those from upper- and middle-class backgrounds. But, as we have seen, the extent of these changes tended to be exaggerated and their meaning distorted.

## CURRENT TRENDS IN VOCATIONAL VALUES

The vocational values and attitudes of young people coming of age in the 1980s also differ in a number of important respects from those of their peers in the 1960s and early 1970s. Again, however, there has been a popular tendency to exaggerate the extent of these differences and to misinterpret them. Thus, some current observers assert that in contrast to the presumably anarchic sixties, there has been a dramatic reconciliation with "the system" among youth and a return to pre-1960s roles. As we shall see, the facts, to the extent that we can discern them, are considerably more complex, both among more economically favored college and college-bound young people—the "forerunners" of this generation (178)—and among the larger majority of noncollege adolescents and youth.

### College and college-bound adolescents and youth

Unlike many of their counterparts in the 1960s, who (correctly) saw themselves in demand by potential employers, and took for granted that at least reasonably remunerative jobs were available for the asking, most college-educated and college-bound youth today perceive (again correctly) that they face a very different world. Instead of a shortage of college-educated youth in the 1980s, there is more likely to be a surplus (see pages 492–494). Furthermore, in what at present looks almost like a closely linked social *and* economic revolution, the potential reward patterns associated with a variety of occupations are shifting. In the current era, fewer opportunities are likely to exist for artists, musicians, historians, philosophers, liberal arts college professors, biomedical and behavioral scientists, social workers, child and youth workers, and government workers, among others; more financially rewarding

prospects are likely to be found in such fields as business management, computer programming, finance, some branches of engineering, banking, and the health professions (see pages 488–492). Even in such occupations, however, demands can change almost overnight in our complex, increasingly technological society, as the earlier experiences of aerospace engineers in the 1960s and of teachers in the 1970s amply illustrate.

In addition—and this is possibly the most significant change in terms of its potential impact on today's young people—even what would generally be considered a good, reasonably well-paying job does not appear to provide assurance of access to such elements of the American dream as a home of one's own, a college education for one's children, or financial security in retirement. Young people are only too aware of the fact that inflation, high interest rates, and declining productivity in many areas of the nations's economy are currently putting a first house out of the reach of nine out of ten Americans. In contrast, in the era following World War II, the great majority of young middle-class Americans were able to purchase a home with a minimal down payment, and interest and mortgage payments rarely exceeded a quarter of their incomes.

As a result, it is hardly surprising to find that the percentage of "career-minded" college students—that is, young people "whose major purpose in going to college is to train themselves for a career" (178, *16*)—has steadily increased since the late 1960s, while the number of those who view their college experience primarily as a period of self-discovery and change has declined considerably. Between

1969 and 1981 the percentage of first-year college students in the United States who cited "being very well off financially" as an "essential or very important objective" increased from slightly less than half to two-thirds (6, 7, 8, 110, 111). In contrast, while "developing a philosophy of life" was cited as a very important objective by 86 percent of females and 78.5 percent of males in 1969, by 1981 these figures had declined to 50 percent for females and 47.5 percent for males. In 1969, fewer than half of all entering college students said that "being able to make more money" was a very important reason for going to college; in 1981, 67 percent considered it "very important." Recognition by peers, having administrative responsibility, and being an authority in one's field showed similar increases, while such creatively—but not necessarily financially—rewarding objectives as writing original works, or creating artistic works, declined by as much as 50 percent in some instances (6, 7, 8, 110, 111).

Among high school seniors, too, there have been parallel but less dramatic increases in the number of those for whom "the chance to earn a good deal of money" and to have "a predictable, secure future" was rated as very important in a job (11, 12).

In accord with these changing concerns and values, the percentages of college students enrolling in the arts and humanities and the social sciences have steadily declined, while the percentages of those enrolling in such fields as business, engineering, computer science, and preprofessional programs have increased (6, 8). Recent changes have been particularly evident among women students, though generally in relative, rather than absolute terms. For example, while the number of first-year college women aspiring to be teachers declined by more than two-thirds in the past decade (from 38 to 10 percent), the number planning to become businesswomen or executives more than doubled (from less than 4 to nearly 10 percent) (6, 8).

Deans, longtime faculty, and students themselves, particularly at the most highly selective elite colleges and universities, report a more serious, pragmatic, competitive, and career-oriented set of attitudes and values currently, with less emphasis on intellectual and creative exploration for its own sake. Even at the high school level, particularly in the more affluent middle- and upper-class communities, similar vocationally oriented pressures are increasing (3):

> Many students seem to have assimilated a deep-seated inflationary psychology that tells them there will always be too many people chasing too few goods and services. And they see the competition for jobs unending. As a result, the material hallmarks of success—a nice home, a rewarding job, a comfortable life—appear more and more elusive" [3, 1].

In the words of one high school senior, "It's a real panic mentality. A lot of [students] are scared of not being as well off as their parents" (3, 1). Many parents, in turn, appear to be passing their economic concerns on to their children. While some educators endorse what they view as "a new, nicer generation of kids," others worry about what they see as an increasing concern with "making it," in which studying becomes merely a means to an end (3).

"They worry that adolescents who start 'playing the game' in high school will never learn how to think for themselves, and will always favor the safe bet over new ideas or calculated risks. 'We could find ourselves with a very bland society' " (3, 27).

Still others worry that high school students "lack the maturity and the experience of older students; therefore, they are more apt to make career choices that don't fit their abilities. One result could be an increase in job dissatisfaction among adults in future years" (3, *27*). In the words of one high school senior, however, "that's just the way it needs to be now" (3, *27*).

Of course, there are still many college-bound and college students whose primary interests are in what they are learning and in creative activities. And there remain, as there have always been, other students who are primarily, as one said, "along for the ride," and still others who do not have the emotional reserves needed to deal with often premature pressure, and who drop out in disillusionment or become involved in such escapes as drugs and alcohol—even, in rare instances, suicide.

What does appear clear, however, is that the vocational values of a majority of today's middle- and upper-class adolescents and youth, and their view of the world they face, have shifted since the late 1960s and early 1970s, just as the world that they are entering has changed.

### A new "silent generation"?

But does this mean, as some observers have suggested, that contemporary adolescents and youth are engaged in a return to presixties' vocational values and goals? As we saw in Chapter 6 (see pages 188–190), the 1950s were characterized by what in retrospect emerges as an excessive conformity in social, political, personal, and vocational roles—the era of "the organization man" (44). Young people, too, went along with these values; they became the "silent generation." They showed "an intensive desire for security, both internal and external, the will to be accepted at any price, and an unwillingness to show individual traits . . ." (176, *84*). A study of college students in the late 1950s found them to be "models of the status quo," with few real commitments of their own and a rather uncritical acceptance of the values and practices of social institutions generally, including those of government and big business (71, 178): "On the job, they placed emphasis on getting ahead, making out, and living according to the mores of the corporate structure. (The classic stereotype of this era was the man in the gray flannel suit.) It was then one retreated from the public world to one's private world—to suburbs, home, garden, station wagon, kids, and family" (178, *21*).

Only through such compartmentalization did many young people see a way to reconcile the conflicting demands of society with their personal needs. And in order to support their private world, they were often willing to accept a high degree of conformity and suppression of individual expression in their jobs (44, 176). Today's adolescents and youth, though they are generally more willing to adjust to the demands of the work place, and more ready to accept compromise than were their 1960s predecessors, are far less willing than 1950s youth to suppress their own individuality and needs for self-expression, on or off the job (see Chapter 13). Nor are they as ready or willing to accept a sharp dichotomy between their private lives and their work (178, 179). And they do not see as much need to (44). Although they acknowledge, as we have seen, an increased interest in economic security and getting ahead, they are also more concerned that their work be personally rewarding.

When college-bound American high school seniors in 1980 were asked what things they rated very important in a job, the two most frequent responses were having "interesting things to do" (90 percent) and "using skills or ability" (74 percent). In comparison, 48 percent cited having a "chance to earn a great deal of money," as very important (up from 41 percent as recently as 1976). Only 25 percent stressed "high status, prestige," but nearly two-thirds wanted "good chances for advancement" and a "predictable, secure future" (see Table 11.5).

Unlike their predecessors of the 1950s, only 23 percent of college-bound high school seniors in 1980 considered working for a large corporation as "desirable"—though this figure represents an increase from 14 percent in 1976 (see Table 11.6). At the same time, unlike their predecessors of the late 1960s, only one in twenty considered working in a large corporation unacceptable (11). Possibly reflecting a continuance of the trend toward greater self-expression and self-fulfillment that emerged from the 1960s, by far the largest number of graduating high school seniors (45 percent) in 1980 preferred being self-employed. Consistent, however, with a decreased concern for the welfare of others and of society among youth (and adults) in recent years (6, 44, 111), only 17 percent considered working for a social welfare organization as desirable, down dramatically since the late 1960s and early 1970s (and down from 23 percent just since 1976).

Contemporary adolescents place greater stress on the importance of self-realization and self-expression in their jobs (as in their lives) than did the "silent generation" of the 1950s. Although they are generally more adaptable than 1960s youth, they also do not share the unquestioning faith in big business (and other social institutions) that characterized their 1950s contemporaries (see pages 188–198). For example, 41 percent of college-bound high school seniors in 1980 agreed that there is considerable dishonesty and immorality in the leadership of large corporations, and 29 percent thought that corporations had not been doing a good job for the country; 55 percent felt they should have less influence, and only 9 percent felt they should have more influence (12).

What is perhaps most interesting, and may represent the greatest change in the present decade, is the percentage of youth who apparently feel that job success and self-fulfillment can be reconciled. Among entering college students in 1981, two-thirds or more listed (in order of frequency) "a good marriage and family life," "strong friendships," "finding purpose and meaning in life," *and* having "steady work" in which they can be successful as very important in life. In other words, today's college and college-bound young people appear to be emphasizing the importance to them of combining "challenging work, the ability to express one's self, and free time for outside interests, as well as the money one can earn, economic security, and the chance to get ahead" (178, *20*).

Whether they will ultimately be successful is still a question for the future. However, the changing climate is at least a substantial portion of the current business world—with increased flexibility, somewhat greater recognition of the needs of the individual, and more tolerance of individual tastes, interests, and life-styles (itself a response to the changes of the 1960s)—suggests that their goal of achieving such a synthesis is considerably more realistic than would have been the case two decades ago. In the final analysis, the outcome may depend more on the state of the econ-

**TABLE 11.5** *THINGS RATED VERY IMPORTANT IN A JOB*

| | COLLEGE PLANS: COMPLETE FOUR YEARS | | | | | |
| --- | --- | --- | --- | --- | --- | --- |
| | 1976 | 1977 | 1978 | 1979 | 1980[a] | 1981[a] |
| Interesting to do | 90 | 91 | 91 | 93 | 90 | 91 |
| Uses skills and abilities | 74 | 74 | 74 | 74 | 74 | 74 |
| See results of what you do | 60 | 60 | 61 | 61 | 58 | 61 |
| Good chances for advancement | 54 | 59 | 61 | 64 | 61 | 64 |
| Predictable, secure future | 60 | 60 | 61 | 63 | 63 | 63 |
| Chance to make friends | 55 | 55 | 56 | 57 | 54 | 55 |
| Worthwhile to society | 49 | 48 | 48 | 48 | 48 | 47 |
| Chance to earn a good deal of money | 41 | 41 | 43 | 47 | 48 | 51 |
| A job most people look up to, respect | 34 | 35 | 37 | 37 | 38 | 38 |
| High status, prestige | 20 | 21 | 23 | 26 | 25 | 26 |

omy than upon the attitudes and values of employers and of the business world generally.

### The noncollege majority

Even at the height of the youth culture of the 1960s, and despite a period of rising prosperity, many fewer noncollege than college youth took for granted that they could always be sure of steady and rewarding employment. Consequently, it is not surprising to find that the noncollege majority are currently at least as concerned as their college and college-bound peers about their future prospects, even though college youth generally are more concerned about finding success in the job market than they were in the late sixties and early seventies (6, 8, 11, 110, 178).

At the same time, however, the noncollege majority during the latter 1970s and early 1980s have increasingly adopted many of the values of college youth of the late 1960s, including a greater emphasis on self-fulfillment and individual expression in work and in their lives as a whole (see Chapter 13). They still want good pay and economic security, but also the opportunity to do self-rewarding and interesting work (11, 12). Thus when American high school students in 1980 were asked what they would be looking for in a job, both those planning to go on to 4 years of college and those planning not to gave similar responses on many items. Both groups ranked highest having a job that was "interesting to do," followed by a job that "lets you use your best skills and abilities"—lets you do the things you can do best—and a job where you "don't have to pretend to be a type of person you are not" (see Table 11.7). While both groups were also concerned with having a well-paying job with a reasonably predictable, secure future, the 4-year-college group showed somewhat less concern; however, they were somewhat more concerned

| COLLEGE PLANS: NONE OR UNDER FOUR YEARS | | | | | |
|------|------|------|------|-------|-------|
| 1976 | 1977 | 1978 | 1979 | 1980[a] | 1981[a] |
| 86 | 89 | 88 | 87 | 86 | 87 |
| 68 | 74 | 70 | 70 | 70 | 71 |
| 57 | 57 | 60 | 58 | 59 | 59 |
| 59 | 63 | 65 | 66 | 64 | 70 |
| 63 | 64 | 66 | 66 | 66 | 66 |
| 54 | 57 | 53 | 56 | 53 | 51 |
| 41 | 43 | 39 | 40 | 39 | 41 |
| 51 | 54 | 57 | 60 | 60 | 61 |
| 33 | 34 | 36 | 35 | 35 | 39 |
| 19 | 22 | 25 | 24 | 23 | 29 |

*Source:* J. G. Bachman and L. D. Johnston. *Fewer rebels, fewer causes: A profile of today's college freshmen.* Ann Arbor, Mich.: Survey Research Center, Institute for Social Research, University of Michigan, 1979.

[a] Data from the classes of 1980 and 1981 have been added but have not been referred to in the text.

with having a job that gave them a chance to be creative and to participate in decision making. In most instances, however, the differences were not large.

Unlike their more privileged peers, however, noncollege youth—including those who never completed high school—are less likely to obtain jobs that provide opportunities for self-fulfillment and individual expression. Consequently, they are more likely to encounter frustration and discouragement (178). In one study, only 23 percent of working blue-collar youth asserted that "my work is more than just a job" (178, *32*). These same young people viewed "educational background" and "lack of vocational training" as the two main obstacles to obtaining a desirable job (178).

In a recent representative national survey (118), the work values and job satisfactions of noncollege young men (aged 18 to 22) and of older noncollege male workers (aged 30 to 49) were examined and compared. The great majority of the younger workers wanted job security, "a good salary," and a chance for advancement, but they also rated as "very important" such work-associated values as "doing meaningful things," "a chance to use your mind and abilities," "new challenges," and "a chance for personal growth." Conversely, only a relatively small minority rated as very important such anti-work ethic values as "not having to work too hard," or "having a comfortable routine that is easy to handle" (although about half considered "having enough free time to enjoy things" very important).

However, when asked if their own jobs provided opportunities for meaningful, growth-enhancing, challenging work that enabled them to use their minds and abilities, fewer than one in five rated their own jobs as excellent in these respects (see Table 11.8). Such findings are not due solely to changes in the attitudes and values of today's young people. Although older noncollege workers in this investigation

**TABLE 11.6 DESIRABILITY OF DIFFERENT WORK SETTINGS**

| | COLLEGE PLANS: COMPLETE FOUR YEARS | | | | | | COLLEGE PLANS: NONE OR UNDER FOUR YEARS | | | | | |
|---|---|---|---|---|---|---|---|---|---|---|---|---|
| | 1976 | 1977 | 1978 | 1979 | 1980 | 1981 | 1976 | 1977 | 1978 | 1979 | 1980 | 1981 |
| Being self-employed | | | | | | | | | | | | |
| Desirable | 44 | 43 | 44 | 45 | 45 | 45 | 42 | 42 | 43 | 47 | 46 | 49 |
| Not acceptable | 10 | 10 | 9 | 9 | 7 | 8 | 15 | 14 | 13 | 10 | 10 | 8 |
| A small group of partners | | | | | | | | | | | | |
| Desirable | 21 | 20 | 22 | 24 | 24 | 22 | 17 | 17 | 18 | 17 | 17 | 15 |
| Not acceptable | 9 | 10 | 9 | 10 | 7 | 8 | 13 | 14 | 15 | 14 | 11 | 13 |
| A small business | | | | | | | | | | | | |
| Desirable | 19 | 20 | 20 | 21 | 22 | 19 | 24 | 22 | 23 | 22 | 21 | 20 |
| Not acceptable | 5 | 4 | 4 | 4 | 4 | 4 | 5 | 6 | 5 | 4 | 4 | 4 |
| A school or university | | | | | | | | | | | | |
| Desirable | 28 | 23 | 18 | 21 | 16 | 17 | 9 | 9 | 7 | 8 | 7 | 7 |
| Not acceptable | 14 | 15 | 19 | 15 | 16 | 17 | 34 | 38 | 37 | 34 | 33 | 34 |
| A social service organization | | | | | | | | | | | | |
| Desirable | 23 | 21 | 18 | 16 | 17 | 16 | 17 | 16 | 16 | 15 | 11 | 13 |
| Not acceptable | 14 | 18 | 20 | 17 | 18 | 20 | 21 | 22 | 25 | 23 | 22 | 25 |
| A large corporation | | | | | | | | | | | | |
| Desirable | 14 | 16 | 18 | 23 | 23 | 24 | 13 | 15 | 15 | 16 | 16 | 17 |
| Not acceptable | 9 | 8 | 8 | 6 | 5 | 6 | 10 | 10 | 7 | 6 | 7 | 7 |
| A government agency | | | | | | | | | | | | |
| Desirable | 21 | 19 | 15 | 19 | 16 | 17 | 15 | 16 | 13 | 14 | 14 | 13 |
| Not acceptable | 15 | 14 | 16 | 15 | 18 | 17 | 26 | 26 | 28 | 28 | 24 | 26 |
| A police department | | | | | | | | | | | | |
| Desirable | 14 | 12 | 11 | 11 | 9 | 8 | 15 | 14 | 14 | 13 | 11 | 11 |
| Not acceptable | 24 | 30 | 30 | 29 | 30 | 32 | 29 | 33 | 33 | 31 | 33 | 31 |
| The military service | | | | | | | | | | | | |
| Desirable | 10 | 7 | 6 | 5 | 5 | 6 | 12 | 11 | 10 | 8 | 9 | 10 |
| Not acceptable | 42 | 48 | 47 | 50 | 51 | 51 | 37 | 40 | 43 | 48 | 47 | 43 |

Source: J. G. Bachman and L. D. Johnston. Fewer rebels, fewer causes: A profile of today's college freshmen. Ann Arbor, Mich.: Survey Research Center, Institute for Social Research, University of Michigan, 1979.

**TABLE 11.7** *VOCATIONAL VALUES OF AMERICAN HIGH SCHOOL SENIORS PLANNING AND NOT PLANNING 4 YEARS OF COLLEGE, 1980 (IN PERCENT)*

| | FOUR-YEAR COLLEGE PLANS | | | | | | | |
| --- | --- | --- | --- | --- | --- | --- | --- | --- |
| | YES | | | | NO | | | |
| JOB CHARACTERISTIC | NOT IMPOR-TANT | A LITTLE IMPOR-TANT | PRETTY IMPOR-TANT | VERY IMPOR-TANT | NOT IMPOR-TANT | A LITTLE IMPOR-TANT | PRETTY IMPOR-TANT | VERY IMPOR-TANT |
| See the results of what you do | 0.5 | 7.2 | 34.5 | 57.9 | 0.8 | 7.8 | 32.8 | 59.2 |
| High in status and prestige | 9.4 | 27.5 | 37.8 | 25.3 | 9.0 | 28.7 | 39.5 | 22.8 |
| Interesting to do | 0.4 | 0.8 | 9.1 | 89.8 | 0.6 | 1.8 | 11.7 | 85.9 |
| Good chances for advancement and promotion | 0.8 | 7.8 | 30.3 | 61.1 | 1.2 | 5.8 | 28.9 | 64.0 |
| Opportunity to be directly helpful to others | 2.0 | 13.2 | 37.5 | 47.3 | 2.9 | 14.5 | 35.9 | 46.8 |
| Chance to earn a good deal of money | 1.5 | 11.0 | 39.8 | 47.7 | 1.5 | 5.0 | 33.1 | 60.4 |
| Chance to be creative | 5.2 | 23.1 | 34.6 | 37.1 | 6.5 | 25.2 | 35.4 | 32.9 |
| Skills you learn will not go out of date | 5.0 | 12.7 | 32.0 | 50.3 | 3.7 | 10.6 | 30.2 | 55.5 |
| Chance to make friends | 2.3 | 9.9 | 33.5 | 54.4 | 1.9 | 9.0 | 36.5 | 52.6 |
| Lets you use your best skills and abilities | 0.5 | 2.7 | 22.8 | 73.9 | 0.5 | 3.6 | 25.4 | 70.4 |
| Worthwhile to society | 2.5 | 14.0 | 35.7 | 47.8 | 4.3 | 17.5 | 39.7 | 38.5 |
| More than two weeks' vacation | 20.6 | 36.8 | 25.1 | 17.5 | 20.5 | 35.3 | 27.0 | 17.2 |
| Chance to participate in decision making | 4.0 | 19.7 | 42.3 | 34.0 | 7.0 | 26.4 | 44.3 | 22.4 |
| Leaves lots of time for other things in life | 1.9 | 15.8 | 43.7 | 38.5 | 2.9 | 15.8 | 41.4 | 40.0 |
| Establish community roots | 13.1 | 20.6 | 31.9 | 34.5 | 7.9 | 15.0 | 32.3 | 44.7 |
| Mostly free of supervision | 9.7 | 25.4 | 37.9 | 27.1 | 8.0 | 24.9 | 42.2 | 24.8 |
| Reasonably predictable, secure future | 1.4 | 6.2 | 29.9 | 62.5 | 1.1 | 4.4 | 28.3 | 66.1 |
| Can learn new things, new skills | 1.6 | 13.3 | 39.7 | 45.4 | 0.5 | 9.6 | 39.0 | 50.9 |
| Don't have to pretend to be type of person you are not | 4.0 | 3.9 | 17.7 | 74.3 | 5.2 | 5.4 | 18.4 | 70.9 |
| Job most people look up to and respect | 5.2 | 18.1 | 38.8 | 38.0 | 5.7 | 21.3 | 37.7 | 35.3 |
| Permits contact with a lot of people | 6.7 | 21.8 | 35.3 | 36.3 | 10.6 | 23.3 | 37.2 | 28.9 |
| An easy pace that lets you work slowly | 30.3 | 40.7 | 21.4 | 7.6 | 24.9 | 36.9 | 27.2 | 11.1 |

*Source:* J. G. Bachman, L. D. Johnston, and P. M. O'Malley. *Monitoring the future: Questionnaire responses from the nation's high school seniors, 1980.* Ann Arbor, Mich.: Institute for Social Research, 1980. By permission.

***TABLE 11.8** INTRINSIC WORK VALUES AND JOB PERCEPTIONS BY AGE, INCOME, AND LABOR FORCE STATUS[a]*

| | PERCENT RESPONDING "VERY IMPORTANT" TO EACH INTRINSIC WORK REWARD | | PERCENT RATING OWN JOBS "EXCELLENT" WITH RESPECT TO EACH WORK REWARD | |
|---|---|---|---|---|
| | AGE | | AGE | |
| INTRINSIC WORK REWARDS | 18–22 | 30–49 | 18–22 | 30–49 |
| Doing meaningful things | 63.5 | 65.2 | 16.5 | 27.7 |
| A chance to use your mind and abilities | 71.9 | 72.7 | 19.7 | 30.2 |
| New challenges | 61.2 | 55.1 | 18.7 | 26.6 |
| Intellectual stimulation | 41.9 | 40.9 | 7.3 | 15.2 |
| A chance for personal growth | 63.6 | 58.8 | 18.1 | 17.1 |
| Freedom to decide how to do the job | 54.2 | 57.7 | 18.3 | 32.0 |
| Working for a company you respect | 58.4 | 69.3 | 20.3 | 27.1 |
| Appreciation for a job well done | 59.8 | 60.7 | 15.3 | 20.3 |
| Intrinsic work rewards indexes | $\bar{X}$ 27.74 | 27.68 | $\bar{X}$ 20.29 | 23.00 |
| | $SD$ 4.59 | 4.33 | $SD$ 6.25 | 5.43 |
| | $N$ 256 | 454 | $N$ 169 | 361 |
| | $t$ 0.18 | | $t$ 4.83[b] | |

*Source:* P. Y. Miller and W. Simon. Do youth really want to work: A comparison of the work values and job perceptions of younger and older men. *Youth & Society,* 1979, **10**, 379–404. By permission.
[a] Men earning less than $15,000 a year who are not in school or in the military.
[b] $p < .001$.

tended to be somewhat more satisfied with the opportunities provided by their jobs, they showed many of the concerns of the younger workers (119).

In summary, despite a number of differences, including differences in the jobs they aspire to and that they expect, today's young people—college and noncollege, male and female, white-collar and blue-collar—share many common desires. They want work that provides not only job security and a chance to get ahead financially, but that is also interesting to do, uses their skills and abilities, and offers a chance for self-expression and personal growth.

## VOCATIONAL PROSPECTS IN A CHANGING WORLD

What, then, are the future vocational prospects of today's adolescents and young adults, in terms of overall numbers and in terms of the kinds of jobs that are likely to be available? Between 1960 and 1980, the number of young people aged 15 to 24 rose from 12 percent of the population to over 17 percent (162). This rapid increase in the number of youth of working age, combined with a dramatic increase (from 38 percent to 52 percent) in the labor force participation of women during this same period, presented the labor market with a significant absorption problem (22, 143, 164). Between 1980 and 1990, the number of young people aged 15 to 24 will decline by somewhat over 16 percent, and the rate (but not the total numbers) of labor force participation by women will ease (162, 164).

Whether these trends will help to resolve the problem of absorbing young people into meaningful positions in the labor force is still very much an open question, however. During much of the earlier period when the number of young people was increasing rapidly, the economy of the nation was expanding dramatically and prosperity was at near-record levels. Whether this will happen again in the coming decade, despite the recent (1982) steep recession, is still uncertain.

Furthermore, unemployment rates for young people and minorities have consistently exceeded those for other segments of the population—and the margin has been significant—even in the best of times. From 1960 to 1980, youth unemployment ranged from 2.3 to more than 3 times higher than total unemployment (see Table 11.9). Recently, over 20 percent of all teenagers seeking work, and nearly one out of every two black teenagers, have been unemployed, compared to a still distressing 9 percent of all workers (see Figure 11.1). In some inner-city areas, the teenage minority unemployment rate has run as high as 70 percent or more. It appears clear that even in reasonably prosperous times, provision for entry employment of young people generally (and especially minority young people) has had a relatively low priority in the social order, despite protestations to the contrary. In difficult times they suffer severely, and out of all proportion to their numbers.

In 1979, a large joint federal and private task force under the direction of the vice president was appointed by the White House to develop a comprehensive youth employment policy for the decade of the 1980s (4, 43). Currently, however, rather than creating new approaches, the federal government has markedly reduced or eliminated existing youth employment programs, and prospects for a turnaround in the near future do not appear bright. The problem, of course, is not simply one of numbers of jobs, but also of the kinds of jobs that will be needed in the 1980s. It has become increasingly apparent in the last 20 years that automation and rapid technological change, the consolidation of small businesses and farms into larger ones, and increased urbanization are producing significant shifts in employment patterns. As can be seen in Figure 11.2, the numbers of jobs available to unskilled and farm workers declined between 1972 and 1980; those for professional and technical workers, and for workers engaged in service occupations and clerical and sales positions, rose significantly. These trends are expected to continue through the decade of the 1980s (see Figure 11.3). In particular, industries providing services will continue to employ many more people than those providing goods (see Figure 11.4).

What are the implications of these trends for our emerging young adults? It is clear that poorly educated youth with few skills will find themselves increasingly penalized in the years ahead. For example, among 16- to 21-year-olds in 1980 who were seeking work and not in college, more than twice as many dropouts as high school graduates were unemployed (27.2 percent versus 12.6 percent) (162). In the case of already disadvantaged minority-group members, the figures are particularly

**TABLE 11.9** *MAJOR UNEMPLOYMENT INDICATORS:*
*ANNUAL AVERAGES FOR 1960, AND 1970 TO 1980*

| SELECTED CATEGORIES | 1960 | 1970 | 1971 |
|---|---|---|---|
| Total | 5.5 | 4.9 | 5.9 |
| Males, 20 years and over | 4.7 | 3.5 | 4.4 |
| Females, 20 years and over | 5.1 | 4.8 | 5.7 |
| Both sexes, 16–19 years | 14.7 | 15.2 | 16.9 |
| White | 4.9 | 4.5 | 5.4 |
| Black and other races | 10.2 | 8.2 | 9.9 |
| Householders | (NA) | 2.9 | 3.7 |
| Married men, wife present | 3.7 | 2.6 | 3.2 |
| Married women, husband present | (NA) | 4.9 | 5.7 |
| Female family householder, no husband present | (NA) | 5.4 | 7.3 |

worrisome; less than 20 percent of 17-year-old black male high school dropouts, and almost none of the comparable young women, are employed. Even 7 years later—at age 24—only 67 percent of black male dropouts and 35 percent of black female dropouts are working (162, 164).

What is particularly troubling is that while unemployment among white teenagers has consistently exceeded overall unemployment, the actual rate has increased relatively slowly, from 12 percent in 1954 to about 20 percent in 1982. In contrast, unemployment for many black teenagers has soared during this same period from 16.5 percent in 1952 to about 46 percent in 1982. It would appear that we are in real danger of creating a permanent underclass of black youth, excluded from meaningful participation in society. Why have young blacks fared so badly in the labor market, even during prosperous periods?

**The culture of poverty**   As we have seen, one reason for unemployment is that young blacks tend to be concentrated in the inner-city areas of our larger, and often poorer, cities. They tend, as a result, to be more exposed to inadequate and inappropriate educational facilities and to a climate of social disorganization. Many youth training and job programs have not focused on inner-city areas, and those that have are being systematically reduced or eliminated (43, 44). New job opportunities keep emerging further and further from inner-city areas where they are needed. It appears that for many inner-city youth, their only realistic chance of breaking out of the cycle of poverty and despair is with specifically targeted, adequately funded educational and training programs and accessible initial employment opportunities. Unfortunately, governmental policies are currently moving in the opposite direction (43, 44).

Obviously, opportunities will be much greater for both majority- and minority-group youth who have managed to obtain increased skills and education. The relationship between job opportunity and amount of education and training, however, is

| 1972 | 1973 | 1974 | 1975 | 1976 | 1977 | 1978 | 1979 | 1980 |
|------|------|------|------|------|------|------|------|------|
| 5.6  | 4.9  | 5.6  | 8.5  | 7.7  | 7.0  | 6.0  | 5.8  | 7.1  |
| 4.0  | 3.2  | 3.8  | 6.7  | 5.9  | 5.2  | 4.2  | 4.1  | 5.9  |
| 5.4  | 4.8  | 5.5  | 8.0  | 7.4  | 7.0  | 6.0  | 5.7  | 6.3  |
| 16.2 | 14.5 | 16.0 | 19.9 | 19.0 | 17.7 | 16.3 | 16.1 | 17.7 |
| 5.0  | 4.3  | 5.0  | 7.8  | 7.0  | 6.2  | 5.2  | 5.1  | 6.3  |
| 10.0 | 8.9  | 9.9  | 13.9 | 13.1 | 13.1 | 11.9 | 11.3 | 13.2 |
| 3.3  | 2.9  | 3.3  | 5.8  | 5.1  | 4.5  | 3.7  | 3.6  | 4.9  |
| 2.8  | 2.3  | 2.7  | 5.1  | 4.2  | 3.6  | 2.8  | 2.7  | 4.2  |
| 5.4  | 4.6  | 5.3  | 7.9  | 7.1  | 6.5  | 5.5  | 5.1  | 5.8  |
| 7.2  | 7.0  | 7.0  | 10.0 | 10.0 | 9.3  | 8.5  | 8.3  | 9.1  |

*Source:* U.S. Bureau of the Census, Current Population Reports, Series P-20, No. 363, *Population Profile of the United States: 1980.* Washington, D.C.: U.S. Government Printing Office, 1981.

not a simple one, although it appeared to be so only a few years ago, when job demand for highly educated youth exceeded the supply.

### Women in the work force:
### New opportunities and old realities

As we have seen (see pages 457–460), women are entering the labor market in numbers that far outstrip all earlier projections, with no sign of a letup in the decade of the 1980s. Approximately 60 percent of all women aged 18 to 64 (compared to 88 percent of men) currently work outside the home for pay, and their ranks are being increased at the rate of an additional 2 million women each year (12, 22, 143, 162).

What are their vocational prospects? If one looks only at current statistics for women as a whole, the answer appears to be, not very good. Full-time earnings for women are still only about 60 percent of those for men (see Figure 11.5). Only 7.9 percent of women earn $15,000 or more per year, compared with 40 percent of men (162). Furthermore, the great majority still hold jobs in the same traditional fields in which women were employed in the 1940s, 1950s, and 1960s: "In 1980, about 79 percent of all employed women were concentrated in the four largest occupation groups for women: clerical (35 percent); professional workers and service workers, except private household (17 percent each); and operatives, except transport (10 percent). However, only about 62 percent of all employed men were concentrated in the four largest occupation groups for men: craft and kindred workers (21 percent); professional, technical, and kindred workers (16 percent); managers and administrators, except farm (14 percent); and operatives, except transport (11 percent)" (162, *32*).

Nevertheless, the opportunities for relevantly prepared women are expanding—dramatically in some areas (162, 164). During the 1970s, the percentage of female lawyers, judges, bank officials and financial managers, scientists, engineers,

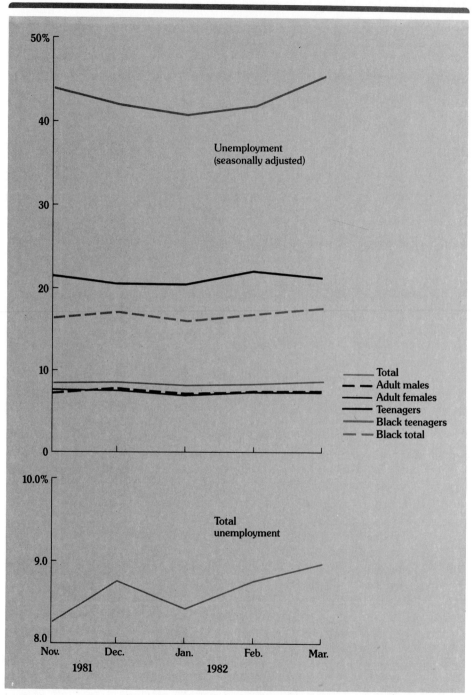

**Figure 11.1** Adult and teenage unemployment rates, 1981–1982. (From U.S. Department of Labor, Bureau of Labor Statistics, 1982.)

electricians, and carpenters doubled (12, 22, 162). During those years the proportion of women accountants rose from 21.7 percent to 36.2 percent, among sales managers in retail trade it has gone from 15.6 percent to 25.7 percent, and among computer specialists it has gone from 16.8 percent to 25.7 percent (see Table 11.10).

Somewhat paradoxically, many of the greatest opportunities for women lie in traditionally masculine fields (which women have frequently been discouraged from considering)—partly because these fields are among those which are expanding most rapidly, and partly to fill affirmative-action goals and redress prior imbalances. These include: engineering, mathematics, advanced computer programming, business administration (at the M.B.A. level), jobs requiring languages such as Russian, Chinese, Japanese, or third world languages, international banking and government, and high technology generally (22, 143). According to the economist Eli Ginzberg, chairman of the National Commission for Employment Policy, academic preparation is a critical factor: "It's a question of what they learned or did not learn in college. If you go through and take a little bit of French, a little history, a little art, you'll be in trouble when you come out. But if you come out with solid training in mathematics, economics, accounting, even biology, you'll have a much easier time" (22, *58*).

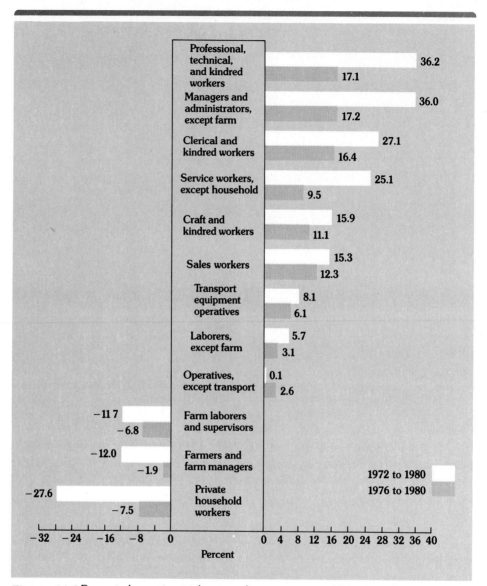

**Figure 11.2** Percent change in employment, by occupation, 1972–1980. (From U.S. Bureau of the Census, Current Population Reports, Series P-20, No. 363, *Population Profile of the United States: 1980.* Washington, D.C.: U.S. Government Printing Office, 1981.)

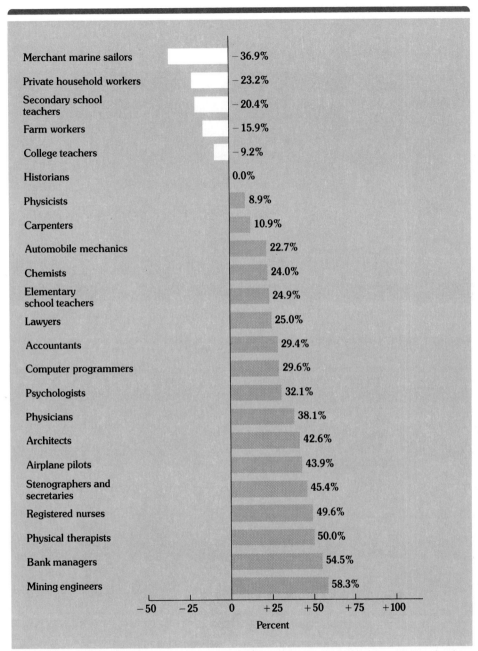

Merchant marine sailors — 36.9%

Private household workers — 23.2%

Secondary school teachers — 20.4%

Farm workers — 15.9%

College teachers — 9.2%

Historians 0.0%

Physicists 8.9%

Carpenters 10.9%

Automobile mechanics 22.7%

Chemists 24.0%

Elementary school teachers 24.9%

Lawyers 25.0%

Accountants 29.4%

Computer programmers 29.6%

Psychologists 32.1%

Physicians 38.1%

Architects 42.6%

Airplane pilots 43.9%

Stenographers and secretaries 45.4%

Registered nurses 49.6%

Physical therapists 50.0%

Bank managers 54.5%

Mining engineers 58.3%

−50    −25    0    +25    +50    +75    +100

Percent

*Figure 11.3* Job requirements and growth, 1978–1990. (From U.S. Department of Labor, Bureau of Labor Statistics. *Occupational projections and training data.* September 1980, Bulletin 2052. Washington, D.C.: U.S. Government Printing Office, 1980.)

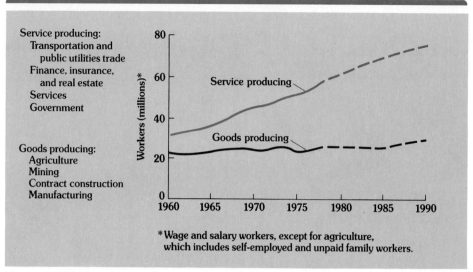

**Figure 11.4** Industries providing services will continue to employ more people than those providing goods. (From U.S. Department of Labor, Bureau of Labor Statistics, *Occupational outlook for college graduates, 1980–81,* Bulletin 2076. Washington, D.C.: U.S. Government Printing Office, 1980 [2nd ed.].)

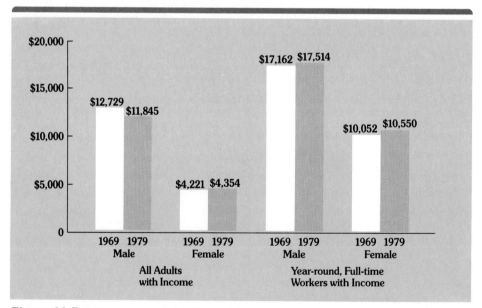

**Figure 11.5** Median income, for males and females 14 years old and over with income, by work experience: 1969 and 1979. (From U.S. Department of the Census, Current Population Reports, Series P-20, No. 363, *Population Profile of the United States: 1980.* Washington, D.C.: U.S. Government Printing Office, 1981.)

**TABLE 11.10** *CHANGES IN SELECTED
EMPLOYMENT PATTERNS FOR WOMEN AND
BLACKS AND OTHER MINORITIES, 1972–1980*

| OCCUPATION | PERCENT FEMALE | | PERCENT BLACK AND OTHER | |
|---|---|---|---|---|
| | 1972 | 1980 | 1972 | 1980 |
| Accountants | 21.7 | 36.3 | 4.3 | 8.2 |
| Computer specialists | 16.8 | 25.7 | 5.5 | 8.0 |
| Engineers | 0.8 | 4.0 | 3.4 | 5.9 |
| Lawyers and judges | 3.8 | 12.8 | 3.8 | 4.2 |
| Life and physical scientists | 10.0 | 20.3 | 7.8 | 9.6 |
| Physicians | 10.1 | 13.4 | 6.2 | 10.8 |
| Registered nurses | 97.6 | 96.5 | 8.2 | 11.4 |
| Social scientists | 21.3 | 36.0 | 5.7 | 5.4 |
| Writers, artists, entertainers | 31.7 | 39.3 | 4.8 | 5.9 |
| Managers and administrators (except farm) | 17.6 | 26.1 | 4.0 | 5.2 |
| Sales clerks | 68.9 | 71.1 | 5.0 | 7.2 |
| Clerical and kindred workers | 75.6 | 80.1 | 8.7 | 11.1 |
| Secretaries | 99.1 | 99.1 | 5.2 | 6.7 |
| Craft and kindred workers | 3.6 | 6.0 | 3.6 | 8.3 |
| Carpenters | 0.5 | 1.5 | 5.9 | 5.7 |
| Electricians | 0.6 | 1.2 | 3.2 | 5.7 |
| Telephone installers | 1.9 | 8.7 | 4.2 | 7.8 |
| Machine operators | 27.0 | 30.7 | 14.4 | 16.1 |
| Bus drivers | 34.1 | 44.9 | 17.1 | 19.9 |
| Laborers (except farm) | 6.3 | 11.6 | 20.2 | 16.9 |
| Construction laborers | 0.5 | 2.8 | 22.4 | 16.6 |
| Gardeners | 2.2 | 5.2 | 20.0 | 16.3 |

*Source:* U.S. Bureau of the Census, *Statistical abstract of the United States: 1981.* Washington, D.C.: U.S. Government Printing Office, 1981 (102nd ed.).

The age at which women begin working and the continuity of their experience also play important roles: "A large part of career development is a function of continuity and experience on the job. If a woman doesn't work from age 28 to 43, she loses relative position in the competition" (22, 59).

Finally, attitudes toward work are important. In the words of Jane Goodin, director of the National Commission on Working Women:

> It is critical that young women understand they have to think in terms of longer-range planning for themselves, and to see one job as a steppingstone to another. Most young women still think the main thing they're going to do is get married and raise a family; they think of their work life as a secondary, incidental kind of thing [22, 59].

The fact, however, is that sooner or later 85 percent of women, for one reason or another, will have to be financially responsible for themselves.

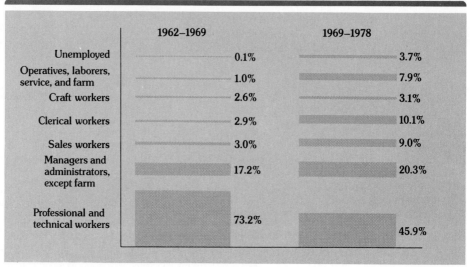

|  | 1962–1969 | 1969–1978 |
|---|---|---|
| Unemployed | 0.1% | 3.7% |
| Operatives, laborers, service, and farm | 1.0% | 7.9% |
| Craft workers | 2.6% | 3.1% |
| Clerical workers | 2.9% | 10.1% |
| Sales workers | 3.0% | 9.0% |
| Managers and administrators, except farm | 17.2% | 20.3% |
| Professional and technical workers | 73.2% | 45.9% |

**Figure 11.6** Jobs entered by college graduates 1962–1969 and 1969–1978, by major occupational group. (From U.S. Department of Labor, Bureau of Labor Statistics, *Occupational outlook for college graduates, 1980–81,* Bulletin 2076. Washington, D.C.: U.S. Government Printing Office, 1980 [2nd ed.].)

### College graduates: Demand and supply in the 1980s

Throughout most of the 1960s, college graduates were almost guaranteed a good job (41, 43, 165, 166). Overall, as students discovered, there were more jobs for which employers were seeking graduates than there were young people to fill them. "Consequently, graduates generally had their pick of jobs and almost all graduates found the kinds of jobs they sought. The job market for college graduates, however, changed dramatically beginning about 1969, and since then, graduates have faced increased competition for the kinds of jobs they wanted" (165, *21*). Slowdowns in the nation's economic growth that occurred in the early and mid-1970s and the early 1980s, and a decrease in the need for new teachers, contributed to this turnaround. However, the main reason for the increased competition faced by college graduates during this period was the rapid increase in the number of graduates seeking jobs. This increase has occurred because of a marked increase in the number of college graduates (which rose from less than 400,000 in 1961 to nearly a million in 1981) and in the proportion of graduates, particularly young women, seeking jobs (165). It is estimated that between 1978 and 1980, the number of college graduates entering the labor force will exceed by 3.3 million the number of openings in jobs traditionally filled by graduates.

As a consequence of this trend, the unemployment rate for recent college graduates, though still significantly lower than that for high school graduates, has nearly tripled in the past decade (from 2.4 to 6.1 percent). In addition, the kinds of jobs entered have also changed; fewer college graduates are now becoming professional or technical workers, and more are becoming clerical, blue-collar, service, and farm workers, not infrequently by outbidding nongraduates (see Figure 11.6). In

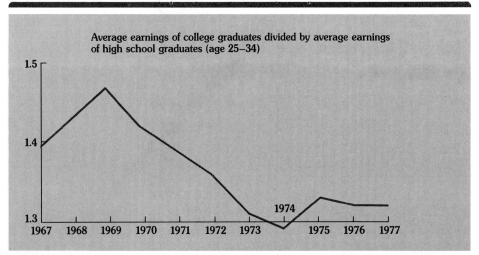

**Figure 11.7** Earnings of college graduates have declined relative to earnings of high school graduates. (From U.S. Department of Commerce, Bureau of the Census, 1980.)

brief, about three out of four college graduates in the 1980s are expected to continue to find the kinds of jobs traditionally filled by graduates; about one in four, however, will need to look to a nontraditional job or face unemployment (165). As a result of both increased competition and the shift in job patterns, the earnings of college graduates relative to those of high school graduates are declining (see Figure 11.7).

Nevertheless, the need for college graduates in the job market is expected to grow faster than the requirements for workers generally in the decade of the 1980s (see Figure 11.8). Furthermore, there are marked variations in projected needs from one occupation to another. For example, as Figure 11.3 illustrates, while the number of secondary school and college teachers is expected to decline in the 1980s, the number of bank managers and mining engineers is expected to increase substantially. Clearly, the relationship to job opportunity of at least the higher levels of education and training will depend as much on the type of training as on its extent. Furthermore, job demands can change rapidly, as rapid fluctuations in the demand for teachers, various kinds of engineers, biomedical and behavioral scientists, and others during the past decade demonstrate dramatically. Indeed, one of the economic problems of a high-technology society is that, on the one hand, it demands highly specialized, frequently nontransferable skills, whereas on the other hand, it also generates rapid shifts in technology and in the economy generally that may make these skills obsolete in a relatively short period of time.

The problem of finding appropriate employment—and even, in some cases, any employment—for young people is not a simple one. And, if anything, it is likely to become more difficult in the future, as our entire society grows more complex, more specialized, more technologically oriented, and more subject to the effects of forces beyond our immediate control. Nevertheless, it is a problem that can and must be solved if we are truly committed to the future of our nation's youth and, indeed, of the nation itself.

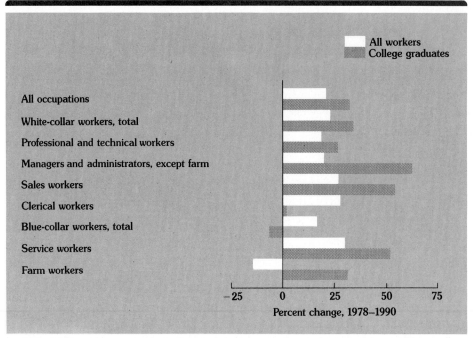

All workers
College graduates

All occupations

White-collar workers, total

Professional and technical workers

Managers and administrators, except farm

Sales workers

Clerical workers

Blue-collar workers, total

Service workers

Farm workers

−25    0    25    50    75

Percent change, 1978–1990

***Figure 11.8*** Requirements for college graduates are expected to grow faster than requirements for all workers. (From U.S. Department of Labor, Bureau of Labor Statistics. *Occupational outlook for college graduates, 1980–81,* Bulletin 2076. Washington, D.C.: U.S. Government Printing Office, 1980 [2nd ed.].)

### REFERENCES
1. Altus, W. D. Birth order and its sequelae. *Science,* 1965, **151,** 44–49.
2. *The American almanac* (The statistical abstract of the United States). New York: Grosset & Dunlap, 1975 (95th ed.).
3. Andrew, J. Getting ahead: In high schools today, youths are absorbed with material goals. *Wall Street Journal,* Wednesday, June 3, 1981, 1, 27.
4. *APA Monitor,* Vol. 10, No. 6, June 1979. Washington, D.C.: American Psychological Association, 1979.
5. Areshansel, C. S., & Rosen, B. C. Domestic roles and sex differences in occupational expectations. *Journal of Marriage and the Family,* 1980, **42,** 121–131.
6. Astin, A. W. Characteristics and attitudes of first-year college students, 1969–1979. *Chronicle of Higher Education,* January 28, 1980, **19,** 4–5.
7. Astin, A. W. *The American freshman: National norms for fall 1980.* Los Angeles: American Council on Education and Graduate School of Education, University of California at Los Angeles, 1981.
8. Astin, A. Freshmen characteristics and attitudes. *Chronicle of Higher Education,* February 17, 1982, **21,** 11–12.
9. Bachman, J. G. *Youth in transition, Vol. II: The impact of family background and intelligence on tenth-grade boys.* Ann Arbor: Institute for Social Research, University of Michigan, 1970.
10. Bachman, J. G., Green, S., & Wirtanen, J. D. *Youth in transition, Vol. III: Dropping out—problem or symptom?* Ann Arbor: Institute for Social Research, University of Michigan, 1971.

11. Bachman, J. G., & Johnston, L. D. *Fewer rebels, fewer causes: A profile of today's college freshmen.* Ann Arbor: Survey Research Center, Institute for Social Research, University of Michigan, 1979.
12. Bachman, J. G., Johnston, L. D., & O'Malley, P. M. *Monitoring the future: Questionnaire responses from the nation's high school seniors, 1980.* Ann Arbor: Survey Research Center, Institute for Social Research, University of Michigan, 1981.
13. Banducci, R. The effect of mother's employment on the achievement, aspirations, and expectations of the child. *Personnel and Guidance Journal,* 1967, **46,** 263–267.
14. Bardwick, J. M. *The psychology of women: A study of bio-cultural conflicts.* New York: Harper & Row, 1971.
15. Bardwick, J. M. *Readings on the psychology of women.* New York: Harper & Row, 1972.
16. Bartol, K. M., & Manhardt, P. J. Sex differences in job outcome preferences: Trends among newly hired college graduates. *Journal of Applied Psychology,* 1979, **64,** 477–482.
17. Baruch, G. K. Maternal influences upon college women's attitudes toward women and work. *Developmental Psychology,* 1972, **6,** 32–37.
18. Baruch, G. K. Maternal role pattern as related to self-esteem and parental identification in college women. Paper presented at the meeting of the Eastern Psychological Association, Boston, April 1972.
19. Bell, A. P. Role modeling of fathers in adolescence and young adulthood. *Journal of Counseling Psychology,* 1969, **16,** 30–35.
20. Below, H. I. Life styles and roles of women as perceived by high-school girls. Unpublished doctoral dissertation. Indiana University, 1969.
21. Benedict, R. *Patterns of culture.* Boston: Houghton Mifflin, 1934.
22. Bennetts, L. Women: New opportunity, old reality. *The New York Times,* National Recruitment Survey, October 14, 1979.
23. Bordin, E. S. A theory of interests as dynamic phenomena. *Educational Psychology Measurements,* 1943, **3,** 49–66.
24. Bordua, D. J. Educational aspirations and parental stress on college. *Social Forces,* 1960, **38,** 262–269.
25. Borow, H. Development of occupational motives and roles. *Review of Child Development Research (Vol. 2).* Chicago: University of Chicago Press, 1966. Pp. 373–422.
26. Borow, H. Career development. In J. F. Adams (ed.), *Understanding adolescence.* Boston: Allyn & Bacon, 1976. Pp. 489–523.
27. Brody, E. B. *Minority group adolescents in the United States.* Baltimore: Williams & Wilkins, 1968.
28. Bronfenbrenner, U. The origins of alienation. *Scientific American,* 1974, **231,** 53–61.
29. Bronfenbrenner, U. *The ecology of human development.* Cambridge, Mass.: Harvard University Press, 1979.
30. Bronfenbrenner, U., & Crouter, A. *Work and family through time and space.* Unpublished manuscript, 1981. A report prepared for the Panel on Work, Family and Community, Committee on Child Development Research and Public Policy. National Academy of Sciences, National Research Council, 1981.
31. Brown, J. D. (ed.). *The hippies.* New York: Time-Life Books, 1967.
32. Burnstein, E. Fear of failure, achievement motivation, and aspiring to prestigeful occupations. *Journal of Abnormal and Social Psychology,* 1963, **67,** 189–193.
33. Caro, F. G. Social class and attitudes of youth relevant for the realization of adult goals. *Social Forces,* 1966, **44,** 492–498.
34. Caro, F. G., & Philblad, C. T. Aspirations and expectations: A reexamination of the bases for social class differences in the occupational orientations of male high school students. *Sociology and Social Research,* 1965, **49,** 465–475.
35. Carter, H. D. The development of interests in vocations. In *Adolescence* (Part I). 43rd Yearbook of the National Social Studies in Education. Chicago: University of Chicago Press, 1944.

36. Cerra, F. Study finds college women still aim for traditional jobs. *The New York Times,* May 11, 1980.

37. Chemers, M. M. The relationship between birth order and leader style. *Journal of Social Psychology,* 1970, **80,** 243–244.

38. Clemson, E. Disadvantaged youth: A study of sex differences in occupational stereo-types and vocational aspirations. *Youth and Society,* 1981, **13,** 39–56.

39. Coleman, J. S. *The adolescent society.* New York: Free Press, 1961.

40. Committee for the Study of National Service. *Youth and the needs of the nation.* Washington, D.C.: Potomac Institute, 1979.

41. Conger, J. J. A world they never knew: The family and social change. *Daedalus,* Fall 1971, 1105–1138.

42. Conger, J. J. A world they never made: Parents and children in the 1970s. Invited address, American Academy of Pediatrics meeting, Denver, April 16, 1975.

43. Conger, J. J. Hostages to fortune: Adolescents and social policy. In H. C. Wallach (ed.), *Approaches to child and family policy.* AAAS selected symposium 56. Boulder, Colo.: Westview Press, 1980. Pp. 75–100.

44. Conger, J. J. Freedom and commitment: Families, youth, and social change. *American Psychologist,* 1981, **36,** 1475–1484.

45. *Denver Post,* September 24, 1979, 1.

46. Derbyshire, R. L. Adolescent identity crisis in urban Mexican Americans in East Los Angeles. In E. B. Brody (ed.), *Minority group adolescents in the United States.* Balti-more: Williams & Wilkins, 1968.

47. Dipboye, W. J., & Anderson, W. F. Occupational stereotypes and manifest needs of high school students. *Journal of Counseling Psychology,* 1961, **8,** 296–304.

48. Douvan, E. Employment and the adolescent. In F. I. Nye and L. W. Hoffman (eds.), *The employed mother in America.* Skokie, Ill.: Rand McNally, 1963.

49. Douvan, E. A., & Adelson, J. *The adolescent experience.* New York: Wiley, 1966.

50. Duvall, E. B. Conceptions of mother roles by five- and six-year-old children of working and non-working mothers. Unpublished doctoral dissertation. Florida State University, 1955.

51. Editors of *Fortune. Youth in turmoil.* New York: Time-Life Books, 1969.

52. Elder, G. H., Jr. Achievement motivation and intelligence in occupational mobility: A longitudinal analysis. *Sociometry,* 1968, **31,** 327–354.

53. Elder, G. H., Jr. Occupational level, motivation, and mobility: A longitudinal analysis. *Journal of Counseling Psychology,* 1968, **15,** 1–7.

54. Elder, G. H., Jr. *Children of the great depression.* Chicago: University of Chicago Press, 1974.

55. Elkind, D. Cognitive structure and adolescent experience. *Adolescence,* 1967, **2,** 427–433.

56. Erikson, E. H. *Identity: Youth and crisis.* New York: Norton, 1968.

57. Fischer, E. H., Wells, C. F., & Cohen, S. L. Birth order and expressed interest in becoming a college professor. *Journal of Counseling Psychology,* 1968, **15,** 111–116.

58. Fitzgerald, L. F., & Crites, J. L. Toward a career psychology of women: What do we know? What do we need to know? *Journal of Counseling Psychology,* 1980, **27,** 44–62.

59. Floud, J. E., Halsey, A. H., & Martin, F. M. (eds.). *Social class and educational oppor-tunity.* London: Heinemann, 1956. Pp. 93–95, 107–108.

60. Forer, L. K. *Birth order and life roles.* Springfield, Ill.: Thomas, 1969.

61. Gallup, G. Gallup youth survey. *Denver Post,* May 29, 1977.

62. Gallup, G. Gallup youth survey. *Denver Post,* April 15, 1979.

63. Gandy, G. L. Birth order and vocational interest. *Developmental Psychology,* 1973, **9,** 406–410.

64. Ginzberg, E. *Occupational choice.* New York: Columbia University Press, 1951.

65. Ginzberg, E. Jobs, dropouts, and automation. In D. Schreiber (ed.), *Profile of the school dropout.* New York: Random House (Vintage Books), 1968. Pp. 125–135.

66. Ginzberg, E. Toward a theory of occupational choice: A restatement. *Vocational Guidance Quarterly,* 1972, **20,** 169–176.
67. Gold, D., & Andres, D. Developmental comparisons between adolescent children with employed and nonemployed mothers. *Merrill-Palmer Quarterly,* 1978, **24,** 243–254.
68. Gold, D., & Andres, D. Developmental comparisons between 10-year-old children with employed and nonemployed mothers. *Child Development,* 1978, **49,** 75–84.
69. Gold, D., & Andres, D. Relations between maternal employment and development of nursery school children. *Canadian Journal of Behavioral Science,* 1978.
70. Goldberg, P. Misogyny and the college girl. Paper presented at the meeting of the Eastern Psychological Association, Boston, April 1967.
71. Goldsen, R., Rosenberg, M., Williams, R., & Suchman, I. *What college students think.* New York: Van Nostrand, 1960.
72. Graduates and jobs: A grave new world. *Time,* May 24, 1971, 49–59.
73. Greenberger, E., & Steinberg, L. D. Part-time employment of in-school youth: A preliminary assessment of costs and benefits. Unpublished manuscript, 1979.
74. Greenberger, E., & Steinberg, L. D. The workplace as a context for the socialization of youth. *Journal of Youth and Adolescence,* 1981, **10,** 185–211.
75. Greenberger, E., & Steinberg, L. D. Sex differences in early labor force experience: Harbinger of things to come. Unpublished manuscript, 1982.
76. Greenberger, E., Steinberg, L., & Ruggiero, M. A job is a job is a job . . . or is it? *Sociology of Work and Occupations,* 1983, in press.
77. Greenberger, E., Steinberg, L. D., & Vaux, A. Adolescents who work: Health and behavioral consequences of job stress. *Developmental Psychology,* 1981, **17,** 691–703.
78. Greenberger, E., Steinberg, L. D., Vaux, A., & McAuliffe, S. Adolescents who work: Effects of part-time employment on family and peer relations. *Journal of Youth and Adolescence,* 1980, **9,** 189–202.
79. Hamilton, S. F., & Crouter, A. C. Work and growth: A review of research on the impact of work experience on adolescent development. *Journal of Youth and Adolescence,* 1980, **9,** 323–338.
80. Harris, L. Change, yes—upheaval, no. *Life,* January 8, 1971, **70,** 22–27.
81. Hartley, R. E. Children's concepts of male and female roles. *Merrill-Palmer Quarterly,* 1960, **6,** 83–91.
82. Hartley, R. E. What aspects of child behavior should be studied in relation to maternal employment? In A. E. Siegel (ed.), *Research issues related to the effects of maternal employment on children.* University Park, Pa.: Social Science Research Center, 1961.
83. Havell, F. M., & Frese, W. Adult role transitions, parental influence, and status aspirations early in the life course. *Journal of Marriage and the Family,* 1982, **44,** 35–49.
84. Herzog, A. R., Bachman, J. G., & Johnston, L. D. *Paid work, child care, and housework: A national study of high school seniors' preferences for sharing responsibilities between husband and wife.* Ann Arbor: Survey Research Center, Institute for Social Research, University of Michigan, 1979.
85. Hetherington, E. M. The effects of familial variables on sex typing, on parent-child similarity, and on imitation in children. In J. P. Hill (ed.), *Minnesota symposia on child psychology* (Vol. 1). Minneapolis: University of Minnesota Press, 1967. Pp 82–107.
86. Hirsch, S. P. Study at the top: Executive high school internships. *Educational Leadership,* 1974, **32,** 112–115.
87. Hoffman, L. W. Early childhood experiences and women's achievement motives. *Journal of Social Issues,* 1972, **28,** 129–155.
88. Hoffman, L. W. The professional woman as mother. *Annals of the New York Academy of Sciences,* 1973, **208,** 211–216.
89. Hoffman, L. W. Effects of maternal employment on the child—A review of the research. *Developmental Psychology,* 1974, **10,** 204–228.
90. Hoffman, L. W. Fear of success in males and females: 1965 and 1971. *Journal of Consulting and Clinical Psychology,* 1974, **42,** 353–358.

91. Hoffman, L. W. Changes in family roles, socialization, and sex differences. *American Psychologist,* 1977, **32,** No. 8, 644–657.

92. Hoffman, L. W. Maternal employment: 1979. *American Psychologist,* 1979, **34,** No. 10, 859–865.

93. Hoffman, L. W. The effects of maternal employment on the academic attitudes and performance of school-aged children. *School Psychology Review,* 1980, **9,** No. 4, 319–336.

94. Hoffman, L. W. Work, family, and socialization of the child. In R. D. Parke, et al. (eds.), *The review of child development research, Volume 7: The family and interdisciplinary perspective.* Chicago: University of Chicago Press, in press.

95. Holland, J. L. Explorations of a theory of vocational choice: Part I. Vocational images and choice. *Vocational Guidance Quarterly,* 1963, **11,** 232–239.

96. Holland, J. L. Explorations of a theory of vocational choice: Part II. Self-descriptions and vocational preferences. *Vocational Guidance Quarterly,* 1963, **12,** 17–24.

97. Horner, M. S. Femininity and successful achievement: A basic inconsistency. In J. M. Bardwick, E. Douvan, M. S. Horner, & D. Guttman (eds.), *Feminine personality and conflict.* Monterey, Calif.: Brooks/Cole, 1970.

98. Horner, M. S. The psychological significance of success in competitive achievement situations: A threat as well as a promise. In H. I. Day, D. E. Berlyne, & D. E. Hunt (eds.), *Intrinsic motivation: A new direction in education.* Canada: Holt, 1971.

99. Huston-Stein, A., & Higgins-Trenk, A. Development of females from childhood through adulthood: Career and feminine role orientations. In P. B. Baltes (ed.), *Life-span development and behavior* (Vol. 1). New York: Academic Press, 1978. Pp. 258–296.

100. Huston, A. C. Sex-typing. In P. H. Hussen (ed.), *Carmichael's manual of child psychology.* New York: Wiley, in press (45th ed.).

101. Kagan, J. The concept of identification. *Psychological Review,* 1958, **65,** 296–305.

102. Kahl, J. A. Educational and occupational aspirations of "common-man" boys. *Harvard Educational Review,* 1953, **23,** 186–203.

103. King, K., McIntyre, J., & Axelson, L. J. Adolescents' views of maternal employment as a threat to the marital relationship. *Journal of Marriage and the Family,* 1968, **30,** 633–637.

104. Kohn, M., & Schooler, C. Occupational and psychological functioning: An assessment of reciprocal effects. *American Sociological Review,* 1973, **38,** 97–118.

105. Kroger, R., & Louttit, C. M. The influence of father's occupation on the vocational choices of high school boys. *Journal of Applied Psychology,* 1935, **19,** 203–212.

106. Kuvelsky, W. P., & Bealer, R. C. The relevance of adolescents' occupational aspirations for subsequent job attainment. *Rural Sociology,* 1967, **32,** 290–301.

107. Lewis, O. *La Vida.* New York: Random House, 1966.

108. Little, J. K. The occupations of non-college youth. *American Educational Research Journal,* 1967, **4,** 147–153.

109. Maccoby, E. E., & Jacklin, C. N. *The psychology of sex differences.* Stanford, Calif.: Stanford University Press, 1974.

110. Maggarrell, J. Today's students, especially women, more materialistic. *Chronicle of Higher Education,* January 28, 1980, **19,** 3.

111. Maggarrell, J. Fewer liberals, more moderates among this year's freshmen. *Chronicle of Higher Education,* February 9, 1981, **20,** 5.

112. Malabre, A. L., Jr. Through good times and bad, joblessness among young blacks keeps right on rising. *Wall Street Journal,* February 1, 1979, 40.

113. Marantz, S. A., & Mansfield, A. F. Maternal employment and the development of sex-role stereotyping in five- to eleven-year-old girls. *Child Development,* 1977, **48,** 668–673.

114. Marcia, J. E. Identity in adolescence. In J. Adelson (ed.), *Handbook of adolescent psychology.* New York: Wiley, 1980. Pp. 159–187.

115. Marini, M. M. Sex differences in the determination of adolescent aspirations: A review. *Sex Roles*, 1978, **4,** 723–753.
116. Mayer, L. A. New questions about the U.S. population. *Fortune*, February 1971, 82–85. Source: U.S. Census, 1970.
117. McCandless, B. *Adolescents: Behavior and development.* New York: Holt, Rinehart and Winston, 1970.
118. Miller, P. Y., & Simon, W. Do youth really want to work: A comparison of the work values and job perceptions of younger and older men. *Youth and Society*, 1979, **10,** 379–404.
119. Miller, S. M. Effects of maternal employment on sex-role perception, interests, and self-esteem in kindergarten girls. *Developmental Psychology*, 1975, **11,** 405–406.
120. Montesano, N., & Geist, H. Differences in occupational choice between ninth and twelfth grade boys. *Personnel and Guidance Journal*, 1964, **43,** 150–154.
121. Morse, N. C., & Weiss, R. S. The function and meaning of work and the job. In D. G. Zytowski (ed.), *Vocational behavior.* New York: Holt, Rinehart and Winston, 1968. Pp. 7–16.
122. Mortimer, J. T. Patterns of intergenerational occupational movements: A smallest-space analysis. *American Journal of Sociology*, 1974, **79,** 1278–1299.
123. Mortimer, J. T. Social class, work, and the family: Some implications of the father's occupation for familial relationships and sons' career decisions. *Journal of Marriage and the Family*, 1976, **38,** No. 2, 241–256.
124. Mussen, P. H., Conger, J. J., & Kagan, J. *Child development and personality.* New York: Harper & Row, 1974 (4th ed).
125. Oberlander, M. I., Frauenfelder, K. J., & Heath, H. Ordinal position, sex of sibling, sex, and personal preferences in a group of eighteen-year-olds. *Journal of Consulting and Clinical Psychology*, 1970, **35,** 122–125.
126. O'Hara, R. P., & Tiedeman, D. V. Vocational self-concept in adolescence. *Journal of Counseling Psychology*, 1959, **6,** 292–301.
127. Palmer, R. D. Birth order and identification. *Journal of Consulting Psychology*, 1966, **30,** 129–135.
128. Pittel, S. M., et al. Developmental factors in adolescent drug use: A study of the psychedelic drug users. *Journal of the American Academy of Child Psychiatry*, 1971, **10,** 640–660.
129. Pittel, S. M., Wallach, A., & Wilner, N. Utopians, mystics, and skeptics: Ideologies of young drug users. San Francisco: Mount Zion Hospital and Medical Center, Department of Psychiatry (prepublication manuscript).
130. Powers, M. G., & Salvo, J. J. Fertility and child care arrangements and mechanisms of status articulation. *Journal of Marriage and the Family*, 1982, **44,** 21–34.
131. Preble, E. The Puerto Rican-American teenager in New York City. In E. B. Brody (ed.), *Minority group adolescents in the United States.* Baltimore: Williams & Wilkins, 1968.
132. Reich, C. A. *The greening of America.* New York: Random House, 1970.
133. Rodman, H. The lower class value stretch. *Social Forces*, 1963, **42,** 205–215.
134. Rosenberg, B. G., & Sutton-Smith, B. Ordinal position and sex-role identification. *Psychological Monographs*, 1964, **70,** 297–328.
135. Schachter, S. Birth order and sociometric choice. *Journal of Abnormal and Social Psychology*, 1964, **68,** 453–456.
136. Seligman, D. A special kind of rebellion. In editors of *Fortune, Youth in turmoil.* New York: Time-Life Books, 1969.
137. Simpson, R. L. Parental influence, anticipatory socialization, and social mobility. *American Sociological Review*, 1962, **27,** 517–522.
138. Singer, J. E. The use of manipulative strategies: Machiavellianism and attractiveness. *Sociometry*, 1964, **27,** 128–150.
139. Sinha, A. K., Prasaa, M. S., & Madhukar, R. P. Extraversion-introversion and rigidity of vocational aspirations. *Guidance Review*, 1964, **2,** 88–94.

140. Smith, D. E., & Luce, J. *Love needs care.* Boston: Little, Brown, 1971.
141. Smith, E. J. The career development of young black females: The forgotten group. *Youth and Society,* 1981, **12,** 277–312.
142. Smith, H. C. *An investigation of the attitudes of adolescent girls toward combining marriage, motherhood and a career.* Doctoral dissertation, Columbia University. Ann Arbor, Mich.: University Microfilms, 1969, No. 69-8089.
143. Smith, R. E. (ed.). *The subtle revolution: Women at work.* Washington, D. C.: Urban Institute, 1979.
144. Steinberg, L. D., Greenberger, E., Garduque, L., & McAuliffe, S. High school students in the labor force: Some costs and benefits to schooling and learning. *Educational Evaluation and Policy Analysis,* in press.
145. Steinberg, L. D., Greenberger, E., Garduque, L., Ruggiero, M., & Vaux, A. The effects of working on adolescent development. Unpublished manuscript, 1982.
146. Steinberg, L. D., Greenberger, E., Jacobi, M., & Garduque, L. Early work experience: A partial antidote for adolescent egocentrism. *Journal of Youth and Adolescence,* 1981, **10,** 141–202.
147. Steinberg, L. D., Greenberger, E., Vaux, A., & Ruggiero, M. Early work experience: Effects of adolescent occupational socialization. *Youth and Society,* 1981, **12,** 403–422.
148. Stephenson, R. Mobility orientation and gratification of 1,000 ninth graders. *American Sociological Review,* 1957, **22,** 203–212.
149. Stephenson, S. P. From school to work: A transition with job-search implications. *Youth and Society,* 1979, **11,** 114–133.
150. Stephenson, S. R., Jr. Young women and labor: In-school labor force status and early postschool labor market outcomes. *Youth and Society,* 1981, **13,** 123–155.
151. Stevenson, W. The relationship between early work experience and future employability. In A. Adams & G. Mangum (eds.), *The lingering crisis of youth unemployment.* Kalamazoo, Mich.: W. E. Upjohn Institute for Employment Research, 1978.
152. Stevic, R., & Uhlig, G. Occupational aspirations of selected Appalachian youth. *Personnel and Guidance Journal,* 1967, **45,** 435–439.
153. Stotland, E., & Walsh, J. Birth order and an experimental study of empathy. *Journal of Abnormal and Social Psychology,* 1963, **66,** 610–614.
154. Sundheim, B. The relationships between achievement, affiliation, sex role concepts, academic grades, and curricular choice. *Dissertation Abstracts,* 1963, **23,** 3471.
155. Super, D. E. A theory of vocational development. *American Psychologist,* 1953, **8,** 185–190.
156. Super, D. E, Starishevsky, R., Matlin, N., & Jordaan, J. P. *Career development: Self concept theory.* New York: College Entrance Examination Board, 1963.
157. Sutton-Smith, B., Roberts, J. M., & Rosenberg, B. G. Sibling associations and role involvement. *Merrill-Palmer Quarterly on Behavioral Development,* 1964, **10,** 25–38.
158. Sutton-Smith, B., & Rosenberg, B. G. *The sibling.* New York: Holt, Rinehart and Winston, 1971.
159. Tangri, S. S. Determinants of occupational role innovation among college women. *Journal of Social Issues,* 1972, **28,** 177–199.
160. Tittle, C. K. Life plans and values of high school students. Paper presented at the annual meeting of the American Psychological Association, Montreal, September 1980.
161. Tittle, C. K. *Careers and family: Sex roles and adolescent life plans.* Beverly Hills, Calif.: Sage Publications, 1981.
162. U.S. Bureau of the Census, Current population reports, Series P-20, No. 363, *Population profile of the United States: 1980.* Washington, D.C.: U.S. Government Printing Office, 1981.
163. U.S. Bureau of Labor Statistics. *Perceptives on working women: A databook.* Bulletin 2080. Washington, D.C.: U.S. Government Printing Office, 1980.
164. U.S. Department of Commerce, Bureau of the Census. *Statistical abstract of the United States, 1981.* Washington, D.C.: U.S. Government Printing Office, 1981.

165. U.S. Department of Labor, Bureau of Labor Statistics. *Occupational outlook for college graduates, 1980–81 edition.* Bulletin 2076. Washington, D.C.: U.S. Government Printing Office, 1980.

166. U.S. Department of Labor, Bureau of Labor Statistics. *Occupational projections and training data, 1980 edition.* Bulletin 2052. Washington, D.C.: U.S. Government Printing Office, 1980.

167. *U.S. News and World Report.* September 6, 1976, 52–53.

168. Vandenberg, D. Life-phases and values. *Education Forum,* 1968, **32,** 293–302.

169. Very, P. S., & Prull, R. W. Birth order, personality development and the choice of law as a profession. *Journal of Genetic Psychology,* 1970, **116,** 219–221.

170. Very, P. S., & Zannini, J. A. Relationship between birth order and being a beautician. *Journal of Applied Psychology,* 1969, **53,** 149–151.

171. Vogel, S. R., Broverman, I. K., Broverman, D. M., Clarkson, F. E., & Rosenkrantz, P. S. Maternal employment and perception of sex roles among college students. *Developmental Psychology,* 1970, **3,** 384–391.

172. Walker, R. H. *Analysis and synthesis of DOL experience in youth transition to work programs.* Springfield, Va.: National Technical Information Service, 1976.

173. Werts, C. E. Social class and initial career choice of college freshmen. *Sociology of Education,* 1966, **39,** 74–85.

174. Werts, C. E. Paternal influence on career choice. *Journal of Counseling Psychology,* 1968, **15,** 48–52.

175. White, K. M., & Ovellette, P. L. Occupational preferences: Children's perceptions of self and opposite sex. *Journal of Genetic Psychology,* 1980, **136,** 37–43.

176. Wolensky, R. P. College students in the fifties: The silent generation revisited. In S. C. Feinstein & P. L. Giovacchini, *Adolescent psychiatry: Developmental and clinical studies* (Vol. 5). New York: Aronson, 1977.

177. Yankelovich, D. *Generations apart.* New York: CBS News, 1969.

178. Yankelovich, D. *The new morality: A profile of American youth in the 1970s.* New York: McGraw-Hill, 1974.

179. Yankelovich, D. *New rules: Searching for self-fulfillment in a world turned upside down.* New York: Random House, 1981.

180. Zajonc, R. B., & Markus, G. B. Birth order and intellectual development. *Psychological Review,* 1975, **28,** 74–78.

181. Zytowski, D. G. (ed.). *Vocational behavior.* New York: Holt, Rinehart and Winston, 1968. Pp. 7–16.

Adolescents and drugs

CHAPTER 12

# Adolescents and drugs

**D**rug use among adolescents and youth increased markedly in the last decade and a half (1, 82, 144). Many adults viewed this increase as a unique, isolated phenomenon—almost exclusively a product of the youth culture of the latter 1960s. Such a view is misleading and hampers attempts to put the problem in proper perspective. Widespread drug use and abuse are not restricted to adolescents, and did not begin with the advent of sixties youth culture. Although there have been, and to some extent still are, significant differences between generations in their patterns of drug use, the fact is that the broader society, of which adolescents are a part, has been developing into a drug culture for many years. For example, one-quarter to one-third of all prescriptions currently being written in the United States are for pep or diet pills (amphetamines) or tranquilizers, such as Valium and Librium. Valium use has nearly doubled since 1964, and it is now the most widely prescribed drug in the nation. It is estimated that 10 to 15 percent of all Americans took this drug in 1980 (55).

Television and radio bombard viewers with their insistent messages that relief for almost anything—anxiety, depression, restlessness—is "just a swallow away." In the words of one 13-year-old, "We're not supposed to take drugs but TV is full of commercials showing people running for a pill because something is bugging them." To the extent that adolescents have adopted this view, they may be reflecting societal and parental models. Indeed, research has shown that young people whose parents make significant use of such drugs as alcohol, tranquilizers, tobacco, sedatives, and amphetamines are more likely than other adolescents to use marijuana, alcohol, and other drugs themselves. As one 15-year-old boy expressed it, "In my house, you can't sneeze without getting a pill. My mother is always taking something for headaches and my father is always taking something to keep awake to get work done at night. They're not drunks but they sure drink a lot. So, now I'm a criminal for smoking pot?"

It is also true that while too many adolescents are becoming serious, high-risk drug users, the majority are not. Despite dire predictions in the latter 1960s about the imminence of an epidemic of adolescent drug use, the epidemic has not materialized. Although use of marijuana, alcohol, and tobacco is widespread among young

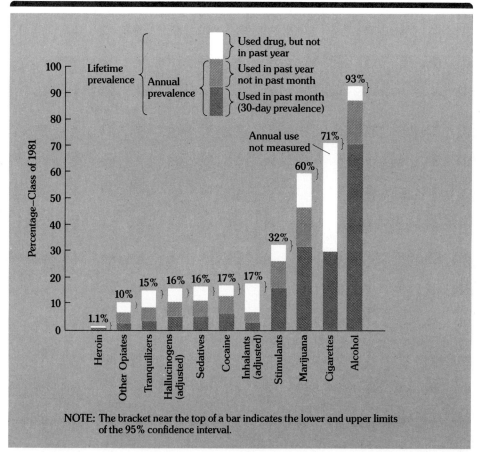

**Figure 12.1** Prevalence and recency of use of eleven types of drugs, class of 1981. *Note:* The brace near the top of a bar indicates the lower and upper limits of the 95% confidence interval. (From L. D. Johnston, J. G. Bachman, and P. M. O'Malley. *Student Drug Use in America, 1975–1981.* U.S. Department of Health and Human Services. Washington, D.C.: National Institute on Drug Abuse, 1981, DHHS Publication No. [ADM] 82-1208.)

people, use of such counterculture drugs as LSD and similar substances, inhalants (e.g., glue), "uppers" (amphetamines) and "downers" (barbiturates), and such more recent entrants into the youthful drug scene as heroin, cocaine, PCP ("angel dust"), and Quaaludes, never exceeded one person in five in the United States (and less in most other Western countries), and many former occasional users have quit (see Figure 12.1).

Furthermore, by 1981, overall adolescent drug use appeared either to have reached a plateau or to have declined (80, 82). Regular use of marijuana (particularly daily use), which had been rising steadily among high school students over the last 15 years, showed a steady decline (from 10.7 to 7.0 percent) between 1978 and 1981 (see Figure 12.2). Decreases also occurred in the annual, monthly, and daily

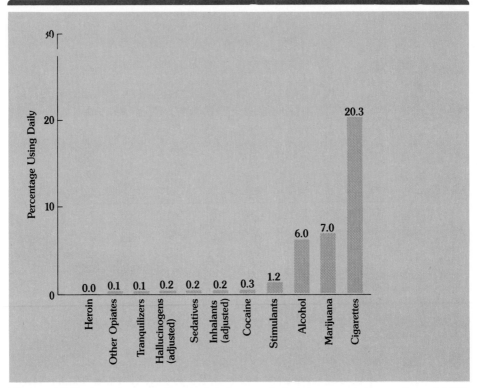

**Figure 12.2** Thirty-day prevalence of daily use of eleven types of drugs, class of 1981. (From L. D. Johnston, J. G. Bachman, and P. M. O'Malley. *Student Drug Use in America, 1975–1981.* U.S. Department of Health and Human Services. Washington, D.C.: National Institute on Drug Abuse, 1981, DHHS Publication No. [ADM] 82-1208.)

use of inhalants, barbiturates, tranquilizers, cigarettes, and alcohol. The use of cocaine among high school seniors leveled off in 1980, following several years of rapid increase, but rose again slightly in 1981. Heroin use, never large, remained steady, as did use of hallucinogens and PCP, and the use of other narcotics declined slightly. In contrast, stimulants (amphetamines) showed a significant increase in 1981 (see Table 12.1).

Nevertheless, there is little room for complacency. As we shall see, almost 10 percent of 14-year-olds are already heavy drinkers. Seven percent of high school seniors reported daily use of marijuana in 1981, down from 10.3 percent in 1979. A small but significant minority of these, according to teachers, are arriving at school "stoned" and smoking again during the school day (82).

The greatest danger in the minds of most of us who work with adolescents is not the young person who occasionally has a few drinks or smokes a marijuana "joint" at a party with friends "for fun"; it is the adolescent or youth who turns repeatedly to drugs in order to cope with insecurity, stress, psychological tension, low self-esteem, feelings of rejection or alienation, conflicts with parents, or prob-

**TABLE 12.1 TRENDS IN 30-DAY PREVALENCE OF SIXTEEN TYPES OF DRUGS**

PERCENT WHO USED IN LAST 30 DAYS

| | CLASS OF 1975 | CLASS OF 1976 | CLASS OF 1977 | CLASS OF 1978 | CLASS OF 1979 | CLASS OF 1980 | CLASS OF 1981 | '80-'81 CHANGE |
|---|---|---|---|---|---|---|---|---|
| Approx. N = | (9400) | (15400) | (17100) | (17800) | (15500) | (15900) | (17500) | |
| Marijuana/hashish | 27.1 | 32.2 | 35.4 | 37.1 | 36.5 | 33.7 | 31.6 | -2.1s |
| Inhalants | NA | 0.9 | 1.3 | 1.5 | 1.7 | 1.4 | 1.5 | +0.1 |
| Inhalants adjusted[a] | NA | NA | NA | NA | 3.1 | 2.7 | 2.3 | -0.4 |
| Amyl and butyl nitrites[b] | NA | NA | NA | NA | 2.4 | 1.8 | 1.4 | -0.4 |
| Hallucinogens | 4.7 | 3.4 | 4.1 | 3.9 | 4.0 | 3.7 | 3.7 | 0.0 |
| Hallucinogens adjusted[c] | NA | NA | NA | NA | 5.5 | 4.4 | 4.4 | 0.0 |
| LSD | 2.3 | 1.9 | 2.1 | 2.1 | 2.4 | 2.3 | 2.5 | +0.2 |
| PCP[b] | NA | NA | NA | NA | 2.4 | 1.4 | 1.4 | 0.0 |
| Cocaine | 1.9 | 2.0 | 2.9 | 3.9 | 5.7 | 5.2 | 5.8 | +0.6 |
| Heroin | 0.4 | 0.2 | 0.3 | 0.3 | 0.2 | 0.2 | 0.2 | 0.0 |
| Other opiates[d] | 2.1 | 2.0 | 2.8 | 2.1 | 2.4 | 2.4 | 2.1 | -0.3 |
| Stimulants[d] | 8.5 | 7.7 | 8.8 | 8.7 | 9.9 | 12.1 | 15.8 | +3.7sss |
| Sedatives[d] | 5.4 | 4.5 | 5.1 | 4.2 | 4.4 | 4.8 | 4.6 | -0.2 |
| Barbiturates[d] | 4.7 | 3.9 | 4.3 | 3.2 | 3.2 | 2.9 | 2.6 | -0.3 |
| Methaqualone[d] | 2.1 | 1.6 | 2.3 | 1.9 | 2.3 | 3.3 | 3.1 | -0.2 |
| Tranquilizers[d] | 4.1 | 4.0 | 4.6 | 3.4 | 3.7 | 3.1 | 2.7 | -0.4 |
| Alcohol | 68.2 | 68.3 | 71.2 | 72.1 | 71.8 | 72.0 | 70.7 | -1.3 |
| Cigarettes | 36.7 | 38.8 | 38.4 | 36.7 | 34.4 | 30.5 | 29.4 | -1.1 |

*Source:* L. D. Johnston, J. G. Bachman, and P. M. O'Malley. *Student Drug Use in America, 1975–1981.* U.S. Department of Health and Human Services. Washington, D.C.: National Institute on Drug Abuse, 1981, DHHS Publication No. (ADM) 82-1208.

*Note:* Level of significance of difference between the two most recent classes: s = .05, ss = .01, sss = .001. NA indicates data not available.

[a] Adjusted for underreporting of amyl and butyl nitrites.

[b] Data based on a single questionnaire form. N is one-fifth of N indicated.

[c] Adjusted for underreporting of PCP.

[d] Only drug use that was not under a doctor's orders is included here.

lems of daily living. One of the important developmental tasks of adolescence is learning to cope with stress, conflict, and frustration; others include the development of cognitive, social, and vocational skills and the establishment of rewarding interpersonal relationships with peers and adults. Failure to master these essential developmental demands during adolescence because of repeated escapes into the world of drugs leaves the young person ill prepared to meet the additional demands of responsible adulthood. Unfortunately, a significant minority of vulnerable adolescents who may think that they are trying drugs only for fun or to experiment are finding that drug use becomes a psychological crutch that is increasingly difficult to renounce.

Our principal aim in this chapter will be to examine the various reasons adolescents take drugs. But first it is necessary to examine the range of drugs available to young people, and their effects. One of the mistakes that adults have made in the past in dealing with adolescent drug use has been to equate one drug with another in dangerousness. Too often, for example, adults (and governments) tried to tell adolescents that marijuana was as harmful and addictive as heroin; when young people discovered for themselves that these adults were exaggerating some of the dangers of marijuana, many were, unfortunately, likely to conclude that the dangers of a variety of high-risk drugs were also being exaggerated.

## ALCOHOL

A few years ago, clinicians and others who work with young people often heard a familiar parental refrain: "I'm becoming concerned that Johnny (or Susie) may be drinking a bit too much. But at least it's better than drugs." What these parents were failing to realize, of course, is that alcohol is just as much a psychoactive drug as is, for example, marijuana, and its dangers for a significant minority have been far more clearly established (40, 124, 163, 164). Furthermore, use of alcohol provides no assurance against the use of other drugs; indeed, prior and concomitant use of alcohol (and tobacco) is more common among marijuana and other drug users than among nonusers (93, 95, 146).

What these parents really appeared to be saying, in the wake of the youth revolution of the sixties and early seventies, was that alcohol was a more familiar phenomenon to them, was more socially acceptable in adult society, and consequently seemed less mysterious and frightening—less likely to indicate a rejection of parental or societal values. As the strength of generational conflicts began to subside in the latter 1970s, and as public awareness of the severity of alcohol problems among a significant minority of adolescents increased, parental attitudes began changing. In recent polls, adults have expressed as great (or greater) concern with alcohol use among adolescents as with marijuana use.

In addition, a number of states have increased their legal drinking ages from 18 to 19, 20, or 21 (largely in an effort to forestall older youth from bringing alcohol to school or other social functions and sharing it with younger adolescents) (160). And the federal government recently budgeted $3.1 million for confronting adolescent alcohol problems. Although the greatest concern is for the minority of youth who will become serious problem drinkers, there is also a concern for the potentially adverse

effects of occasional heavy social drinking. Nine percent of all automobile fatalities in 1977 involved drunken drivers under 20 years of age (124); research has consistently shown that between 45 and 60 percent of all fatal crashes with a young driver are alcohol related (40).

### Adolescent use of alcohol

How widespread is the use of alcohol among adolescents? Virtually all studies agree that the vast majority of young people have at least tried alcoholic beverages by the end of adolescence (3, 82, 126, 136, 144). Among high school seniors in the United States in 1981, 93 percent acknowledged having used alcohol at some time—a higher overall incidence than for any other psychoactive drug, including marijuana. Frequency of alcohol use has been found to vary with such factors as age, sex, social-class status, religious affiliation, ethnic background, geographic area (including rural and urban settings), and personal and social characteristics (3, 7, 40, 78, 82, 124, 136). For example, results of a nationwide study indicated that among seventh graders, 60 percent of boys and 47 percent of girls had at least tried drinking; by twelfth grade, these figures increased to 95 percent for boys and 92 percent for girls (41). Students not planning to complete 4 years of college drink more than those who do. Those living in large metropolitan areas drink more than their rural and small-town peers, and those living in the Northeast and North Central states drink more than those living in the South and West at all ages from 14 to 18 (3, 82, 136).

Alcohol use among adolescents increased dramatically between 1966 and 1975 (e.g., in 1966, only 19 percent of adolescents reported ever having been

drunk; by 1975 the proportion had increased to 45 percent) (124). Between 1975 and 1981, overall alcohol use increased modestly, with slightly more adolescents drinking each year, and at slightly younger ages. For example, during this period the percentage of high school seniors who reported drinking in the past 30 days increased from 68.2 percent to 71 percent; the number of those who began drinking prior to tenth grade increased from 50 percent in 1975 to 57 percent in 1981 (80, 82). Sex differences are decreasing, as are rural-urban and regional differences (3, 82). Among college students, between 70 and 95 percent are active drinkers (40).

It should be emphasized that the majority of adolescents who engage in drinking still are temperate in their use of alcohol, and are likely to remain so (40, 124). What is of far greater concern to clinicians and others who work with young people is the relatively small but important minority who drink frequently and heavily: Six percent of 1981 high school seniors (8.6 percent of boys and 3.5 percent of girls) reported daily use of alcohol in the past month (82). In a related study, 12 percent reported heavy drinking (more than five drinks in a row) three to five times in the past two weeks, while 5.5 percent engaged in heavy drinking six or more times in the same period (80).

In another national study, 21 percent of tenth- to twelfth-grade boys and 8.9 percent of girls were classified as heavy drinkers (defined as drinking at least once a week, typically in large amounts—more than 2.7 ounces of absolute alcohol, or enough to get drunk) (135, 136). Of even greater concern, 4.3 percent of 13-year-olds and 9.7 percent of 14-year-olds were already heavy drinkers (136). If one uses somewhat broader criteria of problem drinking (drunk at least six times in the past year, and leading on two or more occasions to such negative consequences as getting into difficulty with teachers, friends, dates, or the police), 23 percent of boys and 15 percent of girls, grades seven through twelve, fall into the category of problem drinkers (41).

In brief, it appears clear that most adolescents are not problem drinkers and are not likely to become so; nevertheless, the fact that, for example, nearly 10 percent of 14-year-olds are already heavy drinkers can hardly be viewed as reassuring. Furthermore, these nationwide findings are restricted to young people still in school, and the incidence of problem drinking is known to be substantially higher among school dropouts (3).

### The context of adolescent drinking

Most adolescents who begin to drink do so at home under parental supervision (3, 8, 106). Much of this drinking occurs on holidays and other special occasions. "As the teen-ager grows older, more drinking tends to take place outside the home and with less adult supervision. Indeed, the most likely places for teen-age drinking are those where adults are not present" (3, 20). Although the proportion of adolescents at each grade who report drinking at home tends to remain the same, there is an increase in away-from-home drinking with increasing age. The percentage of teenagers who report drinking at night in cars increases through the tenth grade to 50 percent (3).

### Characteristics of student drinkers

In general, adolescent abstainers are more likely than either moderate or heavy drinkers to be conservative, controlled, responsible, studious, cautious, religious, and interested in solitary pursuits; they are less likely to be adventurous, outgoing, socially assertive, impulsive, socially and sexually active, subject to mood swings, critical of society, or tolerant of socially deviant behavior (14, 17, 41, 74, 75, 76, 135). They are also less likely to be depressed or unhappy, or to complain of psychosomatic symptoms, such as headaches, nervousness, rapid heartbeat, or loss of appetite (118, 170). Abstainers are more likely to come from close-knit families, composed of conservative, religious, hard-working, nondrinking parents who place a high value on education (14, 17, 74, 78, 135).

In contrast, adolescents and youth who are heavy or problem drinkers are more likely than either abstainers or moderate drinkers to place a high value on independence, to engage heavily in social activities (such as dances, parties, and dating), to be impulsive and engage in socially disapproved or deviant behavior (such as cutting classes, cheating on examinations, driving too fast, breaking school rules, engaging in sexual "adventurism," using other drugs), and to be dominant and outgoing (17, 41, 76, 135). Heavy drinkers are more likely to experience feelings of exuberance and excitement than are abstainers or moderate drinkers; however, they are also more likely to be pessimistic, unhappy, bored, impulsive, distrustful, cynical, and irresponsible (29, 135, 170). "Male and especially female drinkers reported more frequent feelings of an inability to get going, of boredom, and of vague uneasiness. Furthermore, significantly greater proportions of female heavy drinkers reported feeling lonely or remote from people, angry at some minor frustration, depressed or unhappy, and restless" (118, 357). They are also more likely to complain of psychosomatic symptoms, and to use a variety of medications, ranging from aspirin and vitamins to laxatives and tranquilizers (118).

At all levels, from junior high school to college entrance, problem or heavy drinkers report more difficulties in relations with their parents; they are also less likely to value academic achievement, expect less academic success, and do, in fact, obtain lower grades (17, 74, 94, 118, 135). At the college level, heavy drinkers are significantly less likely than abstainers to major in the biological or physical sciences, and more likely to major in education or the social sciences (118). Not surprisingly, they have a higher rate of academic failure and dropping out (17, 118, 135). Finally, heavy drinkers are more likely to have parents who drink (in a disproportionate number of cases, heavily), as well as friends and best friends who also drink (17, 76, 118, 135).

Variations in adolescent drinking patterns appear remarkably similar in many ways to those of adults (3, 29, 40, 124). As in the case of adolescents, adult drinking has been found to be more frequent among males than females, and among residents of urban areas. It is somewhat more common among younger than among older adults (3, 8, 40). Problem drinking occurs most frequently among older youth and young adults, and tends to decline with age. It is also most common among males; persons who are separated, single, or divorced (in that order); and those with no religious affiliation (3, 123).

### Effects of alcohol

Despite popular notions that alcohol serves as a stimulant, the fact is that it is basically a "primary and continuous depressant of the central nervous system" (33, 85). Further, this depressant effect increases in proportion to the percentage of alcohol in the blood and is greater for more complex and unfamiliar tasks than for simpler and already well learned tasks (36, 124). Even in small doses, alcohol impairs perception and time estimation; reduces reasoning, learning ability, and memory; and produces a relative impoverishment of thought content (36).

Such results can hardly be considered surprising when it is realized that alcohol is basically an anesthetic (163). In higher dosages, increasingly basic brain functions are impaired, resulting in unmistakable abnormality of gross bodily functions and mental faculties, and ultimately, in coma and in some extreme instances, even death (although usually the individual passes out before consuming sufficient alcohol to suspend the operation of basic brain functions regulating breathing, heart action, and the like). In addition to its direct effects on the central nervous system, alcohol may also adversely affect hormonal activity of the pituitary gland and gonads (in males, testosterone production is reduced and estrogen increased); action of the adrenal glands; and kidney, cardiovascular, brain, and liver function (40, 124). In combination with smoking, excessive use of alcohol appears related to the development of certain cancers (40, 124). Heavy drinking during pregnancy can adversely affect fetal development (30, 40, 152). It is currently estimated that *fetal alcohol syndrome* (characterized by retarded growth, physical abnormalities, and intellectual defects) may result from maternal consumption of 3 ounces of absolute alcohol per day (about six drinks). Even smaller doses (1 ounce or more a day) increase the likelihood of low birth weight, developmental delays, physical difficulties (e.g., breathing, sucking ability), and spontaneous abortion (40, 62).

### Alcohol and personality functioning

Most behavioral studies of the effects of alcohol have dealt primarily with the individual's efficiency in the performance of specific tasks. Studies of this sort have definite value, but they leave unanswered many vital questions about the effects of alcohol on the individual's overall adjustment.

To take a simple example, it might well be asked why any individual who has once experienced to a considerable degree the various impairments of function just described would continue to drink. And yet millions of people do—and a small percentage of them to excess. It might also be noted, at least with respect to social behavior, that the change that frequently occurs after a few drinks at an initially rather constrained social gathering would seem to be more aptly described in terms of apparent stimulation than of depression.

Studies of specific psychological factors also tend to be of little assistance in explaining the tremendous variability in the effect of alcohol on different individuals. When Circe gave the same drink to all of Ulysses' shipmates, some of them turned into bears, others into pigs and monkeys. Somewhat similar observations can be made at almost any large cocktail party (36).

### Why do adolescents drink?

As in the case of drug use generally, one may infer that because drinking occurs, it must be motivated; and in instances in which it is continued, it must somehow be rewarded or reinforced. Motives for initial experimentation of young people with alcohol are not difficult to find, nor, for the most part, do they appear particularly complex or puzzling. They may include curiosity, influence of peers (although it should be noted that a majority, even of drinking adolescents, do not disapprove of or reject nondrinkers), identification with parental or other adult models who drink (or, conversely, expressions of independence from, or rebellion against, nondrinking models), or simply a desire to be sociable or to appear grown up (14, 16, 50, 91, 106, 112). For some, particularly males, a desire to seem bold and daring may be involved (8, 14).

Once the drinking response has occurred, its continuance implies that it has proved reinforcing. What is the nature of these reinforcements? Again, in many instances the answers seem relatively simple. First, alcohol tends to reduce anxiety or fear, as well as other sources of tension (34, 35, 109). Decreases in anxiety and tension, manifested in familiar feelings of relaxation and well-being, may be sufficient in themselves to reinforce the drinking response. Drinking may also acquire learned reward value through its association with pleasant personal and social events, such as dates, parties, and celebration of holidays. In other instances, however, the question of reinforcement becomes more complex. Alcohol may serve to resolve conflict situations (34, 35). An adolescent boy may want to ask a girl for a date, or to engage in sexual behavior, but he is afraid to. A young woman may wish to break off a relationship, but is fearful of the consequences. A young man may want to ask his boss for a raise, but fears being rebuffed. If, in any of these situations, taking a drink to bolster one's courage (i.e., to reduce anxiety) is successful, with the result that the previously inhibited response then occurs and is rewarded, the drinking response itself may be further strengthened by a *double reinforcement*—reduction of fear or anxiety and reinforcement provided by the execution of the previously inhibited approach response.

This theoretical model may also help to explain some of the variable effects of alcohol on different individuals. Ingestion of alcohol may lead to aggressiveness in some persons, to dependent responses in others, or to sexual responses in still others. According to this model, such puzzling variability may be explained in terms of individual variations in the previously inhibited response tendencies that are released as a consequence of drinking (and its attendant reduction in anxiety) (35).

If we assume that drinking is learned because it is reinforced, an apparent exception is offered by the adolescent or adult whose drinking has become, at least socially, more punishing than rewarding. The young man who is alienating his employer, his girlfriend, and his friends hardly seems to be socially rewarded for drinking. However, two factors should be considered here. One is the immediacy of reinforcement (see Chapter 2). Immediate reinforcements are more effective than delayed ones. This learning principle is called *the gradient of reinforcement.* It may be that the immediate reduction in anxiety more than compensates for the punitive attitude of the young man's acquaintances the next morning. The other factor is the amount of drive and conflict involved. "The personal anxiety-reducing effects of alcohol may, if the anxiety is great enough, constitute greater reinforcement than the competing social punishment" (35, *303*).

Similar mechanisms may be involved in the excessive use of other potentially destructive drugs, such as speed (amphetamines) or heroin. The immediate effects of mainlining (injecting) speed—the orgasmic sensations, the immediate relief from anxiety, despair, feelings of worthlessness, or even physical pain—may outweigh the increasingly negative longer-term effects of the drug. One of the reasons that a minority of adolescents and adults become addicted to alcohol or to a variety of other drugs, whereas a majority do not, may be that the former have more acute and intense needs for which they are unable to gain relief in other, less destructive ways—whether these needs be primarily psychological, physiological, or some combination of the two (163, 164).

In several recent studies (26, 50), the functions of adolescent drinking were divided into three categories: *positive-social,* in which alcohol is used largely for social activities of a pleasant, convivial nature; *personal-effect,* in which alcohol use is related "to unresolved problems or inadequacies of a psychological nature" (50, *329*), and is used to escape or relieve such problems or to achieve goals not otherwise attainable; and *experiential,* in which alcohol is used to induce pleasant emotional states, religious experiences, self-awareness, and changes in perception. In terms of the theoretical model described here, one would suspect that adolescents who drink for *personal effect* would be more likely to end up in treatment for serious alcohol or other drug problems, and the clinical experience of adolescent drug therapists, as well as research, tends to confirm this expectation.

## *TOBACCO*

Among young people between the ages of 12 and 18 in 1979, some 3.3 million—12 percent of that age group—engaged in cigarette smoking, at least weekly. Although this represented a 25-percent decline from the 1974 incidence of 16 percent, it matched the incidence of 12 percent found in 1968. This does not mean, however, that patterns of adolescent smoking in 1979 were the same as they were in 1968. What happened was that while the incidence of smoking among boys declined significantly during the 1970s, the incidence for girls rose dramatically. For example, among 17- to 18-year-olds, smoking by boys decreased from 31 to 19 percent between 1968 and 1979, while smoking by girls increased from 19 to 26 percent. Reversing long-established patterns, girl smokers began to outnumber boys—1.7 million to 1.6 million. Girls also smoke somewhat more heavily; among high school seniors in 1981, almost 13.8 percent of girls, compared to 12.8 percent of boys, reported smoking more than half a pack of cigarettes daily (82). However, this represents a decrease from 18.9 percent of boys and 18.0 percent of girls in 1978. Furthermore, smoking among both boys and girls continued to decline in the early 1980s (see Table 12.1).

### *Why do adolescents smoke?*

It has been clearly established that smoking substantially increases the risk of heart disease, lung cancer, chronic bronchitis, emphysema, and other ailments, and decreases longevity (151, 173). Furthermore, smoking by pregnant women lowers the birth weight and resistance to illness of their infants (151). It also increases the chances of spontaneous abortion, premature births, and possible long-term consequences in the physical and intellectual development of their children (151). In the words of Julius Richmond, the former U.S. surgeon general, "Smoking is the largest preventable cause of death in America" (151, *ii*). Why, then, do adolescents begin and continue smoking, and why is the rate increasing so dramatically among girls? Clearly, not because of ignorance of the health hazards. Seventy-seven percent of teenage smokers believe it is better not to start smoking than to have to quit; 84 percent believe smoking is habit-forming; and 78 percent believe it can cause lung cancer and heart disease. "Eighty-seven percent of all teenagers and 77 percent of teenage smokers believe that smoking can harm their health" (48, *8*).

Such findings suggest that adolescent smokers do so, not out of ignorance, but despite the personal dangers. Why? In approaching this question, it is necessary to consider *initiation* of smoking separately from *continuation* of the habit. Once established, dependence on cigarettes can be very difficult to overcome, physiologically and psychologically. Largely because of its nicotine content, tobacco can be physiologically addictive, and cessation of smoking can produce symptoms of withdrawal comparable in many ways to withdrawal from narcotics (151, 159). Psychological dependence is fostered by continued use of tobacco in specific circumstances— when one is anxious or bored, trying to concentrate, or attempting to deal with a difficult social situation, or in association with alcohol or coffee.

Neither type of dependence exists initially, however. What factors, then, encourage beginning use? Although we still have much to learn, a number of factors increase the likelihood of smoking. One is parental influence. In families where both parents smoke, 22.2 percent of boys and 20.7 percent of girls also become smokers, compared to 11.3 percent and 7.6 percent, respectively, where neither parent smokes (48, 122). Siblings may exert a similar influence; indeed, if an older sibling *and* both parents smoke, a child is four times as likely to smoke as when there is no model for smoking in the family (122).

Among early adolescents in particular, peer group pressure and conformity to group norms exert a strong influence on smoking behavior. Indeed, several surveys have identified peer influence as the single most significant factor in the initiation of smoking (48, 100, 102). In one such study, having a best friend or group of friends who smoke was found to be the best predictor of smoking in children and adolescents from the fifth through the twelfth grade (102). Other factors that may play a role in encouraging smoking include nonparental adult models, such as teachers, and the mass media, which attempt to portray smoking as sophisticated, sexy, masculine, and so on. The extent of media influence is open to some question, however, since adolescents tend to view cigarette advertising as "hypocritical" and "least-liked" of all advertisements (49).

***Individual characteristics***   Attempts to find personality characteristics that may predispose a young person to become a smoker have had only limited success (48, 100). Young people who become smokers are slightly more likely to be extraverted, tense and anxious, inclined to take risks, and rebellious, and more likely to believe that their fate is determined by external events and chance than by their own efforts (27, 48, 149, 161). However, it appears that personality characteristics are more strongly related to amount smoked, rather than to who will begin to smoke (48). For example, in several studies of smokers, amount smoked has been found to be directly related to degree of anxiety (48, 161).

***Sex differences***   A variety of possible explanations have been offered for the dramatic rise in smoking among girls, at a time when boys' smoking was declining. One is that girls may have felt that they were less likely to develop diseases associated with smoking, such as lung cancer, because the incidence of these diseases is less in women. Recent research, however, has shown an alarming increase in smoking-related diseases among women, as more women have been smoking more. Lung cancer rates for women, for example, have tripled since the early 1960s, and are projected to show a fivefold increase by 1983 (151). In brief, it is becoming clear that "women who smoke like men die like men who smoke" (151, *1*).

Another possibility is that changing sex roles and greater similarity between the sexes is involved. Clearly, smoking was once considered more socially acceptable for men than for women, particularly in public; equally clearly, this is no longer the case: As the manufacturer of one brand of cigarettes targeted toward the younger women's market gratuitously proclaims, "You've come a long way, baby!" It would be ironic to find that women's liberation was helping to "free" female adolescents to develop the same future disabilities as their male peers—especially at a time when smoking among males was declining. At any rate, female adolescents are smoking not only more than males, but earlier and more heavily (68, 173), although fortunately there were suggestions of a decline in girls' smoking in 1981 (see pages 507, 515). One can only hope this trend continues, especially because there is some evidence to suggest that women suffer more severe withdrawal symptoms than men during abstinence, and more of them fail in organized programs to stop smoking (151). It also appears that peer influences may play a greater part in the smoking behavior of girls than of boys (68).

### Prevention

In view of the difficulties involved in giving up smoking, prevention appears to offer the brightest prospect for significantly decreasing tobacco use. Although many traditional approaches to prevention (e.g., lectures on the physical risks of smoking) have proved relatively ineffective, some newer approaches appear promising (48, 49, 110). Generally, these efforts have been directed toward adolescents, beginning about seventh grade; if a person succeeds in avoiding smoking during the adolescent years, the chances of becoming an adult smoker are significantly reduced (68). Although there are individual differences in content, most of these programs tend to emphasize active involvement of the young person in developing strategies to handle pressures to smoke, whether from peers, the media, or adults. For example, in some instances, filmed vignettes showing peer pressure to smoke are presented; the class may then discuss appropriate ways to respond. For example, if a young adolescent is called "chicken" for refusing an offer of cigarettes, he or she might reply, "If I smoke to prove to you that I'm not chicken, all I'll really be showing is that I'm afraid not to do what you want me to do. I don't want to smoke" (110, *653*).

Related approaches may involve role-playing by students of smoking situations, and counseling of junior high school students by high school students. More general techniques for dealing with a variety of stressful life situations that may increase vulnerability to smoking may also be employed—including development of social skills, efforts to improve self-esteem and self-confidence, and assertiveness training. Several studies using these newer approaches have shown significant differences in subsequent smoking between experimental and control groups over 2- to 3-year follow-up periods (68). There is also some preliminary evidence suggesting that "inoculation" against smoking may extend to other drug use, including alcohol (110).

## MARIJUANA

Except for tobacco and alcohol, marijuana is by a considerable margin the drug most widely used by young people. It is derived from the Indian hemp plant *Cannabis sativa* (or *Cannabis indica*), a durable common weed growing under natural conditions in many climates throughout the world. Its earliest recorded use occurs in a Chinese compendium of drugs dated 2737 B.C., and even in ancient times it was a frequent source of controversy. Some warned "that the hemp plant lines the road to Hades" (56, *17*), whereas others maintained that it pointed the way to Paradise.

The active chemical ingredients in marijuana—principally tetrahydrocannabinols, or THC—are contained in a resin present in the topmost leaves and flower

clusters of the female plant (the male plant contains similar substances, but in much smaller amounts). It is these chemicals that appear to be the principal cause of the so-called marijuana high. The strength of the drug may vary considerably, depending on growing conditions, climate, degree of cultivation, the portions of the plant used, and the manner of preparation. The strongest grade of the drug (made from the resin itself, scraped from the tops of mature, well-cultivated plants) is the only grade properly called *hashish,* though the term is often, and incorrectly, used as synonymous with marijuana.

How widespread is marijuana usage in the United States? According to recent surveys, approximately one-fourth of all adults and 40 percent of teenagers have had at least some experience with marijuana. These overall figures, however, tend to be misleading because of the strong relationship between marijuana use and age—ranging from 8 percent use among 12- to 13-year-olds to 59 percent among 17- to 18-year-olds (1, 33, 126, 129). In contrast, fewer than 10 percent of adults over 40 have tried marijuana. Marijuana use is also sex-related, with males at all age levels more likely than females to have used marijuana.

There are recent indications that regular marijuana use may be declining (82). For example, although lifetime use among high school seniors in the United States increased each year from 47 percent in 1975 to 60 percent in 1979, it remained at 60 percent in 1980 and declined to 59 percent in 1981 (79, 80, 81, 82). More importantly, marijuana use in the past 30 days decreased from 37.1 percent in the class of 1978 to 31.6 percent in the class of 1981; daily use declined from 10.7 to 7.0 percent in the same period (80, 82). However, to date the trend toward ever-earlier initial age of marijuana use has not been reversed. In 1972, 10 percent of 14- to 15-year-olds reported some experience with marijuana; by 1981 this figure had increased to about 34 percent (74, 82). Also, there are still wide variations in the extent of marijuana use among youth in different school settings and in different areas of the country. For example, adolescents in the West are more likely to have used marijuana in the past month than those in the South, and usage among adolescents in large metropolitan areas is greater than among those in rural areas and small towns, although in both cases differences are declining (82).

Among college students, overall incidence was higher than among their non-college peers in the late 1960s and early 1970s (1, 63, 125, 126, 129). However, the picture has now changed. While use among all youth continued to increase between 1970 and 1979, use among college students actually declined during the same period. High school seniors currently planning to go to college also have a smaller incidence of marijuana use than those planning no college or less than 4 years (82).

Among both adults and young people, the largest percentage of marijuana users fall in the category of experimenters, and the smallest percentage fall in the category of heavy users (1, 82, 129, 144). For example, although 59 percent of high school seniors in the United States in 1981 reported some lifetime use and 32 percent reported some use in the last 30 days, only about 7 percent—still a large number—reported daily use; 5.3 percent used marijuana more than 40 times a month (81, 82). As will become evident, it is this minority of chronic users who are most likely to have significant drug problems, and about whom psychologists and others who work with young people are most concerned.

### Subjective effects of marijuana

What are the subjective effects of a marijuana high? First of all, the effects are extremely variable, particularly at low dosage levels. Many first-time marijuana smokers have reported feeling only very limited effects, such as difficulties in concentration and remembering what they were saying or thinking; others may find their initial experience anxiety-producing, and still others may find it pleasurable and relaxing. Most social users and clinical observers agree that the subjective effects of marijuana are extremely dependent not only on the strength of dosage, but upon the user's expectations, his or her transient as well as enduring psychological and physical characteristics, and the overall physical and social setting in which use occurs. Thus, an already depressed or seriously anxious person may become more so. One who is relatively more stable emotionally and who is looking forward to a pleasant, relaxing experience in the presence of friends he or she trusts and enjoys may indeed find this to be the case. On the other hand, a suspicious individual taking marijuana furtively in an ugly or distracting setting, or one where there is the possibility of being arrested, may become more suspicious, even at times paranoid.

The subjective effects of marijuana are also significantly influenced by dosage. Most marijuana currently sold in this country has been relatively weak and has functioned primarily as a mild intoxicant, although more potent strains are now becoming increasingly available. However, the effective cannabis chemicals in marijuana, if isolated and given in highly concentrated doses, produce effects similar to those of the more clearly recognized hallucinogenic drugs, such as mescaline and LSD, although the mechanisms of their action on the brain appear to differ. Subjective effects bear a definite relationship to dosage level (69, 70). Thus, for very mild levels of the drug, the most common responses were alterations in mood, feeling happy, silly, and relaxed. With higher dosage levels, colors seemed brighter and hearing keener, the body felt lighter, and alterations in time perception were frequently reported. At still higher levels, all of the above subjective effects were more pronounced and a majority of the subjects reported changes in body image, illusions, delusions, and hallucinations—toxic reactions that occur with excessive dosage of many chemicals that affect the nervous system (33, 124, 167).

The following describes what might be termed a rather typical high at relatively low dosage levels, under favorable social and personal conditions: Alterations in feelings begin within 10 to 30 minutes after smoking marijuana (22, 33). There may be an initial period of anxiety, but the subject soon begins to feel more calm, and "a pleasant sense of warmth suffuses the muscular frame, especially around the shoulder girdle and neck" (33, *103*). Frequently a sensation of lightness in the limbs develops: "Walking becomes effortless. The paresthesias and changes in bodily sensations help give an astounding feeling of lightness to the limbs and body" (22, 167, *321*). The individual is likely to experience "a feeling of contentment and inner satisfaction, free play of the imagination, exhilaration of spirit, the feeling of floating above reality, ideas disconnected, uncontrollable, and free-flowing, minutes seeming like hours, space broadened, near objects seeming distant, uncontrollable laughter and hilarity" (124, *96*). Sensory experiences, such as the sound of music, may seem clearer and more arresting; in addition, for some, "the 'normal' separation between self and nonself may seem less distinct and less necessary" (33, *30*).

The rapid flow of ideas may give the impression of brilliance of thought and observation (22); "the flighty ideas are not deep enough to form an engram that can be recollected—hence the confusion that appears on trying to remember what was thought" (167, *321*). The impression of brilliance may be more illusory than real, as is illustrated by an anecdote told by a successful young businessman:

> One night a bunch of us were somewhat stoned at a restaurant. A man at the next table leaned over and said to his wife, "If there is no view, why don't you frost the windows?" I dutifully informed my table of the remark, and we spent most of the evening on it: it seemed to sum up religion, communism, even drugs. Unfortunately, the next morning it was simply another phrase—a good one, but not something that would knock straight people out for the count [39, *73*].

Although many users typically feel peaceful and relaxed, "they also experience an extraordinary lability, or changeability, of mood. A thought or remark might suddenly plunge the user into sadness, although he can just as rapidly recover, especially if a reassuring friend is present" (33, *31*). Typically, however, the marijuana user's mood is one of quiet contemplation, and he or she is likely to exhibit a warm, live and let live attitude, rather than being aggressive, hostile, or domineering (33, 57). Early propagandistic claims that marijuana produces aggressive acting-out, criminal behavior, or that it stimulates ill-considered, ungovernable sexual desires, stand in rather marked contrast to the facts (33, 107, 129, 130, 134, 144). Sexually experienced partners may feel that the pleasure of sexual relations is sometimes heightened and renewed by marijuana, but many young people report that the often insistent sexual urgings of adolescence are "turned off by grass" (33).

### Adverse effects of marijuana: Fact or fiction?

Despite considerable propaganda and (despite recent progress in a number of states) laws to the contrary, marijuana is not a narcotic and not physiologically addictive (57, 129, 130, 134, 137); nor does it appear likely for most users to lead to the use of hard drugs, such as heroin (93, 137, 138, 143, 158). Its short-term physical effects in normal dosage levels are not particularly remarkable (56, 57, 165): There is an increase in pulse rate, some alteration of blood pressure, and some minimal loss in muscle strength and steadiness (57, 137, 165). Perhaps the most dramatic physical effect is a marked increase in appetite 30 to 60 minutes after ingestion (56, 165).

At least in normal dosages, marijuana appears to have little effect on electro-encephalographic (i.e., brain wave) patterns (141, 169), although one study (141), using highly precise techniques, noted a slight increase in frequency of the alpha waves (which are commonly associated with restful, meditative states).

The degree of impairment of cognitive and psychomotor performance is dose-related, despite wide individual differences. At low dosage levels, and on sim-ple or familiar tasks, impairment is usually minimal, but clearly impaired perform-ance is observable on complex, unfamiliar tasks at higher dosage levels (33, 57, 129, 134, 165, 166, 167). Recent experiments have shown that subjects can usually remember previously learned material while under the influence of marijuana about as well as control group subjects given a placebo. When administered learning tasks while under the influence of moderate dosages of marijuana, short-term, immediate memory seems to be relatively unaffected, although longer-term memory is im-paired (with large doses, both short-term and long-term memory are impaired) (103).

Interestingly, experienced users show less impairment of performance than naive subjects in laboratory test situations, although subjectively they are more likely to report experiencing a high similar to previous social highs (165). Whether these differences between naive and experienced subjects are the result of pharmacologi-cal or of psychological sensitization over time is not known, although most investiga-tors favor the latter hypothesis, emphasizing, as do most users, the importance of psychological "set."

Also of interest is the fact that spontaneous speech, even in the laboratory setting, is more likely to be impaired (e.g., in coherence, complexity, time orienta-tion) than performance on specific assigned tasks (166, 168). This paradox may perhaps be explained by the observation of many users that the effects of marijuana can be suppressed (at least under normal dosages) much more easily than can the effects of alcohol or some other drugs. Investigators speculate that this suppressi-bility may be a function of different actions on the brain (165).

If smoking marijuana is not narcotic and not addictive, and is viewed by most individuals at most times as a pleasurable experience, what, if any, are its dangers? Serious reactions, and even death, may result from the *addition* of unknown sub-stances to marijuana. There have been reports in a number of countries, including the United States, of deaths from marijuana heavily laced with strychnine, and of attempts to create narcotic addiction by giving away, or selling cheaply, marijuana mixed with opiates, without the knowledge of the user.

As already noted, consumption of marijuana under unfavorable circumstances may lead, at least temporarily, to suspiciousness, terror, paranoia, or depression. "Personality factors are also important considerations. A subject who believes that affairs in his life never work out well or that he is not liked by others, has a tendency to experience brief spells of paranoia when under the influence of marijuana" (32, 36–37). Further, as we have seen, marijuana, especially in larger doses, may produce changes in one's body image, subjective sensations, and also a feeling of loss of bodily boundaries or fusion with the surroundings (22, 32, 33). Many users may view this as a pleasurable or even important goal, but in those with either conscious or unconscious fears of loss of control—or more seriously, in whom contact with reality is tenuous—this experience may produce extensive psychological distress.

Although acute toxic psychotic reactions are rare, especially at low dosage levels, they can and sometimes do occur in physiologically or psychologically predisposed individuals (33, 63, 134, 167). However, previous widespread reports of a specific "cannabis psychosis" among users in Asia and the Middle East now appear to be discredited scientifically (19, 56, 108, 129, 134, 142).

Although marijuana is not addictive, psychological dependence upon the drug can become a serious problem for a minority of users. Probably not more than 5 to 10 percent of young people are chronic heavy users. However, for such persons, marijuana can present real dangers, comparable in severity to those of chronic alcoholics. In one clinical investigation of the effects of chronic cannabis intoxication (171), six subjects smoked marijuana freely for 39 days.

> During the first few days, they exhibited euphoria, bursts of spontaneous laughter, silly behavior, and difficulty in concentrating. Later, they showed loss of interest in work, decreased activity, indolence, nonproductivity, and neglect of personal hygiene. All subjects reported subjective "jitteriness" on withdrawal of marijuana, but none showed abstinence signs [167, 323].

If an adolescent boy or girl is using marijuana chronically to escape life's stress, psychological growth is, at the least, likely to be impaired because he or she is not learning how to deal with frustration and with daily problems (130, 134). In addition, as we have seen, marijuana can reduce performance on cognitive tasks and longer-term memory. Thus the minority of students who are arriving at school stoned or becoming stoned during the school day are likely to be endangering their academic performance, and indeed consistent users eventually do appear to suffer academically. Whether prolonged, heavy use of marijuana actually damages the brain's capacity to function is, of course, another matter (see page 523).

Despite earlier propagandistic warnings, the vast majority of marijuana users (approximately 95 percent) do not progress to hard drugs, although many adults still think they do (33, 82, 90, 93, 95, 129, 137, 143, 146). It is not known whether marijuana use plays an etiological role in the case of the small minority who do go on to use other drugs, or whether, as seems more likely, these are simply predisposed individuals who would eventually have used these drugs anyway, given the opportunity. One thing appears clear, however: *Legal classification of marijuana as in the same category with hard narcotics for many years did little to encourage the adolescent to distinguish marijuana from the infinitely more frightening effects of the hard drugs.*

Recent studies of the effects of marijuana and alcohol on driving performance (42, 97, 107, 108) have shown some interesting similarities and differences. Both alcohol and marijuana reduced subjects' reaction times in decision-making driving situations (e.g., whether to pass another car). Marijuana subjects tended to become somewhat more cautious; alcohol subjects, more aggressive (42, 108). On driving-related perceptual tasks, alcohol appeared to interfere with the ability to divide attention—to "time-share"—as demanded by the changing requirements of the situation; marijuana, in contrast, appeared to result in momentary lapses of attention, unknown to the subject (119). Under conditions of stress, however, marijuana subjects (at least at social dosages) appeared more able to compensate effectively for reduced vigilance, while alcohol subjects did not (42). In any event, it appears clear that both marijuana and alcohol, even in social dosages, may impair performance. Inasmuch as a significant percentage of adolescents acknowledge driving under the influence of marijuana, as well as alcohol, it is important to stress that driving under these conditions increases the likelihood of accidents (129, 130, 134).

Finally, we simply do not yet know enough about the possible effects, particularly possible long-term effects, of marijuana usage. It has been rather clearly established that chronic marijuana use can produce impaired pulmonary (lung) function (33, 63, 129, 134). Other investigators have attempted to determine whether marijuana use (particularly chronic use) can produce irreversible changes in brain structure and function, genetic or prenatal damage to unborn children, and suppression of pituitary sex hormones involved in reproductive physiology (19, 33, 63, 64, 98, 129). Significant effects have been reported in all of these areas, only to be challenged in many instances by the results of other studies (19, 33, 63, 130, 134).

In 1982, after a comprehensive study of the available evidence, an advisory committee of the National Academy of Sciences, National Institute of Medicine (33) reported that:

> There is not yet any conclusive evidence as to whether prolonged use of marijuana causes permanent changes in the nervous system or sustained impairment of brain function and behavior in human beings. In the judgment of the committee, widely cited studies purporting to demonstrate that marijuana affects the gross and microscopic structure of the human or monkey brain are not convincing; much more work is needed to settle this important point [123, 9].

Similarly, the advisory committee stated that while animal studies have shown that THC, the major psychoactive constituent of marijuana, lowers the concentration of sex hormones (gonadotropins) in the blood, it is not known if there is a direct effect on reproductive tissues. While marijuana has a modest suppressive effect on sperm production, it is reversible, and there is currently no proof that it affects fertility. Marijuana can interfere with ovulation (at least in monkeys), and its chemicals cross the placental barrier and affect the human fetus. But to date there are no adequate studies of possible permanent effects either on the reproductive system of the mother or on the child (33).

Marijuana does not appear to produce breaks in chromosomes in the judgment of the advisory committee, "but marijuana may affect chromosome segregation during cell division, resulting in an abnormal number of chromosomes in daughter cells. Although these results are of concern, their clinical significance is unknown" (123, 9).

Currently, there is considerable controversy about whether chronic, heavy marijuana use produces "burnout" (63). Professionals who work with young people, as well as parents, have reported that persons involved in such prolonged use may appear blunted, dulled, and mildly confused, with diminished attention span, as well as passive and lacking in goal-directed activity (the "amotivational syndrome"). While there seems little doubt that such effects are seen in a minority of "potheads," establishing causality is more difficult. Did chronic marijuana use lead to the personality changes observed, or did personality change accelerate marijuana use? Furthermore, heavy marijuana use is almost always accompanied by multiple use of other drugs, clouding the picture further (33, 91, 93, 95, 146).

The most reasonable position to take—scientifically and in one's own life—would appear to be that the final chapter on marijuana has not yet been written. It may well be that many fears of physical or physiological damage will prove groundless. But long experience with drugs and chemicals of all sorts that were once considered harmless—from aspirin to thalidomide, from DDT to food additives and estrogenic compounds such as stilbestrol—cannot help but dictate caution, particularly in the case of women who are, or might be, pregnant (129, 130, 134).

In the words of the National Academy of Sciences' advisory committee,

> The scientific evidence published to date indicates that marijuana has a broad range of psychological and biological effects, some of which, at least under certain conditions, are harmful to human health. Unfortunately, the available information does not tell us how serious this risk may be. Our major conclusion is that what little we know for certain about the effects of marijuana on human health—and all that we have reason to suspect—justifies serious national concern [123, 9].

What is most badly needed at this juncture, in the committee's view, is "a greatly intensified and more comprehensive program of research into the effects of marijuana on the health of the American people" (123, 9).

### Why do young people use marijuana?

One way of approaching the question of why young people use marijuana is by asking young people themselves. In a survey of 26,000 college students (117), the most frequent reasons cited for first-time use were "curiosity" (58 percent), followed by "worthwhile for its own sake" (26 percent), for "kicks" (6 percent), and to "help with personal problems" (1 percent). When the 53 percent of all subjects who had not discontinued use were asked why they continued to use the drug, more than two-thirds (68 percent) stated that "it is pleasurable (fun)." In the words of one ghetto 14-year-old, sophisticated beyond his years, "I like pot. It's good. You don't get *too* high. You're cool. It's good to use when you want to cool yourself down. My friends, all of them, use it sometimes. Some are fooling around with stronger stuff, but not me. I see too many people around here that are hooked. They're ruined. They're done, all washed up" (33, 90).

Although much is made in some quarters of the deeper philosophical implications of drug use, only a small percentage of these students cited as reasons for continued use either that "it gives me a greater insight into myself" (7 percent) or "it brings me closer to people and helps me understand others" (4 percent).

Despite the fact that only 1 percent of these students stated that they used marijuana "to help with personal problems," it is difficult to believe that a significant proportion of the 11 percent of young people currently using marijuana daily, or of the 5.3 percent who use marijuana more than 40 times a month (see page 519), do not have personal problems, whether or not they accept the idea.

### Influence of parents and peers

Both parents and peers play a role in youthful marijuana use. Parents influence marijuana (and other drug) use by their own attitudes, values, and behavior, and by the kinds of relationships that they have with their children. Parents who believe strongly that drug use is harmful, socially unacceptable, or morally wrong, and who convey these attitudes to their children are less likely to have children who engage in drug use, including marijuana (23, 73, 76, 91). Parental use of tranquilizers, amphetamines, or barbiturates, as well as alcohol and tobacco, is positively correlated with use of marijuana and other illegal drugs by their children (15, 47, 91, 94, 143, 147). In addition, several characteristics of the relationship between parents and their children increase the likelihood of adolescent marijuana use. These include: absence of emotional closeness; lack of maternal involvement in children's activities: low parental aspirations for their children; and parental passivity, unconventionality, and delinquent or deviant behavior (23, 76, 91, 94).

**Peers**  Peer influences are the strongest predictors of subsequent marijuana use, at least over the near term. Present and future marijuana users report having more marijuana-using friends than do nonusers (23, 25, 66, 73, 77, 87, 88, 91, 94, 140); in fact, most users state that they were first introduced to the drug by a friend (88). Furthermore, the intensity of an adolescent's own use of marijuana varies directly with the prevalence of use among his or her friends. "The heavier the involvement with marijuana, the more likely that one is embedded in a friendship network in which marijuana use is a characteristic of behavior" (73, *342*).

A potential methodological problem of some studies is that they depend on the subject's own report of parental or peer drug use, raising the possibility of perceptual distortions on the part of the subject. In a comprehensive study of drug use among public secondary school students in New York State, Denise Kandel and her associates (87, 88) avoided this possible source of error by obtaining independent data from adolescents, their parents, and their best school friends. They found that involvement with other drug-using adolescents is a more important correlate of adolescent marijuana use than is parental use of psychoactive drugs including alcohol. For example, among subjects whose best school friends had never used marijuana, only 15 percent reported using the drug themselves; in contrast, among subjects whose best school friends reported using marijuana 60 times or more, use increased to 79 percent (see Table 12.2). However, parental use of these drugs (especially alcohol) also plays a role, though a more modest one; furthermore, "inter- and intragenerational influences are synergistic" (88, *107*). Thus, the highest rates of marijuana usage were found among adolescents whose parents and best school friends were drug users (see Table 12.3).

Although peers generally emerge as more important influences on adolescent marijuana use than do parents, two qualifications should be noted. First, there are

**TABLE 12.2 ADOLESCENT MARIJUANA
USE BY SELF-REPORTED BEST SCHOOL
FRIEND'S MARIJUANA USE (PERCENTAGES)**

| | USE BY BEST SCHOOL FRIEND | | | | | | |
|---|---|---|---|---|---|---|---|
| | NEVER | 1–2 TIMES | 3–9 TIMES | 10–39 TIMES | 40–59 TIMES | 60 TIMES OR OVER | TAU– BETA |
| Adolescents having ever used | 15 | 50 | 50 | 72 | 77 | 79 | .477 |
| Total *N* | (1181) | (135) | (140) | (124) | (44) | (126) | |

*Source:* D. Kandel. Inter- and intragenerational influences on adolescent marijuana use. *Journal of Social Issues,* 1974, **30,** 107–135. By permission.

clearly individual differences. For example, even where the subjects' best school friends had used marijuana more than 60 times, 21 percent of these young people reported no use themselves. What accounts for such variations in the relative influence of parents and peers? Kandel's data suggest that the strength and quality of the relationship is an important factor. Concordance of use between the subject and his or her best school friend was higher where the subject's friend "is also considered the best friend overall, when the adolescent sees the friend frequently out of school, or when this best-school-friend choice is reciprocated" (88, *125*).

Similarly, adolescents who reported that they were not close to their mothers were more receptive to their friends' influence than adolescents who reported a close relationship with their mothers. In another study (155), it was found that adolescents who are primarily parent-oriented (i.e., who identify primarily with their parents) are less likely to use marijuana, or to use it regularly, than those who are primarily peer-oriented (see Table 12.4).

**TABLE 12.3 ADOLESCENT MARIJUANA
USE BY BEST SCHOOL FRIEND MARIJUANA
USE AND PARENTAL PSYCHOACTIVE DRUGS USE**

| PARENTAL PSYCHOACTIVE DRUG USE | ADOLESCENTS HAVING EVER USED MARIJUANA BEST SCHOOL FRIEND MARIJUANA USE | |
|---|---|---|
| | NEVER USED | USED |
| Never used: | 13% | 56% |
| Total *N* | (385) | (165) |
| Used: | 17% | 67% |
| Total *N* | (327) | (165) |

*Source:* D. Kandel. Inter- and intragenerational influences on adolescent marijuana use. *Journal of Social Issues,* 1974, **30,** 107–135. By permission.
*Note:* Use patterns for each group are self-reported.

**TABLE 12.4 RELATIONSHIP OF PARENT-PEER**
**ORIENTATION AND FREQUENCY OF MARIJUANA USE**

| | FREQUENCY OF MARIJUANA USE | | | | |
|---|---|---|---|---|---|
| ORIENTATION | NEVER | PAST USER | OCCASIONAL | REGULAR | (N) |
| Parent | 66% | 19% | 9% | 7% | (351) |
| Neither | 41% | 28% | 12% | 19% | (58) |
| Peer | 22% | 22% | 23% | 33% | (352) |
| (N) | (336) | (159) | (117) | (149) | (761) |

Source: L. H. Stone, A. C. Miranne, and G. J. Ellis. Parent-peer influence as a predictor of marijuana use. *Adolescence*, 1979, **14,** 115–121. By permission.
Note: $x^2 = 168.47$ with 6 d.f., $p < .0001$, $\tau_b = .41425$.

Recent research also indicates that the greater influence of peers than parents may be more short-lived than previously thought (91). When subjects in two studies were followed up 3 or 4 years later (rather than after 6 months or a year, as in most studies), the relationship between marijuana use and earlier peer behavior tended to dissipate (23, 104).

In Kandel's view, findings on the relative influence of parents and peers on adolescent drug use fit a "cultural deviance" model of behavior (157). The essential notion involved here is that the family can potentially lead the young person toward some form of socially disapproved behavior (e.g., drug use, delinquency) either because the family engages in the behavior itself, and the young person imitates, or because it creates a negative climate in the home from which the young person seeks to escape. Despite the fact that either or both factors may characterize the family, the young person will usually not engage in deviant behavior unless such behavior is present in the immediate peer culture (88, 157). "Peer behavior is the crucial determining factor in adolescent drug use; parental behavior becomes important when such behavior exists in the peer group" (88, *126*). This formulation, although it appears to fit the findings of Kandel and others, still provides no final answer to the question of the extent to which adolescents seek out other drug users to associate with after they themselves have become involved, versus the extent to which they start using drugs because of their association with drug-using friends. Further longitudinal studies directed toward this question are needed, but it appears likely that both processes are involved and that, at least for a majority of experimenters and moderate users, the latter process is the more crucial.

### Personal characteristics of marijuana users
A variety of investigations have attempted to determine whether marijuana users and nonusers differ in personal characteristics (18, 107, 144, 162). If, as has sometimes been the case, the results of such studies are compared without taking into account the potential effects of such variables as extent of marijuana use and the prevailing social climate, the picture is a confusing one (18). Marijuana users may then appear as little different from their nonuser peers (143, 178) or as emotionally

disturbed (21, 111, 178); they may emerge as impulsive, sensation-seeking, and narcissistic (61), or as calm, relaxed, and "open to experience" (65); as good students or poor students (60, 145, 153). But despite the apparent fact that there are many individual differences among persons in any category of marijuana use, a number of fairly consistent findings do emerge *if we differentiate among categories of users.*

**Early users, late users, and nonusers**   One might expect that adolescents who initiate marijuana use early in adolescence, when it is less common and less sanctioned, would differ significantly from late users, as well as from nonusers. In a large-scale longitudinal study of over 12,000 students, grades four through twelve, in the greater Boston area, this indeed proved to be the case (150). Both in peer ratings and on personality test responses, the greatest differences were found between nonusers and early users (prior to ninth grade), with late users (tenth grade or later) falling between the two extremes. Nonusers emerged as most orderly, curious, hard-working, self-confident, determined, persistent, tender-hearted, achievement-oriented, and obedient, and most likely to feel valued and accepted and in control of their lives. In contrast, early users were most likely to be perceived as impulsive, dependent, not responsible or considerate, unable to be trusted consistently, immature in their interests, emotional, talkative, sociable, and pessimistic.

**Extent of marijuana use**   Even more salient is the extent of marijuana use. Clearly, the occasional experimenter and the chronic "pothead" are using marijuana very differently, and may be expected to differ significantly in personality and behavior as well. Experimenters (those who have tried marijuana a few times and either given it up completely or engaged in subsequent use only very infrequently) appear basically similar to nonusers, especially in peer group settings where marijuana use is not a rarity (143, 144, 162, 178). Experimenters may be slightly more open to experience, less conventional and concerned with rules, more interested in creative pursuits, less reserved, less authoritarian, more adventuresome, and more interested in novel experiences (73, 91, 162). (Interestingly, in view of the question of whether such characteristics precede and increase the likelihood of marijuana use, or whether, instead, they result from use, it has been found [162] that experimenters actually manifest such characteristics slightly less than nonusers who think they might want to try marijuana in the future, as distinguished from those who believe they will not.) In general, however, experimenters tend to be motivated primarily by curiosity or the desire to share a social experience, and are generally as "disciplined, optimistic, self-confident, . . . responsible, goal-oriented as nonusers" (138, 44).

As a group, moderate or intermittent users emerge as clearly less conventional, more adventuresome, more independent, less authoritarian, more impulsive, more sensation-seeking, less inclined to delay pleasurable gratification, more concerned with self-expression, and generally more open to experience than either experimenters or nonusers (65, 73, 91, 162, 172). They are also more likely to be uncertain of their future identity, somewhat more anxious, more nonconformist, more rebellious, and more critical of existing social institutions. Studies of high school and college students (61, 73, 76, 90, 91) indicate that moderate users are more likely to manifest anti-Establishment views regarding politics, religion, restraints on personal freedom, and the success ethic. They are also likely to be less religious and more tolerant of deviant behavior generally (73, 76, 91).

Among both male and female college students, users are more likely to have engaged in premarital intercourse. They are more likely to be majoring in the arts and humanities than in the natural sciences, business, or engineering, and are less likely to come from blue-collar families. They are also more likely to feel that a significant generation gap exists between parents and their young (176). In turn, parents of moderate users appear, on the whole, to be more permissive, less capable of appropriate limit-setting, more inclined toward material gratification, and more likely to suppress family conflicts behind a facade of openness (see pages 240–245; see also 15, 101, 145).

Findings regarding the academic performance of moderate marijuana users are conflicting (73, 90, 91). Some studies have found lowered performance (73, 150, 156, 162); others, higher performance (153); and still others, no difference (73, 114, 115). It would appear that moderate marijuana users include bright, creative individuals who, though more unconventional than their peers, nevertheless remain confident of their own goals and at least reasonably disciplined and interested in their academic work. This category also includes significant numbers of individuals who are uncertain of their goals, incapable of delayed gratification, and dissatisfied with school (especially their coursework); some of them may be "functioning below expectancy levels in terms of grades earned" (145, *3279*), others may have more limited ability to begin with. Discrepancies in findings regarding academic performance of moderate users may possibly result from differing proportions of these varied types from one sample to another. For example, lowered performance is a more consistent finding among high school students (4, 73, 101, 150, 162), who are more representative of the general population and younger in age. In contrast, fewer consistent differences in either direction are found among college and medical or law school students, who have had to demonstrate a reasonably high level of academic capability and motivation to gain admission in the first place (60).

The clearest differences from nonusers or experimenters, however, occur among chronic heavy users. It is among the latter group that, for the first time, fairly consistent indications of significant psychological and social disturbance emerge, as distinguished simply from differences in personality or life-style. Significantly, but perhaps not surprisingly, it is also in this group that multiple drug use is most frequent and most extensive (see Figure 12.3). In a number of studies, heavy marijuana use has been found to be associated with "poor social and work adjustment, increased hostility, greater difficulty in mastering new problems, and the desire for a 'psychotomimetic' experience in marijuana use, rather than simple tension reduction or pleasurable stimulation" (162, *78*). Heavy users have been found to score significantly higher (in the direction of pathology) than control subjects on such psychological measures as the Minnesota Multiphasic Personality Inventory (21, 111), and more of them have been found to be anxious, restless, suspicious, depressed, negativistic, insecure, irresponsible, immature, or incapable of sustained intimate social or emotional relationships with others (63, 96, 116, 129, 178).

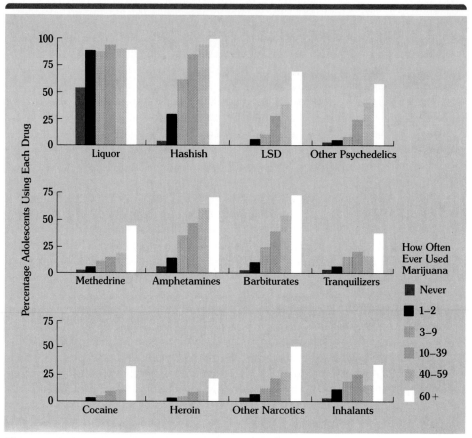

**Figure 12.3** The use of other drugs by frequency of marijuana use (total New York State weighted sample, Wave 1, fall 1971). (From E. Single, D. Kandel, and R. Faust. Patterns of multiple drug use in high school. *Journal of Health and Social Behavior,* 1974, **15,** 344–357. By permission.)

Very heavy users, not surprisingly, tend to lose interest in activities other than drug use, and there may be an extreme lethargy and increasing deterioration of social behavior (20, 32, 138, 144). It should be noted, however, that since heavy marijuana use in American society is typically associated with multiple use of other drugs, one cannot infer that psychological disturbance in this group is directly the result of the heavy marijuana use (73). Furthermore, studies of multiple drug users suggest that heavy drug use is primarily a result of psychological and social disturbance, rather than its cause, although obviously once such drug use has begun a vicious circle may be established.

## OTHER DRUGS

Marijuana is still clearly the drug (other than alcohol and tobacco) most widely used by young people, but smaller percentages of youth have used other drugs as well—

including "the pills" (barbiturates, tranquilizers, amphetamines), hallucinogens (morning glory seeds, mescaline, LSD, PCP), cocaine, and hard narcotics (heroin). In addition, some (principally younger) adolescents have experimented with sniffing glue and a variety of other volatile hydrocarbons ranging from gasoline and paint thinner to dry-cleaning fluid (31).

Rapid increases in the use of these other drugs by junior high and high school students during the 1960s and early 1970s gave rise to fears that they would continue to increase in popularity, eventually approaching the frequency of alcohol and marijuana use. Fortunately, these fears have largely gone unrealized. With the exception of stimulants (amphetamines), which are also used as pep or diet pills, in no case has more than one young person in five been involved, even experimentally (1, 79, 82, 126, 144). Furthermore, as already noted (see Table 12.1 and page 505), by 1980 use of many of these drugs appeared to have stabilized or began to decline. However, adolescent use of several drugs, including cocaine, methaqualone (Quaaludes), and stimulants has continued to increase.

It should be noted that a significant percentage of ever-users of these other drugs either use them infrequently or abandon them entirely after a period of experimentation. Contrary to public opinion, for example, a large majority of opiate ever-users "terminate use of these drugs after experimenting with them one or a few times" (143, *80*). In addition, among all high school seniors in 1981, a substantial majority disapproved of even experimenting with the more serious illicit drugs, as well as of *regular* (as contrasted with occasional) use of all nonprescription drugs, including marijuana, alcohol, and cigarettes (see Table 12.5). Friends were perceived as having similar views (80, 81, 82).

None of this discussion is intended to indicate that use of these other drugs among young people is not a matter of serious, continuing concern. Although we may accurately state that "only" about 5 percent of high school students are current (within the past 30 days) users of hallucinogens (or barbiturates, or cocaine) in each instance, this adds up to over a million young people (80, 82). In addition, the very fact that a substantial majority of contemporary adolescents are apparently wary of these other drugs suggests that the minority who continue to use them, despite their rejection by a majority of their peers, may have more serious problems than if they were simply following peer group influences.

### The pills

The problems posed by the pills—barbiturates, tranquilizers, and amphetamines—vary from one category to another, although all are clearly overused, both by adolescents and adults.

**Sedatives:** *Barbiturates* (*"downers," "yellows," "phennies," "reds"*) The barbiturates (sleeping pills) account for over 3000 accidental or intentional deaths a year in this country alone, but habituation and addiction are far greater problems (148). Barbiturate addiction is characterized by intellectual impairment, self-neglect, slurred speech, tremor, defective judgment, drowsiness, emotional lability, bizarre behavior, and ataxia. Contrary to popular opinion, withdrawal symptoms are even more acute for barbiturate addiction than for heroin; and if withdrawal is abrupt, they

**TABLE 12.5 TRENDS IN PROPORTIONS DISAPPROVING OF DRUG USE**

| Q. Do you disapprove of people (who are 18 or older) doing each of the following?[b] | PERCENT "DISAPPROVING"[a] | | | | | | | | |
|---|---|---|---|---|---|---|---|---|---|
| | CLASS OF 1975 | CLASS OF 1976 | CLASS OF 1977 | CLASS OF 1978 | CLASS OF 1979 | CLASS OF 1980 | CLASS OF 1981 | '80–'81 CHANGE |
| Try marijuana once or twice | 47.0 | 38.4 | 33.4 | 33.4 | 34.2 | 39.0 | 40.0 | +1.0 |
| Smoke marijuana occasionally | 54.8 | 47.8 | 44.3 | 43.5 | 45.3 | 49.7 | 52.6 | +2.9 |
| Smoke marijuana regularly | 71.9 | 69.5 | 65.5 | 67.5 | 69.2 | 74.6 | 77.4 | +2.8s |
| Try LSD once or twice | 82.8 | 84.6 | 83.9 | 85.4 | 86.6 | 87.3 | 86.4 | −0.9 |
| Take LSD regularly | 94.1 | 95.3 | 95.8 | 96.4 | 96.9 | 96.7 | 96.8 | +0.1 |
| Try cocaine once or twice | 81.3 | 82.4 | 79.1 | 77.0 | 74.7 | 76.3 | 74.6 | −1.7 |
| Take cocaine regularly | 93.3 | 93.9 | 92.1 | 91.9 | 90.8 | 91.1 | 90.7 | −0.4 |
| Try heroin once or twice | 91.5 | 92.6 | 92.5 | 92.0 | 93.4 | 93.5 | 93.5 | 0.0 |
| Take heroin occasionally | 94.8 | 96.0 | 96.0 | 96.4 | 96.8 | 96.7 | 97.2 | +0.5 |
| Take heroin regularly | 96.7 | 97.5 | 97.2 | 97.8 | 97.9 | 97.6 | 97.8 | +0.2 |
| Try amphetamines once or twice | 74.8 | 75.1 | 74.2 | 74.8 | 75.1 | 75.4 | 71.1 | −4.3ss |
| Take amphetamines regularly | 92.1 | 92.8 | 92.5 | 93.5 | 94.4 | 93.0 | 91.7 | −1.3 |
| Try barbiturates once or twice | 77.7 | 81.3 | 81.1 | 82.4 | 84.0 | 83.9 | 82.4 | −1.5 |
| Take barbiturates regularly | 93.3 | 93.6 | 93.0 | 94.3 | 95.2 | 95.4 | 94.2 | −1.2 |
| Try one or two drinks of an alcoholic beverage (beer, wine, liquor) | 21.6 | 18.2 | 15.6 | 15.6 | 15.8 | 16.0 | 17.2 | +1.2 |
| Take one or two drinks nearly every day | 67.6 | 68.9 | 66.8 | 67.7 | 68.3 | 69.0 | 69.1 | +0.1 |
| Take four or five drinks nearly every day | 88.7 | 90.7 | 88.4 | 90.2 | 91.7 | 90.8 | 91.8 | +1.0 |
| Have five or more drinks once or twice each weekend | 60.3 | 58.6 | 57.4 | 56.2 | 56.7 | 55.6 | 55.5 | −0.1 |
| Smoke one or more packs of cigarettes per day | 67.5 | 65.9 | 66.4 | 67.0 | 70.3 | 70.8 | 69.9 | −0.9 |
| N = | (2677) | (3234) | (3582) | (3686) | (3221) | (3261) | (3610) | |

Source: L. D. Johnston, J. G. Bachman, and P. M. O'Malley, Student drug use in America, 1975–1981. U.S. Department of Health and Human Services. Washington, D.C.: National Institute on Drug Abuse, 1981, DHHS Publication No. (ADM) 82-1208.

Note: Level of significance of difference between the two most recent classes: s = .05, ss = .01, sss = .001.

[a] Answer alternatives were: (1) don't disapprove, (2) disapprove, and (3) strongly disapprove. Percentages are shown for categories (2) and (3) combined.

[b] The 1975 question asked about people who are "20 or older."

may include nausea, high fever, delirium, hallucinations, and most dangerous of all, convulsions, stupor, and coma that may be fatal.

Except where they may be used as part of a dangerous cycle of "uppers" and "downers"—amphetamines to get high, barbiturates to come down—or for more conventional medical reasons (which may also lead to addiction), barbiturates are taken by adolescents only out of naiveté or in the absence of anything else. As nonspecific general depressants (124), they do not provide a true high, and after a brief period of relaxation, in which tension may seem to disappear, they provide only physical and mental lassitude. Although reliable figures are not available, it appears that the notion of taking barbiturates for kicks is most prevalent among younger, more indiscriminate users. Less than 7 percent of high school seniors in 1980 reported using barbiturates in the previous 12 months, and less than 3 percent in the previous 30 days (82), a significant decrease from prior years.

***Methaqualone*** Usually known on the street as Quaalude (one of its commercial names) or "Ludes," methaqualone is a nonbarbiturate sedative hypnotic (148). "As a 'downer,' methaqualone appears to have an inordinate capacity to produce a dissociative 'high' and ultimately a compelling addiction. Users describe a loss of physical and mental self" (127, *103*). As one adolescent stated, "It's like being hit with four joints at once." The drug also has a reputation among some young people as an aphrodisiac, and has been referred to as "the love drug" (9). The feeling of well-being it produces is associated with ataxia and paresthesias of the legs, arms, fingers, lips, and tongue (127). A sense of invulnerability can lead to accidents (2).

At least initially, most youthful users did not believe that methaqualone was addictive ("It's not a barbiturate"). But in fact it is, and it may produce serious withdrawal complications. Furthermore, tolerance to the drug develops, and as this occurs "the quantity needed for a 'high' gets closer to the lethal dose" (127, *104*). Overdoses may result in coma, heart failure, convulsions, and death. Fortunately, it appears that youthful users and potential users have begun to understand the serious dangers of this drug, which has already accounted for a significant number of deaths among street people and students here and abroad (127). In 1981, less than 7.6 percent of high school seniors reported having used Quaaludes in the previous 12 months, up from 5.1 percent in 1975 and 5.9 percent in 1979 (82).

***Amphetamines*** The amphetamines ("bennies," "dex," "meth," "speed," "copilot," "pep pills") belong to a class of drugs known as sympathomimetics, which "produce effects resembling those resulting from stimulation of the sympathetic nervous system, a part of the nervous system which has primary control over bodily functions" (124, 141). In various forms (e.g., Benzedrine, and the more potent Dexedrine [dextroamphetamine] and Methedrine [methamphetamine]), they are widely, and much too frequently and irresponsibly, prescribed or taken both by adults and adolescents to suppress appetite, to restore energy, and to elevate mood. Indeed their excessive medical use has recently led to warnings by the Food and Drug Administration, and there are current efforts to limit production of the drug (in 1977, over 10 billion amphetamine pills were produced, "about 50 tablets for every man, woman, and child in the United States"), and to restrict use to a very limited number of specific conditions, such as treatment of narcolepsy (44, 46). Despite the fact that over 70 percent of adults 18 and over considered them dangerous, 33.5 million people reported use of amphetamine-based pep and diet pills in 1978 (44).

Although amphetamines do not produce true physiological addiction, they may be psychologically habituating and extremely dangerous physically. In contrast to the majority of central nervous system stimulants, they may produce a high degree of tolerance (i.e., rapid physiological adaptation) that affects various systems selectively (124). Thus, although "increased dosage levels may be necessary to maintain improvement of feelings of energy and well-being, the same dosage level may result in marked increases in nervousness and insomnia" (124). An alternating vicious cycle between amphetamines and barbiturates ("runs and crashes") frequently characterizes heavy users. Continued heavy usage may produce impairment of judgment and intellectual functioning, aggressive or violent behavior, and incoordination and hallucinations, as well as extreme irritability and suspicious or paranoid feelings ("speed freaks") (32, 44, 59, 124).

Toxic dosages vary widely from one person to another, depending on individual sensitivity. Toxic effects may include restlessness, dizziness, insomnia, headache, anginal pain, circulatory collapse, nausea, vomiting, diarrhea, and abdominal cramps. Overdoses may result in convulsions, coma, and cerebral hemorrhage (44, 59). As the hippie slogan of the late 1960s succinctly and correctly stated, "speed kills." Although approximately 24 percent of college students, 26 percent of senior high school students, and 7.2 percent of junior high school students have reported use of amphetamines (1, 12, 79, 82, 126, 144), many use them infrequently and at relatively low dosages, often for such traditional purposes as staying awake when studying or driving (a typical adult use as well). Approximately one in four high school seniors in 1981 reported use in the past 12 months, and only one in six used them in the last 30 days (82).

Of course, use of the multitudinous pills of our time is not restricted to adolescents, but is widespread among adults, as the statistics already cited make clear. In addition, over 400 *tons* of barbiturates (3.6 billion normal doses) are produced each year in the United States alone (44). If ours is getting to be a drug culture—it is not simply an adolescent phenomenon.

### LSD and other hallucinogens

The hallucinogens (i.e., drugs capable of producing hallucinations or distortions of reality in one or more sensory systems) vary in strength from mild (e.g., marijuana, nutmeg) to moderate (e.g., psilocybin, mescaline, peyote) to highly potent (e.g., LSD–25). LSD in its pure form is an odorless, tasteless white crystalline powder, readily soluble in water and of enormous potency (33). It was originally derived from a fungus growing on wheat and rye, and was first used scientifically as a psychotomimetic research drug (that is, a drug thought to produce a model psychosislike state experimentally). In the 1960s it also became the basis of a new philosophical-religious cult led by Timothy Leary, a former Harvard psychologist.

Youthful experimentation with LSD and other hallucinogens grew rapidly in the latter 1960s, appeared to reach a plateau in the early 1970s, and has since declined (1, 79, 82, 144). In 1980, only about 9 percent of high school seniors had ever used LSD, and less than 5 percent had used it in the past year; about equal numbers had used other moderate to strong hallucinogens, such as mescaline, psilocybin, or peyote (82). Many former users have discontinued use of LSD because of fear of physical damage or psychological harm and emotionally upsetting experiences with the drug.

There are many variations among LSD users, ranging from those for whom hallucinogenic experiences are esthetic, religious, and mystical (an expansion of consciousness and a deepening of insight into themselves), to those who view these experiences simply as an explosive way of becoming high or getting their kicks, or as a novel experience. For some users, at some times, the chemical disturbances in brain functioning produced by LSD may lead to experiences of a sense of timelessness, vivid panoramic visual hallucinations of fantastic brightness and depth, a heightening or blocking of sensory experiences, the feeling that superior and lasting insights are emerging, and feelings of a loss of individual identity, together with a feeling of unity with other human beings, animals, inanimate objects, and the universe in general (12, 33). For other individuals, or at other times, however, an LSD trip may produce bizarre and frightening images, a sense of isolation and depersonalization, acute panic, and paranoia. In psychologically unstable individuals, it may sometimes precipitate an acute psychosis (167).

Furthermore, there is still no clear understanding of possible long-term physiological or psychological effects of LSD trips, including the still unresolved question of genetic or prenatal damage to one's offspring (71, 120). Long-term, steady users of LSD tend to view themselves as less constricted, less anxious, more relaxed, more creative, more loving, and generally more open to experience. On the other hand, to outside observers, many of these presumed assets are viewed differently; many long-term users appear to others as showing poor judgment and inappropriate euphoria. Not only may they be less anxious in responding to what previously were neurotic sources of anxiety; they also fail to respond appropriately to more realistic sources of concern or danger, such as the possibility of arrest, loss of a job, or exploitation by others (12, 15). In the words of one former user,

> Just taking LSD doesn't insure that you get any insight out of it. . . . To step out [of the established social structure can be] a pleasant experience. For some people getting out is an end in itself. That's all they're interested in doing. They keep stepping out, and stepping out, and stepping out.
>
> Each time they do, they give up their personality, or ego, or whatever you want to call it. They see shedding their ego as a virtue because it feels good. They have set up a structureless personality for themselves. That leaves them to become relatively passive people, who don't have the perimeters of a personality. They have what might be referred to as "blown minds" [175, 255].

**Mescaline** Ingestion of the mescal bud of the peyote cactus has long been used ritually by members of the Native American Church in the Southwest. Its active ingredient, synthesized and called *mescaline,* has also been employed by youthful drug experimenters, although less so in recent years. It is much milder and far less dangerous than LSD, but it is also a hallucinogen, and markedly distorts and intensifies sensory (primarily visual) perceptions (33, 44). "Objects take on more vivid, vibrant, and intense qualities with heightened color and a fluidity or plasticity of form, which makes them seem to change their shape or color, often quite rapidly" (33, 69). It is far less likely than LSD, however, to cause the individual to lose contact with reality, and he or she usually recognizes the perceptual distortions and hallucinations as such. Although the typical mood is one of mild euphoria, under unfavorable personal or social circumstances the user may encounter anxiety, depression, and even panic. Sometimes sadness, uneasiness, and a sense of detachment may last for several days.

Other naturally occurring drugs, such as psilocybin (from the Mexican mushroom of the same name) and morning glory seeds, also act as hallucinogens. In addition, a number of synthetic hallucinogens (e.g., DMT, MDA) have appeared over the past decade. Some are *relatively* mild and similar to mescaline or peyote in their effects, whereas others are far stronger, more dangerous, and more similar to LSD.

***PCP (phencyclidine)*** Also known as angel dust, Krystal, or DOA (dead on arrival), PCP is another street drug that has recently achieved notoriety. Originally developed as an animal tranquilizer, it has no known medical function for humans. One of its principal dangers is the variability of its effects, which may vary from a pleasant, dreamlike state to extreme confusion, paranoia, psychotic states, and assaultive behavior. PCP may also lead to loss of bodily orientation in space, incoordination and muscle rigidity, and inability to sense imminent danger (131, 132). Increasing numbers of homicides, suicides, and accidental deaths have recently been related to PCP use (131, 132). In large doses PCP has also been known to produce comas and death when combined with other drugs. There are some indications that long-term use may produce memory loss and inability to concentrate, and withdrawal may lead to depression.

Among all adolescents aged 12 to 17, PCP use doubled from 3 percent to approximately 6 percent between 1976 and 1977; use among 18- to 25-year-olds increased from 9.5 to 14 percent in the same period (1). Fortunately, there are some indications that PCP use *may* at last be declining; at least among high school seniors in the United States, annual use of PCP within the past 2 years dropped from 7 percent in the class of 1979 to 4.4 percent in the class of 1980, and 3.2 percent in 1981. (82). In any case, it is an extremely dangerous and unpredictable drug, which can have tragic consequences for some users.

### Inhalation

Confined largely to younger adolescents and children (some as young as 8 or 9), sniffing of glue and other volatile hydrocarbons (gasoline, cleaning fluid, paint thinner), although sometimes producing a sense of euphoria and dizziness, may also produce severe headache and vomiting. Many of these substances also can produce permanent damage to body organs such as the kidneys, brain, and liver; and acute poisoning can, and frequently has, resulted in death (31, 33, 45, 51, 144). Fortunately, only about 12 percent of young people have ever engaged in inhalation, most do so rarely, and there has been no apparent increase in recent years (1, 81, 82).

## Cocaine

Except among some disadvantaged ghetto residents, particularly blacks (for historical and geographic reasons), cocaine played a minimal role on the drug scene until the past decade. Since 1970, however, its use has increased significantly, especially among middle-class youth and "swinging" young adults (1, 82). Between 1975 and 1981, the percentage of high school seniors who reported having tried cocaine increased from 9 to 16.5 percent, and the number of young adults 18 to 25 who have used this drug currently is at least one in five, up from about 14 percent in 1975 (1, 80, 82). Of the former group, 12.4 percent have used cocaine in the past year, and 5.8 percent in the past 30 days (82). Overall use of cocaine would probably be greater were it not for its high cost.

Cocaine (also known as coke, C, snow, uptown, lady) is an alkaloid derived from the coca plant that grows in the Andes in Peru and Bolivia. In pre-Spanish Peru, the chewing of cocaine-containing leaves was a jealously guarded privilege of the Incan aristocracy, and the substance was valued more highly than gold and silver (174). Sigmund Freud, the father of psychoanalysis, played an important role in modern times in the popularization of cocaine in Europe (174). Having heard of the drug from a German army doctor, who spoke of its energizing effects on soldiers, Freud tried it himself and reported that it produced

> . . . exhilaration and lasting euphoria, which in no way differs from the normal euphoria of the healthy person. . . . You perceive an increase of self-control and possess more vitality and capacity for work. . . . In other words, you are simply normal, and it is soon hard to believe that you are under the influence of any drug [174, *118*].

Freud subsequently became disillusioned with the drug when friends and patients to whom he had recommended it for pain, fatigue, and depression began taking progressively larger doses. The results were convulsions, insomnia, tactile hallucinations (e.g., bugs or snakes crawling on the skin), a variety of eccentric behaviors, and, in at least one instance, death (83).

Cocaine is a powerful stimulant to the central nervous system, producing general activation or excitement similar in a number of respects to the effects of amphetamines. "In high doses, heart rate may be decreased or irregular in pattern, respiration depressed or irregular in pattern, and pupils continue to be dilated. The acute toxic manifestations of high doses usually take the form of delirium, often followed by convulsions, respiratory depression, and cardiovascular collapse" (174, *136*). As Freud noted, repeated high dosages of cocaine may produce both visual and tactile hallucinations (more frequently the latter). Paranoia, reflected in such fears as that of being spied upon by police ("bull horrors"), is often associated with chronic cocaine use (174). Increasing hostility, impulsiveness, introversion, social withdrawal, and general deterioration of behavior may also result. Prolonged use can inflame or destroy nasal tissue or cause perforation of the septum separating the nostrils, although this occurs less frequently than was previously thought (58).

The most striking initial effect of a moderate dose of cocaine is a state of euphoria (although, paradoxically, the euphoria may be accompanied or followed by anxiety or apprehension). Feelings of enhanced and accelerated mental and physical abilities are characteristic. Although the effects of isolated experimentation with co-caine appear to be slight, and although the drug is not physiologically addictive like heroin, the powerful lure of the euphoria it produces may be psychologically rein-forcing and lead to increased use, especially among vulnerable individuals who are seeking an escape from the realities and demands of existence, psychological or otherwise (58).

### Heroin

Until the 1960s, use of heroin and other hard narcotics was confined largely to the most depressed sectors of our society. With considerable socioeconomic and psychological justification heroin has been described as the drug of despair—a drug used not to "turn on" to the neglected beauty of the surrounding world or to expand one's consciousness, but rather to shut out physical pain, mental anguish, and a sense of emptiness in an all too brief euphoria and release of tension characterized externally by apathy, listlessness, and inertia.

As such, and because of the danger of addiction, heroin traditionally had little appeal for adolescents or adults outside the ghetto. Beginning in the latter half of the 1960s, however, experimentation with heroin spread to middle-class, suburban high schools and junior high schools in many parts of the country (33, 72, 144, 146). By 1972, approximately 1.5 million persons, or 6 percent of all young people aged 12 to 17, acknowledged having at least tried heroin (86, 138, 144). Fortunately, by 1975 this figure had declined to 2.2 percent, and by 1978 to 1.6 percent (79, 80). From 1979 to 1981, 1 percent of high school seniors had ever used heroin, and most of these had used it only one or two times (81, 82). Although the numbers of users of hard narcotics has never represented more than a small minority of total adolescents, it is difficult to exaggerate the potential dangers of these drugs.

Heroin is a strong semisynthetic drug derived from morphine, an alkaloid chemical found in opium, which in turn is obtained from a milky fluid in the seedpod of the poppy plant. When dissolved in water and injected into a vein (mainlining), it may produce an acute episode of nausea and vomiting ("a good sick"), and height-ened feelings of physical warmth, peacefulness, and increased self-esteem and con-fidence—some have described the initial feelings as somewhat similar to a prolonged orgasm (33, 105, 124). When sniffed (hence, the term *snort*) or injected under the skin (skin-popping), the effects are somewhat attenuated (33).

In the words of one of the young street people in San Francisco, heroin is

> the mellowest downer of all. You get none of the side effects of speed and barbs. After you fix you feel the rush, like an orgasm if it's a good dope. Then you float for about four hours; nothing positive, just a normal feeling, nowhere. It's like being half asleep, like watching a movie: nothing gets through to you, you're safe and warm. The big thing is, you don't hurt. You can walk around with rotting teeth and a busted appendix and not feel it. You don't need sex, you don't need food, you don't need people; you don't care. It's like death without permanence, life without pain [105, 10].

After about 4 hours, the effects taper off. If the individual is not already addicted, the aftereffects may be confined to a slight irritability and a return of whatever psychological or physical pain may have preceded the experience. However, if the individual is strongly addicted, within 12 hours or so he or she will begin to experience withdrawal symptoms—yawning, sweating, sniffling, and watering of the eyes, followed within another 24 hours by twitching and shaking, cramps, feeling cold, vomiting, diarrhea, and, occasionally, convulsions (33, 105).

The potential danger of addiction to heroin is very real, despite the fact that, contrary to public opinion, all users do not become addicts (87, 139). Tolerance for the drug develops quickly and ever-larger doses may be needed to maintain its effects and to avoid withdrawal symptoms. Because of this, and because of its expense, a habit can easily cost $100 to $200 a day. For most youthful users, this means resorting to criminal activity—most frequently robbery, muggings, and the like among men and prostitution among women (although male prostitution also occurs). It also frequently means becoming a small-time pusher oneself. Heroin acts as a strong depressant, and large doses may slow respiration to as little as two or three breaths a minute, starving the brain for oxygen and leading to deep sleep, coma, shock, and even death. Other complications may include pneumonia or edema (i.e., waterlogging) of the lungs (33, 84, 144).

**Psychological characteristics** The heroin-dependent person has been variously described as immature, resentful of authority, passive-aggressive, emotionally labile, sexually inadequate, anxiety-ridden, and socially isolated (5, 6, 133, 144). He or she is also likely to have low frustration tolerance and a need for immediate gratification, low self-esteem and a need to be manipulative:

> The heroin dependent person can be viewed as an individual totally uncomfortable with and alienated from himself and his surroundings, who must constantly maintain control over the frustrations, anxieties, hostility and aggression. At the same time, because his dependence requires his preoccupation with drug-using and drug-seeking behavior, he has neither the time nor the inclination to form stable social relationships. His low self-esteem and perceived inadequacies push him further into isolation from friends and relatives [144, *170*].

It is sobering to find that the median age for initial heroin experience in some urban ghettos is about 13 years for males and 15 for females (10, 144), and that introduction to usage is overwhelmingly by peers rather than adult pushers (10). It is important that young people be made aware that heroin is an extremely dangerous drug with which to experiment, and that it always carries the possibility of becoming "a one-way road to nowhere." In view of its infinitely greater danger compared to marijuana use, the tendency until recently of our laws, and of many law enforcement officials, to link the two drugs certainly did not help to convince the skeptical adolescent of the dangers of heroin. Under the circumstances this tendency can only be viewed as socially irresponsible.

Finally, we must remind ourselves that though heroin was relatively unknown among middle-class, suburban adolescents until the 1960s, it is a tragically old phenomenon among many of their ghetto-dwelling peers. Perhaps one can do no better in concluding this section than to consider the words of the young street person quoted before: "I never really belonged in this world. . . . I've seen a lot of scenes,

man, but I've never been part of one. People have treated me like an animal as long as I can remember. Dope meant hope once . . . but, you know, sometimes I think it'd be better for everyone if I just overdosed and died" (105, *10*).

## PATTERNS OF MULTIPLE DRUG USE

Thus far we have been discussing use of each of a variety of drugs separately. There is increasing evidence, however, of multiple drug use among adolescents (33, 86, 91, 93, 94, 144, 146). In general, users of one drug are more likely to use another drug that is similar with respect to its legal status and pharmacological properties than they are to use a dissimilar drug. Thus, in one extensive study (146), the correlation between marijuana use and use of hashish was .78, and the correlation between heroin and cocaine was .48. In contrast, the correlation between use of beer or wine and use of heroin was only .046. Furthermore, heavy use of any one drug markedly increases the likelihood of use of any other drug, legal or illegal (93, 144, 146).

Young people who had used marijuana only once or twice were unlikely to be involved in using any other drugs, with the exception of alcohol (146). However, as marijuana use increased, the likelihood of using other drugs increased rapidly. Thus, among heavy marijuana users (sixty or more times), 84 percent also reported use of the pills (methedrine, amphetamine, barbiturates, or tranquilizers), 78 percent used LSD or other psychedelics, and 62 percent used cocaine, heroin, or narcotics other than heroin. Other investigators have obtained similar results (77, 85, 113).

For those young people who do become involved in use of a variety of drugs, there generally appears to be a chronological progression. It has been known for some time that most users of heroin or other hard drugs have previously used marijuana; indeed, this fact was interpreted for many years by federal authorities and others to indicate that marijuana use leads to use of heroin. Several points need to be made in this regard, however: (1) Few adolescent marijuana users (9 percent or less) have ever tried heroin; and (2) prior use of marijuana among heroin users does not establish a causal relationship. It seems more likely that the person who is predisposed to heroin use, for whatever reasons, will also be predisposed to trying other drugs.

Nevertheless, it is interesting to note that where multiple use occurs, there appears to be a statistically significant order. Beer and wine are most likely to be tried first, tobacco and hard liquor second, and marijuana third—followed in chronological rank-order (for the minority that progress that far) by the pills, psychedelics, tranquilizers, methamphetamine, cocaine, and heroin. If one were to accept the "first fatal step" theory formerly asserted by narcotics authorities, it would appear that cigarettes and alcohol would lead the way or at least share the limelight with marijuana as major menaces. Needless to say, for reasons more political and social than scientific, this was not the case historically, despite the fact that use of marijuana rarely takes place without prior use of liquor, tobacco, or both (143, 144).

## WHY DO ADOLESCENTS TAKE DRUGS?

The reasons adolescents take drugs vary widely. So does the seriousness of their drug use. There is a world of difference between the curious young adolescent who tries marijuana at a party with friends, and the lonely, despairing young person in an urban ghetto who has been hooked on heroin as "an escape to nowhere," in the words of one 14-year-old ex-addict.

One reason adolescents may try a drug is simply because it is there. As we noted at the beginning of this chapter, our entire society has, to a large extent, become a drug culture; we take drugs to relax, to restore energy, to sleep, to relieve anxiety and depression, to relieve boredom. Perhaps it should be no surprise that many adolescents, like adults, conclude that they can find "better living through chemistry."

Furthermore, all manner of drugs are readily available to young people. Almost nine out of ten high school seniors in the United States recently reported that they could obtain marijuana "very easily" or "fairly easily." A majority have the same view regarding the amphetamines, barbiturates, and tranquilizers, although less than half say that they could easily obtain such drugs as cocaine, LSD, and other psychedelics (80, 81, 82). However, among recent users of the various drugs, these figures are consistently higher; thus from 75 to 98 percent of users of most drugs except LSD, heroin, and other opiates say they can obtain them fairly easily (compared to 50 percent for the latter drugs). Unlike the average young person of 50 years ago, whose opportunities for illicit drug use were limited in most countries to alcohol and tobacco, today's adolescent faces a cornucopia of drugs from which to choose, both those sold in pharmacies and those available only on the street.

Adolescents characteristically are curious about their expanding world, and are far more inclined than most adults to take risks—probably partly to prove their boldness ("not being chicken") and sense of adventure, and partly because they do not really believe, at least initially, that anything disastrous can really happen to *them*. Thus, for many adolescents, some experimentation with drugs may take place merely because of curiosity, a sense of adventure, and opportunity. Furthermore, in limited amounts, some drug use—an occasional marijuana cigarette, or as older adults may more readily recognize, an occasional social cocktail, can be "fun"— which is not to say it is desirable (38).

### Peer pressure

As we saw in the case of marijuana, adolescents may also try drugs because of peer group influences (28, 91). Pressures for conformity to peers increase for most adolescents as they move from the shelter of the family and seek a similar sense of belonging in the wider world of peers (see pages 326–330). Adolescents themselves acknowledge the importance of peer group influences. In a national survey, young people, aged 13 to 18, were asked why young people used alcohol and other drugs; the most frequently cited reason was peer group pressure: "It's the thing." In the words of a 15-year-old ninth-grade girl, "People my age sometimes follow the group so they won't be outcasts. They try to enjoy themselves, but then things get out of hand" (52).

Other young people may experiment with drugs to please a special boyfriend or girlfriend. Girls who have been led to believe that having and keeping a boyfriend is an urgent social necessity may be especially vulnerable (28). This appeared to be the case with a 14-year-old California girl: "I smoked pot with my boyfriend and then he wanted to try LSD. I was scared but he told me that if I didn't go along with him, he'd find a girl who would. Other kids told me there wasn't anything to worry about—that you just see lots of colors and different shapes, like the posters you see around" (28, *18*).

### Rebellion against parents

Another reason that some young people try drugs is as a way of rebelling against the constraints of adults, particularly parents (28, 38). All adolescents, at one time or another, need ways of asserting their independence from their parents. But whether this will take the form of *serious* drug use appears to depend a good deal on the kind of relationships the adolescent has had with his or her parents. For the child of democratic, authoritative, loving parents (especially those with relatively traditional values), who allow their children gradually increasing, age-appropriate opportunities to test their wings, the risk of serious drug involvement is generally low (7, 28, 76). But for the child whose parents have not been loving, and who are either neglectful, overly permissive, or—in contrast—authoritarian and hostile, the risk of significant drug use is much greater (13, 14, 15, 76, 91, 162). In the words of one 17-year-old girl, "I got involved because I was trying to rebel against my father because he never let me do anything that I wanted. You know I couldn't talk to boys until this year. It was really upsetting, and I just turned to drugs for an escape" (99, *106*).

Another angry adolescent said of his parents, "They're always telling me what to do, like I don't have any mind of my own. And like my father is sitting around having his third martini before supper, and telling me like he's some big expert, and I'm an idiot, about how marijuana will destroy my brain. Well, the hell with him!"

An adolescent girl, on the other hand, seemed mostly to be trying to get some response—any response—from her parents as a sign that they cared: "I've been on drugs since I was twelve. My parents think I'm rebelling about something, but they don't know what. It's them. Not that they're strict. It's just that they're not really there and you feel you have to jump up and down and scream before they really notice" (28, *24*).

### Escape from the pressures of life

Another reason cited frequently (26 percent) by adolescents themselves for drug use is escape from tension and the pressures of life, or from boredom (52). Ironically, this is also a major reason why adults use drugs. The bored, depressed suburban housewife who has a few drinks to get her through the day, and the highly pressured corporate executive who takes alcohol and barbiturates to relax or sleep, and pep pills to combat fatigue, have much in common with the tense, jittery, insecure adolescent girl who tries to relax with marijuana, downers (barbiturates), and alcohol, or the boy who takes a few bennies (amphetamines) or cocaine to relieve his feelings of inadequacy and low self-esteem and give himself—if only briefly—a feeling of power, competence, and well-being.

One of the greatest dangers of drug use by adolescents is that it can become a substitute for one of the most important developmental tasks all adolescents face, learning to deal with the daily problems and inevitable frustrations of living. As the former director of the National Institute of Mental Health in the United States has stated:

> Patterns of coping with reality developed during the teen-age period are significant in determining adult behavior. Persistent use of an agent which serves to ward off reality during this critical developmental period is likely to compromise seriously the future ability of the individual to make an adequate adjustment to a complex society [177, *28*].

### Alienation

Some adolescent drug use may reflect alienation—a profound rejection of the values of an adult society that these young people perceive as increasingly impersonal, often cruel, and lacking in concern for the individual. This was not infrequently the case during the troubled decade of the 1960s (particularly in America), when a significant minority of adolescents and youth renounced the "rewards" of organized society and turned inward to the self-preoccupied world of mind-altering drugs (conspicuously, marijuana and the psychedelic drugs, such as LSD, mescaline, and peyote) in order—mistakenly or not—to seek a renewal of wonder, trust, beauty, and meaning (43, 162, 163, 164).

### Emotional disturbance

For other young people, particularly heavy multiple drug users, reliance on drugs may reflect emotional disturbances of varying degrees of severity, and an inability to cope with the demands of living or to find a meaningful personal identity. In some such cases, we need to look to significant disturbances in family relationships during the course of development for clues to the young person's difficulties (38, 99, 163, 169). Among adolescents in residential treatment centers and half-way houses for alcohol and drug users (usually in combination), common themes acknowledged by both the staff and recovering users are feelings of parental rejection or indifference; lack of acceptance by peers; emotional isolation; and low self-esteem, which they felt a need to conceal behind a defense of "appearing cool" (38).

Some young people, who have been using alcohol or drugs steadily since preadolescence, acknowledge that they had never known any other way to cope with anxiety, boredom, depression, fear of failure, or lack of purpose. Poignantly, an important aim of one treatment program, in addition to helping young people to learn to deal with their personal problems and establish genuine friendships with peers, was simply to teach them something many did not know how to do, have fun without drugs (38)!

### Societal rejection

In some cases an indifferent society must share much of the blame. Too many disadvantaged adolescents in many Western countries face the future without hope. Confronted with economic, social, and racial discrimination, with impossible living conditions, often with untreated physical ills, and with a breakdown in their social environment and in their own families, they may give up the search for meaning and a sense of ego identity entirely and seek escape in the oblivion of hard narcotics.

In brief, there are many reasons why adolescents may take drugs, with varying outcomes. The fact remains, however, that although drugs may produce oblivion or temporary escape, or even in more positive instances, a feeling of greater appreciation for simple beauty in the world, there is little evidence that they have, in themselves, produced a long-term sense of well-being or true creativity, and considerable evidence that they have impaired them.

Furthermore, drugs have not produced a better and more responsible world in which all people have an opportunity for food, shelter, health, joy, and a sense of purpose. The challenge to adolescents, and to adults as well, is not to turn on with drugs and drop out of life, but to find a way to make life itself more just, more creative, and more generally meaningful, so that the individual can turn away from the myriad drugs of our age, "turn on" with life itself, and drop out of social isolation and personal anonymity, or hopelessness and despair.

## THE ROLE OF PARENTS

In an era when the availability and use of drugs is widespread, even the most enlightened, sensible parents cannot guarantee that their children will not become involved with some drug experimentation. There are, however, a number of steps that parents can take to minimize the likelihood of adolescent drug use, or to limit its seriousness. In particular, they can seek to keep the lines of communication open between parents and children, to be fair, and to encourage their children to participate in family decision making (37). In a recent study (53), it was found that parents of drug-abusing (and emotionally disturbed) adolescents were far more inclined than parents of normal adolescents to engage in *scapegoating*—blaming family problems and difficulties in decision making on the adolescent. Furthermore, they were far less likely to consult with the young person about his or her views, and more likely simply to tell the adolescent what to do. There was also much greater freedom in the normal families for all members to express themselves openly, as well as greater clarity of communication and more equal participation by all family members.

Parents can also encourage their children, long before the onset of adolescence, to begin learning to become more independent and to take increasing responsibility for their own actions. Obviously, such learning experiences should be geared to the age of the child, and should be expanded only as the child becomes more mature. Parents who think that they can continue—sometimes indefinitely—to run the lives of their adolescent young, and to protect them from any adverse consequences of their actions, are not preparing them for coping with exposure to drugs—or with life itself.

In addition, parents need to remember that they are role models, and that their children take their cues from what parents do, as well as what they say. If parents present models of stable, responsible, problem-solving behavior, their young are likely to do the same (see pages 243–244). With respect specifically to drug use, we have already seen that drug-using parents are more likely to have drug-using children, even though the actual drugs may (or may not) differ (38, 87). If their parents use drugs rarely, and only for responsible, well-defined purposes, adolescents are much more apt to do the same than if their parents are forever running from one drug to another—to sleep, to stay awake, to relax, to cope with anxiety or pressure, or to "pick up their spirits."

It is important for young people to know that their parents have basic values, and that they are making a real effort to live by them. Whether the young person disagrees with some of these values is far less important than the knowledge that the values exist. In the end, this knowledge provides young people with a sense of trust and security, encourages them to think through their own basic values, and promotes respect for parents and a willingness to listen to their views (38).

Finally, adolescents need to know that their parents really care about them, not just in the abstract, but in concrete, demonstrated ways: by shared family activities, and by knowing about and taking an interest in their children's schoolwork, hobbies, friends, social life, goals, and dreams. None of these parental efforts can guarantee that a young person will not become involved in drug experimentation, but they can do much to lessen its likelihood, and to minimize the seriousness of the adolescent's drug use, should it occur.

### REFERENCES

1. Abelson, H. I., et al. *National survey on drug abuse, 1977: A nationwide study—Youth, young adults, and older people.* Rockville, Md.: National Institute on Drug Abuse, 1977. DHEW Publication No. (ADM) 78–618.
2. Ager, S. A. "Luding out." *New England Journal of Medicine,* 1972, **287,** 51.
3. *Alcohol and health: New knowledge.* Second special report to the U.S. Congress, National Institute on Alcohol Abuse and Alcoholism, Department of Health, Education

and Welfare. Washington, D.C.: Superintendent of Documents, U.S. Government Printing Office, No. 1724-00399, June 1974 (preprint edition).

4. Annis, H. M., & Watson, C. Drug use and school dropout. *Conseiller Canadian,* 1975, **9,** 155–162.

5. Austin, G. A., Macari, M. A., & Lettieri, D. J. *Research Issues Update, 1978.* Rockville, Md.: National Institute on Drug Abuse, 1978.

6. Baber, T. F., Meyer, R. E., & Mirin, S. M. Interpersonal behavior in a small group setting during the heroin addiction cycle. *International Journal of the Addictions,* 1976, **11,** 513–523.

7. Bachman, J. G. *Youth in transition, Vol. II: The impact of family background and intelligence on tenth-grade boys.* Ann Arbor: Institute for Social Research, University of Michigan, 1970.

8. Bacon, M., & Jones, M. B. *Teen-age drinking.* New York: Crowell, 1968.

9. Baumgold, J. Down at the juice bars. *New York Magazine,* 1972, **5,** 51–61.

10. Bernstein, B., & Shkuda, A. N. *The young drug user: Attitudes and obstacles to treatment.* New York: Center for New York City Affairs, New School for Social Research, 1974.

11. Blum, R. H. *Utopiates: The use and users of LSD-25.* New York: Atherton, 1964.

12. Blum, R. H. Youthful drug use. In R. I. Dupont, A. Goldstein, & J. O'Donnell (eds.), *Handbook on drug abuse.* Washington, D.C.: U.S. Government Printing Office, 1979. Pp. 257–269.

13. Blum, R. H., et al. *Society and drugs, Vol. 1: Social and cultural observations.* San Francisco: Jossey-Bass, 1970.

14. Blum, R. H., et al. *Society and drugs, Vol. II: College and high school observations.* San Francisco: Jossey-Bass, 1970.

15. Blum, R. H., et al. *Horatio Alger's children.* San Francisco: Jossey-Bass, 1972.

16. Braucht, G. N. A psychosocial typology of adolescent alcohol and drug users. Paper presented at the Third Annual Alcoholism Conference, National Institute on Alcohol Abuse and Alcoholism, June 1973.

17. Braucht, G. N. Problem drinking among adolescents: A review and analysis of psychosocial research. In National Institute on Alcohol Abuse and Alcoholism, *Special Population Issues.* Alcohol and Health Monograph No. 4. Rockville, Md.: The Institute, in press.

18. Braucht, G. N., Brakarsh, D., Follingsted, D., & Berry, K. L. Deviant drug use in adolescence. *Psychological Bulletin,* 1973, **79,** 92–106.

19. Brecher, E. M., & the Editors of Consumer Reports. The health questions. *Consumer Reports,* March 1975, 143–149.

20. Brill, N. W., & Christie, R. L. Marijuana use and psychosocial adaptation. *Archives of General Psychiatry,* 1974, **31,** 713–719.

21. Brill, N., Crumpton, E., & Grayson, H. Personality factors in marijuana use. *Archives of General Psychiatry,* 1971, **24,** 163–165.

22. Bromberg, W. Marihuana intoxication. *American Journal of Psychiatry,* 1934, **91,** 303–330.

23. Brook, J. S., Lukoff, J. F., & Whiteman, M. Initiation into adolescent marihuana use. *Journal of Genetic Psychology,* 1980, **137,** 133–142.

24. Brunswick, A. F. Initiation of smoking in adolescent girls. In *Smoking and health: A report of the Surgeon General.* Washington, D.C.: U.S. Department of Health, Education and Welfare, 1980.

25. Brunswick, A. F., & Boyle, J. M. Patterns of drug involvement: Developmental and secular influences on age of initiation. *Youth and Society,* 1979, **11,** 139–162.

26. Carman, R. S. Expectations and socialization experiences related to drinking among U.S. servicemen. *Quarterly Journal of Alcohol Studies,* 1970, **32,** 1040–1047.

27. Cherry, N., & Kiernan, K. Personality scores and smoking behavior: A longitudinal study. *British Journal of Preventive and Social Medicine,* 1976, **30,** 123–131.

28. Child Study Association of America. *You, your child, and drugs.* New York: Child Study Press, 1971.

29. Clark, W. B., & Midanik, L. Alcohol use and alcohol problems among U.S. adults. In National Institute on Alcohol Abuse and Alcoholism, *Alcohol consumption and related problems.* Alcohol and Health Monograph No. 1. Rockville, Md.: The Institute, in press.

30. Clarren, S. K., & Smith, D. W. The fetal alcohol syndrome. *New England Journal of Medicine,* 1978, **298,** 1063–1067.

31. Cohen, S. Inhalants. In R. I. Dupont, A. Goldstein, & J. O'Donnell (eds.), *Handbook on drug abuse.* Washington, D.C.: U.S. Government Printing Office, 1979. Pp. 213–220.

32. Coles, R., Brenner, J. H., & Meagher, D. *Drugs and youth: Medical, legal, and psychiatric facts.* New York: Liveright, 1970.

33. Committee to study the health-related effects of cannabis and its derivatives. National Academy of Sciences, Institute of Medicine. Marijuana and health. Washington, D.C.: National Academy Press, 1982.

34. Conger, J. J. The effects of alcohol on conflict behavior in the albino rat. *Quarterly Journal of Studies on Alcohol,* 1951, **12,** 1–29.

35. Conger, J. J. Reinforcement theory and the dynamics of alcoholism. *Quarterly Journal of Studies on Alcohol,* 1956, **17,** 291–324.

36. Conger, J. J. Perception, learning, and emotion: The role of alcohol. *Annals of the American Academy of Political and Social Science,* 1958, **315,** 31–39.

37. Conger, J. J. Parent-child relationships, social change and adolescent vulnerability. *Journal of Pediatric Psychology,* 1977, **2,** 93–97.

38. Conger, J. J. *Adolescence: Generation under pressure.* New York: Harper & Row, 1979.

39. Cory, C., et al. Pop drugs: The high as a way of life. *Time,* September 26, 1969, 68–79.

40. DeLuca, J. R. (ed.). Alcohol and health: Fourth special report to the U.S. Congress. Rockville, Md.: National Institute on Alcohol and Alcohol Abuse, 1981.

41. Donovan, J. E., & Jessor, R. Adolescent problem drinking: Psychosocial correlates in a national study sample. *Quarterly Journal of Studies on Alcohol,* 1978, **39,** 1506–1524.

42. Dott, A. B. *Effect of marihuana on risk acceptance in a simulated passing task.* PHS publication, U.S. Government Printing Office, Washington, D.C. 1972.

43. Douglas, R. L. Youth, alcohol, and traffic accidents. In National Institute on Alcohol Abuse and Alcoholism, *Special population issues.* Alcohol and Health Monograph No. 4. Rockville, Md.: The Institute, in press.

44. Drugs '78: The great American roller coaster. *Playboy,* September 1978, 157 ff.

45. Dworkin, A. G., & Stephens, R. C. Mexican-American adolescent inhalant abuse. *Youth and Society,* 1980, **11,** 493–506.

46. Ellinwood, E. H. Amphetamines/Anorectics. In R. I. Dupont, A. Goldstein, & J. O'Donnell (eds.), *Handbook on drug abuse.* Washington, D.C.: U.S. Government Printing Office, 1979. Pp. 221–231.

47. Ellis, G. J., & Stone, L. H. Marijuana use in college: An evaluation of a modelling explanation. *Youth and Society,* 1979, **10,** 323–334.

48. Evans, R., Henderson, A., Hill, P., & Raines, B. Smoking in children and adolescents: Psychosocial determinants and prevention strategies. In *Smoking and health: A report of the Surgeon General.* (DHEW Publication No (PHS) 79-50066, U.S. Department of Health, Education and Welfare.) Washington, D.C.: U.S. Government Printing Office (No. 017-000-00218-0), 1979. Chapter 17, pp. 1–30.

49. Evans, R. I., Rozelle, R. M., Mittlemark, M. B., et al. Deterring the onset of smoking in children: Knowledge of immediate physiological effects and coping with peer pressure, media pressure, and parent modeling. *Journal of Applied Social Psychology,* in press.

50. Forslund, M. A. Functions of drinking of Native American and white youth. *Journal of Youth and Adolescence,* 1978, **7,** 327–332.

51. Freedman, A. M., & Wilson, E. A. Childhood and adolescent addictive disorders. *Pediatrics,* 1964, **34,** 282–292.

52. Gallup, G. Gallup youth survey, *Denver Post,* May 29, 1977.
53. Gantman, C. A. Family interaction patterns among families with normal, disturbed, and drug-abusing adolescents. *Journal of Youth and Adolescence,* 1978, **7,** 429–440.
54. Gilbert, D. G. Paradoxical tranquilizing and emotion-reducing effects of incentive. *Psychological Bulletin,* 1979, **86,** 643–661.
55. Goyan, J., U.S. Food and Drug Administration, cited by United Press International, April 3, 1980.
56. Grinspoon, L. Marihuana. *Scientific American,* 1969, **221,** 17–25.
57. Grinspoon, L. *Marijuana reconsidered.* Cambridge, Mass.: Harvard University Press, 1971.
58. Grinspoon, L., & Bakalar, J. B. Cocaine. In R. I. Dupont, A. Goldstein, & J. O'Donnell (eds.), *Handbook on drug abuse.* Washington, D.C.: U.S. Government Printing Office, 1979. Pp. 241–247.
59. Grinspoon, L., & Hedblom, P. *The speed culture: Amphetamine use and abuse in America.* Cambridge, Mass.: Harvard University Press, 1975.
60. Grossman, J. C., Goldstein, R., & Eisenman, R. Openness to experience and marijuana use: An initial investigation. *Proceedings of the 79th Annual Convention of the American Psychological Association,* 1971, **6,** 335–336 (summary).
61. Grossman, J. C., Goldstein, R., & Eisenman, R. Internal sensation seeking and openness to experience as related to undergraduate marijuana use. Presented at the annual meeting of the Eastern Psychological Association, Boston, April 1972.
62. Hanson, J. W., Streissguth, A. P., & Smith, D. W. The effects of moderate alcohol consumption during pregnancy on fetal growth and morphogenesis. *Journal of Pediatrics,* 1978, **92,** 457–460.
63. *Health consequences of marihuana abuse.* Hearings before the Select Committee on Narcotics Abuse and Control, House of Representatives, 96th Congress, July 17 and 19, 1979. Washington, D.C.: U.S. Government Printing Office, 1979.
64. Heath, R. G. Marihuana, effects on deep and surface electroencephalograms of man. *Archives of General Psychiatry,* 1972, **26,** 577–584.
65. Hogan, R., Mankin, D., Conway, J., & Fox, S. Personality correlates of undergraduate marijuana use. *Journal of Consulting and Clinical Psychology,* 1970, **35,** 58–63.
66. Huba, G. J., Wingard, J. A., & Bentler, P. M. Beginning adolescent drug use and peer and adult interaction. *Journal of Counseling and Clinical Psychology,* 1979, **47,** 265–276.
67. Igra, A., & Moss, R. H. Alcohol use among college students: Some competing hypotheses. *Journal of Youth and Adolescence,* 1979, **8,** 393–406.
68. Institute of Medicine. *Summary of conference on "Smoking and behavior."* Washington, D.C.: Institute of Medicine, National Academy of Sciences, 1980.
69. Isbell, H., Gorodetsky, C. W., Jasinski, D., Claussen, U., Von Spulak, F., & Korte, F. Effects of $(-)\Delta^9$trans-tetrahydrocannabinal in man. *Psychopharmacologia* (Berlin), 1967, **11,** 184–188.
70. Isbell, H., et al. Studies on tetrahydrocannabinal. I. Method of assay in human subjects and results with crude extracts, purified tetrahydrocannabinals and synthetic compounds. Unpublished manuscript, University of Kentucky Medical Center, 1967.
71. Jacobs, B. L., & Trulson, M. E. Mechanisms of action of LSD. *American Scientist,* 1979, **67,** 396–404.
72. Janssen, P., et al. High schools in trouble. *Newsweek,* February 16, 1970, 66–67.
73. Jessor, R. Marihuana: A review of recent psychosocial research. In R. I. Dupont, A. Goldstein, & J. O'Donnell (eds.), *Handbook on drug abuse.* Washington, D.C.: U.S. Government Printing Office, 1979. Pp. 337–356.
74. Jessor, R., & Jessor, S. L. *Problem drinking in youth: Personality, social and behavioral antecedents and correlates.* Publication 144. Boulder, Colorado: Institute of Behavioral Science, University of Colorado, 1973.
75. Jessor, R., & Jessor, S. L. Adolescent development and the onset of drinking: A longitudinal study. *Journal of Youth and Adolescence,* 1975, **36,** 27–51.

76. Jessor, R., & Jessor, S. L. *Problem behavior and psychosocial development: A longitudinal study of youth.* New York: Academic Press, 1977.

77. Johnson, B. *Marihuana users and drug subcultures.* New York: Wiley, 1973.

78. Johnston, L. *Drugs and American youth.* Ann Arbor, Mich.: Institute for Social Research, 1973.

79. Johnston, L. D., Bachman, J. G., & O'Malley, P. M. *Drug use among American high school students 1975–1977.* Rockville, Md.: National Institute on Drug Abuse, 1978. DHEW Publication No. (ADM) 78-619.

80. Johnston, L. D., Bachman, J. G., & O'Malley, P. M. *Drugs and the class of '78: Behavior, attitudes, and recent national trends.* Rockville, Md.: National Institute on Drug Abuse, 1979. DHEW Publication No. (ADM) 79-877.

81. Johnston, L. D., Bachman, J. G., & O'Malley, P. M. *1979 Highlights, drugs and the nation's high school students: Five year national trends.* Rockville, Md.: National Institute on Drug Abuse, 1979. DHEW Publication No. (ADM) 80-930.

82. Johnston, L. D., Bachman, J. G., & O'Malley, P. M. *Highlights from student drug use in America, 1975–1981.* Rockville, Md.: National Institute on Drug Abuse, 1981. DHHS Publication No. (ADM) 82-1208.

83. Jones, E. *The life and work of Sigmund Freud* (edited and abridged by L. Trilling and S. Marcus). New York: Basic Books, 1961.

84. Jones, K. L., Shainberg, L. W., & Byer, C. O. *Drugs and alcohol.* New York: Harper & Row, 1969.

85. Josephson, E. Indicators of change in adolescent marihuana use. In E. Josephson & E. Carroll (eds.), *The epidemiology of drug abuse.* Washington, D.C.: Winston, 1974.

86. Josephson, E., & Carroll, E. E. *Drug use: Epidemiological and sociological approaches.* New York: Wiley, 1974.

87. Kandel, D. The role of parents and peers in adolescent marijuana use. *Science,* 1973, **181,** 1067–1070.

88. Kandel, D. Inter- and intragenerational influences on adolescent marijuana use. *Journal of Social Issues,* 1974, **30,** 107–135.

89. Kandel, D. B. Similarity in real life adolescent friendship pairs. *Journal of Personality and Social Psychology,* 1978, **36,** 306–312.

90. Kandel, D. B. (ed.). *Longitudinal research on drug use: Empirical findings and methodological issues.* Washington, D.C.: Hemisphere Publishing Corporation, 1978.

91. Kandel, D. B. Drug and drinking behavior among youth. *Annual Review of Sociology,* 1980, **6,** 235–285.

92. Kandel, D. B., Adler, I., & Sudit, M. The epidemiology of adolescent drug use in France and Israel. *American Journal of Public Health,* 1981, **71,** 256–265.

93. Kandel, D. B., & Faust, R. Sequence and stages in patterns of adolescent drug use. *Archives of General Psychiatry,* 1975, **32,** 923–932.

94. Kandel, D. B., Kessler, R. C., & Margulies, R. Z. Antecedents of adolescent initiation into stages of drug use: A developmental analysis. In D. B. Kandel (ed.), *Longitudinal research on drug use: Empirical findings and methodological issues.* Washington, D.C.: Hemisphere Publishing Corporation, 1978. Pp. 73–99.

95. Kandel, D. B., Single, E., & Kessler, R. C. The epidemiology of drug use among New York State high school students: Distribution, trends, and changes in rates of use. *American Journal of Public Health,* 1976, **66,** 43–52.

96. Keeler, M. H. Motivation for marijuana use: A correlate of adverse reaction. *American Journal of Psychiatry.* 1968, **125,** 386–390.

97. Kielholz, P., Goldberg, L., Hobi, V., Ladewig, D., Reggiani, G., & Richter, R. Hashish and driving behavior, an experimental study. *Deutsche Medizinische Wochenschrift,* 1972, **97,** 789–794.

98. Kolansky, H., & Moore, W. T. Toxic effects of chronic marihuana use. *Journal of the American Medical Association,* 1972, **222,** 35–37.

99. Konopka, G. *Young girls: A portrait of adolescence.* Englewood Cliffs, N.J.: Prentice-Hall, 1976.

100. Kozlowski, L. T. Psychosocial influences on cigarette smoking. In *Smoking and health: A report of the Surgeon General.* (DHEW Publication No. (PHS) 79-50066, U.S. Department of Health, Education, and Welfare.) Washington, D.C.: U.S. Government Printing Office (No. 017-000-00218-0), 1979. Chapter 18, pp. 1–31.

101. Lawrence, T. S., & Velleman, J. D. Correlates of student drug use in a suburban high school. *Psychiatry,* 1974, **37,** 129–136.

102. Levitt, E. E., & Edwards, J. A. A multivariate study of correlative factors in youthful cigarette smoking. *Developmental Psychology,* 1970, **2,** 5–11.

103. Loftus, E. F. Alcohol, marijuana, and memory. *Psychology Today,* March 1980, 42 ff.

104. Lucas, W. L., Grupp, S. E., & Schmitt, R. L. Predicting who will turn on: A four-year follow-up. *International Journal of Addiction,* 1975, **10,** 305–326.

105. Luce, J. End of the road. *Behavior: San Francisco Sunday Examiner and Chronicle,* November 8, 1970, 8–10.

106. Maddox, G. L., & McCall, B. C. *Drinking among teenagers: A sociological interpretation of alcohol use by high-school students.* Monograph No. 4. New Brunswick, N.J.: Rutgers Center of Alcohol Studies, 1964.

107. *Marihuana and health.* Third annual report to Congress from the Secretary of Health, Education and Welfare. Washington, D.C.: U.S. Government Printing Office, 1974.

108. *Marihuana and health.* Fifth annual report to Congress from the Secretary of Health, Education and Welfare. Washington, D.C.: U.S. Government Printing Office, 1975.

109. Masserman, J. H., & Hum, K. S. An analysis of the influence of alcohol on experimental neuroses in cats. *Psychosomatic Medicine.* 1946, **8,** 36–52.

110. McAlister, A. L., Perry, C., & Maccoby, N. Adolescent smoking: Onset and prevention. *Pediatrics,* 1979, **63,** 650–658.

111. McAree, C., Steffenhagen, R., & Zheutlin, L. Personality factors in college drug users. *International Journal of Social Psychiatry,* 1969, **15,** 102–106.

112. McCluggage, M. M., et al. *Attitudes toward the use of alcoholic beverages among high school students in the Wichita metropolitan area and in the nonmetropolitan areas of eastern Kansas.* New York: Sheppard Foundation, 1956.

113. McGlothlin, W. H., Jamison, K., & Rosenblatt, S. Marijuana and use of other drugs. *Nature,* 1970, **228,** 1227–1229.

114. Mellinger, G. D., Somers, R. H., Bazell, S., & Manheimer, D. I. Drug use, academic performance and career indecision: Longitudinal data in search of a model. In D. B. Kandel (ed.), *Longitudinal research on drug use: Empirical findings and methodological issues.* Washington, D.C.: Hemisphere (Halsted-Wiley), 1978. Pp. 157–177.

115. Mellinger, G. D., Somers, R. H., Davidson, S. T., & Manheimer, D. I. The amotivational syndrome and the college student. *Annuals of the New York Academy of Science,* 1976, **282,** 37–55.

116. Mirin, S., Shapiro, L., Meyer, R., Pillard, R., & Fisher, S. Casual versus heavy use of marijuana: A redefinition of the marijuana problem. *American Journal of Psychiatry,* 1971, **127,** 54–60.

117. Mizner, G. L., Barter, J. T., & Werner, P. H. Patterns of drug use among college students. *American Journal of Psychiatry,* 1970, **127,** 15–24.

118. Moos, R. H., Moos, B. S., & Kulik, J. A. College-student abstainers, moderate drinkers, and heavy drinkers: A comparative analysis. *Journal of Youth and Adolescence,* 1976, **5,** 349–360.

119. Moskowitz, H. A comparison of the effects of marihuana and alcohol on visual function. In M. F. Lewis (ed.), *Current research in marihuana.* New York: Academic Press, 1972.

120. Mussen, P. H., Conger, J. J., & Kagan, J. *Child development and personality.* New York: Harper & Row, 1979 (5th ed.).

121. Nahas, G. G., & Paton, W. D. M. *Marijuana, biological effects: Analysis, metabolism, cellular responses, reproduction, and brain.* Elmsford, N.Y.: Pergamon Press, 1979.

122. National Institutes of Health. Teenage smoking: National patterns of cigarette smoking, ages 12 through 18, in 1972 and 1974. U.S. Department of Health, Education and

Welfare, Public Health Service, National Institutes of Health, DHEW Publication No. (NIH) 76-931, March, 1977.

123. *New York Times,* February 27, 1982, 9.
124. Noble, E. P. (ed.). *Alcohol and health: Third special report to the U.S. Congress.* Rockville, Md.: National Institute on Alcohol Abuse and Alcoholism, 1978 (preprint edition).
125. O'Donnell, J., Voss, H. L., Clayton, R. R., Slatin, G. T., & Room, R. G. W. Non-medical drug use among young men in the United States: A nationwide survey. Unpublished manuscript, portions released to the press, National Institute on Drug Abuse, October 1, 1975.
126. Parry, H. J. Sample surveys of drug abuse. In R. I. Dupont, A. Goldstein, & J. O'Donnell (eds.), *Handbook on drug abuse.* Washington, D.C.: U.S. Government Printing Office, 1979. Pp. 381–394.
127. Pascarelli, E. F. Methaqualone: The quiet epidemic. In R. P. Shafer et al., *Drug use in America: Problem in perspective* (Appendix, Vol. 1). Second report of the National Commission on Marijuana and Drug Abuse. Washington, D.C.: U.S. Government Printing Office, No. 5266-00004, 1973. Pp. 102–105.
128. Petersen, R. C. Cocaine. Statement before the Select Committee on Narcotics Abuse and Control, U.S. House of Representatives, July 24, 1979. Rockville, Md.: National Institute on Drug Abuse, 1979.
129. Petersen, R. C. *Marihuana and health: Seventh annual report to the U.S. Congress from the Secretary of Health, Education, and Welfare.* Rockville, Md.: National Institute on Drug Abuse, 1979.
130. Petersen, R. C. Marijuana: The continuing dilemma. Keynote address, American Academy of Pediatrics annual meeting, San Francisco, October 14, 1979.
131. Petersen, R. C., & Stillman, R. C. *Phencyclidine (PCP) abuse: An appraisal.* NIDA Research Monograph 21. Washington, D.C.: U.S. Government Printing Office (No. 017-024-00785-4), 1979.
132. Pittel, S. M., & Oppedahl, M. C. The enigma of PCP. In R. I. Dupont, A Goldstein, & J. O'Donnell (eds.), *Handbook on drug abuse.* Washington, D.C.: U.S. Government Printing Office, 1979. Pp. 249–254.
133. Platt, J. J. "Addiction proneness" and personality in heroin addicts. *Journal of Abnormal Psychology,* 1975, **84,** 303–306.
134. Pollin, W. Health consequences of marijuana use. Statement before the Subcommittee on Criminal Justice, Committee on the Judiciary, U.S. Senate, January 16, 1980. National Institute on Drug Abuse, Rockville, Md., mimeographed.
135. Rachal, J. V., Maisto, S. A., Guess, L. L., & Hubbard, R. L. Alcohol use among adolescents. In National Institute on Alcohol Abuse and Alcoholism, *Alcohol consumption and related problems.* Alcohol and Health Monograph No. 1. Rockville, Md.: The Institute, in press.
136. Rachal, J. V., et al. *A national study of adolescent drinking behavior, attitudes, and correlates.* Research Triangle Park, N.C.: Research Triangle Institute, 1975.
137. *Report of the National Commission on Marijuana and Drug Abuse.* Washington, D.C.: U.S. Government Printing Office, 1972.
138. Response Analysis Corporation. Survey on drug use, prepared for the National Commission on Marijuana and Drug Abuse. Washington, D.C., May 1972.
139. Robins, L. N. Addict careers. In R. I. Dupont, A. Goldstein, & J. O'Donnell (eds.), *Handbook on drug abuse.* Washington, D.C.: U.S. Government Printing Office, 1979. Pp. 325–336.
140. Robles, R. R., Martinez, R. E., & Moscosco, M. R. Predictors of adolescent drug behavior: The case of Puerto Rico. *Youth and Society,* 1980, **11,** 415–430.
141. Rodin, E. A., Domino, E. F., & Porzak, J. P. The marihuana-induced "social high." Neurological electroencephalographic concomitants. *Journal of the American Medical Association,* 1970, **213,** 1300–1302.

142. Rubin, V. *Marihuana in Jamaica.* Research Institute for the Study of Man. United States Public Health Service Contract No. HSM 42-70-97, 1973.

143. Shafer, R. P., et al. *Marihuana: A signal of misunderstanding. The official report of the National Commission on Marihuana and Drug Abuse.* New York: New American Library, 1972.

144. Shafer, R. P., et al. *Drug use in America: Problem in perspective.* Second report of the National Commission on Marijuana and Drug Abuse. Washington, D.C.: U.S. Government Printing Office, No. 5266-00003, 1973.

145. Shetterly, H. Self and social perceptions and personal characteristics of a group of suburban high school marijuana users. *Dissertation Abstracts International,* 1971, **31**(7–A), 3279.

146. Single, E., Kandel, D., & Faust, R. Patterns of multiple drug use in high school. *Journal of Health and Social Behavior,* 1974, **15,** 344–357.

147. Smart, R., & Fejer, D. Drug use among adolescents and their parents: Closing the generation gap in mood modification. *Journal of Abnormal Psychology,* 1972, **79,** 153–160.

148. Smith, D. E., Wesson, D. R., & Seymour, R. B. The abuse of barbiturates and other sedative-hyponotics. In R. I. Dupont, A. Goldstein, & J. O'Donnell (eds.), *Handbook on drug abuse.* Washington, D.C.: U.S. Government Printing Office, 1979. Pp. 233–240.

149. Smith, G. M. Personality and smoking: A review of the empirical literature. In W. A. Hunt (ed.), *Learning mechanisms in smoking.* Chicago: Aldine, 1970. Pp. 42–61.

150. Smith, G. M., & Fogg, C. P. Psychological predictors of early use, late use, and nonuse of marihuana among teenage students. In D. B. Kandel (ed.), *Longitudinal research on drug use: Empirical findings and methodological issues.* Washington, D.C.: Hemisphere Publishing Corporation, 1978.

151. *Smoking and health: A report of the Surgeon General.* (DHEW Publication No. (PHS) 79-50066, U.S. Department of Health, Education and Welfare.) Washington, D.C.: U.S. Government Printing Office (No. 017-000-00218-0), 1979.

152. Sokol, R. J., Miller, S. I., Debanne, S., Golden, N., Collins, G., Kaplan, J., & Martier, S. The Cleveland NIAAA prospective alcohol in pregnancy study: The first year. Paper presented at the NIAAA Fetal Alcohol Syndrome Workshop, Seattle, 1980.

153. Steffenhagen, R., McAree, C., & Zheutlin, L. Social and academic factors associated with drug use on the University of Vermont campus. *International Journal of Social Psychiatry,* 1969, **15,** 92–96.

154. Stephens, R. C. (ed.). Ethnicity and adolescent drug abuse. *Youth and Society,* 1980, **11,** 395–396.

155. Stone, L. H., Miranne, A. C., & Ellis, G. J. Parent-peer influence as a predictor of marijuana use. *Adolescence,* 1979, **14,** 115–121.

156. Suchman, E. The "hang-loose" ethic and the spirit of drug use. *Journal of Health and Social Behavior,* 1968, **9,** 146–155.

157. Sutherland, E., & Cressey, D. *Criminology.* Philadelphia: Lippincott, 1970 (8th ed.).

158. Tec, N. Some aspects of high school status and differential involvement with marihuana. *Adolescence,* 1972, **7,** 1–28.

159. Technical review on cigarette smoking as an addiction. National Institute on Drug Abuse, August 23–24, 1979.

160. The latest teen drug. *Newsweek,* January 8, 1979, 43–44.

161. Thomas, C. B. The relationship of smoking and habits of nervous tension. In W. L. Dunn, Jr. (ed.), *Smoking behavior: Motives and incentives.* Washington, D.C.: Winston, 1973. Pp. 157–170.

162. Victor, H. R., Grossman, J. C., & Eisenman, R. Openness to experience and marijuana use in high school students. *Journal of Consulting and Clinical Psychology,* 1973, **41,** 78–85.

163. Wallgren, H., & Barry, H., III. *Actions of alcohol, Vol. 1: Biochemical, physiological, and psychological aspects.* Amsterdam: Elsevier, 1970.

164. Wallgren, H., & Barry, H., III. *Actions of alcohol, Vol. 2: Chronic and clinical aspects.* Amsterdam: Elsevier, 1970.
165. Weil, A. T., Zinberg, N. E., & Nelson, J. M. Clinical and psychological effects of marijuana in man. *Science,* 1968, **162,** 1234–1242.
166. Weil, A. T., & Zinberg, N. E. Acute effects of marihuana on speech. *Nature,* 1969, **22,** 434–437.
167. Wikler, A. Clinical and social aspects of marihuana intoxication. *Archives of General Psychiatry,* 1970, **23,** 320–325.
168. Wikler, A. Drug dependence. In A. B. Baker & L. H. Baker (eds.), *Clinical Neurology,* 1971, **2,** 1–53.
169. Wikler, A., & Lloyd, B. J. Effect of smoking marihuana cigarettes on cortical electrical activity. *Federation Proceedings,* 1945, **4,** 141–142.
170. Williams, A. College problem drinkers: A personality profile. In G. L. Maddox (ed.), *The domesticated drug: Drinking among collegians.* New Haven, Conn.: College and University Press, 1970.
171. Williams, E. G., Himmelsbach, C. K., Wikler, A., Ruble, D. C., & Loyd, B. J. Studies of marihuana and pyrahexyl compound. *Public Health Reports,* 1946, **61,** 1059–1083.
172. Wogan, M., & Elliott, J. P. Drug use and level of anxiety among college students. *Journal of Youth and adolescence,* 1972, **1,** 325–331.
173. *Women and smoking: Report of the Surgeon General.* Washington, D.C.: U.S. Public Health Service, Department of Health, Education and Welfare, January 1980.
174. Woods, J. H., & Downs, D. A. The psychopharmacology of cocaine. In R. P. Shafer et al., *Drug use in America: Problem in perspective* (Appendix, Vol. 1). Second report of the National Commission on Marijuana and Drug Abuse. Washington, D.C.: U.S. Government Printing Office (No. 5266–00004), 1973. Pp. 116–139.
175. Yablonsky, L. *The hippie trip.* New York: Pegasus, 1969.
176. Yankelovich, D., et al. What they believe. In L. Banko and editors of *Fortune* (eds.), *Youth in turmoil.* New York: Time-Life Books, 1969.
177. Yolles, S. Statement before the Subcommittee on the Judiciary, U.S. Senate, September 16, 1969 (mimeographed).
178. Zinberg, N., & Weil, A. A comparison of marijuana users and nonusers. *Nature,* 1970, **226,** 119–123.

# Moral development and values

## CHAPTER 13

# Moral development and values

**A**t no time in life is a person as likely to be concerned about moral values and standards as during adolescence. That this should be the case is not surprising. In the first place, rapid cognitive development—particularly an increased capacity for abstract thinking—tends to make adolescents more aware of moral questions and values, and more capable of dealing with them in a relatively sophisticated way. In addition, the social expectations and demands confronting young people, and the experiences they are undergoing, are changing at an accelerated rate during these years. As Erik Erikson notes, this is especially true in America: "This is the country of changes; it is obsessed with change" (18, *29*). Furthermore, seldom has change, and our preoccupation with it, been greater than in the last two decades (24, *132*). As a consequence, the developing adolescent is likely to be exposed to a multiplicity of shifting, sometimes conflicting, values and standards of behavior among which he or she must make choices. Furthermore, the task is not made any easier by the fact that there is a discrepancy between adolescents' increasingly sophisticated cognitive capacity for comprehending moral issues (which may equal, or even exceed, that of their parents), on the one hand, and their still very limited experience in dealing with moral issues and their very real consequences in everyday life, on the other hand.

Nevertheless, moral choices must be made. Under circumstances where diversity and change are the order of the day, the problem of developing a strong sense of identity cannot be separated from the problem of values. If young people (and adults) are to be able to maintain some stability in their conception of self and in internal guides to action in a changing world, they must be faithful to some basic values. They may have to adopt new ways of implementing these values to meet changing circumstances. But if the values are there, and are sound, young people will be able to be flexible in adapting to change while remaining constant in their conceptions of self and faithful to central values.

In Erikson's words:

> I would . . . claim that we have almost an instinct of fidelity—meaning that when you reach a certain age you can and must learn to be faithful to some ideological view. Speaking psychiatrically, without the development of a capacity for fidelity the individual will either have what we call a weak ego, or look for a deviant group to be faithful to [40, *30*].

Although there is little debate about the importance of moral issues and values to adolescents, there is considerable controversy about the nature of moral development, its maturational course, and the factors influencing this development. There have been basically three approaches taken to understanding moral development: cognitive, affective, and social (133). The cognitive view of moral development focuses on moral reasoning and considers cognitive development to be the necessary stimulus for changes in moral development, with changes occurring in predictable stages paralleling cognitive change. The affective perspective on moral development focuses primarily on the role of empathy, sympathy, and guilt. The affective aspect is thought to be influenced primarily by socialization. The social perspective on moral development views morality as linked primarily to peer experiences and the related sense of community. Although each of these aspects is probably involved in moral development, each is based on somewhat different assumptions and theoretical orientations, as we shall see.

Morality is highly complex. Fully developed morality has been described as involving: (1) recognition of, and sensitivity to, a given social situation leading to an awareness that a moral problem exists; (2) moral judgment, in order to determine what ought to be done in a given situation; (3) values and influences that affect one's plan of action consistent with moral ideals, but consider nonmoral values and goals that the situation may activate, as well as the influence of situational pressures; and (4) execution and implementation of moral action, involving behavior consistent with one's goals despite distractions, impediments, and incidental adjustments (21).

Too often there has been a tendency to view morality in terms of a single component. For example, some have argued that morality involves the ability to think adequately about a moral situation. Others have construed morality as primarily involving values. Still others have argued that it is mainly involved with what people do, rather than what they think or believe. It seems clear, however, that morality involves all of these components. Similarly, failures in morality can be due to failure in any of these components. A person may fail to act morally because of a failure in sensitivity to the needs of others, because of limited cognitive capacities, because of constraints in the situation (e.g., threats from others), or because of some limitation preventing the person from carrying out the appropriate behavior (e.g., not knowing how to swim when someone is drowning).

## COGNITIVE GROWTH AND STAGES OF MORAL DEVELOPMENT

Piaget's (104) conceptualization of moral development stimulated much of the subsequent work on this topic. He argued that the organizing principles of the child's world are different from those of the adult's world, with a coherent structure of their own. This view contrasted sharply with the other dominant view of the time (31) in which moral development was viewed primarily as a process of socialization whereby the moral standards of the adult world were taught to children and eventually internalized by them. Although Piaget did not dispute the importance of socialization, he demonstrated that the organizing principle of the morality of younger children was quite distinct from that of older children and adults. Younger children based their moral judgments upon objective aspects of the situation, whereas older children considered more subjective aspects.

One method Piaget used in his investigations of morality was to present subjects with a pair of hypothetical stories. One such story depicted a boy who knocked over fifteen cups while coming to dinner; the other story depicted a boy who broke one cup while attempting to sneak some jam out of a cupboard. Younger children were more likely to consider the first boy naughtier, because he broke fifteen cups while the second boy broke only one. Older children consistently viewed the second boy as naughtier because he was trying to sneak some jam.

The major work extending the conceptualizations of Piaget has been that of Lawrence Kohlberg, a psychologist at Harvard, and his associates (22, 79, 80, 81). Kohlberg posited six stages of moral development. In addition, he and his colleagues also developed Piaget's method by presenting a more complicated set of moral dilemmas involving twelve basic moral concepts, values, or issues. Subjects are asked to describe what the actor in the moral dilemma ought to do, and to justify that course of action. For example, in order to gain information about a subject's conceptualization of "the basis of moral worth of human life," he or she is asked such questions as why a druggist should give a life-saving drug to a dying woman when her husband cannot pay for it, and whether it is better to save the life of one important person or the lives of a lot of unimportant people. On the basis of the responses obtained, these investigators have concluded that children and adolescents tend to progress through "six stages of moral thought . . . divided into the three major levels, the *preconventional,* the *conventional,* and the *postconventional* or autonomous" (83, *1066*).

During the early preschool years (corresponding approximately to Piaget's "preoperational stage," characterized by "symbolic, intuitive, or prelogical thought"), the child has not yet reached a formal stage of moral development. At this point behavior is governed mostly by whatever he or she wants to do at a particular moment.

With the beginning of concrete operational thinking, however, the child may enter the first of two preconventional stages of moral development (see Table 13.1). During this stage, the child is responsive to cultural labels of "good" and "bad," but interprets these labels largely in terms of their physical consequences (i.e., reward or punishment). Behaviors that are punished are perceived as bad and to be avoided, and there is likely to be an "unquestioning deference to superior power" (83, *1067*). During the second preconventional stage, some progress is made beyond this rather simplistic notion. At this juncture, the child is more likely to conform in order to obtain rewards, have favors returned, and the like (83). "Human relations are viewed in terms like those of the market place. Elements of fairness, reciprocity, and equal sharing are present, but they are always interpreted in a physical, pragmatic way. Reciprocity is a matter of 'you scratch my back and I'll scratch yours,' not of loyalty, gratitude, or justice" (83, *1067*). For example, when asked "Should Joe tell on his older brother to his father?" (for going somewhere he was not supposed to), one boy replied, "I think he should keep quiet. He might want to go someplace like that, and if he squeals on Alex [the older brother], Alex might squeal on him" (78, *243*).

By the time the average child in our society reaches adolescence, his or her thinking about moral issues has already shifted away from the most basic preconventional mode, in which the child is governed by literal obedience to rules and authority with the aim of avoiding punishment (see Table 13.1). Furthermore, a majority have at least begun to shift away from the second preconventional stage, characterized by a rather simply conceived doctrine of reciprocity—acting to meet one's own needs and letting others do the same, and doing what is "fair" or what constitutes an equal exchange (22, 81). The moral orientation here is still primarily *individualistic* and egocentric, and the rights of others are seen rather concretely as coexisting with one's own rights (81).

With entrance into adolescence, conventional moral thinking tends to become dominant. In conventional morality, the primary focus on societal needs and values take primacy over individual interests. Initially, this is likely to involve a strong emphasis on being "a good person in your own eyes and those of others" (81, *34*), which means having good motives, and showing concern about others. Typically, there is considerable emphasis on conformity to stereotypical images of what is majority or "natural" behavior (81, 83). Reflecting increased cognitive development, at this stage the intention behind behavior becomes of major importance, not simply the behavior itself; one seeks approval by "being good." This approach is subsequently expanded to include an "orientation toward authority, fixed rules, and the maintenance of the social order. Right behavior consists of doing one's duty, showing respect for authority, and maintaining the given social order for its own sake" (83). At this stage, a *social perspective* takes precedence; there is concern not only with conformity to one's social order, but also with maintaining, supporting, and justifying this order (22, 81, 83).

Contrary to earlier assumptions (7, 8, 79, 80, 84) it appears that many adolescents (and adults) may not advance beyond this level—although recent research results are conflicting (22, 33, 81, 83, 120, 121). Some, however, do advance to what Lawrence Kohlberg (81) calls postconventional or principled thinking. At this level, particular societal arrangements are seen as deriving from a broader moral perspective, which the rational, moral individual has to develop for herself or himself; Kohlberg calls it a "prior-to-society" perspective (22, 81). Reflecting the acquisition of formal operational thinking, this level is characterized by a "major thrust toward abstract moral principles which are universally applicable, and not tied to any particular social group." In the most advanced, and least often achieved, stage of formal principled thinking, there is an "effort to formulate abstract ethical principles appealing to logical comprehensiveness, universality, and consistency" (83).

With more advanced, less concrete cognitive and moral development, the adolescent—particularly the brighter and more sophisticated adolescent—may no longer be able to adopt, without questioning, the social or political beliefs of his or her parents in the happy conviction that solely because the parents have particular beliefs, all right-thinking persons must necessarily share them (36, 38). There is a new-found "relativism of personal values and opinions and a corresponding emphasis upon procedural rules for reaching consensus" (83, *1067*). When asked whether a husband should steal an expensive black-market drug from an exploitative druggist to save his wife's life, Steve, age 16, answered, "By the law of society he was wrong

### TABLE 13.1 THE SIX MORAL STAGES

| LEVEL AND STAGE | WHAT IS RIGHT | REASONS FOR DOING RIGHT | SOCIAL PERSPECTIVE OF STAGE |
|---|---|---|---|
| **Level I: Preconventional**<br>Stage 1: Heteronomous morality | To avoid breaking rules backed by punishment, obedience for its own sake, and avoiding physical damage to persons and property. | Avoidance of punishment, and the superior power of authorities. | *Egocentric point of view.* Doesn't consider the interests of others or recognize that they differ from the actor's; doesn't relate two points of view. Actions are considered physically rather than in terms of psychological interests of others. Confusion of authority's perspective with one's own. |
| Stage 2: Individualism, instrumental purpose, and exchange | Following rules only when it is to someone's immediate interest; acting to meet one's own interests and needs and letting others do the same. Right is also what's fair, what's an equal exchange, a deal, an agreement. | To serve one's own needs or interests in a world where you have to recognize that other people have their interests, too. | *Concrete individualistic perspective.* Aware that everybody has his own interest to pursue and these conflict, so that right is relative (in the concrete individualistic sense). |
| **Level II: Conventional**<br>Stage 3: Mutual interpersonal expectations, relationships, and interpersonal conformity | Living up to what is expected by people close to you or what people generally expect of people in your role as son, brother, friend, etc. "Being good" is important and means having good motives, showing concern about others. It also means keeping mutual relationships, such as trust, loyalty, respect and gratitude. | The need to be a good person in your own eyes and those of others. Your caring for others. Belief in the Golden Rule. Desire to maintain rules and authority which support stereotypical good behavior. | *Perspective of the individual in relationships with other individuals.* Aware of shared feelings, agreements, and expectations which take primacy over individual interests. Relates points of view through the concrete Golden Rule, putting yourself in the other guy's shoes. Does not yet consider generalized system perspective. |

| Stage | What is right | Reasons for doing right | Social perspective of stage |
|---|---|---|---|
| Stage 4: Social system and conscience | Fulfilling the actual duties to which you have agreed. Laws are to be upheld except in extreme cases where they conflict with other fixed social duties. Right is also contributing to society, the group, or institution. | To keep the institution going as a whole, to avoid the breakdown in the system "if everyone did it," or the imperative of conscience to meet one's defined obligations. (Easily confused with Stage 3 belief in rules and authority; see text.) | *Differentiates societal point of view from interpersonal agreement or motives.* Takes the point of view of the system that defines roles and rules. Considers individual relations in terms of place in the system. |
| **Level III: Postconventional, or principled**<br>Stage 5: Social contract or utility and individual rights | Being aware that people hold a variety of values and opinions, that most values and rules are relative to your group. These relative rules should usually be upheld, however, in the interest of impartiality and because they are the social contract. Some nonrelative values and rights like *life* and *liberty*, however, must be upheld in any society and regardless of majority opinion. | A sense of obligation to law because of one's social contract to make and abide by laws for the welfare of all and for the protection of all people's rights. A feeling of contractual commitment, freely entered upon, to family, friendship, trust, and work obligations. Concern that laws and duties be based on rational calculation of overall utility, "the greatest good for the greatest number." | *Prior-to-society perspective.* Perspective of a rational individual aware of values and rights prior to social attachments and contracts. Integrates perspectives by formal mechanisms of agreement, contract, objective impartiality, and due process. Considers moral and legal points of view; recognizes that they sometimes conflict and finds it difficult to integrate them. |
| Stage 6: Universal ethical principles | Following self-chosen ethical principles. Particular laws or social agreements are usually valid because they rest on such principles. When laws violate these principles, one acts in accordance with the principle. Principles are universal principles of justice: the equality of human rights and respect for the dignity of human beings as individual persons. | The belief as a rational person in the validity of universal moral principles, and a sense of personal commitment to them. | *Perspective of a moral point of view from which social arrangements derive.* Perspective is that of any rational individual recognizing the nature of morality or the fact that persons are ends in themselves and must be treated as such. |

*Source:* L. Kohlberg. Moral stages and moralization. In T. Lickona (ed.), *Moral development and behavior.* New York: Holt, Rinehart and Winston, 1976. By permission.

but by the law of nature or of God the druggist was wrong and the husband was justified. Human life is above financial gain. Regardless of who was dying, if it was a total stranger, man has a duty to save him from dying" (78, *244*). A number of studies (83, 113, 124, 125) have shown that a certain level of cognitive development is necessary, but not sufficient for a given level of moral reasoning.

Because the method of scoring the moral dilemmas developed by Kohlberg is so complicated and requires a great deal of training (22, 82), another method of assessment, called the Defining Issues Test (DIT), was developed by James Rest, a psychologist at the University of Minnesota. It is based on the same theoretical perspective as Kohlberg's method, but uses a multiple-choice format and can be objectively scored (94, 109, 110, 111). In addition to these format differences, the DIT is a recognition task involving the identification of the way of thinking most like that of the subject's, whereas Kohlberg's test is a production task requiring the subjects to generate a line of reasoning on their own. Consequently, the results of these two methods are not identical. Correlations between Kohlberg's most recent scoring method and the DIT range from .6 to .7 (21, 46). Nevertheless, these differences appear to be more methodological than conceptual, and the results produced by the two methods seem to be generally similar.

Using both of these methods, the six-stage model of moral judgment has been validated in cross-sectional as well as longitudinal studies (22, 28, 74, 79, 82, 110). There seems to be a clear effect of formal schooling, since scores plateau once subjects leave school. Change from one stage of moral development to another appears to be gradual and slow, with considerable overlap between stages (21). Although some longitudinal studies indicate that about 7 percent of the study participants actually move downward in moral level at some juncture, most of the movement is upward. Kohlberg and his colleagues at Harvard have recently completed a 20-year longitudinal study that finds a gradual change in all subjects, with no subjects skipping a stage (22). Similar results have been found in other societies (Mexico, Taiwan, Kenya, the Bahamas, Honduras, Carib, India, Nigeria, Israel, Thailand, Turkey, Britain, Canada, New Zealand, and the Yucatan), although development tends to be slower and more limited in more traditional, lower-class, and rural areas (22, 33, 57, 121, 128).

Although level of cognitive development is strongly related to level of moral judgment, these two dimensions are not identical. Studies have shown, however, that a certain level of cognitive development may be necessary but not sufficient for a given level of moral reasoning (124, 125). Thus, children who have advanced cognitive capacity will not necessarily demonstrate moral reasoning at the corresponding level (113). Furthermore, one study (61) looking separately at males and females found correlations between cognitive functioning and Kohlbergian reasoning only for males (see pages 570–571). It has generally been found that advancements in cognitive functioning typically precede advancements in moral reasoning, in naturalistic as well as intervention studies (21).

The link between cognitive and moral reasoning stages might lead one to question whether these are distinct. However, the specificity of moral reasoning has been demonstrated in several kinds of studies showing that measures of moral thinking are more related to each other than to measures of cognitive ability (110). When general intelligence or ability is controlled in studies, moral judgment continues to play a significant role with appropriate predictor variables such as delinquency.

### Influences on change in moral development

Piaget suggested that change in moral judgment was produced by cognitive disequilibrium and experiences of cooperation with peers. Because advanced morality is desirable in society, the question of how to produce it becomes very important. There is some evidence to support both of Piaget's proposed explanations for change in moral reasoning. Although the results of interventions aiming to enhance moral reasoning capacities are somewhat confusing (21), programs employing peer discussion of controversial issues do generally appear to enhance reasoning capacity (89, 90). These programs would appear to include both components suggested by Piaget: cognitive disequilibrium produced by ideas new to an individual as well as peer influence and reciprocity. It has been difficult, however, to identify exactly what aspects of these programs lead to successes or failures. The argument of classic cognitive developmentalists that the mechanism of change is primarily a function of self-discovery has not been well supported by research; however, the shaping of the social environment is clearly important (14, 96).

## CHANGING SOCIETAL DEMANDS

Although level of moral development is influenced by a variety of factors, including cognitive development, preoccupation with the problem of moral values is likely to be fostered by changing societal demands during the years of adolescence. The younger child typically lives in a world that is relatively more homogeneous, more immediate, and more limited than that of the adolescent. As a result, the child faces fewer demands for making moral choices. Living according to a fairly circumscribed set of rules, established for the most part by parents, the child and his or her peers learn to find satisfaction of their needs from day to day within this context. Granted, the child must learn to establish internal controls as a necessary part of the socialization process and, certainly, controls are related to the problem of values. But establishing controls is not synonymous with learning to make value decisions, often under ambiguous circumstances (30, 99).

In contrast, the adolescent boy or girl *must* make choices. Not only is he or she changing, but the immediate social world, and his or her relations with it, are changing too. As they move further into adolescence, young people are confronted with an increasingly diverse world in which the opportunities and the necessity for choice are multiplied. They find, for example, that there are many ways to live their lives and that they must make choices. How will they earn a living? What sort of person do they eventually want to marry—if, in fact, they want to marry at all?

Such choices cannot be made independently of personal values, although, of course, many other factors are also involved. If an adolescent is strongly convinced of the importance of helping others, that young person may make a different career choice than if he or she places a high valuation on material success. If he or she believes more in freedom and autonomy than in security, different choices may also be made. If young people believe that honesty is the best policy, they may be less likely to enter certain occupations than if they believe that there is a sucker born every minute, and that the main responsibility (hence the main value of a person *as a person*) is survival in a social jungle.

As we have seen, the time perspective of adolescents, as contrasted to that of children, becomes greatly extended (particularly into the future); this, too, increases the urgency of developing a set of values. The adolescent who is beginning to look forward to an entire lifetime is much more in need of a set of guiding moral principles—if his or her life is to have a semblance of order, consistency, and meaning—than the child whose principal preoccupation at a given moment may be whether he or she is going to an amusement park the next day or to the dentist.

Furthermore, the adolescent is confronted with a wider range of conflicting pressures in the adoption or modification of personal values than is the average younger child. The peer group may be urging one set of values and the parents another. The adolescent may be motivated to conform to the values of peers in order to gain acceptance or to avoid rejection. Increasingly, too, other influences enter the arena of moral choice—teachers, books, television, and representatives of conflicting groups in the broader society.

Such conflicting pressures have long characterized the adolescent period, but it appears that they have increased significantly during recent decades, as the divisions among both adults and adolescents have been magnified, and as our society is confronted with more and more issues on which consensus is difficult to attain. This has made the transition from a "father knows best" sort of preadolescent moral thought to the beginning of postconventional thought, with its emphasis on social consensus, more difficult (120). And it appears to have increased the danger, for some adolescents, of falling into an extreme, essentially directionless, and sometimes chronic kind of moral relativism at this critical juncture in their development. There is similar peril in the other extreme—that of adopting a very rigid moral stance, as is seen among some cults popular with a small percentage of adolescents.

## INTRAPSYCHIC CONFLICT, MORAL VALUES, AND MORAL DEVELOPMENT

To complicate matters further, the adolescent may need to become engaged in wrestling with broad questions of moral value judgments not simply for their own sake, but also as a way of coping with more personal, but no less real, problems (30, 39, 43, 44). Value conflicts are often "'chosen' by adolescents for internal and usually unconscious reasons" (30, *85*). For example, preoccupations with the moral issues of war and peace, or the nature of aggression, may reveal a perfectly rational concern with these important matters for their own sake. But they may also reflect a concern with being able to handle aggressive feelings, partly related to increased size and strength typical of adolescents, as well as increased expectations of assertion and dominance, particularly for boys. Similarly, the involvement of adolescents in cults or restrictive religious groups may be partly a way of resolving moral dilemmas, by letting the group dictate the adolescent's values and behavior. Presumably, objective differences with parents about moral or political values and beliefs may more truly reflect efforts to establish an independent identity of one's own, or to express a deep resentment toward hostile or indifferent parents.

In brief, the increased preoccupation with moral values and beliefs that characterizes many (though by no means all) adolescents is likely to have its roots in expanded cognitive development, in increased—and often contradictory—societal demands, and in intimate (often unconscious) intrapsychic concerns and conflicts.

### Moral relativism, ego identity, and social change

The ability of an adolescent to progress from conventional moral reasoning—with its rather simplistic, absolutistic conceptions of what is right and true, and its dependence on socially accepted stereotypes and respect for authority—to principled moral reasoning is dependent on the development of the capacity for formal operational thought. This includes the ability to think hypothetically—to compare what is with what might be, and to consider a variety of possible alternative solutions to problems, rather than simply looking for the one "right" answer.

This ability to think hypothetically, so obvious in intellectual problem solving, extends equally to moral problems. In some ways, it can be a two-edged sword. On the one hand, it can help free the young person from rigid, arbitrary, stereotyped thinking, and promote flexibility and adaptability in the search for values that will be internally consistent, principled, and *right for him or her*. On the other hand, it may simply overwhelm. Freed from previously unquestioned conventional morality, the adolescent may find himself or herself adrift in a sea of seemingly infinite possible alternatives, and may conclude that there is no way of choosing between them—that one set of beliefs or values is no better and no worse than another set.

The danger of this transitional period in cognitive and moral development, then, is one of what Kohlberg calls *extreme relativism* (83). It is well illustrated in the following statement by one of Kohlberg's subjects, an upper-middle-class high school student:

> I don't think anybody should be swayed by the dictates of society. It's probably very much up to the individual all the time and there's no general principle except when the views of society seem to conflict with your views and your opportunities at the moment and it seems that the views of society don't really have any basis as being right and in that case, most people, I think, would tend to say forget it and I'll do what I want [83, *1074*].

### Relativism and ego identity

Adolescents differ significantly from one another, both in whether they undergo a period of moral relativism and, for those who do, whether it is transitional and brief, or prolonged and sometimes chronic. As might be anticipated, these varying response patterns are related to the problem of identity. In one approach to studying identity development (81), college students were divided into four identity status categories: (1) identity achievement (those who had gone through an identity crisis, had resolved it, and had found new commitments); (2) psychosocial moratorium (those who were still in an identity crisis with only vague commitments); (3) identity foreclosure (those who had experienced no crisis, but were committed to goals and values of parents or significant others); (4) identity diffusion (those who had no commitment regardless of crisis) (93, 106).

Subjects were also grouped (on the basis of an independent set of measures) according to their level of moral development: conventional (stages 3 and 4), principled (stages 5 and 6), and transitional. The last group was further subdivided into those who manifested a combination of conventional and principled thinking and those who were extreme relativists (i.e., they rejected conventional thought and appeared to be operating on the basis of a rather regressive [stage 2] "instrumental hedonism").

It was found that two-thirds of the principled subjects had an identity achievement status. Forty percent of conventional subjects also fell in this group, and the remainder fell primarily in the identity foreclosure group. None of the morally transitional subjects fell in the identity achievement group, and very few in the identity foreclosure group.

> Essentially, then, morally transitional subjects were in transition with regard to identity issues as well as moral issues. Stated slightly differently, to have questioned conventional morality you must have questioned your identity as well, though you may continue to hold a conventional moral position after having done so [83, *1078*].

However, as this research also indicates, many morally conventional students have never encountered a period of identity crisis or questioning.

> An adolescent stage of identity crisis and its resolutions, then, is a picture dependent upon attainment of formal logical thought and of questioning of conventional morality. It fits best, then, the picture of adolescence in the developmentally elite and needs further elaboration for other adolescents [83, *1078*].

Subsequent studies obtained similar results (75, 113). In one study (75), however, students in the moratorium identity status also had high moral reasoning scores, like the identity achievement students; both groups of students had higher moral reasoning scores than those with foreclosed or diffused identities.

## SOCIALIZATION TECHNIQUES AND MORAL DEVELOPMENT

Thus far the primary emphasis has been on factors that sensitize the adolescent to questions related to moral values and that influence the degree of sophistication with which he or she is able to conceptualize moral problems. But there is another side to the broad issue of moral development—the extent to which, and the manner in which, cognitive understanding is reflected in behavior (19, 64, 71, 72). It is clear that a person may be able to conceptualize moral issues with considerable sophistication and to formulate the proper moral course to take, but may not always act in accordance with this formulation (41, 62, 71, 72, 85, 88). In addition, morality may be distinct from understanding of and adherence to social convention (119).

In one study (118) when subjects were first asked "Why should people follow rules?" they were then asked, "Why do *you* follow rules?" In responding to the latter question, most middle-school children and adolescents showed a shift toward earlier, more "primitive" levels, although they were cognitively capable of understanding loftier reasons and subscribed to these. For example, although only 3 percent of older adolescents said that people *should* follow rules "to avoid negative consequences" (see Table 13.2), 25 percent said they personally *would* do so.

**TABLE 13.2 WHY SHOULD PEOPLE FOLLOW RULES? (PERCENTAGES BY AGE)**[a]

| CATEGORIES | EDUCATIONAL GROUP | | | COMPARISONS (BY $T$ TEST) | |
| | PRIMARY (1) | MIDDLE SCHOOL (2) | COLLEGE (3) | $(1) \times (2)$ | $(2) \times (3)$ |
| --- | --- | --- | --- | --- | --- |
| Avoid negative consequences | 50% | 13% | 3% | $p < .01$ | $p < .05$ |
| Authority | 5 | — | — | | |
| Personal conformity | 35 | 13 | 9 | $p < .05$ | |
| Social conformity | 10 | 53 | 25 | $p < .01$ | $p < .01$ |
| Rational/beneficial/ utilitarian | 5 | 27 | 51 | $p < .05$ | $p < .05$ |
| Principled | — | — | 5 | | |

Source: J. L. Tapp and F. J. Levine, Compliance from kindergarten to college: A speculative research note. *Journal of Youth and Adolescence,* 1972, **1,** 233–249. By permission.

[a] This question is multiple coded; therefore, percentages may total over 100 percent. Where answers were idiosyncratic or uncodable, the categories were omitted from the table.

Similarly, in another study (127), adolescents were asked to respond to one of two kinds of stories: (1) one in which they were asked to take the perspective of a fictitious other or (2) one in which they were to respond as they would do themselves. Those responding from the self-involved perspective demonstrated increased concern about punishment and consequences as well as less mature moral reasoning than those adolescents responding from the fictitious-other perspective.

Some adolescents may show a reasonable degree of adherence to personal moral principle, even under considerable duress, but others may yield rather quickly to temptation or to group pressure. Still others may appear to be guided almost solely by the possibility of external sanctions, rather than by internalized standards. In short, knowledge alone, even sophisticated knowledge of moral standards, does not guarantee an effective conscience (66).

A very interesting study (16, 56) examining the effects of a moral confrontation on moral reasoning illustrates the limitations of knowledge of moral standards on moral behavior. In this study, twenty-four young women (15 to 33 years of age) were interviewed twice: once while they were deciding whether or not to terminate a problematic pregnancy and again one year later. The interviews focused on the actual pregnancy dilemma as well as four hypothetical dilemmas, one about abortion and three that constitute the Standard Kohlberg interview (Form A). A scale was developed to rate the occurrence and direction of changes in life circumstances.

Three groups of women emerged from this longitudinal study. One group resolved the actual crisis at a *higher* stage of reasoning than that seen initially in the hypothetical Kohlberg dilemmas; at follow-up one year later, these women had matured and were experiencing improved life circumstances. A second group reasoned at the *same* stage about the actual abortion decision and in the hypothetical Kohlberg dilemmas; at follow-up, their stage of moral reasoning and their life circumstances remained unchanged. A third group of women reasoned at a *lower* stage about the pregnancy resolution than in the Kohlberg interview; one year later, these women were unhappy both about the decisions they had made and about their current life circumstances. These results show that 90 percent of those with improved moral judgment had engaged in high conflict over the decision, suggesting that confrontation may develop more mature reasoning. In addition, it is clear that an individual must be able to grow at that time, since the reverse outcome—that of less adequate reasoning than one is actually capable of—was also seen. A subsequent study of college students by one of the authors in the previous investigation provides further evidence for the power of an actual experience with moral conflict and choice in stimulating postconventional moral development (98).

### Factors affecting conscience development

The development of conscience (or superego) begins long before adolescence. Indeed, even during the preschool years "the child begins to show evidence of this development, that is, of having a set of standards of acceptable behavior, acting in accordance with these standards and feeling guilty if he violates them" (99, *404*).

How does conscience develop? In Freud's view, conscience is a product of identification (see pages 72–74): "When, by the process of identification he demands from himself conformity to a standard of conduct, the superego is said to be making its appearance" (97, *543*). The young child's behavior tends initially to be hedonistic—that is, basically determined by external rewards and sanctions. Gradually, however, the child begins to *internalize* moral standards and prohibitions in the same way that he or she adopts other parental attributes. "The adoption of parental standards makes him feel similar to his parents and, therefore, strengthens his identification with them" (97, *404*). "He then begins to punish himself, or to feel anxious or guilty, whenever he does (or thinks) something for which he believes his parents might punish him" (129). Stated in psychoanalytic terms, ". . . through identification with the parent, he has taken over and incorporated within himself the attitudes of condemnation of those who transgress" (97, *541*).

Many psychological theorists and researchers have investigated, and frequently elaborated, various elements implicit in Freud's basic formulation (e.g., cognitive aspects, modeling, social learning) (6, 64, 69, 116, 126). It has been found, for example, that the kind of model a parent provides, and the kind of discipline he or she employs, will influence the extent and nature of the child's developing conscience. In general, as we shall see, parents who appeal to positive, growth-enhancing motives in the child through their disciplinary techniques appear to foster positive identification and genuine moral maturity to a greater extent than those who appeal to negative motivations (cited by some psychoanalytic writers as motivational bases for identification), such as fear of losing the parent's love or of parental aggression (69).

### Effects of child-rearing practices

Martin Hoffman, a psychologist at the University of Michigan, notes that two basic parental disciplinary patterns affecting moral orientation can be distinguished, *power-assertive* and *nonpower-assertive* (68, 69). Nonpower-assertive discipline can be divided into two main subtypes: *love withdrawal* and *induction* (in which the parent provides explanations or reasons for requiring certain behaviors from the child).

In power-assertion techniques, the parent does not rely on the child's inner resources (e.g., guilt, shame, dependency, love, or respect), or provide the child with information necessary for the development of such resources, to influence the child's behavior (64). Instead, the parent seeks to accomplish this end by punishing the child physically or materially, or by relying on fear of punishment. Power assertion tends to be related to "a moral orientation based on fear of external detection and punishment" (69, *322*). The child or adolescent is less likely to act on the basis of internalized moral norms and more likely to continue to be influenced by external sanctions (64, 66). Not surprisingly, a pattern of power assertion is frequently found among the parents of some kinds of delinquents (see pages 626–627).

The parent employing love-withdrawal techniques "simply gives direction but not physical expression to his anger or disapproval of the child for engaging in some undesirable behavior" (64, *285*). Such a parent may ignore the child, refuse to speak to him, express dislike, or threaten to leave him. As Hoffman observes, "Like power assertion, love withdrawal has a highly punitive quality. Although it poses no immediate physical or material threat to the child, it may be more devastating emotionally than power assertion because it poses the ultimate threat of abandonment or separation" (64, *285*). Love withdrawal is not consistently related one way or the other to the child's development of positive, mature, internalized moral standards, although he or she, motivated largely by anxiety, is more likely than the child of power-assertive parents to confess to violations and to accept blame. Furthermore, love withdrawal disrupts communication (and hence learning opportunities) between child and parent, and fails to make use of the child's capacity for empathy (64). There is some evidence that love withdrawal may contribute to inhibition of anger (69).

*Induction* involves using techniques in which the parent gives explanations or reasons for requiring certain behaviors of the child, such as pointing out the practical realities of a situation, or explaining how inappropriate behavior may be harmful to the child or others. Unlike either of the other two approaches, induction is also likely to include appeals to the child's pride and strivings for maturity or to be "grown up" (64). Inductive techniques, in addition to promoting positive identification, ". . . help foster the image of the parent as a rational, nonarbitrary authority. They provide the child with cognitive resources needed to control his own behavior" (64, *331*). Not surprisingly, inductive discipline, combined with affection, has been found most likely to result in advanced moral development, as evidenced by an internal moral orientation and self-induced guilt about violations of internal standards (68, 69).

Few, if any, parents employ one type of discipline exclusively (69). For example, even a parent who endorses the importance of inductive techniques for the child's long-term development is likely to resort to power-assertive techniques (e.g., "Stop that, right this minute!" "Go to your room!") or to express strong disapproval (e.g., "How could you do an irresponsible thing like that?" "You can't treat your sister like that. It's hurtful, and wrong, and I won't have it!"). As Martin Hoffman

points out, such disciplinary techniques may be necessary to get children to stop what they are doing and pay attention. "Having attended, children will often be influenced cognitively by the information contained in the inductive component and thus experience a reduced sense of opposition between their desires and external demands" (69, *324*).

Obviously, mature moral development involves not only avoidance of prohibitions, but also motivation toward positive, altruistic, helpful, or—as it is currently termed—*prosocial* behavior (34). Much of the recent research on moral development has focused on factors leading to prosocial motivation and behavior, in contrast to prior concentration on avoidance of negative behavior (65). It is not enough, in a world as impersonal, directionless, and morally confusing as ours is presently, simply to avoid prohibited behaviors. Individuals need to be secure in their own personal values and standards, resistant to deviant pressures (from the lowest to the highest levels of society and government), *and* positively concerned, as a moral necessity, with the welfare of others as well as of themselves. Clearly, parental patterns that involve both unconditional love and inductive disciplinary techniques are most likely to produce adolescents and adults who are truly inner-directed, concerned, and morally mature (64, 66, 70, 86, 103, 114, 115).

### Sex differences in moral internalization

The belief in sex differences in morality was clearly articulated by Freud: "I cannot evade the notion (though I hesitate to give it expression) that for women the level of what is ethically normal is different from what it is in man. Their superego is never so inexorable, so impersonal, so independent of its emotional origins as we require it to be in men. Character-traits which critics of every epoch have brought up against women—that they show less sense of justice than men, that they are less ready to submit it to the great exigencies of life, that they are more often influenced in their judgments by feelings of affection or hostility—all these would be amply accounted for by the modification in the formation of their super-ego which we have inferred above" (45, *257–258*). As Carol Gilligan, a psychologist at Harvard, has noted, similar observations about the nature of morality in women appear in the work of Piaget and Kohlberg. Kohlberg (80) identified a strong interpersonal orientation in the moral judgments of women, which—using his criteria—leads them to be more often classified at his conformist stage of moral maturity. Gilligan has criticized Kohlberg's theory and method because of this rather narrow view of interpersonal issues in morality. She, as well as Norma Haan (60), argues that interpersonal morality is not evidence of moral reasoning at a conformist stage, but rather constitutes a separate dimension along which to consider moral reasoning.

Gilligan (54, 55) outlines a series of stages considering moral aspects of interpersonal relationships. Level one involves an orientation to self and individual survival, followed by a transition from selfishness to responsibility, leading to a second level involving moral judgment that relies on shared norms and expectations requiring self-sacrifice. This level is followed by a transition from concern with conformity to a new inner judgment. The third level of moral reasoning involves elevating nonviolence—the injunction against hurting—to a principle governing all moral judgment and action. This sequence appears to be more valid for the responses of girls and women to Kohlberg's moral dilemmas.

Although most of the research on moral development has not examined sex differences in studies where boys and girls have been identified, differences have often been observed. In general, adolescent girls appear to be more likely than boys to internalize their moral orientation and to show more principled reasoning (53, 66).

What might account for these sex differences? Martin Hoffman (67) asserts that one possible explanation may lie in differences in child-rearing practices for boys and girls (15, 66, 70). He has found that mothers tend to express more affection toward girls, as well as more induction and less power assertion, which together may be more likely to foster an internalized, humanistic moral orientation. He also suggests that such sex differences may be partially explained by "differentiated sex-role socialization as well as by increasing pressure on males over the life cycle to achieve and succeed, which may often be in conflict with concerns about the welfare of others" (67, *720*). Indeed, less sex-typed adolescents appear to function at higher levels of moral reasoning (87).

## THE GROWTH OF POLITICAL IDEAS

As in the case of moral and religious values, the development of political thought in adolescence is significantly influenced by the level of the young person's cognitive development (1, 2, 3, 4). Ordinarily the boy or girl "begins adolescence incapable of complex political discourse—that is, mute on many issues, and when not mute, then simplistic, primitive, subject to fancies, unable to enter fully the realm of political ideas" (1, *1013*).

By the end of adolescence, however, a dramatic change is frequently evident;

the grasp that many adolescents have of the political world is now recognizably adult:

> His mind moves with some agility within the terrain of political concepts; he has achieved abstractness, complexity, and even some delicacy in his sense of political textures; he is on the threshold of ideology, struggling to formulate a morally coherent view of how society is and might and should be arranged [1, *1013*].

Although cognitive change is clearly implicated in the growth of political ideas, facile application of a Piagetian structural approach would tend to obscure the examination of the processes involved. In order to explore the processes by which the transformation in political ideas takes place, Joseph Adelson and his colleagues conducted an ingenious series of investigations in the United States, in West Germany, and in England (1, 2, 3, 4, 51). In order to avoid conventional stereotypes and differing degrees of factual information, and to make the results more comparable from one country to another, the investigators avoided questions about existing political systems and presented their subjects with a series of questions following a statement of the premise: "Imagine that a thousand people venture to an island in the Pacific to form a new society; once there they must compose a political order, devise a legal system, and in general confront the myriad problems of government" (1, *1014*).

They then explored their subjects' thinking on a variety of relevant issues (e.g., the purpose of government, law, and political parties). Proposed laws were suggested, and problems of public policy explored.

In general, we tried to touch upon the traditional issues of political philosophy—the scope and limits of political authority, the reciprocal obligations of citizen and state, the relations between majorities and minorities, the nature of crime and justice, the collision between personal freedom and the common good, the feasibility of utopia, and so on [1, *1014*].

In the second of these studies, questions were added about urban tensions, such as the sources and outcomes of poverty, the relations between citizens and the police, and the proper channels for citizen protest (3).

There were some national differences—primarily in social outlook—but very few differences associated with race or sex. Age differences, however, were dramatic. Between the onset of adolescence (age 11 or 12 years) and late adolescence (by 18 years of age), when the process seemed essentially completed, several profound shifts occurred in the character of the average young person's thought.

### Changes in cognitive mode

There was a significant developmental shift in the direction of greater abstractness of thought. For example, when asked what is the purpose of laws, one 12-year-old replied, "If we had no laws, people could go around killing people." In contrast, a 16-year-old replied, "To insure safety and enforce the government." Another commented, "They are basically guidelines for people. I mean like this is wrong and this is right and to help them understand" (1, *1015*).

Lacking the capacity for clearly formulating such abstract concepts as law, society, equal representation, individual rights, and the like, the younger adolescent's political thought tended to be personalized:

When we ask him about the law, he speaks of the policeman, the judge, the criminal. . . . When we mention government, he speaks of the mayor, or the President, or the congressman, and much of the time none of these but rather a shadowy though ubiquitous set of personages known as "they" or "them." ("They do it, like in schools, so that people don't get hurt.") [1, *1015–1516*].

The use to which older adolescents were able to put their increasing capacity for abstract thought was well illustrated by a question in which the subjects were told that 20 percent of the people on the island were farmers and that they were concerned that laws might be passed contrary to their interests. They were then asked what might be done about this. The youngest adolescents could usually do little more than assert that people wouldn't want to hurt farmers, or that the farmers should fight, or move to another part of the island—if, indeed, they could present any answer at all. Slightly older adolescents made such suggestions as, "The farmers should talk to the rest of the people and make their problems understood."

By mid-adolescence, however, many subjects were able to suggest such solutions as forming a union to press for their collective rights, or electing legislators to defend their interests (1, 2, 4). Older adolescents were also more capable of an extended time perspective (i.e., looking ahead to future as well as present consequences of various political alternatives) and of taking motivation into account as a significant factor in social and political behavior.

Adelson considers the nature of the cognitive transitions during adolescence in terms of five characteristics: abstractness, time, change, costs and benefits, and principles. Abstractness appears to be strongly linked to the development of abstract reasoning. The concept of time—from a focus on the present to a consideration of time past and time future—also strongly parallels time perspective in cognitive development. A consideration of change varies in that the political universe of the young adolescent is static whereas the older adolescent "increasingly recognizes and accepts the tractability of all things human, of human disposition, of the laws men make and the social forms they create. Politics and government become, increasingly, exercises in experiment" (2, 69). The young adolescent also has little sense of relative costs and benefits whereas the older adolescent "recognizes that politics involves competing interests, their inevitable collision, and their necessary compromise" (2, 69). Finally, older adolescents, but not younger adolescents, have developed a grasp of principles, based not only on increasing knowledge of political principles but also on increased cognitive capacity to judge particularities in terms of universals.

### Components of social thought

From this research emerged five topics having central importance to social thought: the conceptions of community, and of the law; the growth of principles; the grasp of human psychology and of social reality. In each of these topics significant changes in understanding were seen during the adolescent years.

**The community**   The idea of government and similar concepts of collectivity are not well understood by most young adolescents (11 or 12 years old). Table 13.3 shows the distribution of cognitive complexity of responses, by grade, to the question, "What is the purpose of government?" As can be seen clearly, most young adolescents give concrete responses to this question (speaking in terms of specific and tangible persons, events, and objects), with a shift to responses demonstrating a low level of abstraction by middle adolescence; by later adolescence, a strong majority of youngsters demonstrate a high level of abstraction in their responses. The young adolescent does not understand the mutuality joining the individual and the larger society. "He does understand power, authority, coercion; indeed, he understands those all too well, in which his spontaneous discourse on 'government' and the like relies heavily—at times exclusively—on the idea of force, authority being seen as the entitlement to coerce" (3, 8). A consistent finding across several kinds of questions pertaining to the issue of community is that the adolescent years witness a shift from a personalized, egocentric mode to a sociocentric mode of understanding social, political, historical, and moral issues. "The sociocentric outlook is essentially absent at the beginning of adolescence—that is, when the child is ten, eleven, or twelve; yet it is more or less universal by the time the child is seventeen or eighteen, with most of the movement taking place . . . somewhere between thirteen and fifteen years of age" (3, 8).

**The law**   Adelson (3) reports surprise at the extreme methods proposed by some youngsters to maintain the law. "Perhaps the most unnerving discovery we

**TABLE 13.3 ABSTRACTNESS OF
RESPONSES TO "WHAT IS THE PURPOSE
OF GOVERNMENT?" OVER ADOLESCENCE**[a]

| | GRADE | | | |
|---|---|---|---|---|
| RESPONSE TYPE | 5 | 7 | 9 | 12 |
| Concrete | 57% | 24% | 7% | 0% |
| Low-level abstraction | 28 | 64 | 51 | 16 |
| High-level abstraction | 0 | 7 | 42 | 71 |

*Source:* J. Adelson. The development of ideology in adolescence. In S. E. Dragastin and G. H. Elder, Jr. (eds.), *Adolescence in the life cycle: Psychological change and social context.* New York: Wiley, 1975. By permission.

made upon first reading the interview transcripts was that a substantial minority of our youngest respondents were capable, on occasion, of the moral purview of Attila the Hun. On questions of crime and punishment, they were able—without seeming to bat an eyelash—to propose the most sanguinary means of achieving peace and harmony across the land. Here are three examples, all from the discourse of nice, clean-cut middle-class American thirteen-year-old boys, telling us their views on the control of crime:

> (On the best reason for sending people to jail): Well, these people who are in jail for about five years must still own the same grudge, then I would put them in for triple or double the time. I think they would learn their lesson then.
>
> (On how to teach people not to commit crimes in the future): Jail is usually the best thing, but there are others . . . in the nineteenth century they used to torture people for doing things. Now I think the best place to teach people is in solitary confinement.
>
> (On methods of eliminating or reducing crime): I think that I would . . . well, like if you murder someone you would punish them with death or something like this. But I don't think that would help because they wouldn't learn their lesson. I think I would give them some kind of scare or something" [3, 9].

This view of society gives way over the adolescent years to an entirely different view of the purpose of law. Generally by the time that adolescents are 15 or 16 years of age, and certainly by age 18 years, the dominant stress upon violence and injury has begun to diminish markedly. The idea that laws are a code through which human conduct is guided becomes more prevalent in the later adolescent years.

Two other motifs similarly signal the end of the early adolescent period in terms of views of the law. One of these is the tendency to see laws as benevolent rather than restrictive, as designed to help people. Another motif links law to the larger notion of community, and sees law as providing a means for interpersonal harmony, either among competing social groups or in the nation or in the state as a whole. These changes, which range from a purely restrictive to a benevolent or normative view of law, appear to be as predictable as the cognitive shift from the concrete to the abstract. This shift, showing the gradual abandonment of an authoritarian, punitive view of morality and the law, is demonstrated in Table 13.4.

**TABLE 13.4 RESPONSES TO "WHAT IS
THE PURPOSE OF LAWS?" OVER ADOLESCENCE**[a]

| CATEGORY | GRADE | | | |
|---|---|---|---|---|
| | 5 | 7 | 9 | 12 |
| Restriction | 73% | 68% | 44% | 20% |
| Restrictional benefit | 12 | 18 | 33 | 38 |
| Benefit | 7 | 9 | 20 | 41 |

*Source:* J. Adelson. Rites of passage. Personal communication, 1982. By permission.
[a] N = 326, cross-national sample.

**Principles**  The adolescent's capacity to make use of moral and political principles—ideas and ideals—in organizing his or her thinking about social issues also changes during this age span. During adolescence, we first see the emergence of systems of belief, as the adolescent begins to use principles in coming to legal, moral, political, and social judgments. The first signs of this capacity seem to emerge between ages 14 and 16 years, and the use of principles does not make itself apparent until the end of adolescence (3).

Principled reasoning is demonstrated in the following example in response to the question of what the government ought to do about a religious group opposed to compulsory vaccination.

> Well, anyone's religious beliefs have to be tolerated if not respected, unless it comes down to where they have the basic freedoms. Well, anyone is free until he starts interfering with someone else's freedom. Now, they don't have to get their children vaccinated, but they shouldn't have anything to say about what the other islanders do, if they want to have their children vaccinated. If they're not vaccinated, they have the chance they may infect some of the other children. But then that's isolated, that's them, so if they don't get vaccinated, they don't have anyone else to blame. (Do you think that the government should insist these people go along with what the majority has to say, since they're such a small minority?) No, I don't think that the government should insist, but I think that the government should do its best to make sure that these people are well-informed. A well-informed person will generally act in his own best interest. I never heard of religion that was against vaccination. (There are religions that are against blood transfusions.) If they want to keep their bodies pure . . . well, like I said, I think that a well-informed citizen will act in his own best interest. If he doesn't, at least he should know what the possibilities are, you know, the consequences. So I think the government's job is to inform the people. In that case, at least, to inform them and not force them [3, *10*].

Younger adolescents find it difficult to reason in their attempts to respond to this question. If they are able to respond at all, they frequently assert some principlelike phrase, such as "freedom of religion."

Adelson proposes that these principles are acquired ". . . by the most mundane processes of learning, in the classroom or through the media, or in the church or at home. At moments one can almost see the civics or history textbook before the child's inner eye as he struggles with the question" (3, *11*). In addition, it is almost certain that the mode of discourse involving principles also depends on the growth of cognitive capacity. As evidence of the importance of cognitive capacity, Adelson cites examples of inadequate responses in children who have been exposed to the fundamental ideas involved. Youngsters may use appropriate terms at the same time that they demonstrate their lack of understanding of the concepts involved.

**Understanding human behavior**   In order to understand the psychology of malfeasance, one of the questions in this study proposed that some percentage of people need laws to keep them from getting into trouble, while others "follow their own consciences naturally and do not need laws" (3, *12*). The investigators then asked what accounted for the difference between these two types of people in the adolescent's capacity to talk about human psychology, a shift that seemed to take place fairly early in adolescence, between the ages of 11 and 13. Eleven-year-olds responded with confusion and gaps in discourse, demonstrating that the concept is out of the child's grasp. For example,

> Well . . . it could be that the person who thinks that they were law-abiding, I mean the criminals, they see things wrong. (How do you mean?) Well I mean they see . . . I can't explain it [3, *12*].

Although young adolescents occasionally present some rudimentary theories of behavior, they generally have no stable conception of personality, nor an understanding of motives beyond the most simple. The impact of situations upon the personality also are absent at this age. There is no recognition of incentives beyond simple coercion, and symbolic or indirect effects of rewards and punishments are absent from their thinking. By the time a young person is 13, and no later than 15 years of age, human behavior is discussed with adequate attention to its complexity.

**Appraising social reality**   As with the understanding of human psychology, the comprehension of social reality involves problems in classification and in time perspective. Both issues also reveal a "thinness of texture"; the young adolescent does not seem able to grasp ambiguity, complexity, or interaction.

    To address the topic of social reality, questions were asked about the idea of "political party". This topic was chosen since almost all children raised in democratic countries are exposed to political parties, and as an institution, it is likely to provide fairly uniform experiences to developing youngsters.

    At the beginning of adolescence, children know very little about the nature and purpose of the political party. They certainly are exposed to this concept—in the mass media, at home, and in school—therefore ruling out the possibility of little or no exposure. "Nevertheless, a distinct majority of children at the age of eleven, twelve, and thirteen cannot give satisfactory answers to straightforward questions on the purpose and functioning of political parties. . . . Either they cannot answer the questions at all (about 15% at age eleven) or else give answers that are either too diffuse to be coded or plainly in error" (3, *13*). The most common error made by those young adolescents who do venture an opinion is to confuse the functions of the political party with those of government as a whole.

The next stage in thinking about this issue is marked by an accurate though rudimentary grasp of institutional function. Compared with later development, however, it is marked by "thin texture." Descriptions with thick texture often involve the capacity to describe multiple aspects or functions of the institution being discussed. The most complex of responses involves a synthesized conception of the topic stands somewhat apart from that conception. The most sophisticated responses depend upon an ability to look past the here and now, to trace out events in the future as a function of tradition established today. It is the equivalent in the realm of social thought of the hypothetical-deductive reasoning that Piaget and other cognitive theorists have demonstrated to be involved in advanced modes of reasoning in relation to scientific problems (3). For some reason, it appears that such complex reasoning in the social-political realm appears to be much more difficult than similar reasoning associated with mathematical and scientific problems. Only a few exceptional adolescents demonstrated such complex thinking in the realm of social and humanistic ideas in this study, and even in that exceptional group, it was not seen until the age of 18 years.

### National differences

In the work of Adelson and his colleagues, some distinctive national differences between adolescents emerged. German adolescents were more likely than their American and British counterparts to stress a need for "order, clarity, direction," which led them to look toward a single strong benevolent leader who could be relied on to provide guidance, prevent anarchy and chaos, and obviate the need for making individual decisions. Thus, at age 13, German adolescents preferred one-man rule twice as often as American or British youth. Even when a young German chose a representative system of government, he or she was likely to employ a similar rationale: "If each person decided individually, there would almost certainly be a tremendous chaos, and when only a certain number of people rule, then they guide the people much better. They realize what's important for individual people" (1, *1040*). Views of governmental authority as paternal, wise, and benevolent, and of the citizen as a rather weak and dependent child, so frequent among German adolescents, were rare among their British and American peers.

American adolescents were the most concerned of the three groups with the need to achieve a sense of the citizen's connection to, and harmony with, the community—what Adelson calls "an other-directed politics, a politics of togetherness." Relatively great stress was placed by the Americans on achieving a proper balance between the rights of the individual and those of the community as a whole. Like British, but unlike German adolescents, they also displayed an ambivalence about authority—admiration for accomplishment, but also a lurking resentment that in a presumably equalitarian society, some people, like the residents of Orwell's *Animal Farm*, should be more equal than others.

Most complex were the British adolescents. Of the three national groups, they were most likely to judge the effectiveness of government principally in terms of its contribution to the individual, rather than to the community as a whole. The principal collective responsibility of government was seen as ensuring that others do not deprive one by getting "more than their fair share." Part of the British adolescents' ambivalence about authority appeared to stem from the suspicion that government leaders themselves may not be above trying to obtain an overly large "slice of the pie." In sum, British adolescents emerged, on the one hand as the most devoted to "rugged individualism," the most tolerant of eccentricities and individual differences, and the most dedicated to the preservation of personal liberty. On the other hand, they also emerged as the most self-oriented and least concerned, despite support of welfare concepts, with the community as a whole—a tendency characterized by Britishers themselves in the familiar slogan "I'm all right, Jack," indicating that as long as one's own interests are being served, there is little motivation for broader social concern.

One of the significant methodogical accomplishments of the research described here is that by dealing with a hypothetical political system, the investigators were able to avoid being blinded to the actual cognitive processes underlying adolescent political thought by facile parroting of learned but ill-understood political thoughts and values acquired from others. As a result, the strong dependence of the quality of adolescent political thought (like that of moral values generally) on the individual's level of cognitive development is dramatically highlighted.

In one recent study (35) of the personality and socialization antecedents of sociopolitical liberalism and conservatism, high school students were found to show distinct patterns depending on their political leanings. Conservative adolescents were more conventional, responsible, dependable, orderly, neat, organized, successful, and ambitious than liberals. Liberals were more rebellious, independent thinking, introspective, sympathetic, loving, and tender. They also reported more conflict with parents and emphasized the negative aspects of their interactions, although they also *reported* that their parents emphasized the development of independence, personal responsibility, and emotional control. Conservatives reported good relationships with parents and perceived them as understanding, helpful, and affectionate, stressing conventional and approved behavior, conformity with authority, and making a good impression.

### Other recent studies

A number of other investigators (26, 27, 32, 47, 91, 95, 108, 117) have recently conducted studies on the development of political thinking in children and adolescents, with results generally comparable to Adelson's but differing somewhat in emphasis. In one investigation (27), which employed a similar but somewhat less structured procedure than that of Adelson and his colleagues, children and adolescents were presented with a collection of jacks and told to think of them as people or groups going to a new island somewhere "where they want to make up a new government or country where everyone can live together as well as anyone ever could" (27, *108*). They were then asked, "What kind of government do you think they should have?" and told to use the jacks to set it up. Based on their responses, the subjects were categorized into four fairly distinct groups:

**TABLE 13.5** DISTRIBUTION OF POLITICAL TYPES BY AGE[a]

| | AGE | | |
| TYPE | 8 (N = 18) | 11 (N = 18) | 16 (N = 18) |
| --- | --- | --- | --- |
| I | 16 | 2 | 0 |
| II | 2 | 14 | 3 |
| III | 0 | 2 | 10 |
| IV | 0 | 0 | 5 |

*Source:* W. C. Crain and E. F. Crain. The growth of political ideas and their expression among young activists. *Journal of Youth and Adolescence,* 1974, **3**, 105–133. By permission.
[a] Symmetrical $d = 0.82$.

1. *Concrete personalists.* These subjects generally tended to ignore government, unless it was brought up by the investigator; their societies tended to be thought of in concrete terms, largely built around a "life-supportive system" (e.g., clearing land, building houses and stores, growing food).
2. *Discrete structuralists.* These subjects brought in political figures and governmental institutions, but in a concrete way, without much discussion either of their functions or interrelationships between them (e.g., "Here's the President, he makes the laws, and the Vice-President, he helps. Uh, the Senators, and the Governors are over here. . . ." (27, *110*).
3. *Systematic structuralists.* These subjects were able to "organize institutions systematically," and they did this with an eye toward making society as a whole work. They tended to emphasize such themes as "keeping things organized" and achieving "order." For the most part, however, they were not greatly concerned with the application of broader principles.
4. *Idealists.* In contrast, idealists attempted to form their governments as a way of carrying out a consistent set of (mostly democratic) principles (e.g., "My government would be based on the principle that the government is there to serve the people, rather than the other way around, so I would, of course, have all the offices elected") (27, *111*).

The distribution of the four types by age is shown in Table 13.5. As might be anticipated, most 8-year-olds were concrete personalists, and most 11-year-olds were discrete structuralists. A majority of 16-year-olds were systematic structuralists, but somewhat over a quarter were idealists.

## COGNITIVE DEVELOPMENT AND CHANGING RELIGIOUS BELIEFS

In most religions, adolescence is marked by some kind of religious ritual, which recognizes—as do other societal rites of passage—that an important developmental transition is taking place. Thus, it is during adolescence that many Christian youth

**TABLE 13.6 PERCENT RELIGIOUS BY GRADE**[a]

| | PERCENT RELIGIOUS BY GRADE | | | | |
|---|---|---|---|---|---|
| RELIGIOUS ITEM | 4 | 5 | 6 | 7 | 8 |
| Sometimes or often read Bible or religious writings | 57.6 | 56.6 | 56.8 | 55.4 | 43.7 |
| Attend religious services or Sunday school every week | 68.4 | 71.7 | 68.2 | 63.4 | 58.9 |
| Pray once a day or more often | 75.9 | 73.0 | 67.9 | 66.0 | 55.9 |
| Believe Ten Commandments and other rules must always be followed | 66.0 | 59.7 | 53.1 | 49.4 | 44.6 |
| Bible is always right and its facts are true | 73.8 | 69.8 | 55.5 | 57.2 | 49.2 |

*Source:* H. M. Nelsen, R. H. Potvin, and J. Shields. *The religion of children.* Copyright © 1977. Publications Office, United States Catholic Conference, Washington, D.C. By permission.
[a] $N = 3000$.

formally enter into church membership through *confirmation* ceremonies. Similarly, Jewish youth become adult members of their congregations through *Bat* or *Bar Mitzvah* ceremonies.

As in the case of moral values generally, the religious beliefs of adolescents also reflect their increasing cognitive development. The young person's religious beliefs are likely to become more abstract and less literal between the ages of 12 and 18 (38, 63, 99, 101, 107). For example, God comes to be seen more frequently as an abstract power and less frequently as a fatherly human being. Religious views also become more tolerant and less dogmatic (99). Table 13.6 shows some of the age-related changes in religious practices and beliefs. The last statement, "The Bible is always right and its facts are always true," shows particularly strong effects of age-change (101).

The developmental changes in religion have been organized into a series of stages of faith (42). These stages have been labeled: (1) intuitive-projective, (2) mythic-literal, (3) synthetic-conventional, (4) individual-reflective, (5) paradoxi-cal-consolidative, and (6) universalizing. The first two stages are typical of child-hood, the third of adolescence, with the remaining three possibly—though infre-quently—seen in adulthood (42). The stages parallel cognitive development, with the last three requiring formal reasoning. Other approaches to religious thinking sug-gest, however, that this sort of thinking was influenced more by religious training than cognitive capacity (73).

There may also be some decline in the stated importance of religion—at least of formal religion—during adolescence, although reports of widespread changes ap-pear exaggerated (107). Significantly more high school than college-age young peo-ple believe that religion is important to them, and more of them attend church regularly (116, 131). However, in a set of recent studies (76) examining change in religiosity as students pass through the college years, the only consistent finding was that students reported attending church more frequently as freshmen than as seniors. The author interprets the difference in these results from earlier studies that found substantial change on a number of religious dimensions—doubts about religious beliefs, extent of reaction to religious practices and observances, agreement with family beliefs and practices, importance of religious beliefs, and specific religious beliefs—to a plateauing of the societal decline in religiosity seen during the early 1970s. In addition, the major period of change currently may be from high school to college, with little subsequent change during college.

### Cultural changes

Cultural as well as age changes in religious views also appear to be at work. There was a steady decline during the 1970s in the religious behavior and beliefs of adolescents (29, 107, 130, 131). Interestingly, the decline was greatest among that part of the population in which religious concerns formerly were highest—namely, young people not attending and not planning to attend college. In 1969, for example, 65 percent of noncollege youth, but only 39 percent of college youth, considered religion a very important personal value. By 1973, the comparable percentages had declined to 42 percent for noncollege youth and 28 percent for college youth. Thus, although both groups had declined in the intervening years, and although it was still true that more noncollege than college youth continued to consider religion very important, the magnitude of the difference decreased dramatically. As with other values (see pages 585–590), there has apparently been a rather rapid value diffusion during this period from a minority of economically and socially privileged youth to the working-class majority of their peers.

The change in religious views over the past 50 years among adolescents can be seen in the follow-up study in 1977 of all the high school students in a midwestern community, "Middletown," first surveyed in 1924–1925. The changing views about religion over this half-century are shown in Table 13.7. The authors of the initial study had "reported that the 'old time religion' that characterized Middletown in 1890 had been severely eroded by 1924 and they expected the process of secularization to continue" (20, 4). As is seen in Table 13.7, the secularization has continued, but in selective ways. There has been little change in views regarding the purpose of religion (item 5). There is more decline (about 20 percent) in belief in the basic tenets of Christian fundamentalism (items 3 and 4)—a change partly due to an increase of Catholics in the community. The other items show more substantial changes. This study also showed that "although the numerical differences between the sexes are quite small in both sets of responses, female respondents in 1924 showed more religiosity on every item than male respondents, whereas in 1977 there are essentially no differences by sex in the religion items except for the item on evolution" (item 1) (20, 7). In 1977, 55 percent of the boys and 45 percent of the girls agreed with this item. A comparison of the responses in 1977 of adolescents whose fathers were white collar or blue collar in social class similarly showed nearly identical responses. This lack of difference may reflect the change toward increasing class similarity discussed above.

At least part of this decline of interest in religion seems clearly related to chang-

**TABLE 13.7 PROPORTION OF MIDDLETOWN HIGH SCHOOL STUDENTS AGREEING WITH STATEMENTS ON RELIGION, 1924 AND 1977**

| ITEM | PERCENT ANSWERING "TRUE" (1924) OR AGREEING (1977) | |
| --- | --- | --- |
| | 1924 ($N = 556$) | 1977 ($N = 886$) |
| 1. The theory of evolution offers a more accurate account of the origin and history of mankind than that offered by a literal interpretation of the first chapters of the Bible. | 28% | 50% |
| 2. Christianity is the one true religion and all peoples should be converted to it. | 94 | 38 |
| 3. The Bible is a sufficient guide to all the problems of modern life. | 74 | 50 |
| 4. Jesus Christ was different from every other man who ever lived in being entirely perfect. | 83 | 68 |
| 5. The purpose of religion is to prepare people for the hereafter. | 60 | 53 |
| 6. It is wrong to go to the movies on Sunday. | 33 | 6 |

*Source:* T. Caplow and H. Bahr. Half a century of change in adolescent attitudes: Replication of a Middletown survey by the Lynds. *Public Opinion Quarterly,* 1979, 1–18. Copyright 1979 by the Trustees of Columbia University. By permission.

ing values among young people, and a perception on the part of many of them that religion—at least formal, institutionalized religion—is failing to reflect these changes. For example, rightly or wrongly, approximately half of all 13- to 19-year-old boys and girls in a representative national survey stated the belief that "Churches teach that enjoyment of sex is sinful" and that churches are not doing their best to understand young people's ideas about sex (116). More boys than girls and more nonvirgins than virgins subscribe to these views. Many more contemporary adolescents attribute understanding attitudes about sex to God than to institutionalized religion (116). A clear majority of adolescents believe that churches could be a considerable help to young people trying to find themselves, could play an important role in sex education, and could help to focus attention on "the really important things that we need to get done in this country," but that, for the most part, they are not doing so (17, 116). A number of young people, particularly in the women's movement, also feel that the Catholic Church and some Protestant denominations are not according full status and recognition to women; and a majority of Catholic youth disagree with the Church's position on birth control, annulment and divorce, and the right of priests to marry (17).

There is also some indication that today's adolescents are placing more emphasis than previous generations on personal rather than institutionalized religion

(17, 58, 116, 130). This is consistent with the greater stress among adolescents generally on personal values and relationships and on individual moral standards, with less reliance on traditional social beliefs and institutions.

At the same time there has been increased interest in more conservative religious traditions, among youth as well as in the broader society. While traditional denominations have remained at lower levels established after the decline in their memberships during the 1970s, evangelistic forms of worship have increased their rolls. One estimate places the current number of Evangelical Christians in the United States at 50 million (18). Nearly half of all Protestant teenagers, and 22 percent of their Catholic peers, report a "born again" experience—a turning point in their lives by making a personal commitment to Christ (52). These figures are similar to those obtained with adults.

### Sects and cults

The new religious sects—such as the so-called Jesus Movement, Hare Krishna, and Children of God—that emerged in the late 1970s appear to be remaining vital and perhaps even increasing in membership (17, 102, 105, 112; 48, 49, 50). Current membership in these groups is estimated at 2 to 3 million in the United States (5). Some of these groups tend to be informal, loosely structured, and held together principally by a concern for others, disillusionment with materialistic values (or the apparent absence of *any* strong personal values) in contemporary society, and a belief—often simple, direct, and sometimes fundamentalist—in personal salvation (102, 105). Other groups tend to be highly authoritarian in structure and to require the surrender of all individual autonomy and complete conformity, both in behavior and belief, to the rigid, frequently simplistic dictates of leaders (17, 112). The emergence of some of these movements might appear to contradict earlier assertions about an increase in abstract conceptualizations of religion during adolescence as a function of the advent of formal operational thought. It is possible, however, that what is primarily involved here for many young people is a disillusionment with more rationalistic approaches as spiritually empty, and a turning back, whether regressive or not, to a more comfortable, secure, conventional mode of moral thought. In this connection, it is interesting to note that a considerable number of these young people, particularly those involved in the more authoritarian movements, have enlisted as a result of sudden and total conversion experiences following a period of rootlessness and identity confusion. There is often a prior history of extensive drug use, sexual exploration, and life "on the road" (17, 105). In addition, there is some evidence that some youth in the more restrictive groups experience decreased confusion as well as decreases in alcohol and drug use as a result of their membership (49, 50). Other people, particularly in less authoritarian movements, may simply be expressing a satisfying, and for them workable, set of simple, straightforward values in an otherwise chaotic society. Finally, for at least some young people, joining a particular movement may be merely another fad, and one having the advantage of confounding conventional middle-class parents.

**Religion and other behavior** Religiosity does appear to play a role in the behavior of adolescents. In their longitudinal study of the development of problem

behavior in youth, Richard and Shirley Jessor, psychologists at the University of Colorado, found that expressing more religious beliefs and attitudes—strongly linked to church attendance—was related to less involvement in marijuana use, less deviant behavior generally, and less problem behavior among high school students (77). Religiosity was unrelated, however, to drinking or to school performance. Among college students religiosity remained linked only to marijuana involvement for both males and females and problem behavior among females only (77).

## CURRENT TRENDS IN ADOLESCENT VALUES

As with so many other aspects of adolescent development, the greatest danger in discussing trends in adolescent values is that of overgeneralization. In the middle and late 1960s, much was made of a so-called revolution in the values of young people. They were, it was said, developing a "counterculture"—a set of values, beliefs, and life-styles so different from that of their more traditional elders that a profound "generation gap" had developed. There is no question that the advent of the troubled, violence-ridden decade of the 1960s was followed by major changes in the values of some adolescents. Significant minorities of young people became increasingly disillusioned by a society they viewed as unjust, cruel, violent, hypocritical, superficial, impersonal, overly competitive, or, in the broadest sense of the term, immoral. They reacted to this state of affairs in a variety of ways. Some became social dropouts; others began vigorous efforts to institute social change—efforts that ran the gamut from conventional political activity within the system to extreme revolutionary tactics (see Chapter 14).

Where many observers of that era, and especially representatives of the mass media, erred was not in the essential accuracy with which they identified a significant social change in values, beliefs, and behavior among young people, but in their assessment of its extent, both in numbers and in the degree of change. In its most dramatic manifestations, the counterculture of the 1960s was largely confined to a conspicuous, often highly articulate minority of young people on high school and college campuses, in the streets, and in films and the arts. Social commentators, however, like many parents and even many adolescents, tended to view adolescent culture as monolithic, despite the fact that they acknowledged a growing diversity and polarization of beliefs within the adult society of the period. Consequently, they too often attributed to young people in general the values, attitudes, beliefs, and modes of behavior of the more visible minorities. The fact of the matter, however, is that adults were—and are—not alone in their heterogeneity. During the late 1960s, in particular, the diversity among adolescents was at least as great as among adults, and in all likelihood greater. And although the values of the average adolescent of that period did change in a number of important respects, the extent of the changes was far more circumscribed than popular stereotypes suggested. Indeed, in many ways, the values, attitudes, and beliefs of the majority of adolescents of this era remained surprisingly unsurprising.

It now appears, as we enter the 1980s, that we are in danger of falling into another trap of overgeneralization. Whereas social observers of the 1960s tended to exaggerate the impact of the so-called youth revolution on the average adolescent and youth, many commentators in the early 1980s are misinterpreting the meaning of current trends toward a greater concern with materialism and financial security, a sharp decline in political activism, and a diminishing interest in the welfare of others. In the minds of some critics, these trends are the harbingers of an across-the-board return to pre-1960s attitudes, values, and beliefs. However, such is not the case. This should hardly be considered surprising, if for no other reason than that the world of the 1980s in which young people are coming to maturity, and which inevitably helps to shape their values and expectations, is, as we shall see, vastly different from the world of the 1950s and early 1960s (24, 132).

What then are the facts regarding contemporary adolescent values? To what extent, and in what directions, have they changed in the past decade, and to what extent have they remained relatively constant? As we shall see, the issue is more complex than some critics have been able or willing to recognize. Much of our discussion will focus on older adolescents—partly because their views have been more extensively studied, but also because the attitudes and values of older adolescents and youth are generally more highly differentiated, wider ranging, and more articulate. This reflects their higher level of cognitive development, their longer time perspective, their more advanced education, and their increased exposure to the broader world about them. But it also appears to reflect the differing developmental demands faced by younger and older adolescents.

Younger adolescents, although far from unmindful of society and the problem of their future place in it, continue to be deeply involved in establishing new and still changing parental relationships, and in adapting to their peers, who have become increasingly important as the direct role of the family diminishes. The older adolescent, in contrast, is faced with the imminence of his or her entrance into the broader adult world and the need to establish a continuing social identity as a member of that world—whether as worker, marriage partner, parent, or citizen (10, 11). For the older adolescent, as for the adult, the need to have fidelity to some continuing values is essential to the development of a stable ego identity (40).

Even in the case of older adolescents, however, the question of what their current values are, and the extent to which they have changed in the past decade, cannot be answered meaningfully in terms of global generalities. We need to make explicit what kinds of values we are talking about, and among what group of young people. The available evidence clearly indicates that there are marked differences in value trends from one category of values to another. It is also clear that contemporary values are not identical even for all major groups within the adolescent and youth population. In particular, there are differences between middle- and upper-class college or college-bound young people, on the one hand, and the majority of their working-class noncollege peers—although current differences between these groups are much smaller now than was the case during the late 1960s.

### College and college-bound adolescents and youth

Although college (or college-bound) young people comprise a minority of all young people, their value trends will be considered first because they tend to be trend setters—because any shifts in the values of this group are likely to have a subsequent influence on the values of young people generally. What then do we know about the value trends of this important minority?

In many respects, of course, contemporary adolescents and youth have needs and values that are far from new: self-esteem; feelings of competence; respect from parents, peers, and society; recognition of accomplishment; growing independence; some close friendships; someone to love; some idea of where they are headed, and what they are going to do with their lives, including how they are going to earn a living. The ways in which these traditional needs and values are expressed, and the importance they are given, may vary, however, with social, economic, and political change.

Indeed, what sometimes seem to be dramatic changes in values may actually represent newly aroused concerns for dormant values brought on by social changes that threaten these values. At any rate, it would be difficult to make progress in understanding recent changes in expressed attitudes and values without reference to changing social and economic conditions.

### Social and economic values

Although the extent of the shift has sometimes been exaggerated, there has clearly been an increase over the past dozen years (from the late 1960s to the early 1980s) in concern of adolescents and youth for personal well-being and a diminished concern for the welfare of others—particularly the less advantaged—and of society itself (7, 8, 24, 25, 92). This concern with material values and success in their chosen field of work is much higher among today's high school and college students than it was a little over a decade ago. For example, "being very well off financially" was cited as "a very important objective" by 49 percent of entering college students in the United States in 1969; by 1981 that figure had increased to 65 percent (7, 8, 9). In 1969 fewer than half of all entering students said that "being able to make more money" was a very important reason for going to college; in 1981, 67 percent considered it very important. Recognition by peers, having administrative responsibility, and being an authority in one's own field showed similar increases (7, 8, 9). Among high school seniors, too, there have been parallel but less dramatic increases in the number of those for whom "the chance to earn a good deal of money" and to have "a predictable, secure future" was rated as very important in a job (10, 12, 13). The percentage of college-bound high school seniors considering working for a large corporation desirable increased by 43 percent just between 1976 and 1980 (only 6 percent currently consider such a job unacceptable), while the number considering working for a government agency or social service organization desirable dropped by 25 percent (12).

In contrast to an increased concern with personal well-being and material success, the decade of the 1970s and early 1980s was witness to a marked decline in political and social activism (see Chapter 14), and such limited activist movements as have emerged recently have tended to emphasize issues, such as student financial aid or draft registration, that are directly related to immediate personal concerns, or that are shared broadly in society (e.g., defense expenditures, nuclear proliferation). Less than one-fifth of today's college-bound high school seniors and first-year college students consider "making a contribution to society" or "participating in community action" a very important value (13). And among entering college students, "keeping up with political affairs" was cited as very important by 32 percent fewer young women in 1981 than in 1969 (50 percent versus 34 percent), and by 14 percent fewer young men (52.5 percent versus 45 percent) (7, 8, 9, 92). Even at a more personal level, the number of college students who considered "helping others in difficulty" to be a very important objective declined in the past decade from 58 percent to 54 percent among males, and from 75 percent to 71 percent among females (7, 92).

This relative shift in emphasis from social to personal concerns has been accompanied by a decline in political liberalism. A decade ago, 33.5 percent of entering students described themselves as liberals; in 1981, only 18 percent did so (7, 8, 9, 92). Although the number considering themselves conservative remained constant, the middle-of-the-road group rose sharply—from 45.4 percent in 1970 to 60 percent in 1981. Does this relative shift in recent years away from political and social liberalism indicate, as some have suggested, an across-the-board retreat from the so-called new values that rose to prominence in the 1960s and early 1970s and a return to the status quo ante of the 1950s? The available evidence indicates otherwise.

For one thing, today's young people (and adults as well) are more—not less—skeptical about the infallibility, or even at times the morality, of major social institutions and their values, including big business, big labor, Congress, the executive branch of government, the courts, the schools, law enforcement agencies, and so on, than they were in the late sixties. For example, only about 20 percent of current high school seniors think that Congress has been doing a good job on the whole, and almost 40 percent think there is considerable dishonesty and immorality in Congress (13). Big business, big labor, and the executive branch of government do not fare a great deal better. Colleges and universities, churches, the press, and—in surprising contrast to the late 1960s—the military, fared better, with at least half of all students thinking they are doing a pretty good job (12, 13, 23).

### Personal and moral values

In personal and moral values, too, today's young people show little resemblance to those of the 1950s. The so-called sexual revolution among middle- and upper-class adolescents and youth was a major aspect of the "new morality" of the late 1960s, and one of the most enduring (see Chapter 8). Not only has there not been a return to a more traditional sexual morality, but previous trends are still accelerating. For example, in 1971, 30 percent of all 15- to 19-year-old girls had engaged in premarital intercourse. But by 1976, incidence had increased to 43 percent, and by 1979, to 50 percent (see page 285). The number of unmarried couples under age 25 living together in a household, although still relatively small, increased more than tenfold between 1970 and 1980 (122, 123). The 1960s trend toward considering sexual behavior more a matter of personal decision than a subject for socially imposed moral codes has also increased in the past decade. The percentage of students who consider having an abortion, relations between consenting homosexuals, or having children outside marriage as morally wrong all declined between 1969 and 1981 (7, 8, 12, 13, 92). When American high school seniors in 1980 were asked their reactions to "a man and a woman who live together without being married," only one in five or less said either that they were "experimenting with a worthwhile lifestyle," or that they "were violating a principle of human morality"; in contrast nearly half (48 percent) stated that they were "doing their own thing and not affecting anyone else" (13, *190*).

Most adolescents and youth still look forward to getting married and having children, but their numbers have declined slightly in the past 10 years (7, 9, 12, 13, 131). Perhaps more significant, having children is increasingly seen "as a matter of individual choice—neither a duty to society nor an indispensable life value" (131, *59*). Between 1969 and 1981, the percentage of entering college students who considered raising a family to be a very important objective declined from 78 percent to 67 percent for females, though it declined less than one percentage point (to 66 percent) for males (7, 8, 9), and males and females are now very similar on this attitude.

More broadly, fulfilling oneself as a person and having an opportunity for self-expression (two other important hallmarks of the new values of the 1960s) also have remained strong. Support of freedom, self-determination, and equality for women—an issue that was only beginning to emerge among young people in the 1960s—received increasingly broad support in the 1970s and early 1980s. Discrimination on the basis of age (both the young and the old) is also currently under siege, politically, culturally, and legally (24).

In accordance with the continuing emphasis over the past decade on the "freedom to be me," many young people showed a heightened interest in their own physical well-being—in jogging, conditioning programs, and concern for nutrition (24, 25). Others became involved in self-improvement programs and a variety of psychological "therapies"—from est and being Number One to meditation and relaxation programs (see pages 195–197). Self-realization—physical, psychological, spiritual, or material—appeared to be the predominant message.

The appropriate question, in our view, is not whether 1980s adolescents and youth are engaged in an across-the-board retreat from the values of the 1960s and early 1970s. Rather, it is whether the extension and expansion of such personal, moral, and sexual values of the 1960s as self-fulfillment and self-expression into the 1980s is psychologically growth-enhancing without a corresponding sense of commitment to the welfare of others and of society itself. "Greater self-realization and self-awareness can be positive goals, but if they become a person's only goals they can lead only to the kind of banality that has characterized so many of the current fads in religion, self-improvement books and seminars, and so-called therapies—or even worse, to self-destructiveness" (24, *1480*).

In what can be productive efforts to reexamine old stereotypes about social, sexual, and vocational roles—to realize oneself—it is important to understand that self-realization is not synonymous with self-indulgence, and that concern for others is a necessary concomitant of concern for self (24).

## THE BLUE-COLLAR "REVOLUTION"

One major error of many social observers in the 1960s was, as we have noted, a tendency to ascribe to a majority of young people the values and behaviors of a relatively small avant-garde minority. Even to college campuses, the views of the great majority of students, although influenced by minorities of social activists, the New Left, and advocates of alternative life-styles, nevertheless changed more slowly and remained somewhat more traditional. In turn, the views of noncollege working-class youth remained markedly more conservative than those of college youth in many areas, ranging from attitudes toward greater sexual freedom, use of drugs, and conformity in dress to views on the Vietnam war, business and government, minority rights, and law and order. Clearly, in the late sixties, adolescents and youth, like adults, had their own "silent majority" (24, 130, 131).

Interestingly, however, a significant change occurred during the 1970s, so that by the mid-seventies the values of noncollege adolescents and youth were, "to an almost uncanny degree" (131, *23*), just about where those of college youth were in the late 1960s—whether in the areas of sexual morality, religion, patriotism, politics, work, family, or attitudes toward business and government (131). For example, in 1969 the traditional belief that "hard work always pays off" was held by only 56 percent of college youth, but by 79 percent of noncollege youth. By the mid-seventies, however, the percentage of noncollege youth subscribing to this belief had decreased dramatically to 56 percent—identical to the 1969 percentage for college students. In short, there was a rapid transmission of values from a minority of college youth to youth in general (131).

In the early 1980s, these trends appear to be continuing (13, 24, 132). In most areas, differences between college or college-bound young people and those of their noncollege peers remain considerably smaller than was the case in the 1960s. For example, high school seniors with and without 4-year college plans share generally similar views with respect to couples living together prior to marriage, race relationships, drug use, the role of women in the work force, and the importance of marriage and family life (13), although the latter group (especially males) still tends to be somewhat more traditional about what they consider appropriate family roles for men and women. Members of this group also express considerably less interest or concern about "what's going on in government" (13, *155*) or about "social problems of the nation and the world and about how they might be solved" (13, *172*).

Of particular interest, college and noncollege youth show increasingly similar vocational values (see pages 478–482). Overwhelming majorities of both groups consider as very important: a job that is interesting to do, that lets you make the best use of your skills and abilities, and that provides an opportunity to learn new skills (12, 13). The diffusion of many of the values of the late 1960s and early 1970s to noncollege youth in the 1980s poses a potential problem. Despite the fact that noncollege youth are now more concerned with work that is "more than just a job," as a result of the increasing importance for them of such values as personal fulfillment, creativity, and greater self-expression, they are less likely than more highly educated youth to be able to find such work. Only about one-quarter of employed noncollege youth currently express the view that "my work is more than just a job," and only one-third feel that they have a chance to develop their skills and abilities. As we noted in Chapter 11, a major challenge of our era is to find work for youth generally that offers some opportunity for self-fulfillment and personal growth, as well as for adequate pay and economic security. For minorities, where fully half of all youth seeking work—any work—are unemployed, the problem is already reaching epidemic proportions.

The task will not be easy, and will require a far greater commitment to the welfare of youth on the part of society than has been evident to date. Nevertheless, neither college nor noncollege youth have given up. Although fewer of the latter group feel they are in control of their future, still nearly two-thirds do. And among both groups, three-quarters feel that, all in all, "my own life is going well," nearly two-thirds say they are "pretty happy," with an additional 20 percent saying they are "very happy," and six out of ten state that they anticipate "no difficulty in accepting the kind of life society has to offer" (13). In short, the majority of all youth do not currently appear deeply alienated, either within themselves or in their relations with society. However, although their numbers have decreased markedly since the height of the youth revolt of the late 1960s, a significant minority still do feel alienated to varying degrees, as we shall see in the following chapter.

### REFERENCES

1. Adelson, J. The political imagination of the young adolescent. *Daedalus*, 1971, **100,** 1013–1050.
2. Adelson, J. The development of ideology in adolescence. In S. E. Dragastin & G. H. Elder, Jr. (eds.), *Adolescence in the life cycle: Psychological change and social context.* New York: Wiley, 1975. Pp. 63–78.
3. Adelson, J. Rites of passage: How children learn the principles of community. *American Educator*, Summer 1982, 6 ff.
4. Adelson, J., & O'Neil, R. The development of political thought in adolescence: A sense of community. *Journal of Personality and Social Psychology*, 1966, **4,** 295–308.

5. America's cults gaining ground again. *U.S. News & World Report,* July 5, 1982, **93,** 37–41.

6. Armsby, R. E. A re-examination of the development of moral judgments in children. *Child Development,* 1971, **42,** 1241–1248.

7. Astin, A. Characteristics and attitudes of first-year college students: A 10-year comparison based on data gathered in national surveys of freshmen in 1969 and 1979. *The Chronicle of Higher Education,* June 28, 1980, **20,** 4–5.

8. Astin, A. Freshman characteristics and attitudes. *The Chronicle of Higher Education,* February 17, 1982, **23,** 11–12.

9. Astin, A. *The American freshman: National norms for fall 1981.* Los Angeles: American Council on Education and University of California at Los Angeles, 1982.

10. Bachman, J. G. *Youth in transition, Vol. II: The impact of family background and intelligence on tenth-grade boys.* Ann Arbor: Institute for Social Research, University of Michigan, 1971.

11. Bachman, J. G. *Youth looks at national problems: A special report from the youth in transition project.* Ann Arbor: Institute for Social Research, University of Michigan, 1971.

12. Bachman, J. G., & Johnston, L. D. Fewer rebels, fewer causes: A profile of today's college freshmen. *Monitoring the future.* Occasional Paper 4. Ann Arbor: Institute of Social Research, University of Michigan, 1979, 1980.

13. Bachman, J. G., Johnston, L. D., & O'Malley, P. M. *Monitoring the future: Questionnaire responses from the nation's high school seniors, 1980.* Ann Arbor: Survey Research Center, Institute for Social Research, University of Michigan, 1981.

14. Bandura, A. *Social learning theory.* Englewood Cliffs, N.J.: Prentice-Hall, 1977.

15. Beech, R. P., & Schoeppe, A. Development of value systems in adolescents. *Developmental Psychology,* 1974, **10,** 644, 656.

16. Belenky, M. F., & Gilligan, C. Impact of abortion decisions on moral development and life circumstance. Presented at the American Psychological Association meeting, New York, 1979.

17. Bengston, V. L., & Starr, J. M. Contrast and consensus: A generational analysis of youth in the 1970's. In R. J. Havighurst & P. H. Dreyer (eds.), *Youth: The seventy-fourth yearbook of the National Society for the Study of Education, Part I.* Chicago: University of Chicago Press, 1975. Pp. 224–266.

18. Benson, P. L., & Williams, D. *Religion on Capitol Hill: Myths & realities.* New York: Harper & Row, 1982.

19. Blasi, A. Bridging moral cognition and moral action: A critical review of the literature. *Psychological Bulletin,* 1980, **88,** 1–45.

20. Caplow, T., & Bahr, H. M. Half a century of change in adolescent attitudes: Replication of a Middletown survey by the Lynds. *Public Opinion Quarterly,* 1979, 1–17.

21. Carroll, J. L., & Rest, J. R. Moral development. In B. B. Wolman (ed.), *Handbook of developmental psychology.* Englewood Cliffs, N.J.: Prentice-Hall, 1982.

22. Colby, A., Kohlberg, L., Gibbs, J., & Lieberman, M. *A longitudinal study of moral development.* Cambridge, Mass.: Center for Moral Education, 1980.

23. The Committee for the Study of National Service. *Youth and the needs of the nation.* Washington, D.C.: The Potomac Institute, Inc., 1970.

24. Conger, J. J. Freedom and commitment: Families, youth, and social change. *American Psychologist,* 1981, **36,** 1475–1484.

25. Conger, J. J., Youth needs "a stable future." *U.S. News & World Report,* July 5, 1982, **93,** 50.

26. Connell, R. W. *The child's construction of politics.* Victoria, Canada: Melbourne University Press, 1971.

27. Crain, W. C., & Crain, E. F. The growth of political ideas and their expression among young activists. *Journal of Youth and Adolescence,* 1974, **3,** 105–133.

28. Davison, M. L., Robbins, S., & Swanson, D. B. Stage structure in objective moral judgments. *Developmental Psychology,* 1978, **14,** 137–146.

29. Dickinson, G. E. Changing religious behavior of adolescents 1964–1979. *Youth and Society,* 1982, **13,** 283–288.
30. Douvan, E. A., & Adelson, J. *The adolescent experience.* New York: Wiley, 1966.
31. Durkheim, E. *Moral education.* New York: Free Press, 1961 (originally published, 1925).
32. Easton, D., & Dennis, J. *Children in the political system: Origins of political legitimacy.* New York: McGraw-Hill, 1969.
33. Edwards, C. P. The comparative study of the development of moral judgment and reasoning. In R. Monroe, R. Monroe, & B. B. Whiting (eds.), *Handbook of cross-cultural human development.* New York: Garland, 1977.
34. Eisenberg-Berg, N. Development of children's prosocial moral judgment. *Developmental Psychology,* 1979, **15,** 128–137.
35. Eisenberg-Berg, N., & Mussen, P. Empathy and moral development in adolescence. *Developmental Psychology,* 1978, **14,** 185–186.
36. Elkind, D. Cognitive development in adolescence. In J. F. Adams (ed.), *Understanding adolescence.* Boston: Allyn & Bacon, 1968. Pp. 128–158.
37. Elkind, D. *Children and adolescents: Interpretative essays on Jean Piaget.* New York: Oxford University Press, 1970.
38. Elkind, D. *A sympathetic understanding of the child from six to sixteen.* Boston: Allyn & Bacon, 1971.
39. Erikson, E. H. *Identity: Youth and crisis.* New York: Norton, 1968.
40. Evans, R. I. *Dialogue with Erik Erikson.* New York: Harper & Row, 1967.
41. Fodor, E. M. Delinquency and susceptibility to social influence among adolescents as a function of level of moral development. *Journal of Social Psychology,* 1972, **86,** 257–260.
42. Fowler, J., Keen, S., & Berryman, J. *Life maps: The human journey of faith.* New York: Humanities Press, 1976.
43. Freud, A. *The ego and the mechanisms of defense.* New York: International Universities Press, 1946.
44. Freud, A. Adolescence as a developmental disturbance. In G. Caplan & S. Lebovici (eds.), *Adolescence: Psychosocial perspectives.* New York: Basic Books, 1969.
45. Freud, S. Some psychical consequences of the anatomical distinction between the sexes. In J. Strachey (eds.), *The standard education of the complete psychological works of Sigmund Freud* (Vol. 19). London: Hogarth Press, 1961 (originally published, 1925).
46. Froming, W. J., & McColgan, E. B. Comparing the Defining Issues Test and the Moral Dilemma Interview. *Developmental Psychology,* 1979, **15,** 658–659.
47. Furth, H., & McConville, K. Adolescent understanding of compromise in political and social arenas. *Merrill-Palmer Quarterly,* 1982, **27,** 413–427.
48. Galanter, M. The "relief effect": A sociobiologic model for neurotic distress and large-group therapy. *American Journal of Psychiatry,* 1978, **135,** 388–591.
49. Galanter, M. Psychological induction into the large group: Findings from a contemporary religious sect. *American Journal of Psychiatry,* 1980, **137,** 1574–1579.
50. Galanter, M., Rabkin, R., Rabkin, J., & Deutsch, A. The "Moonies": A psychological study. *American Journal of Psychiatry,* 1979, **136,** 165–170.
51. Gallatin, J. Political thinking in adolescence. In J. Adelson (ed.), *Handbook of Adolescent Psychology.* New York: Wiley, 1980.
52. Gallup, G. Gallup youth survey. *Denver Post,* January 15, 1978, 50.
53. Garwood, S. G., Levine, D. W., & Ewing, L. Effect of protagonist's sex on assessing gender differences in moral reasoning. *Developmental Psychology,* 1980, **16,** 677–678.
54. Gilligan, C. In a different voice: Women's conception of the self and of morality. *Harvard Educational Review,* 1977, **47,** 481–517.
55. Gilligan, C. Woman's place in man's life cycle. *Harvard Educational Review,* 1979, **49,** 431–446.

56. Gilligan, C., & Belenky, M. F. A naturalistic study of abortion decisions. In R. Selman & R. Yando (eds.), *Clinical-developmental psychology.* San Francisco: Jossey-Bass, 1982.
57. Gorsuch, R. L., & Barnes, M. L. Stages of ethical reasoning and moral norms of Carib youths. *Journal of Cross-Cultural Psychology,* 1973, **4,** 283–301.
58. Greeley, A. Jesus freaks and other devouts. *The New York Times Book Review,* Part II, February 13, 1972, 4ff.
59. Gutkin, D. C. The effect of systematic story changes on intentionability in children's moral judgments. *Child Development,* 1972, **43,** 187–195.
60. Haan, N. Two moralities in action contexts: Relationships to thought, ego regulation, and development. *Journal of Personality and Social Psychology,* 1978, **36,** 286–305.
61. Haan, N., Weiss, R., & Johnson, V. The role of logic in moral reasoning and development. *Developmental Psychology,* in press.
62. Hare, R. T. Authoritarianism, creativity, success, and failure among adolescents. *Journal of Social Psychology,* 1972, **86,** 219–229.
63. Havighurst, R. J., & Keating, B. The religion of youth. In M. Strommen (ed.), *Research on religious development.* New York: Hawthorne Books, 1971.
64. Hoffman, M. L. Moral development. In P. H. Mussen (ed.), *Carmichael's manual of child psychology* (Vol. 2). New York: Wiley, 1970.
65. Hoffman, M. L., Developmental synthesis of affect and cognition and its implications for altruistic motivation. *Developmental Psychology,* 1975, **11,** 228–239.
66. Hoffman, M. L. Moral internalization, parental power, and the nature of parent-child interaction. *Developmental Psychology,* 1975, **11,** 228–239.
67. Hoffman, M. L. Sex differences in moral internalization and values. *Journal of Personality and Social Psychology,* 1975, **32,** 720–729.
68. Hoffman, M. L. Development of moral thought, feeling and behavior. *American Psychologist,* 1979, **34,** 958–966.
69. Hoffman, M. L. Moral development in adolescence. In J. Adelson (ed.), *Handbook of adolescent psychology.* New York: Wiley, 1980.
70. Hoffman, M. L., & Saltzstein, H. D. Parent discipline and the child's moral development. *Journal of Personality and Social Psychology,* 1967, **5,** 45–57.
71. Hogan, R. Moral conduct and moral character: A psychological perspective. *Psychological Bulletin,* 1973, **79,** 217–232.
72. Hogan, R. The structure of moral character and the exploration of moral action. *Journal of Youth and Adolescence,* 1975, **4,** 1–15.
73. Hoge, D. R., & Petrillo, G. H. Development of religious thinking in adolescence: A test of Goldman's theories. *Journal for the Scientific Study of Religion,* 1978, **17,** 139–154.
74. Holstein, C. B. Irreversible, stepwise sequence in the development of moral judgment: A longitudinal study of males and females. *Child Development,* 1976, **47,** 51–61.
75. Hult, R. E., Jr. The relationship between ego identity status and moral reasoning in university women. *The Journal of Psychology,* 1979, **103,** 203–207.
76. Hunsberger, B. The religiosity of college students: Stability and change over years at university. *Journal for the Scientific Study of Religion,* 1978, **17,** 159–164.
77. Jessor, R., & Jessor, S. L. *Problem behavior and psychosocial development: A longitudinal study of youth.* New York: Academic Press, 1977.
78. Kohlberg, L. Moral education in the schools: A developmental view. In R. E. Grinder (ed.), *Studies in adolescence: A book of readings in adolescent development.* New York: Macmillan, 1969. Pp. 237–258.
79. Kohlberg, L. Stage and sequence: The cognitive-developmental approach to socialization. In D. Goslin (ed.), *Handbook of socialization theory and research.* Skokie, Ill.: Rand McNally, 1969.
80. Kohlberg, L. From is to ought: How to commit the naturalistic fallacy and get away with it in the study of moral development. In T. Mischel (ed.), *Cognitive development and epistemology.* New York: Academic Press, 1971.
81. Kohlberg, L. Moral stages and moralization: The cognitive-developmental approach. In T. Lickona (ed.), *Moral development and behavior.* New York: Holt, Rinehart and Winston, 1976.

82. Kohlberg, L. *The meaning and measurement of moral development.* Clark Lectures, Clark University, 1979.

83. Kohlberg, L., & Gilligan, C. The adolescent as a philosopher: The discovery of the self in a postconventional world. *Daedalus,* 1971, **100,** 1051–1086.

84. Kohlberg, L., & Kramer, R. Continuities and discontinuities in childhood and adult development. *Human Development,* 1969, **12,** 93–120.

85. LaVoie, J. C. Punishment and adolescent self-control. *Developmental Psychology,* 1973, **8,** 16–24.

86. Leahy, R. L. Parental practices and the development of moral judgment and self-image disparity during adolescence. *Developmental Psychology,* 1981, **17,** 580–594.

87. Leahy, R. L., & Eiter, M. Moral judgment and the development of real and ideal androgynous self-image during adolescence and young adulthood. *Developmental Psychology,* 1980, **16,** 362–370.

88. Leizer, J. I., & Rogers, R. W. Effects of punishment, and timing of test on resistance to temptation. *Child Development,* 1974, **45,** 790–793.

89. Lieberman, M. Evaluation of a social studies curriculum based on an inquiry method and a cognitive-developmental approach to moral education. Paper presented at the annual meeting of the American Education Research Association, Washington, D.C., April 1975.

90. Lockwood, A. L. The effects of values clarification and moral development curricula on school-age subjects: A critical review of recent research. *Review of Educational Research,* 1978, **48,** 325–364.

91. Lonky, E., Reihman, J. M., & Serlin, R. C. Political values and moral judgment in adolescence. *Youth and Society,* 1981, **12,** 423–441.

92. Magarrell, J. Today's new students, especially women, more materialistic. *The Chronicle of Higher Education,* January 28, 1980, 3.

93. Marcia, J. E. Development and validation of ego identity status. *Journal of Personality and Social Psychology,* 1966, **3,** 551–558.

94. Martin, R. M., Shafto, M., & Van Deinse, W. The reliability, validity, and design of the Defining Issues Test. *Developmental Psychology,* 1977, **13,** 460–468.

95. Merelman, R. The development of policy thinking in adolescence. *American Political Science Review,* 1971, **65,** 1033–1047.

96. Mischel, W., & Mischel, H. N. A cognitive social learning approach to morality and self-regulation. In T. Lickona (ed.), *Moral development and behavior.* New York: Holt, Rinehart and Winston, 1976.

97. Murphy, G. *Personality.* New York: Harper & Row, 1947.

98. Murphy, J. M., & Gilligan, C. Moral development in late adolescence and adulthood: A critique and reconstruction of Kohlberg's theory. *Human Development,* 1980, **23,** 77–104.

99. Mussen, P. H., Conger, J. J., & Kagan, J. *Child development and personality.* New York: Harper & Row, 1979 (5th ed.).

100. Mussen, P. H., & Eisenberg-Berg, N. *Roots of caring, sharing, and helping.* Englewood Cliffs, N.J.: Prentice-Hall, 1980.

101. Nelsen, H. M., Potvin, R. H., & Shields, J. *The religion of children.* Washington, D.C.: U.S. Catholic Conference, 1977.

102. Ortega, R. *The Jesus people speak out.* New York: Pyramid Books, 1972.

103. Parikh, B. Development of moral judgment and its relation to family environmental factors in Indian and American families. *Child Development,* 1980, **51,** 1030–1039.

104. Piaget, J. *The moral judgment of the child.* New York: Free Press, 1948.

105. Plowman, E. E. *The Jesus movement in America.* New York: Pyramid Books, 1971.

106. Podd, M. H. Ego identity status and morality: The relationship between two constructs. *Developmental Psychology,* 1972, **6,** 497–507.

107. Potvin, R. H., Hoge, D. R., & Nelsen, H. M. Religion and American youth: With emphasis on Catholic adolescents and young adults. Washington, D.C.: U.S. Catholic Conference, 1976.

108. Rebelsky, F., Conover, C., & Chafetz, P. The development of political attitudes in children. *Journal of Psychology,* 1969, **73,** 141–146.

109. Rest, J. Longitudinal study of the Defining Issues Test of moral judgment: A strategy for analyzing developmental change. *Developmental Psychology,* 1975, **2,** 738–748.

110. Rest, J. *Development of judging moral issues.* Minneapolis: University of Minnesota Press, 1979.

111. Rest, J., Cooper, D., Coder, R., Masanz, J., & Anderson, D. Judging the important issues in moral dilemmas—an objective measure of development. *Developmental Psychology,* 1974, **10,** 491–501.

112. Rice, B. Messiah from Korea: Honor thy father Moon. *Psychology Today,* January 1976, **9,** 36ff.

113. Rowe, I., & Marcia, J. E. Ego identity status, formal operations, and moral development. *Journal of Youth and Adolescence,* 1980, **9,** 87–99.

114. Santrock, J. W. Father absence, perceived maternal behavior, and moral development in boys. *Child Development,* 1975, **46,** 753–757.

115. Saraswathi, T. S., & Sundaresan, J. Perceived maternal disciplinary practices and their relation to development of moral judgment. *International Journal of Behavioral Development,* 1980, **3,** 91–104.

116. Sorensen, R. C. *Adolescent sexuality in contemporary America: Personal values and sexual behavior ages 13–19.* New York: Abrams, 1973.

117. Tapp, J. L., & Kohlberg, L. Developing sense of law and legal justice. *Journal of Social Issues,* 1971, **27,** 65–92.

118. Tapp, J. L., & Levine, F. J. Compliance from kindergarten to college: A speculative research note. *Journal of Youth and Adolescence,* 1972, **1,** 233–249.

119. Turiel, E. Distinct conceptual and developmental domains: Social-convention and morality. *Nebraska Symposium on Motivation,* in press.

120. Turiel, E. Conflict and transition in adolescent moral development. *Child Development,* 1974, **45,** 14–29.

121. Turiel, E., Edwards, C. P., & Kohlberg, L. Moral development in Turkish children, adolescents and young adults. *Journal of Cross-Cultural Psychology,* 1978, **9,** 75–85.

122. U.S. Bureau of the Census, Current population reports, Series P-20, No. 363. *Population profile of the United States: 1980.* Washington, D.C.: U.S. Government Printing Office, 1981.

123. U.S. Department of Commerce, Bureau of the Census, *Statistical abstract of the United States, 1981* (102 ed.). Washington, D.C.: U.S. Government Printing Office, 1981.

124. Walker, L. J. Cognitive and perspective-taking prerequisites for moral development. *Child Development,* 1980, **51,** 131–139.

125. Walker, L. J., & Richards, B. S. Stimulating transitions in moral reasoning as a function of stage of cognitive development. *Developmental Psychology,* 1979, **15,** 95–103.

126. Weiner, B., & Peter, N. A cognitive-developmental analysis of achievement and moral judgment. *Developmental Psychology,* 1973, **9,** 290–309.

127. Weiss, R. J. Understanding moral thought: Effects on moral reasoning and decision-making. *Developmental Psychology,* in press.

128. White, C. B. Moral development in Bahamian school children. A cross-cultural examination of Kohlberg's states of moral reasoning. *Developmental Psychology,* 1975, **11,** 535–536.

129. Whiting, J. W. M., & Child, I. L. *Child training and personality.* New Haven, Conn.: Yale University Press, 1953.

130. Yankelovich, D. *Generations apart.* New York: CBS News, 1969.

131. Yankelovich, D. *The new morality: A profile of American youth in the 1970s.* New York: McGraw-Hill, 1974.

132. Yankelovich, D. *New rules: Searching for fulfillment in a world turned upside down.* New York: Random House, 1981.

133. Youniss, J. Moral development through a theory of social construction: An analysis. *Merrill-Palmer Quarterly,* 1981, **27,** 385–403.

Alienation and delinquency

CHAPTER 14

# Alienation and delinquency

**A**s we saw in the previous chapter, despite a lack of enchantment with many of the policies, practices, and values of government and other social institutions, a majority of adolescents and youth in the early 1980s do not appear to be deeply troubled personally and most feel that their own lives are going reasonably well. Most feel "pretty happy," have a positive attitude toward themselves, and feel that they will be able to be successful in life (13). When asked recently if they thought their lives would be better in 5 years, about eight out of ten American high school seniors said they would. In contrast, three out of five expected things to get worse for this country—and the world—during this period (8, 12, 13). Their outlook is apparently shared by adults; nearly two-thirds of a recent cross section of Americans agreed with the statement: "Americans should get used to the fact that our wealth is limited and most of us are not likely to become better off than we are now" (189, *24*).

Although many young people wish they had more good friends (not just acquaintances), would like greater opportunities for self-expression and self-fulfillment, and feel somewhat "fearful and anxious" about the future of the economy and such problems as nuclear proliferation and the possibilities of war (9, 13, 39, 190, 191), the majority nevertheless expect to be able to find a rewarding life for themselves within the existing social order. For some, this appears to involve a more pragmatic emphasis on achieving a rewarding personal life-style, with less concern than characterized their predecessors of the sixties and early seventies about the well-being of society in general, and the poor and otherwise disadvantaged in particular (7, 9, 12, 39, 40, 190).

Nevertheless, there remain significant minorities of young people who do not share these relatively optimistic feelings, who feel deeply dissatisfied with either themselves or society, or both. At least 10 percent feel that their lives are not very useful, that they have few friends they can get together with or turn to for help, and that there is little sense in planning for the future because plans hardly ever work out anyway (13). Over 16 percent of college-bound high school seniors (and nearly one-third of those not planning 4 years of college) agree or mostly agree that "Every time I try to get ahead, something or somebody stops me" (13, *187*).

Although skepticism toward, and distrust of, governmental and other social institutions have actually increased since the late sixties, among youth and adults in the population at large, the responses provided by this disenchantment have changed markedly. For example, between the early 1960s and the early 1980s, the level of trust that government will do what is right most of the time has been cut in half, from 56 percent to 29 percent (190, 191). Studies by Louis Harris show that "the number of people expressing at least a mild form of political alienation—'what I think doesn't count,' 'those in power don't care what people like me think,' '*They* try to take advantage of people like me'—rose inexorably from one-third minorities in the 1960s to two-thirds majorities by the start of the 1980s" (190, *185–186*). But instead of responding to this perceived state of affairs either with social and political activism aimed at changing "the system," or by "dropping out" in favor of an alternative life-style, as in the case of the short-lived hippie movement of the late 1960s, adolescents and youth in the early 1980s are more likely to respond with political apathy and a decline in social concerns.

There are, fortunately in our view, still young people—and adults—who feel sufficiently disturbed by one or another aspect of current social policies and practices that they are actively engaged in efforts to change them. For some, it is women's rights, spurred on by defeat of the ERA; for others, it is opposition to nuclear proliferation or destruction of the environment; for still others, it is the rights of the have-nots—children, minority adolescents, the poor, the elderly, the handicapped, the mentally ill—against whom they perceive a relentless campaign of attrition being waged, while at the same time, tax breaks and other economic benefits are being generated for the most privileged.

Although these young people differ from one another about the nature of society's ills and the most appropriate responses to them, they are united in the belief that some part of the American dream is being tarnished. And they are not happy about it.

## THE ROOTS OF ALIENATION

In Western culture, the term *alienation* came into its own during the period of the cold war and reached its peak in popular usage during the 1960s. It was used to "explain" all manner of events characterizing that turbulent decade, from student demonstrations and inner-city riots to increased use of drugs and the rise of the hippie movement (38, 158). However, the concept of alienation is far from new (158, 162). Hegel discussed the "self-alienated spirit" in his first book, *Phenomenology of the Spirit,* published in 1807 (80). Subsequently, the term has been employed in a variety of ways by philosophers, theologians, and sociologists, and more recently by psychologists and psychoanalysts (97, 158, 162, 167). Some, like Durkheim, the early Marx, and Robert Merton, emphasized the anomie that results from political and economic exploitation and the separation of people from personally meaningful, productive work. Existentialist philosophers and theologians such as Kierkegaard, Tillich, and Sartre emphasized the painful estrangement of the individual from God, from other people, or from oneself. Others have employed the term in additional ways; not infrequently, in fact, alienation has been used in different, and sometimes conflicting, ways by the same writer (38, 158, 167). What is clear, as the philosopher Richard Schacht observes, is that because the term is employed in connection with so many different phenomena, it enjoys no special association with any of them. "Using the term 'alienation' without explaining any further what one has in mind communicates little more today than does tapping one's glass with one's spoon at a banquet; neither does much more than attract attention" (158, *245*).

Schacht's observation is as applicable to our efforts to invoke alienation as an explanatory concept in developmental psychology as it is in philosophy, theology, or sociology. It became fashionable in the 1960s to refer to young people who in one way or another did not fit in as being alienated. By such labeling we gained the illusion that we were saying something significant about them. However, as Kenneth Keniston (97) has noted, all we were really doing was implying that something was wrong and suggesting the loss or absence of a previously desirable relationship (97, 158). Unless we can go on to specify what relationships the individual has lost, what he or she is alienated *from,* we have accomplished little.

Furthermore, we need to know what new relationships, if any, have replaced those that have been lost. For example, some young people have become alienated from what they perceive as the futility of the corporate "rat race." But those who have reacted with apathy and indifference are in a very different position from those who have attempted to find new and, to them, meaningful alternatives—whether through pursuing private goals and relationships, or perhaps by beginning an entirely different kind of career. In a related fashion, we need to know whether attempts to deal with the alienation are *alloplastic* (i.e., involve an attempt to transform the outside world) or *autoplastic* (involve self-transformation) (97). Finally, it is important to know whether the alienation has been imposed on the individual largely by obvious external forces, as in the case of the disenfranchised poor and a number of minority groups, or whether it is largely chosen by the individual, as, for example, in the case of some of the militant middle- and upper-class youth of the 1960s (38). In brief, then,

> While the concept of alienation in every variation suggests the loss or absence of a previous or desirable relationship, it requires further specification in at least four aspects: (1) *Focus:* Alienated from what? (2) *Replacement:* What replaces the old relationship? (3) *Mode:* How is the alienation manifested? (4) *Agent:* What is the agent of the alienation?" [97, *454*].

Viewed in this manner, it becomes clear that alienation among youth may differ in important ways. Some aspects of alienation are relatively widespread in a particular culture; others tend to be limited to smaller subgroups. With the rapid decline in clearly defined religious faith in the past century, there is a feeling of alienation among many adolescents and adults from what previously appeared to be a meaningful and orderly universe with a personal God at its center. This is particularly likely to be the case for the most highly educated of our young people. This feeling of "existential outcastness" (97, 158, 162), of the essential lack of any absolute meaning in the universe as a whole, can be painful indeed, and can result in feelings of deprivation and outrage—especially among adolescents, with their relatively greater sensitivity, need for absolute values, and relative lack of repressive defenses (38).

Many adolescents also share what Keniston (97) calls "developmental estrangement": a sense of alienation or loss that comes with the abandonment of childish ties to one's childhood self, and, indeed, the whole world of childhood—an egocentric world that, as many of us can recall, seemed to have been created specifically for us, with us at its center. How difficult this sense of estrangement will be to deal with depends in great measure both on the particular kinds of childhood experiences the individual has had, and also on what he or she finds to take their place. The other side of the coin of childhood dependence is emancipation, and for the young person who can find new emotional ties and new challenges and rewards in living, the loss of the world of childhood will be much less painful (38). In a period of rapid social change such as our own, there is likely to be another keenly felt alienation—an acute sense of historical loss: "Most social innovations replace customs, outlooks, or technologies that are in that measure left behind; and those who are most firmly attached to what has been replaced inevitably mourn their loss" (97, 461). The persistent American myth of the small town and the currently popular nostalgia revival bear at least superficial witness to contemporary feelings of historical loss. Alienation may also take the form of a sense of estrangement from what is vaguely felt to be one's real self, as Karen Horney, Eric Fromm, and others have noted (65, 84, 97, 162). Whether as a result of unfortunate developmental experiences or the demands of society, young people may feel that somehow they have lost touch with some inner core of their being, and that much of what they do is empty, flat, and devoid of meaning (97). Such feelings characterize some instances of adolescent depression (see Chapter 15).

Young people may, in varying degrees, show all of these and other forms of alienation. In the 1960s the most prominently emphasized alienation involved an explicit rejection by many middle- and upper-class adolescents and youth of traditional societal values and practices. Although they were often alienated in other ways as well, significant numbers of young people maturing during that troubled decade came to share a common disillusionment with the goals, values, and practices of American society. They reacted against what they perceived as the ultimate futility of an obsessive preoccupation with materialistic rewards and social status, and the shallowness and hypocrisy of many of the values and practices of contemporary society, even though, in some ways, the young people were their beneficiaries. While the intensity and extent of this sort of alienation among privileged youth have diminished sharply in recent years, as we shall see, other more subtle, less publicized forms of alienation have emerged.

## ALIENATION OF
## MINORITIES AND THE POOR

As we have noted, there can be important differences in the sources of alienation and the ways in which it is expressed. Among minorities and the poor—and especially those who fall in both categories—much of the alienation that many feel is largely imposed from without. Quite simply, these young people are prevented by discrimination from sharing in the affluent society that they see all about them and on the ever-present television screen that often occupies a central place in even the

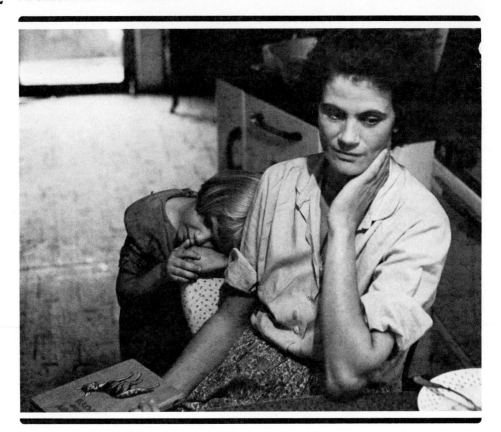

poorest homes. The great majority of adolescents in these disadvantaged groups (e.g., blacks, Spanish-speaking persons of Mexican-American or Puerto Rican heritage, Appalachian whites, American Indians) are born into the "culture of poverty," whether in urban ghettos, in rural slums, or on reservations. Even at birth, the odds are likely to be against them: The infant mortality rate among the estimated 16 percent of Americans living below the poverty level is far higher than of those living above it. Among blacks alone, the infant mortality rate is nearly twice that for whites, and the discrepancy continues till death (104, 171).

In their developing years, the hard-core minority poor are often exposed to hunger and malnutrition; inadequate or nonexistent health care; overcrowded, deteriorated, rat- and vermin-infested housing that is often without heat, electricity, or adequate plumbing; harassment both by police and other authorities and by petty criminals, youth gangs, slum landlords, and gyp merchants. Their parents, often only the mother, are frequently so poorly educated, so worn down, or so powerless to cope with the Establishment that they can be of little assistance in helping their children to cope with an ever more complex society (although some manage to survive, and to help their children to survive, what would seem to most middle- and upper-class adults to be insurmountable obstacles).

Poorly prepared intellectually, psychologically, and socially, disadvantaged children are likely to enter overcrowded, rundown schools. Under these conditions, they may fail to make normal school progress and may drop out of school as soon as they are able. Few jobs are likely to be available at their skill level, and they may find themselves discriminated against even in jobs for which they are qualified. Among all young people currently employed or seeking (and needing) work in this country, nearly 25 percent—one in four—are currently (1982) unemployed. Incredibly, among minority youth generally, this figure rises to one out of every two young people (not counting those who have given up and are no longer actively seeking work), and for those living in the disorganized, dilapidated ghettos of many of our largest cities, unemployment is almost total. The situation shows little indication of imminent change. For such young people, the idea of the American dream becomes a nightmare.

### Alienation, identity, and self-esteem

Still worse, under such circumstances, young people may not only become alienated from the dominant American culture; in some cases, they may also be cut off from the possibility of developing a clearly defined, self-confident personal and cultural identity. Even while resenting the discrimination to which they have been subjected by the dominant majority in society, they may come unwittingly to accept, at least partially, many of its attitudes, values, and beliefs. This may result in a loss of self-esteem, a negative identity and an alienation from the self (49, 50, 57). Although the ascendance of racial and ethnic pride in the 1960s and 1970s, particularly among young people, appears to have played an important part in stemming such negative perceptions and increasing self-esteem, one wonders how long the truly disenfranchised can persevere in the face of a continuing societal rejection that is currently being aggravated by massive federal cutbacks in social, vocational, health, educational, and other programs most needed by the poor and near poor, while taxes for the wealthy are being sharply lowered. Among the programs currently being eliminated or reduced, a number are of particularly urgent concern for young people: youth training and employment programs; nutritional programs for pregnant women and infants, food stamps, Medicaid, child abuse and runaway centers and services, family planning services and counseling for adolescents, and educational and training programs for handicapped children and youth, as well as basic mental health, health, and rehabilitative services.

## ALIENATION AMONG PRIVILEGED YOUTH

In contrast to the alienation of the poor and the victims of racial or ethnic discrimination, which is largely imposed by society, another kind of alienation became increasingly apparent in the turbulent decade of the 1960s—alienation among privileged middle- and upper-class youth. Alienation among members of this group was not as entirely new as it was sometimes proclaimed to be because there have been parallels in earlier youth movements in other countries, as well as in the United States. Throughout history, such movements have arisen when there is a "perceived discrepancy between the individual needs or aspirations of young people and the existing social and political conditions" (22, *560*). During the late 1700s and the early 1800s, for example, the generational continuity of the family was diminished by the advent of the industrial revolution (68). "Large numbers of young people were cut adrift from their homes and occupations as the economy moved from the traditional guild system toward a capitalist society" (22, *560–561*). They were forced to migrate to the cities looking for work, and many began roaming aimlessly across the face of Europe "in search of a more permanent identity" (22, *561*). The historian Samuel Eliot Morison (122) has described the American university student of the 1790s as an "atheist in religion, an experimentalist in morals, a rebel to authority" (22, *585*). Alienated middle- and upper-class youth have long played an important part in the overthrow of political regimes from which they felt alienated (22). Nevertheless, the behavior of the alienated youth of the 1960s represented a dramatic departure from the relative quiescence of the "silent generation" of the fifties; furthermore, the visibility of their alienation was heightened by the rapid increase in the numbers of these young people, their unprecedented concentration in age-segregated high schools and colleges, and the attention they attracted in the media.

There were significant variations in the sources of these privileged youths' alienation and the ways in which it was manifested. For some, the roots of their alienation derived from particular kinds of developmental experiences, such as disturbed parent-child relationships, that would be likely to result in alienation in most societies (38, 39, 97, 134). For others, the special characteristics and conflicts of society played a dominant role. Specific injustices were often involved: racial oppression, economic discrimination, violations of personal freedom, the bitterly opposed war in Indochina. In other instances, alienation was both deep and pervasive, amounting to a rejection of society as a whole, a society they viewed as inimical to their most deeply held values: intimacy ("love," both individual and communal), individuality (freedom to know and be oneself), autonomy (freedom from coercion and freedom to act independently), and honesty (lack of pretense and dissimulation). This meant rejecting relentless competition, obsessive status-seeking, and manipulative role-playing at the expense of others; respect for authority that was based on power rather than on competence or morality; and the traditional Protestant ethic of sacrificing current enjoyment for the sake of a presumably brighter tomorrow (37, 38, 188).

In their view, the goals of technological progress and economic affluence were being ruthlessly pursued without regard to the costs in terms of either human needs or the quality of the environment. Overshadowing all other concerns in the latter half of the sixties (and heightening their feelings of resentment about other issues) was the war in Indochina.

In response to their alienation, some privileged youth chose to continue to work for change within the system; smaller numbers became committed radicals or "revolutionaries" (98, 99, 100, 103, 188, 189). Others withdrew from society as a whole. Sometimes this withdrawal involved deep despair, apathy, or defeat, without any alternative commitment to relieve their feelings of alienation; a number of the youthful psychiatric casualties of the time fell into this category. In other cases, there was a continued search for meaningful private alternatives within themselves or within a separate subculture of likeminded individuals, whether as members of a self-sustaining collective—urban or rural—or as members of the short-lived hippie culture (37, 100, 138, 139).

For the most part, alienated youth during this period tended to come from higher-income families, with high levels of paternal and maternal education (26, 138, 139). Those who became left-oriented activists were found to be generally more autonomous, ascendant, assertive, sensitive, subjective, and socially concerned than nonactivists, and less conforming and in less need of nurturance and support (19, 102, 103, 115). But, contrary to the assertions of a number of early studies (18, 62), *as a group* activists emerged as neither more, nor less, intelligent or emotionally stable than their nonactivist peers (22, 101, 155, 188), and no more, nor less, likely to have positive, rewarding relationships with their parents (15, 20, 155, 188). Clearly, popular stereotypes of the time that all activists were unusually intelligent, mature, and psychologically resilient, or, conversely, that they were—as the psychoanalyst Bruno Bettelheim argued—immature, deeply troubled young people "fixated at the stage of the temper tantrum" (48, *23*)—were both misleading:

> There are obviously many individuals with . . . healthy characteristics who are not activists, just as there are many within the group of activists who do have definite psychopathologies. A variety of individuals with highly diverse talents and motivations are bound to be involved in any social movement; global descriptions are certain to be oversimplified [155, *182*].

## RECENT TRENDS IN ACTIVISM AND DISSENT

By most available measures, as well as common observation, activism and dissent among privileged youth declined markedly following the social convulsions of the 1960s, and particularly following the end of the Indochina war and the draft. By the mid-seventies, substantially fewer young people felt that ours was a "sick society," or that the American system was not flexible enough to solve its own problems (189). Radical politics, sit-ins, student strikes, and protest marches virtually disappeared from college campuses. Between 1969 and 1981, the percentage of first-year college students identifying with either the far left or far right dropped by 48 percent, while those identifying themselves as middle-of-the-road increased by one-third to 60 percent (7, 8, 9).

Despite these trends, many privileged youth, and an increasing number of today's adults, express views that would have seemed astonishing in the 1950s, and that at least superficially do not seem to square with the thesis of a sharp decline in alienation and disenchantment with society (1, 8, 9, 13, 39). Thus among America's high school seniors in 1980, only 29 percent felt that big corporations were doing a good job for the country as a whole; courts and the justice system, the president and the executive branch, and Congress fared even worse, with comparable percentages of 25, 19, and 15, respectively (12, 13). Among entering college students in 1981, over 70 percent felt that government was not protecting the consumer, and nearly 80 percent felt that it was not controlling pollution (8, 9). In brief, although there has been a decline in the number of socioeconomically privileged young people expressing highly critical views of our society, the extent of the decline does not seem sufficient to account for the rather marked decreases that have occurred both in political activism and in personal feelings of alienation.

How can we explain this apparent paradox? Several factors appear to have played contributing roles. First and foremost was the Vietnam war. Other unique events of the troubled 1960s—the rise of the civil rights movement, the inner-city riots, the assassinations of John and Robert Kennedy and Martin Luther King, Jr., the abortive war on poverty—all provoked young people into a more critical view of society and its shortcomings, and inspired disenchantment and protest. But the principal factor that sustained the emotional response of many disaffected youth to these events—that lent them a sense of urgency and of personal identification, despite their own privileged status—was the war. As Daniel Yankelovich comments, "The war and the draft forced an intensely personal link between the students and a far-off war which inspired loathing, fear, and revulsion on campus" (189, 8). Once the war had passed (at least for Americans), much of the feeling of urgency and outrage that it lent to other struggles as well—for civil rights; against poverty, discrimination, and hypocrisy and deception in politics and government—declined significantly. In short, this *feeling* of urgency and personal involvement changed more than young peoples' *perceptions* of what they had come to view as serious flaws in our society.

A second factor that played a part in reducing the emotional thrust toward personal involvement and protest was an amelioration of the so-called generation gap. No longer was adult society sending its young almost exclusively to fight an unpopular, adult-determined war. In addition, the subsequent course of political and military events—the withdrawal from Indochina and the startling revelations of widespread deception, conspiracy, subversion of governmental agencies, and criminal violation of individual rights at the highest level—collectively labeled "Watergate"—produced among a majority of adults a degree of disillusionment and skepticism toward government and other aspects of the Establishment comparable to that of young people (37, 114). Adults now concurred with many of the previously dismissed contentions of concerned young people, thus reducing the need of youth to continue trying to persuade their elders of their validity. Currently, a majority of both youth and adults express the belief that the past looks better than the future (190). Since the early 1960s, the percentage of adults having confidence that those running the government are "smart people who know what they are doing" has dropped dramatically—from 69 percent to 29 percent (190).

Other factors also appear to have been involved. One was the impossibility of maintaining a sense of apocalypse for a sustained period, together with a growing conviction that dramatic, comprehensive, immediate social change was not possible, nor even, perhaps, desirable in some respects (22, 37, 39, 109, 114, 189). Furthermore, as we have already noted, cultural and economic conditions were changing significantly; while liberalization of personal and moral values continued, and even expanded, during the seventies and early eighties, the economy was contracting. Inflation, growing unemployment, high interest rates, a national energy crisis, balance of payment deficits and increasing foreign competition in the production of goods, and the future stability of Social Security, became increasingly worrisome (39, 190). The net result of these additional factors appears to have been a reduction in social concerns, a continued emphasis on self-expression and self-realization, and a growing preoccupation with economic concerns—the hallmarks of what came to be known in pop sociology as the "me-decade" (see pages 195–197).

Finally, it is important to note that the prior life experiences of emerging youth in the 1970s and early 1980s were quite different from those of young people in the 1960s and early 1970s. As Richard Braungart has observed:

> Students attending college during the 1960s were born in the 1940s. What made this generation different from previous age cohorts was that these youth were the products of social and historical forces that developed during the 1950s and extended into the early 1960s [see Chapter 6]. . . . Youth attending college in the mid-1970s were different from those of the previous decade in that they did not experience the direct thrust of many of the historic events that took place in the late 1940s and the 1950s. They did experience, however, the dramatic events of the 1960s, in addition to the excesses of radicalism exhibited by youth groups during that period [22, *567–568*].

Regardless of the relative contribution of these and other factors, what appears to have taken place among the current generation of adolescents and youth is an increasing pragmatism and a greater substitution of private for public concerns. Though not enchanted by the state of society and its institutions (as those who mistakenly perceive a return to the values of the 1950s suggest), these young people currently appear less inclined to view issues as one-sided, less likely to believe that social changes can occur quickly, and more skeptical of the ability of the individual to contribute significantly to them.

Although one may be grateful that there has been an apparent decrease in feelings of alienation since the late 1960s, one may also express some regret that some of the best aspects of the activism of the 1960s—its idealism and genuine concern for other individuals and for the world in which we live—seem to have been attenuated in the process. The number of young people actively in pursuit of needed social goals ranging from work with the poor, the handicapped, or the elderly to concerns with the quality of life generally has, if anything, declined recently. Again, those who are involved are increasingly effective, but their numbers are too limited. Society is still in desperate need of fundamental changes, and of young people willing to make long-term commitments without being discouraged.

## A "NEW" ALIENATION?

Although it is too early to tell whether it will expand, or even to define it with precision, a newer form of alienation appears to be taking root, at least among a minority of adolescents and youth, as well as the young adults who have been both the beneficiaries—and, increasingly, the victims—of the "baby boom" of the 1940s and 1950s (39, 190). This newer alienation—more subtle, elusive, and private than the highly public, multifaceted, intense, and strongly articulated alienation and dissent of the 1960s—appears to be characterized by increased feelings of loneliness, a desire for—but difficulty in achieving—intimacy, feelings of rootlessness, a decreased sense of purpose and direction in life, and a more diffuse sense of self (39, 112, 183, 190).

In part, it appears, this newer alienation can be traced to new economic and political realities. Young people growing up in the early 1960s were part of a continually expanding economy, with a promise of ever-greater affluence. Even such sage social observers as David Reisman, author of *The Lonely Crowd* (147), made the assumption that the economic problem of abundance had been largely solved, at least in terms of production, if not distribution (190). Significant numbers of privileged middle- and upper-class young people debated what kinds of jobs might interest them—not whether appropriate jobs would be available to support the life-styles they aspired to (see pages 470–476). However, as we are all painfully aware, in the 1970s and 1980s the situation changed markedly—with spiraling inflation, declining productivity and technological innovation, increased competition in world markets, and, of course, the enormous increases in OPEC oil prices. As Daniel Yankelovich recently observed, "In a matter of a few years we have moved from an uptight culture in a dynamic economy to a dynamic culture set in an uptight economy" (190, *22*). In brief, a society that appeared at the beginning of the decade of the 1970s to offer ever-increasing social, vocational, and economic options to its youth as a consequence of social and cultural change, had shifted by the early 1980s to a society of increasingly narrowed options. No longer could open and expanding career choices, future job security, money for the children's education and a comfortable retirement—or even for the purchase of a home—be taken for granted. A trend study by the National Opinion Research Center recently found that Americans who felt that their lives would turn out pretty much the way they desired were outnumbered almost two to one by those who felt that their hopes and dreams would not materialize; a generation earlier, opinion on this issue was almost evenly divided (190).

Although new economic realities are unsettling and doubtless play a role in this newer alienation, its principal roots appear to lie considerably deeper (39). As we noted in Chapter 6 (see pages 195–197), the greater "freedom to be me," with its emphasis on self-fulfillment, that was a legacy of the 1960s can be a two-edged sword. Efforts to reexamine old stereotypes about personal, family, sex, social, and vocational roles—"to realize oneself"—can be valuable and productive. But without a corresponding commitment to others and their well-being (which for a time, at least, was also a legacy of the 1960s), this apparent victory can soon become hollow. Psychologically, as well as economically, there is, in reality, no free lunch. Regrettably, in the period of the "me-decade," we did far too little to help emerging youth to understand that "self-realization is not synonomous with self-indulgence, that concern for others is a necessary ingredient of concern for self, and that there can be no freedom without responsibility" (39, *1484*).

Achieving a sense of identity is a crucial developmental task of adolescence, as we have seen throughout this book. But as Erik Erikson notes, maturity also requires the development of a capacity for intimacy—a true sharing of oneself with another that involves caring, trust, and sustained commitment—"come rain or come shine." This is especially true in love, but it is also true in friendship; a "fair weather" friend is just that. A recent survey found that 70 percent of Americans—older as well as younger—"now recognize that while they have many acquaintances they have few close friends—and they experience this as a serious void in their lives" (190, *25*).

Furthermore, two out of five state that they have fewer close friends now than they did in the past.

For a small minority, the situation can be poignant—even, at times, desperate. Beginning in the latter half of the 1970s, we have encountered in our work an increasing number of youth and young adults (as well as some older adults) who had gone through a period of personal "liberation," during which they had concluded that they had been unwittingly the victims of roles assigned by others—as daughter, son, lover, husband, wife, friend, even parent. In a number of instances, they had abandoned these roles—and frequently prior community, social, or vocational responsibilities as well—in the initially heady pursuit of "the freedom to live my own life," only to discover a year or so later that "nobody cared" any longer, and that, in the end, what they had been pursuing was not truly freedom, but loneliness.

### A sense of community

Will these trends be reversed? Currently, we are beginning to see widespread efforts to develop a sense of community, as an antidote to the political, economic, psychological, and social isolation that can afflict contemporary life. Increasing numbers of younger—and older—Americans feel a strong need for mutual identification with others based on interests, special needs, and common concerns (32, 39, 190). In addition to the relatively traditional clubs and societies based on cultural interests, sports, hobbies, and ethnic or religious affiliations, we are witnessing a real burgeoning of mutual support groups whose diversity almost defies description: children of alcoholics, parents without partners, widows, new parents, adolescent drug abusers, families with severely mentally ill children, ex-prisoners, patients discharged from

mental hospitals, overeaters, parents of children with cancer and the children themselves, paraplegics, Vietnam-era nurses, abusing parents, abused children, persons
who have had heart attacks or mastectomies, parents of physically or mentally handicapped children, survivors of natural disasters, men over 40 needing jobs, women
seeking careers, gay and lesbian groups, elders helping elders (39).

The President's Commission on Mental Health estimated that there are currently over a half-million different self-help groups in this country (32). There is a
growing body of research indicating that the availability of community support systems, including mutual self-help groups, can have a significant effect in reducing
stress, facilitating recovery from illness, decreasing depression, reducing angina and
ulcers, and fostering feelings of competence and self-esteem (32).

We can only hope that such trends will continue, and that the kind of new
alienation we have seen developing in the 1970s and early 1980s will decline. As the
poet John Donne wrote several centuries ago, "No man is an island, entire of itself."
In the most profound sense we are all—young and old, rich and poor, of all races
and creeds—"a part of the main," a part of each other, sharing, when all is said and
done, the same basic hopes and dreams, and a common final destiny (39).

### Social dropouts

The hippie movement of the late 1960s—with its aversion to social status,
aggressive competition, and material success, and its widely proclaimed emphasis
on "love," personal freedom and self-expression ("doing your own thing"), and
mystical sensory experience (typically aided by hallucinogenic drugs)—has disappeared from the social scene. This does not mean, however, that the kinds of young
people to whom it appealed no longer exist—although their numbers, particularly
within the middle class, have been markedly reduced. Approximately half a million
young people under 17 still run away from home each year (5), and a like number of
17- to 21-year-olds leave home as well. For many of these young people, their
leave-taking is temporary and not indicative of irreversible alienation from parents
and society. For others, however, the break from their previous way of life is serious
and may be permanent. Often included in this group are adolescents who are escaping from perceived rejection by parents, teachers, or peers; who have been abandoned or expelled from home; or who have been physically or sexually abused (2,
23, 126, 128, 129, 159). Many of these troubled young people can currently be
found in the ranks of the street people still encountered on the fringes of som_
university towns and in urban ghettos (119, 126).

Unlike their predominantly middle-class predecessors in the hippie movement,
an increasing number are truly poor (119). The fact that a hippie culture, in its
original sense, no longer exists serves only to heighten their alienation and to leave
them more powerless and vulnerable. In one year alone recently, over 400 teenage
runaway girls from the Minneapolis area of the Midwest were entrapped into prostitution by New York City pimps (126). Indeed, a fifteen-block stretch of Eighth Avenue porno parlors, strip joints, cheap bars, and fleabag hotels is known to the young
hookers—both male and female—and the drifters, pimps, and addicts who populate
it as the Minnesota Strip.

Thousands of adolescent runaways, male and female, have recently become involved in prostitution, including homosexual prostitution, and in pornographic films and magazines, especially in big city areas such as Los Angeles and New York. Many runaways are robbed, physically assaulted, underfed, or lured into drug use and small-time pushing. Their need for adequate human services—health care, shelter, protection, counseling—is often desperate (126). Temporary shelters, such as Under 21 (run by Covenant House), Independence House, and The Door—A Center of Alternatives in New York City (159) make a valiant, often disheartening, effort to protect and assist young runaways, but they are typically understaffed and underfunded in relation to the increasing size of the problems they face (159). While the current administration recently declared the runaway problem an epidemic, it has also moved to reduce federal contributions to such programs by 70 percent.

Other young people have become drifters, moving from the derelict sections of one city to those of another (110, 119). Some are simply defeated by the lives they have led since childhood. Although they may be alcoholic, they are seldom a threat to anyone but themselves; indeed they are more likely to be victims. Thousands of other young drifters, however, are seriously disturbed emotionally, mentally disorganized, and in some cases, violent and unpredictable. Older hoboes and drifters, who used to think of their established haunts as a kind of haven, are fearful of this new breed of drifters.

Fifteen years ago many would have been residents of youth treatment centers or mental hospitals. With the coming of "deinstitutionalization," however, residential treatment centers and state mental hospitals were deprived of funding and are no longer able to provide care. The original aim of deinstitutionalization was supposed to be "reintegration into the community," but adequate funds for follow-up community care and services were never provided in most states and counties, leaving these individuals adrift. Small wonder that mental health professionals have another name for deinstitutionalization these days: "dumping" (27).

***The hippie movement: a postscript***   What happened to the original hippies—the flower children of the 1967 "summer of love in San Francisco"—who are now young adults? Some, of course, returned to the mainstream of society and the life they once renounced. Some became permanent casualties of a once hopeful revolution—victims of drug abuse, freaked-out, drifting endlessly from one bleak "scene" to another, a few are in jail. Many, however, appear to occupy a middle ground, working at part-time jobs, using fewer hallucinogens but more alcohol and sedatives, establishing more enduring heterosexual relationships, but still indifferent to the political and social system.

What differentiated those who were able to rejoin the mainstream of society from those who remain partly or wholly outside of it? In an analysis by Stephen Pittel and his colleagues of a large sample of hippies followed since 1967, subjects were divided into three broad groups: A *reentry* group (those who had ceased all drug use, were back in school or regularly employed, were not transient, and had a stable relationship with another person, usually of the opposite sex, for at least six months); a *nonreentry* group (regular users of more serious drugs, no regular job, unstable relationships, etc.); and an intermediate *semireentry* group. Of particular

interest were the differences in family background that emerged between these groups. Reentry group members scored significantly higher than members of the nonreentry group on measures of family cohesiveness and happiness, participation in shared family activities in childhood, extent and openness of communication, and, most dramatically, on items dealing with their sense of family belongingness and acceptance. In addition, those subjects who had appeared least disturbed, emotionally and cognitively, at the time of the initial assessment, were most likely to have found their way into the reentry group (139).

## ADOLESCENT DELINQUENCY

Despite the attention it is currently receiving, adolescent delinquency is not a new phenomenon (37, 42). Three hundred years ago John Locke, the great English educator, deplored delinquency in much the same vein as we do today. Six thousand years ago, an Egyptian priest carved on a stone, "Our earth is degenerate. . . . Children no longer obey their parents" (91, *840*). Nevertheless, current rates of delinquency are reason for serious concern, not only in the United States, but in most other countries as well.

Delinquency is basically a legal concept, defined in different ways in different times and places. In our society, the term *juvenile delinquent* is generally applied to persons under 16 or 18 years of age who exhibit behavior that is punishable by law. It is also important to recognize that what we call delinquency includes not only the

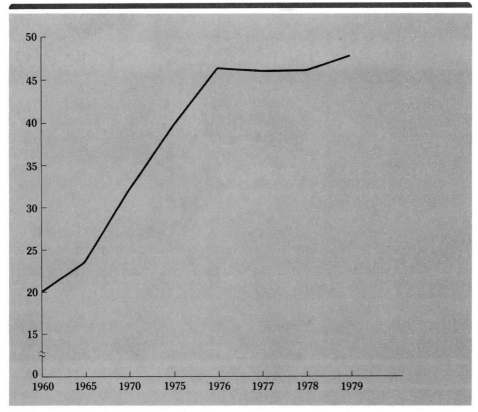

**Figure 14.1** Rate of delinquency cases disposed of by juvenile courts involving children and adolescents 10 through 17 years of age. (From U.S. Bureau of the Census, *Statistical abstract of the United States, 1981.* Washington, D.C.: U.S. Government Printing Office, 1981 [102nd ed.].)

more serious offenses, such as burglary, assault, robbery, and rape, but also "status offenses"— acts such as curfew violation, truancy, running away, sexual activity, or "incorrigibility" that if committed by an adult would not constitute violation of the law.

### Incidence of delinquent behavior

We know a good deal about the incidence of *recorded* delinquency, through various governmental and other compilations (72, 74, 125, 173, 175). After rising rapidly between 1960 and 1976, the delinquency rate reached a plateau between 1976 and 1979 (see Figure 14.1). Whether this relatively steady rate will persist (albeit at a distressingly high level), only time will tell. Even at current levels, recent estimates are that at least 12 percent of all young people (and 22 percent of boys alone) are likely to turn up in juvenile court records before the end of adolescence. Although most delinquents are adolescents when they come to the attention of

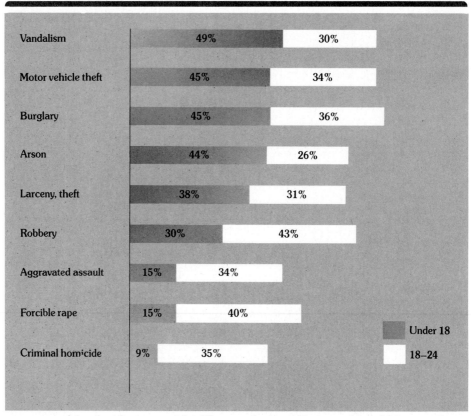

**Figure 14.2** Arrests of persons under 18 years of age, and between 18 and 24 years of age, as a percentage of all arrests. (Adapted from U.S. Federal Bureau of Investigation, *Crime in the United States,* annual; and U.S. Bureau of the Census, *Statistical abstract of the United States, 1981.* Washington, D.C.: U.S. Government Printing Office, 1981.)

authorities, closer examination reveals that for many, delinquent behaviors actually began during middle childhood (41, 69, 70, 72, 74, 153).

Since 1960 the incidence of more serious offenses among young people has been rising at a faster rate than delinquency in general and twice as fast as comparable adult crimes (25, 125, 173). Although in 1980 persons under age 18 comprised only 28 percent of the total population, they accounted for a far higher percentage of many offenses (see Figure 14.2). Furthermore, young people aged 18 to 24, who comprised only 13 percent of the population, were responsible for 35 percent of all serious crime in 1980—a higher offense rate than any other age group (171, 172, 173, 174).

There are clear sex differences in the incidence of recorded delinquency. For many years the ratio of boys' offenses to girls' offenses was four or five to one (72, 173). The most frequent complaints against boys involved active or aggressive behaviors, such as joyriding, burglary, malicious mischief, larceny, auto theft, and, increasingly in the last several years, illegal drug use (particularly marijuana) (59, 72, 91, 173, 175). Girls, on the other hand, were more likely to be reported for such offenses as running away from home, "incorrigibility" (i.e., parental inability to control them), and illicit sexual behavior. It is also interesting to note that according to juvenile authorities, boys were more likely to be apprehended by the police, whereas girls were more likely to be reported to the court by parents (particularly the mother) who asserted that they could not cope with the girl's behavior (41, 19).

In the period between 1967 and 1973, the ratio of girls' offenses to those of boys changed significantly, both in the United States and in other Western countries, such as England (153). During those years, the percentage increase in arrests of girls under 18 in the United States for all offenses was nearly three times that of boys (6, 186). Furthermore, arrests for serious crimes, traditionally more common among males, increased nearly 2.5 times as much for girls as for boys during this period (17.7 percent versus 29.8 percent), although these offenses still continued to occur far more frequently among boys.

As a result, the ratio of boys' to girls' offenses was reduced to about 3.5 to 1. It was suggested at the time that the relatively greater rise in girls' delinquency was at least partially attributable to the fact that girls were becoming more aggressive and more independent in their day-to-day activities (95). It is clear that there was a significant increase among girls during this period in running away from home and increased drug use, often necessitating other crime-related activities, such as shoplifting, robbery, and prostitution (95).

Between 1973 and 1980, however, the ratio of boys' to girls' offenses began to shift back again. Thus, in 1980 boys' total offenses outnumbered those of girls by nearly 3.9 to 1, while for serious crimes alone, the ratio was more than 4.6 to 1 (173). Whether these sex-related trends will continue is difficult to predict at this juncture.

Not surprisingly, reported delinquency rates are also higher among adolescents and youth of lower socioeconomic status, particularly those at the lowest levels, who live in urban ghettos (41, 45, 70, 74, 153, 177).

A number of investigations indicate that at least some of the statistics on reported delinquent behavior may be misleading (11, 71, 72). In particular, it appears that much behavior technically in violation of existing laws either goes undetected, or if detected, is not recorded and does not result in charges filed (21, 55, 72, 153). For example, in one study by Martin Gold and his colleagues (72) an attempt was made to determine the actual frequency of behaviors classifiable legally as delinquent, through the use of detailed interviews with a representative sample of 522 of the 13,200 adolescent boys and girls aged 13 to 16 in a large midwestern city.[1] Repondents reported that police caught only about 15 percent of the 435 adolescents who confessed to one or more chargeable offenses (72). Two points should be noted, however: (1) Many of the offenses included were not particularly serious, and

---

[1] Supplementary use of knowledge informants for validation purposes indicated that approximately 72 percent of young people interviewed acknowledged all offenses known to the informants, and frequently others as well; 17 percent appeared to be "outright concealers," and the remaining 11 percent appeared questionable.

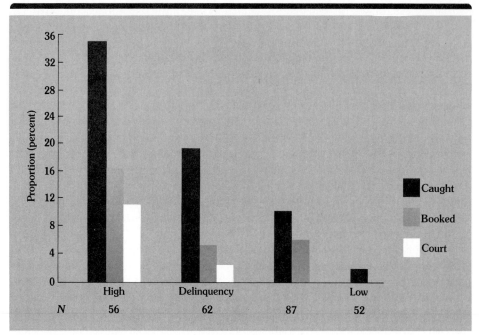

**Figure 14.3** Proportion of boys at each level of delinquency who are caught, booked, and referred to court. (From M. Gold. *Delinquent behavior in an American city.* Copyright 1970 by Wadsworth Publishing Company, Inc. Reprinted by permission of the publisher, Brooks/Cole Publishing Company, Monterey, California.)

(2) adolescent boys and girls with a high level of delinquent activity were far more likely to be caught, booked and referred to court (see Fig. 14.3).

As in the case of recorded offenses, Gold and others have found self-reported delinquent behaviors to be both more frequent and more serious among boys than girls (21, 41, 55, 72, 153). However, unlike the statistics on recorded offenses, girls' self-reported offense patterns did not differ markedly from those of boys by being concentrated in the areas of running away from home, incorrigibility, and sexual delinquencies (72, 74). Indeed, Gold found in his investigation that boys committed such acts almost as frequently as girls. He suggests that a more appropriate question than "Why do girls, rather than boys, commit these particular offenses?" is "Why do girls commit less delinquency of all kinds compared to boys, with the exception of these offenses?"

Despite recent social changes, delinquent behavior generally, especially active or aggressive behavior, is still more strenuously discouraged among girls than boys— not only by parents, but by society and even their peers (52, 77, 123, 153). On the other hand, adolescent girls are, if anything, more affected by family conditions than boys (see Chapter 7), and hence are at least as likely to respond *directly* to unsatisfactory family circumstances through running away, conflict with parents, and sexual behavior. In the last case, other investigators (17, 63, 169, 178) have found much adolescent sexual delinquency on the part of girls to involve an acting-out rebellion against parents or a search for substitute sources of affection, or, in some cases, both. Support for these hypotheses concerning sex differences in delinquent behavior is also found in the fact that most of the more serious and aggressive delinquent acts (e.g., armed robbery) still are committed by boys (153, 173, 174).

**Social class and self-reported delinquency** In contrast to sex differences, there is far less agreement among investigators about the extent—or even the existence—of social-class differences in self-reported delinquencies. A number of studies show considerably smaller social-class differences than do official delinquency reports, and some investigators report finding no social-class differences (11, 21, 55, 75, 82, 153). This has recently led some prominent sociological theorists to conclude that the presumed relationship between social class and delinquency is "a myth" and that significant social-class differences in official delinquency records are due largely to discrimination against lower-class youth by juvenile authorities and society generally, or are the result of inaccurate reporting (21, 55).

A careful examination of the available evidence, however, suggests that the presumed myth is itself somewhat mythical. Many self-report studies, especially those showing few or no social-class differences: (1) are based on small numbers and inadequate sampling techniques, (2) characterize as delinquent such relatively minor acts as cutting classes and disobeying parents (sometimes omitting more serious crimes), (3) employ broad social-class categories, or (4) are limited to nonurban youth (21).

In contrast, significant social-class differences emerge when large, representative samples are used, when urban areas are included, when the focus includes the more serious offenses, and when truly lower-class, socioeconomically disadvantaged adolescents and youth are differentiated from working-class and middle-class peers. Thus, in one recent study (55) a representative national sample of 1726 adolescents, aged 11 through 17, were given carefully structured, detailed interviews. It was found that "predatory crimes against persons" (e.g., sexual assault, aggravated assault, robbery) occurred three times more often among lower-class than among middle-class youth, and "predatory crimes against property" (e.g., burglary, auto theft, vandalism) nearly twice as often. However, generally "victimless" offenses, such as public disorder offenses (drunkenness, disorderly conduct, marijuana use, hitchhiking), status offenses (see page 613), or serious drug use (e.g., hallucinogens, heroin, cocaine) show no significant social-class differences. Similarly (and probably related), black-white race differences were also found—although the size of the difference for crimes against persons was smaller, and for crimes against property larger, than for social class (see Table 14.1).

Still more interestingly, the higher the level of delinquency (number of offenses), the greater were the social-class differences (see Table 14.2). In brief, it appears that there are, in fact, significant social-class differences in crime and delinquency. Nevertheless, a sizable and growing proportion of minor *and* more serious offenses are committed by middle-class delinquents (21, 72, 74, 137). Consequently, theories of delinquency, while they cannot ignore relationships between

**TABLE 14.1 MEAN FREQUENCY OF
SELF-REPORTED DELINQUENCY BY RACE AND CLASS**

| | TOTAL SELF-REPORTED DELINQUENCY | PREDATORY CRIMES AGAINST PERSONS | PREDATORY CRIMES AGAINST PROPERTY |
|---|---|---|---|
| *Race* | | | |
| White | 46.79 | 7.84 | 8.93 |
| Black | 79.20 | 12.96 | 20.57 |
| Probability | ≤.01 | NS | ≤.001 |
| *Class* | | | |
| Lower | 60.42 | 12.02 | 13.50 |
| Working | 50.63 | 8.04 | 9.40 |
| Middle | 50.96 | 3.32 | 7.25 |
| Probability | ≤.05 | ≤.05 | NS |

**TABLE 14.2 PERCENTAGE OF
RESPONDENTS REPORTING SPECIFIC
LEVELS OF DELINQUENCY BY RACE AND CLASS**

| | TOTAL SELF-REPORTED DELINQUENCY | | | | |
|---|---|---|---|---|---|
| | RACE | | CLASS | | |
| NUMBER OF OFFENSES REPORTED | WHITE % | BLACK % | LOWER % | WORKING % | MIDDLE % |
| 0–24 | 71.8 | 67.6 | 71.7 | 72.3 | 70.9 |
| 25–49 | 11.0 | 8.1 | 10.6 | 9.4 | 11.5 |
| 50–199 | 13.1 | 15.4 | 11.4 | 14.4 | 14.4 |
| 200+ | 4.1 | 9.8 | 6.3 | 3.9 | 3.2 |

| | PREDATORY CRIMES AGAINST PROPERTY | | PREDATORY CRIMES AGAINST PERSONS | | |
|---|---|---|---|---|---|
| | RACE | | CLASS | | |
| NUMBER OF OFFENSES REPORTED | WHITE % | BLACK % | LOWER % | WORKING % | MIDDLE % |
| 0–4 | 70.6 | 70.7 | 77.3 | 80.0 | 84.6 |
| 5–29 | 24.1 | 22.7 | 18.2 | 16.1 | 13.8 |
| 30–54 | 3.4 | 2.4 | 1.7 | 2.1 | 0.8 |
| 55+ | 1.9 | 4.2 | 2.8 | 1.8 | 0.8 |

*Source:* D. S. Elliott and S. S. Ageton. Reconciling race and class differences in self-reported and official estimates of delinquency. *American Sociological Review,* 1980, **45**, 95–110. By permission.

| ILLEGAL SERVICE | PUBLIC DISORDER | HARD DRUG USE | STATUS OFFENSES |
|---|---|---|---|
| 1.85 | 14.98 | 1.26 | 14.84 |
| 1.71 | 16.50 | 0.18 | 16.19 |
| NS | NS | NS | NS |
| | | | |
| 2.19 | 14.32 | 1.20 | 14.27 |
| 1.36 | 16.21 | 0.73 | 14.47 |
| 1.56 | 13.81 | 1.37 | 15.66 |
| NS | NS | NS | NS |

*Source:* D. S. Elliott and S. S. Ageton. Reconciling race and class differences in self-reported and official estimates of delinquency. *American Sociological Review,* 1980, **45,** 95–110. By permission.

poverty or social deprivation and delinquency, also cannot be built solely around these relationships (21, 41, 153).

In cases where official statistics show large social-class differences in delinquency, one or more of the following factors may be present: differences in *actual* rates of delinquent behavior, discrimination against lower-status youth by juvenile authorities and society generally, and greater difficulty in finding nonlegal (e.g., parental) solutions to the problems posed by delinquent behavior (41, 72, 91, 153). Not all social-class differences in the way delinquency is treated are the result of discrimination, especially in the case of more serious offenses (21, 41, 55). Although this is undoubtedly—and inexcusably—sometimes the case, in other instances, the motivation is quite honestly the protection of the young person himself or herself (41, 72, 91). It may be, for example, that a lower-class youth will be remanded to the custody of the court because of adverse family conditions (e.g., no stable home; alcoholic, irresponsible, or delinquent parents), while an upper-class youth with a similar offense will be remanded to his or her parents' custody, without formal charges.

## SOCIAL CHANGE, DEPRIVATION, AND DELINQUENCY

Current high rates of delinquency appear to be related at least in part to changes in the structure of society; our increased mobility as a people, with a consequent disruption of well-established cultural patterns and family ties; the increased population growth and social disorganization that has occurred in large metropolitan areas; and the lack of a clear sense of national purpose and concern with social problems. Recent reductions in social programs for the most needy in our society, combined with substantial decreases in taxes and increased benefits for the most wealthy, have increased a sense of deep frustration, even despair, among many of those at or below the poverty level, who cannot feed their families properly, find adequate shelter, obtain even essential health care, and—most critically—find a job paying a minimally adequate wage (121, 145). The recent increase of unemployment among all black youth actively seeking work to more than one in every two should be intolerable in a democratic society.

Interestingly, recent research has indicated that economic deprivation is most likely to lead to crime and delinquency when it is associated with marked inequality in the distribution of society's resources (21). In one study, a number of indices of inequality were used to predict average crime rates on the Uniform Crime Report Indices in 193 cities over a 6-year period. "The income gap between the poor and the average income earner was shown to be a significant predictor of crime rates, while the proportion of the population below the poverty line in the city was not" (21, *48*).

Increases in delinquency, as well as in other adolescent difficulties, appear most likely to occur where a sense of community solidarity and the integrity of the extended family have been most seriously disrupted (e.g., in urban ghettos and in some of the more affluent suburban communities). They are least likely to occur where these ties have been preserved (e.g., some small, traditional, stable, relatively isolated small towns and cities) (24, 25, 36). In the past decade, the greatest increase in the juvenile crime rate has occurred in the suburbs (more than double the urban increase and more than four times the increase in rural areas). Furthermore, within the suburbs, increases appear to be greatest in communities and among families characterized by a high degree of social and geographic mobility and a lack of stable ties to other persons and social institutions (125, 136, 137, 174, 175).

Nevertheless, the absolute rates of delinquency are still highest in deteriorated neighborhoods near the centers of large cities (21, 41, 70). In such areas, which are characterized by economic privation, rapid population turnover, and general disorganization, delinquency is often an approved tradition and there are many opportunities for learning antisocial behavior from delinquent peers (21, 34, 86, 153). Consequently, prior to the 1970s, the steady migration of Americans—particularly disadvantaged, poorly prepared, rural minority-group members—to the central cities was a matter for serious concern. Between 1970 and the 1980s, however, the overall population of the central cities has remained relatively static, while that of nonmetropolitan areas has grown rapidly. It is true that the black population of our central cities increased 13 percent during the decade, while the white population shrank 11.5 percent. However, most of the black increase came from children born to those who were already residents, rather than from in-migration (172). In contrast, among other racial and ethnic groups (principally Spanish-speaking groups and Asians), migration to the central cities increased dramatically during the decade of the 1970s, though their overall numbers are, of course, much smaller (172).

Delinquency occurs about twice as frequently among the children of immigrants as among those of native-born parents (41, 160). Furthermore, among native-born minority groups, it is more frequent among the children of parents moving

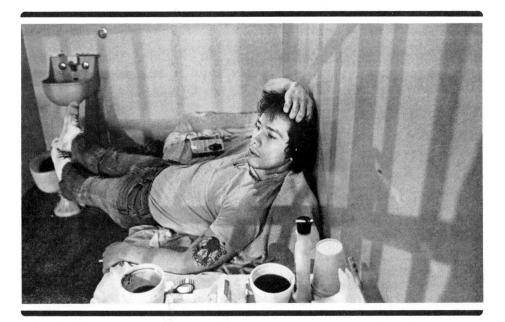

from a relatively simple rural environment to crowded cities than among children of parents already long established in the city environment.

> Children of parents in both groups experience a great deal of conflict produced by the contrasting standards of their homes, on the one hand, and the neighborhood and school, on the other. Moreover, the prestige of these children and their parents in the community may be relatively low [41, 5].

In addition, such families are more likely to live in deteriorated neighborhoods, and thus the children are more likely to be exposed to delinquent practices. Finally, in all too many cases, such parents may themselves lack the knowledge and skills necessary to deal successfully with their environment, and hence may serve as inadequate role models for their children. They also may be too preoccupied or defeated by their own problems to give their children adequate attention (39, 41, 145, 168).

Traditionally, lower-class youth in urban ghettos have been more likely to join delinquent gangs (35, 108, 120, 154, 163). Although these groups were likely to encourage delinquency, the better organized and less violent often helped in meeting needs common to all youth—a sense of personal worth, a meaningful social life and peer-group acceptance (33, 34, 35), and self-preservation (73, 154, 165). Although there appeared to be some decline during the 1960s in the importance of large-scale organized gangs and a rise in small-group and individual crime (166), any such trend has clearly been reversed. Furthermore, contemporary gangs have become far more violent and socially destructive. In a study conducted for the Justice Department, Walter B. Miller of the Center for Criminal Justice at Harvard Law School reported a steady rise in gang activity in the 1970s, particularly in the ghetto areas of our largest cities, such as New York, Chicago, Los Angeles, Philadelphia, and San Francisco. In these five cities alone, 525 gang-related murders were recorded in a 2-year period (120).

Unlike the gangs of the 1950s, which typically relied on such relatively primitive weapons as homemade zip guns, current gangs are likely to be armed with high-quality handguns such as the Smith and Wesson .38 caliber police revolver and semiautomatic weapons. As a result, youth gang violence is more lethal than ever. Although gang members in a number of major cities have terrorized apartment houses and school buildings and killed or wounded scores of teachers, elderly citizens, and nongang youth, 60 percent of the current victims of gang violence are themselves gang members (120). What kind of life is this for a 14-, 15-, or 16-year-old adolescent? In the words of one 16-year-old boy, "Man, I've been on the outlaw trail most all my life. Can't help it. What else you got for me? . . . The only real world is what I got in my hand. Everything else is makeup" (166, *91*). Or in the words of a 14-year-old, "The human race stinks, man. I'm glad I ain't in it" (166, *91*).

Of course, even in high-delinquency areas, many adolescents do not become delinquent. Conversely, many adolescents who are not economically deprived, who come from well-established middle-class homes, and whose parents are neither culturally displaced nor members of struggling minority groups, do become delinquent (56, 74, 86, 153). Indeed, although the absolute rate of delinquency remains lower among middle-class suburban youth, the greatest increase in rate in recent years has occurred in this group.

## PERSONALITY AND DELINQUENCY

Why does one child from a particular neighborhood, school, social class, and ethnic background become delinquent, whereas another, apparently subject to the same general environmental influences, does not? In approaching this problem, investigators have typically used a research design in which delinquents and nondelinquents from the same general background are compared with respect to personality characteristics and parent-child relationships at various ages. The average delinquent scores somewhat lower on tests of intelligence—an average difference of about 8 points (41, 82, 83, 153, 179). When only recidivists are included, the difference rises to as much as 12 points (153). There is also a somewhat higher incidence of mental retardation among delinquents than the population at large. Nevertheless, most delinquents are at least average in IQ (41, 118, 153), and low intelligence in and of itself does not appear to be a primary factor in delinquency in a majority of cases (30, 41, 118). Interestingly, to the extent that intelligence and delinquency are related, the initial effect emerges early; in one longitudinal study (179) when troublesome behavior at ages 8 and 10 years was controlled for, the relationship of intelligence and later delinquency disappeared. Several studies (31, 46, 85) of children adopted shortly after birth have found that delinquency and adult criminality are related to such behavior on the part of the adoptees' biological parents, but not their adoptive parents, suggesting that genetic factors may play some role in increasing an individual's predisposition to develop delinquent behavior (153). However, family and peer relationships, together with other psychological influences, appear to play a far more critical role.

Delinquents have generally been found to be more likely than matched groups of nondelinquents to have attentional problems, to be socially assertive, defiant, ambivalent to authority, lacking in achievement motivation, resentful, hostile, suspicious and destructive, impulsive, and lacking in self-control (3, 29, 41, 47, 58, 64, 70, 74, 76, 153, 170, 179). Many of these traits appear defensive in nature, reflecting impaired self-concepts and feelings of inadequacy, emotional rejection, and frustration of needs for self-expression (3, 41, 42, 73, 79). Delinquents are significantly more likely than nondelinquents to perceive themselves, consciously or unconsciously, as "lazy," "bad," "sad," and "ignorant." According to their own self-concepts, delinquents are "undesirable people; they tend not to like, value, or respect themselves. In addition, their self-concepts are confused, conflictual, contradictory, uncertain and variable" (60, *81*). Although delinquent behavior may increase the young person's conscious self-esteem, it does not increase his or her unconscious self-esteem (41, 74, 153).

As we shall see, the differences between nondelinquents and delinquents in social behavior and personality characteristics are likely to be manifested early in their development, even though clearly defined delinquent behavior may not begin until later.

### *Delinquent boys*

A number of longitudinal investigations have indicated that differences between delinquents and nondelinquents emerge in the early school years and continue and expand over the years (41, 58, 74, 152, 153, 179). For example, several studies have found future delinquents to differ from nondelinquents by age 10 in peer ratings of honesty, troublesomeness, daring, and unpopularity, in teacher ratings of "aggressive maladjustment,"in behavioral problems, and attentional difficulties and school problems (41, 58, 148, 174).

In one extensive study (41), spanning the period from kindergarten through the ninth grade, investigators at the University of Colorado School of Medicine found that by the end of the period from kindergarten through third grade, future delinquents were already viewed by their teachers as more poorly adapted than their classmates. They appeared less considerate and fair in dealing with others, less friendly, less responsible, more impulsive, and more antagonistic to authority. In return, they were less liked and accepted by their peers.

In their schoolwork, they were much more easily distracted, daydreamed more, and, in general, had greater difficulty in maintaining attention and sticking to the task at hand until it was completed. They were less likely to display any special ability or interest. Not surprisingly, these social and academic problems appeared to reflect underlying emotional problems, and in the opinion of their teachers, future delinquents more often came from a disturbed home environment and were considered overly aggressive.

Although this general picture continued into the period covering fourth to sixth grades, some additional differences and some changes in emphasis emerged. Thus, in the middle-school years inconsistent academic performance among delinquents became increasingly evident. They were more likely to be viewed as underachieving and showed poorer work habits. Future delinquents demonstrated less leadership ability and had a narrower range of general interests—although, relatively, they were becoming more and more attention-seeking. On the other hand, resentment toward and rejection of school authority began to differentiate less clearly between delinquents and nondelinquents at this age, "possibly because problems with authority are *generally* more common at this age than among school beginners" (41, *186*).

By the end of the ninth grade, when these boys were entering the period in which delinquent acts are most common, the delinquents manifested differences from their nondelinquent peers in virtually every area of personality functioning and behavior measured through either personality tests or teacher ratings and comments. They continued to display significantly less respect and consideration for the rights of others than the nondelinquents. Not surprisingly, they were much less cooperative in observing school rules and regulations and in meeting their responsibilities as members of a social group. Moreover, at this age the delinquents showed a much greater antagonism toward authority in comparison with nondelinquent peers than was true in fourth to sixth grades. Apparently in the years between middle childhood and adolescence the attitudes of the nondelinquents toward authority improved considerably, while among delinquents they continued to deteriorate.

Peer relations remained significantly poorer among the delinquents in adolescence. The delinquents were less friendly and pleasant toward classmates and, in return, were less well liked and accepted by their peers. In their academic activities, the delinquents continued "to have greater difficulty than their nondelinquent matches. Their work habits were still significantly poorer; they were more careless in their work, appeared more often to be working below their capabilities, and needed much more supervision from teachers. Attendance was more often a problem among these youths" (41, *187*). The delinquents appeared more distractible; they manifested much less capacity for sustained attention, daydreamed more, and, when challenged academically, tended to give up more easily.

In adolescence, the delinquents were rated as less well adjusted generally, more lacking in self-confidence and self-respect, less cheerful and happy, less able to get along with members of their own and the opposite sex, and more attention-seeking. Again, delinquents were much more likely to have a "disturbed home environment" mentioned spontaneously by their teachers as a significant problem. Interestingly, these impressions of poorer adjustment among the delinquents seemed to find support in the reports of the boys themselves, as judged from the psychological testing at the end of junior high school. In the various group tests, the delinquents emerged as clearly less well adjusted.

In particular, they appeared to feel less capable of establishing close personal relationships with either peers or adults, especially the latter. They described themselves as having fewer interests in life, and emerged as generally lacking in enthusiasm. Not unexpectedly, they appeared significantly less impressed by the dominant ethical values and goals of American middle-class culture than their nondelinquent matches. Perhaps somewhat more surprisingly, in the areas of emotional stability, general maturity, and behavior symptomatology, the delinquents also tended to view themselves in much the same way as their teachers had pictured them. Thus the delinquents emerged in the testing as more egocentric, childishly demanding, inconsiderate, thoughtless, and given to petty expressions of pique (although they might not have cared to use these particular labels for the implicit and explicit attitudes they expressed). They also acknowledged feelings of depression and discouragement, mood swings, daydreaming, and oversensitivity more frequently than their nondelinquent peers. And they admitted more often to a variety of somatic and behavioral expressions of anxiety and hypochrondriacal preoccupations. Finally, they also appeared significantly more likely than the nondelinquents to respond to environmental pressures (particularly from parents or other authority figures) with hostility, rejection, or simply withdrawal from the situation, rather than by acceptance, either for their own sake or that of others (41).

### Delinquent girls

Somewhat similar results were obtained for girls, significant differences between future delinquents and nondelinquents becoming evident as early as the period from kindergarten to the third grade. Increasingly, it became evident that future delinquents were significantly less well adjusted socially, emotionally, and academically than their nondelinquent matches. They were less poised and more unstable emotionally; less likely to be cheerful, happy, or friendly; and less likely to possess "a good sense of humor." They had more difficulty in relating to same- and opposite-sex peers. They were less likely to show respect and consideration for the rights of others and, in return, were less well liked and accepted by others.

The delinquent girls also displayed significantly more antagonism toward adult authority of any kind, including the school, and were much less cooperative in observing rules and regulations. At the same time, they appeared to have greater difficulty in learning to think for themselves and in developing a clear set of values of their own or realistic, planful goals. They showed less creative ability generally and fewer special abilities or interests. Their work habits were significantly poorer than those of their nondelinquent peers.

Many of these differences are similar to those obtained for boys. There did, however, appear to be some variations in emphasis. Thus the largest differences between delinquent and nondelinquent girls appeared in the areas of emotional adjustment and conformity; among boys, the largest delinquent-nondelinquent differences occurred in the areas of conformity, creative ability, self-reliance, and relations with peers. Furthermore, though differences were somewhat smaller, negative affect (i.e., feelings of unhappiness, moodiness, humorlessness, and discouragement) differentiated significantly for girls, but not for boys, whereas leadership ability differentiated for boys but not for girls. On self-reports (group psychological tests), many more differences emerged for boys than for girls. This is consistent with the findings of other investigators (78) that delinquent girls are more likely than delinquent boys to be aware of social expectations and to respond on self-reports and psychological tests in terms of these expectations—even though their actual behavior, feelings, and attitudes may be quite different.

## PARENT-CHILD
## RELATIONSHIPS OF DELINQUENTS

A representative national study of the family backgrounds of tenth-grade boys (11) showed that the single most predictive indicator of actual—not simply recorded— adolescent delinquency was the boy's relationships with his parents: "We . . . find a strong inverse association between family relations and delinquency: the better a boy reports getting along with his parents, the less delinquency" (11, *171*). This general finding supports the results of a number of several less extensive, but more intensive, studies of the home backgrounds and family influences of delinquents and nondelinquents (3, 16, 41, 70, 79, 82, 117, 153, 168, 179).

With remarkable consistency, these investigations indicate that the early disciplinary techniques to which delinquents have been subjected are likely to be lax, erratic, or overly strict, and to involve physical punishment, rather than reasoning with the child about misconduct (3, 16, 43, 44, 70, 117, 140, 153). Recent research (131, 132, 151, 175) indicates that a particularly critical factor may be the extent and adequacy of parental supervision. In one recent study in England (175), the family variable most strongly associated with delinquency was "weak parental supervision"—as indicated by such items as not having rules requiring children to say where they were going when they went out, and when they would return home; allowing children simply to roam the streets; and parents' not knowing where a child was much of the time.

Similarly, Gerald Patterson (131, 132) in his work with families of aggressive and delinquent children at the Oregon Social Learning Center (see pages 623–633) has identified four aspects of family interaction as associated with delinquency: a lack of "house rules" (so that there is neither any predictable family routine for meals or chores, nor any clear expectations about what children may and may not do); a lack of parental monitoring of their children's behavior (so that the parents do not know what a child is doing or how he or she is feeling, and tend not to respond to deviant behavior because they have not themselves seen it); a lack of effective contingencies (so that parents are inconsistent in their responses to unacceptable behavior—tending to shout and nag but not to follow through and not to respond with an adequate distinction between praise for positive social activities and punishment for negative or antisocial activities); and, finally, a lack of ways of dealing with family crises or problems (so that conflicts lead to tension and dispute but do not end up being resolved) (131, 132).

Parent-child relationships of delinquents are far more likely than those of nondelinquents to be characterized by a lack of intimate communication, mutual understanding, and affectional identification between parent and child (82, 117, 153, 179). They are also far more likely to be characterized by mutual hostility; lack of family cohesiveness; and parental rejection, indifference, dissension, or apathy (3, 16, 54, 70, 117, 140, 177). Parents of delinquents are more likely to have minimal aspirations for their children, to avoid engaging as a family in leisure activity, to be hostile or indifferent toward school, to have a variety of personal and emotional problems of their own, and to have police records (3, 45, 148, 149, 153). For example, in one longitudinal study, it was found that 39 percent of boys with criminal fathers became delinquent, compared to 16 percent of those whose fathers had no criminal record; other studies have yielded similar results (58, 179).

More specifically, fathers of delinquents are more likely to be rated by independent observers as cruel, neglecting, and inclined to ridicule their children (particularly sons); and less likely to be rated as warm, affectionate, or passive (16, 70, 117, 140). In turn, their delinquent young, especially sons, are likely to have few close ties to their fathers, and to consider them wholly unacceptable as models for their conduct (70). Mothers of delinquents are more likely to be rated as careless or inadequate in child supervision, and as hostile or indifferent; and less likely to be rated as loving (117, 140). Among girls, delinquents, especially recidivists (i.e., repeaters), more frequently acknowledge hostility toward their mothers, and report that their mothers spent less time with them (54, 176).

Finally, in several studies of delinquency, a broken home was found to be significantly associated with a higher incidence of delinquent behavior (3, 153, 182). However, it has also been shown that the likelihood of adolescent delinquency is far higher in *nonbroken* homes characterized by mutual hostility, indifference or apathy, and a lack of cohesiveness than in *broken* homes (usually mother only) characterized by cohesiveness and mutual affection and support (3).

***Adolescent delinquency and adult criminality***  Does delinquency during the years of childhood and adolescence lead to criminal behavior in adulthood? The answer appears to be that it depends on how early delinquent behavior begins, how serious are the offenses committed, how often they are repeated, and the extent to which delinquent behavior is symptomatic of a generally antisocial life style during adolescence (74, 94, 148, 153). Although it is relatively uncommon for individuals to become seriously criminal for the first time in adulthood (74, 148, 149, 153), it is also the case that most adolescents who have been involved in occasional instances of delinquent behavior—even when the result may have been appearance in juvenile court—do not progress to adult criminal careers (41, 74, 93, 130, 149, 153). A number of studies have shown that the younger the age of first onset of delinquent behavior, the greater the number of rearrests (130, 153, 164), the more the delinquent behavior involves a delinquent peer group (130, 153) or criminal activity of parents (148, 149, 153), and the more serious the offenses the adolescent commits (93, 130, 148, 149), the greater the likelihood that delinquent or criminal activities will continue into adulthood. In brief, most adolescents' delinquent behavior has only a modest relationship to antisocial behavior in adulthood; in contrast, "a record of extremely delinquent behavior in adolescence is singularly predictive of adult pathology" (74, *517*).

## SOCIAL CLASS, DELINQUENCY, AND EMOTIONAL DISTURBANCE

Thus far, we have been considering overall differences in psychological characteristics and parent-child relationships between delinquents and nondelinquents. However, a number of theorists (41, 86, 88, 91, 111) have argued that there may be social-class differences in the kinds of characteristics that differentiate delinquents from nondelinquents. One team of investigators, for example, has postulated that "a nonlower-class youth who becomes involved in delinquency is much more likely to be emotionally disturbed than not" (111, *55*), whereas the opposite, they maintain, is the case with lower-class children. The basic assumption here is that delinquency is much less apt to involve norm-violating behavior in lower-class groups, and thus is less likely to require individual emotional disturbance in order to be manifested. They assert that "the preponderant portion of our 'delinquent' population consists of emotionally 'normal' lower-class youngsters" (111, *55*).

A related, but by no means identical, view has been expressed by Adelaide Johnson (88, 89, 90, 91, 92), in her distinction between what she calls the sociologic delinquent and the individual delinquent. "What makes the sociologic delinquent group is that it is largely molded by community and home forces more or less *consciously* in opposition to the whole other social world" (91, *852*). She cites as an example a youngster who grows up in a gypsy society where stealing from villagers is permissible.

In contrast, the individual delinquent's antisocial behavior is seen as stemming not from an untroubled conformity to parental and social norms, but from disturbed parent-child relationships (66, 91). These frequently may include an unconscious fostering by the parents of defects of conscience and related distortions in the child's capacity to evaluate the environment realistically. Johnson cites clinical examples in which "anti-social acting out in a child is unconsciously fostered and sanctioned by the parents, who vicariously achieve gratification of their own poorly integrated forbidden impulses through a child's acting out" (91, *844*).

Other investigators have distinguished between socialized delinquents (similar to Johnson's sociologic delinquent), psychopathic (unsocialized aggressive) delinquents, and neurotic delinquents—although these categories were not directly tied to social-class variables (81, 144, 153). In one study (81), it was found that these groups did, in fact, differ from each other—and from nondelinquents—in terms of parent-child relationships. In general, the nondelinquents' parents were less hostile and power-assertive (see pages 568–570), had more positive expectations for their children, and were less neurotically involved than parents of delinquents. Among the latter, the family relationships of socialized delinquents appeared the most harmonious and stable. Parents of neurotic delinquents tended to be rejecting, highly restrictive, and anxious about any expression of aggression; parents of psychopathic delinquents also attempted to be highly restrictive about their child's activities, but they encouraged aggression outside the home, while suppressing it in the home.

There is little question that many lower-class youth—particularly those living in urban ghettos—are subjected to greater cultural pressures toward delinquency than their more socioeconomically favored peers. But does this mean that lower-class delinquents as a group are necessarily freer of emotional problems than middle- and upper-class delinquents? In a study of a large group of delinquents, Reiss (146) encountered a type of lower-class delinquent youth (the integrated delinquent) who tended to come from a stable family and who did not appear particularly troubled emotionally. Rather like Johnson's sociologic delinquent, he came from a high-delinquency area and simply tended to adopt the asocial values of the delinquent group with whom he interacted. However, Reiss also found another type of lower-class delinquent who would not be likely to be described as emotionally normal. This type, the defective superego delinquent (similar to the psychopathic delinquent described above), was apt to come from a lower-class background, and would not be likely to be described as emotionally normal. This sort of boy typically grew up in a very unstable family marked by divorce, desertion, alcoholism, and/or consistent lack of nurturance. He shows very little guilt about his asocial behavior. He lacks a well-defined conscience and has no set of goals. There is a great deal of resentment toward the social environment and he expresses his anger through his delinquency.

Other investigators (41, 60, 78, 79, 113, 127, 153) have noted widespread signs of poor emotional adjustment and impaired self-concept across a rather wide range of socioeconomic levels of delinquency. In the longitudinal study at the University of Colorado School of Medicine discussed previously, it was found that *both* lower-class and middle-class delinquents emerged as more poorly adjusted than nondelinquents—either deprived or nondeprived. On some traits, at some ages, and at some IQ levels, deprived delinquents scored more unfavorably than nondeprived delinquents, whereas in some other instances the reverse was true. In general, however, socioeconomically deprived delinquents tended to score more like nondeprived delinquents than like nondelinquents, either deprived or nondeprived.

It would appear more meaningful, and probably more accurate, to emphasize the greater accomplishment—emotionally, socially, and academically—of the deprived youth who manages to remain nondelinquent, in comparison to his or her nondeprived counterpart, than to assert that the nondeprived delinquent is much more likely to be emotionally disturbed than the deprived delinquent, or to assert that the latter is generally "normal" (i.e., similar to nondelinquents generally in his or her degree of emotional stability) (41).

## *PREVENTION AND TREATMENT OF DELINQUENCY*

Although a wide variety of approaches have been employed in efforts to prevent or treat delinquency, the results have not been particularly encouraging (21, 55, 153). Counseling and psychotherapy, transactional analysis, institutional treatment in "therapeutic communities," family casework, street-corner youth workers, foster-home placement, intensive community-based treatments, recreational programs, educational and vocational programs, youth service bureaus, or combinations of these and other approaches (health care, legal aid), have not shown widespread success (3, 51, 106, 116, 124, 140, 161, 187). It should be noted, however, that most approaches—even those attempting to use a combination of possible solutions—have concentrated largely on young people with already serious problems, and mostly have been a matter of too little and too late. Furthermore, in many studies, when the data are examined more closely, it becomes clear that even the intervention techniques that are presumably being used are of poor quality or are inconsistently applied (107, 153, 161). For example, the effectiveness of a group counseling program cannot be said to have been adequately tested when the counselors are poorly trained and poorly motivated, and when the counseling itself is superficial and haphazardly arranged (142, 143). In other instances, studies are frequently so poorly designed that valid conclusions about the meaning of the findings—even where favorable—are simply not possible (153, 161).

On the other hand, there is considerable evidence that imprisonment in traditional "correctional" institutions generally only makes matters worse by subjecting the young person to psychologically traumatic and embittering experiences, frequently including sexual and physical abuse, while providing little or no psychological, educational, or vocational help, and by serving as "finishing" schools for future criminal behavior (96, 141, 181, 185). Not surprisingly, perhaps, reconviction rates among those previously institutionalized generally run between 60 and 70 percent (153).

Although there are clearly instances where institutionalization may be the only practical alternative, particularly for violent or "professional" offenders, in many instances suspended sentences, official and unofficial probation, and formal police warnings are at least as effective in terms of recidivism rates. Indeed, several studies indicated that for first offenders, such noncustodial alternatives resulted in somewhat lower reconviction rates (51, 153).

Nevertheless, in many states, where juvenile courts have wide discretion in dealing with juvenile offenders, without the strict rule of law and constitutional due process required in adult jurisdictions, many adolescents who have committed only status offenses are institutionalized. Thus, in a national study of 722 institutions, conducted by the Law Enforcement Assistance Administration (LEAA) in the 1970s, two-thirds of the girls and one-third of the boys were confined solely because of status offenses. Many of the girls were institutionalized only for sexual activity (185).

Ironically, in contrast, because of the organizational chaos, underfunding and understaffing of the court system for juveniles in large metropolitan areas, such as New York City—and in some instances, anomalies of the laws regarding juveniles—many adolescents and youth who have committed repeated violent offenses serve little or no time in correctional institutions (96).

In Chicago, for example, Johnny, a 16-year-old with a long record of arrests for assault, lured a motorist into an alley, drew a .22 caliber pistol, and killed him with six shots. Johnny was arrested, but released when witnesses failed to show up (191). In New York, a 15-year-old boy recalled why he shot "a dude." "Wasn't nothin'. I didn't think about it. If I had to kill him, I just had to kill him. That's the way I look at it, 'cause I was young. The most I could have got then is 18 months" (191, 19). Such incongruities in the present system of juvenile justice—or injustice—led Senator Edward Kennedy, Chairman of the Senate Judiciary Committee, to comment ironically: "If juveniles want to get locked up, they should skip school, run away from home or be deemed 'a problem.' If they want to avoid jail, they are better off committing a robbery or burglary" (96, 58).

Currently, this situation has also led the Juvenile Justice Standards Project of the American Bar Association, after a decade of research, to conclude that juvenile courts, like all other courts, should be bound by the rule of law (96). Acts that would be crimes if committed by adults should be handled in a similar fashion. In the view of Irving R. Kaufman, County Judge of the U.S. Court of Appeals in New York, "Children whose actions do not amount to adult crimes—should be dealt with outside the judicial system" (96, 58).

## THE VIOLENT WORLD OF PEEWEE BROWN

Harold (Peewee) Brown was born on September 24, 1961, the son of an unemployed alcoholic who left his wife when Peewee was 7 months old and who died when the boy was 14. Peewee's mother, Louise, an articulate woman with a high school education, always worked to support herself and her three sons. She had to be at her job by 8 a.m., so she left them alone at home at 7 a.m. and did not return until 5 p.m. Often, she conceded, she did not know what they were doing while she was gone.

"I told them at school, 'When he gets bad, get your stick,'" Mrs. Brown recalled. "I'd tell them, 'You're the kid's mother and father when you're in school. I can't be there. Whomp his behind. . . .'"

There were many at school who tried to help Peewee. He saw psychologists, was assigned to dedicated teachers, and eventually was sent to a special public school. But his violence only increased. He said it was not uncommon for him to stab someone who had inadvertently hurt his feelings and that he once negotiated the price of a sandwich with one of his many guns.

In the very beginning, there was a tug of war between the world of school and that of the streets, but anyone who ever taught Peewee knew which side would win.

"We knew when he was here he was going to kill somebody and that there was nothing we could do to help him," said Coy Cox, the principal of Public School 369, the special school to which Peewee was sent in the sixth grade.

### A MURDERER AT 13

Over a 4-year period, from the age of 11 to 15, Peewee was arrested fifteen times on charges ranging from sodomy to assault, although the school system—for reasons of confidentiality—was never informed.

He now admits that those arrests were for only a small number of his crimes. For example, he said, when he was 13 he shot and killed a man on a deserted street corner in Brooklyn, but was never caught. He added that he seriously wounded at least six others and committed countless other robberies.

But even those few times he was caught, Peewee went free. Each time he was arrested, Family Court routinely dismissed the charge or put him on probation, releasing him back into his mother's custody in an absurd cycle of crime, capture, and release that continued until, at the age of 15, Peewee shot and killed a Brooklyn grocer.

Just 3 weeks before, according to court and school records, Peewee had been arrested for having taken a loaded revolver to school. Because Family Court records are sealed, it is impossible to know the court's rationale in disposing of the gun case or any of the others.

"All they would do is send him back," said Mrs. Brown, a 41-year-old frame-maker who to this day remains confused by the leniency with which her son was repeatedly treated. "They didn't punish him. I told them: 'He keeps getting into trouble. There should be somewhere he can go.' All they did was send him back to me."

The last time, however, Peewee didn't come back home. Now 20, he has been in prison 5 years for the murder of the Brooklyn grocer.

*Source:* Dena Kleiman. The violent world of Peewee Brown. *The New York Times,* Sunday, February 28, 1982, 1, 22. By permission.

### Behavioral methods

Currently, behavioral approaches appear to have the greatest promise for treatment of delinquency (153). "The basic assumptions underlying these approaches are that behavior is a response to factors in the environment and that behavior may be modified by its consequences" (153). Most frequently employed have been techniques of *operant learning* or *behavior modification* (often in the form of a token economy) in which appropriate behavior is systematically rewarded and inappropriate, negative behavior consistently results either in a lack of reward or unpleasant consequences, such as a temporary loss of some privileges (see pages 38–40). Other behavioral approaches have included observational learning techniques and desensitization (see pages 42–43). Behavioral methods may be applied in an institutional setting, such as a residential treatment center or a correctional institution, in school or community programs, or in the family. Regardless of the setting, however, "an individualized problem-solving approach to intervention is central—meaning that the intervention is planned on the basis of a detailed *functional analysis* of how the individual's behavior is affected by the environment *in actuality* (rather than on the basis of theoretical assumptions)" (153).

***Institutional applications*** One of the most significant developments recently in the application of behavioral approaches to the treatment of delinquents involves placement in small community-based group homes under skilled direction (14, 61, 135). The warm, intimate homelike atmosphere stands in marked contrast to the cold sterility of the typical training school and permits close individual attention and supervision. In one such home, Achievement Place, six to eight boys at a time lived with two professional teaching parents (61, 135). Personal interaction and parental warmth were combined with a token economy approach wherein progress in assumption of personal and social responsibility was reinforced with increasing privileges. Achievement Place boys, when compared with similar adolescents placed on probation or in a traditional training school, showed markedly lower rates of recidivism, higher school attendance, and better grades, at least in the short run. How effective this program will prove over the longer term remains to be seen (105, 153). This experiment also demonstrated the crucial importance of an elusive variable—the quality of the caretakers; when the program was repeated, with the same structure but with colder, less understanding "parents," the success rate dropped significantly (135).

In addition to such attempts to apply behavioral principles to overall institutions, efforts have also been made to employ behavioral principles to individuals within an institutional setting (10, 28, 150, 156). In one such project (156, 157), the principal focus was on training social skills, such as those needed in applying for a job, in resisting peer pressures to engage in delinquent behavior, in personal problem solving, and in planning ahead. Strong emphasis was placed on developing behavioral skills that would be widely applicable in everyday life. Modeling, role playing, and rehearsing future behaviors in problem situations were among the techniques used. Five years later, youth who had participated in this program while in the institution had a recidivism rate of 23 percent, compared to 48 percent—or more than double—for control individuals who had not been part of the program while they were at the institution (156, 157).

***Family interactions*** Still other behavioral approaches have focused on family interventions (153). In one carefully designed series of investigations, Gerald Patterson and his collegues at the Oregon Social Learning Center have employed a behaviorally oriented parental training program (131, 133). Parents are helped to use positive, noncoercive methods of control; to interact more positively as a family; to monitor their children's activities better, and to deal more decisively with deviant behavior. They are shown how to negotiate behavioral contracts with the children; and to develop improved social problem-solving skills. Detailed observations of parental behavior, child behavior, and parent-child interactions in the home are made.

While these carefully worked out procedures have been found to be remarkedly effective in the treatment of overly aggressive children, they appear to have less lasting effects on delinquents. Thus a follow-up study of 28 families of children involved in stealing who had completed the training program found an impressive reduction in stealing at end of treatment; however, by the end of the first year, many children had reverted to their pretreatment stealing behavior patterns (132). Another study (4) of young people referred by the courts primarily for status offenses (e.g., truancy, running away, ungovernable behavior) compared the relative effectiveness of three treatment programs: a behavioral approach aimed at improving family communication (and including behavioral contracts), family therapy discussions but without behavioral techniques, and a no-treatment group. Over a 6- to 18-month follow-up period, overall recidivism rates for the three groups were 26 percent, 57 percent, and 50 percent, respectively; when only actual criminal offenses were considered, the comparable figures were 17 percent, 21 percent, and 27 percent.

In brief, behavioral interventions currently appear to "offer the greatest promise of effective methods of dealing with delinquent behavior" (153, *372*). However, several points need to be stressed. It appears clear that significant short-term effects can often be achieved in a particular treatment setting, whether in a residential treatment center, a group home, or a family. To that extent, as the English psychiatrist Michael Rutter notes, "the claim that 'nothing works' is clearly misleading. There are methods that have, at least, a limited degree of success in affecting delinquent behavior. The problem is not so much in bringing about change as in *wanting* change" (153, *373*). Too often, for example, a young person appears to make real progress in modifying self-defeating, delinquent behavior in favor of a more socially adaptive behavior while in a treatment-oriented residential facility, only to regress when returned to the home and neighborhood in which the delinquent behavior originally developed.

Several implications appear to emerge rather clearly from current research. One is that in the long run, prevention or intervention efforts have little prospect of significant success unless they include a major emphasis on changing the child's or adolescent's home environment and existing patterns of parent-child relationships. Another is that in most instances, efforts to help the delinquent directly need "to be concerned with improving his social problem-solving skills and social competence generally, rather than just seeking to suppress deviant behavior" (153, *373*). Furthermore, such efforts will have to begin early in life, and will have to be part of a much larger program of comprehensive psychological and physical care, education, and training directed toward optimal development.

For some, such goals can be realistic ones. But for many other young people, especially the members of an expanding underclass, growing up—if that is the correct term—in deteriorated urban slums, with defeated, neglectful, or abusing parents (or no parents), more fundamental social changes will have to come first. In the last analysis, delinquency is not a disease, but a symptom of more fundamental problems—social, psychological, economic, educational, vocational, physical (e.g., health care, nutrition), and even philosophical. And the chances for success of patchwork approaches—of attempts to salvage particular groups of children—appear destined to be limited so long as our society, despite pious rhetoric on the part of political leaders, does little to ameliorate the social conditions that are the breeding ground of delinquency: poverty, urban decay, ethnic and socioeconomic discrimination, the breakdown of an effective sense of community among all classes of citizens, increasing paralysis of fundamental social institutions, and ever-increasing demands on today's isolated nuclear families. Without a sense of real commitment to attacking such problems, the rate of delinquency, already staggering, appears likely to rise still higher.

### REFERENCES

1. Abramowitz, S. I., & Nassi, A. J. Keeping the faith: Psychosocial correlates of activism persistence into middle adulthood. *Journal of Youth and Adolescence,* 1981, **10,** 507–523.
2. Adams, G. R., & Munro, G. Portrait of the North American runaway: A critical review. *Journal of Youth and Adolescence,* 1979, **8,** 359–373.
3. Ahlstrom, W. M., & Havighurst, R. J. *400 losers.* San Francisco: Jossey-Bass, 1971.
4. Alexander, J. F., & Parsons, B. V. Short-term behavioral intervention with delinquent families: Impact on family process and recidivism. *Journal of Abnormal Psychology,* 1973, **81,** 219–225.
5. Ambrosino, L. *Runaways.* Boston: Beacon Press, 1971.
6. *The American Almanac: The statistical abstract of the United States* (Bureau of the Census, U.S. Department of Commerce). New York: Grosset & Dunlap, 1975 (9th ed).
7. Astin, A. Characteristics and attitudes of first-year college students: A 10-year comparison based on data gathered in national surveys of freshmen in 1969 and 1979. *The Chronicle of Higher Education,* June 28, 1980, 4–5.
8. Astin, A. *The American freshman: National norms for fall 1981.* Los Angeles: American Council on Education and University of California at Los Angeles, 1982.
9. Astin, A. Freshmen characteristics and attitudes. *The Chronicle of Higher Education,* February 17, 1982, 11–12.
10. Ayllon, T., & Azrin, N. H. *The token economy: A motivational system for therapy and rehabilitation.* Englewood Cliffs, N.J.: Prentice-Hall, 1968.
11. Bachman, J. G. *Youth in transition, Vol. II: The impact of family background and intelligence on tenth-grade boys.* Ann Arbor: Institute for Social Research, University of Michigan, 1970.
12. Bachman, J. G., & Johnston, L. D. Fewer rebels, fewer causes: A profile of today's college freshmen. *Monitoring the future.* Occasional Paper 4. Ann Arbor: Institute of Social Research, University of Michigan, 1979, 1980.
13. Bachman, J. G., Johnston, L. D., & O'Malley, P. M. *Monitoring the future: Questionnaire responses from the nation's high school seniors, 1980.* Ann Arbor: Survey Research Center, Institute for Social Research, University of Michigan. 1981.
14. Bailey, J. S., Montrose, M. W., & Phillips, E. L. Home-based reinforcement and the modification of pre-delinquents' classroom behavior. *Journal of Applied Behavior Analysis,* 1970, **3,** 223–233.
15. Balswick, J. D., & Macrides, C. Parental stimulus for adolescent rebellion. *Adolescence,* 1975, **38,** 253–259.

16. Bandura, A., & Walters, R. H. *Adolescent aggression.* New York: Ronald Press, 1959.
17. Barglow, P., Bornstein, M. B., Exum, D. B., Wright, M. K., & Visotsky, H. M. Some psychiatric aspects of illegitimate pregnancy during early adolescence. *American Journal of Orthopsychiatry,* 1967, **37,** 266–267.
18. Bay, C. Political and apolitical students: Facts in search of theory. *Journal of Social Issues,* 1967, **23,** 76–91.
19. Block, J. H., Haan, N., & Smith, M. B. Activism and apathy in contemporary adolescents. In J. F. Adams (ed.), *Understanding adolescence: Current developments in adolescent psychology.* Boston: Allyn & Bacon, 1968. Pp. 198–231.
20. Block, J. H., Haan, N., & Smith, M. B. Socialization correlates of student activism. *Journal of Social Issues,* 1969, **25,** 143–177.
21. Braithwaite, J. The myth of social class and criminality reconsidered. *American Sociological Review,* 1981, **46,** 36–57.
22. Braungart, R. G. Youth movements. In J. Adelson (ed.), *Handbook of adolescent psychology.* New York: Wiley, 1980. Pp. 560–597.
23. Brennan, T. Mapping the diversity of runaways: A descriptive multivariate analysis of selected social psychological background conditions. *Journal of Family Issues,* 1980, **1,** 189–209.
24. Bronfenbrenner, U. The origins of alienation. *Scientific American,* August 1974, **231,** 53–61.
25. Bronfenbrenner, U. The challenge of social change to public policy and developmental research. Paper presented at the biennial meeting of the Society for Research in Child Development, Denver, April 2, 1975.
26. Brown, J. D. (ed.). *The hippies.* New York: Time-Life Books, 1967.
27. Bryant, T., et al. *Report to the President of the President's Commission on Mental Health, Vol. I.* Washington, D.C.: U.S. Government Printing Office, 1978.
28. Burchard, J. D., & Harig, P. T. Behavior modification and juvenile delinquency. In H. Leiternberg (ed.), *Handbook of behavior modification and behavior therapy.* Englewood Cliffs, N.J.: Prentice-Hall, 1976. Pp. 405–452.
29. Butt, S. D. Psychological styles of delinquency in girls. *Canadian Journal of Behavioral Science,* 1972, **4,** 298–306.
30. Caplan, N. S., & Siebert, L. A. Distribution of juvenile delinquent intelligence test scores over a thirty-four year period (N = 51,808). *Journal of Clinical Psychology,* 1964, **20,** 242–247.
31. Christiansen, I. O. A preliminary study of criminality among twins. In S. Mednick & K. O. Christiansen (eds.), *Biosocial bases of criminal behavior.* New York: Gardner Press, 1977. Pp. 89–108.
32. Christmas, J. J., et al. Report of the Task Panel on Community Support Systems. In J. J. Christmas, et al. (eds.), *Task panel reports submitted to the President's Commission on Mental Health* (Vol. 2). Washington, D.C.: U.S. Government Printing Office, 1978.
33. Clark, J. P., & Wenninger, E. P. Socio-economic class and area as correlates of illegal behavior among juveniles. *American Sociological Review,* 1962, **27,** 826–834.
34. Cloward, R. A., & Ohlin, L. E. *Delinquency and opportunity: A theory of delinquent gangs.* New York: Free Press, 1960.
35. Cohen, A. K. *Delinquent boys: The culture of the gang.* New York: Free Press, 1955.
36. Conger, J. J. A world they never knew: The family and social change. *Daedalus,* Fall 1971, 1105–1138.
37. Conger, J. J. Where have all the flowers gone? Adolescents and social change, 1965–1975. Paper presented at the annual Gold Medal Award Conference, Mt. Airy Psychiatric Foundation, Denver, March 1, 1975.
38. Conger, J. J. Roots of alienation. In B. Wolman (ed.), *International encyclopedia of neurology, psychiatry, psychoanalysis and psychology.* New York: McGraw-Hill, 1976.
39. Conger, J. J. Freedom and commitment: Families, youth and social change. *American Psychologist,* 1981, **36,** 1475–1484.

40. Conger, J. J. Youth needs "a stable future." *U.S. News & World Report,* July 5, 1982, **93,** 50.
41. Conger, J. J., & Miller, W. C. *Personality, social class, and delinquency.* New York: Wiley, 1966.
42. Conger, J. J., Miller, W. C., & Walsmith, C. R. Antecedents of delinquency, personality, social class and intelligence. In P. H. Mussen, J. J. Conger, & J. Kagen (eds.), *Readings in child development and personality.* New York: Harper & Row, 1965.
43. Craig, M. M., & Glick, S. J. Ten years' experience with the Glueck Social Prediction Table. *Crime and Delinquency,* 1963, **9,** 249–261.
44. Craig, M. M., & Glick, S. J. *A manual of procedures for application of the Glueck Prediction Table.* New York: New York City Youth Board, 1964.
45. Cressey, D. R., & Ward, D. A. *Delinquency, crime, and social process.* New York: Harper & Row, 1969.
46. Crowe, R. R. An adoption study of antisocial personality. *Archives of General Psychiatry,* 1974, **31,** 785–791.
47. Davids, A., & Falkof, B. B. Juvenile delinquents then and now: Comparison of findings from 1959 and 1974. *Journal of Abnormal Psychology,* 1975, **84,** 161–164.
48. Dempsey, D. Bruno Bettelheim is Dr. No. *New York Times Magazine,* January 11, 1970, 22ff.
49. Derbyshire, R. L. Adolescent identity crisis in urban Mexican Americans in East Los Angeles. In E. B. Brody (ed.), *Minority group adolescents in the United States.* Baltimore: Williams & Wilkins, 1968. Pp. 157–204.
50. Deutsch, M., Katz, I., & Jensen, A. R. (eds.). *Social class, race and psychological development.* New York: Holt, Rinehart and Winston, 1968.
51. Dixson, M. C., & Wright, W. E. *Juvenile delinquency prevention programs: An evaluation of policy-related research on the effectiveness of prevention programs.* Nashville, Tenn.: Office of Education Services, Peabody College for Teachers, 1975.
52. Douvan, E. A., & Adelson, J. *The adolescent experience.* New York: Wiley, 1966.
53. Dullea, G. Child prostitution: Causes are sought. *New York Times,* September 4, 1979, C-11.
54. Duncan, P. Parental attitudes and interactions in delinquency. *Child Development,* 1971, **42,** 1751–1765.
55. Elliott, D. S., & Ageton, S. S. Reconciling race and class differences in self-reported and official estimates of delinquency. *American Sociological Review,* 1980, **45,** 95–110.
56. Empey, L. T. Delinquency theory and recent research. *Journal of Research in Crime and Delinquency,* 1967, **4,** 27–42.
57. Erikson, E. H. *Identity: Youth and crisis.* New York: Norton, 1968.
58. Farrington, D. P., Biron, L., & LeBlanc, M. Personality and delinquency in London and Montreal. In J. C. Gunn & D. P. Farrington (eds.), *Abnormal offenders: Delinquency and the criminal justice system.* New York: Wiley, 1982.
59. Federal Bureau of Investigation, U.S. Department of Justice. *Uniform Crime Reports, 1960–1972.* Washington, D.C.: U.S. Government Printing Office, 1973.
60. Fitts, W. H., & Hammer, W. T. *The self-concept and delinquency.* Nashville: Nashville Mental Health Center (Research monograph No. 1), 1969.
61. Fixsen, D. L., Phillips, E. L., & Wolf, M. M. Achievement Place: Experiments in self government with predelinquents. *Journal of Applied Behavioral Analysis,* 1973, **6,** 31–49.
62. Flacks, R. The liberated generation: An exploration of the roots of student protest. *Journal of Social Issues,* 1967, **22,** 52–75.
63. Fleck, S. Pregnancy as a symptom of adolescent maladjustment. *International Journal of Social Psychiatry,* 1956, **2,** 118–131.
64. Fodor, E. M. Delinquency and susceptibility to social influence among adolescents as a function of level of moral development. *Journal of Social Psychology,* 1972, **86,** 257–260.
65. Fromm, E. *The sane society.* New York: Fawcett, 1955.

66. Gallenkamp, C. R., & Rychlak, J. F. Parental attitudes of sanction in middle-class male adolescents. *Journal of Social Psychology,* 1968, **75,** 255–260.

67. Gallup, G. Gallup youth survey. *Denver Post,* February 12, 1978, 36.

68. Gillis, J. R. *Youth and history.* New York: Academic Press, 1974.

69. Glueck, S., & Glueck, E. T. *One thousand juvenile delinquents.* Cambridge, Mass.: Harvard University Press, 1934.

70. Glueck, S., & Glueck, E. T. *Unraveling juvenile delinquency.* New York: Commonwealth Fund, 1950.

71. Gold, M. Undetected delinquent behavior. *Journal of Research on Crime and Delinquency,* 1966, **3,** 27–46.

72. Gold, M. *Delinquent behavior in an American city.* Monterey, Calif.: Brooks/Cole, 1970.

73. Gold, M., & Mann, D. Delinquency as defense. *American Journal of Orthopsychiatry,* 1972, **42,** 463–479.

74. Gold, M., & Petronio, R. J. Delinquent behavior in adolescence. In J. Adelson (ed.), *Handbook of adolescent psychology.* New York: Wiley, 1979.

75. Gold, M., & Reimer, D. J. *Changing patterns of delinquent behavior among American 13 to 16 years old—1972.* Report No. 1 of the National Survey of Youth, 1972. Ann Arbor: Institute for Social Research, University of Michigan, 1974.

76. Goldberg, L., & Guilford, J. S. Delinquent values: It's fun to break the rules. *Proceedings, 80th Annual Convention of the American Psychological Association,* 1972, **7,** 237–238.

77. Grosser, G. H. *Juvenile delinquency and contemporary American sex roles.* Unpublished doctoral dissertation. Harvard University, 1951.

78. Hathaway, S. R., & Monachesi, E. D. (eds.). *Analyzing and predicting juvenile delinquency with the MMPI.* Minneapolis: University of Minnesota Press, 1953.

79. Healy, W., & Bronner, A. F. *New light on delinquency and its treatments.* New Haven, Conn.: Yale University Press, 1936.

80. Hegel, G. W. F. *Phenomenologie des Geistes.* J. Hoffmeister (ed.). Hamburg: Meiner, 1952 (6th ed.).

81. Hetherington, E. M., Stouwie, R., & Ridberg, E. H. Patterns of family interaction and child rearing attitudes related to three dimensions of juvenile delinquency. *Journal of Abnormal Psychology,* 1971, **77,** 160–176.

82. Hirschi, T. *Causes of delinquency.* Berkeley: University of California, 1969.

83. Hirschi, T., & Hindelang, M. J. Intelligence and delinquency: A revisionist review. *American Sociological Review,* 1977, **42,** 571–587.

84. Horney, K. *Neurosis and human growth.* New York: Norton, 1950.

85. Hutchings, B., & Mednick, S. A. Registered criminality in the adoptive and biological parents of registered male adoptees. In S. A. Mednick, F. Schulsinger, J. Higgens, & B. Bell (eds.), *Genetics, environment and psychopathology.* Amsterdam: North-Holland, 1974. Pp. 215–227.

86. Jensen, G. F. Parents, peers, and delinquent action: A test of the differential association perspective. *American Journal of Sociology,* 1973, **78,** 562–575.

87. Jesness, C. F., Allison, T., McCormick, P., Wedge, P., & Young, M. *Cooperative behavior demonstration project.* Sacramento: California Youth Authority, 1975.

88. Johnson, A. M. Sanctions of superego lacunae of adolescents. In K. R. Eissler (ed.), *Searchlights on delinquency.* New York: International Universities Press, 1949. Pp. 225–245.

89. Johnson, A. M. Some etiological aspects of repression, guilt, and hostility. *Psychoanalytic Quarterly,* 1951, **20,** 511.

90. Johnson, A. M. Collaborative psychotherapy: Team setting. In M. Heinman (ed.), *Psychoanalysis and social work.* New York: International Universities Press, 1953. Pp. 79–108.

91. Johnson, A. M. Juvenile delinquency. In S. Arieti (ed.), *American handbook of psychiatry.* New York: Basic Books, 1959. Pp. 840–856.

92. Johnson, A. M., & Szurek, S. A. The genesis of antisocial acting out in children and adults. *Psychoanalytic Quarterly*, 1952, **21**, 233.

93. Johnston, L. D., O'Malley, P. M., & Eveland, L. K. Drugs and delinquency: A search for causal connections. In D. B. Kandel (ed.), *Longitudinal research on drug use: Empirical findings and methodological issues.* Washington, D.C.: Hemisphere, 1978. Pp. 137–156.

94. Johnston, L. D., O'Malley, P. M., & Eveland, L. K. Drugs and delinquency: A search for causal connections. In D. B. Kandel (ed.), *Longitudinal research on drug use: Empirical findings and methodological issues.* Washington, D.C.: Hemisphere, 1978. Pp. 469–474.

95. *Juvenile Court Statistics 1970.* Washington, D.C.: National Center for Social Statistics, U.S. Department of Health, Education and Welfare, 1972.

96. Kaufman, I. R. Juvenile justice: A plea for reform. *New York Times Magazine,* October 14, 1979, 42–60.

97. Keniston, K. *The uncommitted: Alienated youth in American society.* New York: Dell, 1960.

98. Keniston, K. *Young radicals: Notes on committed youth.* New York: Harcourt Brace Jovanovich, 1968.

99. Keniston, K. The agony of the counter-culture. *Yale Alumni Magazine,* October 1971, 10–13.

100. Keniston, K. *Youth and dissent.* New York: Harcourt Brace Jovanovich, 1971.

101. Kerpelman, L. C. Student political activism and ideology. *Journal of Counseling Psychology,* 1969, **16,** 8–13.

102. Kerpelman, L. C. Student activism and ideology in higher education institutions. Unpublished manuscript, Department of Psychology, University of Massachusetts, 1971.

103. Kerpelman, L. C. *Activists and nonactivists: A psychological study of American college students.* New York: Behavioral Publications, 1972.

104. Kessner, D. S., et al. *Infant death: An analysis by maternal risk and health care.* Washington, D.C.: Institute of Medicine, National Academy of Sciences, 1973.

105. Kirigin, K. A., Wolf, M. M., Braukman, C. J., Fixsen, D. L., & Phillips, E. L. Achievement Place: A preliminary outcome evaluation. In J. S. Stumphauzer (ed.), *Progress in behavior therapy with delinquents.* Springfield, Ill.: Thomas, 1979. Pp. 118–145.

106. Klein, M. W. The Ladino Hills Project. In M. W. Klein (ed.), *Street gangs and street workers.* Englewood Cliffs, N.J.: Prentice-Hall, 1971. Pp. 238–314.

107. Klein, M. W. Deinstitutionalization and diversion of juvenile offenders: A litany of impediments. In N. Morris & M. Tonry (eds.), *Crime and justice: An annual review of research, Vol. 1.* Chicago: University of Chicago Press, 1979. Pp. 145–201.

108. Klein, M. W., & Crawford, L. Y. Groups, gangs, and cohesiveness. *Journal of Research in Crime and Delinquency,* January 1967, 63.

109. Kreeland, D. E. Youth rebellion of sixties waning. *New York Times,* October 24, 1971.

110. Kreeland, D. E. Uncounted young drifters abandon lives of affluence and responsibility. *New York Times,* April 15, 1981, 11.

111. Kvaraceus, W. C. *Juvenile delinquency and the school.* New York: Harcourt Brace Jovanovich, 1945.

112. Lasch, C. *The culture of narcissism: American life in an age of diminishing expectations.* New York: Norton, 1979.

113. Lefeber, J. A. *The delinquent's self-concept.* Unpublished doctoral dissertation. University of Southern California, 1965.

114. Light, D., Jr., & Laufer, R. S. College youth: Psychohistory and prospects. In R. J. Havighurst & P. H. Dreyer (eds.), *Youth: The seventy-fourth yearbook of the National Society for the Study of Education.* Chicago: University of Chicago Press, 1975. Pp. 93–114.

115. Lipset, S. M. The activists: A profile. *The Public Interest,* Fall 1968, 39–51.

116. Martinson, R. California research at the crossroads. *Crime and Delinquency,* 1976, **22,** 180–191.

117. McCord, W., McCord, J., & Zola, I. K. *Origins of crime.* New York: Columbia University Press, 1959.
118. Merrill, M. A. *Problems of child delinquency.* Boston: Houghton Mifflin, 1947.
119. Miller, J., & Braumohl, J. *Down and out in Berkeley: An overview of a study of street people.* Berkeley: University of California School of Social Welfare, 1974.
120. Miller, W. B. Report to the Law Enforcement Assistance Administration. Department of Justice, May 1, 1976.
121. Morganthau, T. Reagan's polarized America. *Newsweek,* April 5, 1982, 17–19.
122. Morison, S. E. *Three centuries of Harvard.* Cambridge, Mass.: Harvard University Press, 1936.
123. Morris, R. R. Female delinquency and relational problems. *Social Forces,* 1964, **43,** 82–89.
124. Mullen, E. J., & Dumpson, J. R. (eds.). *Evaluation of social intervention.* San Francisco: Jossey-Bass, 1972.
125. National Center for Juvenile Justice, Pittsburgh, Pa.: 1975–1979, unpublished data.
126. *New York Times,* November 14, 1977, 20.
127. Novotny, E. S., & Burstein, M. Public school adjustment of delinquent boys after release from a juvenile corrective institution. *Journal of Youth and Adolescence,* 1974, **3,** 49–60.
128. Nye, F. I. A theoretical perspective on running away. *Journal of Family Issues,* 1980, **1,** 274–295.
129. Orten, J. D., & Soll, S. K. Runaway children and their families. *Journal of Family Issues,* 1980, **1,** 249–261.
130. Osborn, S. G., & West, D. J. Do young delinquents really reform? *Journal of Adolescence,* 1980, **3,** 99–114.
131. Patterson, G. R. *Coercive family processes.* Eugene, Oreg.: Castala Publishing Co., 1981.
132. Patterson, G. R. Some speculations and data relating to children who steal. In T. Hirschi & M. Gottfredson (eds.), *Theory and fact in contemporary criminology.* Beverly Hills, Calif.: Sage, 1981.
133. Patterson, G. R., & Fleischman, M. J. Maintenance of treatment effects: Some considerations concerning family systems and follow-up data. *Behavior Therapy,* 1979, **10,** 168–185.
134. Paulson, M. J., & Lin, T. T. Family harmony: An etiologic factor in alienation. *Child Development,* 1972, **43,** 591–604.
135. Phillips, E. L., Phillips, E. A., Fixsen, D. L., & Wolf, M. M. Achievement Place: Behavior shaping works for delinquents. *Psychology Today,* 1973, **7,** 75–79.
136. Pine, G. J. Social class, social mobility, and delinquent behavior. *Personnel and Guidance Journal,* April 1965, 770–774.
137. Pine, G. J. The affluent delinquent. *Phi Delta Kappan,* December 1966, No. 4, 138–143.
138. Pittel, S. M., Calef, V., Gryler, R. B., Hilles, L., Hofer, R., & Kempner, P. Developmental factors in adolescent drug use: A study of psychedelic drug users. *Journal of the American Academy of Child Psychiatry,* 1971, **10,** 640–660.
139. Pittel, S. M., & Miller, H. *Dropping down: The hippie then and now.* Berkeley, Calif.: Haight Ashbury Research Project, Wright Institute, 1976.
140. Powers, E., & Witmer, H. *Prevention of delinquency: The Cambridge-Somerville youth study.* New York: Columbia University Press, 1951.
141. Prescott, P. S. *The child savers.* New York: Knopf, 1981.
142. Quay, H. C. Psychopathic behavior: Reflections on its nature, origins and treatment. In I. C. Uzgiris & F. Weizmann (eds.), *The structuring of experience.* New York: Plenum, 1977. Pp. 371–383.
143. Quay, H. C. The three faces of evaluation: What can be expected to work. *Criminal Justice and Behavior,* 1977, **4,** 341–354.
144. Quay, H. C. Classification. In H. C. Quay & J. S. Werry (eds.), *Psychopathological disorders of childhood.* New York: Wiley, 1979. Pp. 1–42 (2nd ed.).

145. Reese, M. Life below the poverty line. *Newsweek,* April 5, 1982, 20–28.
146. Reiss, A. J. Social correlates of psychological types of delinquency. *American Sociological Review,* 1952, **17,** 710–718.
147. Riesman, D. *The lonely crowd.* New Haven, Conn.: Yale University Press, 1973.
148. Robins, L. *Deviant children grow up: A sociological and psychiatric study of sociopathic personality.* Baltimore: Williams & Wilkins, 1966.
149. Robins, L. Sturdy childhood predictors of adult antisocial behavior: Replications from longitudinal studies. *Psychological Medicine,* 1978, **8,** 611–622.
150. Ross, R. R., & MacKay, H. B. Behavioral approaches to treatments and corrections: Requiem for a panacea. *Canadian Journal of Criminology,* 1978, **20,** 279–295.
151. Rutter, M. Parent-child separation: Psychological effects on the children. *Journal of Child Psychology and Psychiatry,* 1971, **12,** 233–260.
152. Rutter, M. *Changing youth in a changing society: Patterns of adolescent development and disorder.* Cambridge, Mass.: Harvard University Press, 1980.
153. Rutter, M., & Giller, H. *Juvenile delinquency: Trends and prospects.* Baltimore: Penguin Books, in press.
154. Salisbury, H. E. *The shook-up generation.* New York: Harper & Row, 1959.
155. Sampson, E. E., & Korn, H. A. (eds.). *Student activism and dissent: Alternatives for social change.* San Francisco: Jossey-Bass, 1970.
156. Sarason, I. G. A cognitive social learning approach to juvenile delinquency. In R. Hare & D. Schilling (eds.), *Psychopathic behavior: Approaches to research.* New York: Wiley, 1978. Pp. 299–317.
157. Sarason, I. G., & Ganzer, V. J. Modeling and group discussion in the rehabilitation of juvenile delinquents. *Journal of Counseling Psychology,* 1973, **20,** 442–449.
158. Schacht, R. *Alienation.* Garden City, N.Y.: Doubleday, 1971.
159. Scott, R. M. Coordinating services for runaway youth: The case of New York City. *Journal of Family Issues,* 1980, **1,** 308–312.
160. Sebald, H. *Adolescence: A sociological analysis.* Englewood Cliffs, N.J.: Prentice-Hall, 1968.
161. Sechrest, L., White, S. O., & Brown, E. D. (eds.). *The rehabilitation of criminal offenders: Problems and prospects.* National Research Council Report. Washington, D.C.: National Academy of Sciences, 1979.
162. Seeman, M. Alienation studies. In A. Inkeles, J. Coleman, & N. Smelser (eds.), *Annual review of sociology* (Vol. I). Palo Alto, Calif.: Annual Reviews, Inc., 1975.
163. Short, J. F., Jr., & Strodtbeck, F. L. *Group process and delinquency.* Chicago: University of Chicago Press, 1965.
164. Sinclair, I. A. C., & Clarke, R. V. G. Predicting, treating and explaining delinquency: The lessons from research on institutions. In M. P. Feldman (ed.), *The prevention and control of offending.* New York: Wiley, in press.
165. Smith, D. E., & Luce, J. *Love needs care.* Boston: Little, Brown, 1971.
166. Stevens, S. The "rat packs" of New York. *New York Times,* November 28, 1971, 29ff.
167. Stokols, D. Toward a psychological theory of alienation. *Psychological Review,* 1975, **82,** 26–44.
168. Tait, C. D., Jr., & Hodges, E. F. *Delinquents, their families, and the community.* Springfield, Ill.: Thomas, 1962.
169. Toolan, J. M. Depression in children and adolescents. *American Journal of Orthopsychiatry,* 1962, **32,** 404–415.
170. Tutt, N. S. Achievement motivation and delinquency. *British Journal of Social and Clinical Psychology,* 1973, **12,** 225–230.
171. U.S. Bureau of the Census, Current Population Reports. *Characteristics of American children and youth: 1980.* P-23, No. 114. Washington, D.C.: U.S. Government Printing Office, 1982.
172. U.S. Bureau of the Census, Current Population Reports. *Population profile of the United States, 1980.* Series P-20, No. 363. Washington, D.C.: U.S. Government Printing Office, 1981.

173. U.S. Bureau of the Census. *Statistical abstract of the United States, 1981* Washington, D.C.: U.S. Government Printing Office, 1981 (102nd ed.).
174. U.S. Federal Bureau of Investigation. *Crime in the United States,* annual.
175. U.S. Office of Human Development and Services and U.S. Office of Youth Development, Washington, D.C. 1960–1970, unpublished data.
176. Wattenberg, W. W. *The adolescent years.* New York: Harcourt Brace Jovanovich, 1955.
177. Wax, D. E. Social class, race, and juvenile delinquency: A review of the literature. *Child Psychiatry and Human Development,* 1972, **3,** 36–49.
178. Weiner, I. B. *Psychological disturbance in adolescence.* New York: Wiley, 1970.
179. West, D. J., & Farrington, D. P. *Who becomes delinquent?* London: Heinemann Educational, 1973.
180. Wilson, H. Parental supervision: A neglected aspect of delinquency. *British Journal of Criminology,* 1980, **20,** 203–235.
181. Winslow, R. W. (ed.) *Juvenile delinquency in a free society.* Encino, Calif.: Dickenson Publishing Co., 1976.
182. Wirt, R. D., & Briggs, P. F. Personality and environmental factors in the development of delinquency. *Psychological Monographs,* 1959, **73,** 1–47.
183. Wolfe, T. The "me" decade and the third great awakening. *New York,* August 23, 1976, 26–40.
184. Womack, M., & Wiener, F. A work-study program for socioeconomically deprived delinquent youth. Final report. Washington, D.C.: Office of Manpower Policy, Evaluation and Research, U.S. Department of Labor, October 1968.
185. Wooden, K. *Weeping in the playtime of others.* New York: McGraw-Hill, 1976.
186. *The world almanac and book of facts, 1975.* New York: Newspaper Enterprise Association, 1975.
187. Wright, W. E., & Dixon, M. C. Community prevention and treatment of juvenile delinquency: A review of evaluation studies. *Journal of Research on Crime and Delinquency,* 1977, **14,** 35–67.
188. Yankelovich, D. *Generations apart: A study of the generation gap.* New York: CBS News, 1969.
189. Yankelovich, D. *The new morality: A profile of American youth in the 1970s.* New York: McGraw-Hill, 1974.
190. Yankelovich, D. *New rules: Searching for fulfillment in a world turned upside down.* New York: Random House, 1981.
191. The youth crime plague. *Time,* July 11, 1977, 18–28.

# Psychological and psychophysiological disturbances in adolescence

## CHAPTER 15

# Psychological and psychophysiological disturbances in adolescence

**A**nxiety, frustration, and conflict are part of the human condition, and every young person will encounter some psychological problems in the course of development. Furthermore, there is evidence that psychological problems are more frequent at certain ages than others. For example, referrals to psychiatric and psychological clinics tend to peak in the periods 4 to 7 years and 9 to 11 years during childhood, and from 14 to 16 years during adolescence (7). Each of these age periods represents, in one way or another, a transitional stage wherein accelerations in physical or cognitive development, or rapid changes in parental expectations and general social demands, "give rise to temporary imbalances or maladaptations" (7, 704).

In early adolescence, as we have seen, all these changes are at work simultaneously. Consequently, by its very nature, adolescence in our society involves at least some disruption in whatever psychological equilibrium may have been previously established. There is no doubt that all of adolescence involves major challenges to the individual, requiring change and often stimulating growth (152). The fact that more adolescents than adults report only a low level of happiness suggests that many may experience their lives as too stressful (197). The number of changes required in adolescence, particularly if too many occur at once, may overwhelm the young person. And for some vulnerable young people, any additional stress may be too much. The extent of the disruption experienced by a majority of adolescents, and the difficulties encountered in reestablishing a new, more mature equilibrium, have often been exaggerated (see Chapter 1); nevertheless, psychological and psychophysiological disturbances of varying degrees of severity do occur in a significant minority of young people. How severe a particular individual adolescent's disturbance will be, the form it will take, and the time it will occur will depend on many factors, including the relative success of his or her prior childhood adjustment efforts and the extent of the stresses encountered during the adolescent years. For some adolescents, the disturbance may be relatively minor and transient; for others, it may be severe and refractory, leading to crippling neurosis or even psychosis.

The difficult task when attempting to understand adolescent problems, or those of any other age for that matter, is in differentiating an appropriate response to difficult situations from a maladaptive response with serious implications for future development. While an adolescent in a difficult situation can usually be helped with support, the young person who responds nonadaptively may need more intense, skilled intervention. Because adolescents are often adult in size but still childlike in their capacity to deal with new and difficult experiences, they often can prove to be quite disruptive to those around them. Determining whether a symptom or problem in an adolescent is a manifestation of difficulties in dealing with new demands—a difficulty that will eventually be mastered—or evidence of serious disturbance and a poor prognosis, makes differential diagnosis in adolescence a difficult task, requiring not merely general clinical skill, but extensive experience with this particular age group. On the one hand, it is essential to avoid overemphasizing the importance of symptoms that may prove transitory. On the other hand, it is equally essential to avoid dismissing the warning signs of significant and potential chronic disturbance as "transient adolescent adjustment reaction" or "situational disturbance of adolescence" as is too often done (see pages 23–25).

Our aim in this final chapter will be to consider the origins, symptomatology, and prognosis of some of the more prominent psychological and psychophysiological disturbances encountered in adolescence. As will become apparent, although the roots of these disturbances are usually to be found in earlier periods of development, in many cases they become manifest in or exacerbated during adolescence (171). For example, eating disorders, such as anorexia nervosa and some kinds of obesity, certain kinds of depression, suicide or suicide attempts and accidents, some forms of delinquency, and schizophrenia are all more likely to emerge during adolescence than in earlier periods. Disturbances that were apparent prior to adolescence are likely to be exacerbated by the changes associated with adolescence. In most instances, the emergence or worsening of these disturbances appears to be linked in one way or another to the kinds of rapid physical, physiological, sexual, and cognitive changes that take place in adolescence and that must be successfully dealt with in order to achieve a confident sense of one's own identity as a whole, consistent, separate person. We will also review a number of the therapeutic approaches currently being employed with adolescents, as well as some of the special, age-related problems that treatment of adolescents is likely to present.

## THE NATURE OF SYMPTOMS

Some of the manifestations of psychological problems in adolescence are relatively easily understood. The adolescent whose efforts to establish mutually rewarding relationships with same- or opposite-sex peers have met consistently with rejection or ridicule may become painfully anxious and uncertain in their presence and inclined to withdraw into lonely isolation. The young person who has been subjected to an endless series of injustices or rejection on the part of parents and who, at the same time, has had only harsh, arbitrary, or inconsistent discipline in the course of growing up, and has not developed strong internal superego controls (i.e., a stable, effective conscience), may emerge as angry and destructive—as in the case of some delinquents (see pages 626–627).

It is not difficult to appreciate, at least in a general sense, the transient depression of a bereaved young person who has recently lost a parent, sibling, or close friend; or the acute anxiety and bad dreams of an adolescent who has just been through a terrifying real-life experience. Other kinds of symptoms, however, are not always so easily understood: physically wasting away, as in the case of anorexia nervosa, while still worrying about being too fat; a suicidal attempt that, on the surface at least, seems to have been precipitated by a relatively minor disappointment; acute anxiety, or even panic, that seems to have no source either to outside observers or to the adolescent himself or herself; and psychosomatic symptoms of various sorts.

In many cases, as we saw in Chapter 3, the original source of apparently mysterious or illogical symptoms lies in the adolescent's anxiety about something— fear of loss of love, or separation; of having angry, hostile feelings; of sexual impulses; or of personal inadequacy or concern about having no separate identity of one's own. Frequently, the anxiety also involves guilt, in that the young person's impulses are unacceptable to conscience—that is, to the internal standards that he or she has developed about what is right and wrong, good and wicked. One of the difficulties in understanding such symptoms lies in the fact that the adolescent's underlying concerns are not consciously expressed. Instead, he or she may unconsciously erect psychological defenses against their expression, because allowing such disturbing impulses and feelings to find conscious expression would produce painful anxiety and guilt. As we have already noted, the basic function of the various mechanisms of defense is to help the individual avoid such painful feeling (see pages 64–65). The kinds of defenses people are most likely to employ will vary depending on their individual personality structures and specific learning experiences. A number of defense mechanisms are also likely to be age-dependent. Thus, such defenses as intellectualization and asceticism are more common in adolescents than in younger children because they are generally dependent on a higher level of cognitive development; on the other hand, denial, a more "immature" defense, is more frequent among younger children (see pages 66–67). In some cases, of course, defense mechanisms are ineffective or only partially effective. In such instances, generalized anxiety, either acute or chronic, may result.

## ANXIETY

Anxiety states are characterized by apprehension, fearfulness, and tension, and are often accompanied by psychosomatic symptoms such as muscle tension, sometimes leading to shaking, perspiring, headaches, or stomachaches. Unlike either normal fears of realistically dangerous situations or phobias that are intense and unrealistic, anxiety states may occur under any circumstances and are not restricted to specific situations or objects (6, 143, 212). Every adolescent will inevitably encounter some degree of anxiety in the course of normal development. It is only when the anxiety either is excessively strong and disabling or appears to be becoming chronic that it makes sense to speak of anxiety reaction as a clinically significant disturbance or disorder. Anxiety reactions are more common in adolescence than in middle childhood and their frequency appears to increase in the period between the onset of puberty and early adulthood (33, 183). The most recent diagnostic manual of the American Psychiatric Association emphasizes these major categories of anxiety during childhood or adolescence: separation anxiety, "in which the predominant disturbance is excessive anxiety on separation from major attachment figures or from home or other familiar surroundings" (6, *50*), as in the case, for example, of leaving home to go away to school (6, 212); anxiety aroused by contact with strangers or by social situations, which interfere severely with social functioning with peers (6); and "overanxious disorder," in which the sources of anxiety are generalized and diffuse, and lead to unrealistic worry about future events, preoccupation with the appropriateness of one's past behavior, overconcern with one's competence, and "marked feelings of tension or inability to relax" (6, *57*).

### Acute anxiety

The adolescent with an acute anxiety reaction "feels a sudden fearfulness as if something bad were about to happen to him" (183, *134*). He or she may become agitated and restless, startled easily, and complain of physical symptoms such as dizziness or headache. There may be nausea and vomiting. Attention span may be limited, and the young person may appear distracted. Sleep disturbances are common; there may be difficulty in falling asleep, and sleep itself may be limited and restless, with much tossing and turning, perhaps accompanied by nightmares or sleepwalking (7, 33, 143, 183). The adolescent suffering from an acute anxiety reaction may be puzzled or alarmed about its apparently mysterious source or may attribute it to a wide variety of isolated, external circumstances or incidents. Upon more careful examination, however, it usually becomes clear that far more extensive and more fundamental factors are involved, such as disturbed parent-child relationships, concerns about the demands of growing up, or pervasive fears and guilt regarding sexuality or aggressive impulses, even though the adolescent may not be consciously aware of their role in the disturbance.

For example, an adolescent girl suffered an acute anxiety reaction following a minor automobile accident from which she escaped unhurt (183). In the following several weeks, she suffered from nightmares, complained of being unable to breathe, and became fearful of going anywhere. Obviously, her response was disproportionate to the seriousness of the accident. Upon further, gradual exploration, it was learned that the girl's parents were on the verge of divorce and family tensions were high. Furthermore, it turned out that the girl had recently been upset by the onset of menstruation, for which she had been poorly prepared by her mother. She had also been apprehended with a neighbor boy in sexual play a few weeks before, and was being accused currently by her mother of masturbation because she spent long periods in the bathroom—an accusation she tearfully denied. In fact, she had engaged in masturbation, both alone and with her sisters, but largely because of her mother's reaction, felt guilty and "sinful" about it. Reassurance about her sexual behavior and an opportunity to talk about the difficulties she was having with her mother and about her concerns for the future of the family resulted in a rapid alleviation of the acute anxiety symptoms, although longer-term therapy with both mother and daughter was required to deal with her underlying problems.

### Chronic anxiety

Most of what has already been stated regarding acute anxiety also applies to chronic anxiety. Indeed, chronic anxiety frequently results from acute anxiety that has not been resolved (143, 183). "An important difference between the anxiety reactions of the adolescent and the adult is its immediate relevancy to the causative and precipitating factors. Hence, attempts at intervention and amelioration are potentially more successful with the adolescent" (183, *137*). It is obviously essential to begin intervention while the relevancy of these causal factors is still apparent and can be dealt with, and before chronic anxiety and the individual's response to it (e.g., psychological withdrawal, impairment of schoolwork, continuing physical symptoms such as pains, diarrhea, shortness of breath, and fatigue) become a way of life.

## FEARS AND PHOBIAS

Fears are, of course, not restricted to any particular age group, although they do seem to peak in frequency at around 11 years of age (66). At age 11, specific fears are reported by 40 percent of boys and 52 percent of girls; by age 13 only 4 percent of boys and 21 percent of girls report fears (66). The specific nature of fears, however, is clearly age-related. For example, younger children are more likely to manifest fear of the dark, fear of strangers, fear of animals, and fear of ghosts (101, 142). Although young people may sometimes carry over one or another childhood fear unchanged into adolescence, other fears are likely to emerge either for the first time or in a new form. Many fears arising in adolescence are related to the changing demands of this period (see pages 184–185). The adolescent may have fears related "to growing up, or to meeting new experiences like facing a new peer group, going to camp, promotion in school, or taking a first job" (183, *127*). More advanced cognitive development enables the adolescent to grasp more fully potentially fearful events such as death. Adolescents are also more likely than younger children to have fears related to sexuality, in part due to the common familial taboos about discussing sex between parent and adolescent.

Fears may be either realistic or unrealistic. An adolescent boy with a recurring illness that has frequently endangered his life may fear death. A girl who has been repeatedly rejected by persons close to her may fear further rejections. A young person who has been in two airplane crashes may develop a fear of flying. Such fears are not difficult to understand, and, within limits, may even be adaptive if the person, object, or event feared is, in fact, realistically dangerous or threatening. Other fears, however, are unrealistic and in some cases difficult to understand. Many of the fears held by younger children (about 20 percent) are unrealistic and deal with imaginary creatures, the dark, and being alone (101). Dangerous animals, like lions and tigers, are also frequently named as objects of fear. Interestingly, in responding to questions about their fears, children between the ages of 9 and 12 indicated that they were only moderately afraid of immediate and possible dangers, such as getting hit by a car, but were strongly afraid of remote or impossible events, such as attack by lions or ghosts (55, 142). Unrealistic fears, although less common in adolescence, nevertheless do occur. For example, an adolescent may develop an unrealistic fear of traveling or even of leaving the house (6, 33, 212), or conversely, a fear of being in a confined space.

### Phobias

An intense fear which the individual consciously recognizes as unrealistic is called a *phobia*. When not able to avoid or escape the phobic situation, the individual may become extremely apprehensive and experience "faintness, fatigue, palpitations, perspiration, nausea, tremor, and even panic" (6, *40*).

How can phobias be explained? In general, they can be attributed to fear of some person, object, or event that is too painful and anxiety-producing to be allowed conscious recognition. The fear has been displaced onto some other less unacceptable object or situation, usually one that is in some way symbolic of the original fear. In some cases, the basic source of a phobia may be rather readily apparent to the clinician; in others, it may be difficult to identify. In younger children, because of their less advanced cognitive development and their less complex defense mechanisms, the original source of the phobia is often easier to identify than in the case of older adolescents and adults. For example, fear of attack by ghosts or giants may clearly symbolize unconscious fears of parental punishment. In the case of one adolescent, it was eventually learned that his intense fear of automobiles represented a displaced strong fear of his father (33). In these cases, attempts to reduce the fear of ghosts or automobiles by rational arguments are not likely to be successful. Unlike realistic fears, unrealistic or symbolic fears can best be ameliorated by attacking the actual source of the fear, although desensitization of the individual to the displaced fear through behavior modification techniques may sometimes also be helpful if the displaced fear has acquired independent strength over a period of time (66, 78, 108, 191, 216). Sometimes in such cases, the antidepressant drug imipramine has been found to be helpful in quelling the anxiety, even panic, produced by being in a phobic situation (51).

### School phobias

School phobia—a fear, which may approach panic, of leaving home and going to school—is far more common in younger children but may also occur in adolescents (6, 34, 47, 58, 68, 119, 209, 212). In many adolescents brought for treatment "in connection with anxiety, phobic, and conversion or psychophysiologic reactions (especially headache, abdominal pain, diarrhea, nausea and vomiting), refusal to attend school has been the event that crystallized parental concern" (209, *203*). School phobia in an adolescent is likely to be a precursor of work phobia in adulthood (47, 68, 209).

School phobia should not be confused with the occasional mild reluctance to go to school seen in both normal children and adolescents, nor with realistic fears of going to school (e.g., fear of the class bully, abusive treatment by a teacher). In such cases, the young person is only too aware of the true source of his or her apprehension and of its realistic nature. The school-phobic child or adolescent also has little in common with the typical truant. The truant adolescent usually dislikes or does poorly in school, skips classes on an irregular basis as the fancy takes him or her, and spends truant time in pleasurable activities away from home without knowledge or consent by the parents. "The majority of school-phobic youngsters, in contrast, linger at home with their parents' consent, if not their approval, earn average or better grades, and profess to like school and to value academic pursuits" (209, *205*). Although many problems may be symbolized by a school phobia, it usually indicates a dread of some aspect of the school situation, concern with leaving home, or perhaps more frequently, both. For example, an adolescent boy with unconscious fears of homosexuality may displace "anxiety from a threatening locker-room situation to his previously neutral classroom" (209, *207*). Similarly, the young person who remains overly dependent and is uncertain about his or her sexual identity, or who has fears of heterosexual relationships, may become acutely anxious in school when peers begin to organize their social life around dating, parties, and other heterosexual relationships (209). Children and adolescents in whom concern with leaving home (i.e., separation anxiety) plays a prominent part in their school phobia are frequently excessively dependent (58, 68, 209). Not infrequently in such young people, school phobia may be precipitated by the family's moving to a new home, absence of the parents on a vacation, or an illness among family members (209).

Mothers of school-phobic children and adolescents tend to be threatened by any loss of the child's dependency on them, and many reveal unresolved dependency problems with their own mothers (7, 34, 47, 58, 68, 210). Furthermore, these mothers themselves are likely to see the school as a cold, forbidding place, and to go to great lengths to protect their children not only from it, but also from virtually all the painful facts of existence (110). The child or adolescent, in turn, perceives—at least unconsciously—the mother's real desire to keep him or her dependent and responds accordingly (58). Furthermore, the young person is likely to fear separation from the mother because of both dependent and hostile needs (47, 110). Fathers of young people with school phobias also are likely to contribute to the problem. "In most instances, the father intensifies the problematic mother-child relationship by failing to provide any counteractive balance to his wife's overprotective and fantasizing approach and by undermining her already limited sense of competence" (209, *213*). Some of these fathers are themselves passive, dependent individuals. Others tend to be aggressive, exaggeratedly masculine types, deeply involved in their work or outside interests, and only minimally interested in their families (58, 209). Such fathers are usually not informed enough—or interested enough—to intervene in the maladaptive relationship between mother and child. While there has been little recent work examining patterns of adolescent difficulties in relation to parental sex-role attributes, we expect that research along these lines would now show that issues of self-esteem and the quality of the adolescent-parent relationship would prove to be more important than sex-role and gender-identification issues.

School phobias are equally common for boys and girls (1, 66). It has been suggested that school-phobic children and adolescents commonly overvalue themselves and overestimate their own power and achievements, and then try to hold onto their unrealistic self-image. "When this is threatened in the school situation, they suffer anxiety and retreat to another situation where they can maintain their narcissistic self-image. This retreat may very well be a running to a close contact with mother" (119, *686*). School phobias in adolescents tend to be more resistant to change and to indicate a more serious level of disturbance than is generally the case with younger children (33, 68, 209). This is hardly surprising. For one thing, a greater degree of parental dependence normally characterizes younger children. Furthermore, in several studies of school-phobic adolescents (48, 118), it was found that the beginnings of the disturbance typically went back over a period of years usually to around age 7 or 8, and thus represented a relatively chronic condition. Forcing a child or adolescent with a true, intense school phobia back into the dreaded situation will only aggravate the phobia. Prompt therapy to determine and deal with the real source of the youngster's anxiety is essential, and most cases need to involve not only the child or adolescent, but the parents as well because of their part in the development and maintenance of the disturbance.

## DEPRESSION AND SUICIDE

### Depression

Depressive disorders cover a wide spectrum of severity from relatively mild, temporary states of sadness, often in response to actual loss of a loved person, to severely disturbed conditions that may involve cognitive as well as affective disturbances. Possibly partly because major depressive disorders are rarely seen in children and younger adolescents, many clinicians tended until recently to deny that depression can occur in this age group (2, 114, 123, 145, 196). This view may also have been reinforced by the fact that

> The early adolescent as a consequence of his usual disinclination to express his feelings openly and his tendency to deny negative and self-critical attitudes, is relatively unlikely to exhibit the gloom, hopelessness, and self-depreciation that commonly keynote adult depression [209, *163*].

In addition, as we shall see in a subsequent section, the relatively fluid, unsettled process of adolescent developmental change often leads adolescents to mask their underlying depressive feelings in a variety of disguises from boredom and restlessness to hypochondriacal complaints or acting-out behavior (30, 31, 106, 145, 196). Such masked depression is not, of course, limited to adolescents; many depressed adults behave similarly. Nevertheless, the fact is that depressive symptoms are fairly common among adolescents (63, 106). Indeed, Irene Josselyn, an authority in the treatment of adolescents, asserts: "If there is any emotional state that is universal for this age group, it is depression. It may be transient, though recurrent. It becomes a sign of disturbance requiring intervention when it is the dominant mood" (106, *58*). In a study of normal eighth graders, 25 percent of the boys and 30 percent of the girls reported at least one period lasting 2 weeks or more since sixth grade in which they were "sad, blue, depressed, or lost all interest in things" that they usually cared about. Similar results have been obtained in studies of college students (145).

Other investigations of representative samples of adolescents indicate that as many as 40 percent have experienced significant, though usually temporary, feelings of sadness, worthlessness, or pessimism about the future (1, 2, 125, 145, 147). In a large study of the population of the Isle of Wight, Michael Rutter and his colleagues found that only one in nine 10-year-olds reported moodiness, misery, depression, or feelings of self-depreciation, compared to nearly 40 percent of adolescents aged 14

to 15 years (172). In that study, almost 8 percent reported suicidal feelings. Feelings of misery and depression were more common in these adolescents than in their parents, suggesting that these feelings may peak in adolescence (171). "Among adolescents seen in psychiatric clinics and hospitals, fewer than 10% are diagnosed as primarily depressed, but almost half display such depressive features as melancholia, self-depreciation, crying spells, and suicidal preoccupations or attempts" (209, *221*; 128).

As already noted, even when significant depression occurs among adolescents, the forms that it takes typically differ from adult depression (106, 195, 196, 209). As Josselyn observes, although the classic adult concept of depression as hostility turned inward against the self is sometimes the basis of depression in adolescents, it is rather rare. "The depression characteristically has its core in other, primarily indigenous, psychological difficulties" (106, *59*). She cites two kinds of depression among adolescents. The first is expressed as "a feeling of emptiness, a lack of self-definition that approximates, as verbally described, a state of depersonalization" (106, *59*). The adolescent may complain of a lack of feelings and a sense of emptiness. It is as though his or her childhood self had been abandoned and no growing adult self had replaced it. Frequently, this sense of emptiness engenders a high level of anxiety. This kind of depression resembles a state of mourning, in which the loved person is experienced as part of the self; "adolescents of this group mourn for their childhood identity and cannot find an adult identity to which they can be wedded" (106, 59). This type of depression is the least malignant and most resolvable. Unlike the situation with some adults, whose complaints of feelings of emptiness may suggest the possibility of an underlying psychotic process, it is not so much that the adolescent has no feelings, as that he or she does not know what to do with them, how to evaluate or express them. Consequently, he or she denies having feelings.

A second type of adolescent depression, and one that is often more difficult to resolve, has its basis in long-standing, repeated experiences of defeat (57, 97, 106, 192). These are adolescents who have actually tried many ways to find a solution to their problems and to achieve personally meaningful goals but without success— either because of the failure of others to accept or understand what the adolescent was trying to do, or because personal inadequacies made the goals impossible to achieve (97, 106). As we shall see in discussing adolescent suicide, many—probably a majority—of adolescent suicide attempts are the result not of a momentary impulse, but of a long series of unsuccessful attempts to find alternative solutions to difficulties. Frequently, the final straw in this type of depression is the loss of a meaningful relationship, whether with a parent, friend, or someone with whom the adolescent was in love. "Possibly an adolescent who suffers this type of depression can tolerate failures in every other area if he is sustained by a meaningful relationship" (106, 59). Telling such an adolescent to "snap out of it," a step often urged by well-meaning adults, is likely to be meaningless because the adolescent feels he or she has no alternative solutions left to try. The young person who has reached this stage of hopelessness is probably most in danger of suicide (97, 106, 192, 214).

Clinicians fail to recognize depression in adolescents (and children) not only because of its dissimilarity to adult depression, but because of the varied forms it may take. Younger adolescents, in particular, may reveal feelings of depression through "depressive equivalents" such as boredom, restlessness, or an inability to be alone and a constant search for new activities (30, 31, 116, 145, 195, 196). Obviously these characteristics are found in many adolescents at one time or another, but when they become both dominant and persistent, the possibility of underlying depression should be explored. Escape from feelings of depression and loneliness may also be attempted through frequent and excessive use of alcohol and drugs, or through promiscuous sexual activity (116, 135, 145, 196). Some adolescent delinquents employ the defense mechanism of denial and acting-out behavior as a way of coping with depressed feelings (116, 196, 209). The depressed adolescent may also reveal his or her feelings through bodily complaints, such as waking up tired and fatigued or exhibiting hypochondriacal symptoms and excessive bodily preoccupations (114, 196). Difficulties in concentration and failing school performance are frequently signs of a depressed state in young people (145, 193, 196, 209). In one study of college dropouts, it was concluded that depression was the most frequent and most significant causal factor in the decision to drop out of college, either temporarily or permanently (144).

Studies of depressed adolescents who are hospitalized find that they differ from depressed adult patients in that they are less likely to show the usual symptoms of slowed thoughts, irritability, loss of appetite, or diminished libido (96). Depressed adolescents are more likely than adults to fear social abandonment and experience social frustration and to engage in acting-out behaviors such as running away from home and acts of aggression (132). Thus, although depression manifests itself in some basic ways across the life span, depression in adolescence is affected by the demands, tasks, and developmental characteristics of this stage of life.

### Sex differences in depression

In all age groups, rates of depression are higher for women than for men (211). A comprehensive review of treated cases and community surveys, as well as demographic studies of suicides and suicide attempts, all point to the clear conclusion that women are more likely than men to become depressed. A review of rates of mental illness of all kinds over childhood and adolescence revealed that, while boys were more likely than girls to receive treatment for psychological difficulties prior to adolescence, this trend reversed in adolescence (76); in particular, neurotic, transient, and reactive disorders among adolescents showed a preponderance of girls. Another study (79) found that adolescent girls experienced more *internal* distress—including tension, depression, and psychosomatic problems—than did boys. This difference in internal versus external modes of experiencing distress is supported by the results of a study of defense mechanisms (see pages 64–71) in adolescent boys and girls. This investigation revealed that boys tended to externalize conflict through the use of projection and aggression as defensive reactions while girls relied on defenses that internalize the conflict, primarily through directing aggression inward—with these sex differences emerging in early adolescence and increasing over the adolescent years (49).

There appears to be a growing consensus among investigators and clinicians that females are more likely to manifest depression and related difficulties than are males because of the stresses inherent in the female sex role (36, 76, 77, 156, 211). If so, it would make sense that sex differences in depression would first emerge by the end of adolescence, because of the gender intensification (87)—the narrowing and intensification of sex roles—that tends to occur during this stage (see page 85). If sex roles are currently shifting toward greater flexibility and diversity, then we may see a decline in the relatively greater incidence of depression among girls and women.

### Suicide

Learning of the suicide of a close acquaintance of any age is always distressing, but it is particularly so in the case of an adolescent. We cannot help being aware that through this one irreversible action the young person has renounced all future opportunity to participate in experiences—love, friendships, satisfying work, or raising a family—that for many have lent joy and meaning to life. That such normally rewarding prospects have not been sufficient to overcome feelings of hopelessness and despair is tragic in itself. Even more tragic, however, is the knowledge that, at least for many adolescents, these feelings might have been alleviated if only the suicide could have been prevented—if circumstances had only been different. Furthermore, our empathy for young suicide victims is likely to be increased by personal recollections. When a person's actions seem utterly foreign and incomprehensible to us, we may feel sorry for him or her, but true empathy is difficult. This, however, is not likely

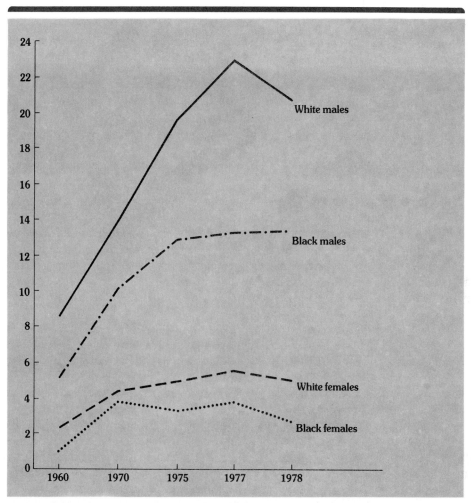

**Figure 15.1** Death rates from suicide among white and black male and female 15- to 24-year-olds, 1960–1978. (From U.S. National Center for Health Statistics, annual.)

to be the case with suicide. For many of us, the likelihood of actual suicide may never have been greater, but many, perhaps most, adolescents at one time or another have "wished that I was dead" and have at least toyed with the thought of suicide.

Suicide is extremely rare in children and almost as infrequent among young adolescents. Beginning about age 15, however, the reported suicide rate increases rapidly, reaching a level of over 20 per 100,000 for ages 15 through 24 among white males, although suicide rates for blacks and females are significantly lower (see Figure 15.1) (23, 199, 200). Furthermore, the overall suicide rate among older adolescents nearly tripled in the three decades from 1950 to 1980 (23). More recently, the suicide rate among younger adolescents has increased in the past decade (200,

201). Although still not common in absolute terms, completed suicide is now the second leading cause of death between the ages of 10 and 20, exceeded only by accidents. There is also evidence that suicide, because of its social unacceptability in our culture and the distress it may cause to friends and relatives, is underreported, especially in the case of children and adolescents (50, 158, 196). Furthermore, many suicides, particularly those disguised as accidents, may go undetected (13, 41, 43, 44, 45, 158, 196). As is the case with all other age groups, *actual* adolescent suicides are more common among males than females, by a ratio of between three and four to one (5, 158, 185). There are also relative differences in the methods employed. Girls are more likely than boys to use passive methods, such as ingestion of drugs or poisons, whereas boys are more likely than girls to use active methods, such as shooting or hanging (99, 123, 149). Among both sexes, however, firearms or explosives account for the greatest number of *completed* suicides, whereas drugs or poisons account for the greatest number of *attempted* suicides (5, 91, 99, 123, 149). Although male adolescents outnumber females in completed suicides, attempted suicides are far more common among females, probably reflecting similar rates of depression. Definitive statistics are lacking, but estimates of the ratio of female to male suicide attempts range from 4:1 to 7:1 (90). Furthermore, suicide attempts may outnumber completed suicides by a ratio as high as 100:1 (99).

**Actual and attempted suicides**    No absolute distinction can be made psychologically between actual and attempted suicides. In some instances, what was intended largely as a suicidal gesture may backfire and lead to death (as in the case of an adolescent girl who takes an overdose of sleeping pills, expecting her parents to come home shortly and discover her, only to have the parents delayed). In other instances, determined suicidal attempts may fail, due perhaps to mistaken ideas regarding the lethal dose level of some drug, or because of unanticipated discovery. Furthermore, the adolescent may not have a clearly delineated aim (a gesture versus certain death); suicidal intent need not be an all-or-nothing matter. In general, however, it seems reasonable to assume that for a larger percentage of completed suicides, death itself was a goal, and that the young person was more despairing and more seriously depressed than the average suicide attempter. Unfortunately, for obvious reasons, investigators know a good deal more about suicide attempters than about completed suicides.

**Why do adolescents attempt suicide?**    In considering the reasons for suicide attempts, it is important to distinguish between immediate precipitating factors and longer-term predisposing factors. Precipitating events may include the breakup or threatened breakup of a romance, pregnancy (real or imagined), school failure, conflicts with parents, rejection by a friend, apprehension in a socially proscribed or delinquent act, loss of a parent or other loved person, fear of a serious illness or imminent mental breakdown, and the like (97, 98, 99, 149, 196). On closer examination, however, it often becomes clear that the adolescent's reaction to such an event is the culmination of a series of mounting difficulties. One study of 154 adolescent suicide attempters found that hopelessness, rather than depression, was most often the critical factor in the suicide attempt (214). Based on his research on adolescent suicide, Jerry Jacobs (97, 98) describes four likely stages in the development of suicidal behavior:

1. A long-standing history of problems (from childhood to the onset of adolescence).
2. A period of escalation of problems (since the onset of adolescence and in excess of those normally associated with adolescence).
3. The progressive failure of available adaptive techniques for coping with old and increasing new problems, which leads the adolescent to a progressive social isolation from meaningful social relationships.
4. The final stage, characterized by the chain-reaction dissolution of any remaining meaningful social relationships in the weeks and days preceding the suicide attempt (97, *64*).

Adolescents who attempt suicide frequently have a long history of disturbed family relationships (see Chapter 7). Marital discord between parents, emotional problems in one or both parents, divorce, death of a parent, stepparents, even abandonment by parents, are all more frequent in the backgrounds of adolescent suicide attempters (98). But even where such obvious signs of family instability may be missing, there is likely to be a *loss of communication* between parent and child. Jacobs, for example, found that the parents of suicide attempters were more than twice as likely as the parents of control adolescents to use such disciplinary techniques as whipping and spanking, withdrawing approval, nagging, and yelling (97). A feeling of inability to understand each other is common both to many suicidal adolescents and their parents (97, 98, 145, 192, 196). Adolescent suicide attempters typically have a long history of escalating family instability and discord, and they have reached a point of feeling alienated from their parents and unable to turn to them for support (94, 98, 192). Frequently, they have struggled to achieve closeness with and emotional support from other people, only to have these relationships also collapse for one reason or another. "Faced with mounting family conflict, dissolving social relationships, and a progressive sense of isolation and helplessness, a suicidal adolescent has gradually come to the conclusion that suicide is the only road left open to him" (210, *222*).

**Prediction of suicide risk**   There is a dangerous myth, among not only laymen but also some clinicians, that a person who talks about committing suicide will not do so. The tragic fact, however, is that many adolescents (and adults) who have threatened suicide and have been ignored—or dismissed as attention-seekers—do subsequently take their own lives. Furthermore, in talking of suicide, adolescents are conveying a message that something is wrong and that they require help, even though they may not yet be seriously intent on suicide as the only remaining solution to their problems. Talk of suicide should always be treated as a potentially serious problem.

Predicting suicidal risk is not easy, but there are a number of warning signals that can help to alert the careful observer to the possibility (13, 97, 158, 209). These include the following:

1. The continuing presence of a depressed mood, escalating to feelings of hopelessness, eating and sleeping disturbances, declining school performance (13, 97, 99, 150, 158, 196, 209, 214).
2. Gradual social withdrawal and increasing isolation from others (2, 97, 98, 192).
3. Breakdowns in communication with parents or other important persons in the adolescent's life (97, 98, 158, 192).
4. A history of previous suicidal attempts or involvement in accidents. Prior suicidal attempts present particularly serious warnings if they appear to have had considerable potential for success (e.g., attempts at shooting oneself or hanging versus superficial wrist scratches or a mild overdose of aspirin) (13, 54, 99, 158, 209).

**Treatment**   Treatment of potentially suicidal adolescents, or those who have already made suicidal attempts, must deal with both the immediate events and life circumstances that are troubling the young person, or that precipitated the suicidal attempts, and also the long-standing problems and conflicts that have brought the adolescent to the point where suicide may appear the only possible solution to his or her difficulties. The therapist must show the kind of warmth and true concern that the suicidal adolescent typically finds lacking in other relationships. He or she must also let the adolescent know that the suicide attempt is being taken seriously, that it indicates a real problem, that problems do have answers, and that it is the therapist's job to help the adolescent to find the answers.

Because disturbed family relationships and breakdowns in communication between the young person and his or her parents play such a prominent role in the ideology of adolescent suicidal attempts, inclusion of parents as well as the adolescent in any psychotherapeutic program is usually required (209). Although an initial period of hospitalization may occasionally be necessary for the self-protection of some seriously depressed suicide attempters, hospitalization itself will not solve the life problems the adolescent is caught up in and in a number of cases is probably neither necessary nor desirable.

## PSYCHOPHYSIOLOGICAL PROBLEMS AND HYPOCHONDRIASIS

Psychological disturbance in an adolescent may be reflected in real or imagined physical symptoms. In the latter case, called *hypochondriasis,* there is an excessive preoccupation with functioning of the body. A hypochondriacal boy may be concerned that there is something wrong with his heartbeat, breathing, or digestion when these are perfectly normal; or he may exaggerate the significance of minor ailments, such as a slightly stuffy nose, a minor stomach upset, or a muscle cramp (110, 183, 210). Hypochondriacal symptoms, though they may occur in childhood, are far more prevalent during adolescence. In view of the fact that the rapid physical and sexual changes of puberty inevitably focus the attention of the adolescent on the physical self, this is hardly surprising. Indeed, a certain amount of what might be considered undue bodily preoccupation in an adult may represent a perfectly normal developmental phenomenon in an adolescent:

> To the adolescent, as to the infant, the body is unfamiliar. . . . In seeking his own identity the adolescent tries to become familiar with the body in which that identity is encased. He responds to new sensations as well as to old ones with a new alertness; by these responses he learns at least who his physical self is [106, *62–63*].

On the other hand, bodily concerns that are excessive and resistant to change may be indicative not of learning about the self, but of underlying disturbances of varying degrees of severity. Hypochondriacal symptoms may serve a number of functions principally related to handling anxiety. All adolescents experience minor transient states of anxiety, which they are generally able to tolerate. But when anxiety becomes intense, and especially when the young person is uncertain of its source, it can be overwhelming, leading at times even to a fear of "going crazy." Being able to find a reason—a source—for the anxiety helps to make it seem rational to the individual, and hence less mysterious or frightening. For some adolescents the focus becomes the body. They will then "not be destroyed by some vague monster the nature of which is unknown, but . . . today by tuberculosis, tomorrow by leukemia" (106, *63*).

The focus of the hypochondriacal adolescent's anxiety may also have a realistic component, even though it is not sufficient in itself to account for the degree of concern. Many adolescents fear that their emerging physical self will not be "a satisfactory home" for their new psychological self (106). General, ill-defined concerns about being unattractive, inadequate, physically immature, or in some way "repulsive" (a persistent term in the lexicon of adolescents) may become pinpointed to one or another aspect of the body or its functioning. A boy may fear that he will never achieve sexual maturity, or that his hips will be too big—too "effeminate." A girl may fear that her breasts will be too small or too big. Because of anxiety or guilt regarding sexuality, a mild prostatitis may convince an adolescent boy that he has acquired a veneral disease, despite objective evidence to the contrary. Feelings of fatigue may lead boys or girls to fear that they have somehow permanently damaged themselves physically, perhaps as a result of masturbation. Hypochondriacal symptoms may also serve as a face-saving way of avoiding certain activities (106). One cannot go to a dance or participate in athletic activities because one is "too weak," when the actual underlying concern is fear of rejection or incompetence.

It is important, however, to keep two general considerations in mind when dealing with what appear to be hypochondriacal symptoms among adolescents. One is that the adolescent's concerns may stem simply from ignorance. He or she may not know that a particular "symptom" is actually a normal event, or that it indicates a condition far less serious than that which is feared. If so, reasonable assurance should allay the anxiety (110, 183). Second, seemingly hypochondriacal symptoms may actually indicate the early stages of a real illness. For example, feelings of fatigue and complaints of a mild sore throat or sensitive glands may actually indicate the presence of that popular adolescent disorder, infectious mononucleosis. Obviously, too, it is important at times to rule out the onset of a more severe psychological disorder, such as schizophrenia, which may be partly manifested by unusual or peculiar physical complaints.

In our brief discussion thus far, it is clear that hypochondriacal symptoms may serve deeper psychological needs (e.g., dealing with anxiety). But other symptoms or defense mechanisms (see pages 64–65) may serve similar needs in other adolescents. Why then does a particular adolescent adopt hypochondriacal symptoms? At least part of the answer usually lies in the adolescent's family background. Children and adolescents who develop hypochondriacal symptoms usually come from families that are preoccupied with health and illness (142, 210). "In such families the slightest physical complaint commands everybody's immediate attention and sympathy. Each member of the family has his own particular brand of aches, allergies, and infirmities, and his own well-stocked shelf of medicines; family conversation frequently revolves around the current status of everyone's latest malaise" (210, *164*). Not infrequently, the symptoms favored by a hypochondriacal adolescent may be based on the model provided by, or an indentification with, a particular parent or sibling. The adolescent whose hypochondriacal symptoms go beyond normal adolescent bodily concerns or prove resistant to change obviously needs psychological help in order to determine the underlying problems that have given rise to these symptoms. Fortunately, once this has been accomplished and the adolescent has begun to deal with the problems, hypochondriacal symptoms usually "disappear with surprising readiness, in contrast to the often stubborn retention of them in therapy with the adult hypochondriac" (106, *65–66*).

### *Psychophysiological disturbances*

Psychological problems may also be revealed in actual disturbances of physiological functioning, either acute or chronic. The latter may lead to an actual psychosomatic (psychophysiological) disorder, sometimes involving structural change, as in the case of peptic ulcer.

Temporary disturbances in psychophysiological functioning are not uncommon during middle childhood and adolescence (7, 33, 65, 183). Psychological stress can have a marked influence on gastrointestinal, cardiovascular, muscular, and central nervous system functioning (33, 65, 143). For example, many gastrointestinal complaints painfully familiar to viewers of television advertisements, such as upset stomach, heartburn, bloating, and vague dyspepsia frequently represent reactions of children and adolescents to emotional distress (33). Similarly, as we have already noted, "paraoxysmal and prolonged rapid heart rate frequently is a physical concomitant of an acute or chronic anxiety state" (33, *227*). An adolescent may complain of a pounding heart or racing pulse, and may even fear that he or she is about to have a heart attack. So-called muscle tension headaches, backaches, chest pains, and discomfort in the extremities may also be precipitated by psychological stress (33). Actual, clearly defined psychosomatic disorders are less frequent than acute or transient disturbances in psychophysiological functioning during childhood and adolescence, but they do occur (7, 33, 110, 183, 213). Among the disorders found during the adolescent years in which psychological factors may play a significant part are these: peptic ulcer and ulcerative colitis, both involving prolonged periods of hyperacidity and hypermotility of parts of the gastrointestinal tract; some skin disorders, such as some cases of urticaria (a vascular reaction of the skin, often accompanied by severe itching); migraine and muscle tension headaches; some cases of asthma; and, as we shall see below, such eating disorders as obesity and anorexia nervosa (33, 60, 65, 85, 213).

Stress may also have long-term effects on the cardiovascular system. Autopsies of young soldiers killed in the Korean and Vietnam wars showed evidence in 45 percent of the cases of significant blocking of the arteries (61, 130). It is now thought that heart disease is developed over a long period of time, probably beginning before adolescence. While behavioral factors are clearly implicated in the development of heart disease—for example, men showing "Type A" behavior (high-pressure, competitive, hostile, and impatient) showed twice the rate of coronary heart disease as men not showing these behaviors (129)—physiological vulnerability is undoubtedly important as well, particularly in interaction with such life-style factors as smoking, consumption of foods related to cardiac risk (e.g., saturated fats, cholesterol, salt, and sugar), and inadequate or irregular exercise. Many of these behavioral patterns begin at an early age, and probably become fairly fixed in adolescence, when adultlike patterns are adopted. One recent study (218) showed that the tendency to behave in ways linked with the "Type A" syndrome increased from age 10 years to 17 years, particularly for girls.

The likelihood that a particular psychosomatic disorder will develop is influenced by constitutional predisposition, and in any particular symptom complex the relative importance of psychological as contrasted to constitutional factors may vary from one individual to another. For example, constitutional differences in pepsinogen (a digestive product of the gastric cells) levels may mean that one individual may develop an ulcer under prolonged psychological stress, whereas another individual subject to the same stress may not (35, 46, 65, 140, 165, 174). Some cases of urticaria are clearly a response to ingestion of allergens or contact with them (60); others are related to emotional stress:

> The connection between emotional stress and urticaria in some children is evident to them and to their parents, and the urticaria sometimes occurs predictably in particular kinds of stressful situations. Urticaria due to emotional stress often occurs on the exposed parts of the body, such as the face, neck and arms, but it may be over the entire body [33, *213–214*].

Similarly, in some children and adolescents with asthma, constitutional factors may be more significant, whereas in others psychological factors may play a more important role (65, 207). Some young people with intractable (i.e., severe) asthma had a rapid remission in symptoms, even without medication, as soon as they were referred to a specialized residential treatment center. Others, however, continued to require maintenance doses of corticosteroid drugs while at the center. A comprehensive series of studies showed that rapidly remitting children and adolescents reported significantly more often than those who were steroid-dependent that emotions such as anger, anxiety, and depression triggered their asthma. Furthermore, both mothers and fathers of rapidly remitting children and adolescents displayed authoritarian and punitive attitudes to a greater degree than the parents of those who were steroid-dependent, according to their responses to a questionnaire (154, 155, 207).

Treatment of psychosomatic disorders typically requires careful attention to all aspects of the disorder—medical, psychological, and social—and, particularly in the case of children and adolescents, to patterns of family interaction, which not infre-

quently are shown to be contributing to or aggravating the problem. In some instances, relaxation training, biofeedback techniques, or meditation (see Chapter 2)
may also prove helpful (78, 148, 157).

## EATING DISORDERS

As already noted in our discussion of physical growth (see Chapter 4), at no other
stage in development is the individual as likely to be preoccupied with physical
appearance as during adolescence. Adolescents may be concerned about their ultimate height, the adequacy of their sexual development, or their general physical
attractiveness. But as Hilde Bruch (26, 27), an expert in the treatment of eating
disorders, has observed, probably the greatest amount of attention and activity centers around concerns about weight. Perhaps paradoxically, it is in affluent societies
like our own that cultural pressures to be thin are greatest, especially during adolescence and young adulthood. Even mild degrees of overweight are likely to be viewed
as unattractive and a sign of self-indulgence (26).

In view of the many rapid physical and physiological changes that follow the
onset of puberty, it is not surprising that many adolescents go through brief periods
in which their weight deviates upward or downward from generally accepted norms.
However, once growth has stabilized, most adolescents will correct their weight
through regulation of their diet. A minority, however, will not. In some cases sustained overeating may lead to serious obesity. In other cases, pathologically prolonged and extreme dieting may lead to serious, sometimes life-threatening degrees
of weight loss. This latter condition, known as *anorexia nervosa*, is most likely to
occur during adolescence and is far more common among girls than boys. An additional eating disorder called *bulimia*, which has recently come into prominence,
involves abnormal eating behavior without abnormal weight loss or gain. Each of
these conditions, and some of the psychological and psychophysical factors that may
be involved, will be discussed briefly.

### Obesity

It is important to distinguish normal variations in weight from serious obesity.
After all, weight, like height or bone width, follows a normal distribution curve. This
might appear obvious, but the preoccupation of Western culture (particularly among
the economically privileged classes) with slimness and the contemptuous attitude
frequently displayed toward any evidence of overweight leads many adolescents to
strive for unrealistically low weight levels, sometimes to a degree that impairs optimal functioning physically and psychologically. This seems especially likely to be the
case where the adolescent, through sporadic crash diets, is continually varying his or
her weight across a relatively wide range.

It is also important to recognize that actual obesity "is a rather complex, far
from uniform, condition with disturbances in many areas" (27, *276*). Hereditary
factors may be involved, as may disturbances in metabolic functioning or endocrine
imbalance, and variations in the number of fat cells in the adipose tissues (24, 26,
27, 88, 187). Overnutrition early in life may produce an excessive number of fat cells
which will remain with the individual throughout life (169). Recent research has also

shown that obese people actually differ from normal-weight people in the way their digestive processes are linked to food cues (162). In a large number of cases, however, psychological and social problems appear to play a major role, and if these problems can be corrected or ameliorated, the individual is likely to be able to reach and maintain a reasonable weight level. This is particularly likely to be the case with excessive weight gains that begin in adolescence (25, 27, 219).

***Psychological factors*** It is necessary to distinguish between psychological characteristics that may play a part in predisposing the adolescent to obesity and those that are a result of societal reactions to the condition. In several studies of obese adolescents (26, 28, 188), it was found that many of these young people reacted to social discrimination and criticism with at least partial acceptance of it as valid. In consequence, they tended to be obsessively preoccupied with being fat and to become passive or timidly withdrawn, eager to please, and tolerant of abuse. In brief, the obese adolescent tends to accept the negative evaluation of others "and settles down to live with it" (27, 277). One study revealed that individuals who were already obese during adolescence (when pressure for peer group conformity is strong and physical appearance is of special concern) were much more likely to be self-derogatory regarding their appearance in later life than those who did not become obese until after they had reached adulthood (188). Nevertheless, even during adolescence, there will be significant variations in the reactions of individual obese adolescents to social criticism. Those who reach adolescence with low self-esteem and a sense of helplessness (often fostered by parental criticism or rejection) will be much less resistant to social criticism than those who have gained self-esteem, competence in a variety of skills, and a sense of autonomy (25, 188).

The psychological and social factors that may *predispose* the adolescent to obesity are not uniform. In some cases, parents may overfeed their children as a way of showing love or, conversely, of expressing unconscious hostility. The child or adolescent may overeat as a way of avoiding pressures for social interaction, athletic participation, or heterosexual relationships, in which he or she feels inadequate. Some may overeat to "fill" a feeling of emptiness or loneliness. Others may do so to give themselves a feeling of "bigness" as compensation for feeling psychologically small or insignificant. Still others may overeat to punish themselves for guilt feelings or to express hostility toward parents. Nevertheless, there do appear to be some common patterns that characterize adolescents who become or remain obese. And there are clearly some psychological characteristics that are essential preconditions for being able to overcome obesity. As Hilde Bruch comments:

> Those who are unable to obtain help, or who cannot make use of it even if it is available, have been disturbed in establishing their own identity, in their ability to relate to others, and in developing a positive self-concept. The problems that face every adolescent appear overpowering to them. Commonly they will withdraw from social contacts, become increasingly inactive, seek comfort in food, and thus grow progressively fatter. Like other youngsters, the obese adolescent needs to emancipate himself and overcome his dependency on his parents. He must redirect his interest, affection, and loyalty toward friends of his own age. He must learn to recognize and pattern his sexual impulses in a way that permits gratification in a dependable form, compatible with his personal ideals and self-concept. Only through

accomplishing these tasks can he find his adult identity and accept the role of an adult [26, *154*].

Clinical and experimental investigations indicate that obese young people are more likely than their nonobese peers to lack a sense of being self-directed, separate individuals with the capacity to identify and control their biological urges, and to define their needs and present them in a way that will enable them to find appropriate rewards (26, 27). Obese adolescents tend to lack discriminating awareness of the signals of bodily urges, and also the sense of emotional and interpersonal effectiveness. They suffer from a conviction that they are "the misshapen product of somebody else's action and do not experience themselves as independent self-directed individuals, with initiative and autonomy" (26, *155*).

The lack of discriminating awareness of the signals of bodily urges has been demonstrated in an ingenious series of experiments (146, 175, 176, 177, 178, 179). In one such experiment (176), Stanley Schachter and his associates had normal and obese students who had not eaten at their previous mealtime come into the laboratory, presumably in connection with an investigation of taste. When the participant arrived, he or she received either a roast beef sandwich or nothing. The person was then presented with five bowls of crackers and asked to rate each kind on such dimensions as salty, cheesy, and the like. During the 15-minute test period, the participant was free to taste as many or as few crackers as he or she wished. It was found that the normal students ate considerably fewer crackers when their stomachs were full from the roast beef sandwiches than when their stomachs were empty. In contrast, the obese students ate as much (and in some instances more) when their stomachs were full as when they were empty (see Figure 15.2). In other experiments, it has been demonstrated that obese individuals eat much more than normal individuals when food is easily available and does not require effort to obtain it; that they eat more than normal individuals when food cues are prominent and less when they are remote (177, 178, 179). In brief, whereas normal individuals regulate their eating primarily by internal physiological cues of hunger, obese individuals do not.

***Treatment of obesity***   Therapeutic approaches to the treatment of obesity have focused on attempts to (1) ameliorate the underlying psychological problems of the individual and to promote personal growth and a sense of identity, autonomy, and control of one's own body; and (2) change the individual's specific eating patterns and his or her responses to cues that previously provoked eating behavior. The former approach is exemplified by psychoanalytically oriented and other relatively traditional forms of psychotherapy; the latter is exemplified by techniques of behavior therapy (see Chapter 2) and by such self-help groups as Weight Watchers (25, 78, 188). Often, combinations of these approaches are necessary, for although the motivation for continued overeating may have deep psychological roots, the continued eating itself is likely to become overlearned as a response to a variety of familiar cues, and substantial relearning is required. In any event, efforts at overcoming obesity appear doomed to failure until, or unless, the individual becomes able to realize that he or she must and can take the initiative for his or her own actions (26, 27).

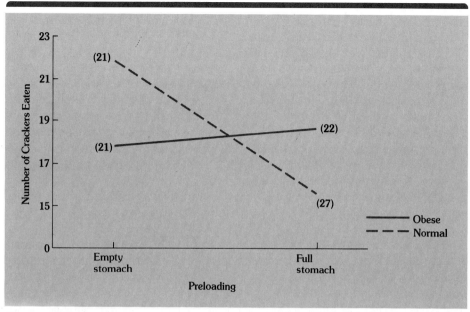

**Figure 15.2** Number of crackers eaten by obese and normal subjects under empty stomach and full stomach conditions. (From S. Schacter, *Emotion, obesity, and crime.* New York: Academic Press, 1971. Copyright 1971, Academic Press. By permission.)

### Anorexia nervosa

Although anorexia nervosa was first generally recognized as a clinical entity only about a century ago, descriptions of the condition are found much earlier. A treatise on "consumption" written in 1689 (141), and cited by Bruch (26), described the case of a 16-year-old girl who

> . . . fell into a total suppression of her Monthly Courses from a multitude of Cares and Passions of her Mind, but without any Symptom of the Green-Sickness following upon it. From which time her Appetite began to abate, and her Digestion to be bad; her flesh also began to be flaccid and loose, and her looks pale . . . she was wont by her studying at Night, and continual pouring upon Books, to expose herself both Day and Night to the injuries of the Air. . . . I do not remember that I did ever in all my practice see one, that was conversant with the Living so much wasted with the greatest degree of a Consumption (like a Skeleton only clad with Skin) yet there was no Fever, but on the contrary a coldness of the whole Body . . . only her Appetite was diminished, and her Digestion uneasie, with Fainting Fits, which did frequently return upon her [26, *211*].

Severe undereating and consequent malnutrition and serious weight loss may accompany a variety of disorders ranging from some schizophrenic conditions to mental retardation, depression, and a variety of undiagnosed organic disorders (26, 27). However, the clinical picture in genuine (primary) anorexia nervosa is remarkably similar from one patient to another. The disorder is most likely to have its onset during adolescence, and is about ten times as likely to occur in females as in males, at least in the United States. (The female-to-male ratio in Japan is much lower.) Though still relatively rare, the incidence seems to be increasing, particularly among girls from affluent, well-educated families (27, 181, 194). Although biological factors may play a part in the etiology of primary anorexia—perhaps an impairment of the release of gonadotropin from the anterior pituitary gland (169) or a defect in the feedback control mechanisms for certain neurotransmitters in the brain (e.g., dopamine) (83)—psychological influences appear predominant. When the backgrounds of anorexic adolescents have been examined by researchers, the initial impression has usually been one not of pathological disturbance, but rather of an unusual freedom from developmental difficulties (26, 27). As children, these patients generally appeared to have been "outstandingly good and quiet . . . obedient, clean, eager to please, helpful at home, precociously dependable, and excelling in school. They were the pride and joy of their parents and great things were expected of them" (26, *255*).

On closer investigation, however, these presumably positive personality characteristics, and the reactions of parents to them, have turned out to have a distinctly negative aspect. First and foremost has been a lack of individual initiative and autonomy—a sense of one's identity as a separate and distinct individual capable of determining and accomplishing one's own goals (26, 95, 184). Instead, at least unconsciously, anorexics are likely to have had feelings of being "enslaved, exploited, and not being permitted to lead a life of their own" (26, *250*). They typically lack a clear sense of emerging selfhood, despite prolonged struggles to be perfect in the eyes of others. Also characteristic is an obsessional need to be in control of every aspect of life, with particular concern about losing control over one's body. Anorexics are preoccupied with thoughts of food and engage excessively in food- and weight-related behavior compared to nonanorexic girls (117).

Not surprisingly, it has been found that parents of female anorexic adolescents were likely to have exerted such firm control and regulation during childhood that the child had difficulty in establishing a sense of identity and confidence in her ability to make decisions by herself; the parents are likely to manifest intrusive concern and overprotection (95, 139), and do not encourage separation and autonomy (184). Parental discomfort with the child's separation leads the parent (usually the mother) to reinforce reliance on her, which stifles the development of the self in the daughter. These parents are likely to have encouraged their children to become perfectionistic overachievers; they also control the child's pleasures (190). Furthermore, such a regulated child may become so focused on external cues and controls as determinants of behavior that, like the obese child, she may fail to learn to respond appropriately to differential cues—physiological and psychological—originating within herself. These results have recently been corroborated by a study using very rigorous methods of assessing family interactions; in addition, this study suggested that the parents of the anorexic are dependent upon her to nurture them, as well as to modulate and inhibit conflict between the parents (73).

Bruch describes three basic symptoms of disordered psychological functioning in primary anorexics (26, 27). First is a disturbance of delusional proportions in the individual's body image and body concept. Even when reduced to a grotesque and pitiful skeletonlike appearance, an adolescent girl may deny that she is too thin, and indeed, continue to worry about becoming fat. Second is a disturbance in the accuracy of the perception or cognitive interpretation of stimuli arising in the body. Rather than a mere loss of appetite, there is a failure to recognize cues of hunger—a failure similar to that occurring in many obese patients, although the result is very different. Failure to recognize bodily cues indicating fatigue is also likely, and despite severe malnutrition the patient may exhibit hyperactivity. Finally, there is usually a paralyzing sense of ineffectiveness—a feeling of acting only in response to the demands of others, rather than to one's own needs and wishes. This feeling of lack of control is typically masked by a surface negativism and stubborn defiance, which tend to conceal it and which, unfortunately, also make treatment difficult.

At least five criteria should generally be met before a diagnosis of anorexia nervosa is made: (1) intensive fear of becoming obese, which does not diminish as weight loss progresses; (2) disturbance of body image (e.g., perceiving oneself as fat even when already emaciated); (3) "weight loss of at least 25% of original body weight or, if under 18 years of age, weight loss from original body weight plus projected weight gain expected for growth charts may be combined to make the 25%" (6, 69); (4) refusal to maintain body weight over the *minimum* normal weight for age and height; and (5) no known physical illness that would account for the weight loss (6).

**Treatment of primary anorexia nervosa** In the past about 10 percent of anorexics actually died of starvation, but this is seldom the case today. Proper management requires both psychological and medical intervention. As in the case of obesity, psychological treatment approaches range from intensive psychotherapy to techniques of behavior modification. The primary psychotherapeutic goal is a personal reorientation so that the patient comes to see herself or himself as having a separate identity from parents and the right to self-respect—an approach advocated by Bruch (26, 27). In behavior modification, a "contract" may be reached between patient and therapist, spelling out increasing rewards (e.g., access to television, smoking, visits with other patients and family) as progress in eating and weight gain occurs (26, 122, 138, 181). The relative long-term success of various treatment approaches is still being evaluated, and often elements of each may be combined. One follow-up study of former anorexics found that 49 percent were cured, 26 percent had fluctuating weight or were obese, 18 percent remained chronically anorexic, and 7 percent had died or committed suicide (180). Of those living at the time of followup, 90 percent were working but only 49 percent had married or maintained an active heterosexual life.

One of the most promising recent approaches appears to be that undertaken at the Philadelphia Child Guidance Clinic by Salvador Minuchin, Lester Baker, and their colleagues (122, 136, 137, 138, 139, 168), in which operant conditioning to initiate weight gain and subsequent family therapy play central roles. It is their view that although the most important goal in the initial stage of treatment is a life-saving one, long-term success without relapses depends on reorganization of maladaptive patterns of family interaction. Of 23 patients treated with this family therapy approach, 85 percent have shown no subsequent eating problem and have established appropriate peer relationships in long-term follow-up (138). Another investigator (182) reported greatly improved results when she moved into total family therapy from an original focus that centered only on the sick child and a "pathogenic" mother.

### *Bulimia*

It has recently been noted that many young women engage alternately in binge eating (gorging) and elimination patterns (purging such as self-induced vomiting or laxative abuse) while maintaining normal weight (6, 20, 83, 194). This disorder, which combines elements of both obesity and anorexia, is called *bulimia*. It is characterized by: (1) episodic binge eating accompanied by awareness that the eating pattern is abnormal, (2) a fear of not being able to stop it voluntarily, (3) depressed mood and self-deprecating thoughts following the eating binges, and (4) repeated attempts following binges to lose or control weight with dieting or purging (6, 83, 104). Between 40 and 50 percent of anorexics develop bulimia, and this eating pattern is associated with a chronic course of the disease (32). Bulimia in anorexia nervosa is also related to greater mood variation and behavioral deviance (69, 170, 186).

What is relatively new is the surprisingly widespread incidence of bulimia among outwardly normal young women (20, 194). In one study initially focused on anorexics and a normal control group, substantial amounts of deviant eating behavior were found among the normally functioning college students (194). A group of these late-adolescent women was then added to the study as a further comparison; they were similar to anorexics in eating behavior but similar to normal women in social adjustment; they fell between anorexics and normals in psychological symptoms.

A new study was initiated recently to obtain further information about bulemics (103, 104). Somewhat to the investigator's surprise, thousands of responses were received to notices placed in several magazines, expressing interest in people who find that they binge and then vomit or use other means to get rid of the food. A preliminary sample of 509 respondents was 99 percent female, 94 percent of whom currently binged and 74 percent of whom met the criteria for a psychiatric diagnosis of *bulimia*. Six percent of the respondents were also classifiable as anorexic (either now or previously) and only 5 percent had *never* purged (vomited or used laxatives).

The respondents tended to have never married (70 percent), were white (97 percent), had some college (84 percent), and a median age of 22 years. Although 62 percent were of normal weight when they responded, 43 percent reported weights during adolescence (at 15 years of age) that were classified as overweight. The average age at which a weight problem was first reported was 15 years, 5 months. Binge eating did not usually begin until later, however, at an average age of 18 years. This age at onset may be linked to living away from home for the first time, primarily at college.

Of the respondents who binged, almost half reported doing so at least daily; the average number of calories consumed per binge was estimated at 4800, usually in the form of sweets (94 percent)! Of those who reported purging (71 percent of the respondents), 69 percent vomited, 39 percent used laxatives, and 26 percent used both. Of those who vomited, 58 percent did so at least daily; about one-fourth of the laxative users took them daily. These bulemic women reported normal sexual interest and experience but unusually low frequencies of alcohol, drug, and cigarette use. They reported that their eating problem had adversely affected their lives in most areas except work, and 73 percent reported adverse effects on their physical health. Sixty percent had sought no treatment for the problem, even though 19 percent had made some kind of a suicide gesture or attempt, and another 51 percent had considered it.

Although more research on bulimia is needed, it clearly is a disorder in need of attention. The medical consequences of bulimia include metabolic changes due to rapid carbohydrate loading, electrolyte imbalances, hernias, ulcers, bowel syndrome, and increased tooth decay (104). It is similar in many respects to other addictive behaviors. It is not yet known what treatment is most effective with bulimia (83).

## ADOLESCENT PSYCHOSES

The term *psychosis* is applied to those disorders that involve severe distortions of cognitive, perceptual, and affective functioning. Frequently, but by no means always, psychotic persons are unaware of the nature of their illness (even though they may be painfully aware of suffering), and their ability to make realistic, rational judgments regarding their own condition or events in the world about them is seriously impaired. As a result, they are usually unable to maintain even minimally adequate personal, social, or work relationships, and to continue responsibility for their own welfare. Some psychoses, such as those stemming from toxic drug reactions or disease, are clearly organic in origin. Others may be primarily psychological in origin or may involve often complex and elusive interactions between psychological and biological (constitutional) influences. Included in the latter category are the major affective disorders (6), such as bipolar (manic-depressive) disorders, severe (major) depression, and schizophrenia, in which cognitive disturbances play a prominent role.

### Adolescent schizophrenia

Among adolescents, schizophrenia is by far the most frequently occurring psychotic disorder. Its incidence, though still relatively rare, increases dramatically from age 15 onward and reaches a peak during late adolescence and early adulthood, leveling off during the end of the third decade (29, 71, 94, 203, 209).

**Symptoms** Although there are individual differences in symptomatology, in type of onset (gradual or acute), in severity of impairment, and in prognosis, adolescent schizophrenia, like its adult counterpart, tends to be characterized by disordered thinking; distortions of, or lack of contact with, reality; limited capacity for establishing meaningful relationships with others; and poor emotional control (16, 29, 208, 209). In its fully developed form, adolescent schizophrenia can usually be identified without much difficulty: The young person's speech is likely to seem peculiar—stilted, overelaborate, disconnected, or even incoherent. He or she may display odd facial grimaces or movements; appear distracted, withdrawn, or confused; and show inappropriate emotional reactions—either failing to respond with appropriate feeling or overreacting in poorly controlled fashion. Proper diagnosis may be difficult in the early stages of the disorder, partly because the symptomatology may be far less obvious or dramatic than later, and partly because some characteristics that might suggest incipient schizophrenia in adults are more likely to occur among non-schizophrenic as well as schizophrenic adolescents. These include "circumstantial thinking, abstract preoccupation, and conscious awareness of blatant sexual and aggressive imagery" (209, *102*), all of which tend to occur more frequently among nonschizophrenic adolescents than nonschizophrenic adults.

This should not appear too surprising when it is realized that adolescence itself is a period of rapid change, when psychological equilibrium may be temporarily disrupted, and when controls on thought and psychological defense mechanisms are more likely to be in a state of flux and not yet firmly established. As a result, so-called primary process thinking that in normal adults is likely to remain unconscious (e.g., illogical or arbitrary reasoning, blatant sexual or aggressive imagery) may emerge occasionally in the nonschizophrenic adolescent's thinking and speech or writing (173, 209). In contrast, it is important, as Irving Weiner points out, "to recognize that these age-related differences do not extend to other patterns of personality impairment associated with schizophrenia" (209, *101*). In particular, he notes that truly disordered thinking—as reflected, for example, in dissociation and blocking—and impaired control—as evidenced by inadequate emotional integration—"have equal significance as clues to schizophrenic disturbance in both adolescents and adults" (209, *101*).

One study (80, 94) of adolescent and young adult schizophrenics found that 17 years was the age of highest risk for the onset of schizophrenia. They found that five features differentiated these young schizophrenics from other psychotic patients of the same age and from matched young people who were not experiencing psychological difficulties. These five features included: (1) difficulties in organizing thought and experiences, (2) a lack of pleasure in experiences, (3) excessive dependency on parents, therapists, or other adults, (4) absence of competence academically and socially, and (5) specific circumstances that seemed to precipitate a psychotic breakdown. These features are similar to those reported in other studies (93, 163, 205, 206). These authors, while acknowledging the importance of biological factors in contributing to individual vulnerability, see evidence that the demands of adolescence create stress on developing young people.

***Sex differences*** Although sex differences in the incidence of schizophrenia are not seen in general, there appear to be different patterns in the onset of this disorder for males and females (53, 120, 121). As with depression, boys are more likely than girls to develop schizophrenia in childhood (166). Unlike depression, this 2.5:1 male to female ratio does not reverse in adolescence. The sex ratios of schizophrenic onset become equal in the mid to late thirties, and by the late fifties, females are twice as likely as males to become schizophrenic (3, 15). It is now thought by some that sex-role norms, with their variations over the life span, may provide the context for making manifest a vulnerability to schizophrenia (3). Thus, boys are more likely than girls to become schizophrenic at younger ages because of the more intense pressure on them to achieve in a variety of ways. Later in life, the argument goes, women are under more stress, not because of too much pressure to achieve, but rather because their function in the traditional stereotype of women's role has ended. If this hypothesis about sex-role strain is accurate, we would expect to see different patterns in the sex ratios of the incidence of schizophrenia if sex-role stereotypes change in our society.

**Precursors**  Although schizophrenia is most likely to become manifest from middle adolescence on, adolescent schizophrenics, along with other adolescents suffering from some form of serious emotional disorder, are likely to have shown earlier evidence of greater than average psychological vulnerability (22, 70, 94, 163, 209). Studies of the earlier adjustment of adolescent schizophrenics have found a higher than expected incidence of shyness, social withdrawal, poor social relationships, difficulty in making friends, "peculiar" behavior, stubbornness, sensitivity, lack of humor, difficulties in concentration, fear of demanding situations, and problems in managing daily life that frequently appear to consist of a series of real or imagined crises (16, 94, 113, 205, 209). In addition, some studies have found precursors in physical health such as having had more infectious illness in early childhood, more physical handicaps, a greater number of eating and sleeping disturbances, and slower motor development (161). It should be noted, however, that such "premorbid" characteristics are not manifested by all young people who become schizophrenic or have schizophrenic episodes during adolescence (21).

**Etiology**  What causes schizophrenia, and why does its incidence rise dramatically during adolescence? There are increasing indications that genetic factors play a role in predisposing the individual to the development of schizophrenia, at least in many cases. Much of the evidence comes from studies of twins. A variety of investigations suggest that the *concordance ratio* for schizophrenia among identical (monozygotic) twins, who share the same genetic endowment, is approximately 50 percent; that is, in cases where one member of the twin pair is schizophrenic, the likelihood of the other twin also developing the disorder is about one chance in two (75, 107, 166, 167). In contrast, among fraternal (dizygotic) twins, the concordance ratio decreases to approximately 12 percent. It is, of course, still lower for other siblings and for parent-child pairs, though higher than for unrelated persons (see Table 15.1).

The most compelling evidence, however, of a genetic contribution in susceptibility to schizophrenia comes from studies of adoptive children (39, 52, 111, 112). One extensive study in Denmark (39, 52, 111) involved two groups of children adopted early in life but studied after they had reached adulthood: individuals who had become schizophrenic in the course of their development and a control group matched for age, sex, age at adoption, and socioeconomic status of the adopting family. The incidence of schizophrenia was then examined among both the biological and adoptive relatives (parents, siblings, and half-sibs) of each group. There was no significant difference in the prevalence of schizophrenic disorders among the adoptive relatives of the two groups. However, schizophrenia was almost six times higher among the biological relatives (11 percent) of those who had become schizophrenic than among their adoptive relatives (about 2 percent), while in the control

**TABLE 15.1 ESTIMATES OF MORBID RISKS FOR SCHIZOPHRENIA AMONG RELATIVES OF SCHIZOPHRENIC PROBANDS (IN PERCENT)**

| | |
|---|---|
| Parents | 4.2–5.5 |
| Children | 9.7–13.9 |
| Children (both parents affected) | 35.0–46 |
| Sibs (all) | 7.5–10.2 |
|    Neither parent affected | 6.7–9.7 |
|    One parent schizophrenic | 12.5–17.2 |
| Half-sibs | 3.2–3.5 |
| Aunts and uncles | 2.0–3.6 |
| Nieces and nephews | 2.2–2.6 |
| Grandchildren | 2.8–3.5 |

*Source:* S. Kessler. Psychiatric genetics. In D. A. Hamburg and S. K. Brodie (eds.), *American handbook of psychiatry, Vol. VI: New psychiatric frontiers.* New York: Basic Books, 1975. Pp. 352–384.

group there were no significant differences in the incidence of schizophrenia between biological and adoptive relatives (52, 111).

It should be emphasized, however, that having close biological relatives with schizophrenia does not mean that one is likely to develop this disorder; indeed, it is unlikely. There may be a variety of reasons for this. In the first place, except in the case of identical twins, relatives do not share all of the same genes. Second, what is called schizophrenia may in fact represent a number of different disorders with similar symptoms. In current reanalyses of the schizophrenic subjects in the Danish study described above, Seymour Kety and his colleagues have divided their subjects into chronic schizophrenics, latent schizophrenics (i.e., those without full-blown symptomatology), and acute schizophrenics (those characterized by rapid onset of schizophrenic episodes, usually of fairly brief duration, preceded and followed by adequate functioning). They are finding that few, if any, of the biological relatives of the acute group were schizophrenic; in contrast, the chronic schizophrenic subjects show the highest rate of schizophrenic relatives, while those classified as latent occupy an intermediate position.

Third, unlike, for example, Huntington's chorea (which is produced by a single dominant gene) schizophrenia may be *polygenic*—requiring the presence of a complex combination of interacting genes to be manifested, even in those instances where genetic factors play a significant role in schizophrenia (67, 134). And fourth, it may be more correct to speak of inheritance not of schizophrenia per se, but of increased *vulnerability to schizophrenia,* in which case whether or not the disorder is precipitated would depend on two factors: how vulnerable a particular individual is to psychological stress and how much psychological or physiological stress he or she is subjected to (59, 111).

If one adopts this paradigm, it may help to explain why some psychologically vulnerable individuals develop schizophrenia while others develop other psychiatric conditions (94). It may also help to account for the dramatic rise in the incidence of schizophrenia during adolescence. As we have already noted, adolescence itself is likely to be a period of increased stress as a result of the rapid physical, sexual, and cognitive changes that accompany the onset of adolescence and to which the individual must adapt, as well as greatly accelerated social demands for independence and personal responsibility. The young person who, though more vulnerable than many of his peers, may have mastered the relatively simpler adaptational demands of middle childhood, but may be unable to cope with the increased demands of the adolescent period.

**Prognosis** Among *hospitalized* adolescent schizophrenics, "it can be anticipated that about one-quarter will recover, one-quarter will improve but suffer residual symptoms or occasional relapses, and the remaining 50 percent will make little or no progress and require continuing residential care" (210, *220*). Unfortunately, similar data are not available regarding the prognosis for milder, nonhospitalized cases of this disorder, although one would anticipate that the percentage of those recovering or showing improvement would be significantly higher.

In addition to the apparent severity of the disturbance and the need for hospitalization, a number of other factors appear to influence the prognosis for a schizophrenic adolescent (210). In general, the older the adolescent is when schizophrenia appears, the better the prognosis is likely to be. Other favorable indications include sudden, rather than gradual, onset of the disturbance; previously good academic and social adjustment; and early response to treatment efforts. Finally, the outlook for improvement will be better if the family is able to accept the disturbance, and if there is adequate planning for future treatment and for school, work, and living arrangements (210).

### Brief reactive psychosis

It is important to distinguish brief psychotic episodes from schizophrenia (6, 64). Although during the episode the individual may exhibit some psychotic symptoms such as incoherence, disorganized associations or behavior, delusions, or hallucinations, these symptoms appear suddenly and are short-lived (varying from a few hours to at most a couple of weeks). The psychotic symptoms typically appear immediately following a severe and recognizable "psychosocial stressor," such as loss of a loved one or a life-threatening event, "that would evoke significant symptoms of distress in almost anyone" (6, *200*). Invariably, there is emotional turmoil, manifested by rapid, generally depressed and anxious mood swings. This disorder, which usually appears first in adolescence or young adulthood, may be followed by feelings of mild depression or loss of self-esteem. But with psychological assistance and support, the young person or adult may be expected to return fully to his or her previous level of functioning (6).

### Major affective disorders

Schizophrenia accounts for the vast majority of psychotic reactions found among adolescents (164, 209). However, contrary to earlier thinking, major affective disorders can occur during adolescence (114, 153). Though relatively rare, there are an increasing number of reports of bipolar (manic-depressive) disorder among adolescents—particularly older adolescents (153). Severe depression (sometimes referred to as major or unipolar depression) may occur at any age (6), although like bipolar depression, it is also found most frequently among adults. Bipolar depression is characterized by periods both of manic excitement (including hyperactivity, excessive euphoria, irritability, inflated self-esteem, grandiosity, and unwarranted optimism) and depression (including a dysphoric mood, decreased energy, loss of interest in life, feelings of worthlessness, and suicidal thoughts).

Of the major mental disorders, bipolar depression appears to have the strongest genetic component. For example, in several studies (111, 215), it was found that if one identical twin had bipolar depression, the chances were three out of four (74 percent) that the other twin would also suffer from this disorder. But in the case of nonidentical twins, the chances of the other twin also developing bipolar depression were less than one in four (23 percent). While sample sizes are still inadequate, it appears that identical twin siblings of bipolar depressives reared apart have a relatively high incidence of the disorder but not as high as that of identical twin siblings reared with the patient (111, 131, 215). Genetic factors also appear to play a role, while not as strong a one, in major (unipolar) depression—a far more common, but less well defined, disorder than manic-depressive illness (114, 215).

It should be emphasized that even in the case of those depressive disorders in which genetic influences appear clearest (i.e., manic-depressive illness), many close relatives of afflicted individuals—even identical twins—do not develop the disorder, suggesting that even here psychological stress or its absence may play an important role. There are also individuals who develop depressive disorders in the apparent absence of family histories of disturbance. In this connection, it is interesting to note that stress itself has been found to produce measurable changes in the levels of certain chemicals in the brain similar to those found in patients with depressive illness (62, 131).

### Other psychoses

Acute and chronic brain disorders, which produce psychotic reactions, may, and do, occur in children and adolescents, as well as in adults. Of these, the most frequent among younger people are toxic psychoses (183).

The term *toxic psychosis* refers to mental disturbances resulting from "an interference with the metabolism of the cerebral cortex" (183, *214–242*). An acute infection with high fever is probably the most common cause among children and adolescents, but there are others, including trauma, hypoglycemia (an abnormally large drop in the glucose content of the blood), and drugs. The latter may include adverse reactions to drugs given as medications, drugs ingested by mistake as poisons, or in recent years, intentional use of a variety of dangerous or illicit drugs in search of "a new high" (10, 183). Especially disturbing has been the recent use by children and younger adolescents of such "deliriant" drugs as ether, nitrous oxide, and various industrial solvents containing hydrocarbons (e.g., glue-sniffing) (38, 40, 56, 72). In addition to producing a toxic psychosis when taken in sufficient quantity, these substances can produce permanent damage to body organs, such as the kidneys, brain, and liver; and acute poisoning can, and unfortunately frequently has, resulted in death for many young people, particularly children (38, 40, 56, 72).

Alcohol may sometimes produce a toxic psychosis (e.g., delirium tremens), as may some psychedelic drugs (10, 11, 89).

The primary symptoms of a toxic psychosis "are defects in the pattern of awareness and in intellectual capacity" (183, *242*). Mental confusion may alternate with some understanding of one's condition. Deterioration of the capacity for abstract thinking, memory, and recall is likely, as are disturbances in orientation (10, 89). Aside from administration of any indicated medication, including counteragents, or other forms of physical treatment, it is vital in dealing with the already confused young person with a toxic psychosis to maintain stability of the environment and to avoid excessive stimulation. It is also important to explain as simply and directly as possible all procedures to which the patient is subjected. As Milton Senn and Albert Solnit of the Yale Child Study Center note, "The altered psychic state of which all patients with a toxic delirium are aware to some extent, is in itself frightening. An adolescent even in his rational mind is easily frightened by the procedure of hospitalization which he experiences" (183, *242*).

## BORDERLINE
## DISORDERS IN ADOLESCENCE

Over the years increasing attention has been focused on a group of adolescents and adults who hover "just across the line from psychosis" (202, *1582*)—hence the term *borderline* personality disorder (74, 86, 109, 115, 126, 202). Probably the most basic characteristics of borderline individuals are instability and unpredictability, whether in interpersonal behavior, mood, or self-image (6, 109, 202). No single feature is invariably present. When facing a crisis, the borderline youth may explode with anger, become argumentative, and try to make others responsible for his or her troubles. "Because both the dependence and hostility are intensely felt, the interpersonal relations of borderline personalities are tumultuous. They can be clinging— sometimes literally so—and very dependent on those to whom they are close" (202, *1583*). However, they can also express enormous anger at those same friends when they are frustrated—with the separate behaviors frequently occurring in quick succession.

At times, in their impulsivity, anger, and need for attention, they may engage in self-destructive acts (e.g., wrist slashings) (6, 109, 202). "In their capacity to manipulate groups of people, borderline personalities have no peer among the personality disordered" (202, *1583*). They typically have difficulty in tolerating being alone, and prefer "a frantic search for companionship, no matter how unsatisfactory, to sitting alone with feelings of loneliness and emptiness" (202, *1583*). Although generally capable of normal intellectual functioning—as measured, for example, by ability testing—they rarely achieve up to the level that one would expect on the basis of their capabilities because of the turmoil in which they live (82, 126, 202).

At the most basic level, borderline adolescents and adults appear to suffer from profound identity problems—with no clear self-image, sexual identity, or long-term goals and values (6, 109, 202). They frequently complain about the lack of a consistent sense of self, and when pressed, describe "how depressed they feel most of the time, despite the flurry of other affects" (202, *1583*). In therapy, borderline patients frequently regress and become extremely demanding and difficult, and sometimes suicidal (202).

The origins of this condition are still poorly understood despite a wealth of hypotheses. Most consistently, perhaps, it is thought that as an infant and very young child the future borderline individual is subjected to unpredictable parental behavior—nurturance alternating with rejection, closeness with perceived abandonment (43, 109). As a result, it is thought that the borderline individual in adolescence or adulthood alternates between hostility and dependency, never developing a confident, consistent sense of self (202), and distorting his or her "present relationships by pigeonholing people into all-good or all-bad categories" (202, *1582*).

A related view focuses on individuation and separation, especially between 18 and 35 months of age (124, 126, 202). In this view, the mother of the toddler-age child can neither allow nor tolerate the separation and individuation of the child as he or she moves in the direction of increasing individuality and autonomy. Her anxiety, stemming from her own borderline childhood, compels her to inhibit her child's growth and to reinforce the child's clinging dependency with her affection and attention while simultaneously punishing movements in the direction of individuation by withdrawal of emotional support.

> Therefore, between the ages of one and a half and three a conflict develops in the child between his own developmental push for individuation and autonomy and the withdrawal of the mother's emotional supply that this growth would entail. He needs her approval to develop ego structure and growth. However, if he grows the supplies are withdrawn. These are the first seeds of his feelings of abandonment, which have such far reaching consequences [126, *22*].

Unable to tolerate an awareness of these painful feelings, the child resorts to such defense mechanisms as denial (see page 66) and "ego-splitting" (which works against the development of a consistent sense of self) in order to keep these feelings from consciousness. Unfortunately, however, the damage is done, and the subsequently borderline adolescent or adult is faced with intense fears of abandonment when attempting to differentiate himself or herself in interpersonal relationships, while still remaining close (124, 126). To date, there have been no definitive efforts to test the etiological hypotheses; however, many of the characteristics of borderline individuals have been demonstrated in careful research (82, 126, 127, 159, 160, 189). In addition, a semistructured diagnostic interview administered to adolescent and adult hospitalized patients has revealed that a borderline group could be successfully differentiated from both a schizophrenic and a neurotic group of patients, despite some similarities to both (81).

## *PSYCHOLOGICAL TREATMENT OF ADOLESCENTS*

Because, like other adolescents, those with significant psychological problems are at a unique stage of development, their treatment presents special challenges as well as special opportunities—whether in individual psychotherapy, in group therapy, or in other approaches (behavior therapy, residential treatment, group homes, and "half-way houses") (4, 14, 17, 18, 78, 148, 159). In the discussion that follows, the primary emphasis is on the treatment of young people during early and middle adolescence. In general, therapy with older youth will more closely approximate that with adults.

### Individual psychotherapy

It is widely agreed that psychotherapy with adolescents is more difficult and demanding than is generally the case with younger children and adults, and many otherwise capable and confident clinicians have assiduously avoided this age group (7, 8, 100, 209). Many adolescent patients, particularly younger adolescents, tend initially to be uncommunicative, skeptical, impatient, uncooperative, and unpredictable; and the course of adolescent therapy, like that of true love, seldom runs smoothly. The young person who seems to be cheerful and making sound progress one day (providing a sense of relief in the therapist) may turn up the next day—if indeed he or she does turn up—moody and depressed, combative and negativistic, or seemingly unaware of insights previously gained. The opposite may also occur: In one therapeutic session, the therapist may find himself or herself struggling with a whole host of adolescent concerns (e.g., no friends, teachers who hate him, imminent school failure, impossible parents), "only to find that the adolescent may have, by the next hour, dramatically reversed his stand in regard to every point he brought up in the previous explosion" (106, *139*). Acting-out behaviors or threats of such behavior (e.g., running away, becoming involved in a sexual adventure, quitting school, taking drugs, committing delinquent acts, making suicidal gestures) are not uncommon in adolescent therapy and may also be a source of considerable concern to the therapist (8, 106). One discouraged psychotherapist compared adolescent therapy to "running next to an express train" (8, *234*).

At the same time, work with adolescents, properly handled by a skilled and experienced therapist, can often be deeply rewarding if one's definition of reward is the adolescent's ultimate psychological growth and improved chances for leading a reasonably effective and happy, though certainly not conflict-free, existence. Because adolescence itself is a period of change and new beginnings, the young person is less likely than an adult to be already fixed in maladaptive patterns that are often resistant to change. Furthermore, despite their surface defensiveness and skepticism, many adolescents at heart remain open to experience and eager to learn from it.

Psychotherapy with adolescents is likely to be complicated by the fact that these young people are typically undergoing independence-dependence conflict with their parents in their everyday lives, and these conflicts tend to be transferred to the therapist, producing alternating cycles of regressive dependence and unrealistic assertions of independence. Furthermore, adolescents—especially younger adolescents—have frequently come to therapy because they have been referred by parents, school authorities, or other adults. As a result, the young patient may be suspicious of the therapist's role and may wonder if he or she is, at bottom, the adolescent's ally and agent, or that of "those adults" (33, 92). "The patient must be convinced that he is not the focus of an adult conspiracy and that his therapist is not in league with his parents to bring him to heel" (8, *243*). Not infrequently, this potentially ambiguous situation may create problems for the therapist as well. The consequence is often a period of probing of the therapist by the adolescent to test the therapist's basic commitment.

It should also be noted that problems of dependence and independence in therapy are not merely a matter of transferring parental conflicts to the therapeutic situation. They also represent extremely important reality problems. Without some trust in the therapist, it is difficult for therapy to proceed satisfactorily. At the same time, however, establishment of autonomy is a critical developmental task of adolescence (see Chapter 7), and the therapist must be alert to the dangers of allowing a regressive dependence on therapy to become a substitute for the adolescent's necessary struggle toward ultimate autonomy and self-reliance. Another way of viewing this problem is to recognize that the adolescent's sense of a clear-cut identity is only just beginning to develop and is still tenuous and potentially in danger of being overwhelmed. The adolescent psychotherapist—like the wise parent, only more so—must be on guard against the sometimes seductive tendency to try to substitute his or her own identity for that of the patient or to prolong therapy unduly.

A comprehensive review of all studies published within one decade that evaluate the outcome of psychotherapy with adolescents found that it was effective 75 percent of the time, compared to a 39 percent improvement rate among comparable youth not seen in psychotherapy (198). After an average follow-up period of 3 years, some effects of the 7 or so months of psychotherapy were still seen: 67 percent of the treated youth compared to 42 percent of those untreated were improved.

**Qualifications of the therapist** In order to handle psychotherapy with adolescents successfully, the therapist needs to have special knowledge of, and experience with, this age group. In addition, however, he or she needs a number of personal qualities that specialized training may be able to foster, but rarely to create—personal warmth, flexibility, openness and honesty, the capacity for candor, confidence in self and the ability to set limits without hostility, a relative lack of defensiveness and reliance on professional status, and, simple though it may sound, just a liking for adolescents. One study found that a key factor in the successful treatment of an adolescent is a positive opinion of the patient for the therapist (102). Adolescents, even more than children, have a particular talent for spotting phoniness—and exploiting it. If the therapist is straightforward, neither minimizing his or her qualifications nor retreating into professional pomposity, the adolescent will usually develop a feeling of trust and respect, though outwardly the patient may still need to make it overly clear that he or she isn't awed by "shrinks."

**The treatment process** We cannot discuss here the numerous technical considerations relating to the handling of specific adolescent disturbances, and adequate discussions are available elsewhere (8, 33, 92, 100, 106). Nevertheless, certain general points are worth noting. Probably first and foremost is the necessity for flexibility (8, 92, 106). The effective adolescent psychotherapist must be prepared to move from listening, to questioning, to reassuring, to clarifying reality, to interpreting, even to arguing and, when necessary, setting limits (92, 106). Willingness on the part of the therapist to yield to argument may indicate to the adolescent a measure of respect for his or her increasing capacity for self-determination; it may also produce an opportunity for both patient and therapist to reduce tension in a constructive rather than a destructive fashion (*argument* is not synonymous with *quarrel*) (33, 61).

**Setting limits**   Setting limits on the adolescent's behavior is sometimes necessary in psychotherapy with this age group. The therapist who fears that any imposition of limits will disrupt the relationship with the patient, or cast him or her in the role of "just another parent," is working with the wrong age group. As Irene Josselyn succinctly observes,

> Adolescents not only need but often want limits imposed. They need externally imposed limits because, as a result of their confused state, they are not able to set their own limits. Many adolescents become frightened when they feel that limits have not been defined. They seek a fence beyond which they cannot go, within which they can experiment and by trial and error and accidental success find a self-concept with which they can feel satisfied [106, *146*].

Donald Holmes provides an amusing but significant example of a positive case of limit setting that clearly went further toward meeting the patient's need at the time than either logical reasoning or anxious compliance on the part of the therapist:

> A 16-year-old girl says, "I'm-going-to-get-out-of-here-and-get-an-apartment-and-get-married-and-you-can't-stop-me!"
> Her doctor replies, "No you're not, and yes I can."
> She acknowledges, quietly enough, "Oh." [92, *110*].

Obviously such directness can be successful only where there is basic trust in the therapist and where the therapist has already made it clear that he or she respects the individuality and worth of the patient. But if the therapist sets limits only where they are necessary for the well-being of the patient, the young person will typically value the therapist because of the security that these limits provide (106).

> The limits are then actually not imposed by the therapist, but are self-imposed by the patient as a result of the strengthening in therapy of the patient's own vague awareness that the limits are valid. He sees the therapist not as a restricting parent figure but as an ally of that side of himself that strives for satisfactory self-identity [67, *147*].

Conversely, in many instances, failure on the therapist's part to set limits when they are essential will be interpreted by the patient as a lack of either real concern or understanding on the part of the therapist.

### The nature of adolescent therapy

In most cases, psychotherapy with adolescents needs to be directed toward personality development and synthesis (33, 106, 209, 217)—toward finding new, more adaptive, and less self-defeating ways of handling current problems or of relating to others; eliminating unnecessary fears and conflicts; and achieving a more workable integration between the young person's basic needs and values, and the demands of reality. In helping the adolescent to achieve these goals, the therapist may note distortions in the adolescent's reactions to people and events in everyday life, including distortions in the relationship with the therapist. He or she may observe that an adolescent girl is "turning off" her peers with critical comments not because these peers are basically stupid or hostile, as claimed, but because the adolescent fears being rejected if she allows them to come close. Or the therapist may note that an adolescent boy's worry about being able to please a part-time employer appears to stem not from any lack of ability on his own part or from the behavior of the employer (who may have made it clear that he was pleased with the adolescent's work), but from the fact that nothing he ever did appeared able to satisfy his father. Similarly, the therapist may wonder if the adolescent's scornfulness toward members of the opposite sex may not really reflect a fear of growing up. In most cases in which such "limited-insight" techniques are employed to help the adolescent boy or girl to reevaluate current unrealistic or self-defeating behavior, the focus is basically on the present (8, 19, 106, 209, 217).

With important exceptions, ontogenetic attempts to achieve deep insights, to strip away psychological defenses, and to reconstruct the past are avoided. For one thing, most adolescents have little patience with rehashing the past (209). Furthermore, the defense mechanisms and patterns of responding of most adolescents are still fluid and changing; they have not, as in the case of many adults, had an opportunity to harden, like arteries, with age (see Chapter 7). The adolescent's main developmental task is to cope successfully with the present, while moving toward the future. As Derek Miller observes, the adolescent is usually correct that present rather than past experiences are more relevant to working out his or her problems: "For an adolescent in search of an identity, overcoming the fears and failures of the moment is much more important than knowing the events which led up to them" (133, 774).

### Group therapy

Group therapy with adolescents, either alone or in combination with individual psychotherapy or behavior therapy (see pages 38–39), may often be an effective way for adolescents to work at "overcoming the fears and failures of the moment." It may be conducted in such nonresidential settings as youth centers, mental health clinics, private offices, or schools; or as part of the total treatment program in a residential treatment center (14, 33, 92, 159).

Group therapy with adolescents has "a natural advantage inasmuch as the forces of identification with a potential peer group can be made to work. The emotional impact of observing one's own experience expressed by someone else in the same situation is quite usually a powerful one and one that facilitates personal involvement and emotional interchanges" (37, 350). Group discussions can range widely and will vary somewhat depending upon the nature of the group. In some groups, there may be discussions of why an adolescent uses drugs, what situations or people are most likely to provoke this behavior, and what its effects—negative or positive—appear to be; in others, there may be a focus on what factors provoke antisocial or acting-out behavior. In most groups of young people, problems in relation to getting along with peers of both sexes are common, as are problems of self-esteem and relations with family members.

Many troubled adolescents, particularly those with more serious disturbances, have had very checkered experiences, frequently going back many years, with parents and parent figures. These may have included divorce, death, separation, or remarriage of one or both parents; rejection, neglect, exploitation, overpossessiveness, seductiveness, physical or sexual abuse, even abandonment (actual or psychological) by parents or parent substitutes; of having had to cope with emotionally disturbed or alcoholic parents or with attempts by one or both parents to manipulate the child as an ally or rival in conflicts with their spouse. Not surprisingly, such experiences may produce profound feelings of loss, anxiety, distrust, depression, or anger and resentment. Under the guidance of a skilled group therapist or therapists (sometimes a mixed-sex pair), adolescents can often help each other considerably to communicate and deal with such feelings, and to provide support through shared experiences.

### Peer counseling

In recent years, several kinds of programs for adolescents have been developed in which adolescents themselves play a major role. The first such programs, called peer counseling, taught adolescents to work with one another on a one-to-one basis (84). Youth are more often called peer leaders or peer teachers in programs where they lead groups. Peer counselors, peer leaders, or peer teachers undergo extensive training by adult professionals. In most programs, they are carefully supervised and supported in their work. Peer programs now exist for problems ranging from smoking and sexuality to depression and general unhappiness (105, 151, 204,

220). The few peer programs (such as smoking prevention) that have been evaluated for their effectiveness demonstrate not only that these programs can change the behavior of adolescents but also that they do so more effectively than other kinds of programs (105). Evaluations of programs focused on other behaviors, such as adolescent pregnancy, are now under way (220).

### Hot lines and free clinics

A development that sprang up in the late 1960s and continues in many places today is that of the "hot line" or "rap line," which provides information and sources of help to troubled adolescents (4, 9, 12). The adolescent may call in confidence (and anonymously if desired) for assistance with specific problems (e.g., drugs, pregnancy, suicidal attempts, sexual concerns, problems with parents or peers, fear of mental illness). Or he or she may be feeling lonely, worried, or depressed, and just want to talk.

A limited number of cities around the country also provide informal and free medical, psychological, and legal services, or simply places to sleep for runaways and youthful street people (see page 610). Many more such facilities are badly needed, however.

## REFERENCES

1. Achenbach, T. M., & Edelbrock, C. S. Behavioral problems and competencies reported by parents of normal and disturbed children aged four through sixteen. *Monographs of the Society for Research in Child Development,* 1981, **46,** 1–82.
2. Albert, N., & Beck, A. T. Incidence of depression in early adolescence. *Journal of Youth and Adolescence,* 1975, **4,** 301–307.
3. Al-Issa, I. Gender and schizophrenia. In I. Al-Issa (ed.), *Gender and psychopathology,* New York: Academic Press, in press.
4. Ambrosino, L. *Runaways.* Boston: Beacon Press, 1971.
5. *The American almanac: The statistical abstract of the U.S.* (Bureau of the Census, U.S. Department of Commerce). New York: Grosset & Dunlap, 1975 (95th ed.).
6. American Psychiatric Association. *Diagnostic and statistical manual of mental disorders.* Washington, D.C.: American Psychiatric Association, 1980 (3rd ed.).
7. Anthony, E. J. The behavior disorders of children. In P. H. Mussen (ed.), *Carmichael's manual of child psychology* (Vol. 2). New York: Wiley, 1970. Pp. 667–764 (3rd ed.).
8. Anthony, E. J. Psychotherapy of adolescence. In G. Caplan (ed.), *American handbook of psychiatry, Vol II: Child and adolescent psychiatry, sociocultural and community psychiatry.* New York: Basic Books, 1974. Pp. 234–249.
9. Baizerman, M. Toward an analysis of the relations among the youth counterculture, telephone hotlines, and anonymity. *Journal of Youth and Adolescence,* 1974, **3,** 293–306.
10. Balis, G. U. The use of psychotomimetic and related consciousness-altering drugs. In S. Arieti & E. B. Brody (eds.), *American handbook of psychiatry, Vol. III: Adult clinical psychiatry.* New York: Basic Books, 1974. Pp. 404–446 (2nd ed.).
11. Barry, H., III. Psychological factors in alcoholism. In B. Kissin & H. Begleiter (eds.), *The biology of alcoholism, Vol. 3: Clinical pathology.* New York: Plenum, 1974. Pp. 53–107.
12. Bauer, J. The Hot Line and its training problems for adolescent listeners. *Adolescence,* 1975, **10,** No. 37, 63–69.
13. Beck, A. T., Resnick, H. L. P., & Lettieri, D. (eds.). *The prediction of suicide.* Bowie, Md.: Charles Press, 1974.
14. Beckett, P. G. S. *Adolescents out of step.* Detroit: Wayne State University Press, 1965.
15. Belle, D., & Goldman, N. Patterns of diagnoses received by men and women. In M. Guttentag, S. Salasin, & D. Belle (eds.), *The mental health of women.* New York: Academic Press, 1980.
16. Bemporad, J. R., & Pinsker, H. Schizophrenia: The manifest symptomatology. In S. Arieti & E. B. Brody (eds.), *American handbook of psychiatry, Vol. III: Adult clinical psychiatry.* New York: Basic Books, 1974. Pp. 524–550 (2nd ed.).
17. Bergin, A. E., & Suinn, R. M. Individual psychotherapy and behavior therapy. In M. R. Rosenzweig & L. W. Porter (eds.), *Annual review of psychology* (Vol. 26). Palo Alto, Calif.: Annual Reviews, Inc., 1975. Pp. 509–556.
18. Berkowitz, I. H. (ed.). *Adolescents grow in groups: Experiences in adolescent group psychotherapy.* New York: Brunner/Mazel, 1972.
19. Blaine, G. R. Therapy. In G. R. Blaine & C. C. McArthur (eds.), *Emotional problems of the student.* Garden City, N.Y.: Doubleday (Anchor Books), 1966. Pp. 257–276.
20. Boskind-Lohdahl, M. Cinderella's step-sisters: A feminist perspective on anorexia nervosa and bulimia. *Signs: Journal of Women in Culture and Society,* 1976, **2,** 342–356.
21. Bower, E. M., Shelhamer, T. A., & Daily, J. M. School characteristics of male adolescents who later become schizophrenic. *American Journal of Orthopsychiatry,* 1960, **30,** 712–729.
22. Bromet, E., Harrow, M., & Kasl, S. Premorbid functioning and outcome in schizophrenics and non-schizophrenics. *Archives of General Psychiatry,* 1974, **30,** 203–207.
23. Bronfenbrenner, U. The challenge of social change to public policy and developmental research. Paper presented at the biennial meeting of the Society for Research in Child Development, Denver, April 2, 1975.

24. Bruch, H. The case for heredity. In H. Bruch, *The importance of overweight.* New York: Norton, 1957.

25. Bruch, H. Obesity in adolescence. In J. G. Howells (ed.), *Modern perspectives in adolescent psychiatry* (Vol. 4). New York: Brunner/Mazel, 1971. Pp. 254–273.

26. Bruch, H. *Eating disorders.* New York: Basic Books, 1973.

27. Bruch, H. Eating disturbances in adolescence. In G. Caplan (ed.), *American handbook of psychiatry, Vol. II: Child and adolescent psychiatry, sociocultural and community psychiatry.* New York: Basic Books, 1974, Pp. 275–286.

28. Cahnman, J. W. The stigma of obesity. *Sociological Quarterly,* 1968, 283–299.

29. Cancro, R. Overview of schizophrenia. In H. I. Kaplan, A. M. Freedman, & B. J. Sadock (eds.), *Comprehensive textbook of psychiatry* (Vol. 2). Baltimore: Williams & Wilkins, 1980. Pp. 1093–1104 (3rd ed.).

30. Carlson, G. A. Unmasking masked depression in children and adolescents. *American Journal of Psychiatry.* 1980, **137,** 445–449.

31. Carlson, G. A., & Cantwell, D. P. A survey of depressive symptoms in a child and adolescent psychiatric population interview data. *Journal of the American Academy of Child Psychiatry,* 1979, **18,** 587–599.

32. Casper, R. C., Eckert, E. D., Halmi, K. A., Goldberg, S. C., & Davis, J. M. Bulimia: Its incidence and clinical significance in patients with anorexia nervosa. *Archives of General Psychiatry,* 1980, **37,** 1030–1035.

33. Chapman, A. H. *Management of emotional problems of children and adolescents.* Philadelphia: Lippincott, 1974.

34. Chazan, M. School phobia. *British Journal of Educational Psychology,* 1962, **32,** 209–217.

35. Cheren, S., & Knapp, P. H. Gastrointestinal disorders. In H. I. Kaplan, A. M. Freedman, & B. J. Sadock (eds.), *Comprehensive textbook of psychiatry* (Vol. 2). Baltimore: Williams & Wilkins, 1980. Pp. 1863–1872 (3rd ed.).

36. Chesler, P. *Women and madness.* Garden City, N.Y.: Doubleday, 1972.

37. Christ, J. Outpatient treatment of adolescents and their families. In G. Caplan (ed.), *American handbook of psychiatry, Vol. II: Child and adolescent psychiatry, sociocultural and community psychiatry.* New York: Basic Books, 1974. Pp. 339–352.

38. Clinger, O. W., & Johnson, N. A. Purposeful inhalation of gasoline vapors. *Psychiatric Quarterly,* 1951, **25,** 557.

39. *Clinical Psychiatry News,* 1977, **5,** No. 5, 1, 40.

40. Coles, R., Brenner, J. H., & Meagher, D. *Drugs and youth: Medical, legal, and psychiatric facts.* New York: Liveright, 1970.

41. Conger, J. J. Accidents. In A. Deutsch (ed.), *The encyclopedia of mental health* (Vol. I). New York: Watts, 1963.

42. Conger, J. J. Parent-child relationships, social change, and adolescent vulnerability. Paper presented at the eighth international conference of the International Association for Child Psychiatry and Allied Professions, Philadelphia, July 28, 1974.

43. Conger, J. J., & Gaskill, H. S. Accident proneness. In A. M. Freedman & H. I. Kaplan (eds.), *Comprehensive textbook of psychiatry.* Baltimore: Williams & Wilkins, 1967.

44. Conger, J. J., Gaskill, H. S., Glad, D. D., Hassel, L., Rainey, R. V., Sawrey, W. L., & Turrell, E. S. Psychological and psychophysiological factors in motor vehicle accidents. *Journal of the American Medical Association,* 1959, **169,** 1581–1587.

45. Conger, J. J., Gaskill, H. S., Glad, D. D., Rainey, R. V., Sawrey, W. L., & Turrell, E. S. Personal and interpersonal factors in motor vehicle accidents. *American Journal of Psychiatry,* 1957, **113,** 1069–1074.

46. Conger, J. J., Sawrey, W. L., & Turrell, E. S. The role of social experience in the production of gastric ulcers in hooded rats placed in a conflict situation. *Journal of Abnormal and Social Psychology,* 1958, **57,** 214–220.

47. Coolidge, J. C., Tessman, E., Waldfogel, S., & Willer, M. L. Patterns of aggression in school phobia. *Psychoanalytic Study of the Child,* 1962, **17,** 319–333.

48. Coolidge, J. C., Willer, M. L., Tessman, E., & Waldfogel, S. School phobia in adoles-

cence: A manifestation of severe character disturbance. *American Journal of Orthopsychiatry,* 1960, **30,** 599–607.

49. Cramer, P., Defense mechanisms in adolescence. *Developmental Psychology,* 1979, **15,** 476–477.

50. Crumley, F. E. Adolescent suicide attempts. *Journal of the American Medical Association,* 1979, **241,** 2404–2407.

51. Davis, J. M. Antidepressant drugs. In H. I. Kaplan, A. M. Freedman, & B. J. Sadock (eds.), *Comprehensive textbook of psychiatry* (Vol. 3). Baltimore: Williams & Wilkins, 1980. Pp. 2620–2630 (3rd ed.).

52. DeFries, J. C., & Plomin, R. Behaviorial genetics. In M. R. Rosenzweig & L. W. Porter (eds.), *Annual review of psychology* (Vol. 29). Palo Alto, Calif.: Annual Reviews, Inc., 1978. Pp. 473–515.

53. Dohrenwend, B. P., & Dohrenwend, B. S. *Social status and psychological disorders.* New York: Wiley, 1969.

54. Dorpat, T. L., & Ripley, H. S. The relationships between attempted suicide and committed suicide. *Comprehensive Psychiatry,* 1967, **8,** 74–79.

55. Dunlop, G. M. Certain aspects of children's fears. Unpublished doctoral dissertation. Columbia University, 1951.

56. Easson, W. M. Gasoline addiction in children. *Pediatrics,* 1962, **29,** 250.

57. Easson, W. M. Depression in adolescents. In S. Feinstein & P. Giovacchini (eds.), *Adolescent psychiatry* (Vol. 5). New York: Aronson, 1977.

58. Eisenberg, L. School phobia: A study in communication of anxiety. *American Journal of Psychiatry,* 1958, **114,** 712–718.

59. Eisenberg, L. The intervention of biological and experiential factors in schizophrenia. In D. Rosenthal & S. Kety (eds.), *The transmission of schizophrenia.* Elmsford, N.Y.: Press, 1968. Pp. 403–412.

60. Engels, W. D. & Wittkower, E. D. Skin disorders. In H. I. Kaplan, A. M. Freedman, & B. J. Sadock (eds.), *Comprehensive textbook of psychiatry* (Vol. 2). Baltimore: Williams & Wilkins, 1980. Pp. 1930–1940.

61. Enos, W. F., Holmes, R. H., & Beyer, J. Coronary disease among United States soldiers killed in action in Korea. *Journal of the American Medical Association,* 1953, **152,** 1090–1093.

62. Fawcett, J. Biochemical and neuropharmacological research in the affective disorders. In E. J. Anthony & T. Benedek (eds.), *Depression and human existence.* Boston: Little, Brown, 1975. Pp. 21–52.

63. Feinstein, S. C. Adolescent depression. In E. J. Anthony & T. Benedek (eds.), *Depression and human existence.* Boston: Little, Brown, 1975. Pp. 317–336.

64. Feinstein, S. C., & Miller, D. Psychoses of adolescence. In J. D. Noshpitz (ed.), *Basic handbook of child psychiatry, Vol. II. Disturbances in development.* New York: Basic Books, 1979. Pp. 708–722.

65. Finch, S. M. Psychological factors affecting physical conditions (psychosomatic disorders). In H. I. Kaplan, A. M. Freedman, & B. J. Sadock (eds.), *Comprehensive textbook of psychiatry* (Vol. 2). Baltimore: Williams & Wilkins, 1980. Pp. 2605–2612.

66. Fodor, I. G. Toward an understanding of male/female differences in phobic anxiety disorders. In I. Al-Issan (ed.), *Gender and psychopathology.* New York: Academic Press, in press.

67. Freud, A. Adolescence as a developmental disturbance. In G. Caplan & S. Lebovici (eds.), *Adolescence: Psychosocial perspectives.* New York: Basic Books, 1969.

68. Gardner, G. E., & Sperry, B. M. School problems—learning disabilities and school phobia. In G. Caplan (ed.), *American handbook of psychiatry, Vol. II: Child and adolescent psychiatry, sociocultural and community psychiatry.* New York: Basic Books. 1974. Pp. 116–129.

69. Garfinkel, P. E., Modolfsky, H., & Garner, D. M. The heterogeneity of anorexia nervosa: Bulimia as a distinct subgroup. *Archives of General Psychiatry,* 1980, **37,** 1036–1040.

70. Garmezy, N. Vulnerable and invulnerable children: Theory, research, and intervention. *Journal Supplement Abstract Service*, MS1137, Washington, D.C., American Psychological Association, 1977, 23 pp.

71. Giovacchini, P. L. Psychiatric treatment of the adolescent. In H. I. Kaplan, A. M. Freedman, & B. J. Sadock (eds.), *Comprehensive textbook of psychiatry* (Vol. 3). Baltimore: Williams & Wilkins, 1980. Pp. 2706–2716 (3rd ed.).

72. Glaser, H. H., & Massengale, O. N. Glue-sniffing in children. *Journal of the American Medical Association,* 1962, **181,** 300.

73. Goldstein, M. J. Family factors associated with schizophrenia and anorexia nervosa. *Journal of Youth and Adolescence,* 1981, **10,** 385–405.

74. Goldstein, M., Baker, B. L., & Johnson, K. R. *Abnormal psychology: Experiences, origins, and interventions.* Boston: Little, Brown, 1980.

75. Gottesman, I. I., & Shields, J. Contribution of twin studies to perspectives in schizophrenia. In B. A. Maher (ed.), *Progress in experimental personality research.* New York: Academic Press, 1966. Pp. 1–84.

76. Gove, W. R., & Herb, T. R. Stress and mental illness among the young: A comparison of the sexes. *Social Forces,* 1974, **53,** 256–265.

77. Gove, W. R., & Tudor, J. F. Adult sex roles and mental illness. *American Journal of Sociology,* 1973, **78,** 812–835.

78. Graziano, A. M. (ed.). *Behavior therapy with children, II.* Chicago: Aldine, 1975.

79. Gregg G. High school— a tough place for girls. *Psychology Today,* 1976, **10,** 36–37.

80. Grinker, R., & Holzman, P. Schizophrenic pathology in young adults. *Archives of General Psychiatry,* 1973, **28,** 168–175.

81. Gunderson, J. G., & Kolb, J. Discriminating features of borderline patients. *American Journal of Psychiatry,* 1978, **135,** 792–796.

82. Gunderson, J. G., & Singer, M. T. Defining borderline patients: An overview. *American Journal of Psychiatry,* 1975, **132,** 1–10.

83. Halmi, K. A. Anorexia nervosa. In H. I. Kaplan, A. M. Freedman, & B. J. Sadock (eds.), *Comprehensive textbook of psychiatry* (Vol. 2). Baltimore: Williams & Wilkins, 1980. Pp. 1882–1891 (3rd ed.).

84. Hamburg, B. A., & Varenhorst, B. Peer counseling in the secondary schools: A community mental health project for youth. *American Journal of Orthopsychiatry,* 1972, **42,** 566–581.

85. Harris, H. I. The range of psychosomatic disorders in adolescence. In J. G. Howells (ed.), *Modern perspectives in adolescent psychiatry.* New York: Brunner/Mazel, 1971. Pp. 237–253.

86. Hartocollis, P. Affects in borderline disorders. In P. Hartocollis (ed.), *Borderline personality disorders: The concept, the syndrome, the patient.* New York: International Universities Press, 1977.

87. Hill, J. P., & Lynch, M. E. The intensification of gender-related role expectancies during early adolescence. In J. Brooks-Gunn & A. C. Petersen (eds.), *Girls at puberty: Biological, psychological, and social perspectives.* New York: Plenum, in press.

88. Hirsch, J., & Knittle, J. L. Cellularity of obese and nonobese human adipose tissue. *Federation Proceedings,* 1970, **29,** 1516–1521.

89. Hoff, E. B. Brain syndromes associated with drug or poison intoxication. In A. M. Freedman & H. I. Kaplan (eds.), *Comprehensive textbook of psychiatry.* Baltimore: Williams & Wilkins, 1967. Pp. 759–774.

90. Hoffmann, A. Adolescents in distress. *Medical Clinics of North America: Symposium on Adolescent Medicine,* 1975, **59,** 1429–1437.

91. Holinger, P. C. Adolescent suicide: An epidemiological study of recent trends. *American Journal of Psychiatry,* 1978, **135,** 754–756.

92. Holmes, D. J. *The adolescent in psychotherapy.* Boston: Little, Brown, 1964.

93. Holmes, D., & Barthell, C. High school year books: A nonreactive measure of social isolation in graduates who later became schizophrenic. *Journal of Abnormal Psychology,* 1968, **73,** 313–316.

94. Holzman, P. S., & Grinker, R. R., Sr. Schizophrenia in adolescence. *Journal of Youth and Adolescence,* 1974, **3,** 267–279.

95. Hood, J., Moore, T. E., & Garner, D. Locus of control as a measure of ineffectiveness in anorexia nervosa. *Journal of Consulting and Clinical Psychology,* 1982, **50,** 3–13.

96. Inamdar, S. C., Siomopoulos, G., Osborn, M., & Bianchi, E. C. Phenomenology associated with depressed moods in adolescents. *American Journal of Psychiatry,* 1979, **136,** 156–159.

97. Jacobs, J. *Adolescent suicide.* New York: Wiley, 1971.

98. Jacobs, J., & Teicher, J. D. Broken homes and social isolation in attempted suicides of adolescents. *International Journal of Social Psychiatry,* 1967, **13,** 139–149.

99. Jacobziner, H. Attempted suicides in adolescence. *Journal of the American Medical Association,* 1965, **19,** 7–11.

100. Jaffe, C., & Offer, D. Psychotherapy with adolescents. In G. P. Sholevar, R. M. Benson & B. J. Bliner (eds.), *Treatment of emotional disorders in children and adolescents.* New York: Spectrum Publishers, 1980.

101. Jersild, A. T., Markey, F. V., & Jersild, C. L. Children's fears, dreams, wishes, daydreams, likes, dislikes, pleasant and unpleasant memories. *Child Development Monographs,* 1933, No. 12.

102. Jesness, C. F. Comparative effectiveness of behavior modification and transactional analysis programs for delinquents. *Journal of Consulting and Clinical Psychology,* 1975, **43,** 758–779.

103. Johnson, C. Personal communication, 1981.

104. Johnson, C. Anorexia nervosa and bulimia. In T. J. Coates, A. C. Petersen, & C. Perry (eds.), *Adolescent health: Crossing the barriers.* New York: Academic Press, 1982.

105. Johnson, C. A., Graham, J. W., & Hansen, W. B. Drug use by peer leaders. Paper presented at the annual meeting of the American Psychological Association, Los Angeles, August 25, 1981.

106. Josselyn, I. M. *Adolescence.* New York: Harper & Row, 1971.

107. Kallmann, F. J. *Heredity in health and mental disorder.* New York: Norton. 1953.

108. Kanfer, F. H., Karoly, P., & Newman, A. Reduction of children's fear of the dark by competence-related and situational threat-related verbal cues. *Journal of Consulting and Clinical Psychology,* 1975, **43,** No. 2, 251–258.

109. Kernberg, O. F. Borderline conditions and pathological narcissism. New York: Aronson, 1976.

110. Kessler, J. W. *Psychopathology of childhood.* Englewood Cliffs, N.J.: Prentice-Hall, 1966.

111. Kessler, S. Psychiatric genetics. In D. A. Hamburg & K. Brodie (eds.), *American handbook of psychiatry, Vol. VI: New psychiatric frontiers.* New York: Basic Books, 1975. Pp. 352–384.

112. Kety, S. S., Rosenthal, D., Wender, P. H., et al. The types and prevalence of mental illness in the biological and adoptive families of adopted schizophrenics. In D. Rosenthal & S. S. Kety (eds.), *The transmission of schizophrenia.* Elmsford, N.Y.: Pergamon Press, 1968. Pp. 345–362.

113. Kleinmuntz, B. *Essentials of abormal psychology.* New York: Harper & Row, 1974.

114. Klerman, G. L. Affective disorders. In A. M. Nicholi, Jr. (ed.), *The Harvard guide to modern psychiatry.* Cambridge, Mass.: Harvard University Press, 1978. Pp. 253–282.

115. Knight, R. Borderline states. In R. Knight & C. Friedman (eds.), *Psychoanalytic psychiatry and psychology.* New York: International Universities Press, 1953/4.

116. Langdell, J. Depressive reactions in childhood and adolescence. In S. A. Szurek & I. N. Berlin (eds.), *Clinical studies in childhood psychoses.* New York: Brunner/Mazel, 1973. Pp. 128–148.

117. Larson, R., & Johnson, C. Anorexia nervosa in context of daily living. *Journal of Youth and Adolescence,* 1982, in press.

118. Levenson, E. A. The treatment of school phobia in the young adult. *American Journal of Psychotherapy,* 1961, **15,** 539–552.

119. Leventhal, T., & Sills, M. Self-image in school phobia. *American Journal of Orthopsychiatry,* 1964, **34,** 685–695.

120. Lewine, R. R. J. Sex differences in age of symptom onset and first hospitalization in schizophrenia. *American Journal of Orthopsychiatry,* 1980, **50,** 316–322.

121. Lewine, R. R. J., Straus, J. S., & Gift, T. E. Sex differences in age at first hospital admission for schizophrenia: Fact or artifact? *American Journal of Psychiatry,* 1981, **138,** 440–444.

122. Liebman, R., Minuchin, S., & Baker, L. The role of the family in the treatment of anorexia nervosa. *Journal of the American Academy of Child Psychiatry,* 1974, **13,** 264–274.

123. Lin, T. Some epidemiological findings on suicide in youth. In G. Caplan & S. Lebovici (eds.), *Adolescence: Psychosocial perspectives.* New York: Basic Books, 1969. Pp. 233–243.

124. Mahler, M. A study of the separation-individuation process and its possible application to borderline phenomena in the psychoanalytic situation. *Psychoanalytic Study of the Child,* 1971, **26,** 403–424.

125. Masterson, J. F. *The psychiatric dilemma of adolescence.* Boston: Little, Brown, 1967.

126. Masterson, J. F. *Treatment of the borderline adolescent: A developmental approach.* New York: Wiley-Interscience, 1972.

127. Masterson, J. The splitting defense mechanism of the borderline adolescent: Developmental and clinical aspects. In J. Mack (ed.), *Borderline states in psychiatry.* New York: Grune & Stratton, 1975.

128. Masterson, J. F., Tucker, K., & Berk, G. Psychopathology in adolescence: IV. Clinical and dynamic characteristics. *American Journal of Psychiatry,* 1963, **120,** 357–366.

129. Matthews, K. A., Glass, D. C., Rosenman, R. H., & Bortner, R. W. Competitive drive, Pattern A, and coronary heart disease: A further analysis of some data from the Western Collaborative Group Study. *Journal of Chronic Diseases,* 1977, **30,** 489–498.

130. McNamara, J. J., Molot, M. A., Stremple, J. F., & Cutting, R. T. Coronary artery disease in combat casualties in Vietnam. *Journal of the American Medical Association,* 1971, **216,** 1185–1187.

131. Mendels, J. Biological aspects of affective illness. In S. Arieti & E. B. Brody (eds.), *American handbook of psychiatry* (Vol. 3). New York: Basic Books, 1974. Pp. 491–523 (2nd ed.).

132. Mezzich, A., & Mezzich, J. Symptomatology of depression in adolescence. *Journal of Personality Assessment,* 1979, **43,** 267–275.

133. Miller, D. C. Short-term therapy with adolescents. *American Journal of Orthopsychiatry,* 1959, **29,** 772–779.

134. Miller, J. P. Suicide and adolescence. *Adolescence,* 1975, **10,** 11–24.

135. Miller, M. L., Chiles, J. A., & Barnes, V. E. Suicide attempters within a delinquent population. *Journal of Consulting and Clinical Psychology,* 1982, **50,** 490–498.

136. Minuchin, S. *Families and family therapy.* Cambridge, Mass.: Harvard University Press, 1974.

137. Minuchin, S. Structural family therapy. In G. Caplan (ed.), *American handbook of psychiatry, Vol. II: Child and adolescent psychiatry, sociocultural and community psychiatry.* New York: Basic Books, 1974. Pp. 178–192.

138. Minuchin, S., Baker, L., Liebman, R., Milman, L., Rosman, B., & Todd, T. C. Anorexia nervosa: Successful application of a family therapy approach. Paper presented to the American Pediatric Society, San Francisco, May 1973.

139. Minuchin, S., Rosman, B. L., & Baker, L. *Psychosomatic families: Anorexia nervosa in context.* Cambridge, Mass.: Harvard University Press, 1978.

140. Mirsky, I. A. Physiologic, psychologic, and social determinants in the etiology of duodenal ulcer. *American Journal of Digestive Disease,* 1958, **3,** 258.

141. Morton, R. *Phthisiologica: Or a treatise of consumptions.* London, 1689 (cited by H. Bruch. *Eating disorders.* New York: Basic Books, 1973).

142. Mussen, P. H., Conger, J. J., & Kagan, J. *Child development and personality.* New York: Harper & Row, 1979 (5th ed.).

143. Nemiah, J. C. Anxiety: Signal, symptom, and syndrome. In S. Arieti & E. B. Brody (eds.), *American handbook of psychiatry, Vol. III: Adult clinical psychiatry.* New York: Basic Books, 1974. Pp. 91–109 (2nd ed.).

144. Nicholi, A. M., Jr. Harvard dropouts: Some psychiatric findings. *American Journal of Psychiatry,* 1967, **124,** 105–112.

145. Nicholi, A. M., Jr. The adolescent. In A. M. Nicholi, Jr. (ed.), *The Harvard guide to modern psychiatry.* Cambridge, Mass.: Harvard University Press, 1978. Pp. 519–540.

146. Nisbett, R. E. Determinants of food intake in human obesity. *Science,* 1968, **159,** 1254–1255.

147. Offer, D. *The psychological world of the teen-ager: A study of normal adolescent boys.* New York: Basic Books, 1969.

148. O'Leary, K. D., & Wilson, G. T. *Behavior therapy: Application and outcome.* Englewood Cliffs, N.J.: Prentice-Hall, 1975.

149. Otto, U. Suicide attempts among Swedish children and adolescents. In G. Caplan & S. Lebovici (eds.), *Adolescence: Psychosocial perspectives.* New York: Basic Books, 1969. Pp. 244–251.

150. Perlstein, A. P. Suicide in adolescence. *New York State Journal of Medicine,* 1966, **66,** 3017–3020.

151. Perry, C. L., & McAlister, A. L. Peer teaching in smoking prevention research: Theoretical considerations in intervention strategies. Paper presented at the annual meeting of the American Psychological Association, Los Angeles, August 5, 1981.

152. Petersen, A. C., & Spiga, R. Adolescence and stress. In L. Goldberger & S. Breznitz (eds.), *Handbook of stress: Theoretical and clinical aspects,* New York: Macmillian, 1982.

153. Preodor, D., & Wolpert, E. A. Manic-depressive illness in adolescence. *Journal of Youth and Adolescence,* 1979, **8,** 111–130.

154. Purcell, K. Assessment of psychological determinants of childhood asthma. In P. H. Mussen, J. J. Conger & J. Kagan (eds.), *Readings in child development and personality.* New York: Harper & Row, 1970. Pp. 345–355.

155. Purcell, K., & Weiss, J. H. Emotions and asthma: Assessment and treatment. In C. G. Costello (ed.), *Symptoms of psychopathology.* New York: Wiley, 1971.

156. Radloff, L. Sex differences in depression: The effects of occupation and marital status. *Sex Roles,* 1975, **1,** 249–269.

157. Reinking, R. H., & Kobb, M. L. Effects of various forms of relaxation training on physiological and self-report measures of relaxation. *Journal of Consulting and Clinical Psychology,* 1975, **43,** 595–600.

158. Resnick, H. L. P. Suicide. In H. I. Kaplan, A. M. Freedman, & B. J. Sadock (eds.), *Comprehensive textbook of psychiatry* (Vol. 2). Baltimore: Williams & Wilkins, 1980. Pp. 2085–2097 (3rd ed.).

159. Rinsley, D. B. Residential treatment of adolescents. In G. Caplan (ed.), *American handbook of psychiatry, Vol. II: Child and adolescent psychiatry, sociocultural and community psychiatry.* New York: Basic Books, 1974. Pp. 351–366.

160. Rinsley, D. Borderline psychopathology: A review of etiology, dynamics, and treatment. *International Review of Psycho-Analysis,* 1978, **5,** 45–54.

161. Robins, L. *Deviant children grown up: A sociological and psychiatric study of sociopathic personality.* Baltimore: Williams & Wilkins, 1966.

162. Rodin, J. The current status of the internal-external obesity hypothesis: What went wrong. *American Psychologist,* in press.

163. Rodnick, E. H., & Goldstein, M. J. A research strategy for studying risk for schizophrenia during adolescence and early childhood. In E. J. Anthony & C. Koupernik (eds.), *The child in his family: Children at psychiatric risk* (Vol. 3). New York: Wiley-Interscience, 1974.

164. Rosen, B. M., Bahn, A. K., Shellow, R., & Bower, E. M. Adolescent patients served in outpatient psychiatric clinics. *American Journal of Public Health,* 1965, **55,** 1563–1577.

165. Rosenbaum, M. Peptic ulcer. In A. M. Freedman & H. I. Kaplan (eds.), *Comprehensive textbook of psychiatry.* Baltimore: Williams & Wilkins, 1967. Pp. 1049–1054.

166. Rosenthal, D. *Genetic theory and abnormal behavior.* New York: McGraw-Hill, 1970.

167. Rosenthal, D. The genetics of schizophrenia. In S. Arieti & E. B. Brody (eds.), *American handbook of psychiatry, Vol. III: Adult clinical psychiatry.* New York: Basic Books, 1974. Pp. 588–600 (2nd ed.).

168. Rosman, B. L., Minuchin, S., & Liebman, R. Family lunch session: An introduction to family therapy in anorexia nervosa. *American Journal of Orthopsychiatry,* 1975, **45,** 846–853.

169. Russel, G. F. M. Anorexia nervosa: Its identity as an illness and its treatment. In J. H. Prive (ed.), *Modern trends in psychological medicine.* London: Butterworth, 1970.

170. Russell, G. F. M. Bulimia nervosa: An ominous variant of anorexia nervosa. *Psychological Medicine,* 1979, **9,** 429–448.

171. Rutter, M. *Changing youth in a changing society: Patterns of adolescent development and disorder.* Cambridge, Mass.: Harvard University Press, 1980.

172. Rutter, M., Graham, P., Chadwick, O. F. D., & Yule, W. Adolescent turmoil: Fact or fiction? *Journal of Child Psychology and Psychiatry,* 1976, **17,** 35–56.

173. Rychlak, J. F., & O'Leary, L. R. Unhealthy content in the Rorschach responses of children and adolescents. *Journal of Projective Techniques and Personality Assessment,* 1965, **29,** 354–368.

174. Sawrey, W. L., Conger, J. J., & Turrell, E. S. An experimental investigation of the role of psychological factors in the production of gastric ulcers in rats. *Journal of Comparative and Physiological Psychology,* 1956, **49,** 457–461.

175. Schachter, S. Cognitive effects on bodily functioning: Studies of obesity and eating. In D. C. Glass (ed.), *Neurophysiology and emotion.* New York: Rockefeller University Press and Russell Sage Foundation, 1967.

176. Schachter, S. Obesity and eating. *Science,* 1968, **161,** 751–756.

177. Schachter, S. The assumption of identity and peripheralist-centralist controversies in motivation and emotion. In M. Arnold (ed.), *Feelings and emotions.* New York: Academic Press, 1970. Pp. 111–121.

178. Schachter, S. Some extraordinary facts about obese humans and rats. *American Psychologist,* 1971, **26,** 129–144.

179. Schachter, S. *Emotion, obesity, and crime.* New York: Academic Press, 1971.

180. Schwartz, D., & Thompson, M. Do anoretics get well: Current research and future needs. *American Journal of Psychiatry,* 1981, **138,** 319–324.

181. Seligmann, J. A. The starvation disease. *Newsweek,* September 3, 1974, 56.

182. Selvini-Palazzoli, M. P. Families of patients with anorexia nervosa. In E. J. Anthony & C. Koupernik (eds.), *The child in his family: Children at psychiatric risk.* New York: Wiley, 1970. Pp. 319–332.

183. Senn, M. J. E., & Solnit, A. J. *Problems in child behavior and development.* Philadelphia: Lea & Febiger, 1968.

184. Sours, J. The primary anorexia nervosa syndrome. In J. Noshpitz (ed.), *Basic handbook of child psychiatry.* New York: Basic Books, 1979.

185. *Statistical Bulletin* (Vol. 55). New York: Metropolitan Life Insurance Company, March 1974.

186. Strober, M. The significance of bulimia in juvenile anorexia nervosa: An exploration of possible etiological factors. *The International Journal of Eating Disorders,* 1981, **1,** 28–43.

187. Stunkard, A. J. Obesity. In H. I. Kaplan, A. M. Freedman, & B. J. Sadock (eds.), *Comprehensive textbook of psychiatry* (Vol. 3). Baltimore: Williams & Wilkins, 1980. Pp. 1872–1882 (3rd ed.).

188. Stunkard, A. J., & Mendelson, M. Obesity and body image: Characteristics of disturb-

ances in the body image of some obese persons. *American Journal of Psychiatry*, 1967, **123**, 1296–1300.

189. Sugarman, A., Bloom-Feshbach, S., & Bloom-Feshbach, J. The psychological dimensions of borderline adolescents. In J. Kwawer, H. Lerner, P. Lerner, & A. Sugerman (eds.), *Borderline phenomena and the Rorschach Test*. New York: International Universities Press, 1980.

190. Sugarman, A., & Quinlan, D. Anorexia nervosa as a defense against anaclitic depression. *The International Journal of Eating Disorders*, 1981, **1**, 44–61.

191. Tasto, D. L. Systematic desensitization, muscle relaxation and visual imagery in the counter-conditioning of a four-year-old phobic child. *Behavior Research and Therapy*, 1969, **7**, 409–411.

192. Teicher, J. D., & Jacobs, J. Adolescents who attempt suicide: Preliminary findings. *American Journal of Psychiatry*, 1966, **122**, 1248–1257.

193. Temby, W. D. Suicide. In G. R. Blaine, Jr., & C. C. McArthur (eds.), *Emotional problems of the student*. Garden City, N.Y.: Doubleday (Anchor Books), 1966. Pp. 147–169.

194. Thompson, M. Life adjustment of women with anorexia nervosa and anorexic-like behavior. Doctoral dissertation. University of Chicago, 1979.

195. Toolan, J. M. Depression in children and adolescents. In G. Caplan & S. Lebovici (eds.), *Adolescence: Psychosocial perspectives*. New York: Basic Books, 1969. Pp. 264–270.

196. Toolan, J. M. Depression and suicide. In G. Caplan (ed.), *American handbook of psychiatry, Vol. II: Child and adolescent psychiatry, sociocultural and community psychiatry*. New York: Basic Books, 1974. Pp. 294–305.

197. Torgoff, I., Torgoff, L., & Ponder, M. Life satisfactions of adolescents. Paper presented at the meeting of the Society for Research in Child Development, San Francisco, March 1979.

198. Tramontana, M. G. Critical review of research on psychotherapy outcome with adolescents: 1967–1977. *Psychological Bulletin*, 1980, **88**, 429–450.

199. U.S. Bureau of the Census. *Statistical abstract of the United States: 1976*. Washington, D.C., 1976 (96th ed.).

200. U.S. Bureau of the Census. *Statistical abstract of the United States: 1981*. Washington, D.C., 1981 (102 ed.).

201. U.S. Bureau of the Census, Current Population Reports, P-23, No. 114. *Characteristics of American children and youth: 1980*. Washington, D.C.: U.S. Government Printing Office, 1982.

202. Vaillant, G. E., & Perry, J. C. Personality disorders. In H. I. Kaplan, A. M. Freedman, & B. J. Sadock (eds.), *Comprehensive textbook of psychiatry* (Vol. 2). Baltimore: Williams & Wilkins, 1980. Pp. 1562–1590 (3rd ed.).

203. Van Krevelen, D. A. Psychoses in adolescence. In J. G. Howell, *Modern perspectives in child psychiatry* (Vol. 4). New York: Brunner/Mazel, 1971. Pp. 381–403.

204. Vriend, T. J. High-performing inner-city adolescents assist low-performing peers in counseling groups. *Personnel and Guidance Journal*, 1969, **47**, 897–904.

205. Watt, N. F. Longitudinal changes in the social behavior of children hospitalized for schizophrenia as adults. *Journal of Nervous and Mental Disease*, 1972, **155**, 42–54.

206. Watt, N. F., Stolorow, R. D., Lubensky, A. W., & McClelland, D. C. Social adjustment and behavior of children hospitalized for schizophrenia as adults. *American Journal of Orthopsychiatry*, 1970, **40**, 637–657.

207. Weiner, H. Respiratory disorders. In H. Kaplan, A. M. Freedman, & B. J. Sadock (eds.), *Comprehensive textbook of psychiatry* (Vol. 2). Baltimore: Williams & Wilkins, 1980. Pp. 1907–1916 (3rd ed.).

208. Weiner, I. B. *Psychodiagnosis in schizophrenia*. New York: Wiley, 1966.

209. Weiner, I. B. *Psychological disturbance in adolescence*. New York: Wiley, 1970.

210. Weiner, I. B., & Elkind, D. *Child development: A core approach*. New York: Wiley, 1972.

211. Weissman, M. M., & Klerman, G. L. Sex differences and the epidemiology of depression. *Archives of General Psychiatry,* 1977, **34,** 98–111.
212. Werkman, S. Anxiety disorders. In H. I. Kaplan, A. M. Freedman, & B. J. Sadock (eds.), *Comprehensive textbook of psychiatry* (Vol. 3). Baltimore: Williams & Wilkins, 1980. Pp. 2620–2630 (3rd 3d.).
213. Werkman, S. L. Psychiatric disorders of adolescence. In G. Caplan (ed.), *American handbook of psychiatry, Vol. II: Child and adolescent psychiatry, sociocultural and community psychiatry.* New York: Basic Books, 1974. Pp. 223–233.
214. Wetzel, R. Hopelessness, depression, and suicide intent. *Archives of General Psychiatry,* 1976, **33,** 1069–1073.
215. Winokur, G. Heredity in the affective disorders. In E. J. Anthony & T. Benedek (eds.), *Depression and human existence.* Boston: Little, Brown, 1975. Pp. 7–20.
216. Wish, P. A., Hasazi, J. E., & Jurgela, A. R. Automated direct deconditioning of a childhood phobia. *Journal of Behavior Therapy and Experimental Psychiatry,* 1973, **4,** 279–283.
217. Wittenberg, R. On the superego in adolescence. *Psychoanalytic Review,* 1955, **42,** 271–279.
218. Wolf, T. M., Hunter, S. MacD., Webber, L. S., & Berenson, G. S. Self-concept, locus of control, goal blockage, and coronary-prone behavior pattern in children and adolescents: Bogalusa heart study. *The Journal of General Psychology,* 1981, **105,** 13–16.
219. Zakus, G., & Soloman, M. The family situations of obese adolescent girls. *Adolescence,* 1973, **8,** 33–50.
220. Zuehlke, M. E., & Rogel, M. J. Adolescent peers as facilitators of contraceptive use. Paper presented at the annual meeting of the American Psychological Association, Los Angeles, August, 25, 1981.

# *Epilogue*

As we noted at the beginning of this book, our society views the adolescent period, and adolescents themselves, in varied and frequently conflicting ways. At this juncture, we hope we can see the adolescent years with a clearer perspective and a greater ability to distinguish myth from reality. Although there has been a widespread tendency to exaggerate the extent of adolescent turmoil in our society, adolescence *is* a complex and often difficult period in development both for adolescents and for their families. It could hardly be otherwise. Confronted by rapid physical, physiological, and cognitive changes, and by an accelerating succession of urgent societal demands, adolescents face formidable challenges in the essential task of deciding who they are, what they are going to be, and how they are going to get there. Furthermore, the difficulties of this period have been increasing, partly as a consequence of continuing changes in the family and most other social institutions, and partly as a consequence of the accelerated rate of these changes. Much of this book has been devoted to a consideration of the kinds of influences—personal, interpersonal, and societal—that facilitate or hinder the adolescent's struggle toward social maturity and a clearly defined sense of his or her own identity.

In the course of our discussion, we have tried to dispel a number of myths. Among these is the view that today's adolescents and youth represent a breed apart, unlike previous generations of young people; or, conversely, that all apparent generational differences are illusory, a matter of form rather than substance. A related popular myth is that there is something monolithic about adolescents and youth as a group, in contrast to adults, whose diversity appears more readily recognized. We are far more likely to hear sententious, blanket statements about "today's youth" than about "today's adults."

If there is one message, however, that comes through loud and clear when we take the trouble to examine the evidence, it is that there is nothing homogeneous or monolithic about contemporary adolescents. As we have seen repeatedly throughout this book, in almost any area one chooses to consider—moral and religious values, social concerns and political beliefs, sexual attitudes and behavior, drug use, intellectual and educational interests, vocational goals, or emotional maturity—the diversity among young people is at least as great as among adults. Furthermore, differences *within* both the adolescent and adult populations are usually far wider than any differences *between* the average adolescent and the average adult. Consequently, sweeping generalizations about today's youth—or adults—should be treated with considerable caution: It soon becomes clear that what is really being talked about is some young people or some adults—if indeed the speaker is talking about real people at all, and not simply projecting his or her own hopes and fears.

Nevertheless, there are important average differences between contemporary adolescents and adults. As we have seen, some of these differences simply reflect differences in the positions that adolescents and adults occupy in the life cycle. Others reflect the effects of very real differences in the worlds into which today's adolescents and their elders were born and in which they developed, as well as profound differences in the futures they face. Clearly, for example, young people are more likely than older Americans to have more liberal views about sexuality, self-determination for women, and family role relationships. They also appear more openly preoccupied with self-fulfillment—"the freedom to be me"—and less concerned with institutional loyalties and more reluctant to assume enduring personal commitments. Paradoxically, they also reflect, if anything, a stronger yearning for intimacy in close personal relationships.

In the decade since the first edition of this book, we have witnessed a decline in society's preoccupations with its adolescents and youth. During the late 1960s and early 1970s, hardly a week went by without a newspaper or magazine article, a new book, or a television special extolling contemporary young people as our last best hope for a more just, more caring, less hypocritical world, or alternatively, as a clear and present danger to long-established values, if not to the basic fabric of society itself. Poll takers vied to keep us abreast of the current attitudes and behavior of the nation's youth (1).

This kind of intense preoccupation is largely absent as we approach the mid-1980s. Why? Obviously, there are a variety of reasons, many of which we have addressed in this book: a decline in youthful activism and dissent, and in alternative life-styles; a narrowing of the so-called generation gap; a shift in the population bulge from adolescents to young adults; a reduced rate of change in social attitudes and behavior, though not in technology; deep concern with unemployment and inflation; and in all likelihood, the need for a period of cultural integration and equilibrium, after the tumult of the 1960s and early 1970s.

In a number of respects, this reduced emphasis on youth can be viewed as positive. In the long run, both young people and adults may benefit from a recognition that the experience of adolescence is not an end in itself (remember the sixties' slogan, "Never trust anyone over thirty!"), but is instead a challenging and, one hopes, exciting stage in a continuing process of personal and social development throughout life. Similarly, a greater sense of generational continuity between parents and children may help to add a deeper meaning to human existence in an unpredictable, frequently chaotic world.

Thus, if this were the sum of the matter, there would appear to be little cause for concern. Unfortunately, however, we suspect that what one historian has labeled "the fading of youth" in contemporary adult society has an added, potentially more troublesome source: Just as the ascendency of youth in our society during much of this century reflected a faith that the young "would not only inherit the future, but make a better future" (2, *15*), so it appears that the relative decline in society's investment in its youth reflects, at least partly, a broader decline in our hopes for continued social and economic progress. "We may be acquiescing to a world in which our young will rise no higher than we, because we have substituted caution for hope in our larger view of the prospects of society" (2, *15*).

Even more troubling, a growing number of today's youth, understandably concerned about their prospects for economic security in an inflationary world of diminishing resources, appear to be going along with this philosophy of lowered expectations, and are narrowing their vision. As we have seen, in the past decade America's youth have become increasingly concerned with personal well-being and material success, and progressively less concerned with making a contribution to society, participating in community action, or even helping others in difficulty.

Nevertheless, a significant minority of young people—and adults—are still actively engaged in trying to create a more human and humane world, whether in personal relationships, in social service activities, in community participation, in school and work, or in politics. Whether this minority will grow or whether there will be a swelling in the ranks of another minority—the disenchanted and alienated—is still an open question.

One thing is certain, however: We can ill afford as a society to abandon the dreams of youth. No matter what the fads or fashions of the moment, or the state of the economy, or the conflicts between nations and the divisions within them, one central fact is inescapable. For better or worse, the future course of our society, and quite possibly, in this interdependent nuclear age, that of the world itself, rests ultimately in the hands of these young people.

If this book has in any degree helped adults to better understand today's adolescents, or today's adolescents to understand more of themselves and their peers, it will have served its purpose.

### REFERENCES

1. Conger, J. J. Freedom and commitment: Families, youth, and social change. *American Psychologist*, 1981, **36,** 1475–1484.
2. Stearns, P. N. The fading of youth. My turn, *Newsweek,* July 25, 1979.

# Index of Names

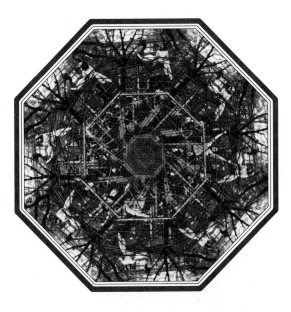

# Index
# of
# Subjects

*83 84 85 86 9 8 7 6 5 4 3 2 1*